STURGIS'
ILLUSTRATED DICTIONARY
OF ARCHITECTURE
AND BUILDING

*An Unabridged Reprint
of the 1901–2 Edition*

Russell Sturgis *et al.*

Vol. III
O–Z

DOVER PUBLICATIONS, INC.
New York

Published in Canada by General Publishing Company, Ltd., 30 Lesmill Road, Don Mills, Toronto, Ontario.
Published in the United Kingdom by Constable and Company, Ltd., 10 Orange Street, London WC2H 7EG.

This Dover edition, first published in 1989, is an unabridged and unaltered republication of the work originally published in 1901–02 by The Macmillan Company, New York under the title *A Dictionary of Architecture and Building: Biographical, Historical, and Descriptive.*

DOVER *Pictorial Archive* SERIES

Manufactured in the United States of America
Dover Publications, Inc., 31 East 2nd Street, Mineola, N.Y. 11501

Library of Congress Cataloging-in-Publication Data

Sturgis, Russell, 1836–1909.
    Sturgis' dictionary of architecture and building : an unabridged reprint of the 1901–2 edition / Russell Sturgis, et al.
        p.   cm.
    Reprint. Originally published: New York : Macmillan, 1901–1902.
    Bibliography: p.
    ISBN 0-486-26025-9 (v. 1)
    ISBN 0-486-26026-7 (v. 2)
    ISBN 0-486-26027-5 (v. 3)
    1. Architecture—Dictionaries.   2. Buildings—Dictionaries.   I. Title.
NA31.S838   1989
720'.3—dc19   89-1350
                                                                    CIP

LIST OF CONTRIBUTORS

TO THE

DICTIONARY OF ARCHITECTURE

CLEVELAND ABBE, Ph.D., LL.D.
Meteorologist U. S. Weather Bureau, Washington, D.C.

WILLIAM MARTIN AIKEN, F.A.I.A.
Architect; New York. Late Supervising Architect of U. S. Treasury Department.

EDWARD ATKINSON, Ph.D., LL.D.
Economist; President Manufacturers' Mutl. Ins. Co., Boston, Mass. Author *Mill Construction: What It Is and What It Is Not; Right Methods of Preventing Fires in Mills.*

CHARLES BABCOCK, M.A., Hon. Mem. A.I.A., Hon. Mem. R.I.B.A.
Emeritus Professor of Architecture, Cornell University, Ithaca, N.Y.

W. J. BALDWIN, Mem. Am. Soc. C.E., Mem. Am. Soc. M.E.
Expert and Consulting Engineer in Heating and Ventilation; New York.

CHARLES I. BERG, F.A.I.A.
Architect; New York.

C. H. BLACKALL, M.A., F.A.I.A.
Architect; Boston, Mass.

EDWIN H. BLASHFIELD, N.A., Hon. Mem. A.I.A.
Mural Painter; New York. Joint Author *Italian Cities;* Joint Editor Vasari.

H. W. BREWER, Hon. Assoc. R.I.B.A.
Author many papers published in the Proceedings R.I.B.A.; London, England.

ARNOLD W. BRUNNER, F.A.I.A.
Architect; New York. Joint Author *Interior Decoration.*

CARYL COLEMAN, A.B.
Ecclesiologist and Decorative Designer; President Church Glass and Decorating Co.

WALTER COOK, F.A.I.A.
Architect; New York. President Soc. of Beaux Arts Architects; President N.Y. Chapter A.I.A.

EDWARD COWLES, A.M., M.D.
Medical Supt. McLean Hospital, Waverley, Mass.; Clin. Instruc. Ment. Dis. Harvard University.

R. A. CRAM.
Architect; Boston, Mass.

FREDERIC CROWNINSHIELD.
Mural Painter and Decorative Artist; New York. Author *Mural Painting.*

FRANK MILES DAY, F.A.I.A.
Architect; Philadelphia, Penn.; Joint Editor *House and Garden.*

CHARLES DE KAY.
Writer on Fine Art; New York. Author *Life and Works of Barye, the Sculptor.*

F. S. DELLENBAUGH.
Painter; Writer and Lecturer on American Archæology and Ethnology; New York. Author *The North Americans of Yesterday.*

WILLIAM DE MORGAN.
Keramist and Designer; London, England.

BARR FERREE, Hon. Cor. Mem. R.I.B.A., Cor. Mem. A.I.A. Writer on Art; New York.

JOHN SAFFORD FISKE, L.H.D.
Alassio, Province of Genoa, Italy. Writer on Fine Art, especially of Italy.

ARTHUR L. FROTHINGHAM, Jr., Ph.D.
Princeton, N.J. Professor Ancient History and Archæology, Princeton University; Late Editor *Am. Journal Archæology;* Joint Author *History of Sculpture.*

WILLIAM PAUL GERHARD, C.E.
New York. Consulting Engineer for Sanitary Works; Cor. Mem. A.I.A.; Author volume on American Plumbing in the *Handbuch der Architektur;* and many works and articles, in English and German, on Sanitary Engineering.

ROBERT W. GIBSON, F.A.I.A.
Architect; New York.

WILLIAM H. GOODYEAR, M.A.
Archæologist; New York. Lecturer Brooklyn Inst. of Arts and Sciences (Curator since 1899); Author *The Grammar of the Lotus; Roman and Mediæval Art; Renaissance and Modern Art.*

ALEXANDER GRAHAM, F.S.A., Mem. Council R.I.B.A.
London, England. Author *Travels in Tunisia; Remains of the Roman Occupation of North Africa.*

A. D. F. HAMLIN, A.M.
Adjunct Professor Department of Architecture, Columbia University, New York; Author *A Text-book of the History of Architecture.*

H. J. HARDENBERGH, F.A.I.A.
Architect; New York.

GEORGE L. HEINS.
Architect; New York.

GEORGE HILL, M.S., C.E., Assoc. Mem. Am. Soc. C.E., Mem. Am. Soc. M.E.
Architect; New York. Author *Office Help for Architects; Modern Office Buildings; Test of Fireproof Floor Arches.*

FRED. B. HINCHMAN.
Architect; New York. Late U. S. Engineer Corps.

WILLIAM RICH HUTTON, C.E., Mem. Am. Soc. C.E., Mem. Inst. C.E., Mem. Inst. C.E. of London.
Civil Engineer; New York.

JOHN LA FARGE, N.A., Hon. Mem. A.I.A.
Mural Painter, Artist in Mosaic and Decorative Windows; New York. Author *Considerations on Painting; An Artist's Letters from Japan.*

v

W. R. LETHABY.
London; England. Joint Author *Sancta Sophia, Constantinople;* Author *Architecture, Mysticism, and Myth;* *Leadwork, Old and Ornamental.*

W. P. P. LONGFELLOW, S.B., Hon. Mem. A.I.A.
Cambridge, Mass. Editor *Cyclopædia of Architecture in Italy, Greece, and the Levant;* Author *Essays on Architectural History; The Column and the Arch.*

ALLAN MARQUAND, Ph.D., L.H.D.
Professor Archæology and the History of Art, Princeton University, Princeton, N.J.; Joint Author *History of Sculpture.*

HENRY RUTGERS MARSHALL, M.A., F.A.I.A.
Architect; New York. Author *Pain, Pleasure, and Æsthetics; Æsthetic Principles.*

GEORGE P. MERRILL.
Head Curator Dept. of Geology, U.S. National Museum, Washington, D.C.; Professor Geology and Mineralogy, Corcoran Scientific School of Columbian University, Washington, D.C.; Author *Stones for Building and Decoration; Rocks, Rock-weathering, and Soils; The Onyx Marbles.*

W. T. PARTRIDGE.
Lecturer on Architectural Design, Columbia University; New York.

CHARLES A. PLATT.
Architect and Landscape Architect; New York. Author *Italian Gardens.*

CORYDON T. PURDY, C.E., Mem. Am. Soc. C.E.
Civil Engineer; New York. Author Pamphlets and Reports on Construction and Fire-proofing.

RUSSELL ROBB, S.B., M.A.I.E.E.
Boston, Mass. Author *Electric Wiring for the Use of Architects.*

W. C. SABINE.
Assistant Professor of Physics, Harvard University, Cambridge, Mass. Engineer for Acoustics, Boston Music Hall (1900).

ALEXANDRE SANDIER.
Architect; Directeur des Travaux d'Art, Manufacture Nationale, Sèvres, France.

JEAN SCHOPFER.
Paris, France. Author many articles on Architecture in American and European periodicals.

MONTGOMERY SCHUYLER, A.M., Cor. Mem. A.I.A.
New York. Author *Studies in American Architecture;* Joint Editor *New York Times.*

F. D. SHERMAN, Ph.B.
Adjunct Professor of Architecture, Columbia University, New York.

EDWARD R. SMITH, B.A.
Librarian Avery Architectural Library, Columbia University, New York.

CHARLES C. SOULE.
Boston, Mass. President Boston Book Company; Trustee Am. Library Assoc.; Trustee Brookline, Mass., Pub. Lib.

R. PHENÉ SPIERS, F.S.A., Mem. Council R.I.B.A.
London, England. Editor Fergusson's *History of Ancient and Mediæval Architecture,* Third Edition; Editor Pugin's *Normandy,* Second Edition.

DANFORD N. B. STURGIS.
Architect; New York.

RICHARD CLIPSTON STURGIS, F.A.I.A.
Architect; Boston, Mass.

ANDREW T. TAYLOR, F.R.I.B.A., R.C.A.
Architect; Montreal. Author *Towers and Spires of Sir Christopher Wren; Dominion Drawing Books.*

EDWARD L. TILTON.
Architect; New York. Late Student and Explorer, Am. School of Classical Studies, Athens, Greece.

T. F. TURNER, B.S.
Architect; New York.

HENRY VAN BRUNT, F.A.I.A. and late President A.I.A.
Architect; Kansas City, Mo. Author *Greek Lines and other Architectural Essays.*

WILLIAM R. WARE, LL.D., F.A.I.A.
Professor of Architecture, Columbia University, New York. Author *A Treatise on Plain and Curvilinear Perspective.*

H. LANGFORD WARREN, F.A.I.A.
Architect; Boston, Mass. Professor of Architecture, Lawrence Scientific School, Harvard University.

EDMUND M. WHEELWRIGHT, A.B., F.A.I.A.
Late City Architect of Boston, Mass. Author *Municipal Architecture in Boston.*

PETER B. WIGHT, F.A.I.A.
Architect; Chicago, Ill. Secretary Illinois State Board of Examiners of Architects.

The Author of ARCHITECT, THE, IN ITALY records his indebtedness for special information to the Commendatore Camillo Boito.

The Author of LAW, — to Mr. Philip Golden Bartlett.

The Author of MUSIC HALL, — to Mr. Theodore Thomas.

The Author of SURVEYING, — to Mr. Edward B. Sturgis.

PREFACE TO VOLUME III., DICTIONARY OF ARCHITECTURE

THE search for accurate definitions for words is one of the most interesting of pursuits ; and when the definitions sought are of tangible things, things interesting in themselves and because of their importance, the search may interest the workman as well as the etymologist. What is, exactly speaking, an arch ? In close relation to that inquiry, what is *not* an arch ? The reader may amuse himself with rearranging or rewording the definitions given in Vol. I. What is the Doric Order in the original and in the derived or secondary sense of the term ? The definitions given in their place assume the preëxistence of the term in the Roman sense, and only its much later application to the order of the Parthenon. Or, to take a more doubtful case, should the word Piazza be given in the sense of Veranda ? A kind correspondent sends, too late for insertion in its place, a history of that word in English, and refers to his own signed letters in the *Nation* (N.Y.), from which it appears that the term Covent Garden Piazza was in use, in London, as early as 1634 ; that thirty years later the term was applied rather to the covered ambulatories fronting on the square, of which some still remain ; that the American use of it for the covered out-of-door extension of a country house was a direct borrowing from those arcades built by Inigo Jones ; that use of the term has been known for two centuries and a half and in all parts of the English-speaking world. If an Englishman were writing home about the strange things seen in the United States, he would name Piazzas rather than Verandas, keeping the later word for India. Piazza used in this sense is a blot on our technical vocabulary, but it must be acknowledged. How, then, concerning *Porte Cochère* in the sense of a covered porch for carriages ? That is a term which ought to be kept out of the language, if possible, and, therefore, either opposed or ignored. A century hence, if it is in the daily use of English-speaking people, it may be necessary to admit it as we now admit Piazza ; but let every accurate writer and speaker avoid it *till then*, and let every dictionary name it with reprehension.

The abuse of trade names threatens the building trades, the decorative arts, and all those human occupations which are seriously modified by the modern race for commercial advantage. It would be well if the architects and mural painters, the trained artists who are concerned in decorative art, would refuse to help confound and corrupt our English vocabulary. We of English speech have to borrow words from the languages of men more versed and more traditionally at home than we are in the things of fine art ; but we may at least take those foreign words in their true senses, and we may use our own English words aright. Let us not force Renaissance to include the Decadence as well ; let us not admit that a Wainscot can be of marble.

In the Preface to Vol. I. there was mention of those contributions to the Dictionary which by their nature could not well be signed. Referring now to those articles which bear their authors' names, it seems advisable to classify, roughly, the work represented by those articles and the character of the information there given. Thus, in the matter of architectural education, Professors Ware and Sherman and Mr. Partridge have treated Drawing, Perspective, Projection, and Shades and Shadows. Mr. Walter Cook has written on the great School of Art in Paris, and Mr. Sandier on other French schools (see Architect in France). Messrs. Blackall, Berg, and Wight must be mentioned in this connection as having written on subjects so nearly akin to education as Fellowship, Photography, and Societies of Architects.

The modern practice of architecture and building has been treated especially by Messrs. Gibson, Sandier, and Fiske in articles on The Architect in England, France, and Italy ; by Messrs. Brunner, Gibson, and Van Brunt in a general way (see Builder, Specification, Superintendent), and by Mr. Marshall, from the point of view of the suggestive reformer of modern practice, in the articles Modelling and Truth in Art.

Immediately connected with this is the large body of work concerning modern construction in all its range, from the simple and realistic subject of Mr. Atkinson (Slow-burning Construction) to the engineering problems treated by Mr. Hutton (Caisson, Centring, Equilibrium of Arches, Excavation, Expansion, Foundation, Iron Construction, Masonry, Steel, Strength of Materials) and the wholly modern scientific considerations which are the subjects of Professor Sabine (Acoustics, Echo, Reflector, Sounding Board, Whispering Gallery, and other kindred terms), Mr. Gerhard (Bath and cognate subjects, Drain, Drainage and House Drainage, Gas Piping and Plumbing, Kitchen, Laundry, Market, and Water Supply), and Mr. Purdy (Fireproofing).

Other departments and other manifestations of this great subject of modern building appliances and building practice are covered by the articles of Mr. Baldwin (Ventilation), Mr. Gibson (Bill of Quantities, Builder, Estimating, Surveyor), Mr. Hinchman (Key, Lock, etc.), Mr. Robb (Electrical Appliances, Elevator [Electric], Warming by Electricity), Mr. D. N. B. Sturgis (Beam, Bolt, Brick, Stair, Step, each with many subtitles), and Mr. Wight (Shoring, which includes house moving and raising). Materials not already mentioned are the special subjects of Mr. De Morgan (Keramics) and Dr. Merrill (Marble with subtitles, Stone with subtitles).

These subjects are often closely interlinked, and it is difficult to classify such work as Mr. Caryl Coleman's, for instance (see Altar, Ambo, Chancel, Font, Reredos, Stall, and similar articles on Ecclesiology ; also Symbology), and to say whether it belongs to the history of architecture or rather to kindred forms of decoration. In the matter of pure decoration, its theory and practice, the articles of Mr. Blashfield on Mural Painting, Mr. Crowninshield on the practical side of the same great art (Distemper, Encaustic, Fresco, Mosaic, Oil Painting, Water Glass, Wax Painting), Mr. La Farge on the subject he has made so especially his own, the Window of decorative glass, and Mr. Lethaby on the nature of Design and the difficulties in the way of originality and significance in the modern industrial epoch, are to be compared with the papers on special topics, such as Robbia Work by Professor Marquand and Keramics by Mr. De Morgan.

Buildings of the modern world, concerning which there has been much semiscientific thought and much discussion, have been treated by Messrs. Abbe (Observatory), Aiken (Post Office), Brunner (Synagogue), Cowles (Hospital), Hardenbergh (Hotel), Hill (Apartment House, Office, Tenement House), Soule (Library), and Wheelwright (Schoolhouse).

Biography has been the work of Mr. Smith, as stated in Vol. I.

Finally, the vast subject of the history of architecture, ancient and modern, European and Oriental, whether treated geographically or by subjects, has been handled by Professor Babcock (Vaults), Mr. Day (the Stoa, the Temple), Mr. Ferree (Church, the summary), Mr. Fiske (Church, the nature of the building), Professor Frothingham (Memorial Arch, Memorial Column), Mr. Goodyear (the Leaning Tower), Mr. Longfellow (Baptistery, Round Church), Mr. Platt (the Villa). Again, this has been examined from another point of view by Mr. Dellenbaugh, who treats American archæology in many papers, Professor Frothingham with Pelasgic and Hittite antiquity, Professor Hamlin with Byzantine Art, Mr. Longfellow who handles Greco-Roman, Latin, Neoclassic, and Romanesque art, Professor Marquand and Mr. Spiers who treat respectively Grecian and Imperial Roman art. The same great subject, treated geographically, has been the business of Mr. Blackall (Belgium, Portugal, and Spain), Mr. Brewer (Austria, Bohemia, Germany, and Hungary), Mr. Cram (China and Japan), Mr. DeKay (Ireland), Mr. Dellenbaugh (Mexico, Central America, and the United States as to their pre-Columbian epoch), Mr. Fiske (Italy, the northwestern provinces), Professor Frothingham (Italy, except the far northwest), Mr. Graham (North Africa), Professor Hamlin (the Balkan Peninsula, Egypt, India, and Scotland), Mr. Schopfer (Switzerland), Mr. Schuyler (the United States), Mr. Spiers (Asia Minor, Persia, Syria), Mr. R. C. Sturgis (England), Mr. Taylor (Canada), Mr. Turner (Mexico), Professor Warren (France, the southern provinces).

The editor cannot close this synopsis of the work of several busy years without renewing his thanks to the contributors who have seconded him so cheerfully. The scheme of the Dictionary has never been disturbed or made difficult by any unwillingness on their part to conform to it. To one who thinks with the present writer that there is no evidence of thorough mastery of a subject more complete than a perfect willingness to present that subject in the form required by a special occasion, — than the absence of intellectual rigidity and a flexibility of spirit such as comes only from long-continued mental exercise, — the evidence thus afforded of the unique merit of the Dictionary's staff of contributors is most complete and convincing.

R. S.

FULL–PAGE ILLUSTRATIONS

DICTIONARY OF ARCHITECTURE

O

OBELISK (in Greek, a spit, ὀβελίσκος, or a pointed weapon, or the like). *A.* A tall and slender decorative structure or piece of material, as a pinnacle-like ornament on a neoclassic building. More especially, a memorial or decorative piece, square in plan, or nearly so, with slightly sloping sides, and terminated at top by a pyramid whose sides slope more rapidly. (See Pyramidion.) The origin of these monuments is to be found in Egypt, where they stood commonly one on either side of the entrance to a temple or palace, their nearly vertical faces affording an admirable opportunity for hieroglyphic inscriptions, easy to read, and of decorative effect. Obelisks are known to have been put up as early as the 4th dynasty of Egyptian kings (3759–3730 B.C. — Flinders Petrie), but none remain of so early a time. The largest obelisk existing is that at Heliopolis, of red granite, and stated to be 66 feet high; this also is the oldest known except some very small ones, as it belongs to the 12th dynasty (2622–2578 — Flinders Petrie). It was customary to cover the pyramidion with metal, perhaps always gilded bronze, with the idea of keeping water from the grain of the stone.

Many obelisks were brought from Egypt to Rome during the days of the great Empire, and some have been carried from Egypt to modern cities, as the obelisk in the Place de la Concorde at Paris (1833), that on the Embankment at London (1878), and that in Central Park, New York (1879).

B. By extension, and with allusion to the sloping sides of the obelisk in its usual sense, any stele or similar upright piece, especially if a monolith. In this sense the term is applied to those modern tombs which have a central structure with sloping sides serving as a background to sculpture, and the like. — R. S.

OBSERVATORY. An establishment erected for the purpose of recording astronomical, meteorological, magnetical, seismological, or tidal phenomena, to be distinguished from a laboratory in which experimental work is the prominent feature. In the former matters, the experimental features are insignificant in comparison with the observational arrangements. The five classes will be considered in detail in the following sections.

Astronomical Observatories. The progress of astronomy has from time to time introduced new instruments and new problems, and corresponding new conditions must be realized in the construction and arrangement of the buildings in order to secure both the desired observations and the necessary accuracy. In general, up to the seventeenth century, the astronomer desired only a clear view of the whole sky from the horizon upward; the oldest observatory of this style now in existence is that founded during the Yuen dynasty, about the year 1300, in Pekin, China, near the location of the present Imperial Observatory; the building was doubtless, in many respects, similar to those of the Arabs, Persians, Greeks, Egyptians, and Chaldeans of most ancient days. The instruments originally in use at the Imperial Observatory are still preserved there, but have been replaced by others made for the Jesuit astronomers at Pekin, between 1673 and 1700. These are all exposed to the heavens, on an elevated granite platform surrounded by a heavy iron railing. Modern European observatories begin with that erected in 1576 for Tycho Brahe, at Uranienborg, on the island of Huen, by the king of Denmark; since then, large instruments have been established in the meridian, and the buildings have been more or less closed in, to protect the astronomer and his apparatus, leaving open slits with movable shutters, or windows, through which to observe the stars. At first, in order to obtain a clear horizon, the instruments were placed in the upper stories of very high buildings, but this is not done now. The Royal Observatory at Greenwich, built in 1675–1676, and the Royal Observatory at Paris, built in 1667, even in their own day scarcely represented the rapidly advancing condition of astronomy. Each of these buildings is still occupied, but has undergone many changes in order to adapt it to modern requirements. At the present time it is generally recognized that each astronomical instrument must have a location and surroundings appropriate to its work; thus, the instruments for observing in the meridian and in the prime vertical should be so located that fixed marks and collimating telescopes can be placed exactly north, south, east, and west of each instrument, and at no great distance therefrom. For all instruments, the stability of their piers, the permanence of their adjustments, the protection from strong wind, the conformity of temperature within the observing room relative to that of the free air outside, the freedom from minute vibrations and jars of the ground, and especially a steady atmosphere, are the fundamental conditions for good work. So far as the buildings themselves are concerned, it is found that these conditions are best secured by giving each instrument its own isolated house; hence modern observatories constitute a cluster of buildings containing offices, residences, and instruments, often scattered over an area of many acres, in order that each may be located as advantageously as possible; it is only in the case of mountain observatories, where space is not available and where it is impossible to go out in stormy weather, that it becomes necessary to crowd several instruments into one building. A complete modern observatory must provide for work both in the exact meridian and upon objects far removed from the meridian. The former is done by meridian instruments whose use requires simply a broad slit open from the zenith down to the opposite sides of the horizon. The extra-meridional work is done with instruments of either the altitude and azimuth type, or the equatorial type; both these types require to be mounted in rooms whose walls and roofs revolve horizontally, so that the broad slit from zenith to horizon, which serves as the observing window, may be brought opposite to any part of the sky that is to be examined through the telescope. The equatorial telescope invented by Fraunhofer has a perfectly free motion around an axis parallel to that of the earth, called the equatorial axis; this can be moved by clockwork, so that an object once brought into the centre of the field of view will remain there permanently. With such apparatus, photographs of faint stars, comets, and nebulæ can be obtained by giving several hours of continuous exposure to the sensitive plate. The eye end of this telescope is near the floor of the room when the observer is looking at the zenith, but may be 20 feet above the floor when he is looking at points near the horizon. In the older observatories, a complex observing chair was needed for the convenience of the observer; but in all the newest ones the floor itself is made adjustable, rising and falling at any moment to suit the needs of the case.

Among the best illustrations of the extent and manifold character of the works undertaken by modern observatories and the consequent necessary expansion of apparatus and buildings, we quote the Observatory of Harvard University, Cambridge, Mass., which now maintains several branch observatories and employs in all about fifty astronomers, physicists, computers, and clerks. Among the great observatories built in recent years with a view to work in some special department in astronomy, we may enumerate the following: The Imperial Central Observatory at Poulkova, near Saint Petersburg (1836–1839); the new Observatory of the University of Vienna; the Observatory at Nice (1885–1890); and, in the United States, the Lick Observatory on Mount Hamilton; the Naval Observatory in Washington, and the Yerkes Observatory belonging to the University of Chicago, but located at Williams Bay, Wisconsin.

Meteorological Observatories. The only building pertaining to meteorology that has descended to us from classic times is the so-called " Tower of the Winds " at Athens, which dates from between fifty and a hundred and fifty years before Christ. Each side of the tower bore a sundial, that is to say, a horizontal stylus projected from the middle of the upper edge of each face; from it radiated the hour-marks chiselled into the smooth marble, and, undoubtedly, at one time filled with red or black pigments. The interior of the tower still bears witness to the fact that it formerly contained a large water clock or clepsydra.

The modern revival of interest in meteorology dates from Galileo and more especially from his pupil, Ferdinand II., Grand Duke of Tuscany, who, in 1653, distributed thermometers to several cloisters and organized a system of daily records, the general oversight of which was committed to Father Luigi Antinori. During the past two hundred and fifty years, the conditions under which satisfactory observations can be made have come to be better understood, and the observatory buildings have undergone corresponding alterations, although observations and records are still made by thousands of amateurs under more or less unsatisfactory conditions. Meteorological observations are frequently combined with seismological and magnetical in one establishment, and in order to respond to these manifold requirements a number of small buildings must be scattered over an area of several acres. If magnetic self-registration is undertaken, it is almost necessarily done in underground or cellar rooms where the temperature can be controlled throughout the year. The first story of the observatory building is devoted to offices and libraries, while the upper story is usually given up to self-recording meteorological apparatus connected with the thermometers, rain gauges, anemometers, sunshine recorders, etc., on the roof. In order to obtain the temperature and moisture of the air, it is considered necessary that the thermometers shall be exposed freely to the wind and yet be perfectly shielded from the sun's rays by day and from their own radiation to the clear sky at night; they are, therefore, enclosed in a shelter of open latticework, which is either elevated high above the roof, or located near the ground, according to the subject under investigation.

PLATE I

OBSERVATORY AT WILLIAMS BAY, WISCONSIN

(See the figures in the text and Plate II)

Interior of the revolving dome. The telescope revolves on an axis parallel to the earth's axis of rotation; it is driven by clockwork so that a star is kept in the centre of the field of vision.

The observing slit is 13 feet wide and extends from the horizon to a point 5 feet beyond the zenith. It is closed by two shutters which work side-wise on rollers, and which move simultaneously. Canvas curtains are mounted on tracks and can be adjusted so as to shelter the telescope from the wind. The floor seen in the figure is arranged so as to rise for a distance of 23 feet vertically; thus enabling the observer to reach the eyepiece of the telescope at all times.

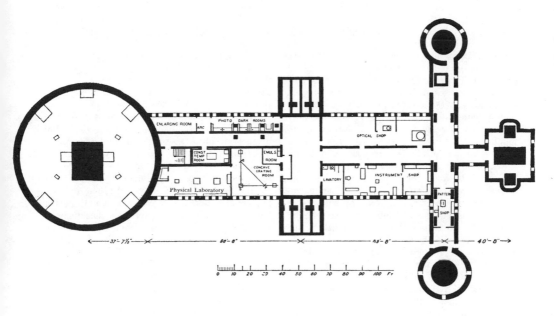

OBSERVATORY AT WILLIAMS BAY (SEE NEXT FIGURE); GROUND FLOOR.

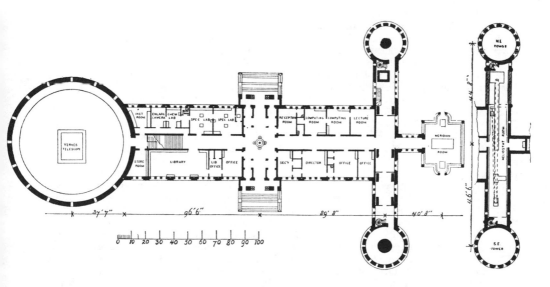

OBSERVATORY AT WILLIAMS BAY, WISCONSIN, BELONGING TO THE UNIVERSITY OF CHICAGO; PRINCIPAL FLOOR; AND UPPER FLOOR OF EASTERN TOWERS.

The Eiffel Tower in Paris was originally designed by its inventor for utilitarian as well as architectural purposes, and since the close of the Paris Exposition in 1889 it has been largely devoted to physical and meteorological purposes. The records of pressure, temperature, and wind taken on it, in mid-air, one thousand feet above the ground, have given a new aspect to certain problems in meteorology. This tower is now known to the scientific world as a meteorological observatory. It responds precisely to a fundamental condition that is not fulfilled by any mountain observatory, namely, that the instruments be placed in free air high above the ocean level, so as not to be affected by the influence of the ground or building which supports them. The records from the Eiffel Tower are more valuable even than those obtained from instruments suspended in the free air by balloons or kites, because they are continued uninterruptedly.

In order to satisfy the same conditions, the Weather Bureau of the United States (and, to a less extent, the bureaus of other countries) elevates its observing stations to the tops of the highest accessible buildings ; but in some cases, from necessity, it takes the observations quite near the surface of the ground.

For climatological studies bearing on vegetable and animal life, it is, of course, necessary to keep records of rainfall and temperature near the surface of the ground, therefore the central stations generally have an auxiliary open field for this purpose. When these stations can be located in such fields with an adjacent grove, the whole constitutes a park, and for economy's sake other scientific institutions are established in the same park. Illustrations of this arrangement will be found in the combination of astronomy, meteorology, and magnetism in Greenwich Park ; of magnetism and meteorology at Pavlosk ; of geodesy, astronomy, meteorology, and magnetism at Potsdam, and the similar combinations at the observatories at Nice and Budapest, and at stations for the study of forestry, agriculture, etc.

In order to explore the upper atmosphere, meteorological observations are frequently established on the summits of hills and mountains. The mountain observatory is usually a very plain structure, and the apparatus is installed with difficulty on the rocky summit. Observations at still higher levels are obtained by the use of balloons and kites. The first of the modern series of buildings combining the needs of a meteorological and magnetic observatory with those of a central station where an extensive collection of records must be preserved and students must be provided for, was the Seewarte at Hamburg, now the *Deutsche Seewarte*, designed by Professor Neumayer as scientist, and G. Kirchenpauer as architect. Next in chronological order, and rivalling it in importance, was

the collection of buildings erected in the Imperial Park at Pavlosk as the technical adjunct to the Central Physical Observatory at Saint Petersburg. The most recent structure of the kind is the magnetic and meteorological observatory at Potsdam, near Berlin, which is established in the park at that place, near other buildings devoted to astro-physical and geodetic research. The Potsdam observatory is the technical observatory and the school of experimental research for the Central Meteorological Institute in Berlin, of which Professor W. von Bezold is director. The meteorological and magnetical observatories at Parc Saint Maur, Montsouris, Pavlosk, and Potsdam respond to the important condition that meteorological observations for general climatological purposes should not be taken in large cities, but in open regions at a distance therefrom. On the other hand, there are many problems that demand special observations made within cities or within forests, or at some other locality for which special stations are needed. The instruments themselves and the methods of their exposure constitute special problems that are rather differently handled in each observatory. The central office of the Weather Bureau at Washington is located on sufficiently high ground to enable the apparatus on its roof to indicate the proper temperature and wind for a large mass of air just above the city. The first floor is 79 feet above sea level, and the anemometer about 60 feet above that; the observer's room, the self-registers, and the barometer are on the top floor of the central tower, but an auxiliary experimental observatory belonging to the Instrument Division is located on an adjoining building. All Weather Bureau stations for storm studies are elevated high above the soil in order to obtain approximately the state of the air at the cloud level.

Magnetic Observatories. The first magnetic observatory, in the modern sense of the term, was that occupied by Gauss and Weber at the University of Gottingen, 1833–1850. The difficulty of carrying on these delicate measures with sufficient frequency led C. Brooke, in 1844, to devise the Greenwich and John Welsh, in 1857, the Kew, system of photographic apparatus for continuous registration ; the so-called Kew system is now in use at about twenty magnetic observatories. Improvements in many details were, c. 1885, made by Mascart, whose apparatus is now in use at about fifteen stations. The latest improvements are found in the three observatories designed in 1900 by Dr. L. A. Bauer, and to be erected by the United States Coast and Geodetic Survey. The conditions to be fulfilled in a magnetic observatory are primarily two : namely, as great a freedom as possible from local magnetic disturbances due to the building, the geological strata, and adjacent industrial electric plants; and as uniform a temperature as possible within the building. This latter condition is now seen to be so important that great efforts are being made everywhere to attain it: self-adjusting furnaces and air driers are provided; the rooms for the self-registering apparatus are placed either in the basements and cellars of large buildings, as at Potsdam, or in smaller adjacent buildings that are covered over entirely with a mound of earth, as at Pavlosk. The latter method was adopted by Wild, and his published records show that there is not a variation of 1° Centigrade in his observing room during the year. In the observatory at Potsdam the cellar and sub-cellar rooms are arranged within double walls and with special furnaces and ventilators in order to secure dry air with a sufficiently constant temperature. At both places there is provided at some distance an additional light, wooden building in which absolute measures may be made as the standard for the correction of the work done underground by the self-registers. The buildings and arrangements adopted at Pavlosk and at Potsdam are recognized as, at present, the most comprehensive and the most appropriate in the world. The buildings at both places are quite plain and small as compared with those of the modern astronomical observatory.

Seismological Observatories. The systematic observation of earthquake phenomena is now carried on at many astronomical, meteorological, and magnetic observatories throughout the world. As the apparatus must be closely connected with the solid ground, it is often placed in the cellars of these larger establishments. The most elaborate apparatus has been devised by the Japanese students of the Seismological Society of Japan, and is to be found at Tokyo; other styles of apparatus are at Geneva, Vesuvius, Parc Saint Maur, Mount Hamilton, California, Washington, D.C., and Cleveland, Ohio. The apparatus devised for Professor Miln's Observatory at Shide, on the Isle of Wight, is now being widely introduced. The whole subject may be said to be still in an experimental stage as regards the instruments and the interpretation of their records. The stations of observation have not generally required the erection of special elaborate buildings. The meteorological observatory founded by Melloni on Monte Somma, on the north flank of Mount Vesuvius, in 1841, has of late years become so prominent in seismic studies as to be frequently called the "Seismological Observatory of Mount Vesuvius." It belongs to the University of Naples, and Professor Luigi Palmieri was the director from 1854 until his death in 1896. Palmieri early introduced his electromagnetic seismograph and, subsequently, other more delicate forms of apparatus, by means of which he was able to study the shocks and tremors and to predict the eruptions of Vesuvius.

Tidal Observatories. Records of the variations in level of the ocean and the great lakes are kept by means of tidal registers, or marographs. The instruments must be located close to the shore so that a float may rise and fall, within a protected well, simultaneously with the surface of the free water. In some cases an open tube runs beneath the ground out to some point a few hundred yards from the shore into deep water, so that the well reproduces the changes in the deeper water and avoids recording violent breakers. Such tubes, however, produce a retardation as to time, and it is preferable to build up a foundation for the tidal register in the deep water itself. The superstructure for the tidal station is simple and inexpensive.

— CLEVELAND ABBE.

OBSIDIAN. A natural glass formed by the rapid cooling of acid lavas. Colours: gray, red-brown, to black. — G. P. M.

OBSTAL. (See Opstal.)

OCTASTYLE. Having eight columns in the front or end row; consisting of a row or rows of eight columns; said of certain classic buildings, and of architectural compositions derived from them. (See Columnar Architecture.)

OCULUS (in Latin, an eye; applied by modern archæologists to round windows, and the like, in Roman monuments). A circular member, as a window or panel (compare Œil de Bœuf); especially, the round opening in the summit of the cupola at the Pantheon, Rome; or, by extension, any opening having a similar character.

ODEION. Same as Odeum.

ODEUM (in Greek, Ὠδεῖον, or Ὠιδεῖον; used by Roman writers for a music hall; Vitruvius, V., 9). A. A Greco-Roman building in Athens said to have been of a very early epoch, and adorned at a later time by Pericles; destroyed by fire during Sulla's siege of Athens, and rebuilt at the expense of King Ariobarzanes of Cappadocia. Herodes Atticus, in the reign of Marcus Aurelius, built an odeum at Athens, the ruins of which still remain at the foot of the Acropolis, and west of the theatre of Dionysos. There is no doubt that this building is nearly, if not exactly, on the site of the older odeum. Such buildings existed in other cities of Greece. They were distinguished from the great theatres in being roofed.

B. In modern times, a music hall or place of intellectual entertainment, rather as forming part of the name of a special building than as a general term.

OECHSEL, JORG; architect.

He was architect of the cathedral of S. Stephen, in Vienna, at the beginning of the sixteenth century, and built the organ over the Peter and Paul altar.

Perger, *S. Stephan in Wien.*

ŒCUS. In Latin, a hall or large room in a dwelling house ; rare in ancient authors, and applied by modern archæologists to a room with columns, or otherwise decorative, as in some Pompeian houses. The room so called was sometimes a dining room.

ŒIL DE BŒUF. In French, a comparatively small round or oval window ; as adopted in English usage, such a window especially when treated decoratively, as in a frieze. (See Eye ; Oculus.)

Salle de l'Œil de Bœuf. The antechamber of the king's apartment in the palace of Versailles ; so called on account of the oval window in one of the walls.

OFFICE. *A.* A room in which work is done, especially work of a professional or intellectual sort, as distinguished from a workshop. Thus, in the house of a physician, the room in which patients are received is the office. In a hotel, a factory, or other establishment where many persons are employed, the room especially reserved for interviews between the proprietor or his representative and persons having business with the concern ; in a shop or store, the compartment, whether forming a separate room or not, in which the clerks and bookkeepers do their work, as distinguished from the salesmen.

In modern cities, the places of business, even of professional men, are so often separated from their residences that offices have come to be rooms or suites of rooms in large buildings, perhaps erected especially for the purpose. (See Office Building.)

B (in this sense, much more common in the plural, as, the offices). The kitchens, storerooms, service rooms, laundries, etc., taken together, as in a hotel or large dwelling house.

— R. S.

OFFICE BUILDING. One intended for renting to tenants for the purpose of transacting clerical or executive business or the practice of a profession.

Development. Prior to 1858, except in a few commercial cities like New York, office buildings were usually converted dwellings, the light, air, heat, and height which were sufficient for living rooms being deemed sufficient also for the office, the plans of new buildings closely following those in use for dwellings. A number of new buildings were erected during the period 1858 to 1865, at which time the elevators began to be common, and led to the use of five- and six-story buildings. About 1880 the speed of the passenger elevator was increased somewhat, and during the next few years buildings of eight and nine stories in height became common ; during the period up to 1890 the elevator speeds were gradually increased, reaching the practicable limit, and since 1890 the development of the office building has been along the lines of the carefully

braced steel skeleton supporting a masonry covering, with an increased number of stories and a decreased size of the office unit.

Plan. It is required to produce a building having the greatest practicable number of rooms of about uniform size, each practically equidistant (in time) from the street, and each well lit and ventilated naturally. For a uniform distribution of light during business hours it is desirable that the direct light should be admitted morning and evening, and diffused light during the middle of the day, a greater dependence being placed upon diffused than upon direct light. It is also desirable that each office should receive a nearly equal portion of light during the day. It is therefore necessary that they should all be symmetrically arranged about an axis. If this axis runs east and west, the offices on the north side of the building receive diffused light only during the early morning and late afternoon in the summer. Those on the south side have the sun directly on them nearly the entire year. The direct sunlight on such offices is too intense to be admitted, and it is therefore necessary to use awnings or shades, which darken the rear of the office. If the axis runs in a northerly and southerly direction, the offices receive the direct sun in the morning, and in the afternoon and during the middle of the day are protected ; shades, therefore, are unnecessary, and the diffused light fills the entire room during the greater part of the day. In courts, the direct light is only available during a small portion of the day ; the balance of the time the reflected light from the sides and the diffused light must be depended on. If the long axis of the court is placed in a northerly and southerly direction, the direct light can reach farther down than would be the case if the axis were placed in another direction, and the reflected light will be much better. This follows as a necessary consequence of the laws of reflection, and can be readily demonstrated by using a candle to represent the sun and a rectangular box having light-coloured sides 1×3 inches in plan and 6 inches high. By placing the long axis of the box in various positions with reference to a meridian, the amount of light can be noted on a piece of tracing paper held at the bottom. To insure the even distribution of the light during the business days, lay off on a full circle the twenty-four hours which compose the day, draw two radii, one to 9 A.M. and one to 5 P.M., and bisect the angle formed by these two with a third radius. This radius should be the approximate bearing of the court axis. The aim being to provide an equal number of unit offices of equal desirability, a unit building is developed by placing two rows of offices on either side of a centre corridor, the offices opening to the street or court. As many unit buildings should be

OFFICE BUILDING; AMERICAN SURETY COMPANY, NEW YORK CITY.

arranged in parallel rows as the lot permits, leaving adequate court space between them and joining them at their northerly ends, unless there is some controlling reason due to the position of the lot or the exceptional length of the building, by means of a cross building containing the stairways, elevators, and connecting corridors. Typical plans are given in Figs. 1, 2, and 3. The size of the office unit depends on local demands and the size of the lot, varying from 9 × 15 feet up to 15 × 25 feet. The corridors should vary from 4 to 6 feet in width, and the walls from 1 foot to several feet in thickness. The unit building will vary in width from 37 to 60 feet or more. The cross corridors should be 25 per cent, and the landing in front of the elevators 50 per cent, wider than the side corridors, with 12 feet as a maximum. The main hall, from the street to the elevators, should be at the street level, 7 feet wide in small buildings and 12 feet wide in larger ones. All of them should receive direct light and air from at least one window. The courts should be from 18 to 25 feet wide. In buildings of an L shape, the elevators can be placed at the angle of the L.

Height. Present practice ranges from ten to twenty stories. The limit is fixed structurally by the smallest dimension of the lot when the building is free standing or designed to be entirely independent of its neighbours, and economically, by reaching the point where the rental value of the additional story is not sufficient to pay the interest on the cost of the story, for the loss of space due to increase in the number of elevators in all the stories, for loss of space in the court, and for increased cost of service. All of these items are serious in amount, but cannot yet be definitely determined. The author believes that the limit is at about sixteen stories, regardless of the size of the lot, and that as the lot decreases in size the height should decrease. The total height of the building is influenced by the height of each story, which should generally be one-half of the depth of the rooms, but never less than 9 feet for the office floors and 12 to 15 feet for the first and second floors. If an excessive height is given to the story, the light is not materially improved, and the cost of the building and of the service of the building are both needlessly increased.

Windows. The windows should occupy an area of from 30 to 50 per cent of the entire area of the exterior walls of the office, being so placed that the top will be no more than 1 foot below the ceiling and practically square-headed. The usual practice is to hang the windows on pulleys and weights, dividing the sash into two parts, with the provision made, in the best practice, to rotate the sash in the frame, thus affording double the opening for ventilation in the summer, and permitting the outside of the glass to be cleaned without danger. Side-pivoted and casement sash are also used to a certain extent. They should be so arranged as to be easily cleaned. Generally, about 35 per cent of window surface in the wall gives a very efficient light. Very large glass surfaces should be avoided in cold climates as the glass radiates externally, the heat of the interior producing the effect of a draught which is difficult to neutralize. Bay windows are used in certain localities and seem to meet the approval of the tenant, but are objectionable on the score of cost, additional fire risk, and are not always efficient in adding to the rentable area of the office. They are always difficult of satisfactory architectural treatment. The reveals of the windows are generally fixed by architectural considerations; any portion of them not required for effect should be placed inside of the windows, and the area of the room increased by reducing the thickness of the wall underneath the window as much as practicable.

Elevators should all be grouped at one point at the end of a court. Good service requires that a car shall be in front of a landing going in each direction every forty seconds. The height of building and speed of car fixes the number, and the number of offices per floor fixes the size. The car should be at least 5 × 5 feet and should not exceed 7 × 7 feet. Some form of automatic indicator operating within 8 feet of a landing must be used in high-speed service to indicate the requirements of passengers on landings. The division of the cars into way and express, or into sections, one section serving the lower portion of the building and the other the upper, is one that on its face seems to be good; but practically it is open to objection as causing delay and congestion at the bottom landing. In buildings of reasonable height this question does not arise.

Stairs are used simply for communication from one floor to another and for emergencies. They should be made entirely of masonry and iron without winders, and if more than 4 feet wide should have a hand rail on each side. They should be protected by their position so as to remain free from flames and smoke in case of fire.

Trimming. The preference seems to be generally for wood floors in the offices, though ground cork on plastic asbestos may soon be in general use; mosaics or marbles in the halls, corridors, and toilets; wood trimming to the windows and doors on the office side, and in the best buildings fireproof, or wood covered with sheet metal on the corridor side. Communicating doors between offices may be fireproof or not, depending upon the character of the building and funds available. The windows, as before mentioned, may be double hung, or may be made casement windows, opening out, there being two sashes in the frames. The doors should always have transoms over them for ventilation. Occasionally the entire upper half of the corridor partition is made with sash and frames. This is objectionable on the score of fire risk, and because in many offices the space is required for bookcases, pictures, large maps, etc. Fireplaces are sometimes placed in the office, but are objectionable, occupying valuable room, thereby decreasing the rental value of the office. In localities where the size of the lot occupied by the building has resulted in very deep offices, fireproof vaults have been introduced, simply to use up the room, as safes are generally preferred. Generally, conveniences of this character which are built in the room are likely to meet with the approval of but a restricted number of tenants, and may profitably be omitted.

Toilets. General toilets for the use of the buildings should be provided on each floor where the number of offices served is large, or where the lot is 100×100 feet or larger. Where the lot is smaller the toilets should be grouped on two floors, and a considerable space devoted to them. All of the closets should be in any case open for the general use of the tenants. Hot and cold water should be supplied to the washbasins, and if the building is of very high grade, cooled and filtered drinking water may also be supplied. All toilet compartments and floors should be of marble, with the compartment-slab lifted at least 8 inches above the general floor level. There should be a marble wainscot 6 feet high. Side walls and ceilings above the marble should be finished in enamelled paint or thin tiles, so that every portion can be washed. The toilets must be placed so as to have one window opening to the outer air and preferably two. Toilets should be proportioned on the basis of one water-closet for every five offices, one washbasin and one urinal for each two closets. Every office should also be provided with a washbasin near the rear, supplied with cold water. All of the fixtures should be of the most approved sanitary form with brass fittings, entirely open, and should be served with plumbing pipe of the most approved form. (See Plumbing.) Where toilets are grouped on two floors, it is necessary to provide at least one washbasin and closet for emergency use on each floor.

Heating should be direct radiation, low pressure steam, with the radiators placed in front of the windows with their tops below the sills. Experience has been had with indirect hot air heating, direct-indirect heating, and various modifications of both, on both large and small scales, and found unsatisfactory. In some cases the steam pipes are concealed in chases in the walls, and in other cases they are left exposed. In some cases the supply is by the usual two-pipe system, and in others by a one-pipe system. In the author's experience, exposed pipes of the one-pipe system for buildings of moderate height are satisfactory. Where buildings are very high the supply mains become so large as to be unsightly and should be hidden. (See Engine Room; Warming.)

Artificial lighting is almost exclusively by means of incandescent electric lights throughout the entire building. Gas is sometimes installed as a reserve for general illumination, and sometimes installed only in the hallways. The illumination of the entrance halls and other portions of the building may be by rows of small lamps at or above the cornices, lighting by means of reflected rays principally, or by clusters of light at the ceiling, shaded on the under side with ground glass. In special places the enclosed arc lamps are used to advantage. All of the ceiling outlets in the public places should be controlled by a switch operated by a key. In buildings operating all night it is economy to run special circuits for hall lights, one for general illumination and the other for the night lights. The lighting of the office should be by means of a small ceiling or lighting outlet, the fixture being placed near the ceiling and controlled by a switch at the entrance door. The desk illumination is provided for by means of a circuit running entirely around the exterior wall of the building in the baseboard or picture moulding, which should be formed with wire channels to act as a moulding, permitting branches to be taken off to any of the side walls desired, bracket fixtures or unsightly cord pendents being entirely avoided. Each floor should be provided with a separate riser controlled by an independent switch in the engine room, placing the lighting of the building under the control of the engineer. (See Lighting, Electric.)

Telephones. Provision should be made for the introduction of the telephone and messenger calls to every office unit, providing one or more cable ways through the building, from which telephones can be extended through the mouldings in the base.

Mechanical Plant. The building should be entirely self-contained, the most economical operation resulting from the combination of good boilers, good engines and generators, economical pumps, exhaust steam heating, and above all a competent chief engineer.

                  — GEORGE HILL.

(For the construction of the high modern office building see Fireproofing; Foundation; Iron Construction; Wind Pressure. See also Legislation.)

OFFSET. Distance or dimension taken perpendicularly to a main line or direction; the amount of a comparatively slight projection measured or considered as at right angles to the main structure or surface. Hence, where such a projection is caused horizontally by a diminution of the thickness of a wall, the surface or piece forming the top of the projecting portion. The several diminutions in horizontal size of a buttress, in Gothic architecture, are properly offsets, but are commonly spoken of as weatherings, which term applies, properly, to the exposed pieces of stone. .

O. G. Same as Ogee (adj. and noun); a common trade term.

O. G. DOOR. A form of stock door common in parts of the United States, so called because made with stock mouldings having an ogee section.

OGEE. A double or S curve; applied especially to the profile of a moulding.

Reversed Ogee. An ogee when used as an overhanging profile convex above and concave below; so designated from association with Cyma Reversa, which is an ogee so placed.

OGIVALE. In French, characterized by the use of the Ogive; the term being applied especially to Gothic architecture, and signifying often merely pointed in style, or having pointed arches. By extension, having a form resembling in outline a pointed arch. (See Ogive.)

OGIVE. In French, properly, one of the diagonal ribs in a Gothic vault. This significance has been maintained by Viollet-le-Duc (*Dict. Archit.*, s. v. *Ogive*), who points out that the term *croix d'augives* meant in the fourteenth century a pair of diagonal ribs. As, however, the term itself carried the idea of curves meeting one another, and as the resulting form which struck the eye was always like that of the pointed arch, it resulted that the term has been generally applied in French writing to an arch made up of two circular curves meeting in a point. Even so accurate and so recent a writer as Auguste Choisy uses the terms *ogive* and *ogival* as applied to a pointed arch. The term seems to be as well established as is the adjective Gothic itself, as qualifying the pointed architecture of the Middle Ages.

OGNABENE, ANDREA; goldsmith and sculptor.

The son of Jacopo, a goldsmith of Pistoja. In 1316 he made the bas-reliefs from the life of Christ in the altar of S. Jacopo at Pistoja signed PER ME ANDREAM IACOBI OGNABENIS AVRIFICEM DE PISTORIO. This famous altar was begun in 1287, continued by Ognabene in 1316, by Giglio in 1353, by Piero of Florence in 1357, and by Leonardo di Giovanni in 1371.

Marcel Reymond, *La Sculpture Florentine*; Alfred Darcel, *Les Autels de Pistoia et de Florence*.

OHLMULLER, DANIEL JOSEPH; architect; b. Jan. 10, 1791; d. April 22, 1839.

A pupil of Karl von Fischer (see Fischer, Karl von). He assisted Klenze (see Klenze)

on the *Glyptothek* in Munich, and built the brick Gothic church in the Au suburb of the same city.

Seubert, *Künstler-lexicon*.

OILET. Same as Eyelet.

OIL PAINTING. That painting which is done with colours mixed with oil — usually linseed oil, with or without a drier.

Although oil painting is mentioned by the monk Theophilus (eleventh century?) and Cennino Cennini, who interprets the methods of the fourteenth and early fifteenth centuries, and though it may have been employed occasionally as a medium for mural painting, both in mediæval and early Renaissance times, certainly its general use does not antedate the great Venetians. Leonardo da Vinci tried it with disastrous results in his "Last Supper," and Sebastian del Piombo was constantly advocating its use, though he failed to convert either Michelangelo or Raphael, who preferred the fresco process.

Oil paintings invariably darken with age, for the following reasons: *Oil* is composed of an oil acid linked with glycerine ether. *Soap* is a compound of an oil acid linked with alkalies or oxides, such as potash, soda, lime, lead, zinc, iron, etc. The white lead used by painters is a strong soap maker; zinc white and the iron oxides less so. While it seems to be certain that soap making, either by the pigment itself with the linseed oil, or by the addition of a drier, improves the solidity and durability of paint, it is equally certain that all soap making has a tendency to redden or yellow. Oil painting cannot be used on fresh plaster, because the caustic lime combines with oil to make an excess of soap which, if the plaster be very wet, will run down the wall together with the paint. But even when the plaster is dry, the wall should be protected by several coats of paint (oil being entirely omitted or reduced to a minimum), or other intervening material, such as canvas (as explained below), if it is to receive oil pictures; for dry plaster (carbonate of lime, or chalk, with sand) changes some pigments, especially if these be exposed to any dampness, which is almost inevitable. Chalk with white lead or zinc white easily produces a yellowish white when mixed with oil. Moreover, oil is saponified by wet chalk. The yellowing of oil is not caused by soap making alone; it is also caused by want of light. The less light there is, the yellower and darker oil-mixed pigments grow with time. The cure — if there be any — is sunlight. No more oil should be used than is absolutely necessary — since oil, especially in combination with white lead, is a darkening agent. Sometimes it happens that decorative conditions exact rich, low-toned pictures, and under such circumstances oil would prove an excellent medium, the lowering of the tone with time

PLATE II

OBSERVATORY AT WILLIAMS BAY, WISCONSIN; VIEW FROM THE SOUTHWEST

(See the figures in the text and Plate I)

OPEN TIMBER ROOF, MIDDLE TEMPLE HALL, LONDON

being of no import. Frequently the painting is not executed on the wall itself, but on canvas, and afterward transferred to the wall. Occasionally this canvas is attached to the wall by means of a stretcher. If the canvas be large this method is not to be recommended, owing to the shrinkage and expansion of the canvas. The process called "marouflage" is preferable, the painted canvas being laid in a bed of white lead, mixed with boiled oil, dammar varnish, and a drier, previously applied to the wall. Even to this process there are objections. The surface of the canvas is never quite so flat as the painted plaster would be, and frequently there are awkward joints. Nor can the canvas be applied to concave or convex surfaces. Moreover, it is probable that the great amount of oil with which the white lead is mixed will, sooner or later, darken the superimposed picture. To obviate this source of danger, oil might be omitted and the white lead mixed with some such medium as dammar varnish. Glue should not be used, if there be any exposure to dampness.

The surface of the finished oil painting is apt to shine in spots. To prevent this, turpentine, or better still, turpentine and wax, should be freely added to the colours with which the picture is painted, or a final coat of wax and turpentine be applied.

— FREDERIC CROWNINSHIELD.

OKTASTYLOS. An octastyle building (Vitruvius).

OLD COLONIAL ARCHITECTURE. (See Colonial Architecture; United States, Architecture of, § II.)

OLIVIERI, PIETRO PAOLO; architect and sculptor; b. 1555; d. 1599.

During the reign of Clement VIII. (Pope 1592–1605) he built the great altar of the transept of the church of S. Giovanni in Laterano, Rome. In 1591 he began the church of S. Andrea della Valle, Rome. The nave was completed by Carlo Maderna (see Maderna). The façade is later. He made the monument of Gregory XI. in the church of S. Francesca Romana.

Gurlitt, *Geschichte des Barockstiles in Italien;* Ebe, *Spät-Renaissance.*

OMODEO (AMADEO), GIOVANNI ANTONIO; architect and sculptor; b. 1447; d. Aug. 17, 1522.

Antonio was born near the Certosa at Pavia, and was attached to the works at that building at the age of nineteen with his brother Protasio. About 1470–1471 he built the chapel of the Colleoni at the church of S. Maria Maggiore in Bergamo. He designed also the monuments in this chapel to Bartolommeo Colleoni and his daughter Medea. About 1478 he returned to Pavia, and in 1490 succeeded Guiniforte Solari (see Solari, G.) as architect of the Certosa.

(For origin of this building, see Bernardo da Venezia.) The façade of the Certosa was carried out by himself, his associates, Benedetto Briosco (see Briosco, B.), the Mantegazza (see Mantegazza), and about thirty others whose names are known. He was at the same time supervising architect of the cathedral of Pavia. From 1499 to 1508, with Giovanni Jacopo Dolcebuono, he directed the work on the central tower of the cathedral of Milan, which they carried to the summit of the octagon.

Calvi, *Notizie;* Calvi, *La Fondazione del Tempio della Certosa;* Müntz, *Renaissance;* Perkins, *Tuscan Sculptors.*

ONOFRIO DI LA CAVA; architect.

He built the aqueduct of Ragusa, Dalmatia, and in 1435 began the Palazzo del Rettore.

OOLITE. Oölitic limestone. A limestone composed mainly of small concretionary granules of lime carbonate, and resembling the eggs, or roe, of fish. Example, Bedford Oölite.

OPAION. *A.* In Greco-Roman archæology, an opening, as in a roof, for smoke to escape.

B. In Greek architecture, same as Lacunar, *B.* This is the Greek term corresponding to *lacunarium* in Latin.

OPEN–TIMBERED (adj.). Having the timberwork exposed; having the wooden framework not concealed by sheathing, plaster, or other covering. (For open-timbered roofs, see Wood Construction, Part I.)

OPERA DEL DUOMO. The workshop of a cathedral; a term common in Italian as describing a building in which certain necessary work is or has been done in connection with a cathedral, and in which important models, historical documents, and the like are sometimes preserved.

OPERA HOUSE. A building intended primarily for the public performance of operas, but hardly to be distinguished architecturally from the Theatre.

OPHITES. *Lapis ophites.* (See Serpentine.)

OPISTHODOMOS. In Grecian archæology, a back or subordinate room or porch: in two general senses : —

A. Same as Epinaos.

B. A smaller division of the whole naos or cella; the treasury; the back room of the temple, sometimes opening into the larger room, sometimes opening only upon a back portico, which is then the epinaos.

OPPEN–OORDT. (See Oppenort.)

OPPENORT (OPPEN–OORDT), GILLES MARIE; architect, decorator, and engraver; b. July 27, 1672 (at Paris); d. March 13, 1742.

Gilles Marie was the son of Cander Johan Oppen Oordt from the province of Guildres in Holland, an *ébéniste* (worker in fine woods) who appears frequently in the accounts of Jules Hardouin-Mansart (see Hardouin-Mansart. J.)

and a *pensionnaire* of the king at Rome. Oppenort was *directeur général des bâtiments et jardins* of the Duke of Orléans, then regent. In 1719 he continued the construction of the church of S. Sulpice, Paris, which had been discontinued since 1675. He completed the church except the portal, which was added by Servandoni (see Servandoni). He built the great altar of S. Sulpice. Oppenort was one of the chief decorators engaged in developing the style associated with the reign of Louis XV. His principal collection of engravings, *Œuvres de Gille Marie Oppenort contenant différents fragments d'architecture et d'ornemens*, has been reproduced in facsimile (1 vol. 4to., Paris, 1888).

Mariette, *Abecedario;* Guilmard, *Les maîtres ornementistes;* Guiffrey, *Comptes de Louis XIV.;* Lance, *Dictionnaire;* Lazare, *Dictionnaire des rues de Paris.*

OPSTAL (OBSTAL), GÉRARD VAN; sculptor; b. 1604 (at Antwerp, Belgium); d. 1668.

He began the practice of his profession in Flanders, and was called to France by Richelieu in 1630. He executed decorative sculpture at the Louvre, Tuileries, Hôtel Carnavalet, the portal of the hospital of La Salpêtrière, the Palais Royale, the Palais de Justice, and the Hotel Lambert, all in Paris. He held the office of *sculpteur ordinaire des bâtiments du roi.*

Lami, *Dictionnaire des sculpteurs français;* Guiffrey, *Comptes de Louis XIV.*

OPTICAL CORRECTION. In architecture, an expedient resorted to for the purpose of correcting a disagreeable appearance of certain lines or masses; thus, a perfectly horizontal beam or girder is apt to look as if it sagged downward in the middle, and an optical correction would be the giving to this beam a camber. Many refinements in design (see Refinements in Design) in ancient and mediæval architecture have been assumed too hastily to be mere attempts at optical correction, but many of them are of this character.

OPUS. In Latin, Work, in the sense of labour or the results of labour; the common term used in composition in the modern European languages for masonry, embroidery, and decorative work of different kinds. Some of these compound terms are taken direct from classical authors, and are applied without a perfect knowledge of the subject to pieces of work left us by antiquity. The piece of work exists, the name is found in a classical author; but it is often uncertain whether our modern application of the given name to the given piece of work is accurate. This is peculiarly the case with the terms borrowed from Vitruvius (II., 8, and elsewhere), whose extremely cursory and undetailed descriptions leave his precise meaning uncertain in too many instances. (See the titles

below; see also Classic Architecture; Masonry; Mosaic; Roman Imperial Architecture.)

OPUS ALEXANDRINUM. (See Mosaic.)

OPUS ANTIQUUM. Same as Opus Incertum.

OPUS GRÆCANICUM. Work done in the Greek manner; apparently a pavement, as of mosaic, or an inlay of marble, supposed to resemble in pattern or in workmanship the work done by the Greeks.

OPUS INCERTUM. Roman masonry, as that of walls, the surface of which displays irregularly placed stones of different sizes, or even bands or other parts of brickwork. The signification appears to be limited to the facework of a wall. (See below Opus Reticulatum; Opus Spicatum; Opus Testaceum.)

OPUS INTERRASILE. Incised ornament; made either by cutting away the pattern and leaving the ground, or by cutting away the ground and leaving the pattern in low relief.

OPUS ISODOMUM. Roman masonry done with regular courses. (See Isodomum.)

OPUS LATERICIUM (LATERITIUM). Masonry of tiles, or faced with tiles. (Compare Opus Testaceum.)

OPUS LITHOSTRATUM. (See Mosaic.)

OPUS MUSIVUM. Same as Mosaic.

OPUS PSEUDISODOMUM. In Roman masonry, a kind of stonework or ashlar in which, while the stones of each course were alike, they differed from those of other courses in respect to height, length, or thickness, so that while continuous horizontal joints were maintained, such joints were not necessarily the same distance apart in the wall. (See Opus Isodomum.)

OPUS RETICULATUM. Roman masonry faced with squared pieces of stone, usually very small, and set anglewise so as to cover the face of a wall, as it were with a net of joints crossing each other at right angles and making an angle of forty-five degrees with the perpendicular. (Compare what is said under Opus Incertum.)

OPUS SECTILE. (See Mosaic.)

OPUS SIGNINUM. Plaster or stucco stated to have been made of fragments of pottery ground up with lime; sometimes, as in Pompeii, used for floor covering, which much resembles Terrazzo Veneziano. The name appears to be derived from the town of Signia in Latium.

OPUS SPICATUM. Masonry faced with stones or tile which are arranged in herringbone fashion or in a similar pattern, producing sharp points or angles. (See what is said above under Opus Incertum.) The adjective *spicatus*, signifying having spikes or ears as of wheat, etc., is applicable to other surfaces than those of a wall. Thus, *testacea spicata* is a pavement laid herringbone fashion.

OPUS TECTORIUM. In Roman building, a kind of stucco used to cover walls in three or four coats, the finishing coat being practically an artificial marble usually polished to a hard surface to receive paintings. The distinction between this and Opus Signinum is not clear (Middleton).

OPUS TESSELATUM. (See Mosaic.)

OPUS TESTACEUM. Masonry faced with tiles. This term, like Opus Incertum and others given above, refers to the face of a wall only, the mass or body of the wall not being considered.

OPUS VERMICULATUM. (See Mosaic.)

ORANGERIE; ORANGERY. A building of the nature of a cold greenhouse (see Greenhouse) used for the storage in winter of ornamental trees in tubs. The frequent employ of orange trees in this way in connection with public and private palaces has caused the use of the term for permanent houses of the sort, which are sometimes of considerable architectural importance. The Luxembourg collection of paintings and sculpture is now housed in the orangerie of the palace, which has received some modifications for the purpose.

ORATORY. *A.* Same as Domestic Chapel (which see under Chapel).

B. A small chapel of any sort, more particularly one intended for solitary devotion ; a place of prayer and not a place for liturgical celebration of any sort. An oratory was often erected as a memorial. At places where it was supposed that a miracle had taken place, or upon the site of the cell or other habitation of a sainted personage, an oratory was often raised, and most of these were extremely simple structures. Some few were of architectural importance. The chapel of a fortress, or a secondary or minor chapel within its walls, is often called an oratory. — R. S.

ORBAIS, JEAN D'; architect.

His name and image were in the Labyrinth of the cathedral at Reims (destroyed 1779).

ORBAY, FRANÇOIS D'; architect; b. 1634; d. 1697.

Son-in-law and pupil of Levau. He worked under the direction of the latter upon the Collège Mazarin, now the Palais de l'Institut (see Institut), and later upon the Louvre. He built other important buildings in Paris, and designed the Porte Peyrou at Montpellier (Hérault), a memorial arch, built 1690–1710, in honour of Louis XIV., and especially of the Revocation of the Edict of Nantes.

ORCAGNA (ANDREA DI CIONE); painter, mosaicist, sculptor, architect, and poet; b. about 1308 (Vasari) ; d. about 1369.

The name Orcagna is an abbreviation for Arcagnuolo. Orcagna is, after Giotto (see Giotto), the greatest Florentine master of the fourteenth century. He was, according to Vasari, a pupil of Andrea Pisano (see Andrea da Pisa), and doubtless came directly under the influence

of Giotto. In 1368 he appears as a member of the Compagnia di San Luca. In 1357 Orcagna competed unsuccessfully with Francesco Talenti for the capitals of the piers at the Duomo, Florence. In the same year he finished the frescoes, including the paradise, of the Strozzi chapel at S. Maria Novella, Florence. Between 1349 and 1359 he was *capomaestro* of Or S. Michele, Florence, and executed the only work of architecture and sculpture which can with certainty be ascribed to him, the tabernacle constructed to contain a miracleworking picture ascribed by Milanesi to Bernardo Daddi. The balustrade was added in 1366 by the goldsmith Piero di Migliore. Orcagna was called in 1359 to Orvieto, where he worked on the mosaics of the façade of the Duomo until Sept. 12, 1362. Vasari probably confuses Andrea di Cione with Benci di Cione (see Benci di Cione) when he ascribes the Loggia dei Lanzi to Orcagna. (See Talenti, Simone.) Orcagna died seven or eight years before this building was begun.

Karl Frey, *Loggia dei Lanzi;* Castellazzi, *Or San Michele;* Luigi Fumi, *Duomo di Orvieto;* Crowe and Cavalcaselle, *Painting in Italy;* Vasari, Milanesi ed. ; Vasari, Blashfield-Hopkins ed. ; Reymond, *Sculpture Florentine;* Perkins, *Tuscan Sculptors.*

ORCHESTRA. *A.* Originally, in a Greek theatre, the place occupied by the dancers and chorus about the altar of Dionysos, and later the circular space reserved for that purpose between the auditorium and the proscenium.

B. In the Roman theatre, a semicircular level space between the stage and the first semicircular rows of seats, reserved for senators and other distinguished spectators.

C. In a modern theatre, music hall, and the like, the space reserved for the musicians.

D. In the United States, by extension from the last definition, the main floor of a theatre or similar place of entertainment. A recent substitute for Parquet. (Compare definition *B* above.) — D. N. B. S.

ORCHYARDE; architect.

Orchyarde built Magdalen College, Oxford, which was founded by Waynflete, Bishop of Winchester, in 1448.

Ackerman, *History of Oxford University.*

ORDER. Primarily, a row, a course of stones, a rank of similar objects. Hence, in architectural practice, two significations, which, though apparently very different, are akin.

A. In masonry, a course of stones, one ring of an arch or the like, considered as part of a larger structure. Especially, in arcuated building, such as the Romanesque of the north of Europe, one ring of an arch which consists of several rings of different thicknesses, horizontally. In some cases there are three or four such rings, but the arrangement of two is more common. A section through the completed arch in such a case is like a double flight of steps, the intrados being much narrower than the extrados, and the arch thickening upward or outward with the offset from each order to the one next above or outside of it.

B. The columns with their entablature of any building; but especially of Greek, Greco-Roman, or neoclassic architecture. In this sense, the term is often limited to a single shaft with its appurtenances as above; for the distinction be-

established five orders, namely: the three above named; the Tuscan, which to Vitruvius would have seemed a plain form of Doric and nothing more; and the Composite, which to the Roman Imperial builders must have seemed merely one of the many varieties which the Corinthian style had to undergo. Neither the classical nor the post-Renaissance writers speak of the Grecian

ORDER, FIG. 1: GRECIAN DORIC; THAT OF THE SO-CALLED TEMPLE OF NEPTUNE AT PÆSTUM.

tween one order and another is marked by the details of one such unit of a colonnade. The orders known to Vitruvius (the only writer on architecture of classical times whose works have survived) are three: Doric, by which he means that Roman style of column and entablature which is found in a few Italian buildings; Ionic, by which he means the Roman Ionic as seen in buildings of his time, which have now disappeared, but which may have been of a style very similar to that of Greece; and the Corinthian. The writers of the sixteenth century

Doric, although the buildings at Pæstum must have been known to the Roman builders, and although it is very different from the Roman Doric. Modern designers in some modifications of the classical styles have made many attempts at designing new orders, and some of these have been effective; but none has been perpetuated or modified by later designers. (See Columnar Architecture; Composite; Corinthian; Doric; Grecian Architecture; Greco-Roman Architecture; Ionic; Neoclassic Architecture; Roman Imperial Architecture; Tuscan Architecture.) — R. S.

Colossal Order. One of a height greatly beyond that of one story of the building within; especially one of nearly the whole height of the building. It has often been stated that this device, unknown to antiquity, tiers of windows between the antique columns and beneath the original entablature. This is a hasty conclusion, as examples existed at an earlier epoch. An early instance is in the two similar fronts of the museum buildings on the

ORDER: GRECIAN DORIC; THAT OF THE PARTHENON: HAVING THE ENTABLATURE MUCH LESS HIGH AND THE ECHINUS MUCH LESS SPREADING, IN PROPORTION, THAN THOSE AT PAESTUM.

orignated in the modern Dogana (custom house) of the city of Rome, which was built late in the seventeenth century on the foundations of an ancient temple, generally called Temple of Neptune, and which has its three Campidoglio (see Capitoline Museum, under Museum; Palace of the Conservators); and the largest one known, that of S. Peter's church at Rome, is hardly later (1550–1580). It was much used in the eighteenth century.

By extension, an order occupying nearly the whole height of a one-story building, if large and high.

Persian Order. One distinguished by the use of draped male statues in the place of columns. The term is found in Vitruvius, I., 1, and the author explains that the victory of the *proportions en architecture;* Normand, *Nouveau parallèle des ordres d'architecture des Grecs, des Romains et des auteurs modernes;* Mauch (German translation of preceding).

ORDER ABOVE ORDER. (See Superimposition.)

ORGAGNIA. (See Orcagna.)

ORGAN. A musical instrument in which sound is produced by the vibration of the air in pipes of wood and metal, and which is played by the keys of a keyboard opening and shutting valves of these pipes. The simplest form of this is the instrument carried in the hand or on

ORDER, IN SENSE *A*: ARCH OF TWO ORDERS, EACH HAVING ITS CARVED HOOD MOULDING, THE VOUSSOIRS OF THE SUPERIOR ORDER OF TWO COLOURS. PISA CATHEDRAL.

ORDER, IN SENSE *A*: LOWER ARCHES OF TWO ORDERS, THE UPPER ORDER HEAVILY MOULDED; UPPER ARCHES OF THREE ORDERS; THE GREAT ARCHES CARRYING THE TOWER OF TWO ORDERS; JEDBURGH ABBEY, SCOTLAND.

the left arm, and played on by the fingers of the right hand, as often seen in ancient paintings. The church organ, as developed in modern times, is a group of instruments rather than a single one, and each group of pipes and stops is often called an organ, separately, and usually with some distinctive epithet, as the swell organ, the solo organ, and the like, the term "great organ" being given to the principal one of these groups, which is generally placed in the middle. The architectural arrangement of a church organ is usually made by placing it in a large wooden case with openings in all its sides and entirely

Lacedemonians over the Persians at Platæa led to the erection (probably at Sparta) of a building called the Persian portico, the roof being supported by richly costumed statues of the barbarians. (See Atlantes; Caryatid; Telamon.)

Chipiez, *Histoire critique des origines et de la formation des ordres Grecs;* Fauré, *Théorie des* open at top ; but the attempt to fit an organ into such a case is often accompanied by a great amount of unnecessary work, the putting up of sham pipes to form symmetrical groups with those real ones which are visible, and the completion of a costly edifice, for the greater part of which there is no utility. Another plan is to arrange the different groups in an organ chamber or organ loft, with strict, or very close, reference to their musical purpose and their connection with the keyboard, and partially to conceal the whole by a screen, which may be as decorative as desired and wholly in accordance with the architecture of the church. This screen, if low, need not even be pierced or opened ; or it may fill the whole openings of an archway, or the like, between the organ chamber and the church proper with tracery and pierced carved work. (See the following terms.) — R. S.

ORGAN CHAMBER. That room or space in which the organ is placed ; often, in a church, a separate structure between the choir and a transept, or beside the choir, with a large open archway between. It is often better, for the musical effect, that the organ should stand almost free under the roof of the church, in which case the space screened off to hold the actual instrument is hardly called the organ chamber. (See Organ ; Organ Gallery.)

ORGAN GALLERY. In many churches, where the organ is placed high above the floor, an upper floor with a parapet, or screen, fronting toward the church, and arranged to receive the organ. It is often extended so as to afford place for the singers as well.

ORGANI, ANDREA DEGLI (DA MODENA) ; architect.

The first architect (ingegnere) employed on the cathedral of Milan (begun 1386). His name appears in a memorandum of Jan. 15, 1387. April 13 he is mentioned as ingegnerio domini (ducal engineer). In October of this year he was appointed to superintend the labourers at the cathedral. In a letter dated Jan. 3, 1400, of the Duke Gian Galeazzo Visconti, he is mentioned as the father of Filippino degli Organi (see Organi, F. degli).

Boito, Duomo di Milano ; Annali del Duomo.

ORGANI, FILIPPINO DEGLI (DA MODENA) ; architect and sculptor ; d. March, 1450.

Son of Andrea degli Organi (see Organi, A. degli). He is first mentioned in a letter of the Duke Gian Galeazzo Visconti, dated Jan. 3, 1400. He was at this time appointed to a position on the force employed in the construction of the cathedral of Milan, and Oct. 12, 1404, became a regular architect (ingegnere) under the direction of Marco da Carona. Sept. 16, 1410, he served on the commission which determined the form of the vaulting and flying buttresses. The upper part of the cathedral was built from the drawings which he made

at this time (secundum designamentum magistri Filippini). In 1417 Filippino became chief architect, and retained that position until 1448. He made the monument of Marco Carelli (now in the nave of the cathedral), probably with the assistance of Jacopino Tradate.

Boito, Duomo di Milano ; Annali del Duomo.

ORGAN LOFT. Same as Organ Gallery.

ORGAN SCREEN. *A.* In England, rarely, a Rood Screen upon which the organ has been placed.

B. An ornamental screen of any sort separating the organ chamber from the body of the church. (See Organ.)

ORIEL. A bay window ; especially, one in an upper story, and overhanging ; carried on brackets or corbels, or upon an engaged column or pier, from which usually a corbelled structure is carried up to the floor of the oriel. This distinction is the one usually made ; but in older writers the word is used for bay windows even of the largest and most massive sort. (Cuts, cols. 35, 36.)

ORIENTATION. Primarily, the state of one who faces, or of a building which is turned, toward the east ; hence, in architecture : —

A. The placing of churches so that the priest at the altar may face the east while he is celebrating Mass. It is thought that in the early days of the Church the priest, in some parts of the Roman Empire, stood on the other side of the altar from the worshippers, and that therefore the body of the church was placed east of the sanctuary ; but that when the priest's position was changed so that he turned his back to the worshippers, then the church also was changed, with its main entrance toward the west and its sanctuary toward the east. (See Apse ; Chancel ; Chevet ; Choir ; Sanctuary.) The practice of orientation in churches is by no means universal ; thus, in Italy, it is much less observed than in the north of Europe. The great church of S. Peter's at Rome, built upon the site of the early basilica, has its narthex at the east end and its sanctuary at the west.

B. The placing of any building with reference, or apparent reference, to any special point of the compass ; thus, the Greek temples have an orientation which involves the placing of the main entrance toward the east, or approximately so ; the larger pyramids of Egypt have their entrances carefully placed in a given special direction, and it is thought that in all these cases the rising point of a certain star, or some as yet unknown and perhaps misunderstood necessity, has determined these forms of orientation. In this sense the term is used very loosely, as when it is said that the builders of Egyptian temples had little care for exact orientation, i.e. placed their buildings on axes not parallel with one another. (See Axis, B. ; En Axe, under Axe.)

— R. S.

ORIEL AT EAST END OF THE CHAPEL, PRUDHOE CASTLE,
NORTHUMBERLAND. PLAN.

ORIEL: SEE THE PLAN, ABOVE.

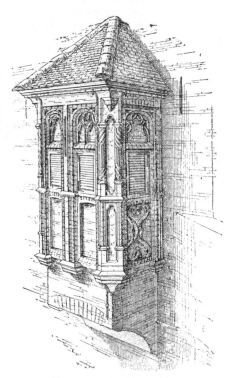

ORIEL, FRONT OF A HOUSE IN BRUGES; c. 1515.

35

ORIEL FORMING CHAPEL; OLD TOWN HALL, PRAGUE, BOHEMIA.

36

ORILLON. Same as Crosset.

ORLE; **ORLET**. A narrow band, or series of small members, or units, taking the form of a border, hence a fillet forming an edging or border. Specifically, a fillet beneath the ovolo of a capital. (See Cincture.)

ORNAMENT. That which is added to a structure of any kind for decorative purposes alone. The term is distinguished from Decoration (see that term and Decorative Art), because denoting something wholly apart from the necessary structure, which structure may be highly decorative, but not ornamental.

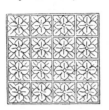

ORNAMENT IN LOW RELIEF. GOTHIC SCULPTURE.

Sculpture in the form of Basrelief (see that term; also Arabesque; Diaper; Relief), painting in the form of patterns when used as a border, diaper, frieze, or the like (see those terms), mouldings and modifications of mouldings (see Billet Moulding; Nailhead Moulding; Dentil; Venetian Dentil), are all spoken of as ornament, rather in contradistinction to representative statuary and painting. Thus, the statues set upon the geison and showing against the tympanum of a Greek temple, or those upon the Bernini colonnade at Rome, showing against the sky, are hardly called ornament; but the half figures in an arabesque, however realistic in treatment, are parts of a piece of ornament. — R. S.

ORNAMENT: ENGLISH ROMANESQUE SCULPTURE; THE SPACES OF AN ARCADE FILLED ALTERNATELY WITH A FIGURE AND A PANEL OF SCROLL-WORK.

ORSENIGO, SIMONE DA. (See Simone da Orsenigo.)

ORSINI, GIORGIO (DA SEBENICO); architect and sculptor.

Giorgio appears to have been born at Zara, Dalmatia. His family was a branch of the noble Roman house of Orsini. April 23, 1441,

ORNAMENT CARVED IN RELIEF; BETOURSA, SYRIA; 5TH CENTURY.

he superseded Antonio di Pietro Paolo (see Antonio di Pietro Paolo) as architect of the great cathedral of Sebenico, Dalmatia (see Dalmatia and illustration). This building is an important example of the transition from the Gothic style to the Renaissance. In 1444 Orsini built a chapel in the church of S. Rainerio at Spalato, Dalmatia, and in 1448 the Gothic altar of S. Anastasio in the cathedral of that city. Between 1451 and 1459 he built the Loggia dei Mercanti and the façade of S. Francesco della Scala at Ancona in Italy. June, 1464, he was associated with Michelozzo Michelozzi (see Michelozzi) in the reconstruction of the Palazzo del Rettore at Ragusa. In 1470 Giorgio was sent on a special mission to Rome. In his contract with the cathedral authorities at Sebenico he was bound to do some of the carving with his own hand. The door of his house at Sebenico, with the bear of the Orsini carved on the lintel, is still in existence.

Pietro Gianuzzi, *Giorgio da Sebenico;* Fosca, *Cattedrale di Sebenico;* Jackson, *Dalmatia.*

ORTHOSTYLE. Arranged in a straight row, as columns; rare, but used in such phrases as an orthostyle plan, or the like.

OSSATURE. In French, the skeleton or framework of any structure; hence, in English, such a framework when of a more elaborate kind, as the steel cage construction of modern buildings.

OSSUARY. A place for the deposit and preservation of the bones of the dead; especially a building for the safe keeping of bones after the desiccation of the flesh, or of such as are found in excavating new graves in a cemetery. (See Charnel House.)

Overdoor Panel; Modern Parisian Work, in Louis XIV. Style.

OSTENSORE, LUCIANO. (See Luciano da Laurana.)

OUBLIETTE. In mediæval times, a pit or shaft constructed or excavated in the masonry or foundation of a castle, or similar building, and in which prisoners were confined as in the most hopeless form of dungeon, or into which their bodies were thrown.

OUNDY. Wavy, or, by extension, zigzag; said of a moulding, a string course, or the like.

OURADOU, MAURICE AUGUSTIN GABRIEL; architect; b. July 24, 1822 (at Paris); d. June 27, 1884.

Ouradou was a pupil of Viollet-le-Duc (see Viollet-le-Duc), whose daughter he married. He entered the *École des Beaux Arts* in 1845. After leaving the school he was appointed inspector of the works at the cathedral of Paris and of the château of Pierrefonds. He was made architect of the diocese of Châlons in association with Eugène Millet (see Millet), *architecte des monuments historiques* in 1865–1870, and architect of the château of Pierrefonds in 1880.

Bauchal, *Dictionnaire.*

OUTBOND (adj.). Bonded, or forming a bond, along the face of a wall; as in the case of stretchers. Composed largely or entirely of stretchers.

OUT OF WIND. (See under Wind.)

OUTPORCH. A porch or outer vestibule; a term having no special architectural significance.

OUTSHOT; OUTSHUT. Originally a shed or small wing built against one end of a house, independently, and, in construction, not forming part of the general framing of the house. In British local usage any small extension.

OUT TO OUT. Same as Over All.

OUTWINDOW. A projecting loggia, or the like. (Compare Bay Window; Oriel.)

OVE. Same as Ovum.

OVER ALL (adjectival and adverbial phrase). Between the edges or boundaries; from the extreme limit at one side to the corresponding point at the other; especially between two imaginary parallel lines, or planes, so disposed as exactly to include all projections on two opposite faces or edges. Said of measurements and dimensions.

OVERDOOR (adjectival term). Occupying a space above a doorway, or above a door frame, even when no doorway is opened within it. The picture panel or the like which fills such a space is known as an overdoor picture, etc., the term being a modification of the French *dessus de porte.* (See Overmantel.) (Cuts, cols. 41, 42; 43.)

OVERHANG. The projection of part of a structure beyond the portion below; the exten-

Plan.

0   1   2   3   4   metres

OVERDOOR WINDOW; PALAIS DE JUSTICE, PARIS.

sion of an inclined structure or member, outside of its base, or any lower portion; the amount by which any part departs from a given vertical line or plane. (See Leaning Tower.)

OVERDOOR PANELLING AND FRONTON, FORMING AN ATTIC; 16TH CENTURY; UPMARK, SWEDEN.

OVERMANTEL (adjectival term). Occupying the space above a mantelshelf, or the front of a chimney-breast of any form and above the open fireplace. Overmantel mirrors, pictures, panels, and the like are spoken of; the term being imitated from the French *dessus de cheminée*. (See Overdoor.)

OVOLO. A convex rounded moulding, quarter round in section, or approximating that form.

OVUM (pl. ova). The rounded member, usually known as an egg, between the darts of an egg and anchor moulding.

OXEYE. A round, or more commonly, an oval window. (Compare Œil de Bœuf.)

OYELET. Same as Eyelet.

P

PACE. A part of a floor slightly raised above the general level; a dais; a broad step or slightly raised space, as about a tomb, altar, or chimney piece, or forming a landing in a staircase. The last meaning appears to be the most specific in modern usage, and in this sense is commonly accepted as synonymous with space. The latter term would seem to be more properly applied to the area at the turning-place of a stair which may be occupied by a landing,—or pace,—or by winders; and it is in this sense that the word space is used

by Mowat. Called also Footpace, although this appears to be obsolescent. (See Landing.)

Halfpace. *A.* A landing where one flight of stairs stops and another begins, the two flights being on the same side of the platform of the landing. A person going up such a stair reverses the direction of his horizontal progress as he reaches and again leaves the landing, making a turn of 180°. Such a landing is, therefore, usually about twice as long as it is wide, and extends the full width of the staircase. (See following subtitles.)

B. A raised platform (see Hathpace).

Half Quarterpace. A landing corresponding to one of the two triangular spaces formed by cutting a quarterpace diagonally at 45°, the other half being commonly filled with winders, so that the stairs will still make a quarter turn as described below.

Quarterpace. A landing in a staircase between two flights which make a turn of 90°. It is, therefore, about one half the size of a half pace, and commonly about square.

—D. N. B. S.

PACKING. Small stones embedded in mortar, used to fill up the interstices between the larger stones in rubble work.

PAD STONE. A stone template such as is used for supporting, in a wall, the end of a girder or of a roof truss.

PADUA, JOHANNES DE. (See John of Padua.)

PÆONIOS OF MENDE (in Thrace); sculptor.

According to Pausanias, he was sculptor of the statues of the eastern pediment of the temple of Zeus at Olympia, fragments of which have been found. His statue of Nike (Victory), described by Pausanias, has also been found in place.

Curtius and Adler, *Olympia;* Pausanias, Frazer's translation.

PAGNO DI LAPO. (See Portigiani.)

PAGODA. A shrinelike building, often of great size, in the religious architecture of Hindustan, Ceylon, Burmah, Siam, China, and lands occupied by Malays, usually in the form of a tower as in China, or of a lofty stepped, pyramidal structure, as, generally, in India. The term is of disputed etymology. (Compare Dagoba; Paoh-Tah; see, also, India, Architecture of.)

PAGOT, FRANÇOIS NARCISSE; architect; b. Aug. 31, 1780; d. Dec. 4, 1844.

A pupil of De la Barre (see Barre), and the *École des Beaux Arts.* In 1803 he won the *Grand Prix de Rome* in architecture. Returning from Rome, he settled at Orléans, became architect of that city, and professor in the local school of Architecture. He built at Orléans the Palais de Justice, the grain market, an abattoir (1823), the library, an insane asylum

PLATE III

PAGODA

That of the temple of Horiuji, in Japan. This
and the Hondo are the only early buildings in this
establishment. They are of the twelfth century
A.D. The lowest roof is a modern addition. For
the construction of this building, see cuts under
Japan.

(1828), laid out the botanical garden, and finished the portal of the cathedral.

Herluison, *Artistes Orléanais;* Lance, *Dictionnaire.*

PAILLETTE. In decorative work, a bit of shining foil used in picking out relief work to obtain a jewelled effect in connection with gilding or other metallic applications. (Compare Paillon.)

PAILLON. Bright metallic foil used in decoration to show through enamelling or through a glazing with transparent colour, so as to modify or emphasize its brilliancy, and bring it into harmony with the general scheme of colour. The term is also extended to gilding, or to parcel-gilding on wood, papier-maché, etc., when the gilding is to be glazed over with transparent colours. (Compare Paillette.)

PAI-LOO. In Chinese architecture, a decorative gateway. The design of these gateways is interesting, because of the general avoidance of the arch, even when the building is massive and on a large scale. (Compare Torii.)

PAINT (n.). Any dry colouring matter, material, or pigment, mixed with a liquid vehicle, so as to be readily applied with a brush to any surface to protect it from the weather or to give it any desired colour. It differs from a *dye* or *stain* in that while the latter is intended to sink into the wood or other surface to which it is applied, the former is devised to give it a superficial non-transparent coating, more or less impermeable. To this end paint is applied in several successive coats, put on over a priming coat, which latter is intended to prevent the other coats from sinking into the substance of the material covered.

For woodwork and other parts of a building, the dry paint is nearly always mixed with linseed oil; and this mixture may be thinned with turpentine, which acts on the oil as a solvent. The more oil there is the more gloss there is in the finished work: hence it is common to use almost pure turpentine for flatted or mat work. White carbonate of lead forms the body of most paint, pure for white work, mixed with other powdered pigments as the desired colour is different from white; a darker pigment is sometimes used pure, or a mixture of two. There are various fireproof paints, waterproof paints, luminous paints, etc.; but the essential function of all of them is, first, practical, to protect the material covered from the effects of exposure; and second, decorative, to give it colour or colours to enhance its æsthetic value as an architectural feature. (See Oil Painting; Painting.) — H. V. B.

PAINTED GLASS. (See Window.)

PAINTING. The work of covering any surface with colours as described under Paint, or with pigments mixed with water and glue, called water colour, kalsomine, or distemper.

The term frequently includes work done with a transparent glaze made with shellac or varnish; the treating of wood with shellac and oil, or with wax and other materials in successive coats, rubbed down between with pumice-stone and oil, to smooth and polish their surfaces and bring out their beauty of grain and natural colour; and the staining of wood surfaces without concealing the grain, as well as gilding or otherwise overlaying them with metallic substances.

Painting should supplement form with colour, making every part of a building æsthetically more fit for its various service of luxury or use. It can, to a great extent, correct errors of form and proportion by a judicious choice and comparison of colours. It can appear to lower a room which is too high, or heighten a room which is too low; on the other hand, it can diminish or even destroy an architectural effect by want of sympathy with it. (See Mural Painting; Encaustic; Fresco; Fresco Secco; Gilding; Intonaco; Kalsomine; Oil Painting; Polish; Staining; Water Colour.) — H. V. B.

PAINTING ROOM. A studio, atelier, or workshop for the use of a painter as an artist. Experience has shown that the local conditions best suited to his work are a room, large and lofty, to accommodate large canvases, and to give ample space for the furniture, models, draperies, and other equipments essential to the practice of the art; it should be most abundantly lighted, mainly from the north, — in north latitude, — so as to give high and low light, governed by screens and shutters; it should have the largest possible extent of clear wall space, and, if possible, galleries or lofts overlooking the area of the room.

PAIR (I.). As used of a staircase, a flight or series of flights from one floor to the next; perhaps derived from a former custom of habitually constructing that portion of a staircase in a pair of flights, returning on each other.

PAIR (II.). In mechanics, two forces, considered collectively, which have different points of application and which are equal, parallel, and act in the same direction. (Compare Couple.)

PALA. (In Italian, anything flat and thin, as the blade of an oar. In ecclesiology, a chalice cover or chalice veil.) An altarpiece. (See the subtitle.)

PALA D' ORO. The altarpiece, or retable, of S. Mark's church at Venice; a magnificent work in silver gilt, jewelled and enamelled; tenth century and later.

PALACE. Primarily, the official residence of any high dignitary; hence, frequently the term is applied to a residence of exceptional magnificence and extent.

The name comes from the Palatium, the Palatine Hill at Rome, which term was extended to the imperial residence during the life of Augustus. (For the residences of Italy, commonly called palaces, see Palazzo; see also Château; Hôtel; Palais.)

PALACE OF THE CONSERVATORS. At Rome, on the square of the Campidoglio; built by Michelangelo and his successors. (See Campidoglio.)

PALACE OF THE SENATOR. At Rome. (See Campidoglio.)

PALÆO CHRISTIAN. Belonging to the early ages of the Christian church. (See Latin Architecture.)

PALÆSTRA. In Greek archæology, and later among the Romans, a public place appro-

still remains. It was greatly enlarged at a later time, and the front, on the Quai d'Orsay, with pediment and dodecastyle portico, was not finished until 1807. Since 1790 it has been mostly used for public purposes, and for the greater part of that time the second Chamber of the National Legislature (now the *Chambre des Députés*) has occupied it.

PALAIS DE JUSTICE. In France, a building devoted to law courts, judges' chambers, and the like, and usually containing a large waiting room for the public (see Salle des Pas-Perdus). The Palais de Justice of Paris consists of a great mass of buildings of many dates, which occupy that part of the Île de la

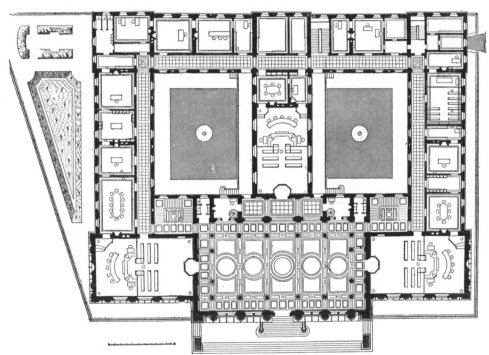

PALAIS DE JUSTICE, HÂVRE. PLAN.

Three court rooms open out of the great vestibule of entrance. The corridors are lighted from the great courts.

priated to athletic exercises or to preparing and training for the public games.

PALAIS. In French, a stately building; used in two general senses:—

A. A palace; that is, the official residence of a sovereign, or the usual and most important residence of a prince of the blood or other great nobleman.

B. A building for the public service, especially when of size and architectural importance.

PALAIS BOURBON. In Paris, on the south bank of the Seine; begun in 1722 as a private hôtel, the entrance gateway of which, on the Rue de l'Université, built by Girardini,

Cité which is between the Pont Neuf and the Pont au Change, and on the south bank of the principal arm of the Seine. The ancient Conciergerie forms a part of it; the round towers and the clock tower (Tour de l'Horloge), on the river, are of the fourteenth century, but they have been frequently rearranged within. The Sainte-Chapelle is enclosed in one of the courts. The main building, having a western front on the Place Dauphine, and a court and main entrance at the east end, was built by the architect Joseph Louis Duc, and was finished in 1869; it is one of the most successful pieces of modern architecture in Europe, and contains some important monuments. —R. S.

PLATE IV

PALAZZO

Palazzo Riccardi, in Florence, originally, and for two hundred years, the Palazzo Medici, and the chief home of the princes of that family. The building is from the design of Michelozzo Michelozzi, and is one of the earliest buildings of the Renaissance. It may be compared with the plate of the Pazzi Chapel (Neoclassic Architecture) for the presence in one case and the absence in the other of classical details. Three-fifths of the building is of about 1440, the part on the right is later.

PALAIS DE L'ÉLYSÉE. (See Élysée.)

PALAIS ROYAL. A mass of buildings in Paris, immediately north of the Louvre, fronting southward on the Place du Palais Royal, and bounded on the east and west by the Rue de Richelieu and the Rue de Valois. The first structure was completed in 1625 by the great Cardinal de Richelieu, and it was afterward much enlarged. Since 1672 the building has always been the property of the family of Orléans, except during the years when it was held by the revolutionary government. The building above described is the palace proper, that is to say, all that stands southward of the Galerie d'Orléans. The buildings which surround

1787, and these form no part of the Palais Royal.

PALAZZO. In Italian cities, a large sepa-

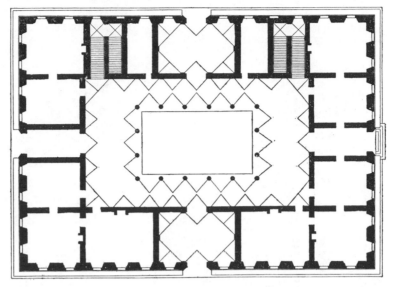

PALAZZO: PLAN OF THE STROZZI PALACE, FLORENCE.

rate dwelling, a term nearly corresponding to the French "hôtel." The Italian term signifies, also, palace, in the strict sense, but as used in Eng-

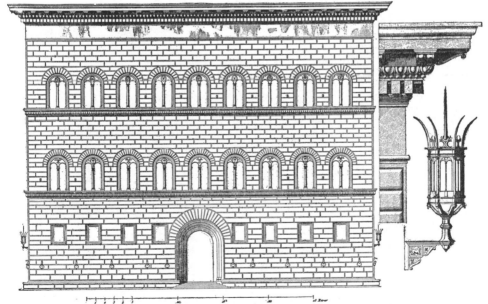

PALAZZO STROZZI, FLORENCE, ITALY; ABOUT 1489. (SEE PLAN.)
The cornicione and one of the lanterns are given on the right.

the great garden (nearly 800 feet long) were built for wholly commercial reasons by the Duc d'Orléans, Philippe Égalité, between 1781 and

lish it has only the meaning above given; thus, we speak of the Palazzo Farnese, but not of the Quirinal, or the Vatican, or the Lateran, as a palazzo. The cities of Italy are adorned by so many noble buildings, private palazzi of the thirteenth and following centuries, that it is impracticable to give the names even of those most important or most celebrated; moreover, it is rare to speak of a palazzo by its name without also naming the city in which it stands. — R. S.

Palazzo Communale, and sometimes by special names, as Palazzo Vecchio.

PALEO CHRISTIAN. Same as Palæo Christian.

PALESTRA. Same as Palæstra.

PALIMPSEST. *A.* A parchment from which one writing has been removed to give place to another; hence, the new writing or manuscript upon such a parchment.

B. By extension from the preceding meaning, an ancient inscribed slab or mediæval brass, which has been turned and engraved with new inscriptions and devices on the other side.

PALING. A fence formed of similar stakes or pickets set vertically, generally with small equal interspaces, to rails supported by posts; a picket fence.

PALISADE. A barrier composed of long stakes driven into the earth close together, sometimes connected by horizontal beams, or bound by osiers interwoven, to form a defence against attack, or for other purposes of secure enclosure. Palisades have always been used in warfare as aids to permanent defences, as well as for temporary defences, as in connection with fortified camps, and the like.

PALLADIAN ARCHITECTURE: PALAZZO THIENE AT VICENZA; ABOUT 1556.

PALAZZO COMMUNALE. In Italy, the building containing public offices, and the like, of a city or town. (See Palazzo Publico.)

PALAZZO PUBLICO. In Italy, a building containing public offices, as of a municipality or a larger community. These are known sometimes as Broletto or Palazzo Signoria, or

PALLADIAN ARCHITECTURE. Relating to the art or style of Palladio. This work belonged to the period of decline in Italian neoclassic architecture, when classic formality and the punctilious observance of rules were

PLATE V

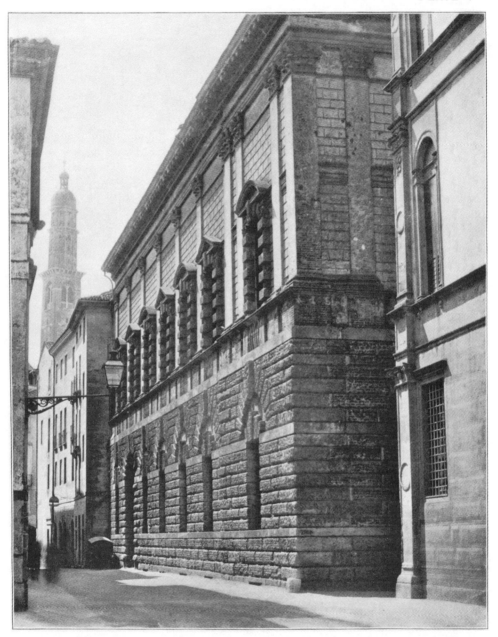

PALLADIAN ARCHITECTURE

The Palazzo Tiene at Vicenza. This is one of the master works of Andrea Palladio, its demerits being merely those attending the wide divergence between utility and design; for the building is arranged with almost a single eye to the exterior effect, and this effect is produced with stucco laid upon brickwork in close imitation of cut stone. It is a most powerful abstract design.

taking the place of the grace, freedom, and life which characterized the earlier period. The classicism of Palladio was noted for a certain cold and correct purity of form. A favourite motive of his, known as the Palladian Motive, was to use a minor and major order of columns in the same composition, the former being used to support the arches which occurred between the latter, as in his two-storied arcade about the mediæval basilica of Vicenza. His writings had the good fortune to be considered the most authoritative exposition of the principles of classic architecture in the seventeenth and eighteenth centuries throughout Europe, and his monuments were models for the classic art of that period ; the name Palladian, therefore, is descriptive of that variety of neoclassic architecture distinguished for cold, inelastic, and unimaginative, but correct, elegant, and studied classicism. It is generally held as true that the English classical revivalists followed Palladio, while the French were rather under the influence of Vignola. There has been some attempt as late as the last decade of the nineteenth century to revive in England the study of Palladian examples. (See England, Architecture of.) See also Inigo Jones and Wren ; or *The Rise and Decline of Modern Architecture in England*, by W. J. Loftie (New York, 1893). (See Classicismo ; Italy, Architecture of ; Neoclassic Architecture ; Pseudoclassic Architecture.)

—H. V. B.

PALLADIO, ANDREA ; architect ; b. about 1518 ; d. August, 1580.

Palladio is supposed to have been the son of a carpenter named Pietro, employed by the scholar and poet, Gian Giorgio Trissino. He became the protégé of Trissino, who gave him the name Palladio (from Pallas, goddess of wisdom), and educated him as an architect. Palladio's first work was the Palazzo Godi at Lonedo in 1540. He visited Rome first with Trissino in 1541, and again in 1544. In 1545 he presented four designs for the reconstruction of the basilica of Vicenza. Work was begun from his model in 1549. Palladio built the Palazzo Pisani at Bagnolo, near Vicenza ; the Palazzo Porto, now Colleoni, in Vicenza, 1552 ; the Palazzo Thiene (Banca popolare), Vicenza, 1556, dated ; the Palazzo Foscari on the Brenta before 1561 ; the Palazzo Pisani, near Padua, 1565 ; the famous Palazzo Chiericati, Vicenza, before 1567 ; the Palazzo Valmarana, Vicenza, after 1566 ; and the Palazzo Porto Barbarano, Vicenza, after 1570. The famous villa, called the Rotonda, which he built for Paolo Almerico, near Vicenza, was begun before 1570 and finished about 1591. The façade of the church of S. Francesco alla Vigna (Venice) was designed by him in 1562. In 1561 he built the cloister of the Convento della Carità (now the Accademia, Venice), on the plan of a Roman house.

It was nearly destroyed by fire in 1650. Palladio built the refectory of the church of S. Giorgio Maggiore, Venice, about 1560, and in 1565 the church itself with its fine façade. In 1570 he designed the cloister of the same building. He began the church of the Redentore, Venice, in 1576 (finished 1592). In the third book of his *Architettura* is given a splendid design for a bridge supposed to have been intended for the Rialto, Venice. In 1571 the loggia of the Piazza Maggiore, Vicenza, was begun from his designs. In February, 1580, he began the celebrated Teatro Olimpico, which was finished after his death by his son Silla and Vincenzo Scamozzi (see Scamozzi, V.). Palladio's treatise on architecture was first published complete, in Venice, in 1570, with the title *I quattro Libri dell' Architettura*. Many of his drawings were published by Lord Burlington (op. cit.) (see Boyle, R.) in 1730, and those on the Roman baths by Bertotti Scamozzi (see Scamozzi, O. B.). A collection of his buildings was published by Bertotti Scamozzi in 1776 (op. cit.). (See Palladian Architecture.)

Magrini, *Memorie;* Zanella, *Vista;* Gualdus, *Vita;* Temanza, *Vita;* Boito, *Andrea Palladio;* Ferrari, *Palladio e Venezia;* Melani, *Palladio;* Lord Burlington, *Fabbriche Antiche;* O. Bertotti Scamozzi, *Fabbriche di Palladio;* Montenari, *Treatro Olimpico;* Rigato, *Osservazioni sopra Palladio;* Rondelet, *Pont de Rialto.*

PALMATE. Having fanlike lobes or leaves, such as characterized the Greek anthemion or honeysuckle, and its derivations in conventional architectural decoration.

PALMETTE. In Greek and Roman architecture, a conventional ornament, frequent in friezes, of which the most characteristic feature is an erect leaf divided into lobes, like a fan or palm leaf; a kind of anthemion. It was either carved or painted. The motive is supposed to have been developed from Oriental origins.

PALUSTRE, LÉON; archæologist and historian of art ; b. Feb. 4, 1838 ; d. 1894.

He succeeded Arcisse de Caumont as director of the *Société française d'Archæologie*, but abandoned this position to devote himself entirely to the study of the French Renaissance. His great work, *La Renaissance en France*, was published, Vol. I. in 1879, Vol. II. in 1881, and Vol. III. in 1885. It was never finished. Palustre published many works on archæology and the history of French art.

Ch. Lucas in *Construction Moderne*, Nov. 3, 1894.

PAMPRE. A running undercut ornament, generally in the form of a vine with grapes, used to fill cavettos and other continuous hollows in a group of mouldings, as in an archivolt, in the circumvolutions of a twisted column, or wherever great luxury of decoration was required.

PAN. *A.* A wall plate (see Pon).

B. A part, larger or smaller, of an exterior wall ; in half-timbered work in England, especially one of those spaces which are left between the upright and horizontal timbers, and which are filled either with plastering on laths, or by rough brickwork, or the like. (Compare the French use of the word *Pan de Bois* and *Pan de Fer* in the sense of one considerable part of the framing of vertical walls in wood or iron ; also *Pan de Mur*, by which is meant generally a piece of any wall from basement to cornice ; also *Pan coupé*, which means a piece of wall forming a cut off corner of a building or a room. Compare also Bay ; Panel, the general definition.)

PANACHE (n.). The triangle-like surface of a pendentive.

PANDROSEION. Same as Pandrosium.

PANDROSIUM. A building or enclosure on the Acropolis of Athens, sacred to the Nymph Pandrosos. It is generally admitted that this

was very near to the Erechtheum (which see). The name is often applied to the south portico of the Erechtheum (see Caryatid) ; but there is not sufficient authority for this attribution.

PANE. Any part or division of the elevation of a building having a plane surface and more or less definite or symmetrical outlines or boundaries. More especially as follows :—

A. Same as Panel, but applied to larger areas, as to one side or face of a spire or tower.

B. A plate of glass, generally rectangular, set in a window, door, or the like.

PANEL. *A.* Primarily, a small plane surface usually sunk below the surrounding surface ; the term is akin to Pane, and both are derived from the term for a small piece of cloth, or the like. The architectural panel is generally rectangular, but in some styles, oval, or circular, or irregular panels are used. (Compare Caisson, II. ; Lacunar ; Tympanum.) The sunken surface of the panel is often charged with ornament. (See Raised Panel, below.)

B. In carpentry and joinery, a thin piece of board, generally rectangular, held at the edges by a frame in such a manner that it is free to

PANEL WITH CARVED DIAPER, AND SECONDARY OR INNER PANEL WITH GOTHIC TRACERY ; c. 1500.

shrink or swell, while prevented from warping by the frame. Such a panel is nearly always sunk below the surface of the frame but may be flush with, or project beyond it. — D. N. B. S.

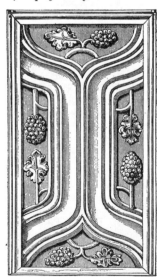

PANEL: LATE TUDOR TRACERY WITH CARVED HERALDIC BEARINGS OR COGNIZANCES ; LAYER MARNEY HALL ; c. 1530.

Fielded Panel. Same as Raised Panel.

Flush Panel. One whose plane surface is flush, *i.e.*, in the same plane, with the stiles and rails which frame it, and which are often beaded with a flush bead on the edges next the panel to mask the joint. Often used in table tops, and the like.

Linen Panel. One carved with the Linen Pattern.

Lying Panel. One which is placed with its greater dimension horizontal.

Raised Panel. One of which the face has a raised plane projecting beyond the edges of the panel, and sometimes beyond the frame or other surrounding surface.

Sunk Panel. One of which the face is recessed from the frame or other surrounding surface. — D. N. B. S.

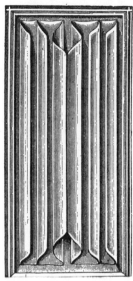

LINEN PANEL; LAYER MARNEY HALL, ESSEX, ENGLAND; CIRCA 1530.

PANEL BACK. Same as Panelled Back.

PANEL BOARD. A drawing board of the kind used by water colour draftsmen, by which the paper can be held flat and in place without the trouble of saturating it with water and so straining it tight. The board is fitted with a frame which can be removed at pleasure, and which, when fitted into place, will hold firmly the edges of the paper which covers the panel. (Called also Frame Board.)

PANELLED BACK. The back lining when panelled; as of a window back (which see; see also Back, *D*).

PANELLING. *A.* The making of a structure in carpentry or joinery by means of frames holding panels. (See Panel, *A*.)

B. The breaking up of a surface by panels.

C. The structure or surface resulting from the processes *A* or *B*; thus, a room may be lined with oak panelling, or a plaster or stone surface may be broken up by panelling. (See Caisson, II.; Wainscot.)

PANEL STRIP. A narrow piece of metal, or moulded wood, or batten, to cover a joint between two sheathing boards, so that several will thereby form panels; or one between a style and a panel, forming a secondary or accessory panel, as in elaborate patterns of panelling.

PANE WORK. The division of the exterior surface of a house into panes or panels, as constructively, in a half-timbered house by the disposition of its visible timbers, whether arranged so as to form rectangular panes, or, by branching and shaping, to enclose other and more or less decorative shapes as quatrefoils, circles, etc. The pane work of the half-timbered manor houses, inns, hospitals, etc., of the Tudor period, emphasized by the strong contrast between the white roughcast of the panes and the weathered blackness of the beams, constitutes their most distinctive characteristic. (See Black and White; Half-Timbered.)

PANNIER. Same as Corbeille.

PANOPTICON. A building, especially a prison, so arranged on a radiating principle that a single inspector or guard can, from a central, common point, look through each of the converging halls. Its use was advocated in England by Jeremy Bentham at the end of the eighteenth century; the most conspicuous early example of the application of this principle of planning is the house of correction at Ghent (Plate 28, Durand's *Parallèle d'Édifices*).

PANORAMA. In architecture, a building arranged to contain a large picture with or without accessories, and of the kind known as cyclorama, diorama, or panorama; those three terms being used without clear distinction in describing the representations themselves. The buildings are seldom of architectural importance, but that built by Davioud in Paris, in 1859, and called *Panorama National*, is of some interest.

PAN PIECE. Same as Pan, *B*.

PANTAGRAPH; PANTOGRAPH. An instrument for the mechanical copying of engravings, plans, diagrams, etc., either on the same scale as the original or on an enlarged or reduced scale.

PANTHEON. In Rome; a circular building with an octastyle portico hardly forming part of the design. The rotunda has walls of immense thickness, in which mass are chambers, some showing as chapels upon the rotunda within, and others concealed and intended merely to diminish the amount of masonry, while allowing of the full spread or depth of the mass to act as a buttress for the cupola. The cupola is the largest existing, the dimension being generally given as 142 feet, which is also almost exactly the height of the interior from the pavement to the top of the dome. The only opening for the admission of daylight is the oculus, nearly thirty feet in diameter. The building is thought to have been built in the reign of Hadrian, and perhaps between 120 and 124 A.D. But it is not doubted that the present building represents an earlier one commonly known as the Pantheon of Agrippa, and built in the reign of Augustus;

see). It was called by this name when, during the first French Revolution, it was taken up by the state to serve as a place of burial and of memorial to distinguished citizens, and when the famous inscription, AUX GRANDS HOMMES

THE PANTHEON, ROME.
Isabelle's restoration, which, however, omits the bronze shutter of the oculus.

and the portico may be a remaining fragment of that building.

Lanciani, *The Ruins and Excavations of Ancient Rome*; for plates, Isabelle, *Les Édifices circulaires et les dômes* (1855); *Parallèle des salles rondes de l'Italie*.

PANTHÉON (properly Le Panthéon de Paris). Same as church of S. Geneviève (which

LA PATRIE RECONNAISSANTE, was put upon the entablature. Under Napoleon III. it was a church once more; but under the third Republic it is once again the Panthéon, and is very elaborately adorned within by memorial paintings of great importance, and by a few sculptures.

PANTRY. *A.* A small apartment adjoining a kitchen, in which provisions and kitchen utensils are kept, knives cleaned, pastry rolled, etc. By extension, often applied to a closet, especially one among the offices of a house or hotel.

B. A small apartment adjoining a dining room, used as a waiting or serving room, where the courses for a meal are laid out for serving, dishes washed, silver, glass, and china kept, etc.; in the United States, specifically, called a Butler's Pantry. (Compare Service Room.)

PAOH-TAH. In China, a temple, especially the towerlike structure of the Buddhists, always of an uneven number of stories. The most celebrated was the Porcelain Tower at Nankin, built in the fifteenth century and destroyed in the Tai-ping Rebellion, between 1853 and 1856. (See China, Architecture of.)

PAOLO DI MARTINO. (See Beccafumi, Domenico.)

PAOLO ROMANO; sculptor and architect. His name appears frequently in the pontifical records. Between 1451 and 1460 he was employed on the triumphal arch of the Castel Nuovo at Naples (see Isaie da Pisa). About 1463 he made the statue of S. Andrea, which stands in a charming Doric shrine near the Ponte Molle, Rome.

Müntz, *Les Arts à la cour des papes;* Müntz, *Renaissance;* Minieri Riccio, *Gli Artisti del Castel Nuovo;* Vasari, Milanesi ed.; Perkins, *Italian Sculptors.*

PAPAKHU. In an Assyrian or Babylonian temple, the most sacred place, the holy of holies. (See Mesopotamia; Temple.)

PAPER. (See Building Paper; Hanging.)

PAPE, SIMON DE; architect; b. June, 1585; d. Sept. 13, 1636.

The son of a silversmith. One of his earliest works was the Korenhuis at Audenarde (Belgium). In 1617 he was appointed *Stads bouwmeester* of Audenarde.

PAPIER-MACHÉ. A composition of paper reduced to a pulp, and mixed with glue, size, or other substances, so that it is readily moulded or cast in any desired form. It lends itself to fine and clean modelling, and, when modelled, is conveniently applied for decorative purposes in low relief on ceilings and walls. It is often especially prepared and made waterproof, to decorate exterior work.

PAPWORTH, GEORGE; architect; b. about 1781; d. March 14, 1855.

In 1806 he settled in Dublin, and in 1831 was elected to the Royal Hibernian Academy. He built the Museum of Irish Industry at Dublin.

Palgrave, *Dictionary of Artists.*

PAPWORTH, JOHN (after 1815, John Buonarroti); architect; b. Jan. 24, 1775; d. June 16, 1847.

He was apprenticed to Thomas Wapshott, and had some instruction from Sir William Chambers (see Chambers). He acquired intimate practical knowledge of the details of construction, and designed a large number of buildings in London, and many country residences. He was much employed as a landscape gardener, and wrote many practical works on architecture.

Wyatt Papworth, *John B. Papworth, architect;* Arch. Pub. Soc. Dictionary.

PAPWORTH, JOHN WOODY; architect; b. March 4, 1820; d. July 6, 1870.

Elder son of John Buonarroti Papworth (see Papworth, J). He entered the Royal Academy as a student in 1839. Papworth contributed many articles for the architectural periodicals, and wrote useful books on architectural subjects. He was largely employed as a practical architect. He was associated with his brother, Wyatt Papworth, in the preparation of the *Dictionary of the Architectural Publication Society.*

Arch. Pub. Soc. Dictionary.

PAPWORTH, WYATT ANGELICUS VAN SANDAU; architect and antiquary; b. Jan. 23, 1822; d. Aug. 19, 1894 (at the Soane Museum in London).

A younger son of John Buonarroti Papworth (see Papworth, J.). He studied with his father, and served in the office of Sir John Rennie (see Rennie, Sir J.). In 1849 he was awarded the silver medal of the Institute of British Architects for an essay, *The Peculiar Characteristics of the Palladian School of Architecture.* In 1867 he revised and edited the *Encyclopædia of Architecture* of Joseph Gwilt (see Gwilt, J.). In 1848 he undertook the formation of the Architectural Publication Society, and in 1852 became editor of its *Dictionary of Architecture,* which was finished in 1892 (8 vols. folio). He published many works on architectural subjects.

Obituary in *Journal of Royal Institute of British Architects,* 1894, p. 618; Stephen-Lee, *Dictionary of National Biography.*

PARABEMA. In buildings of the Greek Church, a room or division closely connected with the bema, differently described by different authorities. It is probable that the signification of the term varies with different epochs and in different countries. In a regularly planned Greek church of the latter time, there were always two parabemata, one on either side of the bema. Thus, in the Coptic churches of Egypt, it is expressly stated by A. J. Butler (op. cit., Vol. I.) that a Coptic church has always three eastern chapels: the prothesis (see Prothesis), on the north of the bema, being the place for the consecration of the elements, while the diaconicon (see Diaconicon) on the south side serves as a vestry and sacristy; while it seems to be evident that the prothesis and the diaconicon are the parabemata.

Butler, *The Ancient Coptic Churches of Egypt.*

PARADISUS. In mediæval architecture, a court or atrium in front of a church, usually surrounded by cloisters, either in whole or in part; sometimes another enclosure; thus, the cloister garth of Chichester Cathedral is still called the Paradise. (See Parvis.) In domestic architecture, a small apartment equivalent approximately to the modern boudoir.

PARALLELOGRAM OF FORCES. A graphical representation of the composition and

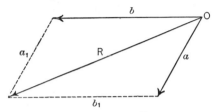

PARALLELOGRAM OF FORCES.

resolution of forces. A force may be represented in magnitude and direction by a line. If two or more forces act upon a body, they may be replaced by a single force called the Resultant, a force which, if reversed, would maintain the body in equilibrium. Suppose two forces applied to the point O represented in magnitude and direction by the lines a b; draw the lines a' b' parallel, respectively, to a and b, and we form the parallelogram of forces, the diagonal of which parallelogram is the resultant, R, and indicates the force which would produce the same effect upon the point O as the two forces a and b, if acting simultaneously. This force, if applied to O in a contrary direction, would balance the two forces a and b. (See Polygon of Forces.)

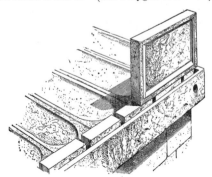

PARAPET OF SOLID SLABS, WITH ROOF AND GUTTER ALL OF CUT STONE; SYRIA; 5TH CENTURY A.D.

PARAPET. A dwarf wall or barrier built on the edge of a terrace, platform, bridge, balcony, or other elevated place, as a protection against falling; also above the cornice of a house, whether built with a steep or with a flat roof. It is characteristically a solid construction, with a plain, straight coping; but as a feature of more or less decorated architecture, it is one

of the first to be emphasized by panelling and tracery, often pierced with great richness and

PARAPET WITH PIECED TREFOILS: S. MARY'S CHURCH, OXFORD; C. 1280.

delicacy of detail; it is sometimes more or less broken with crenelations like a battlement, especially when used as a sky line, and in some domestic work it is corbelled out from the surface of the wall which it crowns, and takes the place of a cornice. (See Blocking Course.) (Cuts, cols. 65, 66.)

PARASCENIUM. In the ancient theatre, a projecting structure or wing flanking the stage on either side, and with the scena, or background, enclosing it on three sides. It included apartments for the actors, and often the passageway, Parodos.

PARASTAS (pl. Parastadæ). That part of the flanking wall of the cella of a Greek temple which projects beyond its front or rear, enclosing walls so as to form an open vestibule; the ends of these walls were treated with bases and capitals (see Anta), and the area enclosed

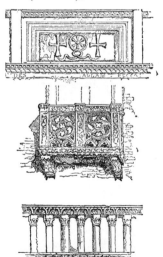

PARAPET: THREE VENETIAN PATTERNS, COMMON IN BALCONIES:

No. 1. Byzantine style, 11th century.
No. 2. Florid Gothic, late 14th century.
No. 3. 14th or 15th century, with baluster columns.

by them with its open screen of columns became a *portico in antis*. The word "parastas" is

PARAPET WITH PIERCED TRACERY; S. MARY
MAGDALENE, OXFORD; A.D. 1337.

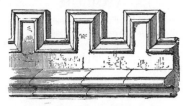

PARAPET CUT INTO SMALL CRENELLATIONS IMI-
TATING BATTLEMENTS; S. PETER'S CHURCH,
DORCHESTER, ENGLAND; C. 1450.

PARAPET, CATHEDRAL OF SANTIAGO DE COMPOSTELLA, SPAIN; 1520 TO 1540.

PARAPET, CATHEDRAL OF SEVILLE, SPAIN; 17TH CENTURY.

 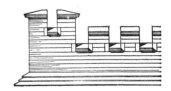

PARAPET: MODERN PATTERNS IN BRICKWORK, WHICH MUST BE CAREFULLY LAID IN STRONG
CEMENT MORTAR.

often used to signify the anta itself, and Vitruvius applies the term to an isolated square pillar. The jamb of a doorway, especially when treated with shaft and capital, is called parastas. (Also written Prostas.)

PARATORIUM ; PARATORY. A place where any preparation is made ; particularly, in early churches, a place for the offerings.

PARCLOSE. A screen, or other enclosing barrier, often richly decorated, to protect a tomb, as at Fifield, Berks (*Oxford Glossary*, pl. 184) ; to separate a chapel or chantry from the main body of the church, as at Winchester, Wells, Saint Albans, Salisbury, etc.; to form the front of a gallery, or for other similar purposes. It is either solid or of open work.

PARETTA. Roughcast with pebbles inserted ; often left in their original colours so as to produce chromatic effect.

PARGET. *A.* Gypsum, or plaster stone.

B. Plaster ; specifically, a kind of mortar formed of lime, hair, and cow dung.

C. Coarse plasterwork in general. The modern facing on rough brickwork, as in the lining of flues.

PARGETTING ; PARGET WORK. Plasterwork of various kinds ; specifically, exterior

PARGETTING, DATED 1642, BUT PRESERVING ELIZABETHAN MOTIVE ; HIGH STREET, OXFORD.

plaster facing, stamped with diapers in low relief, or in ornamental patterns raised or indented ; much used in the interior, and often on the exterior, of English houses of the Tudor period. In interior work it is often delicately executed and highly finished. This sort of work is a marked characteristic in the external enrichment of some Elizabethan half-timbered houses. Sometimes incorrectly called parge work.

PARIS, PIERRE ADRIEN ; architect ; b. 1747 ; d. Aug. 1, 1819.

He was a student at the *École royale d'Architecture* and studied in Rome as *pensionnaire du roi*. In 1778 he was appointed *dessinateur du cabinet du roi*, and in 1780 was admitted to the *Académie d'Architecture*. In 1787 he was appointed architect of the cathedral of Orléans, and finished the towers of that church in 1790. In 1787 he was commissioned to install the Assembly of Notables in the palace of Versailles. He designed the Hôtel de Ville at Neufchâtel, Pas-de-Calais, France. In 1806 he was appointed director of the French Academy at Rome. During his administration he bought the antiques of the Villa Borghese for the Musée du Louvre.

Lance, *Dictionnaire ; Nouvelle biographie générale.*

PARK. *A.* A considerable extent of more or less carefully preserved woodland and pasture attached to a residence. A legally enclosed and privileged domain which is especially defined by old English law.

B. A public reservation for recreation and utility, varying in extent from great government reservations, such as Yellowstone Park, United States, to a small square, or the like, in a city. Those in, or near, cities are commonly treated with great care in some form of landscape gardening. — D. N. B. S.

PARLER, PETER ; architect ; b. about 1333 ; d. about 1397.

Parler came of a stonecutter's family in Cologne (Germany). He was architect of the choir and nave of the cathedral of Prague, in Bohemia, begun 1392. He was assisted and succeeded by his sons, Nicolaus, Johann, and Wenzel. His bust stands in the triforium gallery of the cathedral of Prague. He is also known as Peter von Gmund.

Neuwirth, *Wochenrechnungen des Prager Dombaues.*

PARLIAMENT HOUSE. (See Legislature, House of.)

PARLOUR. *A.* A room for conversation. The term was in use as early as the time of Chaucer, apparently, in a general sense, as meaning any place for the intercourse of a few persons, as distinguished from a large hall. When the term "drawing-room" came into use in a special sense, the word "parlour" in England was applied rather to rooms for the family, as distinguished from rooms for the reception of visitors. In this sense we have "dining parlour" and "eating parlour," and in London private houses, "the parlours," applied to the rooms on the ground floor, one of which might be the dining room and the other the library. When, in *Mrs. Lirriper's Lodgings*, the Major takes "the parlours," this must be taken to be the rooms on the ground or entrance floor, as distinguished from the drawing-room at the head of the first flight of stairs. (Compare Living Room; Reception Room; Sitting Room.)

B. In a monastery or nunnery, the room in which the members of the establishment were allowed to receive visitors. Such a parlour was often divided by a grating, to one side of which the inmates of the monastery or convent were confined, while the guests were received only on the other side; in this sense, an exact equivalent of the French *parloir*, which has retained its original signification of a room especially provided for conversation. — R. S.

PARODOS. In the ancient Greek theatre, one of the two passages separating the stage from the cavea, or auditorium, through which the chorus entered the orchestra, and which served also as entrances for the public. The parodos was sometimes a passageway carried through the parascenium, and sometimes distinct from it.

PARQUET. In a modern theatre, the whole or a part of the principal floor of the auditorium. In France, the term has been appropriated to the part nearer the stage, but this term has been superseded by *orchestre*. In the United States the same change has been made in the naming of parts, though, perhaps, not universally. (See Orchestra; Parterre; Pit.)

PARQUET CIRCLE. In the United States, the space at the rear of the Parquet of a theatre corresponding in extent approximately to the parterre, but arranged with seats, and considered inferior only to the parquet or orchestra. (See Parterre.)

PARQUETERIE; PARQUETRY. A mosaic of woodwork for floors, composed of hard woods of various colours or grains, tongued and grooved together in small pieces, finished flush on the surface, forming ornamental patterns, generally with borders, and always highly polished. It is sometimes composed of thin veneers glued to canvas, so that it can be put down like a carpet; but properly it is of thicker stock glued together and secured to the under flooring, so as to form a solid and permanent structure.

PARSONAGE; –HOUSE. The residence of a parson, that is, of the man holding a living as a clergyman of a parish. (See Manse; Rectory; Vicarage.)

PARTERRE. *A.* The part of the floor of a theatre beneath the galleries, often raised so as to overlook the pit or parquet.

B. A formal portion of a garden, set aside for flower beds of ornamental shapes.

PARTHENON. In Athens, Greece, an octostyle Doric temple dedicated to the goddess Athena. (See Greece, Architecture of.)

PARTHIAN ARCHITECTURE. That of the peoples subjected to the Parthian dynasty, which lasted for nearly five centuries, from 250 B.C. to 226 A.D., and which, during the reign of its greatest monarch, Mithridates (163–140 B.C.), extended its empire over 450,000 square

miles. This does not seem to have been a building race, and were it not for the discoveries made by W. K. Loftus at Warka (Erech), in Mesopotamia, of various decorative features, such as capitals and friezes; and for the descriptions given of the temple and palace of Al-Hadhr, thirty miles north of Mosul, first visited by Dr. Ross and Ainsworth in 1835, and by Sir Henry Layard some ten years later, nothing would have been known of its architectural work.

The remains of the palace at Al-Hadhr consist of a block 350 feet long, 128 feet deep, and from 50 to 70 feet high, which is subdivided into three great reception halls or *aiwans* (one of which forms now the vestibule to a temple at the back), and four sets of smaller rooms, three in number, one behind the other. The aiwans measure two of them 49 feet wide, the third 58 feet, and they occupy the whole depth of the building. All the halls and rooms are vaulted with semicircular barrel vaults, and over the smaller chambers was a second story. The principal front faces the east, and the aiwans and the sets of rooms are entered by arched portals, that of the largest aiwan being 40 feet wide and 60 feet high. The palace is built in the brownish grey limestone of the country, in regular courses with fine joints. The archivolts of the portals have two fascias and an outer moulding, and every alternate voussoir is decorated with a mask in high relief. The imposts carrying the arches are moulded and carved with acanthus leaves. On each of the piers between the arched portals is a semidetached shaft (the upper part of which is broken away, so that it is not known how it was terminated) and on either side of the northern, the largest aiwan, are two shafts.

Over the entrance door to the temple at the end of the south aiwan is a frieze with the heads of the sun god in the centre, and, on either side, doves holding the crescent representing the moon, bulls' heads, and griffins. Similar carvings were found by Loftus at Warka, together with a large number of Parthian coins, as also small capitals with busts in the centre, similar to those found on the voussoirs of the archivolts at Al-Hadhr. Sir Henry Layard and Fergusson attributed the palace to the Sassanian dynasty, but the temple with its doorway and frieze is known to have existed in Hadrian's time. The construction of the palace is also entirely different from Sassanian work. The vaults are semicircular and not elliptical, like those of the latter; the masonry is in regular courses with fine joints, whereas the Sassanian masonry is of the coarsest kind, with thick mortar joints, and was always hidden under a layer of stucco; and in no Sassanian building is there any Greek or Roman ornament or sculpture of the kind found at Al-Hadhr.

The two palaces now forming part of the mosque at Diarbekr, and apparently rebuilt partly with old materials, are decorated with columns, the shafts of some of which are richly carved with ornamental diapers similar to those found at Warka.

Communications by Dr. Ross and Mr. William Ainsworth in the ninth and eleventh volumes of the Royal Geographical Society of London ; the description, with plans and drawings, communicated to the Royal Institute of British Architects in 1846 and published in the R. I. B. A. Transactions, Vol. VI., New Series, as a supplement to a paper read by R. Phenè Spiers, December 2, 1890, on Sassanian Architecture ; Prof. Rawlinson's *Sixth Great Monarchy of the Ancient Eastern World, the Parthian* ; and *Travels and Researches in Chaldea and Susiana*, with an account of excavations at Warka, the Erech of Nimrod, by Sir William Kenneth Loftus (8vo, London, 1857).

— R. Phenè Spiers.

PARTING LATH. Same as Parting Strip.

PARTING SLIP. In a cased frame, a thin strip of wood or metal hung from the top between the weights to separate them and prevent their mutual interference. (See Cased Frame, under Frame.)

PARTING STRIP. Any slender, thin piece, — usually of wood, — to separate and maintain a slight distance apart two adjoining members. Specifically, a strip of wood from $\frac{3}{8}$ inch to $\frac{1}{2}$ inch wide, set vertically into or against the pulley stile of a window frame, to separate the upper from the lower sash by forming runways in which they can slide past each other. Called also Parting Bead (which see under Bead ; see also Cased Frame, under Frame).

PARTITION. Originally, any dividing wall. In modern building, specifically, a wall or similar structure separating the rooms or other divisions of a building. In the United States the term is almost entirely limited to structures of wood, hollow brick, or the like, as distinguished from solid masonry ; one of the latter being commonly designated as a partition wall, especially when serving also as a bearing wall. (See Wall.)

Folding Partition. A partition arranged in sections, each closing on the next, so that a large apartment may be readily subdivided and again opened up, at pleasure.

Rolling Partition. One constructed on the principle of a rolling shutter (see Shutter) and serving the purpose described under Folding Partition.

Stud Partition. A partition of studs ; covered usually with lath and plaster.

Trussed Partition. A partition constructed wholly or in part on the principle of a truss, so as to span an interval without intermediate supports. Used to relieve a floor of its weight.

PARTY WALL. A wall built on the line between two pieces of land belonging to different proprietors, the purpose of which is to save room while providing a wall of sufficient thickness and strength. The building of such a wall is a matter of agreement between the two owners ; he who first proposes to build erecting the wall under this agreement, the other owner agreeing to pay for his share of it when he puts up his own building, and rests his floor timbers and roof timbers upon the party wall. The custom and the validity of the agreement has been recognized by courts of law since the Middle Ages.

PARVIS ; PARVISE. *A*. An open space in front of a church, usually surrounded by a balustrade or parapet, often slightly raised, where religious ceremonies were conducted in the open air. (Compare Paradisus and Peribolos.) The term is little used in England or the United States, but on the Continent of Europe is extended to signify the whole of a small square in front of a large church ; and a house may be built fronting on the parvis of a cathedral, exactly as, in London, it may front on " St. Paul's churchyard."

B. A room or porch connected with the main entrances of a church ; in this sense used very loosely. — R. S.

PARVIS TURRET. A small turret built over a church porch ; often occupied as a library or study.

PASCHAL CANDLESTICK. A massive and sometimes fixed and immovable candlestick, arranged in a church to receive the Paschal candle, which is often of great size. In some Italian churches it is placed near the ambo, and is treated architecturally in the same style, as in the well-known instance of the cathedral of Ravello, and that in the Basilica of S. Clemente at Rome.

PASSAGE (I.). A gallery or corridor leading from one apartment, or suite of apartments, to another ; or from one building to another, as in a group of hospital pavilions. More usually a comparatively narrow and subordinate means of intercommunication convenient in the service of a household ; or, in large public buildings, a private footway giving access to remote parts of the edifice for cleaning or repairs, as the gallery made in the thickness of the walls of a church under the nave windows.

PASSAGE (II.). In French and pronounced in the French way even in English speech, an avenue or alley connecting two thoroughfares through the intervening block, accessible to foot-passengers only. Sometimes covered with glass and lined with shops. (See Arcade (II.) ; Galleria ; and compare Wynd.)

PASSAGE AISLE. An aisle made so narrow as to serve only as a passageway, as from one end to another of a church. Such a passage allows all the width of the nave to be used for seats, or to have no more than one passage, as in the middle. (Cut, cols. 73, 74.)

PASTI (or **BASTI**), **MATTEO DE'** ; architect, painter, sculptor, and medalist.

Pasti came from Verona (Italy), and was a pupil of Pisanello, the painter and medalist.

About 1446 he attached himself to the court of Sigismondo Malatesta at Rimini, Italy. The remarkable reconstruction of the church of S. Francesco at Rimini (il Tempio Malatestiano), undertaken by Sigismondo, was undoubtedly executed under the direction of Pasti so far as the interior is concerned. A letter to him from Leon Battista Alberti (see Alberti), dated Nov. 18, 1454, indicates that the exterior was built by Pasti from drawings and directions sent by Alberti from Rome. (See Nuti Matteo and Agostino di Duccio.) As medalist he ranks next to Pisanello.

Müntz, *Renaissance;* Yriarte, *Rimini ;* Geymüller - Stegman, *Die Arch. der Renaissance in Toscana;* Heiss, *Les Médailleurs de la Renaissance.*

PASTICCIO; PASTICHE. *A.* A work of art produced in deliberate imitation of another or several others, as of the works of a master taken together.

B. Especially, in decorative art, the modification for transference to another medium, of any design. Thus, the cover of a book may be the pasticcio of a mosaic pavement.

PASTORINI, PASTORINO; painter, glass painter; b. 1508; d. 1592.

Pastorini was a painter of Siena, a pupil of Guillaume de Marcillat (see Marcillat, Guillaume de), who, at his death, bequeathed to him all his work. After 1531 he painted glass in the cathedral of Siena, and in 1536 restored the windows of the Palazzo Petrucci (Siena). After 1541 he painted glass at Rome from cartoons by Perino del Vaga (see Buonaccorsi, P.).

Müntz, *Guillaume de Marcillat.*

PASTRY ROOM. A room in the service part of a dwelling or hotel appropriated especially to the making of pastry, and furnished generally with marble slabs for the rolling of dough.

PATENT HAMMER. A hammer used to dress stone by cutting series of short parallel grooves. Its head consists of small chisels held together by bolts, and adjustable as to number

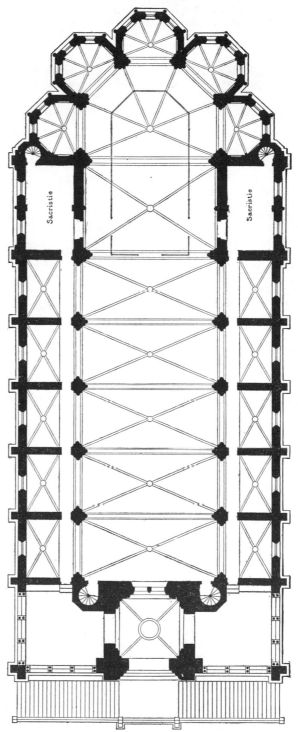

PASSAGE AISLE, CEAPEL OF NOTRE DAME DE LOURDES (HAUTES-PYRÉNÉES).
The aisle is separately roofed, between the nave pillars and the buttress walls which separate the chapels.

and spacing, the series being parallel with the handle.   Called also Patent Axe.

PATENT HAMMER.

PATENT LIGHT.   Same as Pavement Light or Vault Light (which see under Light).

PATERA.   The representation of a flat, round dish or disk, generally more or less decorated in low relief, to ornament a panel, frieze, etc.   The term is improperly extended to rosettes and other approximately circular embellishments bearing no resemblance to disks or dishes.

PATERNOSTER.   An astragal, baguet, or any small round moulding cut in the form of beads, like a rosary or chaplet.   A moulding so cut is also called a pearl moulding or bead moulding.

PATIENCE.   Same as Miserere.

PATINA.   *A*.   The incrustation formed on bronze by natural or artificial means.   Those found originally on ancient bronzes are so admired that they have been imitated by various processes.

B.   By extension, the surface of any work of fine or decorative art, supposed to be the result of time, and, therefore, greatly admired by students.   Thus, an ancient carving in wood, supposed to have its original patina, is worth many times the value of one which has been cleaned by potash and repolished.

PATIO.   In Spain, and Spanish-American countries, an open court, partly or wholly surrounded by the house, but approached directly from without by a door or gateway which is frequently under the upper stories of the house.   (See Court ; Porte Cochère.)

PATROL HOUSE.   In the United States, a building for housing the apparatus, horses, and men constituting a fire patrol ; a uniformed force maintained by insurance companies, whose business it is to attend conflagrations and preserve the building and contents as far as possible from damage by fire, or by water, or the operations of firemen, and from theft.

PATRYNGTON, ROBERT DE; architect. January 5, 1368, he was appointed master mason of York Cathedral (England) and built a great portion of the present choir.   He succeeded W. de Hoton (see Hoton, W. de) and was himself succeeded by Hugo Hedon.

Browne, *York Cathedral*.

PATTE, PIERRE; architect and engraver ; b. Jan. 3, 1723 ; d. 1812.

Patte appeared first as a critic, especially attacking the design of Soufflot (see Soufflot) for the Panthéon (Paris), on account of the weakness of the piers supporting the dome. He erected numerous unimportant buildings, but is best known by his published works.   He continued the *Cours d'Architecture* of Jacques François Blondel (see Blondel, J. F.), and published independently *Discours sur l'Architecture* (Paris, 1854, 8vo); *Études sur l'Architecture en France et en Italie* (Paris, 1755, 20 pls.) ; *Essai sur l'Architecture Théâtrale* (Paris, 1782), etc.

Nouvelle biographie générale ; Lance, *Dictionnaire*.

PATTEN.   *A*.   A stand or movable support, upon a number of which a building can be set without other foundation and without breaking the ground.   In English law this was held to remove the building from the class of realty and, therefore, from the number of improvements which remain for the benefit of the owner. — (A. P. S.)

B.   A stand, support, or foot ; a term used loosely and without accurate signification in English.   Thus, one authority uses it for the stand or foot of a weathercock ; another for the base course of a wall, or the sill of a timber frame.

PATTERN.   *A*.   A model made in some easily worked material, like wood or plaster, to serve as a guide in respect to form and dimensions in the laying out of any piece of work in building requiring accuracy, or to facilitate correctness of outline in stonecutting or stucco work or carpentry ; especially to preserve and secure uniformity in continuous work like mouldings ; to serve as a matrix in casting in plaster, metal, or clay ; or to secure correctness of repetition in all kinds of stamped and stencil work. The making of patterns for castings and for stonecutting constitutes a special trade, requiring unusual intelligence and special training.

B.   A design, considered as a unit, of which an idea can be given by a fragment ; as a diaper pattern, or sprinkled pattern ; or, more in detail, a fleur-de-lis pattern.

PAULUS; architect and mosaicist.

He made the altars, pavement, and mosaics of the cathedral of Ferentino, Italy (1106–1110), and a pavement in the Vatican gardens, which is supposed to have come from the first basilica of S. Peter on the Vatican Hill.   He probably built the cathedral of Ferentino, Italy. An altar in the church of S. Lorenzo at Terra di Cave, near Rome, bears his name and the date 1093.

A. L. Frothingham, Jr., *Roman Artists in the Middle Ages*.

PAUSANIAS; traveller and historian.

Whatever is known of Pausanias is gathered from his writings. He was a contemporary of Hadrian, who died in 138 A.D., and was the author of the famous *Description of Greece*, an itinerary in ten books, which contains a description of Corinth, Laconia, Messenia, Elis, Achaia, Arcadia, Bœotia, and Phocis. It is evident from his works that he travelled widely beyond the limits of Greece and Ionia. He describes a tomb in Jerusalem, saw the pyramids in Egypt, and visited the cities of Campania and Rome. Pausanias was writing his fifth book in 174 A.D.

Introduction to Frazer's Translation of *Pausanias's Description of Greece;* Smith, *Dictionary of Biography and Mythology.*

PAVEMENT. Primarily, a covering of real or artificial stone or tile laid over the surface of a street, road, or the like. Hence, by extension, a floor covering of concrete, marble, mosaic, tile, or the like. In this sense, applied only to large and important floors in public halls, corridors, etc. Thus, we speak of the mosaic pavement of a church, but the mosaic floor of a vestibule.

Pebble Pavement. A pavement formed of closely set water-rounded pebbles, smaller than cobbles, used for light service as in courtyards and gardens; often the natural contrasts of colour in these pebbles were used to form patterns in a sort of coarse mosaic. This practice was common in the forecourts or doorway courts of mansions of the seventeenth and eighteenth centuries.

Venetian Pavement. Same as Terrazzo Veneziano.

PAVEMENT LIGHT. Heavy glass set in a pavement to convey light to a cellar room or vault beneath; hence, usually, the same as Vault Light (which see under Light).

PAVILION. *A.* Originally, a tent or movable habitation.

B. A building more or less dependent on a larger or principal building, as a summer house; more especially, a dependent residential building.

C. A central, flanking, or intermediate projecting subdivision of a monumental building or façade, accented architecturally by more elaborate decoration, or by greater height and distinction of sky line, as in the pavilions of the Louvre in Paris. In this sense the term is used for a department, or group of wards, of a large public institution, as a hospital.

PAVING. *A.* The process of laying a pavement.

B. Same as pavement.

C. Paving material in general.

PAVONAZETTO. Same as Pavonazetto Marble, under Marble.

PAX ROMANA. The Roman Peace. The contrast between the distracted and devastated condition of the ancient world and the peace brought to it at the beginning of the reign of Augustus led to identifying peace and prosperity with Rome. Hence the term Pax Romana, which was current even after the fall of the Empire. Contemporary with Horace's *Carmen Sæculare*, and the first monument by which this fact is commemorated is the Altar of Peace of Augustus (Ara Pacis), erected 13–9 B.C. in Rome by the Senate, and one of the most notable works of combined sculpture and architecture of the reign of Augustus. The altar itself stood on a platform enclosed by a rectangular parapet about 4 metres high, formed of slabs carved on both sides. The basement and architrave brought the total height to over 6 metres. The slabs were arranged in two lines — a lower one with a decoration of vines and flowers intermingled with birds, and an upper one with a sacrificial procession headed by Augustus and his family, in evident imitation of the Parthenon frieze. Both the figures and the bold, yet delicate, ornamentation are among the best products of Greco-Roman art. The ornamentation of the Portico of Octavia and the Baths of Agrippa may be compared with this. In the interior, groups of pilasters connected by festoons hanging on bucranes support an architrave. In a niche or *ædicula* opposite the one door apparently stood the figure of the Earth (Terra). Compare this entire idea with the early Pelasgic idea of out-of-door worship, of which it seems a survival. Other monumental altars were erected as centres of national worship under Augustus, for Gaul at Lyons and for Spain on the northwest coast. — ARTHUR L. FROTHINGHAM, JR.

PAXTON, SIR JOSEPH; landscape gardener and architect; b. Aug. 3, 1801; d. 1865.

The son of a farmer, in 1823 he entered the service of the Horticultural Society, which had leased the gardens at Chiswick (England) from the Duke of Devonshire. In 1826 he was appointed by the Duke superintendent of the Gardens of Chatsworth. In 1836–1840 he built the great conservatory at Chatsworth. Paxton built the Crystal Palace of the great Exhibition of 1851, on the principle of a very large greenhouse, and deserves the credit of the bold innovation. He was knighted in 1851. He designed several important buildings and published many works on botany and gardening.

Stephen-Lee, *Dictionary of National Biography.*

PAZZI CHAPEL. (See Capella dei Pazzi.)

PECKY. Showing the first symptoms of decay, said of timber

PEDESTAL. A substructure upon which a column, a statue, a memorial shaft, or the like, is elevated. It consists in Roman architecture and its derivatives of a base or foot, a die or dado, and a surbase, cornice, or cap; and in classic architecture is subject to especial canons of proportion in relation to the column or pilaster which it supports. A continuous pedestal is called a Podium. The term is commonly extended to a similar feature interposed at long intervals of a balustrade, even when not supporting a vase or the like.

PEDIMENT. The low triangular gable following the roof slopes over the front and rear of a classic building. It is coped by a cornice of the same section as that of the entablature, and in part mitring with it. The triangular tympanum was the field in which was displayed typical sculpture in high relief or detached. In the neoclassic styles the pediment was often given a segmental or more elaborate form, instead of triangular. It was also used to crown subordinate features, such as doors and windows, and in such cases often called Fronton. (Compare Coronet.)

PEDIMENTAL. Relating to, or of the nature of, a pediment; found on a pediment; designed to be used on a pediment; thus the Niobe Group in the Uffizi Gallery is pedimental sculpture.

PEDIMENTED. Provided with a pediment; constructed in the form of a pediment. A pedimented gable is a gable of which the foot of the coping or cornice is connected with the opposite foot by a horizontal string course, thus, in a measure, recalling the classic original.

PEDRO DE COMA (or **CESCOMES**); architect.

According to an inscription on the wall of the presbytery of the cathedral of Lerida, Spain, Pedro was architect of that cathedral in 1203. Viñaza, *Adiciones al Diccionario historico.*

PEEL ; PEEL TOWER. (See Pele.)

PEEN CHECK. (See under Check.)

PEEN JOINT. (See under Joint.)

PELA. (See Lamberti, Niccolò di Piero.)

PELASGIC ARCHITECTURE; BUILDING. In the ancient pre-Hellenic world, a third style beside the two styles of architecture current in the valleys of the Nile and Euphrates. This was less advanced and less differentiated artistically, but was diffused over a far wider territory and adopted by a greater variety of peoples. It ruled the eastern and northern shores of the Mediterranean and all its islands. The bulk of the early population of this region was called Pelasgian by the Greeks, and a part of it was termed by the other Eastern nations Hittite (see Hittite Architecture). Abundant traces of this people are found even in Egypt. These Pelasgic tribes occupied Armenia and northern Syria, colonized Cyprus, Crete, and other islands, making their headquarters in Crete between 2500 and 2000 B.C., and advancing on the one side through Asia Minor, and on the other through Greece and Italy, of which

they occupied the greater part. Their art included the styles known as "Ægean," "Pre-Mycenæan," "Mycenæan," "Post-Mycenæan," and "Homeric," as well as "Early Hittite." The substantial identity everywhere of the culture of these emigrants, although all were not of the same blood, is shown by archæological as well as architectural remains. Even after their political power had been broken — in Asia by the Shemites (especially the Assyrians) and Arians; in Greek lands by the Dorians; in Italy by the Etruscans and Hellenes — their architectural traditions were so firmly established that their style was long perpetuated. In Italy the tribes of Pelasgic blood, such as Sabines and Latins, retained their autonomy the latest, and here also did the style continue longest. It is impressive in its massive grandeur and rugged simplicity, and in the way its monuments are adapted to the picturesque natural sites and become a part, almost, of nature.

The Orient. Never having been excavated, the Pelasgic cities of Asia Minor and Syria are still almost unknown, excepting Troy, whose "Sixth" city (see Grecian Architecture) represents the highest local development of the Pelasgic style. At the opposite end of Asia Minor the province of Cappadocia has the Hittite capital Boghaz Koi, and other cities which flourished from about 2500 B.C., and have been made better known by Perrot and later by Chantre. Nearly every province in Asia Minor shows works of this early architecture. Caria has them at Assarlik and Myndus, — the latter of very primitive Cyclopean style, and Assarlik, remarkable for its tombs with dromos. In Lycia are the ruins of Pinara and of Pidna, with interesting series of square towers. In Lydia are the tombs of Sardes, especially the royal tomb of Alyattes, which rivalled the pyramids in circuit and height. Phrygia has fortresses at Pishmish-Kaleh, and a great variety of sacred and secular ruins of early date and great renown on and about Mt. Sipylos between Smyrna and Magnesia. It only requires excavations to make evident the monumental importance of this region for the pre-Hellenic age.

Farther east was the Hittite confederacy of Syria. Hazar, in Galilee, is a fine example of its architecture previous to the Hebrew occupation. Military architecture was even more highly developed than in Asia Minor, owing to the constant danger from Egypt and Mesopotamia.

Islands. Pelasgic architecture was thoroughly diffused throughout the islands between Asia Minor and Syria and Greece, even in the smallest. It is singular that Cyprus, so soon colonized and so highly civilized, has furnished so little early architecture. At Melos the English school has been unearthing primitive private and sacred architecture. But it is Crete which furnishes the earliest and most numerous series. Gortyna and Knossos, its greatest centres, Præsos, Goulas-Lato, Itanos, Priansos, Phæstos, Axos, Eleutherna, and a host more of the hundred walled cities mentioned by Homer, form such closely packed and, until now, practically untouched groups, with extensive ruins, as to show that here more than in any other part of the Pelasgic world lies the key to this civilization. Already the excavations of 1900 have begun to prove this fact.

Greece. Tradition points to Thessaly and Arcadia as the great early Pelasgic centres in Greece; but the primitive ruins of Cyclopean and polygonal cities, especially numerous in the north, have been only superficially explored. The majority of discoveries have been on the famous sites of Argolis, such as Tiryns, Mycenæ, Argos, Mideia, Vaphio. In central Greece the structures of Arne (Lake Copaïs) are the most monumental; while Attica is ever growing in importance as a late Pelasgic centre (Sparta, Menidi, Thoricos, Athens, and several necropoli).

Italy. Pelasgic ruins are not found in Piedmont, Liguria, Lombardy, Venetia, Emilia, or Upper Tuscany; in fact, not north of a line drawn from Leghorn across to Ancona. But in most of lower Tuscany, Umbria, Latium, Abruzzi, Campania, Apulia, Basilicata, Calabria, and Sicily their cities abound, over one hundred having been located. Of these Sicily and Campania are least prolific; Calabria and Basilicata least explored. South Tuscany and Latium are best known. We do not know in what relation these early tribes stood either to the Hellenes who displaced them on the south or to the Etruscans who occupied many of the important northern cities. (For separate sites, see Italy, Architecture of.)

Megalithic. The megalithic constructions of the Balearic Isles, of Sardinia, Malta, Gozo, Calabria, are to some extent a branch of Pelasgic, especially of Cyclopean, construction. The similarity between the sacred edifices of Malta and Crete is especially striking. (See Mediterranean Islands.)

Classes of Monuments. The kinds of monuments thus far discovered are: (1) citadels (see Acropolis); (2) city walls with their towers, bastions, and gates; (3) palaces of local rulers, one in each city; (4) temples and shrines, sometimes as palace chapels, sometimes as separate structures; (5) private houses, either of grandees (villas) or of modest dimensions; (6) subterranean vaulted chambers and passages, used either as tombs, treasure houses, cisterns, annexes, or in connection with sally ports; (7) forts, bridges, and other works of engineering; (8) small detached settlements, farms, villas.

General Character of Pelasgic Art. While in architecture there is practical unity of style, in other branches of art there is a great diversity. Cretan discoveries show that there during both the pre-Mycenæan Age (12th Egyptian Dynasty) and the Mycenæan Age (18th Egyptian Dynasty) extraordinary perfection was reached in decorative work and other accessories — in fresco painting, stuccoes, sculptures, stone and terra cotta ware. In realism this art surpassed contemporary work in Egypt and Babylonia. While Troy lags far behind, the art of Mycenæ and the rest of Argolis almost equals the earlier art of Knossos. Every trace of it vanished in the later Pelasgic art of Italy, where only the style of architecture remains unchanged.

Materials. The preference for heavy stone construction is universal. However, crude brick was extensively used in Syria, Cappadocia, and Greece, though apparently not in Italy; its use was confined to inside buildings, shrines, palaces, etc., and its disintegration accounts for much of the disappearance of architectural detail. Varieties of limestone were preferred by the builders to the softer stones that required much tooling. For decorative details it is probable that wood, at times with metal sheathing, was often used, for example in columns.

Architectural Forms. There is a great variation according to period. Spaces were covered in two ways; either by wooden beams or by stone slabs. The palaces and houses undoubtedly used the lighter forms; even the lintels of the doors and the window frames were wooden architraves. The earliest city gates were spanned by wooden beams. When stone was used in the gateways four forms occur: (1) the plane architrave of a long single stone; (2) the triangle, either built up from projecting courses, or formed by sloping jambs; (3) the middle form in which the narrower summit is crossed by an architrave; and finally (4) the true arch, seldom found and comparatively late (Boghaz Koï, Ferentino). These various forms are also used in subterranean and open galleries (Tiryns). The true arch, requiring careful tooling and fitting, was hardly ever used except with different materials from those of the Cyclopean or even the polygonal work. For example, the bridge at Cora (Latium) is entirely polygonal except for the single bold arch, which is of the same material and *opus quadratum* as the double gateway of Ferentino. The use of vaulted chambers was common everywhere. They are used as cisterns, storerooms, and tombs (see Tholos; Tomb). The earliest chambers are both rectangular and circular; if rectangular they are covered by course masonry, each course projecting and being either left square or chamfered; if circular they are covered with a dome in the same fashion, which thus takes an extremely pointed outline. In this way the form of the pointed arch and vault is reached, though not the construction. Multitudes of these structures are found in connection with all Pelasgic cities and necropoli. It is in them that we have, until the present Cretan discoveries, been best able to study the details of refined Pelasgic construction and decoration. The most famous are the " royal " tombs of Mycenæ and the tholos at Orchomenos : the door with its lions and columns at the former and the carved ceiling of the latter are thus far unique in their class. Proto-Doric columns have also been found in Crete by Dr. Evans. The type of the megaron, or palace hall, is sometimes with supporting columns (*e.g.* Troy), but the use of the column seems never to have become characteristic or common.

Cities. Pelasgic cities were usually built on naturally strong hills (exceptions, at Tiryns, Boghaz Koï), and were defended by a fortress or acropolis. In Greece, the fortified city is much smaller in extent than in Crete or Italy. The *enceintes* of Troy, Tiryns, and Mycenæ could all be placed within the circuit of Norba's walls, and two Norbas could find room within Vetulonia, five miles in circuit. In Asia Minor and Greece, the main structure inside the acropolis was the royal palace. In Crete and Italy, with larger circuits there were usually two monumental centres — sacred and secular — placed wherever possible on two hills, like the Capitoline and Palatine at Rome. The origin of the city may be found in Crete, where small separate forts were first grouped together, and sometimes within a single wall for common defence. Then, as in a great city like Goulas-Lato or Præsos, there are only three forts within the common enclosure. There were usually several encircling city walls ; sometimes concentric, sometimes intersecting, but never more than three. The walls were defended by projecting circular or rectangular towers at the gates or accessible points. The gates themselves are often deep and double with a court and were supplemented by posterns connected with the interior by long vaulted passages (Boghaz Koï, Norba, Alatri, Ferentino). Broad, well-graded roads, with heavy retaining walls, led up to the gates and connected the network of cities. They were protected at intervals by forts. In plan, these cities are an irregular oval, differing essentially from the prehistoric *terremare*, and the Etruscan cities which use a square plan, with two main streets at right angles like the Roman camp. In Italy there is one city where the lines of streets and sidewalks, different classes of buildings, water supply and drainage, grading system in terraces with huge retaining walls, plan of houses and temples, can be studied : this is Norba in Latium, recently surveyed by the writer for the American School of Classical Studies in Rome. Similar work with excavations is being commenced in Crete by the English, French,

and Italian archæologists. For northern Syria, the Germans have uncovered a typical Hittite city at Sendjirli, which has two circular circuit walls with a hundred small towers and three gateways, some of them decorated with monumental sculptures.

In Crete, the city of Goulas-Lato is even better preserved than Norba and is of far earlier date. There still remain the great gate, and its approach and outworks, the entire city wall with its ramps and towers, the retaining walls of terraces, with stone houses and palaces often preserved to a height of 6 feet, with pavements and door jambs in place. It is now being surveyed, and will probably be excavated by the French. Thus far, Knossos has yielded the best results, although the English explorers, Evans and Hogarth, have had only one campaign of work. The great Palace of Minos has been found to be sacred to Zeus of the Double Axe (Labrys ; hence Labyrinth, which see) and to be the famous Cretan Labyrinth. The relations with Egypt are proved by a statuette of the 12th Egyptian dynasty. There are earlier stages of the palace below the level now being excavated, which may date from about 2000 B.C. The stonework of the chambers and passages is coated with gypsum, and either frescoed or decorated with painted reliefs. This great royal residence of the ruler of the island was not defended by any fortress. It lay, surrounded by the buildings of the city, which reached up to it from the lower level on terraces ; some are villas of considerable extent, enclosed by heavy walls, in part even earlier than the palace (pre-Mycenæan).

Styles of Construction. Certain common traits may have been developed before the emigrations. For example, the so-called " Cyclopean " construction, before the introduction of metal tools for quarrying and dressing stone ; also the use of bricks (especially sun-dried), adopted from the Babylonians and used in early Hittite, Trojan, and Mycenæan palaces, though not for main outer walls of acropolis, city, etc. The distinctions that arose in various countries were due : (1) to racial differences ; (2) to local material ; (3) to individual development.

The methods of wall construction can be roughly classified as follows : (1) Cyclopean, of large unhewn blocks as they come from quarry, the crevices being filled either with chips or a smear of mud or cement ; (2) horizontal scales, also unhewn, in rough courses of small material ; (3) polygonal blocks dressed only where not exposed ; (4) squared blocks dressed in same fashion ; (5) polygonal blocks, and (6) squared blocks, both dressed on exposed as well as on other faces. There are many subvarieties. Roughly speaking, these categories follow in the chronological order indicated. Still, even when the Cyclopean blocks were used, there was a difference made between the outer and inner walls: the temenos and palace walls being of stones of medium size, and fairly uniform and regular shape, thus leading to irregular horizontal courses. Later, when the wooden wedges, by which the Cyclopean blocks and horizontal scales had been quarried and made ready for use, had been supplemented by metal implements, which allowed of squaring and facing the blocks, the older and easier rough methods were continued in the outer walls, while the palace walls, sanctuaries, tombs, treasuries, cisterns, and the like were constructed of tooled stones, sometimes polygonal, but more often in horizontal courses, because this was the most convenient in short wall spaces, broken by openings. It is a mistake to suppose that the use of tooled polygons is earlier than that of similarly tooled course construction, for polygonal walls continued in use until long after Pelasgic artistic traditions had become obsolete. The famous polygonal wall at Delphi (sixth century) is unique for its archaistic use of sinuous lines, and the polygonal wall at Eretria is even later. In Asia Minor the transition to the *opus isodomum* is shown in such course construction with oblique joints as the walls of Isionda in Pamphylia. Archaistic use of polygonal above with *opus isodumum* is shown at Cnidus, in Lycia and Akarnania, and even earlier in the fortifications with curved towers near Iasus; while it occurs in Latium as late as the close of the Roman Republic. Of genuine early polygonal masonry, the finest examples in Italy are the citadel of Alatri and the walls of Segni, Norba, and Ferentino, dating probably between 1000 and 600 B.C.

— ARTHUR L. FROTHINGHAM, JR.

Schliemann, *Ilios, Troja, Mykenæ, Tiryns;* Schuchhardt, *Schliemann's Excavations*, etc.; Perrot and Chipiez, *Histoire de l'Art dans l'Antiquité;* Chantre, Ernest, in *Nouvelles Archives des Missions scientifiques* (Vol. VII., 1897); Papers in Archæological Periodicals, as the *American Journal of Archæology.*

PELE ; PELE TOWER. Along the Scotch and English border, a small fortified tower or keep, common from the early Middle Ages to the seventeenth century. It was the manor house of those districts, and as such formed a place of refuge for tenants and neighbours.

PELLEVOISIN (PELLEVOYSIN), GUILLAUME ; architect ; b. 1447.

Dec. 31, 1506, he was chosen to construct the new tower of the cathedral of Bourges, France, under the direction of Nicholas Byard and Jean Chesneau, and in 1515 was made

sole director of the works at the cathedral. In 1522 he rebuilt the Hôtel Dieu at Bourges.

Chennevières, *Archives de l'Art français.*

PELOURINHO. A monument erected in a public square of a Portuguese city as a sign that the corporation has been invested with municipal rights ; it has usually the form of a decorative column standing on a platform.

PEN. An instrument for drawing or writing with ink or other coloured fluid.

Bow Pen. (See Bow Compass, under Compass.)

Compass Pen. A pen made like a ruling pen and fitted to a pair of compasses, for describing circles in ink. (See Compass ; Drawing Pen, below.)

Dotting Pen. (See Drawing Pen, *B*, below.)

Drawing Pen. Any pen for use in drawing ; specifically : —

A. A metal pen of the usual form, but gen-

PELE TOWER, ON THE ENGLISH AND SCOTTISH BORDER: AYDON HALL, NORTHUMBERLAND.

The undefended doorways opened into the base-court, of which the high wall is now destroyed.

erally harder, and having a sharper point, for free-hand drawing. (See Crowquill.)

B. An instrument for ruling lines in mechanical drawing when guided by the edge of a square, curve, or the like. In its most common form it has two thin, elastic, metal blades, fixed face to face in a handle, of which they form the prolongation. The blades are precisely the same in shape, and have exactly corresponding rounded points, between which the ink is retained by capillary attraction. The distance between the points can be adjusted by means of a screw, which thus regulates the thickness of the line to be drawn.

A double drawing pen has two pairs of such blades, with a third screw, by which the two pairs may be adjusted, so that two parallel lines may be drawn at a given distance apart.

A dotting pen has, between the points of the blades, a small wheel, the circumference of which is indented at intervals, so that, when travelling over the paper, it will describe an interrupted, broken, or dotted line.

Lining Pen. Same as Drawing Pen, *B*.

Railroad Pen. A double drawing pen for describing two parallel lines, and used for drawing railroad tracks. (See Drawing Pen, *B*.)

Right Line Pen ; Ruling Pen. Same as Drawing Pen (*B*), above.

PENARIA. In Roman antiquity, a storeroom ; or, as some modern writers think, a small and unimportant sleeping room opening on a court.

PENCIL. *A*. A small brush for writing or painting, such as, in European countries, are made of camel's-hair, sable fur, and the like, and, in the East, of different vegetable fibres.

B. A piece of lead, plumbago, chalk, or other somewhat hard substance, by which a mark can

PENDANT: WINDOW HEAD CUT INTO RESEMBLANCE OF TWO ARCHES, WITH PENDANT INSTEAD OF MULLION.

be made, whether set in a wooden case or a metal holder, or not.

PENCIL (v. t.). *A*. To produce or describe (as a line) with a pencil.

B. To paint, or otherwise embellish, by means of a pencil ; thus, joints in brickwork are often pencilled in white.

PEND. In Scotland, an arched roof of masonry, not groined ; hence, a vaulted or arched passage through a block of buildings. In the latter sense sometimes in the plural, as the Pends.

PENDANT ; PENDENT. *A*. Anciently, a pendentive.

B. A fixed hanging ornament, frequently richly sculptured ; usually the projecting lower end of a member or a piece of construction, as the bottom of a newel below a ceiling, or the

bottom of a keystone, or the end of a post of a roof truss extended below the tie beam.

C. A hanging ornamental object of any sort ; applied loosely to hanging lamps and lanterns (see also Corona), votive offerings in churches, and the like.

PENDENTIVE. *A*. A piece of masonry construction for filling in the space in the re-entrant angle of two walls, beginning with a point or line at the bottom, and forming a continuous, more or less

PENDANT OF FAN VAULTING ; HENRY THE SEVENTH'S CHAPEL, WESTMINSTER ; A.D. 1510.

triangular surface sloping or curving outward as it rises, until it ends at the top in an arc

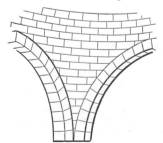

PENDANT, 17TH CENTURY, AT SCHLOSS KALMAR, SWEDEN.

of a horizontal circle or a straight line, in order that a square or polygonal room may be covered by a cupola of circular plan or having more sides than the room. The simplest and typical

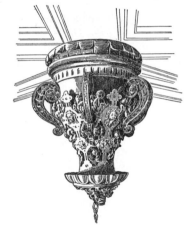

form is the Byzantine, or spherical, pendentive, Fig. 1, the surface of which is part of a sphere

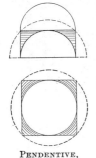

whose diameter is the diagonal of the square to be covered. This half square, or cupola, is supposed to be intersected by four equal barrel vaults whose diameter or chord is the side of the square, or by four vertical planes, and by a horizontal plane tangent to the tops of the resulting semicircles. What is then left of the surface of the sphere makes the surface of four pendentives, intended to carry a smaller cupola whose diameter is that of the square to be covered, Fig. 2. As the pendentive is most commonly built in the spandrels of large arches, which pierce the walls of the room to be covered, so it quite commonly starts at a point above the springing line of its supporting arches, in which case its surface is part of a sphere whose diameter is greater than the diagonal of the square. It may also start from a line or a small circular arc, instead of a point, the corners of the square being cut off, as often occurs in Renaissance buildings, the diameter of the sphere being then less than the diagonal of the square.

PENDENTIVE, FIG. 2.

It is evident that by means of spherical pendentives a dome may cover not only a square,

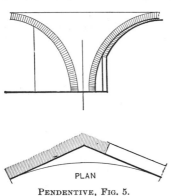

PLAN

PENDENTIVE, FIG. 5.

but a triangle or a polygon of any number of sides, or a rectangle, and examples of hexagonal, octagonal, and sixteen sided occur. There is a peculiar form, Fig. 5, in the baths of Caracalla, Rome, in the angles of an octagon, faced with brick, and doubtless once plastered over or covered with marble. It starts with two straight lines, at an angle of 135°, which, as they rise to describe the surface, become curved, obliterate the angle, and merge into an arc of 45° at the top. In the case of a rectangle which is not a square there are two methods of forming the pendentive. In the first, Fig. 6, the intersecting vaults are in pairs of different diameters,

and the pendentives are run together above the ridges of the smaller vaults, and continued so up to the level of the ridge of the larger, the diameter of the covering dome being then that of the smaller. In the second, the side, or narrower, vaults are stilted so that their crowns are level with those of the main, or larger. The origin of the pendentive which we call Byzantine is not clear. There are apparently one or two Roman examples of it, as in the temple of Minerva Medica, Rome ; but it is quite certain that its general use occurs first in the early Christian architecture of the East, whence it spread to the West. It is very rarely found in the Gothic period, but is common in the Renaissance. For a fuller discussion of the forms see Sir Gilbert Scott's *Lectures on Mediæval Architecture*, Vol. II., and Viollet-le-Duc's *Dictionnaire Raisonné*.

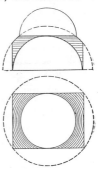

PENDENTIVE, FIG. 6.

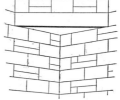

PENDENTIVE, FIG. 7.

B. Less accurately, any device for making the transition, internally, from the corner of a square or polygon to a straight line above across the angle, in order to carry an octagonal vault or a spire, or as preparatory to a circle which shall carry a dome. The forms are various, and will be best understood if arranged as far as practicable in geometrical order.

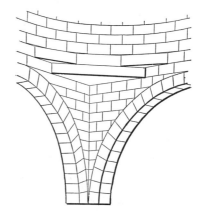

PENDENTIVE, FIG. 8.

A lintel, or several lintels, laid across the angle, Figs. 7, 8. Common in tombs in India, forming an octagon, surmounted by a sixteen-sided polygon, which carries a cone.

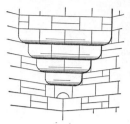

Corbel courses, Fig. 9. Common in England as the support of the four non-cardinal sides of a square tower which has to carry a spire.

A solid with a *plane* surface, Fig. 10, part of an inverted pyramid. An early example occurs

PENDENTIVE, FIG. 9.

at Latakieh, carrying a dome. (De Vogüé, *Syrie Centrale*, Vol. I, p. 76.)

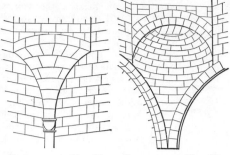

PENDENTIVE, FIG. 17.   PENDENTIVE, FIG. 18.

Fig. 13 is a part of a cone, fan-shaped, spherical, or spheroidal. Fig. 14, domical, S. Julia,

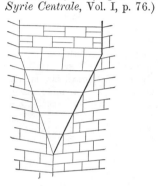

PENDENTIVE, FIG. 10.

PENDENTIVE, FIG. 11.

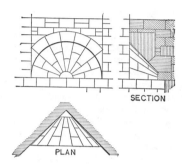

SECTION

PLAN

PENDENTIVE, FIG. 12.

A solid with a *cylindrical* surface, Fig. 11, Spoleto.

A solid with a *conical* surface. Fig. 12 shows

Brescia. Fig. 15, domical, theoretically a variation on the preceding made by carrying up the walls until they intersect the half dome, but really an earlier form. Fig. 16, with a

PENDENTIVE, FIG. 13.

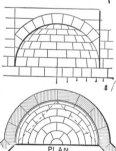

PLAN

PENDENTIVE, FIG. 14.

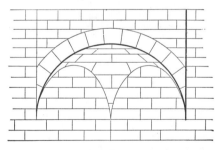

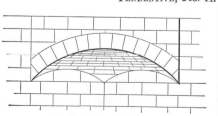

PENDENTIVE, FIG. 16.

the half of a right cone. Very common in French Romanesque, and known as a *trompe*.

PLAN

PENDENTIVE, FIG. 15.

segmental dome. Fig. 17, fan-shaped, from Limburg Abbey. The form, starting from a point, is common in French Romanesque. Fig. 18, cell-shaped, developed from Fig. 14.

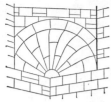

Fig. 19, a transitional form, beginning at the spring as a conical, and passing into a domical surface. It is quite common in French Romanesque. Fig. 20, a barrel vault. A Byzantine form. Common in Saracenic architecture, but the construction is obscured by stalactites or honeycomb ornamentation.

PENDENTIVE, FIG. 19.

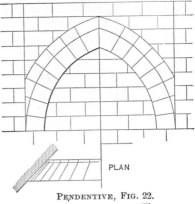

PLAN

PENDENTIVE, FIG. 22.

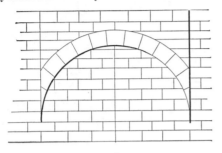

PLAN

PENDENTIVE, FIG. 20.

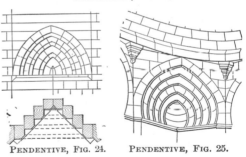

PENDENTIVE, FIG. 23.

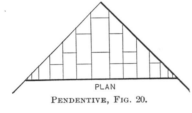

PLAN

PENDENTIVE, FIG. 21.

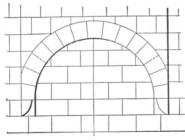

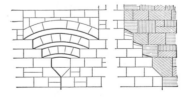

PENDENTIVE, FIG. 24.   PENDENTIVE, FIG. 25.

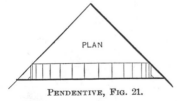

PENDENTIVE, FIG. 26.

Arches, simple or compound, generally called squinches. Fig. 21 is a common arch, whose soffit is *cylindrical*. Fig. 22 shows a splayed arch, whose soffit is a *conical* surface. Fig. 23, an arch whose soffit has an elliptical curve on one face and a circular on the other, the ridge being level; and the surface of soffit *conoidal*. Fig. 24, a series of chamfered or moulded arches. Fig. 25 is from a tomb at Old Delhi, India. Fig. 26, segmental arches, with splayed or conical soffits.

Compound forms: Fig. 27 is a conical, fan-shaped vault, with an arch in front of it. Fig.

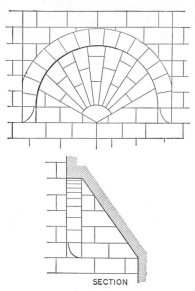

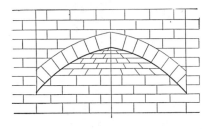

PENDENTIVE, FIG. 27.

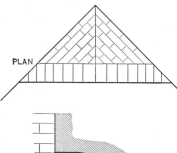

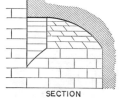

PLAN

SECTION

PENDENTIVE, FIG. 28.

28 is the half of a cloistered vault with an arch in front of it; from the abbot's kitchen at

Stanton Harcourt, England. Fig. 29 is a fan-shaped form, spheroidal, with a squinch above

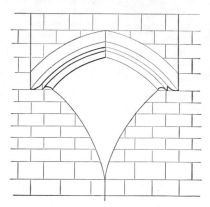

PENDENTIVE, FIG. 29.

PENDENTIVE, FIG. 30.

it; Spanish, Gothic. Fig. 30, a combination of cylindrical, arched, and conical.
— CHARLES BABCOCK.

PENDENTIVE BRACKETING; CORBELLING. Corbelling in the general form of, and discharging the office of, a pendentive. The term is extended to include the apparent construction, common in Moorish and other Mohammedan styles. (Compare Honeycomb Work; Stalactite Work.)

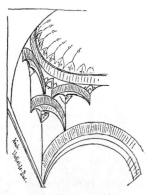

PENDENTIVE BRACKETING: CONJECTURAL RESTORATION OF ROOF OF AN ASSYRIAN CUPOLA, THE FORMS SUGGESTED BY MOSLEM WORK.

PENDICE. Same as PENTICE.

PENETRALIA (pl. n.). The innermost parts of a building, as the inner chambers; hence, in particular, a sanctuary; especially in Roman dwellings, the private chapel or sacred chamber in which the *penates* of a household were enshrined.

PENITENTIARY. *A.* A place for the performance of penance; a small building in a monastic or conventual establishment in which a penitent confined himself or was confined. That part of a church to which penitents were committed during the service.

B. A prison in which convicts are confined for punishment or reformation (see Prison).

PENNETHORNE, SIR JAMES; architect; b. 1801; d. Sept. 1, 1871.

He was a nephew of Sir John Nash (see Nash, J.), and studied also with A. Pugin (see Pugin, Augustus). He visited France and Italy. In 1832 he was employed by the commissioners of metropolitan improvements (London) to devise plans for New Oxford Street, Kensington Palace gardens, Victoria, Kennington and Battersea parks, the Chelsea embankment, etc. He built in London the Museum of Economic Geology, the Stationery Office, Westminster, the west wing of Somerset House, and made many improvements in Buckingham Palace. His most notable work is the building for the University of London.

Stephen-Lee, *Dictionary of National Biography.*

PENNETHORNE, JOHN; architect; b. Jan. 4, 1808; d. Jan. 20, 1888.

A younger brother of Sir James Pennethorne (see Pennethorne, James). In 1830 he made a journey through Europe to Egypt. He was the first to observe the curvature and optical refinements of the Parthenon; and he also observed the curvatures of the temple of Medinet Haboo in Egypt. In 1844 he published privately a pamphlet entitled *The Elements and Mathematical Principles of the Greek Architects and Artists*, in which he set forth a theory of optical corrections. Mr. F. C. Penrose continued these investigations in 1846, and published his *Principles of Athenian Architecture* in 1851 (1 vol. folio). Pennethorne's great work on *The Geometry and Optics of Ancient Architecture* was not published until 1878. He published also a paper in the Transactions of the Royal Institute of British Architects (1878–1879) on *The Connection between Ancient Art and the Ancient Geometry.*

Stephen-Lee, *Dictionary of National Biography.*

PENN PIT. In Great Britain, a primitive dwelling under ground or nearly so; the pit excavated for the purpose being roofed at the level of the surface or, later, somewhat above. (Addy.) (See Pit Dwelling.)

PENTASTYLE. Consisting of five columns, or having a row of five columns in front;

said of a portico or of a building. (See Columnar Architecture.)

PENTASTYLOS. A pentastyle building. The term is modern, made up to correspond with hexastylos, octastylos, etc.

PENTHOUSE. *A.* Primarily, a roof of only one slope; hence, by extension, —

B. A small building or shed with such a roof. In modern times used attributively, as a penthouse roof. Sometimes written Penhouse.

PENTICE. Same as Penthouse; written also Pendice, Pentise.

PEPERINO. A volcanic conglomerate of ashes and gravel found in considerable quantities in the Alban Hills, near Rome, and much used in and near Rome in ancient and modern times. The name is given to other conglomerates found elsewhere in Italy; as it is suggested by the resemblance of the black spots to peppercorns.

PERAC. (See Duperac, Étienne.)

PERCENTAGE CONTRACT. A contract in which the builder binds himself to furnish material and labour at market rates in the construction of a building according to plans and specifications, his remuneration being strictly confined to a stipulated percentage on the value of such labour and material. The main theory of such a contract is to give to the designer a more complete control over the work from day to day. (Compare Day's Work.)

PERCIER, CHARLES; architect; b. Aug. 22, 1764; d. Sept. 5, 1838.

Percier was a pupil of Antoine François Peyre (see Peyre, A. F.), in whose atelier his association with Pierre Fontaine (see Fontaine) began. He was employed also by Chalgrin (see Chalgrin) and Pierre Paris (see Paris, P. A.). In 1786 he won the *Premier Grand Prix de Rome* in architecture. He supported himself during the Revolution by designing furniture and decorations, introducing antique motives from Rome and Pompeii. This may be thought the beginning of the so-called *style empire*, popular throughout Europe in the early years of this century. In 1794 Percier and Fontaine, acting together, replaced Pierre Paris in the direction of the decoration of the Opera in Paris. Between 1802 and 1812 they had charge of the Louvre and Tuileries. They restored the colonnade of the Louvre (see Perrault, Claude), and completed the upper story of the buildings on the court. At the Tuileries they constructed the chapel and theatre, and the buildings adjacent to the Pavillon Marsan in the newly opened Rue de Rivoli. They designed the Arc de Triomphe du Carrousel, and the great stairway of the Museum of the Louvre which was removed by Napoleon III. They designed residences in Antwerp, Brussels, Venice, Florence, and Rome. Percier retired from the association with Fontaine in 1814. He published *Restauration de la Colonne Trajane* (1788), and, in association with Fontaine, *Palais, Maisons et autres édifices de Rome Moderne* (Paris, 1802, folio) ; *Recueil de décorations executées dans l'église Notre-Dame et au Champs-de-Mars* (Paris, 1807,

APPROACH

FISH MOSAIC

GREAT BASE

BARRIER WITH DOOR

BARRIER

BASE OF THE ZEUS

GROUND PLAN RESTORED.
Scale of Metres
0 1 2 3 4 5 6 7 8 9 10 30 40

PERIPTERAL TEMPLE: THAT OF ZEUS AT OLYMPIA.

The peristyle of 84 columns is separated from the naos by the width of the pteroma, and by the wider porticoes at the ends.

Walker & Boutall sc.

1 vol. folio) ; *Choix des plus célébres Maisons de plaisance de Rome et de ses environs* (1809–1813, grand folio) ; *Recueil des décorations intérieurs* (Paris, 1812) ; etc.

Nouvelle biographie générale ; Lance, *Dictionnaire.*

PERCLOSE. Same as Parclose.

PERGAMENE ARCHITECTURE. That of Pergamum or Pergamon, a city of Mysia in Asia Minor, an important centre of Greek civilization and art after the time of Alexander. (See Grecian Architecture.)

PERGOLA ; PERGOLO. A sort of arbour, common in formal Italian gardens or on terraces connected with Italian villas ; formed of a horizontal trellis, vine-covered, and supported by columns of stone or posts of wood. A platform or balcony so protected. The Latin form, *pergula*, is sometimes used in English for such an arbour.

PERGULA. In Latin, a particular member of a larger building, especially of a house, as to the nature of which modern writers differ. Mau's *Pompeii* and Pauly's *Real-Encyclopedie*, make it an upper and slighter construction, a balcony, bay window, or light wooden gallery ; especially the upper story of a shop, as in Pompeii, where the small shops enclosed within the *insulæ* (see Insula), have often upper floors connected with them ; much as, in Paris, the shopkeeper's family live in the Entresol. By extension, a shop in either sense, for selling or working ; a Bottega or Studio. — R. S.

PERIBOLOS. In Greek architecture, a wall enclosing consecrated grounds, generally in connection with a temple. The area so enclosed. In the Middle Ages, the wall enclosing the choir, the atrium, or any other sacred place ; or the other walls surrounding the precinct about a church, and forming the outmost bounds allowed for refuge or sanctuary.

PERICOLI, NICCOLÒ DEI. (See Tribolo.)

PERIDROMOS. The narrow passage around the exterior of a peripteral building behind the enveloping columns. (See Peripteral.)

PERINO DEL VAGA. (See Buonaccorsi Pierino.)

PERIPTERAL (adj.). Surrounded by a single range of columns. Said of a building, especially a temple. (See Columnar Architecture.)

PERIPTEROS. A peripteral building (Vitruvius).

PERISTALITH. A circle or cincture of upright stones, surrounding a burial mound or barrow.

PERISTELE. One of the monolithic upright stones in a peristalith.

PERISTERIUM. The inner or second ciborium ; the Greek term for a hanging tabernacle. — C. C.

PERISTYLAR (adj.). Surrounded by columns; having, or pertaining to, a peristyle.

PERISTYLE. A range or ranges of roof supporting columns enveloping the exterior of a building, as of a peripteral temple; or surrounding an internal court of a building, as in the Peristylium of a Greek or Roman house; or forming a covered ambulatory or open screen around any large open space, partly or wholly enclosing it. Also, by extension, the space so enclosed. (See Columnar Architecture.)

PERISTYLIUM; PERISTYLUM. Same as Peristyle; the original Latin word taken directly from the Greek. By familiar extension in Latin writing, the enclosed garden of a large Roman house, forming a court wholly or partly surrounded by occupied buildings, and having a colonnade on at least three sides.

Rhodian Peristylium. According to Vitruvius, one in which one side is higher than the others. This form is supposed by some to imply a second story colonnade on that side, the upper story corresponding to the second story of rooms.

PERPEND. (Evidently derived from the French *parpaing*.) *A.* A throughstone; a bondstone passing through the whole thickness of a wall and showing on both sides thereof, especially in a wall of squared stones or ashlar. A perpend wall is a wall composed entirely of such stones. Keeping the perpend is a phrase formerly used by masons, referring to

PERPENDICULAR ARCHITECTURE: EARLIEST TRACERY; EDINGTON, WILTSHIRE, A.D. 1361.

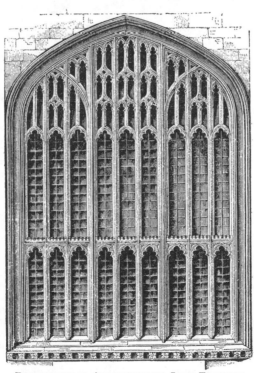

PERPENDICULAR ARCHITECTURE: LATE TRACERY; KING'S COLLEGE CHAPEL, CAMBRIDGE.

keeping the vertical joints over one another in the alternate courses. This use, however, seems to be derived from perpendicular.

B. A vertical joint in masonry; especially in brickwork, in which, when of good workmanship, these joints are supposed to make regular lines perpendicular to the beds.

PERPENDICULAR ARCHITECTURE. That English style which is characterized by perpendicular lines in the common use of that term, more strictly, of vertical lines. The term was introduced by Thomas Rickman for that style of English Gothic architecture which is characterized by window tracery having straight stone mullions, carried vertically not only in the lower parts of the window, and dividing the lights one from the other, but in the decorated, traceried top itself. The style may be considered to begin in 1370, and it never wholly disappears so long as Gothic influence appears in English architecture, which is until a very late period. (See England, Architecture of.) — R. S.

PERPENDICULAR, RESTORING TO THE. The act of correcting a building, or part of a building, which is out of plumb, as in a wall or pier, a tower or spire. This is accomplished in various ways, according to the peculiar conditions of the case: by the distributed pressure of heavy balks of timber applied in the form of props or struts against the affected wall or pier, and bearing at bottom against immovable points and actuated by jack-screws; or by pulling it into place by the use of turn-buckles in heavy iron rods or bolts; or by the driving in of steel wedges in the joints of the masonry; or by iron rods put in place when very hot and exerting a drawing power by contraction while cooling; or by a combination of these devices.

PERRAULT, CLAUDE; physician and architect; b. 1613 (at Paris); d. Oct. 9, 1688.

Claude Perrault was a mathematician, scientist, and practising physician, who acquired a taste for architecture. In 1664 Louis XIV. undertook the construction of the eastern façade of the quadrangle of the Louvre (Paris). The

PERRÉAL, JEAN (JEHAN DE PARIS); b. 1463; d. about 1529.

As early as 1486 he resided at Lyons, France. March 25, 1493, he commenced the church of the Cordeliers in that city, and in the same year was charged with the restoration of the arches of the *Pont du Rhône* at Lyons. In 1494 he accompanied the expedition of Charles VIII. into Italy. In 1499 he was *contrôleur général des bâtiments* of the city of Lyons. For Anne, queen of Louis XII., he designed the monument of François II., Duke of Brittany, for the cathedral of Nantes, which was executed by Michel Colombe (see Colombe, M.), 1502–1556. In 1505 he was commissioned by Marguerite d'Autriche to make the plans of the monastery and church of Brou at Bourg-en-Bresse (Eure-et-Loire), and in 1510 was made *con-*

PERSIAN ARCHITECTURE, PART I.: PLATFORM AND RUINS AT PERSEPOLIS.
View from the east, that is, from a point below and to the left of *A* in the plan. On the left are the winged human-headed bulls of the propylaea *B* in plan. The columns are of the so-called hypostyle hall of Xerxes *E* on the second platform.

designs made by Levau (see Levau) not being acceptable, a scheme was elaborated by Bernini (see Bernini), which was begun Oct. 17, 1665, and soon afterward abandoned. Before the arrival of Bernini, Perrault had presented a plan for the building, which was rejected at the time; but this was presented again in 1667 and accepted. This building, forming the eastern side of the great court, and having on its outer face the famous colonnade of the Louvre, was completed in 1674. The southern façade (the river façade) was also built by Perrault. These buildings were not actually roofed over until 1755. (See Gabriel, J. A.)

Lance, *Dictionnaire*; Bauchal, *Dictionnaire*; Abbé Lambert, *Histoire du Règne de Louis XIV.*

trôleur of the works. In 1513 he was replaced at Brou by the Flemish architect, Van Boghem.

Charvet, *Lyons Artistique, Notices biographiques*; Charvet, *Jean Perréal*; Dupasquier, *Notre Dame de Brou.*

PERRON. A flight of steps, including platform and parapet, forming approach, as to the entrance door of a house or public hall; usually out of doors, but occasionally in an outer vestibule, or the like. (Compare Stoop.)

PERRONET (PERONET), JEAN RODOLPHE; engineer and architect; b. Oct. 8, 1708 (at Suresnes, France); d. Feb. 20, 1794.

He was educated as a military engineer, but abandoned this profession for architecture. In 1745 he rebuilt the choir and spire of the cathe-

PLATE VI

PERSIA

A specimen of Moslem architecture in that country. Courtyard of the great Mosque of Teheran, which dates from the sixteenth century of the Christian era. The decoration is almost wholly in richly coloured enamelled earthenware tiles: a manufacture in which the Persians have always excelled.

dral of Alençon (France), which had been destroyed by fire in 1744. In 1747 he was made director of the *École des Ponts et Chaussées*, Paris, founded in that year. In 1748 he began with Hippeau the great bridge at Orléans, France. In 1763 he replaced Hippeau at his death as *premier ingénieur du roi*. He designed the bridge at Nantes in 1764, the bridge at Nogent-sur-Seine in 1766, the bridge at Neuilly (Paris) in 1768, and the Pont Louis XVI. (now Pont de la Concorde) in 1786. Perronet held the office of *inspecteur général et premier ingénieur des ponts et chaussées du royaume*. He published *Description des projets de la construction des ponts de Neuilly, de Nantes, d'Orléans et autres*, etc. (Paris, 1782–1783, 2 vols. folio; supplement, 1 vol. folio, Paris, 1789.)

Bauchal, *Dictionnaire*.

PERSEPOLITAN ARCHITECTURE.
(See Persian Architecture.)

PERSIA, ARCHITECTURE OF. (See Persian Architecture.)

PERSIAN ARCHITECTURE. That of the lands included in the modern kingdom of Persia, and those immediately adjoining which have received and retained Persian artistic influence. Thus, although the great empire of Cyrus reached the Mediterranean, it left but little impression upon the architecture of Asia Minor and Syria; while within the boundaries of modern Persia that influence is still easy to study, and to judge, at least in part. Architecturally, Persia may be considered under (1) the rule of Darius, Xerxes, and their successors, about 500 to 334 B.C.; (2) the rule of Alexander and his successors, beginning 334, an epoch not identified with known buildings of importance in this region; (3) the Parthian rule in the second and third centuries A.D.; (4) the kingdom of the Sassanians, 226 A.D. until the Moslem conquest; (5) the Moslem rule, resulting about the ninth century in an independent Mohammedan kingdom. The later conquests, as by the Seljuks and by Jenghis

Khan, do not alter the national character of the Persian Mohammedan art. (For these subjects see, in the following order, Persian Architecture, Part I.; Parthian Architecture; Persian Architecture, Part II.; Persian Architecture, Part III.)

PERSIAN ARCHITECTURE; Part I. The origin of the architecture of Persia must be sought for in that of the two countries conquered by her, viz., Babylon and Media. From the former she derived the raised platform, or terrace, on which her palaces were built, — the broad flights of steps which led up to them and to her palaces, — and the winged bulls which

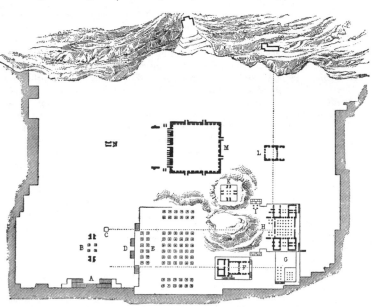

PERSIAN ARCHITECTURE, PART I.: PLATFORMS AND PALACES AT PERSEPOLIS.
The white surface is that of the platforms.

A   Landing of stairs from town to platform.
B   Propylaea on the first plateau.
C   Cistern.
D   Stairs leading to second plateau.
E   So-called hypostyle hall of Xerxes.
F, G, H   supposed royal dwellings (F generally called House of Darius).
I   Gateway.
K   Gateway.
L   Unknown ruin.
M   Throne room, called hall of 100 columns.

flanked the portals of her Propylon. To the Medes she owed her porticoes and halls of columns. Media being a country abounding in timber, the supports of her peristyles and halls were all in that material, protected and decorated with plates of the precious metals in thin laminæ (Polybius). These columns in Persia were copied in stone. The Persian column, twelve or more diameters in height, is a copy of a wooden and not a stone support, and the rich decoration of the campaniform base and the capitals with their vertical volutes on each side suggest a metallic origin.[1] The bracket

[1] In his report on the investigations at Assos 1881, Mr. T. Thacher Clarke observes, p. 120: "The proceeding of the Phœnician artisan was to

capital may also have been derived from the Medes, but its further development into the heads, or, more properly speaking, the torsi of bulls and griffins, is probably owing to the influence of Babylonian or Chaldean art, if indeed the Chaldean sculptor may not be looked upon as the artist who carved the winged bulls of the propylon and the rich balustrades of the flights of stairs.

The earliest Persian palace is the one built at Pasargadæ, by Cyrus, which consisted, according to Flandin and Coste, of a porticus, *i.e.* a building with its roof supported by rows of columns, and, at each angle, a small chamber enclosed with walls which formed the antæ of the entrance porticoes. This type of building may have been the "stoa" referred to by Polybius.

A second Persian work is the Takht-i-Soleiman (throne of Solomon), also at Pasargadæ, an immense platform with a frontage of 730 feet, evidently built in imitation of Babylonian work, but executed in stone with an external wall of fine ashlar masonry with drafted joints. Portions of the wall still rise to the height of 38 feet, some of the stones being 13 feet long, and the courses 3 feet high. This platform is considered to be the terrace on which a palace was intended to be erected, but of which there are no traces to suggest that it was even commenced. It is the earliest example known of regular drafted masonry, and may have suggested that type of architectural embellishment which forms the chief characteristic of the substructure of Herod's temple at Jerusalem. (See Syria, Architecture of.)

From these we pass to the more developed examples at Persepolis and Susa, where, in the palaces of Darius and Xerxes, and in the apadana, or great reception hall, of the latter monarch, we find the masterpieces of Persian architecture. The palaces at Persepolis were built on an immense platform at the foot of a high range of rocky hills, consisting of the natural rock at the back, but on the west and south sides built in blocks of stone of various sizes, not laid in horizontal courses, but fitted to one another with the greatest accuracy, and held together by metal clamps. The approach to the platform on the west side is by a double flight of stairs, 22 feet wide, the steps having a tread of 15 inches with a rise of 4 inches, so that they could be ascended by horses. The first building on the platform (originally, probably, connected

make a model of wood for the relief, or sculpture, in the full round, as the case might be, upon which sheets of metal were secured, and finally beaten to the shape of the carving beneath." "It is natural that the peculiar forms resulting from the technical properties of beaten sheet metal should determine a style which is recognizable even in stone carvings when these were the creation of sculptors familiar with works of this kind."

by low walls with the parapet of the platform, now gone) is the Propylon of Xerxes, a square building with its roof supported internally by four columns, with winged bulls flanking the entrance and rear portals and doorways on the right and probably on the left. The best preserved building on the platform is the palace of Darius, the examination of which will facilitate the inquiry into the restoration of the Hall of Xerxes, respecting which there is so much difference of opinion amongst antiquaries.

The palace of Darius was built on a platform 10 feet high, ascended by flights of stairs at each end. Its principal front faced the south and consisted of a portico of eight columns, in two rows of four each, in antis between wings enclosed with walls. The portico led to a square hall with its roof carried by sixteen columns in four rows, the bases of which only remain *in situ*. There were other rooms on each side with a court and other rooms in the rear, the plan of which has not been made out. The wall between the portico and the hall has a central doorway and two windows on each side; these were built in stone, the doorway in three stones, viz., posts and lintel, and the windows each cut out of a solid block. These blocks of masonry were isolated one from the other, but the toothing left and the mortice holes on each side show that the walls uniting them were of an ephemeral nature, such as crude brick, similar to those found by Mr. Dieulafoy at Susa, and found also in those stone portals at Karnak in Egypt, which were originally flanked by huge crude brick pylons. Of the portico the bases of the columns remain *in situ*, showing their position and the stone antæ of the angle wings. The mortice holes to receive the ends of the epistyle are in advance of the line of columns, which would be inexplicable were it not for reproduction of the palace façade in the tomb of Darius carved in the rock at the rear of the platform. The capitals there carved are double bracketed capitals; parallel with the epistyle are the two bulls' heads, and in between them and at right angles are other brackets projecting forward to carry the epistyle. The lower fascia of the epistyle, in fact, projects nearly a diameter of the column in front of it. To counterbalance their weight in the portico of the palace, a similar bracket inside must have carried the roof beams. It is probable that these were all in timber, and the three fasciæ of that epistyle suggest that it was formed of three separate horizontal timbers projecting one in front of the other; they carried a series of joists, the ends of which projecting forward give the origin of the dentil cornice; the joists not being placed quite contiguous one to the other: these joists carried a platform of boards on which the earth roof was formed.

We may now pass to the great Hall of

Xerxes, one of the most stupendous works of antiquity, and which, though composed only of the simplest elements, viz., a central hall and three porticoes, covered an area greater than that of any European cathedral, excepting that of Milan and S. Peter's at Rome.

The remains of the Palace of Xerxes consist of the platform or terrace, 350 feet east to west, and 246 feet north to south, raised ten feet above the northern terrace, from which it was ascended by four flights of stairs, and of the bases of all the columns, viz., thirty-six in the central group in six rows with six in each, and of three other groups in two rows of six each.[1] In the restoration of this great hall there are many serious differences of opinion among archæologists.

In the east and west porticoes the capitals consist only of the double bull or griffin ; the cross corbels on their backs, being in timber, have disappeared. In the north (principal entrance) below the bulls' torsi are two other features, the upper one consisting of groups of vertical volutes, the lower a calyx with pendent leaves. The ornament of these two features, as well as that of the campaniform bases, resembles the forms taken by thin plates of metal when beaten out on a wooden core, and is therefore probably derived from the Median work already referred to. The columns were fluted, having from forty-eight to fifty-two flutings, of elliptical section, and not semicircular like the Ionic column.

The palace at Susa, first discovered by Loftus in 1850, was similar in plan, design, and detail to that of the great Hall of Xerxes ; it was raised on a platform on the east, north, and west sides, with an inclined ascent leading round up to the higher level. On the south side it was on the same level as the court in front. Here Mr. Dieulafoy found negative evidence of the existence of walls enclosing the central hall, viz., in the lines where the paving stopped. The south side he considers was open to the court ; as, however, its columns were placed between antæ, its restoration would be similar to that of the porticoes and, as usual, the epistyle would project in front of the columns, raising none of those difficulties of design which Messrs. Perrot and Chipiez show in their drawings, and which are in distinct contradiction to the tombs of Darius and of his successors carved in the rock behind the platform at Persepolis. The magnificent frieze of Archers in enamelled *béton*, now in the Louvre, discovered by Mr. Dieulafoy (the preservation of which was due to the fact of the walls they decorated having fallen forward on their face), would seem to have decorated the

two walls in front of the great Hall or apadana. (Mr. Dieulafoy calls them pylons, but as the opening between them was 170 feet, it could scarcely be looked upon as part of a doorway.) The winding ascent referred to was probably the private approach of the king. About 200 feet to the south of these two walls Mr. Dieulafoy found the remains of the great staircase, the steps of which, as that at Persepolis, measured 15 inches tread and 4 inches rise, the balustrade being decorated with enamelled *béton* blocks. Mr. Dieulafoy found also portions of a frieze of lions in the same material, decorating some parts of the palace.

One of the most important discoveries made by Mr. Dieulafoy at Susa lies in the material employed for the walls of the Persian palaces, viz., that of crude brick, protected externally at Susa by blocks of enamelled *béton*, and at Persepolis by burnt enamelled brick.

The only other monumental works of Persian architecture are the tombs ; to those cut in the solid rock we have already referred ; there are two examples of isolated tombs constructed in masonry, built in the form of towers, square on plan. The example at Persepolis, in front of the four royal tombs cut in the rock, measures 24 feet square and is 36 feet in height. It is built in regular coursed masonry, with angle strips in relief, and a dentil cornice between, with stone roof slightly weathered. The entrance doorway is placed halfway up, and was closed originally by stone doors. Besides other recesses in the walls, probably introduced for decorative purposes, there are a series of small sinkings or grooves in the stone, placed at regular intervals, the object of which has never been ascertained.

Except for their peculiar vertical position, there is such a close resemblance between the volutes of the Persian capital and those of the Greek Ionic capital, that it is assumed there may have been some connection between the two. The Greek Ionic capital, however, was fully developed elsewhere : in the archaic Temple of Diana at Ephesus, the capital of which is now in the British Museum. It is probable though that in both cases the features had a metallic origin. At Neandria, an ancient Greek city north of Assos, several capitals have been found of a temple ascribed to the seventh century B.C., with vertical semivolutes, and underneath a calyx with pendent leaves, with much resemblance to those at Persepolis.

— R. Phenè Spiers.

PERSIAN ARCHITECTURE ; Part II., the Sassanian Period. The three principal monuments attributed to the Sassanian dynasty are the palaces of Firouzabad, Serbistan, and Ctesiphon. The approximate dates of the first and last are known, Firouzabad having been erected by the King Firouz (Pheroses, A.D. 460–494), and Ctesiphon by Chosroes Nushirvan

---

[1] One column of the north group, four of the eastern group, five of the western, and three of the central group remain *in situ*, and four bases or foundations of walls between the north and the centre group of columns.

(531–579). Fergusson places Serbistan before Firouzabad, but the plan of the former suggests an advance in its construction, in that, instead of erecting the enormously thick walls we find in the latter, probably derived from the early traditions of Mesopotamia, its builders had learned how to economize their thickness and to provide for the thrust of the vaults by carrying them on piers built within the walls.

Firouzabad also is the only Sassanian building in which we find, internally, reproductions of decorative features copied from those in Persian palaces. The traditions of Mesopotamia are shown likewise in the external breaking up of the wall surfaces, which are decorated with a series of semidetached shafts without base or capital, copied from the ground story of the Babylonian temple.

Serbistan, on the other hand, shows the influence of Roman work in its plan; the side halls, with their piers carried on stumpy columns, and the recesses between, covered with semidomes, recall, though on a much smaller scale, the tepidaria of the Roman baths. The semidetached shafts are here employed to emphasize and give importance to the entrance portals, or aiwans, instead of being distributed along the side walls.

In the great façade of the palace of Ctesiphon, similar shafts are found, apparently superimposed on three levels, in imitation of those of the Roman amphitheatres. The shafts, however, do not stand one on the other, but are set back and rest on ledges, and the design includes other features quite foreign to Roman work, so that it is possible the Greco-Roman work at Seleucia may have suggested the scheme of decoration, which is entirely different to any other known example.

The plans of Firouzabad and Ctesiphon are somewhat similar in arrangement, all the reception halls being in the front, preceded by great portals, and with an open courtyard at the back surrounded with smaller rooms. At Ctesiphon, there is one great aiwan, or reception hall, with a series of long parallel vaulted chambers on each side, so arranged that the thrust of the vaults should be neutralized. This will account for the exceptional thickness given to the lower part of the front wall, viz., 16 feet 6 inches. At the back, the cross walls of other buildings resisted the thrust.

The principal interest in Sassanian architecture lies in its vaulted construction, which, on the one hand, seems to be a revival of the traditional method of constructing elliptic domes as shown in Assyrian bas-reliefs; and, on the other, to run on parallel lines with that development of domes carried on pendentives, as shown in S. Sophia and other churches of Justinian's time.

The chief difference, however, between the Sassanian and Roman or Byzantine vaulted surfaces, is that the former adhered always to the upright elliptical section, a form necessitated by the absence of centring. The value of the upright elliptical section given to a vault lies in the fact that the lower part of the ellipse being of slight curvature, it can be built with horizontal courses. Thus, the great barrel vault of the aiwan at Ctesiphon is 83 feet in span; the bricks are built up in horizontal courses to nearly half the height of the ellipse, leaving a span of only 70 feet. In order to dispense with the necessity for centring, the vault is built with bricks laid flatwise in slanting rings. This system was adopted by the early Egyptians in their vaulted granaries, and is practised down to the present day throughout Egypt and Persia.

The domes over the three central halls of Firouzabad are built on pendentives, consisting of a series of concentric arches, the low one serving as the centring for the arch above.

At Serbistan, the central dome is carried on pendentives erected in a very haphazard manner, which suggest that the Sassanian builder trusted to the excellence of his mortar rather than to any proper constructional method, unless the stone facing has fallen away, exposing only the filling in at the back. This is just possible, because the semidomes over the recesses in the two side halls show considerable knowledge of dome construction.

It is evident, from the coarse quality of the masonry, rubble work of an inferior kind, that it was always intended to cover it over with stucco; in the doorways at Firouzabad are the only remains of stucco which exist in any of these Sassanian palaces.

Beyond this stucco work, there are only two decorative features peculiar to this style: the first is the zigzag (*dents-de-scie*) moulding, a design obtained by placing projecting bricks edgewise to carry a string course, and this is found throughout Firouzabad and Serbistan. The second, found at Ctesiphon, is the introduction of angle shafts, without capital or base, to arched openings and arcades.

Both these features are found in a remarkable building at Ammon, in Moab, attributed to Chosroes, the Sassanian king, and supposed to have been built by him, as well also as in the palace of Mashita, built during his triumphal march to Jerusalem in 14 A.D.

At Ammon, the zigzag decoration is carried round the archmoulds, giving the design of the Norman dogtooth ornament. Both at Ammon and Mashita, the rich decoration of the carved stonework is due to Greek artists, in the former probably the native sculptors, in the latter those sent from Byzantium for that purpose. (See Syria, Architecture of.)

In the rock-cut tombs at Tak-i-Bostan, the Sassanian sculptor shows an acquaintance with the capital as a decorative feature, but not as a constructional one. There are, however, isolated capitals at Bisoutun, illustrated in Flandin and Coste, as also panel sculpture of great beauty and much originality, which causes us to regret that more is not known of their work.

— R. PHENÈ SPIERS.

PERSIAN ARCHITECTURE; Part III., Moslem Architecture. The precise position of Persian art in the history of the Mohammedan styles is still a matter of debate among scholars. Some writers — notably Aug. Choisy in his recently published *Histoire de l' Architecture* — consider it the fountain head of inspiration of all the Moslem styles. Others refuse it this preëminence, while conceding its dominant influence in the Mogul architecture of India and in Oriental ceramic design. The extent to which Arabic and Moorish architecture borrowed from Persia, or it from Bagdad and Cairo, can be finally determined only by a more thorough exploration both of Persia itself and of Persian, Turkish, and Arabic literary sources, than has yet been practicable. To restore, with any approach to completeness, the aspect and details of the earlier phases of Persian-Moslem architecture will always be difficult or impossible, owing to the havoc wrought by the Mongol invaders of the thirteenth and fourteenth centuries. One fact, however, stands unquestioned; the Persians alone among Mohammedan peoples have had from the first an art of their own. In Persia, as perhaps nowhere else except in China, the art of architecture has been actively practised by natives, in their own way, without interruption, from the sixth century B. C. down to our own day, borrowing freely, at times, from other styles, but never without a pronounced national character easily recognized. The probabilities are therefore strongly in favour of its having given to the conquering Arabs in the West far more than it ever received from them.

The history of Persian-Moslem architecture naturally falls into three periods. The first extends from the Arab conquest in 641 to the Mongol invasion under Jenghis Khan in 1221. The second covers the long period of commotion and incessant changes of dynasty from 1221 to the accession of the Sefi dynasty in 1499. The third extends to the present time; for in spite of the decline in taste and architectural enterprise since the extinction of the Sefis by the Afghans in 1694, the more modern works represent no real change of style from those of that dynasty.

Of the first of these periods the remains are too scanty to enable us to reconstruct the earlier phases of the style, and there is hardly an authentic vestige of the period of the Abbasid khalifs and of the great Haroun-al-Rashid. The substructions of a few mosques rebuilt in later years, — as, for example, that of Kazvin, — a considerable number of tombs of descendants

of Ali (the Prophet's son-in-law), known as *imam-zadeh* and preserved with reverence but probably not without frequent restorations, rendering their original aspect a matter of uncertainty, and scattered ruins of other buildings, generally mere fragments, are all that remain of the first period. The most interesting examples are a number of tombs near Bagdad, dating perhaps from the tenth century; not, it is true, in Persia, but clearly Persian and not Arabic in style. They have roofs suggesting pyramidal piles of beehives, each beehive forming internally a niche; and are wholly built of brick, which has always been the favourite building material in Persia. These cellular pyramids suggest an origin for the whole Persian and Arabic system of "stalactite" decoration (see article by R. Phenè Spiers in *Journal of the R. I. B. A.*, Vol. 4, New Series). Two ruined towers at Rhei, the ancient Rhages, give further evidence as to the character of the style. One, faced with enamelled tiles and adorned with a Cufic inscription, has a species of stalactite cornice; the other is faced with rubble, originally plastered; both were once roofed with domes, and both have pointed-arched doors enclosed in rectangular panels. The triangular fluting of the first of these towers, resembling that of ancient Persepolitan bases, illustrates the persistent vitality of style traditions in Persia. At Hamadan, the ancient Ecbatana, are the ruins of an ancient mosque displaying many of these same features. The antiquity of this edifice appears from the fact of its being stuccoed and painted externally instead of being veneered with tiles. The use of brick as the chief building material; the pointed arch, both of the equilateral and the four-centred or Persian type; the enclosing of each arch or feature in a rectangular framework; the exaggeration of the entrance-portal; the exterior decoration by patterns in colour, at first on stucco, later by enamelled tiles; the use of Cufic inscriptions as decoration, and the stalactite cornices, — all these features, so characteristic of the later Persian architecture, are recognizable in these earlier ruins. Several of these are clearly traceable to Sassanian origins, such as the preference for and skill in the use of brick, of the dome and other varied forms of vaulting, the exaggeration of the portal arch, and the general lack of mouldings. It is possible that the pointed arch was a survival from the pointed-arched vaults of Mesopotamia, from which the ancient Persians borrowed many details. These various considerations point to a home origin for most of the essentials of the Persian-Moslem style. The enamelling of tiles (or in some cases even of bricks of *béton*) in brilliant colours for exterior decoration was an art handed down in Persia and Mesopotamia, with occasional interruptions, from the very earliest antiquity.

The second period begins with the overthrow of the Seljûk dynasty at the hands of Jenghis Khan in 1221. In 1387 Persia was overwhelmed by a second Mongol wave under the terrible Timûr. During the interval there was considerable architectural activity; but upon the death of Timûr, who had united all the Persian provinces under a firm central government, there began a century of disorder and bloodshed, caused by the incessant quarrels of rival governors. Yet in one and another centre there were, between these wars, periods of quiet to which we owe most of the important examples of the style of this period remaining to us. Chief among these is the tomb of the Mongol Sultan Oljaïtou Khodabendeh at Sultanieh (1313), a fine ruin, consisting of an octagonal chamber covered by a dome 80 feet in diameter, rising with an ovoid profile to a point 175 feet high, and surrounded by eight slender minarets springing from the angles of the edifice. The sarcophagus is in a smaller chamber behind the octagonal hall. The whole edifice, admirably constructed of brick, is revetted externally with enamelled tiles, and all its details are in excellent taste. A ruined mosque at Tabriz is by some authorities attributed to this period (1313), and is probably in part as old as this, but its style is that of the fully developed Sefi mosques, and it was probably given its final form in the sixteenth century. The Great Mosque (Mesjid-i-Shah) at Kazvin was built, or rebuilt and enlarged, by the Sultans of the Dailamite line in the tenth century upon earlier foundations; to a later part of the period belongs the mosque and tomb of Hussein in the same city. The greater part of the extant monuments of this period are tombs, especially tombs of the descendants of Ali. The Persians belong to the Shiah sect, considered heretical by the orthodox Sunnis (Turks, Arabs, etc.); they regard the descendants of Ali, the son-in-law of Mohammed, as the rightful successors of the Prophet; hence the great number of these revered *imam-zadeh*. They are of various degrees of elegance and size, but nearly all consist of a square or polygonal chamber surmounted by a lofty roof, either pyramidal or bulbous in form, and are decorated externally with a revetment of coloured tiles. At Shiraz the tombs of the poets Sadi and Hafiz belong to the latter part of the period (fifteenth century); they are both open-air structures of no great architectural pretensions, but not without elegance; that of Hafiz is sheltered by a canopy on columns, doubtless comparatively modern.

There are probably many mosques and other edifices of more or less importance originally erected in this period which would deserve mention in a more extended notice; but earthquakes, and the Oriental habit of allowing a building to go to ruin when once it begins to decay, and of then using its ruins as a quarry, have destroyed

great numbers of buildings, and many others have been rebuilt and altered so many times that their original form is not recognizable. The majority, therefore, of the extant monuments of Persia belong to the third period, which begins with the accession of the Sefi (called also Sufi or Sefavean) dynasty under Shah Ismail, whose final triumph over his enemies occurred in 1499. For nearly a hundred years, however, no important buildings were erected; but under the Shah Abbas I., the greatest of Persian-Moslem rulers, a man of great energy and ability, and one of the great builders of history, there was an extraordinary revival of architectural activity, in which the accumulated traditions of the past were developed into a complete and monumental style, and applied to a great variety of buildings, often of great size and richness of detail. Ispahan was restored to its former dignity as capital, and embellished with a remarkable series of splendid buildings; and other cities shared in this renaissance of art. Abbas called to his court many European artists, to whom may in part be due the grandiose planning of some of these great works; but there is no trace of Italian or classic detail discoverable in them. The Shah Hussein was also a great builder. The Sefi dynasty — the first native Shiah dynasty in Persia — was overthrown in 1696 by the Afghans, and it was not until the accession of the present Khadjar line at the beginning of the nineteenth century that architecture experienced another revival. The Shah Feti Ali erected a number of palaces, mosques, and caravanserais, and the art is still practised with no essential change of style, though with less splendour and purity of taste than under the Sefis.

The most important works of the Sefis are at Ispahan, and include the Great Square (Meidan Shah), the adjoining Royal Mosque (Mesjid-i-Shah), the Djouma Mesjid or "Friday Mosque" (corresponding to the Jumma or Jami Masjid of Indian cities, and the Jami of Turkey), a structure of various periods enlarged and completed under the Sefis; the Medress or college and caravanserai erected by Shah Hussein to the memory of his mother (Medresseh-Mader-i-Shah); the Chehil-Soutun palace by the same Shah, and the two splendid bridges across the Zendeiroud, the Allah-Verdi-Khan bridge of thirty-three arches, built under Shah Abbas, and that of Hassan Bey. To the reign of Feti Ali Shah (cir. 1805) belong a number of important palaces, mosques, and tombs: at Ispahan the celebrated Mirror palace (Aineh Khaneh) and Char Bagh pavilion; the great mosque at Koum with its Medress (college) and several tombs; the Kasr-i-Khadjar palace at Teheran; the great caravanserai of Mohammed-Baker at Passaingan, and many bazaars and public baths of no little splendour.

These very varied buildings are treated with remarkable uniformity of style. The great mosques, medresseh, and caravanserais are built around large courts, usually square or rectangular, entered by an imposing vaulted portal, and surrounded by arcades, usually in two stories, which give access to the various chambers, rooms, or cells behind them. The centre of each side of the square is occupied by some especially important feature, such as a portal, or a prayer room, or music gallery, invariably preceded by a colossal portal or deeply recessed arch, enclosed in a square framework of decoration rising high above the two-storied arcades, and frequently flanked by tall and slender round minarets, bearing an arcaded gallery carried on stalactite corbelling. Opposite the chief entrance is usually the main prayer room of the mosque, or the chapel mosque of the college, with a similar portal and minarets, but distinguished by a lofty ovoid-pointed dome, often swelling with a bulbous outline from a high drum. This exterior dome is wholly distinct from the interior vault, which is much lower: an arrangement which may have been introduced by European architects in the reign of Shah Abbas.

As to details, it should be noted that neither the horseshoe nor the cusped arch prevails in Persia. The equilateral pointed arch occurs but rarely; the characteristic Persian arch resembles somewhat the Tudor arch of the perpendicular English style, being four-centred, or, more often, having the upper outline formed by two straight lines meeting at an obtuse angle. The vaulting, generally executed in brick, is often treated with great ingenuity of detail; with complex interpenetrating surfaces, structurally more scientific than the treatment with stalactite decoration. Excellent examples of this are in the Tailor's Bazaar at Ispahan and the bazaar and baths at Kashan. Sometimes, however, stalactite vaults were used, and it is not improbable that this sort of ornament, though less lavishly used by the Persians than farther west, was originally invented in Persia, as already observed.

In the matter of ornament the Persians surpassed the Western Moslems as far in ceramic decoration and in the flowing grace and freedom of their patterns, as they were inferior to them in variety and splendour of ornament. Hardly a moulding is to be met with in Persian exterior decoration, which is effected almost entirely by means of ceramic tiles in beautiful hues of blue, yellow, red, and green, with inscriptions and details often in black. It was Persian artists who carried the art of wall tiling into Turkey, and into Egypt, Sicily, the Moghreb, and Spain. This art underwent a revival consequent upon the importation of Chinese wares and ceramic artists into Persia under Shah Abbas, and is still practised, though

less successfully than formerly. Persian decorative art makes free use of pictures, of naturalistic floral and animal forms, and even of sculpture, differing in this from the more orthodox Moslem art. In the Char-Bagh pavilion at Ispahan, the four slender wooden columns that support the panelled ceiling stand on pedestals formed by grouped caryatides; and pictures are an important element in the decoration of the Hesht-Der Behisht, or "Eight Gates of Paradise." Modern Persian architecture, following, no doubt, an immemorial tradition of which the slender columns of Persepolis were the interpretation in stone, makes free use of wood, both for the supporting columns and for the ceilings of its palaces and houses, and uses it with great elegance, as in the Chehil-Soutun palace at Ispahan, the Kasr-i-Khadjar, the Throne Pavilion at Teheran, and the famous Mirror Hall near Ispahan, in which small panels of looking-glass are inlaid in the mosaic ornament of the columns and other woodwork, with an effect somewhat tawdry perhaps, but not without a certain charm. The Persians are adepts in a certain kind of formal gardening, which adds to the effect of their palaces and squares, and which was carried to India by Persian artists in the train of the Moguls in the sixteenth century. — A. D. F. HAMLIN.

The bibliography of Persian art is scanty. Descriptions by mediæval travellers and the writings of Pietro della Valle and Krusurski of the sixteenth–seventeenth centuries, the travels of Ousely and Malcolm in English, and in handy and popular form the *Story of Persia* and *Persia and the Persians*, by S. G. W. Benjamin, give comparatively little information on the Moslem architecture. For this, dependence is chiefly on French works: Flandin et Coste, *Voyage en Perse;* Coste, *Monuments Modernes de la Perse;* Texier, *Description de l'Arménie, la Perse et la Mésopotamie;* Dieulafoy, *L'Art Moderne de la Perse;* Gayet, *L'Art Persan.* Cf. also in the German *Handbuch der Architektur* (Darmstadt) the volume *Die Baukunst des Islam*, by Franz Pasha; Dieulafoy, *L'Art Antique de la Perse*, Part V; *Monuments Parthes et Sassanides;* Perrot and Chipiez, *Histoire de l'Art dans l'Antiquité*, Vol. V, *La Perse;* Loftus, *Travels and Researches in Chaldea and Susiana;* Fergusson, *Palaces of Nineveh and Persepolis.*

PERSIENNE. A shutter or window blind with slats; either hinged at the side or attached at the top and hanging loosely. (See Blind, and subtitles; Shutter; also description of Halles Centralles under Iron Construction.)

PERSPECTIVE. The art of representing graphically an object as it actually appears to the eye; scientifically, a form of projection by the use of which such a representation may be obtained, or very closely approximated. Also the result obtained by either process.

Perspective as a science is usually understood as meaning linear perspective; that is, the scientific process as distinguished from, for example, the free hand methods of representing nature, or from aerial perspective as considered by painters.

Linear perspective is a branch of Applied Geometry, like Descriptive Geometry, Projection, and Shades and Shadows. But while these discuss the real dimensions and directions of lines, and their projection on plane and curved surfaces by parallel lines, perspective treats of their apparent directions and dimensions as viewed from a certain definite point, and of their projection upon a plane or curved surface by lines converging to a point. This point, called the "station point," is the point supposed to be occupied by the eye of the spectator. This system is sometimes called conical projection, as distinguished from orthographic and isometric projection, because the rays of light, considered collectively, which pass from the outlines of an object to the eye approximate the form of a cone, of which this outline is the base, and the eye the vertex. If this cone is cut by any intervening surface, the line of intersection is the perspective of the given outline, and when viewed from the station point it covers and coincides with the outline in question, and is a picture of it or true representation of its appearance.

When the intervening surface is a plane, it is called the plane of the picture; it is understood to be vertical unless specified to the contrary, and the picture is then said to be drawn in plane perspective. This is the system in ordinary use for the study and exhibition of architectural designs, as in making preliminary studies. The point in the plane of the picture opposite and nearest to the station point is called the centre of the picture, or point of sight. It is the orthographic projection of the station point.

There are two methods of obtaining, in the plane of the picture, the true conical projections of lines. In the first method, which is that of direct conical projection, the aim is to obtain the projection of the points at the ends of the given right lines, and of a sufficient number of points upon the given curved lines. By connecting these points the perspective of any figure can be constructed. In practice this method is commonly used only in the horizontal plane of projection to determine the position of vertical lines as projected in the picture plane. The position of horizontal and inclined lines is then obtained by the second method, the method of infinite lines. In the first method points are first determined and then lines are obtained by connecting the points. In the second method infinite lines are first determined, and points and finite lines are obtained by the intersections of these infinite lines.

In practice, it is usual, in making a perspective drawing of a building, to determine the horizontal dimensions, that is to say, the posi-

tion of vertical lines, by the method of conical projection, using an orthographic plan to represent the building, drawing a line through its nearest corner to represent the plane of the picture, taking a point at a proper distance from it to represent the position of the spectator, or station point, and drawing lines from the different points in the plan to the station point to represent the visual rays. These lines cut the plane of the picture at points which give the position of the vertical lines in perspective. Vertical dimensions are then laid off on the nearest corner and transferred to other vertical lines by drawing the perspectives of horizontal lines from the points so obtained. By the same process the perspective of any line parallel to the picture plane may be found, as it is obviously parallel to the line itself.

To obtain the perspective of a line not parallel to the picture plane, it is necessary to find the perspective of two points of the line. Usually, the two points chosen are the point where the line pierces the picture plane and the extremity of the line supposed to be prolonged to infinity beyond the picture plane. The former point is its own perspective, and is readily found by the process above described. The projector of the latter point, infinitely distant, must necessarily be parallel to the line itself; hence, to find the perspective of the extremity of a line, draw a projector through the station point parallel to the given line. The point so found will be the perspective of the extremity of the given line as well as of all lines parallel to it. Such a point is called a vanishing point; in it the perspective lines of any parallel system meet, and appear to vanish. Architectural designs are largely composed of, or can be reduced to, systems of parallel lines, vertical and horizontal. The former are drawn in perspective by the process first described; the latter by the location of the vanishing points, which are usually two, for the two faces of the building meeting in front of the observer. Furthermore, these two vanishing points serve to obtain the perspective of any other point by means of imaginary lines drawn through the points parallel to either system.

Distortions and Corrections. A perspective drawing looks all right when seen from the station point, but it necessarily appears more or less distorted when seen from any other point. For the apparent size of objects is determined to the eye by their relative angular dimensions, and their position by their angular distance from the point opposite the spectator. But in plane perspective drawing the distance of points from the centre of the picture is determined, not by this angle, but by its tangent, and the size of an object is made proportional, not to its apparent angular dimensions, but to the differences of the tangents of the angles. It follows that dimensions become more and more exaggerated as they are more and more distant from the centre. This is not very noticeable within an angle of twenty-five or thirty degrees. Beyond that it becomes intolerable. Even within this range the unavoidable distortion of circular, cylindrical, and spherical objects becomes offensive. In fact, as is readily seen, the outline of objects drawn in plane perspective is exactly similar to that of their shadows cast upon a screen parallel to the plane of the picture by a candle occupying the station point. Such shadows are notoriously distorted. It is only at the centre that they are of the same shape as the objects that cast them.

A practical remedy for this distortion is found by limiting the range of perspective drawing to fifty or sixty degrees, and then " doctoring " the difficult objects, such as spheres, columns, and round towers.

For similar reasons the human figure is never put into perspective, but is always drawn in orthographic projection, as if at the centre. This is sometimes difficult to manage when other objects, such as chairs, tables, etc., are drawn in plane perspective.

Another way to avoid these distortions is to draw things just as they appear, in their apparent angular dimensions. This, of course, could be exactly accomplished only upon the interior surface of a hollow sphere. But for objects of no great height, so that only horizontal angles have to be considered, a cylindrical surface answers as well. (See Curvilinear Perspective, below.)

Angular Perspective. A method of perspective in which a rectangular parallelopiped would be so set that four of its edges are parallel to the plane of the picture, and eight inclined, and that four of its faces are inclined, and two normal.

This is the most common case, buildings being generally drawn with their corners vertical, and parallel to the plane of the picture, while their floors are level and the eaves and other horizontal lines are directed right and left to their vanishing points. Such an object has two vanishing points and has three horizons, one horizontal and two vertical. The station point may be anywhere upon a semicircle, of which the line joining the two vanishing points is the diameter.

If an object is set so that its sides are very nearly forty-five degrees with the plane of the picture, it had better be taken exactly so. A horizontal square then has one of its diagonals normal to the plane of the picture, with its vanishing point at the centre, which is now halfway between the right- and left-hand vanishing points. The other diagonal will have its perspective horizontal.

Bird's-Eye Perspective. A method of perspective for which the eye is taken at a considerable height above the ground, so as to look down upon the objects to be represented, thus having an extended range of vision. It is thus not a separate branch of the science of perspective, but may make use of any of the systems here described.

Curvilinear; Cylindrical Perspective. A method of perspective in which the surface of projection is a hollow vertical cylinder, with the spectator at a point on the axis ; the picture is then said to be made in cylindrical, panoramic, or curvilinear perspective.

Panoramas are painted upon such surfaces, and such a surface is virtually employed in sketching from nature. But when it is developed, that is to say, flattened out, the perspectives of all the straight lines appear curved, as may be seen in some of Turner's pictures, and in photographs taken with a revolving camera.

In the construction of such drawings the perspective of every right line is properly a certain geometrical curve ; parallel lines appear as a group of such curves, all of which have the same origin, which is their vanishing point. But by substituting their tangents for the curves themselves, at any place an object can be drawn, as in plane perspective, without serious error ; and by a continuous series of such plane perspectives a very close approximation to curvilinear may be obtained. Properly, curvilinear perspective should include also spherical perspective ; that is, a method involving the use of a spherical surface as the surface of projection. This process is, however, hardly available for practical use, as the surface of a sphere cannot be developed upon a plane.

Diagonal Perspective. Angular Perspective in which the principal faces of an object are shown as if at forty-five degrees to the picture plane ; one set of diagonals of the square in plan vanishes then at the centre of vision, halfway between the right and left chief vanishing points, and the other is parallel to the picture.

Linear Perspective. (See main article, above.)

Oblique Perspective. That in which a rectangular parallelopiped would be so set that all its faces and all its edges would be inclined to the plane of the picture. There are three vanishing points and three horizons. The station point is fixed, and is at the vertex of a triangular pyramid, in front of the picture, of which the three horizons form the base. The centre is at the point in the plane of the picture where the three perpendiculars dropped from the three vanishing points upon the opposite horizons meet and cross.

Oblique perspective is used when an object is not vertical, or when the plane of the picture is itself inclined, as sometimes happens in photography, as when a camera is directed upward at a tall building, the sides of which will then appear to approach.

One Point Perspective. Same as Parallel Perspective.

Panoramic Perspective. Same as Curvilinear Perspective.

Parallel Perspective. A method of perspective in which the principal plane face of the object is assumed as parallel to the picture plane. When a rectangular parallelopiped is so situated that four of its faces and four of its edges are normal to the plane of the picture, and the others parallel to it, it is said to be in parallel perspective, or one point perspective, since only these four edges have a vanishing point. This is at the centre of the picture, which is the vanishing point of all normal lines.

Parallel perspective is much used for interiors, street fronts, etc., especially if vertical circles occur in the object, since if these are parallel to the picture they can be put in with compasses.

If an object is very nearly in parallel perspective it had better be drawn exactly so. Otherwise, both the horizontal vanishing points may come on the same side of some portion of it, which is intolerable, as may often be seen in photographs, especially of interiors.

Plane Perspective. (See main article, above.)

Spherical Perspective. (See Curvilinear Perspective.)

Three Point Perspective. Same as Oblique Perspective.

Two Point Perspective. Same as Angular Perspective. — W. R. WARE.

A great number of text books on perspective have been published, which are useful for the the study of the usual methods of perspective drawing, but for a full scientific treatment of the subject in all its branches, consult *Modern Perspective* by Prof. W. R. Ware, 1 vol. text, 1 vol. plates. See also Herdman, *Curvilinear Perspective in Nature.*

— R. S.

PERU, ARCHITECTURE OF. (See South America, Architecture of.)

PERUCCI. (See Peruzzi, Baldassare.)

PERUGINO. (See Vanucci, Pietro.)

PERUZZI (PETRUCCI, PERUCCI), BALDASSARE; painter and architect of Siena, Italy ; b. Mar. 7, 1481 ; d. Jan. 6, 1556.

Peruzzi was probably born at Volterra, Italy, the son of a Florentine weaver, and was brought up in Siena. He went to Rome about 1503, and under the patronage of the famous Sienese banker, Agostino Chigi, devoted several years to study. One of his earliest buildings was Chigi's villa, now called the Villa Farnesina, finished about 1510. After the death of Raphael, Peruzzi was associated with Antonio (II.) da San Gallo (see San Gallo, Antonio II.) in the superintendence of the works at S. Peter's church, and held that position intermittently from Aug.

1, 1520, until his death. During the reign of Adrian VI. (Pope 1522–1523) he was invited to Bologna by the *presidenti* of the church of S. Petronio to design a façade for that church. A drawing in the Gothic style now in the sacristy is attributed to him. Peruzzi in 1525 built the Ossoli palace in Rome. At Siena he was twice made *architetto del publico* on petition of citizens. The little court of the oratory of S. Caterina and the Villa Belcaro date from this time ; and in 1529 he was made *capomaestro* of the cathedral. He began the famous Palazzo Massimi (*Alle Colonne*) at Rome in 1535, the year before his death. He began also the palace of Angelo Massimi (now Palazzo Orsini).

In painting, Peruzzi was at first a pupil of Pinturicchio (see Pinturicchio). He afterward assisted Raphael in Rome. Among his many works are the paintings of the choir of S. Onofrio (Rome), much of the decoration of the Farnesina, and the decoration of the Capella Pozzetti at S. Maria della Pace (Rome, 1516). He frequently designed fêtes and processions, and painted many façades. His notes and designs were used by Serlio (see Serlio) in preparing his books. Peruzzi was buried in the Pantheon near Raphael.

Rudolf Redtenbacher, *Baldassare Peruzzi und seine Werke ;* Vasari, Milanesi ed.: Vasari, Blashfield-Hopkins ed.; Müntz, *Renaissance ;* Suys et Haudebourt, *Palais Massimi ;* A. Venturi, *Farnesina ;* Donati, *Elogio ;* Gaye, *Carteggio.*

PEST HOUSE. (See Lazar House.)

PETER OF COLECHURCH; priest and architect ; d. 1205.

London Bridge was destroyed and rebuilt in 1091, 1136, and probably at many other times. All these early structures were of wood. According to Stow (op. cit.) the last wooden bridge was built by Peter, curate of S. Mary Colechurch (London), in 1163. The first stone bridge was begun by Peter of Colechurch in 1176 and finished in 1209. It was constructed on twenty arches with nineteen piers, and houses were built upon it.

Knight, *London ;* Knight, *Cyclopedia of London ;* Stow, *Survey of London ;* Redgrave, *Dictionary of Artists ;* Thomson, *London Bridge.*

PETIT, FRANÇOIS ; architect.

A son of Guillaume Petit, *maître des œuvres* of the city of Beauvais. May 3, 1578, he was chosen to conduct the works at the Pont Neuf (Paris) with his brother Jean, Guillaume Marchand (see Marchand, G.), and others. March 7, 1600, he contracted with others to build the western portion of the *Grande Galerie du Louvre.* (See Chambiges, Pierre, II.)

Berty, *Topographie, Louvre et Tuileries.*

PETRUS DE MARIA; architect and mosaicist.

Petrus de Maria built the cloister at Sassovivo

near Foligno, Italy, finished in 1229. This cloister is similar to that of the Lateran.

Frothingham, *Cloister of the Lateran.*

PETRUS GULIMARI. (See Gulimari da Piperno, Petrus.)

PEW. Originally, an enclosed and slightly elevated place fitted with a desk and more or less complete conveniences for writing ; the place for a cashier or paymaster, a clerk who had business with the public, or any one who needed a certain separation or enclosure, while still remaining accessible. Lawyers formerly received their clients in public places where each attorney had his own pew. Later, a box in a theatre ; and, in the same way of extension, an enclosed space with one or more seats in a church held by one person or family, as distinguished from the open benches, which were free. The pews of the seventeenth and eighteenth centuries had often seats on three sides of a space about 5 by 7 feet, enclosed with wooden partitions 4 feet or more high. The nineteenth century pew is generally long and narrow, with back and ends 3 feet high or less, and fitted with one long bench only, the

PEW: BINHAM PRIORY, NORFOLKSHIRE; C. 1340.

occupants of which all face the pulpit or reading-desk. (Cuts cols. 126, 127, 128.) — R. S.

PEW CHAIR. A hinged seat, attached to the end of a church pew, to afford accommodation in the aisle when additional seats are required. (United States.)

PEYRE, ANTOINE FRANÇOIS; architect and painter ; b. April 5, 1739 ; d. March 7, 1823.

A brother of Marie Joseph Peyre (see Peyre,

125

M. J.). In 1762 he won the *Grand Prix de Rome* in architecture. Returning to Paris, he was appointed *contrôleur* of the buildings at the château of S. Germain and of Fontainebleau. He designed the electoral palace and chapel at Coblentz (Rhenish Prussia). Under the Empire he was architect of the administration of the hospitals. He published several works on architecture.

PEW IN CHURCH AT ELKSTONE, GLOUCESTERSHIRE; C. 1280.

Quatremère de Quincy, *Notice sur A. F. Peyre ; Nouvelle biographie générale.*

PEYRE, ANTOINE MARIE; architect ; b. 1770 ; d. May 24, 1843.

A son of Marie Joseph Peyre (see Peyre, M. J.). Under the Directoire he was appointed *architecte des bâtiments civils* and took charge of the construction of the Observatoire and of the installation of the Musée des Monuments Français in the convent of the Petits-Augustins under the direction of Marie Alexandre Lenoir (see Lenoir, M. A.). In 1809 he was appointed architect of the Palais de Justice (Paris), and made extensive additions to that building. In 1800 he built the old Gaîté theatre in Paris (now destroyed). He built also the theatre at Soissons and a theatre at Lille. He published several works on architecture.

Nouvelle biographie générale ; Bauchal, *Dictionnaire.*

PEYRE, MARIE JOSEPH; architect ; b. 1730 ; d. Aug. 11, 1788.

He won the *Grand Prix de Rome* in architecture in 1751. In 1767 he was admitted to the *Académie d'Architecture.* In 1772 he was associated with De Wailly (see Wailly) as supervising architect of the château of Fontainebleau, and with him built the Odéon theatre in Paris.

Bauchal, *Dictionnaire.*

PHAROS. *A.* A lighthouse or beacon tower which anciently stood on the Isle of Pharos, at the entrance of the port of Alexandria. Hence, —

B. Any lighthouse for the direction of seamen ; a watch tower or beacon, especially when of a more or less monumental character.

126

PHIDIAS (PHEIDIAS); sculptor and architect.

Phidias began as a painter. He was one of the three great pupils of Agelaidas (see Agelaidas). His earliest recorded work was a chryselephantine statue of Athena at Pellene in Achaia, Greece. About 459 he made a statue of Athena Areia for a temple at Platæa in Bœotia. To this early period may be ascribed his Aphrodite Ourania, the Apollo Parnopios, the Hermes Pronaos, and the Amazon at Ephesos. Before the end of the administration of Cimon (d. 469 B.C.)

PEW IN CHURCH AT KIDLINGTON, OXFORDSHIRE; WITH ABBREVIATION OF THE NAME OF JESUS (I.H.C.: SEE ARTICLE I.H.S.).

Phidias made the bronze statue of Athena Promachus which stood on the Acropolis. The history of the great chryselephantine statue of Zeus in the temple of that god at Olympia is obscure, but it was probably dedicated about 448 B.C. After this time Phidias was attached to the administration of Pericles at Athens, and Phidias, according to Plutarch, was made superintendent of all the public buildings. The colossal chryselephantine statue of Athena which stood in the Parthenon was consecrated in 438 B.C. (See Elgin Marbles; Greece, Architecture of; Parthenon.)

PEW: CHURCH AT STEEPLE ASTON, OXFORDSHIRE; C. 1500.

Collignon, *Histoire de la Sculpture Grecque;* Collignon, *Phidias;* Waldstein, *Essays on the Art of Pheidias;* Story, *Phidias and the Elgin Marbles;* Peterson, *Die Kunst des Pheidias;* Michaelis, *Der Parthenon;* Hamilton, *Lord Elgin's*

Pursuits in Greece; Plutarch, *Pericles; Pausanias,* (Fraser's Trans.).

PHENGITES. Same as Phengites Marble; under Marble.

PHILON; architect.

Philon was included by Varro among the seven greatest architects of Greece. His best known building was the arsenal at the Peiræus (the port of Athens). This building was erected between 346 and 328 B.C., and was burned by the Roman general Sulla. Philon wrote books on proportion and a description of the arsenal. An inscription has been found giving an accurate description of this building. (Choisy, op. cit.)

Choisy, *Études épigraphiques;* Thos. W. Ludlow, *The Athenian Arsenal of Philon* in *American Journal of Philology.*

PEW: CHURCH AT MILVERTON, SOMERSETSHIRE, A.D. 1540.

The upper panel has the royal escutcheon, with the Garter, Tudor Rose, and a Pomegranate.

PHOTOGRAPHY. The art and the process of making pictures by the action of light upon chemically prepared surfaces, as of paper, glass, metal, etc. The application to the study of architecture dates from about 1849, at which time Ponti, of Venice, was making paper prints of important buildings in Venice. The prints made at this time, though somewhat faded, are still useful. E. D. Baldus, of Paris, was making large and very splendid pictures of French cathedrals as early as 1854, and these pictures are still in excellent condition.

The great majority of architectural photographs which are purchased by travellers in Europe are taken with a view to giving a general picture of an agreeable sort; carefully taken pictures giving less visited buildings, and especially views of details on a large scale, are often difficult to procure. In this respect there is a very great difference between one town and another.

Great collections of architectural photographs

have not very commonly been made, one reason being the difficulty attending their accumulation, owing to the absence of a well-organized trade with its catalogues, its advertisements, and its trade methods. The necessity of providing much space for the accommodation of photographs and the difficulty of their organization and cataloguing, and the constantly increasing number of books illustrated by photography, have also counted against the making of these collections. It is probable that the formation of a complete collection of architectural photographs would involve the immediate purchase of 70,000 or 80,000 prints and the taking of hundreds of new ones yearly, besides the necessary taking of many pictures for which special orders would have to be given. A photograph of a building or part of a building should be taken without the slightest reference to the artistic effect of the picture. The object of the picture being to convey to the student all the facts possible, concerning the work of architectural art, the photograph should be considered as a faithful mirror in which those truths are preserved. On this account many operators prefer an overcast day which, by avoiding strong shadows with sharp edges, enables the student to see the details of the building even in its recesses. On the other hand, there are those students of architecture who insist upon the intention of the designer to use shadows as the chief element in his architectural design. It is to be observed in relation to this that designing in shadow is rather an ideal of the theorizer upon architectural designing than a practical matter; as is made evident by the fact that the details of the north flank of a building, where the sun seldom strikes, are not often very unlike those of the south side. The practice, therefore, of taking photographs in cloudy weather is to be commended, the resulting photographs being much truer and softer, and with careful stopping down of the lens and giving a longer exposure, the details, in the shade and high light as well, will be strong and brilliant. Until within the last few years the photographs of interiors have not been successful, owing to the halation or fog which would appear around all windows facing the direct light; but with the introduction of the non-halation plate much of the trouble is obviated. The flash light is hardly to be recommended for architectural reproduction, as long exposure of the plate will give best results except in interiors where light does not penetrate at all.

Photography, as applied to the rendering of architectural subjects, may be divided into two divisions, — prints by direct process, and prints which are photo-mechanical.

Direct process is where the negative is used for making a positive print by the action of light on a sensitized surface.

Photomechanical is where the negative is a means only to produce either another negative or a positive on some hardened surface, on which printer's ink can be spread for the purpose of mechanical printing.

Prints by direct process may be made by direct contact with the negative, thus giving the same size picture as the negative, or may be enlarged by solar or arc light projections on to the sensitized paper; or a large negative of the desired size can be made from the small negative, from which direct printing can be done without the further necessity of a projecting or enlarging camera; where a large number of prints are to be made this is the best method. For direct printing there are many papers, as silver, aristo, vera, blue print, platinum, carbon, bromide, velox, etc. For detail, such as is required for architectural subjects, carbon and bromide give the best results, and especially are adapted for enlargements.

Mat surface papers are, on the whole, to be recommended over the glazed papers, as avoiding the annoying reflecting surfaces, though for accuracy and clearness of detail the glazed papers may be preferred.

The various papers above mentioned can be divided into three classes, — those which print out after exposure to the light, through the negative, those which print but faintly or where the image is scarcely discernible, and those which show no image; the two latter classes must be developed after the exposure is made before the full image appears.

Silver, aristo, vera, and blue print are of the first class, platinotype of the second class, and bromide and carbon of the third class.

Of the papers in the two latter classes, *i.e.* those which do not print out, platinum is to be recommended both for the results obtained, the extreme facility for working, and for permanency; it yields a soft gray print, but lacks brilliancy of detail in the half tones and shadows; it might be said that it is to photography what the impressionist school is to painting.

The platinum print is thoroughly appreciated for pictorial work where softness and effect are sought and minute detail is not required.

Of the processes belonging to the second division, the photomechanical, there are as many varieties as there are papers in the first division; those most in use are the collotype, photogravure or heliogravure, half tone, or photo-electrotype.

The collotype process is worked on a film of bichromated gelatine, which, when exposed under a negative, may, when washed and dried, be treated in the same manner as a lithographic stone; that is, the parts acted on by the light refuse to absorb water, but take the greasy printer's ink, while the parts not acted on absorb water and refuse the inks.

The collotype process is used largely in all countries, and worked under various names. In Germany as *Lichtdruck*, in France as *phototypie*, and in England and America as collotype, phototype, albertype, and various other fancy names. The heliotype is a slight modification of the collotype process, the principal feature being that the gelatine film can be hardened with chrome alum, and afterward detached from the support on which it was originally prepared. It then forms a tough and flexible skin of gelatine, which can be used at any time for printing from by attaching to a zinc plate or to a cylinder.

For the reproduction of architectural sketches for illustrative work, either line drawings or coloured sketches, the photo-electrotype process is most in vogue, and is one of the earliest processes of engraving with the aid of photography. If a black and white line drawing is to be reproduced, a sheet of chromotized gelatine is exposed under the negative, the effect being that the parts most affected by the light shining through become insoluble and incapable of absorbing water, while the parts not affected become readily soluble when treated with warm water or an acetic acid bath, so leaving the insoluble parts to form an image in relief; from these, moulds in wax and plaster are made, from which the copper relief block is made for typographic printing. If the drawing to be reproduced is either in wash or in colour, we have to deal with what is known as tone work, and the negative must be made through a fine lined screen, about two hundred lines to the inch; this breaks the light up into little dots and squares, producing what is generally termed a " half tone."

If a reproduction is to be made from a photograph, the photograph should be made on silver paper, and not too glossy.

In summing up, as to the most desirable method for the reproduction of architectural subjects, it must be stated that it depends entirely on the use or purpose to which the reproduction is to serve.

Where a large number of prints are to be made of the same subject, one of the photomechanical processes must be accepted; while if time and number of prints or reproductions do not enter into the question, it is safe to say that the best results are from the carbon print, its superiority over other papers being its brilliancy and softness of detail in high light, shades, and shadows, also the latitude it affords for rendering different tone, to which must be added its permanency.

Of the photo-mechanical processes, the photogravure is undoubtedly the most satisfactory in every way, giving the most exquisite detail; its range is so great that the softest or hardest materials will come out in their true value; the

stone corbel or the carefully wrought grille will, at a glance, show in true contrast with the delicately veined polished marble columns and the soft plush draperies, and it is in this very particular that the half-tone process is so inferior, texture being almost absent. In fact, the one should hardly be compared with the other. The former is a hand process, where each picture is pulled from the copper plate, while the latter is the direct result of the "rapid fire" multiplying printing machine, and naturally the least expensive.

In enumerating the various methods above, the American synonym is given in each case.

The *Encyclopædic Dictionary of Photography*, by Walter E. Woodbury, is a most valuable work, capable of furnishing aid to every student of the subject.

       — CHARLES I. BERG.

PIANO NOBILE. In an Italian residence, the principal story containing the apartments of ceremony and reception, usually one flight above the ground, but often situated above an intermediate entresole or mezzanine. (Compare Premier Étage, under Étage.)

PIAZZA. *A.* In Italian cities, an open square more or less surrounded by buildings; the open area made by the intersection of several streets.

B. In the United States, same as Verandah.

PICCONI, ANTONIO. (See San Gallo, Antonio II., da.)

PICK DRESSING. The first rough dressing, or facing, of granite or other hard-quarried stone by means of a heavy pick or wedge-shaped hammer. Pick dressing produces a result suitable for heavy foundations or underpinnings where smooth work is not required.

PICKET HUT. A rude dwelling made by driving stakes, or "pickets," into the ground, and roofing them. The Mexican jacál construction is a form of picket hut. (See Jacál.)

       — F. S. D.

PICTOU STONE. An olive-gray, fine-grained, carboniferous sandstone from Pictou Harbour, Nova Scotia. — G. P. M.

PICT'S HOUSE. In Scotland, a rude dwelling built often upon the side of a hill, so that parts of the house are excavated, while others are enclosed by walls of unhewn stones. The rude stonework was carried up in a conical or domical shape until the roof was completed; then the earth was heaped above it, or a layer of turf or peat was used to cover everything. These buildings were sometimes large, containing many chambers.

Wilson, *Prehistoric Annals of Scotland.*

PICTURE GALLERY. A hall planned and provided with regard to wall spaces, area of floor, and lighting by day or night, for the

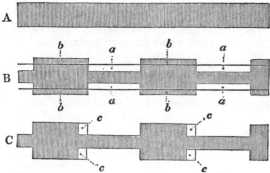

PIER: THEORY OF PIERS AS EXPLAINED BY RUSKIN.

A is a wall, hardly strong enough; *B* contains the same cubic contents gathered up into piers, *b*, and curtains, *a*. This will be so very much stronger than *A* that the material *c, c* can be removed with safety. This is true of very many conditions.

most convenient exposition of pictures. (See Gallery, *C*.)

PICTURE PLANE. In perspective drawing, the plane of projection, generally vertical. (See Perspective.)

PIECE WORK. Work done and paid for by measure of quantity at a fixed rate, according to a previous estimate of value; *i.e.* at an agreed price per thousand for a certain quality of bricks laid in a specified manner, or, in the case of stonework, at a given price per perch, etc., in contradistinction to work done and paid for by the measure of time, or by lump sum. (See Contract; Day's Work.)

PIEDROIT. A pier partly engaged in a

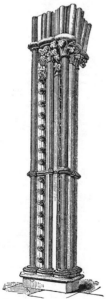

CLUSTERED AND BAND-
ED PIER: CHOIR,
LINCOLN CATHE-
DRAL; c. 1200.

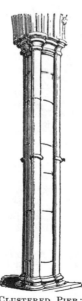

CLUSTERED PIER:
ONLY THE
VAULTING
SHAFTS BANDED.

133

PIER: NAVE ARCADE; ISLIP
CHURCH, OXFORDSHIRE; c.
1180.

wall; perhaps to be distinguished from a pilaster, as having no cap and base. A term of loose application, adapted from the French *Pied-droit*. (Compare Pilaster Mass.)

PIEN ; PIEND. An arras; a salient angle. Compound terms result from this meaning; as pien hammer, a hammer having a cutting edge; pien rafter, in Scotland, a hip rafter. (See Pien Check, under Check.)

PIER. *A*. Any more or less isolated mass of masonry, generally acting as a support; as the portion of a wall between two openings; the supports — larger than mere columns — of vaulting in mediæval churches, the projecting buttresses or stiffeners along the flanks of Romanesque and Gothic churches, the masonry and

PIER: CLUSTERED AND BAND-
ED PIERS; LINCOLN CATHE-
DRAL; 13TH CENTURY.

grillage under a column in modern construction. (See Column; Clustered Column; Pilaster and following titles.)

B. A structure like a bridge or dyke, projecting from the land into deep water to allow of the loading and unloading of vessels, or more rarely to protect an anchorage or the entrance to a harbour. (See Embankment; Fondamenta; Jetty; Landing; Molo; Quay; Riva.)

Compound Pier. Any pier composed of several members grouped together, as distinguished from one having a simple square, cir-

134

PIER: CLUSTERED PIER; OLD, NORTHAMPTONSHIRE; c. 1450.

PIER: CLUSTERED PIER OF LATEST TYPE, WITH ONE CAPITAL FOR THE WHOLE. STOGUMBER, CHURCH OF S. MARY, SOMERSET; c. 1500.

cular or polygonal section. The term thus includes all clustered pillars or piers, and those having a cruciform or stepped cross section. They constitute a distinguishing feature of mediæval church architecture, through almost its entire history from the tenth to the fifteenth or sixteenth century.

Recreation Pier. (See under R.)

PIERCED WORK. Decoration which consists mainly or partially of perforations. The essential character of this kind of decoration depends on whether the perforations are intended to be seen

PIERCED WORK: STONE WINDOW SLABS; CENTRAL SYRIA.

PIERCED WORK: SWITZERLAND, 17TH CENTURY.
Fascia below string course in wooden house; each piercing bordered by light coloured paintings.

as accentuated points of light against dark or of dark against light.

PIETRA NEPHRITICA. (See Nephrite.)

PIETRASANTA, GIACOMA DA; architect and sculptor.

Many of the buildings in Rome, which are attributed by Vasari to Giuliano da Maiano (see Giuliano da Maiano) and Baccio Pontelli (see Pontelli), were probably built by Pietrasanta. Among others, the church of S. Agostino, built in the reign of Sixtus IV. (Pope 1471–1484). In 1452 he made several marble doors for the Capitol, and in the records of Pius II. (Pope 1458–1464) he is mentioned as superintendent of the construction of the loggia of the Benediction, with the title "Superstes fabricæ pulpiti." In 1467 and 1468 he appears as director of the works at the Vatican and the Palazzo di S. Marco (Rome).

Müntz, *Les Arts à la cour des papes.*

PIETRO DA CORTONA. (See Berretini, Pietro.)

PIETRO DI MINELLA. (See Beccafumi, Domenico.)

PIGALLE, JEAN BAPTISTE; sculptor; b. Jan. 25, 1714 ; d. Aug. 20, 1785.

At the age of eight he was employed in the atelier of Robert le Lorrain (see Lorrain, R. le), and at twenty entered the academy of painting and sculpture in Paris. He studied in Rome, and on his return made the beautiful statue of Mercury, now in the Louvre. One of his most important works is the tomb of the Maréchal de Saxe in the church of S. Thomas at Strasburg (Elsass, Germany).

Gonse, *Sculpture française.*

PIGEON HOUSE. (See Colombier ; Dovecote.)

PIG LUG JOINT. Same as Dog Ear Joint (which see under Joint).

PIGTAIL AND PERIWIG STYLE. In German, *Zopf und Perücke Styl,* the fantastic late neoclassic of Germany, a term of ridicule corresponding to Barock (for which see Barocco Architecture). The style is more commonly designated *Zopf*

Styl simply, and this abbreviated form is rather common even in serious writing.

PILA. In Italy, a holy-water font, consisting of a bowl mounted on a shaft or foot, as distinguished from a font secured to or hanging from a wall or pier. (Compare Bénitier.)

PILASTER. An engaged pier with a more or less flat face, projecting slightly from a wall surface, and furnished with a capital, base, etc., as if to correspond with a column ; the shaft may be in a single piece, or it may be built up in courses with the masonry of the wall of which it forms a part. It was a Roman expression of the Greek Anta, but, unlike the anta, its capital was made as nearly as possible like the capital of the corresponding column, with which in Roman work it was nearly always associated as a respond, but rarely used independently in Roman work. But in the Renaissance, the function of pilasters became greatly enlarged, and they were often used, without the detached columns from which they were derived, to express upon a wall face an order of architecture or a superimposition of orders in flat-relief as it were, taking the place of the engaged column as used in the practice of the Romans. The engaged piers in Romanesque architecture are sometimes, by extension, called pilasters. — H. V. B.

PILASTER MASS. An engaged pier built up with the wall : usually without the capital and base of a pilaster ; an undeveloped buttress, as in Romanesque work. (Compare Piedroit.)

PILASTER STRIP. Same as Pilaster Mass, but generally applied to a comparatively slender pier of slight projection.

PILASTRATA. In Italian, and by adoption in English, a row, series, or order of pilasters. (Compare Colonnade.)

PILE. A post, or similar member of wood or metal sunk or driven into the soil to form a foundation for a superstructure or to form a retaining wall or dam. Most commonly used in series in soft and yielding soil, or in water as a support for walls, piers, and the like, whose pressure would be too great for the soil. When in place, a pile may reach a hard substratum and thus serve as a column or post to transmit the pressure of the superstructure through the softer material to a firm foundation ; or it may resist the imposed pressure by the friction of the material against its sides. (See Foundation.)

Close Pile. One placed in immediate contact with another, as in the construction of a coffer dam.

False Pile. A pile, or similar member, placed on top of a pile or piles, after driving, to reach a desired level. (See Follower Pile, below.)

Fender Pile. A pile used at water fronts to act as a guard or fender between boats and

a landing. The most notable examples are those of Venice, which are mentioned here on account of their decorative effect. They are adorned with simple painted decorations, recalling the colours of some heraldic achievement.

PIGEON HOUSE : SHIRLY, VIRGINIA, U.S.

(Compare cuts under Colombier.)

Filler or Filling Pile. One driven between gauge piles after these have been placed.

Follower Pile. One used, in driving, as an extension to a pile which has been driven to its full length without reaching a hard bottom or meeting with sufficient resistance. (See False Pile, above.)

Gauge or Gauged Pile. One of several carefully placed by accurate measurement, as a gauge for the rest of a series. The tops of gauge piles are commonly connected by a horizontal ledge, or wale, on each side, between which the Filling Piles are driven.

PILASTER : ROMAN DORIC, WITH NAMES OF THE DETAILS.

PILASTER OF DECORATIVE INTERIOR : PERISTYLE, HOUSE OF THE FAUN, POMPEII.

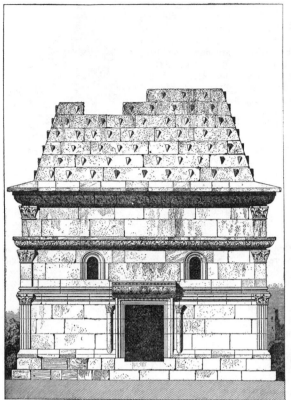

PILASTER: EARLY ROMANESQUE FORMS, 5TH CENTURY: EL BARAH, SYRIA.

Screw Pile. A pile terminating in a screw at its lower end, by which it is forced into very hard material when revolved.

Sheet Pile. One of a series of accurately cut and squared timbers — generally broad and thin, as planks — driven in close contact, as for forming a temporary wall about a deep excavation. In its best form, a sheet pile is tongued and grooved, and its foot is bevelled so as to form a point or sharp edge at the side which is to come against a pile which is already in place: in driving, the pile is thus wedged close. The form known as the pug pile has a tongue and groove of dovetail section by which it is tightly locked to its neighbours.

Sheath Pile. Same as sheet pile; a corruption, possibly in confusion with sheathing, which such piling resembles. — D. N. B. S.

PILE DRIVER. A machine by which a heavy weight (about 1200 pounds) is raised to a height and then allowed to fall suddenly. The windlass may be turned by hand, or by a small steam engine; the weight or hammer is commonly released by the automatic action of a hook which is thrown out of a ring when it reaches a certain height.

PILE DWELLING. A house built upon piles, especially when surrounded by water or swamp, the piles being long

Hollow Pile. A hollow metal cylinder used as a pile and commonly sunk from its interior.

Hydraulic Pile. A form of hollow pile, inside of which excavating is carried on by means of a jet of water.

Pneumatic Pile. A form of hollow pile which is forced into place by atmospheric pressure when the air within is exhausted, bringing with it the displaced soil. (See Caisson I.)

Pug Pile. (See Sheet Pile.)

Sand Pile. A preparation for foundation in soft soil — a substitute for a wooden pile — by a filling of sand in a deep round hole; usually formed by driving a wooden pile, withdrawing it, and ramming sand into the opening. (See Foundation.)

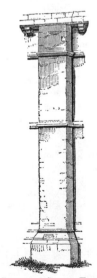

PILASTER: LATE NEO-CLASSIC, WROUGHT INTO FORM OF GAINE; SCHLOSS TORPA (WESTERGOTT-LAND), SWEDEN.

PILASTER IN DECORA-TIVE WOODWORK: 17TH CENTURY; WAD-STENA, SWEDEN.

PILASTER STRIP: FOUN-TAINS ABBEY; C. 1170.

enough to hold the house with its platforms and accessories at some distance above the surface. Such dwellings were very common in Europe previous to the development in each region of organized society, the isolated position and the surrounding surface of water or marsh serving as a defence. They are still in use in tropical regions, as in certain of the Pacific islands. A village composed of such dwellings is known as a lake village or a swamp village. Much of our knowledge of prehistoric archæology is obtained from the remains found on the lake bottom or buried in the swamp on the sites of such villages.

Some of these villages seem to have been of the nature of communal dwellings; in others a complete street of rough woodwork or of wattle seems to have been faced on either side by the dwellings, each independent of all the others. — R. S.

PILE TOWER. Same as Pele Tower.

PILING. The process, and the result, of driving piles.

PILLAR. Properly, any isolated vertical mass, whether monolithic or built up in courses, as an isolated pier, or the like. The term is hardly a technical one, and is very loosely applied; thus, the mass of coal left in a mine to carry the rock above is so

PILLAR: SQUARE AND ROUND ONES (COMMONLY CALLED PIERS AND COLUMNS), KOKANAYA, SYRIA; 5TH CENTURY A.D.

PILLAR: NAVE ARCADE PIERS IN THE FORM OF SIMPLE PILLARS; FOUNTAINS ABBEY, YORKSHIRE, ENGLAND; c. 1180.

called; and the English Bible (Gen. xix. 26) speaks of a pillar of salt. In architecture, the term is applied to a vertical supporting member which is not a column nor a pier, in the usual senses of those words; also, to large memorial columns.

Compound Pillar. Same as Compound Pier, under Pier.

Midwall Pillar. (See Midwall Column, under Column.)

Pompey's Pillar. A large memorial column of red Egyptian granite, in Alexandria, Egypt, erected by Pompeius, a prefect, in honour of Diocletian, in the fourth century A.D. (See Memorial Column.)

PILLAR OF VICTORY. A pillar-like

PILLAR, OCTAGONAL: CHURCH OF ORTON-ON-THE-HILL, LEICESTERSHIRE; c. 1350.

structure devoted to the commemoration of a victory, the term being sometimes extended to buildings like eastern pagodas, which arc hardly pillars in any strict sense. The rostral column (see Columna Rostrata) of the Romans, and all those columns mentioned under Memorial Column as being commemorative of military triumph, as well as the rude cathstones or megalithic pillars of the North, are included under this title.

PILLARET. A small pillar.

PILLOW WORK. The decorative treatment of any surface with pillow-like projections; more especially of any member of an order, usually flat, with a continuous cushion-like swell or bulge. (See Cushion.)

PIN IN VISIBLE AND DECORATIVE FRAMING: A SWISS CHALET.

The diagonal brace is halved and notched into the upright, and is held with two pins with ornamental heads.

PILON (PILLON), GERMAIN; sculptor and architect; b. 1535 (in the Faubourg Saint-Jaques, Paris); d. Feb. 3, 1590.

In 1558 Pilon received payment for eight figures in relief for the vault of the monument of Francis I., at Saint-Denis (see De l'Orme, Philibert), one of his earliest and best works. He superseded Domenique Florentin and Geronimo della Robbia (see Robbia, Geronimo della) as sculptor of the monument to Henry II., at Saint-Denis, and made all the statues of this monument. The bas reliefs of the base are by Laurent Regnauldin (see Regnauldin) and Fremyn Roussel. Pilon made the monument to Guillaume du Bellay de Langey at the cathedral of Le Mans (finished in 1557), and the monument to Birague in the Louvre. One of his most celebrated works is the group of Three Graces which supports a vase intended to contain the heart of Francis I. This work, made for Catherine de' Medici in 1561, is now in the Louvre.

PINNACLE: OXFORD CATHEDRAL; C. 1220.

Lami, *Dictionnaire des sculpteurs français;* Palustre, *Renaissance;* Gonse, *Sculpture française.*

PIN. A cylindrical or slightly conical or wedge-shaped peg or bolt, generally of wood, used to connect two or more pieces together.

It is most widely used in mortise-and-tenon framing, and the like. (Compare Bolt.)

PINACOTHECA. In classic architecture, a building for the preservation or exhibition of pictures; in modern use, a gallery of painting. (See Pinakothek.)

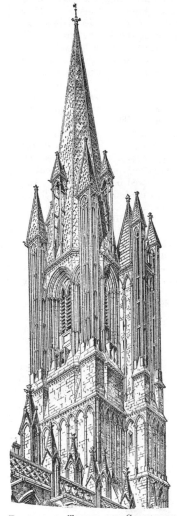

PINNACLE: TOWER OF COUTANCES CATHEDRAL, NORMANDY, ABOUT 1130, WITH PINNACLE OF UNUSUAL SIZE.

The roof of the stair turret has also two pinnacles closely combined with its mass.

PINAKOTHEK. A building for the exhibition of paintings, the term having been put to use in Munich to denote the two important picture galleries known, respectively, as the New and the Old Pinakothek. (Compare Pinacotheca.)

PINNACLE. A subordinate vertical structure of masonry, generally more or less taper-

PLATE VII

PINNACLE

A part of the chevet of the cathedral at Reims. The importance of these pinnacles is in their colossal size, for each from the level surface at the top of the great buttress rises 80 feet to the finial upon its spire, and includes a solid basement pierced only by the waterway leading to the gargoyle, an open niche containing the great statue on its pedestal, and the spire, which itself is accompanied by four minor pinnacles. The gargoyles are ruined in effect by the modern water-leaders.

ing, rising above the neighbouring parts of a building. It is generally used to crown a buttress, or the like, to which it gives additional weight; also, at each of the four corners of a square tower, to fill the space left by an octagonal spire above, and to complete the proportion. In some examples, the pinnacle consists of an open pavilion supporting a spire, the whole being of great relative size. (See Buttress; Flying Buttress; Gothic Architecture.)

PINNING IN. The closure of open joints in rubble work or rough walling by small wedges or spalls of stone fitted into the interstices and bedded solidly in mortar, especially to avoid hollow spaces in the interior of a wall; but it is customary, in specifying for the face work of such a wall, that there shall be few spalled joints.

PINNING UP. The operation of securing the solid horizontal bearing of timbers or lintels on walls or piers of masonry by the insertion of thin wedges of stone or layers of slate or metal; the operation of driving in metal wedges or blades to bring the superstructure to bear fairly upon the substructure, or to restore to the perpendicular a wall which is not plumb. (See Perpendicular, Restoring to the; Shim.)

PIN STOP. A metal pin inserted in any turning member to stop it at a certain point, as in the key of a gas fixture.

PINTELLI, BACCIO. (See Pontelli, Baccio.)

PINTLE. A pin forming an axis or pivot to secure two parts or members, while leaving one or both free to revolve; especially, a combination of such a pin with another part, by which it is held more or less at right angles, forming a sort of hook.

PINTURICCHIO, BERNARDO; painter; b. 1459; d. 1513. Pinturicchio painted frescoes at the Sistine Chapel (Rome), which still exist; the Borgia apartments at the Vatican, recently restored; and the decorations of the library of the cathedral of Siena.

Crowe and Cavalcaselle, *History of Painting in Italy;* G. W. Kitchen, *Piccolomini Library;* Volpini, *Appartimento Borgia del Vaticano.*

PINNACLE: PETERBORO' CATHEDRAL, A.D. 1238.

PIPE. A long, generally cylindrical, hollow body, used for the conveyance of a fluid, as a drain, or a steam, water, or gas pipe. The material of pipes differs according to the service which they have to perform. To quote some examples: —

for soil and waste pipes; heavy cast iron, asphalted and galvanized wrought iron, brass, and heavy lead for short branches;

for vent pipes; heavy cast iron, galvanized or lead-lined wrought iron, heavy lead and brass;

for drain pipes; earthen, cement, and extra heavy cast-iron pipes;

for supply pipes; heavy drawn lead, plain black, galvanized, enamelled, lead-lined, tin-lined, and glass-lined wrought iron, tin-lined lead, tinned brass, and copper;

for suction pipes from cisterns and wells; tin-lined lead and block-tin pipes;

for illuminating gas; black or plain wrought iron, galvanized wrought iron, and for exposed work, brass pipes;

for steam; plain black wrought-iron pipes;

for gas and water street mains; heavy asphalted cast-iron pipes, asphalted or cement-lined wrought-iron pipes,

for water; wooden log pipes.

(See Gas Fitting; House Drainage; Joint; Plumbing.) — W. P. GERHARD.

Supply Pipe. The pipe by which the public gas, water, or steam service is con-

PINNACLE: WEST END OF ST. FRANCIS, PAVIA, 13TH CENTURY, WITH PINNACLES OF WHOLLY DECORATIVE PURPOSE, AND UNUSUALLY HIGH.

nected with private or especial service. In plumbing, the supply service precedes the service of special distribution.

PIPE BOARD. A board secured over a sink or the like, commonly fixed to the wall; to which the various plumbing pipes for supply

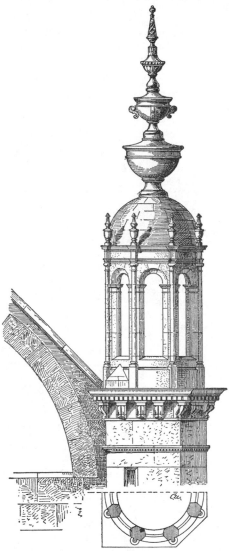

PINNACLE: SPANISH RENAISSANCE; CATHEDRAL
OF LEON; 1520–1550.

or tell-tale purposes, with their faucets, are attached.

PIPPI, GIULIO (Giulio Romano); painter and architect; b. 1492; d. 1546.

As the principal assistant of Raphael (see Santi, R.) he was associated with him in executing the frescoes of the Stanze of the Vatican. He also superintended the execution of the fres-

coes in the loggia of the Farnesina (finished about 1518). He assisted in the decoration of the Loggia of the Vatican, and of the Villa Madama, near Rome. In 1525 he designed the Palazzo del Te (abbreviation for Tejetto, a sluiceway or canal) at Mantua (finished 1528). Giulio built his own palazzo, which still stands in Mantua, and the tomb of Baldassare Castiglione in the church of S. Maria delle Grazie (Mantua).

Stiller, *Palazzo del Te*, in *Allgemeine Bauzeitung*, Vol. XLIX.; Bottani, *Palazzo del Te*; Carlo d'Arco, *Vita ed opere di Giulio Romano*; Müntz, *Renaissance*; Vasari, Milanesi ed.; Gaye, *Carteggio*; Gruner, *Specimens of Ornamental Art*.

PIPPI D'ANTONIO DA FIRENZE; sculptor and architect.

After 1491 he was associated with Ambrogio d'Antonio da Milano in the construction of the portico of the cathedral of Spoleto.

PIRANESI, GIOVANNI BAPTISTA; architect and engraver; b. 1720, at Venice; d. Nov. 9, 1776.

He was the son of a mason and went to Rome at the age of eighteen to study architecture. His plates were published under the following titles: *Antichità Romane*, 4 vols. folio, first ed. 1756, second ed. 1784; *Monumenti degli Scipioni*, 1 vol. folio, 1785; *Sciographia quatuor Templorum Veterum*, dedicated to Pope Pius VI., 1 vol. folio, 1776 (Part II. contains the Pantheon); *Della Magnificenza ed Architettura de' Romani*, 1 vol. folio, dedicated to Clement XIII.; *Opere Varie di Architettura*, etc., Rome, Year VIII. of the Republic; *Lapides Capitolini*, 1 vol. folio, dedicated to Clement XIV.; *Il Campo Marzio dell' Antica Roma*, 1 vol. folio, Rome, 1762; *Antichità d'Albano e di Castel Gandolfo*, 1 vol. folio, dedicated to Clement XIV.; a volume of plates on the column of Trajan, a volume of plates on the ruins of Pæstum, various engravings of Roman vases, candelabra, etc.

Biography compiled from a manuscript memoir of Piranesi by one of his sons in *Library of Fine Arts*, 1831.

PIRCA. A kind of construction found in Peruvian ruins where round stones are laid in mortar, forming a sort of rubble. — F. S. D.

PISANO, ANDREA. (See Andrea da Pisa.)

PISANO, GIOVANNI. (See Giovanni da Pisa.)

PISANO, NICCOLÒ. (See Niccolò da Pisa.)

PISANO, TOMASO. (See Tomaso di Andrea Pisano.)

PISAY. Same as Pisé.

PISCINA. A shallow basin or sink, supplied with a drain pipe, generally recessed in a niche, which is often elaborately decorated. In modern churches, generally situated in a canopied niche in the sanctuary wall, on the Epistle, or south side of the altar, and east of the Sedilia, used to receive the water in which the priest washes his hands at the Mass, and also that in which the sacred vessels are cleansed.

Mallet, *D'Archéologie Réligieuse*, 2 vols., Paris, 1887.

—C. C.

PISÉ. A building material (see Pisé Masonry, under Masonry.)

This material is much used in parts of Central and South America. A kind of pisé work was used by some American Indians, a good example still existing in the noted ruin, Casa Grande near Florence, Arizona, and also others in Mexico. Another variety was in use in the Salado Valley, Arizona, where an examination of

PISCINA: IN DWELLING-HOUSE AT OAKHAM, RUTLANDSHIRE; 13TH CENTURY.

many ruins discloses a method of ramming the clay between two lines of wicker work bound together by cross sticks. (See Cajon; Clay Walling; Tapia.) — F. S. D.

PISON; architect.

Pison, *Maître d'œuvre*, constructed, at the close of the tenth century, the old cathedral of Le Puy (Haute Loire), central France, of which vestiges appear in the present building.

Bourasse, *Cathédrales de France*.

PIT. In a theatre, or the like, the main portion of the floor of the auditorium, situated at a lower level than the dress circle or boxes which originally enclosed it on three sides. Commonly separated from the boxes by a sunken aisle. The term is now, in Great Britain, applied to the inferior seats in whatever part of

PISCINA: COWLING CHURCH; c. 1260.

the floor of the house, and in the United States has been superseded by the term Orchestra or Parquet.

PITCH (I.). The amount of slope given to any member, as a roof, or part of a roof; thus, a pitch may be stated as of 2 to 3 (viz. 2 feet or inches upright to 3 feet or inches horizontal) or of a given angle (30 degrees, 45 degrees, etc.). An ingenious instrument is sold, devised for the easy determination of the pitch of roof and much used by carpenters, surveyors, and the like. It is furnished with a spirit level, and by the use of this, a glance will determine either the angle of the pitch or the number of feet of rise or vertical height which corresponds with a given length of slope, or, at pleasure, with a given horizontal length.

PISCINA: BLYTHFORD CHURCH, SUFFOLK; c. 1300.

The pitch of roofs has generally been determined by two considerations taken together; one, the amount of rainfall or snowfall which is to be expected during the year, or any season of the year; the other, the material with which the roof is covered. A roof made of sheets of tin plate, zinc, or other metal soldered together, may be much more flat than a roof of shingles; this, again, somewhat less steep than a slate roof — all without danger of leakage so long as the roof is in good repair. Other considerations, such as those of architectural effect, have, however often affected the question; thus, the sixteenth century architects of France inherited from the Gothic church builders a taste for very steep and high roofs, requiring very lofty chimneys, which, together with proportionally large dormer windows, became an important feature of the Renaissance building of France. A hundred years later this taste had disappeared, and the influence of classical and pseudo-classical traditions coming from Italy caused the adoption of roofs of very low pitch and almost entirely concealed behind blocking courses, parapets, and the like. The flatter roofs may have required somewhat greater care in their construction; but the change from one to another was wholly caused by local and temporary change in taste of design. — R. S.

PITCH (II.). The distance from centre to centre of rivets in iron construction.

PITCH-FACED. In stonework, having the edges of the face trimmed down to a true arris or angle all around (see Draft), so that, when laid up in the wall, the central part of the visible face of each stone is left projecting and rough as it came from the quarry, or but slightly dressed into shape with the pick, while the joints are narrow, true, and all on the same plane. A pitch-faced wall, therefore, is a rough wall of squared stones with fine joints somewhat below the general surface. (See Rock Faced; Stone Dressing.)

PITCH HOLE. A recess or depression occurring in the surface of a stone which has otherwise been more or less dressed to a true face for setting.

PITCHING PIECE. Same as Apron Piece.

PITCH OF AN ARCH. The versed sine, or height, from the springing line to the highest part of the soffit or intrados.

PIT DWELLING. A residence wholly or in part under ground and formed by an excavation. Records of houses which appear to have been entirely subterranean are not uncommon, and there exist in the south of England (Addy, op. cit.), in several parts of Italy, and upon the sites of different Gaulish cities many pits which must have been from 4 to 6 feet deep and from 12 to 14 feet in diameter or width, all of which were evidently, from the remains within them, used for human habi-

tation. The wall, if any was needed for greater height, was built up of rough stones, or by screens of wattle covered with mud, but the roof seems to have been in every case a pyramid or cone of boughs. It has been pointed out that there still remain many English cottages of which the floor (of beaten earth, or of stones laid upon the earth) is a foot or more below the surface, and allusions to this will be found in literature. It is claimed that houses were warmer in winter if built in this way. (See Pennpit.)

Addy, *The Evolution of the English House;* Hamerton, *The Mount and Autun;* Helbig, *Die Italiker in der Poebene.*

PIVOT. A pin on which any object is free to revolve; it may be stationary or attached to the revolving object. In antiquity, used in the place of hinges for doors and the like; fixed near to the jamb in the sill and lintel; or fixed to the door and revolving in sockets. In modern times, heavy sash with large sheets of plate glass have sometimes a pivot in the middle of the top and bottom rail; pivots are also used for hanging fan lights and other sash, being secured to the middle of the side stiles and having their sockets in the jambs, or sides of the frame.

PIVOT LIGHT. A glazed sash supported on pivots so that it may be opened and closed by revolving, either horizontally or vertically; a common arrangement for fan lights.

PLACARD. *A.* Pargetting; parget work.
B. The decoration of the door of an apartment, consisting of a chambranle crowned with its frieze or gorge. — (A. P. S.)
C. In French use, a small, shallow cupboard.

PLAFOND. A ceiling in the sense of the under side of a floor. The French term used in English, especially when such a feature is made decorative.

PLAIN TILE. (See Tile.)

PLAN. A drawing which geometrically represents an object in horizontal projection, as distinguished from those representing vertical sections or elevations; it may represent the exterior of the object as seen from above, as in a roof plan, or any part of its interior as shown by a horizontal section, as a floor plan.

As the horizontal section has the advantage, over vertical sections and elevations, of being able to set forth the shapes, dimensions, and mutual relation of all the apartments in a building and the character of its intercommunications, the plan is generally considered as the basis of every architectural composition.

Plans, in the plural, commonly, any set of graphic delineations intended collectively to describe an object or objects, even including vertical projections and perspective drawings. (See Planning.) — D. N. B. S.

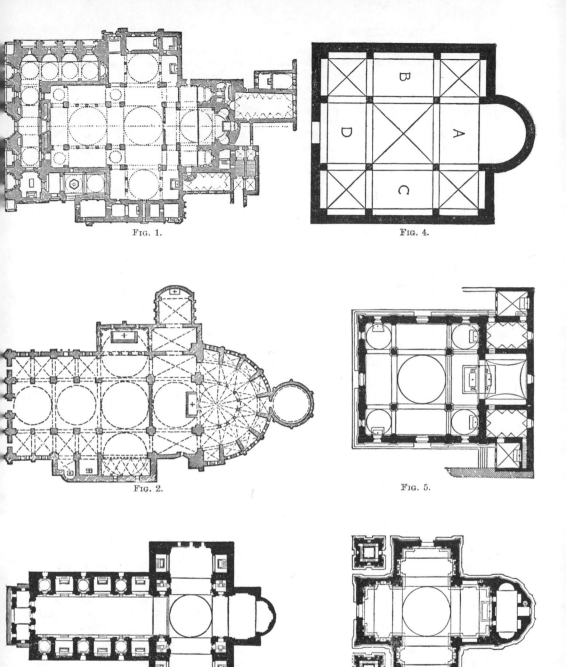

FIG. 1.

FIG. 4.

FIG. 2.

FIG. 5.

FIG. 3.

FIG. 6.

PLAN: A COMPARISON OF THE SYSTEMS OF THE FORMS OF CHURCH PLANS OF DIFFERENT EPOCHS. FOR THOSE OF THE BASILICA TYPE, OF ROMANESQUE, GOTHIC, RENAISSANCE, AND CINQUECENTO, SEE UNDER CHURCH AND SUBTITLES.

Fig. 1: Church of S. Mark, Venice, the typical Byzantine Greek cross with five cupolas with a narthex carried around the three sides of the western arm ; the southern branch of this cut off as a chapel. Fig. 2: S. Antonio, Padua, first half of thirteenth century ; a combined Romanesque and Byzantine style, though contemporaneous with the earlier Gothic buildings of North Italy ; the Greek cross is lost in the prolongations to east and west. Fig. 3: S. Andrea, Mantua ; c. 1475. One of the earliest Renaissance churches of wholly novel plan. The piers between the chapels serve as buttresses. Fig. 4: General scheme of Renaissance church plan in Middle Italy. A, B, C, D, are roofed by barrel vaults, the apse by a semidome, the five compartments either by groined vaults or cupolas. Compare Church of S. Fantino (plan under Church ; interior under Renaissance). Fig. 5: Church of S. Maria Nuova, Cortona, Tuscany, the plan resembling Fig. 4 but with the chancel square-ended, covered by a cupola with lunettes flanked by sacristies. Fig. 6: S. Biagio, Montepulciano, Tuscany. The type plan Fig. 4 with the corner compartments omitted ; therefore reduced to the simplest terms, a Greek cross enclosed by walls as simple as a box, a single cupola, and four barrel vaults.

Block Plan. A plan giving the general mass or outlines without subdivisions; as when it is desired to exhibit the relations of a building, as a whole, to surrounding buildings or grounds; or when the general distribution of rooms is indicated roughly without minor details, as doors and windows.

Ground Plan. That one of a set of architectural drawings which shows the ground story of a building, or, in some cases, of the basement story. It is usual to consider the ground plan as the primary drawing to which others must be made to conform, and this because it is commonly the one first laid out and the one in which the general lines of construction are first considered and more or less determined.

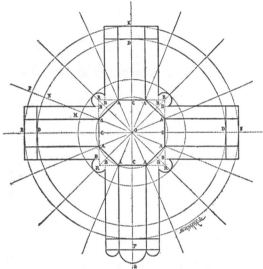

PLANNING: CHURCH AT KALAT SEM'AN, SYRIA; 5TH CENTURY.

O, column of S. Simeon Stylites. The circle *A, A, A*, fixes the Hypaethral octagon. The circle *R, R*, fixes the exterior of the absidioles. The circle *D, D*, fixes the length of the three great porches north, south, and west. The circle *H, K, S*, fixes the width of the outer narthex to each porch and the length of the nave of the church proper at the east. Lines drawn through *C, C*, are the axes of the church and porticoes. The sides of the naves and aisles being made parallel to these axes. Lines drawn through *R, R*, are the axes of the absidioles.

Perspective Plan. A plan drawn in perspective; used as a preliminary process of drawing in perspective, but rare.

PLANCEER. The soffit or underside of any projecting member as a cornice. Also, a plank; a floor of wood; sometimes called plancher, or corrupted into plansheer.

PLANE (v.). To smooth as with a plane, said of wood more especially, but also of stone of such qualities as will bear fine dressing, and of forging of iron and steel. In architecture, as in ship building, even the heaviest timbers were finished by the hand plane until about 1830; at that time the planing mill became common, and this has received great improvements. Planks and boards are said to be mill-planed when they are of that smoothness which is obtained by the planing machine. (See Woodworking Machinery.)

PLANE OF A COLUMN. The surface of a longitudinal section made on the axis of the shaft of a column. In some Greek peristyles and porticoes the planes of the columns incline inward slightly. (See Refinements in Design.)

PLANE TILE. (See Tile.)

PLANK. A piece of timber, the thickness of which is small as compared with its width. In the United States it is always more than one inch in thickness. In construction, only such pieces as are laid flat or nearly so; thus a timber, 3 inches × 10 inches, laid as in flooring, is called a plank; but when set on edge would be a beam or joist. (See Slow-burning Construction.)

PLANNING. The laying out and developing the general scheme of a building, referring especially to its ground plan and floor plans as the basis of every architectural composition. This process involves the adjustment of the building to the site and a consideration of the grades and their effect upon the plan; the size, shape, and proper mutual disposition of the halls, rooms, chambers, corridors, staircases, and offices of all degrees, having in view, first, the adaptation of each to its especial use in all respects of practical comfort, convenience, and accessibility; second, the best construction compatible with proper economy; third, the reconciliation of the upper stories with the lower, so that there may be no unnecessary, costly, or awkward concessions; fourth, the possible exterior developments, in respect to height, fenestration, division into pavilions and proportions generally; and fifth, beauty, harmony, and distinction of style by proper subordination or emphasis of each part in accordance with its just relative importance, so that a complete unity may be established throughout the whole fabric. In this process the establishment and observance of axial or centre lines and lines of vista are often made to play an important part. (See Plan; also Architecture; Drawing.)

— H. V. B.

PLANT (v.). To attach by glueing, nailing, or otherwise securing to a surface, particularly in carpentry; usually with *on*. A moulding when not worked in the solid is said to be planted on. (See Stick.)

PLAQUE. A tablet or distinctly flat plate, generally of metal, whether plain or ornamented, for exterior or interior wall decoration, or to be inserted or inlaid in a panel. (Compare Patera.)

PLASTER. In building: —

A. Same as Plaster of Paris.

B. A mixture, either of lime or of lime and

plaster, in sense *A*, with sand and water, and sometimes with short cattle hair or vegetable fibre, in considerable quantity, used while wet for covering surfaces of walls, or the like, where it hardens with a smooth surface. This is the only common use of the term in building, as other preparations serving the same purpose are rarely called by this name. (See Arriccio; Chunam; Gatch; Gauge Mortar, under Mortar; Gauged Work; Intonaco; Rough Cast; Staff; Stucco; see also Plastering.)

PLASTERING. The art and the practice of mixing and applying plaster in sense *B*, including the occasional use of plaster in sense *A*. It is customary to apply plaster in three or in two coats. For three-coat work the first coat is generally rather coarse mortar made of lime and sand with much hair mixed in the paste. This is put on wet, and rubbed hard with the trowel or float so as to form a good key upon the lathing or the masonry, while it is deeply scratched or scored to allow the second coat to make a key. The second coat, called the browning or floated coat, is of lime and sand, and is floated smooth. The third coat, called finishing coat, may be a hard finish, and is then composed of selected lime and fine white sand or marble dust, and is rubbed very smooth; or else it is of sand finish, and is then made like the second coat, but with selected and washed sand, and is floated true and smooth. Mouldings are made by running nearly pure plaster, in sense *A*, along the line to be followed, and then shaping the soft material by a pattern or templet, or by casting them in pieces of some size which are then nailed in place. Raised ornaments are of this material, sometimes stiffened with glue, or of papier maché; they are put up while the first or second coat is still wet, and keyed well into it, the finishing coat being worked around them afterward.

Sand finish is employed when the wall is to be painted, and when the peculiar depth and glow of colour caused by the rough surface is desired. Hard finish is much more common in modern times. Where painting is to be very elaborate, special treatment of the plastered surface is needed, unless plaster, in the strict sense, is replaced by some cement. (See Stucco.)

Plastering was used by the Romans both separate and in combination with stucco; it was used also throughout the Middle Ages, though what remains of this is generally a fine and apparently pure gypsum (plaster in sense *B*). It was in the sixteenth century that the use of flat, plastered ceilings began to replace the visible soffits of the floor beams and girders; and as this was nearly contemporaneous with the classical revival in the north, the Elizabethan and Jacobean English buildings offer examples of very elaborate moulded and patterned ceilings made of plaster. Colour was

mixed with the plaster very often, and different colours used in the same piece of work, with deliberate search for polychromatic effect.
— R. S.

PLASTER OF PARIS. *A.* Gypsum; so called because first discovered in the tertiary of the Paris basin.

B. Gypsum deprived of its natural moisture by heat, which, when ground to powder and diluted with water into a thin paste, sets rapidly, and expands at the instant of setting, a peculiarity which causes it to take sharp and delicate impressions from a mould. (See Plastering.)

PLAT. (See Plot, n. and v.)

PLATBAND. *A.* Any flat or square faced moulding of slight projection in comparison to its width, forming a contrast or rest in a group of mouldings of curvilinear section, as a fascia in an architrave.

B. A flat arch (which see, under Arch).

PLATE. *A.* A member intended to serve as the immediate support of isolated pressures, its especial advantage being to distribute those pressures widely throughout the mass of masonry or the row of separate uprights of iron or wood which support it. (1) A timber, plank, or piece of scantling used in this way (for which see sub-titles, Ground Plate; Pole Plate; Wall Plate). (2) A piece of metal or a block of stone of even surface and of uniform thickness, often not very much larger than the end of a beam, girder, or truss which rests upon it. (See Templet.)

B. A flat slab or piece of material of any sort intended, not for constructional purposes, but as an accessory. (See the sub-titles, Hand Plate; Push Plate.)

Bearing Plate. A plate in sense *A*; especially one used to carry a great and concentrated weight, as one end of a heavy truss.

Deck Plate. A purlin plate in cases where the upper slope of the roof is so nearly flat as to be called a deck.

Ground Plate. The lowest plate in a timber frame, resting upon the foundation of masonry or the piers which replace it; therefore, usually the same as sill, as in the framing of houses, and the like.

Hand Plate. A flat piece of hard, and often glazed and washable, material, intended to be fastened upon a door at the point where it is apt to be handled in opening and shutting. In old-fashioned houses its place is sometimes taken by a black painted parallelogram or other figure upon the lighter surface. (See Push Plate, below.)

Pin Plate. A form of Bearing Plate; so called because, when cast in iron, it is made with a pin intended to project downward into the masonry and steady the plate in its place.

Pole Plate. A plate for the support of the ends of the common rafters; specifically, such a plate laid across, and resting upon, the tie beams, and acting in place of a purlin.

Purlin Plate. A purlin in a roof which takes a new set of rafters, as where there is a break in the inclination of the roof, the upper part being less steep than below. (See Curb; Gambrel Roof, under Roof.)

Push Plate. A thin piece of metal, porcelain, or similar hard and washable substance applied to a door at a point where it is frequently pushed by hand or foot; especially the somewhat ornamental piece set below the knob and keyhole, and, more rarely, above these. (See Hand Plate.)

Raising Plate. In carpentry, any continuous horizontal timber laid upon the top of a wall or upon a timber framing, to support the heels of rafters or any other superincumbent frame work; a wall plate.

Wall Plate. A plate resting upon the wall and carrying the timbers of a floor or roof; more especially the piece which supports the ends of the rafters of an ordinary roof, and which is often spoken of as "the plate," without qualification. — R. S.

PLATEA (pl. plateæ). In Latin, an open space, as a street; hence, in Roman archæology, a passage in a theatre, amphitheatre, or other large building.

PLATE BEAM. (See under Beam.)

PLATE GLASS. (See under Glass.)

PLATERESQUE ARCHITECTURE. That supposed to resemble silversmiths' work in its ornamental details, viz., a delicate and elaborate tracery or massing of fine sculptured detail. This style is peculiar to Spanish architecture from about 1520. (See Spain, Architecture of.)

PLATFORM. In architecture: —

A. A natural or artificial raised piece of ground, more or less level and regular in shape; especially as prepared for the reception of buildings, as the great even surfaces retained by heavy walls from which rose the palaces of the Assyrians. (See Mesopotamia, Architecture of.)

B. A floor raised above or sunk below the ground or the general level of the floor of a room or hall; as a stair landing, a dais.

C. A grillage, bed of concrete or similar construction prepared to receive a pier.

D. A row of beams on top of a wall to support the timber work of a roof. (See Wall Plate.) — D. N. B. S.

PLATFORM RESIDENCE. A house or group of houses of American Indians built on an artificial platform, or terrace of earth. Such platforms in Florida were 20 to 50 feet high and sometimes nearly 2000 feet in circumference, surmounted by houses of the chief and his family. The steep sides were ascended by means of steps cut in the earth and covered with wood. It is probable that some of the mounds of the so-called Moundbuilders were of this nature. (See Mound.) — F. S. D.

PLATING. In stained glass work, the lining or doubling of one piece of coloured glass by another piece with the purpose of modifying its colour or diminishing its intensity. (See Window.)

PLAZA. In Spanish, an open place in a town. The term is being gradually adopted with a similar meaning in parts of the United States.

PLEASANCE. Anciently a garden or part of a garden intended for ornament and for enjoyment.

PLEXIFORM (adj.). Having the appearance of network, weaving, or plaiting, as in Romanesque and Celtic ornamentation.

PLINIUS CÆCILIUS SECUNDUS, CAIUS (Pliny the Younger); writer; b. 61 or 62 A.D.; d. 116 A.D.

A nephew of Plinius Secundus, author of the *Historia Naturalis* (see Plinius Secundus, Caius). He is best known by the ten books of his letters (*Epistolæ*). A letter from him to Gallus (Book II., Ep. XVII.) describes his Laurentine villa sixteen miles from Rome, and a letter to Apollinaris (Book V., Ep. VI.) describes another villa in Tuscany. Numerous attempts have been made to reconstruct these villas from his description. In 106 A.D. he succeeded Frontinus (see Frontinus) as superintendent of the Roman aqueducts.

Smith, *Dictionary of Greek and Roman Biography; Arch. Pub. Soc. Dictionary;* Castell, *Villas of the Ancients;* Marquez, *Delle ville di Plinio.*

PLINIUS SECUNDUS, CAIUS (Pliny the Elder); writer, b. 23 A.D.; d. 79 A.D.

The *Historia Naturalis* of this famous Roman writer is one of the chief sources of information regarding antique art, especially the thirty-fifth and thirty-sixth books. He was killed by the eruption of Vesuvius in 79 A.D.

Smith, *Dictionary of Greek and Roman Biography.*

PLINTH. *A.* The plain, continuous surface under the base moulding of any architectural member, and connecting it with the ground or floor. In the classic orders, the low square block under the base mouldings of a column, pilaster, or pedestal. The term is extended to include a course of stone or brick in which an offset is cut, as where a wall diminishes in thickness. The Doric abacus has been called a plinth erroneously and because of its square and simple form.

B. In joinery, interior finish, and the like, a flat and plain member at the bottom of any architrave, dado, or the like; or the broad and flat part of a Base Board or Skirting.

Sub Plinth. A plinth placed under the principal plinth and of slightly greater projection.

PLINTH BLOCK. A plinth used to prevent the mouldings of a door or window frame from reaching the floor. (See Plinth, *B*; also Base Block.)

PLINTH COURSE. A course of stones, forming a continuous plinth. Specifically, the first projecting course of stones above the underpinning, forming the base or part of the base of a building. (See Base Course; Water Table.)

PLINY. (See Plinius.)

PLOT (n.). *A.* A piece of ground, as for building, generally small.

B. A map or plan as laid out or plotted.

Ground Plot. Same as Ground Plan; nearly obsolete and connected with Plot (v.) in the sense of drawing plans.

PLOT (v.). To make a drawing of a plot or ground plan; to map; specifically, to lay out a map from a surveyor's notes.

PLOUGH. (See Plow.)

PLOW (v.). To cut grooves or channels, as in dadoing and housing.

PLOWED AND TONGUED. (See Tongued and Grooved.)

PLUG (n.). *A.* A wedge or peg of wood driven into a joint of a wall of brick or stone and then sawn off flush to afford a hold for nails, so that furring strips or other woodwork may have firm attachment in preparation for interior finish.

B. In plumbing, a branch from a water-supply pipe threaded at the outlet for coupling to a hose. It is generally closed by a screw cap.

PLUG AND FEATHER. A combination of three pieces, usually of iron, for splitting stone. It consists of two half-round bars which are placed in a hole drilled in the stone for the purpose, and between the flat sides of which is driven the third piece having a wedge shape. This last appears to be generally known as the Plug, although Feather would seem more appropriate from the general meaning of that term.

PLUMB (adj.). Vertical, as shown by a plumb line.

PLUMB (n.). A plummet; hence, by extension, the verticality of a line supporting a plummet. (See the sub title.)

Out of Plumb, not vertical; said of any member or face; and especially of one that ought to be truly vertical.

PLUMB BOB. The weight used for a plumb line; hence, by extension, the plumb line and weight used together. (See Plumb Line; Plumb Rule.)

PLUMBING. Formerly the trade and art of working in lead; nowadays the trade of fitting up in buildings the metal pipes, traps, tanks, and fixtures of different materials used for water supply, drainage, gas illumination, and for gas cooking and heating; also the pipe

system and apparatus used for the conveyance of water, sewage, and gas.

As implied by the name, plumbers used at one time principally lead in their work. Soil pipes were made from sheet lead rolled into cylindrical forms and soldered at the edges. Cisterns, tanks, and sinks were lined, and roofs of buildings were covered, with sheet lead. Handmade traps, rain-water heads, gutters, leaders, and flashings were made of this metal. Later on, cast-lead pipes came into use, and are now superseded by drawn lead pipes, bends, and traps. The tedious work of bending pipes by hand is done away with; drawn traps have no sand holes from casting and do not open at the soldered seams.

With progress in manufacturing, better and stronger materials became available for the plumbers' work. Cast and wrought iron pipe, for water, sewage, and gas, and copper and brass pipes, fittings, and traps for the waste and supply system of plumbing appliances, have to a large extent replaced lead and given to plumbing work an entirely different character. Comparatively little lead is used in the modern American plumbing, whereas in England and France lead soil, water and gas pipes, are still in use. In the case of very soft waters lead as a material for supply pipes should be avoided, as there is some danger of the water acting on the lead and causing, when used for drinking, lead poisoning. (See Pipe; Water Supply.) The journeyman plumber of to-day must understand wiping soldered joints in lead pipe, making screw joints in wrought-iron pipe, lead-caulked joints in cast-iron pipes, and the joining of brass, block tin, and copper pipes.

Plumbers' work comprises the running of soil, vent and waste pipes and house sewers of various materials, the tapping of street mains, bringing the water service pipes into buildings, and running supplies to plumbing fixtures, tanks, and hot water boilers; the fitting up of water metres, and the setting and connecting of hand lift and force pumps, hot air pumping engines, steam and gas pumps, electric and fire pumps. Plumbers fit up cooking ranges for coal or gas fuel, and make the connections of waterbacks or pipe coils, and must know how to obtain perfect hot water supply and circulation. They provide fire protection appliances, such as fire pumps, standpipes, valves, and hose, and fit up water sterilizers and pressure filters. They must know and understand the setting of the numerous kinds and types of plumbing fixtures, such as water-closets, urinals, sinks, basins, and tubs, and how to connect them with the soil and waste pipes in such a way as to secure the safe removal of sewage and perfect exclusion of sewer air. (See House Drainage.) The plumber also fits up buildings with gas pipes for lighting, cooking, heating, and power purposes.

The most important appliance from a sanitary point of view is the water-closet. Numerous types have been devised, many of which, after a brief trial, have been abandoned. The pan closet was the one to hold out the longest, notwithstanding its universal condemnation. At the present writing (1900), the pan, valve, and plunger closets are fast disappearing. Cheap wash-out closets and a few of good make are still in great demand, although not free from defects. In well-appointed bath rooms and toilet rooms, the all-porcelain siphon and siphon-jet closets are preferred. For institutions, schools, and servants' closets, pedestal washdown closets make a thoroughly sanitary fixture, in particular those with deep trap seal. In some situations a flushing-rim hopper closet works satisfactorily.

Wash basins are made in a variety of patterns. Those with outlet closed by a plug, and those with standpipes or with metal plugs operated by a lever, are much better than bowls with secret waste valves, or tip-up basins.

Bath tubs are made of wood lined with copper, of solid copper, of steel lined with copper, and of enamelled iron and earthenware. In hospitals for the insane and in people's baths, overhead inclined douches or sprays are substituted for tub baths, being more economical and sanitary. A great variety of hand sprays, needle and shower baths are made, as also foot baths, sitz baths, and bidets for bathing parts of the body.

Urinals have been improved, and a good pattern for single stalls is a flushing-rim bowl, holding water, flushed by a cistern and emptied by siphonic action. In public places, railroad stations, etc., and for factories and schools, continuous troughs of enamelled iron, slate, soapstone, or white glazed stoneware, with automatic intermittent flush, are used.

Wooden washtubs have been superseded by soapstone, slate, and artificial cement tubs for cheaper dwellings, and white or yellow glazed roll-rim earthenware tubs are used in more expensive residences.

Slop sinks for emptying chamber slops, and washing bedpans and other sick-room utensils for hospitals, are made in strong fire clay, and have a top flushing rim supplied from a cistern.

Sinks for kitchens, sculleries, and pantries are obtainable in painted, galvanized, or enamelled iron, in copper, soapstone, slate, and white or yellow stoneware. The latter are the best from a sanitary point of view, and recent improved methods of manufacture at American potteries have enabled the makers to reduce the price appreciably. In kitchens of large hotels and institutions, grease from dish washing and cooking operations is intercepted in grease traps, to prevent stoppages of waste pipes.

While much progress has been made in the art of fitting up buildings with plumbing con-

veniences, the manual work of the plumber has not advanced as much. Future improvement seems to lie in the direction of more accurate and mechanical workmanship, *i.e.* plumbing work should be laid out and fitted in the shop in much the same way as machinists turn out their work, thus enabling a more rapid and accurate putting together of the parts at the building.

Gerhard, *House Drainage and Sanitary Plumbing*, 7th ed. ; F. W. Tower, *Plumbers' Textbook ; Plumbing and House Drainage Problems*, from the *Sanitary Engineer ; American Plumbing Practice*, from the *Engineering Record* (formerly the *Sanitary Engineer*) ; Gerhard, *Recent Practice in the Sanitary Drainage of Buildings ; Sanitary Engineering of Buildings*, Vol. I. published, Vol. II. in preparation ; Gerhard, *Guide to Sanitary House Inspection ;* Waring, *How to Drain a House ;* Hellyer, *Lectures on Sanitary Plumbing ;* Gerhard, *Entwaesserungs-Anlagen amerikanischer Gebaeude* (Part X. of *Fortschritte der Architektur* of the *Handbuch*).

— W. P. GERHARD.

PLUMB LINE. The line which supports a Plumb or Plumb Bob.

PLUMB RULE. An instrument for determining verticality, consisting of a narrow board with straight parallel edges, having a plumb line attached to one end and a hole at the other end large enough to allow the plumb to swing freely. The verticality of its edges is known when the plumb line coincides with the centre line of the board, as marked on its face.

PLUMMET. Same as Plumb (n.).

PLUTEUS. In Roman architecture, a dwarf wall or parapet ; especially such a wall closing the lower portion of the space between the columns of a colonnade.

PNYX. A public place of assembly in ancient Athens ; known to have had little architectural character or formal arrangement. It is generally identified with a bare rocky platform west of the Acropolis.

POCKET. A hollow or recess, as in a wall ; generally comparatively small. Specifically :—

A. In a window frame for hung sash, an open space behind a pulley stile to accommodate the weights, particularly the lower portion of such a space to which access is had by means of a movable piece in the pulley stile.

B. A box made of thin boards, and built into a partition or wall to receive a sliding door when open.

C. A recess in the interior jamb of a window to receive a folding shutter or blind when open.

D. That part of a flue which is below the opening into it of a stovepipe or the like, where soot may accumulate and may be removed through a special opening.

POCKET PIECE. A movable part of a pulley style of a window frame for sliding sash ; the purpose of which is to enable the workman to reach the weight and sash cord within.

PODIUM. *A.* A continuous pedestal with die, cap, and base, such as is used in elevating an order of columns or a monument above the ground, or a dome above the roof. (See Crepidoma ; Stylobate.) A Roman temple was often set upon a podium, in contradistinction to the stepped platform of the Greek temple.

B. A wall, generally composed of concrete faced with marble, about 12 feet high, surrounding a Roman amphitheatre ; upon the platform above this wall the seats of the nobles were placed, while the other spectators occupied the ranges of seats rising behind, to the boundary walls.

PŒCILE. (Greek Ποικίλη, parti-coloured or painted ; applied to a portico in Athens.) A portico, or by extension any public building richly adorned with paintings on its interior walls. The original structure in Athens has not been identified in modern times. It is known that it was close to the Agora. It is thought that there were statues within the building, but the paintings of the taking of Troy, of the war with the Amazons, of the battle of Marathon, are especially identified with the building, the pictures being by Polygnotos, Mikon, and Panainos.

POERLAERT, JOSEPH; architect; b. 1816 (in Brussels); d. Nov. 3, 1879.

In 1849 he won the competition for the monument of Belgian independence at Brussels. He restored the *Grand Théâtre* at Brussels, and built the church of S. Catherine in Brussels and the royal church at Laeken (Belgium). In 1866 he began his most important work, the monumental Palais de Justice in Brussels, which was finished after his death, and inaugurated Oct. 15, 1883.

Meyer, *Konversations Lexicon ; Nécrologie* in *l'Émulation*, 1880.

POIKILE. Same as Pœcile.

POINT (n.). Same as Pointing Tool.

POINT (v. t.). (**I.**) To fill up and finish carefully, and with more or less elaboration, as the joints at the face of a piece of masonry, or about the edges of slates or tiles of a roof. Such finishing may be done during the progress of the work, or — as is more usual in good work, when greater elaboration is desired — after the completion of the masonry, or other structure. In the latter case, the process is generally understood as including both the operation of raking and of stopping. The purpose of such work is better to preserve the masonry from the effects of weather, — the joints being filled with a superior kind of mortar, — and also to obtain a certain decorative finish, either by the use of mortar colour, or by the particular form of modelling given to the faces of the joints as described under Pointing (I.).

POINT (v. t.). (**II.**) To dress stone roughly with the point, by which its faces are brought to approximately plane surfaces. (See Stone Dressing.)

POINTED ARCHITECTURE. That which is distinguished by the use of the pointed arch. The term seems not to have been used except in this sense, though steep roofs, spires, and the like might justify its application to buildings not furnished with pointed arches. It is not uncommon to use the term as synonymous with

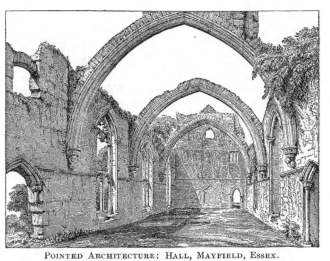

POINTED ARCHITECTURE: HALL, MAYFIELD, ESSEX.
A building of the best Gothic period, but not intended for vaulting, and therefore not of Gothic Architecture in the strict sense.

Gothic ; and it is also not uncommon to discriminate between the Gothic style, properly so called, with its elaborate system of vaulted construction, flying buttresses, etc., and that which, having pointed arches but no Gothic construction, can only be called Gothic by a rather liberal extension of the term: such as the modern churches and halls which have wooden roofs and no provision for vaulting. The term is applied less frequently to buildings of Moslem styles.

POINTED WORK. *A.* The surface finish of hard stone which has been roughly shaped for use by the pointing tool or pick, only the coarsest projections having been removed. (See Pick Dressing.)

B. Masonry, the joints of which have been raked out and pointed with mortar. (See Pointing Tool.)

POINTEL. (See Poyntell.)

POINTING (**I.**). The process, and the result, of finishing a joint or joints, as defined under Point (I.).

Bastard Pointing; Bastard Tuck Pointing. Similar to, but more simple than, Tuck Pointing; a portion of the stopping being made to project in the form of a fillet along the centre of a thick joint, the section being rectangular. The mortar joint is sometimes coloured as in Tuck Pointing.

Flat Joint Pointing. The simplest form, the mortar being finished flush with the face of the masonry. The term is commonly restricted to mean such pointing when done during the progress of the masonry. (See Hick Joint Pointing.)

Flat Joint Jointed Pointing. Flat joint pointing, in which the joints are further embellished by narrow grooves along their centre lines; or by grooves at top and bottom, next to the bricks; or by both.

Hick Joint Pointing. Pointing with flush joints, but with a superior sort of mortar used as stopping after raking out the joint; thus distinguished from Flat Joint Pointing.

High Joint Pointing. Pointing done during the progress of the work, while the mortar is still soft, by first trimming the joints flush with the face of the wall, and then scraping grooves along the edges of the brick at both sides of the joint. Subsequently, the mortar joints are usually grooved along the centre lines also.

Key Joint Pointing. A form in which the soft mortar is pressed and worked into shape by means of a jointer having a rounded convex edge, so that the face of the joint has the form of a cavetto.

Mason's V-Joint Pointing. That in which the mortar is given a projecting profile like a flattened $>$; perhaps having also a flat fillet at top and bottom.

Tuck Pointing; Tuck and Pat Pointing. Pointing in which the ordinary pointing mortar is finished with narrow grooves along the centre of the joints, this being afterward filled with a projecting ridge of fine lime, putty, or the like, perhaps coloured. This projecting fillet is supposed to be finished with accurately ruled and trimmed edges and faces; and it is common to colour the rest of the joint to match the brick, so that the joints appear to be only of the thickness of the fillet.

POINTING (II.). The process and the result of dressing stone as defined under Point (II.).

POINTING TOOL. A stonecutter's implement, having a narrow, wedge-shaped, chisel-like edge, and this usually worked upon a solid bar of steel, which is struck directly by the stone mason's mallet. It is used for rough tracing of surfaces which may either be left "pointed" or "dressed with the point," or may be finished afterward with other tools. It is used also to cut across the face of the stone, from edge to edge, incised lines which are brought into the true plane of the four arrises, and thus help to determine the future surface of the stone when dressed.

POINT OF SIGHT. The position from which anything is observed, or is represented as being observed; the position of the eye of the observer. Also called point of vision, point of view, centre of projection, centre of vision, etc. (See Perspective.)

POINT OF SUPPORT. In the plan of a building, a space of small dimensions where the superincumbent weight of structure is gathered together and met. Columns, pillars, and piers form points of support. In a plan of foundations, those places where, by reason of the conditions of the structure above or of the soil below, it is necessary to concentrate weight, are points of support; and, in order to avoid dislocations in the superstructure through unequal settlement, the area of such spaces must be exactly adjusted to the weight which each is to transmit to the soil, according to the ascertained capacity of the soil to bear weight.

POLAND, ARCHITECTURE OF. The buildings of the ancient kingdom of Poland, extending, in the seventeenth century, over those parts of Europe which stretch from the river Oder eastward to within a hundred miles of Moscow. These have been so little studied that their treatment as a national architecture is as yet impracticable. The buildings of the earlier states of Lithuania and Poland proper, with the work of the eastern Russians and German military orders on the Baltic, would have to be studied, and even the fascinating and picturesque city of Danzig would form a part of that field. (For

POLAND: ARCHITECTURE OF KRAKAU (CRACOW), CHURCH OF S. MARY.

the principal buildings of this region, see Germany, the Eastern Provinces, and Russia.)
— R. S.

POLICE STATION. The headquarters, or district headquarters, of a police force. It contains, usually, sleeping accommodations for the force and for prisoners, and frequently room for a patrol wagon and stabling for horses.

POLISH (v. t.). To bring (any surface) to a state of great smoothness. The term is generally limited to the producing of such smoothness for decorative effect as for bringing out the colour and veins of marble or wood, or by giving metallic brilliancy to a surface. A surface may be polished either by simply scraping and rubbing without any application, as where in Japan-

POLYCHROMY: MARBLES OF VARIED COLOUR; SPAN-
DRIL OF DOGE'S PALACE, VENICE.

POLYCHROMY: INLAY OF WOOD OF DIFFERENT
COLOURS (TARSIA).

POLYCHROMY: INLAY OF MARBLES AND COLOURED
AND GILDED GLASS; BASILICA OF S. CLEMENTE,
ROME.

POLYCHROMY: PAINTINGS OF HISTORICAL SUBJECT UNDER THE ROOF AND OF HERALDIC
SUBJECT ON EACH SIDE OF THE TRIPLE WINDOW COMBINED WITH COLOURED
TREATMENT OF THE HERALDIC AND OTHER CARVING AND A SOLIDLY GILDED
ROOF; INNSBRUCK, TYROL.

PLATE VIII

POLYCHROMY IN EXTERNAL ARCHITECTURE. CHURCH OF S. PIETRO,
PISTOJA, TUSCANY

ese interiors delicate woods are left with their natural veining shown ; or by means of some

POLYCHROMY: PAINTING ON A FLAT CEILING OF STOUT PLANK ; SWEDISH ; 17TH CENTURY.

varnish, as where mahogany and rosewood furniture is covered with a transparent coat of copal varnish ; or by means of a dressing which is put upon the surface and then rubbed off so that but little of it remains, and that little fills up the hollows of the surface merely, without covering the whole. It is not customary to speak of polishing sandstone, limestone, and the like, as nothing that can be done to them will bring them to a lustrous surface, but granite, marble, and hard wood are polished when it is intended to show the full beauty of the material.

POLLAJUOLO, ANTONIO. (See Benci, Antonio di Jacopo.)

POLLAJUOLO, SIMONE DEL. (See Il Cronaca.)

POLYCHROMY. Colouring with many colours ; elaborate decoration in colour. It seems to have been the uniform practice of builders in all ages, in Europe previous to the classical revival in the fifteenth century, and in non-European lands even to the present time, to seek for effects of colour as well as those of form. There is an apparent exception to this general rule in the practice of the stone-building races of India, with whom the play of light and shade secured by deep and strong modifications of surface exposed to a brilliant sun seem to have taken the place of chromatic effects produced by the direct agency of man. Modern Europe has retained this taste, or desire, for colour only for interiors, the efforts at external

coloration having been either connected with the admitted revival of some bygone style of art, or else sporadic and individual efforts.

Such exterior colour effects as are produced by keramic painting have been treated under that term. (See also Tile.)

The use of natural materials to produce a contrast or modification of colour in the exterior of a building is more common in mediæval art than elsewhere. Several important styles of architecture — the Romanesque of France, the Romanesque and Gothic of Italy, and the Mohammedan of Egypt and Syria — employed for this purpose the materials with which their walls were faced. (See France, Part VIII. ; Moorish Architecture ; Moslem Architecture ; Romanesque Architecture.) The Italian buildings of Verona have the most elaborate and most effective of coloured brick work combined with marble : those of Lombardy the most successful terra-cotta enrichments ; those of Tuscany the most tasteful combinations of white marble with marble or other stones of greenish black, dark gray, and the like. The Moslem work has this peculiarity, that the forms of the stones in an arch or a horizontal frieze are often elaborate, increasing the complexity of effect.

In the English Gothic revival, beginning about 1850, the influence of Italian art in this respect was strongly felt, and some of the architects interested in that movement employed coloured materials with excellent results. It may be considered one of the characteristics of Victorian Gothic, properly so called, that external colour is used with some freedom.

POLYCHROMY: PAINTING ON A PLASTER CEILING ;
17TH CENTURY NORTHERN WORK.

But the pattern is derived from the endless supply of diapers and sowings in Italian and Spanish tiles and stencil work.

The most important form of polychromy is that produced by painting with its accessory, gilding. This was the practice of antiquity in all those lands where keramic materials were not constantly used. (See Egypt, Architecture of; Grecian Architecture; Greece, Architecture of; and for contrasting use in keramics, see Mesopotamia, Architecture of; Persian Architecture, Parts I. and III.)

In the European Middle Ages painting was applied with less skill than in European antiquity or in the East, but it was applied continually. There is very little of it preserved. The famous doorway of Reims cathedral, which had been closed, — boarded up for centuries, — and which had preserved its painting intact, is the best single instance we have of mediæval painting freely applied to an exterior. It is well known, however, that large numbers of the Gothic cathedrals were painted elaborately; the porches with their sculpture, and similar prominent members of the building; and this was evidently a survival from a Romanesque practice of still more general polychromatic treatment.

As regards the colour decoration of interiors, this has been treated under Mural Painting. (For the processes employed, see Encaustic; Fresco; Fresco-Secco; Oil Painting.) — R. S.

POLYCLITUS; sculptor; flourished between 470 and 400 B.C.

A younger contemporary of Phidias (see Phidias), who was probably born at Sicyone and settled at Argos, Greece, and a pupil of Agelaidas (see Agelaidas). His most important work was the chryselephantine statue of Hera, in the Heraion at Argos, which replaced the old temple destroyed in 423 B.C.

Friederichs, *Der Doryphoros des Polyklet*; Waldstein, *Excavations at Argos*; Rayet, *Monuments de l'Art Antique*; Collignon, *Histoire de la Sculpture grecque*.

POLYCLITUS THE YOUNGER; sculptor and architect.

Polyclitus, the son of Patrocles, flourished between 370 and 336 B.C., and built the Tholos (round temple) and theatre at Epidauros, in Greece. He is not to be confounded with the great sculptor Polyclitus, of Argos.

Defrasse et Lechat, *Epidaure*; Collignon, *Histoire de la Sculpture grecque*.

POLYFOIL. Same as Multifoil. (See Foil.)

POLYGNOTUS; painter.

He was a native of the island of Thasos, in the Ægean Sea, and probably came to Athens about 463 B.C. He was employed by Cimon (d. 449 B.C.) to decorate the temple of Theseus, the Anaceium, and the Pœcile at Athens. He painted the so-called Lesche at Delphi. About 435 B.C. he was engaged on the decoration of the Pinacotheca, on the Acropolis at Athens. He painted the walls of the temple of Athena Areia at Platæa. Polygnotus was contemporaneous with Phidias. (See Phidias.)

Brunn, *Geschichte der Griechischen Künstler*; Bertrand, *La peinture dans l'Antiquité*; Girard, *La peinture antique*.

POLYGONAL BUILDING. Masonry laid up with irregular polygonal-faced stones fitted together. This construction was employed in those Mediterranean lands where the earlier forms of Pelasgic architecture had been previously current. It was a modification due mainly to new implements and improved methods. (See under Pelasgic Architecture where it follows "Cyclopean" and "Mycenæan.")
         — A. L. F., Jr.

POLYGON OF FORCES. A graphical representation of the composition and resolution of forces when there are more than two such forces, and when, therefore, the parallelogram of forces (which see) cannot be used. Let

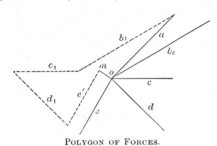

POLYGON OF FORCES.

O be the point acted upon, and the different forces be denoted by the lines a, b, c, d, e, the lengths of which lines indicate their intensity. Draw b' parallel to b, c' in prolongation of c, d' parallel to d, e' parallel to e, the line a itself serving to form the polygon. There is now required to close and complete the polygon a line connecting the extremity of e' with the point O. Draw this line m. This line is, then, the resultant of all the other forces, and the force which it represents would maintain the point O in equilibrium if acted upon at once by the forces a, b, c, d, e.

POLYSTYLE. Composed of many columns.

POMEL; **POMMEL.** A knob, knot, or boss; especially a ball-shaped terminal used as a finial for steep conical or pyramidal roofs, pinnacles, etc.; also for the similar decoration of furniture.

PON. Same as Wall Plate; a local English term.

Addy, *The Evolution of the English House*.

PONCE, JACQUIO; sculptor.

An Italian sculptor who was employed on the monuments of François I. and Henri II. in the church of S. Denis. (See Pilon, Germain.)

Lami, *Dictionnaire des Sculpteurs français*.

PONCET, JEAN; sculptor and architect.

Aug. 31, 1450, he contracted to build the

tomb of King René, at Angers (France). He probably designed the retable of the church of S. Pierre at Saumur.

Lecoy de la Marche, *Comptes du roi René.*

PONCET, PONS; architect and sculptor.

A son of Jean Poncet (see Poncet, Jean.) After the death of his father in 1542 he was called to continue the works of the tomb of King René, at Angers (Maine et Loire, France). June 24, 1459, he contracted to build the great altar of the church of the Carmelites at Angers.

Lecoy de la Marche, *Comptes du roi René.*

PONS; monk and architect.

He rebuilt the abbey of Montierneuf at Poitiers (France), which was dedicated Jan. 24, 1096.

Bulletin Monumental, Vol. IX., p. 391.

PONT. In French, a bridge; sometimes, in combination, forming the proper name of an important bridge which is not connected with the geographical name of the place. (See the following titles.)

The bridges which cross the Seine at Paris are all, or nearly all, of great celebrity and of importance in French history and French art. They are very numerous; but the most important are, Pont d'Austerlitz; Pont Sully in two branches like the Pont Neuf and connecting the Île Saint Louis with both banks; Pont de la Tournelle; Pont d'Arcole; Pont Notre Dame; Pont S. Michel; Pont au Change (the last four crossing one arm only of the Seine); then the Pont Neuf (which see below). Below these are, spanning the whole river, the Pont des Arts, a footpath only; Pont du Carrousel, called also and more frequently, Pont des Saints Pères; Pont Royal; Pont Solférino; Pont de la Concorde; Pont Alexandre III. (built before 1890 for service during the great exhibition of that year); Pont des Invalides; Pont de l'Alma; Pont d'Iéna.

PONT D'AVIGNON. Same as Pont S. Bénezet, but under the geographical name enters into French proverb and song.

PONT DU GARD. An aqueduct bridge across the river Gard, in the south of France, and which was built under the Roman Empire as part of the aqueduct of Nemausus (Nîmes). A modern roadway has been built along one side of it.

PONTE. In Italian, a bridge. (See what is said under title Pont; see also following titles.)

PONTE DEI SOSPIRI. Same as Bridge of Sighs (which see).

PONTE DI PAGLIA. In Venice; the small bridge spanning the mouth of the Rio, or small canal, which is also spanned by the Bridge of Sighs, and which separates the Doge's palace from the prisons. It forms a part of the walk along the sea front.

PONTE DI RIALTO. The bridge connecting the two great islands of Venice, one of which, known as the Rialto, gives its name to the bridge. This was for very many years the only bridge spanning the Canalazzo, or Canal Grande; a wooden building was removed in the seventeenth century and replaced by the present most interesting structure. (See Bridge.)

PONTE, GIOVANNI DA. (See Giovanni Da Ponte.)

PONTELLI (DE PUNTELLIS) or PINTELLI, BACCIO (BARTOLOMEO); architect, engineer, and wood worker (intarsiatore); d. after 1492.

Pontelli was a pupil of Francione (see Francione). The earliest notice of him is as intarsiatore at Pisa (Italy), where he was employed in 1471. 1475–1477 he made the stalls in the choir of the cathedral of Pisa. In 1479 he went to Urbino, where he came under the influence of Francesco di Giorgio Martini. (See Martini, Fr. di G.) After the death of Federigo da Montefeltro, duke of Urbino, in 1482, he went to Rome. July 27, 1483, he was sent to inspect the work of Giovannino dei Dolci (see Dolci, G.) at Città Vecchia, and in 1484 himself directed the construction of that citadel. During the reign of Innocent VIII. (Pope 1484–1492) he was placed in charge of all the fortresses in the Marches. Nothing is known of him after 1492.

Müntz, *Les Arts à la cour des papes,* Vol. III., p. 66; Müntz, *Renaissance;* C. Rocchi, *Baccio Pontelli e la Rocca d'Ostia.*

PONTE MOLLE. At Rome; the ancient Milvian bridge (Pons Milvius); largely rebuilt in modern times.

PONTE VECCHIO. Literally, the old bridge, a name given to several important structures in Italy, the most interesting being that which crosses the Arno at Florence.

PONTIFS, GUILLAUME; architect.

May 27, 1462, he succeeded Geoffray Richier as *maître d'œuvre* of the cathedral of Rouen. Between 1463 and 1467 he completed the *portail de la Calende* and the *tour Saint Romain.* In 1484 he built the portal of the *cour des Libraires* and in 1485 commenced the *tour de Beurre,* of which he built one story. He built the screen of the choir and the sacristy.

Deville, *Revue des architectes de la cathédrale de Rouen.*

PONT NEUF. In Paris; in two divisions, ealding from the north bank of the Seine to the Île de la Cité, and from that island to the south bank. It was begun under Henri III. and finished under Henri IV. about 1610.

PONT S. BÉNEZET. At Avignon; built in the twelfth century. (See Bénezet; see also for the fuller title of the monastic Order of Bridge Builders, Pont S. Esprit.)

PONT S. ESPRIT. On the Rhône above Avignon, built between 1265 and 1295 ; five-eighths of a mile in length with twenty-two arches. This, like the Pont S. Bénezet, has an angle or elbow in the wider branch of the river. This was the last bridge of importance built by the Frères Hospitaliers Pontifes, founded by S. Bénezet.

PONT VALENDRÉ (VALENTRÉ). At Cahors in southern France ; built about the middle of the thirteenth century and still retaining its curious towers of defence.

POOP. Same as Poppyhead. — (C. D.)

POPPY-HEAD: Clifton Campville Church, Staffordshire ; Rude 14th Century Work.

POORHOUSE. A public institution for the care and support of the helpless poor ; especially in some states of the United States such an establishment kept up by the township. (See Almshouse ; Workhouse.)

POOR, RICHARD ; bishop.

He was bishop of Salisbury (England) from 1217 to 1228. He removed the cathedral and its offices from the old fortress of Sarum to a plot of ground called Merrifield, where, on April 28, 1220, the foundations of the existing church were begun. On Michaelmas Day, 1225, the church was sufficiently advanced for the celebration of divine service. In 1228 he was transferred to Durham.

Britton, *Cathedral Antiquities*, Vol. II.

PÖPPELMANN, MATTHÄUS DANIEL; architect ; b. 1662 ; d. Jan. 17, 1736.

Pöppelmann held the offices of *Baukondukteur* (1696), *Landbaumeister* (1705), and *Ober-*

landbaumeister (1718) in Dresden, Saxony. In 1711 he began the famous baroque palace called the Zwinger (Dresden). He built also the *Schloss Moritzburg* near Dresden (1722–1730) and the old *Holländische Palast* (1715–1717), which was transformed by Von Bodt (see Bodt) and is now called the *Japanische Palast* (Dresden). Pöppelmann built numerous fine residences.

POPPY-HEAD: All Soul's Chapel, Oxford; c. 1450.

Gurlitt, *Baroque-Stil in Deutschland;* Schmidt-Schildbach, *Der Zwinger in Dresden ;* Schuman, *Barok und Rococo.*

POPPY; POPPY-HEAD. An ornament generally used for the finials of pew or bench ends and other similar pieces of furniture in churches. It is sometimes merely cut into the form of plain Fleurs-de-lis or in some other simple decorative shape, and chamfered, but frequently it is richly carved with leaves and figures. The name is apparently derived from the French *poupée*, the bunch of flax on a staff, not from the flower or plant.

POPPY-HEAD: Christ Church, Oxford; c. 1520.

PORCH. A covered place of entrance and exit attached to a building and projecting from its main mass ; it may, when so projecting, be in more than one story and may form the lower

PLATE IX

PORCH

That of the church of S. Germain l'Auxerrois, opposite the east front of the Louvre, in Paris. This porch dates from 1431, and its design is ascribed to Jean Gaussel.

PORCH: CHURCH AT BARNACK, NORTHAMP-
TONSHIRE; C. 1250.

PORCH: CHURCH AT BERNIÈRES (CALVADOS); C. 1250.

PORCH: TIMBER CONSTRUCTION, ALDHAM, ESSEX; C. 1350.

PORCH: KIDLINGTON CHURCH, OXFORDSHIRE; c. 1350.
The inner doorway is much earlier.

PORCH: ALL SAINTS, STAMFORD, LINCOLNSHIRE;
c. 1500.

PORCH: WOODEN CANOPY WITHOUT PILLARS; 15TH CENTURY.
HOSPITAL AT BEAUNE IN BURGUNDY.

183

PORCH: AMERICAN "OLD COLONIAL" OR GEORGIAN ARCHITECTURE; LITCHFIELD, CONN.

184

story of a tower or the like. In Elizabethan houses in England the projecting porch is often extended to the full height of the main building forming a pavilion, the upper stories having so-called porch chambers, the porch proper occupying the lower story.

Historically, the porch of the early Christian churches and basilicas was a narthex, furnished for religious uses with piscinas or lavatories and baptismal fonts, and contained tombs. It was used as a place in which the newly converted were prepared for entrance into the church proper. Of porches of this character, that of the church of Vézelay is perhaps the most important remaining to us. A conspicuous example of the later Gothic porch is that of S. Germain l'Auxerrois at Paris. The characteristic porch of modern times was foreshadowed in the simpler constructions, projecting often from the side doorways of parish churches, especially in England, and not unusual in domestic work. The term "porch" is somewhat inexactly applied to an open arcade or loggia forming the first story of a building and giving sheltered entrance to it ; also to a classic portico with columns. But the veranda of modern American houses, where it serves to give entrance to them by a principal doorway, is a true porch.
— HENRY VAN BRUNT.

PORCH CHAMBER. In a two-storied porch or advanced projecting building, of which the ground story forms a porch, the room occupying the whole or the greater part of an upper story.

PORINOS. (See Antistates.)

PORPHYRY. Any igneous rock containing comparatively large and conspicuous crystals lying in a fine-grained, often dense and compact, ground or base.
— G. P. M.

Green Antique Porphyry ; *Marmor Lacedæmonium viride* of Pliny. An igneous rock of the nature of a diabase porphyrite, consisting of a compact, deep greenish black ground, thickly studded with greenish feldspars in all

sizes up to an inch in diameter, and which are often cruciform or octagonal in outline and show a zonal structure. Much used by the Greeks and Romans for pavements and general inlaid

PORTE COCHÈRE AT TOULOUSE: C. 1580.

decorative work. The source of the material is near Levetsova, Laconia, in southern Greece.
— G. P. M.

PORTA, GIACOMO DELLA. (See Giacomo Della Porta.)

PORTAIL. The same as Portal.

PORTAL. An entrance or gateway of a monumental character ; specifically, an entrance which is emphasized by a stately architectural treatment, such as may make it the principal *motif* in an entire façade.

PORTCULLIS. A strong door sliding vertically, usually a grating heavily framed of wood with pointed iron bars at the bottom. It is arranged so as to be dropped suddenly and thus protect an entrance in case of a surprise. The portcullis was a constant feature in mediæval fortification, there being sometimes two or three in the same passageway.

PORTE COCHÈRE: RUE BOURDONNAIS, PARIS; 16TH CENTURY
STYLE OF LOUIS XIV.

PORTE COCHÈRE. In French, a doorway large enough to accommodate wheeled vehicles. Such entrances are a common feature of private houses of France, and generally open into driveways which lead through the building, from the street to the interior court. From this passage the entrance to the staircase and that to the ground story generally open, so that there is sometimes a footway or sidewalk beside the carriage road. The doorway itself, and the woodwork of the door, are often very richly decorated.

The use of the term, common in the United States, to signify a carriage porch, is erroneous.

PORTICO. A porch or vestibule roofed and partly open on at least one side, as one section of a peristyle or a cloister; but specifically and more exactly, an ambulatory or vestibule covered by a roof supported by columns on at least one side, such as is characteristic in Greek, Roman, and Neoclassic architecture. It properly includes the pronaos and epinaos of a temple, enclosed by a screen of columns between its projecting side walls (portico in antis); any vestibule or pronaos formed by one or more rows of columns standing clear of a cellar and in front of it (see Prostyle; Amphiprostyle); any one side or face of an ambulatory or pteroma formed by a single row of columns entirely enveloping the temple on the sides and ends (see Peripteral; Dipteral); or any other form of a columnar ambulatory or vestibule, whether connected with a religious or secular building, or standing clear (see Columnar Architecture).

PORTICUS. In Latin, usually, same as Portico, but employed in a somewhat larger sense (compare Cryptoporticus).

PORTIGIANI, PAGNO DI LAPO; sculptor and architect of Fiesole, Italy; b. 1406; d. 1470.

Pagno assisted Michelozzo at the church of the Annunziata in Florence. In 1428 he worked on the front of S. Giovanni at Siena, and in 1460 made the plans for the Bentivoglio palace at Bologna. His best work is the monument of Giovanni Cellini, in the church of S. Jacopo at S. Miniato al Tedesco, between Florence and Pisa.

Geymüller-Stegman, *Die Architektur der Renaissance in Toscana;* Vasari, Milanesi ed. (Vita di Michelozzo), Vol. II., p. 445.

PORTLAND STONE. A light-coloured Jurassic limestone from the Isle of Portland, off the English coast. Used in the construction of S. Paul's cathedral, London.— G. P. M.

PORTUGAL, ARCHITECTURE OF. That of the modern kingdom, occupying part of the western seacoast of the Iberian peninsula. Although there are a few buildings here which date from the tenth century, it is almost impossible to trace through them any continuous architectural development, for the numerous earthquakes and hostile invasions have made

PLATE X

PORTUGAL, ARCHITECTURE OF. PLATE I

Belem, near Lisbon; church of the monastery of S. Jerome (S. Hyronimo). The porch, which is the main entrance, is in the south flank and dates from the earlier years of the sixteenth century. The design is recognized as individual, resembling that of no other land, and it is called "Manuelino" from the name of the sovereign under whom it was erected.

PORTE COCHÈRE: RUE MÉNARS, PARIS; 19TH CENTURY.

189   190

havoc. At Braga, in the extreme northern portion of the country, is a cathedral which is the most ancient existing edifice in Portugal, dating from 1112. In plan it consists of a single three-aisled nave with square termination and square of Portugal, a convent church which was built in 1222, consisting in plan of a very long nave with a row of square-ended chapels and a semicircular chevet which was added in 1676. The church was built from French plans, but in de-

PORTE COCHÈRE SEEN FROM WITHIN; ENTRANCES TO THE HOUSES AT LEFT AND RIGHT; MODERN PARIS.

chapels and only very slightly marked transepts. The plan of the cathedral of Oporto is of interest from its square eastern termination, recalling some of the English types, but neither of these structures offers any noticeable exterior effect. At Alcobaça, a small village sixty miles north of Lisbon, is the largest religious edifice sign it does not show a very strong French influence. It is early Gothic in style, carried out in a very severe, subdued spirit, except in the chapel in the south transept, where there is a tomb which is cited as the most beautiful piece of carving in the kingdom. Twelve miles beyond Alcobaça is the hamlet of Batalha, possess-

PLATE XI

PORTUGAL, ARCHITECTURE OF. PLATE II

Monastery of Batalha, south flank of the church with a part of the
unfinished chapel (Capella Imperfeita) at the east of the choir. All
this work was done before 1515, and is, therefore, contemporary with
the church at Belem, which, however, is in a different style.

ing a monastery and church erected in 1388. In plan the church suggests Alcobaça, but the design, as far as relates to the façade at least, was inspired by that of York Cathedral, and is directly ascribed to an English architect, Stephen Stephenson, who went to Portugal in the suite of Queen Philippa. The west front is in a late Perpendicular style, well proportioned and free from vagaries, and a large octagonal chapel on the south is in appearance not unlike the exterior of Henry the Seventh's Chapel, in Westminster Abbey. Adjoining the church on the north is a large cloister, with some most marvellously elaborate stone carving filling the heads of the arches.

The cathedral of Lisbon was built in 1147, but has suffered so repeatedly from earthquakes and has been renewed at so many different periods that its original Gothic character has been quite obliterated, though the same general disposition has always been preserved. This is the Portuguese church which in plan most nearly approaches the perfect Gothic type as it was understood in France, and is the only one which possesses the fully developed circular apsis with radiating chapels.

The most interesting group of buildings in Portugal is in the suburb of Belem just outside of Lisbon, comprising an extensive monastery and a small chapel or church flanked on one side by cloisters. The church was built in the fifteenth century to commemorate the discovery by Da Gama of the passage around the Cape of Good Hope. It is the one building in the country which in all its details seems to be thoroughly Portuguese. In plan it has a three-aisled nave with square transepts. A small semicircular apsis is a late Renaissance alteration. The church is covered by a triple line of vaulting of very daring construction, somewhat on the lines of the English fan work, except that the fans are not cotangent, and they make complete circuits about the slender piers, the three aisles being all of the same height, and the lines of the fan work connected by a species of flat cloister vaulting. This work is balanced so cleverly that during the great earthquake, though the church was violently shaken, not a stone was dislodged. In exterior appearance the design is Gothic in general scheme, though early Renaissance in detail. An elaborate side porch, built entirely of beautiful cream-coloured sandstone, has a wealth of excellent detail which is interesting of itself and forms a part of a very harmonious grouping. The cloisters immediately adjoin the church at the north and are in the same style but with details more pronouncedly Renaissance in character.

About three-quarters of a mile west of the Belem church, on a bit of sandy beach stretching out into the Tagus, is an interesting piece of Gothic military architecture dating from the early part of the sixteenth century, consisting of a tower and a wide terrace, the whole forming a part of the military defences of Lisbon. The tower of Belem shows in style a crude Gothic, marked by English influence in some of its details. It is about the only piece of military architecture existing in the country.

At Thomar, a little town about eighty miles northeast of Lisbon, is the celebrated Convent of Christ, considered to be the most remarkable in Portugal, after that at Batalha. It dates from 1180, but the interesting part is three hundred years later in date and is a most elaborate example of the possibilities of Portuguese decoration. The apsis of the chapel attached to the church has sculpture of a character which one can only compare to some of the carvings of the Hindus. Indeed, this convent work and the cloisters of Batalha and Belem have a very strong flavour of the qualities which make the East Indian work so attractive, though curiously mingled with reminders of late English Gothic. The Spanish element seems to be strangely lacking in all this work. Another striking bit of detail is found in the church of S. Clara at Coimbra, a town about midway between Lisbon and Oporto, which has a pulpit carved from a single block of marble built into the walls of the church, with an elaborate profusion of details, interesting as a composition in both mass and detail to an extent which entitles this to rank as the *chef-d'œuvre* of Portuguese work.

Eighteen miles to the northwest of Lisbon is the palace, monastery, and church of Mafra, the Escorial of Portugal, an immense structure erected by the Braganza family in 1717, in a severe, restrained variation of the style of Louis XIV. The entire façade measures over 700 feet in length, and the whole edifice is planned on a most magnificent scale.

At Cintra, a few miles to the west of Lisbon, is an interesting old convent castle picturesquely grouped on the summit of a steep, rocky hill, and presenting a mixture of Gothic, Moorish, and early Renaissance. It is a curious picture of what a fortified mediæval Portuguese monastery might have been.

There is a decorative feature of Portuguese architecture which deserves mention, namely, the extensive use of wall tiling. Nearly all of the houses in Lisbon are faced on the exterior with enamelled tiles, often painted in bright colours, and in some of the older work, notably at Cintra and at Coimbra, this species of decoration is carried to a considerable extent with interesting results.

The strictly modern architecture of Portugal presents nothing worthy of study.

— C. H. BLACKALL.

POSADA. In Spain, or Spanish America, a tavern.

POST. In general, any stiff, vertical, more or less isolated upright, whether of timber, metal, or stone; whether solid or hollow; whether homogeneous or composite. A post may support a superstructure, as a lintel, or may afford a firm point of lateral attachment, as for a gate or for fence rails, or may stand alone for any purpose. Any main vertical member in timber framing is especially called a post, as in the subtitles, Prick Post, King Post. For the specific technical sense of the term, see Truss.

Broach Post. Same as King Post, below.

Crown Post. A vertical post in a roof truss, whether a king post or a queen post. It is sometimes a joggle piece. These are both rare in the United States.

Door Post. One of the uprights which enclose a doorway; especially, in framing of wood or iron, such a piece which forms part of the structure as distinguished from the jamb piece, casing, or other covering member. The term is less often used for stone uprights which are at once a part of the structure and a part of the external architectural composition.

Hanging Post. *A.* In carpentry work, a tie resembling a post, such as the king post and queen post. (See also Truss; Wood Construction, Part I.)

B. In framing, that post of a door frame which is to receive the hinges of a door.

Heel Post. *A.* A post serving as a newel or the end support of any partition; as, in a stable, the stout one set up at the end of each partition between the stalls.

B. The hanging post, as of a door; in this sense, rare and local.

Jamb Post. Same as Door Post or window post.

King Post. In a truss, as for a roof, a vertical member connecting the tie beam with the point of meeting of the two principal rafters. Properly, it is not a post but a tie. The name probably comes from the early mediæval practice of supporting the ridge piece by a vertical post resting upon the very heavy transverse timber below or upon the top of the stone vaulting. (See Cuts under Roof.)

Newel Post. (See under Newel.)

Pendent Post. In decorative open timber roof trusses, a short post set against the wall, bearing at bottom on a stone corbel or capital and supporting, generally with the aid of a curved brace, the wall end of the tie beam or hammer beam of the truss.

Prick Post. A secondary or intermediate post; in a roof truss, a side post.

Purlin Post. In a roof truss, a post inserted at the point where a purlin meets a rafter.

Queen Post. In a truss, as for a roof, one of two vertical members or side posts between the principals and the lower chord. Properly,

it is not a post but a tie, the name being derived from the mediæval English roof construction, in which the principals were supported by two queen posts standing on a heavy girder which carried directly the weight of the roof. (See King Post, above.)

Tree Post. Same as King Post, above.

Trellis Post. A post constructed of trellis-work between slender uprights; especially in ironwork, where a stiff but light structure is produced by slender angle irons with a trellis of wirework between; often used to support the roofs of verandas, and sometimes on a much larger scale.

POST, PIETER; architect; b. 1608; d. 1669 (at Haarlem, Holland).

The architect of Prince Maurice of Orange. He went with the prince to Brazil. He erected a church and other buildings at Olinda and rebuilt the fortifications of Pernambuco. Among his principal works in Holland are the *Huis ten Bosch* at The Hague, the *Sael van Oranje*, the Swanenburg situated between Amsterdam and Haarlem, the palace at Rijxdorp, the *Stadhuis* at Maestricht, and the *Waag* (weighing house) at Gouda. A collection of engravings of his buildings was published at Leyden in 1715. (See bibliography.)

Galland, *Holländische Baukunst;* Immerzeel, *Hollandsche en Vlaamsche Kunstenaars;* Pieter Post, *Ouvrages d'Architecture.*

POST AND LINTEL CONSTRUCTION. That which is composed of the simplest elements, namely, uprights carrying horizontals as distinguished from Arcuate (which see). (Compare Trabeate.)

POSTERN. A subsidiary door or gate; in military architecture, such a gate in a part of a work remote from the main gate; in domestic architecture, often a small door near a larger one, as a door for foot passengers adjoining a porte-cochère.

POST HOUSE. A wayside inn where relays of vehicles for a journey may be hired, and where horses are kept for the convenience of travellers. Called also Posting House.

POSTICUM; in Roman archæology: *A.* A back door, à postern. *B.* Same as Epinaos. *C.* Same as Opisthodomos, in sense *B.*

POSTING HOUSE; POSTING INN. (See Post House.)

POST OFFICE. A building, or sometimes a room, or set of rooms, devoted to the purposes of the receipt and delivery of letters, newspapers, and other mail matter.

The sixteenth century marks the commencement of modern postal systems. The coffee-house or tavern, which was the point of departure and arrival of the stagecoach or post wagon, was often the post office where private letters were left and called for; but public sorting offices date from the close of the seventeenth century in England, and were established at even an earlier date in Germany.

The first plans of government buildings had little to distinguish them; but gradually there have been evolved two main types, each with its own modifications, and which may be called the European, or Continental, and the American; for the English post office possesses some of the characteristics of each of the other two. The main point of difference between the two types is in the use of the central court or cortile. In the European or Continental plan the mail wagons generally enter the court to receive and deliver mail; in England and the United States the mail bags are handled from the mail dock or platform at the rear of the building, and in certain other respects the cortile is not emphasized in England as it is on the Continent. In Continental cities a great proportion of the central court is given to the public, and the surrounding space is divided into a series of offices for the administration. In the United States there are exterior corridors for the public, with an interior working room for the employees. On the Continent the cortile may or may not be roofed over with glass, according to the climate; in the United States the fact that the clerical force occupy this space and that the upper portion of the building is generally occupied by other departments of the Federal Government, requires that this working room shall always be shut off absolutely from other portions of the building. In Canada and Mexico the general arrangement is more like that of the United States. Throughout Europe, in the English colonies, and in Japan, the telegraph and telephone service is under government control, and is generally housed in the same building, as is also the service for the expressage of packages of merchandise.

In the United States the building is generally denoted officially as the United States Post Office and Custom House, or United States Post Office and Court House, and is occupied jointly with the departments of the Treasury, of the Interior, and of Justice, — offices being provided on the upper floors for the Collectors of Customs and of Internal Revenue, for the Land Office, United States and Pension Commissioners; also in cities of a certain size and population, for the District, Circuit, and Appellate Courts, but only Federal offices are entitled to accommodation in the building.

Formerly the outline of the average post office plan was a rectangle; or a rectangular first story with a hollow square for the superstructure, — in this respect following the precedent of European post offices, — but since 1895 the plan of the hollow square for stories above the ground floor has been modified so as to enclose only three sides of the square, as it affords better light and air not only for those stories, but more

satisfactory sky light for the post office working room below. In the basement is situated the heating and ventilating apparatus, elevator machinery, and sometimes the electric light plant, with the necessary coal storage; also the lavatories and toilet rooms for employees, and a waiting room, with outside entrance, for the use of mail carriers when not on duty, as they are not allowed at that time in the working room. On the first floor are the public corridors, entered from and next to the streets upon which the building faces; in the embrasures of the windows, or in a lobby, are writing desks for the use of the public; at one end of a corridor is a lobby or anteroom giving access to the money order and registry division.

The postmaster's private office is placed at or near the end of another corridor, and opens both into the corridor and into the working room, and is provided with private lavatory. As he is frequently the custodian of the entire building, the staircase to the upper floors is near by, but is closed with a grille or gate after the cessation of business on those floors.

If the business of the office is such as to warrant the appointment of an assistant postmaster, he is usually also the cashier, and has his room next to the money order and registry division, and there are safes or vaults built into the walls between the rooms; the stamp clerks are placed where they may have windows or wickets upon the corridor, not far from a public entrance, and are also provided with vaults or safes.

Between the corridors and working room is the post-office screen, the upper part of which is of glass, and the lower, 7 feet, is subdivided for lock boxes (letters above, papers and periodicals below), with open backs and metal and glass fronts; drops are provided to receive outgoing letters, papers, and packages; and wickets are placed at intervals for the general delivery of mail, the sale of stamps and envelopes, and for the transaction of other business; in the most modern buildings the screen has no door giving access from the corridor directly into the working room. Within are tables and cases for sorting letters, cancelling-machines, racks (for papers and periodicals), and frames (for holding bags while the mail is being made up), and all the other necessary furniture of the establishment. Wire screens, not solid partitions, are used to separate the various departments.

As the relative importance of each of these details has been gradually developed by the requirements of the postal service in the United States, the following facts have been demonstrated: that the space assigned to the clerical force should be as compact as possible, and the space assigned to the public should permit of direct access from, and egress to, the street, and of unimpeded circulation within the building; that the most expeditious and economical handling of the mail is accomplished by aggregating the various subdivisions of the service within, or in close proximity to, a central working room; and that the public can be served to the best advantage by its use of exterior corridors.

— WILLIAM MARTIN AIKEN.

POST–RENAISSANCE ARCHITECTURE. The architecture, if classical in character, of any period succeeding that of the Renaissance proper. Thus, in French practice, the term "Renaissance" being strictly limited to the epoch beginning with the reign of Louis XII. and ending with the wars of religion under Henry III., all the styles of neoclassic architecture which follow the reign of Henry III., and which are commonly called in France by the reigns of the sovereigns, as Louis Treize architecture, and the like, may properly be called post-Renaissance architecture. In Italy the Renaissance (*Rinascimento* or *Risorgimento*) begins nearly a century earlier than in France; and in like manner it is considered by Italian writers that the epoch of it closes, and the classicismo, or extreme classic, style begins, about the middle of the sixteenth century. Any neoclassic style of architecture belonging to a later date than the limits of the Renaissance in any country, as above given, may properly be considered as a post-Renaissance style. (See Barocco; Cinque Cento; Classicismo; Decadence; Decadenza; Lombardesque; Lombardic Architecture; Renaissance; Rococo; see also articles on the architectures of France; Germany; Italy.)

— R. S.

POT CHIMNEY: AS BUILT BY INDIANS IN THE N.W. OF THE U.S.

POT CHIMNEY. A roof chimney made of earthen cooking pots, the bottoms of which have been cut out or broken. Used in Pueblo villages of the southwestern United States. (See Communal Dwelling.) — F. S. D.

POT CONSTRUCTION. A method of constructing vaults and domes with earthen pots fitted together in a succession of rings diminishing in diameter upward to form the concave; this expedient was common in Oriental countries from the earliest times as a substitute for heavier and more costly materials, such as brick, stone, and concrete, to diminish the weight upon the supporting walls. Domes so constructed, though thin and apparently fragile, have endured the vicissitudes of centuries, and have proved as stable and permanent as fabrics much more massive and monumental. A conspicuous example of its use in Romanesque work is in the dome of S. Vitale at Ravenna.

POT METAL. Glass coloured thoughout its substance while melted. (See Glass; Window.)

POTSTONE. A soft stone of the nature of steatite or soapstone, used mainly by primitive people in making pots. — G. P. M.

POULTRY HOUSE. A structure furnished with accommodations for the protection and rearing of poultry; a henhouse or chicken house.

POUNCE. A fine powder of dark or pronounced colour, which is used to transfer a drawing by being forced through holes pricked in the original upon the surface which is to receive the transfer.

POUNCED. *A.* Decorated with indentations or perforations. (See Pounced Work.)

B. Made as a transfer of a drawing by means of Pounce.

POUNCED WORK. Ornamentation executed by means of a punch, which might have its point cut into a unit of a pattern, as a circle, cross, or the like.

POURTOUR. In French, a circuit; a gallery or passage allowing of movement around a central hall or the like; especially, in churches, the aisle which nearly surrounds the apse or chevet, passing along the north and south sides and curving around the east end. (See Deambulatory.)

POWDERING. *A.* A surface enrichment produced by sprinkling one colour upon another, as gold or silver upon a tinted background. In heraldry, a surface adorned with powdering is said to be *semé.*

B. By extension from the preceding definition, the ornamentation of a surface by the frequent repetition thereon of a small figure or pattern, as a rosette or star, not connected, as in a diaper, but isolated and regularly or irregularly disposed.

POWDERING ROOM. In the eighteenth century a chamber or anteroom especially adapted to powdering perukes, and, later, the hair.

POWER HOUSE. A building in which steam power, water power, or the like, is generated, and from which it is conveyed for the operation of machinery or other purposes, as to the other buildings of a large factory, or to the vehicles on a trolley or cable railway.

POYNTELL; POYNTILL. A pavement, generally of tiles, formed of small pieces, but differing from mosaic in that the pieces form a set pattern rather than a picture. Also written pointel or pointal.

POZZO. *A.* A well; the Italian term. Not used in English except in combination.

B. In Venice, a cistern; one of the numerous water-tight structures below the pavements of courtyards, public and private, in which is stored the water brought from the mainland. This water is drawn from the natural stream of the Brenta, on the western shore of the lagoon, and in other places. (See Vera da Pozzo.)

POZZO, ANDREA ; painter and architect ; b. 1642 ; d. 1709.

His real name was probably Brunnen (Puteus in Latin, Pozzo in Italian). His work was in perspective illusions, and his chief monument is the decoration of S. Ignazio at Rome.

Ilg, *Der Maler und Architekt, P. A. dal Pozzo.*

POZZUOLANA. A volcanic sand, first found at Pozzuoli at the foot of Mount Vesuvius, whence the name ; and also in abundance in the neighbourhood of Rome, and extensively disseminated throughout Europe. When pulverized and mixed with slaked lime, the compound will harden under water like the more energetic hydraulic cements. Before the introduction of the so-called Roman and the Portland cements, it was extensively used in sea works. Trass, a similar volcanic product found in the valley of the Rhine and in Holland, possesses the same qualities. Both pozzuolana and trass are composed of silica and alumina, the former largely in excess of the latter.

The substances composing these mortars, which mutually react, being separate, cannot be brought into contact except by the use of a sufficient quantity of water. — W. R. HUTTON.

PRÆCINCTIO. In a Roman theatre, a passage running parallel with and on a level with one of the steplike seats of the cavea. Generally the slope of the lower ranges is broken at the præcinctio by a wall, from the top of which the seats slope upward to the outer wall of the theatre. This wall of the præcinctio contains doors giving access to the vomitoria, or passages of exit and entrance. In the Flavian Amphitheatre there was an intermediate *zona* or passage, parallel with the seats, between the arena and the præcinctio. It is sometimes called balteus, and is equivalent to the Greek *diazoma.*

PRÆTORIUM. That part of a Roman camp or garrisoned post in which the quarters of the general were placed ; the official residence of the prætor or governor of a Roman province ; a hall of justice, presided over by the prætor.

PRAYER CHAMBER ; ROOM. In a mosque, that part of the roofed and enclosed building which is used for the prayers of the faithful and for listening to the exhortations from the mimbar ; (1) in the sense of the whole large building, perhaps several hundred feet in every direction, which is distinguished from the galleries and ambulatories which connect with it and surround the court ; and (2) the place screened off by a partition and especially reserved to those who are engaged in devotions, and forbidden to others, called Maksoorah, though this term has other significations.

PRECEPTORY. A subordinate religious establishment of the Order of Knights Templars ; a place of residence, instruction, and discipline, presided over by an officer called a knight preceptor, one of the more eminent members of the fraternity. The cells in the Temple, or chief house of the Knights in London, were called the preceptories. (Compare Commandery.)

PRE–COLUMBIAN ARCHITECTURE. That of the United States, Mexico, and neighbouring countries, sometimes of South America, of a period assumed to be earlier than 1492 A.D. (See United States, Architecture of, § I., and the references given under Prehistoric Architecture.)

PREDELLA. *A.* The footpace of an altar. (See Altar.)

B. One of a series of seats or steps raised one above another ; a gradin or gradine. (See Altar ; Altar Step ; Footpace under Pace.)

C. An altar ledge ; one of the series of ledges or shelves surmounting an altar to accommodate a crucifix, candlesticks, vases, etc., or a painting. (See Altar Ledge, Retable.)

D. By extension, a painting, mosaic, or bas-relief, forming the front of *B.*

PREHISTORIC ARCHITECTURE. That of epochs which on account of their relative antiquity cannot be determined ; that is to say, whose apparent date goes back of all certain records of the country or district in which they exist. (See Pre-Columbian Architecture ; Communal Dwelling ; and also, for further information, Aztec ; Etruscan ; Inca ; Maya ; Mexico, Architecture of, § I.; Toltec ; United States, Architecture of, § I.)

PRELIMINARY STUDIES. Drawings and models made by artists in the way of preparation for elaborate work. According to the schedule of charges approved by the American Institute of Architects, " Drawings, such as ground plan, one upper floor plan, and elevation or perspective view of exterior," as distinguished from " Preliminary drawings, which include the above, and such additional elevations, plans, and sections as are necessary to illustrate the general scheme without working drawings." (See Drawing.)

Beyond this purely commercial usage, the phrase is employed very generally to describe the technical method adopted by the architect in the formulation of his thought, and the forms which he employs to represent to himself his designs as they are at first crudely conceived, and to fix them provisionally, so that his imagination may have full play in determining the final arrangements of plan, proportion of parts, etc.

A large part of these preliminary studies are made, for convenience, in pencil on paper, by the employment of plans and elevations and sections " in projection " (see Projection). These are translated in the mind of the artist as he studies, so that they represent to him the building which he intends to construct.

As he proceeds with his work he finds it desirable to enlarge his use of the methods thus introduced, for the instruction of the artisans who are employed under his supervision in constructing the buildings he designs, geometrical projections of plans and sections and elevations being invaluable in connection with the work of the builder.

No one, however, who thinks at all of the subject will question the fact that the architect is able to use these geometrical methods only as ready means of representing in a practical manner what the drawings do not in any way express; in all cases these drawings must be translated in the artist's mind into other terms if he is to gain from them any conception of the way his building will look when it is finished; they must be translated in imagination into terms of solid form and colour mass, and it is the constant and serious concern of the thoughtful and experienced architect to assure himself that he is making this translation correctly; it is the constant, and too often the false, assumption of the tyro in architecture that his translation is perfect and exact. Note, for instance, the clever designs "in elevation" one sees in our exhibitions and illustrated architectural journals — designs which too often make the heart of the experienced practitioner sink within him, as he considers how certainly they would prove unsatisfactory if they were built. One finds often, for example, the geometrical projection of a dome, or of some other massive central *motif*, which, in the constructed building, could not possibly be seen together with the façade, used, nevertheless, as a unifying element in the composition of this façade as it is presented in elevation.

The architect is wont to assume that these geometrical projections, so useful to the artisan who develops the artist's designs, are *necessary* tools for himself also; and although, in fact, it must be agreed that in all probability they will always be used because of their convenience, yet it is evident that architecture, even in this day, could, on a pinch, get along without them. This is clearly shown by the work of the architects of past ages; for, although we know little of the methods of design employed by the earliest architects, it is reasonably certain that, had they made as much use of geometrical projections as we do in our time, more record of this use would appear than has been discovered by the archæologists. But even if it be assumed that the ancient masters did employ these geometric tools exactly as we do, we must note that the matter of tools and of methods is of insignificant import. The great architects of the past have been those who have thought and studied in masses — in colour masses; it is this fact that has made them great architects, whatever has been their method of work, otherwise they would not be looked upon by us as masters of their art. A really artistic architect is one who constructs well-proportioned and properly decorated masses; if he fails in realizing this end, he has failed to do more than build.

There is much reason for believing that the greatest danger in connection with modern architectural practice — the gravest error in modern architectural teaching, the cause of most of the modern failures to produce really beautiful buildings — lies in the fact that so much time is given by the architect to the study of those geometrical tools of his. He constantly is tempted to forget the translation into solid form, and to think only of the thing he sees on the paper before him. It requires a touch of real genius in a man to enable him to make the translation from the drawing to the solid form correctly in any event, and men of ordinary talent and indolent habit soon learn to forget to make the attempt.

The architect's position in this respect is not unique, for every artist finds himself subject to special limitations determined by the character of the material in which he works — limitations which compel the invention of methods and tools, and the adoption in each case of a special technique which is highly complex and difficult of acquirement. Thus, every artist who is in earnest is compelled to spend a great amount of time in preliminary training, which consists in little else than the process of familiarizing himself with the technique of his chosen art — the learning how to use his elaborate tools.

Mere technical skill thus becomes a most important acquisition for the artist, and, in the effort to gain it, in proportion as he is in earnest, he must necessarily find himself deeply interested in mere technique *per se* — in the mere tools he is to use. The human mind is so constituted that when a man becomes deeply interested in any given subject he is likely to overestimate its importance, and thus it happens that all artists are subject to one and the same danger: they run the risk of becoming so much interested in their technique — in the tools of their art — that they are led to overlook altogether the end they should have in view, led to forget that their aim should be the production of works of beauty.

In music we see this danger exemplified in the triumph of formalism, against which Wagner preached so eloquent a lesson in his masterly *Meistersinger*. In literature we see it in the failure of writers who bend their efforts overmuch to the formalism of, or to the perfection of, style: or of others who aim to express some doctrine, — realism, for instance, — instead of endeavouring to produce perfect works of beauty. In painting we see it in the devotion to partial ends, in the exclusive attention which the artist gives perhaps to "values," careless of the necessity of composition, and of perfection of drawing, and of the other elements which go to make the painter's masterpiece.

Architects are especially prone to err in this way. Their art products are buildings, and these buildings nowadays cannot be erected without preliminary processes which involve the construction of the most elaborate of tools. They must make representative studies, and constructional drawings, and large scale details, and then full-size developments of these details. All of these, however, must be recognized to be mere tools of their guild, means to an end, that end being the production of a work of beauty in solid form. But the mere making of these tools themselves requires so much of their attention that they are all too likely to concentrate their interest upon them rather than upon the work for which they are created.

The danger is greatly aggravated by a discovery we have made, — the discovery that the same technical geometrical drawings of which we are speaking, as applied to the representation of the outside of a building, do actually give a very fair conception of the building as it will appear if it can be seen from a very great distance, and provided the observer can stand exactly on the middle line drawn perpendicular to the plane of its façade. Furthermore, we have devised a scheme of colouring and of technical shadows, by the use of which we deceive ourselves with the belief that we can thus equally well conceive the appearance of the future building, whether it is to be seen from a great distance or from a short distance. And, behold, his method saves the architect a great amount of time and trouble : no longer is he compelled to bother himself with attempts to study parts that are not shown on projections, to sketch such perverse things as reëntrant angles, for instance ; no longer does he have to go through the tedious process of drawing in perspective ; no longer is he compelled even to think in perspective.

All this carelessness as to the actual effect to be produced is of course unconscious to most architectural students, but it cannot fail to be a fact for most of them, when so much time in their offices and so very large a proportion of the study in the architectural schools is devoted to the consideration of these mere drawings on plane surfaces. That this habit of thinking in surfaces rather than in solid form is one which is very apt to be acquired cannot be doubted; for the architect in judging a building naturally finds himself tempted to consider it, not as it appears at all, but rather as it would appear if he could translate what he sees back into terms of the working drawings with which he is so familiar ; he finds himself asking how the building really appeared in "elevation" in the architect's studio. He is likely to think, and even to formulate, the thought in words, "This effect is not satisfactory as it exists, but it is produced by such and such compositions and proportions which must have appeared well in elevation ; " and on this ground he all too often condones

ugliness, or actually commends a design which fails of all beauty as it really appears. One hears architects, young and old, constantly expressing judgments based upon such translation ; and one of the leading architectural journals has lately not only acknowledged editorially that the majority of architects judge buildings in this way, but has actually upheld the view that on the whole it is the best way to judge them.

It is self-evident, however, that a building which is beautiful only to the technically trained architectural translator, and not to the average highly cultivated man, is not a work of architectural art at all ; at most it can claim to be no more than the means of suggestion of beautiful forms to those who are skilled in this species of translation. Similarly, the skilful musician is able, by casting his eye upon the score of an opera, to get the greatest delight out of the mere reading apart from imagined production ; but no one for a moment would think of considering the printed score as a work of art in itself ; it is looked upon justly by the musician as a means to an end, as a mere tool. Modern architects, however, have become so infatuated with their tools that they actually treat them as works of art in themselves. The architects spend a great amount of time, which might better be given to the study of solids, in the perfecting of drawings in "elevation," which they gather together and exhibit as though they were proud of them. But if these drawings have any value as works of art, it is surely a most ephemeral one. There is nothing in them that can appeal to the world at large, nothing that can stimulate permanently the sense of beauty in men. What is properly demanded of the architect is that he make a beautiful building. He, however, seems too often to overlook altogether the propriety of this demand, and is content to treat his drawings in a way in which the painter would treat his brushes did he carve their handles delicately and then ask us to admire these carvings as part and parcel of his work as an artist painter.

All this points a moral to which careful heed should surely be given. If it is true that architects tend to overemphasize the importance of geometrical projections, and thereby tend to lose the capacity to think in the solid, evidently it should be the aim of the thoughtful men amongst them to break down all methods of instruction which lead to this overemphasis, and to minimize all habits of practice which encourage it.

The exclusive use of drawings "in elevation " and the discouragement of studies in perspective, as this discouragement is seen in the best of the schools of architecture to-day, is nothing less than an artistic scandal. Of course elevations must be used for preliminary compositional studies, as well as for working purposes ; but surely no great advance in the instruction of young men can be hoped for under a system which deliberately discourages the habit of thinking in cubic scale by encouraging the exclusive use of studies in superficial scale.

Theoretically this trouble may be obviated by the architect if he will make his preliminary studies in perspective. (See Perspective.) But it must be acknowledged that there are difficulties in connection with such use of perspectives, although they are difficulties which are in all cases instructive to the designer. The work involved in the construction of a perspective, if it is to be true to fact, is very tedious, and even when the greatest care is taken the danger of error in its production is very great. On the other hand, although the perspective draughtsman may cheat his client, if he wish to do so, he can scarcely cheat himself if he be a serious worker, unless he is a loggerhead ; and the great difficulty with the current method to which objection is here made is that it tends systematically to instruct the architect how to cheat himself.

The great difficulty with the use of perspectives for preliminary study lies in the fact that few architects in active practice have time to develop the perspectives themselves, but must trust to their assistants to work out the problems for them ; they are thus liable to fail to detect serious errors which are easily made by the perspective draughtsman. Furthermore, each perspective gives us but one point of view, and to gain a proper notion of the appearance of a future building so large a number of perspectives would be required that no architect could afford to give the time or labour necessary for their construction.

There is, however, a better way to avoid the dangers which we are discussing than by the use of perspective drawings, and one which is particularly adapted to study purposes, viz., sketch modelling. The architect's artistic product is to be presented to the world in solid form as much as is the sculptor's ; why should he not study in the solid as the sculptor does ? Imagine the scorn that would be heaped upon the sculptor who never modelled in his studio, but who, instead, gave drawings to artisans who, from these drawings, prepared the finished work. Yet the architect all too often contents himself with the preparation of technical geometrical drawings, and thinks his duty done when he turns these drawings over to contractors of reputation. Have we any right to expect truly artistic solids to be constructed so long as this practice is common ? It must make of us a race of commonplace builders ; it cannot make of us a race of artistic architects.

Sketch models, such as are referred to above, are very simple to construct. They may be made in paper or wood or wax or clay ; but the disadvantages of working in these materials

are considerable, and this fact doubtless goes far to account for the little use that has been made of them in daily practice. Of late, however, certain clay preparations have been discovered in which inexpensive models can be made which do not easily lose their form, and which do not need to be kept wet during preparation or afterward. After they are fully formed they can be given coatings of shellac, and then painted in oil with the colours which are to be given to the finished buildings. They can be placed in the sun from time to time during the process of the work upon them, and properly oriented, so that one can study in them the real shadows to be cast by roofs and projections, and not merely the forty-five degree shadows of convention ; and furthermore, they may be photographed from many points of view, the photographic prints being used in place of, and much better than, elaborately " rendered " drawings, to explain to clients the appearance of the buildings they propose to erect.

The writer of this article has used such models in his practice for many years, and with the greatest satisfaction. He finds them less expensive than properly prepared perspectives, and much more useful to himself and to his clients, because they give an indefinite number of perspectives as the result of only one process. They tend to render self-deception on the part of the architect impossible. They enable him to study his lights and shadows and colour masses with great accuracy, and to see instantly, and to alter and amend easily, forms which do not appear at all upon geometrical projections, and which few, if any, practitioners have time to study in perspective drawings.

It is, of course, conceded that it may be best, and to some extent necessary, to use geometrical drawings in conjunction with the models to aid in one's study ; but the great advantage of the model lies in the fact that it keeps the designer constantly thinking in the solid, whereas drawings in projection keep him constantly thinking in the flat. The advantage connected with this use of models in presenting a definite project to one's client are of course self-evident ; so self-evident, indeed, that we often see carefully prepared models of proposed buildings made for the public gaze after they have been studied in projection, and determined in form by use merely of the deceptive study " in elevation " ; but it is the use of models for purposes of preliminary study which is here urged upon the profession.

It is a most significant fact that during the time of the Renaissance in Italy the great architects, to whom we look back with admiration and reverence, are known to have used sketch models very freely. Geometrical or pictorial drawings were not felt to suffice in the proper study of a projected building. These sketch models were often made in wood, and some of them are still extant, *e.g.* that of the Strozzi palace in Florence. Michelangelo is said to have modelled his buildings, in all cases, in clay. (Müntz, *Renaissance*, Vol. II., p. 320; also Vol. III., p. 301.)

The working drawings of most important buildings of that age, as we know from many examples still existing, were often little more than figured sketches, sufficient to indicate to the workman what he was to do, but entirely inadequate for purposes of such study as must have been given to the designs by the artist-architects.

But for the difficulties connected with the use of clay, which have happily now been removed, there is no doubt that the use of geometrical drawings would never have become as universal as it is to-day; could the habit of their use be overcome, there can be no doubt that the model would, to a great extent, take their place.

To be of value to the architect in determining the forms of his constructions, these sketch models must of course be made to a definite scale, so that the different parts may be measured by draughtsmen in preparing the necessary geometrical working drawings; but it will be perceived that the process suggested is the reverse of that now usually adopted in practice, which is to prepare the geometrical drawings first, determining the design in connection with study of them only, and then, after all is determined, work out from them such perspectives as are demanded by the client, or such models as are occasionally made for the fascination of the public.

For ordinary buildings the scale of the models may be relatively small, as they are especially valuable to the artist in enabling him to see clearly and quickly the masses of his proposed work. Ordinary details can usually be worked out directly in projection, although it will often be found to be most advantageous to the architect, economically as well as artistically, to model these details also on a large scale. In larger, more monumental buildings, models on a large scale may well be made, being built up in the first instance by mere mechanical enlargement of the smaller model by unskilled hands. Having been thus enlarged, the whole scheme can then be restudied with ease, and the important details of architectural ornament and sculpture decided upon in a manner which is likely to produce better results than are usually obtained by the methods now employed. This process, it will be noted, corresponds accurately with the practice of the architect's coworker in the arts of solid form, the sculptor, who habitually sketches in pencil, then makes a small scale model, which, being enlarged, is studied in greater detail; this enlargement, finally reproduced almost mechanically in full size, being again restudied in the clay before being cast in bronze or cut in marble.

— HENRY RUTGERS MARSHALL.

PRESBYTERIUM. *A.* That part of a church in which the high altar is placed and which forms the eastern termination of the choir, above which it is generally raised by a few steps for distinction, and so that it may be visible from the nave; it is occupied exclusively by those who minister in the services of the altar, and its western boundary is the end of the choir stalls or choir proper. The use of the word "choir," as including the presbyterium, is common but inexact.

B. The dwelling of a clergyman; rare.

PRESBYTERY. Same as Presbyterium.

PRESENCE CHAMBER. A reception room; especially, in modern usage, the principal hall of ceremony or state in a palace, containing the throne; an apartment for the formal reception of those entitled to admission on certain occasions.

PRESERVATION. In building, the protection of building materials from such forces as would tend to destroy them, as wood from rotting, stone from disintegration, plaster from separating from the key and crumbling or falling in larger pieces, and iron from rust. This may be of two kinds, either the covering of one material by another, which is considered proof against the destructive force which is feared; or the filling, partially filling, or coating a material with some application which will make it much more resistant. The preservation of stone and brick from moisture is generally attempted by coating the material with a liquid application which permeates its substance to a greater or less depth; in the latter case a fat of some kind, usually liquefied by heat, is allowed to soak into the surface of the finished masonry; and there are contractors who undertake the preservation of finished brick walls and stonework, applying the fat in a semiliquid condition, and then bringing a high degree of heat to bear immediately upon the surface so filled with the fat, which in this way is supposed to find its way more freely into the pores of the material, and to be more firmly fixed there. The preservation of wood by means of chemicals, which are allowed to soak into the vessels of the wood, is not very much in use, although many plans have been proposed, some of which are known to be efficacious. It is necessary to dry the wood very thoroughly, and this fact is in part the cause of the reluctance of builders to use these prepared woods; for it is well known how little thoroughly seasoned wood is to be obtained, the constant and constantly increasing demand for it preventing the storing of large quantities in advance. If, however, seasoned wood is placed in contact with hot oil, or the like, it will

absorb it rapidly; and if the wood is placed in a receiver and the oil is forced into the receiver with considerable pressure, the rapidity of the process is increased. The practical use in building of wood prepared in this way is almost limited to the fireproof wood which came into use toward the close of the nineteenth century; but even this is, as yet, very unusual in buildings. Its fireproofness does not reach the degree of absolutely resisting combustion; but the combustion is slow, and the wood chars and crumbles without bursting into flame, and therefore without tending to spread the conflagration.
— R. S.

PRESIDIO. A frontier fort of Spanish America. This was generally the beginning of a town. A ditch was dug making a rectangular enclosure of about 500 or 600 feet on a side. A rampart was built around within the ditch, enclosing church, quarters, barracks, dwellings, storehouses, etc. — F. S. D.

PRESS BED. A bed permanently built in a recess and more or less enclosed by woodwork, as frequently in the houses of peasants in Holland and Germany; so called from the outward resemblance of the structure to a press or cupboard. (See Bed Place.)

PRESSED CLAY CONSTRUCTION. (See Adobe; Cajon; Pisé, etc.)

PRETORIUM. Same as Prætorium.

PRICKET. A vertical spike or point on which a candle is stuck and held upright; hence, such a point together with its base or stand; a candlestick; often called pricked candlestick. (See Candle Beam.)

PRICKING UP. The first coat of plaster in three-coat work on laths, sometimes called the rough coat, scratch coat, or scratching, from the custom of scoring it in various directions before it is dry, so as to afford a better hold for the second coat. (See Hard Finish, under Finish; Plastering.)

PRIEST'S DOOR. A door by which the priest enters the chancel or nave from without, or the chancel from the robing room or vestry. Any small, low door in the flank of the church, especially on the south side, is often called by this name.

PRIEUR, BARTHÉLEMY; sculptor; d. October, 1611.

Prieur was probably a pupil of Germain Pilon (see Pilon, G.). He made the monument to the Constable Anne de Montmorency (d. 1567), fragments of which are now in the Louvre. He worked on the château of Ecouen and carved the figures in the spandrels of the arches of the *Petite Galerie du Louvre*. In 1573 he made the vase containing the heart of Montmorency, and its supporting column, now in the Louvre.

Lami, *Dictionnaire des Sculpteurs;* Berty, *Topographie, Louvre et Tuileries*, Vol. II.

PRIMATICCIO (PRIMATICE), FRANCESCO; painter, sculptor, and architect; b. 1490 (at Bologna, Italy); d. 1570.

Primaticcio was associated with Giulio Romano (see Pippi Giulio) at Mantua, and in 1531 was called to France by François I. and was employed at Fontainebleau. He was at first associated with Il Rosso (see Rosso), at whose death he assumed sole charge of the decoration of the palace. In 1554 he was made abbé of S. Martin de Tours. Aug. 3, 1559, he replaced Philibert de l'Orme (see De l'Orme, Ph.) as superintendent of the royal buildings. About 1562 he assumed direction of the construction of the monument of Henri II. at Saint Denis (see Pilon, Germain). The construction of portions of the palace of Fontainebleau is ascribed to him. In 1562 he assumed the title *commissaire général des bâtiments du roi*, and had large power over the artistic productions of his time in France.

Pfnor, *Monographie du palais de Fontainebleau;* Pfnor, *Guide artistique au palais de Fontainebleau;* Guilbert, *Description de Fontainebleau;* Haynes, Williams, *Fontainebleau.*

PRIMATICE. Same as Primaticcio; the French form of his name.

PRIMING. In painting, the first layer or coat of paint, size, or other material applied to any surface as a ground in preparation for succeeding coats. (See Painting.)

PRINCESS. (See Slate.)

PRINCIPAL (the adjective used substantively). In a framework, floor, or the like, one of the main members as distinguished from a less important and subordinate one; especially one forming, wholly or in part, a main support as distinguished from a similar intermediate piece. Often one truss of several, as in a roof.

PRIORY. A religious house governed by a prior or prioress. (See Abbey and references.)

Alien Priory. A small monastery dependent upon a larger one which is in another country.

PRISM LIGHT. Prisms of glass, either made separately and set collectively in iron frames for pavement lights, or made connectedly in sheets and placed vertically or at an angle in or over window openings, or the like. The angles of the prisms are so adjusted as to intercept the rays of light from the sky, and to direct them into rooms otherwise imperfectly illuminated.

PRISON. A building for the detention of persons duly convicted and ordered by law to undergo this form of punishment. The detention of persons awaiting trial and of witnesses is not generally in a prison in the proper sense.

Ancient prisons were not commonly built for the purpose. Even where the imprisonment was itself not the punishment inflicted, but a mere detaining of the prisoner until his punishment should begin, or until his judgment should be declared, the buildings used were unwholesome and unfit for habitation. The dungeons of antiquity (see Mamertine Prison, below) and those of the Middle Ages (see Dungeon; Oubliette) are interesting to the builder only as forming part of the strong fortified buildings in which they are placed. Modern prisons hardly date back of the closing years of the eighteenth century, and in the nineteenth century very great changes were made, first in one direction and then in another, as differing ideas of prison discipline and prison management succeeded one another. On the whole, the cell system, with either solitary confinement or separate confinement, the prisoner being in every case isolated at hours of meals and of repose and of exercise in the open air, has gained acceptance; and the prison buildings which are of interest are those in which the arrangement of the cells, the corridors which connect them, the yards in which exercise is taken, and the like, are elaborately arranged according to some definite theory. Workshops and yards in which work is done by convicts in each other's presence, but under the close supervision of foremen, wardens, and sentinels, are not very different from ordinary yards and sheds.

That which is desired is easy access to the cells and a complete supervision of the interior of each, while the opportunities of escape are reduced to a minimum. With a view to this the cell itself is commonly a single small room with a window in the outer wall, and the door at the other end opening upon a narrow open balcony. Any number of stories of cells, each with its own balcony, may be built one upon another; but the balconies all open upon a single great corridor the whole height of the building. In some prisons of the United States the reverse of this plan is tried: each cell has a window and door, side by side, opening upon the balcony, and the balcony is between the prisons and the outer wall. This is brought about by building one very large hall with lofty windows, and by erecting within this the pile of cells in any number of stories, thus leaving on either side of the walls a long open corridor of the whole height of the building, upon which corridor the balconies project. The only objection to this system is that the window of the cell does not open directly into the open air; but this objection seems not serious in view of the ease with which a perfect system of forced ventilation may be adopted and of the abundant light obtainable.

The Panoptikon is much used in prisons in different parts of Europe; the system is applied not merely to the long corridors from which cells are entered on either side, but also to the yards of exercise. The system is carried even into the chapels and the rooms in which the persons in authority may address the prisoners; each prisoner having a separate enclosed seat so contrived with a partial roof that his next neighbour in the rear, looking over the top of his enclosure, will be unable to communicate with him except by rising entirely out of his own compartment and of necessity attracting notice; and these enclosures being so arranged as to radiate from a point occupied by the priest at the altar or by the speaker.

The question of washing conveniences, baths, water-closets, window sashes or casements, and their fastenings, and of the fitting up of each cell with bedstead only available at night, table, chair, shelves, cupboard, and the like, is of extreme interest, and somewhat complex, so very many different expedients having been tried under so many different influences and to meet so many different requirements. (See cut, cols. 215–216.)

Handbuch der Architektur (Darmstadt), Part IV, Halb-band 7, Kapitel (Chapter) II, and the full bibliography appended. — R. S.

Mamertine Prison. A very ancient dungeon in Rome, at the northernmost corner of the Forum and near the Capitoline Hill. The name is not antique; it appears to have been derived from a statue of Mars near by.

PRISON RUSTIC WORK. Rustic work of which the larger surface is more or less deeply pitted, with the purpose of producing an effect of rugged strength.

PRIVY. A private or secluded place. Specifically, a water-closet; a latrine.

PRIZE OF ROME (French, *Prix de Rome* or *Grand Prix de Rome*). The highest prize given to competing students of the *École des Beaux Arts*. (See School of Architecture.)

PRO-CATHEDRAL. A church used as the cathedral church of a diocese while the proper church remains unfinished or is under repair.

PROCOPIUS OF CÆSAREA; historian.

He accompanied the campaigns of Belisarius in 527 A.D., and held high office at Constantinople under the Emperor Justinian (b. about 483; d. November, 565). He described the wars of Justinian, and wrote a book on his architectural undertakings, the *Ktismata* or *Procopi Cæsariensis de Ædificiis Domini Justiniani libri sex*.

PROCURATIE NUOVE. In Venice, on the south side of the Piazza di S. Marco. The two lower stories were built by Scamozzi, and are a continuation of the Library of S. Mark (which see). These are now the lower stories of the Palazzo Reale (see Procuratie Vecchie).

PROCURATIE VECCHIE. In Venice, on the north side of the Piazza di. S. Marco; begun in 1496 by Pietro Lombardo; served as public offices until the Procuratie Nuove were built, and are now private property.

PRODOMOS. A lobby of entrance, a vestibule, usually the same as pronaos.

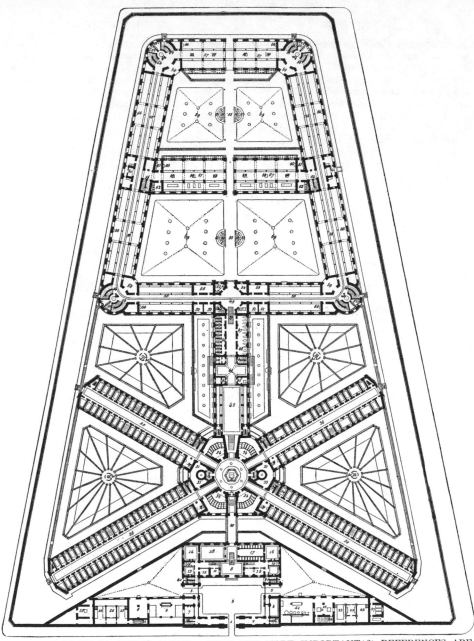

PRISON: RUE DE LA SANTE, PARIS; ONLY THE MORE IMPORTANT(?) REFERENCES ARE
HERE GIVEN.

4. Waiting room.
6, 6. Guard room for fifty men.
7. Officer's room.
9, 10. Stairs going down to the prison of those condemned to death.
11. Search room.
13. Room for the priest.
14. Room for judges.
15. Office of secretary and registrar (Greffier).
16. Office of the superintendent.
17, 18. Rooms for accused and condemned persons arriving at the prison.
21, 22. Kitchen and dependencies.
27. Room for bodies of the dead.
28. Room for punishment.
30. Entrance to prison of the accused.
31. Room for distribution of the meals.

32. (One in each wing) room for legal counsel.
33. Storehouse for clothing.
34. Parlour with separate cells for prisoners.
35. Altar at which divine service is held ; 34 and 42 command view of it.
36. Cells of the accused and corridors.
40. Watch tower at centre of separate courtyards for exercise of prisoners.
42. Hall where condemned prisoners can see divine service performed.
49. Entrance to prison of the condemned.
51. Halls for Jewish worship.
55. Protestant oratory.
56. Library.
58. (Four large halls) refectories.
66, 66. Sinks with running water.
67. Workshops.

215   216

PROFILE. An outline, especially such as is revealed by a transverse section. Specifically : —

A. The outline of a moulding, group of mouldings, or the like.

B. The outline of the surface of the ground as shown by a vertical section (see Sky Line).

PROJECTION. A. The salience or protrusion of a portion of a building from the general surface, as of a pavilion, a cornice, or stringcourse, from the mass of façade.

B. The act, and the result, of projecting or throwing ; as the projection of a shadow upon a bright surface, the width, depth, and character of the shadow varying with the object which casts it and the nature of the surface upon which it is cast ; hence,

In mechanical drawing, the graphical representation of such a process. The projection of any point on a given surface is obtained by drawing a straight line through the point to the surface, the point of intersection so obtained being the projection of the given point. Such a line is called a projector. The projection of an object upon a surface is the figure obtained by means of straight lines drawn to the surface, according to a fixed law, from points of the object or from the predetermined points of an imaginary object. The surface is supposed to be a plane unless specified to the contrary.

There are three systems of projection in common architectural use ; namely, (1) Perspective, — sometimes called conical projection, — where the projectors diverge from a single point, and in which the surface in question is sometimes curved (see Perspective) ; (2) Parallel Projection, where the projectors are parallel to one another (see Shades and Shadows) ; (3) Orthographic or Right Line Projection, where they are parallel to one another and perpendicular to the plane of projection. The term " projection " is commonly understood to mean that system of orthographic projection which makes use of a vertical and a horizontal plane, forming a diedral angle, which is turned toward the observer. It is this system which is treated here (compare Descriptive Geometry, below).

The complete presentation of a solid object requires its projection upon two planes, since upon one plane only two of its dimensions can be shown. In practice, these are taken at right angles to each other, one being horizontal and the other vertical. They are denoted by HP

and VP, respectively. Their intersection is a straight line called the ground line, denoted by GL.

Plans ; Elevations. The projection upon HP is called the horizontal projection, or plan ; that upon VP, the vertical projection, or elevation. The plan and elevation of a building are its projections upon these two planes.

Let a sheet of paper be folded at right angles along a line GL as shown in Fig. 1, so that one part is horizontal (HP) and the other vertical

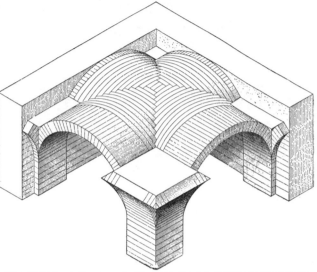

PROJECTION: A BYZANTINE GROINED VAULT SHOWN IN ISOMETRIC PROJECTION.

(VP). Upon HP let any object, such as a rectangular block, be placed, and let lines be drawn through all of its points perpendicular to HP, giving its plan, and other lines perpendicular to VP, giving its elevation.

If now the paper be pressed out flat, the plan and elevation of the block will appear, as shown in Fig. 2. This is the conventional method of representing the planes of projection and the projections upon them.

The plan of an object is seen by looking at it *vertically downward ;* the elevation, by looking at it *horizontally forward* (Figs. 1 and 2). In Figs. 3 and 4 are shown the plan and two elevations of a block house. Fig. 5 shows an oblique elevation and plan. The dotted lines are the projectors.

Section. It is often necessary to determine more than the simple plan and elevation of the outside surfaces of an object. When, for example, it is desired to show the internal arrangement and construction of a building, — walls, doors, staircases, etc., — several plans and elevations are needed. These are obtained by using supplementary planes of projection, parallel or perpendicular to HP and VP. Figs. 6, 7

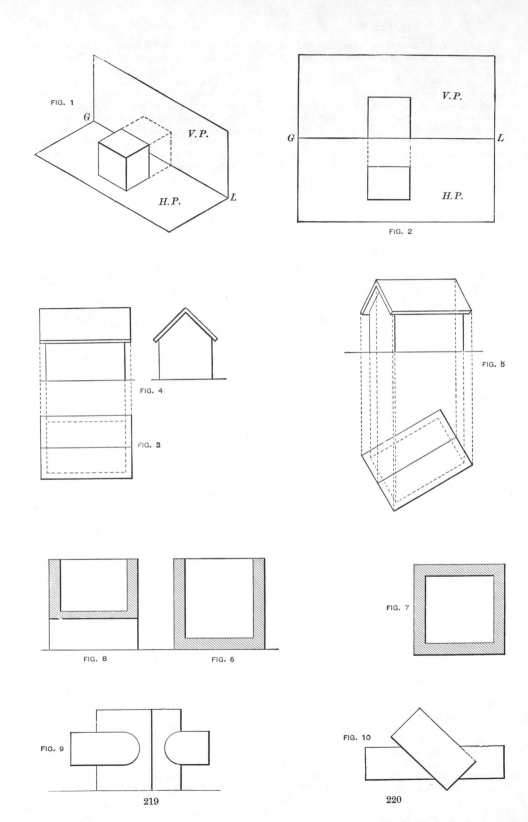

FIG. 1

G

V.P.

H.P.

L

FIG. 2

V.P.

G   L

H.P.

FIG. 4

FIG. 3

FIG. 5

FIG. 7

FIG. 8

FIG. 6

FIG. 9

FIG. 10

219

220

and 8, show vertical, horizontal, and oblique sections of a cubical box. The portion of the box between the supplementary plane and the eye is supposed to be removed. The projections upon these planes are called Sectional Plans and Elevations, or, briefly, Sections.

Intersections. When two objects intersect, it is sometimes desirable to know the character of the line of intersection common to their surfaces. If any auxiliary plane perpendicular to HP or VP be passed through both objects, it will determine two linear sections of their surfaces; the points where these linear sections intersect will be points of the required line of intersection. Figs. 6, 7, and 8 show the intersections of a solid by a plane; Figs. 9 and 10 show the intersection of one solid by another. In every case, it is not the *line of intersection* itself that is obtained, but its projections. The auxiliary planes are generally taken perpendicular to HP and VP, so as to get the easiest and simplest sections of the objects. Sometimes the same result is obtained by revolving the section until it is parallel to one of the planes of projection.

Descriptive Geometry. This is a more elaborate form of projection; also a branch of practical geometry in which the shapes and dimensions of lines, surfaces, and bodies are determined by means of two planes at right angles to each other, one horizontal and the other vertical. These planes, called planes of projection, by their intersection form four right diedral angles, called the 1st, 2nd, 3rd, and 4th angles. Their line of intersection is called the ground line.

The process of investigation in descriptive geometry is an extension of that employed in the more elementary work of "projection." It employs all four diedral angles, and consequently four planes of projection, while in projection only one angle and two planes are used. It is thus a branch of orthographic projection, although practically unused in architectural practice.

Isometric ; Isometrical Projection. A method of projection based upon the following principle: If three mutually perpendicular lines, such as edges of a cube, be equally inclined to a plane of projection, their projections on this plane will be three lines making equal angles with one another ($120°$); moreover, the lengths of these projections bear a common ratio to the given lines ($\sqrt{2} : \sqrt{3}$).

Strictly speaking, only such objects as are rectangular can have isometric projections; but since it is always possible to refer an object bounded by inclined or curved lines to three mutually perpendicular lines, any object may be said to be drawn *in isometric*. In this case, the measure of all lines other than those lying in the three principal directions is obtained by

referring them to lines in their own planes which are truly isometric.

The isometric drawing of a building when taken from above, as is usual, produces an effect resembling what is popularly known as a bird's-eye view; but the representations of parallel lines do not approach one another, as in perspective. As the name imports, equal objects are shown of the same size in all parts of the drawing.

Farish, *Isometrical Perspective*, 8vo., Cambridge, 1820 ; Jopling, *Practice of Isometrical Perspective*, London, 1835 ; Sopwith, *Treatise on Isometrical Drawing*, London, 1834 ; Church, *Elements of Descriptive Geometry;* Miller, *Elements of Descriptive Geometry*, London, 1878 ; Ocagne, *Cours de géométrie descriptive et de géométrie infinitésimale*, Paris, 1896 ; Watson, *Course in Descriptive Geometry for the Use of Colleges and Scientific Schools*, London, 1880 ; Gillespie, *Elements of Perpendicular Projection*, 1897.

PROJECTOR. (See Projection).

PROJECTURE. The same as Projection, *A.*

PROJET. The original design or scheme of a building. In the system of the School of Fine Arts at Paris, the *projet* is the first sketch of a design, portraying its specific character in outline or general terms, to be after developed in detail in the final study.

PROMENADE. A place suitable for walking for pleasure, as a sidewalk, a terrace, a portico, or mall, with a more or less elegant or attractive environment.

PRONAOS. The open vestibule in the front of the naos or cella of a temple; usually opposed to epinaos, but if the treasury or rear part of the temple is under consideration, the vestibule leading to this is sometimes called the pronaos to the treasury, though it remains the epinaos of the whole structure.

PROPERTY ROOM. The room in a theatre in which are kept the stage properties, such as costumes, furniture, or any other accessories of a dramatic performance.

PROPORTION. In an architectural composition, the relation of one part to another and to the whole, especially in respect to size and position ; the relative dimensions and arrangement of parts, as of a room in regard to its height, width, and length ; of a pavilion in regard to the whole façade ; of a capital in regard to the shaft ; of an entablature in regard to the column ; or of the different members of the entablature in regard to one another. Good proportion in a design depends upon the relative importance given to its subdivisions, or the degree of subordination of its parts, not only in respect to dimensions, but in respect to comparative emphasis of architectural treatment, according to the just value of each in the general scheme, and upon their mutual disposition, so as to secure harmony and balance by agreeable contrasts. Thus, in the proportions of the classic column and its entablature, the study of successive generations of great artists upon the problem finally brought the Greek orders to such perfection of proportion that they constituted a sensitive organism, which could not be varied in any essential particular without a shock to the whole system.

With the conviction that correct proportion in architecture, as in music, should be the result of some scientific method, rather than of artistic feeling alone, many attempts have been made to discover some arithmetical formula or geometrical figure of such properties that, when applied to an architectural composition, the proper relative dimensions of its parts, and their proper harmonic relations to the whole, might be determined and proved. Among these attempts, those of Viollet-le-Duc have been pursued with more sympathy for purely artistic conditions than the rest, and with more diligence and ingenuity. Like Cresy and Hay, he based his somewhat empirical investigations on a geometrical figure; and, assuming the triangle, or vertical pyramidal section, to be the expression of stability, he persuaded himself that in the equilateral triangle, the isosceles right-angled triangle, and the triangle of which the base has 4 parts and the vertical $2\frac{1}{2}$ parts, were concealed the true generative principles of proportion. In his *Entretiens* and *Dictionnaire Raisonné*, he published diagrams showing the application of these figures to various monuments of Egypt, Greece, Rome, and the Middle Ages, whose proportions had long challenged the admiration of mankind; taking care, however, that these applications should not be made in a spirit so mathematical and uncompromising as to prevent the artistic instinct from correcting the results in certain details, especially where such corrections were obviously needed, in view of the phenomena of perspective. These experiments exhibit many coincidences so remarkable, as to make it appear that the dimensions and details of each of these monuments have indeed certain mutual harmonic relations, resulting in general harmonic unity, dependent on some other laws than those of statics, and established on some definite principles which had protected them from the aberrations of caprice, taste, or accident.

But while beauty, in line and mass, may sometimes seem to be curiously confirmed by such tests as these, it may be doubtful whether it can be created by them; for elasticity, life, and freedom seem to be the essential qualities of true art. — HENRY VAN BRUNT.

PROPOSAL. In building, the offer made by a contractor to furnish certain material and labour at a certain price.

PROPYLÆA; **PROPYLAIA** (Προπύλαια; also occasionally in the singular, Προπύλαιον;

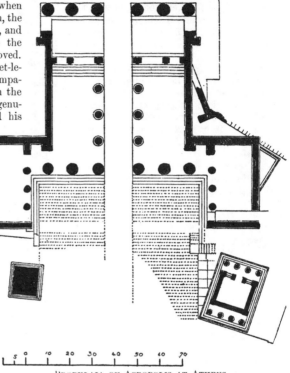

PROPYLAIA OF ACROPOLIS AT ATHENS.

The dotted lines show steps which were probably absent in classical times. The path through the middle seems to have been kept open for beasts of burden. The three columns on each side of this path are Ionic: all the rest of the building is Doric. The little building on the right is the Ionic temple of the Wingless Victory.

strictly the space *before* the gate). The name used by the Greeks to designate a porch or entrance of architectural importance; such as the one at Corinth, mentioned by Pausanias (II., 3), the one at the sanctuary of Æsculapius at Epidaurus, the two leading into the sacred precinct at Eleusis. By ancient writers, the name is applied almost exclusively to the building which marked the principal entrance to the Acropolis of Athens. It was a structure of singular beauty and originality, built of Pentelic marble at the time of Pericles, from the designs of the architect Mnesicles. It was begun 437 B.C., and was provisionally completed five years later, although the original intentions of its architect were never fully carried out. Its central portion contained the portal proper, a wall pierced by five openings, of which that in the middle was wide enough to permit the passage of chariots, the others being for pedestrians only. These openings were provided with gates. Facing the open area of the Acropolis, to the eastward of this wall, was a Doric hexastyle portico of admirable proportions, but with a central intercolumniation, which, for the same reason as the middle doorway, was of unusual width. To the westward of the wall containing the gates, and therefore before, or outside of it, was a covered hall, walled on three sides, the marble roof of which, so greatly admired by Pausanius (I., 22), was carried by six Ionic columns of great beauty, arranged in two rows, between which ran the roadway leading to the central entrance. The

The chief work especially devoted to the building is Bohn's *Die Propylaen der Akropolis zu Athen*, 1882, with complete drawings and citation of earlier authorities. Dr. Dörpfeld's masterly discussion of the original plan of Mnesicles, and of the modifications which it underwent in execution, will be found in *Mittheilungen der deutschen archeologisches Instituts zu Athen* (1885), pp. 38–56 and 131–144. His argument is given in Miss Harrison's *Ancient Athens*, and in Frazer's *Pausanias*, Vol. II., p. 250. The drawings of the Propylæa in Penrose's *Principles of Athenian Architecture* are of great accuracy. An excellent account of the structure, with plans and elevations, may be found in Baumeister's *Denkmäler der klassischen Altertums*, pp. 1414–1422.
— FRANK MILES DAY.

PROPYLON. In ancient Egyptian architecture, a monumental gateway, preceding the main gateway (see Pylon) to a temple or sacred

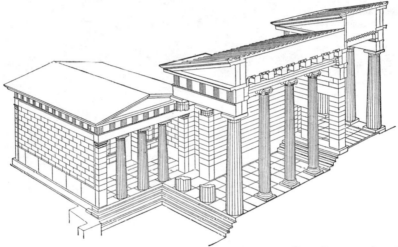

PROPYLAIA AT ATHENS: PERSPECTIVE SECTION SHOWING NORTHERN HALF RESTORED (SEE PLAN).

western front of this hall was formed by a portico similar to the one which faced eastward on the Acropolis. To the north and south of this portico, and at right angles with it, were smaller porticoes, of three columns in antis, the northern one of which had behind it a nearly square chamber, which was probably the room containing the pictures described by Pausanius (I., 22), and now frequently called the *pinakotheke*, or picture gallery.

This building belongs to the highest type of Athenian architecture. In ancient times, just as to-day, it was esteemed a work of equal interest and importance with the Parthenon itself. The structure seems to have remained nearly as Mnesicles left it, until about the year 1656, when an explosion of gunpowder caused its partial destruction. Even in spite of such an accident and the subsequent neglect of almost two centuries, the greater part of the building is still standing.

enclosure. The isolated masses of masonry on both sides of the passage were built in the Egyptian manner, with battering faces, so that the whole was of the general form of a truncated pyramid, the whole being crowned with a massive cavetto cornice ; or in some cases, the gateway was flanked by two solid and unpierced masses of buildings of that form, as in the pylon itself. These stood singly, or in a series of several, before the actual entrance or pylon of the temple, in order that the approach should be invested with dignity and ceremony.

PROSCENIUM. The platform or *logeion* of an ancient Greek theatre, upon which the actors enacted their parts, in front of the rear wall, which was treated like a façade forming the background, the *skene*. It corresponds with the modern stage and the Roman *pulpitum*. In the modern theatre, that part of the house which lies between the curtain and the orchestra, including generally the proscenium arch.

PROSCENIUM ARCH. *A.* In a theatre or similar building, the arch above the opening in the proscenium wall, at the front of the stage. In the United States, as usually constructed, the arch is a relieving arch above a lintel composed of iron beams ; hence, —

B. The imitation arch formed by means of furring, or the like, beneath such a lintel ; the opening, of whatever form, which allows the performance to be seen by the audience.

PROSCENIUM BOX. In a theatre, or similar building, a box in or near the proscenium, as distinguished from those more removed from the stage.

PROSCENIUM WALL. In a theatre, or similar building, the wall separating the stage and the auditorium ; usually of masonry and very solid. It is in this wall that the proscenium arch is opened.

PROSTAS. An antechamber ; a vestibule ; according to Vitruvius, the portion of the front of a temple included between the antæ or parastades of a portico in antis.

PROSTASIS. That which is put before a place to conceal it ; a screen.

PROSTOON. Same as Portico.

PROSTYLE. In Greek architecture, having a columnar portico in front, and not on the sides or rear. (See Amphiprostyle ; Columnar Architecture.)

PROSTYLOS. A prostyle building (Vitruvius).

PROTHESIS. In church buildings of the Greek Church, a Chapel immediately connected, generally on the north side of the bema. (Compare Parabema.)

PROTHYRID ; **PROTHYRIS.** Same as Ancon (Vitruvius, IV., 6).

PROTHYRON ; **PROTHYRUM.** In Greek, something before the door. It is stated by Vitruvius (VI., 10) that the Greeks used the term for a vestibule, but the Latin writers for a railing, or perhaps for the gate itself, like the Greek word Διάθυρα. Commonly used in the plural, prothyra.

PROTO-DORIC. Of a style apparently introductory to the Doric style ; said of any building or feature of a building which is considered to have contributed anything toward its evolution, as the Proto-Doric columns of the tomb at Beni-Hassan in Egypt.

PROTO-IONIC. Of a style apparently introductory to the Ionic style ; said of any building or feature of a building which is considered to have contributed anything toward its evolution, as the footings of the columns of Nineveh in relation to the Ionic base, the Assyrian helix to the Ionic volute, the characteristic Oriental lintel of palm timber to the Greek epistyle, etc. The capital discovered by the American archæologists at Assos in Asia Minor is an excellent example of Proto-Ionic style. (See Ionic ; Grecian Architecture.)

TOMB WITH COLUMNS AT BENI-HASSAN, NUBIA.

PROTRACTOR. A flat, generally semicircular, piece of metal, paper, celluloid, or the like, upon whose perimeter are marked the degrees of the circle, for use in laying off any desired angle at any given point in a drawing. In some cases a pivoted arm is attached for ruling the required line.

PROUT, SAMUEL ; water colour painter ; b. Sept. 17, 1783 (at Plymouth, England) ; d. Feb. 10, 1832.

He assisted John Britton (see Britton, John) in his topographical work, and was also employed by the publisher Ackerman. In 1818 went to Normandy and began the water colour drawings of picturesque architecture which are well known. In 1824 he visited Venice and afterward Germany. Among his published volumes of lithographed drawings of architectural subjects are sketches made in France and Germany (1833) ; sketches in France, Switzerland, and Italy (1839) ; all are of singular fidelity to the general aspect and character of the monuments represented, although the appearance of picturesque rudeness is exaggerated.

Redgrave, *Dictionary of Artists.*

PROVES. (See Broebes.)

PRYTANEIUM. In an ancient Greek city, the hall in which the magistrates took their meals in state at the public charge, received foreign embassies, entertained strangers of distinction, honoured citizens of high public merit, and in general exercised the rites of official hospitality. It was consecrated to Vesta, and in her honour a perpetual fire was maintained in it, which, in the colonies, was originally brought from the famous Prytaneium of Athens, the mother city. — H. V. B.

PSEUDISODOMUM. In ancient masonry, composed of layers or courses alternately thick and thin (Vitruvius, II., 8). (See Isodomum.)

PSEUDOCLASSIC ARCHITECTURE. That phase of neoclassic architecture which marked the most stilted period of post Renaissance art, when, under the influence of Vitruvius' writings and those of his modern disciples, the

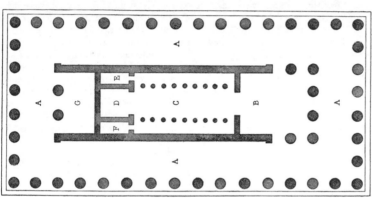

PSEUDO-DIPTERAL TEMPLE AT SELINUS, SICILY: 5TH CENTURY B.C.

most formal imitation of Roman architecture prevailed, and it was the aim to revive the whole art of Rome. (See Neoclassic Architecture.)
— W. P. P. L.

PSEUDO-DIPTERAL. In classical architecture, having an arrangement of columns similar to dipteral, but with the essential difference of the omission of the inner row, thus leaving a wide passage around the cella.

PSEUDO-DIPTEROS. A pseudo-dipteral building (Vitruvius).

PSEUDO-PERIPTERAL. In classic architecture, having a portico in front or with porticoes in front and rear, but with the columns on the sides engaged in the walls instead of standing free, as, in the case of Greek temples, that of Olympian Zeus at Girgenti, ruins of the ancient Akragas, or the nine-columned edifice at Pæstum, or, in the cases of Roman temples, that of Fortuna Virilis at Rome, or of the Maison Carrée at Nimes.

PSEUDO-PROSTYLE. In classic architecture, prostyle, but without a proper pronaos, the columns of the portico being set less than the

width of an intercolumniation from the front wall, or being actually engaged in it.

PTEROMA. In classic architecture, the passage along the side of the cella of a temple or other building, referring generally to the space behind its screen of columns, or pteron. In modern practice, often used for this space on the front and rear as well as at the sides.

PTERON. In classic architecture, that which forms a side or flank, as the row of columns along the side of a temple, or the side wall itself.

PUDDLE (n.). Same as Puddling, *B.*

PUDDLING. *A.* The act of filling a cavity with clay mixed with water, with or without sand, and rammed or tamped in successive layers to a certain condition of solidity, especially to prevent the infiltration of water, as behind sheet piling in a cofferdam, against the back of a retaining wall, etc.

B. The material used in such operations.

PUDSEY, HUGH; bishop.

He was Bishop of Durham from 1153 to 1194, and built the unique chapel called the Galilee at the western end of that cathedral, an interesting specimen of late Norman architecture, erected for the use of women, who had been hitherto excluded from the church. It was altered in the early English and perpendicular periods.

PUEBLO. In Spanish, a town or village; especially in the United States, an Indian village (and its inhabitants) of the Southwest, — Arizona and New Mexico. Village Indians have existed in many parts of the United States; indeed, except that their communal houses were of frailer material, and perished as soon as they were abandoned, the Indians of the more eastern parts of the country and of the northwest coast were as completely settled in communities as those of the so-called Pueblos. (See the following titles.)

PUEBLO ARCHITECTURE. That of those American Indians who are called Pueblo Indians, Pueblos, or Puebloans. (See Pueblo; Pueblo House.)

PUEBLO HOUSE. A communal dwelling of the village Indians called Pueblos. (See Pueblo.) These houses were, and still are, built of stone, adobe, jacál, etc., sometimes on the mesas, or tops of clifflike hills; sometimes in clefts or hollows of the cliff face ; sometimes excavated in the solid material of the cliff; sometimes on a plain or in a valley. In this article it is proposed to treat only those which are built independently of natural aid, reference being made under Communal Dwelling to other types.

The Pueblo dwellings consist of a group of flat-roofed chambers combined in a single structure that resembles a pile of receding packing cases. Several of these piles, with spaces and courts between, form a village. These villages were not absolutely permanent, but were frequently abandoned, and others built elsewhere, though in some instances the same site has been built on for centuries. Ruins of these communal dwellings extend northward in an ever narrowing region as far as the 40th parallel, and the known area dwindles to a mere point along Green River. Southward it widens, to embrace nearly the whole of Arizona and New Mexico, and scatteringly vanishes in the uncertain knowledge we have of northern Mexico. Within this immense tract permanent communal dwellings were built almost everywhere, on plain and mountain slope, in valleys and cañons, and even in the bottom of the Grand Cañon of the Colorado. Single houses are common, but the majority are buildings of a semifortress type : lower stories without entrance on the ground, and terraced upper stories reached by ladders easily removed. There was also, sometimes, a defensive wall. Before the acquisition of horse and gun, assault on one of these strongholds by predatory tribes or by a neighbouring community was difficult.

The inhabited dwellings of to-day consist, as did the ruins, of numerous rooms built in juxtaposition, or superimposed, the upper opening on terraces formed by the roofs of those below. There is generally no prearranged plan. The beginning is in one or two single-room structures, to which others are added as required. This seems to have been a frequent method, even in many of the elaborate buildings of the Mayas and the Aztecs. Formerly the ground-floor rooms in Arizona and New Mexico were entered only by a hatchway in the roof, a method still in vogue at Oraibe, which, with the other towns of the Moki, exhibits the nearest approach to pre-Columbian conditions. Frequently the house group formed a barrier around a court opening to southward, the rear wall insurmountable, and without entrance, the houses being terraced down inside to the court, and this protected by a defensive wall or a line of one-story buildings. Fortresses of this kind are seen in the ruins in Chaco Cañon, in northwestern New Mexico, and at other places. The court was always a feature, and is so still. It generally has one end closed, or at least entered through a covered way or passage beneath buildings. Where adobe was not used the building

material was stone slabs, usually sandstone. The arid nature of the country not only compelled the use of other materials than wood, but supplied these materials, ready to hand in profusion in the disintegrating cliffs and in the enormous reaches of argillaceous soil.

The Moki, in building, fixes the four corners by placing at each a prayer feather under a stone. A doorway is marked by placing food on each side of it. Other ceremonies are performed before the dwelling is occupied. The walls are of the usual stone slabs, roughly squared, and raised to a height of 6 to 8 feet. They are generally plastered inside and out with adobe mortar, and the inside is further finished by a coat of whitewash. This wash is sometimes applied outside as well. At the pueblo of Zuñi, and throughout the Rio Grande valley, adobe is largely used as building material, but at the Moki towns the material is almost exclusively stone. Doorways were originally of the notched variety (see Notched Doorway, under Doorway), where they opened on a roof, and there were hatchways through the roof, as mentioned ; but now, in Zuñi and the Rio Grande pueblos, and even in most of the Moki towns, there are commonly entrances on the ground. Formerly blankets or curtains formed the only doors, but now there are wooden doors hung to wooden frames, the doors being usually merely boards roughly nailed together. The Moki use frequently the old wooden latch with the string running through a hole in the door. On one side of the frame an opening a few inches square is left, through which the door may be securely propped inside, and the hole then plastered up till the return of the owner. Frequently the sill is raised a foot or more, while over the top is often an open transom, probably a smoke outlet. Windows were rectangular openings, barely differentiated from doors. No glazed windows existed until modern times, though mica and selenite were used early at the suggestion of the Spaniards, but only to a very limited extent. Small windows are now glazed to some extent in all the pueblos. At Zuñi there are also hatchways in the roof used as skylights. The masonry work is usually done by women, though the stones are brought by the men. A woman will sometimes work singly and alone in a desultory way that almost escapes observation, as no tools are used. Plumb line, level, and square were apparently not known to aboriginal America. The hand was the trowel and the thumb was the rule ; yet some of the angles and corners are quite regular, and appear to be vertical.

North of the Maya region the roof was always what may be called typical American construction, because it was used in principle by widely different tribes. The principle was simply a support of boughs or poles, which were finally covered with earth. In the Pueblo construction tree trunks without bark and 6 or 7 inches diameter are laid across the tops of the walls. Outer ends when too long are permitted to project beyond the walls, sometimes being finished into a kind of portico. Smaller poles are laid across the first, somewhat separated, and then comes a layer of slender willows or reeds, with next a layer of twigs or grass, though in some old buildings the grass was omitted. In one of the Chaco ruins thin, narrow, split boards took the place of the layer of small poles. On the grass layer a quantity of adobe mortar is spread, and then earth laid on and trodden down. The final finish is another layer of adobe mortar. Sufficient slope is given to carry off water, but not enough to create a current that would injure the surface. The walls are built up to the level of the top of the roof, and frequently somewhat above it, and a coping of thin slabs put on with their outer edges flush with the wall face. Through this parapet outlets are made for the rain, and drains are put in to carry the water clear of the walls. In the ordinary storms of the arid region these roofs answer well, but continued wet weather saturates them and causes dripping inside. Floors are constructed in the same way, the floor of one chamber being the roof of the one under it.

There are no stairways within, all mounting being done outside by ladders and by steps built on end projections of walls. The ladders are easy for the inhabitants, who go up and down, even with a load, without touching the sides or the rungs with their hands, and the dogs find no barrier in them, running over the roofs at will. The original ladder, used also by other tribes, was a notched log. There was, too, another form made of a Y-shaped tree or branch. Present ladders are similar to our ordinary kind, except that they have very long ends rising above, and held together by crosspieces. Floors are sometimes paved with irregular slabs of sandstone, and this feature has been noted in very old ruins. When of adobe the floor is kept in repair by occasional applications of very thin adobe mortar, but moccasined feet do not injure it much. A hole is left at one corner or one side of the chamber for a chimney, which is a modern affair, having been unknown before the appearance of the Spaniards. The chimney top is stone, adobe, or broken earthen pots placed one above the other. Within there is a hood across the corner built of sticks plastered with adobe, which begins about 4 feet above the floor where the hearth is laid. A mat of reeds or a slab of sandstone forms the covering for the hatchway, when necessary, and in cold weather a sheepskin is frequently placed over the top of the chimney when the fire has died out, and

held there by a large stone. The end of a terrace is often roofed over, forming a sort of porch, where cooking is frequently carried on, a fireplace being built in one corner. At Zuñi, the dome-shaped oven in use is often built on the roof. The house walls vary in thickness from 16 to 22 inches, but some of the old walls were much thicker. The rooms are generally small, some used for baking being no more than 7 × 10 feet; 12 × 14 feet would be a fair average. The interior height is barely 6 feet, and often less. In going southward rooms increase in size and in height. — F. S. DELLENBAUGH.

PUGET, PIERRE; sculptor, architect, and painter; b. Oct. 31, 1622; d. Dec. 1, 1694.

Puget was born at Marseilles (France). He was apprenticed to a shipbuilder, and was at first employed to decorate galleys. He came especially under the influence of Pietro da Cortona (see Berretini), Jean Bologne (see Bologne), Algardi (see Algardi), and Bernini (see Bernini). In 1655–1657 he made the famous caryatids of the portal of the Hôtel de Ville at Toulon. In 1660 he settled in Genoa, where, among other works, he made the colossal statues of S. Sebastien and S. Ambrose in the church of the Carignan. His practice as an architect was considerable. About 1664 he was occupied with the Arsenal, the *Halle de la Poissonnerie*, the *Chapelle de l'Hospice de la Charité*, and the *Portail des Chartreaux* at Marseilles, and the *Hôtel d'Aiguilles* at Aix, and with the decoration of galleys at Toulon. Some of these decorations of ships are in the Louvre. He is best known as a sculptor of full statues and groups.

Lagrange, *Pierre Puget*; Gonse, *Sculpture Française*; Rioux-Maillon, *Pierre Puget, Décorateur*.

PUGGING. *A.* Coarse mortar, or similar material, used to fill the spaces between beams, studs, and similar places, as in partitions and floors, intended to act as deafening.

B. The operation of filling with clay or puddle.

PUGIN, AUGUSTUS; architect and archæologist; b. 1762 (in France); d. Dec. 18, 1832.

Pugin went to England during the French Revolution. He was educated at the Royal Academy and began to exhibit there in 1799. He was employed for over twenty years in the office of John Nash (see Nash, J.). For Ackerman the publisher he illustrated *Microcosm of London* (1808–1811), *Views in Islington and Pentonville* (1813), etc. He published *Specimens of Gothic Architecture: selected from Various Ancient Edifices in England* (London, 1821, 2 vols. 4to), *Examples of Gothic Architecture* (1831, 2 vols. 4to), *Gothic Ornaments* (London, 1831, 1 vol. folio); with John Britton (see Britton, J.), *Illustrations of Public Buildings in London* (1825–1828, 2 vols. 4to); with Le Keux, *Specimens of the Architectural Antiquities of Normandy* (London,

1827, 1 vol. 4to), etc. These works laid the foundation for much that has been accomplished in the revival of the Gothic style in England.

Ferrey, *Recollections of A. N. Welby Pugin and Augustus Pugin;* Redgrave, *Dictionary of Artists.*

PUGIN, AUGUSTUS NORTHMORE WELBY; architect and designer; b. 1812; d. 1852.

He was taught to draw by his father, Augustus Pugin (see Pugin, A.), and was, like him, an enthusiastic admirer of mediæval art. At the age of fifteen he was employed to make designs for furniture and goldsmith's work. At the age of twenty he took up the study of architecture, and interested himself in stained glass, metal work, embroidery, and the like. He built many Catholic churches and the cathedral in Saint George's Fields, London. At Ramsgate, England, he built much; and he worked on the houses of Parliament under Sir Charles Barry (see Barry, Sir C.). He published *Contrasts, a Parallel between the Noble Edifices of the Fourteenth and Fifteenth Centuries and the Present Day* (1836, 1 vol. 4to); *The Present State of Ecclesiastical Architecture in England* (1843, 1 vol. 8vo); *Design for Iron and Brass Work in the Style of the XV. and XVI. Centuries* (1836, 1 vol. 4to); *Details of Ancient Timber Houses of the Fifteenth and Sixteenth Centuries* (1836, 1 vol. 4to); *The True Principles of Pointed or Christian Architecture* (1841, 1 vol. 4to); *Glossary of Ecclesiastical Ornament and Costume* (1848, 1 vol. 4to).

Ferrey, *Recollections of A. N. Welby Pugin;* Redgrave, *Dictionary of Artists; Avery Architectural Library Catalogue.*

PUG PILE. (See under Pile.)

PULL. A fixture to be grasped by the hand, and to receive the fingers in opening or shutting a door, shutter, or drawer. Generally used in composition, as door pull.

PULLEY. In architectural practice, the simplest form of wheel with a grooved or hollowed surface; used especially to receive the cord or chain which supports at one end the counterpoise of a vertically sliding sash, and is secured at the other end to the sash itself.

PULLEY CASE. (See Cased Frame, under Frame, I.)

PULLEY MORTICE; STILE. (See under Mortice; Stile; also Cased Frame, under Frame, I.)

PULPIT. A stand, especially an enclosed stand, prepared for a speaker, generally limited to such a stand in or attached to a church. The pulpit is especially the place for the preacher of the sermon, as distinguished from the officiant who reads the Gospel or the Epistle (see Ambo; Lectern; Reading Desk).

Pulpits in the open air are sometimes built upon the church wall, as in the famous example

of the cathedral of Prato in Tuscany, the beautiful design of Donatello, and sometimes a separate platform, as was common in England

PULPIT: S. MINIATO, NEAR FLORENCE; INLAY OF BLACK AND WHITE MARBLE; DESIGN PROBABLY OF 12TH CENTURY.

during the sixteenth and seventeenth centuries. In the interior of a church the pulpit may be

PULPIT: ENTRANCE FROM STAIRWAY IN THE WALL, BEAULIEU, HANTS; c. 1260.

on one side, as is most common in Roman Catholic churches, or at the end directly opposite the audience, and connected in some way with the reading desk, as is most common in Protestant churches. In the former case the pulpit is commonly built upon one of the pillars between the nave and the north aisle, and these are often of extraordinary richness and beauty, such as the beautiful marble one at S. Croce in Florence, and the richly carved wooden pulpits in the churches of Belgium. When such pulpits are entirely independent of the structure,

churches and some others, and especially in the United States in recent times, the pulpit is a large platform with a solid parapet in front, combined with a reading desk of some sort, and is occupied by the clergyman throughout the service.

PULVINAR; **PULVINATE**, **-ED** (adj.). Rounded convexly, as a Cushion, or as in Pillow Work.

PULPIT: CHURCH OF S. GIOVANNI PISTOIA; c. 1270.
The sculptures by Niccolò Pisano or his pupils.

PUMP (I.). A mechanical appliance for lifting liquids. For raising water for purposes of water supply to buildings, many different forms of pumps are in use, such as ordinary suction, hand lift and force pumps, chain pumps, pumps driven by animal power, hot air and gas pumps, windmill and steam pumps, electric pumps, hydraulic rams, waterwheels, and turbines. Steam and electric pumps are either of the rotary or the plunger type. (For electric pump, see Electric Appliances.) —W. P. G.

PUMP (II.). A large timber set vertically under the wall or pier of a building which is to be lifted or altered in its lower parts. (See Shore; Shoring.)

PUMP ROOM. In England, in connection with a mineral spring, a room in which the waters are drunk; it is sometimes an open

and stand on columns as at Siena cathedral, in the Pisa baptistery, or S. Lorenzo at Florence, they may be still more magnificent in design and still richer in sculpture. The pulpit at the end of the church, and facing the audience as they are seated, is often in Great Britain, until recent times, a two-storied structure, the lower story being occupied as reading desk and the upper as the pulpit proper; or it had three stories, the lowermost story being occupied by the clerk, the second as a reading desk, and the third as the pulpit proper. In Congregational

pavilion, and sometimes, as in the famous example at Bath, an assembly room of a more or less monumental character. (Compare Kursaal.)

PUNCHED WORK. Same as Pounced Work.

PUNCHEON. In carpentry, a short piece of timber, especially : —

A. In framing, a stud, queen post, or the like, and which is unusually short for its thickness.

B. A piece of split timber, as a slab or hewn plank roughly dressed as by the adze, such as is used in the absence of sawed boards.

PULPIT IN FRAUENKIRCHE, NUREMBERG: 14TH CENTURY.

PUNTELLIS, DE. (See Pontelli, Baccio.)

PURFLED. Ornamented with a fine decoration like lacework or embroidery, especially as applied to borders or margins. The term is transferred to any lacelike effect in stone or woodwork, as in tabernacles and shrines, treated profusely with miniature pinnacles, finials, buttresses, and tracery.

PURLIN. In carpentry, a horizontal timber laid across the principal rafters or trusses to support the jack rafters.

PURLIN BRACE and other compounds. (See the special nouns.)

PUSH BUTTON. (See Electrical Appliances.)

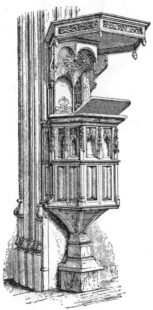

PULPIT OF OAK: FOTHERINGAY CHURCH, NORTH-
AMPTONSHIRE; A.D. 1440.

PUT LOG. In scaffolding, for building walls of masonry, one of the horizontal pieces of timber four or five feet long, set at right angles with the wall, and bearing on it at one end, while the other rests upon the ledges or ledger-boards which form part of the upright temporary framework of the scaffold or stage; upon the put logs are laid the floor planks upon which the masons work until they have carried the wall out of reach, when a new line of put logs is laid at a higher level. (Called also put lock.)
— H. V. B.

PUT LOG HOLE. One of a horizontal series of holes left by the masons in a wall to receive the wall ends of put logs. These holes are supposed to be filled up when the scaffolding is removed; but in many brick buildings of Italy they remain open, and their dark checker adds to the picturesque effect of the plain, square campanili.

PUTTY. *A.* A plastic composition made of whiting and linseed oil, sometimes mixed with

PULPIT: EXTERNAL, ADJOINING DOORWAY OF
BAPTISTERY, PISTOIA; c. 1350.

a small amount of white lead, worked together until it has a tough pasty consistency; in this state it is used by glaziers in setting panes of glass in the frames of windows, and by painters in filling or stopping accidental holes and cracks in woodwork preliminary to painting it. It has the quality of growing hard by exposure, and of not shrinking. A composition of this sort is sometimes used in decoration after it has been formed in moulds into ornamental shapes fit to

painter and decorator; b. Dec. 14, 1824; d. Oct. 24, 1898.

The greater part of his education as painter was received from Henri Scheffer, a brother of Ary Scheffer. He studied for brief periods with Delacroix and Thomas Couture. His life was occupied with a series of mural paintings, the most important of which are scenes from the life of S. Geneviève at the Pantheon of Paris, the decorations of the museum at Lyons, of the museum of Amiens, of the Sorbonne (Paris), and of the Public Library, Boston.

Gaul, *Puvis de Chavannes;* Vachon, *Puvis de*

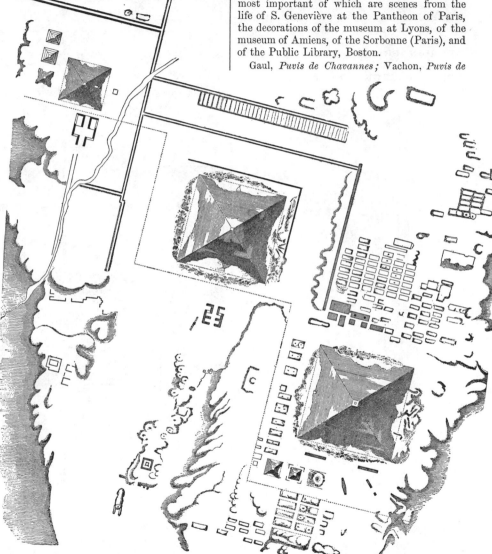

PYRAMIDS OF GIZEH: PLAN OF THE MODERN CONDITION OF THE SITE.

be glued to the surface of wooden panels or friezes. Such decorations are called putty ornament.

B. A mixture of gypsum and lime, used for the finishing coat of fine plastering. Usually called lime putty or plaster putty.

PUVIS DE CHAVANNES, PIERRE;

Chavannes; Buisson, *Puvis de Chavannes; Kunstchronik ; Chronique des Arts.*

PYCNOSTYLE. In classical architecture, according to the Vitruvian formulæ, having an intercolumniation less than that usually employed, generally equal to one diameter and a half of the columns. (See Columnar Architecture.)

PLATE XII

PYRAMID

(Upper figure.) The three near Gizeh, seen from the southwest. The third pyramid, that of Menkaura, is in front next the second pyramid, that of Schefren, and the Great Pyramid, that of Cheops or Chufu, is the most distant and seems the lowest.

(Lower figure.) That which marks the tomb of Caius Cestius outside the walls of Rome and close to the Porta Ostiensis, or gate which leads to Ostia. The casing is of white marble; the mass of the building of solid rubble masonry in which is reserved a burial chamber once richly decorated. The height is given as 118 feet.

PYLON. In ancient Egyptian architecture, the portal of a temple. Characteristically, it was composed of two lofty wall masses built in the usual manner of the Egyptians, with battering wall surfaces profusely covered with countersunk bas-reliefs and hieroglyphics, the doorway being a lower structure between these two masses. (See Propylon.)

PYRAMID. Primarily, an Egyptian tomb of the well-known shape, four-square at the base and tapering upward nearly to a point; the term being Greek and signifying pointed like a flame of fire. In modern times any object of the same shape. A very small pyramid, especially when terminating a structure, is called pyramidion (see that term and also Obelisk).

The pyramids of Egypt are, in the first place, the tombs of kings. The use of this type has been alleged to cease with the 6th or 7th dynasty (3400 or 3200 B.C.); but they exist of a much later date and probably this form of royal tomb remained common until the complete

have gained their great size from continual enlarging and recasing during a long reign; but this is improbable. At the same time it is not clear how a pyramid, begun on a great scale during the author's life, could have been finished in case of his early death.

The pyramids are mainly cairns, i.e. they are solid masses of stone, or of brick masonry; but

PYRAMID : TOMB OF CAIUS CESTIUS AT ROME.

establishment, for all classes, of the grotto tomb during the Middle Empire. Even at a still later time the same form was used on a small scale for private persons.

The royal pyramids are numerous; but none have been made the subject of architectural study except the larger, which are also the more ancient buildings. That of Medum (probably 4000 B.C.) seems to have been built upon and around a mastaba; but it was sheathed with masonry and brought to a pyramidal form. The great pyramids of Gizeh have been supposed to

each has a chamber or several chambers with long passages leading to them, which passages were always carefully concealed; while false passages exist, intended to deceive plunderers. The sarcophagus of a king was placed in the tomb chamber before this was built, and the superstructure carried on.

The great pyramids were of the Kings Khufu, Khafra, and Menkaura (3969–3784 B.C. — Flinders Petrie). The latest very large one known to us is much less perfectly preserved; it is near the Fayum at the place called Illahun.

A still later one, built by Amenemhat III., at Hawara in the Fayum, was of brick, cased with limestone; it enclosed a tomb chamber hollowed in a single block of quartzite and roofed by three blocks of the same material. This brings the history of the larger pyramids to the 12th dynasty and about 2600 B.C., and with this the now ascertained history of the more important royal tombs ceases.

The pyramid form was used for tombal structures elsewhere than in Egypt, such as the tomb of Caius Cestius built into the city wall of Rome. In modern times it has been indicated in tombs built against the walls of churches (but see Obelisk, B.). — R. S.

PYRAMIDION. A small pyramid, especially when completing a larger form, as the apex of an obelisk; it was often sheathed with metal.

PYTHIUS; architect and sculptor.

Vitruvius mentions Pythius as architect of the temple of Pallas Athena at Priene in Ionia, built about 329 B.C., and as one of the architects and sculptors employed on the Mausoleum at Halicarnassus in Caria, begun 348 B.C. He made the four-horse chariot with attendant figures which crowned the Mausoleum.

Vitruvius, ed. Marini; Brunn, *Geschichte der Griechischen Künstler.*

Q

QUAD. In the University of Oxford, a college court; one of the large open spaces upon which front the college buildings, which enclose it on all four sides with usually one or two gateways of entrance. The term is extended to the few courts which are not completely enclosed. The term hardly extends to Cambridge, in which university the word Court is used.

Tom Quad. A great court of Christ Church College (which see under College).

QUADRANGLE. A rectangular or nearly rectangular court, usually large and surrounded by buildings of some importance, as in a college, a royal palace, or governmental building (see the abbreviated form, Quad).

QUADREL. A square tile, or the like; a quarrel.

QUADRIPARTITE. Made up of four; fourfold. Quadripartite vaulting is the commonest form of groined and also of ribbed vaulting.

QUANTITIES. (See Bill of Quantities.)

QUARREL. A square or lozenge-shaped piece of material. Especially a piece of glass of such a shape, set diagonally, as in a latticed sash. By extension the opening left or prepared for such a square, as in a window.

QUARREL PANE. (See Quarrel.)

QUARRY (I.). (See Stone.)

QUARRY (II.). Same as Quarrel.

QUARRY BED. (See under Bed; see also Masonry.)

QUARRY-FACED. Having a rough face as if that obtained by splitting from the quarry; said of stone.

QUARTER. In British usage, same as Stud.

QUARTER CUT. Same as Quarter-sawed.

QUARTERED. (See Quarter-sawed.)

QUARTER HOLLOW. A concave moulding or cavetto, of which the transverse section is an arc of about ninety degrees; the converse of a quarter round or ovolo.

QUARTER PARTITION. Same as Stud Partition (which see, under Partition; see also Quarter).

QUARTER ROUND. A convex moulding or ovolo, of which the transverse section is a quadrant, or approaches a quadrant; the converse of a quarter hollow or cavetto.

QUARTERS. Places for lodging taken collectively, or any one such place; especially: —

A. One of soldiers of any rank; more often used with regard to commissioned officers, as in such phrases as, "You will find the captain in his quarters."

B. The cabins of the negroes on a Southern plantation during the time of slavery, and, to a certain extent, since the emancipation of the slaves, the term being applied rather to the whole colony or village of cabins than to any house or number of houses taken separately. (See Cabin.)

QUARTER-SAWED. In lumber working, sawed into quarters longitudinally; — said of a log so cut in preparation for the subsequent making of boards which are cut at 45° with the first cuts, and hence more or less parallel with the medullary rays. By extension, boards cut in such a manner or by any system of approximately radial cuts. Boards so produced have a rich grain, especially in oak, when it is called the silver grain, and are less subject to shrinkage and warping.

QUARTZ. Crystalline silica. A hard, brittle mineral breaking with a glasslike fracture, and usually transparent to translucent, and colourless, or of a white, pink, and amethystine hue. — G. P. M.

QUATREFOIL. (See Foil.)

QUATREMÈRE DE QUINCY, ANTOINE CHRYSOSTOME; archæologist and writer on art: b. 1755 (at Paris); d. 1850.

In 1785 he won the prize of the *Académie des Inscriptions et Belles-lettres* (Paris) by an essay on the influence of Egyptian upon Greek art. In 1791 he was elected to the *Assemblée legislative.* In 1824 he was made dramatic censor and professor of archæology at the *Cabinet des Antiquités* of the Bibliothèque Nationale (Paris). He published many works on archæology and art. Among the most important are *Canova et ses Ouvrages*, etc. (Paris, 1834, 8vo) ; *De l'Architecture Égyptienne considerée dans son origine . . . et comparée sous les mêmes rapports à l'Architecture Grecque* (Paris, 1803, 4to) ; *Dictionnaire historique d'Architecture*, etc., at first forming part of the *Encyclopédie Méthodique*, and published separately in 1832 (2 vols. 4to) ; *Histoire de la vie et des ouvrages des plus célèbres architectes, ou l'Art de la Sculpture antique considéré sous un nouveau point de vue* (Paris, 1815, folio) ; *Restitution des deux frontons du temple de Minerve à Athènes* (Paris, 1825, folio).

Larousse, *Dictionnaire ;* Vapereau, *Dictionnaire des Litératures ;* British Museum, *Catalogue of Printed Books.*

QUATTRO CENTO. In Italian, the fifteenth century, or, more strictly, the years which have fourteen in their number, viz. from 1400 to 1499. (See Cinque Cento.)

QUAY. *A.* The marginal space around or along the water front of a dock or still harbour, a river landing, a canal, or the like, and generally supported by retaining walls, paved, lighted, drained, and used for the loading, unloading, storage, and shipment of merchandise. The quay of an important port generally requires a large equipment of machines for unloading and handling cargo, storehouses for its care, and generally a system of railway tracks for the prompt reshipment of inland freights.

In New York the quays are largely replaced by piers covered with sheds, for the receipt and temporary storage of goods, warehouses for local freights being built off the immediate water front.

Quay walls, which must resist the pressure of the earth behind them, and of the weight of structures and goods upon them, vary with the conditions of each case. (See Foundation ; Retaining Wall.)

B. A permanent landing place or landing stage of any sort, as at the side of the tracks at a railway station. — W. R. HUTTON.

QUEEN. (See Slate.)

QUEEN ANNE ARCHITECTURE. The architecture existing in England during the short reign of Anne, 1702 to 1714. The more important structures of the reign were generally the completion of designs fixed in all of their parts before her accession, and but little that was monumental was begun in her time. Wren's work upon Greenwich Hospital and Hampton Court was still going on, and he built many churches in London and elsewhere, of which S. Bride's, Fleet Street, is a good example. The most elaborate single building begun in Anne's reign was Blenheim, the palace by Sir John Vanbrugh, built by the nation for the Duke of Marlborough. The buildings which are especially associated with the style are the minor country houses and many houses in the suburbs of London, built frequently of red brick, and characterized by sculpture in relief, moulded or carved in the same material. A certain picturesqueness of treatment, like a revival of Elizabethan, or even of mediæval styles, in mass, in sky line, and in such details as chimneys, gables, and dormer windows, is noticeable in these ; and, although all is on the same moderate scale, and nothing is very massive or imposing, the style has considerable attraction when applied to dwelling houses. It was this character of the buildings of Anne's reign which caused their acceptance by some architects of the years from 1865 to 1885, in England, as types for modern designing, and country houses of this character were built in considerable numbers. A feeble imitation of these modern buildings was also attempted in the United States, but usually on a very small scale, and with such inappropriate materials as those used in the ordinary frame constructions.
— R. S.

QUEEN CLOSER. (See Closer.)

QUERCIA, GIACOMO DELLA. (See Giacomo Della Quercia.)

QUESEVEAU. (See Coysevox.)

QUESNEL, FRANÇOIS ; architect and painter.

With Claude de Chastillon he made the plans of the hospital of S. Louis (Paris), which was built in 1607. Quesnel was the author of the first geometrical plan of the city of Paris.

Bauchal, *Dictionnaire.*

QUESNOY. (See Duquesnoy.)

QUINCUNX. An arrangement of five points, four of them being at the corners of a square, and the fifth in the centre. A quincunxial arrangement is a series of quincunxes forming collectively equally spaced points at the intersections of crossing diagonal lines, used especially in tree planting and gardening.

QUINTEFOIL. Same as Cinquefoil. (See Foil.)

QUIRK. *A.* A piece taken out or set aside for some specific purpose, especially from one corner of a room or plot of ground. In some old English houses, and in the Hôtel de Cluny, an enclosed vestibule projecting into the room, allowing of passage between two other rooms by cutting off a corner.

B. In English provincial use, a quarrel or lozenge of glass.

C. A groove in a group of mouldings, as on either side of a countersunk or flush bead in matched and beaded sheathing, or in a beaded angle or arris. (See also Quirk Moulding, under Moulding.)

QUOIN. *A.* One stone helping to form the corner of a wall of masonry, especially when accentuated by a difference in the surface treatment of the stones forming the corner from that of the rest of the wall mass ; one of the stones forming such a corner.

B. A wedge to support and steady a stone ; a pinner.

Rustic Quoin. A quoin or corner treated with sunk joints, the face of the quoins being generally roughened, and raised above the gen-

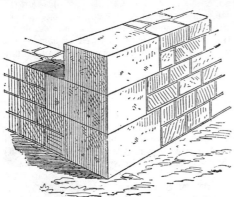

QUOINS OF CUT STONE FORMING THE ANGLE OF A WALL OF SMALLER MATERIALS.

eral surface of the masonry so as to form a contrast with it and give an appearance of more or less rugged strength to the angles, corners, or reveals so treated.

R

RABBET. A continuous small recess, generally understood as having a right angle included between its sides, especially one whose sides enclose a relatively restricted area ; one formed by two planes very narrow as compared with their length, such as the small recess on a door frame, into which the edge of a door is made to fit, the recess of a brick jamb to receive a window frame, and the like.

RABE, MARTIN FRIEDRICH ; architect ; b. 1775 ; d. 1856 (at Berlin).

From 1801 to 1804 he was employed on the Schloss at Weimar (Germany). In 1810 he was appointed professor at the Academy of Architecture in Berlin, and from 1829 to 1842 was architect of the Schloss in Berlin.

Bormann, *Denkmäler von Berlin.*

RACQUET COURT. A court or area in which the game of racquet or racquets is played ; also written raquet and racket. (Compare Tennis Court, Fives Court.)

RAD AND DAB. In England, a coarse substitute for brick nogging between the studs or quarters of partitions ; formed of clay and chopped straw filled in upon a rough lathing. Also called rab and dab.

RADIATING PRINCIPLE. In planning, a system used especially in prisons, and, some-

times, to a certain extent in hospitals, in which, from a central guard room or administration building, galleries radiate in four or more directions. ,(See Panopticon ; Prison.)

RADULPHE (RAOUL) ; abbots and architects.

The name of several abbots of the monastery of Mont Saint-Michel (France). Radulphe (I.) built four pillars and the base of the tower, between 1048 and 1060. Radulphe (II.) built three bays of the nave and the porch, between 1160 and 1184. Radulphe (III.) (d. March 18, 1218), continued the *Merveille* about 1212.

Héricher-Bouet, *Mont Saint-Michel.*

RAFFAELLO DA MONTELUPO ; sculptor ; b. 1505 ; d. 1557.

A fragment of Montelupo's Autobiography is published by Gaye (op. cit., Vol. III., 581), and translated by Perkins (*Tuscan Sculptors*, Vol. II., p. 72). Montelupo is best known as one of the chief assistants of Michelangelo Buonarroti (see Buonarroti). He made, under his direction, the statue of S. Damiano in the new sacristy of S. Lorenzo in Florence (for the statue of S. Cosmo, see Giovanni Montorsoli). Feb. 27, 1542, he contracted to finish three statues for the tomb of Julius II., by Michelangelo. He made several bas-reliefs for the Casa Santa at Loreto. Montelupo assisted Bandinelli in the completion of the tomb of Leo X., at the church of S. Maria Sopra Minerva in Rome, and designed the monument of Baldassare Turini at the cathedral of Pescia. He assisted in defending the Castello di S. Angelo during the siege of Rome in 1527. He died at Orvieto while assisting Sanmicheli (see Sanmicheli, M.), and Simone and Francesco Mosca in the construction of the altar of the Magi in the cathedral.

Müntz, *Renaissance ;* Vasari, Milanesi ed. ; Perkins, *Tuscan Sculptors ;* Gaye, *Carteggio ;* Fumi, *Il Duomo di Orvieto.*

RAFTER. A roof beam ; one of those which are set sloping, the lower end bearing on the wall plate, the upper end on the ridge piece or its equivalent.

Angle Rafter. In English usage, strictly the principal rafter under the hip rafter ; it carries the purlins, on which rest the jack rafters and hips.

More commonly, in the United States, any rafter at the angle of a roof, whether principal or secondary.

Auxiliary Rafter. In a truss, a rafter used to stiffen the principal rafter as by doubling it, or, as in a queen post truss, to go from the tie beam to the queen post, thus doubling the sloping chord of the truss in that place.

Binding Rafter. A timber to support rafters at a point between the plate and the ridge. It may be a purlin.

Common Rafter. A rafter to which the roof sheathing is nailed, as distinguished from the main rafters or truss rafters, and from hip, valley, and other special rafters. In trussed roofs they are ordinarily carried by the purlins, and spaced 16, 20, or 24 inches on centres; their scantling varies greatly according to the character of the roof.

Compass Rafter. In an ornamental roof truss, or the framing of a gable, a rafter cut to a curve, either at both edges (inner and outer) or on the inside only.

Crook Rafter. Same as Knee Rafter.

Cushion Rafter. Same as Auxiliary Rafter.

Jack Rafter. One reaching from the angle rafter to the ridge, and therefore short.

Knee Rafter. One taking the place of a Knee, *i.e.* of a brace fitted into the angle between a principal rafter and the tie beam or collar beam.

Kneeling Rafter. Same as Knee Rafter.

Principal Rafter. The diagonal member of a roof truss or principal.

RAFTER PLATE. (See Plate.)

RAG WORK. Rough masonry built with undressed flags or flat stones.

RAIL. In carpentry, any horizontal member mortised or otherwise secured between or upon two posts, forming a frame or panel, as, first, in fencing, whether the closure is made by several parallel rails or by only two to give nailing to palings; second, as a coping to a balustrade, when it is called a hand rail; third, in panelling, doors, and the like, being the horizontal member of the frame in which the panels are set, the vertical members being the stiles. The rails of massive stone, elaborately sculptured, which form the ceremonial enclosures of ancient Buddhist topes, temples, etc., in India, are among the most characteristic and important features of Buddhist architecture.

Clamp Rail. In carpenter work, a piece receiving the ends of a number of boards in a piece of ceiling, a platform, trapdoor, or the like. The clamp usually has a groove run along the edge into which the ends of the boards fit with tongues or tenons. In the United States, called more often Cleat or Batten.

Frieze Rail. In a framed door or the like, that next below a frieze panel.

Hanging Rail. In a door, window sash, or shutter, hung with hinges at the top or bottom, that rail to which the hinges are attached. (See Hanging Stile, under Stile.)

Lock Rail. In a framed door, that rail which comes nearest to the place for the lock, and, therefore, generally about three feet from the ground.

Meeting Rail. (See under M.)

RAILING. Primarily, any structure or member composed mainly of rails; in common use, a parapet, enclosure or the like made with slender bars and of no great size. Such a parapet, whether consisting of balusters (see Baluster) or of a trellis of wire or laths, or of iron bars equal or nearly so in thickness, or parallel or nearly so, is called a railing, but the term does not commonly include balustrades or the like of stone.

RAILWAY BUILDING. Any structure especially prepared for the business of a railroad or railway; especially such a building as is of peculiar fashion and construction, as fit for that service only, or chiefly. (See Baggage Room; Dépôt; Engine House; Round House; Station; Waiting Room.) Freight sheds and car sheds are not peculiar in design.

In addition to these the central offices of railroads require a great number of rooms, which are contained in very large and costly buildings; but these differ in no important respect from other large office buildings. There are, in some cities, hotels combined with terminal stations, but these, also, are merely ordinary hotels built between the car sheds and the street.

RAIMOND (RAIMONDUS); architect.

Raimond, *maître d'œuvre* of Carcassonne (France), planned the cathedral of Lugo (Spain), and commenced its construction in 1169.

Bauchal, *Dictionnaire.*

RAINALDI, CARLO; architect; b. 1611; d. 1691.

Carlo was a son of Girolamo Rainaldi (see Rainaldi, G). He was the leading architect of the great church of S. Agnese, in the Piazza Navona, Rome. One of his best buildings, and a fine example of the baroque style, is the church of S. Maria, in Campitelli (1665). He also built the façade of the church of S. Andrea delle Valle (see Pietro Paolo Olivieri), and the twin churches of S. Maria de' Miracoli and S. Maria di Monte Santo, in the Piazza del Popolo (about 1662). All the works mentioned are in Rome.

Gurlitt, *Geschichte des Barockstiles in Italien;* Ebe, *Spät-Renaissance;* Strack, *Baudenkmäler Roms.*

RAINALDI, GIROLAMO; architect; b. 1570; d. 1655.

A pupil of Domenico Fontana (see Fontana, D). He was much employed as engineer, especially in laying out the harbour of Fano (Italy). About 1623 he built the church of S. Luca at Bologna. Rainaldi was one of the many architects called upon to make designs for the façade of the church of S. Petronio (Bologna). He was also employed by the Farnese and Este families, at Parma, Modena, and Piacenza. He returned to Rome in 1650, and built the Palazzo Pamfili, in the Piazza Navona.

Gurlitt, *Geschichte des Barockstiles in Italien;* Ebe, *Spät-Renaissance.*

RAINALDUS; architect.

One of the architects of the cathedral of Pisa : the façade finished about 1100.

RAINERIUS (RANUCIUS) ; architect.

He made the central window of S. Silvestro in Capite, Rome. Works of his sons Nicolaus and Petrus are dated 1143 and 1160.

RAISER. Same as Riser.

RAISING. *A.* In the technical sense, the process of lifting a building, or part of a building, by means of screws, the hydraulic press, or other mechanical appliances. The subject is treated at length under Shoring.

RAM. *A.* A large weight for driving piles, and the like.

B. A machine for raising water. (See Hydraulic Ram, below.)

Hydraulic Ram. A mechanical device, operating automatically, for raising a small quantity of water by utilizing the force obtained by the fall of a large body of water, the height to which the water is raised being often many times greater than the fall. The water lifted may be either from the same source which furnishes the power operating the machine, or from a different source, and the ram is called either single or double-acting. The

RAMPART CARRYING AN INNER AND AN OUTER CRENELATED PARAPET, ALLOWING OF TWO LINES OF BOWMEN, ETC. WALLS OF POMPEII, CAMPANIA, ITALY; PROBABLY C. 200 B.C.

B. Same as Rearing.

RAISING PIECE. In carpentry, a piece of timber like a wall plate. (See Bolster.)

RAKE. Inclination or slope, as of a roof or of a flight of steps in a staircase. (See Pitch.)

RAKE; **RAKE OUT** (v. t.). In masonry work to remove, as by scraping, the mortar joints at the face of the work to a slight depth, in order that they may be finished by pointing. In masonry intended to receive very heavy pressure, such raking is done during, or immediately after, the completion of the wall or pier, in order to relieve the outer edges of the stones or bricks from the subsequent strains which might otherwise cause the material to spall at the face. (See Point.)

raising power is given by the elastic reaction of a confined volume of air, which is compressed by the falling water.

RAMESSEUM. A group of buildings in Egypt, among the ruins of Thebes, believed to serve as a memorial to Ramses (Rameses) II., and including an enormous gateway with pylons, two great courts surrounded by colonnades, and one large hypostyle hall, with many smaller though still important rooms.

RAMP. An inclined plane, as of a floor rising from a lower to a higher level, taking the place of steps ; specifically, a concave connecting sweep in a vertical plane, as on a coping or hand rail, where it turns from a sloping to a horizontal direction, or rises from one level to a higher level.

RAMPART. A wall of defence. In ancient and mediæval fortification, a wall of masonry, thick and solid enough to resist the ram or the pick for a long time, and to afford a broad platform on the top for the defenders; and high enough to give these a great advantage over the assailants; (see Battlement; Hoard; Machicolation; Parapet). In modern fortification, a bank of earth, showing grassed slopes to the assailant, but often faced with masonry below. The top of the rampart is always faced with a parapet, which, in this sense, was crenelated before the use of gunpowder, then broken by embrasures, and finally left with a uniform horizontal top.

RANCH; **RANCHE** (from the Spanish *Rancho*). In the western United States, a tract of grazing land, including also the house upon it; also an ordinary farm not devoted to stock raising. The forms rancho and rancheria have also been used. — F. S. D.

RANCHERIA. A collection of herdsmen's huts or an Indian village of a temporary nature in the southwestern United States and Spanish America; not applied to stone or adobe structures of the Pueblo type, but to clusters of frailer shelters like those of the Gila Pimas. The term "rancho" had a similar application. (See Ranch.) — F. S. D.

RANCHO. (See Ranch; Rancheria.)

RANCONVAL or **RANGUEVAUX, JEHAN**; architect.

A son or pupil of Henri Ranconval, *maître des œuvres* of the city of Metz (Lothringen, Germany). In 1468 he was architect of the cathedral, and about 1473 succeeded his father as *maître des œuvres* of the city of Metz. In 1477 he designed the tower of La Muette at the cathedral. In 1481 he commenced the church of S. Symphorien at Metz.

Bauchal, *Dictionnaire.*

RANDLE BAR. An iron bar built into the jamb of an open fireplace, and projecting so that pots may be suspended from it for cooking over the fire. (See Chimney Hook, under Hook.)

RANDOM COURSED WORK. Masonry laid in regular courses, which differ one from the other in height.

RANDOM RANGE WORK. (See under Range.)

RANDOM TOOLED. Wrought to a surface with irregular tooling; said of stone work.

RANDOM WORK. Same as Random Range Work.

RANGE (I.). In masonry, a row or course, as of stone. This is an attributive term, used alone or in composition, to express the amount of regularity of the face work.

Random Range Work. Masonry of rectangular stones not laid in regular courses, but broken up by the use of stones of different heights and widths fitted closely; otherwise called broken ashlar or random work.

Broken Range Work. Masonry of stones laid in courses, but not continuously, the courses being of different heights, and any one course being broken at intervals into two or so that three courses correspond with two, or the like.

RANGE (II.). An apparatus by which cooking is done, having one or more compartments in which fire is maintained, one or more ovens and arrangements for the accommodation of the various cooking utensils, pots, saucepans, etc. In their simpler forms, ranges are hardly to be distinguished from cooking stoves, except as being more permanently installed.

RANUCIUS. (See Rainerius.)

RAOUL. (See Radulphe.)

RAPHAEL. (See Santi, Raffaello.)

RATH. A primitive fort, of which many remains exist in Ireland, consisting of a rude rampart of earth or stone, or both, enclosing, generally, one or more huts.

RATHHAUS. In Germany, a building for government purposes, especially of a municipality; a term corresponding nearly with Hôtel de Ville or Mairie, City Hall, Palazzo Communale (see those terms). Since about 1880 generally Rathaus.

RATHSHAUS. A building belonging to the municipality of a city or town, to whatever purpose it may be put. Since about 1880 Ratshaus.

RATHSKELLER. Primarily, a cellar of the Rathhaus or Rathshaus; hence, as the term was taken as a name for places of popular resort, a beer house; a German restaurant or Kneipe when occupying a basement.

RAUCH, CHRISTIAN DANIEL; sculptor; b. Jan. 2, 1777; d. Dec. 5, 1857.

Rauch was a pupil of J. G. Schadow (see Schadow, J. G.), in Berlin, and of Ruhl, at Cassel. In 1811 he made the reclining statue of the Queen Louise for her monument at Charlottenburg. He made, in 1815, statues of the Generals Scharnhorst and Bülow, in Berlin, and in 1826 statues of Blücher for Breslau and Berlin. He designed also the Dürer monument at Nuremberg, about 1829. About 1833 Rauch made six statues of "Victories" for the Walhalla, near Ratisbon (see Klenze). His most important work is the monument to Frederick the Great in Berlin.

Eggers, *Christian Daniel Rauch;* Cheney, *Life of Christian Rauch.*

RAYMOND DU TEMPLE; architect; d. about 1404.

He seems to have been employed on the old Louvre (Paris) as early as 1364. At that date he built a stairway on the south side of the north wing of that building. He made extensive additions to the palace in the reign of Charles V., which included the *Tour de la*

RATHHAUS, BREMEN, NORTH GERMANY; c. 1610.

Librairie, where the king's manuscripts were stored. Within the palace he built the *Salles du roi et de la reine*. In 1370 he appears as *maître maçon* of the cathedral of Paris, probably succeeding Jehan le Bouteillier (see Bouteillier); in 1370–1385 he built the chapel of the *collège de Beauvais*. He was employed, in 1387, on the royal palace on the Ile de la Cité (Paris). In 1401 he made a visit of inspection to the cathedral of Troyes (France). Du Temple is undoubtedly the author of the château and chapel of Vincennes, near Paris, which was built for Charles V. about 1379.

Berty, *Topographie;* Christine le Pisan, *Faits et bonnes Mœurs du Sage roi Charles;* Bauchal, *Dictionnaire.*

RAYMOND, JEAN ARMAND; architect; b. April 9, 1742 (at Toulouse); d. Jan. 29, 1811.

Raymond was a pupil of Jacques François Blondel (see Blondel, J. F.) and Leroy, and in 1766 won the *Grand Prix de Rome* in architecture. In 1787–1788 he was appointed architect of the province of Languedoc. He went to Paris after the Revolution, and was associated with Chalgrin (see Chalgrin) in designing the Arc de Triomphe de l'Étoile. His design was accepted at first, but was afterward replaced by that of Chalgrin. Raymond retired from the association with Chalgrin Oct. 31, 1808. He was employed on the Louvre, the Bibliothèque Nationale, and the Opéra.

Thierry, *Arc de Triomphe de l'Étoile;* Lance, *Dictionnaire.*

RAYONNANT. Radiating; referring, in decoration, to any system dependent upon the radiation of lines from a centre. The term is specifically applied to a certain character of tracery prevalent in French Gothic from the end of the thirteenth century to the end of the fourteenth.

READING DESK. In ecclesiology, that which is used to support in a proper position the book of the Gospels or of the Epistles, or, in some forms of worship, the lectionary, the antiphonary, and other service books. (See Ambo; Lectern.)

READING PEW. In Protestant churches, a pew appropriated to the reading of a part of the service; used instead of a lectern. This term is sometimes extended to the clerk's desk below the pulpit. (See Pulpit.)

READING ROOM. A room in a club, library, hotel, or public institution, especially adapted and appropriated to reading. In a library, often wholly separate from the rooms used for the storage of books.

READING STALL. A chancel pew for the use of the priest, situated between the choir stalls and the chancel rail, and from which the lessons and notices are read.

— C. C.

REARING. The process, now almost obsolete, of erecting a building by raising the separate frames of the walls, etc., each of which has been previously framed, wholly or in part, in a horizontal position. Formerly, an occasion of ceremony. Hence, a frame building was commonly known as *reared*, to distinguish it from those of masonry. In the United States, the operation and the occasion is known as Raising.

REBATE. Same as Rabbet.

RECEPTION ROOM. An apartment especially adapted for the formal reception of guests. In a small establishment, the parlour or drawing-room serves this purpose; but in a club, large residence, or the like, these apartments would be distinct, and, frequently, on another floor.

RECITAL HALL. A hall intended for the giving of concerts with a few performers, soloists, quartettes, and the like. (See Concert Hall; Music Hall.)

RECREATION PIER. A waterside pier or wharf, part of which is set apart for open air recreation and entertainment. In the eastern United States such piers have usually two stories and a roof, the lower story, level with the street, being used for wharfage, and the upper part open to the public.

RECTORY. In England, the residence of a rector. (See Manse; Parsonage.)

RED ANTIQUE PORPHYRY. Same as Rosso Antico.

RED BRICK. (See under Brick.)

REDUCT. A small piece, or a quirk, taken out of a larger piece for the sake of conformity, symmetry, or balance, as in a room, a corner replaced by a diagonal wall to correspond with a corner fireplace or window.

REED. *A.* One of the members in reeding.

B. Same as Cable, *B.*

REEDING. A series of small, similar, convex or beaded mouldings used to decorate a plane surface, as a panel or frieze, or a curved surface, as a column; a surface ornamentation the reverse of fluting; cabling. The lower portion of the flutes in a series is frequently occupied by reeding set in the concavities. (See Cable, *B.*)

REEL AND BEAD. A bead moulding broken into short lengths, so that one elongated section or piece of the beading, from two to five diameters long, alternates with two or three spherical, nearly spherical, or angular sections. These pieces are sometimes represented as strung together by a much more slender rounded moulding.

REEPER. In the East, a piece split lengthwise from the fibrous trunk of a palm tree, used for building purposes. By extension, a wall or screen made with a succession of such sections.

REFECTORY. An eating room; specifically, a hall in a convent, monastery, or public secular institution where the meals are eaten, or one building of a group of buildings appropriated to this use.

REFERENCE LINE. On a drawing, plan, or the like, a line used to indicate the direction and limitation of any measurement or dimension which may be noted in figures.

REFERENCE POINT. In drawing, a point showing the limit of a measurement or dimension, as indicated by a crowfoot at the end of a Reference Line.

REFINEMENTS IN DESIGN. Intentional deviations from mechanical exactness in architectural design.[1] These refinements do not relate to such general disposition of the masses nor to such shaping of the details as come under the head of architectural composition; they are elaborate devices, tending to give subtile artistic variety and interest to the architecture, by delicate curvatures of apparently straight lines, by slight differences in sizes of corresponding parts otherwise presumably equal, and by a great number of variations and modulations too slight to attract attention as irregularities and yet sufficient to produce an agreeable effect.

The engineer's point of view, as it may be called, is that in a building straight lines should be mathematically straight and vertical and horizontal surfaces and lines actually vertical and horizontal; also that apparently parallel surfaces and lines should be actually parallel: in a word, it assumes mechanical or mathematical accuracy of construction as a standard of excellence. The artist, however, is influenced in his ideals by what he sees in nature. His is the primordial or natural ideal and is fundamentally dependent upon free-hand work. The very irregularities inseparable from the most perfect free-hand work become agreeable to the trained artistic sense, and just so far is the dull monotony of machine work repellent. The painter will prefer for a subject an old house with picturesque variations and delicate modulations given by time to a new villa freshly painted, which is, of course, lacking in such modulations.

It is interesting to note in Greek ornament how rarely any form is exactly repeated. The opposite leaves of an anthemion will not be duplicates, one turn of a scroll will be almost invariably a trifle larger than another, and even in the most perfectly finished scrolls, breaks in the exact continuity of curves will occasionally be noticed. The Greeks unquestionably designed their buildings as well as their decorative patterns from the artistic standpoint, and shaped them with the free

[1] The term is capable of other interpretations; but the peculiar importance of the recently observed and surprising deviations named in the definition above require special examination.

hand; hence their work was full of animation and interest, their walls, their spacing having a charm and grace which is utterly lost in the dull copies of classical porticoes made a generation ago in ignorance of the higher qualities of Greek art.

If, then, these peculiarities are hardly observed in modern architectural practice or in the instruction given to the modern architect, it is to be observed that such practice and instruction are so largely based upon drawings that, first, the student is a student not of Greek building, but of drawings of it, in which the refinements could not be given, even if the draughtsman cared for them; and, second, that the architect's career is more dependent upon the agreeable effect of his drawings upon his employer than upon the effect of his completed building. The architect to-day does not carry his free-hand design into execution, but passes it through the ordeal of mechanical draughtsmanship; whereby, as every practitioner knows, it loses immediately almost all its charm and the freshness of the original sketch, and tends to become hard and uninteresting. This tendency existed to a great extent in the time of the Renaissance; and still more generally during the Cinque Cento. The fifteenth century student of art studied and measured the remains of antiquity, and this unquestionably brought new ideas into architectural design, but he did not acquire the age-long traditions of the earlier art. Neither did he always retain the traditions of his own past, of the mediæval art in which his masters had worked. Such traditions would, with the natural decadence of art, become confused, misunderstood and overlaid with eccentricities; and it is but natural that when the rich and alluring vista of classical art opened before men's eyes, they should hasten to discard all hampering traditions, the good with the bad. In this way, while the traditions of the Greeks or the Greco-Roman builders were not to be recovered, those of the Middle Ages were of course neglected.

As to those traditions which classical antiquity cherished, it is only since exact measurement has proved the existence of a great number of refinements in classical work that the statements of Vitruvius (III., 3) concerning the horizontal curves have been appreciated and generally believed. Stuart and Revett measured the Parthenon in 1756, but they observed no refinements, not even the entasis in the columns, which, indeed, was first discovered by Cockerell in 1810. Lord Elgin did not notice the curves in the entablatures when he had the sculptures removed in 1801. Donaldson in 1829 discovered that the axes of the columns were inclined inwards from the vertical, and later measurements of the drums showed that the slope of 1 in 131 was provided for very exactly in the stone cutting. In 1837 Penne-thorne discovered the convexity of steps and entablatures; and at the same time Hofer and Schaubert reached similar conclusions inde-pendently. Penrose, in 1845, 1846, and 1847, observed a great number of refinements which, with later discoveries, form an imposing series; thus, of two neighbouring capitals the abaci are not of the same size, no two adjacent columns are of equal diameters nor any adjacent metopes equal, and no two adjacent intercolumniations are equal. The faces of the entablatures and even of small fillets are rarely vertical, the architrave, frieze, and tympanum lean back ward, the antefixes and faces of fillets, forward. The side walls have a slight batter, the door jambs and the pilasters at the angles lean forward, the main, apparently horizontal lines are all curved, and the four corners of the build-ing coincide perfectly with the free-hand habit of work. Most of them are too delicate to be visible at all on the architect's customary scale drawing, and they would probably never have been thought of if the Greeks had worked under the disadvantages of the modern methods of architectural designing.

Most of the Greek buildings, particularly temples, show analogous refinements. The temple at Pæstum has vertical curves in the cornice under the pediments, but the cornice on the side is curved outward on the horizontal plane. The Maison Carrée at Nîmes has hori-zontal curves in the cornice; and the base is also curved horizontally, but in a less degree. In Egypt also the courtyard of the temple of Medinet Habou has horizontal curves in the cornices, which curves are undoubtedly of origi-nal construction.

After the discovery of these refinements in Greek art and before their existence in later work was suspected, various attempts were made to suggest an adequate motive for their introduction. Perspective illusion, that is to say, a desire to give an apparently increased size to the building; the desire to correct that delusion of human sight which makes a hori-zontal cornice under a gable seem to sag; artistic preference; all were suggested, but a closer examination of the evidence seems to show that the third is not an accidental but the principal motive. It would seem that the theory of perspective illusion has very little to support it, and the theory of visual correction even less. If, however, we can give a satisfac-tory reason why a column should have an entasis, that same reason will suffice to account for all the other refinements as yet known to exist, at least in classical work. The only satisfactory explanation of them is that the entasis and other such refinements were intro-duced from artistic preference, from delight in the abstract beauty which results from their use.

With regard to mediæval buildings, the ex-istence of apparently deliberate irregularities in measurement was pointed out by Ruskin in *The Seven Lamps of Architecture*, published in 1849, and in *The Stones of Venice*, pub-lished in 1851; and Viollet-le-Duc in the *Dictionnaire de l'Architecture Française*, s.v. *Trait* (Vol. IX., first published 1868), deals with the same subject. There has been, however, no such comprehensive investigation as that undertaken by Professor W. H. Good-year, of which the results were published in part in the *Architectural Record* (Vols. IV., VI., VII., IX.; New York).

In such investigations great discretion must be exercised. It is evident that thrust and settlement may produce unexpected results; masonry is, moreover, plastic to a certain ex-tent, and stone may be appreciably distorted by long-continued pressure. There is, too, the element of mere carelessness and incapacity for accurate work to be considered. The case is further complicated by the fact that these re-finements are not universal in mediæval build-ings. They are usually present in direct ratio to the amount of Byzantine influence visible in the work. Where they exist it is generally in larger and richer churches rather than in the poorer ones — and this has evidently some bearing upon the question whether they are the results of carelessness or of design. Where the same irregularity occurs on both sides of a church in corresponding places, where a cornice has an even and regular curvature, and examina-tion shows that the stones were originally cut to fit the curve, where a curve in plan is regular from the base of the walls up, with no opening of joints, or where a striking irregularity of arrangement is found repeated in a large number of instances, the conclusion seems irresistible that these particular deviations were intention-ally put in. The objection that one feels to the belief that the leaning tower of Pisa, for instance, was intentionally built with so marked a slant does not hold in the case of in-conspicuous irregularities, and this idea of incon-spicuousness is part of the essential character of refinements in design. It is evident how inconspicuous they generally are when we con-sider the surprising fact that irregularities so large as some which have been pointed out should have remained unnoticed by thousands of visitors until revealed by careful measure-ment.

Mr. Goodyear cites many cases of schematic variations in spacings of nave arches, of con-verging walls or piers, of distorted plans, of cross arches set at different levels, and of slop-ing floors; the instances are to be counted by scores; and all this in Italy alone. No indi-vidual cases in mediæval work are known where all the means tending to produce false perspective are used at once. For a church interior, these means would be, first, placing the choir on a different axis with that of the nave; second, an upward slope of the floor toward the choir; third, converging walls or piers; fourth, a falling line of the capitals and of the nave arches or of the ceiling; fifth, regularly diminishing spacing and size of columns in the nave arcade. All these devices never occur in any one example; but several are combined in some cases. Thus, in the basilica of S. Pietro at Assisi, the upward-sloping floor is accompanied by the fairly regular drop of the levels of the capitals. Many other churches have also upward-sloping floors; such are S. Maria in Ara Coeli, S. Saba and S. Sabina at Rome, and the cathedral of Genoa. Convergence toward the choir is shown in S. Stefano at Venice, S. Antonio at Piacenza, and S. Giorgio in Velabro, at Rome, where the nave narrows about a foot toward the crossing. Curvature in plan is seen in the fronts of S. Mark's at Ravenna, where the nave columns are set on parallel curves six inches off the straight line; this curve being convex to the nave on the right hand and concave on the left, and the curvature extends up through the clearstory wall upon which are the original mosaics. The divergences in Pisa cathedral are most marked and striking; note the last item in bibliography. Even in the fourteenth century, and in the elaborate Gothic church of S. Ouen at Rouen, both walls of the church and both lines of piers are set on a curving plan; and the late cathedral of Orvieto has both gallery walls curved concave to the nave. Refinements in the spacing of nave arcades occasionally take the form of successive increase of dimension toward the choir.

It is probable that further research will show that, throughout the Middle Ages, and as long as traditional methods prevailed in any country, such devices were employed by masons and by roofers, working without direction from professed architects. Thus, the slater or roof tiler, who diminishes the size of his tiles or slates as he approaches the ridge, is evidently carrying out a simple old device for securing a proportion or balance between the top and the bottom; just as the scales of a fish diminish with the girth. So the stone masons who put up a tall pole in the axis of the spire they are building, and who diminished the height of this pole from day to day, building always so that the slope of the spire was directed toward the upper end of the pole, were giving the same entasis to the slope that a Greek artist gave to his shafts. (See Entasis; Grecian Architecture; Leaning Tower.)

(See Bibliography under Grecian Architecture; especially the works of Cockerell and Penrose.) Pennethorne, *Geometry and Optics of Ancient Art*,

1878; Hofer, in *Wiener Bauzeitung* for 1838; Schaubert, *Die Akropolis von Athen nach den Neuesten Ausgrabungen*, 1839; *The Architectural Record*, as mentioned in the text; Thiersch, *Optische Täuschungen auf dem Gebiete der Architectur*, in *Zeitschrift für bauwesen*, v. 23, p. 9; Boutmy, *Le Parthénon et le Génie Grec*, originally issued as *Philosophie de l'Architecture en Grèce*; Hauk, G., *Die subjective perspective und die horizontalen Curven des Dorischen Styls*, Stuttgart, 1879; Ruskin, *Seven Lamps of Architecture*, 1849; *Stones of Venice*, 1853; Goodyear, *A Lost Art*, in *Scribner's Monthly*, August, 1874; the same (*The Field of Art*), September, 1898; Smithsonian Report for 1894; J. H. Middleton, in *The Nineteenth Century*, about 1896; C. J. MacCarthy, *Some Intentional Irregularities in Italian Mediæval Architecture*, in *The Irish Builder*, Feb. 1, 1899, a Lecture before the Royal Institute of the Architects of Ireland; George Coffey, in *Archæological Journal*, December, 1900, Lecture before the Royal Archæological Institute of Great Britain and Ireland. Also, soon to be published, *Memoirs of the Museum of the Brooklyn Institute of Arts and Sciences.*
— George Louis Heins.

REFLECTION. (See Lighting.)

REFLECTOR. *A.* In acoustics, a sounding-board; a hard surface behind and above the speaker or orchestra, serving to give an immediate instead of a more distant reflection of the sound to the audience. Its service is twofold: that of strengthening the sound, and that of preventing distinct and disturbing echoes. It is sometimes flat, as illustrated by the great reflector over the orchestra in the present Boston Music Hall. When the source of sound is localized, as in a pulpit, the reflector is generally concave. However, its exact form, spherical, ellipsoidal, or parabolic, is a matter of but little importance, especially for the lower notes. The extremely high notes, being less diffracted, obey more definitely the ordinary laws of reflection. (See Music Hall; Sounding-board.) — W. C. S.

B. In lighting, a polished surface of metal or glass arranged to reflect or give any desired direction to rays of sunlight, as mirrors, or to rays of artificial light by the use of plane, parabolic, elliptical, or other concave or convex surfaces.

REFRACTION. (See Lighting.)

REFRIGERATOR. A box or chest, whether portable or fixed, a chamber or apparatus, designed to keep its contents at a low temperature, being provided with a compartment for ice (or receiving cold air currents from an ice or freezing machine) and other compartments readily accessible for the storage of perishable provisions.

REGISTER (I.). A contrivance connected with a duct, arranged either to control the inward passage of warmed air or fresh air, or to allow foul air to escape. It is usually a pierced screen, behind which slats are arranged, rotating or sliding, and controlled by a handle in front of the screen.

PLATE XIII

RENAISSANCE

Interior of S. Lorenzo in Florence; the first church built by Brunellesco after his declarations of principles with regard to the revival of classical architecture. He felt obliged to set an entablature upon the capital of each column, although the entablature itself was to carry the abutment of two arches; but he reduced the entablature in every dimension so that it is in fact a secondary or upper capital. Brunellesco's connection with the church dates from 1440.

REGISTER (II.). Same as Metre.

REGLE. In building, a groove or channel by which the movement of anything, as that of a sliding or lifting door or sash, is guided.

REGLET. In architecture, any fillet or small flat-faced projection, such as is used in a fret moulding, or to cover the joint between two boards; a batten.

REGNAULDIN, LAURENT; sculptor; d. about 1570.

A sculptor of Florentine origin, whose name figures in the accounts of the château of Fontainebleau from 1534 to 1550. In 1541 he was associated with Pierre Lescot (see Lescot) and Jean Goujon (see Goujon) in the construction of the choir screen (jubé) of the church of S. Germain l'Auxerrois in Paris. In 1564 he was employed on the monument of Henri II. at S. Denis.

Lami, *Sculpteurs de l'École française.*

REGRATING. In masonry, re-dressing or tooling the outer surface of an old stone to give it a new face — a treatment which when practised on an ancient architectural monument has destroyed many a venerable weather stain, and has ruined the historical significance and value of many an ancient moulding and bit of carving.

REGULA. In the Doric entablature, one of the series of short fillets beneath the tænia, each corresponding to a triglyph above. Each regula has a row of guttæ on the under side.

REIGNIER WORK. Delicate woodwork of the nature of Marquetry, dating from the reign of Louis XIV. and named after a cabinet-maker of the time. It is not dissimilar to Boule Work (which see).

RELEVÉ (part.). In French, taken off, made up from observation; especially in the talk of ateliers, obtained from measurements, as a drawing made from an existing building. Used substantively, the result in drawings, with or without a written treatise, of careful measurements made from an ancient building or part of a building. Hundreds of such studies are preserved by the *École des Beaux Arts;* many have been published, as in the two works called *Archives de la Commission des Monuments Historiques.*

RELIEF. That which is raised or embossed on a more or less uniform surface; raised work. A bold embossing is called high relief, *alto rilievo;* a low embossing is called low relief, or bas-relief, *basso rilievo;* a middle or half-relief is called *mezzo rilievo.* In high relief the figures or objects represented project at least one half their natural rotundity or circumference from the background, parts of the figures sometimes being undercut and solid like statues, as in pediment sculpture; in low relief the projection of the figures is but slight, no part being entirely detached; a very flat relief, such as is seen on some coins, is called *stiacciato rilievo.*

An Egyptian form of relief is counter sunk, *i.e.* it does not project above the general surface upon which it is wrought. This is known as *cavo rilievo* or *intaglio rilevato;* also hollow relief or cœlanaglyphic sculpture. The outlines are incised, and the relief is thus contained in a sunk panel no bigger than itself. Relief work executed in thin metal may be done by *repoussé* work, or by chasing; or may be copied by the electrotype process. Other relief in metal is done by casting. Relief work of the best periods did not represent its subject pictorially, and the surface upon which subject and action were depicted was recognized as the actual background, no attempt having been made at perspective illusions. But in later art, this proper condition of relief work was less uniformly respected, and as in the panels of the arch of Titus, and in those of the bronze gates of the Baptistery at Pisa, actual pictorial subjects were attempted with distant backgrounds.

RELIEVE (v.). To assist any overloaded member by any device of construction, as, in the case of a lintel, by building over it a discharging or relieving arch to transfer the burden to the piers or beams of iron or steel to receive the imposed weight, or by placing between the lintel and the supporting pier a bolster or raising piece, or by the use of a brace, etc.; or, in the case of a pier or section of wall, to spread the weight of a girder or beam bearing upon it over a larger surface by interposing a plate of metal or wood; or, in the case of a beam or girder in wood construction, bearing a wooden partition or any portion of the frame, to build in the partition or frame a truss with suspension rods or suspension timbers to transfer the weight to the piers or walls; or, in the case of the soil under a foundation pier, to ease it from the great concentration of burden by broad levellers of stone or concrete, by inverted arches connected with other piers, etc.

REMIGIUS; bishop; d. 1092.

Remigius was a monk of Fécamp in Normandy who was appointed bishop of Dorchester, England, in 1067, by William the Conqueror. After 1075 the see was removed to Lincoln, where it could be under the protection of the castle then being constructed. He began at once to build his cathedral, which was completed in 1092. Of this original Norman building almost the entire western front remains and the lower stories of the western towers.

Wild-Britton, *Cathedral Church of Lincoln.*

RENAISSANCE. *A.* A new birth; especially such a change in the state of learning, of literature, of fine art, or of all these things together, as is assumed to be a great improvement and advance, carried on according to principles formerly existing, long neglected, or supposedly lost. The term has been applied for many years almost exclusively to the advance in classical learning in Italy and the contemporaneous changes in forms of fine art during the earlier years of the fifteenth century, together with the years immediately following ; and, by extension, to the corresponding epochs in other parts of Europe, which epochs, however, are later by many years than that of the Renaissance proper in Italy. It is, however, customary, in the critical writing of our own time, to speak of the thirteenth-century Renaissance, of the eleventh-century Renaissance, etc., each of these denoting an important advance in learning, thought, and fine art in one or another nation of Europe. It is extended in like manner to non-European nations; thus, an advance in the art of painting or architecture in China or Japan is spoken of as the Renaissance of such and such a century, or of such and such a reign.

B. (Used adjectively.) Belonging to the Renaissance ; and, when the term occurs alone (as in the phrase, the Renaissance of Venice shows Byzantine influence), that absolute use of it is to be taken as meaning Renaissance Architecture (which see). This is to be discriminated from Italian Architecture in the special sense given under that term, and from the styles described under Barocco Architecture ; Henri Quatre ; Louis Quatorze ; Louis Quinze ; Louis Seize ; Louis Treize ; Pigtail and Periwig ; Post Renaissance ; Rococo ; Zopf. The nature of the distinction is described under the special terms ; but it should be kept in mind that the term "Renaissance" denotes the beginning of a change and that alone, and that the development into high perfection can be included only by forcing its meaning, while all times of degeneracy are of necessity excluded. (See, besides the terms given above, Cinque Cento ; Classicismo ; Decadence ; Decadent ; Decadenza.) — R. S.

RENAISSANCE ARCHITECTURE. *A.* That of Italy from 1420 to about 1520 (for which see Neoclassic Architecture ; Renaissance ; Italy, Architecture of).

B. That of France, of Germany, Spain, and other nations of the continent of Europe, which was based upon or suggested by the Italian Neoclassic style above alluded to, but which began generally at a much later period. In Spain, indeed, some buildings with Neoclassic feeling date back to the second half of the fifteenth century, but in France and Germany nothing of the kind appears before 1510, except, indeed, in small tombal monuments or similar pieces of decorative work which are generally thought to have been made by Italian artists. (See France, Architecture of ; Germany ; Spain.)

There can hardly be found a Renaissance style in England. (See Elizabethan ; Jacobean ; also England, Architecture of.)

The reader should note that in this, and in other articles of this Dictionary, the term "Renaissance" is used in the limited sense employed by the French critical writers for the same word, and by the Italian writers for the corresponding terms *Rinascimento* and *Risorgimento*. It is more usual for English writers to speak of Renaissance architecture as of the whole epoch from the beginning of Neoclassic

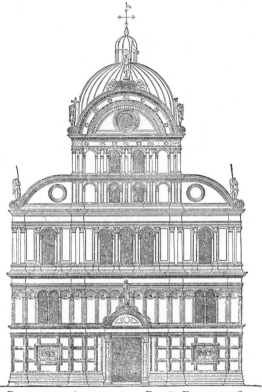

RENAISSANCE ARCHITECTURE, FIG. 1: FAÇADE OF S. ZACCARIA, VENICE; C. 1490.

work, at least to the outbreak of the French Revolution ; but the same writers would hesitate to call these centuries, taken together, the time of the Renaissance in anything except architecture. A building is often said to be of Renaissance architecture even if built in the later years of the nineteenth century, and under purely classical influences ; but such usage is to be avoided. In exact writing it is as erroneous to call the front of S. Peter's at Rome (1605 and later) or S. Paul's Cathedral in London (1675 and later) Renaissance buildings, as to call Cervantes or Newton Renaissance authors. — R. S.

RENDER. *A.* In building, to apply plaster directly to brickwork, stonework, tiles, or slate; said especially of the first coat, the application of the final coat being described by the term *to set*, and an intermediate, when used, by *to float* (which see). Two coat work is hence often called render and set, or render-set work; while three coat is known as render float and set.

B. In drawing, to give to a mechanical drawing, as an elevation, a more or less com-

RENNIE, JOHN, F.R.S., F.S.A.; engineer; b. June 7, 1761; d. Oct. 4, 1821.

He was born in Scotland and educated in Edinburgh. In 1780 he removed to London. Rennie built in London the Waterloo Bridge, begun Oct. 11, 1811, and dedicated on the second anniversary of the battle of Waterloo, June 18, 1817; whence its name. He built the Southwark Bridge, London, begun 1814,

RENAISSANCE ARCHITECTURE, FIG. 2: THE MANOR HOUSE OF THE MERCHANT ANGO, NEAR VARENGE-VILLE, SEINE INFÉRIEURE, FRANCE; C. 1530.
Early French Renaissance manifested in simple country buildings.

plete indication of shades and shadows, whether in ink, colour, or other medium.

RENDERING CEMENT. A tough and strong cement plaster, taking the place of lime and hair mortar in the plastering of walls and ceilings, not liable to crack or swell, capable of being applied directly to a surface of masonry or laths, and not needing finish coats; it has the property of drying and hardening rapidly.

and designed the new London Bridge, which was built after his death by his son Sir John Rennie (see Rennie, Sir J., and Peter of Colechurch).

Smiles, *Lives of Engineers;* Knight, *London;* Knight, *Cyclopædia of London;* Cresy, *Treatise on Bridge Building.*

RENNIE, SIR JOHN, F.R.S.; engineer; b. Aug. 30, 1794; d. Sept. 3, 1874.

RENAISSANCE ARCHITECTURE, FIG. 3: CHÂTEAU BUSSY-RABUTIN, ARCADE ON COURT; C. 1540.

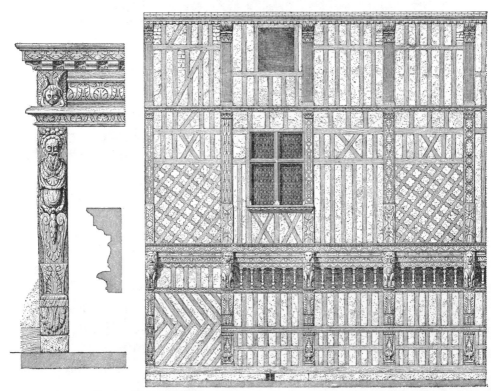

RENAISSANCE ARCHITECTURE, FIG. 4: HOUSE AT BEAUVAIS; C. 1560.
French Renaissance seen in wood-framed street architecture.

Son of John Rennie. He was associated with his father in the construction of Waterloo

RENAISSANCE ARCHITECTURE, FIG. 5: HOUSE AT ROUEN; C. 1581.

This and Fig. 6 are of the latest epoch of Renaissance; the *style Henri Quatre* succeeds it immediately.

and Southwark bridges, London, and built new London Bridge from his designs. He was knighted on the completion of London Bridge

in 1831. Rennie was employed in many important works.

Rennie, *Autobiography;* Obituary in *Building News*, Vol. XXVII., 1874.

RENWICK, JAMES; architect; b. 1818 in New York; d. 1895.

He graduated from Columbia College at the age of seventeen, and devoted himself to engineering and architecture. He was employed on the Erie Railroad and the Croton Aqueduct, and built the reservoir, Forty-second Street and Fifth Avenue, New York City. He built Grace Church in New York, and designed the Smithsonian Institute and Corcoran Gallery in Washington. His plans for a Catholic cathedral in New York City were accepted, and Aug. 15, 1858, the corner stone of that building was laid. It was dedicated May 25, 1879. The spires were added in 1887. He planned and built numerous other buildings of importance in New York.

American Architect, Vol. XLVII., p. 125.

REPOSITORIUM. A place for the disposition or storage of anything; especially, in a Roman temple, a place of votive offerings and treasure; in a church, an Ambry.

REPOUSSÉ WORK. Relief work in thin metal wrought by being beaten up with hammers on the reverse side; the art of modelling and decorating the surface of plaques or vessels of gold, silver, copper, or other thin malleable metals, by hammering the metal on the underside with special tools so as to bulge it in patterns of any desired ornamental character, forming reliefs on the upper side. In fine work the pattern thus raised is modified, dressed, and finished by placing the metal face uppermost upon a yielding bed and beating it back so as more clearly to define the subject and correct its outlines, and by chasing and engraving it.

REPTON, HUMPHREY; landscape gardener; b. May 2, 1752; d. March 24, 1818.

He was the first to adopt the title of Landscape Gardener, and published numerous works on parks and gardens. A great part of this material was republished in one volume by Loudon (see Loudon) in *Repton's Landscape Gardening and Landscape Architecture*, 1 vol. 8vo., 1840.

Biographical Notice in Loudon's *Repton*.

REREDOS. A screen or wall at the back of an altar, more or less ornamented, either forming part of the retable or standing by itself. In the Middle Ages it was sometimes called a postabula, retrotabularium, and retro-altar. The reredos was not in use to any great extent before the eleventh century, and when first introduced was a movable object; moreover, it could not have been used in connection with the high altars of cathedrals until after the change in their orientation; which did not begin much before the twelfth century, as it would have hidden the priest from the people; nevertheless, there is no reason to suppose that

ciborium. During the later Middle Ages this hanging reredos was changed with every change of the sacerdotal vestments, so as to conform to the colour requirements of the various castes. When this form gave way to something more substantial, the reredos was movable, and was only used on great solemnities and the principal festivals of the ecclesiastical year. Such is the

RENAISSANCE ARCHITECTURE, FIG. 6: HOUSE AT AMIENS, 1593; SEE FIG. 5.

it was not employed at a very much earlier period with side or secondary altars, and with the altar of an oratory. The earliest form of the reredos, outside of those in the catacombs and crypts, was probably that of the *dossal*, a hanging of silk, damask, or textile fabric; this curtain was suspended, above and back of the altar, from hooks in the wall or ceiling of the sanctuary, and in some cases from the arch rod of the

Pala d'Oro, the reredos of the high altar in S. Mark's at Venice; another, the golden reredos of Bale, now in the Cluny Museum at Paris. Toward the end of the sixteenth century the movable reredos went almost entirely out of use, fixed ones taking its place, even in conjunction with the high altars of cathedrals. These reached their finest development in Spain, many of them extending across the entire east end of the sanctuary, in some cases following the wall line of the apse, and often attaining a height of over fifty feet ; as a rule, they are a mass of the most intricate, at the same time delicate, Gothic carvings, endless in detail, with numerous figures of angels and saints, scenes from the life of

REREDOS, FIG. 1: SOMERTON, OXFORDSHIRE; c. 1400.
In this case, as in Fig. 2, the altar has been moved, but the reredos keeps its ancient place.

Christ, and symbols. The fixed reredos in Italy and France usually formed a frame or setting for a painting, a bas-relief, or a group of sculpture ; in Germany and the low countries it was usually in the form of a triptych ; in England it was largely architectural, made up of niches, tabernacle work, buttresses, crockets, and pinnacles.

Rohault de Fleury, *La Messe*, 8 vols. folio, Paris, 1888 ; Mar. Barbier de Montault, *Construction de l' Ameublement et de la Décoration des Églises*, 2 vols. 8vo, Paris, 1878 ; *Transactions of the S. Paul's Ecclesiological Society*, Vol. III., Plate IV., London, 1884 ; Articles by Caryl Coleman in the *Architectural Record*, New York, 1895.
— CARYL COLEMAN.

RESIDENCE. A place of residing or abode ; a dwelling ; a habitation. The official home of a British resident at the court of an Indian prince is called The Residency.

RESIDENZ. In German, a residence, especially that of a sovereign ; applying equally to a royal or other palace and to the city in which it is situated. Used also in combination in each of the above senses. Thus, in Munich, the royal palace or *Königliche Residenzgebäude* consists of two chief parts, *Die alte Residenz*, or old palace, and *Die Neue Residenz*, which

is called also *Der Königsbau*. So, in Braunschweig (Brunswick), in Schwerin, and in Neu Strelitz, the palace of the reigning or formerly reigning Grand Duke is called *Residenzschloss*. The city in which one of these palaces stands is called officially *Die Haupt und Residenzstadt*.

RESIDUAL SOUND. The vibration of the air in a confined space that continues after the source has ceased, until absorbed by the walls, the furniture, the drapery, and the clothes of the audience. (See also Acoustics.) — W. C. S.

RESISTANCE. The power of any substance, as building material, to resist forces, such as Compression, Cross Breaking, Shear, Tension, Torsion. (See Strength of Materials.)

RESOLUTION OF FORCES. See Parallelogram of Forces.

RESONANCE. The phenomenon that occurs when a periodic force, applied to an elastic

REREDOS, FIG. 2: S. THOMAS'S CHURCH, SALISBURY; c. 1450.

body, has a frequency agreeing with the natural rate of vibration of the body. In architectural acoustics, the increased loudness of a note whose vibration frequency agrees with one of the natural rates of vibration of the air contained in the room. (See Acoustics.) — W. C. S.

RESPOND. A pilaster, anta, or half pier taking the place of a column in a colonnade, or of an impost pier in an arcade at the point where the colonnade or arcade terminates and is connected with the wall, as in a portico, and at the east and west ends of the nave arches in a church. In Renaissance architecture, every column having relations with a wall has a respond in the wall in the form of a pilaster.

RESPONSIBILITY FOR ACCIDENTS. (See Legislation.)

RESSANT. Same as Ressaut.

RESSAUT. In French, a projection, as of a pilaster, a chimney breast, or any other feature, from a wall, or of one moulding from another. A projecting member is *en ressaut*.

In English, especially, a decorative device in Roman and neoclassic art : the breaking out of a certain length of an entablature, with two returns, with a pilaster, a column, or a pair of columns supporting the projecting part. (See cuts, S. Fantino under Neoclassic : and Scuola ; also Plate IV., Vol. I. ; Plates XXVIII. and XXIX.,Vol. II. The larger projecting pieces of entablature, as in Plate XXXII., Vol. I., and Plate XXVIII., Vol. II., are not often called ressauts.)

RESTAURANT. A place where meals are served ; an eating room or house. Specifically, in a hotel, an apartment where meals are served, at any hour to order, in contradistinction to the dining room, where guests are served with regular meals at stated hours.

RESTING PLACE. A landing ; a half- or quarter-pace in a staircase.

RESTORATION. *A.* The process of renovating a building so that it shall wholly or in part regain its original character. Such work was never undertaken until the present century. When admiration for ancient buildings became common, and their nature and character began to be studied, there was also manifested a strong desire to remove from them such additions as were of a different character from the general design of the original structure. Thus, it was natural to remove from a church of the thirteenth century an organ loft which had been put up in the eighteenth century, and pews of the nineteenth century. It was also natural to scrape off plaster in hopes of finding painting underneath ; and when such painting was found, it was natural to seek to repaint the parts which had suffered the most grievously, or had disappeared almost altogether. When works of fine art of considerable importance were found in a building of an earlier date, it was often hard to decide what should be done with them ; thus, a seventeenth century monument in a mediæval church had an individuality of its own, and a vested right to its place. On the other hand, singing galleries, altars, and similar accessories of the church itself had a less powerful hold upon the respect of the authorities, and many of them were removed, some hastily and carelessly, others with some respect, in order that they might be sold to museums.

Some of the restorations undertaken during the years following 1850 were very intelligently managed, with great respect shown to the original structure and a strong desire to retain all its existing parts unimpaired. Other such undertakings were reckless and destructive, and consisted in an almost complete rebuilding of the original structure according to what the architect in charge, or his bishop, or the municipality might think was the way in which such a building ought to have been carried out. In either case, however, this very serious difficulty has resulted, namely, that there is now no longer a ready means of distinguishing between the genuine work and its imitation. The most aggravated instance of this is in the west fronts of English cathedrals where statues have been put up by the scores in niches which had been standing empty for many years. The new statue being put in place and being found to differ somewhat from the ancient ones, there has been too strong a disposition to scrape and clean the older ones to match the new. It is therefore of the greatest importance that the documents should be studied and the memories of architects and artisans consulted before it is too late, and that a complete account of the restorations carried out be compiled and made accessible to all students of the monuments in question. If one goes to Wells Cathedral as a student, he should have a ready means of ascertaining just which statues, which pew heads, which details of the sculptured exterior and interior, are wholly modern, which have been scraped and cleaned, and which remain intact.

The restorations of the great French cathedrals have been on the whole judicious, because the respect felt in France, by every local community for its own monuments, is so great that the newly cut stones which are inserted to make good decaying or broken stones of the old fabric, are most carefully copied from the originals ; and such work as cannot be copied, such as the elaborate sculpture of the porches, is preserved in its existing state with pious care. One can study the cathedral of Chartres or Reims without much fear that those parts which no modern hand could touch without destroying have been renovated. There are, however, remarkable exceptions. One which may be named is the rebuilding of the important and exquisite church of S. Front at Périgueux. This building has been entirely rebuilt, and it is not unfair to say that the attempt has been, not to preserve the old church, but to build a new one according to the architect's notions of a Romanesque church of the date of S. Front. This will be found very completely and carefully described in the book entitled *A Visit to the Domed Churches of Charente*, published by the London Architectural Association after 1875 ; see the preliminary chapter, and also the description of the plates of that church. The Romanesque church at Auteuil, in Paris, has been restored in a similar radical way, that is to say, rebuilt from its basement. The cathedral at Valence, on the Rhône, has been rebuilt in a similar fashion. The famous strong castle of Pierrefonds was restored by Viollet-le-Duc at the expense, it is understood, of the Emperor Napoleon III., and here, while the repair of the walls and the fortifications, roofs, and the like can be justified in every important part, the artist has allowed himself almost a free hand in the decorative sculptures and paintings. The fortress is trustworthy as an example for the modern student of military architecture, but the decorated halls are mere *pastiches*.

As regards the restoration of buildings in towns, it is to be observed that those who reside in the place have a feeling toward one of their local monuments somewhat different from that held by visitors. Thus, to the Venetian who walks every afternoon on the Place of S. Mark and takes coffee under the arcades, it seems absurd that his familiar Ducal Palace, Church of S. Mark, Procuratie Vecchie, and the rest should be left shabby and defaced by time merely to please travellers. To him it seems important that the church should be firm, and square-set, and neat-looking; and that the palace should seem elegant, whole, and free from flaws and defacements. He cannot understand that it is of vital importance to the whole world of students that every capital that can possibly be left in the arcades should remain unaltered from that which time and accident has left it. This love of local monuments is not to be ignored merely because of the fact that sometimes fine old buildings are destroyed to make room for a wide street; this also is a part of the local love of neatness, elegance, spaciousness, and the appearance of high cost and free expenditure.

There is, however, but one true doctrine, and that is that buildings should be held together by iron ties, if necessary; that they should be stayed up, fastened together, held in place; that it should be clearly understood that no modern work whatever shall be put upon them in the way of rebuilding, carving, painting, or the like. It is the most important thing that a rich man could do for the study of art that he should purchase fine old buildings all over the world and see to it that they are left unaltered by modern restorers.

The influence of the French *Commission des Monuments Historiques* (see Historical Monuments) has been extremely beneficial. A society was founded in England under the influence of the late William Morris, who was its first honorary secretary, and this, entitled the Society for the Protection of Ancient Buildings, has also been of value. (See Architect; Architect in England; France; Italy.) The student is also referred to the books on William Morris by Aymer Vallance; *The Art of William Morris,* folio, and *William Morris; His Art, His Writings, and His Public Life;* octavo.

B. The process of making drawings or models, or both, showing how, in the opinion of the designers, a now ruined building might probably have appeared when perfect; also the drawings, etc., so made. Many such restorations have been published; and it is to be noted that all our modern ideas of Greek and Roman buildings are the results of just such drawings and models, for none of them is so nearly intact as to convey any just architectural impression to the beholder. (Compare Relevé.)
— R. S.

RESURRECTION GATE. A Lich Gate; so called from the frequent occurrence of representations of the Resurrection carved or painted upon such structures.

RETABLE. A decorative screen set up above and behind an altar, generally forming an architectural frame to a picture, bas-relief, or mosaic, which are included in the term. It is sometimes a movable feature resting on the back of the altar, and is often made of precious materials. The retable sometimes includes a shelf or shelves. (See Altar Ledge; Reredos; Super-Altar, under Altar.)

RETAINING WALL. A wall erected at a place where a difference of level occurs in the soil and intended to retain the higher soil and prevent it from sliding.

Benjamin Baker, C. E., *The Lateral Pressure of Earthwork;* Professor William Cain, C. E., *Practical Designing of Retaining Walls.*

RETICULATE. Crossed with a network of lines; decorated on a basis of regularly intersecting lines, as on a surface ornamented with an interlacing of fillets or reglets like network, presenting a meshed appearance. This species of ornamentation is common in the Byzantine and Romanesque styles.

RETREAT. A falling back, retirement, or withdrawal, as of one surface behind another in a panel, or of a part of a building, or of a whole building, behind or to the rear of another.

RETROCHOIR. A projection behind the choir or east end of a church, forming a separate division or chapel; if there is a lady chapel, it is interposed between the lady chapel and the choir.

RETURN. A surface turned back from a principal surface, as the side of a pilaster, the jamb of a window or door opening. A return forming an oblique angle is called a splayed return. (See Splay.)

RETURNED MOULDING. A moulding continued in a different direction from its main direction, as in mediæval architecture, a drip, hood, or label moulding over an arch, when, at the springing point on either side, it turns and assumes a horizontal direction, either for a short distance or continuously, as a string course. (See Dripstone, and the figures under that term.)

REVEAL. That portion of the jamb of an opening or recess which is visible from the face of the wall back to the frame or other structure which may be placed between the jambs. Thus, the windows of an ordinary brick building have usually reveals of some four inches; that being the width of each brick jamb visible outside of the window frames.

RIB, FIG. 1: EARLY RIBBED VAULTING WITH ONLY THE ESSENTIAL RIBS, VIZ., DIAGONAL RIBS (OGIVES) MEETING AT THE CENTRAL BOSS; TRANSVERSE RIBS SEPARATING THE VAULTING SQUARES; WALL RIBS (FORMERETS) ON RIGHT AND LEFT; THE COMPARTMENT IN THE DISTANCE IS, IN PART, IN SEXPARTITE VAULTING; SALISBURY CATHEDRAL.

REVERBERATION. The process of reflection of sound by the walls whereby it is returned into the room, as distinguished from transmission or absorption. This results in a prolongation of the sound, or, if the source continues to act, in cumulative intensity. It is to be carefully distinguished from resonance. (See Acoustics.) — W. C. S.

REVESTRY. Same as Vestry; the old form.

REVETMENT. In masonry, a facing intended to afford a better or more fitting surface, as the facing of a rubble or concrete wall with thin slabs of marble according to the Roman manner, or, in interior work, with marble, stone, wainscoting, or any other material in the service of decoration.

REVETT, NICHOLAS; architect; b. about 1721; d. June 3, 1804.

He visited Rome in 1742 and met James Stuart (see Stuart, J.), with whom he went to

Athens in 1750. He was associated with Stuart in the preparation of the *Antiquities of Athens*, 4 vols. folio, 1762–1816. He also prepared the drawings of Parts I. and II. of the *Antiquities of Ionia* (1769–1797, folio) published by the Society of Dilettanti. He designed and decorated various residences in England.

Redgrave, *Dictionary of Artists.*

REYNAUD (REGNAULT) DE CORMONT. (See Cormont, Reynaud de.)

REYNAUD, FRANÇOIS LÉONCE; engineer and architect; b. Nov. 1, 1803, at Lyons; d. Feb. 14, 1880, at Paris.

He went to Paris in 1818, was a pupil at the *École polytechnique* and of Durand (see Durand). In 1824 he entered the *École des Beaux Arts* as a pupil of Huyot (see Huyot). He studied in Italy and in 1835 became an engineer in the *Service des Ponts et Chaussées.* In 1842 he was appointed professor of architecture at the *École des Ponts et Chaussées.* March 7, 1883 he was associated with Vaudoyer and Viollet-le-Duc as *inspecteur général des édifices diocésains.* He became *inspecteur général des ponts et chaussées* in 1867, and in 1869 director of the *École des Ponts et Chaussées.* He was one of the founders of the *Société centrale des architectes.* He is best known by his *Traité d'Architecture* (text 2 vol. 4to, plates 2 vol. fol., 1850–1858).

Charvet, *Architectes Lyonnais.*

REZ-DE-CHAUSSÉE. In French buildings, the story on a level with the ground (see Étage and sub-titles).

RHODONITE. A silicate of manganese of a pink or red colour, frequently streaked and spotted. Hard and tough, and with a close texture. Little used in America, but a favourite material with the Russians. Found in commercial quantities only in the Urals.   — G. P. M.

RHOEKOS. (See Theodoros.)

RIALTO, BRIDGE OF THE (Ponte di Rialto). The ancient bridge which connects the Rialto with the other large island of Venice, Isola di San Marco. (See Bridge.)

RIB. A moulding on an arched or flat ceiling; but specifically and more properly, in mediæval vaulting, an arch, generally moulded, forming part of the skeleton upon which rest the intermediate concave surfaces which constitute the shell or closure of the vault. The crowning intersections of these arches or ribs are adorned with sculptured bosses. In quadripartite vaulting the main diagonal ribs are called by that name and also *arcs ogives* (see Ogive); each transverse rib is called *arc*

PLATE XIV

RIALTO BRIDGE

At Venice; connecting the two large islands, that of San Marco on the right and that of the Rialto on the left. This was the only bridge across the Canalazzo previous to the nineteenth century. There is a double row of shops, and a sidewalk between each of these and the outer parapet of the bridge, and a broader walk between. The building with arches on the left is the Palazzo dei Camerlenghi; that on the right with a parapet of separate battlement-like pieces is the Fondaco dei Tedeschi. It was built toward the close of the eighteenth century and replaced a bridge of wood.

doubleau, and each longitudinal rib, *arc for-meret*. To this fundamental system of ribs supplementary and subordinate ribs were afterward added, dividing the concave of the ceiling into many panels, but in general these had no function in the construction. (See Lierne Rib.)

Diagonal Rib. In a ribbed vault, one of the two intersecting ribs extending from one corner of the compartment to that diagonally opposite. In Gothic vaulting, the diagonal ribs were generally semicircles; so that the wall ribs (*formerets*) and cross ribs (*arcs doubleaux*) were naturally pointed to avoid the cupola-like form which would result from too great a difference in their respective heights. When the diagonal ribs were thus pointed, the cross ribs and wall ribs were naturally given the form of a more acute pointed arch. (See Ogive.)

Laminated Rib. Same as Laminated Arch (which see under Arch).

Lierne Rib. (See under L.)

Ridge Rib. A longitudinal rib sometimes used at the apex of mediæval vaulting.

Wall Rib. That one of the two formerets which is closely attached to the exterior wall of

RIB, FIG. 2: VAULTING OF 1260 WITH MANY RIBS USED FOR ORNAMENT ALONE, AS THOSE AT THE RIDGE OF THE VAULT, AND ALL THE OTHERS NOT FOUND IN FIG. 1; WESTMINSTER ABBEY.

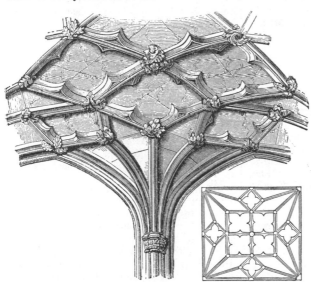

RIB, FIG. 3: ROOF WITH RIBS LARGELY NON-CONSTRUCTIONAL; ENGLISH PERPENDICULAR STYLE; LIERNE VAULT, S. MARY REDCLIFFE, BRISTOL; A.D., 1413.

the vaulting square in question; therefore, parallel with and opposite the other formeret which is a part of the nave arch or the open arch leading into some other vaulted compartment.

RIBAND. Same as Ribbon.

RIBBET. Same as Rebate: Rabbet.

RIBBING. Decorating with ribs; the results of such treatment, especially as shown in the later vaulting of the Middle Ages, when non-constructive ribs were multiplied for the sake of decorative effect, and in the arabesques formed by intersecting ribs in the stucco ceilings of the Tudor period in England.

RIBBON. *A.* A narrow belt of decoration in any material or in colour alone.

B. In carpentry, a thin strip of bent wood, such as is used in shaping convex or concave surfaces. In ship carpentry, where it is more frequently used, it is called rib band.

C. A thin grooved strip of lead used in glazing stained glass windows, or in setting the quarrels or panes in leaded sashes. (See Window, Part II.)

D. In the balloon frame construction of the United States, a light girt or similar piece secured to the faces of the studs, and forming a continuous tie around the building and supporting the ends of the beams.

RICAMATORI, GIOVANNI DE' (**Giovanni da Udine**); painter and decorator; b. 1487; d. 1564.

According to Vasari, he studied with Giorgione in Venice about 1508. He was especially successful in decorative painting and stucco work, and was the chief assistant of Raphael at the Loggie of the Vatican and in painting accessories in the Loggia of the Farnesina, Rome. The decoration of the Villa Madama, Rome, is ascribed to him.

Crowe and Cavalcaselle, *Raphael;* Franceschini, *Elogio di Giovanni da Udine;* Maniago, *Storia delle belle arti friulane;* Vasari, Milanesi ed.

RICCHINI (RICCHINIO) FRANCESCO MARIA ; architect.

From 1605 to 1638 he was supervising architect of the cathedral of Milan. He was also employed at the Ospedale Maggiore where he built the portal on the Via Ospedale. His greatest work is the Palazzo di Brera, the court of which is one of the finest in Italy. He built also the Palazzo della Canonica and many other buildings in Milan.

Gurlitt, *Geschichte des Barockstiles in Italien;* Ebe, *Spät-Renaissance;* Boito, *Duomo di Milano.*

RICCIARELLI, DANIELLO DE' (DANIELO DA VOLTERRA) ; painter and sculptor ; b. 1509 ; d. 1566.

Ricciarelli was influenced by Sodoma, Peruzzi (see Peruzzi), Perino del Vaga (see Buonaccorsi), and Michelangelo (see Buonarroti). He was a laborious painter and left many pictures in the Roman churches. The most important is the Descent from the Cross in the church of S. Trinità del Monte, supposed to have been designed by Michelangelo. He assisted Michelangelo in much of his work.

Müntz, *Renaissance.*

RICCIO, ANDREA. (See Briosco, Andrea.)
RICCIO, ANTONIO. (See Rizzo, Antonio.)
RICHARD DE GAINSBOROUGH. (See Gainsborough, Richard de.)

RICHARDSON, CHARLES JAMES; architect.

A pupil of Sir John Soane (see Soane, Sir J.). He published numerous architectural works, the most important of which are : *Architectural Remains of Elizabeth and James I.* (1836, 1 vol. folio), and *Studies from Old English Mansions* (4 vols. folio 1841–1848).

Redgrave, *Dictionary of Artists.*

RICHARDSON, HENRY HOBSON; architect ; b. Sept. 29, 1838 ; d. April 27, 1886.

Richardson was born in Louisiana. In 1860 he entered the *École des Beaux Arts* under the direction of L. J. André. The outbreak of the Civil War having destroyed the resources of his family, he secured through André a position as draughtsman in a government office in Paris. Returning to America in October, 1865, his first commission was for a Unitarian church in Springfield, Massachusetts. This was followed by the construction of the offices of the Boston and Albany

railroad in Springfield and a church in Medford, Massachusetts. October 1, 1867, he formed a partnership with Charles Gambrill. In July, 1870, Richardson's design for the Brattle Street Church in Commonwealth Avenue, Boston, was successful. This Romanesque church is noted for its fine tower, bearing a frieze sculptured with colossal figures. The best known of his works is Trinity Church in Boston, begun in 1872 and finished in 1877. In 1876 he was associated with Leopold Eidlitz and Frederick Law Olmstead in the completion of the State Capitol in Albany. Richardson built the Allegheny Court House (which see), Sever Hall in Harvard University, and numerous public and business buildings. In most of his works he followed a style of his own based on the Romanesque architecture of southern France.

Van Rensselaer, *Henry Hobson Richardson and His Works.*

RICHIER, GEOFFROY; architect.

February 17, 1451, Richier succeeded Jehan Roussel as *maître de l'œuvre* of the cathedral of Rouen. About 1458 he began the archbishop's palace at Rouen.

Deville, *Revue des architectes de la Ville de Rouen.*

RICHIER, GÉRARD; architect and sculptor.

A son of Ligier Richier (see Richier, L.). In 1511 he made the fireplace of the Salle des Grands Jours at Saint Mihiel (Meuse), France. In 1580 he went to Nancy, and in 1581 made the tomb of Perrin Lecuver in that city.

L'Abbé Souhaut, *Les Richiers.*

RICHIER, JEAN ; architect and sculptor.

Probably a son of Gérard Richier (see Richier, G.). In 1609 he was associated with Michel Pierre in constructing the sepulchral chapel of the dukes of Lorraine for the church of the Cordeliers at Nancy. In 1614 he assisted in the fortification of that city.

L'Abbé Souhaut, *Les Richiers.*

RICHIER, LIGIER ; architect and sculptor ; b. probably in 1506 at Saint Mihiel (Meuse), France ; d. April 11, 1567, at Geneva, Switzerland.

His first work is the Nativity of Haton-Châtel (1523). In 1532 he executed for the church of S. Étienne at Saint Mihiel the famous group of the Sepulchre, his most important work. In 1544 he made the monument of the Prince of Orange for the cathedral of Bar-le-Duc (Meuse), France, and in 1545 that of René de Châlon for the church of S. Pierre in that city. In 1547 he made the monument of the duchess of Philippe de Gueldre for the Cordeliers at Nancy. In 1549 he made a design for the chapel of the Collegiate church of S. Maxe at Bar-le-Duc, and in 1555 decorated this chapel with sculpture.

Jos de Lisle, *Abbaye de Saint Mihiel;* Gonse,

Sculpture française; Bauchal, *Dictionnaire;* Tremblaye, *Solesmes.*

RICKMAN, THOMAS, F.S.A. ; architect ; b. June 8, 1776 ; d. January, 1841.

In 1813 he was elected professor of architecture in the Liverpool Academy. His best-known work, *An Attempt to discriminate the Styles of English Architecture,* was first printed separately in 1817. He built a very large number of churches in England.

Redgrave, *Dictionary of Artists.*

RIDGE. The line of meeting of two opposite roof slopes, especially the nearly horizontal edge which is seen against the sky and is often decorated by a Ridge Ornament or Cresting.

RIDGE AND FURROW TILING. (See Pan Tile, under Tile.)

RIDGE ORNAMENT. A cresting following the ridge of a roof often elaborately moulded or having floral ornamentation of pottery or of lead over an iron skeleton.

RIDGE PIECE ; — POLE. The board or plank at the apex of a roof against the sides of which the upper ends of the rafters abut ; sometimes called ridgeplate. Sometimes a second plank, called a false ridgepole, is secured above the ridgepole so as to form a cresting or a foundation for metal cresting.

RIDGE SPIKE. A finial at the end of a ridge crest, made of the same material as the crest (compare hip knob).

RIDING HOUSE. A building specially fitted up for riding horseback indoors. The essential part of the structure is the great hall which will generally be high in the middle because of the construction of the roof, and may be ventilated and also lighted in part from the centre of the roof. The floor is usually covered with some soft material easy for the horses' feet, and preventing noise. There will also be arrangements for bars for practice in leaping, and places reserved for spectators usually in the form of raised galleries. Some of these halls are very large ; one at Moscow is said to be 550 feet long, and one at Darmstadt has a roof given as 319 feet long by 157 feet broad in a single span. These buildings seem, however, to be connected with military training.

RIGGENBOCH, CHRISTOPH ; architect ; b. 1810 at Basel ; d. 1863.

He was a pupil of Moller (see Moller) at Darmstadt and studied also in Berlin and Munich. He superintended the restoration of the minster at Basel, Switzerland, and built the Elizabeth Kirche in that city.

Seubert, *Künstler-lexikon.*

RIGHT LINE PEN. (See under Pen.)

RIGHT OF WAY. (See Law ; Legislation.)

RILE, GÉRARD VON. (See Gérard von Rile.)

RILIEVO. (See Relief.)

RINASCIMENTO. In Italian, a rebirth ; especially in the sense of Renaissance, the Italian movement of the fifteenth century. The term is used for the rebirth of literature, scientific investigation, and fine art, while Risorgimento (which see) is often the term for the epoch historically considered.

RINGHIERA. (Connected with Italian *Arringa,* a public address.) In Italian art, any place from which it was customary to speak in public ; especially the balcony projecting from the principal front of the Palazzo Publico, Palazzo Communale, Broletto, and the like.

RING STONE. One of the stones of an arch which show on the face of the wall, or the end of the arch ; one of the voussoirs of the face forming the archivolt.   — W. R. H.

RINK. A building enclosing a large unobstructed area and used for some form of skating.

The skating floor for ice skating should be at least 74 feet x 170 feet, insulated with at least 8 inches of cork and then made water tight either by planking covered with tarred felt or asphalt mastic ; it should be made tight along the sides so as to have a maximum depth at the drainage points of 12 inches and at the sides of 7 inches. The top inch should be protected against cutting by means of a wooden strip. The refrigerating pipes should be carried by means of strips placed parallel with the short axis of the floor with semicircular depressions in them for the support of the pipes. There should be at least one drainage point from which connection should be made to a sewer controlled by means of a valve. The entire skating surface should be 4 feet below the level of the spectators' platform, this in conjunction with a 2-foot railing affords a depression in which the cold air lies and makes it easy to maintain the ice hard and without fog, and to maintain as well an agreeable temperature for the spectators.

The artificial ice is made by flooding the floor and freezing by either the compression or the absorption system, using either direct ammonia expansion or cold brine circulation, the latter being very much safer and very much less troublesome.

The light must be very brilliant, a skating floor such as is described requiring at least five hundred 16 c.p. lamps.

With a high roof and windows at the sides no especial provision need be made for ventilation. If the conditions are different, then a fan should be provided, discharging cold air into the skating-floor pit near the ice surface through ducts under the spectators' gallery, at four points, at least.

The rink for roller skating is arranged in the same way except that the skating floor should be made of sugar maple in 2-inch strips, well nailed and planed smooth. — GEORGE HILL.

RIO. A stream or canal; the term is an abbreviation of the Italian *Rivo* and is in use especially in the city of Venice, where it is applied to all the smaller water streets, that is to say, to all except the Canalazzo and Canareggio.

RIOTERRÀ. (Apparently a Venetian abbreviation of *Rivo* (*rio*) *terrazzato*.) A street made by the filling up of a canal; especially in Venice, where, during the last forty years, a number of old canals have been turned into streets which are generally wider and straighter than the old *calli*.

RIPLEY, THOMAS; b. about 1685; d. 1758.

In 1705 he obtained the freedom of the Carpenters' Company. Favoured by Sir Horace Walpole, he became chief carpenter of the king, 1721, a place previously held by Grinling Gibbons. He built Houghton Hall, Norfolkshire, from the designs of Colin Campbell, and from 1724 to 1730 Wolterton House in the same shire. At about the same time he built the Admiralty, in London, except the façade.

Stephen-Lee, *Dictionary of National Biography*.

RIP RAP. Broken stone more irregular in shape and size than Rubble; used in walls and foundations.

RIP RAP WALL. A stone wall without regularity of structure; as used in deep water.

RISE. *A.* The vertical distance between two consecutive treads in a stair; sometimes, the entire height of a flight of stairs from landing to landing. (See Riser.)

B. The vertical height of the curved part of an arch, that is the distance measured vertically, as in an elevation, from the springing line to the highest point of the curved intrados.

RISER. *A.* The upright of one step, whether the step be in one piece as a block of stone, or built up. In the former case, the riser is the surface alone (compare Jamb; Soffit). In the latter case, the riser is the board, plate of cast iron, or similar thin piece which is set upright between two treads.

B. By extension, the same as Rise. A stair in which the treads are separate planks, slabs of slate, plates of iron, or the like, is sometimes built without risers. (See Open Riser below.) In this case, an incorrect extension of the term is used, and such a stair is said to have open risers.

Open Riser. The space between two adjoining treads in a stair when such space is not filled with a solid riser. (See Riser.)

RISING JOINT HINGE. (See Rising Hinge, under Hinge.)

RISING LINE. In plumbing and gas fitting, the main which carries water or gas vertically or nearly so; the term often including the minor pipes and branches attached.

RISORGIMENTO. (See Rinascimento.)

RIVA. A piece of ground along the edge of the water; a quay or terraced road at the water's edge. The word is used for one of the larger water-side streets of Venice, especially the *Riva degli Schiavoni*.

RIVET. A short bolt or pin of wrought iron, copper, or other malleable metal, formed with a head, so that when inserted in a hole passing through two pieces of metal, the point or end projecting on the other side having been hammered flat, a second head is formed and the junction made thus permanent and effectual. Except when the rivets are small, this hammering out of a second or inner head is done while the rivet is hot, so that by shrinking in the process of cooling it may bind more closely the pieces which it is intended to unite. In this closer and more effectual bond exists the principal advantage of rivets over bolts and nuts.

RIVETTING. The process of uniting the various parts of any structural member or framework of stone or iron by the use of hot or cold rivets, whether driven and headed by machines or by hand. (See Iron Construction.)

RIVOLTATURA. (See Mosaic.)

RIZZO (RICCIO), ANTONIO DI GIOVANNI. (The Antonio Bregno of F. Sansovino); sculptor and architect; d. about 1498.

Antonio Rizzo should not be confounded with Andrea Briosco (see Briosco, Andrea) called Riccio. Antonio Bregno of Como, sculptor of the monument of the Doge Francesco Foscari in the church of S. Maria dei Frari, in Venice, is probably also a different person. The only work which bears Rizzo's signature is the statue of Eve on the Arco Foscari, at the Doge's Palace, Venice, but the Adam and other statues on the Arco are doubtless by him. Sansovino (op. cit.) ascribes to him the monument of the Doge Niccolò Tron in the Frari. Rizzo's chief work was the reconstruction of that portion of the court of the Doge's palace which was destroyed by fire Sept. 14, 1483. He held the office of *Soprastante* of this work until 1498. At the Doge's Palace, Rizzo built the northern half of the eastern wing (on the Riva), including the façade upon the court and that upon the canal. The Giants' Stair (which see, under Stair) was also built by him.

Bernascone, *La vita e le opere di Antonio Rizzo;* Paoletti, *Rinascimento;* Müntz, *Renaissance;* Perkins, *Italian Sculptors;* Cicognara, *Fabbriche di Venezia;* Meyer, *Das Venezianische Grabdenkmal;* Zanotto, *Palazzo Ducale;* Sansovino, *Venetia.*

ROBBIA, ANDREA DELLA; sculptor; b. Oct. 28, 1435; d. Aug. 4, 1525.

A nephew of Luca della Robbia (see Robbia, Luca della), and assisted him in developing the art of colouring terra cotta with stanniferous glazes. The scheme of colour employed by Luca was always simple, and Andrea usually confined himself to blue and white for the figures, reserving polychromatic decoration for the accessories. He is less severe and elevated in style than Luca. The only work which can with certainty be ascribed to Andrea is the retable of the church of S. Maria delle Grazie at Arezzo (see Benedetto da Maiano). The works of the members of the family can hardly be distinguished (see Robbia Work).

(For bibliography, see Robbia, Luca della.)

ROBBIA, GIOVANNI DELLA; sculptor; b. May 8, 1469; d. about 1529.

One of the seven sons of Andrea della Robbia (see Robbia, A. della), of whom five appear to have assisted him in the development of the family specialty of colouring terra cotta with stanniferous glazes. (See Robbia, Luca della; Robbia Work.)

(For bibliography, see Robbia, Luca della.)

ROBBIA, GIROLAMO (JÉRÔME) DELLA; sculptor and architect; d. Aug. 4, 1566.

Girolamo was the youngest son of Andrea della Robbia (see Robbia, Andrea della). Nothing is known of him until he went to France, probably between 1525 and 1528. In a document dated Feb. 5, 1529, *Jerosme de Robia, tailleur d' ymages et esmailleur* is mentioned as associated with Pierre Gadier, *Maistre Maçon* in the construction of the Château du Bois de Boulogne (known as the Château de Madrid, and destroyed in the eighteenth century). He appears in the records of the building until 1553, and he was either its architect or the designer of the terra-cotta decoration, which was destroyed with the building.

Marquis de Laborde, *Le Château du Bois de Boulogne;* Marquis de Laborde, *La Renaissance des Arts;* Palustre, *La Renaissance en France;* Jacques Androuet du Cerceau, *Les plus excellents bastiments de France.*

ROBBIA, LUCA DELLA; sculptor; b. 1399 or 1400; d. Feb. 20, 1482.

The principal member of a family of sculptors in Florence in the fifteenth century. He was apprenticed to a goldsmith. The best known of his works and the earliest which can be dated with certainty is the marble cantoria which was formerly in the cathedral of Florence and is now in the Museo Nazionale (Bargello). It was begun in 1430 and finished about 1440. The companion piece is by Donatello (see Donatello). Between 1437 and 1440 Luca made five bas-reliefs, completing the series begun by Giotto (see Giotto) in the first story of the Campanile, Florence. The bronze doors of the sacristy of the cathedral of Florence were begun by Luca with the assistance of Michelozzi (see Michelozzi) in 1447, but not placed until 1474. In 1455 he began the marble monument of the bishop Bonozzo Federighi in the church of S. Francesco di Paolo near Florence (finished 1451).

To Luca is due the application of the art of glazed terra cotta to figure sculpture and to elaborate architectural decoration. He was assisted and succeeded by various members of his family (see Robbia Work). Luca's earliest work in Robbia ware, of which the date is known, appears to be the bas-relief of the *Resurrection* over the door of the sacristy of the cathedral of Florence (1443). The *Ascension* also in the cathedral was made between 1446 and 1450. A series of medallions on the façades of Or S. Michele (Florence) are among his earlier works. The works of Luca are more severe in style and more simple in colour than those of his successors.

Marcel Reymond, *Les della Robbia;* Cavallucci Molinier, *Les della Robbia;* Stegmann, *Die Bildhauerfamilie della Robbia;* Marquand, *Hunting della Robbias in Italy;* Vasari, Milanesi ed.

ROBBIA WORK. Glazed terra-cotta work of the Della Robbia family.

This decorative material, though known to the ancient Egyptians, Babylonians, Assyrians, and Persians, seems to have been introduced into Europe by the Saracens and applied by them only to the minor arts. It assumed monumental importance in the hands of Luca della Robbia, a Florentine sculptor of unusual skill and refinement. Work in this material became the exclusive occupation of his nephew Andrea, five of whose sons were sculptors. These sons spread their productions in various quarters of Italy. Giovanni sent examples of his art into many small towns of Tuscany, Fra Ambrogio to the region about Siena, Fra Mattia to Umbria and the Marches, Luca the younger to Rome, and Girolamo to France. Giovanni was succeeded by Benedetto Buglioni and by Santi Buglioni (1494–1576), who continued the practice of the art until late in the sixteenth century. A south Italian sculptor, Maestro Jacopo da Benevento, is represented by a signed altarpiece of glazed terra cotta, and there are many monuments of the fifteenth and sixteenth centuries made of this material which cannot be assigned to any member of the Robbia School. Some care is sometimes required to distinguish this class of Renaissance sculptures from the similar works and copies made by Bastianini, Novelli, and Graziani in the early part of this century or by the Cantigalli or Ginori companies of the present day.

The glazes used by the different members of the Robbia School varied in quality. Luca's glazes were hard and brilliant, while those of his successors proved to be in many cases less durable. Luca's handling of coloured glazes was masterly, and the results harmonious and refined. Andrea's attempts at polychromy were less successful and Giovanni's frequently atrocious.

The Robbia family applied glazed terra cotta to many kinds of architectural decoration.

Pavements were made by the elder Luca for the palace of Piero di Cosimo dei Medici, by Andrea for the chapel of S. Lorenzo in the Collegiata at Empoli and by the younger Luca, after designs by Raphael, for the *loggie* of the Vatican. The earliest Robbia pavements showed some trace of Saracen influence, which, however, was soon replaced by more distinctively Italian designs. Glazed terra-cotta ceilings were made by Luca for the Medici palace, for the rotunda of the porch of the Pazzi chapel, and by Andrea for the porch of the cathedral at Pistoia. Some of these may be viewed as substitutes for the marble-coffered ceilings of classic architecture, others for the mosaic-covered vaults of Byzantine type, but the designs have in addition the charm which comes from the naturalism of the early Renaissance. Medallions, not infrequently set in frames representing fruit and flowers, decorated the centre and corners of vaults, as in the Portogallo chapel at San Miniato, or the spandrils of the arches of an arcade as in the porches of the Innocenti hospital in Florence or the Ceppo hospital in Pistoia, or were arranged in horizontal lines, as in the Pazzi chapel. Medallions, rectangles, and other simple forms were frequently used for heraldic emblems.

The minor towns of Tuscany contain on the walls of their public buildings hundreds of coats-of-arms in glazed terra cotta by the Robbia School. Continuous friezes were not commonly made of this material. Luca attempted them on a small scale on two baldachinos at Impruneta, and Andrea made a terra-cotta frieze around the interior of the dome of S. Maria delle Carceri at Prato. It was reserved for the pupils of Giovanni to make the very striking frieze of the Ceppo hospital. Not a few lunettes were made by the Robbias, as, for example, the pointed-arched lunettes at the Florence cathedral by Luca, the round-arched lunette over the entrance of the cathedral at Prato by Andrea, and the polychromatic lunette by Giovanni, recently acquired by the Brooklyn Institute.

Many magnificent altarpieces in glazed terra-cotta may be credited to this school. Their pilasters and capitals and friezes and mouldings are charming examples of Renaissance architectural design. It would be difficult to find a more exquisite monument of its kind than Luca's tabernacle, which serves as an altarpiece in the chapel of the Holy Cross at Impruneta. Andrea is, however, much more abundantly represented by beautiful altarpieces in many Italian towns outside of Florence, especially at Arezzo and La Verna. Perhaps the most perfect of his altarpieces is the Coronation of the Virgin in the Osservanza near Siena. A good example of such altarpieces is the Assumption

of the Virgin in the Metropolitan Museum, New York. Many inferior, highly coloured but partially glazed altarpieces were made by the pupils of Giovanni for the smaller villages of central Italy. The figured composition in these altar-pieces are in high relief. Sculptures in the round, like the beautiful group representing the Visitation, which Luca made for the church of S. Giovanni at Pistoia, were not common.

Pavements, ceilings, lunettes, friezes, medallions, altarpieces, statues, by no means exhaust the list of the applications made by the Della Robbia family of glazed terra cotta. The churches of central Italy are abundantly supplied with Robbia tabernacles, and Robbia fonts, candelabra, and vases are not rare. Thus the new technique was applied systematically in many directions, where previously more expensive methods of marble and metal sculpture, of mosaic and tempera painting had prevailed.

— ALLAN MARQUAND.

ROBERT DE COUCY; architect; d. 1311.

The architect of Reims cathedral, after the the fire of 1211, was either Robert de Coucy or Hue Libergier (see Libergier), who began the church of S. Nicaise at Reims in 1229. The Robert de Coucy known to the records became architect of S. Nicaise at the death of Libergier in 1263. He was also architect of the cathedral of Reims at this later time.

Gonse, *L'Art Gothique;* Cerf, *Notre Dame de Reims;* Tarbé, *Notre Dame de Reims;* L'Abbé Tourneur, *Description de Notre Dame de Reims;* Bauchal, *Dictionnaire.*

ROBERT DE LUZARCHES. (See Luzarches, Robert de.)

ROBIN, PIERRE; architect.

He made the plans of the church of S. Maclou at Rouen about 1437 and conducted the works on that building until 1450.

Bauchal, *Dictionnaire.*

ROBUSTI, JACOPO. (See Tintoretto.)

ROCAILLE (n.). A system of decoration supposed to be founded upon the forms of rocks, or upon the artificial rock work of the seventeenth-century gardens to which were added shells sometimes of real, sometimes of imaginary shapes. The ornament soon passed into a system of scrolls combined with abundant floral and other carving, with gilding used freely, and paintings in panels. This system of ornamentation was used equally for the wood-lined interiors of handsome residences and choirs of churches and for the smallest objects of familiar ornamentation, such as the little boxes of gold, ivory, and tortoise shell used for snuff and bon-bons, small toilet articles and the like. The essence of the style is that these curves shall never be continuous for more than a short distance, nor make more than one double curve like the letter S, without breaking off to begin again abruptly. (See Meissonier, and the collective edition of his works cited.) — R. S.

ROCK-CUT BUILDING. Excavation in

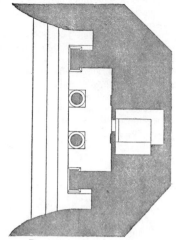

ROCK-CUT BUILDING: TOMB AT TELMISSUS, ASIA MINOR; PLAN.

native rock without the aid of masonry, or with but little masonry. Tombs so excavated are common in Egypt, Lycia, Petra, Etruria, and Jerusalem, generally presenting an architectural front only, with dark interior cham-

Ellora, they are entirely isolated from the native rock mass from which they were cut, presenting within and without all the appear-

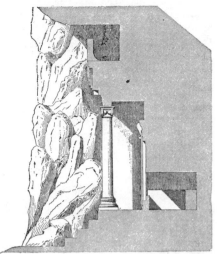

ROCK-CUT BUILDING: TOMB AT TELMISSUS; SEE PLAN.

ance of structural buildings, though actually monolithic. — H. V. B.

ROCK FACED. Same as Quarry Faced. (See Stone Cutting.)

ROCK-CUT BUILDING: UNDERGROUND KITCHEN, VILLAGE OF MONDJEBIA, SYRIA.

bers, of which the sections are supported by masses of stone left in the form of solid pillars. Temples so excavated occur in Nubia, as at Ipsamboul, and in modern India, where, as at

ROCK TEMPLE. (See Rock-cut Building.)

ROCK WORK. A rough and purposely irregular combination of stones, broken bricks, and other hard materials, with cement mortar poured over it, and earth, pebbles, and the like filling the cavities, sometimes having grass and small plants growing upon it; the whole intended as a garden decoration in what was supposed to be a naturalistic style. This device was common in the eighteenth century, and its prevalence is supposed to have had to do with some of the features and with the names of the decorative styles of the time. (See Rocaille; Rococo.)

ROCOCO ARCHITECTURE. The archi-

ROCOCO ARCHITECTURE: EARLIEST TYPE; DOORWAY AT TOULOUSE, FRANCE.

tecture of the century beginning about 1660 A.D. in so far as it is marked by a certain excess of curvature and a lack of firm lines and formal distribution. The term is of French origin, in spite of its Italian appearance, and was apparently derived from the term Rocaille. The characteristic decoration of the style is hardly seen in the exteriors of buildings, or at least hardly in the walls, porticoes, etc., but these are characterized by great boldness in deviation from the classical orders as described

and drawn by Vignola and other authorities. The capitals of columns assume new forms; wreaths and festoons adorn the Ionic capital; the entablature is sometimes cut into pieces, or wholly changed in its proportions to allow of a story of windows; there is a tendency toward setting piers and flanking buttresses, with an angle projecting in front, so that the plan of the buttress is approximately triangular; there is a disposition to use irregularly curved window heads and door heads, and to open windows of round and oval shape in unusual places; the balconies have commonly wrought-iron railings, and these are of fantastic curvature both in plan and vertically; sculpture of human figures, either complete or used as caryatids and telamones, is very much diversified in pose and gesture. The characteristic interior decoration is composed of scrolls which pass into each other abruptly, as described under Rocaille. There is also in the interiors a singular indifference to the constructive character of the design, the walls passing into the flat ceilings through a very large cove, which is not limited to horizontal lines either at top or bottom, but when seen from below is difficult to determine as to size and exact location. These strange coves are often filled with very elaborate and highly finished painting, a continuation often of the composition with which the ceiling is filled. Openings also fill the wall above doors and windows. (See Overdoor; Dessus de Fenêtre; Dessus de Porte; also Churrigueresque.) — R. S.

ROD. A piece or strip of wood, such as could be cut out of a plank; that is to say, about 2 inches square; as used by carpenters for setting out their work. Such a strip of wood, marked with feet and half feet, and sometimes with inches and half inches for a part of its length, is generally cut exactly 10 feet long, and is then called by the workmen the Ten-foot Rod.

Lightning Rod. (See under L.)

Picture Rod. A rod serving the same purpose as a Picture Moulding (which see under Moulding).

ROESNER, KARL; architect; b. June 19, 1804; d. 1867.

He was educated at the Academy of Vienna and in Italy, and was appointed Professor of Perspective at the Academy in Vienna. Professor Roesner was especially attracted to early mediæval architecture and built many Romanesque churches.

Seubert, *Künstler-lexikon.*

ROGER (I.); Archbishop of York.

Roger, Archbishop of York from 1154 to 1181, began in 1171 to build the original Norman choir of the cathedral of York (England), of which the crypt remains.

Brown, *Metropolitan Church of S. Peter, York.*

ROGER (II.), abbot.

The eleventh abbot of Mont Saint-Michel. He repaired the nave of the church of his abbey, which had fallen in 1103. After the conflagration of 1112 he repaired the buildings of the abbey, and erected the constructions to the north of the nave of the church. The

études iconographiques et archéologiques (Tours, 1874, 2 vol. folio), *La Messe, études Archéologiques sur les Monuments* (Paris), 1883–1889, 8 vols. 4to); *La Sainte Vierge, études archéologiques et iconographiques* (Paris, 2 vols. folio, 1878, etc.).

Bellier de la Chavignerie, *Dictionnaire;* Bauchal, *Dictionnaire.*

ROHAULT DE FLEURY, HUBERT; architect; b. 1777; d. 1846.

A pupil of Durand (see Durand). He won the *premier grand prix de Rome* in 1802. In 1806 he was appointed inspector of the works at the Arc-de-Triomphe de l'Étoile.

ROCOCO ARCHITECTURE: EARLY AND GOOD DECORATION FROM A CHÂTEAU AT BERCY, PARIS; NOW DESTROYED.

Merveille, usually ascribed to him, was not erected until the beginning of the thirteenth century.

Héricher, *Mont Saint-Michel;* Corroyer, *Mont Saint-Michel.*

ROHAULT DE FLEURY, CHARLES; architect; b. Sept. 22, 1801; d. Aug. 12, 1875.

A son of Hubert Rohault de Fleury (see Rohault de Fleury, below). He was educated at the *École Polytechnique* and the *École des Beaux Arts* (Paris). In 1833 he was appointed architect of the hospitals of Paris, and about 1837 built important works at the *Jardin des Plantes.* He was associated with Hittorff (see Hittorff) in designing the houses in the Place de l'Étoile (Paris). Charles Rohault de Fleury is best known by his important works on Christian archæology: *L'Évangile,*

From 1817 to 1833 he was architect of the hospitals of Paris. He built important public edifices in Paris.

Bellier de la Chavignerie, *Dictionnaire;* Lance, *Dictionnaire.*

ROLL. *A.* A nearly cylindrical member, comparatively small; especially a rounded strip of wood fastened to and continuous with a ridge or hip of a roof; a false ridge pole. (See Ridge Piece; — Pole.)

B. In a roof of lead or other metal, one of a series of rounded strips of wood secured at regular intervals along the slope, and extending from the ridge to the eaves, over which the ends of the roofing plates are turned and lapped, thus preventing the crawling of the metal by alternate expansion and contraction.

C. A similar rounded piece made by the

metal sheathing alone, or with the support of a wooden batten.

ROLL AND FILLET. A round moulding, larger than a bead, with a fillet on the face of it — characteristic in string courses and labels of the middle and late mediæval periods.

the Roman. The name has been most commonly restricted to the distinct and homogeneous style that was evolved in Western Europe in the ninth, tenth, eleventh, and twelfth centuries, leaving the name of Latin (see Latin Architecture) for the transitional style which

ROCOCO ARCHITECTURE: PERFECTED INTERIOR DECORATION; c. 1760; BRUCHSAL ON THE RHINE.

ROLLED IRON. Iron pressed while in a heated state into sheets or bars of any form by passing between heavy steel rollers in a rolling mill.

ROLLOCK. One ring of a rollock arch (which see under Arch); or one solid of such a ring.

ROMANESQUE ARCHITECTURE. Generally the architecture of Europe between the Roman period and the Gothic ; a term applied to it long ago, because this architecture was recognized as a closely related variation from

had intervened between the breaking up of the Roman in the fourth century and this ; but it may be broadly used to cover the interval from the fourth century to the appearance of Gothic in the latter half of the twelfth. The Romanesque was emphatically the architecture of the round arch and the vault, as the Greek had been that of the order and the lintel, and the Roman a compromise between the two. It took its start, it has been said, elsewhere (see Latin Architecture) from the time when the column was first used as the direct support of the arch rather than of the entablature, to which it was inseparably joined in the Classic styles, the earliest known example being in Diocletian's palace at Spalato (see Greco-Roman Architecture). But the change remained barren till the ninth century, and the development from the union of the arch and column, and the use of vaulting in common with them which gave the new style its character, did not begin till then. The style has been called Lombard where it appeared in Italy, and has been ascribed to the builders of the Lombard kingdom in Italy; but its beginnings did not appear till that kingdom had been destroyed by Charlemagne, and it was practically worked out simultaneously under Teutonic influences in Italy, France, and Germany, one country being now in the lead and now another, and with considerable local differences in detail, yet with an all-pervading unity. In the eleventh century it spread into England, where it appears as the style often called Norman, and later into the Scandinavian countries.

Up to the ninth century the basilican plan, adopted in Italy and derived from there, was the typical plan for churches throughout Europe, wherever the influence of the Byzantine empire did not reach, although there were churches of a different type, round or polygonal, such as Charlemagne's at Aachen (Aix-la-Chapelle), S. Vitale at Ravenna, and others of the kind (see Round Church). These last were exceptional; the basilican was the type which had been developed with the ritual of the Western Church,

ROCOCO ARCHITECTURE: STOCKHOLM, SWEDEN.

and out of which the architecture of the Middle Ages was evolved. In the ninth century the storm of invasion, which had lulled for two centuries, was renewed over a great part of Europe by the Northmen, the Saracens, and the Huns, more destructive than the earlier invaders; churches were destroyed by hundreds, and the progress of architecture was checked. The tenth century was a period of general depression and poverty, of political confusion, of disorder in the church. But before the end of the century the condition of Europe had begun to mend, and with the opening of the eleventh came a great architectural fervour which was to last for centuries, and in which new forms of building were rapidly developed. The steps of transition are obscure, but from this time the Romanesque type of church, which set the form for the Middle Ages, began to take shape. This was the cruciform type, which, being continued on a great scale through the twelfth century, was followed in its main lines by the Gothic of the thirteenth and fourteenth, and so fixed the type for the whole of the Middle Ages. The basilican plan was not cruciform, though it is often so called. In the cruciform the nave and transept interpenetrated; the nave, continued across the transept, made the eastern arm of a Latin cross, and the square space in which they met, which we call the

ROMANESQUE ARCHITECTURE: VAULTING COMMON IN GERMAN ROMANESQUE CHURCHES.

M N, transverse arches; *A C*, springing line of the smaller arch of the vault; *P*, crown of the smaller arch; *X*, triangle of vaulting which is curved in the direction *O* to *P* as well as in the opposite way.

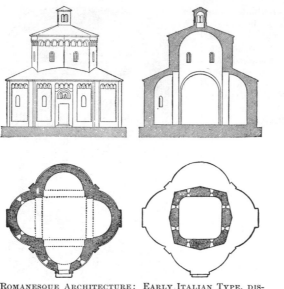

ROMANESQUE ARCHITECTURE: EARLY ITALIAN TYPE, DISTINGUISHED FROM LATIN ARCHITECTURE; CHAPEL AT BIELLA, PIEDMONT; 8TH CENTURY A.D.

ROMANESQUE ARCHITECTURE: EARLY FRENCH; CHURCH OF VIGNORY (MARNE); 10TH CENTURY; PLAN.

7

10

6

12

ROMANESQUE ARCHITECTURE: BYZANTINE TYPE; CAPITALS FROM VENICE AND MURANO.

311   312

crossing, belonged architecturally to both. In the basilica the apse was cut off from the nave by the transept, in which the service was performed; in the cruciform, when the nave, prolonged through the transept, made the eastern arm, the apse was joined to it, so that the two together made the choir, which only when much space was needed for the clergy was prolonged across it, or even down into the western arm. Thus the nave, by virtue of its continuity, gained the predominance which had belonged to the transept. The two were usually built on the same system and of the same dimensions except as to length, so that the crossing became square. The aisles, too, were sometimes continued across the transept, flanking the continuation of the nave, and in the twelfth century even round the apse. The orientation of the basilicas was followed, except in some parts of Italy, the churches facing the west, with their apses to the east, and occasionally smaller churches were built without transepts, like the smaller basilicas.

But a difference as marked as the change in plan from basilican to cruciform, and even more important to the construction and aspect of churches, was the change in covering them. The basilicas were roofed and ceiled with wood; their construction was proportionally slight; they often fell to pieces, and great numbers of them were burned. The desire for more permanent and more monumental buildings grew with wealth and architectural experience. As early as the eighth or ninth century vaulted crypts were built under

in the round churches. It was done in Roman fashion, with barrel vaults and groins; but the difficulty of vaulting the irregular oblique divisions of the aisles of the octagonal churches led to dividing the vaults into small compartments by cross ribs. This system, extended to the aisles

ROMANESQUE ARCHITECTURE: CHURCH OF VIGNORY; SEE PLAN.

and finally to the naves of the long churches, led to dividing them throughout into regular bays which could be built one by one, and greatly facilitated the construction of vaults. In early experiments barrel vaults, both longitudinal and transverse, were freely used, but they were heavy and uncomely, and soon gave way to groined vaults, which, by collecting the thrust at their points of support, could be stayed by there increasing the thickness of the wall and pier. In the course of the eleventh century the habit of groin vaulting the aisles in square bays became general in the north, and probably in that part of Italy where the Teutonic influence was controlling. The greater difficulty of vaulting the naves led to various efforts and many failures. It was necessary to increase greatly the weight of the clearstory walls, and elaborately contrabut the thrust of the high vaults. In the middle of France by the end of the eleventh century a method was devised of covering the nave with a barrel vault, round or pointed, and abutting it by half-barrel vaults over the aisles, whose crowns reached nearly to the springing of the nave vault. There are examples in S. Étienne at Nevers, Notre Dame-du-Port at Clermont-Ferrand, and in the abbey

ROMANESQUE ARCHITECTURE: ENGLISH, C. 1140; CHURCH AT NORTHAMPTON.

churches at first barrel vaulted, afterward groined in Roman fashion; but it was long before the mediæval builders got skill to vault the parts above ground. It is difficult to trace out the line of progress in times and places, but it is clear that the aisles, being lower and narrower, were first vaulted, and that this was first done of Fontenay. For the same purpose were used barrel vaults, whose axes are at right angles with the axes of the aisles. But the thrust of the main vault along the whole clearstory wall was still difficult to meet; the clearstory was darkened or wholly closed by the aisle vaults, the interiors were heavy and dark, and the system did not prevail.

story walls, rising high above the aisles without a trace of buttressing, and so thick that an arcaded gallery is carried through them under the eaves above the springing of the vaults. The French builders, more inventive, tried every means to lighten their construction. Sometimes they tied the vaults across with iron, stiffening the clearstory walls with tim-

ROMANESQUE ARCHITECTURE: A DOMED CHURCH; S. FRONT AT PÉRIGNEUX (DORDOGNE); 13TH CENTURY.

Here the divergence of the French builders from the German and Italian is conspicuous. The Germans and Italians, averse to buttressing, trusted, in Roman fashion, to sheer weight of masonry, using thick walls, massive piers, and narrow openings, maintaining even to the thirteenth century the aspect of massive breadth, dignity, and repose that marked their early Romanesque. In the cathedral of Speyer the thick-shelled vaults, a hundred feet high, are balanced by the mere weight of the clear-

bers, which in time rotted away. Sometimes they relied on buttresses applied to the clearstory, and those, too, at first betrayed them. At last they invented the flying buttress, set across the aisles at the springing of the main vault above the piers. They built their vaults on independent ribs, transverse, diagonal, and longitudinal, which bore them like a permanent scaffolding. They lightened the shells of their vaults and the clearstory walls between their buttresses as much as possible, expanding the windows, and shortening the bays of the naves; and finally, equalizing the height of the ribs and levelling the crown of the vaulting by the use of the pointed arch, they led the way to the wonderful development of Gothic in the thirteenth century.

This was not achieved without many failures; the chronicles of the eleventh and twelfth centuries are full of stories of churches which fell down soon after they were built, or were soon destroyed to make way for new experiments. The cruciform shape and the arrangement of aisles and transept being presupposed, the church was designed to suit the vaulting compartments, so that these became the units of the plan, and it has been said that mediæval churches were planned from the top downward. In Roman architecture, wherever an entablature, an arch, or the pendant of a vault abutted against a wall, a column or a pilaster was provided to receive it. This principle, carried out in Byzantine architecture and in the round and polygonal churches of the early Romanesque, produced the compound pier, and, where arches met at right angles, the cruciform pier. In the north, and in Italy when the supply of columns that could be got from the Roman buildings was exhausted, piers were the natural supports of the arcades. The plain square pier, when a pilaster was added to it on one side to receive the cross rib of the aisle vault, took the shape *A*, and when the main archivolt was broken into steps by adding a sub arch,

the shape *B*. As the workmen gained skill half columns were substituted for the pilasters, and the forms *A'* and *B'* resulted. When pilasters or shafts were carried up on the side of the nave to receive cross arches or vaulting ribs, or sometimes even the roof trusses, the piers took the forms *C* and *D*, which last may be taken as a typical form of pier in a developed Romanesque church. As the style pro-

gressed the plan of the piers grew varied and complicated; a representative of every subdivision of the arches and every vaulting rib was gathered into it. The compound pier came

ROMANESQUE ARCHITECTURE: PORCH, KELSO ABBEY, SCOTLAND; c. 1160.

to be used even in churches which were not intended to be vaulted, as we may see in S. Miniato in Florence. On the other hand, in churches here and there columns continued in use, increasing in size, and bearing on their capitals the groups of shafts and the stepped archivolts above them, set either continuously, or oftener alternately with piers. The charm of an alternating arrangement of piers and columns, or of lighter and heavier piers, seems to have early caught the eye of the German and Italian builders, though the French made little use of it. The German system found in this exactly the provision of supports it needed, for it was based on equal vaults intersecting in square compartments, the natural result of the Roman system. Their naves being twice as wide as their aisles, the bays of the nave were twice as large as those of the aisles, and each of them covered two arches. It followed that while every pier or column carried a shaft from a groin of the aisle, every alternate one carried also a shaft from the nave vault. Hence every other pier was a heavy one, and the alternate ones were lighter, or in many cases were replaced by columns. This arrangement gives a peculiar charm to many interiors in the German Romanesque or so-called Lombard style, and to some in England.

The intersection of nave and transept in the cruciform church gave special architectural importance to the crossing, which before long came to be covered with a dome, or at least with a vault higher than the rest, perhaps in reminiscence of the Byzantine method. Over it a large tower was often built, a habit which lasted long a triforium, was in some cases itself vaulted, and made a second story aisle, like those in some of the Latin churches and many of the Byzantine, which served to increase the capacity of the churches and to divide the worshippers,

in the churches of Normandy of a later style. It early became a habit to carry an interior gallery above the main arcades and under the aisle roofs, opening into the nave through an arcade of small arches, usually borne on colonnettes, and treated with greater richness than the principal arches below. This gallery, called — men from women or monks and nuns from the laity, — and answered to the Gynæceum of the Eastern churches, from which it was doubtless derived. This upper gallery or aisle appears here and there all over Europe, for instance, in S. Ambrogio in Milan, in the Abbaye aux Hommes at Caen, the cathedral at

Peterborough, and the Münster at Aachen. The triforium itself, usually a mere open arcade, became almost universal in churches of importance, a very effective element of their interior composition, whose triple vertical division, into two contrasting arcades with the windowed clearstory above, was the theme of endless picturesque variations.

The exteriors of churches developed in correspondence with the interiors. Instead of the single detached campanile of an Italian church a characteristic group of towers grew up about a German church, all intimate parts of its design. Usually there was a tower at the crossing with a lantern, often a pair at the west end, often a pair flanking the eastern arm, sometimes a second lantern over the narthex, which in German churches was often in two stories, and at times all these were combined in one building, as we may see in the abbey of Laach, or the cathedral of Speyer. The massive walls needed to stay the vaults, and hardly reënforced with buttresses, were divided by flat pilaster strips, which often merged in round-headed panels enclosing the round-arched windows, or were continued up till they were lost in the arcaded and corbelled cornices running up the gables with which the fronts of naves and transepts were finished, and were a marked characteristic of the style. The towers, lighted by small windows which multiplied with the ascending stories, in groups divided by small colonnettes, were at first mostly round or octagonal; the later ones more commonly square, and in Germany

ROMANESQUE ARCHITECTURE: CAPITALS OF PORCH, ST. PETER'S CHURCH, NORTHAMPTON; C. 1160.

and Italy they were regularly covered with pointed roofs, conical or pyramidal. The French builders were more sparing of towers than the German, and were apt to employ only a pair, or a single one which they commonly placed over the crossing or the west porch. Upon this they lavished great richness, developing the roof into a stone spire, decorated with pinnacles and lucarnes, which even before the transition to the Pointed style became a beautiful and elaborate composition.

The favourite ornamental features of the Romanesque builders were arcades and colonnettes. Arcades were used in the utmost profusion, especially in the north of Italy and along the Rhine. Open or blind, they were carried about the sides of cloisters, along blank walls, over the fronts and even the flanks of churches, under eaves, and up and down the slopes of gables. Colonnettes were multiplied unceasingly; clustered about doors and windows, and supporting every

arcade, occasionally set in rows for their own sake alone with no arches to carry, as on the front of the Pieve at Arezzo. The decorative instinct of the workmen expressed itself chiefly in ornamental sculpture, neglecting the early Christian art of pictorial mosaic, and making painting subordinate, as it had been in classic times. The carving, which was chiefly accumulated upon capitals and string courses and about doorways, and which at first was based on classical and Byzantine models, took a new direction under northern influences, abandoning the classical types, the acanthus and basket work, for a lavish development of animal forms, human faces and figures, even narrative scenes, and florid interlacing foliage. A kind of capital which is called the cubic or cushion capital, in its underlying form a cubical block with its lower corners rounded away to meet the shaft, and which was originally a Byzantine form, as we may see in S. Sophia at Constantinople and many other Byzantine churches, was adopted by the Germans both in the north and in Italy, probably at first because of its simplicity, and elaborated into a thousand richly decorated forms. It is a distinct mark of the Lombard style, in Italy and Germany, and though banished from the centre and south of France, is found abundantly in Norman churches both on the continent and in England. The doorways were adorned with peculiar richness, their jambs crowded with shafts, the arches with decorated mouldings, the tympanums sculptured with Biblical or legendary stories. In Italy elaborate projecting porches were built over them, carried by columns which commonly rested on lions or fabulous beasts.

It is difficult to trace the transition from Latin architecture to Romanesque. Though the two styles were continuous in development, they were the products of different conditions and of different races. The basilican was of southern origin; it is its peculiarity that it scarcely changed during the five centuries in which it was practised. Born perhaps in the East, it was developed in Italy; its monuments are found there, and have influenced the forms of many later churches. It was evidently the work of secular builders. Italy was a land of cities, and well provided with builders, who were formed into guilds or something like them even in the days of the Empire, and were succeeded by the Lombard masons, whose reputation was great through the Middle Ages. The churches in Italy, founded by bishops or secular princes, or even by colonies of monks, were doubtless built by these secular workmen. The condition of Gaul at first was approximately that of Italy. The coasts and the valleys of the Rhône and the Rhine had a fringe of Roman cities and civilization; the invasions of the fifth century left things here very much as in Italy, and their early Christian architecture was an echo of the Italian. But in Germany, between the Rhine and the Baltic, there were no cities before the reign of Charlemagne. He and his successors founded a few towns; but the settlement of Germany was practically the work of the monks, whose monasteries, established for the conversion of the natives, became the nuclei of communities from which most of the cities sprang. The invasions of the ninth century threw back civilization in Gaul, and left it almost as bare of churches as Germany. The evolution of a new architecture began alike in both countries and in the Germanized parts of Italy at the hands of the invaders. To apportion among the three countries their shares in the working out of the new style is not easy. Up to the Carlovingian period Italy was the leader; the north looked to her both for example and workmen. When, at the end of the tenth century, building revived, it was with an astonishing fervour, which continued all over Europe for three centuries, and the leaders seem to have been for a century at least the monastic builders of the north. The Benedictine Order in its two great branches, first the Clunisian and afterward the Cistercian, spread its monasteries with great rapidity over Europe, and in the north filled the vacant districts with its communities. North of the Alps and away from the large cities the monks, and especially the Benedictines, were the builders of Europe, which was bestrewn with their churches. Isolated and self-dependent, they gathered about them great companies of workmen, whom they organized into regular schools or guilds, and among whom the art of building progressed very fast. There grew up among them a body of lay brothers, affiliated but not cloistered, and untonsured, subject to the Order, who migrated from place to place, building churches and convents. Through the

ROMANESQUE ARCHITECTURE: ABBEY CHURCH AT MAULBRON.
See the ground plan under Monastic Architecture.

ROMANESQUE ARCHITECTURE: CATHEDRAL OF SPEYER (SPIRE); INTERIOR, 1165–1190; LATEST ROMANESQUE, CONTEMPORARY WITH THE EARLY GOTHIC OF FRANCE.

eleventh and twelfth centuries the monks were the chief guardians of literature and the arts

ROMANESQUE ARCHITECTURE: CAPITAL IN CHURCH OF MAURSMÜNS-
TER NEAR STRALSBURG.

south, until the formation of the communes in the twelfth century, political confusion prevailed, and naturally the progress of the arts was slow.   It was natural that with hundreds of thousands of monks eagerly absorbed in building their churches, and with their bands of workmen carrying their experience and their methods from convent to convent and from country to country, monastic architecture should lead the evolution of the Romanesque style.

This style as we have described it was the work of the Teutonic races, and in its general characteristics is the same in Lombard Italy, in Germany, France, England, and in Spain so far as it existed there.   In the south of Italy and on the Adriatic shore it was greatly modified by the influence of the Byzantine Empire and the forms of its architecture, which indeed left their traces wherever commerce with Constantinople was habitual, on the Mediterranean coasts and in the middle of France, and even in some degree northward along the course of the Rhine.   In the south of France, which while it was Gaul had been pervaded by Roman influence almost as completely as Italy, the effects of the classic style lingered long, and left conspicuous traces in the new architecture as late as the twelfth century.   In the neighbourhood of Rome, which never forgot the traditions of the Empire, the Romanesque style was never implanted.   In the northwest of Italy, in Tuscany and Liguria, the Lombard kingdom was not fairly established, and even under the Frankish, the population never was thoroughly Germanized, nor lost its old instincts.   Here when the cities grew prosperous in the eleventh century a style grew up which was isolated and peculiar to itself, of which the cathedral of Pisa is the most conspicuous example.   Though it has been called Romanesque, it is rather the Latin style

north of the Alps, and building seems to have absorbed most of their active energy.   In the

modified by the example of the neighbouring Lombard.   The churches are basilican, unvaulted, and columnar. They show a distinct fondness for classic form in the prevalence of horizontal lines, the parti-coloured banded walls, the survival of traces of the classic entablature, with which are combined the multiplied shafting, the elaborate doorways, the continued arcades of the Lombard Romanesque, all carried out with a peculiar refinement and delicacy of detail which is difficult to account for, and which is not found in the contemporary Romanesque. — W. P. P. LONGFELLOW.

Adamy, *Architektonik des Muhamedanischen und Romanischen Stils;* Adler, *Mittelalterliche Backstein-Bauwerke des Pruessischen Staates;* Choisy, *Histoire de l'Architecture,* Vol. II., chapters 13 and 15; De Dartein, *Étude sur l'Architecture Lombarde;* Fergusson, *History of Architecture in All Countries,* 1893, Part II., Book I., and parts of Books II.-VIII.; *Handbuch der Architektur* (Darmstadt), Part II., Vols. 3 and 4; Inkersley, *An Inquiry into Romanesque and Pointed Architecture in France;* King, *Study Book of Mediæval Architecture and Art;* Mallay, *Essai sur les Églises Romanes et Romano-Byzantines du département du Puy de Dôme;* Revoil, *Architecture Romane du midi de la France;* Robert, R., *L'Architecture Normande aux XI. et XII. siècles;* Schnaase, *Geschichte der bildenden Künste im Mittelalter,* Vols. III., IV., Book 2, 4, 5, 6, 7; Scott, Sir G., *Lectures on the Rise and Development of Mediæval Architecture;* Viollet-le-Duc, *Dictionnaire;* Vogüé, *La Syrie Centrale.* Also see bibliography under Byzantine Architecture.

ROMANESQUE, ENGLISH. English Romanesque, more commonly referred to by English authorities as the Norman style, was not wholly an innovation introduced by the Conqueror. The close relation between England and Normandy had been increased and strengthened by intermarriage. Edward saw in his cousins across the channel far more unity of interests than he could see in the Danish usurpers in England. When, after his exile, he again held sway, he brought with him Norman ideas and perhaps Norman workmen.

Notwithstanding the turbulence of the times and the necessity for fortified castles and towns, the ecclesiastical buildings were still by far the most important architecturally. That in England they followed very closely on the work across the channel is most natural, but there was too much native energy to allow the English merely to copy.

The French and English Normans were always alike in their general aims and ambitions; the vault and its support, the development of the openings, the size and magnificence of their structures. Therefore we see close parallels in Caen, Sens, and Canterbury. As the conquerors became more and more at home and united with the conquered, they became differentiated from the French Norman, and their buildings took on special characteristics. The proportion of the plan was altered by giving it unusual length, and we find among the very early

churches lengths of 556 feet and of 480, respectively, at Winchester and Peterborough. In proportion to their width the parish churches were equally long, often six or eight times the span of the nave. No special ambition was shown in the constructural problems which interested the Continental builders. The English were often content with aisle vaults, leaving the nave to be spanned with timber. The long vista of nave and choir and the network of timber carved and decorated in colour almost compensate for the lost beauty of the main vault. On both sides of the water the recessed orders were rich in ornament, chiefly of geometrical character; but the English used ornament also with much profusion on plain surfaces, enriching them with arcades, plain and interlaced, and with various forms of surface ornament, of which the towers of Norwich Cathedral and of the little church at Castor near Peterborough are good examples. Finally, they laid great stress on their central towers. The unvaulted nave was comparatively low, and being also very long afforded an excellent opportunity for contrast in a tower of even moderate height. This opportunity was eagerly seized.

To sum up: the English features are the great length, the central tower, and the lack of ambition in scientific construction. (See England, Architecture of.)

The introduction of the pointed arch in the twelfth century marked but a phase in the development of Romanesque. The keynote of Gothic, the balance of parts, the thrust and counterthrust, had not yet made its impress on England, and even in France it was as yet but a blind groping after the Gothic principle. The aims of the eleventh century remained the chief aims of the twelfth. This period is generally spoken of by English writers as "Transitional." — R. CLIPSTON STURGIS.

ROMAN IMPERIAL ARCHITECTURE. That of the Roman dominion in Europe, Asia, and Africa, ending with the fourth century A.D. With the exception of fragments of walls and of a few simple buildings, Roman architecture is represented by those monuments which were erected *during the Empire,* and as the style was first developed in Rome and then spread throughout the various countries subjugated, with such modifications as the materials of the country and the labour to be obtained required and as the climate suggested, the term "Roman Imperial architecture" has been adopted as setting forth more fully the scope of this article.

Under Etruscan Architecture reference has already been made to the first source of what may be called the elements of the Roman Imperial style, and in one sense the most important. It was mainly through her paved roads that Rome was able to bring into connection all the chief cities of the Empire, by the solid construction of her walls to render the cities she founded secure against attack, and by the employment of arched construction to roof over her buildings with an imperishable material, to build bridges and aqueducts (the latter of basilica; the thermæ (from the Greek Gymnasium, a group of halls for athletic exercises, would seem to have been the prototype of the public baths), and lastly the orders of architecture, Doric, Ionic, and Corinthian.

ROMAN IMPERIAL ARCHITECTURE: THERMÆ OF CARACALLA; C. 215 A.D.
Viollet-le-Duc's restoration of the great hall (tepidarium).

vital importance in all her Eastern possessions), and lastly to drain off water from marshy districts.

The second source was that of Greek architecture, from which were derived the temple with its peristyle or portico and its outer enclosure; the porticus or stoa of her fora, and the

These orders, when employed in those structures which were Greek in their origin, underwent but little change; the great scientific advance however made in the quarrying of stone and marble, and in the transport of large masses of stone, enabled the Roman architect to substitute the monolith for the Greek column built in several courses, and the greater display of richness in the Corinthian order led to its almost universal adoption. In those buildings however in which was carried out the full development of the arch and vault, in the theatres and amphitheatres, in the thermæ and in palaces raised to great height and of several stories, the orders were utilized as apparently an

away, and probably in provincial towns such as Pompeii and Herculaneum, the Tuscan order was never employed. The Doric order also did not meet with much favour with the Roman Imperial architect, and, besides Pompeii and the exceptional temple of Cora near Rome, which, barring the attenuation of its columns, may be put down to Greek influence, there are

ROMAN IMPERIAL ARCHITECTURE: A HALL OF THE THERMÆ OF DIOCLETIAN; C. 300 A.D.

The groined vault has lost its ornaments, but the walls and piers are nearly as originally designed. (This is now the church of S. Maria degli Angeli.)

afterthought, to break up and decorate the wall surface, and without any connection with their origin as constructional features.

The so-called Tuscan order, which was derived from the Etruscans, was of a primitive nature not far removed from the wooden post; the columns also were so widely interspaced that the epistyle they carried was in wood. The employment of this ephemeral material was not in accordance with Roman Imperial custom, and except in domestic work which has long passed

but few examples known. It is found in Asia Minor at Pergamon, in the agora of Aizani, and in a few instances in North Africa and Syria, where probably the want of sculptors to carve the decorative features of the Ionic or Corinthian capitals led to its adoption. (Reference is now to the use of the Doric order as a detached constructional feature and not to its application as a decoration only to a wall surface.)

The Ionic order followed the same fate, and is found in only two temples in Rome, the temples of Fortuna Virilis and of Concord. Two portions of the colonnaded streets of Gerasa in Syria are flanked by Ionic columns, and also, but of a very degraded type, many of the smaller temples in the same country. There is a modified type of Ionic capital found in Pompeii, in which the volutes are retained at each angle and consist of fine spirals which suggest the

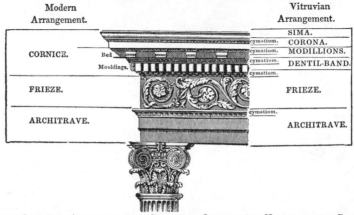

Modern Arrangement.   Vitruvian Arrangement.

	cymatium.	SIMA.
CORNICE.	cymatium.	CORONA.
	cymatium.	MODILLIONS.
Bed Mouldings.	cymatium.	DENTIL-BAND.
	cymatium.	
FRIEZE.		FRIEZE.
ARCHITRAVE.	cymatium.	ARCHITRAVE.

ROMAN IMPERIAL ARCHITECTURE: COMPOSITE ORDER WITH NAMES OF THE PARTS.

work of a Greek artist. It is possible also that the uncertainty which prevails in the spacing out of the triglyph in the Doric frieze and in the choice between the cushion or the angle volute of the Ionic capital may have led to rejection of those orders.

With the Corinthian capital it was otherwise, and its magnificence appealed much more to the

ROMAN IMPERIAL ARCHITECTURE: IONIC CAPITAL, TEMPLE OF SATURN IN THE ROMAN FORUM.

instincts of the Roman Imperial architect; moreover, it presented the same design on all four faces and could be equally well employed in the rectangular or circular temple or for the hemicycle peristyle which in Roman Imperial architecture plays so important a factor in the setting out of the plan. The Greek Corinthian capital, though very varied in design and in many cases of great beauty, was never completely developed in Greek architecture, and it remained for the Romans to systematize the double range of

leaves which surround the lower portion of the base and to give a greater sense of support to the abacus by the accentuation of the spiral tendrils at the four angles. In the carving of the acanthus leaf the section was made flat in the place of the V-shaped section of each lobe found in Greek work. This rule applies to all the principal examples in Rome, with two or

three exceptions. In Syria, where the Greek artist would seem to have been mostly employed, the V-shaped section of the leaf is almost universally adhered to, except where, as in Baalbec and Palmyra, works of such importance were being carried out as to call for the employment of Roman sculptors. There is, however, a second type found at Pompeii and in the Temple of Vesta at Tivoli, where the treatment of the leaf resembles more that of the crinkled cabbage. In these two cases the capital is only one diameter high, instead of one and a quarter, as in the portico of the Pantheon and the Temple of Castor and Pollux. The complete order of this last example is the finest Roman Imperial example known. In the entablature of this temple, the enrichments of the various fasciæ, which in the Greek temples were usually painted in gold and colours, are here elaborately carved.

In the Roman Corinthian entablature a very important addition was made by the introduction of modillions. These may have had their origin in the mutules of the Doric cornice; they consist of small brackets or corbels which suggest a better support to the corona of the cornice and break the line of shadow as projected on the frieze. In the temples of Syria these corbels are further supported by consoles or ancones underneath, which rest on the upper moulding of the architrave and constitute an original but overcharged decoration for the frieze.

There is one other order introduced by the Romans, the composite, which may originally have been derived from a desire to add leaf decoration to the Ionic capital, or by the substitution of the Ionic volute for the Corinthian volute to give a better support to the angles of the abacus. It is in fact a mixture of the two orders with, however, the Corinthian entablature. The earliest example is found in the Arch of Titus. In two of the theatres of Asia Minor it is found in the proscenium. (See Composite Order.)

The earliest example of the superimposition of orders is found in the Theatre of Marcellus in Rome (44–13 B.C.). Here there are only two orders superimposed, the Doric and Ionic, both much purer in design than any later examples. In the theatre at Orange, France, the order is confined to the lower story only; the outside face of the stage wall, 340 feet long and 116 feet high, is one of the finest masses of masonry in existence.

The conjunction of the arcade with the order and the superimposition of the orders as decora-

ROMAN IMPERIAL ARCHITECTURE: COLUMNS FROM THE TEMPLE OF DIANA, EVORA, PORTUGAL.
An illustration of principal and declining style.

tive features on a wall surface, as in the Theatre of Marcellus, the Coliseum, and other amphitheatres, may in a sense be looked upon as a new

order, inasmuch as the relative proportion of the features employed followed a fixed rule. Thus whilst the proportions of the column and entabla-

ROMAN IMPERIAL ARCHITECTURE: CORINTHIAN CAPITAL WITH IMAGERY; PRESERVED IN THE LATERAN MUSEUM, ROME.

ture and the tapering of the shaft are the same as in an ordinary peristyle, the intercolumniation varies from five to six diameters. Again, the upper diameter of the shaft of the lowest order becomes the lower diameter of the shaft of the order superimposed. Thus, given the diameter of the lowest order of columns, the proportions of the whole of the rest of the design is governed by the intercolumniation.

As the Roman Imperial style was first developed in Rome, and then adopted with various modifications throughout the Empire, some brief account of the materials employed in the city is first necessary. In the time of Augustus there were three methods of building, — in cut and squared stone, in compact masonry of small stones and cement mortar, and in crude bricks. Though Vitruvius lays great stress on the care which should be taken in the preparation of material for the second method named, it is doubtful whether, even in his time, it was much employed (his treatise is said to have been written in the early part of his career); but his description of pozzuolana (II., 6) shows that already the special value possessed by this material had been recognized, though not to its full extent. The fact is, as Dr. Middleton observes (*The Remains of Ancient Rome*, I., 7), "This pozzuolana more than any other material contributed to make Rome the proverbial 'eternal city.' Without it a great domed building like the Pantheon would have been impossible, as would also the immense vaulted thermæ and a wide-spanned basilica such as that of Constantine." It is true that this valuable material is not found in other parts of the Empire, but the great conceptions of the Roman Imperial style were evolved in Rome, and they owe their chief magnificence to the immense size of the vaults which spanned the halls of the Imperial palaces and thermæ. Without the pozzuolana they would have scarcely been feasible, and this is borne out by the fact that no vaults approaching the span of those in Rome are found in any other part of the Empire.

That which first strikes the inquirer in the development of Imperial Roman architecture, when compared with the history of more ancient styles, is the immense variety of buildings of every type. To describe adequately even a fraction of these would be impossible in a general article of this kind; therefore consideration is confined here to the principles which seem to have guided the architects of Imperial Rome in the laying out of their cities and towns, and in the planning of the palaces and thermæ which

Romans, and in this case the first course was to run two main streets, lying north and south and east and west respectively, intersecting in the middle of the site and running from gate to gate in the walls built round the town. In one of the angles thus formed by the intersection would be placed the forum, with the principal temple at one end and the senate house, basilica, treasuries, and other public buildings around. The natural level of the ground would suggest the best position for the citadel on an eminence commanding the town, the side of a hill would be utilized for the position of the theatre, and in the lower part of the town, near the river, if one existed, would be established the thermæ. The next consideration in the Roman Imperial mind would be the

ROMAN IMPERIAL ARCHITECTURE: CAPITALS OF LATE EPOCH USED BY THE MOORISH BUILDERS OF THE MOSQUE AT CORDOVA.

formed the foundation of the style and of its development.

Just as in the present day the first course taken to extend civilization is to provide easy means of communication with settlements at convenient distances, so in the first three centuries of our era the Romans extended their power and influence by the formation of paved roads, so well selected in their direction, and so solidly carried out, that they still serve as the main lines of communication, even in those countries where the increase of population might have led, centuries ago, to their being discarded in favour of new roads, whilst in the more distant portion of their empire, as in North Africa and Syria, they form at the present day the only roads in existence. The direction taken by their roads in Syria suggests that, when laid out, they were intended to connect cities or towns, already existing; but so far as the actual existence of any remains prior to the Roman occupation goes, the evidence is negative. There are, however, instances in which the towns would seem to have been founded by the

supply of water, the very essence of existence in the East, and even in Rome looked upon as one of the most important requirements.

The maintenance of a central axis with buildings symmetrically arranged on either side, constituted the leading principle in Roman Imperial design, and it was on this principle that the Imperial fora was laid out. Of these the largest and most important was the Forum of Trajan, lying to the northwest of the old Forum, and in the most crowded part of Rome. To obtain a level area for the immense group of buildings, a large ridge of tufa rock had to be cut away at an immense cost of labour. The forum consisted of three parts: the forum proper, to which entrance was obtained through a magnificent triple archway (from which the bas-reliefs now on the arch of Constantine were taken) which was surrounded with a lofty porticus or stoa; the Ulpian basilica beyond, with immense apsidal terminations on either side for the courts of justice; and at the further end, the Temple of Trajan enclosed in a court with porticoes around. Between the two in an open court was placed the famous column with the bas-reliefs recording the Dacian victories carried around in spiral form. The temple was erected probably on the site of the cliff which had been cut away. On either side of the basilica and the forum, preëxisting streets ran at various angles, their junction with the basilica being masked by the two apses referred to ; a similar expedient was adopted with the forum, where two immense hemicycles were built one on each side ; these in their play of light and shade as seen through the open porticus on each side must have been of magnificent effect. Later on when speaking of the palaces of the Cæsars on the Palatine Hill, reference will again be made to the adoption of similar features to mask the junction of blocks of buildings inclined at slight angles to one another. There were, of course, instances in which this symmetry could not always be maintained, as in the case of the old Forum, where the sites of the earlier temples and other buildings dating from the first settlements were necessarily retained.

In the more important temples, whether in Europe or the East, the Romans adopted the peristyle of the Greeks ; but they gave greater importance to the pronaos, and they omitted the posticum. In by far the larger number, however, the cella occupies the full width of the portico, and the order around the temple is represented only by semidetached columns against the cella wall. The temples at Nîmes and Vienne in France are the best still existing examples in Europe. Unlike the Greek temple the temples were rarely orientated in Rome. They were looked upon as monumental features and faced the fora or piazza in which they were built. So little regard was paid to orientation in the great capital that in one instance the temples of Venus and of Rome are placed back to back, both enclosed in the same peristyle ; the cellas of these temples were covered with barrel vaults. It is not known for certain whether the Temple of Jupiter at Baalbec was vaulted ; there are two small temples in the palace of Diocletian at Spalato which were covered with vaults ; in Rome there is the remarkable example of the Pantheon built by Hadrian, and at Nîmes in France the so-called Baths of Diana (see Nymphæum) had barrel vaults with transverse ribs ; otherwise the timber roofs of the Greeks seem to have been generally adopted in all Roman temples ; an advance, however, having been made by the introduction of the system of trussing the principals with tiebeams and king-posts.

By far the greatest development in Roman Imperial architecture is that which, in the thermæ and palaces, is found in the employment of the barrel vaults, the intersecting barrel vault, and the dome. These features led to the

erection of buildings entirely homogeneous in the material employed, and of so lasting and durable a nature that, but for earthquakes and the destructive action of mankind, they might all have remained perfect to the present day. The barrel vault constructed with regular stone voussoirs had already for six centuries been employed by the Etruscans, but only for passages of comparatively small width underground, or for gateways of towns where the side walls served as ample abutment to the thrust, but the Romans already, in the Baths of Agrippa (24–25 B.C.), had employed it to vault over wide spans of considerable height, requiring therefore walls of great thickness to resist the thrust. With the barrel vault these walls must have been continuous throughout the whole length, and windows or openings could only have been made below the level of the springing so that the vault would have been comparatively dark. The Romans introduced therefore what is known as the intersecting barrel vault (see Groined Vault), in which two vaults running at right angles to one another intersect and form groins at the angle of intersection ; along these groins the thrust of the vault is carried down to the pier from which it springs, thus concentrating on a series of piers that thrust which in the ordinary barrel vault necessitated a continuous wall. The earliest example of this solution of the problem is found in a tomb at Pergamon in Asia Minor, built by the Attalide kings, in 150 B.C. Though not of great dimensions, it is constructed entirely in stone and shows a considerable knowledge of stereotomy in its execution. It is doubtful, however, whether in the early years of the Roman Empire, the employment of stone for such great spans as those in the Baths of Agrippa would have been possible ; it would certainly have been very costly, involving the employment of highly skilled workers.

Mr. Choisy, in his work, *L'art de bâtir chez les Romains*, has shown how the Romans adopted a construction which was not only the most lasting and solid ever conceived, but which in its execution was the most economical, both in labour and material. Centring trusses were built at intervals and on the cross lines of the quoins, and planks laid across from truss to truss. On these was constructed a shell vault of flat bricks or tiles set in pozzuolana mortar, which added considerably to the strength of the centring. Over the trusses they built arches of brick which relieved the trusses and acted as permanent ribs, with horizontal ties of brick at intervals to connect the brick arches. When the construction thus formed had set, they filled up the haunches with rubble masonry built in horizontal layers until the level of the top of the brick arches was reached. According to the width of span, one, two, or three courses of brick rings were employed for the arches. The centring was removed to a second section as soon as the first vault was built. Eventually the upper surface was sloped down on either side, and the exterior covered with tiles or metal plates. The whole vault built with pozzuolana concrete consolidated into so hard and homogeneous a mass that it rested like the lid of a crockery bowl on the walls, and it became only necessary to build piers or walls of sufficient size to carry the weight. The Romans, however, did not apparently realize the splendid nature of the material employed, and built as if it were also requisite to provide against the thrust.

The walls or piers were built in the same material as the vault, and by somewhat similar means. Thus not only was the whole structure homogeneous, but by the shifting and raising of the centring and the posts and planking, the construction was of the most economical kind, and could be done, under proper supervision, by unskilled labourers.

From Rome as a centre, the principle of plan and design extended to all parts of the Empire. It is true that pozzuolana could only be found in Rome and in the south of Italy, but the fine quality of the Roman mortar throughout the Empire is proverbial, and the immense fallen masses which are found in the large temples of Syria, where sometimes in the core of the wall the mortar exceeds in bulk the stones it holds together, testify to the great value the Romans attached to it. It is true we do not find vaults there with a span equal to those in Rome, but the same principles of design obtain in all Roman Imperial architecture, so that from one end of the Empire to the other we find similar monuments, varying only in size, and, outside Rome, in a somewhat more liberal interpretation of the Roman Imperial style than would have been tolerated in the capital, where the principles of Vitruvius were more rigorously adhered to.

The thermæ of Caracalla may be taken as the leading type of all the Roman baths. The "motif" of the great central block of the baths proper, which covers a site of about 730 feet by 380 feet, is to be found in the central hall known as the Tepidarium. This hall, 170 feet long by 82 feet wide, was covered by an intersecting barrel vault of three bays, carried by immense piers 30 feet deep, placed at right angles to the hall and contrived not only to carry the superstructure but to resist the thrust of the vault. The windows to light this hall were placed above the springing of the vault, so that halls of less height could be provided around it; the spaces on either side between the piers were utilized as exedræ, with baths in them, and at each end spacious vestibules divided from the hall by columnar screens, so that a vista 380 feet in length was obtained. With the vestibules, the tepidarium covers an

area of about 380 feet by 150 feet. On the east and west sides are open courts surrounded with peristyles. The frigidarium is placed on the north side with vestibules, dressing rooms, etc., and the caldarium on the south side with a series of halls for exercises opening into the xystus, all of these, however, derive their axial lines and setting out from the principal hall, the tepidarium, which, as we have said, is the "motif" of the whole structure, and with minor variations is to be found in all the Roman thermæ. In the palaces on the Palatine a similar principle is adopted. The tablinum or throne room, the bibliotheca or library, and the triclinium or dining room, are lofty halls taking their light above the roofs of the adjoining rooms, and they give the key to each group, which is here varied by the great peristyle court inside, with temples or circular shrines in their midst. In speaking of the Forum of Trajan, we referred to the two hemicycles which seem to have been introduced to mask the junction of Hadrian's work with preëxisting streets which joined it at various angles. The palaces of the Cæsars on the Palatine Hill (see Restoration, by Mr. Deglane, *Moniteur des Architectes*, and *The Builder*, Feb. 22, 1890) show numerous instances of this device. The various blocks were erected by succeeding emperors on sites which necessitated their being built at a slight angle one to the other. Each block appears to be symmetrically arranged with centre axis, but this applies only to the leading features, viz., the principal halls and the peristylar courts. The rooms on either side vary in their dimensions, but they are always contrived to balance one another; where the axis of the block is placed at a slight angle with a second block, its junction is marked by a semicircular or segmental niche. This seems to have been the principle adopted by the Romans, not only in the setting out of their palaces, but also in those of all the cities of the Empire.

So far we have dealt only with the main lines of the plans and the structures. The scheme of the decoration must have been conceived from the first, which is evidenced by the numerous recesses left in the walls to receive the blocks of marble forming the cornices. Owing to the value of the materials, which has led to their removal, there are but few instances in which any of it remains to bear witness to the magnificence of its design and colour. The rich marble decoration of the Pantheon is probably in the main not far removed from the type which was adopted in the great thermæ and palaces.

The appliqué nature of the decoration was a necessity because of the materials of the structure of these great Roman baths, and this becomes the more evident when we compare the palaces, the temples, and baths in Rome with those which are found throughout Syria. Here quarries of excellent stone existed in all parts of the country, and the core of the walls and the external face were homogeneous and constructed with the same material. In a few instances the walls were decorated with pilasters or semidetached columns, the latter frequently found in the interior of the cellas, but plain ashlar masonry in courses of from 2 to 3 feet in height was used as a general rule. There is one exceptional feature in Syria to which great importance was always attached, viz., the great entrance doorways of the temples, which were enriched with bands of carving. Some of these were of immense size, the great door in the Temple of Jupiter at Baalbec measuring 20 feet wide by 41 feet high. The lintel of this doorway was voussoired, the voussoirs being carried through both architrave and frieze. The peristyle of this temple, 9 feet between columns and wall, is covered over with single slabs of stone of segmental curve underneath and enriched with sunk coffers similar to those which, in the basilica of Maxentius at Rome, were sunk in the brickwork of the great arches of the aisles. Although contrary to Roman custom, the employment of Phœnician labour of the country probably led them to the quarrying and fixing in position of those enormous blocks which form the substructure of the great temple of Jupiter Sol. Three of these blocks, known as the "trilithon," measure from 62 to 64 feet, each one 12 feet high and 11 feet thick, and so close are the joints that it is impossible to insert a sheet of note paper in the same. As these blocks are raised on a foundation of smaller stones which Mr. Renan attributes to the Seleucidæ, he is of opinion that the large blocks must have been quarried and placed in their positions by the Romans.

The dome of the Pantheon was originally covered with tiles of gilt bronze (stripped off in 663), part of which still exists, as also does the bronze rim of the central opening with its enriched bronze mouldings. The inner ceiling of the portico was also in gilt bronze, supported by a system of bronze tubular girders; this was all taken away in 1626 to make the cannon for the Castel Sant' Angelo, and the great baldachino of S. Peter's.

The frigidarium of the Baths of Caracalla was covered over with a lattice-work ceiling formed of two T-bars, riveted together and then cased in bronze, showing that the Roman Imperial architect was acquainted with a type of iron construction which it was thought belonged only to the nineteenth century.

Among the other monuments of Imperial Rome the basilicas come next in importance, more, however, owing to their immense size and the magnificence of the materials employed in their construction and decoration than for any

special novelty in their design. They were evidently copies of the Greek stoa, and from the ephemeral nature of their timber roofs have long since passed away. The basilica Ulpia, which formed part of Trajan's forum, covered an area of 30,000 square feet. The central area, 180 feet by 54 feet wide, was enclosed with double aisles with galleries above, and was probably covered with a flat ceiling with deep coffers between the trussed beams, and lighted by clearstory windows above the gallery story.

The great basilica of Constantine commenced by Maxentius, but left unfinished at his death in 312 A.D., is a reproduction on a slightly larger scale of the tepidarium of the Baths of Caracalla. It was covered with an immense groined vault, over 80 feet in width, divided into three bays; with three deep recesses on each side which, communicating one with the other, form the aisles.

Although in the palaces of Rome we find a strict adherence to axial lines and symmetrical disposition, the description given by Pliny of his Laurentian villa, and the actual remains of the villa of Hadrian near Tivoli, show that away from Rome and in the country aspect and prospect would seem to have been the chief consideration. In these instances, as in all those where there were great differences of level in the ground, the Roman Imperial architect availed himself of natural eminences where he placed the most important halls, grouping other buildings around them, much in the same way as round the tepidarium of the Bath, though on different levels.

Under the heads of Syria and Asia Minor, the colonnaded streets which formed the main thoroughfare of the chief cities have received attention. In these features the Romans recognized the customs of the country, and developed on a larger scale and with greater magnificence the colonnades of the city of Antioch built by the Seleucidæ, but now known only from descriptions.

To works of a purely utilitarian character, such as the great aqueducts which still exist across the Campagna of Rome, in the north of Africa, in Syria, and in Asia Minor, the Romans probably attached but little architectural character. There are, however, a few instances (and particularly in Rome where the aqueduct crosses a thoroughfare) in which the engineer has attempted to make a display by an appliqué of the orders, and this as usual is unsatisfactory. In cases, however, where the Roman engineer confined himself to his legitimate sphere, viz., solid and economical construction, he has produced results which, from the æsthetic point of view, could not be surpassed. The Pont-du-Gard near Nîmes, built across a deep ravine, with two lower ranges of great arches carrying a third range of small arches, above which is the aqueduct channel, is not only from a constructive but from an artistic point of view one of the finest conceptions of Roman Imperial architecture.

The same can scarcely be said of those favourite examples of Roman Imperial architecture, the Arches of Triumph, which are found from one end of the Empire to the other, and were by the Romans probably regarded as their most successful masterpieces. Just so far as they were decorated with bas-reliefs representing the victories of the Empire, and in their superb construction, they have a definite object which they fulfil; but the assemblage of attached and detached columns and entablatures becomes monotonous and displays poverty of design.

It is, however, the one example which, whether in Europe or eastern countries, remains very much the same in design, except that in the latter, owing to want of sculptors, there are very seldom any bas-reliefs. In Palmyra and other eastern towns this was met by an elaboration of ornament which, executed by Greek artists, is sometimes of great beauty.

Amongst the numerous triumphal arches, the example of Trajan at Benevento is one of the most pleasing, as the Corinthian columns are only semidetached and serve as a frame to the bas-reliefs which decorate it. In arches of a more utilitarian character, such as those forming the entrances of towns, as the two at Autun, the Gateway of Saintes, or of the bridge at Saint Chamas in France, and the gateways of Ancona and Verona in Italy, the architectural result, though simple, is more satisfactory. The great arch at Palmyra, one of the largest in existence, is triangular on plan, and is one of those designs dear to the Roman Imperial mind which was conceived to mask the angle of two colonnaded streets, viz., the main thoroughfare of the town leading from west to east and the street to the western propylon of the great Temple of Jupiter.

More originality and variety is shown in other examples of Roman Imperial monuments (see Memorial Column). Of Hadrian's mausoleum we have only the kernel in the Castel Sant' Angelo (which see), but with its several tiers of peristyles, it must have been one of the most splendid examples of Roman architecture. The tomb of Cecilia Metella and others of the Via Appia in the Street of Tombs, which extends four miles outside Rome, are in too ruinous a condition to judge of their pristine beauty, and the same may be said of those in the Street of Tombs at Pompeii. In France and Germany they seem to have met with a better fate, and the tomb of S. Remy near Tarascon and the Igel tomb near Trèves are well-preserved examples of considerable interest.

— R. PHENÈ SPIERS.

347

R. Adam, *Ruins of the Palace of the Emperor Diocletian at Spalatro in Dalmatia;* Baumeister, *Denkmäler des klassischen Altertums;* Bender, *Rom und Römisches Leben im Alterthum;* Comparetti and De Petra, *La Villa Ercolanese;* Ferrero, *L'Arc d'Auguste a Suse;* Lanciani, *The Destruction of Ancient Rome; The Ruins and Excavations of Ancient Rome; Ancient Rome in the Light of Recent Discoveries; Pagan and Christian Rome;* Martha, *Archéologie Étrusque et Romaine;* Mau, *Pompeii, its Life and Art;* Mazois, *Les ruines de Pompei;* J. H. Middleton, *The Remains of Ancient Rome* (2 vols.); Nissen, *Pompejanische studien zur Städtekunde des Alterthums;* Normand, *Essai sur l'existence d'une architecture métallique antique,* etc., *Encyclopédie d'arch.,* 1883; Overbeck, *Pompeji in seinen Gebäuden, Alterthümern und Kunstwerken;* W. C. Perry, *Greek and Roman Sculpture;* Peterson and Von Domaszewski, *Die Marcus-Säule;* Ramsay, *Manual of Roman Antiquities,* revised by Lanciani (see above); Reber, *Geschichte der Baukunst im Alterthume; Restaurations des Monuments Antiques* (a series; Thermæ, Trajan Column, etc.); Smith, *Dictionary of Greek and Roman Antiquities,* 3d ed., 1890; Taylor and Cresy, *Architectural Antiquities of Rome;* Uchard, *Architecture de Pompei — ordre ionique — Revue gén. de l'arch.,* 1860; *ordre Corinthien — Revue gén. de l'arch.,* 1862; Vitruvius, *De Architectura* (or Gwilt's Translation); Weichardt, *Pompeji vor der Zerstoerung* (a study of restorations of the ancient buildings); Wickhoff, *Roman Art* (Macmillan; a translation from an extra volume of the *Jahrbuch der kunsthistorischen Sammlungen des österreichischen Kaiserhauses;* Robert Wood, *Ruins of Palmyra and Balbec.* See also the bibliography under Etruscan Architecture, and Jules Martha, *L'Art Étrusque.*

ROMANO, GIULIO. (See Pippi, Giulio.)

ROMAN ORDER. The peculiar system introduced by the Romans of late Republican or early Imperial times, by which an arched construction is given some appearance of Greek post-and-lintel building. In the illustration under Alette, in each story an engaged column carries, in appearance, an entablature. The abutments and the arch which they carry, and the wall upon this arch, are, however, the real structure, and the entablature is merely an ornamental balcony. The structure is really a highly adorned arcade. (See Roman Imperial Architecture, tenth paragraph.)

RONDELET, JEAN BAPTISTE; architect; b. June 4, 1743; d. Sept. 28, 1829.

In 1763 he came to Paris to study under J. F. Blondel (see Blondel, J. F.) and later assisted Soufflot (see Soufflot) as inspector of the works at the church of S. Geneviève, afterward the Panthéon (Paris). In 1783 he obtained a royal pension and visited Italy. In 1785 he superintended the construction of the dome of the Panthéon under Brebion (see Brebion), who had succeeded Soufflot. In 1799 he was appointed professor at the *École des Beaux Arts.* Rondelet published *Traité théorique et de l'art de bâtir* (Paris, 1802, text 5 vols. 4to, pls. 2 vols. folio), *Mémoires historiques sur le dôme du Panthéon français* (Paris, 1 vol. 4to,

348

ROOD SCREEN (JUBÉ): S. MADELEINE AT TROYES; 1508 A.D.

1814), *Traduction des commentaires de Frontin sur les aqueducs de Rome*, etc.

Bellier de la Chavignerie, *Dictionnaire;* Lance, *Dictionnaire.*

ROOD. A cross or crucifix, especially a large crucifix placed at the entrance of the choir or chancel in mediæval churches, often supported on the rood beam or rood screen, and, in later examples, accompanied by images of the Virgin Mary on one side and of S. John on the other, the Crucified being in the middle.

ROOD ALTAR. An altar standing against the nave or outer side of a rood screen.

ROOD ARCH. The central arch in a rood screen, the rood being over it. (See Rood Screen and Rood.) The term is sometimes applied to the arch between the nave and chancel, the rood in that case being under it.

ROOD BEAM. A horizontal beam extending across the entrance to the choir or chancel of a church to support the rood ; generally at the line of the springing of the choir or chancel arch.

ROOD LOFT. A gallery or elevated platform established upon the rood screen, with pierced parapets, pinnacles, and images culminated in the central rood. From this loft the Epistles and Gospels were sometimes read to the people assembled in the nave, and sermons were occasionally preached.

ROOD SCREEN. A screen, open or partly closed, of wood, stone, or wrought iron, erected in mediæval churches between the nave and the choir or chancel supporting the rood in the centre ; it was sometimes double with vaulting between and rood loft over, and frequently richly adorned with niches, statues, tracery, and other architectural details. The jubé of the church of the Madeleine at Troyes is among the richest of the remaining examples in wrought stone. (See Choir Screen and references ; Jubé ; Rood ; Rood Loft.)

ROOD SPIRE. A spire or steeple built externally over the intersection of nave and transepts, because that point marks the entrance to the choir and the position of the rood. It was generally of wood, as at Amiens and Paris ; but the term is extended to great central spires, as at Lichfield.

ROOD STAIRS. Stairs by which the rood loft was approached. These were placed at the ends of the rood screen, were often spiral, and of beautifully sculptured open work and tracery.

ROOD STEEPLE. Same as Rood Spire.

ROOD TOWER. A tower built externally over the entrance to the choir from the nave, or over the intersection of nave and transepts.

ROOF. That part of the closure of a building which covers it in from the sky. Upon this part of a building depends in large measure the character of its design as a work of architecture. Roofs are distinguished : (1) By their form and method of construction ; as, the flat roof, characteristic of dry tropical countries, and much used in modern commercial buildings in the United States ; the sloping roof, including gabled, hipped, penthouse, mansard, and gambrel-roofs with their varieties (see Pitch). (2) By the character of their covering ; as, thatched, shingled, battened, slated, tiled, metal-covered, tarred, asphalted, gravelled, etc.

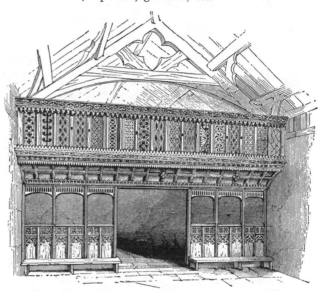

ROOD LOFT: LLANEGRYNN, MERIONETHSHIRE; C. 1500.

The cross (rood) is no longer in place ; perhaps removed during the Puritan supremacy.

In carpentry, the term refers to the timber framework by which the external surface is supported. This, in sloping roofs, consists usually of a series of pairs of opposite rafters or couples, of which the lower ends are tied together in various ways to prevent spreading ; or, where the span is too great for such simple construction and there are no intermediate upright supports, of a series of rafters supported by longitudinal horizontal purlins, which are generally carried on a system of transverse timber frames or trusses, spaced from 8 to 20 feet apart. In modern practice, the typical forms of these trusses are indicated in figures 1 and 2, showing principal rafters or principals, of which the lower opposite ends are tied together by tiebeams hung in the centre from a king-post, as shown in figure 1 ; or, at two points, from queen-posts, as shown in figure 2 ; from the lower part of these suspension members, braces or struts may be extended to stiffen the principals. To suit various conditions of shape of roof and area to be covered, these typical and elementary forms are, in modern usage,

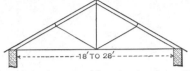

subjected to innumerable structural modifications and extensions, some of which are illustrated in the figures of this article and in Wood, Construction in ; Part I.

One of the most marked distinctions in the historic styles consists in the pitch or inclination of the roof. Thus in the Greek temple the slope of the pediment varied from 15° to 16½° ;

Traité pratique de la Construction Moderne et description du Matériel employé par les constructeurs, Paris, 1887, 2 vol. folio.
— H. Van Brunt.

Barrel Roof. *A.* Same as Barrel Vault (which see under Vault). *B.* A roof or ceiling

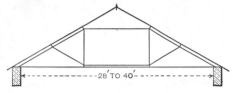

which has within the appearance of a Barrel Vault ; a ceiling of nearly semicircular section.

Compass Roof ; Compass-headed Roof. (See Cradle Roof below ; also Compass (II).)

Coupled Roof. A ridged or double pitched roof of the simplest construction, often without

Roman roofs had a slope of from 22° to 23½° ; Romanesque roofs followed closely the Roman slope ; the Gothic pitch was much steeper, sometimes reaching 50° or even 60°. In the Renaissance era there was in Italy a revival of the Roman pitch with the other classic features ; but the French builders of this era retained the steepest slopes of the mediæval sky lines, especially in the conical roofs of their round towers and in the pyramidal roofs with which they characteristically covered each separate division of their buildings. These lofty roofs, with their high dormers, chimneys, and crestings, constitute a distinctive characteristic of the French Renaissance, the peculiar steep roof of double slope, known as the mansard roof, being a development from these French traditions. The structural conditions from which the steep mediæval pitch was evolved are explained in Wood, Construction in ; Part I., where also may be found some notice of the flat terraced roofs of tropical or semi-tropical countries.

Denfer, J., *Couverture des Édifices ; Ardoises, Tuiles, Métaux, Matières diverses. Chênaux et descentes*, Paris, 1893, 1 vol., 4to ; Lanck, Leopold,

tiebeam or collar beam, depending upon the stiffness of the walls for its permanence, and, therefore, of small span.

Roof of Stone; Slabs resting on Cross Walls carried on Arches.
For similar transverse arches see cuts Monastic Architecture; Pointed Architecture.

ROOF: CHURCH OF S. MINIATO, FLORENCE; TYPICAL BASILICAN ROOF; A WOODEN
GALLERY RESTS UPON THE TIE BEAMS.

Cradle Roof. A form of timber roof much used in the Middle Ages for churches and large halls, in which the rafters, collar beams, and braces of each truss were combined into an approximately arched form, and sometimes indeed had their soffits cut to the curve of an arch, producing internally the effect of a series of arches; or, when the arched members were ceiled, of a cradle vault.

kind are the metal-covered roofs of Europe and America in which the slope is often half an inch to a foot or one in twenty-four. The plates of metal in these cases must be soldered together with care.

French Roof. A curb roof with sides set at a very steep angle so as sometimes to approach verticality, while the top above the curb may be nearly flat or may have a visible slope though

Roof: with Collar Beams and Braces (Knee Rafters), 13th Century; Hall of Stokesay Castle, Shropshire.

Curb Roof. One in which the slope is broken on two or four sides; so called because a horizontal curb is built at the plane where the slope changes (see Curb, *D*; Gambrel Roof; French Roof; Mansard Roof; which are forms of curb roof).

Flat Roof. *A.* One whose surface is actually horizontal or with no perceptible slope, as in the mud, earth, or cement roofs of tropical countries and the roofs of brick or terra cotta supported by iron beams and covered with water-tight material which are characteristic of modern fireproof buildings.

B. A roof having a slope so slight that one can walk or sit upon it as upon a floor. Of this

much less steep than the lower slope. The term is of United States origin, and applies especially to a form of roof which, beginning about 1865, became very common all over the country.

Gable; Gabled Roof. A ridge roof which terminates at each end in a gable, as distinguished from a hipped roof. A gambrel roof is a form of gable roof.

Gambrel Roof. A curb roof with only the two opposite sides sloping; it is therefore a gabled curb roof. This form is common throughout New England, New Jersey and eastern New York, having been adopted by the earlier colonists of the Northern states, and being much more frequently seen there than in the countries whence the colonists came.

Hip ; Hipped Roof. One having hips by which the projecting angles between two adjacent slopes are squared. Thus, a pyramidal roof is one which has four hips ; and in some cases a roof, as on a building of irregular plan, may have more hips than four and often alternating with valleys.

gables, each of which is truncated halfway up or thereabout so that the roof is hipped above. It may be otherwise explained as a hipped roof, of which the hips starting from the ridge are too short to reach the eaves, so that the roof below becomes a gabled roof of which the gables are truncated.

Lean-to Roof. One with a single slope ; as where the aisle of a church is usually roofed

Roof: Early English; Solar of House at Charney, Berkshire; c. 1270; with Cambered Cross Beams supporting Posts and a Purlin Plate by Direct Resistance to Pressure; 13th Century.

Homogeneous Roof. One in which the same mass of material furnishes the outer pitch for shedding rain water and the surface exposed within ; that is to say, a roof forming a solid shell either of compact masonry, as often in Byzantine art, or of slabs of stone, as in Syria and in a few churches of Europe. (See cut Sebenico, under Dalmatia.)

Jerkin Head Roof. A ridge roof of which the ridge is shorter than the eaves, having two

with a single slope from the wall of the clearstory outward.

M Roof. One in which two ridges parallel or nearly so to one another are separated by a receding or dropping valley, gutter, or the like ; a device sometimes resorted to for diminishing the height of the roof, as in supposed necessities of the architectural style, and sometimes resulting from the building of an addition when it is not desired to disturb the earlier roof.

Mansard Roof. A curbed roof with dormer windows of some size; that is to say, such a roof as will best provide for habitable rooms within it. This is the roof common in neoclassic and modern châteaux and public buildings in France, the deck or upper slope being usually small in proportion to the lower slopes, whereas in the French Roof (see subtitle above) the reverse may be the case.

Pavilion Roof. A roof hipped on all sides so as to have a pyramidal or nearly pyramidal form.

Penthouse Roof. A roof with one pitch like that of a shed or of the aisle of a church in the ordinary distribution.

Pyramidal Roof. One in the form of a pyramid or, by extension, a hipped roof in which the ridge is relatively short so that the sloping sides end nearly in a point.

Ridge; Ridged Roof. A double-pitched roof, the two slopes of which meet at a horizontal ridge.

Saddleback Roof. A gable roof in some peculiar position, as when a tower is roofed in this way instead of terminating in a flat terrace or in a spire.

Shed Roof. Same as Penthouse Roof.

Single-framed Roof. A roof framed without trusses, the opposite rafters being tied together by the upper floor frame or by boards nailed across horizontally to serve as ties or collars.

Slab Slate Roof. A roof covered with slabs or flags of slate, as in cottages built in the neighbourhood of slate quarries.

Span Roof. A roof composed of two equal

ROOF: WITH CAMBERED CROSS BEAMS CARRYING A DECORATIVE SYSTEM OF BRACES AND STRUTS.

slopes, as a nave roof, in contradistinction to one having one slope, as an aisle roof or penthouse roof.

Terrace Roof. A flat roof in sense *A*; especially when the roofing is of masonry and the surface allows of free use of the roof as a place for walking and taking the air.

Trough Roof. Same as M Roof.

Truss Roof. A roof, the rafters of which are supported on a truss, or a series of trusses, by means of purlins.

Valley Roof. One which covers a building so arranged with projecting wings or pavilions, nearly on the same level as the main roof, that there are valleys at the junction of the two parts of the roof. The term is hardly applied to roofs which have merely the valleys of dormers and small gables.

ROOF COVERING. The closure laid upon a roof frame, including the wood sheathing or boarding, and the outside protection or weathering by metal, slate, tiles, shingles, painted

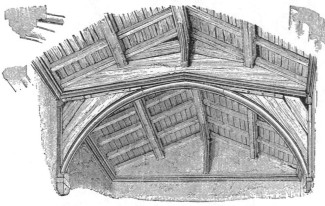

ROOF: FRAMED LIKE A FLOOR: HEAVY CROSS BEAMS CARRYING PURLINS, AND STIFFENED BY BRACES CUT TO A CURVE WHICH IS COMPLETED BY MOULDINGS PLANTED ON; KIDDINGTON, OXON; c. 1350.

canvas, tarred paper, thatch, by any composition of tar, bitumen, asphaltum, etc., with gravel, or any other form of protection

ROOF: LIKE THAT AT CHARNEY, BUT MUCH LIGHTER AS BEING WORK OF A SKILLED CONSTRUCTOR; HIGHAM FERRERS, NORTHAMPTONSHIRE; C. 1350.

against the weather. In the few cases of absolutely incombustible construction (see Fireproofing) the slates or tiles are tied by lead wire

ROOF: OF STAIRCASE, THORNTON ABBEY, LINCOLNSHIRE; C. 1370.

to iron laths; or, the roof being filled up solid with brick, terra cotta, or cement blocks, large sheets of copper, zinc, or lead may be nailed upon it, lapping over one another like slates, and left free at the lower end to allow for ex-

pansion and contraction; or, in flat roofs, large slabs of slate or stone are bedded in cement. In the more usual cases, roofs of any pitch may be covered with metal, which is nearly always of tin plates in the United States; though tern plates are used, and, much more rarely, zinc, as in France, lead, as often in Great Britain, or copper. The term, The Leads, applied in England to a nearly flat roof which may be used as a floor, is unknown in the United States, where such a roof would be covered with tin plates or with tar and gravel. Steep roofs alone may be covered with tiles, slate, or shingles, laid in the usual way, without any filling or cementing of the joints; and it is to be noted that rain and snow may beat in through the crevices to a slight degree without serious damage. (See the separate terms: also Flashing.)

ROOF GARDEN. A garden formed upon a flat roof, especially prepared for the purpose by arranging thereon growing plants and shrubbery in pots, tubs, and boxes, and occasionally by accumulating thereon sufficient soil to sustain grass and other small vegetation; specifically, a place of public entertainment in the open air upon a roof, provided with facilities for vaudeville performances, partly sheltered by awnings and adorned with a few ornamental plants.

ROOF GUARD. A device to prevent snow from sliding off a roof without interfering with its watershed; it is fencing or openwork of wood or iron at the foot of the slope, or of stiff wire bent into the form of loops, laid in with the slate or shingles, and forming projections distributed over the roof surface so as to arrest the tendency of snow to slide.

ROOF: ELABORATE HAMMER-BEAM CONSTRUCTION; S. STEPHEN'S CHURCH, NORWICH; c. 1480.

ROOFING. The materials of which a roof is composed; the art of constructing a roof. (See Roof Covering.)

ROOFING SLATE. (See under Slate.)

ROOF PLATE. A Wall Plate (see under Plate), which carries roof timbers.

ROOF STAGING. A scaffolding used by roofers in working on a roof slope. It automatically holds fast to the roof by means of barbed rods or claw plates.

ROOF TREE. Same as Ridge Piece — Pole. Sometimes used figuratively, referring to the whole roof as a shelter.

ROOF TRUSS. In carpentry, one of the transverse timber frames composed of principals, ties, struts, and suspension rods, used in roofs of wide span to support common rafters by means of longitudinal purlins.

ROOM. An enclosure or division of a house or other structure, separated from other divisions by partitions; an apartment, a chamber; as a drawing-room, parlour, dining room, or chamber in a house, a stateroom in a ship or railroad car, a harness room in a stable.

ROOT, JOHN WELLBORN; architect; b. 1851; d. 1891.

He was born in Atlanta (Georgia), and in 1864 was smuggled through the Federal lines and sent to England. Returning to America after the war, he graduated at the College of the City of New York and entered the office of James Renwick (see Renwick). He afterward became an assistant of John B. Snook, and under his direction superintended the construction of the Grand Central Station in New York City. In 1872 he entered the office of Drake & Wight in Chicago, and later formed a partnership with Daniel H. Burnham. Root held the important office of consulting architect of the World's Fair Commission in Chicago.

Harriet Monroe, *John Wellborn Root.*

ROPE. A roll moulding decorated with a twist like the strands of a rope, common in Romanesque architecture; a cable moulding. (See Cabling.)

RORITZER, KONRAD (THOMAS and **WOLFGANG);** architects.

Konrad Roritzer was architect of the cathedral of Ratisbon (Regensburg) from 1459 to 1465, and built also the choir of the Lorenz Kirche at Nuremberg between 1459 and 1477. Thomas Roritzer was cathedral architect at Ratisbon (Regensburg) in 1482 and Wolfgang

Roritzer held that office in 1514, when he was decapitated for sedition.

Popp, *Les Trois Âges de l'Architecture Gothique;* Seubert, *Künstler-lexikon.*

ROSACE. Same as Rosette (I.).

ROSACE FROM A HOUSE AT BETOURSA, SYRIA;
5TH TO 6TH CENTURY.

ROSE. *A*. A conventional representation of the flower in its original or wild state, much used in Gothic sculpture and especially in late English Gothic and Elizabethan art. One form of it is especially suggestive of English political changes. (See Tudor Rose below.)

B. A circular or nearly circular ornament. (Compare Rosace, Rosette, Roundel.)

C. A diaphragm of woven wire or of a plate of metal pierced with holes to stop solid matters which might clog a pipe.

Tudor Rose. (Originally, in heraldic use; hence common in architecture.) A combination of two or three single wild roses, red and white, one above another, expressing the marriage of Henry VII. of England with Elizabeth of York, and the resulting peace between York and Lancaster. In the Deanery at Worcester the flower is seven-petalled: sometimes it is six-petalled; usually it is, as in nature, five-petalled. It has always five small, sharp "rays," representing the leaves of the calyx.

ROSENGARTEN, ALBERT ; architect : b. 1809.

In 1839 he won a three years' travelling scholarship and went to Paris to study with the architect Labrouste (see Labrouste). After a sojourn of two years in Italy, he established a large practice in Hamburg, Germany. He published *Die Architektonischen Stylarten* (1874, 1 vol. 8vo).

Seubert, *Künstler-lexikon.*

ROSETTE (I.). A decoration common in all the historical styles, treated as a flower, a knot of foliage, or as a patera with conventional or geometrical detail, generally approaching circular in form, but sometimes square. In Roman architecture, it occurred in the centre of ceiling or soffit panels, and as a central ornament on the Corinthian abacus. In mediaeval architecture, rosettes of square form were frequent in the decoration of mouldings, as a knot of foliage in the centre of foliated panels, etc. In early Italian work, rosettes

appeared often as geometrical inlays of coloured marbles. — H. V. B.

ROSETTE (II.). (See Electrical Appliances.)

ROSE WINDOW. A window which is of circular form, especially a large one and filled with tracery such as those of the west and north and south transept fronts of Gothic churches. In these, however, the circular form of the window, although distinguishable, is sometimes, in later work, a part of the tracery of a still larger window with pointed head. When a rose window has the tracery bars arranged in decidedly radiating order it is often called Wheel Window, and by a popular extension, Catherine Wheel Window. (See cols. 1093–1098.)

ROSS, LUDWIG ; philologist and archæologist; b. July 22, 1806 : d. Aug. 6, 1859.

Ross studied in Kiel, Copenhagen, and Leipzig, and in 1832 went to Greece. In 1834 he was appointed chief conservator of the antiquities of Greece and in 1837 professor of archæology at the University of Athens. With Schaubert (see Schaubert) and Christian Hansen (see Hansen, H. C.) he restored the temple of Nike. Apteros on the Acropolis at Athens. In 1843 he made a journey among the Greek islands and in Asia Minor. In 1845 he was appointed professor of archæology at the University of Halle, Germany. He published *Die Akropolis von Athen . . . der Tempel der Nike Apteros* (1839, 1 vol. folio) ; *Reisen auf den Griechischen Inseln* (1840–1852, 4 vols.) ; *Das Theseion und der Tempel des Ares zu Athen* (1852).

Brockhaus, *Konversations Lexikon.*

ROSSELINO. (See Gambarelli.)

ROSSI, DOMENICO ; architect ; d. 1742.

A pupil of Baldassare Longhena (see Longhena). He built the façade of the church of S. Eustachio, the church of S. Maria dei Gesuiti (1715–1728), the Palazzo Corner della Regina (1724), and the Palazzo Saudi (1721), all in Venice.

Gurlitt, *Geschichte des Barockstiles in Italien.*

ROSSI, GIOVANNI BATTISTA DE (*il Commendatore*) ; archæologist ; b. 1822 ; d. 1894.

Il Commendatore G. B. de Rossi was the historian of Christian and subterranean Rome, and published a remarkable series of works on this subject: *Inscriptiones Christianæ urbis Romæ*, (1857–1885, 3 vols.); *Roma Sotterranea cristiana* (1864–1877, 3 vols. folio); *Mosaici cristiani e Saggi di pavimenti delle chiese di Roma* (1878). He was also editor of *Bulletino d' Archeologia cristiana* (1863). He assisted Henzen and Mommsen in the direction of the *Corpus Universale Inscriptionum Latinarum.*

Nécrologie in *Construction Moderne*, Sept. 29, 1894.

ROSSO, IL (Giovanni Battista di Jacopo; called in France, Maître Roux); painter and decorator; b. 1496 (at Florence, Italy); d. 1541.

Rosso was one of the young men who studied from the cartoons of Michelangelo (see Buonarroti). In 1530 he went to France and was employed with Primaticcio (see Primaticcio) in the decoration of the palace of Fontainebleau. He decorated the *Grande Galerie* and the *Chambre de Madame d'Estampes* at Fontainebleau.

Vasari, Milanesi ed.; Palustre, *Renaissance;* Pfnor, *Monographie de Fontainebleau;* Rouyer et Darcel, *L'Art Architectural.*

ROSSO ANTICO (*Porfido Rosso Antico*). This is, according to Delesse, a porphyrite; *i.e.* a basic eruptive rock, consisting essentially of a compact reddish felsitic base, in which crystals of hornblende and rose-coloured plagioclase feldspar are porphyritically developed. The stone was used by the ancient Egyptians for making statues of the deities and for other ornamental purposes, and later by the Romans. The original source of the rock was the Dokhan Mountains on the west shore of the Red Sea, in Egypt. — G. P. M.

ROSTRA. (See Rostrum, *B.*)

ROSTRAL COLUMN. (See under Column; also see Memorial Column; Rostrum.)

ROSTRUM (pl. Rostra). *A.* The beak or prow of a ship, used as a ram in the naval conflicts of the Greeks and Romans; it consisted of a beam or beams armed with heavy pointed irons, the whole being affixed to the bows of the war galleys above or below the water line. Captured rostra were preserved as symbols of victory.

B. In the plural (Rostra), a platform elevated in the Roman Forum, so called because its basement or podium was decorated with the rostra of ships captured in the first naval victory of the Republic; from this platform orations and pleadings were delivered to the Roman populace.

C. Any pulpit or platform from which addresses are made.

ROT. (See Dry Rot.)

ROTUNDA. A circular hall, especially one covered by a cupola like the Pantheon or the central hall of the Capitol at Washington. The frequent application of this term to any large central area in any public building, as the " office " of a hotel, which is neither circular in plan nor covered by a dome, is improper.

ROUBILLAC (**ROUBILIAC**), **LOUIS FRANÇOIS**; sculptor; b. 1695 (at Lyons, France); d. Jan. 11, 1762.

A pupil of Balthazar, sculptor to the Elector of Saxony and probably also of Nicolas Coustou (see Coustou, N.). He won the second *Grand Prix* at the Académie Royale in 1730. He appears first in England in 1738, when he made a statue of Handel for Vauxhall gardens, London. In 1743 he made the monument of John Campbell, Duke of Argyll (Westminster Abbey), in 1753 the monument to Admiral Sir Peter Warren (Westminster Abbey), in 1758 the statue of Shakespeare (British Museum), in 1761 the well-known Nightingale monument (Westminster Abbey).

Walpole, *Anecdotes;* Stephen-Lee, *Dictionary of National Biography.*

ROUGH CAST; **HARD CAST.** A kind of plaster made with strong lime mortar and sand, mixed with clean gravel until it resembles a concrete, used for the exterior faces of rough masonry walls, as of small country houses. In different parts of Great Britain and the United States different processes are used. Sometimes the mortar is very hot when the gravel is mixed with it. Commonly the whole mixture is thrown or dashed forcibly against the wall when freshly plastered. The surface is often coloured by a wash while still wet.

ROUGHING-IN. Any coarse mechanical process preliminary and preparatory to final or finished work, as the rough coat of mortar forming a foundation for one or more coats of fine plaster, or, in a scheme of decoration, the necessary mechanical groundwork of colours or modelling. Specifically, in plumbing, the establishment of the system of pipes for supply and waste, done while the house is preparing for plastering, and before the pipes are connected with the fixtures.

ROULETTE. Same as Dotting Pen. (See Drawing Pen, *B*, under Pen.)

ROUND CHURCH. One whose plan is a circle or is symmetrical about a centre, and not

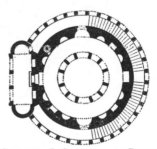

ROUND CHURCH: S. COSTANZA AT ROME; PLAN.

arranged upon a defined axis. Polygonal churches, and those which consist of equal arms radiating from a central point, are included in this term. Such buildings are apt to differ radically from longitudinal churches in that they are centred upon some monument or feature which is set in the middle, and for whose protection or accommodation the church is planned. The baptisteries were buildings of this kind (see Baptistery), being planned to receive a central font or basin.

The round plan for buildings belongs, with variations, to most styles and periods of architecture. It was a favourite among the Romans and common among the Greeks, especially for mortuary and commemorative structures; and from these evidently the Christians adopted it. The circular type prevailed with the Romans — on a large scale as we see it in the mausoleums of Hadrian and Augustus, on a small scale in many lesser tombs. It was a favourite form for temples to lesser divinities and heroes; for example, the temples of Vesta and Her-

is the same. The niches were continued in Christian architecture, especially in baptisteries, but the round form gradually prevailed in them over the rectangular. The Roman tombs, and rotundas that appear to have been tombs, were most commonly domed, and are often lighted, like the Pantheon, through a round opening in the crown of the dome. This last treatment appealed to the Christian sentiment; we are expressly told that the rotundas that Constantine built at Jerusalem, to commemorate the Holy Sepulchre and the place of Christ's

ROUND CHURCH: S. COSTANZA AT ROME; SEE PLAN.

cules at Rome and of Vesta at Tivoli, and still more for important tombs. This last use commended it to the Christians for memorial buildings. The most characteristic Roman type was a cylinder with a thick wall, in which niches were cut inside, most commonly eight, usually square and semicircular in alternation. We see this type at Rome in the so-called Torre dei Schiavi and the Mausoleum of Helena, at Tivoli; in the Madonna della Torre, and on the largest scale, with some complication, in the Pantheon. In what is known as the Temple of Jupiter at Spalato, the building is octagonal without and circular within, an Eastern fashion that became characteristic of Byzantine work, but the arrangement of niches

ascension, were in the middle left open to the heavens into which he had ascended. Others of the earliest Christian buildings seem to have been built in this way. Some authorities have believed it of S. Costanza at Rome, S. Maria Maggiore at Nocera, and the Baptistery of Constantine. The baptistery at Mujelia in Syria was apparently uncovered in the middle; and in the great church or group of churches consecrated to S. Simeon Stylites at Kalat Siman, the central octagon from which the four arms radiate, and in which was preserved the pillar on which the saint had stood, was characteristically left unroofed. (See cut under Planning; also under Syria.)

Round churches were not naturally adapted

to the liturgical worship of the Church; the very early custom of setting the clergy conspicuously aside from the congregation did not allow of their officiating in the middle of the church, but required them to stand apart toward the east. This orientation at once established a longitudinal axis in the church that was at variance with the centralized plan of the round church. This fact of the orientation of the liturgical churches divided the buildings into two classes, one symmetrical about a line, the other about a point. The need of separating the central feature, tomb or font, from the body of the spectators in the round building naturally led to dividing the building into a central nave, as it were, and a surrounding aisle — which was, in fact, as some writers have noticed, the infusion of the basilican idea into the round structure, for the central space must needs be lighted by a clearstory. The separation of this space from the aisle, whether by a range of columns or by an arcade, soon almost enjoined the substitution of a polygonal plan, with piers or columns at the

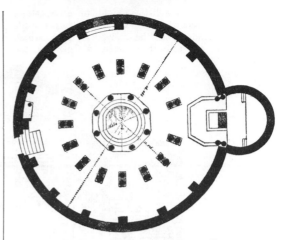

ROUND CHURCH: S. MARIA AT NOCERA, SOUTH ITALY; 6TH CENTURY A.D.; PLAN.

angles, for the round. The difficulty and awkwardness of applying arcades to a circular plan is conspicuous in S. Costanza and in the baptistery (S. Maria Maggiore) at Nocera. The smaller the building and the sharper the curve, the greater the difficulty. We have no chronological series of securely dated round buildings by which we can trace their progress continuously, but it is clear that there was in the first Christian centuries a rapid change from the circular plan, which the R o m a n s preferred, to the polygonal form. By the time of Justinian, and even earlier, if we may judge from the remains in central Syria, the straight-sided shape had prevailed for the main lines, though the round outline was retained in niches and apses. We see both combined in S. Sofia and SS. Sergius and Bacchus at Constantinople, and in S. Vitale at Ravenna, where the main constructive arches of the building are set in the straight walls of a polygonal enclosure, while the arcades of the apses, which are merely decora-

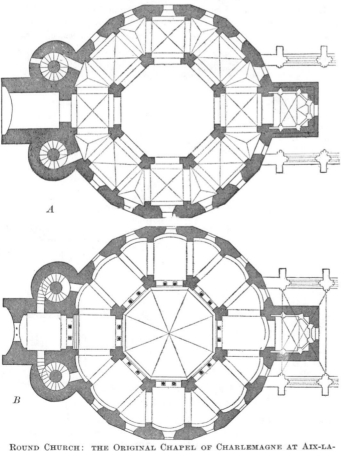

_A_

_B_

ROUND CHURCH: THE ORIGINAL CHAPEL OF CHARLEMAGNE AT AIX-LA-CHAPELLE; _A_, GROUND STORY; _B_, UPPER STORY.

tive, and have little weight to carry, stand on a circular plan. The effort to reconcile the arcade, and the polygonal plan which suited it, with the dome, which was the

space than were covered by any other form of roofing in masonry. This invention, giving commanding importance to the central feature of the plan, and shown in its greatest develop-

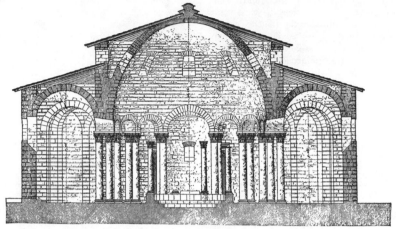

ROUND CHURCH: S. MARIA AT NOCERA; SEE PLAN.

favourite covering of the Romans, and to which the Eastern builders clung tenaciously, led to the great invention of pendentives, by which

ment in S. Sofia, became the leading influence in shaping Byzantine churches (see Byzantine Architecture). These, nevertheless, though the

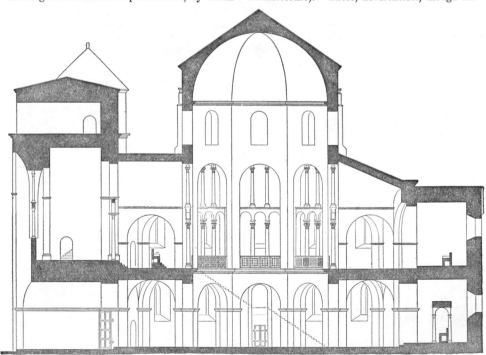

ROUND CHURCH: AIX-LA-CHAPELLE; SEE PLANS.

the dome could be hung even over a square plan, leaving the floor under it unobstructed, except by four piers at the corners of the square, and opening vaster areas of interior

square or nearly square plan prevails in them, with a central dome, are intended for liturgical worship, and so are built on an axis, and to be classed, not as round churches, but as longitudinal. The Byzantine church was thus intermediate between the round and the cruciform.

Round churches were built here and there over Europe through the early Christian period and the Middle Ages, though they were few, and grew rarer in the later periods, compared with those of basilican and cruciform types, which were almost imperative for the needs of great congregations. The two churches of S. Costanza at Rome and S. Maria Maggiore at of uncertain date, shows the masonry of a century or two later. It was doubtless meant originally for a baptistery, for which the unusually large font still occupies the centre. Both were evidently converted into churches for liturgical worship some time after their building, for the apses in both are later additions. S. Stefano Rotondo, the other great early round church of Rome, is of basilican structure, far slighter than these two, being roofed with

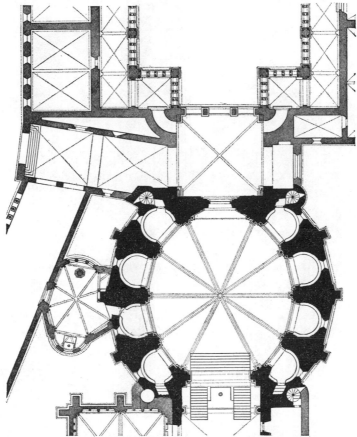

ROUND CHURCH: S. GEREON'S AT COLOGNE; THE OLDER PART NOW ALTERED INTO A GOTHIC ROTUNDA; ITS PLAN IS OF UNKNOWN ANTIQUITY; PROBABLY 4TH CENTURY A.D.

Nocera, already mentioned, the second an obvious imitation of the first, are of peculiar form. A circular arcade, in the one case of twelve arches and in the other of fifteen, whose columns are in pairs set across the wall, and therefore radially, encloses a central space some 40 feet wide, which is domed, and surrounded by an aisle under an annular vault. S. Costanza, built, we are told, in the fourth century as the mausoleum of the sister and the daughter of Constantine, is of brick and concrete in the Roman style of that day, but the dome is raised on a clearstory. The church at Nocera, wood, with concentric aisles round a central rotunda some 70 feet in diameter, which now at least contains the altar. Essenwein's theory that S. Stefano was built in imitation of Constantine's church of the Holy Sepulchre, and that the middle was at first open to the sky, is at least plausible; the fact that it was dedicated to the protomartyr lends some colour to it. It is clear that the round form of the Holy Sepulchre had much influence on the building of round churches among the early Christians, and that this influence was revived in the West during the crusades. The great rotunda whose foundations remain in the church of S. Bénigne at Dijon was apparently an imitation of it, built in the eleventh century ; the form and the name are recalled in the church called S. Sepolcro among the complex of chapels known as S. Stefano at Bologna. The churches built by the Knights Templars over Europe, of which the Temple Church in Lon-

Christians added to the Roman form. SS. Angeli at Perugia and the old rotunda of S. Gereon at Cologne, rebuilt in the thirteenth century, both buildings of uncertain date, are furthur instances. S. Vitale of Ravenna, already noticed, contemporary of S. Sofia, set the example of a more complicated structure radiating from a polygonal centre. It was

ROUND CHURCH: S. GEREON'S AT COLOGNE, FROM THE S.E.; SEE PLAN.
The smaller accessory buildings are not shown.

don is one, are later examples, as is the smaller one at Cambridge called S. Sepulchre, and that of Neuvy-Saint-Sépulcre in France. The Rotonda in Brescia, if it belongs to the eleventh century, is probably due to the same influence, and it repeats the same type. S. Michael's at Fulda was a German example of the same. S. George of Thessalonica is also a round building with a surrounding aisle, by some attributed to the Roman Empire, but probably a Christian building, and has the clearstory which the

imitated by Charlemagne in his Münster at Aachen (Aix-la-Chapelle), and recopied from that in similar churches at Essen and Ottmarsheim. But the practical value of the cruciform type for all the uses of the Latin worship made it prevail through all Western Europe ; on it was spent the progressive effort of the builders of the later Middle Ages, and Gothic churches of round form are very few. The architects of the Renaissance, enamoured of the dome, under which Brunellesco introduced the new style in Florence, reverted to the round church. Bramante's famous Tempietto in S.

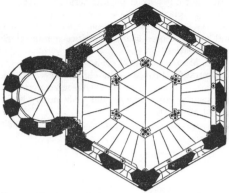

ROUND CHURCH: MATHIAS KAPELLE AT KOBERN ON THE RHINE; PLAN.

Pietro in Montorio at Rome led the way; the Madonna della Consolazione at Todi, the In-

ROUND CHURCH: MATHIAS KAPELLE; SECTION SHOWING INTERIOR ONLY; SEE PLAN.

coronata at Lodi, both ascribed to Bramante, were the forerunners of a long line of round churches, of which the well-known Salute at

Venice is one of the most picturesque examples, and the Liebfrauenkirche at Dresden one of the later. But the great achievement of the Renaissance architects in church building was the union of the central type with the cruciform by setting over the square crossing the dome built on pendentives, after the manner of S. Sofia, which culminated in S. Peter's, and fixed the dominant form for Renaissance architecture, as the development of the groined vault had for mediæval. — W. P. P. LONGFELLOW.

ROUNDEL. *A.* A small circular panel or window; specifically, a circular niche deeply recessed, often decorated with a bust in high relief, or, in late neoclassic design, filled by a free standing bust.

B. In glass making, or glazing, a bull's-eye or circular light, like the bottom of a bottle.

ROUNDHOUSE. *A.* In the United States, an engine house, in sense *B*, which, in plan, is constructed on a circular arc, from which radial tracks converge toward a turntable near the centre of the arc. The turntable also connects with one or more branches of the railway, so that an engine is readily transferred from the house to the railway line, or *vice versa*.

B. A police station house or other place of temporary confinement for persons arrested; popular and without exact significance.

—(C. D.)

ROUND TOWER. *A.* In early Christian architecture, a building of a peculiar type with few windows and those generally so small that bells would hardly give out their sound freely; very slender, and commonly furnished with conical stone roofs. Of these there are more than one hundred in Ireland; and there are known to be more than twenty-two in other countries of Europe. Although it is probable that they were used rather for defence and for lookout purposes than for the placing of bells, yet a tower of this type is commonly called Bell House. (See Ireland, Architecture of.)

B. In the Southwestern United States the work of American Indians of the Pueblo type. Some stand alone but the greater number are near, or connected with, other ruins of rectangular form. Two or three concentric walls exist in some, separated by from 2 to 6 feet, the outer interval being divided by transverse walls on radial lines into small chambers. The diameter of the inner circle varies from 10 to 20 feet or more. Walls were of roughly dressed stone. Those near other ruins are generally classed as kivas; isolated ones may have been lookouts. (See

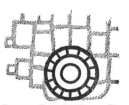

ROUND TOWER (DEF. *B*).

Communal Dwelling; Kiva; Watch Tower, under Tower.) — F. S. D.

Stokes, *Early Christian Art in Ireland.*

ROUSSEL (ROUXEL), JEHAN; architect. He was *maître d'œuvre* of the city of Rouen. Sept. 21, 1447, at the death of Jehan Salvart (see Salvart), he succeeded him as architect of the cathedral of Rouen, and held that office until 1451.

Deville, *Revue des architectes de la Cathédrale de Rouen.*

ROUX, MAITRE. (See Rosso, Il.)

RUBBLE. *A.* Rough stones of irregular shapes and sizes, broken from larger masses, either naturally by geological action, or artificially by quarrying. The term is used very loosely, covering all between dimension stone and cobble stones or gravel. (See definition *B* and sub-titles.)

B. Masonry built of such stones.

Coursed Rubble. Rubble in sense *B*, in which the stones have faces with square corners and nearly parallel sides, and beds nearly horizontal and vertical.

ROUND TOWER (DEF. *A*): ARDMORE, IRELAND.

ROVER. In architecture, any member, as a moulding, which follows the line of a curve.

ROVEZZANO, BENEDETTO DA. (See Benedetto da Rovezzano.)

ROW; **ROWLOCK.** (See Rollock.)

ROYERS DE LA VALFENIÈRE, FRANÇOIS DES; architect; b. August, 1575; d. March 22, 1667.

The chief member of a family of architects which was employed at Avignon, and at Lyons in the seventeenth century. In 1636 he was appointed architect of the Chartreuse of Ville-neuve-lèz-Avignon, which he enlarged and decorated. In 1646 he finished the Palais de Justice at Carpentras, and in 1647 made the plans of the abbey of the Dames de S. Pierre (now Palais des Arts) at Lyons.

Charvet, *les La Valfenière;* Monfalcon, *Histoire Monumentale de la ville de Lyon.*

Snecked Rubble. Rubble laid up with rough or irregular stones, but so fitted as to secure an effective bond.

RUDE, FRANÇOIS; sculptor; b. 1784 (at Dijon, Côte d'Or, France); d. Nov. 3, 1855.

Rude was the son of a coppersmith of Dijon. He studied art at the excellent school of Devosge in Dijon. In 1807 he went to Paris and was employed on the *Colonne de la Grande Armée* (Colonne Vendôme). In 1812 he won the *premier grand prix*, but on account of the political disturbances of the time did not visit Rome. He went to Brussels (Belgium) where he made the Caryatides of the Théâtre Royal, the pediment of the Hôtel des Monnaies, etc. He returned to Paris in 1827, and in 1828 exhibited his statue of Mercury at the *Salon* (now in the Louvre). Rude executed a part of the frieze of the Arc de Triomphe de l'Étoile (Paris).

In 1832 Abel Blouet (see Blouet) succeeded Huyot (see Huyot) as architect of the arch. For him, largely at the suggestion of M. Thiers, Rude made four designs for the sculpture of the piers representing four subjects illustrative of war: *Le Départ, Le Retour, La Défense du Sol,* and *La Paix.* These drawings are now in the Louvre. *Le Départ,* the only one of the four which was carried out by Rude, is probably the most important monument of French sculpture. The three other groups were made by Cortot and Etex (see Etex). In 1836 Rude made his statue of Maréchal de Saxe, now in the Louvre. In 1852 Rude opened an atelier for the instruction of pupils, which formed many important sculptors. Among his many works are the monument to Napoleon in a park at Fixin (France), the splendid reclining statue of Godefroy Cavaignac in the cemetery of Montmartre (finished 1847), and statues of Monge, Bertrand, and Ney.

Fourcaud, *François Rude;* Gindriez, *François Rude;* Gonse, *Sculpture française.*

RUGERUS. (See Theophilus.)

RUGGIERI, FERDINANDO; architect. Ruggieri rebuilt (1736) the interior of the church of S. Felicità, designed the façade of the church of S. Firenze (1715), and assisted Carlo Fontana (see Fontano, Carlo) in the construction of the Palazzo Capponi, all in Florence. He is best known by his *Studio d'Architettura Civile.*

Gurlitt, *Geschichte des Barockstiles in Italien.*

RUIJSBROECK, JAN VAN; architect. A Belgian architect of the fifteenth century who made the plans for the *Stadhuis* at Brussels. The first stone of this building was laid in 1444.

Immerzeel, *Hollandsche en Vlaamsche Kunstenaars.*

RULE. A strip of wood or metal with a straight or true edge, used to assist workmen in making straight or true work, as in plastering, to assist in keeping a surface in plane. When graduated and correctly marked with foot divisions and subdivided into inches, and into halves, quarters, eighths, and sixteenths of an inch, and made to fold in two or four sections for convenience of carriage, the tool becomes a carpenter's rule.

Diminishing Rule. A board or the like used to lay out or determine the curvature of the swelling of a column; its edge being cut with a concave curve.

Foot Rule. Similar in make and form to Two-foot Rule, but half as long, and, therefore, half as long when folded up.

Two-foot Rule. A carpenter's rule as defined above, two feet long, and folding usually into four six-inch lengths. This is much the most common form of rule used by mechanics,

architects, and all persons engaged in the building trades. — R. S.

RULER. (See Straight Edge.)

RULING PEN. (See under Pen.)

RUMFORD, COUNT. (See Thompson, Benjamin.)

RUN. In the United States, same as Going.

RUNIC KNOT. A form of interlacing common in the ornamentation of jewels, implements, and in stone and wood carving generally among the early Northern races of Europe. — H. V. B.

RUSKIN, JOHN; writer on Fine Arts; b. 1819; d. 1900, Brantwood, Coniston, Lancashire.

While engaged in the study of painting, especially landscape painting of early Italians and modern English, he studied also the mediæval architecture of Europe, and made many accurate drawings, engravings from some of which illustrate his published works. In 1849 was published *The Seven Lamps of Architecture,* a series of essays; and, in 1851–53, *The Stones of Venice,* one chapter of which, "The Nature of Gothic," has been reprinted separately. He published also lectures and detached essays.

RUSSIA, ARCHITECTURE OF. That of so much of the modern empire of that name

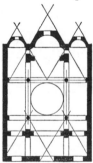

RUSSIA, FIG. 1: A GREEK BYZANTINE CHURCH-PLAN, ILLUSTRATING THE TYPE COMMON IN RUSSIA ALSO; THE CUPOLA IS COMMONLY LIKE THAT SHOWN IN FIG. 2.

as lies west of the Ural Mountains. In this vast region there are many remains of ancient building showing great capacity for art of a semibarbaric sort, and much of that picturesqueness which comes from massive building of unusual height and expressive outline, as in fortification. Thus, the watch towers, which serve also as places of defence, which exist in great numbers in the region of the Caucasus, are as effective as Scottish Pele Towers or the border towers of the Pyrenees, and the wooden houses and churches of all the forest-covered parts of the country exhibit a power of design not surpassed by the log churches of Norway (see Scandinavia) or the chalets of Switzerland. That influence which was to change the character of church architecture throughout the empire seems to have come into Russia not earlier than the twelfth century. This was the

Byzantine influence coming partly from the monasteries of the Greek church in the south, such as those of Mt. Athos, and partly from Constantinople direct; but it was largely influenced,

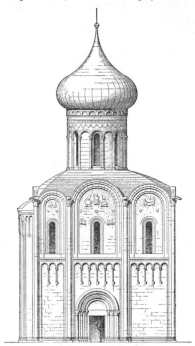

RUSSIA, FIG. 2: CHURCH OF THE INTERCESSION OF THE VIRGIN AT POKROVA; SEE THE GREEK PLAN, FIG. 1.

at least in decoration, by a more purely Oriental spirit which is manifested in earlier Russian manuscripts, jewellery, and other minor arts of decoration. The immediate result of this was that the cities of the empire were filled with churches built with central cupolas in the Byzantine taste, but also much smaller than the churches of Constantinople; hardly larger than those in the towns of the Peloponnesus or of Attica (see Greece, Architecture of), and taking their essential characteristics largely from the conventual churches which were often small, because of the small size of the religious communities. Thus, a relatively important church in a good-sized town may be only 20 feet square within the four main piers which carry the cupola, with a surrounding aisle not over 6 feet in width, so that the congregation of 150 people would crowd it.

The constructional features of these buildings are: first, a very simple and straightforward plan of vaulting with either brick or stone, and a great abundance of mortar, generally in the Byzantine manner; second, an almost universal disposition with a square compartment supported by four piers carrying a cylindrical drum which might be finished in a

bulbous cupola, or an octagonal tower generally finished with a blunt spire; third, a marked disproportion of height to size of plan, a peculiarity undoubtedly resulting from the conventual church within its crowded enclosure, but very effective in cities; fourth, a disposition to carry up the central tower or drum unbroken within, so that mural painting could be carried out over the whole of the somewhat high funnel-shaped or cylindrical tower above the heads of the congregation; fifth, a tendency to make much of the entrance, by means of a porch often crowned by a low tower, an elaborate flight of steps leading to a second porch communicating with the much loftier bell tower, and a final inner narthex leading directly to the place of worship. There are many minor peculiarities, but the above which are generally found in the churches from the twelfth to the eighteenth centuries are strongly marked and suffice by themselves to explain the notable individuality of Russian church architecture.

Above the roof the drum of the cupola was often raised to an exaggerated height, many times higher than the bulb itself, and pierced by slender windows. The bulb might be more or less prolonged into an onion-shaped, upward-pointing form, evidently of Persian origin, and this bulb might be covered with metal or with brilliant coloured tiles. The octagonal tower and spire which sometimes replace this cupola and drum have the unique feature of coming inward from the sides of the tower to the starting of the spire by means of a series of small arches rising one upon another, like the squinches of Western towers but in three or four horizontal rings; these arches showing on the exterior produce an effect as novel as it is thoroughly constructional and logical. The same system

RUSSIA, FIG. 3: TOWER OF CHURCH OF VASILI BLAJENOI, MOSCOW; RECEDING ARCHES DIMINISHING SIZE OF CENTRAL OPENING.

is applied to larger towers which rest on the ground, as in the really noble tower of S. John Chrysostom at Korowniki, a tower which though only 125 feet high has a most stately appearance. The chapel of the convent of S. Nicetas has a blunt, octagonal spire built in a more familiar western style, but of equally good form. The church of the Virgin of Kasan at Markowo, near Moscow, has the roof itself carried up on a moderate slope by means of this system of squinch-like arches, these showing on the outside of the roof like blind dormers with rounded tops or like eyebrows (see that term *B*), of which the window openings are stopped. In this church, as in those of less importance, the peculiarity of an elaborate system of vaulting, an effective exterior, and a brilliant mural painting within applied to a church which could not hold over 200 worshippers is as notable as in still smaller churches. The church of the Resurrection at Rostow has its tower arched up high with a special cupola reaching a height of 85 feet, and this is covered with figure painting of generally cool and dusky tones but with warm colour in the costumes. The church of the Trinity and of the Virgin at Moscow has an important tower over the entrance like the gateway pagodas in India. In this church the chapels, of which there are several, are nearly as large as the church proper. All these buildings of the seventeenth and eighteenth centuries are of the character described above, but there are also churches the plan of which is a marked Greek cross, which cross is roofed by its cupola, except the apse. A modification of this, again, shows a plain parallelogram without on three

sides, the fourth side broken by three apses, but the plan within is not so different from the plans cited above, the piers dividing the church into a cross.

The ancient buildings of the Kremlin in Moscow, though much altered externally, retain, within, their halls of curious vaulting of many types. The willingness of the Russian builders to close the roofs even of their very large rooms with masonry, and their apparent interest in the different systems within their reach, point to a natural readiness for architectural achievement which the existing buildings, interesting and suggestive as they are, do not quite verify. The extremely backward social condition of the empire through the ages which were most fruitful of architectural work in Europe and in the nearer East, must be held as the cause of this backwardness. Ancient Russian architecture is rather a series of curious complex tendencies and admirably intended results than a triumphantly successful result. All Europe may go to Russia to study, but not to copy.

The simple log buildings of the peasantry,

including churches as well as large and small residences and village houses, are extremely attractive because of their successful combination of some truly architectural treatment with the simple structure (see Chalet; Loghouse; Scandinavia, Architecture of). The practice followed in Russia even to the present day of hollowing the under surface of each log, that it may more nearly fit upon the log below and thus be capable of more perfect chinking, points to a use of this kind of structure in buildings of some importance and considerable cost.

Beginning with the reign of Peter the Great, buildings of modern European form have been imitated in Russia, and palaces for the sovereign and for the nobles have followed the neoclassic style of the epoch, but generally without fortunate result. The taste is often barbarous without being effective, the exteriors pompous without being stately. An exception is, however, the great church of S. Isaac, the cathedral of Saint Petersburg, which was the hobby of several succeeding emperors, the plan having been changed frequently, and the present one dating from 1817. The church is considered to rank in size, cost, and importance next after S. Peter's of Rome and S. Paul's of London. It has four octostyle porticoes, two of them being much deeper than the others and having inner columns on the principle of the famous portico of the Pantheon at Rome, and the parallelogram from which these porticoes project is roofed by a central cupola of great size accompanied by four smaller ones at the four principal angles of the central square. The cupola is built entirely of cast and wrought iron, an admirable achievement for permanence and successful combination of parts; but when viewed in the light of modern engineering, unnecessarily costly, the material being used in enormous masses. There is a great abundance of decorative sculpture in bronze, although part of what seems bronze is confessedly electrotype. The great doors are designed in the most exaggerated taste with human figures in high relief, seeming like statues in niches, and of a scale much greater than life.

     L. Rusca, *Recueil des Dessins de différents bâtimens construits à Saint Pétersbourg et dans l'intérieur de l'empire de Russie;* Fedor Rikliter, *Monuments of Ancient Russian Architecture,* 1850; A. Ricard de Montferrand, *Église cathédrale de Saint-Isaac;* A. Weltmann, *Description du nouveau Palais Impérial du Kremlin de Moscou,* 1851; Demidoff, *Voyage pittoresque et archéologique en Russie;* Souslow, *Monuments*

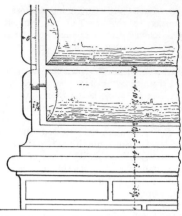

RUSTICATION: BASE OF PALAZZO STROZZI, FLORENCE; 15TH CENTURY.

de l'ancienne architecture Russe, 26 Pl., St. Petersbourg, 1895; Alexis Martinow, *Anciens Monuments des environs de Moscou,* 1889; Nöhring and Von Löwis, *Die Städtische Profanarchitektur der Gothik, der Renaissance und des Barocco in Riga, Reval und Narva,* Lübeck, 1892; Fabricius, *Le Kremlin de Moscou,* 1883; Valérien Kiprianoff, *Histoire pittoresque de l'architecture en Russie,* 1864.

                   — R. S.

RUSTICATED. In stone masonry, distinguished from smooth ashlar by rustication.

RUSTICATION. In stone cutting, that done with joints sunk in some sort of channel, the faces of the stones projecting. The above is what is meant generally when rustication is spoken of, but the face of the stones is usually roughened artificially to form a contrast with ordinary dressed ashlar; and this roughening may be carried so far as to include vermiculation, or may consist of a regularly cut series of projections and sinkings. This is sometimes imitated in brickwork; and then sometimes, and perhaps in stonework also, in horizontal grooves without verticals.

RUSTIC WORK. *A.* Decoration by means of rough woodwork, the bark being left in place, or by means of uncut stones, artificial rockwork, or the like, or by such combination of these materials and devices as will cause the general appearance of what is thought to be rural

RUSTICATION: PALAZZO WIDMAN, VENICE, ITALY; CLOSE OF 16TH CENTURY.

in character. Where woodwork is used it is customary to provide a continuous sheathing as of boards, upon which are nailed the small logs and branches with their bark, moss, etc., carefully preserved; but these strips of wood are often arranged in ornamental patterns, causing anything but a rural appearance.

B. In cut stone; same as Rusticated Work.

S

S. The abbreviation for saint (English and French); *sainte* (French, feminine); *san* (i.e. *santo*), *santa*, *santi* (Italian and Spanish). (For the plural form and the superlative, see SS.)

SABINE. (See Savine.)

SACRAMENT CHAPEL. A chapel especially reserved for the preservation of the host.

SACRAMENT HOUSE. An ambry; used especially for the keeping of the sacred wafer.

SACRARIUM. *A.* In Roman archæology, a place of deposit for sacred objects, a chapel or shrine.

B. In Christian ecclesiology, the sanctuary, the choir, the sacristy, a piscina, a sacrament house; the late Latin word being employed in various meanings.

SACRED TENT; TIPI. A tent erected by American Indians to shelter some sacred object. Especially, one of three tents or tipis, of the Omaha, used for the Sacred Pole, a stick of cottonwood eight feet long, said to be over two hundred years old, the Sacred White Buffalo-cow Skin, and the Sacred Bag consecrated to war. These sacred tents and all they contained are now in the Peabody Museum at Cambridge, Massachusetts. See the contributions of Dorsey to the reports of the United States Bureau of Ethnology.
— F. S. D.

SACRISTY. A place reserved near the high altar and sanctuary of a church, usually a single room, but sometimes of great proportions. It is the place where priests and deacons vest for the service and unvest again, and where ecclesiastical garments are stored; and where much of the business of the church is done, as the reception and registration of requests for masses or prayers. There is of necessity a lavatory, and there should be a separate piscina for washing altar vessels and the like; also permanent presses and cupboards; and all these fittings are commonly made architectural and are often adorned very richly. In some old sacristies there were ovens for baking the bread intended for consecration; in others the church muniments are kept in a special press by themselves.

SADDLE. *A.* The cap of a doorsill, or the bottom piece of a door frame, forming a slightly raised ridge, upon which the door, when shut, fits rather closely. The object is to give the under side of the door such height above the floor as to prevent its striking or binding when thrown open. Saddles are made of wood, cast-iron, brass, marble, etc. In England, some carefully built houses have no saddles for the

SACRISTY: CATHEDRAL OF LE MANS (SARTHE), FRANCE.

interior doors, the carpets of two adjoining rooms meeting under the doors, the theory being that the floor is so perfectly levelled and built that saddles are unnecessary.

B. Anything used to interpose a vertical support and the foundation or the load upon the support; especially in temporary work, as in Shoring.

SADDLE-BACKED. Sloping equally on either side from a ridge. (See Saddle-backed Roof, under Roof.)

SADDLE BAR. A horizontal bar of iron across a window opening, sometimes to stiffen the slender stone mullions; more often to secure the leaded glass by means of wires twisted around it.

SADDLE STONE. The stone set at the apex of a gable built of masonry, and forming the capstone of the coping.

SÆPTA. Same as Septa.

SAFE. A place for the safe keeping of money, plate, papers, and other valuables. Safes are intended to be fire-proof, burglar-proof, or both. When built with the building as an integral part of it, they are commonly built from the foundation with solid masonry to the first floor, and with brickwork above in double walls, and are commonly called vaults. When extended through several stories, the structure is called a stack of vaults. The floor and ceilings in each story are generally constructed with light iron beams and railroad bars laid far enough apart to permit a solid closure of brick laid upon the flanges with a covering of brick or cement; or fewer beams are used, and arches of brick are laid between them. In each story the doorway, or doorways, are of bevelled steel frames built into the masonry, forming a vestibule closed with outer doors of iron and steel, and lighter inner doors, all provided with burglar-proof bolts. In fire-proof buildings these safes or vaults are not necessarily built from the foundations, but may be started from the steel framework of any floor, wherever required. Safes of this kind, though fire-proof, are not considered burglar-proof unless lined with steel and provided with other securities against intrusion. For banks and other public institutions these structures are built with greater care and with ampler interior space, and often with two stories of safes on each floor. Good safes have outer and inner doors, both provided with burglar-proof locks. A patent for fire-proof safes provides an outer and inner steel lining between which alum is packed. When exposed to heat the alum gives off its water of crystallization, which becomes steam at ordinary atmospheric pressure, thus enclosing the contents in an envelope of steam at 212 degrees F., which is maintained until the water is all expelled, and which thus greatly delays the burning of contents. (See Godown; Kura.)

— HENRY VAN BRUNT.

SAFE–DEPOSIT VAULT. A vault in sense *B*, to provide safe storage for documents, bullion, jewels, plate, coin, and other valuables. Public safe-deposit vaults are large basement rooms or vaults of solid masonry, lined with burglar-proof boxes of various sizes, which are severally accessible only to those who rent them. Such places are provided with every possible appliance of safety and protection, and include a series of small rooms or compartments, wherein those who rent the boxes can be secluded while examining their property or consulting their papers.

SAIL OVER. Any projection or jutting beyond the general wall surface. Also, sale over, oversale, oversail. A term connected with salient. (See Overhang.)

SAINTE CHAPELLE. In French, a holy chapel, that is, one of especially sacred character; a term used peculiarly for those which contain some relic of great sanctity, as any one of those which relate especially to the Passion of Christ. The structure of a double building, with a lower and a higher church, is especially identified with these buildings throughout the Middle Ages in France. It is found in the celebrated Sainte Chapelle of Paris, once forming part of the royal palace in the Ile de la Cité and at Vincennes, but this has no special significance, its purpose being rather to add to the height and dignity of the structure.

SALLE DES PAS PERDUS. A large hall forming a monumental vestibule or waiting room to smaller halls or apartments, as in courts of justice and other public buildings in France.

SALLY. A projection; the end of a timber, as the foot of a rafter, cut with an internal angle to fit over a plate or horizontal beam.

SALOMON DE CAUS. (See Caus, Salomon de.)

SALOON. *A.* A spacious or elegant apartment for the reception and entertainment of company; a hall of state or ceremony.

B. In the United States, specifically, a bar-room.

SALT IN BRICK WALLS. (See Efflorescence.)

SALTPETERING; SALTPETRING. (See Efflorescence.)

SALUTATORIUM. In mediæval building, a porch or a portion of the sacristy of a church, where the clergy and the people could meet and confer.

SALVART, JEHAN; architect.

March 13, 1398, he replaced Jehan de Bayeux as architect of the cathedral of Rouen (Seine Inférieure, France). In 1407 he restored the west portal of the cathedral. From 1400 to 1411 he was employed on the château of Tancarville (France). In 1430 he enlarged the windows of the choir of the cathedral of Rouen. In 1432 Salvart appears as *maître d'œuvre* (city architect) of the city of Rouen.

Deville, *Revue des Architects de la Cathédrale de Rouen;* Bauchal, *Dictionnaire.*

SALVI, NICCOLÒ; architect; b. 1699; d. 1751.

Salvi was a pupil of Antonio Cannevari. His most important work is the fountain of Trevi (which see) in Rome (1735–1762).

Gurlitt, *Geschichte des Barockstiles in Italien;* Milizia, *Memorie.*

SALZBURG, ARCHITECTURE OF. (See Austrian States, Architecture of.)

PLATE XV

SALUTE

The church of the Madonna della Salute (or of Health or Salvation, the Italian word having both meanings). The view is taken from the Molo, that is, the church is seen from the northeast; the low building on the left is the Dogana del Mare, and the church without tower on the right of the Salute is S. Gregorio. Fender piles (pali) are numerous, and one carries a lantern marking a Traghetto or ferry of gondolas.

SALZENBERG, WILHELM; architect.

He was a pupil of Schinkel (see Schinkel). During the restoration conducted by Fossati (see Fossati) at the church of S. Sophia in Constantinople, in 1847–1848, Salzenberg was commissioned by the king of Prussia to examine the construction and decoration of the building. He published his results in 1854, under the title, *Alt-christliche Baudenkmale von Constantinople* (1 vol. folio). This won for

France). He built the fine western portal of the church of S. Michel at Dijon. The signature on the bas-relief of the tympanum is supposed to be modern. Other works at Dijon are ascribed to him.

Chabent, *Dijon.*

SAMMICHELE, SAMMICHELI. (See Sanmicheli.)

SAMPLE ROOM. *A.* A room where commercial samples are kept and shown, as by a travelling merchant in a hotel.

B. A place where liquor is sold by the glass; a barroom.

SANCHEZ, UNFRO; sculptor.

He built the stalls of the choir of the cathedral of Seville (Spain). An inscription on this work bears his name and the date, 1475.

Bermudez. *Diccionario.*

SAINTE CHAPELLE: S. GERMER NEAR BEAUVAIS (OISE), FRANCE; AT EAST END OF CHURCH.

him the silver medal of the Royal Institute of British Architects in 1855.

Seubert, *Künstler-lexikon.*

SALZMANN, MAX; architect; b. about 1850; d. Feb. 7, 1897.

Architect of the cathedral of Bremen, Germany. At the time of his death he had finished the towers and the decoration of the northern side of the building.

Nekrologie, in *Kunstchronik*, Feb. 18, 1897.

SAMBICHE. (See Chambiges.)

SAMBIN, HUGUES; architect.

Architect of the city of Dijon (Côte d'Or,

SANCTUARY. A place considered sacred, especially in connection with the idea of safety from pursuers. Thus the innermost and least public part of a temple, or of a Christian church, the separate shrine of a divinity or saint, a region within which all the trees, buildings, monuments, etc., and the soil itself was held sacred to a divinity, or an asylum in sense *A* is a sanctuary; and there is no clear distinction between the different uses of the term.

Especially, in a Christian church, the place where the principal altar is set, distinguished from the choir (see Choir, *A*), or from the outer part of the chancel.

SANCTUARY SCREEN. Any partition which separates the sanctuary proper from the larger part of the choir. (See Chancel Screen; also Choir Screen and the references.)

SANCTUS BELL. A bell hung in an exterior turret or bell cot over or near the chancel arch, which was formerly rung to fix the attention of those not in the church to the service of the mass; this notice is now usually limited to the ringing of a hand bell in the sanctuary.

SAND. Small particles of stone formed sometimes by the trituration of stones or rocks when carried by water, sometimes by the decomposition of the cementing substance of crystalline rocks. Sand for building purposes is generally found in the beds of streams or in beds, or pits, in the earth, as well as on the seashore.

It should be silicious, gritty, not too fine, and should be perfectly clean and free from loam. Sand formed by the trituration of finely grained or amorphous rocks, really fine pebbles, may be used for mortar, if of hard material, and no other can be obtained. Silicious material is to be preferred. — W. R. H.

SANDBY, THOMAS; architect; b. 1721; d. June 25, 1798.

He was appointed architect to King George II. of England in 1754, and in 1755 was one of the committee which considered the formation of a public academy. At the formation of the Royal Academy, in 1768, he was made a member, and the first professor of architecture.

William Sandby, *History of the Royal Academy.*

SAND FINISH. (See Plastering.)

SAND FOUNDATION. A platform or bed of sand, natural or artificial, prepared for the erection of a building. (See Foundation.)

SANDING. The sprinkling of fine sand on fresh paint to obtain a granulated surface resembling sandstone.

SANDSTONE. A stone consisting of consolidated silicious sands. (See Stone.)

SAN GALLO, SANGALLO, ANTONIO (I.) DA (GIAMBERTI); b. 1455; d. 1534; architect, engineer, and woodcarver.

Antonio Giamberti, brother of Giuliano da San Gallo, began life as a woodworker. He went to Rome about 1492, and was employed by Alexander VI. (Pope 1492–1503) to remodel the Castel Sant' Angelo, and build the gallery connecting it with the Vatican. · He appears in the records as *murator*. About 1496 he was appointed *Capomaestro* of all the works of the Signoria of Florence, Italy, including the improvement of the Palazzo Vecchio and the fortresses of Firenzuola and Poggio Imperiale. He enjoyed a large practice as military engineer until about 1518, when he seems to have settled at Montepulciano, where he built the Cervini, Tarugi, and Bellarmini palaces and the important church of the Madonna di S.

Biagio. The palace of the cardinal, Del Monte (Palazzo Communale), and the *Loggia del Mercato*, at Monte San Savino, are attributed to Antonio. He built also the nave of the church of the Annunziata at Arezzo. (See San Gallo, Giuliano da.)

Lamberti, *Madonna di San Biagio ; Mémoires de la Société des Antiquaires de France*, 1884, p. 222.

SAN GALLO, SANGALLO, ANTONIO (II.) DA (ANTONIO PICCONI); architect; b. 1485; d. Oct. 3, 1546.

Antonio II. was the son of a sister of Giuliano and Antonio (I.) da San Gallo. His name was Picconi. He was employed by Bramante (see Bramante) as a draughtsman, and assisted Giuliano da San Gallo at S. Peter's church, and in 1517 was made Raphael's associate in the superintendence of that building. May 1, 1518, he was appointed architect of the church and the Vatican palace, and retained that office until his death. The model which he made for S. Peter's is still in existence. Antonio was for many years the leading architect in Rome, and controlled a large military and civil practice. He had in hand at one time the fortresses of Florence and Ancona, the completion of the buildings at Loreto (see Sansovino, Andrea), the enlargement of the Vatican, and the fountain and aqueduct at Orvieto. The villa Madama, Rome, is attributed to Raphael by Vasari, but existing drawings by Antonio and his brother, Battista, indicate that much of the work was done by them about 1530 (Geymüller, op. cit., p. 59). About 1542 he built for Paul III. (Farnese, Pope 1534–1549), the Pauline chapel in the Vatican, which was decorated by Michelangelo (see Buonarroti). For the same pope, also, he began the famous Farnese palace in Rome. At about the beginning of the third story, the work was transferred to Michelangelo, whose design for the cornice was preferred. A long list of Antonio's palaces and churches is given by Vasari (Vita di A. San Gallo the Younger). Many of his drawings are in the gallery of the Uffizi (Florence).

Bertolotti, *Nuovi documenti ;* Ravioli, *Notizie ;* Redtenbacher, *Baumeister der Renaissance ;* Müntz, *Renaissance ;* Vasari, Milanesi ed. ; Vasari, Blashfield-Hopkins ed. ; Geymüller, *Raffaello Sanzio come architetto.*

SAN GALLO, SANGALLO, ARISTOTELE. (See Sangallo, Bastiano da.)

SAN GALLO ; SANGALLO, BASTIANO DA (ARISTOTLE); painter and architect; b. 1481; d. 1551.

Bastiano was a son of the younger sister of Giuliano and Antonio (I.) da San Gallo, and a cousin of Antonio (II.) da San Gallo. He was apprenticed to the painter Perugino (see Vanucci, Pietro) in Florence, and studied the great cartoon of Michelangelo Buonarroti. He earned the name, Aristotele, by his intelligence and application. With his brother, Giovanni Francesco, he was employed to build the Pandolfini palace, in Florence, from the designs of Raffaello Santi (see Santi, R.). The building was not finished until after 1530. He attached himself to the court of Cosmo I. de' Medici ; San Gallo, Battista (il Gobbo) ; architect ; b. about 1496, a brother of A. (II.) da San Gallo, assisting in much of his work.

SAN GALLO, SANGALLO, FRANCESCO DA ; sculptor and architect ; b. 1494 ; d. 1576.

Francesco was a son of the great architect, Giuliano da San Gallo (see San Gallo, Giuliano da). His best work is the recumbent statue of Bishop Bonafelde, at the Certosa, near Florence. Between 1531 and 1559, he made with Antonio Solesmo the monument to Piero de' Medici at Monte Cassino (Tuscany).

Vasari, Milanesi ed. ; Müntz, *Renaissance*.

SAN GALLO, SANGALLO, GIULIANO DA (GIAMBERTI) ; architect, engineer, and woodcarver.

Giuliano was born in Florence ; the oldest son of Francesco Giamberti, a woodworker who trained his sons to his own trade. Francione was also his teacher and associate. Milanesi derives the name San Gallo from his residence near the Porta di San Gallo in Florence. In 1465 he was in Rome, and was employed by Paul II. (Pope 1464–1471) on the palace of S. Marco, the tribuna of S. Peter's, and the Vatican (Müntz). In 1848 he fortified and defended, unsuccessfully, the city of Castellina against Ferdinand I. of Naples. For Lorenzo de' Medici Giuliano designed the octagonal sacristy of S. Spirito in Florence (begun 1489), and the famous villa of Poggio a Cajano (about 1485–1489). His *chef-d'œuvre*, the church of the Madonna delle Carceri at Prato, was built between 1485 and 1491. Dec. 9, 1507, Giuliano was chosen *Capomœstro* (chief architect) of the Duomo, Florence. The cloister of S. Maddalena de' Passi, in which he copied an Ionic capital found at Fiesole, was begun in 1479. The Palazzo Gondi (Florence) is ascribed to Giuliano by Vasari. For the Cardinal della Rovere, afterward Julius II., he restored the fortress of Ostia (1484), and built the palace of Savona (1494). On one of the sketches of the Barberini collection is written an account of a journey to France in 1496. Giuliano built the dome of the church at Loreto, Italy (1497–1500), and was employed as civil and military architect in many Italian cities. During the reign of Leo X. (Pope 1513–1521), he was associated with Raphael as architect of the Vatican and S. Peter's (see Santi, R). July, 1515, he returned to Florence. Several of the designs which he made in competition for the façade of S. Lorenzo in 1516 are still preserved at the Uffizi Gallery. A list of his buildings is

published by Milanesi in his Vasari. The San Gallo had a *botega* (shop) in Florence for woodcarving and sculpture. The wooden crucifix at the Annunziata, and a part of the high altar at the Duomo (Florence), and other works at Perugia and elsewhere, are attributed to Giuliano. Del Badia, in the Fabbriche di Firenze, has shown that between Sept. 19, 1489, and Feb. 6, 1490, Giuliano da San Gallo was paid 115 lire, 10 soldi for the model, still in existence, of the Strozzi Palace (Florence), of which he was undoubtedly the designer, instead of Benedetto da Maiano (see Maiano, Benedetto da), as Vasari asserts. There is an album of his sketches in the Barberini Library (Rome). Another collection is in the library at Siena. They contain drawings of monuments in Italy, France, and Greece, which have disappeared.

Dr. Hans von Stegmann in *Die Architektur der Renaissance in Toscana ;* Ravioli, *Notizie ;* Müntz, *Les Arts à la cour des papes ;* Müntz, *Renaissance ;* Vasari, Milanesi ed. ; Mazzanti del Badia, *Fabbriche di Firenze ;* Müntz, *Giuliano da San Gallo et les monuments du midi de la France ;* De Laurière, *Observations sur les dessins de Giuliano,* etc. ; V. Geymüller, *Documents inédits sur les Manuscrits,* etc.

SANITARY ENGINEERING. A branch of the science and art of civil engineering, relating to such works of civil engineering as tend to promote public and individual health, to remedy unsanitary conditions, and to prevent epidemic diseases. Sanitary engineering, although a new profession, comprises a great many subjects, and much more than is usually understood by the term. The practice of sanitary engineering embraces water supply, sewerage, sewage and garbage disposal for cities, the prevention of river pollution, street paving and cleaning, laying out cities, municipal sanitation, sanitary surveys, regulation of noxious trades, disinfection, cremation, and the sanitation of buildings.

The requirements of modern buildings are numerous and complex. They have given rise to several departments of engineering work, of which the sanitary is not the least important. The sanitary engineering of buildings comprises sewerage, removal and disposal of waste matters, water supply, lighting and ventilation, plumbing work, subsoil drainage, dry foundation walls and cellars, and sewage disposal for country houses ; furthermore, sanitation of schools, hospitals, prisons and military barracks, erection of public baths, fire protection of institutions and safety measures for theatre audiences ; sanitation of factories, workshops, summer hotels and resorts, and railway and ship hygiene.

Part of the work of the sanitary engineer relates to sanitary inspections of old or new buildings, and building sites ; it includes expert services in court, and special work arising during epidemics, in war time and after floods or inundations, etc.

It is not the special province of the sanitary engineer to enter into the question of diseases and their cause, neither does he profess to have an intimate knowledge of medical science and biology, yet he must be well acquainted with general health axioms, for upon these all practical sanitary progress is based.

Quite often the term "sanitary engineer" is improperly used, and applied to plumbing inspectors; and even tradesmen have misappropriated the name. There is a large and growing field for the sanitary engineer's services, and conscientious, accurate, and intelligent work, coupled with a broad general culture, is the key to success in this, as in other professions.

Edw. S. Philbrick, *American Sanitary Engineering;* Mansfield Merriman, *Elements of Sanitary Engineering;* Wm. Paul Gerhard, *Sanitary Engineering.*

— W. P. GERHARD.

SANMICHELI, MICHELE; architect and military engineer; b. 1487; d. 1559.

Sanmicheli was born at Verona (Italy). About 1500 he went to Rome, where he came under the influence of Bramante and Raphael. As early as Nov. 27, 1509, he is mentioned as cathedral architect at Orvieto, Italy, and appears in the records of that building until 1528. Michele built the altar of the Three Kings in this cathedral. His earliest independent work is the church of the Madonna delle Grazie at Montefiascone (1519). After the sack of Rome in 1527, Sanmicheli was employed by Clement VII. (Pope 1523–1534) to assist Antonio (II.) da San Gallo (see San Gallo, Antonio II.) in the fortification of several Italian cities, notably Parma and Piacenza. This was a beginning of an immense practice as military engineer, which included the construction of the defences of Milan, Urbino, and Naples, and the superintendence of the entire system of fortifications for the territory under Venetian rule in Italy, Dalmatia, Crete, and Cyprus. He is said to have invented angular bastions. The most architecturally important of his military works are the fort of S. Andrea di Lido, Venice, the bastions of Verona, and the superb series of semi-military portals in the walls of Verona; the Porta Nuova, the Porta Palio (or Stuppa), the Porta S. Zenone, and the Porta S. Giorgio. The most important of his palaces are the Bevilacqua, the Canosa, the Pompeii, Versi, and Gran-Guardia in Verona, and the Grimani (on the Grand Canal), and the Cornaro Mocenigo (in the Campo S. Paolo) at Venice. The architecture of these palaces is in the main a development of the type established by Bramante in the so-called palace of Raphael (now destroyed) in Rome; heavy rustication below

crowned by a single order above (Sturgis; op. cit., p. 453). Sanmicheli designed the domical church of the Madonna di Campagna, the famous circular chapel of S. Bernardino, the façade of the church of S. Maria in Organo, and portions of the church of S. Giorgio in Braida, all in Verona. He designed the monument of Alessandro Contarini in the church of S. Antonio at Padua.

Camuzzoni, *Discorso per l' inaugurazione del monumento a Sanmicheli;* Salva, *Elogio di Michele Sanmicheli;* Ronzani-Luciolli, *Fabbriche di Sanmicheli;* Vasari, Milanesi ed.; Müntz, *Renaissance;* Burckhardt, *Renaissance in Italien;* Burckhardt, *Cicerone;* Sturgis, *European Architecture;* Gsell-Fels, *Ober-Italien;* Fumi, *Duomo di Orvieto.*

SANSAVINO. (See Sansovino.)

SANSOVINO (SANSAVINO), ANDREA (ANDREA CONTUCCI); sculptor and architect; b. 1460; d. 1529.

According to Vasari, Andrea was the son of a labourer of Monte San Savino in Tuscany, and his first teacher was Antonio Pollajuolo (see Benci, Antonio da J.). His earliest known work is a terra-cotta altar with figures of S. Lorenzo, S. Sebastiano, and S. Rocco, now in the monastery of S. Chiara at Monte San Savino, Italy. In 1480, on the recommendation of Lorenzo de' Medici (b. 1448; d. 1492), he was invited to Portugal by King John II. A bas-relief and a statue by him are still in the church of the monastery of S. Marco, near Coimbra (Portugal). In 1490 he returned to Florence, and was employed in the decoration of the church of S. Spirito. In 1500 Andrea was commissioned to execute the marble statues of Christ and S. John Baptist over the door of the Baptistery (Florence). The statues of the Madonna and S. John Baptist in the cathedral of Genoa were finished by him in 1503 (signed *Sansovinus faciebat*). His earliest work in Rome appears to be the monument of Pietro da Vicenza (dated 1564) in the church of Ara Coeli. His chief work, the monument of the Cardinal Ascanio Sforza, brother of Ludovico il Moro, Duke of Milan, at S. Maria del Popolo, was finished in 1506. The similar monument of the Bishop Hieronimus Bassus in the same church was begun in 1507. The monument of the Cardinal Johannes Michaelius and his secretary Antonio Orso in the church of S. Marcello (Rome) is by Andrea. Among his works in his native city (San Savino) is the cloister of S. Agostino, which is especially interesting on account of optical refinements introduced to correct the effect of its irregular plan. He built the great stairway between the cathedral and the bishop's palace at Arezzo.

Schönfeld, *Andrea Sansovino;* H. Semper, *Hervorragende Bildhauer-Architekten;* Müntz, *Renaissance;* Perkins, *Tuscan Sculptors;* Facco-Sacconi, *Loreto.*

SANSOVINO, GIACOMO. (See Sansovino, Jacopo.)

SANSOVINO (SANSAVINO), JACOPO or **GIACOMO (JACOPO TATTI)**; sculptor and architect; b. 1486; d. Nov. 27, 1570.

Jacopo was born at Caprese, near Florence. He attached himself to the sculptor Andrea Sansovino, from whom he received his name and artistic training. About 1467 he went with Giuliano da San Gallo (see San Gallo, Giuliano da) to Rome, where he met Bramante and entered the service of Julius II. Sansovino made a design for the façade of the church of S. Lorenzo (Florence), which was not executed (see Buonarroti). He designed the church of S. Giovanni dei Fiorentini in Rome, which was continued by Antonio (II.) da San Gallo. The façade is by Alessandro Galilei (see Galilei). After the sack of Rome (1527) Sansovino went to Venice, where he remained the rest of his life. He had charge of the church, campanile, and Piazza di S. Marco, and the adjacent public buildings except the Doge's Palace. The Palazzo Cornaro della Ca' Grande appears to be one of his earliest Venetian buildings. In 1535 the Council of Ten (Venice) commissioned him to build the Zecca, in which he used a fireproof iron construction. Sansovino's greatest work is the library of S. Mark. He began the loggietta of the Campanile (Venice) about 1540. Sansovino built also in Venice the church of S. Francesco della Vigna in 1534, façade by Palladio (see Palladio), the church of S. Giorgio dei Greci about 1550, the church of S. Salvatore (restored), the church of S. Maria Mater Domini about 1540, and the façade of the Scuola di S. Giorgio dei Schiavoni about 1551. He made the monument of the Doge Francesco Venier (d. 1556), with the fine statues of Hope and Charity, in the church of S. Salvatore (Venice), and the monument of Livio Podocataro, archbishop of Cyprus, in the church of S. Sebastiano (Venice). He built also the Palazzo Delfini, now Banca Nazionale, and began the Procuratie Nuove continued by V. Scamozzi (see Scamozzi, V.). Dec. 18, 1545, the great vault of the Libreria fell. Sansovino was held responsible for the loss, imprisoned, and fined. He was restored to his position Feb. 3, 1548. His most important works of sculpture at Venice are the statues of the loggietta, the colossal figures of Mars and Neptune which give its name to the Giant's Stairway at the Doge's Palace, the evangelists over the choir screen of S. Marco, and the famous bronze door of the sacristy of S. Marco (begun 1546, finished 1569). He made also a bas-relief for the church of S. Antonio at Padua. He was much assisted by Alessandro Vittoria (see Vittoria, Alessandro).

Temanza, *Vita di Sansovino;* Mosler, *Sansovino u. s. w.;* Müntz, *Renaissance;* Vasari, Mi-

lanesi ed. ; Sturgis, *European Architecture;* Perkins, *Tuscan Sculptors.*

SANTI (SANCTIUS, SANZIO), RAFFAELLO ; called Raphael ; painter and architect ; b. March 26 (or 28), 1483 ; d. April 6, 1520.

Raphael was born at Urbino (Italy), the son of Giovanni Santi, a painter. About 1499 he entered the atelier of Perugino (see Vanucci, Pietro), at Perugia, and probably assisted in the decoration of the Cambio at Perugia, which was done at this time. According to Vasari, he also assisted Pinturicchio (see Pinturicchio) in decorating the library at Siena, begun in 1502. He visited Florence in 1504, and spent much time in that city until 1509. Raphael was called to Rome by Julius II. (Pope 1503–1513) in 1509, to assist in the decoration in fresco of a suite of apartments (*stanze*) in the Vatican already begun by Sodoma, Perugino, and others. The first *stanza* was finished in 1511. The second *stanza* was painted between 1511 and 1514 ; much of the execution was deputed to his assistants. The third *stanza*, still less the work of Raphael, was finished about 1517 by Giulio Romano (see Pippi, Giulio). The decorations of the loggie of the Vatican were begun in 1517 (see Loggie of the Vatican). In 1514 he painted at the Villa Farnesina (Rome) the fresco of "Galatea," and later made the designs for the "Marriage of Cupid and Psyche." The splendid sibyls in the Chigi chapel at the church of S. Maria della Pace (Rome) were painted at about the same time as the "Galatea." When Bramante died (March 11, 1514), Raphael succeeded him as architect of S. Peter's ; with him were associated Fra Giocondo (see Giocondo) and others. Raphael's principal innovation was to substitute a Latin for the Greek cross of Bramante. His reputation as architect rests mainly upon obscure statements by Vasari. He may have designed those portions of the Villa Madama (Rome) which were built before 1520, although existing measured drawings for that building are by Antonio (II.) and Battista da San Gallo. The Pandolfini palace (Florence) is ascribed to Raphael, but was begun after his death. The Farnesina villa was undoubtedly the work of Baldassare Peruzzi (see Peruzzi). Raphael may have designed the Chigi chapel at the church of S. Maria del Popolo and the palace of Giovanni Battista dell' Aquila (Rome), which has disappeared.

By a brief dated Aug. 27, 1515, of Leo X. (Pope, 1513–1521) Raphael was authorized to inspect and purchase all marbles in the ruins within ten miles of Rome. This enabled him to institute an extensive series of important excavations. He began a work on the topography of Rome, the text of which, by Andreas Fulvius, was published in 1527. The plates were never completed.

Crowe and Cavalcaselle, *Raphael;* Müntz, *Raphael;* Passavant, *Raphael von Urbino;* Springer, *Raphael und Michelangelo;* Gruyer, *Les Fresques de Raphael;* Von Geymüller, *Raffaello come Architetto;* Vasari, Milanesi ed. ;

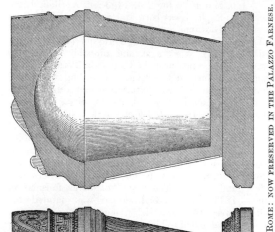

Sarcophagus of Roman Imperial Time from Tomb of Cecilia Metella near Rome; now preserved in the Palazzo Farnese.

Vasari, Blashfield-Hopkins ed. ; Bigot, *Raphael et la Farnesine;* Pontani, *Opere architettoniche di Raffaello Sanzio;* E. Müntz, *Histoire de la Tapisserie en Italie;* Waagen, *Treasures of Art in England.*

SANZIO. (See Santi, Raffaello.)

SAPWOOD. (See Heartwood.)

SARACENIC ARCHITECTURE. The architecture of the Saracens, that is, of the Mohammedans considered as the conquering people whose power gradually extended to the lands of the Mediterranean. It is in this sense that the word "Saracen" has come into the English language. The term "Saracen," as applied to the Mohammedan arts of design is, therefore, much more nearly accurate than the term Arab, Arabian, or Arabic. Thus, it would be obviously erroneous to speak of the Mohammedan architecture of India as Arabian, and the term Saracenic Indian or Indo-Saracenic may be used. In this connection see the title of Mr. Stanley Lane-Poole's book, *The Art of the Saracens in Egypt,* which is a useful book, but too brief. See also the same author's book, *Cairo, Sketches of the History, Monuments, and Social Life.* (See also bibliography under Moslem Architecture.)

— R. S.

SARCOPHAGUS (pl. Sarcophagi). A stone coffin. The term having been originally a Latin adjective, "flesh devouring," and applied to a certain stone from Asia Minor (Pliny's *Natural History,* XXXVI., 17). It was applied substantively in later Latin to any tomb or coffin.

The use of sarcophagi was common in Egypt from the time of the builder of the great pyramid. Greeks and Romans seem not to have used them often before the time of Trajan ; although the famous sarcophagi of Sidon in Syria are thought to be of the time of Alexander the Great, and the Scipio tomb in the Vatican is undoubtedly of the third century B.C. ; but afterward they were extremely common, and the museums of Europe contain many very richly sculptured. In the Middle Ages the Gothic tombs of Italy often included a sarcophagus (see Tomb), and the Renaissance brought back the use of them in a more nearly antique way, standing free. Perhaps the most celebrated are those in the smaller sacristy or Capella dei Depositi, at the church of S. Lorenzo, in Florence, having Michelangelo's magnificent recumbent statues on their lids. — R. S.

SARDINIA, ARCHITECTURE OF. (See Mediterranean Islands, Architecture of.)

SARKING. In Scotland and the north of England, thin boards for lining, sheathing, etc.

SARRASINE. A portcullis.

SARRAZIN, JAQUES; sculptor and painter ; b. 1538 (at Noyon, Picardie, France) ; d. 1660.

Sarrazin was a pupil of Nicolas Guillain in Paris. In 1610 he went to Rome and studied there for eighteen years. For his patron, the Cardinal Aldobrandini, he made the figures of Atlas and Polyphemus at his villa at Frascati. Returning to Paris about 1628, Sarrazin made the sculptured decoration of the Tour d'Horloge at the Louvre (see Lemercier, Jaques). The Caryatides supporting the pediment of this building are his best work. About 1643 he made the monument to contain the heart of Louis XIII., the sculpture of which is now in the Louvre, and about 1646 the monument to contain the heart of Prince Henri I. of Condé, now at Chantilly. In 1654 he was appointed *recteur* of the Académie royale de peinture et de sculpture (Paris).

Lami, *Dictionnaire des sculpteurs de l'École française;* Gonse, *Sculpture française;* Babeau, *Louvre.*

SARTO, ANDREA DEL. (See Andrea del Sarto.)

SASH. A frame to hold the glass of a window; especially in English usage of a sliding window as distinguished from a swinging window (see Casement). Such a sash is said to be *hung*, that is, by its sash cord or chain; and *double-hung* when it has a sash cord on each side. In the United States the term "sash" is often applied to the movable woodwork of a casement or glazed door. (See Cased Frame.)

SASH BAR. One of the cross bars of a sash, subdividing it for convenience of glazing. (See Muntin.)

SASH CHAIN; SASH CORD. (See Sash Line.)

SASH FASTENER. Same as Sash Holder.

SASH FRAME. The window frame in which a sliding sash is hung; the vertical parts (usually pulley boxes) are made hollow (boxed or cased) to contain the balancing weights. In the United States, also, any window frame.

SASH HOLDER. Any contrivance for holding the sash of a window so that it cannot be opened from outside, or so that it will not fall if it is not hung with weights; especially an appendage like a bolt or revolving latch which holds the meeting rails of two sashes together, preventing either from being opened.

SASH LINE. The cord, chain, or metal ribbon by which the sliding sash is attached to its balance weights.

SASH POCKET. The upright side of a sash frame when made hollow to receive the balance weights. By extension, a movable section in the style enclosing the above, intended to give access to the sash weights and lines.

SASH RIBBON. (See Sash Line.)

SASH WEIGHT. A cylindrical casting of iron or lead hung by the sash cord in the pocket or box of a sash frame to balance the sliding sash.

SASSANIAN ARCHITECTURE. (See Persian Architecture, Part II.)

SAW CURF; SAW IN. (See Kerf.)

SAW MILL. A mill in which lumber is split or divided by saws run by power machines. (See Woodworking Machinery.)

SAXON ARCHITECTURE. *A.* Architecture of Saxony; first, as a larger state, electorate, and kingdom, down to the Napoleonic wars; second, as a smaller kingdom, since the Peace of 1815 and the cessions to Prussia; third, as a province of the kingdom of Prussia, including the districts annexed by Prussia in 1815, and other lands. (For all the above, see Germany, Architecture of, Part II.)

B. The architecture of England and southern Scotland before the Norman Conquest. (For this see England, Architecture of; Scotland, Architecture of.) There is much uncertainty as to the date of the earliest mediæval buildings existing in England and Scotland, and there is no building of which it is certainly known that it dates from the period previous to 1066. — R. S.

SCABBLE. In stone working, to dress a surface with a broad chisel or heavy-pointed pick after rough pointing or shaping, and preliminary to finer finishing. Also Scapple. (See Stone Cutting; Stone Dressing.)

SCABELLUM; SCABELLON. In Roman and neoclassic architecture, a high pedestal for the support of a bust, often shaped like a Gaine.

SCAFFOLD. In building, a temporary wooden framework, put together with nails or ropes, to afford footing for workmen in erecting the walls of a building, or in giving access to ceilings and other parts which cannot be reached from the floors.

French Scaffold. *A.* A scaffold built on the system prevalent in France. A double row of poles or squared timbers is set up along the whole frontage to be built, and stiffened by X-bracing, continuous girts are lashed or bolted to the uprights and support cross sleepers, on which planks are placed at convenient levels; a species of tower with a pulley serves for hoisting material, which is trundled over the scaffold to its destined position.

B. A term applied in England to scaffolds built of squared timbers framed together by bolts, collars, fish-joints, etc., and capable of being taken down and reërected without injury; called also Jenny Scaffold.

Jenny Scaffold. Same as French Scaffold, *B.*

SCAGLIOLA. In Italian, an interior surface decoration for columns, walls, and floors, composed of white plaster and glue, mixed in various ways with metallic oxides, or with insertions of coloured stucco, generally in imitation of marbles, the whole being rubbed and finely polished.

SCALA CORDONATA, or A CORDONI. A ramp or inclined plane formed into paved steps from 18 inches to 3 feet tread, with only

1 to 4 inches rise, each step being thus inclined somewhat less than the general slope. The risers or fronts of the steps are of stone, and constitute the *cordoni*. Such ramps are used for animals as well as pedestrians, and are common in Italy.

— A. D. F. H.

SCABELLUM WITH DECORATIVE VASE; MODERN FRENCH.

SCALE. *A.* A straight line divided into feet and inches, or metres and centimetres, or the like, according to a definite and stated proportion to reality, as one forty-eighth (or four feet to one inch), one one-thousandth, etc. Drawings of all kinds when made by mathematical instruments (see Drawing) are made

to scale; and the scale may be laid down on the drawing, or may be on a separate piece of paper or wood (see definition *B*).

B. A rule, generally of metal, ivory, or wood, marked with a scale in sense *A*, or several such scales, to facilitate the making of drawings and diagrams to any convenient scale.

C. In architectural drawings, the size of the drawings as compared with the actual size of the object delineated, as one-quarter of an inch to the foot.

D. In architectural design, the proportions of a building or its parts, with reference to a definite Module or unit of measurement.

SCALLOP WORK. The cutting of a fascia or edge into a series of similar convex lobes, as frequently in Romanesque mouldings. (See Imbrication.)

SCAMILLUS. In classic and neoclassic architecture, — *A*, the slight bevelling of the outer edge of a bearing surface of a block of stone, making the part visible by a slight incision, as occurs between the necking of a Doric capital and the upper drum of the shaft.

B. A plain block placed under the plinth of a column, thus forming a double plinth.

SCAMOZZI, GIOVANNI DOMENICO; architect; b. about 1530; d. 1582.

From a simple carpenter he became an accomplished architect. He visited Budapest and Warsaw, where he reconstructed the royal palace. Giovanni made the index (*indice copiosissimo*) of the edition of Serlio's works, which was published in Venice in 1584 and 1619. (See Serlio.) In his introduction to this edition, Ludovico Roncone mentions some of Giovanni's buildings.

Roncone, Introduction to Serlio edition, 1584; Zanella, *Vita di Palladio*, p. 102.

SCAMOZZI, OTTAVIO BERTOTTI; writer and editor.

His most important undertaking was the publication of Palladio's designs (see Palladio). His *Il Forestiere isstruito delle Cose pia di Architettura e di Alcune Pitture della Città di Vicenza* was published at Vicenza in 1761, and *L'Origine dell' Accademia Olympica di Vicenza* in 1790.

Larousse, *Dictionnaire.*

SCAMOZZI, VICENZO; architect; b. 1552 (Vicenza); d. 1616 (Venice).

The name Scamozzi is derived from *Camoccio* (*Camoscio*), chamois leather, indicating some ancestral occupation. Vicenzo was a son of Giovanni Domenico Scamozzi (see Scamozzi, Giovanni Domenico), and a pupil and rival of Andrea Palladio (see Palladio). He studied mathematics under the Padre Clavio, who was employed by Gregory XIII. in reforming the calendar. Scamozzi made a thorough study of the Roman monuments. In 1582 he went to Venice to continue the Libreria di S. Marco, begun by Sansovino (see Sansovino, J.). Scamozzi added the *Anti Sala*. He also continued the Procuratie Nuove, begun by Sansovino, adding a third story (see Longhena, B.). In 1593 Scamozzi designed and began the fortress of Palmanuova in Friuli (Italy). In 1600 he accompanied a Venetian embassy to France, Germany, and Hungary. An autograph account of the visit, with drawings, is in the museum at Vicenza. He built a casino at Lonigo, another at Castelfranco near Treviso, the Palazzo Trenta at Vicenza, the Palazzo

opere ed. 1838; Zanella, *Vita di Palladio*, p. 103; Mosler, *Sansovino u. s. w.*; Quatremère de Quincy, *Les plus célèbres Architectes;* Milizia, *Memorie.*

SCANDINAVIA, ARCHITECTURE OF. That of the great peninsula now occupied by the two kingdoms of Sweden and Norway. The Scandinavian lands are sometimes held to include Denmark, which is treated separately.

The western half of the peninsula, now the kingdom of Norway, contains a score of very ancient timber churches, the construction of which is not unlike that somewhat familiar in

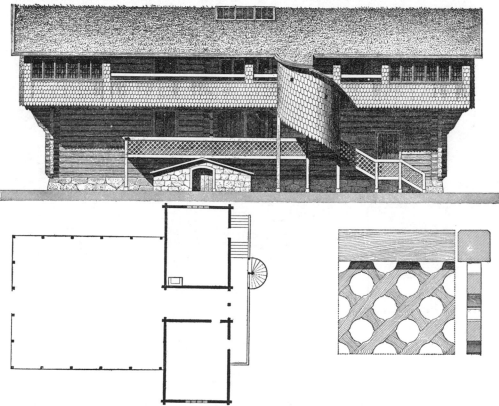

SCANDINAVIA, FIG. 1: HOUSE IN WHICH GUSTAVUS WASA TOOK REFUGE IN 1529; NEAR UPSALA, SWEDEN.
The structure is of solid timber like a log house, or a châlet of type *a*. Part of upper story and screen of stairs are covered with large, matched shingles.

Trissino at Vicenza, the Palazzo Verlato at Villaverla (1574), the Palazzo Raveschieri at Genoa, and the second story of Buontalenti's Palazzo Roberto Strozzi in Florence. About 1604 he designed the cathedral of Salzburg (Austria) and a part of the *Schloss* at Prague (Bohemia). Scamozzi published *Discorsi sopra l'Antichità di Roma* (Venice, 1582), and *Dell' Idea dell' Architettura universale* (2 vols., Venice, 1615). There is a modern edition, *Pubblicata per cura di S. Ticozzi e L. Masieri* (2 vols 8vo, Milan, 1838).

Temanza, *Vita;* Ticozzi, *Vita*, in Scamozzi

New England in the seventeenth and eighteenth centuries, viz. a frame filled in with slabs or thick upright planks (see Wood, Construction in, Part I.). These churches are peculiar in plan and general arrangement, but especially unique in their absence of architectural treatment of windows (see Fenestration), this depending largely upon the severity of the climate, combined with an apparent absence of window glass at the time of their construction. They are generally thought to be of the years between 1100 and 1250. They are built, like the semi-Byzantine churches of Russia, with a central nave and an aisle surrounding it on either side with lean-to roofs, but the whole surface above the aisle roof is not a clearstory in the proper sense, because containing no windows, or at most small ventilating apertures. There is often a second and lower aisle surrounding the whole of the building, with a second lean-to roof; this outer aisle is almost wholly a continuous narthex or porch, and is in part enclosed with solid slab walling, in part opened in wooden colonnades with a semblance of arched construction. Although partly open, its purpose is mainly additional shelter and warmth.

One of their characteristics is, however, so much respected in Norway that they are not likely to be injured in this way; the carved scrollwork, which is called runic scrollwork, dragon ornament, and the like, and which is extraordinarily effective and suited alike for covering large surfaces and for the ornamentation of pillars, square or round, is generally in wood, but there are instances of similar work in stone, and even the earliest wrought iron-work is studied from the same sources.

Romanesque stone vaulted churches are not unknown. There are two very good ones in

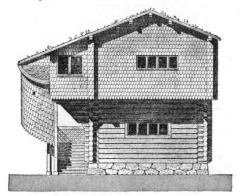
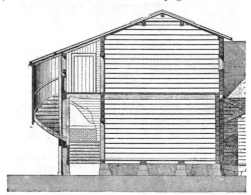

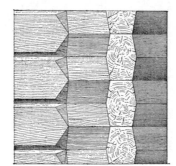

SCANDINAVIA, FIG. 2: HOUSE OF GUSTAVUS WASA; SEE FIG. 1.

The exteriors of these churches show very few and very small windows, perhaps two of six square feet each on each side, and no more. It is probable that in winter the chief light of the interior came from the lighting of the altar, aided, perhaps, by other lamps burned in the nave or at the entrance.

Of these churches, the large one at Hitterdal has been illustrated in popular books and is well known; those of Burgund and Urnes in Bergen, at Timd in Tellemark near Hitterdal, and at Ringebu, Gol, Vang, Kaupanger, and at Torpe, near Nybgaarden, are equally important to students and are illustrated in books named below. Restoration, destruction, and in one case the moving of the church to a new site, have interfered greatly with the study of these buildings.

Norway, at Throndenaes and Ibestad. Moreover, the great cathedral at Trondhjem, though it has never been completely rebuilt since ruinous fires, is most interesting in plan and has admirable Romanesque and late Gothic work in all its parts. A nave with aisles and two western towers, a transept without aisles, and a choir with aisles much narrower than those of the nave lead to a curious octagonal structure which serves as the chancel, though it is more like a separate chapel; and a Romanesque chapter house of oblong form of great interest adjoins the choir on the north. The great arcades of the choir show a marked divergence, the whole choir widening from the crossing toward the east end; the lady chapel, moreover, is not set on the axis nor yet parallel with the north wall of the choir (see Refinements in Design, where the general subject of these divergences is treated).

The cathedral at Lund is an excellent

SCANDINAVIA, FIG. 3: SWEDISH HOUSE, CLOSE OF 17TH CENTURY.
The roofing has been carried over the coping of the gable, injuring the outline : compare Fig. 4.

Romanesque church apparently completed in the eleventh century, but injured in its original features by restoration. The cathedral of Upsala is of the thirteenth century, and of in-

SCANDINAVIA, FIG. 4: 17TH CENTURY DOORWAY, CASTLE TORPA, WESTGÖTLAND, SWEDEN.
The heraldic achievements are unusually well disposed.

telligent Gothic building, although carried out in the unusual material of brick, in this resembling some admirable buildings in North Germany (see Germany, Architecture of, Part IV.). The cathedral at Linköping is also a

Gothic church ; this and the church at Lund are of stone.

Early wooden houses are not rare, and an excellent system of log house building has been used for these, sometimes combined in the same building with the slab construction mentioned above. Round logs were used even for the roof timbers, but generally set lengthwise and heavy enough to carry the whole stretch of roof. Most of those of undoubted antiquity are small, one story high, or with a partial upper story ; but a farmstead at Biolstad contains a seventeenth century house of considerable size, and barns of

SCANDINAVIA, FIG. 5; SWEDISH DECORATION OF INLAID WOOD; PALACE AT KALMAN.

the nineteenth century built carefully in the ancient manner.

The neoclassic architecture of Scandinavia is largely a matter of the residences of the nobility, though there is an admirable brick church at Christianstad. Some of these residences are of extraordinary interest, containing a character of bold pseudo-Renaissance design reminding one of good seventeenth century German work, but of still greater independence and daring in the treatment of the semiclassical details. The heavy timbered roofs and the plastered walls, both elaborately painted in polychromatic designs, the unusually elaborate wooden dadoes and doorpieces, make the interiors interesting, and the exteriors of such buildings as the Crown Prince's palace at Stockholm and the castle of Gripsholm are as picturesque as anything on the mainland of Europe. The close of the seventeenth century and the eighteenth century have left civic buildings of graver and more sedate aspect, and the admirable cathedral church at Kalmar in Sweden has to be studied by all interested in church architecture.

J. C. C. Dahl, *Denkmale einer sehr ausgebildeten Holzbaukunst aus den frühesten Jahrhunderten in den innern Landschaften Norwegens;* Dietrichson und Munthe, *Die Holzbaukunst Norwegens in vergangenheit und gegenwart,* Berlin, 1893 ; P. A. Munch and Schirmer, *The Cathedral of Throndheim,* published by order of the Norwegian government, Christiania, 1859 ; H. J. Kumlien, *Svenska Herrgårdar och Villor af Svenska Arkitekter,* Stockholm ; Upmark, *Die Architektur der Renaissance in Schweden;* Von Minutoli, *Der Dom zu Drontheim und die mittelalterliche Christliche Baukunst der Scandinavischen Normannen.*
— R. S.

SCANTLE. A gauge by which slates are cut to the proper length.

SCANTLING. *A.* In carpenter work, the measurements of timber in its breadth and thickness, as in the phrase, a timber of 4 by 10 inches scantling. By extension, the timber itself ; more especially the pieces of common sizes as commonly obtainable in the market. Thus, studs 4 by 4, rafters 2 by 8, and the like are scantling, when very heavy timber would not be so designated. (See Lumber.)

B. In stone cutting and dressing, the length, breadth, and thickness. In this sense rare in the United States.

SCAPE. Same as Apophyge.

SCAPPLE. Same as Scabble.

SCARF. The oblique joint by which the ends of two pieces of timber are united longi-

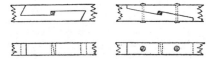

tudinally so as practically to form one piece ; the two parts being usually cut with projections and recesses which mutually fit one another, and these are sometimes forced together and tightened by keys or wedges in various ways, and secured by iron straps and bolts. Also the part cut away and wasted from each timber in shaping it to form this joint.

End Scarf. One formed by the insertion of one end into the other in a manner approaching a mortise and tenon.

Hook Butt Scarf. One in which the timbers form, in part, butt joints with one or more oblique cuts, by which they are hooked together.

SCARFING. The process of connecting two pieces of timber by a scarf joint.

SCARPAGNINO. (See Abbondi, Antonio.)

419

SCENOPHYLACIUM. Same as Diaconicon.

SCHADOW, ALBERT DIETRICH; architect ; b. 1797 (in Berlin) ; d. Sept. 7, 1869.

He was trained in Italy, and on his return in 1835 was made *Hofbaumeister* in Potsdam (Prussia), and in 1839, *Schlossbaumeister* in Berlin. With Stüler he built the *Schlosskapele* (Berlin).

Seubert, *Kunstler-lexicon;* Borrmann, *Denkmäler von Berlin.*

SCHADOW, JOHANN GOTTFRIED; sculptor ; b. May 20, 1764 ; d. Jan. 27, 1850.

He was a pupil of the Dutch sculptor Tassaert in Berlin, and in 1785 went to Rome. In 1788 he superseded Tassaert as court sculptor and secretary of the Academy in Berlin. In 1793–1794 he made the marble statue of Frederick the Great at Stettin (Germany), and in 1795 began the quadriga and metope reliefs of the *Brandenburger Thor* in Berlin. He made the statue of Luther in Wittenberg in 1821. Schadow was in 1816 director of the Academy in Berlin. He published *Lehren von den Knochen und Muscheln* (1830) and *Polyklet oder von den Maasen des Menchen* (1833, text 1 vol. 8vo, 1 vol. folio), etc.

Friedlaender, *Gottfried Schadow;* Dobbert, *Gottfried Schadow in Zeitschrift für Bauwesen,* 1887.

SCHAUBERT, EDWARD ; architect ; b. 1800.

He studied in Breslau and Berlin, and in 1830 went to Greece, where he held several public offices. He was associated with Ludwig Ross (see Ross, L.) and Christian Hansen (see Hansen, Chr.) in the restoration of the temple of Nike Apteros on the Acropolis and in the publication of *Die Acropolis von Athen . . . der Temple der Nike Apteros* (1839, 1 vol. folio).

Seubert, *Künstler-lexicon.*

SCHINKEL, KARL FRIEDRICH ; architect ; b. March 13, 1781 ; d. Oct. 9, 1841.

In 1797 he entered the Academy in Berlin and studied under David and Friedrich Gilly (see Gilly, F.). In 1820 he was appointed professor in the Academy at Berlin and in 1839 *Oberlandbaudirector.* He visited Italy, including Istria and Sicily, France and England. In 1834 he made a design for a royal palace on the Acropolis at Athens which, fortunately, was never executed. Among the most important of his buildings are the museum in Berlin (1824–1828), the Royal Theatre in Berlin (1819–1821), the fine *Nicolai Kirche* at Potsdam, the *Königs-Wache* in Berlin (1818), the *Schloss-Wache* in Dresden, the fine architectural school in Berlin, the *Charlottenhof* and Casino at Potsdam, etc. Schinkel was much interested in the construction of Protestant churches in

420

the Gothic style, the most important of these being the *Werder Kirche* in Berlin. He made a design for the completion of the cathedral of Cologne, which was never executed.

Wolzogen, *Schinkel als architect, Maler und Kunstphilosoph;* Ziller, *Schinkel (Künstler-Monographien);* Kugler, *Schinkel* (in *Kleine Schriften);* Waagen, *Schinkel* (in *Kleine Schriften);* Krätschell, *Schinkel,* in *Seinen Verhältniss zur gothischen Baukunst.*

SCHLOSS. In German, the residence of the feudal lord of the soil, a term corresponding closely to " château," and containing the significance of the two English words, " castle " and " manor house."

SCHLÜTER, ANDREAS; sculptor and architect; b. May 20, 1664 (in Hamburg); d. 1714.

After the death of his father, Gerhard Schlüter, a sculptor, Andreas became a pupil of the sculptor Sapovius in Danzig (West Prussia). Between the ages of twenty and thirty he visited Italy, and in 1691 entered the service of Johann III. Sobieski, King of Poland, at Warsaw. Here he attracted the notice of Prince Friedrich of Prussia (afterward Elector Friedrich III. and in 1700 King Friedrich I.), who in 1694 made him court sculptor at Berlin. After 1696 Schlüter built the greater part of the palace of Charlottenburg in Berlin. In 1697 he made the model of the equestrian statue of the Elector Friedrich III. in Königsberg. The famous equestrian statue in Berlin of the Great Elector Friedrich Wilhelm was begun by Schlüter about 1698 and placed in position in 1705. Schlüter superintended the sculptural decoration of the *Zeughaus* (Berlin), and made the series of twenty-one masks of dying warriors in the inner court of that building. About 1699 he was made architect of the *Schloss* in Berlin, and held that office until 1706, when he was superseded by Eosander (see Eosander). In 1713 he was chief architect of the Russian court and died the next year in Saint Petersburg.

Seubert, *Künstler-lexikon;* Adler, *Aus Andreas Schlüter's Leben;* Mosler, *Schlüter in Sansovino u. s. w.;* R. Dohme, *Die Masken Sterbender Krieger.*

SCHMIDT, FREIDRICH FREIHERR VON; architect; b. Oct. 22, 1825; d. Jan. 23, 1891 (in Vienna).

He was educated at the Polytechnische Schule in Stuttgart under Mauch, and made a special study of stereotomy and stone cutting. In 1843 he was employed as a stone cutter on the cathedral of Cologne. In 1856 he passed the state examination in architecture in Berlin. Schmidt devoted himself especially to the Gothic style and built many churches in Germany. In 1859 he won first prize in the competition for the *Rathhaus* in Berlin, but did not carry out that work. He was made professor of architecture at the Academy of

Milan in 1857, and began the restoration of the church of S. Ambrogio in Milan, which was interrupted by the war of 1859. In this year Schmidt was appointed professor at the Academy in Vienna, and in 1862 was made architect of the cathedral of S. Stephen in that city, the tower of which church he finished in 1864. He designed the *Rathhaus* in Vienna, which was finished in 1883.

Reichensperger, *Friedrich, Freiherr von Schmidt;* Farrow, *Recent Developments in Vienna;* Meyer, *Konversations-Lexicon.*

SCHOLARSHIP IN ARCHITECTURAL TRAINING. (See Fellowship, *B.*)

SCHOOL. In Architecture, same as Schoolhouse, *A.*

SCHOOLHOUSE. *A.* A building devised, or appropriate for use as a school.

B. The dwelling house provided for the use of the schoolmaster or schoolmistress, generally attached to or adjoining a school (Great Britain).

The graded class system in the schools of the United States has been developed essentially from that of the Teutonic countries of Europe, rather than from the school systems of England and France, which, while varying one from the other, differ radically from the Teutonic systems. While in Germany and Austria there are no rooms, as in the United States, in which the whole school, or several classes of the school, are assembled for general exercises, and for entertainments of various kinds, such assembly halls, used for the same purpose, are not an unusual feature of Swiss schools. In Germany and Austria the " Aula " is used only for the annual examinations. So far as the disposition of the plan is concerned, however, these examination halls are as suggestive as if their use were the same as that of the American "Assembly Halls." The German " Aula " is generally given a rich monumental treatment, as if to express the dignity of the state, while, as a rule, the " Assembly Halls " in the United States have had little more architectural character than the class rooms. In Switzerland, the assembly halls are primarily provided as places for recreation, and are handsomely finished.

Since in Germany and Austria there are no collective exercises, each graded class remains in the class room assigned to it, except when it passes as a class to the rooms assigned to instruction in drawing, music, and other special studies, or when the class goes, either in a body or in sections, to its gymnastic exercise or to the shower baths, as is required three times a week of every pupil in Prussian schools of the lower grades.

As far as coeducation of the sexes affects the planning of schools, we find in Switzerland practically the same conditions as in the United States; but in Germany and Austria, as in

France, no coeducation exists, and consequently the plans show an absolute, and, as even some educators of these very countries maintain, an undesirable, division of the sexes. In the United States, division of the sexes in the primary and grammar grades is mainly confined to the basement ; and in many cases is besides only an imaginary line in the playground.

In Switzerland, as in the United States, and more recently in England, the advantage of providing the pupils with fresh and pure air appears to be equally well appreciated, and this consideration brings into school construction features rarely found in Germany and Austria. For the past twenty years in Switzerland, and the past fifteen in the United States, the best schools have been planned so that the pupils' out-of-door clothing should not only be excluded from the class rooms, but from the corridors. Special enclosures with outside light, thoroughly warmed and specially ventilated, called in the United States " wardrobes," are built immediately adjoining each class room.

Until but recently few German schools have been so planned that especially assigned alcoves are provided off the corridors in which the out-of-door clothing can be hung ; previously all wraps were hung on pegs about the class rooms. The hanging of clothing in corridors is an alleviation, not a correction, of a poor condition ; for, as the movement of air is naturally from the colder corridors to the warmer class rooms, especially where warmed fresh air is artificially supplied to the class rooms, the foul odours from the clothing must find their way to the class rooms.

In the United States, hat and coat hooks are set only on the side walls of the wardrobes ; the top row of hooks is placed, in primary schools, 4 feet, in other schools, 5 feet, above the floor. The minimum hanging space is 30 running feet for a class of fifty-six pupils. Above the upper row of hooks, or immediately above the baseboard, is set a shelf for overshoes, etc. ; and umbrella stands are provided. The width of these enclosures is not less than 4 feet ; they have a door from the corridor and one from the class room.

Class rooms of Europe and in the United States are usually 32 feet in length ; those of high schools in the latter country are sometimes even 8 feet longer. A greater length than 32 feet makes it difficult for the teacher's voice to reach without strain the pupils in the last row of seats, and at a greater distance the pupils' work on the blackboards at the end of the room cannot be readily seen from the platform. On the Continent, as in Germany, for instance, 32 feet is the generally adopted length of a class room, although 30 feet is preferred by most of the European authorities on school construction. In the German schools analogous to those of the grammar grades in the United States, the class rooms are generally 32 feet long, 22 feet wide, and 13 feet high, and accommodate, upon forms seating four each, fifty-six pupils, giving a floor area of $12\frac{1}{2}$ square feet and an air enclosure of 163 cubic feet for each pupil. In the schools more recently built in Prussia, as in the *Gemindeschule*, No. 204, of Berlin, most of the class rooms are approximately 32 feet long, 20 feet wide, 13 feet high, and accommodate forty-six pupils, giving a floor area of 14 square feet and an air enclosure of 182 cubic feet for each pupil.

The grammar class rooms built within recent years in Boston, Massachusetts, and in many other cities of the United States, are 32 feet long, 28 feet wide, $13\frac{1}{2}$ feet high, accommodating fifty-six pupils, seated at single desks, giving a floor area of 16 square feet and an air enclosure of 216 cubic feet for each pupil.

While the areas above noted are much in excess of those found in the latest and best Prussian schools, they fall far short of those advised by Dr. Risley, the most recent medical writer upon this subject, who advises a class room 32 feet long, 24 feet wide, 15 feet high, to accommodate forty-five pupils of the grammar grade, seated at single desks, giving a floor area of 19 square feet, and an air enclosure of 250 cubic feet for each pupil,

The seating of the pupils of American schools at individual desks, which elsewhere obtains only in Switzerland, and there, the writer understands, in none except the upper grades, is not likely to be discarded in America. In the best practice the minimum floor area and the minimum cubical area of air for each pupil, 16 square feet and 216 cubic feet respectively, should be maintained, and, with these factors determined, the question of the satisfactory lighting of the class rooms remains the principal consideration.

The code of rules established by the French government for the construction of schools fixes the minimum allowed height of a class room at 13 feet, and where the light comes from one side only, requires that the minimum height of the room shall be two thirds of its width, measured from the inner wall to the face of the outer wall of the building, In a brick school fitted with double sash, a class room lighted from one side only, 32 feet long, 28 feet wide, accommodating fifty-six grammar school pupils, would require a height of 19 feet ; a room of the same length, $24\frac{1}{2}$ feet wide, would accommodate forty-eight pupils, and would require a height of 17 feet ; a room of the same length, 21 feet wide, would accommodate forty pupils and would require a height of 14 feet. It will be seen that this French rule requires a greater height of ceiling than that recommended by Dr. Risley, *i.e.* 15 feet in height for a room 32 feet long, 24 feet wide, accommodating forty-five pupils. It is probable that in the clear atmosphere of the United States a room would have on the average throughout the year much better lighting than would a room of like dimensions in any part of the north of the Continent of Europe, or in England. Even rooms 28 feet wide are fairly well lighted by the four windows on one side of a room but $13\frac{1}{2}$ feet high. It is probable, therefore, that if the class rooms in the American grammar schools were given a width of $24\frac{1}{2}$ feet, they would be well lighted if given a height of $13\frac{1}{2}$ feet. Providing, of course, that adequate lighting can be given by other means, extreme height of stories and hence of stairways should be avoided; but it is possible that the standard of 14 feet 3 inches, adopted in the more recently built schools in the city of New York, may be that finally adopted in the grammar schools of the United States, especially in those of several stories in height. With this ceiling height, economy of space can be gained by placing two tiers of toilet rooms in the height of a full story. In the United States, with ceiling height noted above, class rooms with windows on one side only, and 28 feet wide, would probably be found not to be ill lighted; but American architects should not be content with the lighting which can be given a room lighted from one side only, 28 feet wide, with 13 feet of ceiling height, which are the customary dimensions of grammar grade class rooms in the United States, the ceilings in the primary grades being 1 foot lower.

The dimensions given the best American class rooms for the grammar grade assure ample light only for the corner rooms, where, disregarding theoretical objections, a good diffusion of light can be gained by taking it from the backs as well as from the left-hand sides of the pupils. The inside rooms, even in most of the best designed schoolrooms of the United States, are planned to accommodate the same number of pupils as the corner rooms, under conditions of lighting which are approved by no authority on the subject. Dr. Cohn says, " There never can be too much light in a schoolroom," and he has in this opinion the support of all who have given practical consideration to the lighting of schoolhouses.

In writing exercises it is advantageous to have most, if not all, of the light from one side only, and that on the left of the pupil, but otherwise the quantity of the light and not the direction from whence the light comes is the important consideration. It is, therefore, better with corner class rooms 28 feet wide to have four windows in the long wall, and at least two, if not three, in the other outside wall. A window directly opposite the teacher's desk is objectionable, and hence, as is often done in France, and sometimes in the United States, the portion of the wall directly opposite the teacher's desk

should be blank, and the windows on either side of this space should be placed as near the corners of the room as the construction makes possible, or as may be advisable for the external appearance of the building. In the schools of the Continent, the class rooms are seldom more than 22 feet wide, and the regulations generally provide the lighting of class rooms from one side only; but this regulation is respected in the majority of, but not in all, cases.

From the foregoing it would appear that, as far as the lighting of the corner rooms of American schools is concerned, they might retain their present large dimensions; but that, if their height is not increased to 14 or 15 feet, they should have, in the rooms which have light from one side only, not more than $24\frac{1}{2}$ feet of width, and in such rooms forty-eight instead of fifty-six pupils should be accommodated. Class rooms in primary schools, if given a ceiling height of 13 feet, should be 32 feet long by 22 feet wide, and thus furnish accommodations for fifty-four instead of fifty-six pupils.

In Germany light from the north is permitted at the backs of the pupils; in France additional windows are permitted in the wall opposite that through which the main light comes, but light is shut off from these windows when the room is occupied. The common-sense view of the lighting question appears to be that all possible light should be gained for a class room, providing that, if from a side of the building exposed to the sun, the major part of the light comes from the left-hand side of the pupils, and that none comes in their faces, and that on a side of the building exposed to the sun there should be no windows directly opposite the teacher's desk. The conditions seldom exist which permit the construction of a school with the orientation which its designer would give if the choice of location were to be made by him.

There is by no means a unanimous opinion in regard to the best method of placing such buildings so that they may have the most advantageous exposure to the sun. Most authorities agree that the eastern exposure is that most desirable for class rooms, but others whose opinions are also authoritative maintain that the northern light is preferable for these rooms, providing the windows are furnished with double sash, and that the rooms are thoroughly warmed and ventilated. Probably most would agree that greater advantages would be gained in a building whose main façade had a southeastern exposure, by which the sun could shine on three faces of the building for the greatest part of the year. There is substantial agreement that, on the whole, a westerly is less desirable than a northerly exposure, providing the building is well heated and ventilated. An easterly exposure is the best for class rooms;

the question of the relative merits of the northerly and southerly exposure for class rooms may be left to be decided, as the advantages of a steady, clear, northern light, or that of the healthful and cheerful light from the south, may be given the greater importance.

In the United States class room windows are, in the best practice, made 4 feet wide between jambs; the window stools are usually set 3 feet above the floor. Sometimes in that country, and generally in Germany, the window stools are set at a height of about 4 feet to prevent the pupils from looking out of the windows, and to that end the lower sash of some latest German schools are glazed with ribbed glass; on the other hand, in some of the Swiss cantons the stools are set $2\frac{1}{2}$ feet high, with the object of making it easy for the pupils to look out-of-doors.

In all well-designed schoolhouses the top of the windows is placed as near the ceiling as the finish will admit. Transom bars should not be permitted, both because such features cut off too much valuable light, and because opening of windows by the teacher is thereby facilitated. In a well-designed and properly regulated warming and ventilating system the introduction of outside air by such means is unnecessary, and it is detrimental to the working of a good system. Windows evenly distributed in the class room walls give a better diffusion of light than that given by groups of mullioned windows of equal glass area. Where arched windows are used, their height, and consequently the height of the room, should be increased that the glass area may equal that of the square-headed windows of height proportionate to height and width of such a room. Double runs of sash are desirable to aid in economizing fuel, to check draughts from the windows, and to help shut out dust and noise. Under normal conditions of site, the basement windows should have a minimum height between masonry jambs of 4 feet, and preferably $4\frac{1}{2}$ feet. The basement windows should be stepped down with the grade to give greater height of window wherever feasible.

In the United States a movable platform 5 or 6 feet by 10 feet is provided for the teacher, for whom also a wardrobe 1 foot 4 inches in depth, and a bookcase 10 to 12 inches in depth, is built, if possible, flush with the wall, and placed as convenient as is possible to the platform.

Black slate is the best material for blackboards. In the United States the blackboards are usually $4\frac{1}{2}$ feet high, and are set upon all available wall surface of class and recitation rooms, in primary schools 2 feet 4 inches, and in other schools 3 feet above the floor, with a chalk receiver $2\frac{3}{4}$ inches wide.

Sheathed dadoes are often found to be infected with vermin; those of "gauged mortar," with wooden chair rail, and plain ogee hospital baseboards run out of 3-inch plank have been found cleanly and serviceable. Concaved angles of plastered walls and of walls and ceilings facilitate the cleaning of the building. Inaccessible dust ledges should be avoided. As little wood finish as possible should be used, and to that end Keene's cement for door and window trims is advisable. In short, it is as fully important to take precautions against dust lodgment and the use of absorbent surfaces in a schoolhouse as it is in a hospital.

Rift Georgia or Florida pine or maple are held in the United States to be the best upper flooring for schools.

Doors should open toward corridors, and should have a glass panel set with bottom 4 feet above floor, and transom lights over.

A picture moulding should be set on the walls of all class rooms, recitation rooms, and assembly halls.

Light shades of blue-gray or green-gray are required for the wall painting of class rooms by some German authorities, and these are probably the best colours for the purpose. Plastered walls should be painted in oil to the top of the blackboards; above this height the walls and ceilings may be tinted with water colour, with ceilings a very light buff or ivory-white water colour tint. Corridors should have walls painted in oil colour $5\frac{1}{2}$ feet high.

In the United States a master's office is requisite for large schools, and private rooms, with toilet rooms adjoining, for teachers of both sexes, should be provided in all schools.

It is held by some authorities that no toilet rooms should be placed in the basement, but that all plumbing should be in a separate, well-warmed building. The writer is not alone in his opinion that there is no need of thus increasing the cost of schoolhouse construction, providing a strong and certain ventilation to an ample aspirating shaft through the plumbing fixtures themselves is provided. The toilet rooms, when placed in the basement, should immediately adjoin the playrooms for each sex, and should always be shut off therefrom by fly doors with spring butts. Where space permits, the basement may well be used for gymnasiums and for rooms for manual training and cooking schools. In the German schools portions of the basement are used for bathing rooms, provided with shower baths only, each scholar being required to take such a bath three times a week. In a very large school, if the size of the lot permits, the boiler and coal room may be well assigned to a separate building adjoining the school. In schools of moderate size, such an arrangement has not sufficient advantage to warrant the increased cost of construction.

Except for boiler and coal rooms, where brick pavement laid on edge should be used, and for rooms used for gymnasiums or for school purposes, there is no better flooring for basements than the best brands of asphalt, $\frac{3}{4}$ inch thick, laid on a concrete bed. Wooden floors in the basement should be without air space, laid on screeds bedded in concrete, with waterproof paper between the upper and lower floors. If the site is damp, as, for instance, on "made land" in Boston, a coat of hot asphalt, or, at least, of tar concrete, may well be laid on the concrete before laying the screeds.

In European schools living apartments are provided for the janitor in the large schools, and in many cases, and even quite generally in the smallest rural schools, like provision is made for the master. There is no advantage apparent in assigning space in a school building for the master's housekeeping; he can rent his habitation elsewhere for much less than the sum which should be deducted from his salary to compensate the city or town for the interest on the expenditure on the portion of the school building he would occupy.

In addition to the main entrance, there should be outside separate entrances to the basement for each sex, and there should not be less than two exits from the first floor, and not less than two staircases from the top to the first floor of every school building.

A sheltered porch, or, better, a vestibule of ample dimensions, should be provided, in which early comers may find shelter, without being given admission to the building proper. In Switzerland such vestibules are required for all schools. In the United States, basement entrances are sometimes arranged so that the pupils may have access to the playroom and toilet rooms before the hour at which the school exercises begin. All entrance doors should open outward to guard against disaster in case of fire or panic. Outer vestibule doors should be hung with double action swing butts. Ten feet is the minimum width for a school corridor; 12 feet is preferable. Corridors should be given all the light which the conditions of the plan and of the economical construction of the bounding walls permit. The basement should be shut off by tinned doors fitted with spring butts or doorchecks; the staircases also might be well shut off on each floor by like protection from fire.

Staircases should preferably be of masonry, or metal construction throughout; but, if the cost of the building must be kept within strict limits, and staircases of wooden construction are used, they should be thoroughly fire-stopped with brick or with terra-cotta blocks; as the minimum precaution against fire danger, the soffit should be wire-lathed.

The treads of iron stairs should be covered with rubber mats, or, better, with combined steel and lead treads, not less than $5\frac{1}{2}$ inches

wide, set into a rebate cast in the metal tread. In primary schools the height of risers should be 6 inches, and in other schools not more than $7\frac{1}{2}$ inches. Posts and balusters should be of the plainest and most readily cleaned design. Hand rails of $2\frac{1}{2}$-inch iron piping have proved serviceable and of sufficiently good appearance. Hand rails on the walls, except at platforms, are requisite. Some authorities hold that school staircases should not be wider than $3\frac{1}{2}$ feet, so that only two files of pupils, each provided with a hand rail, can pass, and so that the possible crowding between the files, in case of panic, should be prevented. The excellent discipline of American school children, which has been proved by alarms of fire, justifies, however, the retention of the more comfortable width of 5 feet, which has generally been adopted in the schools of the United States. There appears to be no advantage in a greater width than this. There should not be more than fifteen and not less than three risers between landings, and landings should not be less than 4 feet between steps.

When structural steel is low in cost, it would not appear to be extravagant to advise that the first floor of all schools of more than one story in height should be built of incombustible materials; not even the narrowest appropriation justifies the construction of such a building without a wire-lathed basement ceiling. How much further "fireproof" construction should be carried is a matter of judgment in each case. The main danger from fire in a schoolhouse is not from outside, but from the inside, and that danger again is practically confined to the basement. If the basement ceiling is properly protected, the staircases thereto shut off by fire doors, and if the plastering of the walls is directly on the brickwork, and with the partitions, if not solid, as is preferable for the exclusion of vermin as well as for fire protection, at all exits properly fire-stopped, there is little danger from fire to the inmates of the school. The danger from panic makes it advisable that schools of over three stories in height should have their floors constructed of incombustible materials, as the knowledge of such precaution increases the confidence of the inmates.

Twenty years ago the warming and ventilating system used in the Swiss schools was in advance of anything to be found in any other country. The writer does not know whether Switzerland has retained the same relative superiority in this respect; but it is probable that the scientific warming and ventilating of schoolhouses has, with the use of the plenum fan in ventilation, been more perfected in the United States than elsewhere. Experience shows that in the United States a school building is best warmed by direct radiation, without reliance upon an increased temperature from the air delivered by the fan, and that this machine should be employed for the sole purpose of supplying an adequate amount of fresh air warmed to 70° Fahrenheit. This method of warming and of supplying fresh air is advisable, except perhaps in schools of six or less rooms, and even in such cases a plenum fan run by a gas engine may be advantageously used.

With such a system of warming and ventilating, the direction and velocity of the wind cannot, from time to time, affect the evenness of result which is the paramount condition of success in a warming and ventilating system. With a system of warming and ventilating by "indirect radiation" a uniform certainty of result cannot always be attained, and with such a system, the first cost of which is less than in the "direct heat" and "fan" air supply system, the consumption of fuel to give a satisfactory result is greater under even conditions.

In *Gemindeschule* No. 204, Berlin, the summer and winter vent outlets in a class room accommodating forty-six pupils have an area of .35 metres square, *i.e.*, about 1.72 square feet. This building is warmed by direct radiation, there is no special supply of warmed fresh air for each room ; such fresh air as is supplied to the inmates must come from cracks in the windows or from the corridors in which are hung the pupils' clothing. In a well-warmed and well-ventilated American class room which accommodates fifty-six pupils, the air inlets and outlets are $4\frac{1}{2}$ square feet for the lower rooms, ranging up to 6 square feet in the third story. Where the plenum fan is used for supplying warm fresh air, the air outlets remain as above, but the air inlets are reduced in area 25 per cent to 30 per cent. Air outlets should be arranged on inner walls wherever found most convenient.

The upper of the two air outlets is provided with a register which is opened in the summer only, and is set as close to the ceiling as possible, while the lower outlet is fitted with a register face and is set as close to the floor as the baseboard will permit. Air inlets are set with bottom of register face not less than 7 feet above the floor ; 8 feet is a preferable height for these openings.

The construction of the Latin and English High School building in Boston, Massachusetts, begun in 1877, marks an important period in the school architecture of the United States, as it was the first application in that country of sound principles of planning adapted to the needs of graded schools. The construction of this building was not, however, beneficial in so far as it affected the system of instruction or the plan of the high school, at least as those needs had been up to that time understood in that country. The plan of this Boston school was avowedly based upon that of the *Akademishe Gymna-*

sium at Vienna. This type of plan meets well, in the principal features, the necessities of American schools of the primary and grammar grades, but its adoption for a high school tended to divert the natural development of the academic schools of the United States, whose traditional systems were based upon that of England ; pupils of several classes being congregated in large schoolrooms, wherein certain recitations are heard, while other pupils are busy with their studies, or pass from this large room to other rooms for recitation in special subjects. This was a system which permitted somewhat of the freedom of a collegiate institution, and it would appear to develop the self-reliance and broaden the experience of the pupil.

The adoption of the gymnasium type for the Boston high school, from the mere copying of its features of plan in new high school buildings, appears to have changed this system of academic construction, with the result that the American high school in most cases exhibits to-day in plan and arrangement an elaborate development of the graded grammar school. We generally find in high schools "wardrobes" adjoining each class room, a feature derived from the necessities of discipline for pupils of the primary and grammar grades, and not in harmony with the freer spirit which had been characteristic of the academic schools.

In the Cambridge High School, built about 1887, the building which, above all others, most affected for good the architectural design of American schools, is a marked example of the effect of the above-mentioned Boston school upon the American high school type. This Cambridge school has no feature of its plan which differs from that of an American grammar school of the highest type of to-day, except that the class rooms of the former school are 28 by 40 feet, instead of being, as in grammar schools, 28 by 32 feet.

Neither has the Brookline High School, begun in 1894, or the Springfield High School of about the same date, or the Cambridge Latin School, begun about 1897, any feature especially characteristic of an academic school, and all could as well be used for a large graded grammar school, except for the greater length of class rooms, as for the purpose for which they were designed. It need not be said that the responsibility for this condition rests entirely with the several school boards, and not upon the architects of the several buildings. There has lately appeared in the United States a tendency in high schools to revert to the former academic type. Rooms for the pupils' out-of-door clothing, fitted with individual lockers, are being provided wherever found convenient, in place of the wardrobes immediately adjoining each schoolroom. There is again a tendency to assign large schoolrooms for the accommodation of at least two classes, instead of placing each graded class in a separate room.

In the Mechanic Arts High School of Boston the writer believes the first tendency was shown, in the eastern United States at least, to differentiate the high from the grammar school type. This tendency does not appear in the introduction of hand training as complementary to the usual mental training, but in the building of large "locker rooms" in place of "wardrobes," and that of schoolrooms seating seventy or more pupils of two or more grades instead of class rooms for a more or less number of pupils of the same grade. This school was begun in 1893. In 1894 the Brighton High School was begun, and the feature of locker rooms, derived directly from the Mechanic Arts School, was introduced, but the class rooms were designed only for single graded classes. In 1898 the South Boston High School was begun, which has also the locker room method, and provides also four "double class rooms."

It thus seems probable that the American high schools will gradually become again differentiated from the graded grammar schools, and that the American high school systems will again follow the academic methods from which they appear to have been turned, mainly by the enthusiastic admiration of a single superintendent of schools for Teutonic school methods and school plans.

In the United States the institutions for the special training of teachers are called Normal Schools. These schools are modelled essentially upon the early system of the high schools of that country,— the academic system. The students of the several classes have their desks in a large general room, and pass thence for recitations to special class rooms for laboratory practice, or to lectures. For practice in the art of teaching, "model departments," composed of class rooms for pupils in the kindergarten, primary, and grammar grades, are either placed in the same or an adjacent building, or in conveniently located public schools of the city or town.

While manual training in its restricted sense has been much less widely introduced in the United States than it has in England and on the Continent of Europe, the most important and most characteristic development of the American school system is the "Manual Training" or "Mechanic Arts" schools. In these schools manual skill is not taught for its own sake; the object is to encourage intellectual activity through the knowledge of materials, of natural forces, and of the use of tools as well as through books. Manual training is but one, and that not the most important, part of the instruction which is given in American schools of this class.

Machinery for wood and metal working, car-

penters' benches, forge shops, and, in some cases, moulding and modelling rooms are provided, but there are also draughting rooms, laboratories, recitation rooms, and schoolrooms; these latter rooms are not all arranged for a single graded class, but for pupils of different grades of advancement, thus, as noted above, reverting in a measure to the academic system of high school instruction, which the people of the United States inherited with their English traditions, and which is essentially the system which prevails to-day in all grades of English schools.

— EDMUND M. WHEELWRIGHT.

SCHOOL OF ARCHITECTURE. In modern times, an institution for the professional training of architects. (See Architect, The, in England; France; Italy.) This article is devoted to the *École des Beaux Arts*, which is the principal institution in France for art education, occupying the buildings of the *École* on the *Quai Malaquais* and the *Rue Bonaparte* in Paris. These buildings are principally the work of the architect Duban and his successor Coquart, and occupy the site of the former *Musée des Petits Augustins*. In 1884 the *Hôtel de Chimay* was acquired and added to the school.

The school is divided into three sections, those of painting, sculpture, and architecture. The present article is confined to the last-named of these.

The origin of the School of Fine Arts is coincident with the foundation, under Mazarin, of the *Académie de Peinture et de Sculpture* in 1648, and of the *Académie d'Architecture* under Colbert in 1671. Instruction in architecture was given by the members of the latter until the abolition of all the academies during the Revolution. After the foundation of the *Académie des Beaux Arts* (as a section of the *Institut de France*) in 1803, instruction was given by the academicians; and it was not till 1819 that regular courses in architecture were established in the school.

The regulations of 1819 have been repeatedly modified since then. The most important change perhaps has been the institution of the official, or school, ateliers, in 1863, a movement which met at the time with much opposition. The school is placed under the direction of the Minister of Fine Arts. Its immediate administration is now in the hands of a director, appointed by the minister. This position has been held since 1878 by the sculptor Paul Dubois.

The organization of the school is strictly that of a university; that is, it prescribes the work to be done in its various courses, provides lectures and instruction in these, institutes and judges competitions in design, drawing, and modelling, conducts all examinations, and gives all awards. It does not, however, compel attendance on its courses, or any but a minimum of participation in its competitions or examinations. It is sufficient, during a year, to render two competitive designs, or to attend two examinations in the sciences; or to render one design and attend one examination, for a student's name to remain on the roll. At thirty the limit of age is reached, and he is dropped. Accordingly there is no fixed number of years for the course, and the *Bemooste Haupt* of the German universities is a familiar figure.

To enter the school the student passes examinations in elementary design, drawing from the cast, modelling, arithmetic, algebra, elementary and descriptive geometry, and history. Of late years the great number of applicants has induced the administration to increase gradually the difficulty of these entrance examinations.

The courses of the school are gratuitous, and foreigners are admitted on the same footing as Frenchmen. Recently, however, so many foreigners have presented themselves that the number admitted has been limited to a certain percentage of the entering class.

While the intent of this article is to speak principally of the study of design as pursued by the students of the school, it is necessary to speak briefly of the course in general. The standing of the student depends on the number of "*valeurs*" which he obtains. A certain number of points is attached to each recompense given either in design or in examination. The student on entering the school becomes a member of the second class. He is obliged to obtain a certain number of these *valeurs* before admission to the first class. There are at present six in architectural design, one in archæology, two in drawing from the cast or the figure, one in modelling, one each in descriptive geometry, stereotomy, perspective, and mathematics, and two in construction.

The time requisite for this work varies very much in different cases; except where the previous preparation has been exceptionally thorough, between two and three years is the average.

In the first class the student's time is mostly given to the study of design, with some archæology, modelling, and drawing from the figure. When five "*valeurs*" in this class have been obtained, and under certain other conditions, he may obtain the "*Certificat d'Études de l'École.*"

The highest honour given is the "*Diplomé d'Architecte.*" To be eligible for this the student must have obtained in the first class at least ten *valeurs* in architecture, one in drawing from the figure, and one in modelling. He must also have passed at least one year in superintending the construction of a building under a government architect.

The examination for the diploma itself comprehends the complete working drawings and specifications of a projected building, the subject of which the student may select, subject to approval; and a searching examination on the different parts of this project, on the elements of physics and chemistry as applied to construction, on the history of architecture and the law relating to building.

Of the total number admitted to the school, less than half enter the first class, and a small minority receive the diploma. From 1819 to 1893 the total number of students was about 4000; of students of the first class about 1500, and of *diplomés* somewhat over 300.

The number of foreign students at the school has been very considerable, Switzerland and the United States furnishing the greatest number.

The honours and awards of the school are, in general, open to Frenchmen and foreigners alike, as are also the special prizes, of which there are about twenty-five. The exception to this is the *Grand Prix de Rome*, which is, however, not properly a school prize, although awarded by the school. This greatest honour of the French architectural student is open to all Frenchmen between the ages of fifteen and thirty, whether members of the school or not, and is given to the victor in a competition in design only — the project of a monumental building. Founded (for the architects) in 1720, it entitles its winner to a stay of three years in Rome at the expense of the government, and the certainty of a position as government architect thereafter.

It has already been said that the organization of the school was that of a university. Until the institution of the three school ateliers in 1863, there was no actual designing done within its walls, every student being necessarily the pupil of some outside instructor. At present, the pupil of one of the three school instructors is absolutely on the same footing with those belonging to the outside ateliers, of which there are now about a dozen. Each atelier has its instructor — *patron*. These *patrons* are practising architects, of recognized standing, who give up a portion of their time to this work. The atelier is thus the important unit of this federal system; its members are animated by the strongest *esprit du corps*, are bound by the strong bond of custom to help each other in their work, and are united in loyalty to the ideas of the *patron*. The triumphs are triumphs of the atelier, which cast a lustre on all its members.

There are six architectural competitions (*projets*) a year in each class. On the appointed morning the students of each class meet in the court of the school, answer to their names, are handed a programme prepared by the Professor of Theory, and are then imprisoned in stalls (*loges*) for twelve hours, or as much less as they please. During this time each one makes a sketch on a small scale of the proposed building, without access to books or advice. This sketch is handed in and numbered, the student himself keeping the tracing. The next day he presents this at his atelier, where it is subjected to a severe criticism on the part of the *patron*. The rendered design must agree in all essentials with this sketch ; if it is too unpromising on examination, the student is counselled to drop it and take up other work. More often he is advised as to its possibilities of development, referred to examples, and encouraged to make what he can out of it.

This system has been found successful in many respects. It insures a certain individuality in the work, and prevents the possibilities of blind copies. It confines the work of the student also within certain fixed limits, — those of a certain conformity to his sketch, — avoiding the successive trial of one general scheme after another. And these artificial limitations imposed by the school take the place of real limitations which occur in architectural practice — those of cost, special conditions, or the idiosyncrasies of the client.

The usual time given for each *projet* is two months. Of this time from one to two weeks only are given to making the actual drawings, the remainder being taken up with the study of the problem. The French methods of study have been so generally imitated in other schools, especially in those of the United States, that it is hardly necessary to describe them. Nowhere is tracing paper held in more honour : beginning with the smallest scale, a great number of successive studies are made, and roughly rendered before the final drawings are touched. These studies are made with the advice and criticism, not only of the *patron*, but (especially in the case of the less advanced students) of the better men of the atelier ; and there are often warm informal discussions in which all take part. The aid of the elder men is given as a matter of course, and when the final drawings are made, all hands turn to and help. The younger men, especially, pay for the advice they have received by working for their elders ; and many a one in his turn has had a difficult bit of rendering helped out by more skilled hands than his own.

The study of the plan is especially insisted on, and in the awards great weight is always laid upon it. It is, too, an article of faith, that while the handsome plan is not necessarily good, the good plan will generally be handsome. Accordingly, much study is given to the presentation of the plans, so that they may be easily read, and that the results of so much study may be at once apparent.

It is held that as the actual studies of the architect must be largely in elevation, the finished drawings should be so presented, and that an important part of architectural education consists in the ability to translate these elevations into their solid forms. It is only exceptionally that perspectives are required in the rendering of a *projet*, although in the ateliers partial perspectives, as aids to study, are often made. The conventional shadows are always used, both in studies and finished drawings, and their correct projection is always demanded.

The completed drawings of any given *projet* are delivered at the school at the appointed time, and exhibited. The awards are given by a jury consisting of the eight architects, members of the Institut, twelve other permanent members, and nine who are renewed from year to year. Finally, the Professor of Theory delivers a lecture on the problem, often containing criticisms of the premiated designs.

These exhibitions are occasions of the greatest interest to the students who have taken part, and they are fundamentally different to those in other schools. For here are gathered together, not simply the individual efforts of students, all working under one influence, and seeking the solution of a given problem, but those of some fifteen different architectural schools, eager rivals, representing different ideas, and all prepared to criticise the successes and failures of the other ateliers, and to profit by them. The awards, too, have a special value and interest, because they are given by an independent body, in which the *patrons* are in a minority.

It cannot be too strongly insisted upon, that in the atelier system lies the essence of the School of Fine Arts, and that to it is due, in large measure, its success, and the enthusiasm felt for its teaching by so many of its old students. The atelier, as has been said, really antedates the school, which accepted them as it found them ; and to change this feature would be to change the entire character of the school. The opposition to the establishment of the school ateliers in 1863 only ceased when it was firmly established that these were to have no precedence or advantage over the others, and that there was no intention on the part of the administration to place architectural education in a few official hands. It is significant that the student signs himself " Pupil of M. —— and of the School of Fine Arts."

It may be added to this sketch, necessarily incomplete, of the training of the school, that it is common for the student, during a portion of the time that he spends at it, to devote some time to work in an architect's office, not infrequently in that of the *patron*.

The roll of the pupils of the school includes the names of nearly all the prominent French architects of the last seventy-five years, and not a few well-known names of foreigners. This roll, with other information, is contained in *Les Architectes Elèves de l'École des Beaux Arts*, by David de Penanrun, Roux-et-Delaire, (Paris, 1895), to which the writer acknowledges his indebtedness. — WALTER COOK.

SCHULZ, FRANZ; architect; b. 1838; d. Oct. 22, 1870.

Educated at the Academy of Vienna under Friedrich von Schmidt (see Schmidt, F. von), he devoted himself to the study of mediæval art. He published *Profanbauten des Mittelalters in Rom und umgegend; Die Baudenkmäler auf Majorca.*

Seubert, *Künstler-lexikon.*

SCHWANTHALER, LUDWIG MICHAEL; sculptor; b. Aug. 26, 1802; d. Nov. 28, 1848.

His father, Franz Schwanthaler, came to Munich, Bavaria, in 1785, and was made court sculptor. Ludwig was educated at the Munich Academy. In 1826 he won a travelling stipend, and visited Italy, where he attracted the attention of Thorwaldsen. In 1834 he was appointed professor at the Academy in Munich. Among his most important works are the decoration of the Glyptothek, Munich; the pediment group on the Walhalla near Regensburg (Ratisbon) representing the Hermann Schlacht, the decoration of the Propylæa in Munich; the Mozart monument in Salzburg, Austria; the Goethe monument in Frankfort; the colossal statue of Bavaria in Munich, and other works.

Raczynski, *L'Art Moderne en Allemagne.*

SCIALBO. Same as Intonaco.

SCISSOR BEAM. The tie of the Scissor Beam Truss (which see under Truss).

SCKELL, FRIEDRICH LUDWIG; landscape gardener; b. Sept. 13, 1750; d. 1820.

Studied landscape gardening in Paris, and in 1773 went to England and worked under the influence of Brown and Chambers (see Chambers). Returning to Germany, he laid out many parks and gardens, and in 1804 was made *Hofgartenintendant* at Munich, Bavaria. He laid out the park at Nymphenburg and the English garden in Munich under the direction of Count Rumford (see Thomson, B.).

Seubert, *Künstler-lexikon.*

SCOINSON ARCH. An arch carrying a part only of the thickness of a wall, as behind a window frame; or one of slight reveal forming a flat niche or recessed panel.

SCONCE (I.). *A.* Any construction which ·gives shelter by screen or roof, as a shed or covered stall. (Compare Booth; Cabin; Cot; Hut.)

B. A seat in an open chimney place (Scotch).

SCONCE (II.). A candlestick or group of branches, each forming a candlestick, springing from an applique, so that the whole shall seem to project from the wall upon which the applique is hung.

SCONCHEON. The part of the side of an aperture from the back of the exterior reveal to the inside face of the wall, usually forming in the masonry a rebate or internal angle in which the wooden frame is set. (Compare Scoinson Arch.)

SCOPAS; sculptor and architect.

Scopas was born in the Island of Paros in the Ægean Sea. In 352 B.C. he assisted in the sculptural decoration of the mausoleum of Halicarnassos. He built and decorated also the temple of Athena Alea at Tegea, which replaced the old sanctuary destroyed in 395 B.C. Some of the sculpture of the pediments of this building was discovered in the excavations made in 1879. A passage in Pliny, which has been doubted, indicates that he was employed in the decoration of the columns of the Artemision at Ephesus. A famous statue by Scopas was a Bacchante in the great theatre at Athens. The temple of Apollo on the Palatine in Rome, contained an Apollo Citharœdos by Scopas, which is probably represented by a statue in the Vatican.

Urlichs, *Skopas, Leben und Werke;* Collignon, *Histoire de la Sculpture Grecque;* Furtwängler, *Meisterwerke* (translated as *Masterpieces of Greek Sculpture*).

SCORING. Same as Scratching.

SCOTCH CROWN. The peculiar termination of the tower of S. Giles's church at Edinburgh, consisting of eight pinnacles, from each of which a sloping bar carried on a half arch and resembling a flying buttress rises, the whole eight meeting in the middle and supporting a central pinnacle. The term is applied to other terminations of towers in which only four sloping bars occur; and this form is not peculiar to Scotland. It occurs in S. Dunstan's in East London. and elsewhere.

SCOTCHING. Same as Scutching.

SCOTIA. A hollow moulding; especially, such a moulding used in the base of a column in Greco-Roman architecture and its imitations (called also Trochilus). (See Attic Base, under Base.)

SCOTLAND, ARCHITECTURE OF. That of the modern kingdom, united with England in 1707. This may be considered as a provincial school or branch of English architecture. At times it has shown wide departures from the contemporary phases of the English type, both in spirit and detail; but these departures hardly constitute a distinct style. Differences as great separate the Gothic schools of the Ile-de-France and Brittany, or of North and South Germany. The long-continued political independence of Scotland operated less effectively than one would imagine; Scotland acknowledged the ecclesiastical primacy of Canterbury and York, and Scotch

PLATE XVI

SCOTLAND, ARCHITECTURE OF. PLATE I

The church of Jedburgh Abbey, seen from the southeast. The central tower is unroofed, as is also the nave. The low arches seen on the left are those of the south aisle, and traces of the cloister are also visible between the trees.

architecture has in general been more English than it has been anything else. But it has been English with a difference: more rugged and picturesque, less consistent, less elegant; and, owing to scantiness of resources as much as to any other cause, deficient in grandeur and richness. Scotland has always been less wealthy than England, and is, therefore, not only less rich in civic and scholastic buildings of importance, but less opulent and sumptuous in the extent and adornment of its religious and domestic edifices. Frequent invasions by the English, especially under Edward I., Edward II., and Richard II., resulting in a terrible de-

are a few round towers resembling those of Ireland, in one case — at Egilsey on Orkney — forming an integral part of the church edifice (Abernethy, 865 A.D.; Brechin, 1000; Egilsey cir. 1100). The square towers of Restennet priory and of S. Regulus ("S. Rules") at Saint Andrews mark the transition to the Normanized style of the twelfth century.

The reign of David I., who ascended the throne in 1124, was marked by an extraordinary activity in the founding and enlargement of monasteries; an activity which continued through a large part of the century, and was stimulated on the architectural side by Norman

SCOTLAND: ABBEY OF IONA, SOUTH AISLE OF CHOIR; DIVIDED INTO THREE COMPARTMENTS BY TWO FLYING BUTTRESSES OF PRIMITIVE TYPE.

struction both of castles and of monasteries with their churches, covered Scotland with ruins, many of which are now preserved for their picturesqueness and their historic associations.

Previous to the Norman conquest the larger churches were generally of wood, the convents mere assemblages of rude cells. While there are many ruins of stone churches of the seventh-eleventh centuries, they are too small and rough to merit the name of architectural works (S. Ronan's chapel; Teampull Beannachadh; Eilean Mor; S. Carmaig; chapels in the Orkneys). The monasticism of these centuries was purely Celtic, and long resisted all effort to assimilate it to Roman systems and ideas. More important as the chief monuments of this Celtic period

influences from the south. Parish churches were still insignificant, but the conventual churches were often of imposing size, with vaulted side aisles and massive square towers having either flat or "saddleback" roofs. Most of these churches are in ruins, but the finest of them all, S. Magnus's cathedral at Kirkwall on Orkney, is in perfect preservation. It is. however, a purely Norwegian work of cir. 1137, a fine example of the Northern Norman style, vaulted throughout. Dunfermline Abbey (1125, nave only extant), with its massive western towers; Kelso Abbey in Linlithgowshire, built at the end of the twelfth century, with a cruciform plan, a long choir, and a tower over the crossing; and Jedburgh, near Kelso, a complete design with vaulted aisles, transepts, wooden-roofed nave and choir, presbytery, and central tower, — are the most important purely Scotch churches of this period, severe and massive externally, with sparing ornament, but vigorous and consistent in design. As compared with English churches the Scotch examples are smaller and simpler; the choir, often longer than the nave, has usually no side aisles; the details are less rich, the composition more massive. Sometimes, however, the aisle vault ribs and the arch mouldings are richly carved, and wall ar-

cades of interlacing arches are not uncommon (Dalmeny church, Linlithgowshire; Leuchars, near Saint Andrews, etc.). In the Transition, which followed a little later than in England, many Norman elements were persistently retained, and round arches are not uncommon even in Early Pointed work (Coldingham priory — ruins partly embodied in modern parish church; Dryburgh Abbey, Berwickshire; and many others; the conventual buildings at Dryburgh are less ruinous than the church itself, which dates from 1230). To the Early Pointed period belong a number of fine churches, partly or wholly ruined. Of S. Andrew's cathedral, Fifeshire (1160–1275, ruined 1559) the west and

east ends and part of the south side are alone extant. Arbroath Abbey in Forfarshire (1176–1233) is in much the same condition. Both show a large admixture of Norman details. Holyrood Abbey church near Edinburgh, one of the most elegant and important examples of the style, built in the first half of the thirteenth century, and of which only the ruined nave has survived the vandalism of the sixteenth century, also displays Norman interlacing arcades in certain parts. Dunblane cathedral, Perthshire, was the first important church to be completely built in the Pointed style. Its one-aisled choir with its flanking lady chapel is still perfect and in use. It is not surpassed by any Gothic church in Scotland except Melrose Abbey and S. Mungo's cathedral at Glasgow, which is slightly later in date, with a central tower of the fifteenth century. This cathedral, commonly called Glasgow cathedral, is a complete Gothic design 330 feet long with three aisles in both nave and choir, but no transepts; and with a fine sacristy and an especially beautiful lower church (usually miscalled the crypt) below the choir (1233–1258). The ribbed vaulting of this lower church is remarkably fine, and equal to anything of the kind and period in Great Britain. The nave and choir of the cathedral have wooden ceilings; the aisles are vaulted. Elgin cathedral (Morayshire), an almost equally fine church with a beautiful octagonal chapter house, is now completely ruined, and little is left of Brechin cathedral but its Celtic tower, west front, nave arches, and fragments of the choir. Pluscarden priory is also a notable ruin of a fine church.

It is to the rebuilding of churches ruined in the Border Wars that we are chiefly indebted for examples of the Decorated or Middle Pointed style of the fourteenth and early fifteenth centuries. The most conspicuous and beautiful example of the style is the ruined abbey of Melrose. No trace remains of its monastic buildings, some of which were no doubt very ancient. The church, whose ruins are of exceptional beauty, was erected by order of Robert Bruce, after his death in 1329; ravaged by Richard II. in 1385, and finally ruined in 1544; the present ruins date chiefly from the reconstruction after 1385. It has three aisles, with a southern row of chapels, transepts, and a short choir. The traceries of the east window and south aisles and transepts, the rich buttress pinnacles, niches, and canopies, the elaborate vaulting of choir and nave (the latter replaced in 1618 by an ugly pointed barrel vault) and the elegant details of almost all its parts, give this church a place among the most beautiful in Great Britain. Its style is nearer to that of English late Decorated churches than is that of any other Scotch edifice of the period. Although its chief mason, Morrow, was born in Paris, he appears to have been

PLATE XVII

SCOTLAND, ARCHITECTURE OF. PLATE II

Kelso Abbey ; the upper figure gives the view from the northeast, the short northern arm of the transept ending in a wall with the complete gable on the right.   The other high wall is the southern wall of the tower seen from within, and the arches on the left are those of the south wall of the choir. The lower figure shows what remains of the west front of the short nave, the western wall of the tower rising above it, and the south transept on the right.

of Scotch blood, and there is little or nothing to suggest French design in the building. Very different in character is the contemporary church of S. Giles, Edinburgh (1387 ; enlarged in the fifteenth century), almost Doric in its severity of detail. Its massive central tower was in 1500 adorned with the famous "Scotch Crown" (which see). This very elegant feature is peculiar to Scotch architecture (King's College, Aberdeen ; S. Nicholas, Newcastle, probably by Scotch builders ; others formerly at Linlithgow and Haddington). The most complete example of the style is S. Michael's at Linlithgow, a late

Scotland. The fifteenth century seems to have brought to Scotland, not only a decline in taste, but a decline in craftsmanship as well. In the art of vaulting, this retrogression is especially notable, as shown by the reversion to plain round or pointed barrel vaulting, even for the middle aisle. So emphatic was the aversion to groins that the transept vaults were stopped against solid gable walls in the planes of the nave clearstory walls, in order to avoid the groined intersection with the nave vault. Most of the churches of this period are parish churches and relatively uninteresting. The cathedrals of

SCOTLAND: KELSO ABBEY; NAVE AND SOUTH TRANSEPT FROM N.E.

Decorated church perfectly preserved and in use ; it shows something of the same contrast of severe and almost rude masses with bits of highly ornate detail as S. Giles. The ruins of New or Sweetheart Abbey and of Lincluden College may also be mentioned.

With the close of the fourteenth century the Decorated style passed into the Perpendicular, but in the monuments of this later style there was, with one or two exceptions, none of that elaboration of fine detail which characterized the corresponding English style. The huge windows filled with Perpendicular tracery, the rich traceried panelling, and the elegant fan vaulting of England have no counterpart in

Paisley (mostly 1445–1459), Dunkeld (nave, 1406–1464 ; choir mostly modern), and Aberdeen (S. Machar, nave only extant, 1422–1440) were the largest churches of this period. The first two have the characteristic Scotch plan, with three-aisled nave, short transepts, and long choir without side aisles ; Paisley is the most elegant in details, S. Machar the most rugged and simple of the three. At Perth the church of S. John is a large and well-preserved church, but uninteresting in design. Far richer than any of these is the incomplete but perfectly preserved collegiate church of Roslyn near Edinburgh, built in 1446. The choir, which with the sacristy was the only portion erected, is 60 feet long, with side aisles and a double aisle across the east end. The whole is barrel vaulted, the aisle bays having transverse vaults sprung from straight-arched transverse lintels, an inartistic and very un-Gothic arrangement, only tolerable in a small edifice. The interior, though profusely carved, hardly merits the praise it commonly receives; the execution is somewhat coarse, and hardly supports the allegation often made that the builders were Spanish or French.

Of the civil and domestic architecture of the Celtic period and twelfth and thirteenth centuries there are no remains, and the history of Scotch military architecture begins only with the Norman period. Even the most important castles of this period, such as Dunstaffnage, Bothwell, Yester, Carlaverock, etc., were of the simplest character — mere heavily walled enclosures with angle turrets and a keep. It was not until the fourteenth century that notable advances were made in castle building. The majority of the Scotch castles were small but massive and compact strongholds — a keep or tower, or a simple L-shaped edifice. In the fourteenth century there took place a general enlargement of these into castles with courtyards, and many new castles were built (Balvaird, Roslyn, Ruthven, Edinburgh, Linlithgow, Dirleton, Tantallon, and Stirling). Of these Stirling is the finest, with its parliament hall, and Linlithgow, long the favourite royal residence, comes next in architectural interest; but they are hardly comparable with the magnificent contemporary castles of England and France. In the sixteenth century castle building took on a more artistic and domestic character, in which the idea of the fortress, no longer impregnable against artillery, gradually disappeared, a change which became complete in the seventeenth century. Until the time of Charles I., however, and even later, many mediæval features were retained; such were the round corner turrets corbelled out at the top to a square plan, stepped gables, circular stair towers in the angle of two wings, and a general severity of mass and detail. Fyvie castle, in Aberdeenshire, begun in 1400 but much altered in later centuries; Glamis castle (mostly 1578–1615), and Thirlstane castle (middle of seventeenth century) are interesting examples of this treatment. Meanwhile the fashions of the Renaissance were making their way in Scotland, coming in from England, and gradually replacing the corbelled parapets and stepped gables of the Scotch castles with the pilasters, pediments, round arches, and cornices of the Anglicized classic style, and, above all, introducing a new element of regularity and symmetry into the plans. But the formal classicism of Inigo Jones, and later of Christopher Wren, found little favour in Scotland, and even in the later castles there is a picturesqueness

wanting in the English examples. Drumlanrig castle in Dumfriesshire well illustrates the style. Its chief later monuments are Holyrood palace (begun 1528 by James IV., extended by James V., burned 1650, finally rebuilt by Charles II., 1671); Heriot's hospital, Edinburgh (1628–1659), a quadrangular structure with central court, very effective in the massing of its bays, pavilions, and chimneys, and adorned with corbelled parapets, angle turrets, Gothic details associated with Elizabethan "strap-work," and a very rococo portal; and the now demolished Glasgow College, a rambling pile in much the same style, but less successfully handled. These buildings are less interesting internally than externally, and generally inferior to the great English residences and colleges in grandeur and elegance of interior disposition and adornment.

There was but little church building done during the seventeenth and eighteenth centuries, and the ecclesiastical work of this period is almost wholly confined to minor structures, such as the richly carved gallery fronts of Pitsligo and Bowden churches (1630 and 1661), and elaborate canopied tombs in black, white, and red marble, e.g. the Montgomery monument at Largs (1636). The Renaissance in Scotland was as emphatically provincial as the mediæval styles had been; this is shown in the persistent retention of old-time and out-of-date details, and the mixture of incongruous elements long after the style had in England and elsewhere reached a harmonious and definite form. Moreover, the severity of Scotch taste or the poverty of the Scotch artistic imagination rendered impossible that sumptuousness of decorative detail which seems essential to the best results in Renaissance design. Until recent years very few buildings in Italian or classic style had been erected in Scotland; by far the best known is the college of Edinburgh University, by the brothers Adam (1789), a dignified but rather uninteresting pile.

Since the beginning of the nineteenth century Scotland has shared in the general development of British art, and the chief difference to be noted between the more recent architecture of the two countries is seen in the effort to retain the picturesque and semi-mediæval features of the Scotch castles of the seventeenth century in many of the modern Scotch buildings, e.g. Inverness castle, the municipal buildings of Aberdeen, and many large country seats. The classic revival is represented by the works of Sir Thomas Hamilton and W. H. Playfair; among its most notable productions are the High School (1825, Hamilton) and Royal Institution (Playfair) at Edinburgh, both remarkably successful and elegant designs; the Royal Exchange and Justiciary Courts at Glasgow; and the somewhat affected and singular, but interesting efforts of Alexander Thomson ("Greek Thomson") to

PLATE XVIII

SCOTLAND, ARCHITECTURE OF. PLATE III

The quadrangle of the "United Colleges" at Saint Andrews, that is, the two colleges of S. Salvador and S. Leonard. The buildings are modern and replace those which had become ruinous in the early part of the present century.

adapt Greeks details to modern Protestant church design. Most of the churches erected since then have been in the revived Gothic style, and in nowise different from contemporary English work; *e.g.* S. Mary's cathedral, chapter house, and library, at Edinburgh (Sir G. G. Scott), S. Andrew's cathedral, Inverness (Alexander Ross), S. Benedict's Monastery at Fort Augustus (P. P. Pugin), and many parish churches. Other examples of the Victorian Gothic are the Scott monument, Edinburgh (1844, by George Kemp), and the very ambitious and elaborate Glasgow University buildings by Sir G. G.

Architecture of Scotland. Of a more popular character are H. C. Butler's *Scotland's Ruined Abbeys* and A. H. Millar's *The Historical Castles and Mansions of Scotland.* The larger and more celebrated monuments are described in monographs and in the works of Billings (*Baronial and Ecclesiastical Antiquities of Scotland*), Britton, and others.

— A. D. F. HAMLIN.

SCOTT, SIR GEORGE GILBERT; architect; b. 1811; d. March 27, 1878.

In 1827 he was articled to James Edmeston, and in 1832 entered the office of Henry Roberts. In 1844 he won first prize in the competition

SCREEN, FIG. 1: LOW BRONZE RAILING, AIX-LA-CHAPELLE; PROBABLY 5TH CENTURY, AND FROM ITALY.

SCREEN, FIG. 2: SEE FIG. 1.

Scott (1870). This revived Gothic has been of late years, as in England, largely supplanted by free versions of the Renaissance styles, inclining sometimes toward the Italian and sometimes toward the French in general character. As early as 1861 the Edinburgh Post Office (Matheson) was erected in the Italian style. The most elaborate and successful among recent public buildings in Scotland is perhaps the Municipal Building of Glasgow (1880, Wm. Young) in a style based upon the Venetian Renaissance. In general it may be said that architecture as now practised in Scotland is in no essential different from that of England.

For the earliest Scotch architecture, rude monuments, and stone crosses, see Skene, *Celtic Scotland;* Anderson, *Scotland in Early Christian Times;* and Fergusson, *Rude Stone Monuments.* For the general history of Scotch architecture, Macgibbon and Ross, *The Ecclesiastical Architecture of Scotland* and *Castellated and Domestic*

for the church of S. Nicholas at Hamburg, Germany, to replace the building burned in 1842. This he built in the German Gothic style of the fourteenth century, with a tower 475 feet high. In 1847 he was appointed architect of Ely cathedral, and architect of Westminster Abbey in 1849, where he restored the chapter house, monuments, and northern portal. His *Gleanings from Westminster Abbey* was published in 1862. After competition he was appointed in 1858 architect of the building of the War and Foreign offices, London. His first designs were Gothic, but he was required by Lord Palmerston's government to substitute a design in the style of the Italian Renaissance, according to which the building was erected (begun 1861). He afterward completed this block of buildings by erecting the Home and Colonial Offices. Between 1863 and 1868 Scott designed and built the Albert Memorial in Hyde Park, London.   In 1866 he was one of the six competitors for the Royal Courts of Justice in London (see Street, Sir G. E.).   He won the gold medal of the Royal Institute of British Architects in

Fig. 4.

SCREEN, FIG. 4: SEE FIG. 3 OF WHICH THIS IS A
PARTIAL ENLARGEMENT.

1859, and was president of that body from 1873 to 1876.   He was appointed professor of architecture at the Royal Academy in 1868.   His lectures were published under the title *Mediæval Architecture* (2 vols. 8vo, 1879).

Sir Gilbert Scott, *Recollections;* Stephen-Lee, *Dictionary of National Biography.*

SCRATCHING.   The roughening of the first coat of plaster, when fresh, by scratching or scoring its surface with a point so that the next coat may adhere to it more firmly.   Also called scoring.

SCREED.   A narrow strip of plastering brought to a true surface and edge, or a strip or bar of wood, to guide the workmen in plastering the adjoining section of the wall surface.

SCREEN.   Any structure of any material having no essential function of support and serving merely to separate, protect, seclude, or conceal.   In church architecture, specifically, a decorated partition of wood, metal, or stone, close or open, serving to separate, actually or in sentiment, a chapel from the church, an aisle from the nave or choir, the chancel from the nave, etc.   In this sense, a screen replaces the Jubé in small churches.   In early houses of some importance, a partition by which the entrance lobby is separated from the great hall.   An open colonnade or arcade, if serving to enclose a courtyard, or the like, is sometimes called a screen.   (See Chancel Screen; Choir Screen; Sanctuary Screen.)

Pardon Screen.   A screen surrounding or placed before a confessional, to hide the penitent from public view during the act of confession.

SCREEN CHAMBER.   An apartment formed by a screen separating it from a larger area.

SCREEN WALL.   A screen of some solidity as differing from one which is pierced, especially in the intercolumniations of a colonnade.

SCREW.   A solid cylinder having a ridge wound around it in a spiral direction evenly;   though sometimes the piece has rather the look of a thread being cut into the solid cylinder.   In building this is used in the form of a Bolt (which see, sense *A*) and in the form of a Wood Screw (which see below).

Wood Screw.   (Often by abbreviation simply Screw, which is the term in use among carpenters.)   A screw used to replace a nail, usually intended to be driven by a screwdriver, for which purpose it has a slot in the head, which may be flat or rounded.   Gimlet screws are those wood screws which have a sharp pointed end so that they can be driven, at least into soft wood, without the preparatory boring of a hole.

SCREW JACK.   Same as Jack Screw.

SCRIBBLED ORNAMENT.   Decorative effect produced by lines, curves, and scrolls carelessly distributed over a surface.

SCRIBE (v.t.).   To mark with an incised

SCREEN OF OAK: NORTHFLEET CHURCH, KENT; c. 1300.

line, as by an awl; hence, to fit one piece to another of irregular or uneven form, as a plain piece against a moulded piece, or as in shaping the lower edge of a baseboard to fit the irregularities of the floor.

SCRIPTORIUM.   In mediæval Latin, a writing room; specifically, the room assigned in

SCREEN, FIG. 3: SEE FIGS. 1 AND 2, THIS BEING A DETAIL OF A THIRD AND VERY SIMILAR SCREEN.

SCREENS OF OAK: *A*, SHOTSWELL, OXFORDSHIRE; C. 1350. *B*, GEDDINGTON, NORTHAMPTONSHIRE; C. 1360.

SCREEN OF OAK: HANDBOROUGH CHURCH, OXFORDSHIRE; c. 1480.

a conventual establishment for the copying of manuscripts.

SCROLL. An ornament composed of curved lines like volutes, and sometimes of double flexure passing on from one volute to another.

Vitruvian Scroll. A scroll of great simplicity, without leafage or the like, but generally having the section of a flat band.

Wave Scroll. Same as Vitruvian Scroll. So called because of a suggestion of sea waves in regular succession.

SCULLERY. A room, generally annexed to a kitchen, where dishes are washed.

Plate Scullery. In Great Britain, a separate scullery for cleaning plate. It should connect directly with the butler's offices. — (Kerr.)

SCULPTURE. The art and the practice of carving in hard material, whether in relief or in intaglio. By extension, the producing of forms in soft material, as by modelling, but always with a view to artistic or semiartistic results, the copying of natural forms, or the embodying of design in form. The distinction between the mere incising of lines on a smooth surface and sculpture is not capable of being fixed exactly; the enlargement and unequal widening of the incised lines passes insensibly into sculpture in low relief, or in concavo-convex relief. In general,

however, that form of relief which has a decidedly rounded and varied surface approaching thereby somewhat more nearly to the look of natural form, together with all production of form in the round, as it is called (see Relief), is considered sculpture. The Egyptian and most other concavo-convex relief is of this character, the figures being as freely rounded as in ordinary bas-relief, although they do not project beyond the general surface of the material.

Relief sculpture of the kind above named is the most common form used by the Egyptians. It lends itself peculiarly to decoration in polychromy, and is capable of great excellence in the way of narrative and expression. By means of it Egyptian architecture was more immediately helped by its sculpture than was any architecture previous to the time of the later Romanesque or even that of the Gothic styles.

In the Assyrian and other buildings of Mesopotamia it seems that the sculpture can hardly have decorated the exteriors very much, nor even the interiors in the true sense of the term "to decorate," that is by increasing the general

SCREEN OF CUT STONE DIVIDING A CHAPEL: CATHEDRAL OF AIX-LA-CHAPELLE; 14TH CENTURY.

splendour of the apartments more than the presence of portable objects of beauty would decorate them. The chief specimens which have come down in fair preservation to modern times are sculptured slabs, the work being in very low relief upon a soft alabaster-like stone. In this the work is of extraordinary interest and of expressional merit. The well-known winged and human-headed bulls and similar creatures of religious significance are really relief sculpture, a huge block being worked on at least two of its sides in such a way that a view of it taking in the front and long side would show the semblance of a statue in the round.

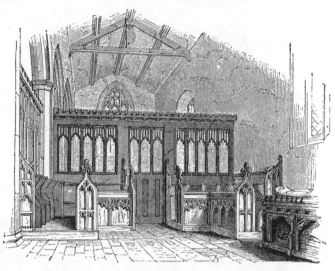

SCREEN SERVING AS CHOIR SCREEN: FYFIELD CHURCH, BERKSHIRE; c. 1480.

Persian sculpture of the early kingdom seems to have been much of the same general character. The artistic differences are very great, but the relation which the sculptures bear to the buildings is not unlike in kind. The bull-headed have only relief, and that of no strictly architectural character, and some free statues like those found in Cyprus. The critical and historical inferences hitherto drawn from it are not to be considered final. It is obvious that the only

SCULPTURE, FIG. 1: ASSYRIAN (SEE MESOPOTAMIA): ALABASTER SLAB FROM SENNACHERIB'S PALACE, MOUND OF KOUYUNJIK.

half capitals which mark the architecture of Persepolis are a nearer approach to sculpture in the round than anything we have of Assyrian or Babylonian work used in connection with buildings.

Of Hittite and other Phœnician sculpture we works which would remain are first the very few separate statues and busts which have been buried in the ground, and second, those reliefs which are so large and are worked upon such massive bases of native rock or of walling, that the centuries have spared them. Our ideas of

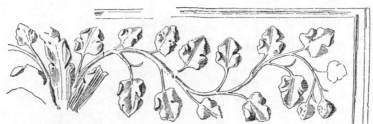

SCULPTURE, FIG. 2: ROMAN FRIEZE PROBABLY OF TIME OF AUGUSTUS; IN THE LATERAN MUSEUM, ROME.

SCULPTURE, FIG. 4: ITALIAN ROMANESQUE, 12TH CENTURY; CHURCH OF S. ANDREA, PISTOJA.

SCULPTURE, FIG. 13: FRENCH GOTHIC; BOURGES CATHEDRAL; WINDOW OVER WEST PORTAL.

the power of the western Asiatic nations to decorate buildings by means of elaborate sculpture are likely to be changed at any moment by the making of new discoveries, and even the Lycian tombs and other proto-Greek works point to a freer use of sculpture, at least in the adorn-

Very different was the feeling of the Romans under the Empire during that great period beginning, apparently, with the early days of Augustus, or even a little before it, and ceasing with the Great Plague and the political disturbances of the last Antonine emperor, — a period

SCULPTURE, FIG. 3: SYRIAN ROMANESQUE, SHOWING MUCH ORIENTAL INFLUENCE; LINTEL OVER DOORWAY, KHARBET-EL-BEIDA.

ment of external walls, than anything common in the great days of Grecian or of Greco-Roman art.

This is true of Greek sculpture as well; it is one of the earliest in which relief is worked freely upon the walls of buildings, and here with the culmination of Greek architecture, on the one hand, and of Greek sculpture of the human form on the other hand, the student finds an almost complete separation between that sculpture which is decorative in the usual sense, and that which has for its chief object the telling of a story or the expression of a religious or devotional purpose. The sculpture of Greek temples is divided sharply into the simplest and most formal sculpture of mouldings with conventionalized leaf-form and of flat surfaces of rigid anthemion designs in low relief on the one hand, and on the other hand, human subject worked to its highest pitch of artistic perfection. The consequence must have been that the sculpture in the pediment and even that in the metopes of a rich temple could hardly have seemed an essential part of the structure. Even the resulting use of polychromatic painting would seem to have failed of necessity in uniting the thought of the sculpture of incident and representation and the half-architectural, half-sculpturesque forms which we know as anthemions, egg and dart mouldings, ivy leaf pattern, meanders, and rosettes. A building without the sculpture of human figure would have been still a highly organized, and in a sense completed, temple or portico, and the sculpture would have been associated with the same and no greater feeling for its necessity than we should feel as to the putting up of a group in a modern city park.

of just two centuries. During this period the great memorial arches and other monumental buildings were adorned with relief sculpture of great significance, both as matter of record and in the decoration of the buildings. The most important instance of this is the Arch of Trajan, at Benevento. A comparison of this building with those arches which are devoid of sculpture seems to show how completely the general scheme of the building was connected in the designer's mind with the free use of elaborate sculpture. The extreme refinement of the Greeks as to all the parts of their architecture, their thought about the minutest details of curvature and projection, and of proportion carried to the smallest subdivisions, was not imitated by the Romans, who were content to get a fairly happy general result and then to glorify the whole with sculpture sometimes

SCULPTURE, FIGS. 5 AND 6: GERMAN ROMANESQUE; CHURCH AT BRAUWEILER ON THE RHINE.

elaborately painted in bright colours, sometimes much less fully adorned in that way. A memorial arch, also, is to be considered rather as the base for a great system of sculpture to be rested upon its top than as a gateway (see Memorial Arch); and although these sculptures have in every case disappeared, the representations given on Roman medals are sufficient to explain to us the Roman feeling toward them. Even in the decline of the Empire, and in the complete collapse of the once great power over sculpture possessed by the Roman artists, the Arch of Constantine is adorned with fragments taken from the previous building dedicated to Trajan, and they are combined in a new memorial building in a not unsuccessful way.

Recent discovery and the comparison of fragments leave no doubt of the existence of a

SCULPTURE, FIG. 7: GERMAN ROMANESQUE; 12TH CENTURY; PORTRAIT EFFIGY; ABBEY OF ARNSTEIN ON THE RHINE.

highly differentiated non-Greek school of sculpture, as partly shown by Wickhoff (op. cit.). Fig. 2 illustrates the kind of leafage characteristic of this school, which flourished at least from 25 B.C. until the decline of the Empire in the second century. In sculpture of human subject, the extraordinary draped figures in the

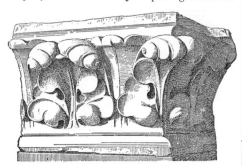

SCULPTURE, FIG. 8: FRENCH GOTHIC CORNICE; 13TH CENTURY.

friezes in the Lateran Museum are the best examples. In many of the best qualities of sculpture this school is unsurpassed. One modification of the sculpture of the imperial school is that which is found so abundant among the stone-built buildings of Syria. There is a Greek and also an Oriental influence to be found in this, shown especially in Fig. 3, but there is also a strongly Roman influence shown

by some of the capitals figured under Syria, Architecture of.

The architecture of the far East has always depended very largely upon sculptured form, which often invades what the European world

SCULPTURE, FIG. 9: FRENCH GOTHIC CORNICE; 13TH CENTURY.

has thought the architectural province proper; and supporting members such as pillars, as well as those less essential to the building's life, are found carved into extremely spirited and often, to our eyes, grotesque forms of conventionalized humanity and of imagined beast and bird. The rock-cut buildings of India, and the stone-built Buddhist and Jaina structures of the same peninsula, are distinguished by very extraordinary abundance of sculpture, an abundance which, to the unaccustomed eye, seems disagree-

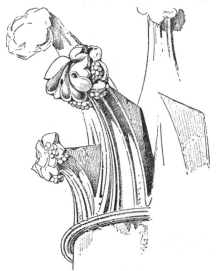

SCULPTURE, FIG. 10: FRENCH GOTHIC; BURGUNDIAN SCHOOL; CROCKETS OF A CAPITAL.

able as affording no relief — no reserved spaces to separate part from part of the highly wrought representative design. This feeling never fails to disappear to a great extent as custom diminishes the strangeness of the dispositions. It is caused, so far as India is concerned, largely by the absence of any necessity of sheltering sculpture from the weather. In a much less degree the same shock of strangeness is produced when masonry buildings not highly decorated are found in the West Indies, standing safely

without copings and similar devices against the ruinous effect of moisture which will freeze after percolating the joints and pores of the structure. The Indian stonemason, free from any such anxiety, and working in a gentle climate amid the most generous and ample forms of plant and animal, has developed a school of sculpture from which the Western world can learn a great deal whenever it seeks new paths.

Of China we know little; that country must have possessed an architecture as abundant, as

its few remaining or traditionally known monuments are important and curious (see China, Architecture of). In Japan, on the other hand, the ancient art has been wonderfully preserved, and this has for us the curious lesson that

sculpture, in what we consider perishable materials, is practically everlasting if it is cared for. The temples and palaces of Japan are built of wood, and the sculpture is of panels carved in relief or often pierced, the carving showing on both sides relieved partly against flat background and partly against empty space. The climate is not unlike that of the Eastern United States, varying between the climatic conditions of Boston and Charleston. The carved panels are therefore set where rainwater

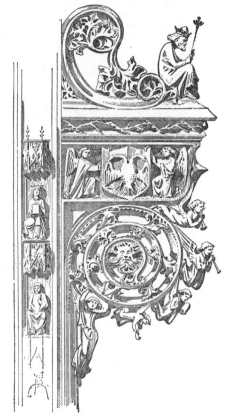

will not reach them easily, and they are, furthermore, protected by different appliances which the extraordinary skill and patient care of the Japanese workmen have taught them to use; but the sculptures are from one thousand to some six hundred years old, and apparently as well preserved in all essential particulars as could be wished. Indeed, the more elaborately protected pieces have suffered the most, as we now see them, because of the gradual peeling off of the carefully laid coats of gesso or its equivalent. Where lacquer of the true sort has been used this ruin has, perhaps, not taken place; but highly finished pieces of lacquer-work are generally kept for interiors. More recent times in Japan have developed a system of carved and pierced panelling for the decoration of buildings other than temples. There is also a certain tendency toward the use of the admirable pottery of Japan, both glazed and unglazed, in the production of friezes and panels of this sort, and specimens of these exist even in our museums, their effectiveness greatly diminished by the indoor light and by the disappearance of their proper surroundings.

In Europe a long epoch, from the beginning of the third to the close of the tenth century — eight hundred years — is, indeed, not unmarked by the production of important works of decorative art, but this decoration seldom

landscape painting in its later development was in the nineteenth, is shown first in Italy ; and such sculptures as shown in Fig. 4, in their mingling of clumsy and unreal modelling with well-developed effect, are partly expressive of a vast and widespread tendency. At a time hardly later, the German stonecutters were producing capitals like those shown in Figs. 5 and 6, and the same spirit shows itself throughout the world of Western Europe, the churches, porches, and cloisters of which were often very completely wrought into carvings of expressional value. In all of this there is no classical feeling at all. The treatment of the human figure at this time was not more essentially nonclassical than the treatment of animal and leaf form (see Fig. 7), but it is more easy to recognize ; and the tendency toward portraiture, toward record of the nature of portraiture, though not including precise likenesses, and the abundant supply of legendary detail in the form of bas-relief, taking its most perfect development in the middle of the thirteenth century, was carried on without pause or check and with constantly developing skill, if with less artistic variety, for two hundred and fifty years.

The leaf sculpture of the Gothic

SCULPTURE, FIG. 15: LATE ITALIAN GOTHIC ; CLOSE OF THE 14TH CENTURY ; VITERBO, ITALY.

takes the form of sculpture in any true sense, and still more seldom takes the form of architectural sculpture following any natural development. A few buildings have sculptures even of considerable size, in which a certain Roman Imperial influence, or even an influence from the Byzantine empire (at the height of its artistic power during the years previous to the iconoclastic fury at the beginning of the eighth century) survives, as in the church at Cividale (see Italy, Architecture of, Part IV.). As European society refines and strengthens itself, and what are called the Dark Ages become less dark, sculpture is the last of the arts to show any advance. When, however, it does begin to have life, this is not the old life — the sculpture is not classical at all. The feeling which was as modern a thing in the eleventh century as

epoch is famous because nothing like it was ever before achieved by man, and because it offends no one to see the forms of vegetation treated in a conventional manner (see Figs. 8 to 13) ; but the use of animal form, and even of the human form, is equally seen and demonstrably as excellent for its purpose as the use of leaves and flowers. In every case, the sculptors of the day were the greatest masters of artistic abstraction that we know. Not that the individual merit of this or that piece of work can exceed that of Egyptian or even of some Assyrian pieces, but that the amount produced was so incredibly great, and that this vast amount of delicate art was produced at a time when Europe was thinly populated, ill governed, and poor beyond anything that we can now imagine.

The use of Gothic sculpture by the Italians

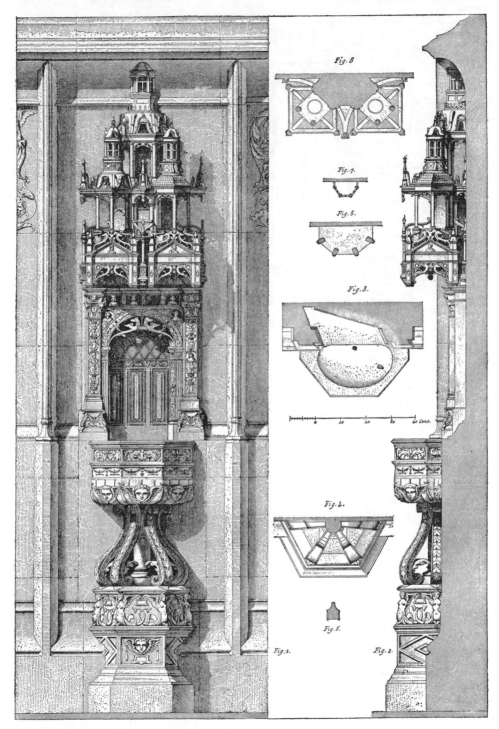

SCULPTURE, FIG. 17: PISCINA AND NICHE; EARLY 16TH CENTURY; CHURCH OF LA FERTÉ BERNARD

Fig. 1. Front elevation.   Fig. 2. Section through wall and side elevation of piscina and canopy.   Fig. 3. Plan above piscina.
Fig. 4. Plan below piscina showing consoles of base.   Figs. 5, 6, 7. Small details.   Fig. 8. Plan above large niche showing the
open tabernacles set diagonally.

SCULPTURE, FIG. 16: FRENCH RENAISSANCE; EARLIEST PERIOD; TOMB OF PHILIPPE DE COMINES; ABOUT 1510.

was never so thoroughly combined with architectural design as in the North, but in itself, this sculpture, as it remains to us, is of surprising beauty. The presence of many and rich sculptured details is that which makes attractive and even irresistibly charming many a building whose constructional merit is slight, and whose value as a piece of proportion, of composition, from whatever point of view it is considered, is but slight. Figure 15 gives a single instance of the way in which figure sculpture is combined with leafage and both with the architecture of an elaborate fifteenth century portal, and the presence of the painting in the tympanum of the doorway exemplifies further the combination of these representative arts with the constructional art of building in the truly characteristic Italian way.

The sculpture of the Renaissance in Italy assumed at once entirely new form. The delicate scrollwork which invests the faces of pilasters, the belt courses, and the encrusted panels, is the study of Roman painted originals; and it is evident that the Renaissance builders, when they began to build somewhat in the Roman taste, had ready at hand a school of sculpture which had taken form previously (see Renaissance). The art of the sculptor took its new form before the "revival of art" had its say in architecture. It was long indeed before any serious attempt was made to reproduce Roman forms with any completeness, and at no time was the secret of Roman decorative sculpture learned or even guessed, as far as their works can show it, by the neoclassic architects. In the North the Renaissance, beginning nearly a century later than in Italy, retains traces of the mediæval feeling of the builders in sculpture as well as in plan and the arrangement of interiors. Figure 16 shows a piece of work which is certainly not Gothic, and yet which would never have existed in its actual form but for the influence of the Gothic sculpture. This tendency is shown curiously in Fig. 17, where the delicate architectural carving of a niche and its very complex series of canopies is so combined with actual representative sculpture that no one can say where the architectural limit is overpassed. Here the forms are entirely neoclassic and the details of the sculpture are so equally, but the dash and abundant freedom of the whole is far enough from anything which classical influence would have inspired in the Northern mind. It is not until the century is well rounded, since the beginning of the classical revival in Italy, that anything in the North becomes classical in its disposition. Figure 18 gives one of the earliest instances of such classical feeling, for in this, though the action of the figures, especially of the S. Martin in the niche, is partly mediæval, the disposition of the architectural parts and even the grouping of the

SCULPTURE, Fig. 18: FLEMISH, 1533; RETABLE IN CHURCH OF NOTRE DAME, HAL, BELGIUM.

figures in the rondels show Southern feeling at least — a strong influence from Italy which is, at one remove only, a Greco-Roman influence.

The tendency away from truly decorative processes, which is characteristic of European peoples since 1780 or thereabout, shows itself in architecture at a somewhat earlier day. Even the buildings of the earlier years of the eighteenth century show a tendency to very slight and thin architectural sculpture properly so called ; decorative enough in the somewhat fantastic way of the Rococo style, but limited to few parts, to low relief, and to thin and bare designs. This was helped out by the use of almost free standing statues modelled with extraordinary skill for their places on the front or interiors of buildings, but these figures have no minor sculpture leading up to them, they are set upon the buildings as if with the builders of Greek temples the eighteenth century artists had decided that a building had no use for sculpture except to hold it up in a favourable point of view. Since the return of prosperity and tranquillity after the Napoleonic wars there has been no real progress in the way of architectural sculpture. The really surprising work of the French sculptors has been almost wholly confined to the putting up of statues on pedestals, on brackets, or in niches. And when a building is undertaken in a style such that surface decoration in scrollwork and patterns can hardly be omitted, the copying from ancient work of the same style is hardly disguised and is never to be ignored. The English more than other nations have produced sculpture that had newly imagined forms combined closely with the building in its structure ; but as there is but a comparatively feeble school of representative and expressional sculpture in England, this excellent work of their architectural sculptors has not obtained that influence over other nations that might well be desired. If the French would for a while build frankly in the style of their own Renaissance, accepting the necessity of covering large parts of their buildings with delicately wrought sculpture, great things might ensue ; but the difficulty caused by the very high price of trained manual labour in the twentieth century seems likely to make that impossible. Something, however, may result from the freer use of terra cotta.
— R. S.

Collignon, *Histoire de la Sculpture Grecque*, 2 vols.. Paris. 1892 ; Furtwängler, *Masterpieces of Greek Sculpture*, New York, 1895 ; Gardner, *Sculptured Tombs of Hellas*, 1896 ; Gonse, *La Sculpture Française depuis le XIV. Siècle*, Paris, 1895 ; H. S. Jones, *Select Passages from Ancient Writers, illustrative of the History of Greek Sculpture*, 1895 ; Mitchell, *A History of Ancient Sculpture ;* Overbeck. *Geschichte der griechischen Plastik*, Leipzig, 1881 ; W. C. Perry, *Greek and Roman Sculpture*, 1882 ; Wickhoff, *Roman Art*, 1900.

SCULPTURE GALLERY. A room especially provided for the exhibition of sculpture (see Gallery, *C*). It is generally found that sculpture is best seen by a well-diffused light, as even that modelled under the "studio light" of the artist's workroom is handled as if with a view to being put out of doors, — this being traditionally and properly so. Diffused light, however, is hard to get by means of a skylight, and even the light of a lantern or of a clearstory, though partaking of the nature of window light, comes generally from a point too high above the piece and falls upon it in too strongly marked a beam to show sculpture to the best advantage. This applies especially to sculpture in the round ; relief sculpture may be fairly well seen in a picture gallery of the usual sort unless the relief is very high.

The old halls of the central museum at Athens, plain, bare rooms with windows on one side and high up, afford the best possible light for the pieces set near the wall opposite the windows. Similar dispositions are used in the Naples museum. In some of the rooms of the Munich Glyptothek (which see) the same thing is done for both sides and with fair success, but this building is so elaborately wrought out with a view to its architectural effect that the most was not made of its capacity as a sculpture gallery. The ideal arrangement seems to be to build a large and high room with windows high in the wall on the two opposite sides, and to shelter the pieces backed against each wall from such rays of light as might filter upon them directly from above — a thing which can be done by simple architectural devices. — R. S.

SCUNCHEON. Same as Sconcheon.

SCUTCHEON. Same as Escutcheon.

SCUTCHEON: PIERCED AND WROUGHT IRON; c. 1450; BEAUCHAMP CHAPEL, WARWICK.

SCUTCHING. A method of finely dressing stone with a hammer, the head of which is composed of a bundle of steel points. Also scotching. (See Dress, the verb ; Stone Cutting ; Stone Dressing.)

SEABROOKE, THOMAS ; abbot.
Elected Feb. 16, 1450, abbot of the cathedral

of Gloucester, England, he began the beautiful tower of that church which was finished after his death by Robert Tully. Seabrooke repaved the choir of his cathedral.

Britton, *Cathedral Antiquities*.

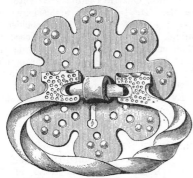

SCUTCHEON OF SHEET IRON WITH WROUGHT IRON DROP HANDLE; c. 1480; RYARSH CHURCH, KENT.

SEALING. *A.* Fixing, as a piece of wood or iron in a wall, with cement, plaster, or other building material, or with melted lead or sulphur; for staples, hinges, etc.

B. Closing the chinks, as of a log house, with plaster or clay.

SEAR. Same as Saw Curf. (See Kerf.)

SEASONING TIMBER. The process of drying or hardening timber by removing its natural sap by exposure to the sun and air, or by placing it in a kiln. Kiln-dried wood is the only wood fit for interior finish.

SEAT. *A.* A place of abode, a residence. Rarely used in modern times except in combination (see the sub-titles); though such phrases as "seat of the Marquis of Blank" are common in England.

B. Any structure affording a place for a person to sit. Especially, in architectural usage, such a structure when much larger than a chair or stool, so as to accommodate two or more persons; and commonly fixed.

C. A bed, surface, or piece of material arranged to support any member of a structure; as the bearing of a beam, the foot of a column, or the like.

Country Seat. In Great Britain, a rural residence of some importance. The use of the term generally implies a complete establishment with offices, stables, kennels, and an enclosed park in addition to the family house proper. In the United States the term is more loosely used of any country house or villa of some pretensions. (See Château; Villa.)

Hunting Seat. (See under H.)

SEATING. *A.* Seats, in sense of Seat, *B*, taken collectively; especially, a quantity of seats more or less carefully arranged, as for an audience. (See Seating Capacity.)

B. Same as Seat, *C*; especially the flat bed of that part of a sill which is cut with a lug so as to leave a horizontal space at each end to receive the jamb stone or brick jamb.

C. The process of securing a proper seat or bearing; as for the foot of an iron column by planing off the bearing surface so that every point may do its equal share of work in sustaining the superincumbent load. An iron plate or shoe arranged to provide against lateral movement, and to enlarge the bearing area, is generally interposed between the foot of the column and the foundation piece on which it rests.

SEATING CAPACITY. The fitness of a building or a room to accommodate an audience properly placed on benches or chairs, or in boxes, stalls, or the like, perhaps also in different divisions, according to the classes of the audience. In ordinary calculations, to determine the seating capacity of a room, it is customary to consider a width from elbow to elbow of each person's seat and the distance from back to back of the chairs or benches; thus, 2 feet 6 inches by 3 feet is liberal, and a more common arrangement would allow 2 feet 2 inches of width with 2 feet 9 inches from back to back of seats. If, now, to this space of 6 square feet for each person be added the necessary lobbies and the like, it may be safe to allow $7\frac{1}{2}$ square feet for each person to be accommodated on the floor. This, at least, is the way such calculations are made.

When private boxes are to be arranged in a theatre the question of seating capacity disappears, as each box is treated as a private room, with or without a lobby, and with weight given to other considerations.

SEA WALL. A retaining wall set where the land has to be protected against the waves of the sea.

SEBASTIANO DI GIACOMO; of Lugano; architect.

In 1504 Sebastiano undertook the completion of the church of S. Giovanni Grisostomo. In 1505 he contracted to build the choir of the church of S. Antonio di Castello, and in 1507, in association with Leopardi (see Leopardi), presented a model for the Scuola della Misericordia, all in Venice.

Paoletti, *Rinascimento*, Vol. II.

SEBENICO, GIORGIO DA. (See Orsini, Giorgio.)

SECOS. Same as Sekos.

SECTION. *A.* The surface or portion obtained by a cut made through a structure or any part of one, in such a manner as to reveal its structure and interior detail when the part intervening between the cut and the eye of the observer is removed.

B. The delineation of a section as above defined. In general scale drawings, sections usually represent cuts made through a structure on vertical planes, in contradistinction to cuts made on horizontal planes, which are Plans.

SEDILIA. A low-backed seat or bench, within the sanctuary, to the south of the altar, for the use of the officiating clergyman at the Eucharistic celebration ; wide enough not only for the celebrant to be seated, but also for the deacon and subdeacon. The back is made low in order to allow the vestments to hang over,

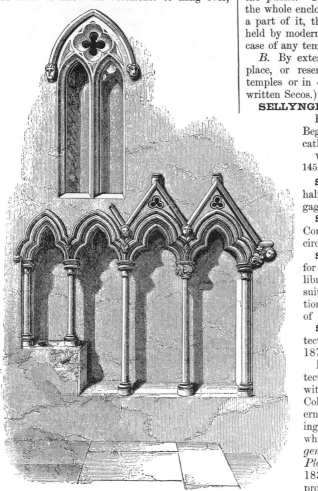

SEDILIA WITH PISCINA; c. 1200; RUSHDEN CHURCH, NORTHAMPTONSHIRE.

so that the clergymen will not injure them by sitting upon them. — C. C.

SEFFRID ; bishop.

Seffrid, second of that name, was bishop of Chichester, England, from 1180 to 1204. In 1186 the church was greatly injured by fire. The repairs, which extended through eleven years, were so considerable that the church was rededicated in 1199.

Winkle, *Cathedral Churches of England and Wales.*

SEGGIO. In Italian a chair; a seat in sense *B*.

SEICENTO. Belonging to those years numbered from 1600 to 1699 ; that is, in general, of the seventeenth century. (Compare Cinque Cento ; Quattro Cento ; Tre Cento.)

SEKOS. *A.* In Greek archæology, the sanctuary ; a place more or less forbidden to the public. The term is sometimes used for the whole enclosure of the naos, sometimes for a part of it, this depending upon the opinion held by modern scholars as to the usage in the case of any temple or sacred enclosure.

B. By extension, a sanctuary, shrine, holy place, or reserved chamber, as in Egyptian temples or in early Christian churches. (Also written Secos.)

SELLYNGE, WILLIAM ; prior.

Prior of Canterbury, England. Began the central tower of the cathedral of that city in 1472.

Wharton, *Anglia Sacra*, Vol. I., p. 145.

SEMICOLUMN. A column half engaged in a wall. (See Engaged Column.)

SEMIDOME. A half dome or Conch, such as occurs over a semicircular apse.

SEMINAR ROOM. A room for study ; especially, in a college library, a room provided for the pursuit of a particular line of investigation by students, under the direction of a professor.

SEMPER, GOTTFRIED ; architect ; b. Nov. 29, 1803 ; d. May 15, 1879.

He went to Paris to study architecture, and was later associated with Gärtner in Munich and Gau in Cologne. In 1830 he visited southern Italy, Sicily, and Greece, studying the use of colour in architecture, which he published in *Bemerkungen über bemalte Architektur und Plastik bei den Alten* (Altona, 1834). In 1834 he was appointed professor of architecture in the academy at Dresden. He built the Synagogue in Dresden (1838–1840), and the Hoftheater (1838–1841). Other buildings in Dresden by Semper are the Gothic fountain in the Post platz (1843–1844), and the Villa Rosa (1839). In 1847 he began the new museum at Dresden. Semper left Dresden during the political disturbances of 1848–1849 and settled in London, where he supported himself as a designer for metal work and decoration, and wrote some of his smaller essays on art and architecture. In 1855 he was appointed director of the architectural section of the *Polytechnische Schule* in Zurich, Switzerland. In Zurich he built the Polytechnicum (1858), the observatory (1861), the city hospital, and other buildings. He built also the Rathhaus in Winterthur. During this period he wrote his important work, *Der Stil* (2d ed. Munich, 1878–1879, 2 vols., 8vo). In 1871 Semper was made architect of the new Museums and the Hofburgtheater in Vienna. He made the plans for these buildings, which were, however, executed by Baron von Hasenauer (see Hasenauer), who changed them considerably. The exterior of the two museums is probably much as Semper designed them.

Sommer, *Gottfried Semper* in *Zeitschrift für Bauwesen*, Vol. 36, pp. 305–402; *Die Söhne Sempers; Die K. K. Hofmuseen in Wien*; Farrow, *The Recent Development of Vienna;* Harvey, *Semper's Theory of Evolution in Architecture.*

SENATE CHAMBER. A hall for the accommodation of a legislative body; specifically, in the United States, a hall for the sittings of the higher branch of a legislature. (See Legislature, House of.)

SENATE HOUSE. A building in which a legislature holds its sessions. (See Senate Chamber; also, for the Roman Senate, Curia and following titles.)

SENAULT, GUILLAUME; architect.

City architect (*maître d'œuvre*) of the city of Rouen, France. March 12, 1500, he took part in the deliberations concerning the construction of the Pont Notre Dame in Paris. He appears for the first time in the records of the château of Gaillon, near Rouen, in 1502, and worked on that building until December, 1507. The part of the château called the "Grant Maison" which he built is still in existence without its decoration. In 1506 he was consulted concerning the construction of the *Tour de Beurre* at the cathedral of Rouen.

Deville, *Comptes de Gaillon; Revue des Architectes de la Cathédrale de Rouen.*

SENS, WILLIAM OF. (See William of Sens.)

SEPARATOR. In iron framing, a small casting placed between two beams which are connected by bolts passing through the casting to maintain them at a fixed distance apart. — W. R. H.

SEPTA. (Latin, *Septum;* an enclosure or bounding wall.) A large enclosed and covered area or porticus, serving for a bazaar or exchange; especially, the Septa Julia near the Campus Martius, which was a magnificent

building decorated with many statues and divided into seven aisles by rows of columns, with rostra for public orations, booths for shops, etc. Its remains lie under the Palazzo di Venezia, and thence northward for 1100 feet. (Also Sæpta.)

SEPTIZONIUM. A building in Rome built by Septimius Severus, and known to form that part of the imperial palace on the Palatine Hill which rose above the Forum at its northwestern extremity. The word "septizonium" indicates a building with seven bands, but there is no evidence that there were really seven orders of columns, one above another, as is often assumed. The earliest modern records of the

SEDILIA: C. 1250; UFFINGTON CHURCH, BERKSHIRE.

building are drawings by sixteenth century artists, and these show only three superimposed orders. The building was wholly destroyed in 1588–1589. — (Lanciani.)

SEPTUM. (See Septa.)

SEPULCHRAL. Having to do with a tomb or other burial place, or with a cenotaph.

SEPULCHRAL ARCHITECTURE. That whose purpose is to give magnificence or beauty to tombs upon which large sums are to be expended, and to give fitness and good taste to the smallest tombs, and, by extension, to headstones or slabs. Some architectural styles have been especially rich in splendid tombs, but according as these are independent structures standing in the open and visible from all sides, or as they are placed within large buildings such as churches, do they assume, in the one case, an effect of ponderous solidity, of which much the most striking example is given by the pyramids of Egypt, and, in the other case, do they appear rather as decorative appendages most commonly attached to the inner face of the wall, and more rarely standing free upon the pavement. The largest and most sumptuous sepulchral monuments are rarely spoken of as tombs. Thus, neither the pyramids, nor the Taj Mahal, nor the wonderful buildings erected in memory of the Mohammedan rulers in northern India (see India, Architecture of, and Moslem Architecture), nor the Mausoleum at Halicarnassus are generally called tombs, and the memorial church built essentially for the purpose of covering a monument or several monuments, such as the church of Brou at Bourg-en-Bresse in southeastern France, could not properly be considered a tomb. All these buildings, however, come under the head of sepulchral architecture, and it will be noted by a comparison of their designs with the other buildings of their times, that no peculiar manner of building or of decorative treatment, nor even of sculpture and inlaid detail, has ever been appropriated to sepulchral as distinguished from ecclesiastical or civic architecture. In fact, sepulchral architecture on a large scale, and treated with great splendour, can only differ from other buildings of the same epoch in the comparative freedom of its plan and arrangement. As its chief object is splendour, and as it rarely needs to be appropriated to practical uses in any way, there is, on the one hand, a great freedom allowed the designer, which, if he is very able, and is of an epoch of growth and of intelligence, may result in a building of great magnificence. On the other hand, there is no suggestion in the plan itself, the result of which may well be, especially in times not of the most prosperous and vigourous artistic life, that the designer will be deprived of that suggestion which the necessary plan and structure of the building afford, and will produce a meaningless work. It is from this reason that modern large tombs and other memorial buildings are seldom of much artistic interest. — R. S.

SEPULCHRE. *A.* A tomb; a cave or structure for purposes of interment.

B. A receptacle for relics, especially, in a Christian altar.

C. Same as Easter Sepulchre, below.

Easter Sepulchre. A shallow arched recess or niche in the north side of the chancel, for the reception of the sacred elements between their consecration on Maundy Thursday and the Easter High Mass.

Holy Sepulchre. The sepulchre in which the body of Christ lay between his burial and resurrection. Its supposed site is marked by a church at Jerusalem.

SEPULCHRE LIGHT. A special lamp suspended in the Holy Sepulchre, and in all churches built to recall that sacred place.

SERAGLIO. *A.* An enclosed or protected place; hence, a Harem.

B. A palace; The Seraglio, used as a

proper name, the great palace at Constantinople.

Several different etymologies are given, and this term, as well as Serai and Serail, is used indifferently in many senses. Sir Richard Burton, deriving the word from the Portuguese *cerrar*, writes it Serraglio.

SERAI; SERAIL. Same as Seraglio in both senses. In sense *A* it has been applied to a Caravanserai or Khan.

SERDAB. A small chamber connected with an ancient Egyptian tomb. (See Mastaba.)

SERLIO, SEBASTIANO; architect and writer on architecture; b. Sept. 6, 1475 (at Bologna, Italy); d. before 1555 (at Fontainebleau, France).

The date of Serlio's birth is established by the records of the church of Tommaso della Braina in Bologna. About 1515 he went to Rome and was intimately associated with Baldassare Peruzzi (see Peruzzi), who, at his death in 1536, bequeathed to him his notes and drawings, which were afterward used by Serlio in the composition of his books. He seems to have gone to Venice about 1532. He measured the ancient monuments of Verona, and was the first to draw the ruins at Pola in Istria. In 1541 he was established in France by Francis I. as consulting architect at Fontainebleau. Neither in Italy nor in France is there any building of importance which can with certainty be ascribed to him. — (Müntz, *Renaissance*, Vol. III., p. 298.)

Serlio commenced the publication of his works with the fourth book, entitled, *Regole generali di Architettura di Sebastiano Serlio Bolognese, sobra le cinque maniere degli edifici . . . Venezia, 1537.* The third book appeared next with the title, *Il terzo libro di Sebastiano Bolognese nel quale si figurano e si descrivono le antichità di Roma . . . Venezia, 1540.* The first book followed : *Le premier livre d'Architecture de Sébastien Serlio Bolognois, mis en langue française par Jéhan Martin . . . 1545, Paris.* The second book was published with the first, *Le Second livre de Perspective de Sébastien Serlio Bolognois, mis en langue française par Jéhan Martin.* The fifth book was published next : *Quinto libro di Architettura di Sebastiano Serlio nel quale si tratta di diverse forme di Tempj . . . à Paris, 1547.* The sixth book was published at Lyons : *Extraordinario libro di Architettura di Sebastiano Serlio . . . trenta porte di opera Rustica mista con diversi ordini . . . in Lione, 1551.* The seventh book was bought by Strada the Antiquary, and was published after Serlio's death : *Il settimo libro d'Architettura di Sebastiano Serlio Bolognese, nel quale si tratta di molti accidenti, etc., . . . Francofurti ad Moenum, 1575.* An eighth book, on military architecture, was also bought by Strada with Serlio's collection of drawings, but appears not to have been published. The first complete editions of his works was printed at Venice in 1584. (See Scamozzi, Giovanni Domenico.)

Charvet, *Sébastien Serlio* ; Léon Palustre, *La Renaissance en France* ; Müntz, *Renaissance* ; Amorini, *Elogio di Sebastiano Serlio* ; Promis, *Ingegneri e Scrittore militari Bolognesi* ; Redtenbacher, *Architektur der Italienischen Renaissance* ; De Laborde, *Comptes des Bâtiments du Roy.*

SERPENTINE. An altered rock consisting essentially of a hydrous silicate of magnesia. Used to some extent for building purposes and the finer grades as marbles. (See Verdantique Marble, under Marble.) — G. P. M.

SERVANDONI, JEAN NICOLAS ; architect and painter ; b. May 22, 1695 (at Florence); d. Jan. 19, 1766 (at Paris).

Servandoni studied painting under Penini and architecture under Giovanni Rossi, and later was established in Paris as director of decorations at the opera. In 1732 he won the first prize in the competition for the construction of the façade of the church of S. Sulpice in Paris. (See MacLaurin and Chalgrin.) At S. Sulpice also he built the organ loft and decorated the chapel of the Virgin. In 1742 he built the great altar of the cathedral of Sens (Yonne, France), and in 1745 that of the cathedral of Reims, and about the same time that of the church of the Chartreux at Lyons. In 1752 he took part in the competition for the creation of the Place Louis XV., now Place de la Concorde, in Paris (see Gabriel, J. A.). In 1755 Servandoni was made court architect of King Augustus at Dresden, Saxony. He built the great staircase of the new palace at Madrid, Spain, and was employed at Brussels. Servandoni was especially successful in organizing fêtes, processions, and the like.

Chennevières, *Servandoni* in *Revue des Arts décoratifs ;* Marlette, *Abecedario ;* Lance, *Dictionnaire.*

SERVANTS' HALL A room where the servants of an establishment take their meals and may meet socially.

SERVICE PIPE. The pipe by means of which water, gas, steam, or other fluid is carried from a street main into a building. (See Water Supply.) — W. P. G.

SERVICE ROOM. A room used for the service of the table, usually in immediate connection with a dining room, as in a large house. Called also sideboard room. It should be easy of access from the dining room and from the kitchen, and is commonly fitted up with closets or dressers for crockery, glass, table linen, etc., and with tables for carving, and also for the adorning and arranging of dishes. In the United States, the room used in this way is generally called Butler's Pantry.

SERVING ROOM. Same as Service Room.

SET (v. t.). To set in position, as stones in a wall.

SET (v. i.). To become hardened or permanently fixed, as plaster.

SET. The form assumed by any piece of material or simple structure when it has yielded to pressure so as to have lost in part its original form. Commonly used only in the sense of Permanent Set (which see below).

Permanent Set. The permanent form assumed by a piece of material whose elasticity has been overcome by long-continued pressure or by a simple structure, as a truss or built beam under the same conditions.

SET-OFF. Same as Offset.

SET SQUARE. A draughtsman's tool, used with a T square, for drawing lines at right angles. (See Triangle.)

SETT. Same as Set (n.).

SETTIGNANO, DESIDERIO DA. (See Desiderio da Settignano.)

SETTING COAT. The second or third coat, *i.e.*, generally the final coat, in painting.

SETTING-OUT. The work of correctly locating a building upon the site which it is to occupy, according to the actual shape and dimensions of its ground plan, or of laying out any part of the work on a building.

SETTING-OUT ROD. (See Rod.)

SETTLE. *A.* A seat or bench ; specifically, a wooden bench with high back and arms for two or more people, placed near the chimney or at the foot of a bed, and often provided with a chest or coffer underneath.

B. A part of a platform lower than another part, as one of the successive stages of ascent to the great altar of the Jewish Temple.

SETTLEMENT. A gradual sinking of any part of a building, whether by the yielding of the foundation, the rotting of timber, or other imperfection. (See Leaning Tower.)

SETTLING Same as Settlement.

SETT-OFF. Same as Set-off (see Offset).

SEVERY. One bay of a vaulted structure, that is, the space within two of the principal arches (see Transverse Arch, under Arch, and Arc Doubleau). The term is evidently derived from the Latin *ciborium*, which term, from its original meaning of a covered receptacle, took first the significance of a rounded canopy (see Ciborium), then of a covered vessel or closet to hold the Host (see Ciborio), and also of a dome-shaped structure of any kind, whence comes the present meaning of a compartment of vaulting, whether dome-shaped or not. (Written also cibory and civery.)

SEWER. A conduit of brickwork, or a vitrified cement or iron pipe channel, intended for the removal of the liquid or semiliquid wastes from habitations, including in some cases the rain water falling upon roofs, yards, areas, and courts. We may distinguish street sewers and house sewers, the former being laid in the public streets, and intended for all the houses and lots composing a city block or blocks, the latter being the lateral branches for each building. The New York Building Department defines the house sewer as " that part of the main sewer of a building extending from a point two feet outside of the outer face of the outer front vault or area wall to its connection with a public or private sewer or cesspool." (See House Drainage.) — W. P. G.

SEWERAGE. A system of sewers for villages, cities, and towns. Where sewers receive household wastes only, the system is called a "separate system," and where rainfall and sewage are removed in the same channels the system is called the " combined system." — W. P. G.

SEWER GAS. More properly Sewer Air. The contaminated air of sewers, house drains, soil, waste, and vent pipes. It is a mechanical, ever-varying mixture with common air of a number of gases due to the decomposition of animal and vegetable matter, such as carbonic dioxide, carbonic oxide, ammonia, carbonate and sulphide of ammonia, sulphuretted hydrogen, and marsh gas. Sewer air also contains organic vapours, and some microscopic germs or bacteria.
— W. P. G.

SEXFOIL. (See Foil.)

SGRAFFITO. The scratching or scoring of a surface, as of fresh plaster, with a point to produce decorative effects. Sometimes, in plaster work or pottery, the scoring is done so as to reveal a surface of different colour beneath. The process is sometimes carried far, even to the decoration of large wall surfaces. (See Graffito.)

SHACK. A rude hut erected for camping. Also applied to more substantial though still rude structures of logs, boards, or even stone, frequently roofed with earth. — F. S. D.

SHADE. Same as Blind (n.), *B.*

SHADES AND SHADOWS. That branch of descriptive geometry which has to do with the laying out and representation, on a drawing of any object, of the shadows and the resulting shades formed by or on the object ; the position of the source of light being assumed at pleasure.

When an opaque object is exposed to the sunlight, a portion of its surface is illuminated, and is said to be in light. The portion turned away from the light is dark, and is said to be in shade. The line upon the surface which separates the light side from the dark side is called the line of shade.

The dark space beyond, from which the light is cut off, is called the object's shadow in space, or invisible shadow. The invisible shadow of a solid or of a plane figure is taken as a prism or cylinder ; of a right line, a plane ; and of a curved line, a cylindrical surface. The invisible shadow of a point is a right line, a line of

shadow which has the same direction as the rays of light.

If a second solid object intercepts this shadow in space, a portion of its surface is darkened. This is called the cast shadow or visible shadow. The cast shadow of a solid object, or of a surface cast upon a surface, is a surface ; of a line, a line ; of a point, a point. If the surface that receives the shadow is a plane, then the cast shadow, if a right line, is a right line, being the line of intersection of two planes. No surface which is in shade or in shadow can receive a cast shadow.

The shadow cast by one object upon the surface of another is its projection upon that surface, the rays of light being the projectors (see Projection). When the source of light is at a finite distance, the shadow is a radial projection, or perspective (see Perspective). When it is at an infinite distance, the shadow is a parallel projection. Shadows cast by the sun are, practically, parallel projections ; all others are radial projections.

It is obvious that the line of shade upon the surface of an object determines the shape of its shadow in space, which is bounded by the invisible shadow of the line of shade ; and also the shape of the cast shadow, which is bounded by the visible shadow of the line of shade. To find the cast shadow of a body it is sufficient, therefore, first to find its line of shade, and then to find the shadow of this line.

The rays of light are commonly assumed to be parallel, as if coming from the sun, and their direction to be such that they make the same angles with the planes of projections that the diagonal of a cube makes with its sides (35° 15' 50"). The projections of such rays upon the planes of projection are at 45° with the ground line. The advantage of this is that where one portion of an object projects in front of another portion, the width of the shadow shows exactly the amount of projection, thus giving information as to the third dimension.

The shadow of a point upon either plane of projection is found by drawing the projections of its line of invisible shadow and finding the point where it pierces that plane. The shadow of a line is found by determining the shadow of a sufficient number of points in it. For the shadow of a right line cast upon a plane surface, it is sufficient to find the shadows of its terminal points. The shadow will be the right line that connects them.

The shadow of a surface is bounded by the shadow of the line that encloses it, and that of a solid by the shadow of its shade-line. When the solid is bounded by planes, the shade line is made up of right lines, and its shadow is easily found. When the solid is bounded by curved surfaces, a special device is used to find the line of shade and its shadow. Auxiliary planes are passed through the object, parallel to the direction of the light and perpendicular to the horizontal plane of projection. Each of these planes cuts the horizontal plane in a line at 45°, and cuts the vertical plane in a vertical line. The section of the object itself is an oval, or other closed figure, set edgewise to the light. The shadow in space of this section is a plane figure lying wholly in the auxiliary plane, and bounded by the lines of invisible shadow cast by the extreme points of the section, those, namely, at which the rays are tangent to the section. These are two points in the required shade-line upon the surface of the object.

The projections of these two tangent rays, in the vertical plane of projection, are lines at 45°, tangent to the projection of the section. The cast shadow of the section lies wholly in the vertical line in which the auxiliary plane cuts the vertical plane of projection, and occupies so much of this line as is included between these two rays. The points in which they pierce this plane are two points in the cast shadow of the shade-line.

The shadow cast upon the horizontal plane of projections may be found in the same way, and the auxiliary planes taken parallel to the rays of light may, if more convenient, be taken normal to the vertical plane instead of to the horizontal one.

When the shadow cast by an object falls, not upon one of the planes of projection, but upon another object, each auxiliary plane is made to cut them both. As both sections lie in the same vertical plane, and stand edgewise to the light, the shadow of the first will fall exactly upon the edge of the second, and the shadow cast by the two extreme points in the shade-line of the first object will give the extreme points of the shadow cast by it upon the second. All four points can be determined in the vertical plane of projection, by drawing tangent rays at 45° from the projection of the first section to that of the second. If the object is of such shape that one part of it throws a shadow upon another part, the two parts are treated as separate objects.

When a right line and a cylindrical surface are both parallel to one plane of projection, and one is normal and the other is parallel to the other plane, the projection, upon the first plane, of the shadow cast by the line upon the cylindrical surface is a true section of that surface.

When a right line is normal to either plane of projection, the projection of its shadow on that plane is a right line at 45°, irrespective of the form of the surface upon which it falls.

In the case of curves, mouldings, rings, etc., it is convenient to use auxiliary plans perpendicular to the one plane, and at 45° to the other, and either by the use of a supplementary plane of projection, or by the process of revo-

lution (see Projection) to find the true sections made by each of these planes. The tangent rays which determine these planes of shade and shadow are drawn upon these sections at an angle of 35° 15′ 50″.

In architecture the objects are for the most part made up of parallelopipeds, cylinders, cones, and spheres, and their shadows are mostly cast upon plane surfaces, parallel to the planes of projection. The shapes of their shadows present, accordingly, but little variety, and can easily be learned by heart, so that they can be drawn from memory. — F. D. SHERMAN.

SHAFT. *A.* An upright object, high and comparatively small in horizontal dimensions. The term is applied to a building, as when a tower is said to be a plain shaft; to an architectural member, as when a high building is said to present a more elaborate basement and a less adorned shaft above; or to a single stone, an obelisk, menhir, cathstone, or the like. Even a classical column like "Pompey's Pillar," made up of capital, shaft, and base, is called in popular writing "a tall shaft." In modern usage, often, a straight enclosed space, as a well extending through the height of a building, or through several stories, for the passage of an elevator, to give light to interior rooms, or the like. Commonly, in combination, as elevator shaft; light shaft.

B. Specifically, the principal part of a column; that which makes up from two thirds to nine tenths of its height, and which is comparatively simple and uniform in treatment from end to end. The shaft of an Egyptian column was often diminished in size at the bottom, like the under side of a cup, and set without a base; then tapering to the neck. In Mycenæan art the shaft was often smallest at bottom, increasing

SHAFT OF DOUBLE FUSIFORM SHAPE, CARVED WITH LEAFAGE: CLOISTER AT BELEM, PORTUGAL.

in size upward by an even taper; and this form, though often spoken of as whimsical and sure to be abandoned, has its prototype in the trunks of certain palm trees, which, when used

MIDWALL SHAFT: WINDOW IN CHURCH OF GERNRODE, GERMANY.

as veranda posts and the like, are of very happy effect. The shafts of Doric columns of the sixth century B.C. are about six times as high as they are in greatest diameter; and these have an entasis showing a very visible curve. (For the shafts of the developed Grecian and Greco-Roman columns, see those terms, and references under them.) In the earlier Middle Ages, classical columns were so often taken for the new buildings, that their forms were inevitably copied in new work; but the result of Romanesque work, in making common the semi-cylindrical buttress piers within and without brought in a change, and free columns also were made cylindrical, without taper or swell. This custom prevailed without change throughout the epoch of Gothic architecture; and was only replaced, not modified, by the reintroduction of classical forms in the fifteenth and sixteenth centuries. — R. S.

(For the proportions of neoclassic architecture determined by the diameter of the shaft, see Intercolumniation; also Columnar Architecture and references.)

Angle Shaft. (See under A.)

Elevator Shaft. (See Shaft above, definition, *A*.)

Jamb Shaft. One of several slender columns, serving for the adornment of a deep jamb,

as of a Gothic or Romanesque portal. Less often a single column, set at the angle between the jamb and the face of the wall.

Midwall Shaft. (See Midwall Column, under Column.)

SHAFTED IMPOST. In mediæval architecture, an arrangement of shafts, wrought in the mass of a pier or jamb, so that corresponding groupings of archivolt mouldings may start from their caps at the impost line.

SHAFTING. In mediæval architecture, the system of grouping shafts in a clustered pier, or in the jamb of an aperture.

SHAFT RING. In mediæval architecture, a moulded band encircling a shaft; common in early English work. (See Annulated.)

SHAKE (I.). A rough split shingle about 3 feet long, usually of ash. Used on the roofs of log cabins, especially in New York. — F. S. D.

SHAKE (II.). A crack due to natural causes, occurring in the interior of a tree or log. The term is commonly but erroneously used also as synonymous with check.

Cup Shake. One occurring between two annual rings.

Heart Shake; Star Shake. One radiating from the centre of the trunk.

SHALE. A fine-grained, thinly bedded arenaceous rock. — G. P. M.

SHAMBLES. A slaughter house; by extension, the stalls on or in which butchers expose meat for sale.

SHANK (I.). One of the plain spaces between the channels of a triglyph in a Doric frieze. Called *femor* by Vitruvius.

SHANK (II.). The shaft of a column; obsolete. — (C. D.)

MIDWALL SHAFT: ABBEY OF MÜNSTERMAIFELD, RHENISH PRUSSIA.

SHANTY. A hut; a small temporary building of a rough character.

SHARPE, EDMUND, M. A., F. R. I. B. A.; architect; b. Oct. 31, 1809; d. May 8, 1877.

Received the degree of B. A. at S. John's College, Cambridge, in 1833, and M. A. in 1836. In 1832 he was elected travelling Bachelor of Arts for the University, and spent three years in the study of architecture in France and Germany. He became a pupil of John Rickman (see Rickman), and in 1836 established himself at Lancaster, England. He was a profound student of mediæval architecture, and published many important works on that subject: *Architectural Parallels* (1848, 1 vol. folio with supplement); *Decorated Windows* (1 vol. 8vo, 1849); *The Seven Periods of English Architecture* (1 vol. 4to, 1851), and numerous articles in architectural periodicals.

Stephen-Lee, *Dictionary of National Biography.*

SHAW, HENRY, F. S. A. ; architectural draftsman; b. July 4, 1800; d. June 12, 1873.

Employed by John Britton (see Britton) to illustrate his *Cathedral Antiquities of Great Britain*, making especially the plates for Wells and Gloucester. He published *Dresses and Decorations of the Middle Ages* (1843, 2 vols.); *Decorative Arts of the Middle Ages* (1851, 4to); *Details of Elizabethan Architecture* (1839, 4to); *Encyclopœdia of Ornament* (1842, folio); *Specimens of Ancient Furniture* (1836, 4to).

Redgrave, *Dictionary of Artists; Avery Architectural Library, Catalogue.*

SHEALING.   Same as Sheiling.

SHEARING FORCE; SHEARING LOAD.   Same as Shearing Weight.

SHEARING STRENGTH.   (See Strength of Materials.)

SHEARING WEIGHT.   That kind of breaking weight or force which acts by shearing; *i.e.* by pushing one portion of a member or material past the adjoining part, as by a pair of shears. (See Strength of Materials.)

SHEATHING.   In carpentry, a covering or lining to conceal a rough surface or to cover a timber frame. In general, any material, such as tin, copper, slate, tiles, etc., prepared for application to a structure, as covering.

SHEATHING BOARD.   A board prepared for sheathing purposes, often with tongue and groove for jointing.

SHEATHING PAPER.   A coarse paper specially prepared in various grades and laid with a lap under clapboards, shingles, slates, etc., to exclude weather, or between the upper and under flooring, for deafening. When made with asbestos or with magneso-calcite it is used for fireproofing.

SHED.   A roofed structure, usually open on one or more sides, for storage and for shelter of workmen and material; especially one with a lean-to roof.

SHED LINE.   The summit line of high ground, as being that at which the watershed begins; hence the ridge of a roof.

SHED ROOF.   Same as Penthouse, Def. *A.*

SHEETING; SHEET PILING.   (See Excavation; Pile.)

SHEILING.   A hut for temporary shelter. Especially, a rough shelter for shepherds and sheep in Scotland. (Also Shealing.)

SHELF.   Any ledge, wide or narrow, made of a board or other thin material, set edgewise and horizontally, for supporting small objects; as in closets for house linen, china, glass, etc. In general, a flat ledge, wherever or however occurring.

SHIM; –ING.   A piece of wood or thin iron used sometimes to raise a part to the proper level, sometimes to fill up a bad joint.

SHINGLE.   Originally, a thin parallelogram of wood (in the United States generally 6 inches by 18 to 24 inches), split and shaved, and more recently sawn, thicker at one end than the other; used for covering sides or roofs of houses, about 4 or 5 inches of its length being exposed. Shingles are now sometimes made of metal in the form of tiles.

SHINGLE–ROOFED.   Roofed with shingles.

SHINTO; SHINTOO.   The moral code or system of Japan. Shinto shrines are plain wooden structures, without images, thatched, and approached by passing under one or more torii, or porches composed of two posts bearing one or more cross beams, generally carved. The latter are accepted as symbols of Shinto.

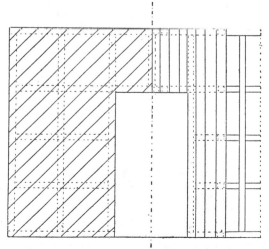

SHEATHING, DIAGONAL AND VERTICAL, AS WITH ROUGH BOARDS ON A FRAME OF STUDS AND TIES; THE SCHEME SHOWN IS GERMAN.

SHIPPEN; SHIPPON. In local British usage, a stable for cattle.

SHOE. A piece of stone, timber, or, more commonly, of iron, shaped to receive the lower end of any member; either to protect the end, as in the case of a pile which is to be driven into hard ground, or to secure the member at its junction with another. In this case, commonly adapted to prevent the penetration or rupture of one member by the other, as in the case of a plate under the end of a post or under the nut of a tie rod.

SHOOT (n.). *A.* The thrust of an arch.

B. Same as Chute.

SHOOT (v.). In carpentry, to dress an edge; especially to trim two adjoining edges with great care, so as to make a close joint. (Compare List, v.)

SHOOTING BOARD. *A.* A slab of wood or metal used by carpenters, and provided with a device for holding an object while it is being shaped for use.

B. An inclined board fitted to slide material from one level to another.

SHOOTING BOX. A building intended as a dwelling for persons engaged in the pursuit of deer, wild birds, or the like. The term includes the necessary outbuildings. (See Hunting Box.)

SHOOTING GALLERY. A long room with a target at one end, arranged for practice with firearms.

SHOP. *A.* A place where goods are offered for sale; in this sense, employed in Great Britain for large and elegant as well as small establishments; rare in the United States, but perhaps increasing in frequency in the Eastern cities. In the British colonies the tendency seems to be, as in the United States, toward the use of the word Store. The term Shop Front is in common use in America for the glass door, show windows, etc., of what is otherwise called a store. This has become an important part of street architecture in modern cities, although it cannot be thought to have been treated successfully except in a very few cases. The interior and exterior of modern shops are often costly and treated with a good deal of architectural pretension, but the conditions are against the introduction of anything of permanent value into the constructive architecture or the added decoration.

B. A place in which work is done; usually distinguished from a factory by the smaller number of workmen employed or the less extensive use of machinery. Thus, a carpenter shop is supposed to be a place where much work is done by hand or by the aid of the simplest machines. In this sense, often used in combination, as machine shop, workshop, repair shop, and the like.

C. By extension of the usage *B*, the work-

men employed in a shop, including foreman and master; as when a certain establishment is spoken of, or a principal is said to have established an excellent shop.

SHOP FRONT. That portion of the front of a building which is especially arranged to afford extensive show windows for a shop or store; characteristically, it is a screen of windows, glazed with large sheets of plate glass, the door being in a recessed vestibule, and the structural supports being reduced to a minimum, so as to give the greatest possible space for display of goods.

SHORE. A piece of timber to support a wall, usually set in a diagonal or oblique position, to hold the wall in place while the under part of it is taken out for repairs, or for the cutting of larger window openings, or the like. (See Shoring.) — R. S.

SHORE UP. To hold or support by means of Shores. (See Shoring.)

SHORING. The process of supporting a building or part of one upon Shores.

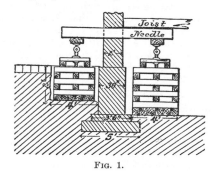

FIG. 1.

Under this head will be included the process of raising buildings, and the process of moving buildings from place to place.

The ordinary method by which buildings are shored is shown in Fig. 1, which is a cross section of a wall held by needles through the medium of jack screws resting upon temporary wooden blocking. In supporting a small weight, — as in the case of removing a single pier between two windows, — one or two upright timbers may take the place of the crib work shown. Many other methods of shoring parts of buildings are used, such as by pumps, or large square timbers having jack screws inserted in the lower end, which bear on temporary foundations of timber, their upper ends being inserted either under the walls, or in notches cut in them. It is also customary to hold isolated piers or iron columns by cramping them with timbers and belts, depending upon friction and utilizing any convenient indentation, or bars passing through holes that have been drilled.

A part of a building raised to position with

the screws removed is shown in Fig. 2. If the wall is only to be underpinned, the new sub-structure is built up between the needles, which are about four feet apart, according to circum-

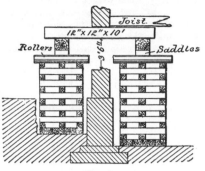

FIG. 2.

stances; then wedged with iron or slate and left for the mortar to harden until the needles can be removed. The holes thus left are then filled in with masonry.

If the building is to be removed, long inter-mediate needles are introduced, running from wall to wall so as to hold the building to-gether. These are supported on very heavy string timbers, shod with hardwood saddles on the under side. Rollers of beach or maple are inserted, resting on the temporary platform or wooden cribbing, and then the screws and short needles are removed. If there is room enough to get them in, the long needles are inserted first, and the raising is done by screws under them until the proper height is reached for in-serting the stringers and rollers. These expe-dients have to be varied constantly according to circumstances, and it is necessary always to bring the whole weight upon the long stringers, so that when the power is applied to them they will carry the building along without straining. Allowances are always made for settlement in the foundation platform over which the build-ing is to be moved, so that it is always going slightly up hill. The apparatus generally used for moving is a capstan or windlass operated by one or two horses, and sometimes two cap-stans are used. The chain, which is given a good hitch around the windlass, is a long one, running through many pulleys attached to the stringers, and other pulleys fastened to iron bars which are driven in the ground. This equalizes the strain on all parts of the building and furnishes the multiplication of power that is necessary.

Shoring is oftener required for making re-pairs or alterations to buildings than as a pre-liminary step to moving them. The alterations may involve a considerable raising of the whole superstructure. The trussed roof of a beer storage house in Milwaukee was raised 30 feet,

the masons following the house raisers until the desired height was reached. Some extraordinary alterations have been made in buildings that have been shored up. The entire original Chamber of Commerce Building at Chicago was held on temporary foundations and steel needles until the steel and concrete foundation of the present fourteen-story building were put in. In the Chicago Opera House block, which is a comparatively new twelve-story building, but was built with coursed foundations of con-crete and stone under the interior columns, a tier of iron columns was held up and new foundations of concrete and steel built under them, so as to insert basement columns and provide a clear open cellar, without disturbing the business of the first story.

For the shoring and raising of wooden build-ings, wooden screws were first used about 1840; the method in which these were employed is shown in Fig. 3. The post shown performed the office of the modern pump, and was placed under any part of the building requiring tem-porary support. This primitive apparatus was supplanted by the use of wrought-iron screws about the year 1850. It was soon found that, by reason of the softness of the metal and the knocking about and rough handling to which they were subjected when not in use, the threads became injured and would not work in the nuts or sleeves, and they were abandoned. Next, cast-iron screws came into use, and as they were rough and the joining of the mould had to be obliterated to make them work, their threads were cut by machinery. But this was too expensive, and some one invented a way of casting seamless screws which were so smooth and perfect that they could be used just as they

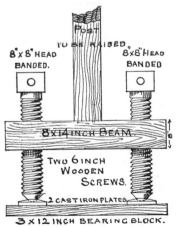

FIG. 3.

came from the sand. These screws are still the standard for all ordinary work. An illustra-tion is given in Fig. 4. They are $2\frac{3}{4}$ inches in diameter and 2 feet long; the pitch is $\frac{3}{4}$ inch, and they have a raising distance of 14 inches without shifting. Their lifting power is five tons to one man with a 4-foot lever, which is an ordinary iron bar with one end slightly bent to regulate the distance that it enters the head. It is only in exceptional cases that steel screws with cut threads are used for lifting; but long steel screws $2\frac{3}{4}$ inches in diameter have been used with pumps during the last ten years for pushing horizontally, in cases where buildings have to be turned on a pivot, or pushed into places where a windlass cannot be used.

Hydraulic jacks are used only in connection with screws at extra heavy points. The most expert house raisers will not use them unless they can catch the weight on screws in case of accident to the jacks. They were employed many years ago at San Francisco for raising entire buildings. In 1862 the Franklin House at Chicago was raised with hydraulic power. One pump was used for all the jacks, which were set in the walls. This method has gone entirely out of use.

The moving of frame houses through the streets has been a matter of very common oc-

24x3x¾-inch Pitch.
FIG. 4.

currence, especially in the large cities of the western part of the United States which have grown so rapidly during the last forty years. Where property increased so rapidly in value and there was always a demand for cheap buildings in outlying districts, it was very economical to move the light balloon frame buildings occupying central lots which demanded improvements. The construction of elevated viaducts for railroads has been the cause for moving great numbers of buildings of a heavier character.

The new foundations of the Chamber of Commerce Building, at Chicago, were put in in the winter of 1890 and 1891, and this is the first time that steel beams were used for needles. They were 27 feet long between bearing points and the following sizes were used: 15-inch, 50 lbs. per foot, regular pattern; 8-inch, 60 lbs. per foot, special pattern; 12-inch, 60 lbs. per foot, special pattern; and 15-inch, 80 lbs. per foot, special pattern. Iron beams had been used for this purpose as long ago as 1875, the contractors preferring Belgian beams rolled to extra thickness so as to provide against the possibility of their breaking down in the web.

One of the most important uses of shoring is in preventing the settlement of old buildings

caused by the erection of new ones on adjoining lots where the soil is compressible. When this is done a new foundation is built for both buildings, after shoring up the old one in the usual way: Fig. 5. The weight of the old building is then transferred to the new foundation by placing a row of short pumps and screws on it, directly under the wall and as the new building settles the screws are turned upward from time

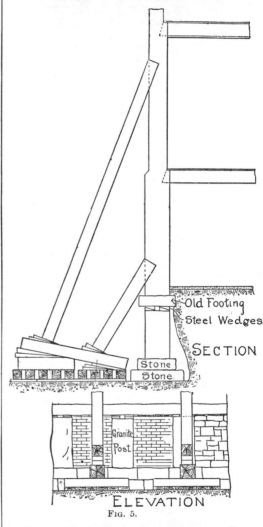

Old Footing
Steel Wedges.
SECTION
Stone
Stone
Granite
Post
ELEVATION
FIG. 5.

to time until all the settlement has ceased. Then the pumps are gradually removed and the wall underpinned: Fig. 6.

It is believed that brick buildings were first moved in 1850 at Boston, Massachusetts, in the widening of Tremont, Washington, and Hanover streets. This work was done by James Brown. He afterward took into partnership James Hollingsworth. Together they first devised the method now in use for turning buildings on pivots. Buildings are not supported entirely on pivots for this process, but the pivot is used for keeping them in position, the main weight being on the rollers. The power used is mainly applied by long steel screws, set at various points about the building. Brown and Hollingsworth moved to Chicago in 1857, and the first brick building raised in Chicago was the Thayer building in Randolph Street, between State and Dearborn, in that year. The second was at the corner of Madison and Market Streets, raised in the spring of 1858. The third brick building raised and underpinned in Chicago was the Commercial College building, State and Randolph Streets, in the spring of 1859, and was done under the direction of the writer of this article. The Tremont House, the largest hotel in that city, was raised 9 feet in 1861; and this was the largest undertaking of the kind up to that time. This feat was described and published all over the civilized world. After that nearly all of the brick and stone buildings then standing in the business section of Chicago were raised to the new grade of the city, which was established to admit of effective sewerage.

Many buildings have been moved over water. Frame buildings at Chicago are moved on floats across the rivers that intersect the city and to considerable distances on the same. At Eureka, California, also, many buildings have been moved across the water. Many of the state buildings at the World's Columbian Exposition were moved away entire, and the Delaware state building was moved across Lake Michigan on floats.

The following are among the most remarkable instances of house moving: —

In the winter of 1887–1888, the Brighton Beach Hotel at Coney Island, near New York, which was gradually being undermined by the sea, was moved back from the beach 595 feet. This building was of wood heavily framed, three and four stories high, having five large towers six and seven stories high, and weighed 5000 tons. It was 460 feet long and 210 feet deep, and was broadside to the sea. It was first raised by screws and then lowered upon 112 flat cars standing on 24 parallel railroad tracks which were built between the blocking. To each of these cars was given a nearly equal weight of 44 tons. The 24 trains of cars were coupled together rigidly. The transfer of the weight to the cars was made by hydraulic jacks. The building was moved by an arrangement of falls and sheave blocks, there being 34 of the latter and 12 sixfold purchases, the main block of each purchase being attached to the cars, while the opposite block was fastened by chain slings to the track on which the car rested about 100

feet distant from the building; the power employed was from six locomotives standing on two tracks in trains of three each. Six ropes were attached to each train. The building was moved 117 feet on the first day, and on other days at about the same rate. The whole was planned and executed by Benjamin C. Miller, of Brooklyn, New York.

In October, November, and December, 1895, the Emmanuel Baptist Church on Michigan Boulevard, Chicago, was moved 50 feet south. It was built of stone, covering 93 by 161 feet, the greatest height of the roof being about 100 feet. The stone tower with slated wooden spire was 24 by 24 feet and 225 feet high, weighing 1430 tons, the whole weight being 6652 tons. It was first raised by 175 30-ton steel screws

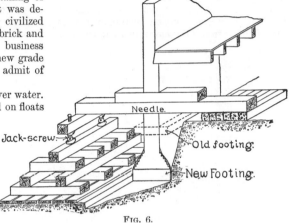

FIG. 6.

under the tower and 1100 5-ton cast iron screws under the rest. The bed on which it was moved was formed of 60-lb. steel rails on a heavy grillage of timber. The rails were bunched in threes, fours, and fives. Sixteen hundred steel rollers were used, and this was the first use made of them for the purpose, as hard wood rollers would have been crushed. They were 25 inches long and 2 inches in diameter, being tempered to correspond with the rails. The weight of the building was carried on 15-inch I beams, in bunches of two and three respectively, but the rollers were not in contact with the under side of these beams. They were separated from them by linings of Bessemer steel $\frac{1}{2}$ inch thick by 12 inches wide and 2 feet long. These linings were forged with a bevel of 2 inches at each end so as to permit the feeding of the rollers, and were cushioned to the I beams with heavy carwheel paper. The illustration (Fig. 7), which shows two sections of the work under the tower, will serve to show these dispositions, as well as the method of applying the motive power. The steel rail runners had a rise of 1 to 360 to allow for settlement. Extra heavy timbers were fastened parallel to the north wall of the church to serve as a resting base to moving force. Heavy iron chains at 10 feet intervals held these to the ground sills, transferring the moving force to the compressed ground under the building. Sixty long steel screws, in pumps, with capacity of 5 tons each, were used to apply the moving force, with one man to each screw. They were placed between the abutting timbers and the upper timbers of the superstructure. The 50 feet of movement was covered in 6 days with 60 men. After moving, all the parts of the church which were out of plumb before anything had been done were straightened and the whole left better than ever before. The contract was taken by H. Sheeler, and the calculations and supervision were by Charles H. Rector.

In 1893 the Normandy apartment building, a three-story brick and stone structure at 116 to 122 Laflin Street, Chicago, which happened to

of each with one hundred tons of sand to balance them. They were successfully put together on the new foundation, anchored, and finished off as a new building which has never shown any effects of the operation. The necessity for preserving the proper level of the platform and providing against its gradual settlement in this case will be readily appreciated, but the whole operation was conducted without failure or accident. This is the first time that a brick building has been cut in two and united again. This work was done by L. P. Friestedt under the direction of the writer.

There are two remarkable facts connected with the art of house shoring and moving. One is that it is purely an empirical art. Those who have practised it most and brought it to its present condition are not what are considered scientific men, or men of mathematical or theoretical training. The most of mathematics that is employed is in estimating the weight to be lifted and the necessary area of the temporary

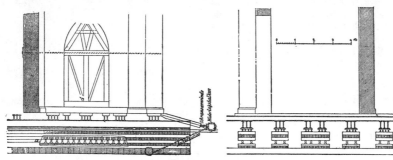

FIG. 7.

be on the right of way of the Metropolitan Elevated R. R. Co., was moved backward, turned 90 degrees, and made to face on Van Buren Street, which is at right angles to the street on which it had stood. The building was 94 by 84 feet and estimated to weigh 8000 tons. The work was successfully done by L. P. Friestedt.

One of the most remarkable instances of house moving was in the case of the three-story apartment building at Chicago, moved from 147 and 149 Centre Street, to 171 and 173 Sheffield Avenue. It was on the right of way of the Northwestern Elevated R. R. Co. There was no possible direction in which the building could be moved as a whole on account of obstructions, for it was 49 by 72 feet in size, so the building, which was a comparatively new one, was cut into two vertically through its greatest axis, and moved in two sections, one following the other, on the same platform; the aggregate distance travelled was nearly 800 feet and three corners had to be turned by each section. The sections had brick walls only on one side, and it was necessary to load the floors

foundations required. Everything else is the result of repeated experiment. Another fact is that there are no records of any disasters that have followed attempts to move or raise heavy structures. One reason for this is that the system followed is such that, if any piece of material used fails, there is always another to take the strain, and it is one that necessarily requires the constant shifting of loads from one point to another in order to carry on the work. When it is understood that a large part of the work of house shorers is to make safe buildings which give evidence of insufficient supports or foundations, it will be realized that the house raiser is constantly obliged to face dangers caused by the mistakes of others, and caution is almost an instinct with him.

Very little work of this kind has been done in European countries, though the greatest interest in what has been done in the United States has been excited abroad, and the most reliable accounts of them can be found in foreign journals. Notwithstanding many instances in which American contractors have been consulted in other countries, where their services might have prevented much destruction of property, there is no record of any of them having been thus employed.[1] The reason is that such matters are first referred to engineers, who cannot understand, without mathematical deductions, how the American operations have been carried on, and consequently cannot be convinced that they are safe.

Furthermore there are no published treatises on this subject to which reference can be made. (For work done in Europe in the way of supporting buildings while they are in course of alteration or repair, see footnote and Underpinning. See also Shore; Needle.)

— Peter B. Wight.

SHOT. Having its edges straight and true, said of a board or plank.

Riley, *Building Construction.*

SHOT TOWER. A high building for the manufacture of shot, which are formed by dropping molten lead from an upper story or platform into a cistern of water at the bottom. The mass of lead subdivides into drops during the descent, and the size of the shot is frequently regulated by perforated screens or sieves, having openings of various sizes, through which the lead is poured.

SHOT WINDOW. In Scotland, an unglazed window, generally circular.

SHOULDER. The projection or break made on a piece of shaped wood, metal, or stone, where its width or thickness is suddenly changed, as at a tenon or rebate, the break being usually at right angles.

SHOULDERING. The raising of the upper edge of a slate with mortar so that at the lower edge it may make a closer joint with the slate which it overlaps.

SHOULDER PIECE. A piece of material secured to another part or parts so as to form a shoulder.

SHOW ROOM. A room especially adapted to the effective display of objects on sale.

SHOW WINDOW. A Shop Window, arranged for the display of goods to persons in the street.

SHREAD HEAD. Same as Jerkin Head.

[1] Since this was written information has been received that in carrying out the extensive municipal improvements lately instituted in Budapesth, Hungary, there has been secured the assistance of L. P. Friestedt, of Chicago, who performed the remarkable feat of moving a large brick building, in two sections, and reuniting the same. The changes in street lines included the ground occupied by several important buildings, some of them monuments of mediæval art. These have been successfully saved by moving them, while others at this writing are being moved and reconstructed. The authorities would not allow the work to be done until very heavy surety bonds were given.

— P. B. W.

SHREADING; SHREDDING. Light furring strips of wood secured to the under side of rafters to give nailing to sheathing or laths.

SHRINE. In architecture, a receptacle for sacred relics, most often the body of a saint. The shrine is then a tomb in a Choir, Chapel, or Crypt, such as that of S. Edward "the Confessor" in Westminster Abbey. Portable shrines are made for smaller relics, often of very rich material and splendidly adorned.

SHRINKAGE. The contraction of materials by cooling, as metal, or by drying, as timber. In the latter case, shrinking is at right angles with the direction of the grain. (See Seasoning Timber; Wood Construction.)

SHRIVING PEW; SHRIVING SEAT. (See Confessional.)

SHROUDE. Same as Crowde.

SHUTE. Same as Chute.

SHUTTER. A movable screen, cover, or similar contrivance to close an opening, especially a window. In the United States the term is commonly made to include all varieties of hinged and swinging Blinds, as well as any solid or nearly solid structure to close an opening tightly at the outside. These latter would not be spoken of as blinds.

Box Shutter. An inside folding shutter, so contrived that when not in use it can be folded back into a recess provided for it in the deep window jamb. Usually the upper and lower sections are separate, for independent opening and closing.

Louver Shutter. One fitted with louver boards, *i.e.* with slats set diagonally and immovable, as distinguished from adjustable slats. (See Rolling Blind, *B*, under Blind; Rolling Slat, under Slat.)

Rolling Shutter. A shutter made of thin, slender strips secured edge to edge by hinge-like joints, so that the whole combination results in a flexible structure which can be rolled and unrolled, usually at the top of the opening. These may be of wood, but are most often of iron or steel, and used to protect openings from fire, burglars, etc. Rolling shutters, an invention of the second half of the nineteenth century, are wholly distinct from shutters with rolling slats.

Venetian Shutter. One with slats; either with rolling slats held together by a strip which causes them all to move or to "roll" simultaneously, or a Louver Shutter.

SHUTTER BAR. A bar for locking a pair of window shutters on the inside, generally pivoted on one leaf and dropping into a socket on the other.

SHUTTER LIFT. A small shutter bar with a handle for convenience in opening or closing and locking shutters.

SHUTTING SHOE. A device of iron or stone with a shoulder, sunk in the middle of a gateway, as in a carriage drive, against which the gate is shut and secured.

SIAM, ARCHITECTURE OF. (See Farther India, Architecture of.)

SICARD VON SICARDSBURG, AUGUST; architect; b. Dec. 6, 1813; d. June 11, 1868. A pupil of Edward Van der Null (see Null), and was associated with him in all his principal undertakings, especially the *Hofoperahaus* in Vienna.

Allegemeine Deutsche Biographie.

SICILY, ARCHITECTURE OF. Although Sicilian monuments are very distinctive, they have a great deal in common with those of the nearer provinces of the mainland. Of the prehistoric peoples the remains are mainly not architectural. Phœnicians and Siculi left polygonal and other primitive constructions at Cefalù, Mt. Eryx, and Motye, or Motya. The series of pure Hellenic monuments begins earlier here than in other parts of the Hellenic world, and comprises the largest groups of Greek temples. The Doric order is used consistently, no example of Ionic being known previous to the Roman period. Through Sicilian temples and those of the southern mainland at Tarentum, Pæstum, Metapontum, and Croton, a consecutive idea of the development of the Doric style is obtained, from its beginnings c. 600 B.C. to its close in the second century B.C. This region is the real home of Doric. The existing monuments in Greece proper are less numerous and consecutive. After the proto-Doric of the early Megaron of Demeter, near Selinus (c. 600), the earliest examples of the colossal monumental style are two temples at Syracuse — the Olympieion and the Appolonion — with their contemporary at Tarentum. They are of the peripteral hexastyle type that ever after ruled in Sicily and on the mainland, with but few exceptions. Selinus furnishes in temple C of the Guidebook an almost contemporary example (c. 600–575), the oldest of a series of nine temples on this site, which, although badly preserved, are historically of the greatest value. The next in date at Selinus is temple D; then temple F; both probably earlier than 550. With them should be classed the finely preserved temple at Pæstum called the "Basilica," and the fragment of the old temple at Pompeii. A trifle later are the temple of "Ceres" at Pæstum and the two temples at Metapontum. These latter presage the adoption of new forms; but the transition from the archaic into the developed or canonical Doric is best exemplified by the colossal temple G at Selinus (cf. temple of Hercules, Akragas), and the equally colossal and unusual temple of Zeus, or Olympieion, at Akragas (Girgenti), — works of the close of the sixth and beginning of the fifth centuries. Up to this time no real standard prevailed for proportions and forms, but a growing tendency toward uniformity and harmony shows itself in these transitional buildings. Then commenced the style aptly termed "canonical," because henceforth certain canons were to obtain. The earliest examples are three of the temples at Selinus, A, O, and E, the temple near Himera, three temples at Akragas (Athena, Hera, and Ceres), and the later parts — especially the west front — of the temple G at Selinus. (Cf. Temple of Gela.) These are all anterior to c. 450. Then comes, in the latter half of the fifth century, the last important group — the temples of Segesta, of Concord at Akragas, that upon which the cathedral of Syracuse is built, and that of Poseidon at Pæstum — all posterior to the Parthenon. After this there are straggling monuments, such as the propylon to the Megaron at Selinus, three temples at Akragas (Dioscuri, Vulcan, and Asklepios), and even later, a few that conform to the Hellenistic style of the third and second centuries, such as the little prostyle temple B at Selinus, the prostyle at Taormina, the Corinthian-Doric temple at Pæstum, and the Ionic-Doric oratory of Phalaris at Akragas.

For unity's sake temples of the mainland are enumerated and characterized with the Sicilian. Certain general facts emerge from the series. The earliest temples had a single façade to their cellas, the "canonical" had two by the addition of the opisthodomos. The earliest allowed the irregularity of a wider metope at the corners; "canonical" counteracted it by narrowing the corner intercolumniation. The disposition to regularity in the later style is shown, for instance, in placing the columns of the peristyle on the axis of the cella walls, and the tendency to lightness is shown in the increasing height of the columns in relation to their diameter and the change in the shape of the capitals. Certain local distinctions must also be recognized. All the temples of Selinus had an *adyton*, or holy of holies, behind the main cella, perhaps of early Greco-Oriental origin. It was also used in some very early temples elsewhere (*e.g.* "Basilica" at Pæstum), but soon abandoned, except at Selinus, which appears to have been conservative. As mentioned above, the rule was to have 6 columns on the ends, and 13 or 14 on the sides, but the earliest temples were more oblong, having sometimes 15–17 columns (*e.g.* Apollo and the Olympieion, Syracuse; Hercules, Akragas; C and E, Selinus). In the whole group three temples alone have more than 6 columns on the ends, the "Basilica" at Pæstum (9–18), temple G at Selinus (8–17), and the temple of the Olympian Zeus at Akragas (7–14). These temples also are the most colossal known in the Doric order, and have other revolutionary peculiarities. Already in temple C, and the Megaron at Selinus, the mysterious nature of the worship was accentuated by the closing of the pronaos, and afterward at temple F, Selinus,

PLATE XIX

SICILY, ARCHITECTURE OF. PLATE I

La Cuba, at Palermo; a building of the Norman kings of Sicily, dating from the twelfth century. The pointed arches are not evidence of the building being Gothic in its structure. They are like the similar details of Cairene mosques of the same and earlier epochs; their forms appeal to the semi-Oriental population of Sicily. There is a hall in the building which retains traces of decoration closely copied from that of the Moslems. A similar building though with round arches is La Zisa; the two are of 1165-1185.

this was made more prominent by the unique expedient of closing up the intercolumniations by a high screen of stone slabs, thus creating a closed deambulatory. But the climax was reached in the temple of Zeus at Akragas. Here the peristyle is changed into a pseudo-peristyle by a solid wall with engaged half columns, between which stands the famous colossal Atlantes, while the interior thus formed is divided into three aisles by two rows of square piers, which stand where the cella walls usually were. This interior, so different from the regular small cella, is the closest approach to a colossal sacred hall that Greek antiquity has given us. Two other temples have cellas of a size larger than the customary, also divided into nave and aisles, namely, temple G at Selinus, which has the clumsiness of a first attempt at such an innovation, with aisles of the same width, an adyton inside the cella, and a rich pronaos with independent columns; and the temple of Poseidon, at Pæstum, where the theme is treated far more harmoniously. Before this three-aisled scheme had been developed the division of the cella into two aisles by a single line of supports had been attempted at the "Basilica" at Pæstum, and at Metapontum, but never appears to have reached Sicily, and was soon abandoned. Of all Sicilian temples the best preserved are those of Juno and Concord at Akragas, and the unfinished temple at Segesta, which rival in condition those of Poseidon, Ceres, and the basilica at Pæstum. At Syracuse the temple at the cathedral is in fair condition. Nearly all the rest are extremely ruinous. The quarries for the stone with which all these temples were built are in several cases known. That near Selinus still has lying in it some shafts cut out of the mass for temple G, and the methods used are clearly exemplified.

The other Greek remains in Sicily, though not without importance, may be dismissed briefly. They are mainly of two classes : (1) fortifications ; (2) theatres. Of military architecture two works of primary importance remain, both of the fifth century, at Syracuse and at Selinus. Fort Euryelus at Syracuse defended the west end of the city, where the north and south walls converged, and comprised four massive towers defending a great court, with outlets for cavalry and infantry ; connected with it was the great circuit wall of Epipolæ At Selinus the north end of the city was strongly fortified, especially just after the disaster of 409. It was here that were recently discovered some interesting round arches of c. 407 B.C. The immense bastion in the form of a demilune that formed the avant corps of the defensive system, with its round towers, and that has been mistakenly dubbed a theatre, is the most remarkable feature. Cf. walls at Himera, Tyndaris, Eryx.

Sicily was the favourite home of Greek plays ; the love for them was almost a mania, and found expression in superb theatres. The largest was that of Syracuse, with a diameter of about 500 feet, and some 60 tiers of seats with 9 cunei and one broad and one narrow præcinctio. It was built by Demokopos under Hiero I. (478–467), and restored by Hiero II. (276–215). In far better preservation is that of Taormina (Tauromenion), with a diameter of 357 feet. Its stage, one of the finest known, was entirely remodelled by the Romans, as the stages of nearly all Greek theatres were, in order to suit the new customs of presenting dramas. The retaining walls also are a Roman reconstruction. Even less that is Greek remains in the theatres of Catania (diameter, 318 feet, 9 cunei, 2 præcinctiones) ; Tyndaris (diameter, 212 feet, 9 cunei, 27 tiers) ; Segesta (diameter, 205 feet, 7 cunei, 1 præcinctio), and the smallest of all at Acræ.

The Romans did very little but plunder Sicily, and left there hardly any monuments of interest. They occasionally erected an odeon next to the theatre, as at Acræ and Catania ; an amphitheatre (Termini, Catania, Syracuse) ; an aqueduct (Catania, Termini, Adernò) ; baths (Acireale, Catania, Taormina) ; or even an entire town (Soluntum). But their constructions are now in far poorer preservation than the Greek, and present no special features.

Of the early Christian churches for which Sicily was famous nothing remains ; the Mohammedan invaders destroyed them all. The only pre-Norman church is the little Byzantine structure at Malvagna. The superb works of Arabic architecture, glowingly described by writers, have also perished. The second great group of Sicilian monuments commences with the Norman conquest. Its characteristics are derived from various sources. The pointed arch universally used, one form of the dome, the high plain outer walls, some forms of the mosaic and marble decoration, are Mohammedan, presumably Cairene-Sicilian. The figured mosaics, heavy apsidal grouping, domical arrangement, narthex, are Byzantine. The plan of nave and aisles with columns, carved decorations and mouldings, occasional use of porches and towers, are mostly Norman-Lombard. The school is unique in architectural history for its combination of elements from so many diverse styles. There appears not to be a single normal Romanesque structure in Sicily of either the vaulted or roofed types. Beside the Cistercian church of S. Spirito at Palermo, c. 1170, a mere importation, the nearest approach to pure Romanesque is the first large church built by the Normans after the conquest, the cathedral at Troina (1078), showing the hand of Lombard architects from the mainland trained in the simplest style of Benedictine architecture

—square piers, square apses, wooden roof. At about the same time S. Giovanni dei Lebbrosi (Palermo) was built on a pure Byzantine scheme, but without decoration. The use here of the pointed arch indicates its prevalence in previous Saracenic monuments. In several earliest Norman works round and pointed arches were used together, but in the twelfth century the round arch was abandoned. In the cathedral of Catania (1075–1094) and other of the earliest churches Lombard forms still prevail (cf. cathedral at S. Agostino, Messina). The Byzantine plan, with central dome on four columns, is used at the same time, as at La Nunziatella dei Catalani at Messina, but even here the details of arcades and decoration are mostly Northern. During this same period (1071–1110) a great mass of civil and military constructions arose, less important for art than for engineering, as at Mazzara, Aderno, Paterno, and Alcamo, the latter with Arabic elements. A new period began with Roger II., who frankly subordinated Northern to Arabic and Byzantine influences. Now begins the series of really important monuments. The earliest were the palaces, in which the Moslem type of palace of the Mohammedan emirs was followed. Palermo was encircled by them ; parts of a few remain in Palermo itself, at Altarello di Baida (called Minenio), and at Favara. Rows of long, slender, pointed windows form the principal exterior decoration. Each has a beautiful chapel and a court. Saracenic vaulting and Cufic decorative inscriptions are used. In the churches built soon after these palaces, there is still a mixture of styles. The most considerable is the cathedral of Cefalù, which represents the highest point of achievement (1131–1148). It shows that in this part of the island the Norman and Lombard element still predominated, even though the pointed arch and Arab false arcade were used. In the façade the two heavy towers remind of Normandy ; the three-arched porch between them is borrowed especially from Benedictine churches of the middle South (*e.g.* Cathedral Piperno, S. Clemente in Casauria, S. Angelo in Formis) ; the plan is a Latin cross, with almost no projection of the transept, a scheme that became popular in Sicily. The arches of the nave are low-pointed, supported on sixteen columns. The adjoining cloisters are beautiful, and give the type soon followed everywhere in Sicily (S. Carcere at Catania, Eremitani at Palermo, Monreale). The mosaics of this church are the most beautiful in Sicily, and evidently executed by Greek artists.

In and around Palermo the Oriental element was stronger. Here the gem of art was the chapel of the palace (Cappella Palatina): stilted pointed arches with capitals part antique, part Lombard, part Saracenic ; an elaborately decorated and painted stalactite ceiling by Moslem

artists ; a series of figured wall mosaics by Greek Byzantine artists ; decorative mosaics and marble slabs in dadoes and furnishings, such as throne and ambone, perhaps by Cairene artists ; a central dome and tunnel vaults over the transepts. Such are the heterogeneous elements in this typical structure. The interesting church of S. Giovanni degli Eremiti, supposed to be contemporary (1132–1148), has a nave formed of two square bays, each covered by a horseshoe dome on pendentives, crossed by a transept with three smaller domes. Here the style is so thoroughly Cairene, devoid even of Byzantine decoration, that it seems as if it might be a remodelled mosque. The cloister, however, is of the regular Norman type (cf. Cefalù). A thoroughly Byzantine church, on the other hand, is S. Maria dell' Ammiraglio, called La Martorana (1128–1143), also at Palermo, with the usual dome on four columns, with both tunnel and cross vaults over aisles, and a typical atrium. Though most of the Sicilian churches of this period have one or more towers at the façade or transept, they are mainly of Moorish or Byzantine types, and that of the Martorana is the first to show rich Norman decorative details. There is here also progress in the dome, and in general a tendency to harmonize the various elements of Sicilian architecture. S. Cataldo combines Byzantine and Apulian styles (1161). The civil architecture of this generation was interesting : some fine bridges with pointed arches (*e.g.* Ponte dell' Ammiraglio), large baths (Termini, Cefalù), palaces, and castles. Perhaps the climax in palace architecture was reached under William I. (1151–1166), who built the famous " La Ziza." Its façade was 90 × 63 feet, with a main pointed portal 30 × 15 feet, flanked by two smaller portals. Above were two stories of blind pointed arcades in narrow windows, both single and double, which are opened. The interior has a symmetrical grouping of halls on two main floors all vaulted with domes, tunnel vaults, and especially domical cross vaults, with abundant use of the Moorish stalactite niche ornament. This is the best-preserved type of the Arabo-Norman palace, of which " La Cuba " is a later and smaller example, under William II. (1166–1189), who also favoured Mohammedan art. The state of church architecture under the latter is best shown by the cathedral of Monreale (1173–1182), which, while it lacks in the treatment of details the perfection of the earlier Cappella Palatina and the cathedral of Cefalù, is richer in its architecture and shows a final harmonious welding of styles. This is probably due to the existence toward the close of the twelfth century of a national school of Sicilian artists educated by Mohammedan, Greek, and Italian masters. The plan com-

PLATE XX

SICILY, ARCHITECTURE OF. PLATE II

Monreale ; nave of the cathedral, seen from the northwest. The choir includes the crossing of the transept, which is very short, and the central apse, which is but of slight projection. There are eight free columns on each side of the nave beside the two responds.

bines the wooden-roofed, thin-walled basilica in the nave and aisles, with the Greek church in the heavy transept and choir. The columns are antique; capitals antique or classic imitations; arcades pointed everywhere; Norman zigzag combined with Cairene battlement design and Byzantine-Moorish geometric designs in stone inlay and relief. The fashion of inlaying the smaller columns with mosaics was now introduced, as shown in the cloister at Monreale — most interesting, perhaps, of Italian cloisters — and the tombs of the kings (*e.g.* crypt cathedral, Palermo). Had it remained unruined by the barbarous Fuga (1781–1801), the cathedral of Palermo would have exhibited the same style as Monreale, with later parts showing transition to Gothic. The Normano-Byzantino-Arab style thus constituted reacted upon the mainland in Campania and other southern provinces. Even after the German dynasty under Henry VI. succeeded the Norman, the style continued unaffected, though for a while (1189–1215) political disorders hindered art production. The Badiazza at Messina shows the continued strength of the Byzantine dome and plan, with Norman profiles and ornament. But parts also, of c. 1225–1235, especially the side portals, show the transition to Northern Gothic. To help the change in style came the Cistercians, Dominicans, and Franciscans, though these orders were less prominent here than in any part of Italy. The era of great religious structures is past; only small churches are built henceforth under the German and Spanish princes. Under these dynasties, architecture lost some of its insular characteristics, gradually eliminating most Byzantine and Saracenic elements during the first half of the thirteenth century (*e.g.* stilted arches and domes), and retaining the Norman elements. The proto-Renaissance style of Frederick II. found temporary lodgment, especially in civil and military architecture (*e.g.* Syracuse, Catania, Rocca Orsino).

The Gothic forms did not eject the Norman until the fourteenth century, and then found their finest expression in civil architecture throughout the island. Sicily has a superb mass of little-known houses, palaces, fortresses, castles of the Middle Ages, illustrating every phase from the early Norman to decadent Gothic. Entire towns, such as Randazzo, are mediæval. Middle Gothic palace architecture is best represented by two rival palaces in Palermo, — Chiaramonte (1307–1380) and Sclafani (1330), — with fine arcaded courts and lines of three and four light windows. The cathedral of Taormina shows the Gothic supremacy to be complete at c. 1330: compare the contemporary palaces of S. Stefano and Corvaja at Taormina and the later parts of the cathedral, Messina. Throughout the

fifteenth century Gothic continued to reign, with scarcely a trace of earlier local styles, but with strong elements both of French (House of Anjou) and German and even English Gothic. Its details were more elegant and clean-cut than in most of the mainland schools. As the style was late in arriving, so it was very late in departing. The two rival palaces in Palermo — Aiutamicristo (1485) and Abatelli (1495) — are fine instances of late Gothic. The richly sculptured ruins of S. Maria at Militello (1501) show some traces of Renaissance forms. But throughout the island Gothic was used universally as late as c. 1525, and sporadically much later. In the latest Gothic churches the hall type was used, either in three aisles of equal height (S. Maria della Catena, Palermo) or in a single nave.

Not becoming popular in Sicily until after 1550, neoclassic architecture produced very little before the barocco period. Palermo was its centre, with some examples at Catania and Messina. The "Porta Felice" at Palermo shows barocco in 1582. At Palermo, S. Eulalia dei Catalani has a good façade; S. Giorgio dei Genovesi (1591) has a remarkable interior, with each arch supported by four columns. With the development of a particularly florid barocco throughout the seventeenth century a number of interesting buildings were erected. At Palermo, S. Salvatore (1628), by Amato, has an oval interior with three niches, and its rich marble decoration is paralleled at S. Giuseppe dei Teatini. The aim at the colossal is best exemplified by S. Domenico (1640) at Palermo, and by the Benedictine monastery of S. Nicola at Catania (1693), supposed to be next to the most colossal monastery in Europe.

A. L. FROTHINGHAM, JR.

SICULO-ARABIAN. Having the characteristics of the Moslem conquerors of Sicily, who subdued the island during the ninth century, and occupied it without much interruption for a hundred years. The term is inaccurate in so far as anything Arabian in a national sense is assumed to exist in the artistic work of Sicily (see Arabian Architecture). Siculo-Moslem would be a more accurate term, but has not as yet found currency.

SIDEBOARD. A serving table in a dining room, often permanently fixed, provided with lockers and drawers beneath, and with shelves above, sometimes partly closed, the whole being treated as a conspicuous decorative feature.

SIDE TIMBER; **SIDE WAVER**. (See Purlin.)

SIDING. The covering, or material for covering, the exterior walls of a frame building, and forming the final finished surface, as distinguished from the sheathing, on which, when used, the siding is nailed.

Novelty Siding. In the United States,

wooden siding of which the boards have rabbets, or grooves, at the lower edges to lap over corresponding tongues along the upper edges, thus permitting all the boards to be nailed flat against the frame. (Compare Clapboard.)

SIGNORELLI, LUCA; painter; b. about 1441; d. 1523.

A great mural painter.

Vasari, Blashfield-Hopkins ed.; Müntz, *Renaissance*; and in the general bibliography, Bryan, Crowe and Cavalcaselle, Nagler, Scribner's *Cyclopædia*, Seubert, Vasari.

SIKRA. A peculiar form of tower in northern India. (See India, Architecture of, col. 473.)

SILE. Same as Syle.

SILL. The lowest member of a frame, usually a horizontal, uniting two or more verti-

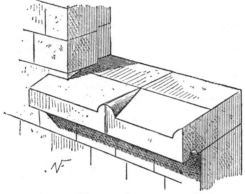

SILL FOR A WINDOW OPENING: OF STONE CUT WITH A WASH, WITH LUGS UNDER THE JAMB STONES AND SADDLE JOINTS.

cals, and, in a large structure, often forming a level base on which the uprights are erected; also a similar member, of any material, forming the lower side of an opening whether part of a frame or not.

In the former sense a sill is an integral part of the construction, and the term applies equally to the series of long horizontal timbers laid on a foundation wall to receive the uprights of a wooden house, and to a similar member beneath a window opening, uniting the jamb pieces and corresponding to the head above. In the latter, and more restricted, sense, the term designates any horizontal member making a finish to the bottom of an opening, and in this sense is used in connection with masonry as well as framing.

The doorsill of interior doors is covered by the saddle, or is shaped into a form of a saddle. The doorsill of a door at the head of a flight of steps, or one which gives entrance to a story raised above the outside surface, is practically the same thing as the top step. Thus, in an ordinary porch, or stoop, to a city house, there are said to be so many steps beside the sill. Door and window sills alike, when of stone or

terra cotta, are usually cut or moulded with a slight slope or wash on the upper surface, and this slope should be stopped at each end against a lug (see Seating). In cheap and hasty buildings the lug is often omitted, and the brick wall is rested upon this sloping surface, the crevice being made good with mortar or spawls of stone.

Groundsill. That sill of a framed structure which is nearest the ground; as, usually, the principal sill of a framed house, which is laid on the foundation wall two or three feet above the level of the ground.

Mudsill. A sill laid on the ground for the support of the structure above; as in very slight sheds and outhouses.

SILL COURSE. *A.* A string course or belt course which is placed so as to include and extend the sills of a window, or row of windows; or rarely of both doors and windows. The sills may be of the same height as the whole sill course, but the wash or slope and the mouldings by which the sill projects from the face of the wall and drips the rain water are not continued throughout the course.

B. A belt course set immediately below the window sills, and upon which these latter seem to rest.

SILOÉ, DIEGO DE; sculptor and architect.

A son of Gil De Siloé. He erected, partly from his father's designs, the cathedral of Granada (Spain), at the beginning of the sixteenth century.

Stirling-Maxwell, *Annals of the Artists of Spain*; Bermudez, *Diccionario*.

SILVA, JOAQUIM POSSENDONIO NARCISSO DA; b. May 17, 1806; d. 1896.

Da Silva spent his childhood in Brazil, and returned to Lisbon in 1821. In 1827 he entered the *Académie des Beaux Arts* in Paris. In 1833 he was appointed court architect at Lisbon. He transformed the convent of La Pena into the residence of the king, Dom Ferdinand, and restored the palace of the Duke of Palmella.

Construction Moderne, April 18, 1896.

SILVE, GIL DE; architect and sculptor.

Originally from Burgos (Spain). Gil is known by the fine tombs of King Juan II. and the Infante Don Alonso, which were placed in the presbytery of the Chartreuse of Miraflores (Spain) by Queen Isabella. They were begun in 1489 and finished in 1493, and are among the latest and finest of the Gothic monuments of Spain.

Stirling-Maxwell, *Annals of the Artists of Spain*; Bermudez, *Diccionario*.

SILVER GRAIN. In certain woods a peculiarly brilliant grain and very decorative in effect, obtained by cutting in the direction of the medullary rays; that is, by sawing the boards or planks in the direction of the radius of the section of the log. It is peculiarly attractive in oak, partly because of the openness of the other grain, with which the broad and smooth stripes of the silver grain contrast. (See Quarter ; Wood.)

SIMA. Same as Cyma.

SIMONE DA ORSENIGO ; architect.

Simone came to the construction of the cathedral of Milan March 1, 1387. In a memorandum of October in the same year he is called *inzignerio fabricae.* He seems to have been the first supervising architect of the cathedral. It is possible that the building was designed by him.

Boito, *Duomo di Milano : Annali del Duomo.*

SIMONI. (See Buonarroti-Simoni, Michelangelo.)

SINAN, ABDULLAH, PACHA ; architect.

The most important Turkish architect. He is credited with a large number of mosques, minarets, schools, palaces, etc. His three principal works are the mosque of Sultan Selim I. (built 1521–1527), the mosque of Sultan Suleiman I. (built about 1550), and the mosque of the Sultana Valideh, built for the mother of Sultan Murad III. ; all at Constantinople.

Edhem Pacha, *L'Architecture Ottomane ;* Evlya, *Narrative.*

SINGING GALLERY. A gallery for singers, often, in churches of the Italian Renaissance, richly decorated with carving ; also cantoria. (See Gallery, *B.*)

SINGLE FRAMED FLOOR ; ROOF. One having only a single tier of beams, or joists, or rafters ; that is, a floor without girders or binding beams, or a roof without principals, having only common rafters. It follows from the simplicity of construction that in large spans the beams or rafters have to be trussed or in some way strengthened ; hence the common use of the term to denote a roof in which the rafters are separately braced as with tie rods and a central pin or post to each.

SINGLE HUNG. (See Hung.)

SINGLE MEASURE. In England, having no mouldings on either side ; said of a door. When moulded on one side only it is accounted a measure and a half. When moulded on both sides it is a Double Measure.

SINK. A receptacle for waste water, often set under a faucet or tap. In modern plumbing, a fixture, usually rectangular, and connected by a trapped waste pipe with a soil or drain pipe. Sinks are fitted up in kitchens, sculleries, pantries, and housemaids' closets. Sinks for the emptying of slop water are deeper than ordinary sinks, and are known as slop sinks. (See Plumbing.)—W. P. G.

SINKING. Same as Settlement.

SINKROOM. In the United States, a room in which a sink is placed ; often having

the water of a neighbouring spring brought in by pipes or bored-out scantling.

SINK TRAP. A trap for a sink arranged to permit the discharge of water without allowing sewer gases to escape into the room.

SITTING ROOM. A room arranged for the use of a family or an association of friends for private and sociable gatherings, distinguished from a room reserved for the receiving of company in a more formal way.

SIZE. An important element in architectural design. Dimensions, as quoted in a table, are frequently misleading, because a low or a slightly built building may be much longer than one of many times its mass, its constructive importance, or its architectural beauty. At the same time statistics of dimension are of value if properly understood ; for design in a very large building cannot be compared with design in a small one unless the comparison of size be also made with care. The buildings of antiquity had rarely great comparative height, but the two great Pyramids of Gizeh and some temples of Mesopotamia were remarkable in this respect ; and in any comparison of interior heights the Roman imperial vaulted halls are important. Horizontal dimensions, however, were sometimes very great among the Egyptians, and also among the Romans.

The Great Pyramid of Gizeh in Egypt covers a square surface of about 754 feet on each side, but was about 770 feet square when the outside sheathing was complete. The second pyramid is about 700 feet square on the plan. These measurements are not to be compared with the horizontal measurements of most great buildings, because these pyramids are almost solid masses of stone, probably built around and upon a native rock, but in the main a cairn of piled blocks of limestone. The thirteen acres or more thus covered with a single mound of stone is to be compared with the six acres occupied by the Coliseum, itself considered a very massive building, although open to the sky and composed of an elliptical ring of seats supported on vaulting.

The great tombs and temples of the plains on the Euphrates and Tigris (see Mesopotamia, Architecture of) do not seem to have rivalled the Egyptian buildings in size, and their mass was evidently of unburnt brick, with a facing of hard brick, and only a substructure of stone. The restoration by Chipiez of the Chaldean temple in successive stages gives a base of 330 feet square for the actual nearly pyramidal mass.

Although the above-named solid piles of material affect no special architectural interest as towerlike masses, imposing by their easily felt height, their actual vertical dimensions are very great. The Great Pyramid of Gizeh may be described as 485 feet high to the apex of the sheathing, its present height to the irregular platform of the top being 451 feet. This is higher than the magnificent spire of Strasburg cathedral, of the modern church of S. Nicholas at Hamburg, of S. Stephen's at Vienna, or of the Landshut church in South Germany; and only two masonry buildings are known to reach a greater height. (See the table of heights below.)

The Roman thermæ covered vast tracts of ground; and although this was partly open, in race grounds and promenades, and partly covered by low porticoes and other one-story buildings of no great pretensions, there were also magnificent vaulted halls whose interior dimensions are unsurpassed. The thermæ of Diocletian have been described under Thermæ. The thermæ of Caracalla have a great central mass 390 feet broad by 740 feet long, without including the apselike projection of the circular caldarium. Much of this central mass was at least two stories in height, the ground story itself being of very great dimensions. The largest vaulted room was the tepidarium, 82 feet by 170 feet in its general dimensions, and with projecting transepts and apses. As for its height, the estimates differ; it may best be judged by comparison with the building next mentioned. Thus, the basilica of Maxentius and Constantine can be rather closely estimated as to its size. The span of its great hall between the walls was 82½ feet, but the projecting columns with the ressauts above them diminish the span of the actual vault to 76 feet. This vault gave to the hall an interior height of 125 feet and some inches, which is somewhat less than the height of the nave of Cologne cathedral, with this consideration, that Cologne cathedral is, like all Gothic buildings, light and slender, built of small separate stones, a somewhat elastic construction, the vaults held in place by the counter pressure of other vaults or of flying buttresses; while the Roman building is of prodigious massiveness and built so as to form a solid shell hardly capable of exercising a thrust upon its ponderous buttress piers.

The largest cupola in existence is that of the Pantheon in Rome, 143 feet span, and having a height from the pavement within to the oculus very nearly equal to the horizontal dimension.

The interior width of some large buildings in Europe should be compared with that of the basilica of Maxentius above. The naves of great churches are nearly as given below. The widths are in the clear between the piers: Beauvais cathedral, the nave, 42 feet 6 inches.

Albi cathedral in the south of France, 62 feet.

Gerona in northeastern Spain, 73 feet (much the largest Gothic nave. It was built long after the great French cathedrals, and was the special effort of a great builder, comparable for originality with the cupola of Florence cathedral).

S. Paul's cathedral, London, 49 feet.

S. Peter's church, Rome, 88 feet. (The style of these neoclassic churches excludes all attempts at great spans of vaulting; massiveness and a large proportion of supports to clear spaces is rather their purpose. The great width of the nave of S. Peter's is a part of its unapproached greatness of scale.)

It is curious how nearly the proportions of great classical, Gothic, and recent neoclassic buildings, when their transverse dimensions are considered, seem to have been inspired by the same idea of proportion. Thus the nave of the basilica of Constantine, given above, should be compared with S. Peter's church at Rome, 88 feet wide by 148 feet 6 inches high, and this with the loftiest of all Gothic naves, Beauvais, 42 feet 6 inches wide, 153 feet 6 inches high. These are the extremes; most Gothic churches would show greater width in proportion to their height.

Table of heights : —

Washington Monument, Washington, a plain obelisk . .	555 ft.
Cologne cathedral, two equal steeples to top of cross . .	511 ft.
Philadelphia " Public Buildings," or City Hall, to be . .	510 ft.
Hamburg, Germany, church of S. Nicholas . . .	475 ft. 6 in.
Strasburg Cathedral . .	465 ft.
Landshut, South Germany, church of S. Martin . .	462 ft.
Chimney of furnace on the River Mulde, opposite Freiburg, Saxony	453 ft.
Great Pyramid to top of existing platform	451 ft.
Vienna, church of S. Stephen, south tower . . .	450 ft.
Rome, S. Peter's church, including cross	435 ft.
Antwerp cathedral, north tower .	407 ft. 6 in.
Salisbury cathedral, central tower	400 ft.
Florence cathedral to top of lantern of cupola . . .	352 ft.
Chartres cathedral, south tower, completed in the thirteenth century	340 ft.

Buildings entirely of metal are not to be compared with those of masonry. Thus, the central tower of the cathedral of Rouen, of cast iron, is given as 488 feet, and the Tour Eiffel, commonly called La Tour de trois cent mètres, is commonly rated at 1000 feet.

Of modern American business buildings it is to be noted that they resemble in external appearance the massive fortress towers of the past, of which the famous one of Coucy is 180 feet 5 inches in height from the bottom of the paved ditch, while the modern buildings are light of structure, their real framework being of metal.

New York, the Park Row building
to top of angle towers . .   392 ft.
Same to top of level cornice . .   338 ft.
New York, The American Surety
Co.'s building to top of level
cornice .   .   .   . 308 ft.
Chicago, the Masonic Temple . 265 ft.

(It does not appear to which cornice this measurement is made.)

Finally, the aggregate dimensions of some very large groups of buildings, such as palaces, should be given. Thus, the palace of the Vatican, at Rome, has an extreme length from north to south of 1392 feet. This includes the whole façade on the Vialone di Belvedere, along which visitors pass to enter the museum. Extreme width from east to west, including the high buildings about the court of S. Damaso, 670 feet, the southernmost of the two great courts, 211 by 488 in the clear. It is impossible to measure along any axis because of the irregularity of the plan ; the perimeter may be estimated at 4292 feet.

The Louvre at Paris : the front on the Seine, east and west in general direction, 1891 feet, and that on the Rue de Rivoli about the same. Perimeter, as if the Tuileries were still in place between the Pavillon Marsan and the Pavillon de Flore, 4974 feet. The length along the axis of the great galleries and through the different pavilions, as if the whole building were extended in a single line, 8475 feet, or much more than a mile and a half. The length of the colonnade of the east front, 540 feet ; the Great Court as fixed in the sixteenth century, about 400 feet square, inside dimensions.

Windsor Castle : length in one line from the Curfew Tower to the angle at the east terrace, nearly east and west, about 1460 feet ; perimeter, 3670 feet.

The Trocadéro Palace at Paris, opposite the Champ de Mars. measured in a straight line northeast and southwest, from out to out of the curving wings, 1452 feet. Measured along the convex curve of the northwestern wall, 1782 feet.

The Capitol at Washington : length north and south, 751 feet. The building covers about three acres, or less than a quarter of the surface covered by the Great Pyramid.

S. Peter's Church at Rome : from outside the narthex, nearly westward, to outside the principal apse, 712 feet.

Westminster Palace, London, including House of Parliament and Westminster Hall : total length on the river, including the Speaker's residence and Blackrod's residence, 885 feet. There are eight courts surrounded by buildings which are generally five or six stories high. — R. S.

SIZE (v.). To apply size or sizing, as in preparation for painting and gilding.

SIZE (n.). Any glutinous covering matter

applied to the surface of plaster and sometimes to wood as a preparation for painting, or more especially for gilding with gold leaf. The purpose of it is to provide a perfectly uniform surface and one as little porous as possible.

Gold Size. Such a glutinous application (see Size ; Sizing) as is found convenient for the subsequent application of gold leaf in gilding. This is applied to the plaster or wood, and allowed to dry, partly, before the leaf is put on.

SIZE DOWN. To diminish, continually and regularly, the size of members of a series. Thus, slates are sized down from the eaves to the ridge, in order to increase the apparent extent of the sloping roof, and to add a picturesque charm to it.

SIZING. *A.* The same as Size (n.).

B. The application of such sizing in sense *A.*

SKELETON. A frame of wood or iron without the covering.

SKELETON CONSTRUCTION. That which depends for its strength upon a skeleton ; especially, in modern building beginning about 1885, a manner of building in which, while the exterior is of masonry, the whole structure is of iron or steel which supports the exterior walls as well as the roof. It is common to carry these exterior walls by means of cantilevers upon which one story or two stories of such walls are built up at a time ; so that the structure may be completed and the roof put on before any part of the walls are in place. The walls may even be built in the tenth story before those of the eighth and ninth stories are completed, and so on. (See Iron Construction ; Office Building.)

SKEW VAULT OR ARCH: THE TRIANGLE IN THE PLAN CORRESPONDS TO THE ELABORATE HORIZONTAL MOULDINGS IN THE VIEW, WHICH ARE THE CORBELLING TO CARRY THE WALL ABOVE.

SKEW (adj.). Set sloping ; inclined in any direction, but most commonly in a horizontal plane. A Skew Arch or Skew Vault is an arched opening or passage the axis of which makes an oblique angle with the face of the wall (see Skew Arch, under Arch). The term Skew Back, below, is made up in the same way from the obsolete term "back."

SKEW. Any member cut or set so as to present a sloping surface ; especially for other necessary parts of a structure to butt against, as in a gable or the abutment of an arch.

SKEW BACK. That portion of an abutment which is arranged to receive the thrust of

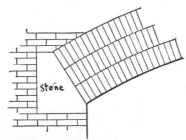

SKEWBACK OF STONE IN ONE BLOCK, FOR A
BRICK ARCH IN THREE ROLLOCKS.

a segmental or flat arch, having an inclined face corresponding with the adjoining voussoir.

SKEW CORBEL. Same as Kneeler, *A* ; but especially one which projects considerably beyond the side wall. Two such stones, one on each side, widen the gable effectively at its base ; and the corbel-like projections serve as stops for the eave gutters or wall cornices.

SKEW PUTT. Same as Skew Corbel.

SKIFFLING. (See Knobbing.)

SKIM COAT. (See Skimming.)

SKIMMING. The process of finishing the surface of plastering with a thin coat of lime and sand putty, or plaster of Paris. Also the coat so produced.

SKIRREH. In surveyors' work, a cord wound upon a reel or prepared in another way, for convenient delivery and recovery, used in laying out foundations, trenches, and the like. (See Surveying.)

SKIRT. An apron-piece or border, as the moulded piece under a window stool, or the plinth board or mopboard of a room or passage, which last is in the United States called base or baseboard.

SKIRTING; SKIRTING BOARD. Same as Base, *C*. (See also Skirt.)

SKYLIGHT. A glazed aperture in a roof, whether a simple glazed frame set in the plane of a roof, or a structure surmounting a roof with upright or sloping sides and perhaps an independent roof ; the entire structure consisting wholly, or in large part, of glazed frames. In its more elaborate forms, a skylight may be constructed as a Lantern (which see), or may have the semblance of a dormer window from

which it is sometimes hardly to be distinguished. The term is, however, only applicable to such lights when overhead, *i.e.* located decidedly above, rather than at the sides of, the space immediately covered by the roof, although, perhaps, extending considerably down the lateral slopes of the roof. The frame is either of wood, or, preferably, of metal, braced or tied with iron rods, if of large size, the metal sash bars being shaped with gutters to carry off the water of condensation, and glazed with sheets of fluted or rough plate glass, varying from 12×48 inches and $\frac{3}{16}$ of an inch thick to 20×100 inches and $\frac{6}{16}$ of an inch thick ; if ordinary double thick glass is used, the sheets are from 9 to 15 inches wide, and from 16 to 30 inches long. In metal sash bars or muntins these sheets are set without putty. Skylights are often provided with ventilators arranged to be opened or closed by cords from below, and a flat decorated inner skylight is frequently placed beneath the outer skylight in a ceiling panel, when it is desired to make this feature an element in an architectural composition as seen from beneath. Sometimes, as in the covering of interior courts, winter gardens, exposition buildings, conservatories, marquises or canopies, and horticultural buildings, the entire roof is a skylight, and is emphasized as an especial architectural feature, the frame in such cases being of iron or wood. (See Greenhouse.) Occasionally smaller skylights are in the form of glazed scuttles arranged to be opened for access to the roof. — H. VAN BRUNT.

Double Skylight. One in which a lower and usually horizontal glazed frame completes the ceiling of a room or gallery, while the space between this and the skylight proper serves for ventilation.

Raised Skylight. One in which a curb or coaming of some height raises the skylight proper above the level of the roof.

SKY LINE. The upper outline or silhouette of a building as seen against the sky.

SKY SCRAPER. A name derisively applied, but generally accepted, referring to one of the tall many-storied office buildings which have become characteristic in the large cities of the United States.

SLAB. Any piece of material of considerable breadth and little thickness as compared to its length ; more specifically, an outside plank as sawn from a log, having one rounded side and consequently of very unequal thickness.

Except in the last sense the term is more frequently applied to stone than to other materials. (See the following titles.)

SLAB BOARDING. A rough covering with slabs as in some rural sheds.

SLAB DASHING. Rough casting a wall with coarse mortar and pebbles. (Also written Slap Dashing.)

SLAB HOUSE. A house built of wooden slabs or rough-hewn planks. Especially applied to houses so made by the Indians of northern California and the Northwest coast. Planks were split out of cedar or other wood with elk-horn and wooden wedges driven by stone mallets. They were reduced to any required thickness by adzing. In size the planks were something extraordinary at times, reaching such dimensions as 4½ by 24 feet. Some tribes built houses with a roof of one slope while others put up a ridge or double ridge and made two or more slopes. Several families lived under one roof, and often a whole community had but a single house. The dimensions were sometimes as great as 75 feet long by 40 wide and 15 high. The rafters were supported by heavy posts set in the ground, and the planks were tied horizontally on the sides between upright posts, while those on the roof ran with the slope and were grooved and overlapping. The family apartments were separated by partitions about 2 or 3 feet high and often higher. North of the Strait of S. Juan de Fuca the slab houses become even more massive, with carving on the posts in front and sometimes within. The totem posts set up in front are elaborately carved. (See Assembly House; Communal Dwelling; Totem Post.)
— F. S. DELLENBAUGH.

SLAB PLASTERING. Coarse plastering such as was used in filling between the beams on the exterior of half-timbered houses in England. Also Slap Plastering.

SLAG ROOFING. A plastic material made by mixing coal tar, asphalt, or a similar material with finely divided slag and sometimes other hard material. This, when properly applied, serves well for roofs of very low pitch.

SLAG WOOL. Same as Mineral Wool.

SLAP DASHING. Same as Slab Dashing.

SLAP PLASTERING. Same as Slab Plastering.

SLAT. A flat and thin board or strip, especially if relatively narrow, usually of wood.

Rolling Slat. A slat in a Shutter, or a Blind in sense *A*, which with the others in the same panel is fitted into the frame by pivots, and secured loosely to a rod, so that all the slats are adjustable together.

SLATE. In building, Roofing Slate; that is to say, a fissile variety of argillite used mainly for roofing and, in more solid masses, for sinks, floor tiles, mantels, and the like.
— G. P. M.

Roofing Slate is obtained by splitting the larger masses into thin slabs, which are then trimmed to certain standard dimensions. It was formerly divided in Great Britain into regular sizes known by arbitrary names. The sizes most often used are Countess, 10″ × 20″, and Duchess, 12″ × 24″. Other sizes are given as follows : —

Double, 7″ × 13″.   Empress, 16″ × 26″.
Lady, 8″ × 16″.   Imperial, 24″ × 30″.
Viscountess, 9″ × 18″.   Rag, 24″ × 36″.
Marchioness, 11″ × 22″. Queen, 24″ × 36″.
Princess, 14″ × 24″.

It does not appear that these terms have ever been common in the United States. It is more usual to specify the sizes, which do not vary greatly. Thus, 8″ × 16″ is a good size for smaller surfaces, and 10″ × 20″ for large slopes of a roof. The varieties of slate are very great, and the preference for this or that quarry has varied from time to time, partly according to the colour in vogue or called for by the building in question, and partly by the favour shown to a particular surface with or without gloss and the like. Purple, green, and red are the common colours, and each of these colours is often very agreeable; moreover, it has been found easy to make somewhat effective patterns of their combination. On the other hand, the very darkest slate, that which approaches black, is preferred by many architects, and some of the best qualities of slate are of this colour.
— R. S.

Riley, *Building Construction for Beginners*, 1899.

SLATE BOARDING. The covering of walls with slate, as if with boards or shingles.

SLATING. The applying of roofing slate to the sheathing boards or battens or strips which are nailed to the rafters. As the slating must overlap for a definite proportion of its length, the distance apart of the places for nailing can be determined beforehand. Thus, if slates 24 inches long are used, and if it be required that each slate overlap the one below it for 14 inches (leaving 10 inches "to the weather" in each course) then the rows of nails will be 10 inches apart. Nails may be driven near the centre of each slate or near the head; it is rare that both methods are used, as two nails to a slate of ordinary size is considered sufficient. Nails should be of copper or be in some way protected by a non-corrosive metal composition, and the holes through which they are driven must be made in advance, which is done usually by the sharp point of the slater's hammer.

SLAUGHTER HOUSE. A place, building, or group of buildings intended for the slaughter of domestic animals used for food.

The object of the public abattoir, or highly organized slaughter house, is to do away with the nuisance and evils of scattered private slaughtering places. In ancient Rome, under the emperors, a guild of butchers existed who were privileged to do slaughtering in special buildings. In modern times, the organized public abattoir originated in the beginning of the nineteenth century. Napoleon I., recognizing the sanitary, commercial, and economical advantages of centralized public abattoirs, authorized in 1810 their construction in the suburbs of Paris, and decreed that private slaughter houses be forbidden. In 1815 five public slaughter houses were opened, covering thirty-eight acres of ground. Since then large cities and many of the smaller ones have followed the example of Paris. In the United States large abattoirs exist, particularly in the large Western cities, which are centres of the cattle market. Some of these are immense establishments, fitted up with elaborate machinery for rapid and humane killing of a large number of animals, and with well arranged auxiliary buildings intended for the sanitary and commercial disposal of the offal incident to slaughtering.

In Europe municipal abattoirs are the rule; in the United States many abattoirs are built by butchers' associations. Public abattoirs, erected by a city, offer the best solution of the problem of the sanitary control of the meat supply; cleanliness and sanitation can be enforced, and the slaughter stands or compartments rented to butchers form a source of revenue to the city. Abattoirs must be located in the outskirts of a city; good facilities for the transportation of the cattle, by rail or by water, and by the country roads, where the adjoining rural districts are devoted to cattle raising, are required. For the conglomeration of buildings a large area of suitable ground is required, and future extension must be considered in the original lay-out. Markets for cattle to be slaughtered are best placed adjacent to abattoirs, for by combining the cattle market with the slaughter house, the sanitary inspection of the meat supply of a city is rendered more concentrated and efficient.

A public abattoir consists of many buildings, namely stables, large sheds and pens for the animals to be slaughtered, subdivided again into stables for oxen, calves, sheep, and pigs; separate slaughtering houses for each of the animals named; covered yards for dressing of carcasses; buildings for diseased or suspected animals, for storage of fodder for the animals, for cold storage of meat, for the cleaning of entrails, and for the commercial utilization of the offal (fat-rendering and bone-boiling establishments); an administration building, with offices, rooms for the butchers, for the sanitary inspectors and veterinary surgeons, laboratories for the microscopical examination of the pork; toilet rooms, bath houses, restaurants, etc.; finally, a boiler and engine house, with pumps, dynamos, and refrigerating plant. To this is sometimes added a wholesale meat market (see Market). The generally low-roofed one-story stable structures present no features differing from rural cattle stables (see Stable). The roadways between the sheds and all open yards must be well

paved with durable pavement (like the Belgian block pavement) and must have good surface water drainage.

There are two types of arrangement of the halls for slaughtering: in one there is only a large common slaughtering hall; in the other two rows of smaller compartments are arranged, one on each side of a central aisle, each compartment being rented to one or several butchers. The first-named type facilitates official inspection. The outer walls of the slaughter houses may be of brick, or of iron with glass roofs and sides. It is essential that the inside walls, to a height of at least five feet, should be made impervious, so that dried blood and scraps of flesh adhering to them can be removed by means of warm water. Walls may be faced with glazed brick, or be of brick coated with asphalted varnish; the woodwork, if there is any, is treated in a similar manner. Floors should also be impervious, hard, durable, and not too smooth or slippery. Asphalted and concrete floors have proved to be but partly successful, for asphalt is apt to become soft in summer time, and cement floors crack, or become chipped or broken by the axe of the butcher. A good pavement is formed of two layers of hard-burnt brick laid on edge in cement or concrete. Many butchers prefer a wooden floor, of heavy planks, of Georgia pine, thoroughly calked at the joints in the manner of a ship's deck; but as this becomes splintered by the blows of the axe in slaughtering or dividing up the killed animals, it is necessary to put down two layers of plank. The upper parts of the walls and the ceilings should be frequently whitewashed. The sanitary features of a slaughtering house include a very ample and liberal supply of cold water, for the watering and washing of the cattle, for floor washing, fire protection, etc.; a supply of hot water; proper sewerage and floor drainage; sometimes a chemical purification of the sewage, slaughtering waste, and blood; plenty of ventilation; good lighting and special arrangements for removal of offal, animal manure, blood, fat, entrails; well-paved yards and streets, etc.; modern German abattoirs are frequently provided with a rain bath (which see under Bath) for the butchers' employees. The interior equipment of slaughter houses comprises hoisting machinery, cranes, truck, and iron tanks on wheels for the manure and hides; barrels for the blood; weighing scales; hydrants for watering and flushing; also a refrigerating plant. The noxious vapours and gases arising from the pans and kettles should be passed through condensing tanks and then under the fires of the boiler, and discharged through the main chimney stack of the boiler house. The disposal of the manure from stable yards, cattle pens, hog pens, etc., should be carried out with regularity; the streets and boulevards of the abattoir must be swept and washed, and buildings in which diseased animals are kept require disinfection.

Oscar Schwarz, M.D., *Bau, Einrichtung und Betrieb öffentlicher Schlachthäuser und Viehhöfe*, Second Edition, Berlin, 1898 ; *Handbuch der Architektur*, Part IV., Vol. III., 2 ; *Gebäude für Lebensmittel-Versorgung*, Second Edition ; Dr. Theo. Weyl, *Handbuch der Hygiene*, Vol. VI., Part B ; G. Osthoff, *Markthallen und Schlachthäuser ;* Stevenson and Murphy, *Treatise on Hygiene and Public Health ;* article on Slaughter Houses, by E. W. Hope, Vol. I., 1892, Fifth and Sixth Annual Reports of Massachusetts State Board of Health. Also the following papers contained in the Transactions American Public Health Association, viz. : Vol. II., 1876, Dr. Janes, on Abattoirs, H. G. Crowell, on Abattoirs ; Vol. VI., 1880, Dr. James, "Abattoirs," Dr. G. Devron, "Abattoirs " ; Vol. XV., 1889, Dr. Salmon, "Meat Inspection " ; Vol. XXII., 1896, Dr. Bryce, "Municipal Meat Inspection " ; Vol. XXIII., 1897, Dr. Pearson, "Meat Inspection." Also *Zeitschrift des österr. Ingenieur und Architekten-Vereines*, Vol. LII., No. 28, article by G. Witz on "Municipal Abattoirs."

W. P. GERHARD.

SLEEPER. A piece of timber laid directly on the ground as a base or support for a superstructure, especially to carry the flooring of a cellar or ground story. Sleepers are taken from timber which resists decay : in the United States, locust or chestnut.

SLEEPING ROOM. A bedroom.

SLIDING POLE. (See Engine House.)

SLIP (I.). *A.* A narrow passage, as between two buildings.

B. A bench or open pew in a church.

SLIP (II.). A small and slender strip, as of wood. The more usual term in the United States is strip ; thus Parting Slip (A. P. S. ; Riley) is always called in the United States Parting Strip. (Compare Lath.)

SLIP PIECE. A strip of wood attached to a sliding member to serve as a wearing surface ; specifically, a strip playing in a dovetailed groove to hold the object in place.

SLIP SILL. A sill no longer than the distance between the jambs of an opening, so that it can be set in the aperture after the walls are built, instead of extending into the wall on each side beneath the jamb.

SLODTZ, ANTOINE SÉBASTIEN. (See Slodtz, Michel.)

SLODTZ, MICHEL (MICHEL-ANGE) ; sculptor ; b. 1705 ; d. 1764.

He was a son of Sébastien Slodtz, sculptor, and was of Flemish origin. He studied long in Rome. There is a statue of S. Bruno by him at S. Peter's, and a monument to the Marquis Capponi in the church of S. Giovanni dei Fiorentini (Rome). Returning to France, he made the two monuments of the cardinals of Auvergne, at Vienne (Isère). In 1747 he returned to Paris, and in 1750 made the monument to the Abbé Lanquet de Gerzy at the church of S. Sulpice, Paris, his chief work, and decorated the Chapelle de la

Vierge. He was assisted in much of his work by his brother, Antoine Sébastien Slodtz.

Gonse, *Sculpture française ;* Seubert, *Künstlerlexicon.*

SLODTZ, SÉBASTIEN. (See Slodtz, Michel.)

SLOPE OF A ROOF. (See Pitch.)

SLOW – BURNING CONSTRUCTION. Any construction designed to diminish as far as possible the facility of ignition, and to hinder the spread of fire, while consisting entirely or in large part of combustible material.

This system, sometimes called Mill Construction, has been developed by the Factory Mutual Fire Insurance Companies of New England, with a view to bringing the construction of cotton and woollen factories, paper mills, and metalworking establishments to the safest conditions which can be made consistent with the use of wood ; also to give stability and strength coupled with adequate light, air, and ventilation ; and finally, at the least cost by the unit of the square foot of occupied floor, giving due regard to the respective uses to which the building is to be put. It has been a gradual development of many years, proceeding wholly from the interior motive or use of the property, without regard to architectural display. The customary method of construction at the present day is as follows : —

The basement floor is laid on well-drained ground covered with a tar or asphalt concrete in which heavy timbers may be placed, overlaid with plank and board floors without danger of decay. Cement concrete, being hygroscopic, does not serve the purpose, but permits or promotes the rapid decay of the wood laid in or upon it. Asphalt concrete is also a non-conductor of heat and is warm to the feet ; cement or stone floors keep the feet cold, hence the common use of wooden clogs or soles in the stone-floored weaving sheds of foreign countries.

The superstructure may be of one or more stories in height. The modern textile mill seldom exceeds three stories for the preparation and the spinning of the stock, one story for weaving. The modern machine shop is more often one story in height than in excess. There is a moderate relative difference in the cost by the unit of the square foot of floor between the one-story or many-storied building, a building of two or three stories in height being on the whole cheapest.

The structure consists preferably of brick walls with the maximum of window space, the top of the window being carried between the timbers flush with the underside of the floor or roof so as to give the maximum of top light. Within these walls heavy timbers are carried 8 feet or 10 feet 4 inches or rarely 11 feet on centres, preferably 22 feet span from wall to post and from post to post ; the sizes of timber vary according to the proposed weight of machinery and stock to be placed upon them, the weights in a textile factory rarely exceeding seventy pounds to the square foot at any point. Upon these timbers are laid planks grooved and splined, of not less than 3 inches in thickness, on 8-foot spans, — 4 inches or more on the wider spans, — covered first with rosin-sized paper or a fire retardent or waterproof material, then a top floor, now in the North customarily of birch or maple.

The spaces between the timbers may be sheathed solid or close upon the planks, or may be in some instances protected by sheet metal, Air Cell Asbestos Board, or Sackett Wall Board, which retard ignition ; or it may be covered with a porous wash or water paint. Beams should never be oil painted under less than three years, lest they should be exposed to dry rot.

The roof, of one-half inch pitch, is constructed in the same manner, covered usually with composition roofing of the best kind. In certain cases, like the roofs over the Fourdrinier machines in paper mills, where there is a very great condensation of moisture, a coating of 1-inch mortar is sometimes placed between the plank and the outer boarding of the roof, and the ceiling is sheathed solid within, making a roof of at least 6 inches in thickness, which is sufficiently proof against cold when properly ventilated to be free from condensation. Varnish of the common kinds is never used on any part of these wooden surfaces, on account of the extreme hazard of a fire passing rapidly over it.

It is not held that this construction of timber and plank is free from the danger of fire, unless suitably guarded according to the degree of hazard of the contents within. This solid method of construction is, however, free of the customary danger which affects hollow walls, hollow floors, and hollow roofs, since in the wooden flues of what is sometimes called " combustible architecture " fire may pass from cellar to attic fully protected from water.

In the mill of slow-burning construction automatic sprinklers placed between the timbers sweep the ceiling with water on both sides of the timbers whenever called upon by the occurrence of a fire. Hose streams thrown from either side may also sweep the fire completely from the ceilings between the timbers.

The next most important point in slow-burning construction in a building of many stories is that each floor shall be absolutely cut off from every other floor by avoiding all open ways. Staircases are placed in towers, preferably outside the main building ; if within, cut off by fire walls, the doorways being protected by suitable fire doors made of wood encased in tin, with lock joints, the nail heads being covered. Belts or ropes for driving the machinery are also carried in separate towers without openings into the main mill. The sanitary and other appliances are also constructed in separate towers without any open way from floor to floor ; adequate fire escapes being attached at suitable points outside the mill.

This factory floor has never been burned through by any fire occurring in the working department of the factory. All fires that have passed from one story to another have either passed through belt holes or by open passageways. In two instances of storage in large quantity, where stock has taken fire at the bottom of the pile, the heavy floor has been burned through.

The tendency in modern days has been, especially in cotton mills, to adjust the size of the floor to certain elements of the mechanism. The modern cotton factory is usually 126 to 128 feet in width by any suitable length, that width giving free play to the mule spinning machine of the size that will give full employment without overwork to one spinner. In other words, the plans for placing the machinery are made before the floor spaces are laid out.

Another method of construction is to put up a self-sustaining timber frame, the outer post being recessed in a pilastered wall wholly free of any fixed connection with the wall itself, a band or tie being placed across the recess in the pilaster and across the post but not attached to the post itself. Every post is given its own support on its own separate pier, the foundation of the wall, which may be very light, being separated. In this way, if there is any shrinkage or settling of the wall, which is apt to occur, especially in high buildings, it does not throw the alignment of the timbers out of level. The adjustment of shafting therefore takes much less time and is much more certain. In this method of construction the substance of the wall may be almost veneer, the greater part consisting of windows.

It is now customary to glaze these windows with fine ribbed glass in true curves, inverse and obverse, twenty-one ribs to the inch, ribs set vertically. This type of glass diffuses the light throughout a very wide building, giving daylight free of shadows — a most important factor, especially in weaving. When the inside work is dusty, the ribs are placed outside. Where the outer side of the window is exposed to smoke or soot, the ribs are placed inwardly. In special places prismatic glass is used in place of the factory ribbed glass.

After this building is constructed, the greatest care is taken not to fill it up with combustible shelves, wooden partitions, or other dangerous elements in construction. Incombustible material is chosen as far as possible for these purposes. Closets, cupboards, and concealed spaces are avoided to the utmost, the purpose being that there be no place either in roof, floor, or wall, or within the building, in which fire may be protected from water, or in which vermin of any kind can lurk.

What is called slow-burning construction should never be adopted without due regard being given to all the principles of mill construction: the separation of each floor from every other, the avoidance of open ways, the avoidance of varnish upon inside finish, of combustible shelving, and yet more without giving full regard to adequate apparatus for the extinction of fires. Wood will furnish material for fire, however disposed. All that is claimed for slow-burning construction of wood is that its adoption gives readier opportunity to extinguish a fire than any other at a low cost.

Whether or not this method of construction is better or worse than the modern steel construction, depends upon many conditions which cannot be dealt with in this treatise. Unless the steel is protected adequately from the heat generated in the ignition of the contents of the building, the complete destruction of the steel frame building may not follow, but so long as it stands, it serves to hold the contents under conditions which will assure their complete, or nearly complete, destruction by fire. Slow-burning mill construction in its place and for the purposes for which it has been developed, has proved to be cheaper, safer, and better than any form of so-called fireproof mill yet invented. The losses by fire on many hundred million dollars' worth of factories constructed on these rules, and fully protected with apparatus for extinguishing fires, have, for five years, October, 1895, to November, 1900, inclusive, been less than four cents per annum on each hundred dollars of risks carried by the Senior Factory Mutual Fire Insurance Companies, or less than twenty cents per one hundred dollars — for five years' insurance on over $600,000,000 worth of so-called "special hazards."

— EDWARD ATKINSON.

SLUSH (v.). In masonry, to throw mortar on top of a course to form a bed for the next course. Slushed work permits bricks to be laid dry on such a bed in the interior of a wall, and makes inferior work. Shoved work requires each brick in the interior of a wall to be surrounded with mortar so as to avoid any dry or open joints. (See Shove Joint, under Joint.)

SLUTER, CLAUX (NICOLAS); sculptor (*imagier*); d. 1404 or 1405.

Philippe le Hardi, Duke of Burgundy, founded the Chartreuse of Champmol at the gates of Dijon (Côte-d'Or, France), in 1383. To build and decorate this monastery, with its church and his own monument, he called together many of the best architects and sculptors of his time, chief of whom were André de Dammartin (see Dammartin, A. de), Jean de Marville (see Marville, J. de), and Claux Sluter. Jean de

Marville directed the sculptors until his death in 1389, when Claux Sluter of the Comté d'Hollande took control. The earliest of the sculptures of the Chartreuse are the figures on the portal of the church. Of these the Madonna is probably by de Marville, but the splendid statues of Philippe le Hardi, his Duchess Marguerite de Flandre, S. Jean and S. Marguerite are by Sluter. Sluter's most characteristic work is the so-called *Puits de Moïse* (Well of Moses). This was intended to be the base of a Calvary (crucifixion group) which stood in the cloister of the Chartreuse. The design of this work is by Sluter. · He was assisted by his nephew, Claux de Werwe (see Claux de Werwe), who in 1398 began to take control of the work. The great monument of Philippe le Hardi in the museum at Dijon was undoubtedly designed and begun by Sluter, but the sculpture itself, especially the famous *pleurants* (mourners) about the base, is the work of Claux de Werwe. In 1404 Sluter retired to the Abbey of S. Étienne at Dijon, where he died.

Gonse, *Sculpture française;* Gonse, *L'Art gothique;* Chabeuf, *Dijon Monuments et Souvenirs;* Brownell, *French Art;* Marquis L. De Laborde, *Les Ducs de Bourgogne.*

SLYPE. Same as Slip (I., *A*); written in this form, which it retains from the fifteenth century, it is used in ecclesiological writing.

SMIDS, MICHAEL MATTHIAS; architect; b. July 11, 1626 (in Rotterdam); d. July 24, 1692 (in Berlin).

He was court architect of the great Elector Friedrich Wilhelm, and rebuilt the Marstallgebäude (Berlin) about 1666.

Borrmann, *Denkmäler von Berlin.*

SMILIS; sculptor and architect.

Smilis was probably from Ægina, Greece. He flourished in the sixth century B.C., and was associated with Theodorus (see Theodorus) and Rhoecuss in the construction of the labyrinth at Lemnos and the Temple of Hera at Samos. He made the statue of Hera in that temple, and a group of the *Hours*, which was preserved in the Heraion at Olympia.

Collignon, *Histoire de la Sculpture grecque.*

SMIRKE, SIR ROBERT; architect; b. 1781; d. April 18, 1867.

In 1796 he entered the office of Sir John Soane (see Soane, Sir J.), then occupied with the building of the Bank of England, and in the same year became a student of the Royal Academy. In 1799 he won the gold medal for design. He visited Athens in 1803, while Lord Elgin was removing the sculpture from the Parthenon. He also visited Sicily and made drawings of the architectural remains there. Smirke was employed on the Mint, London, in 1809; and in 1845 was placed by Sir Robert Peel on the commission for London improvements. He built

Lowther Castle and Eastnor Castle, and in 1808 rebuilt Covent Garden Theatre (burned in 1858). One of his most important works is the main façade of the British Museum (London).

Edward Smirke, *Memoirs of Sir Robert Smirke; Arch. Pub. Soc. Dictionary.*

SMIRKE, SYDNEY; architect; b. 1799; d. Dec. 8, 1877.

A brother of Sir Robert Smirke (see Smirke, Sir R.). In 1828 he was clerk of the works at S. James's Palace (London). At the British Museum, about 1855–1857, he designed and built the great circular reading room.

Arch. Pub. Soc. Dictionary.

SMOKE EXTRACTOR. Any device, as a hood or ventilator at the top of a chimney, by which an upward draught is maintained or accelerated.

SMOKE TOWER. Any high construction, more important than a chimney stack, used to convey smoke from a building to the outer air, as in some churches.

SMOKE VENT. An opening in a roof, generally of some primitive dwelling or hut, by which smoke may escape.

SMOKING ROOM. An apartment set aside for the use of smokers.

SNACKET. In Scotland, a latch, hasp, or catch for a door.

SNECK. A latch; local British; the term applied especially to one of several ancient forms of thumb latch.

SNECK (v., I.). To fasten with a sneck.

SNECK (v., II.). To dress stone roughly. (See Snecked Rubble, under Rubble.)

SNOW BOARD. A continuous board secured at the foot of a roof slope to serve as a snow guard.

SNOW GUARD. Any device intended to prevent snow from sliding off a sloping roof; especially, in the United States, one of several patented contrivances intended to be arranged in successive regular rows across the slope, commonly formed of a loop of wire.

SNOW HOUSE. A habitation built of snow. (See Iglugeak.) — F. S. D.

SOAKER. In Great Britain, a piece of metal used in flashing, each piece being of the size of one of the slates or tiles of the roofing, and the soaker being laid with the slates or tiles in their courses. In the United States, called step flashing.

SOANE, SIR JOHN; architect; b. Sept. 10, 1753; d. Jan. 20, 1837.

His name was originally Swan. He changed it to Soan, and afterward to Soane. He was the son of a bricklayer, and in 1768 entered the service of the younger George Dance (see Dance, G., II.). He afterward studied with Henry Holland (see Holland), and at the schools of the Royal Academy. In 1776 he won the gold medal of the Academy, and a travelling stipend which enabled him to spend three years in Italy. From 1788 to 1833 he held the office of architect and surveyor to the Bank of England. The façade of this building is one of the best of his works. Between 1791 and 1794 he was clerk of the works at S. James's palace, the Houses of Parliament, and other public buildings in Westminster, and in 1807, clerk of the works at the Royal Hospital, Chelsea. In 1802, Soane was made Royal Academician, and in 1806, professor of architecture at the Royal Academy. In 1836 he built the State Paper Office, destroyed in 1862. His house in Lincoln's Inn Fields and his large collection of art treasures were left to the nation, and constituted by act of parliament the Soane Museum.

Fergusson, *History of the Modern Styles of Architecture;* Stephen-Lee, *Dictionary of National Biography.*

SOAPSTONE. A soft stone having a soapy feeling, composed largely of foliated talc, or steatite, and used in making sinks, stationary washtubs, etc. (See, also, Potstone.)

— G. P. M.

SOCIETIES OF ARCHITECTS. (That is, composed wholly or in part of architects.)

The Academies of Europe, which have existed in great numbers for three hundred years, were known under various names signifying devotion to different departments of fine arts, many of them including architecture. These Academies of Fine Art were sometimes organized only to afford instruction, while others were associations of professional artists of different classes. It will be endeavoured in this list to include only those in which professional architects were associated. Many societies are composed of architects and engineers, like most of those in Germany and Austria-Hungary, and others are societies of architects and archæologists. There are also many societies of archæology, composed mostly of architects; but in most archæological societies, such as exist in nearly every European city of any consequence, and a few in America, the influence of architects does not predominate. As compared with them, the number of purely architectural societies is very limited. The fine art societies, first referred to herein in each country, are those in which professional architects are believed to have had administrative functions. Then will follow, more specifically, architectural societies in each, most of which are of comparatively modern origin.

Austria-Hungary. An Academy of Painting, Sculpture, and Architecture was founded in Vienna in 1705. There are also Societies of Architects and Engineers in Vienna and Prague, and in Budapest, where there has recently been a great revival of architecture.

Belgium. The Central Society of Architecture of Belgium was founded at Brussels in 1872. Its monthly publication is called *L'Émulation.* It has a defensive league like that of the Central Society of Architects of France.

Canada, Dominion of. There is a Quebec Institute of Architects, which has recently been instrumental in having a law passed by the Parliament of the Province of Quebec requiring the official registration of architects, somewhat similar to that now in force for examining and licensing architects in the state of Illinois. The headquarters of the Institute is at Montreal. There is also an Institute of Architects in the Province of Ontario, with headquarters at Toronto.

France. The Academy of Architecture was founded in 1671, and existed down to the breaking out of the revolution of 1789. In 1819 the now existing Academy of Fine Arts was definitely founded. This is one of the five great divisions of the Institute of France; it consists of the five sections : painting, sculpture, architecture, engraving, and music, and is composed of forty members. Its chief duty toward the art or profession of architecture is in directing certain competitions, giving the prizes, including the great Prize of Rome (which see), and nominating candidates for professorships and the like. The Academy of France at Rome, which also was founded in the seventeenth century, still continues to occupy the Villa Medicis, which it has held ever since the beginning of the present century ; but this is rather a school than a society.

Of distinctively architectural societies in France, the Central Society of Architects, founded in 1840, takes the lead. It not only holds regular meetings, but periodical congresses, to which all the Architects of France and visitors from other countries are invited. Its first bulletin was issued in 1851, and its *Annales* in 1875, since which time it has conducted the congresses just mentioned. It now has 500 members. The congresses have been held annually since 1873. Its publications are : *Manual of the Laws of Buildings* (Paris, 1878–1881), and *Price Lists Applicable to Buildings* (1883–1893). Under its auspices was established in 1884 the Architects' Mutual Defense Association, of which there are 340 members, a sort of mutual assurance against the rigorous provisions of the French laws concerning the personal responsibilities of architects. The National Society of Architects of France was founded in 1872, and in 1891 it was changed to the Professional Union of the Architects of the Department of the Seine, with 150 members. It publishes a fortnightly journal called *The Architect.* A society was organized in 1877 called the Friendly Associ-

ation of Architects Honoured by the Government, comprising those who had obtained the diploma of "Architect" from the National School and those who had obtained the Grand Prize. There are 230 members. It is a sort of *Corps d'Élite* of French architects, and publishes an annual bulletin. The *Union Syndicale* of French architects was formed in 1890, composed of architects, inspectors, designers, decorators, and the better class of operatives, comprising the independents or free lances of the profession. There are thirty-two local societies in France, among which is the Academic Society of Architecture of Lyons, the oldest of all existing French Societies, and which stands first in importance, founded Dec. 18, 1829. Connected with it is a society of assistants and students called the Architectural Union of Lyons. Of other departmental societies are the Provincial Society of Architects of the North of France, The Provincial Society of Architects of the Southeast of France, and a provincial society with headquarters at Lyons, which comprises the members of twenty local societies. (See Architect, The, in France, for the laws regulating the practice of the profession, and col. 140 for French societies.)

Germany. The Royal Academy of Arts was founded in Berlin by Frederick I. of Prussia in 1699. After the failure of the academies that had been established in Munich in 1759 and 1770, the present Royal Munich Academy was established by Joseph I. of Bavaria in 1808. The following German cities have mixed societies : Berlin, Architects and Engineers, founded 1857 ; Constance, Architects and Builders, founded 1881 ; Dresden, Architects and Engineers ; Hanover, Architects and Engineers ; Munich, Architects and Engineers. German architects have held congresses since 1853.

Great Britain. In England the Royal Academy is supposed to deal with all the arts, and has always included architects in its membership. The committee which petitioned the King (George III.) had for its chairman Sir William Chambers, architect, Dance, architect of the Mansion House, also being a member. Sir Joshua Reynolds was the first president, and Sir William Chambers, treasurer. Architectural drawings are shown at its annual exhibitions.

There is in Edinburgh a Royal Scottish Academy of Painting, Sculpture, and Architecture, founded in 1825 and incorporated under royal charter in 1838.

Of distinctively architectural societies the *Royal Institute of British Architects* (called R. I. B. A.) stands first. It was organized in 1834 as the *Institute of British Architects*, and chartered by William IV. in 1837, and subsequently, through the influence of the late

Prince Albert, the Queen permitted it to prefix the word " Royal " to its name, and instituted the " Royal Gold Medal for the Promotion of Architecture." A new charter was granted in the fiftieth year of the reign of Victoria (March 28, 1889), under which it is now conducted. Under the existing by-laws " Any non-metropolitan architectural society in the United Kingdom, or in any colony or dependency of the United Kingdom, consisting in whole or in part of professional members, may, subject to such regulations, limitations, and restrictions as may from time to time be prescribed by resolution of the Royal Institute, be allied with the Royal Institute." The Institute in 1899 had 618 Fellow members, 993 Associate members, 46 Honorary Associates, comprising a total subscribing membership of 1657.

The Architectural Association (London) is incorporated under the authority of the Literary and Scientific Institutions Act, 1854. The objects of the Association are, " to provide and afford facilities for the study of architecture, and to serve as a medium of friendly communication between the members and others interested in the study and progress of architecture." The president is *ipso facto* a member of the Council of the R. I. B. A. Many of its members are Fellows or Associates of the R. I. B. A. Its membership, like that of the Institute, is not confined to London, but comprises also architects from other parts of the United Kingdom. (See Architect, The, in England.)

Of local societies not affiliated with the R. I. B. A. are those at Oxford, 1837, and Edinburgh, 1850. The Cambridge–Camden Society was once a great power in connection with the Gothic revival during the middle of the century. It was composed of High Church clergymen and architects, and issued many valuable publications. It was mainly instrumental in reviving the ancient forms of worship in the churches of the establishment, vestments, church furniture, and fittings, and decorative work allied to Gothic architecture.

The Society of Architects, London, is independent of the R. I. B. A. It was founded in 1884, and incorporated under the same authority as the Architectural Association in 1893. Its objects are similar to those of the Architectural Association, but have a more practical turn and concern more the practice of architecture. It also has a very thorough educational department, and requires an educational test for membership. In 1899 it had 509 members, 17 honorary members, 10 associates, and 15 students. It publishes a monthly journal.

There is also in London a Society of Antiquaries, famous for its periodical *Archæologia*, which was incorporated as early as 1751. This society is still in existence, and commenced a movement in November, 1888, to bring about the union of all the archæological societies of the United Kingdom. A consultative central body was formed by it in 1890, composed of representatives of all the county societies. *The Society of the Dilettanti* was founded in 1734. In 1769 it published a folio volume on Ionian antiquities, and later, in 1797, supplemented the investigations of Stuart and Revett (to which it had contributed material support) by another volume entitled *Antiquities of Ionia.* In 1817 it published a still later volume entitled *Unedited Antiquities of Attica.* There is also a society for the preservation of ancient buildings. (See Restoration.)

There is also the Royal Archæological Institute of Great Britain and Ireland, and the society which publishes the *Archæological Journal*, and the British Archæological Association, which publishes its own journal.

There is an Architectural Institute of Scotland located in Edinburgh, which publishes transactions, and a Society of Antiquaries of Scotland.

In Ireland are similar associations ; The Royal Institute of the Architects of Ireland, and the Historical and Archæological Association of Ireland.

Italy. An Academy of Architecture was established as early as 1380, in Milan, by Galeazzo Visconti. The Society of S. Luke, of Florence, is also one of the oldest art societies in the world and is still in existence. It was founded by one of the Medici family in 1350. There was an earlier Academy of the Fine Arts established in Venice in 1345 also named S. Luke. The Academy of S. Luke at Rome was founded in 1595, and is still in existence. The French academy is somewhat related to it by tutelage and descent. Of modern societies the *Institut de Corrispondenze Archæologica*, of Rome, was established in 1830 for the investigation of the ancient monuments of Italy, and has been mainly supported by the Prussian government. It has issued many valuable publications. (See Architect, The, in Italy.)

Japan. There is an Institute of Japanese Architects, with headquarters at Tokio, which has a large membership.

Netherlands. The Society for the Encouragement of Architecture was founded at Amsterdam in 1819, and reorganized in 1830, after the separation of Belgium from the monarchy of the Netherlands. It has about a thousand members.

Russia. In 1674 Peter the Great founded and endowed an Academy of Sciences, in which the Empress Elizabeth (r. 1741–1762), at the suggestion of Count Shuvaloff, established an Imperial Academy of Fine Arts at Saint Petersburg. Catherine II. increased its revenues and built the present academy, which educates architects as well as other artists. It is an immense establishment, and supports its students from childhood until they graduate. The Moscow Archæological Society recently opened a museum. An Archæological Congress has also been instituted in the same city.

Spain. In Madrid an Academy of Painting, Sculpture, and Architecture was founded in 1752 by Philip V., and is still in existence. Madrid also has a Central Society of Architects.

Sweden. There is a Royal Academy in Stockholm founded by Linnæus in 1739, under royal charter.

Switzerland. In Switzerland there are societies of architects and engineers at Basel, Lausanne, and Zurich.

United States. The *National Academy of Design*, located in New York, was founded January 15, 1826. Three architects were among its founders, and it set out to encourage architecture as well as the other fine arts. It long since ceased to give recognition to it, and there are now no architects in its membership.

The first specifically architectural society in the United States was known as the *American Institution of Architects*. It was organized in Philadelphia, Dec. 7, 1836, and comprised twenty-three professional, two associate, and twenty-five honorary members. It had a desultory existence for twenty years.

The American Institute of Architects was organized in New York, Feb. 23, 1857, and held regular meetings at New York up to the breaking out of the Civil War in 1861. The meetings were resumed in 1864, and continued up to the time of the reorganization of the Institute into a federal body, composed of local chapters in the several cities. The first chapter, that at New York, was organized March 19, 1867, with thirty-two Fellows and four Associates. Since then the Institute has only met in annual convention, the first convention having been held Oct. 22 and 23, 1867. Up to October, 1897, there had been thirty-one conventions. There is, since November, 1898, a house in Washington, D. C., called "The Octagon," which is occupied by the Institute, and in which is the office of its secretary and treasurer. In 1889 an important event in the history of the A. I. A. was the consolidation with it of the *Western Association of Archi-'ects*, which was accomplished at the annual convention in Cincinnati. The Institute now has (1899) 22 local chapters, 418 fellow members, and 60 associate members, besides honorary and corresponding members. Each chapter may have members, associate or junior, who are not fellows or associates of the Institute.

The Western Association of Architects was organized at Chicago in 1884, and has a large membership. In 1889 it was consolidated with the *American Institute of Architects*, as above stated.

The Architectural League of America was organized at Cleveland, Ohio, June 2, 1899, by a convention of representatives delegated by nearly all the architectural clubs in the United States and one in Canada. It holds annual conventions in different cities, to which delegates are regularly accredited by the clubs composing the league. Its main work is the regulating of exhibitions of architecture and the allied arts, which take place successively at the seats of the several clubs. The architectural clubs of Pittsburg, Washington (D. C.), Toronto (Canada), Cleveland, Detroit, Chicago, and Saint Louis, the Architectural League of New York, the T-Square Club of Philadelphia, the Chapters of the Institute at Pittsburg and Cincinnati, and the Architects' Club of the University of Illinois are in the League.

The Archæological Institute of America was organized in Boston in 1879, and has made much progress in architectural research in classic lands as well as in America. Archæological societies in the different cities are affiliated with this body. The American schools at Rome and Athens are supported by associations organized for that purpose, which are closely connected with the *Archæological Institute of America*. It publishes quarterly *The American Journal of Archæology.*

The Art Institute of Chicago supports a school of architecture in conjunction with the *Armour Institute.*

The Boston Society of Architects, founded a few years earlier, was affiliated with the *American Institute of Architects* as a chapter in 1868, but still retains its separate name.

The Architectural League of New York is a strong body of architects, mural painters, sculptors, and decorative workers who have to do with building. It was organized in 1881 and reorganized in 1886. It is both professional and social, and has annual exhibitions. Boston, Philadelphia, Cleveland, Detroit, Chicago, Cincinnati, Denver, San Francisco, Washington (D. C.), Pittsburg, Toronto (Ontario), and Saint Louis also have architectural clubs composed mostly of the younger members of the profession, and to which draughtsmen are admitted. Many of them hold annual exhibitions.

The Chicago Architects' Business Association, now three years old, is the first of the kind ever organized; (but see above the *Union Syndicale* in France, and the Society of Architects in Great Britain). It was instituted for the purpose of regulating the business affairs of architects and their relation to various parties with whom they are brought into contact, to watch legislation affecting architects, and to enforce professional morality. It has (1900) 151 members and is rapidly increasing.

Encyclopedia Britannica, s.v. *Academy* (*Societies*); also American Supplement of same, s.v. *Archæology; Encyclopédie de l'Architecture et de la Construction*, P. Planat ; Paris, Dujardin et Cie., 1888–1890 ; Cummings, *Historic Annals*, N. A. D. address of S. F. B. Morse, p. 37, George W. Childs, Philadelphia, 1865 ; Transactions of the American Institute of Architects, 1869, *The Architectural and other Art Societies of Europe*, by A. J. Bloor ; Proceedings of the A. I. A., 1890, Paper by A. J. Bloor ; *The R. I. B. A. Kalendar*, published annually at 9 Conduit St., Hanover Square, London, W. ; *Year Book of the Society of Architects*, published annually at S. James's Hall, Piccadilly, London, W.

— PETER B. WIGHT.

SOCKET. A depression or cavity, shaped to receive and hold in place the foot of a column or beam, or the end of a bolt ; or, in the case of heavy doors or the like, a revolving pivot.

SOD. The thin layer of soil matted together by the roots of grass and other small herbs which forms the surface of a lawn or grassy field ; also, with the article, a small piece of this layer.

Turning the First Sod. A ceremony akin to laying the corner stone. (See Break Ground, under Break, and Corner Stone.)

SOD HOUSE. A habitation of sod or of earth, — stones and sod together. The roof is generally of poles or logs, covered with earth and sod. For that used by the Eskimo, see Turner, Eleventh Annual Report United States Bureau Ethnology. (See also Dugout.)

— F. S. D.

SOFFIT. The under side of a structure, especially of comparatively limited extent. Thus the under side of an arch or lintel and the sloping surface beneath a stair would be called soffits. — W. R. H.

SOIL PIPE. A vertical pipe which receives the discharge from water-closets with or without wastes from other plumbing fixtures. (See House Drainage.) — G. P. M.

SOISSONS, BERNARD DE. (See Bernard de Soissons.)

SOISSONS, JEAN DE. (See Jean de Soissons.)

SOLAR. An upper story ; hence a separate or private room, as in an early English dwelling house. (See Solarium.)

SOLARI, CRISTOFORO (il Gobbo) ; sculptor and architect.

An architect of the school of Bramante (see Bramante) in Milan. His most important building is the church of S. Maria della Passione (Milan). He is supposed to have worked on the façade of the Certosa at Pavia and the tombs of the Visconti and Sforza in that monastery. In 1495 he entered the service of Lodovico Sforza (il Moro), Duke of Milan, and made the monument to his duchess, Beatrice d'Este, which was originally placed in the church of S. Maria delle Grazie (Milan). He was employed upon the sculpture of the cathedral of Milan until 1519, when he was appointed super-

vising architect of the cathedral. Solari was probably related to Pietro Lombardo (see Lombardo, Pietro).

Müntz, *Renaissance;* Perkins, *Italian Sculptors;* Boito, *Il Duomo di Milano;* Paoletti, *Rinascimento in Venezia.*

SOLARI, GUINIFORTE; architect and sculptor ; d. about 1481.

One of the Milanese family (see Solari, C.). He succeeded Filarete (see Filarete) as architect of the Ospedale Maggiore in Milan, Italy, and was at one time architect of the Certosa of Pavia.

Müntz, *Renaissance;* Boito, *Il Duomo di Milano.*

SOLARIUM. In Roman archæology, a part of a house exposed to the sun, generally taken to be the roof of a portico or other place serving the purpose of a modern balcony, and easy of access from the upper stories. Hence, in mediæval Latin, the second-story room or rooms. From this is derived the English solar.

SOLARO. (See Lombardo.)

SOLDER. An alloy of varying composition, but always easily fusible, employed in joining pipes or surfaces. Solder for making wiped joints in lead pipe consists of three parts lead and two parts tin. — W. P. G.

SOLDERING. The process of uniting metallic substances, as in tinware, by solder, dropped when molten on the parts to be joined, and then run together with a hot iron which keeps it fused.

SOLLAR; SOLLER. Same as Solar.

SOMER. (See Summer.)

SOMERSET HOUSE. In London. A building for public offices on the site of the old palace of the Protector Somerset. The present structure is of 1776–1786, the work of Sir William Chambers.

SOMER STONE. Same as Summer (II.).

SORBONNE (LA). In Paris, a great educational and religious institution, named from Robert de Sorbon, who founded an institution for poor students of theology in the thirteenth century. The buildings have been frequently rebuilt, and quite recently have been greatly enlarged, enclosing several courts, and including many rooms, large and small, in addition to a very well-designed lecture hall, where is a great painting by Puvis de Chavannes. The church of the Sorbonne was built before 1659, and is, though small, one of the most interesting neoclassic buildings in Europe.

SOSTRATOS ; architect.

He built the Pharos (lighthouse) at Alexandria about 320 B.C.

Brunn, *Geschichte der griechischen Künstler.*

SOTTO PORTICO. In Italy, a public way beneath the overhanging upper story and behind the columns of a building or a series of buildings. There are many such covered streetways in Venice, especially along the water fronts.

SOUFFLOT, JACQUES GERMAIN; architect; b. 1709; d. Aug. 29, 1780.

After a journey to Asia Minor he returned to Lyons (France) about 1737, where he built the church of the Chartreux, and enlarged the Hôtel Dieu. In 1752 he took part in the competition for the creation of the Place Louis XV., now Place de la Concorde, in Paris (see Gabriel, J. A.). In 1754 he was charged with the reconstruction of the cathedral of Rennes, and in the

and *Œuvres ou Recueils de plusieurs parties d'architecture* (Paris, 1767).

Lance, *Dictionnaire*; Jal, *Dictionnaire critique*; Charvet, *Architectes Lyonnais*.

SOULAS (SOLAS) JEAN; sculptor.

There is a contract between Jean Soulas, sculptor in Paris, and one Jean Tronsson for an Entombment and a Resurrection in the chapel of Notre Dame at the church of S. Germain-l'Auxerrois (Paris). He appears also

SOMERSET HOUSE, LONDON: VESTIBULE; AFTER 1776 A.D.

same year the theatre of Lyons was begun from his plans. In 1755 he designed the Hôtel de Ville at Bordeaux, and in that year replaced Cailleteau as *contrôleur* of the works at the château of Marly. In 1756 he designed the École de Droit (Paris). Soufflot made the plans for the church of S. Geneviève, afterward called the Panthéon, in Paris, in 1764, and carried the building to the spring of the cupola. In 1772 he was appointed *contrôleur général* of the embellishments of the city of Lyons. Soufflot published *Suite de plans, coupes, etc., de trois temples antiques . . . à Pestum* (Paris, 1764),

in a contract of Jan. 2, 1519, for the execution of certain figures of the screen which surrounds the choir of the cathedral of Chartres (see Texier, Jean le).

Lami, *Dictionnaire des Sculpteurs Français*.

SOUND. Audible vibration communicated to the air or other surrounding media by the sounding body. It consists of a train of waves, alternately of condensation and rarefaction, propagated with a velocity dependent on the elasticity and density of the medium. Any portion of the air moves to and fro over a very minute path in the direction in which the sound is being propagated, its motion being, therefore, what is known as longitudinal vibration. (See Acoustics.) — W. C. S.

SOUND BOARD; BOARDING. Pieces of board put in between joists of a floor to form a horizontal surface to receive deafening.

SOUNDING BOARD. *A.* A large surface of wood or other resonant material, by means of which a vibrating string or other small source of sound communicates its motion to the air. Very little sound is produced by the string of a violin or piano directly ; for the air, instead of being compressed by the forward motion of the string, flows around it. The string cuts the air without compressing it, and

board. It does not itself vibrate, or rather in so far as it does vibrate it is inefficient. (See Reflector.) — W. C. S.

SOUND, PROPAGATION OF; REFLECTION OF; RESONANCE OF; VIBRATION OF. (See Acoustics.)

SOUTH AMERICA, ARCHITECTURE OF. *Ancient Architecture.* The most interesting architectural development of the continent of South America was achieved in the period previous to the conquest of Peru by the Spaniards under Francisco Pizarro in 1532. The extent of this period and the time of its beginning are not known. At the time of the Spanish invasion, the entire western territory

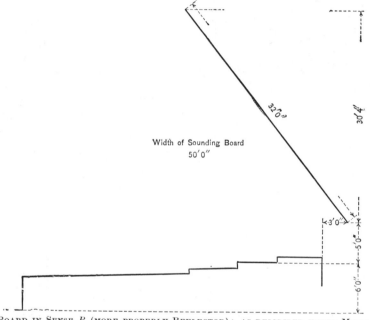

Width of Sounding Board
50′0″

SOUNDING BOARD IN SENSE *B* (MORE PROPERLY REFLECTOR): AS DESCRIBED UNDER MUSIC HALL (5); THE DIMENSIONS ARE GIVEN IN FEET AND INCHES.

therefore without producing sound. If, however, the string is properly attached, as in a harp, or, as in a violin, made to press by means of a bridge or sounding post against a board or other elastic surface of sufficiently large extent, a portion of its motion is communicated to this, and by this in turn to the air. While the ultimate source of sound is the vibrating string, the immediate source is the sounding board, and this is, therefore, of very great importance in determining the musical quality of the instrument.

B. A reflector placed behind and above the speaker or orchestra, for the purpose of strengthening the sound to the audience. It is unfortunate that the term " sounding board " has also been applied to this, for the action of a reflector is very different from that of a true sounding

of South America was in possession of the Inca dynasty. Many writers suppose that there was an extensive civilization in the Peruvian highlands before the rise of the Incas, and ascribe several monuments of great importance to that civilization which Markham (op. cit.) calls the Megalithic. Many of the monuments mentioned by him cannot, however, be very clearly differentiated from true Inca work. Those of Tiahuanaco, however, south of Lake Titicaca, in the great plateau between the Andes and the Cordilleras, in northern Bolivia, are quite different in style from the recognized Inca work. The monuments of Tiahuanaco are fully described and drawn in detail by Strubel and Uhle (op. cit.). The ruins are grouped about the village of Tiahuanaco, which lies in an arid and desolate plain south of Lake Titicaca, and

13,000 feet above the sea. They do not appear to have constituted a city, or even a group of residential palaces, but rather a series of structures erected for public or ritualistic purposes. The ruins cover a large area, and have been used as a quarry for three centuries. Beautifully cut stones are found built into the rude houses of the village. The picturesque Jesuit church of Tiahuanaco contains many. The materials for the cathedral of La Paz, in Bolivia, were derived from this source. There are, however, still scattered over the area of nearly a square mile vast masses of splendidly worked sandstone, trachyte, and basalt. The names given to the different ruins by the Spanish historians are still used in describing them. The "Fortress" is an immense rectangular mound of earth, 620 feet long by 450 feet wide and 50 feet high, which was originally composed of terraces, each terrace supported by massive walls of cut stone. More interesting than the "Fortress" is the "Temple," an area 388 by 445 feet, defined by lines of erect stones, somewhat irregular in shape and size, from 8 to 10 feet high, 2 to 4 feet broad, and 20 to 30 inches thick, placed about 15 feet apart from centre to centre. They were connected by slabs of stone laid on their edges. The *terre pleine* supported by these walls had on its western side an apron or lower terrace 18 feet broad. Along the central part of the outer border of this lower terrace are ten great stone posts, the largest of which is 14 feet high by 4 feet 2 inches wide by 2 feet 8 inches thick. West of the "Temple" is the "Palace," a rectangle, 280 feet long by 190 feet wide, enclosed, like the other monuments, by blocks of finely cut trachyte. Another ruin described by D'Orbiquy (op. cit.) as the Hall of Justice has nearly disappeared. One of the monolithic doorways now forms the entrance of the cemetery of Tiahuanaco. The most important of all the remains of Tiahuanaco is the great monolithic doorway which stands within the enclosure called the "Temple." The block stands seven feet above ground, and is 13 feet long and 1½ foot thick. The surfaces of one side of the stone above the lintel are covered with sculpture, the centre being formed by a figure boldly cut in high relief. On either side three tiers of kneeling figures in very low relief, forty-eight in all, face toward the centre of the composition. A great part of this work at Tiahuanaco is characterized by extreme precision and complexity of stone-cutting.

With the ruins of Tiahuanaco, Markham classes other colossal monuments, notably the fortresses of Sacsahuaman and Ollantay tombs. These are, however, strictly within the territory covered by the early Inca civilization, and will be described with the Inca remains.

The dynasty of the Inca, that being the

name by which sovereigns of the Quichrea tribes of Peruvian Indians were known, had its origin, according to tradition, in the basin of Lake Titicaca, but established its capital very early at Cuzco, in the plateau adjacent to that of Titicaca, on the north. Inca architecture is characterized by distinctively stone construction. There is no suggestion of wooden types as in Greece and Egypt. Everywhere are found low walls of porphyry, granite, basalt, and brick, the bricks being works usually of large size. The jambs of the doors incline as in Egypt. Long walls are frequently decorated with niches constructed like the doors. Buildings are sometimes of two or three stories, but there appear to have been no stairways or other internal communication between them. The apartments of a large building usually open directly into a central court. The most important monuments are characterized by a high degree of finish and precision in the treatment of the stone. The roofs were high and pointed, and made of thatch. One of these thatched roofs, near the village of Azangaro, north of Lake Titicaca, is still intact. The houses of the common people were built of rough stones laid in clay. They were probably stuccoed and painted yellow and red. There was little sculpture in Peru, only an occasional carved lintel. The mountainous country of the Incas was terraced to the limits of cultivation. Every foot of ground reclaimed in this way was carefully irrigated and cultivated. The splendid retaining walls of the terraces are still intact, the water courses made by the Incas are still in use, and the terraces are still under cultivation. To connect the extremes of their enormous territory, they built a splendid system of military roads, usually constructed of large stones, carefully fitted, and lined on either side with larger stones placed on edge.

The most interesting remains of the civilization of the Incas are in the city of Cuzco. When Francisco Pizarro entered that city, Nov. 15, 1533, he found it composed of long, straight streets, forming right angles with each other, and finely paved. A great central, open square, called Huacapata, was surrounded by enormous temples and palaces. The three small streams which pass through the city were confined between walls of fine masonry, and covered by bridges built of large slabs of stone laid horizontally, which are still in use. Enormous masses of the old masonry, cut and fitted with extreme precision, but with extremely little sculptured decoration, still line the narrow streets of Cuzco. The Inca ruins of Cuzco are all of large palaces or public buildings, the houses of the people having disappeared entirely. The palaces and temples are built around courts. The entrances are high, covered by stone lintels, which, in a few instances, are elaborately carved. The stones are laid for the most part in regular courses, fitted with the utmost precision. Occasionally they are cut away at the joints so as to form a rustication similar to that of the Italian palaces. In the circular wall of the temple of the Sun, the lines of contact of the stones are true radii of the circle of the plan. The walls are sometimes 35 or 40 feet high. The great temple of the Sun, at Cuzco, was the finest building in the territory of the Incas. It stood on the bank of the little intramural stream called Huatenay. The garden which lay between the temple and the river was composed of a series of terraces with carefully built retaining walls. The temple proper, which was 296 feet long by 52 feet wide, occupied one side of an immense court. It had a flat wooden ceiling, but its roof of thatch was high and pointed. According to the Spanish chroniclers, large portions of this building were decorated with plates of gold. Specimens of these plates as thin as note paper are still to be seen in museums. The site and ruins of the temple of the Sun are now occupied by the church and convent of S. Domingo. Next in importance to the temple of the Sun is the palace of the Virgins of the Sun, the ruins of which are occupied by the convent of S. Catalina. The outside wall of the enclosure, still standing, is 750 feet long and 20 or 25 feet high, the end wall is 180 feet. The palace of Huayna Capac lay between the palace of the Virgins of the Sun and the great square called Huacapata. It was an immense enclosure, 800 feet long. It is now occupied by the convent of the Jesuits, the barracks, and the prison. The remains of fourteen of these immense palaces are to be found in Cuzco. On the site of the cathedral of Cuzco stood an immense covered hall or basilica.

The great fortress of Sacsahuaman stands on a rocky bluff near Cuzco on the north, the face of which is precipitous and impassable. The farther side descends gradually to a plateau which is accessible from the valleys on either side. Across the end of this plateau, near the bluff, are built three enormous walls 1800 feet long and parallel. These walls are built in zigzag, with projecting and entering angles, always exposing their faces to a parallel fire. The outer wall is 27 feet high and supports a terrace 35 feet wide. Above this terrace rises the second wall, 18 feet high. This, in turn, supports a terrace 18 feet wide, above which rises the third wall, 14 feet high. The total elevation of the entire fortification is 59 feet. The stones used in the outer wall are of great size, one of the largest being 27 feet high, 12 feet wide and 10 feet thick. The stones are levelled at the joints. All this material is taken from a quarry of blue limestone at the farther end of the plateau. There

are entrances at either end of this line of defence, and a narrow passage in the middle. There was a high wall along the face of the rock toward the city which has been nearly destroyed. Traces of building within the enclosure are also to be seen. Water was carried into the fortress by subterranean channels.

The island of Titicaca in the lake of that name was the reputed cradle of the Inca dynasty and was always held sacred. There were important buildings upon the island, ruins of which are still to be seen. The so-called palace of the Inca is surrounded by terraces which originally supported beautiful gardens. The building forms a rectangle 51 by 44 feet. The front, facing the lake, has two doors and two niches. Above these, on the second floor, is an esplanade or terrace from which is a superb view of the lake. The palace has twelve small rooms 13 feet high. The walls were covered with a kind of stucco which was painted yellow on the outside of the building and red on the inside. The second story does not correspond in plan with the first, and has no connection with it. The "Temple of the Sun" stands on the crest of a ridge on the eastern side of the island. It is a rectangle 105 feet long and 30 feet wide, and has five doors with two windows between each pair of doors. It is built of rough stones laid in clay, stuccoed and painted inside and out. The sacred rock at Manco Capac and the fountain of the Incas at Titicaca are also interesting. The island of Coati in Lake Titicaca which was sacred to the Moon contains an important ruin called the palace of the Virgins of the Sun. It stands on the uppermost of a series of seven terraces supported by retaining walls of cut and uncut stones. The building occupies three sides of an oblong court. It is 180 feet long and 80 feet wide, built of rough stones laid in clay and carefully stuccoed. The courtyard is surrounded by a series of interesting niches and doorways leading into various apartments. The outside was painted yellow except the niches and cornice, which were red. There was a second story and a sharply pitched roof. The temple of Viracocha, situated in the southern part of the same plateau as the city of Cuzco, is remarkable for a wall of adobe 40 feet high, which appears to have been the central wall of a building 300 feet long and 87 feet high. Near this temple is a series of small Inca houses in good preservation. Along the valley of the river Vilcanota, which is the beginning of the Amazon, and in the passes leading into it, are numerous interesting ruins. The mountains also on either side of the valley are terraced in the usual skilful Inca fashion to the height of about 2000 feet. The most important monuments of this region are the three great fortresses of Ollantay Tambo, which lie outside the pass which separates the territory of the Incas from the savage tribes of the Amazon Valley. The walls of the chief fortress are about 25 feet high, built of rough stones stuccoed inside and out. Within the walls is a confusion of buildings, among which are a series of immense blocks of porphyry perfectly cut and finely polished. One of these blocks is 18 feet high, 5 feet wide, and 2 feet thick. These stones are brought from a quarry more than two leagues distant and 3000 feet above the valley. The work at Ollantay Tambo shows some resemblance to that at Tiahuanaco and is ascribed by Markham (op. cit.) to his Megalithic period. A typical Inca house well preserved and in use is to be seen at Ollantay Tambo.

Numerous remains in the Titicaca basin have no resemblance to Inca work, and appear to have belonged to a contemporary civilization of the Aymara tribes who were later conquered by the Quichrea followers of the Incas.

The Inca dynasty which originated in the Titicaca basin at first governed only the Quichrea Indians of the plateau about Cuzco. As they grew more powerful they increased their dominion until, just before the advent of the Spaniards, they had acquired control of the entire continent of South America west of the Andes.

The last to yield to the Inca domination were the tribes governed by the great Chimu, a name which probably stands for an Indian dynasty which had its seat on the northern coast of Peru, near the Spanish city of Truxillo in the valley of the river Moche. The ruins at this place cover an area about fifteen miles long and five miles wide. There appears to have been a surrounding wall, several miles of which still stand. From this wall others extend into the city, apparently dividing it into districts. Much of the area thus enclosed has never been built upon. It was, however, carefully cleared of stones and irrigated, and was undoubtedly used for parks and gardens. Within and without the walls is an interesting series of enormous mounds called *huacas*. Of these the most important is the huaca of Obispo, which is built of rough stones and adobe. It covers an area 550 feet square or about eight acres, and is 150 feet high. Another immense mound is called the huaca of Toledo, from Don Garcia de Toledo, who extracted an immense treasure from it. It is now very much in ruins. The great pyramid of Moche at Chimu is a rectangular structure about 800 feet long and 470 feet wide, forming a plateau about 100 feet high, above which rises a square pyramid to the extreme height of 200 feet. Other smaller huacas resemble those described. The most important of these ruins is the so-called palace of the great Chimu. It covers a large area divided into courts and

chambers. The most important feature of the palace is the Hall of the Arabesques, about 62 feet wide and probably twice as long. The walls are covered with effective and intricate patterns in stucco relief.

The Indian tribes along the coast of Peru, which were all finally conquered by the Incas, had considerable civilization and left many important monuments which resemble very much those of Moche. The most important of these ruins are at Pachacamac, twenty miles south of Lima. The Incas also erected a temple of the Sun at Pachacamac.

Modern Architecture. The most interesting monuments of modern architecture in South America are situated in Peru, and were built soon after the conquest of that country by the Spaniards. The city of Lima was founded by the conqueror, Francisco Pizarro, Jan. 6, 1535. The feast of Epiphany falling on this day, the new city was named Ciud de los Reyes, or City of the Kings. Lima, which is a corruption of Rimac, the name of the river on which the city is situated, has taken the place of the original name. The first stone of the cathedral in the Plaza Mayor at Lima was laid by Pizarro Jan. 18, 1535. It was consecrated ninety years later. The cathedral was nearly destroyed by the great earthquake of 1746, but was afterward rebuilt. The building is of stone, except the towers, which are of stucco. The interior has five aisles and is much decorated, but is poorly lighted. The old palace of Pizarro, on the south side of the Plaza Mayor, has also been much rebuilt. The episcopal palace was built by the order of Francisco Pizarro near the cathedral. The University of S. Marcos was founded by royal decree in 1551, and finished in 1576. The Chamber of Deputies now occupies the great hall, formerly chapel, of the University. The old hall of the Inquisition, in the Plaza de la Constitution, is now the Senate House. It has a famous ceiling imported from Spain in 1560. The convent and church of S. Francisco, founded in the same year as the city, 1535, are very extensive. Immense areas of the interior are covered with tiles beautifully designed. The building of the International Exhibition at Lima was designed in 1870 by Dr. Don Manuel a Fuentes. There is a fine old bridge across the Rimac at Lima.

One of the most interesting Spanish buildings in Peru was the cathedral of Arequipa, which was designed by an architect named Andrea Espinosa, and finished in 1656. This church was burned, but rebuilt. It was destroyed again by the great earthquake of 1868, which nearly obliterated the city of Arequipa. The fine church of the Jesuits at Arequipa was destroyed at the same time. At Callao, the port of Lima, the old fortress of Real Telipe, which was built in 1770, is very interesting.

At Cuzco, the old capital of the Incas, the convent of S. Domingo was built on the ruins of the temple of the Sun. The palace of the Virgins of the Sun became the convent of S. Catalina. The church of the Jesuits, one of the finest buildings in South America, occupies the ruined palace of Huayna Capac, and the cathedral was built on the site of an immense hall constructed by the Inca Viracocha for the festivals of the people. The church of La Merera at Cuzco has a fine tower and a cloister of white stone. The city of Truxillo, in northern Peru, was founded in the same year as Lima, 1535; the cathedral and churches are picturesque, but it has no public buildings of importance. In the early days of their prosperity, the Jesuits built many small churches of good architectural design in the valley of Lake Titicaca; one of the best of these is the church and shrine of Unestra Senora at Copacabana, on the shore of Lake Titicaca. A dominical shrine in the fore court of this church is especially interesting.

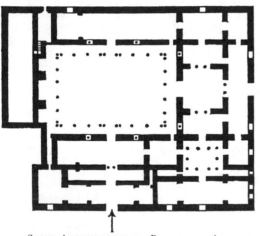

SPAIN, ARCHITECTURE OF: PLAN OF THE ALCAZAR, SEVILLE. MOORISH IN ORIGIN, ILLUSTRATING THE USE OF THE PATIO FROM WHICH LARGE ROOMS ARE ENTERED AND TAKE DAYLIGHT.

The architecture of Brazil is quite recent, and includes few monuments of importance. The larger buildings in the cities of Rio de Janeiro, Bahia, Pernambuco, have frequently been designed by European architects of note (see Silva, and Grandjean de Montigny). The buildings are mainly of brick, the splendid woods of the country being used in the interior. An exhaustive discussion of the domestic architecture of Brazil is to be found in Vol. XI. of *Revue de l'Architecture* (1853). The most imposing structure in Rio is the great aqueduct leading from the Morro de Santa Theresa to the Morro de Sant' Antonio. Like the cities of Brazil, those of Venezuela, Colombia, Chili, the Argentine Republic, and other South American countries are quite modern and built in the current European fashion. — R. S.

Squier, *Peru;* Prescott, *Conquest of Peru;* Markham, *History of Peru;* Nadaillac, *Prehistoric America;* Hutchinson, *Two Years in Peru;* Stubel and Uhle, *Die Ruinen;* Stalk, *Von Tiahuanaco;* Brehin, *Das Inca Reich;* Angrand, Article in *Rev. de l'Architecture*, Vol. XXIV.; D'Orbigny, *Voyage dans l'Amérique Méridionale; Revue générale de l'Architecture*, Vol. XI., Vol. XXIV.; Don Manuel a Fuentes, *Guia de Lima;* Curtis, *Capitals of Spanish America.*

SOYNERE (SUNERE), HEINRICH; architect.

The first architect of the cathedral of Cologne, Germany. The first stone of the choir was laid Aug. 15, 1248.

Faline, *Baumeister des Kölner Domes.*

SPACE. The area at the corner of a turning stair, limited approximately by lines drawn through the newel or angle perpendicular to each of the two strings, or by such a line and one drawn in prolongation of the string. Commonly used as synonymous with Pace (which see for the probable distinction).

Foot Space.
Half-Quarter Space. | (See Pace and sub-
Half Space. | titles.)
Quarter Space. |

SPAIN, ARCHITECTURE OF. The Iberians, or pre-Roman inhabitants of Spain, left no surviving monuments beyond a few slightly known structures in the northern Basque provinces. Of the constructions of the Roman period, there is an aqueduct at Segovia carried across a valley in a double tier of stone arches; at Merida, in the province of Badajoz, there are some remains of a temple of Mars, together with fragments of an aqueduct, a so-called Arch of Triumph and a temple of Diana; at Tarragona, on the Mediterranean, there is a fragment of Roman wall superimposed upon a construction of cyclopean masonry, the latter being ascribed to the Iberian period; and at Italica, near Seville, there are the remains of an amphitheatre. All of this work, however, is in very fragmentary condition, and the invasion of the Visigoths or Vandals in the fifth century appears to have swept away nearly all the architecture then existing, while the conquest by the Moors, in the early part of the eighth century, in its turn obliterated most of the remains of the Visigothic work. There are some exceptions, however; and the few scattered remains of the mediæval buildings, dating from anywhere between the second and the eighth century, present a curious analogy, in style, plan, and arrangement, to some of the Roman or early Christian work of Syria. The slight remnant of national life which was left in the northern provinces after the Moorish invasion developed by growth, conquests of the invaders, and amalgamation of the rival interests, into

PLATE XXI

SPAIN, ARCHITECTURE OF. PLATE 1

Toro (Leon); the Collegiate Church (Colegiata); interesting Romanesque work, and one of the three or four serious attempts made in Spain to produce a cupola-like roof to the crossing of a church.

the mediæval kingdom of Spain, culminating in the capture of Granada in 1492. The seat of government being fixed about Madrid, the Renaissance style, which was imported from Italy and fostered by constant intercourse with foreign artists, was naturally at its best on the central plateau. The north was not a fashionable part of the kingdom, consequently the Gothic remains which had grown up there during the early centuries of the monarchy were little disturbed, while in the central portion most of the mediæval work disappeared to make room for the Renaissance palaces. In the south the

There does not appear to be in Spain a very well-defined development or consecutive growth from the mediæval to the modern styles. Rather, each style appears to be broadly and frankly borrowed outright, the only essentially Spanish factors being displayed in a few peculiarities of plan and in the spirit of the detail, the noticeable lack being in inventive progression rather than in ability to adapt. Of the mediæval work there are a few examples in the province of Catalonia, such as the very interesting convent of San Pablo at Barcelona, in the style of the Romanesque of the south of

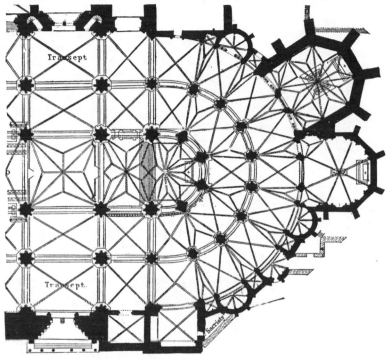

SPAIN, ARCHITECTURE OF: CHOIR AND AISLES OF TOLEDO CATHEDRAL; BEGINNING OF THE 14TH CENTURY. THE ALTERNATION OF SQUARES AND TRIANGLES IN THE VAULTING OF DEAMBULATORY IS VERY RARE; IT OCCURS ALSO IN THE CATHEDRAL OF LE MANS IN FRANCE.

Moors found little to preserve when they first entered the kingdom, and the architectural work that they did was of such manifest value as to strongly impress the Christian conquerors, so that as the Moslems were driven out and the Christian influence gained the ascendence, the Moorish work in the south was, on the whole, very little disturbed, resulting in our finding it in its present condition to-day, with but a slight admixture of the Renaissance. The existing architectural remains of Spain, therefore, present, in their geographical distribution, a curious analogy to the conditions of the soil and climate, the Gothic and Romanesque being chiefly found in the north, the Moorish in the south, and the neoclassic along the central plateau.

France. There is also a striking interior arrangement in the cathedral and in the church of S. M. del Mar at Barcelona. The best of the Romanesque work, however, is found at Salamanca, Zamora, and the neighboring cities in the west of Spain, and in the old province of Leon. There are three buildings in this locality which exhibit a certain progression, and were undoubtedly successive improvements upon an original motive. The dome of the Zamora cathedral comes first, a low cupola resting upon a continuous arcade, with gabled pavilions at the four faces, and circular conical roofed turrets at the angles. The old cathedral at Salamanca is a second step. In this instance the cupola is raised considerably, there is more elaboration in the detail, and the style of the work approximates closely to that of the Romanesque of Aquitania, without, however, losing its decidedly Spanish decorative treatment. The third structure is the Collegiata at Toro, a few miles east of Zamora, presenting little architectural interest except for the large tower over the intersection, which is sixteen-sided in plan, with a double row of arched windows, with round turrets at the corners, the whole crowned in its present condition by a flat tiled roof, though there is every evidence that the intention was to superimpose a stone cupola or roof in the style of the Salamanca cathedral.

SPAIN, ARCHITECTURE OF; ARCADES ON PATIO; PALACE AT GUADALAJARA; ABOUT 1465 A.D.

These churches show a development of Romanesque architecture which is manifestly French in its origin. Indeed, there is evidence, more or less vague, that the cathedral at Zamora was built by a French architect, the character of the detail and the arrangement of the cupola all suggesting French work, while the north transept has a bold, well-proportioned portal which is thoroughly in the style of the southern French Romanesque. This building is believed to be one of the earliest purely Romanesque structures existing in Spain. The motives of the Spanish Romanesque were very few and exceedingly simple, but the decorative sense of getting the very utmost out of the play of light and shadow over a plain wall surface, emphasized by a few sharp bits of detail, is a peculiarity which runs through nearly all the Spanish work. The church of the Magdalena at Zamora is another early Romanesque work, which, however, is less distinctively Spanish.

At Avila, a short distance from Salamanca, in the province of Old Castile, are several noteworthy Romanesque structures, especially the church of S. Vincente, the principal portal of which is undoubtedly the richest and most fully developed specimen of the style in Spain. It is, however, so completely in the spirit of the work at Arles, in Provence, that it has less purely Spanish significance. In the little church of S. Pedro at Avila there is a more perfect development of the Spanish tendencies, as manifested by the treatment of the west front and by the brilliant decorative character of the details.

A somewhat isolated example of the Romanesque is found near the extreme northwest point of Spain, in the cathedral at Santiago de Compostella, dating from 1082, which forms one of the earliest examples of a complete Spanish cathedral. It is modelled quite closely after S. Sernin, of Toulouse. The western portal, known as La Gloria, has been considered one of the greatest achievements of Christian art, fairly ranking with the north porch of Chartres.

Of the strictly Gothic work the best is found farther north, at Burgos, in Old Castile, and at Leon, in the province of that name, the two cities lying near the northern seacoast. The Burgos cathedral is three-aisled, with transepts and chevet, and the intersection is crowned by a high dome. The exterior of the church has a rather simple west front, with two towers with openwork spires, strongly suggestive of the spire of Freiburg, in Breisgau (Würtemburg). The interior presents one of the noblest efforts of Gothic architecture, with combinations of decorative effects in the carving, and truly scenic dispositions of light from the tall central cupola such as have seldom been surpassed, and which, together with the elaborate enclosure of the choir, the theatrical effect of the altars, and the richness of the side chapels, combine to make this one of the great cathedrals of the world. The effect of the interior, however, does not bear analysis. In an architectural sense it is illogical, and where it follows precedent it goes astray, but as a work of art, as a combination of motives and details which were used with only indifferent appreciation, it is remarkably successful, though entirely an unacademic creation. The cathedral at Leon is much more rigid in its adherence to the canons of northern Gothic architecture. The details are correct, the proportions are on the whole pleasing, and isolated portions of the architecture seem like a page from the Ile de France. The interior, however, shows more Spanish feeling in arrangement of the plan and in the disposition of the choir. All of the Spanish Gothic work is imitative, having less distinctive character than the Romanesque;

elaborate stonework, sometimes merely a high metal railing or grille. In the design and in the elaboration of this choir enclosure the Spanish architects developed a remarkable ability, and in nearly all of the large churches these are worthy of careful study.

The cathedral of Oviedo, near the north coast, has a very interesting tower in the late Gothic style. The cathedral of Pamplona, in Navarre, among the spurs of the Pyrenees, has

SPAIN, ARCHITECTURE OF: PALACE OF CHARLES V., GRANADA; BEGUN ABOUT 1530 A.D.; NEVER FINISHED.

and, indeed, the only peculiarly Spanish feature about the Gothic churches is in the plan. In Spain the church is built primarily for the clergy, consequently the space occupied by the priests includes, not only the portion to the east of the intersection, which is specifically designated as the choir, but also a large space reaching out into the nave of the church, and often including a good deal more than half of the total area (see Trascoro). This space is furthermore usually separated from the rest of the building by a high screen, sometimes of

a successful interior arrangement, and there are quite a number of smaller Gothic churches which present many points of interest. At Saragossa, in Aragon, the cathedral of Lo Seo has some of the best vaulting in Spain, somewhat on the style of the German hall churches. Architecturally the interior is chiefly noteworthy, however, for its magnificent carved choir enclosure in the style of the Renaissance.

In the central region the most interesting example of Gothic work is afforded by the cathedral of Toledo, in New Castile, a short

distance south of Madrid, which, in some respects, is quite as remarkable as the cathedral
of Burgos. The western towers recall quite
strongly some of the perpendicular English
Gothic work in its treatment of the wall surfaces, though the design of the spire with its
triple crown of thorns in the form of huge rays
is unique and peculiarly Spanish in its effect.
The interior of Toledo cathedral is one mass of
richness. The grille work enclosing the choir
is a marvel of elaborate wrought work, and the
contents of the chapels, the sacristy, and the
choir are of the fervid theatrical type which
lends such a character to so many of the Spanish churches, rich in gilding and elaborate
carving, full of colour, and, though often inco-
herent in design, certainly very splendid in

and was built as the chosen residence of the
Moorish kings. The Moorish architecture was
peculiarly a matter of decoration. The exteriors of all the structures of the Alhambra are
mere huge unformed masses of masonry, while
the interiors were most elaborately decorated
with stucco and tiling, the rooms being arranged around open courts and connected by
colonnades, which let the light and air in everywhere. Only a small portion of the original
structures is at present in repair, but enough
remains to give one a very fair realization
of the decorative motives and the general
arrangement.

The mosque at Cordova is a structure which
was erected, in 770, on the general plan which
characterizes the mosques of Northern Africa, a

SPAIN, ARCHITECTURE OF: CATHEDRAL OF JAEN, BEGUN 1532. THE WEST FRONT AND TOWERS,
THIRTY YEARS LATER; ONE OF THE FINEST NEOCLASSIC DESIGNS.

effect. The Spanish idea of these churches
seems to have been to get the rich effect, no
matter how it was obtained, and, as the additions made to these cathedrals during the Renaissance period were always carried out with
a lavish hand and no lack of resources, the
results, while radically different from the grand,
dignified treatment of the northern Gothic
churches, is fascinating by its bewildering
richness.

At Seville, in Andalusia, in the far south, the
cathedral is of architectural interest chiefly for
the elaborate grille work about the choir and
in front of some of the chapels. The architecture, *per se*, has little distinctive charm.

Of the Moorish remains, the Alhambra is a
collection of semi-detached structures disposed
irregularly along the summit of a hill jutting
out into the valley above the city of Granada,

huge rectangle divided by interior columns into
small bays, each crowned by a brick vault, and
the whole preceded by a large garden. The
columns which support the vaulting, together
with their capitals, are mostly spoils from
Roman or early Christian buildings, and were
put in place apparently without much attention
to special fitness, varying in material and somewhat in size. The vaulting is in red and
white brick, or red brick and stucco, and is
one of the few examples remaining in Spain
of Moorish masonry vaulting. All the ceiling
effects in the other Moorish buildings are obtained with plaster or wood. In the very
centre of the mosque has been built a late
Gothic or early Renaissance cathedral, which is
sufficiently uninteresting by comparison with
the Moorish work. The old Moorish sanctuary
has been preserved and restored, and the deco-

PLATE XXII

SPAIN, ARCHITECTURE OF. PLATE II

Burgos ; the cathedral seen from the southwest. The western towers are copies of northern work of the same character and epoch, but the great lantern (cimborio) which covers the crossing, though very late in epoch (1567), is extremely in-teresting in its mass and general treatment in con-nection with the cathedral roof, and even its detail is fine. The flat roofs of nave and transept are characteristic of Spanish work of the time : they are covered with heavy stone flags.

rations put, as nearly as possible, in their original shape, so that this part of the mosque presents an extremely brilliant effect of the Moorish decoration applied to the architectural forms.

There are several examples of Moorish construction afforded by some of the Toledo churches. S. Cristo la Luz is a part of an earlier Moorish structure, and contains a considerable portion of the original brickwork, while the interior of the church of S. M. la Blanca is a part of an old mosque in which the Moorish construction and the decoration have been on the whole pretty carefully preserved.

The third most important of the Moorish remains is the Alcazar at Seville, a structure which was erected under the direction of the

all carried out in plain brick, the upper part blooming into an elaboration of arched forms, and crowned at present by a later Renaissance cupola and balustrades, while a weather vane in the form of a gigantic figure of victory caps the whole. However much this tower may have suffered by recent changes, it still presents the effect of Moorish work. The Renaissance work at the top has not sufficed to destroy its character, and it is quite probable that all of the lower part is in essentially the condition it was before the Christian conquest.

There are a number of other examples of the Moorish construction in brick and stone which have survived to our days. The Puerta del Sol at Toledo is a part of the old Moorish fortifications, and an interesting combination of brick

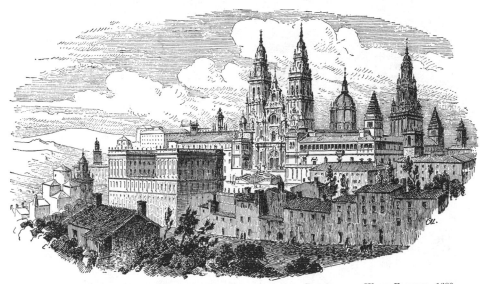

SPAIN, ARCHITECTURE OF: SANTIAGO DE COMPOSTELLA: CATHEDRAL, WEST FAÇADE, 1680.

Christian conquerors after the Moorish kingdom had been destroyed; but the work, the design, the decoration, were all intrusted to Moorish captives, and though it is not as pure in style as the Alhambra, it is on the whole in better preservation, and is of very considerable interest. The only strictly Moorish portions are the entrance pavilion adjoining the garden, and the interior work. The gardens also are believed to be of Moorish origin, though they have been modified in the Renaissance period so as to lose their original character.

The Giralda tower of the cathedral of Seville is another of the peculiarly Moslem remains, and though forming a part of the cathedral it was, originally at least, begun as a feature of the mosque which stood upon this site. It is a magnificent structure, almost entirely of brick, combining a perfectly plain wall surface in the lower part with a species of encrusted tracery

and stone. Then in the Leaning Tower of Saragossa there is an example of the sort of brickwork which the Moors used, though this structure was built in 1504. The tower is a little over 40 feet square at the base, constructed entirely of brick, but with a variety of forms, ornaments, and details recalling both the Gothic and the Moorish styles. There are also several other smaller towers in Saragossa which show the character of the Moorish brickwork, such as that of the churches of S. Pablo, of S. Gil, and S. Miguel.

There is a little structure in Seville, known as the Casa de Pilatos, which was erected during the Renaissance period, in the interior of which the Moorish workmen were evidently given a pretty free hand, with the result of producing an interior decorated almost entirely in glazed tiles and elaborate stucco work.

The influence of the Moorish art made itself

felt through all the succeeding Spanish work. The so-called Mudejar style, which was a combination of Gothic and Moorish motives and construction, continued down well into the period of the sixteenth century, and in later examples there is often an added mixture of Renaissance flavor which produced most charming combinations. Examples of Mudejar work are scattered all through the southern provinces and in Toledo. The convent of S. Paula at Seville illustrates the latter phase of this style, wherein glazed tile, enamelled terra cotta, and moulded brick are used as Moorish details in combination with

SPAIN, ARCHITECTURE OF: COURT OF THE ROYAL PALACE AT MADRID; ABOUT 1730 A.D.

faience work, which is almost Della Robbia in style, the whole added to a construction, especially about the doorway, which is essentially Gothic. This type of work it is, by the way, which was carried from Spain by the conquerors into Mexico and Central America, though in the cisatlantic work the Renaissance element is more predominant in the details. To the Mudejar style also belongs the church of S. Marco at Seville. This style may be said to have begun in the eleventh century, and to have reached its highest development in the fifteenth, and it, together with the Plateresque style, of which a description will be given later, are two most peculiarly Spanish developments, which seem less influenced by external direct impor-

tations than the Gothic, Romanesque, or the Renaissance.

During the sixteenth century Spain was at the height of her power. Her king ruled, as Emperor of Germany, over the greater portion of civilized Europe. Within her borders there was peace from one end of the land to the other, while the discoveries made by her voyagers in the west opened the way for a flood tide of wealth which was as lavishly expended upon internal improvements, palaces, magnificent churches, and convents, as it was plentifully received. By her possessions in southern Italy, Spain was in touch with the dominant artistic race of Europe, and her constant intercourse with Italian art made the introduction of the Italian Renaissance a natural sequence, while the lavish profusion with which the Spanish nobles dispensed their easily acquired gains brought to Spain some of the most skilful artificers and the most able designers. That the Renaissance in Spain falls short of the artistic excellence of the work of the corresponding period in Italy was due to the spirit of the Spanish themselves, who were not content with merely importing their art of architecture, but endeavoured to extend and perfect it to their own taste, and under the hothouse influences of the Spanish temperament the Renaissance bloomed in Spain into a style which, while owing all its antecedents and traditions to foreign influences, and while far from Italian perfection, was at its best thoroughly Spanish in feeling, and showed many of the better qualities which had characterized the earlier Romanesque and the later Mudejar styles. As a style it deserves special study, because of the intensely decorative qualities of the work, the manner in which the detail is treated in mass rather than as mere detail, and the extremely effective disposition of masses of light and shade. All of these qualities are made conspicuously manifest in the hospital of S. Cruz at Toledo, a structure dating from about 1500, and in some respects one of the most unique and characteristic productions of Spanish art. The lingering influence of Gothic or Mudejar art is shown in the mouldings each side of the entrance, the disposition of the arch, and the concentration of ornament. The details themselves will bear pretty close inspection; they are well executed, strongly accentuated throughout, and answer their decorative purpose admirably; while the scheme of the façade, with its elaborate entrance, its less elaborate upper windows, simple cornice, and absolutely plain wall surface, form a kind of combination which can be typified as

Spanish. The interior of the hospital has some excellent work of its kind, though less striking than the exterior. There is a stairway with details strongly recalling some portions of the pulpit in the Siena cathedral.

The Spanish Renaissance did not, however, arrive at one bound at work such as the S. Cruz hospital. The line between the late Mudejar and the Renaissance was an irregular one, and is occupied by buildings such as the Casa de las Conchas in Salamanca, which derives its name from the pilgrim cockle shells disposed at regular intervals as projecting bosses over the otherwise plain surface of the wall, a clever decorative treatment which has seldom been so successfully carried out as in this instance. The doorway of this house is essentially Gothic in spirit and mass, though the details are strongly Renaissance. The courtyard of S. Georgio at Valladolid is another of the early Renaissance structures wherein the Gothic influence is even more pronounced, the columns being fluted spirally, and the capitals of the superimposed work a bizarre mixture of the old and the new. There are a number of private houses of the transition style which are of great interest, such as the Casa de los Momos at Zamora, the so-called House of Maria la Brava at Salamanca, and the street front of the Casa de Pilatos at Seville, the latter being interesting in showing how effectively a plain wall and little ornament will set off each other. Of the more pretentious public buildings the Lonja, or Exchange, at Valencia shows a persistence of the Moresco-Gothic motives with an adornment of the Renaissance forms. The exchange at Saragossa is a design of a very different type, in which the only influence of the early work is manifest in the details of the main cornice. As regards proportion, disposition of openings, and general mass, this building has caught very thoroughly the style of the Roman Renaissance, and is one of the most dignified, restrained public buildings in Spain. The interior, however, which contains a large hall, reverts to the Gothic type, the vaulting being supported on isolated columns, which, though rudely Renaissance in character, are essentially Gothic in construction.

The palaces of the Renaissance period naturally afford an opportunity for all the lavish display which was so peculiarly Spanish. At Guadalajara, about fifty miles northeast of Madrid, is the palace of the Infantados, one of many which can be found in out-of-the-way towns, set in the midst of the most squalid surroundings now, and generally in a more or less dilapidated condition. The motive of the exterior of this palace recalls the Palazzo Bevilacqua in Bologna, in its rustications and arrangement of the openings. Another interesting palace, purer in type and of more merit in mass, is the palace of the Counts of Monterey at Sal-

amanca; and in Saragossa there is the palace of the Infanta, or more popularly Casa Japorta, with a simple exterior crowned by a cornice, recalling that of the Bigallo at Florence, and with a richly elaborated interior courtyard and stairway.

There are a few buildings in which the Italian influence is predominant, while the Spanish taste is only manifest in a certain portion of the detail, of which the Ayuntamiento of Seville is a type. This is a perfectly straightforward Italian design, both in mass and in disposition of openings, recalling some of the best of the northern Italian work; but the Spanish exuberance crops out in the treatment of the arabesques which fill the pilaster panels, and in the detail of the ornament throughout.

The name Plateresque, or the style of the silversmiths, has been used specially to designate the superabundant over decorated work of the middle Renaissance in Spain. The name is a perfectly fitting one. The work shows a sense of light and shade, a feeling of chiselled elaboration, which is eminently characteristic of the work which we assume to be peculiarly adapted to silversmiths' designs. That a great deal of it is overdone and thoroughly bad goes without saying, but the best of the Plateresque work is certainly very effective; and if we can forget for a moment the manifest incongruities of the detail in a historical sense, and think of it only as a Spanish production, it must be given a very creditable place in judging of its worth. There is a bit of grille work in the sacristy of the Salamanca cathedral which is wrought in iron in the most perfect manner, and certainly merits the appellation of being preëminently Plateresque. It is a mere enclosure around a sanctuary, but it is one of the richest pieces of metal work in the peninsula. Also, in a private house in the centre of the commercial district of Barcelona, there is a perfectly charming stairway leading up two sides of an open court, which is visited by every artist who knows where to find it, and is a most typical and perfect example of the Plateresque, with the added merit of the details of the carving being very purely designed and admirably executed, and quite free from the grotesque distortion which is manifest in so much of the Spanish work. There is also a most marvellous grille about the royal chapel in Granada cathedral, and some of the most interesting work in Seville and Toledo cathedrals is in the elaborate Renaissance wrought grilles about the chapels and the choir.

It will be remembered that during the Renaissance period Spain was noted for its universities. At Alcala de Henares, Cardinal Ximenes caused to be built, about 1497, a group of buildings for the university, which are of considerable architectural interest, both by their arrangement and design. Of about the same time is the work in the University of Salamanca, the principal entrance to which shows, considered in detail, some of the choicest carvings of the period. Though this work was executed over four hundred years ago, the soft, yellowish sandstone has preserved all its sharpness and character, and the details seem as clear and crisp-cut as though executed yesterday. The merit of this work is in the decorative quality of its carving. As a design, the whole lacks coherence and purpose. The Irish College in Salamanca is a much more sober and a later example, the chief interest centring in a splendid arcaded courtyard, around which are grouped the buildings. At Leon, the city which also possesses the magnificent Gothic cathedral, there is a very remarkable group of buildings, forming a part of the convent of S. Marcos. The main front of the buildings forms a most interesting composition, with a succession of very elaborate arched openings along the central portion, flanked on the right by the unfinished façade of the convent church, while on the extreme left the lines of the structure are carried out by a low bridge. The elaboration of detail about the central portion of this structure is most remarkable. Carvings, statuettes, bas-reliefs, abound at every conceivable point, and the mechanical execution is so excellent one can almost forget the absence of any real architectural feeling in mass.

Of the Renaissance churches of the middle period the two which are most worthy of interest are the new portions of the cathedral at Salamanca, which, though retaining very strong traces of the Mudejar, are most elaborately carved in Renaissance motives and details, and the Church of S. Domingo or S. Estaban at Salamanca, the entrance to which is simply a tremendous display of fine carvings and figure work crowded about a single central doorway, the carvings being, as is so often the case in Spanish work, excellently wrought, beautiful of themselves, but lacking in appropriateness and not forming a part of a comprehensive scheme. The cloisters of S. Estaban are of more positive architectural merit, without being so rich or so essentially Spanish. The arcades of the cloister are in the style of the early Renaissance of Toulouse, while the vaulting is a species of fanwork which is seldom found in Spain.

The military architecture of Spain is not without considerable interest. It is not easy to make any exact classification of it as to architectural style. Of the early Gothic period there are some interesting brick constructions, such as the old castles at Coca, near Segovia, and at Medina del Campo, in Leon, a few miles south of Valladolid, both of which are constructed entirely of brick and recall the effect of some of the work about Albi in southern France. Of the early period, also, are the fortifications about

Avila, which are picturesque in the extreme and are still in use as an enclosure, though the city has grown somewhat beyond them. Of a later period is the picturesque Alcazar at Segovia, and still later is the Alcazar at Toledo, which has a courtyard with interesting details and a simple but quite effective treatment of a plain exterior wall, while the arch of Gonzales at Burgos, dating from 1539, is one of the latest semimilitary city fortifications still existing. There are also scattered through various parts of Spain very interesting bridge constructions, most of which show the lingering influence of the Roman domination, or perhaps more truly the Moorish interpretation of Roman constructions, notably the Alcala bridge at Toledo, and the long structure which crosses the river just beyond the Mosque, at Cordova.

The palace of the Escorial, which was built by Philip II. in the mountains to the north of Madrid, is in a class by itself. Its architectural value is often ignored, but some of the interior work, though unquestionably copied outright from Italian models and with a notable lack of any particularly Spanish feeling, is quite effective. The library, in the style of the library of the Vatican, is interesting and effective, and the interior of the church, which forms a part of the palace, is impressive with a sombre grandeur which falls but little short of being good architecture.

It is but natural that, given the love of ostentatious display, the desire to keep up the appearance of one's ancestors, and the artificial life of the Spanish courts, the late Renaissance should degenerate into the most meaningless abnormal growths. As the work of the middle Renaissance is designated as the Plateresque, so the developed exuberance of the later neoclassic, the riot of form, is characterized by the name of an architect who is perhaps unjustly credited with most of the late abominations, Josef Churriguera, who died in 1725. Notwithstanding the utter abandonment of good taste which marks the very late work, and the lack of any attempt at coherent design, as is shown in the front of S. Pablo at Valladolid, in the Cartuja of Miraflores at Burgos, or the similar interior at Granada, there still lingered in the late work some traces of the grandiose, pompous, theatrical effects which are so interesting in the best of the Plateresque. The cathedral at Jaen, in Andalusia, north of Granada, is not without some of the good qualities which, transplanted across the ocean, bore fruit in Mexico in the cathedral of Chihuahua and the church at Lagos, though it must be confessed the American examples on the whole are rather more satisfactory. And the homely, uninteresting exterior of Cadiz cathedral encloses an interior which, for theatrical effect and pomp, is hardly equalled throughout Spain. The Spanish archi-

PLATE XXIII

SPAIN, ARCHITECTURE OF. PLATE III

Convent of Miraflores, near Burgos; interior of the church, with tombs. The choir with its carved wooden stalls is in the middle of the picture. The double tomb is that of King Juan II. and his queen, Isabelle of Portugal. The wall tomb on the extreme right is that of their son, Alonzo, who died in youth. These monuments are ascribed to Gil de Siloé, and their epoch is about 1490. The iron railings are entirely modern; they destroy the intended effect of the sculptured surfaces.

tects never quite lost the original traditions. To the present day they will occasionally show the appreciation of the decorative qualities of ornament, and are able to catch the light and shade on their work in a manner which recalls their ancient triumphs.

Of the eighteenth century work, the only structure of any value is the Royal Palace at Madrid, which is a dignified, well-balanced composition, free, on the exterior at least, from any of the exuberance of the mediæval work, and quite equal in design to much of the best of the seventeenth century work of Northern Europe. — C. H. BLACKALL.

Carderera y Solano, *Iconografía Española*, 1855–1864 ; Ford, *Handbook*, 3d ed., 1855 ; Girault de Prangey, *Essai sur l'Architecture des Arabes*, 1842 ; Grangaret de Lagrange, *Les Arabes en Espagne*, 8vo., Paris, 1824 ; Murphy, *Arab. Antiq.*, folio, 1813 ; Parcerisa, *Recuerdos y Bellezas de España*, 1839 ; Spanish Government, *Monumentos Arquitectonicos de España*, 1859–1880 ; Stirling Maxwell, *Annals of the Artists of Spain*, 1848 ; Street, *Gothic Architecture in Spain*, London, 1865 ; Taylor, *Voyage Pittoresque en Espagne*, 1826–1832 ; Villamil et Escosura, *L'Espagne Artistique et Monumentale*, Paris, 1842 ; Villamil y Castro, *Ant. prehistoricas de Galicia*, Madrid, 1868 ; Waring and Macquoid, *Architectural Art*, 1850 ; Wyatt, *Architect's Note-book in Spain*, 1872.

SPALL (n.). A splinter of stone either accidentally removed by irregular pressure as of superincumbent masonry, or by a blow of the hammer. Spalls are used to fill interstices in wall building ; or may be used to make, with abundance of mortar, a kind of rubble masonry, which is called also Spauled and Spawled Rubble.

SPAN. The interval between two terminals of any construction ; the distance apart of two consecutive supports, especially as applied to the opening of an arch or the width of a space covered by an unsupported length of a joist or rafter or truss. As ordinarily understood, the term applies to the clear opening ; but it is frequently used of the distance between the centres of the supports.

SPANDREL. *A.* The quasi-triangular space included between the extradoses of two adjoining arches and a line approximately connecting their crowns, — or the space equal to about half of this, in the case of a single arch,— with whatever piece of masonry or other material fills that space. In decorative styles of architecture this is a favourite place for sculpture or inlaid ornament.

B. In steel skeleton construction, the space between the top of the window in one story and the sill of the window in the story above. (Compare Allège.) — W. R. H.

SPANDREL WALL. A wall or partition erected on the extrados of an arch filling in the spandrels.

SPANNER. A horizontal cross brace or collar beam.

SPARE ROOM. In the United States, a Guest Chamber.

SPARK ARRESTER. (See Electrical Appliances.)

SPAR. *A.* A bar used for fastening a door or gate.

B. Same as Common Rafter. From the use of unhewn timber in primitive or rough building.

SPAUL. Same as Spall.

SPAVENTO, GIORGIO DI PIETRO ; architect ; d. 1509.

Spavento succeeded Antonio Celega as *inzegnerius prothus dominorum procuratorum Sancti Marci*. He built the new sacristy of S. Marco in Venice (begun August, 1486), and at the same time the church of S. Teodoro and that of SS. Filippo e Giacomo in Venice. About 1498 he restored the Sala del Gran Consiglio at the Doges' Palace. He assisted in the construction of the Palazzo della Ragione at Vicenza in 1500, and at the Ponte delle Nave at Verona in 1502. At the same time he built the Capella di S. Niccolò at the Doges' Palace. In 1506 he made the model for, and began the construction of, the church of S. Salvatore in Venice, but was superseded the next year by Pietro and Tullio Lombardo (see Lombardo, P. and T.). In 1507 he was again employed at the Doges' Palace.

Paoletti, *Rinascimento ;* Lorenzi, *Monumenti ;* Ongania, *San Marco.*

SPAWL. Same as Spall.

SPEAKING TUBE. A tube, generally of metal, extending from one part of a building to another, to facilitate intercommunication by the voice.

SPECCHI, ALESSANDRO ; architect.

In coöperation with Francesco de' Sancti he built in Rome between 1721 and 1725 the immense stairway leading from the Piazza di Spagna to the church of S. Trinità de' Monti, the façade of which was built by Domenico Fontana. He built the stalls of the Palazzo Quirinale, Rome.

Gurlitt, *Geschichte des Barockstiles in Italien.*

SPECIFICATION. *A.* A formulation in words of all those items of information regarding a proposed building which cannot be graphically set forth in the drawings. It is consequently supplementary to the drawings and is necessary to define the especial conditions, limitations, and requirements to be observed by the contracting parties in carrying them into execution, and, specifically, the character and quality of the material and workmanship to be employed.

Specifications generally open with the statement of certain general propositions common to most building-contracts, including the requirement that the party of the second part, generally called "the contractor," is to furnish all apparatus and utensils necessary to the carrying on of the work ; that all materials are to be the best of their several kinds unless expressly set forth to the contrary ; that the work is to be carried on promptly, in order, and without unnecessary delays ; that it is to be completed and ready for use at a certain date ; that the drawings are to be followed exactly according to their true intent, not only the general drawings which have been signed as a part of the contract, but those detail and full-size drawings which are to be subsequently furnished in further explanation of the original drawings. After a page or two of preliminaries of this general kind, the more specific items of work and material are briefly recited as far as possible in the order of execution, and each in a separate paragraph with a distinctive title. These include, for example, the special requirements as to excavation, drainage, and grading ; the character of footings, foundations, and underpinnings ; of all cut stonework, brickwork or terra cotta ; of chimney stacks and all other special constructions in masonry ; of all framing, whether of timber, iron, or steel ; of all partitions and furrings, whether fireproof or otherwise ; of all boarding, flooring, and roofing ; of plastering and stucco work ; of interior finish in all departments ; of doors and windows, stairs, wainscottings, and tiling, marble and metal work ; electric wiring and electric connections of all kinds ; gas piping, plumbing, and plumbing fixtures ; heating and sanitary provisions ; elevator service ; painting, polishing, and decorating of all degrees and kinds ; builders' hardware and all the devices of construction and equipment necessary to the perfecting of the scheme.

As, with the progress of civilization, the requirements of convenience, comfort, use, and economy or luxury of every degree have become more exacting, and as the appliances to meet these exactions have become more complicated and scientific, the function of the specification in building contracts has greatly increased in importance. The modest instrument of a dozen or twenty pages, which amply sufficed our fathers to secure good work and material according to their standard, has expanded into a formidable document often of more than a hundred. The progress of invention is so active, and methods and material of building are so constantly changing and enlarging, that the architect cannot properly develop his specification upon established formulas or comfortable routine, but is constrained to a constant vigilance lest in his latest work he should fail to avail himself of the best which science and invention is constantly lavishing upon the art of building.

In order to avoid the danger of omissions and to facilitate the work of the architect in the important department which we are now considering, model blank specifications have been prepared by skilful hands with the intention of including every item necessary to the modern building in construction, material, and appliance ; but these, though in some cases and to some practitioners useful, are generally found cumbersome in practice, and rather to complicate than to simplify the task of the architect.

The architect of active practice finds it on the whole safer and more convenient to perfect his specification out of the fulness of his own experience and observation, using perhaps, as a guide and monitor, his specification for some previous structure which has produced the best results with the least conflict of interpretation.

Under these conditions, the greatest virtues of the modern specification are comprehensiveness, order, clearness and compactness of definition, and the utmost brevity consistent with these qualities ; avoiding unnecessary enlargements, repetitions, and all that sort of generalization which may mean much or little according to the point of view, which rather confuses than instructs the builder, and is therefore fruitful in disputes. Moreover, the overburdened specification may be and often is greatly relieved, without in any way impairing the force and intelligibility of the contract, by omitting such items as can be inscribed upon the drawings themselves and in immediate connection with the delineation of the details which they are intended to explain.

—HENRY VAN BRUNT.

B. In law, the whole body of description and direction under which a building is erected ; in this sense including the drawings as well as the specification in sense *A*, including also such orders or decisions of the architect or other superintendent as may have controlled in part the character of the work. (See Law Concerning Building, *C*, 8.) — R. S.

Bower, *Specifications; a Practical System for writing Specifications for Buildings*, New York, W. T. Comstock.

SPECUS. In Roman architecture, the channel of an aqueduct elevated above the ground, and covered by an arch, or slabs. Sometimes the same arcade carried several of these channels, one above another.

SPEER. Same as Spier.

SPEISET, FRIEDRICH. (See Egl., Andreas.)

SPEOS. In Greek, a cave, especially a large or deep one ; hence in archæology, a cave-temple or a large tomb ; a large and architectural chamber, excavated in the rock. (Cut, cols. 577 and 578.)

SPHÆRISTERIUM. In Roman architecture, an enclosed place adapted to ball playing. The *sphæristeria* were often adjuncts of baths, gymnasia, and important villas. (Compare Fives Court ; Tennis Court.)

SPHINX. A creature made up of parts of a lion (but see below) and of another natural animal, though the artistic conception may be thought rather to include the whole nature of each. In Egyptian antiquity, the human-headed sphinx is always male; and of this nature is the Great Sphinx, which is one of the very earliest of existing monuments. It is near the great pyramids of Gizeh, partly cut from the rock, partly built up of masonry, with a temple or shrine built against the breast, the path to which leads between the fore paws. The height to the top of the head is 66 feet.

forming a Quirk. In each sense obsolescent. Also Speer, Sper ; called also Enterclose.

SPIGOT. A plug to close the aperture of a faucet and control the flow of liquid. The spigot itself may be perforated for the passage of the liquid. A mere perforated cork or stopper fitted with a peg is a faucet and spigot. By extension, these terms are applied, in the plumbing and kindred trades, to various contrivances and parts intended respectively for the reception of, or the insertion into, another part. Thus, each length of ordinary iron drain pipe is made with one end abruptly enlarged to form a socket for the reception of the small end of the connecting length, the small end being known as the spigot end, the larger as the faucet end.

SPIGOT AND FAUCET JOINT. A joint between two lengths of pipe, made by the insertion of the spigot end of one into the faucet end of the other, as explained under Spigot ; called also Spigot Joint.

SPIKE. A pointed bar or strip, commonly of iron, as in a grille or the cresting of a wall. In the United States, more commonly a very large nail.

SPILE. *A.* A peg or plug used to fill a nailhole, as a spigot.

B. Same as Pile.

SPILLWAY. A channel for superfluous water, as from an overflow of a dammed and walled lake, reservoir, or tank. In some in-

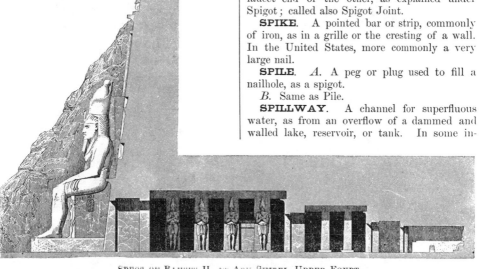

SPEOS OF RAMSES II. AT ABU SIMBEL, UPPER EGYPT.

The name given to this image is transliterated Hu, or more fully, Horemkhu, a word having connection with the god Horus, and other androsphinxes seem to have received the same name. Such images cut out of single blocks of granite and of all sizes up to 8 feet in length, were sometimes arranged along a roadway or approach to a temple, forming a double avenue. (See Androsphinx ; Criosphinx ; Hieracosphinx.)

In Greek and Greco-Roman antiquity the sphinx is always female, with human head and breast. In some coins, etc., the forms are of the dog rather than of the lion.

SPIER. A permanent screen ; especially in a hall, as of a manor house, or English college, or London Company, the architecturally treated partition cutting off a part, as described in Vol. I., col. 346. Apparently, also, a partition

stances this takes the shape of an aqueduct of architectural character.

SPINA. The wall or other barrier extending along the middle of a Roman circus, and about the ends of which the contestants turned.

SPINDLE. A member round in one direction, as if revolved upon one axis. The term fusiform, which means spindle-shaped, implies a form larger in the middle and approaching a point at each end ; but the word spindle is applied more loosely, as to the small pieces of turned wood which make up the grating of the Meshrebeeyeh, and equally to the turned part of a post, baluster, or other piece fashioned in the lathe.

SPINTHAROS ; architect.

He built the latest temple of Apollo at Delphi, in Greece. This building was not begun before 536 B.C.

Pausanias, ed. Frazer ; Brunn, *Geschichte*.

SPIRE OF CHURCH: BERNIÈRES
(CALVADOS); 13TH CENTURY.

SPIRE OF SOUTH TOWER, CHARTRES CATHEDRAL: c. 1175;
HEIGHT ABOUT 350 FEET.

579

580

SPIRA. The mouldings at the base of a column.

SPIRE. In general, any slender, pointed erection, surmounting a building. Its distinctive form was generated from the steep tower roofs characteristic, especially, of the secular buildings of the Middle Ages in France and Germany; but when the roofs were transferred to churches, they gradually submitted to architectural modifications, so important, that a new type of form was finally developed, even as early as the twelfth century, to which the name of spire has been specifically attached. In fact, the feature became the natural termination of every church tower from the thirteenth to the sixteenth century, and, whether built or not, it was provided for in the design and construction of every such tower. These modifications of the original steep roof included an increase in the height so considerable that it was often equal to the whole height of the supporting structure, and was rarely less than two-thirds of it.

Spires in their most common and simplest form, as in parish churches, arose from the tower cornice, where they could obtain direct support, and, as they were octagonal in plan, the diagonal sides were built up from corbels or squinches, which were developed from the interior corners of the towers; on the outside these corners were occupied by steep pyramidal constructions of triangular plan, rising from the tower cornice and sloping back to the diagonal or canted faces of the spire. The variations of, and departures from, these simple and beautiful types are very numerous, and were entirely influenced by the desire to obtain variety and enrichment of sky line, and by the desire to reconcile the tower with the spire, so that together they might form one harmonious composition with no visible line of demarcation, as in the south tower of Chartres, and in those of Senlis, Reims, Laon, etc. To this the spire ribs were broken into rich crockets, tall gabled spire lights grew up on the faces, in emulation of the pinnacles crowded around the base of the spire; often an octagonal open lantern was interposed between tower and spire, and pinnacles were built on the unoccupied corners of the tower, flanking the lantern as at Freiburg in the Breisgau. The sides of the spire were often pierced by foliated openings, and sometimes, as in Freiburg in the Breisgau, Burgos in Spain, etc., the whole structure became a mere open-work of tracery. In these enrichments of the primitive type, every device of design was used to obliterate the line of demarcation between tower and spire, and the general pyramidal effect of the combined structure was secured by the successive offsets of the tower buttresses, so that the tapering effect, as especially at S. Stephen's at Vienna, began at the ground, and one feature melted into the other by insensible transition.

581

SPIRE OF NORTH TOWER, CHARTRES CATHEDRAL:
FINISHED 1513: HEIGHT ABOUT 380 FEET.

582

In other and later varieties, especially in England, the spire arose from the roof of the tower behind a mask of ornamental battlements and pinnacles, confessing itself as a separate structure. In these cases the spire was often of wood. In some of the later mediæval spires in the sixteenth century, the ambitious builders lost sight of the primitive type, and a general pyramidal effect was obtained by the superimposition, as at Strasburg, of a diminishing succession of highly enriched vertical steps. When, in the Renaissance period, the church towers climbed in this way to their final consummation with classic detail ingeniously disposed, as in the famous churches of Sir Christopher Wren in England, the constructions ceased properly to be spires and became steeples, though the latter term is sometimes loosely applied, even to examples so pure as that of Salisbury.

— HENRY VAN BRUNT.

SPIRELET. A small spire, as of a pinnacle or turret.

SPUR: ENGLISH ROMANESQUE; ROCHESTER CATHEDRAL; c. 1120.

SPIRE LIGHT. A window in a spire, generally in the form of an attenuated dormer, with a steep roof or gable, used less to give light to the interior than in conjunction with pinnacles to enrich its outlines. (See Spire.)

SPLAY. Any surface, larger than a Chamfer or a Bevel, making an oblique angle with another surface; specifically said of the oblique jamb of an opening, as in a window or doorway.

SPLINE. *A.* A thin, narrow board, corresponding generally to boards used for ceiling, and the like.

B. Same as Loose Tongue (which see under Tongue).

C. In drawing, a thin strip of some elastic, flexible material, used as a guide in drawing curves, by being bent to the desired form and held in place by weights or pins.

Feather Tongue Spline. A spline in sense *A*, but cut to a bevel. (See Clapboard.)

SPLIT PIN. A pin, as a spike, split at the point, so as to spread when it is driven in, giving somewhat the form of a dovetail, and making it difficult to extract.

SPRING. *A.* The line or plane at which the curve of an arch or vault leaves the upright or impost.

B. Resilience, as of a floor; its elasticity when compressed.

SPRING (v.). To leave its impost by rounding upward and outward, said of an arch or vault. In making elevation drawings and section drawings, the horizontal plane at which this takes place is represented by a horizontal line; hence, the common term, Springing Line, which is used even when the building itself is under consideration, as when it is said by a person looking at a vault: The springing line is about nine feet above the pavement.

SPRINGER. A stone or other solid which is laid at the impost of an arch. (See Skew and following titles; also Spring, v.)

SPRING HOUSE. A building erected over a natural spring to protect it from injury or impurities; sometimes decorative, or large enough to contain fixed seats; or used as a place for cooling milk, or the like, in the cold water, as frequently on American farms, where the house is roughly built of wood.

SPRINGING COURSE. (See Spring, v.; Springer.)

SPRINGING LINE. The line marking the level from which an arch springs. (See Spring, v.)

SPRINKLER. A system of perforated pipes extending through a building, and at frequent points connected with a water supply, controlled by fusible plugs, which, when melted by an accidental fire in their neighborhood, automatically turn on the water and start the sprinklers to extinguish the flames.

SPUDD AND RING. A metal ring or ferrule combined with a projecting pin, and applied to the foot of a wooden post, or the like, to secure it to a stone base or sill, the pin being inserted into the stone. — (A. P. S.)

SPUR. *A.* In timber framing, a diagonal brace between a post and a tie beam or rafter.

B. A buttress or similar projecting piece of walling.

C. In mediæval architecture, specifically, the carved claw or griffe projecting from the lower torus of a column, so as to cover one of the projecting corners of the square plinth beneath.

SPUR BRACE. Same as Spur, *A.*

SQUARE. *A.* An open space, generally

more or less rectangular, in a town, formed at the junction of two or more streets, or by the enlargement of one for a short distance ; especially, such a place provided with a park or parks.

SPUR: ENGLISH GOTHIC, EARLIEST TYPE; S. CROSS, WINCHESTER.

B. Same as Block, *E.*

C. An instrument intended primarily for laying out right angles, consisting usually of two arms fixed, or capable of being accurately adjusted, perpendicularly to each other.

Carpenters' Square. A steel implement forming a right angle with a shorter and a

sense *C*, having a long blade attached at about the centre of a shorter crosspiece. In use, the latter is moved along the edge of a drawing board, holding the long blade in successive parallel positions. Some T squares have adjustable blades, which can be set at different angles with the head.

SQUARE (v.). To provide by an instrument, or otherwise, that the angles of a piece

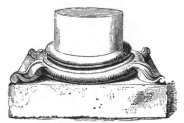

SPUR: ENGLISH GOTHIC; 13TH CENTURY; STOCK-BURY, KENT.

of work or material are right angles ; or to ascertain the amount of their deviation from right angles.

SQUARE END. The end of a piece of timber when cut off square, in contradistinction to an end prepared for framing with a tenon or otherwise.

SQUINCH: OXFORD CATHEDRAL; C. 1240.

longer arm, each divided into feet and inches or other measurements.

Set Square. In drawing, same as Triangle.

T Square. A draughtsman's square, in

SQUARE-FRAMED. In joinery, framed with square and not moulded pieces.

SQUARE-HEADED. Having a straight horizontal lintel or a flat arch, said of a doorway, or window opening.

SQUARE STAFF. A wooden rod, square in section, set flush in an external angle of plastered surfaces to secure the corner from injury. When moulded it is called a staff bead. (See Shaft; Staff, *B.*; also subtitles Angle Bar; Bead.)

of the high altar from a point where it would otherwise be invisible. (See Hagioscope.)

SS. *A.* The abbreviation for *santissimo, -ma, -mi* (Italian), or *sanctissimus, -ma, -mi* (Latin). The most holy; a title generally reserved for the Trinity or the persons of the

SQUINCH: SALISBURY CATHEDRAL; c. 1300.

SQUINCH. An arch, a lintel, corbelling, or system of such members, built across the interior corner of two walls, as at the top of a tower, to serve as foundation for the diagonal or canted side of a superimposed octagonal spire or lantern. The squinch performs the functions of a Pendentive (which see).

Trinity and their attributes, including the Host, the Assumption, the Cross. Used even in English writing in the same sense.

B. The abbreviation of *santi, i.e.,* saints, in cases where a church is dedicated to two saints;

SQUINT: CRAWLEY CHURCH, HAMPSHIRE; 13TH CENTURY; THE SILL SERVES AS A PISCINA.

SQUINT: S. MARY MAGDALEN, TAUNTON; 14TH CENTURY.

SQUINT. An aperture pierced askew through the interior walls of a church, often on the side of a chancel arch, so as to give a view

as (in Italian) SS. Giovanni e Paolo. In the same sense (in English), used to replace the word "Saints," though rarely.

STAB (v.). To roughen the surface of a brick wall by light blows with a point, so as to make a hold for plastering. (See Key, *C.*)

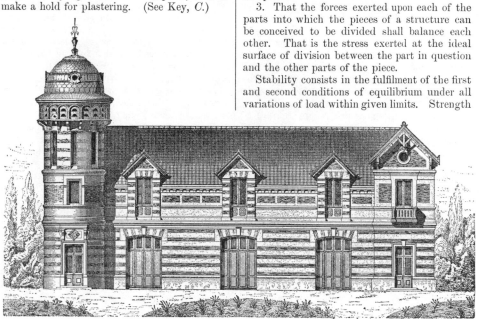

STABLE AT MÂCON (SÂONE-ET-LOIRE), FRANCE.

resistances, or stresses, exerted at the joints of the piece.

3. That the forces exerted upon each of the parts into which the pieces of a structure can be conceived to be divided shall balance each other. That is the stress exerted at the ideal surface of division between the part in question and the other parts of the piece.

Stability consists in the fulfilment of the first and second conditions of equilibrium under all variations of load within given limits. Strength

STABILITY. As applied to structures, the property of remaining in equilibrium without change of position, although the externally applied force may deviate to a certain extent its mean amount or position. The conditions of equilibrium of a structure are these : —

1. That the forces exerted on the whole structure by external bodies shall balance each other. The external forces are the force of gravity, causing the weight of the structure, the pressures exerted against it by bodies not forming part of it, and the supporting forces, or resistances of the foundations.

2. That the forces exerted on each piece of

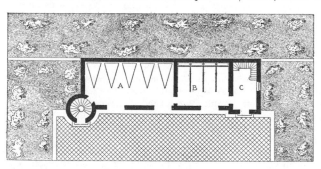

GROUND STORY: *A*, CARRIAGE HOUSE; *B*, STABLE: *C*, HARNESS ROOM.

a structure shall balance each other. These forces are the weight, the external load, and the

consists in the fulfilment of the third.

—W. R. H.

STABLE. A place where horses are housed,

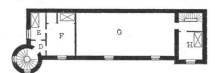

UPPER STORY: *D*, LANDING; *E*, *F*, *H*, BED ROOMS; *G*, FODDER LOFT.

fed, and cared for, and, incidentally, where vehicles, horses' equipments, and feed are kept for use, and sometimes where coachmen or grooms have their lodgings; also, in composition, a place provided for other domestic animals, as cow stable. Stables for horses may be distinguished as private, club, livery, breeders' or trainers', farm, sale, delivery, and racing stables.

The principal features in the plan of a private stable are (1) the stable proper, allowing an area about 10 by 10 feet each for box or loose stalls, and about 5 by 9 feet each for common stalls, with a sufficient common space for stable service in grooming and tackling, ventilation in the ceiling, connecting by a trunk through the loft above with a ventilator on the roof, drainage for each stall, high windows, a watering trough, and feed ducts of various sorts from the loft above for grain and hay ; (2) the carriage or coach room, allowing about 100 square feet for each vehicle, and a sufficient clear space for entrance and exit and for harnessing and unharnessing, the carriage room being generally the vestibule of the establishment ; (3) the wash stand for washing carriages, which is either an annex to the carriage house, occupying 350 to 400 square feet, with floors shedding the water to a single drainage point, or a depression in the floor of the carriage house with similar drainage facilities and covered by a grating ; (4) a harness room, opening generally from the stable directly or indirectly, and containing various hanging devices for harness, together with some means for heating ; (5) an enclosed yard connected with the stable ; (6) a dung pit, generally in the yard ; and (7) an open shed for the temporary shelter of carriages. The second story is connected with the first by an enclosed stairway, and contains over the stable a grain and hay loft with an exterior door for taking in feed of all sorts, provision for ventilation by the vent trunk before mentioned, and often lodging rooms for coachmen or grooms. A cow stable and tool house often form a part of this group. The stable proper contains the stalls, of which the partitions are of plank about four feet high, surmounted by a ramp, generally of open ironwork. The stable floor is of wood, clay, asphaltum, vitrified brick, or artificial stone, sloping to drainage gutters and extending into the stalls ; sometimes the stall floors are of compact clay or earth, and a stout wood grating is often placed over the stall paving. In the country, the various parts of the stable are often in separate but connected buildings, or in distinct wings of one long, low building ; but in the city, where space is valuable, there is a far greater compactness of plan than is necessary or desirable elsewhere.

Club stables, as they are generally built in crowded localities, are compact forms of large private establishments, but with more ample accommodations, the washing place being often in a covered courtyard, placed between the coach house and the stables.

Livery stables are generally an enlarged but inexpensive form of club stables, without their luxury or completeness of appointment and finish, and often without adequate ventilation. The stalls are generally narrower, and are often placed either in a basement or in a second story, with access by inclined planes ; and, in general, every device of economy is used in their construction and equipment consistent with the decent keeping of horses and vehicles, and prompt service.

In breeders' and trainers' stables, convenience and economy of service are obtained in large, well-built, barn-like structures, generally provided with a broad central passage like a nave, the stalls being ranged on either side, generally facing inward with passages behind, and the hay and other feed stored in lofts of half stories above. Special provisions are made for ventilation by louvres, clearstories, or lanterns, and for cleanliness ; and separate accommodations are provided in loose boxes for breeding mares and colts. In those parts of the United States, especially in Kentucky and the southwestern states, where the breeding and training of high-bred horses form an active industry, this great barn, with its offices, is often the principal building in a group of subordinate structures for hospital service, farriery, etc., with ample stable yards for airing, well-watered pastures, and often a private track for the training of racers and roadsters.

In sales stables, where provision must be made for several hundred animals constantly changing, the stalls are disposed in a series of long ranges, head to head, with broad passages between. A counting room, and generally a salesroom with seats in successive grades on one side, a pulpit for the auctioneer on the other, and an area between for the display of the stock under sale, form an essential part of such an establishment ; and the whole is contained under a wide roof sloping on two sides, supported on posts between the stalls, with a louvre or clearstory at the top provided with numerous windows for ventilation and light.

On the Continent of Europe the château or Schloss in the country, or the hôtel in the city, generally has its stable in the buildings surrounding the quadrangle, to which access is obtained by a gateway in the enclosing wall.

Cattle stables are rarely provided on a large scale in the great cattle-raising regions of the United States, except for the protection of high grade stock. In the neighborhood of great abattoirs and packing houses, immense feeding stables are sometimes established, in which the herds, which have been reared on the open ranges, may be fattened for the market more readily and conveniently than in the pastures. These sheds occur not infrequently as part of the plant of large breweries, the grain, after having been deprived of its alcoholic properties, being transmitted hot through trunks to long feeding troughs, which have ranges of covered stalls on either side. Stables for blooded stock do not differ materially from those provided for the breeding of horses. The rural farm stable for milk cattle is a long and often rough structure, without much distinctive character. The farm stock is often housed in a part of the hay barn, on the main floor or in a basement with access from the rear. — HENRY VAN BRUNT.

STACK. *A.* Of a chimney. (See Chimney Stack.)

B. For the storage of books in a library. (See Bookstack ; Library ; Stackroom.)

STACKELBERG, MAGNUS, FREIHERR VON ; architect ; b. 1787 ; d. 1837.

Educated in Dresden, and from Dresden went to Rome, and in 1810 to Greece, where he assisted in the excavation of the temple of Athena at Ægina (see Cockerell, C. R.). He published *Der Apollo tempel zu Bassæ in Arcadien* (Rome, 1826, folio), and *La Grèce, vues pittoresques et topographiques* (Paris, 1834, folio).

Seubert, *Künstler-lexicon.*

STACKROOM. A room in a library provided for the bookstacks. Usually, in public libraries, such rooms are not open to the public, the books being served from the room by the attendants.

STACKSTAND. A structure intended to receive a haystack, usually consisting of a circular frame with uprights which lift it 2 feet or more above the ground, for the purpose of keeping off dampness and vermin.

STADDEL ; STADDLE. *A.* A prop or post, such as may be used for temporary purpose, as in scaffolding.

B. Same as Stackstand.

STADHUIS. In the Netherlands, a town house or city hall.

STADIUM. In Roman archæology, an open area for the foot race and for the exercises of athletes ; often made architectural by its association with Thermæ or the like.

STAFF (I.). *A.* A piece used to close the joint between a wooden frame, as a window or door frame, and the masonry in which it is set.

B. A piece used to strengthen or protect an external angle in plastering ; often called Angle Staff.

STAFF (II.). A kind of stiff plastering held together with any fibrous material, and generally used for exterior surfacings and mouldings, as in temporary buildings.

STAFF BEAD. Same as Angle Staff (see Staff, *B*).

STAGE. A platform in a theatre, auditorium, or similar place, on which the performance is carried on.

STAGE DOOR. A door giving access to the stage and to that portion of a theatre which is for the use of the actors and other employees.

STAGGER (v.). To arrange in alternate order, as bolts connecting two members of a frame which are often set zigzag ; or as beams resting upon a wall, where there are two sets, one on each side, and those on one side are set halfway between those on the other side. By extension, to dispose floors so that each one

is not continuous throughout the building, but so that they are arranged in two or more vertical series, each with its own independent system of heights.

STAGING. Same as Scaffolding.

STAIN. *A.* A colouring liquid or dye for application to any material — most often wood. It differs from paint as being thinner and readily absorbed by the pores of the material, instead of forming a coating on the surface, so that the texture and grain of the material is not concealed. In America stain has been used for exteriors of frame houses, the shingles and clapboards taking on a rougher and far more picturesque look than if painted.

B. Any ingredient which is used to change the colour of a material by chemical action, as in the case of glass, in which a deep blue is got by means of protoxide of cobalt, and a

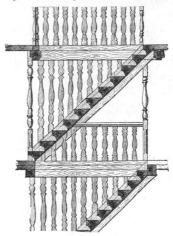

STAIRS IN A HOUSE AT WOLFENSCHIESSEN, SWITZERLAND. EACH STEP IS A SOLID TIMBER: ITS ENDS FRAMED INTO THE STRING PIECES.

green by copper and by iron, as in the production of pot metal (see Glass). Silver Stain (see subtitle) is more properly an enamel applied to the surface without changing the colour of the mass.

Silver Stain. In decorative glasswork, a yellow enamel introduced into Europe in the fifteenth century and immediately accepted by the makers of decorative windows. (See Window, Part III.)

STAINED GLASS. (See Glass ; Window.)

STAINING. (See Stain.)

STAIR. A series of steps, or of flights of steps, connected by landings, for passing from one floor or other principal level to another, or to several other successive floors or levels. Thus, a series of steps from one floor to another in a house would be called a stair, as well as the entire series connecting the successive floors from the lowest to the uppermost. The term Flight is often used as synonymous with stair in designating the structure contained between two floors; this use is only correct, however, when no landings intervene. No absolute distinction can be made between stairs and ladders; a simpler form of construction or a steeper pitch being often the only feature of a flight of steps which would cause it to be designated as a ladder, as in ships.

As regards their construction, stairs may be classified as Newel Stairs and Geometrical Stairs

CATHEDRAL OF SENS (YONNE). STAIRCASE TO UPPER SACRISTY. TRANSITION; 12TH CENTURY.

(see subtitles); as regards their general plan, they are designated as quarter-turn, half-turn, three-quarter-turn, and one-turn, implying that, in their progress from top to bottom, they pass through one, two, three, or four right angles. Such turns may be made by a continuous series of winders, or by straight flights and winders, or by straight flights and paces or landings. Thus, a quarter-turn stair may accomplish the turn by a plan constructed on a quarter circle with risers radiating from its centre; or it may be composed of two straight flights at right

angles with a pace or with winders in the quarter space; or again, it may be a single straight flight terminating with two or three winders at top or at bottom.

The stair has undergone a marked change from early times to the present in location and disposition as well as in construction; and in no class of building so much as in the residence. It is quite a modern idea, that of providing but one staircase for the chief apartments, and of treating this one as an all-important and prominent feature. A back stair, or two, there may be for domestic service; but, except for these, there is rarely more than the one flight or series of flights for communication between floors. And this disposition and treatment marks strongly the difference in the modern stair and that of the Middle Ages and earlier part of the Renaissance. A mediæval castle, of even a small and unpretentious sort, would have a number of staircases at frequent intervals, and these comparatively small and placed in a rather retired situation, in small towers, corner turrets, or in the thickness of a wall or buttress, so that the dwelling was divided vertically into suites of rooms. The motive for such a disposition was, of course, primarily security and the facility of defence, the building being divided vertically into towerlike compartments by more or less massive walls, two adjoining compartments having little or no lateral communication. Large and important stairs there were, but not for very general communication: rather in the way of outside perrons or their equivalent in a vestibule or somewhat isolated tower.

This general arrangement of many isolated stairs continued in vogue long after the abandonment of the original reason for such a provision in the way of vertical communication, and was even retained when the more modern practice began of lateral intercommunication by means of passages on each floor. (See House, Figs. 5 and 6.) This is to be seen in such buildings as the late châteaux of France and the great Elizabethan houses; although here, already, the modern idea of one "main stairway" began to find expression, but still not to the exclusion of several other subordinate ones. Such "grand staircases" were at first rather a part of the state apartments — to be used

PLATE XXIV

STAIR

In the north transept of Burgos cathedral, Spain, leading to the external doorway called the Puerta Alta ("high portal"), this height being made nec-essary by the slope of the ground. This work dates from the sixteenth century, and is ascribed to Diego de Siloé.

on occasions of ceremony — than a means of general communication. In recent times the restricted size of building lots in cities makes the provision of several staircases impossible, beyond the putting in of a service stair near the dining room or pantry ; but this feature does not appear to be generally adopted even in the spacious and costly country residences of late years, or in the large city houses, where economy of space is not of first importance.

As regards this last necessity, — economy of

not always have when opening only on the general passages and main stairway.

In its modern construction, the stair of common usage in Great Britain and the United States has become less an integral part of the general construction, and more of a separate piece of light framing set up after the completion of the main structure — often in large part completed before being brought to the site. This requires, in its construction, great skill in joinery, built, as it usually is, of light and

STAIRCASE AT PÉRIGUEUX (DORDOGNE): NEOCLASSIC OF 17TH CENTURY, WITH LOCAL PECULIARITIES OF DETAIL.

space, — much is to be said in favour of the spiral stair, — or some modification of a turning stair, — when not too restricted in its dimensions. This again was an early feature retained until quite recent times, its great advantage lying in the fact that comparatively little space was required horizontally ; a landing in the run of the stair would answer the purpose of the elongated passage as now usually provided to connect two flights.

On the whole, then, it is perhaps a question whether the modern practice of providing one central stair has not caused the abandonment of a valuable feature. An additional retired stair might often give a certain privacy and retirement to a set of rooms which they would

slender parts, secured together with systems of slight concealed bracing and blocking and with much use of glue. The necessity for such highly trained labour has indeed developed a special class of joiners, and a wooden stair of some elaboration is now almost invariably supplied by a stair-builder, who makes such construction his only business. This is the more necessary in the case of curved and winding stairs, where great skill is required in building up and shaping the wreaths and other curved portions, and in so securing the various members together to make the stair, as a whole, self-supporting, at least between its terminal bearings. In the greater part of the

STAIR: PALAIS DE JUSTICE, PARIS; ABOUT 1880.   THE CUT-STONE STRING PIECE FOLLOWING THE SWEEP AND THE TURNS OF THE STAIR IS OF VERY GENERAL USE IN FRANCE; THE PARAPET IS GENERALLY OF METAL, AS HERE.

Continent of Europe the old traditions obtain of erecting solid stairs of stone at the same time with the surrounding masonry, wood not being very generally used except in those localities where it abounds and where construction

Perhaps the most important point in considering the planning of a stair is the pitch, or, in other words, the relation between the riser and tread. In buildings of an unpretentious sort the pitch is often restricted, owing to other

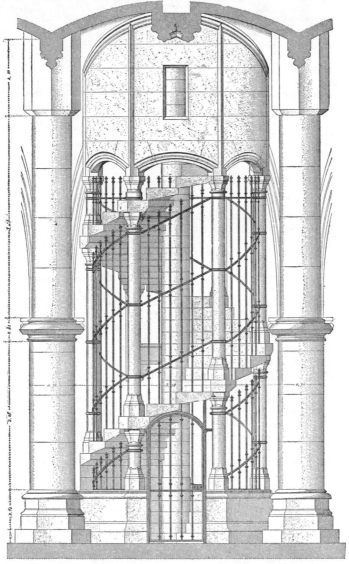

PALAIS DE JUSTICE, PARIS. THE CAGE IS CYLINDRICAL, AND PIERCES THE VAULTED FLOOR BELOW AND ABOVE. THE IRONWORK IS INTENDED TO SEPARATE THE STAIRWAY COMPLETELY FROM THE CORRIDORS; THERE IS A GATE AT EVERY LANDING.

in that material is traditional. Even then it is commonly treated in a massive and substantial way, with larger and solid parts put together by methods of more genuine framing: even the solid step is not altogether unknown, cut from one piece after the manner of a stone step so as to form both tread and riser.

exigencies in the floor plan; but, under ordinary circumstances, the requirements of the surrounding features should yield so far as to allow of ample horizontal space for the stair in order to avoid a steep ascent. Several rules are prescribed for determining the relation of the riser and tread. In the United States their sum is generally taken as between 17 and 18 inches, and the riser made as little over $7\frac{1}{2}$ inches as possible, in the ordinary stairs for dwellings.

Another rule gives the quotient of tread and riser as between 70 and 75 inches. In Great Britain this quotient is commonly prescribed as 66 inches, based on the assumption that a step $5\frac{1}{2}$ inches high by 12 inches wide is a proper average step. Another British method of proportion is based on the same assumed standard, and provides that, for every inch of tread added to or subtracted from 12 inches, the $5\frac{1}{2}$ inch riser should be decreased or increased by $\frac{1}{2}$ inch, or vice versa. Thus we should have :

For a 13 inch tread a 5   inch riser
    "   12   "   " $5\frac{1}{2}$ "   "
    "   10   "   "   7   "   "

It is worthy of note that, from the above rules, the total length of step assumed as correct for British usage is noticeably less than the standard assumed in the United States. For instance, by the first British rule cited above, a riser of $7\frac{1}{2}$ inches would require a tread of $66 \div 7\frac{1}{2} = 8\frac{4}{5}$ inches, whereas this would rarely be less than 10 inches in the United States, except for a back stair or the like. A rule adopted from the French gives results more nearly equivalent to the American custom — twice the riser, added to the width of tread, should be between 24 and 25 inches. The German rule for stairs of ordinary pitch is substantially the same, but is not considered altogether practical when applied to a riser of less than 14 cm. or more than 19 cm. ($5\frac{1}{2}$ and $7\frac{1}{2}$ inches respectively). In the former case, the product of tread and riser is taken as 47 cm. ($18\frac{1}{2}$ inches); in the latter case, the width of tread is obtained by dividing the coefficient 500 by the given riser. This coefficient being prescribed for centimetres, its equivalent for inches would be $77\frac{1}{2}$. These formulæ are as given in the Darmstadt *Handbuch*, and give results substantially equivalent to the dimensions of American practice.

The foregoing dimensions for treads do not, of course, include the nosing, which is not considered in determining the size of steps. For ordinary purposes a riser of 7 to $7\frac{1}{2}$ inches with a tread of 10 inches makes a very comfortable ascent. If, however, the stair is long, it will be desirable to make the riser much less in proportion to the tread, thus lessening the pitch of the stair. It is also well, in the case of a long stair, to introduce one or more landings. It should be noted, however, that for stairs out of doors a much longer step is practical, and even quite desirable, especially as where a short flight is introduced in the course of a footpath or at the break of a terrace. In such cases the longer step, especially with a low riser, accommodates itself more pleasantly to the impetus and longer stride naturally gained by a person walking a distance out of doors.

The pitch of the stair being assumed, it is desirable that it be altered as little as possible during the ascent. The riser, of course, once determined, remains unchanged : the tread also should be as nearly constant as possible. That is, if winders become necessary, they should be introduced as Balanced Steps (see under Step); and this change of plan should be as gradual as possible, as described under Winder. It is, of course, a modern axiom that winders are to be avoided in a stair of any pretension, except in a case of circular stairs of long radius, or similar stairs laid out on a very extended sweep, as is typical of the stone staircases of the more recent French châteaux. It is to be observed, however, that the prejudice, where such exists, against a winding stair of a smaller and less spacious sort, is of quite modern origin ; as the circular staircase was the common form in mediæval and later architecture, as has been pointed out above. A winding stair offers one advantage which, although of no great importance, is, perhaps, worth consideration : by the triangular form of the tread the step accommodates itself to different lengths of stride, according to the distance of a pedestrian from the axis. The width of landings, where these occur in a straight stair, is almost equal in importance to the width of tread, and should be designed to conform to an average length of step ; say, the width of the tread plus 24 inches, or a multiple of 24. (See Scala.)

In addition to the following terms, various specific names are applied to stairs derived from the construction of certain parts, their meaning being self-evident from the use of the attributive term, as in Open Riser Stair, Closed String Stair. (See Landing ; Newel ; Pace ; Riser ; Step ; String.) — D. N. B. S.

Back Stair. Any stair situated at the rear, that is, at the back, of a building, as for domestic service or other subordinate purpose. Hence, any retired and unimportant stair for a similar use, wherever situated.

Box Stair. One made with two closed strings, so that it has a boxlike form of construction, and may be more or less completely finished before being set up on the site.

Close String Stair. (See Close String, under String.)

Cocklestair. From Cochlea ; a helical or corkscrew stair.

Cut String Stair. (See Cut String, under String.)

Dog-leg ; Dog-legged Stair. A half-turn stair consisting of two parallel flights, their strings and hand rails being in the same vertical plane. The hand rail of the lower flight commonly butts against the under side of the string of the upper flight, there being no well hole.

Geometrical Stair. One which is constructed without the use of newels at the angles or turning points. The intersecting strings and hand rails are, therefore, usually joined by means of short curved portions called wreaths.

Giants' Stair (*Scala dei Giganti*). A perron or out-of-door stairway in the court of the Doges' Palace at Venice. The name is derived from the two statues, Mars and Neptune, which stand on pedestals at the head of the stair, and are the work of Jacopo Sansovino. It consists of thirty steps, and a plat-

STALACTITE WORK IN WOOD AND PLASTER: THE ALHAMBRA, GRANADA, SPAIN.

form divides these into two flights. It was designed by Antonio Rizzo, and built during the last few years of the fifteenth century.

Halfpace Stair. (See Halfpace, under Pace.)

Half-turn Stair. (See main article above.)

Hollow Newel Stair. (See Hollow Newel, under Newel.)

Newel Stair; Newelled Stair. One constructed with newels at the angles to receive the ends of the strings, as distinguished from

STAIR TURRET: CHURCH OF S. WULFRAN, ABBEVILLE (SOMME).

a geometrical stair. The term is sometimes, with no apparent reason, limited to a dog legged stair.

One-turn Stair. (See main article above.)

Open Newelled Stair. A newelled stair which is built around a well; apparently, a term adapted to distinguish such a stair, which is "open" as regards the existence of a well, from a dog-legged stair, which has no well. Each are newelled.

Open Riser Stair. One in which there is no riser in the sense of a solid board, metal casting, or the like, but the whole rise between tread and tread is left open. When this arrangement is followed in costly staircases of elaborate buildings, it is usually to allow light to pass, as from a window.

Open String Stair. (See Open String, under String.)

Quarterpace Stair. (See Quarterpace, under Pace.)

Quarter-turn Stair. (See main article above.)

Screw Stair. A circular stair; especially, one in which the steps radiate from a vertical post or newel.

Straight Stair. One which rises in one direction only, without turns.

Three-quarter-turn Stair. (See main article above.)

cles *Escalier, Perron*; W. and A. Mowat, *Treatise on Stairbuilding*, etc. — D. N. B. S.

STAIRCASE. *A.* Properly, the structure containing a stair; a stair together with its enclosing walls.

B. Improperly, but in common usage, a stair or series of stairs; *i.e.*, the complete me-

STALLS OF S. GEREON, COLOGNE: 14TH CENTURY; TYPICAL GOTHIC ARRANGEMENT AND DESIGN; THE HEAVY SEAT IN EACH STALL IS A MISERERE.

Water Stair. Stairs or steps communicating between any water level, as of a river, lake, or harbour, and the land, for convenience of embarkation or debarkation.

Winding Stair. Any stair constructed wholly or chiefly with winders. (See Screw Stair.)

O. Schmidt and E. Schmidt in *Handbuch*, Part III., Vol. III.; Viollet-le-Duc, *Dictionnaire*, arti-

chanical structure of a stair or set of stairs with its supports, hand rails, and other parts.

STAIR TURRET. *A.* A building used to contain a winding stair which usually fills it entirely. Such a turret is often added to a larger tower, as of a church, and this is frequently at one angle of a large tower, making a picturesque addition to its mass.

PLATE XXV

STAIRCASE

Venice; a tower with open arcades connecting with other arcades, which connect with the rooms beyond; the whole a fifteenth-century Venetian building, fronting on an out-of-the-way court which visitors seldom reach. The arcaded front formed part of the ancient Palazzo Minelli, in the Corte del Maltese, south of the new Piazza Manin.

STALL IN THE CATHEDRAL OF
AMIENS: ONE OF THE FOUR COR-
NER PIECES WHICH RISE HIGH
ABOVE THE REST. THERE ARE 110
STALLS. THE WHOLE WORK IS
OF CARVED OAK, WITH HUNDREDS
OF HUMAN FIGURES; 1508–1520.

609

STALL: DETAIL OF THOSE OF AMIENS; SEE PREVIOUS
CUT.

610

B. A domical or hoodlike protection for the top of a stair which is carried through the platform or flat roof of a tower, or the like. Such

STALLS: S. MARGARET'S CHURCH, LEICESTERSHIRE;
c. 1450.

small structures rise above the large mass of a building and are frequently great additions to its beauty.

STALACTITE. One of the pendent cones of lime carbonate found attached to the roofs of caves. — G. P. M.

STALACTITE WORK. A system of corbelling of peculiar form or the imitation of such corbelling in wood and plaster. So called from a fancied resemblance of its form to those of natural stalactites. (See Honeycomb Work.) (Cut, col. 605.)

STALAGMITE. One of the deposits of lime carbonate on the floor of caves, and which may or may not be in the form of upright pillars corresponding to pendent stalactites. — G. P. M.

STALK. In the Corinthian capital, the representation of the stem of a plant, sometimes fluted, from which the volutes spring. (See Cauliculus.)

STALL. *A.* In an ecclesiological sense, a fixed seat, enclosed at the back and sides. Rows of such stalls for the use of the clergy, acolytes, and choristers are usually arranged on the north and south side of the choir; they are separated from each other

STALLS, CARVED OAK: MONTRÉAL (YONNE), BURGUNDY; EARLY RENAISSANCE; c. 1520.

STAKE OUT (v.). To designate or mark with stakes the plan and position of a future building upon its site.

by high projecting arms, and have their seats hinged so as to fold against the back when the occupant wishes to stand in the stall. On the under side of each seat there is a bracket upon which the occupant can rest when standing (see Miserere). In the larger churches the stalls are often surmounted by canopies; and in the monastic and some other churches the choir stalls return at the west end of each row.

B. In a stable, one of the divisions, averaging 4 to 5 feet wide and 9 feet deep, separated by partitions, open in the rear, and provided with appliances for feeding and drainage, for the accommodation of horses and cattle. (For the larger stall, called loose stall, or loose box, see Box, *C.*)

C. In a theatre, originally, a seat separated from others by arms or rails; now, usually, one of the seats in the front division of the parquet (sometimes called orchestra stalls); but the application of the term is variable. (Cuts, cols. 607, 608, 609, 610, 611, 612, 614.)

Loose Stall. Same as Loose Box. (See Box, *C.*)

STALL BOARD. One of a series of boards or shelves upon which soil is pitched successively in excavating. (See Bench, *C.*)

STALL POST. The post at the foot of the partition between stalls in a stable, used to hold and protect the ends of the partition boarding.

STAMBA. A pillar standing alone and serving as a memorial or a votive offering. There are many of these in India, and it is found that they have been erected at all epochs from the third or fourth century B.C. down to the commencement of the European conquest and settlement of the peninsula. Some of these are elaborately built up of many courses of stone and arranged with a spreading capital to support some larger culminating structure, as a table or roofed recess for holding a lamp. The Lantern of the Dead should be compared with these. (See Lat; Minar.) Spelled also sthamba.

STANCHION. An upright prop or support; a Puncheon; a Mullion.

STAND. A structure, usually temporary, or at least slight and unarchitectural, as (1) a booth for a shopkeeper; (2) a platform for speakers; (3) an arrangement of seats for an out-of-door exhibition of some kind, as a race or a ball game. (See Grand Stand.)

STANDPIPE. A pipe, usually vertical, intended to facilitate the supply of water to elevated points. Thus, at certain points along an aqueduct, a standpipe may be used into which water is forced by mechanical means, thus providing a pressure sufficient to raise the water supply higher than the normal level. In architectural practice, chiefly, a pipe intended to facilitate the extinction of fires. It is sometimes on the exterior of a building, and sometimes within, with branches in the different stories; but always with a mouth near the street and outside, and a coupling to which the hose of the fire engine can be attached. — W. P. G.

STANZA (plural Stanze). In Italian, a room or chamber; as the *stanze* of Raphael in the Vatican palace.

STAR ANCHOR. (See under Anchor.)

STARLING. *A.* A breakwater formed of piles driven closely side by side as a protection in hydraulic constructions.

B. One of the piles so used. (Also written sterling.)

STALLS IN THE CHURCH OF NOTRE DAME, PARIS; 17TH CENTURY.

STAROFF, IWAN IGOROWICH; architect.

A Russian architect who built about 1790 the Alexander Newski church in Saint Petersburg, also called the Pantheon. He built, according to the designs of Guadagni, the church of S. Sophia in Saint Petersburg.

Seubert, *Künstler-lexicon.*

STATE HOUSE. In the United States, a building appropriated to the government and legislation of one of the states. (See Capitol.)

STATICS. Force acting by balancing other forces. — W. R. H.

STATION. (See Railway Building.)

STATION HOUSE. *A*. The headquarters or office of the police force of a district. (See Police Station.)

B. In the life-saving service, a house on the seacoast, furnished with boats and other appliances for the service.

STATUARY. That form of sculpture which deals with figures in the round as distinguished from figures in relief, especially with figures of the human body complete, either singly or in groups. Such figures are used in architecture in two general ways. (1) In immediate connection with the building, as in cathedral porches of the thirteenth century, and commonly in niches and under canopies (see Vol. I., pl. VII.). (2) Set upon a building, but without apparent connection with its architectural design. Thus, in the pediment of a Greek temple the statues were designed for their place as so far above the eye and likely to be seen from so great a horizontal distance; but the tympanum of the pediment is used merely as a convenient background and the geison as a convenient shelf to support them. A similar arrangement seems-to have existed in Roman theatres and amphitheatres, where the great open arches of the structure which supported the rising tiers of seats were often occupied by statues and groups well seen against the comparatively dark interior. In memorial arches, statues are set upon ressauts of the main order, and thus relieved against the attic. In the Renaissance and post-Renaissance styles statues appear against the sky ranged upon the pedestals of the parapet, as in the library of S. Mark in Venice, and the great colonnade by Bernini in the Piazza S. Pietro at Rome. This last-named arrangement involves the difficulty that the light of the sky eats into the outline of the statue, which can hardly be seen aright unless illuminated by the sun from behind the spectator, or unless seen against a very sombre background of clouds. It is partly to avoid this that there has been a partial return, as in highly decorated buildings in the United States, to the front of the attic as a place for statues; and other buildings have porticoes of slight projection chiefly to afford the same opportunity.

STATZ, VINCENZ; architect; b. 1819 (in Cologne).

About 1841 he was associated with Zwirner on the works of the cathedral at Cologne. He became diocesan architect in 1863, and in twenty years built about sixty churches in the Gothic style, most of them in the archbishopric of Cologne. He published *Gothische Einzelheiten* (eight parts, folio, 1874), and with Ungewitter, *Gothisches Musterbuch* (Leipzig, 1856).

Seubert, *Künstler-lexicon*.

STAY. Anything that stiffens or helps to

maintain a frame or other structure, as a piece of timber or iron acting as a strut or brace; or a tie of any material.

STEAM HEATING. (See Ventilation; Warming.)

STEE. In local British usage, a ladder or steep stair of simple form.

STEEL. A compound of iron with from .01 to 1.5 per cent of carbon. It also contains minute quantities of silicon, sulphur, phosphorus, etc. The processes of making steel may be classed under two heads, — by adding carbon to wrought iron, and by abstracting carbon from cast iron. The former is used for making steel for cutting tools and other fine purposes. The latter class of processes is adapted to making large masses of steel rapidly and cheaply.

Blister steel is made by packing bars of wrought iron in layers, each surrounded by charcoal, hermetically sealed, and subjecting them to intense heat for two or three days. The bars absorb carbon and are converted into highly crystalline steel.

Shear steel is made by breaking the bars of blister steel into lengths, hammering or rolling them at a welding heat. If the process is repeated the metal becomes "double shear" steel.

Crucible cast steel is produced by melting bars of blister steel in a crucible with a small quantity of oxide of manganese and of ferromanganese. The carbon is sometimes varied by mixing wrought iron with the blister steel.

Bessemer steel is made by pouring molten iron into a bottle-shaped vessel lined with refractory material, and blowing air through the iron until the carbon and silicon are burned out. The combustion of the carbon and silicon produces sufficient heat to keep the mass thoroughly melted. If the lining of the vessel is silicious or acid, all the phosphorus and sulphur remain in the steel. By the Thomas Gilchrist method a basic lining is used, and the steel is made free from phosphorus.

Open hearth or Siemens-Martin steel. After the invention of the Siemens gas furnace, it was utilized by Martin to melt steel in bulk upon a sand bottom. It was found that the sulphur and phosphorus remained in the steel. A basic bottom of dolomite or magnesite was substituted for the acid (silicious) sand bottom, and phosphorus was eliminated better than by the basic Bessemer, and a better steel was made.

— W. R. HUTTON.

STEEL CAGE. The frame of the modern building of "steel skeleton" construction, as described under Iron Construction, Vol. II., col. 515.

STEEL CONSTRUCTION. (See Iron Construction.)

STEENING. The brick or stone lining, often laid dry, of a well, cistern, or cesspool.

STEEPLE. *A.* A tall ornamental construction surmounting a tower and composed usually of a series of features superimposed and diminishing upward, as the steeples of Sir Christopher Wren's churches, in contradistinction to a Spire, which is properly a tall pyramid uninterrupted by stories or stages.

B. A tower terminated by a steeple in sense *A*, or by a spire, the term covering the whole structure, from the ground up.

STEINBACH, ERWIN VON. (See Erwin von Steinbach.)

STEEPLE OF A CHURCH NEAR CAEN IN NORMANDY: C. 1160.

STELE. In Greek and Greco-Roman art, a pillar or upright monument composed of one or two stones and simple in its outline and general character, although it may be adorned with very elaborate carving. The more common forms were a slender cylinder, and a flat slab, higher and more narrow than a modern gravestone. These were set up as boundary stones; thus a law, or edict, or a treaty between two nations, would be recorded in an inscription upon a stele set up in an appropriate place. In some cases a sunken panel is filled by a bas-relief of a few figures, such as some in the Acropolis at Athens. The largest stelai known were erected on the graves of individuals, and these were sometimes

sculptured with superb bas-reliefs, like those found in the graveyard at the Dipylon at Athens, and now in the Central Museum there. (Also written stela.) — R. S.

STEEPLE OF S. STEPHEN'S CATHEDRAL, VIENNA, AUSTRIA.

STENCH TRAP. In plumbing, any form of trap which, by means of a water seal, is intended to prevent the passage of noxious gases from the sewers into a house.

STENCIL; STENCIL PLATE. A thin plate of metal, or sheet of paper, perforated with any desired pattern or device, so that, when held against the wall and scumbled with a brush of colour, the pattern is transferred through the perforations to the surface to be decorated.

STEP. A vertical break formed by a sudden change of level between two more or less horizontal surfaces. Especially, in architecture, such a break when only a few inches in height, and disposed (singly or in series) for the convenient ascending or descending of persons passing from one level to another. Hence, a small structure or block of material with a flat upper surface, — a platform of very limited extent, — placed at such a change of level. In the broad general sense, the change in level produced by the retaining wall of a terrace may be spoken of as a step, especially when it is one of a series of such breaks by which an inconvenient slope of ground may be modified. The term may be used in connection with any structure formed into a series of breaks (see Crow Step, Stepped Gable),or a masonry foundation wall which is enlarged toward its base by successively projecting courses. In the more especial sense, a rough, approximately flat, stone forming the sill of a doorway which is somewhat above the level of the ground adjoining would properly be called a step; as also one of a number of horizontal boards supported in a vertical or inclined series.

A series of steps designed for the accommodation of persons passing from one level to another is called a Flight or a Stair. (See the terms.) The flat upper surface of such a step is the tread ; the vertical surface, the riser; these terms designating also the pieces of material which form those respective surfaces where the step does not consist of a solid block. A step included between two parallel risers, which are also perpendicular to the general direction of a flight, is a Flier ; where a flight makes a turn, risers must necessarily approach each other at one side and diverge at their opposite ends, and each step, therefore, receives a somewhat triangular shape and is then known as a Winder. (See Balanced Step below ; also Flier ; Stair ; Winder.) — D. N. B. S.

Balanced Step. A winder included between two risers which are not normal to the curve. Thus, in a stair of ordinary construction, a quarter-turn is brought about by three or four winders with risers radiating from a common centre ; but in a stair of superior plan the change of ninety degrees is accomplished more gradually by a series of balanced steps formed by slightly decreasing the regular width at the inside of the curve and a corresponding increase on the outside, and this disposition begins before reaching the actual turn, and is continued beyond the curve.

Bullnose Step. A step — usually at the

foot of a flight — of which one or each end is shaped to a semi-circle projecting beyond the string, and, perhaps, surrounding the newel. Sometimes, a step having one or each end shaped to a quarter round, the curve terminating against the newel or the riser above. (Compare Curtail Step.)

Commode Step. One of a combination of two or more steps at the foot of a flight, which have curved ends projecting beyond the string and surrounding the newel, which apparently stands on the upper or uppermost step of the group.

Curtail Step. A step, usually at the foot of a flight, of which one or each end is given a scroll or spiral shape, this portion projecting beyond the string. This projecting scroll commonly supports a newel composed of a curved row of balusters following the outline of the step and continuing the line of balusters above. (Compare Bullnose Step.)

Dancing Step. Same as Balanced Step.

Hanging Step. One of a flight of stone steps which is built into a wall at one end and has no other support except what it may derive by slightly overlapping the stone step next below.

Scroll Step. Same as Curtail Step.

Spandrel Step. A solid step — as one worked from one piece of stone — having more or less the section of a right-angled triangle, the hypothenuse forming part of the sloping soffit of the flight. (Compare Square Step.)

Square Step. A solid step — as one worked from a single piece of stone — of which the section is more or less rectangular, so that the soffit of the flight is formed into steps similar to the upper surface. (Compare Spandrel Step.)
— D. N. B. S.

STEP LOG. A kind of ladder made by cutting notches into the side of a log. The first ladder of the American Indians.
— F. S. D.

STEREOBATE. The top of a foundation or substructure, forming a solid platform upon which the columns of a classical building are set. That part of it which comes immediately beneath the columns is distinguished as the Stylobate.

STEREOCHROMY. Painting by means of, or secured by, water glass (which see under Glass).

STEREOTOMY. In architecture, the science and art of stonecutting. Scientifically, that branch of Descriptive Geometry which has to do with the graphical representation of the forms and dimensions of stones which are to be prepared for building purposes.

STERLING. Same as Starling.

STEVENS, ALFRED ; sculptor, architect, painter, and decorator ; b. 1818 ; d. May 1, 1875.

He spent nine years in Italy studying the entire field of art, painting, sculpture, architecture, and decorative design. In 1841–1842 he was associated with Thorwaldsen in Rome. In 1850 he became chief designer to the firm of Hoole and Company, metal workers, at Sheffield, England. A very large part of his finest

STILTED ARCH: CHURCH OF S. FOSCA, TORCELLO.

work was done in the decoration of silverware, bronzes, cutlery, stoves, and other objects of utility. In 1856 he entered the competition for the proposed monument to the Duke of Wellington in S. Paul's cathedral. He received the commission for this work in 1858, and was occupied with it during the remainder of his life. This monument was placed in the cathedral in 1892. The original model is in the South Kensington Museum, and is important because of changes made in the finished work. Among the best of his decorative works are those of Dorchester House, London, including the splendid chimney piece of the dining-room, with its famous crouching caryatides.

Stannus, *Alfred Stevens and his Work ;* Armstrong, *Alfred Stevens, a Biographical Study.*

STEW. A heated room, as in a Turkish bath ; a hothouse ; a stove.

STIACCIATO. In Italian decorative art, very flat; said of relief sculpture.

STICK (v.). To run, strike, or shape with a moulding plane ; by extension, to shape, as longitudinal mouldings, splays, and the like, by the moulding mill. (See Plant, v.)

STILE. Any plane surface forming a border. Specifically, in carpenter work and in joinery, one of the plane members of a piece of framing, into which the secondary members or rails are fitted by mortise and tenon, as in panelling. In framed doors, and the like, it is nearly always a vertical member.

Diminished Stile ; Diminishing Stile. In a glazed door, a stile whose upper part above the middle rail is narrower than the lower part, in order to admit of a sash wider than the panelling below.

Falling Stile. Same as Shutting Stile, below.

Gunstock Stile. A diminished stile in which the reduction in width is made by a long slope, usually of the whole width of the lock rail.

Hanging Stile. *A.* In the framing of a door, a hinged casement window, or the like, that stile to which the hinges are secured, and by which, therefore, the door, etc., is hung to the jamb or doorpost. *B.* Same as Pulley Stile.

Hinge Stile. (See Hanging Stile, above.)

Meeting Stile. (See Meeting Rail.)

Pulley Stile. That surface of the box frame of a window, against which the sashes slide up and down ; it receives its name from the sash pulleys which are set into it near the top, and through which the sash cords or chains are passed.

Shutting Stile. In a hinged door, the stile opposite the hanging stile, being that one which strikes the rebate of the jamb when the door is shut.

STILL ROOM. Originally, a room in which distilling can be carried on, as in a country house ; hence, in a large establishment, an appendage to the kitchen, usually for making tea, coffee, and chocolate and preparing the more delicate dishes.

STILTED. Raised higher than is normal, or usual, or seeming to be so raised, a term almost wholly limited to the arch, which is

a   *b*

STILTED ARCHES IN VENICE; *a.* CALLE DEL PISTOR; *b.* SALIZZADA S. LIO.

said to be stilted when the curve does not spring at or close to the top of the capital or of the moulded or otherwise strongly marked impost. The term is extremely vague, as many arches have no architecturally marked impost, and as it is considered an error to start the curve immediately upon such an impost in any case; but those arches are called stilted which have a vertical jamb or intrados below the curve more than about one quarter of their total rise. Thus, Fig. 1 shows an arch whose rise is one half its span; its springing line is raised above the mouldings of the impost by nearly $1\frac{1}{2}$ times its span, and hence it is said to be much stilted.

STINASH. The Modoc term for house lodge. In Klamath it means a willow-framed lodge (see Latchash).

STIPPLING. In painting, the production of effects of gradation by fine dotting with brush-point or other implement; a process imitated in engraving by the stipple graver.

STIRRUP; **STIRRUP IRON**. A piece of iron forged or cast in the shape of a loop or shoe, which, when hung to a timber, as a header, affords resting for the end of a joist framed at right angles to the timber, or when secured to the top of a tie or plate, forms a resting for the lower end of a brace or rafter. It is a substitute for a mortise and tenon joint of any sort, and preserves the full strength of the timbers.

STOA. A portico used by the ancient Greeks as a shady promenade or meeting place, where conversation might be held or speakers heard. The stoa took the form of a roofed structure, the length of which was great as compared with its depth. Ordinarily, there was at the back an enclosing wall, and in front, facing the street or public square, a colonnade. The floor of the stoa was generally raised a few steps above the street.

In early examples the depth was so slight that the space between the wall and the colonnade was covered by a single span, and the roof sloped in one direction only; but later, with greater depths, one or more lines of supports had to be introduced between the wall and the outer colonnade, to assist in carrying the roof, which then frequently had a double slope. Pausanias describes a deviation from the more usual forms in the case of the Corcyræan colonnade at Elis, of which he says (Bk. VI., Ch. XXIV.): "The colonnade . . . is double, for it has columns both on the side of the market place and on the side away from the market place. In the middle the roof of the colonnade is supported, *not* by columns, but by a wall; and there are statues beside the wall on either side." Sometimes such porticoes were divided by two rows of columns into three aisles, or in one case by four rows into five aisles.

The stoa of Attalos at Athens was, according to Vitruvius, two stories in height, the columns of the lower story being of the Doric order, those in the upper Ionic (see Adler, *Die Stoa des Königs Attalos II.*); nor was this the only example of the two-story stoa, as witness those at Pergamon and Epidauros. Stoas were frequently adorned by statues of celebrated per-

sons, and in certain cases the rear wall was decorated with paintings.

For descriptions of the more important buildings of this character, and for references to the literature of the subject, see Durm's *Die Baukunst der Griechen*, p. 340.

— FRANK MILES DAY.

STOCKADE. *A.* Same as Palisade.

B. An enclosed space surrounded by a palisade. In this sense, the term carries with it the idea of a complete defensible work, however small and simple, the term "palisade" being limited to the line of stakes itself.

STONE. *A.* The material of which rocks are composed.

B (used with the article). A fragment of a rock.

C. Any aggregate of mineral matter, natural or artificial, as in the terms "precious stone," "artificial stone."

The kinds of stone utilized for purposes of construction or for general interior, decorative, monumental, or art work, may be roughly grouped under five general heads: granites, sandstones, marbles, limestones, and slates.

Granitic and Allied Rocks. The term "granite," in its strict scientific sense, is made to include only a class of eruptive rocks, consisting essentially of quartz and feldspar, with usually minerals of the hornblende or mica group, and which are consequently known as hornblende or mica granites. They are tough, hard rocks, massive and strong, of a pronounced granular structure, and vary in colour through all shades of gray; pink and red colours are, however, not uncommon. Until a comparatively recent period, rocks of this type had been used almost wholly in the more massive forms of construction. The introduction of steam power into stone working has, however, brought them into very general use.

Granites, of a type suitable for general purposes of construction, occur in nearly every state bordering along the Appalachian chain, but have been most fully developed in New England, owing to the fact that abundant quarry sites are found within easy reach of tide water, thus enabling the material to be shipped comparatively cheaply, even to the most remote points. Maryland, Virginia, the Carolinas, and Georgia have, of late years, furnished no inconsiderable amount. The region of Minnesota and Wisconsin is supplied from granitic rocks within the glaciated areas of those states. Chicago, St. Louis, and neighbouring cities derive an abundant supply of a coarse red granite, suitable for general building, from isolated areas of igneous rocks in Iron and St. François counties, Missouri. Small areas of syenitic rocks in the vicinity of Little Rock and Magnet Cove, Arkansas, are also becoming important sources of supply.

Light gray granite from Concord, New Hampshire, was used in the construction of the new National Library building at Washington, D.C. ; similar stone from Hallowell, Maine, in the State Capitol at Albany, New York ; dark Quincy (Massachusetts) granite in King's Chapel, the United States Court and Custom Houses, Masonic Temple, and many other buildings in Boston; a pink epidotic granite from Dedham, Massachusetts, in the Trinity Church building, Boston ; gray granite from Vinalhaven in the Masonic Temple, Philadelphia ; fine gray granite from near Richmond, Virginia, in the State, War, and Navy Department buildings in Washington, etc. Red and pink granites are quarried at Red Beach and Jonesboro, Maine ; Grindstone Islands, New York ; Westerly, Rhode Island ; Leetes Island, Connecticut ; and in Missouri and Texas, as already noted. The Grindstone Islands' granite is represented by two magnificent columns in the senate chamber of the State Capitol building at Albany, New York. A beautiful coarsely crystalline deep red granite from Lyme, Connecticut, was used in the Chaney Memorial Church at Newport, Rhode Island, but the material is not regularly quarried.

Gray granites of the ordinary type occur in many parts of British North America, but reference need here be made only to the pink and red stone from the vicinity of St. George, Kings County, in New Brunswick. This is the stone used in the large granite vase east of the Capitol in Washington and in the additions made in 1897 to the Natural History Museum in New York City.

Among the more noted of foreign granites are the gray and red so-called Scotch granites from near Aberdeen in Scotland, and the gray coarsely porphyritic Shap granite from Cumberland in northern England. The coarse red varieties from near Peterhead have been used in London, for the interior columns of S. George's Hall in Liverpool, and those of the provincial Bank of Ireland, in Dublin. Their use in America is limited mainly to polished columns and monumental work. It was from the gray granite of Aberdeen that were so largely constructed the buildings of the city of Aberdeen proper, described by Hull as perhaps the cleanest and freshest looking city in the British Isles. Other granites of local importance occur in Kirkcudbrightshire, Argyleshire, and the Isle of Arran. The principal English granite quarries are situated in Cornwall and Devon, the majority of the material being coarse-grained and of a gray colour. The so-called Shap granite is stated to vary in colour from light to deep gray, pink, red, and purple. The so-called Luxullianite, from which was made the sarcophagus of the Duke of Wellington, is a coarse red and black stone composed of red orthoclase, gray quartz, and black tourmaline. It is found only in boulders. What is probably the most extensive granite district in the British Isles stretches from Dublin, Ireland, southward through Wicklow and Carlow counties into Kilkenny and Wexford. None of the Irish granites seem, however, to have been fully developed, though many of the large buildings in Dublin are made from Wicklow materials. Stone from the Bessbrook quarries in Newry was used in the new Town Hall in Manchester.

The granite used by the Egyptians in the construction of so many columns, obelisks, sarcophagi, etc., is a coarse, red, hornblende-mica variety, found in large quantities in Upper Egypt, near Ancient Syene ; hence the name syenite, first given it. This is historically one of the most interesting of granitic rocks, the huge size of the blocks obtained, their sculptured hieroglyphics, and the great distances they have been transported having excited the wonder of people in all subsequent ages. Pompey's Pillar in Alexandria, and Cleopatra's Needle, now in Central Park, New York, as well as the companion obelisk, now in London, are of this material. The same stone was used in the linings of the interior of the great pyramid of Gizeh, and in the obelisk of Luxor, in the *Place de la Concorde*, in Paris.

The principal granite used in Saint Petersburg is the coarse, red, so-called Rapakivi stone from the Finnish coast, between Wiborg and Lovisa. This is the material used in the Alexander column in Saint Petersburg, and also in the magnificent monolithic columns in the cathedral of S. Isaac, in that city. It is a beautiful coarse red stone ; the large orthoclase crystals, sometimes three or four inches in diameter, being of an oval outline and surrounded by a darker translucent border of oligoclase. This stone leaves little to be desired, so far as colour and structure are concerned ; but its durability, when exposed to the atmosphere, is a matter of very grave doubt. In the basement extension of the cathedral of the Saviour, in Moscow, there was used a beautifully complex granite-gneissoid rock, of a prevailing reddish colour, with black streaks, and often a fine faulted and brecciated structure. This is also from Finland.

The granite so largely employed in Italy, particularly in the cities of Milan, Turin, and Florence, is stated to be mainly from near Baveno, on the western bank of Lago Maggiore. It is fine-grained and of a warm, pinkish tinge, and is seen to good advantage in the columns of the restored basilica of S. Paolo fuori le Mura in Rome ; there are also columns of the stone on either side of the main porch of the cathedral, and supporting the dome of the church of S. Carlo Borromeo, Milan.

Granites from Elba and Sardinia have also found a limited use in Italian cities. The eight columns supporting the dome of the baptistery of Pisa are stated by Hull to be of pink granite from Elba.

Granitic rocks from the vicinity of Fingspong, Sweden, in the form of monuments and turned columns, find their way to the American and other markets in considerable quantities. The most striking and desirable of these is a red granite with peculiar amethystine opalescent quartz.

Igneous rocks of the nature of diorite, diabase gabbro, and basalt have been but little utilized for constructive purposes, owing in part to their sombre colours and in part to poor working qualities. In the United States very dark diabasic rocks are used to some extent for monumental work. The coarse gabbro of Keesville, New York, a dark gray rock with iridescent feldspars, has been utilized for monumental work, and to some extent for polished interior work, with good effect. A coarser variety, with larger, purplish iridescences, is exported from quarries near Fingspong, Sweden. A stone similar to this, from near Kiev, has been used with fine effect in panelling the lower interior walls of the church of the Saviour in Moscow. Other igneous rocks, of lighter, somewhat inferior colours, are used for general building, though most of the material of this nature is utilized for Belgian blocks in street pavements. A mica diorite (kersantite) from the Brest roads has been quarried and utilized for building for many years, and many of the Gothic churches in Brittany have been constructed from it.

There are yet other types of eruptive rocks which need mention in this connection, though they are but little used. Under the name of *Porphyry* is included a class of rocks varying widely in chemical composition, but having in common what is known technically as a porphyritic structure, that is, they show crystals of quartz or feldspar, porphyritically developed in a fine-grain ground mass. When, as is frequently the case, the porphyritic crystals are of a different colour from the ground mass, the effect is striking and often very pleasing. The so-called *Marmor Lacedæmonium viride*, or green antique porphyry, is a porphyritic diabase from Laconia, in southern Greece, while the red antique porphyry, or *rosso antico* of the modern Italians, is a porphyritic diorite occurring in the Dokhan mountains. Rocks of similar grain, but varying colours, occur in many parts of the world, but are little used, owing to their great hardness. Nevertheless, they acquire often a fine polish, and their colours are such as to make them eminently desirable for turned columns and works of art. Materials of a high grade of this nature occur in various

parts of America, and the red varieties found near Hingham, Massachusetts, and in the Franconia Mountains of New Hampshire, are well worthy of consideration. In spite of the refractory nature of the material, rocks of this type were used by the ancient Egyptians, Greeks, and Romans much more extensively than to-day, and modern museums contain abundant illustrations of the patience and skill of the people in fashioning from it statues and other works of art.

In the western portion of the United States, and in other volcanic regions, a considerable variety of the younger eruptive rocks, called *Lavas*, are locally utilized, but mainly for purposes of rough construction.

Mention should also be made of certain altered forms of igneous rocks, like the impure *Serpentines* of southern Pennsylvania and northern Maryland. These are of a dull greenish colour, soft, and somewhat porous, but fairly durable. These have been used extensively in New York, Philadelphia, and Baltimore, mainly in coursed rubble work.

The Sandstones and Quartzites. Under this head are grouped a widely varying series of rocks, having only in common the one property of being composed of more or less consolidated sands. They are made up of the silicious fragments derived from the disintegration of older crystalline rocks which have been rearranged through the mechanical action of water. The material by which the individual particles of a sandstone are bound together is, as a rule, of a calcareous, ferruginous, or silicious nature, though sometimes argillaceous. The substance, whichever it may be, has been deposited between the granules by percolating water, or during the process of original sedimentation, and forms a natural cement.

Upon the character of this cement is dependent quite largely the colour of the stone, and its working and lasting qualities, as will be noted later. Stones containing any considerable amount of ferruginous cement are nearly always of a yellow, brown, or red colour. Several varieties of sandstones are popularly recognized, the distinctions being founded upon colour or working qualities. Thus the name "brownstone" is applied to a sandstone containing so large a proportion of ferruginous cement as to be of a brown or red colour, like those of Connecticut and New Jersey. The term "freestone" is applied to any sand or limestone of sufficient uniformity of texture to work freely in any direction. The terms "calcareous," "ferruginous," "silicious," and "argillaceous" are often applied to sandstones in which these constituents play the rôle of cementing materials. Many sandstones contain scarcely an appreciable amount of cement, but owe their consistency wholly to the pressure to which they have been subjected. Silicious sandstones which have undergone metamorphism, like those of Potsdam, New York, and Sioux Falls, South Dakota, are known as quartzites. From a geological standpoint the sandstones are known as Triassic, Carboniferous, or Silurian, etc., according to the period during which they were formed. According to the size and shape of their constituent particles they are known as sandstones proper, or if the grains are large and rounded like a consolidated gravel, as conglomerate. When these large granules are angular, instead of rounded, the stone is known as breccia.

Sandstones and limestones are to be found in any and all of the states of the American Union, but naturally in not all are they of such quality and colour as to make them desirable for constructive purposes. Throughout the triassic areas of the Eastern states are found important beds of brown red sandstone, or so-called "brownstone," which has been used from a very early period in American history for general constructive purposes, as is well exemplified in the monotonous rows of brownstone fronts in New York City.

Connecticut, Massachusetts, New Jersey, Pennsylvania, and Maryland have been thus far the chief producers of this class of material, though somewhat similar stones are now brought from near Flagstaff, Arizona, Verte Island in Lake Superior, and from near L'Anse in Michigan. Fine blue-gray and buff sandstones of the carboniferous age occur throughout many regions in the Mississippi Valley, as near Berea and Amherst, Ohio, and have furnished and still may furnish an almost unlimited quantity of these materials for general purposes of construction. Thin-bedded blue-gray Devonian sandstones from New York and Pennsylvania, known commercially as Hudson or North River Bluestones, Wyoming Valley stone, or simply Bluestone (which see), are largely utilized for flagging, and the better varieties for steps, sills, and lintels.

Owing to their abundance, variety, and relative cheapness in the United States, sandstones of any kind are brought from abroad to a very limited extent. The so-called Dorchester stone, from Shepody Mountain, New Brunswick, finds a limited application in the Eastern cities. It is of an olive-gray colour and fine texture. Scotch sandstone of gray and red-brown colours from near Craigleith, Scotland, used in many of the public and private buildings of Edinburgh, and to a less extent in London, was formerly imported into New York.

In England carboniferous sandstones of a light brown colour, from near Yorkshire, have, in connection with jurassic stones of a similar colour, been utilized in the construction of Whitby Abbey, the new library building at Cambridge, and many other buildings of less

importance. Triassic (Lower Keuper) sandstones of gray to red-brown colour have likewise, according to Hull, been largely employed in the construction of churches and private dwellings in the midland counties.

In France the most important quarries of sandstone are presumably those of Villerz, which have furnished the stone used almost exclusively in Carcassonne. The castle of Heidelberg, Germany, is of a reddish sandstone corresponding to the triassic; the cathedral of Cologne, of bunter sandstone from the Black Forest.

In this connection mention should be made of a series of elastic rocks composed of the reconsolidated fragmental matter ejected from volcanoes, and technically known as tuffs. These as a rule are soft, light, and porous, and, though enduring in Mexico or Italy, are totally unfit for exposure in cold and wet climates.

Soft, light gray volcanic tuffs, known as peperino, or piperno, were anciently used in Rome, and those from the near vicinity are used almost exclusively for building materials in Naples now as in the past. Similar tuffs were largely used in Herculaneum, Pompeii, and ancient Rome.[1]

The volcanic tuffs of Douglas County, Colorado, have been utilized to some extent in Denver. The stone is light and fairly strong, but its durability, even in a dry climate, is yet to be demonstrated.

The Calcareous Rocks: Limestones and Marbles. Under this head is included a series of rocks composed essentially of carbonate of lime alone, or of carbonate of lime and magnesia, though frequently rendered quite impure through the presence of clayey matter, iron oxides, free silica, and silicate minerals. They have originated through the induration, and, in some cases, metamorphism of beds of calcareous mud, shell, and coral remains, formed on ancient sea bottoms.

Many varietal names are given to these rocks, according as they vary in composition, colour, structure, or even uses to which they are put. The terms "argillaceous," "silicious," and "ferruginous" are applied to such as carry an appreciable quantity of those substances. Hydraulic limestone is an impure silicious and argillaceous variety used for making hydraulic lime. Often a part of the lime is replaced by magnesia, giving rise to magnesian limestones, or if the magnesia occurs to the amount of 45 per cent the stone is called a *dolomite*. An oölitic limestone is one in which the individual particles are of rounded, nearly spherical shape, like the roe of a fish. The so-called Bedford (Indiana) stone is of this type. A fossiliferous limestone is one carrying fossils; a coral or shell

[1] This tuff must not be confounded with the calcareous tufa or travertine of Tivoli, used in the construction of the Coliseum, the exterior walls of S. Peter's, and other public and private buildings in Rome.

limestone, one containing coral or shell remains, etc. Many limestones or dolomites have undergone just the right amount of induration or metamorphism to impart to them such colours and textural qualities as make them desirable as marbles. In short, a marble properly is but a limestone or dolomite of such appearance as to make it suitable for decorative or the finer grades of building work. Many marbles, as noted below, are so coarsely crystalline and of such colour as to make them unsuited for decorative purposes, though they may be eminently suited for fine structural or monumental work.

The colour of marbles, and of limestones in general, is quite variable. A pure limestone or dolomite is white; gray or blue-gray and black colours are common. Such are due to the presence of organic matter, *i.e.* carbon.

The pink and red or green colours are due as a rule to the presence of iron in some of its forms. In many marbles, and particularly the dolomitic varieties, the impurities have crystallized in the form of some variety of amphibole, pyroxene, or mica, or as free quartz, magnetite, iron pyrites, graphite, etc. Such minerals as a rule exert a detrimental effect, as noted in the remarks on Weathering.

In structure the stones classed under these names are by no means constant. Those which have undergone little metamorphism are often so fine-grained as to seem quite amorphous, and may carry numerous more or less conspicuous fossil remains. Metamorphism itself is almost invariably productive of crystallization, and all grades of texture from that which is too fine to be visible to the unaided eye to stones in which the individual particles are an inch or more in length are common.

Occasional calcareous rocks are met with in which the beds have been, by earth movements, shattered like so much glass, and the fragments again cemented into a more or less solid mass, forming thus breccia marbles, which are often of great beauty. Many of the so-called Numidian marbles are of this type. In other cases the original limestone beds have been broken into fragments, and the individual particles tumbled about by wave action until more or less rounded like the pebbles on a beach, and the whole, in the form of a coarse gravel, once more cemented by calcareous matter to form beds sufficiently firm for the production of marbles. The beds of calcareous triassic conglomerate near Point of Rocks and elsewhere in Maryland and Virginia are of this type. When blocks of this stone are sawn into slabs they show rounded and angular pebbles of a great variety of colours and sizes, forming an ornamental stone of no mean quality. Colours and structure change abruptly, so that a slab but a few feet in length may show on one half well-

rounded pebbles such as shall cause it to be classed as conglomerate, while in the other half the fragments are mainly angular and the stone classed in consequence as a breccia.

The most noted of American limestones is the oölitic variety from the subcarboniferous beds having an extensive development in Indiana, and to a less extent in Iowa, Illinois, and Kentucky.

The stone is of a light gray colour, uniform texture, works readily in any direction, acquires readily a sharp and pleasing relief, and is beyond question an excellent material for carved work and ordinary sills, trimmings, etc., in all but the most exposed of situations. It is of the same general type as the well-known jurassic oölite of Bath (England), used so extensively in English ecclesiastical architecture during the thirteenth, fourteenth, and fifteenth centuries, but is of a darker shade, somewhat more compact, harder, and in the trying climate of the Eastern and Northern United States doubtless would prove much more durable. The Caen stone of Normandy, used in the cathedral of Canterbury and Westminster Abbey, belongs to the same geological horizon as this last, and is to be considered in the same connection, though lacking the oölitic structure. This stone, however, while unsurpassed for colour and other physical qualities, lacks enduring powers in our trying climate, and is passing out of use.

Marble. The most noted marbles of the United States are the whites, blue-grays, and greenish grays of Vermont, used mainly for interiors and for monumental work; the red or chocolate and white mottled dolomitic varieties, — the so-called "Winooski" marble, — of Mallets Bay, in this same state, used mainly for wainscotings and tilings; the white granular dolomitic building marbles of Lee (Massachusetts), used in the United States Capitol building at Washington; the very coarse "snowflake" marble of Westchester County, New York, used in S. Patrick's cathedral on Fifth Avenue, New York; the pink, gray, and chocolate-brown and white mottled varieties of East Tennessee, used mainly for interiors and furniture; and the coarse white, white clouded, and pink varieties of northern Georgia, which are used both for general building and decorative work, though best adapted for the former.

Crystalline granular marbles, suitable for general building, are found in abundance in the provinces of Ontario, Canada, as in Hastings County, and a deep red stone, veined with white, is found near the Calway River in the province of Quebec.

The better-known of the foreign marbles are mentioned below.

Africa. The so-called Numidian marbles from the provinces of Mauritania and Africa, in Algeria, are the principal stones needing mention. These vary from drab and yellow through light pink to deep red in colour, and are often beautifully brecciated. The commercial names by which they are known are given under the definition of Numidian marble (see Marble), the "Jaune Antique Doré" being that found in Roman ruins, and called *Giallo antico* by the Italians.

These all take an enamel-like surface and polish, and, with the exception of the Italian siena, are the most sought of all marbles for interior effects. Statuary, pink, green, and bluish violet-veined marbles are reported from Lower Umzinkula, Natal, South Africa, though such has as yet been little exploited. The onyx marbles, or Oriental alabasters of Algeria and Egypt, are mentioned elsewhere.

Australia has thus far produced but little in the way of marbles, and apparently nothing of such quality as to be of more than local consequence. The national collections at Washington show a small series of crystalline, granular marbles from New South Wales, varying from whitish with ochreous lines through dull yellow-grays to blacks. The last-named varieties are mottled with darker blotches, often slightly yellowish.

Austria. Pure white and slightly gray crystalline granular marbles occur near Salzburg, in the Tyrol, and also very compact, sometimes brecciated and fossiliferous, varieties. The compact varieties are of beautifully delicate and warm tints of cream, yellow, pink, and chocolate-brown or red. They acquire an excellent surface and polish, and are well worthy of consideration for interior decoration. They have been utilized in the monolithic columns of churches in Munich, but seem to have never been introduced into the American markets. Verd antique marbles are found at Sterzing in the Tyrol.

Belgium is noted for its black marble from Golzines and the environs of Dinant, and also from Saint Anne, the latter being, however, a blue-black variegated with white. There are also red marbles from Cerfontaine and Merlemont, but which are less brilliant than the French griottes. There are no white marbles in the country.

France. The most noted of the French marbles are the griottes and the Languedoc from the Pyrenees. These are of a brilliant red, almost scarlet colour, and have no competitors so far as colour alone is concerned, save the red Numidian varieties from Algeria. Other French marbles are the rose marbles from Cannes and the *Vert Moulin* or *Griotte Campan Vert* or *Mélange.* A brocatelle of a light yellow body traversed by irregular veins and blotches of dull red is found in the Jura.

Germany. Aside from the Formosa and Bougard marbles, described elsewhere, Germany proper produces nothing in the way of marbles that needs consideration here.

Great Britain. The English marbles are scarcely known in the American markets. This is presumably due to their high price, incidental to cost of working, since the cut stone, as supplied by dealers, is somewhat uneven in texture and bears evidence of shearing such as has developed incipient flaws. The textures as a whole are fine, the stones compact, of good colour, and acquiring a good surface and polish. They are seemingly well worthy of a more extensive use. Gray and drab varieties mottled with pink, of soft, warm, and pleasing colours, are quarried at Petit Tor; dark gray bird's-eye varieties at Ashburton; dull red mottled with white and gray fossiliferous stones, with fine red threadlike veins at Ogwell, and beautiful drab with lilac tints merging into red at Radford. There is also a black marble with white gashlike veins at Pomphlett. All these localities are in Devon.

A dark blue or grayish compact limestone diversified with white fossil shells and known as Purbeck marble is found at Durdlestone Bay in Dorsetshire, England. This was formerly much used in shafts, columns, and monuments in the south of England churches and cathedrals. A compact variety of gypsum or alabaster, of a prevailing white colour with rust-red streaks and clouds, is found in Devonshire, and has been introduced into the American markets, but is too soft for the uses to which it has been put. The English serpentines are mentioned under the head of Verd Antique Marbles.

Of the Irish marbles the black marble of Kilkenny and Galway is perhaps the most noted, with the possible exception of the Connemara green mentioned in this article in section Verd Antique Marbles.

Greece and Italy are the countries which above all others have been famous for the wealth and variety of their marbles from a very early period.

The Grecian marbles are best known to the world through the granular statuary varieties from Mount Pentelicus and the island of Paros, used in the construction of the Parthenon and statues too numerous to mention. Veined varieties, however, occur, including pink, chocolate, brown, and yellow colours. A beautiful breccia consisting of whitish fragments in a red ground is well worthy of note.

The Italian Apennines, in the vicinity of Carrara, Serravezza, and Massa, furnish marbles of a variety and colour not equalled in any other part of the globe. Most noted among these are the pure white saccharoidal statuary, the blue-veined *bardiglio*, the yellowish and drab of Siena, the black and gold of Palmaria, and the yellows of Verona. Perhaps the most prized of these for other than statuary purposes is that of Siena. This is a very compact stone of almost waxlike appearance, sometimes brecciated, and, as noted, of a beautiful yellow colour, varying to drab. The yellow is the kind most sought, but as the colour is not uniformly distributed throughout the mass, it becomes necessary, in high grade work, to select carefully blocks or sawed slabs of the desired hue from a considerable amount of poorer material. Examples of this stone in American buildings are to be found in the vestibule of the new Public Library building in Boston and the rotunda of the National Library building in Washington.

Japan has crystalline granular white and variegated marbles, some of which, from Hitachi province, are blue-veined like the Italian *bardiglio*. Others from Mino province are breccias composed of black fragments in a white ground.

Portugal. (See Spain below.)

Russia. No marbles of more than local interest have thus far been reported from Russia proper, though the white and clouded varieties used in the cathedral of the Saviour, in Moscow, are said to have been brought from somewhere in the Urals.

Spain and Portugal. The best-known of the Portuguese marbles is the so-called Lisbon yellow, from Estremoz, which compares fairly well with the Italian siena, though lacking its waxy, almost translucent appearance. Mottled white and pink to red marbles, close-grained and compact, are found in Beira province. A variegated conglomerate marble, resembling in a general way the "Calico" marble from Maryland, occurs in the Sierra de Arrabida. Fine compact marbles of a dull reddish hue, veined with drab, are found in Saragossa province; red and yellow mottled stones in Murcia province, and black in Alicante. Few if any of these now find their way into the American markets.

Verd Antique Marbles. Under the name of "verd antique marble" is included a class of rocks consisting essentially of serpentine, but often variegated with veins of calcite and magnesian carbonates, iron oxides, etc. Such are metamorphic rocks resulting, for the most part, from the alteration of magnesian eruptives. The prevailing colours are green, but sometimes oil-yellow, red, and nearly black, variegated as noted above. The lines of veination are almost invariably lines of weakness, and the stone, as a rule, is fragile in the extreme. Marbles of this type, from Prato and Genoa, Italy, came into early use during Grecian and Roman civilization, and material from the same source under the name of *Verde di Pegli, Verde di Genoa,* and *Verde di Prato* is still to be found in American markets. Other noted serpentines, or verdan-

tiques, are the so-called "Irish Green" or "Connemara marble" from West Galway, Ireland, and from Cornwall, England, the latter being often of a red colour, and very beautiful.

In America, high grade material is found in Roxbury and Cavendish, Vermont; Westfield, Massachusetts; Milford, Connecticut; Harford County, Maryland, and the adjacent portions of Pennsylvania; near Marietta, Georgia; San Bernardino County, California; and a beautiful, evenly banded variety on the Middle Gila River, New Mexico.

The Argillites, or Clay Slates. The rocks here included may be best briefly described as indurated clays. But, inasmuch as the clays vary greatly in composition, so, too, do the slates. The most pronounced characteristics of the argillites, as a whole, are their fineness of grain, smooth, almost gritless feeling, and argillaceous or claylike feeling when wet, or breathed upon. The prevailing colours are some shade of gray, blue gray, or nearly black, though sometimes greenish, purplish, or even red. Through a process of dynamic metamorphism, a squeezing and shearing such as often accompanies the uplifting of mountain chains, many of the argillites have become converted into finely fissile slate, which split readily and evenly along certain definite, parallel lines, into thin sheets, suitable for roofing and other purposes. The less fissile varieties are utilized for flagging, billiard tables, sinks, etc. The production of roofing slates has, up to date, been limited in America almost wholly to the states in the Appalachian area. In fact, no beds of more than local importance have thus far been exploited outside of this area, although it is possible that such may exist. Roofing slate of a blue-black colour is quarried extensively in Piscataquis County, Maine; of a blue-black, greenish, and purplish colour in Rutland and Bennington counties, Vermont; red and greenish slates in Washington County, New York; deep blue-black in Northampton and Lehigh and York counties, Pennsylvania, and in Harford County, Maryland, the last-named furnishing the well-known Peach Bottom slate. Slate quarries have also been worked to some extent in Buckingham County, Virginia; Polk County, Georgia; near Huron Bay in Michigan; and in Carlton County, Minnesota. Excellent slates in large quantities have been produced in Richmond County, Province of Quebec, Canada. The importation of Welsh slates, from Wales, has now almost entirely ceased, while at the same time there has been built up a very considerable export trade in American materials.

The Essential Qualities of Building Stone. The suitability of any stone for structural purposes is dependent mainly upon the four essential qualities here mentioned in the order of their importance: first, durability; second, permanency of colour; third, crushing strength and elasticity; and fourth, cheapness.

The durability of any stone depends to a very large extent upon its ability to withstand, unharmed, the constant expansion and contraction due to temperature variations, and the expansive force of water in passing from the liquid to the solid state. A stone is a complex body made up of a large number of particles, which may or may not be of the same mineral nature, and which are essentially in actual contact with one another. Constant expansion and contraction of these particles, through diurnal and annual temperature variations, is sure to bring about, in time, a weakening and consequent disintegration. How great this disintegration may be is dependent upon the natural tenacity of the rock, its absorptive properties, and the extremes of temperature variation. In addition to this mechanical disintegration, stones in the walls of buildings are subjected to the corrosive action of more or less acid rains. Amongst the purely silicious rocks this corrosive action amounts to very little, but with the calcareous rocks it is often a matter of very serious importance, particularly in large cities, where the natural acidity of the rain is augmented by the acid gases from the furnaces of manufacturing establishments and dwellings.

The permanency of colour of a stone is dependent upon physical as well as chemical processes.

Provided there are no chemical changes taking place, nearly any stone is likely to become slightly bleached on the outer surface by exposure, merely owing to physical changes, such as the opening up of cleavage planes and minute rifts, though this change is often so slight as to be quite inconspicuous. Stones containing pyrite or iron bisulphide are likely to become discoloured through the oxidation of this mineral. Stones taken from below the water level nearly always undergo mellowing in tint, due to the change in the condition of the combined iron, which may be either a sulphide or carbonate, and which gradually passes into the sesquioxide. Where the colouring constituent is finely disseminated, such a change is by no means injurious, in fact, if anything, is often beneficial; but where the material is segregated in spots and veins, the matter is much more serious, and whole fronts may be sadly disfigured through such causes.

The matter of the crushing strength of stone is one which has received a very great amount of attention on the part of architects and engineers, but the importance of which, as the present writer has often asserted, is greatly overestimated. There are few stones in the market which will not be found by actual test

to bear tenfold more than is likely ever to be required; and, excepting so far as indicating tenacity and hence power to withstand the action of the frosts, a strength of over fifteen thousand pounds to the square inch is of very little importance. The matter of elasticity is of much greater import, since this property has a direct bearing upon the power of a stone to resist the expansions and contractions of ordinary temperatures. The figures given below, which are the averages of a large number of tests made by engineers of the United States army and others, will serve to show the strength and weight in pounds, of the ordinary type of stone used for constructive purposes:—

DESCRIPTION.	Strength in Pounds, per Square Inch of Surface.	Weight in Pounds, per Cubic Foot.
Granite	15,000 to 25,000	165 to 170
Trap (diabase) . .	20,000 " 30,000	175 " 185
Marble (crystalline limestone) . . .	6,000 " 12,000	165 " 170
Marble (crystalline dolomite) . . .	8,000 " 13,000	168 " 175
Limestone	5,000 " 14,000	145 " 170
Sandstone	5,000 " 17,000	130 " 160

The adaptability of a stone for structural purposes depends in no small degree upon its weathering qualities, that is to say upon its power to withstand, for centuries even, exposures in the walls of a building, without serious discoloration, disintegration, or solution, through the causes noted above. It will be well then to consider briefly the weathering qualities as displayed by the various types of rocks. A more complete discussion of the subject by the present writer may be found elsewhere.[1]

Granites and gneisses, possessing very low ratios of absorption, and being made up so largely of silica and silicate minerals, are very little affected by freezing and solution. The chief causes of disintegration with rocks of this class are temperature changes, such as produce granulation. Aside from a weakening of the cohesive power between the individual constituents, the feldspars may split up along cleavage lines, and a disintegration follows which may be sufficiently evident to cause small spawls to fall off along the joints between the blocks, or perhaps to ruin fine carvings. In some instances deleterious minerals like pyrite are present in sufficient quantity to cause unsightly discoloration.

[1] See *Rocks, Rock-Weathering and Soils,* The Macmillan Company, New York; and *Stones for Building and Decoration,* Wiley and Sons, New York.

All things considered, a fine-grained, homogeneous rock will be found more durable than one that is of coarser grain. Also a rock in which the individual particles are closely interknit, dovetailed together, as it were, will resist disintegration longer than one that is of a granular structure at the start. The same remarks hold good for the basic eruptive rocks, though such are, as a rule, less durable than those of the granite type possessing the same structure.

Serpentines are likewise only slightly absorptive, and, where homogeneous, little affected by solution. Nearly all serpentines, of such quality as to be used as verd antique marble, contain, however, veins and spots of calcite, dolomite, or magnesite, and many dry seams. Such rocks therefore weather unevenly, lose their polish, and shortly crack and split along these dry seams when exposed to the weather. These marbles should then be used only in protected situations. Crystalline limestones and dolomites (marbles) are extremely variable in their weathering qualities, are likely to carry pyrite, and great care needs always to be exercised in their selection. A limestone marble, *i.e.* one composed essentially of lime carbonate, is likely in time to suffer from solution, whereby corners become rounded, surfaces roughened, and perhaps inscriptions obliterated. The mechanical agencies are here also operative as in granites, so that as a rule a stone of this class is less durable than a good granite. The pure white stones are generally more granular and weaker than the gray and blue-gray varieties. Dolomites, being less soluble than limestones, might at first thought seem to promise greater durability than the limestones. Unfortunately this is not altogether the case, since such stones as a rule possess a more granular structure than do limestones, and hence suffer more from disintegration. This rule is not without important exceptions. The light colours characteristic of most marbles render iron stains peculiarly objectionable, and as pyrite is a very common constituent of such rocks, much care is necessitated in their selection. The ordinary, unmetamorphosed limestones, like the deep blue-gray varieties from the Trenton formations, are scarcely at all absorptive and weather fairly well, but their sombre colours are a drawback.

Sandstones, on account of the widely differing character of the materials of which they are made up, variation in texture, degrees of porosity, etc., are perhaps, as a whole, more unreliable in their weathering qualities than any other class of rocks. In order fully to appreciate this, one has but to remember that we have to do here with what are but beds of indurated sand; that they are made up of sand particles held together by simply being closely compacted by finer materials, or by means of a

cement composed of lime carbonate, iron oxides, or silica. Where the sand is loosely compacted, or the sand granules are interspersed with much finer clayey matter, the stone will absorb comparatively large amounts of water and is likely to become injured on freezing. Where the cementing matter is carbonate of lime, rain water trickling over the surface will in time remove it in solution, leaving the stone to fall away, superficially, to the condition of sand once more. Ferruginous cements are likewise slightly affected, though in a much less degree. The silicious cement is least affected of all, and, provided the amount of induration be the same, a purely silicious sandstone, cemented by a silicious cement, is one of the most indestructible of natural building materials.

Methods of Testing Stone. It is evident from what has been said under the head of essential qualities of building stone, that some system of testing stone, for the purpose of ascertaining how far it may possess such qualities, is eminently desirable. The following is an outline of the methods ordinarily employed : —

(1) Tests to ascertain permanency of colour.

But two tests are commonly employed : the one, the chemical test for sulphur (indicating the presence of pyrite), and the other, made with a view of accelerating the ordinarily slow processes of oxidation by means of artificial atmospheres. In this last-named test, prepared samples are placed under bell glasses, where they are subjected to fumes of nitric acid and chlorine. Pyrite or ferruginous carbonates are quickly attacked, and their presence made known by ferruginous discolorations and efflorescences.

(2) Test to ascertain resistance to corrosion.

This is necessary only on calcareous rocks, or on sandstones containing a calcareous cement. Prepared samples, carefully weighed, are suspended in a glass vessel of water, through which carbonic acid is kept constantly bubbling, the water being changed occasionally. The extent of corrosion is indicated by the loss in weight during the time of testing.

(3) Test to ascertain resistance to abrasion.

This is necessary only in cases where, as in steps and walks, the stone is to be subjected to the friction of feet, and in dams and breakwaters. In certain exposed places the action of wind-blown sand may be an important consideration. The ordinary method pursued consists merely in subjecting a block of stone, under constant pressure, to wear on a grindstone or horizontally revolving iron bed such as is used by stone workers.

(4) Tests to ascertain absorptive powers.

Rectangular specimens, with smoothly ground faces, thoroughly dried and weighed, are immersed in water for a period of three or four days — preferably in a porcelain dish. They are then removed, dried by blotting paper, and weighed immediately. The increase in weight indicates the amount of water absorbed.

(5) Tests to ascertain resistance to freezing.

The preliminary proceedings are the same as in the last case, the cubes being repeatedly frozen and thawed while saturated with water. After the freezing and thawing, the specimens are dried and reweighed. The loss in weight indicates the amount of material disintegrated through the expansive action of the freezing water. Attempts at substituting solutions of salts, which by crystallizing in the pores of a stone shall simulate the action of freezing water, have not proven satisfactory.

(6) Test to ascertain ratio of expansion and contraction.

Carefully measured bars of stone are immersed in water at 32° Fahr., which is then raised to 212°, and then gradually lowered once more to 32°. The total expansion at the highest temperature is noted. The object of lowering the temperature once more to 32° is to ascertain the amount of permanent expansion which has taken place, it having been found that the stone, on such lowering, did not at once regain its former dimensions, but showed a slight permanent swelling or set. Tests of this nature seem, at first sight, of the greatest importance; but in attempting to judge of their value, one should not lose sight of the fact that a loose-textured stone, like a friable sandstone, would probably show less actual expansion than one of closer grain, owing to the interspaces of the particles; hence the poorer stone might give apparently the better results.

(7) Test to ascertain resistance to crushing.

This is made on carefully prepared cubes with smooth, parallel surfaces, crushed between steel plates. The size of cubes operated upon is variable, but, all things considered, one 2 inches on a side seems most desirable. The results, as tabulated above, are given per square inch of crushing surface.

(8) Test to ascertain elasticity.

This is best made upon prisms some 4 inches by 6 inches by 24 inches, the loads for compressibility being applied parallel to the direction of the long side. The transverse tests are made on similar bars supported at the ends and the load applied in the middle.[1]

(9) Test to ascertain resistance to shearing.

This is made by supporting a prepared prism, at each end, by blocks, and applying pressure in the centre by means of a plunger of such dimensions as to leave a clearance space of half an inch between the sides of the plunger and the blocks at the ends.

[1] For details of these processes, see Reports of the "Tests of Metals and Other Materials," made at Watertown Arsenal, 1890, 1894, and 1895, Washington Government Printing Office.

(10) Test to ascertain fireproof qualities.

This is made by heating the stone in a furnace and noting its condition on cooling, and also, in extreme cases, after the heated stone has been plunged into cold water.

(11) Test to ascertain specific gravity.

The prepared specimen is first weighed in the air, and then in the water, the air from the pores of the stone being removed by boiling or by means of an air pump. The weight in air, divided by the loss of weight in water, gives the specific gravity. The weight per cubic foot, if desired, can be obtained by multiplying the figures denoting the specific gravity by 62.5, which represents, in pounds, the weight of a cubic foot of water.

— GEORGE P. MERRILL.

Artificial Stone. Any hard material made in imitation of stone, usually by mixing strong cement mortar with sand as for a very fine concrete, but without the chips or larger fragments of stone or granite. Blocks of concrete in its different forms are used freely for building and more especially for under-water foundations and the like, but the term "artificial stone" is commonly used for such material as is prepared as a substitute for flagging. Thus, the sidewalk or footway of a street or the broader walks in a park or garden are, since 1870, very commonly covered with this material, which is often scored with deep lines to imitate the joints between flags. The basins of fountains, heavy curbstones, and copings, as of retaining walls, are also modelled in this material.

Semi-Precious Stone. That which is of value for decorative and art work, but which, owing to rarity or high cost of working, is not used for ordinary building. Of these only the more important are described in detail.

The onyx marbles, owing to their variegated colours, banding, and translucency, as well as easy working qualities, have long been favourites and have been in use for interior work and household utensils since a very early period. As early as the second Egyptian dynasty we find the Egyptians using the translucent, light straw-yellow or amber material from rifts and caves in the eocene limestones of the Nile Valley for making canopic vases, urns, and amphoræ for holding offerings to the gods, ashes of the dead, ointments, cosmetics, etc. Tombs and shrines were built from it, the sarcophagus of Seti I., the father of Rameses II., being hollowed from a single block. The exterior walls of the celebrated alabaster mosque at Cairo are of the same material.

Since these days down to the present the stone has continued a favourite for the finer grades of decorative work, as well as for table tops, small columns, etc. The present sources are: (1) The region about Pueblo, in Mexico;

(2) San Luis Obispo, California; (3) Yavapai County, Arizona; and (4) Blad Recam, in Algeria.[1]

The Mexican varieties are of a white, amber-yellow, green, and red colour, as are also those of Arizona. Those of California are mainly white, and those of Algeria white and amber. The stalagmitic forms are never green or red, but usually amber and white. At the present time the latter are not regularly worked, nor have they any constant value, although properly treated they might be made very effective.

Quartz and the cryptocrystalline varieties of silica grouped under the general name of chalcedony are, in America, in very little demand except for the cheaper forms of jewellery and for making small ornaments, as paper weights, etc. The clear glassy form is utilized by the Japanese in making the quartz spheres and small objects of art for which Japanese collections are noted. Quartz traversed by thread-like needles of rutile or amphibole, and known as Thetis hair stone, is used for similar purposes. The cryptocrystalline and amorphous forms are used for a great variety of purposes, from the making of jewellery, as with opal and agate, to the manufacture of pottery and gun flints, as is the case with flint commonly so called.

The principal varieties of these cryptocrystalline forms are defined below. It may be well to premise their description, however, with the statement that as a rule none of the varieties is to be had in pieces of more than very moderate dimensions, while the great hardness and toughness of the mineral renders it very difficult, and consequently expensive, to work. Nearly all the systematic work of this nature now carried on is done in German, Japanese, and Russian workshops.

The most important source of chalcedony or jasper, for commercial purposes, within the limits of North America, has been the so-called fossil forest near Holbrook, Arizona. Here are found numerous fallen tree trunks in which all organic matter has been replaced by silica, sometimes with and sometimes without the preservation of the original wood structure. The prevailing colours are red and yellow variegated with white and gray. The material takes a beautiful surface and polish, and has been used to some extent in the manufacture of small ornamental columns, tops of stands, etc., as well as for paper weights and other small objects.

Of all modern people the Russians have shown most skill and enterprise in working the refractory materials on a large scale. In the museum of the Hermitage in St. Petersburg is an enormous shallow oval vase of green gray polished chalcedony some 12 feet by 8 feet in

[1] See *Stones for Building and Decoration,* by George P. Merrill, 2d ed., pp. 120–175.

diameter and 3 feet in depth, supported upon a base some 4 feet high and this resting on a rectangular block of the same material 6 by 5 by 2 feet.

It is to be regretted that a more extended use cannot be made of materials of this class. At present our manufacturers and dealers decline to handle any stone the supply of which cannot be considered as constant, or the individual peculiarities of which are such that special care and taste must be exercised in its preparation. For this reason, many a fine piece which in proper hands might be worked up into something really unique and artistic is allowed to go to waste. Beautiful masses of clear or rose quartz go to the making of road materials or abrasives. Occasional blocks of stalagmite from the limestone caves of the South might be made to yield beautiful columns, urns, or vases. In reality such are neglected simply because the material cannot be quarried by the ton, sawed into slabs like so many mill logs, and used for wall linings. In ancient times, before the advent of the labour unions, stones of these types were used much more extensively in proportion to wealth and population than to-day. While the present high valuation set upon labour might be a drawback to their extensive use under the old hand methods, the introduction of machinery would seemingly have equalized matters, and one can but feel that it is the artistic sense that is lacking.

It is a little singular that the art of working these refractory materials, if indeed they are worked at all, should be limited, to-day, so largely to people whom we do not regard as representatives of the highest types of civilization. The best work in nephrite that has ever been done is Chinese; the best now being done in chalcedony, rhodonite, and malachite is Russian; and the best in stalagmite, Egyptian. The art as practised by the French and Germans during the fourteenth century and the Italians during the sixteenth seems almost wholly lost. Since the decay of Roman civilization there has been nothing done with the beautiful antique green and red porphyries, and the use of jasper by any people has long since practically ceased. — GEORGE P. MERRILL.

STONE, NICHOLAS; sculptor, architect, and master mason; b. 1586; d. Aug. 24, 1644.

Stone was a pupil of Isaac James, a mason, and assisted Hendrick van Keyser (see Keyser, H. van) at Amsterdam. In 1614 he returned to England and executed many works from the designs of Inigo Jones (see Jones, I.), such as the Banqueting House, Whitehall (1619–1622), the portico of old S. Paul's; the water-gate at York Stairs, and the fine portal of S. Mary's, Oxford. He was appointed master mason at

Windsor by Charles I., and was employed in the execution of a vast number of monuments. He was assisted and succeeded by his sons Henry, Nicholas, and John.

Stephen-Lee, *Dictionary of National Biography*; Rymer, *Fœdera*; Blomfield, *Renaissance in England.*

STONE CUTTING. The art and practice of preparing stone for its place in a building,

STONE CUTTING, FIG. 1: WITH JOGGLED JOINTS, GIVING GREAT SOLIDITY TO THE WORK; SYRIA, 4TH CENTURY.

including in the largest sense the rough shaping of Rubble and the like, and also the finishing of the faces as well as the beds and joints of stones for building. The scientific part of it, as the drafting and calculation, is called Stereotomy. The finer tooling of the faces, beds, etc., is also called Stone Dressing (which see); and the term "stone cutting" is often limited to the work of shaping Cut Stone (which see) as distinguished from rubble and the like. Under

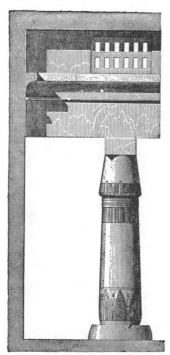

STONE CUTTING, FIG. 2: DETAIL OF A TEMPLE AT THEBES.

Masonry the different processes are described. It is proposed to give here a brief historical account of building by means of stone, and,

therefore, Stone Setting (which see) must be considered together with stone cutting, because the practice of the two arts is very closely connected.

Thus, in Fig. 1, the stones are so fitted together that great solidity may be given to the wall in a country where earthquakes are frequent. The stones are cut with Joggles as

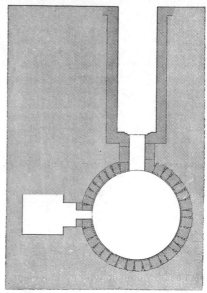

STONE CUTTING, FIG. 3: THAT OF THE PRE-HELLENIC EPOCH. A THOLOS AT MYCENÆ; A VERY LARGE TOMBAL CHAMBER, WITH DROMOS, ALL FACED WITH STONE.

shown, with the immediate intention of fitting each stone carefully to the neighbouring stones above or below, and such work is usually done on the spot, a common superintendence of the cutters and the setters insuring accurate work. Figure 2 shows such stone cutting as was done by the Egyptians, the building represented being of the 18th dynasty; but buildings of much earlier times show a similar skill in shaping and dressing and setting the stone. The separate stones are in Egyptian work not often of very great size, except when they are used as obelisks or in similar monolithic work; but in the temples and palaces the number of rather large stones is very great, and the skill in jointing, shaping, and surfacing the stones is equal to anything that is known to exist. It is to be observed that the public buildings of Egypt, though generally built of stone only, are yet thought to have taken some part of their form and many of their details from an earlier structure of reeds and light woodwork covered with coatings of Nile mud. (See Egypt, Architecture of.)

The pre-Hellenic work of Greece is very inferior to the Egyptian work in finish and in

STONE CUTTING, FIG. 4: THOLOS AT MYCENÆ; SEE PREVIOUS CUT. THE BLOCKS OF STONE ARE SET WITH HORIZONTAL BEDS, AND THE BEE-HIVE SHAPE IS GOT BY CORBELLING.

STONE CUTTING, FIG. 5: EARLY GREEK WORK IN SOFT SANDSTONE, INTENDED TO BE COATED WITH STUCCO, BUT INCOMPLETE. TEMPLE AT SEGESTA, SICILY.

architectural character, though much less ancient than the latter, but it is peculiar in this, that it has no reference in its forms to other material than stone. Thus, the tomb at Mycenæ, illustrated in Figs. 3 and 4 (see Treasury of Atreus), is built as men would build who thought of no other material than stone; and in this respect it resembles megalithic and other prehistoric work (see Cyclopean; Pelasgic Architecture); the stones are as large as a man can handle conveniently, they are rudely cut

again more simple. The Greek temple, as illustrated by that at Segesta, shown in Fig. 5, is built entirely of stones laid one upon another, and keeping their place by dead weight, unless aided by metal clamps within, as a partial defence against the vibrations caused by earthquakes. The temple at Segesta was never completed by its builders, and hence it has been a valuable study to modern archæologists. It does not follow, from the refusal of the Greeks of the fifth and the fourth centuries B.C. to use

STONE CUTTING, FIG. 6: BARREL VAULT OF PECULIAR CONSTRUCTION; NYMPHÆUM AT NÎMES, SOUTH OF FRANCE; ROMAN IMPERIAL WORK.

to an approximately uniform size, and are selected so that the stones of one course shall be of the same size throughout, constituting what is known as coursed work. Each successive course is then set somewhat in advance of the next lower course, all the work being corbelled inward in such a way that gradually the size of the rotunda diminishes until a single stone caps it at the top, the resistance of the very stones of the ring or course preventing one stone from falling inward, on the principle of an arch laid horizontally. The Dromos, or passageway, leading to the tomb is built of larger stones, generally set on their smaller faces, and the whole is covered with earth, much on the principle of the tumulus. It is to be noticed then how much more elaborate this work is, considered as stone cutting and as stone setting, than the more magnificent work of Egypt, confined to plain trabeated construction.

With the classical epoch of Grecian architecture, the character of stone cutting becomes

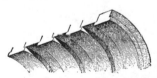

STONE CUTTING, FIG. 7: DETAIL OF NYMPHÆUM, NÎMES. SEE CUT ABOVE.

the arch in any form, that they were wholly unacquainted with its nature and possible uses. They, with the Egyptians and the Indians of the early time, seem to have thought the arch too dangerous and untrustworthy to form a part of dignified architecture, of which architecture repose should be an essential character. The constant tendency of an arch to thrust out its abutments and to destroy the work of which it forms a part was enough to account for this refusal, at a time when the value and interest of interior architecture had not been studied.

To the Romans of the Empire, however, the interior seemed of equal importance with the exterior, and the arch is in continual use, both singly, as in a wall, and as extended to the vault over a large apartment. Figure 6 shows one of the few Roman vaults which, out of Syria, are known to have been built of cut stone throughout, for the Roman practice was usually to build these roofs with small stones laid in a bath of mortar. Figure 7 shows the detail of the construction of this very curious

STONE CUTTING, FIG. 8: FRENCH GOTHIC WORK OF THE BEST PERIOD; CHURCH OF S. EUSÈBE, AUXERRE: 13TH CENTURY.

roof, in which the thicker bands of stone forming parallel arches have served no purpose except to enable the planner of the work to simplify it by giving his workmen one arch or ring of voussoirs at a time. These being cut and set, the other slabs could be filled in between, with some unusual expenditure of labour, but with some facility for the work of ignorant workmen. Many examples of the cut stone work of the later Empire can be found in the illustrations under Syria.

In the mediæval epoch, stone was the material most convenient to the workmen, because

it could be handled easily, two or three men at a time cutting a certain number of pieces out of a quarry and dressing them at once, preparatory to transporting them a short distance and to placing them immediately in the work. To have built on a large scale with brick or rubble and abundance of mortar would have involved a long term of preparation and more abundant resources ; but any bishop, abbot, or baron who could command the services of two or three stonecutters and of twenty labourers, could find a quarry in his neighbourhood from which sufficient material could be got to carry his building a few courses higher, or to turn one more arch of the nave. It is noticeable that throughout the Middle Ages the stones used are of moderate size in all parts of the building, there being but few which can have needed any elaborate machinery for hoisting them into place, and the greater number being so small that each one could be carried on a man's shoulder up a ladder and along a scaffold. Figure 8 shows an instance of such mediæval work, and it is evident that whether the large stones of the arch on the right and of the wall above it are, as here shown, too heavy to be handled as above described, there would be nothing to prevent the building of all parts of the structure by stones of forty pounds weight and under. The lintels which stretch across the triforium gallery are the only pieces requiring larger size, and these might be replaced by other devices. Figure 9 is a piece of the French interior decorative work of the sixteenth century, in which the extraordinary skill gained during the long epoch of Gothic art was applied by the builders in a different way. Simplicity of construction having succeeded, under the Renaissance, to great complexity, the ingenuity of the stonecutters was then shown in their details, the niches, colonnades, and friezes of this tomb having been evidently intended by the workmen as a rare masterpiece, challenging comparison with any other work known to the artists ; while the intimate relation maintained between the figure sculpture and that which is purely decorative carries still further the Gothic scheme, in which there was no sharp line of distinction between the religious portrait statue and the ornaments composed of mere zigzags and nailheads.

The later stone cutting, as that of the post-Renaissance styles in Europe, affected a solidity and simplicity fully equal to that of the

Roman Imperial builders, and included even some methods of work not familiar to them, so far as we know from the ruins. The groin vaulting of the seventeenth century, especially in Italy and Spain, is far in excess of anything left us by the Romans, both in elaborateness and in the stone cutting skill displayed. In fact, it is only with the later years of European work, begun about 1450, and then only in the south of Europe, that stone cutting is attempted which

blocks ; in that case, the stone is dressed with a slightly receding or hollowed bed, and the edges of the faces of the stones may almost touch, no mortar being visible. Such joints as these require cutting as careful as that of the faces, but the actual surface should always be more or less rough, in order to afford a good hold for the mortar.

As for the face, the simplest way of work, compatible with a uniformly vertical or uniformly sloping wall, is what is known as rock-

STONE CUTTING, FIG. 9: FINELY FINISHED WORK OF THE FRENCH RENAISSANCE.

can be called elaborate in our modern sense of the word. — R. S.

STONE DRESSING. That part of stone cutting which relates to the surface of stones prepared for building. Thus, the beds and joints of the stone may be hammer dressed, or where finer work is required and the joints are to be made as thin as possible, they may be worked with the point, for it is rare to carry them farther. Sometimes the actual thickness of the mortar joint is required to be greater than the external and visible joint between the two

faced or pitch-faced work, in which the joints being first determined and the external edges of the stone established (see Out of Wind under Wind), a drove chisel, or a pitching chisel of stouter make, is set with its edge upon this determined angle of the stone, and with a blow a rough splinter is broken off, the operation being repeated until the face of the stone is at its edges true and vertical, whatever rough projections there may be on the face beyond the joints. The finish may then be carried farther by establishing a draft on all four edges of the stone, or at pleasure along the horizontal edges only, this process emphasizing the coursed look of the whole. In the case of drafted work, however, it is less usual to use a wholly rock-faced finish, the larger projection being then commonly knocked off, so as to bring the stone to approximate uniformity of surface. When chisel work is to be used, the workman begins with the Point or Pointing Tool (see those terms), a straight bar of steel, square or octagonal, with a four-sided pyramidal point, or sometimes a very short edge. With this point the workman cuts channels across the face of the stone diagonally, and across each other, all these channels being carefully kept in the same plane by reference to the edges and the use of the wooden straightedge. The spaces between, where the rugged stone still projects, are then gone over with the point until the whole has an approximately uniform surface. This can be carried so

entering the groove on one side and leaving it on the opposite side. The toothed chisel can be used with great effect on soft stone, if applied much as the lines of cross hatching are applied in ordinary drawing; the edge blow of the tool gives seven or eight short parallel lines; if the successive blows are at different angles, a surface is procured generally uniform and sufficiently smooth, but without a regular tool mark which can be counted, and with a very happy result. Hammer-finished work is done by blows directly upon the surface, which bring a uniformly lined or finely grained surface, but these implements are hardly applicable to soft stone. The steps and platforms for stairs of marble or granite are nearly always hammer-dressed, and for this the coarsest hammer, or that which has the fewest blades, is used. A hammer with six blades gives what is called six-cut work, and from six to twelve-cut work is the limit. Other varieties

STONEHENGE, NEAR SALISBURY, WILTSHIRE, ENGLAND.

far, and the lines cut by the point made so regular and fine, that the stone is considered presentable for face work. It is then said to be Broached, the rough projections between the lines made by the point being never more than three-quarters of an inch wide, nor projecting more than one-quarter of an inch. Instead of cutting parallel lines by the point, short and irregularly spaced, lines may be cut, producing what is called pointed work, and sometimes rough pointed work, a surface very effective in granite, especially if having many party-coloured ingredients in its mass. If, however, it is intended to use the chisel of any form, the point is laid aside after the first evenness of surface is obtained, and then, according to the quality of the stone — hard, soft, fine, or coarse in grain — there may be used either the Toothed Chisel, the edge of which is cut into blunt teeth, having about eight in an edge of three inches, or the Drove Chisel, which has a uniform straight edge, or the Patent Hammer, or Bush Hammer, the two last being used for harder rock, the two former for the softer sandstones and limestones. Drove work is done by the drove chisel, which cuts shallow grooves sidewise, the edge of the tool

of dressing are known; thus, Picked, or Sparrow-billed, Work has a somewhat uniform surface produced by the blows of a sharp point, so that it resembles pointed work of considerable regularity. A similar effect is produced with less labour by means of the Crandall. Vermiculated work is that sometimes seen in neoclassic buildings, in which the surface looks as if worms had eaten their way about the surface without going below a certain fixed depth; it is an awkward way of expressing the effect of rough stone, which could be better done by some form of rock-faced work. Rusticated work is merely the sinking of the joints, or, more properly, the raising of the larger part of the face of each stone beyond the joint. — R. S.

(See Axe, II.; Boast; Chase; Dab; Draft; Hammer-dressed; Nig; Nobble; Quarry-faced; Rock-faced; Scabble; Scutching; Skiffling.)

STONEHENGE. A prehistoric and megalithic monument in Wiltshire, England, not far from Salisbury. It is the most imposing megalithic monument in existence, though not covering as much ground as those at Carnac, in Brittany.

STONE LIME. Lime made by calcining limestone or marble in a proper kiln. The quality of the lime varies with the amount of sand, clay, or silicates mixed with the pure calcareous element of the stone.

STONE SETTING. The art and practice of putting into permanent place the stones prepared for building, including the preparation and spreading of mortar, if used, the laying of lead joints where needed (as between bases and shafts, or shafts and capitals), and the exact turning of arches made up of wedge-shaped solids (see Voussoir), and similar work. (See Stone Cutting.)

STONEWARE. Potter's ware made of very silicious clay, or of clay and flint, which, when properly mixed, moulded, and fired, becomes vitrified throughout. It is often moulded to form copings, chimney tops, etc.

STOOL. *A*. Same as Seating.

B. The small moulded shelf under the sash of a window, serving as an interior sill.

STOOP. *A*. In New York and in those cities which have followed New York in this respect, an out-of-door flight of stairs with a platform at the top, the whole constituting the means of approach to the front door.

B. By extension, in parts of the northeast United States, a porch, veranda, platform, or terrace of any sort. Thus, the inhabitants of a small frame house in a village speak of the front stoop and the back stoop, meaning anything from a flight of three steps and a small platform to a veranda covering the whole side or end of the house. (Also written Stoup.)
— R. S.

Box Stoop. In New York, since 1880, a stoop making a quarter turn, having a platform, and presenting the side of the lower flight to the street. This structure requires a vertical wall and parapet on the outer side, whence the name.

STOP (n.). Anything serving to keep a door or casement from swinging past its proper plane when shut or open ; or to keep a sliding sash, shutter, or door in its proper grooves ; or to stop a door or drawer from going too far into the frame in which it slides. Stops may be permanent or temporary, and the permanent ones may form a part of the structure or be inserted afterward at pleasure.

STOP BEAD. A continuous strip or moulding, usually shaped into a half round on one edge, whence its name, bead, and serving to keep a sliding sash or similar member in its place. When such a sash has to be taken out for repairs, or the like, the stop bead is usually removed ; it is therefore in good work often held by screws only.

STOPCOCK. (See Cock.)

STORAGE BATTERY. (See Electrical Appliances.)

STORAGE BUILDING; WAREHOUSE. (See Warehouse.)

STORE. *A*. A place for the storing of goods of any kind ; in this sense, nearly equivalent to Storehouse. (Compare also Warehouse.) Stores in this sense are not usually the subject of careful architectural treatment ; they are apt to be extremely plain and bare buildings of greater or less strength in the floors and walls, according to the material expected to be deposited in them.

B. A place for the exhibition and sale of goods ; a shop. In this sense, common in the United States and in many of the British colonies. Buildings designed for stores in this sense have been erected during the second half of the nineteenth century in the great cities of Europe and the United States, and some of these buildings are of very great size and cost. Buildings for Departmental Stores (see below) have been erected covering 100,000 square feet of ground and six or seven stories high ; the whole being occupied by salesrooms and the workrooms for persons who receive and deliver goods, unpack, pack, and repair them, and in other ways serve the salesrooms to which the public has access. It does not appear, however, that as yet careful architectural thought has been given to the problem of the planning and construction of these buildings. In the plural, Stores, see Coöperative Store below.
— R. S.

Coöperative Store. A store in sense B, kept up by a coöperative society, to enable its members to procure goods cheaply by eliminating profits. In Great Britain, often called the Stores, in ordinary conversation.

Departmental Store. An establishment for the sale of goods of many varieties. The staff of employees being very great, and the goods offered for sale being of many widely different sorts, there have to be established departments almost wholly independent of the others, and each having a superintendent.
— R. S.

STORE FRONT. Same as Shop front.

STOREHOUSE. A building used for the storage of goods ; the general term. (See Storage Warehouse, under Warehouse.)

STOREROOM. A room for the convenient storage of goods or reserved stock, not exposed for sale, in connection with a shop or store ; or of domestic supplies in a dwelling house.

STORM CELLAR. In countries where tornadoes are to be feared, a structure partly or wholly underground, intended for shelter and safety when a tornado threatens to pass over the spot. In the middle west of the United States the tornadoes travel eastward or northeastward, and the rule is, when you see the black cloud approaching, to run northwesterly from what appears to be its course. As, then, the tornado approaches from the west or southwest, it is usual to place the storm cellar northwest of the house, and connected with the cellar under the house by a tunnel.

STORM DOOR. Same as Weather Door, (which see, under Door).

STORY. *A.* The space in a building comprised between the top of a floor and the top of the floor next above; hence, one of the structural subdivisions in the height of a house. (See Attic; Entresol; Étage; Mezzanine; Piano Nobile; Rez-de-Chaussée.)

B. A tier, a horizontal row of windows, or the like, forming a large architectural detail, and making up one of several successive stages, even where no floors exist.

STORY POST. In stories open to the street, as in some shops or sheds, one of the posts under the beam which supports the exterior wall.

STORY ROD. A rod cut to the exact height of a story, from top of floor to top of floor, used to ascertain the proper height for the risers of the staircase by dividing the rod into as many equal subdivisions as there are steps.

STOSS, VEIT; sculptor and engraver; b. about 1447 (in Krakau, Poland); d. 1533.

He was a well-known master as early as 1472, in which year he finished the great altar of the King Kasimir in the cathedral of Krakau. In 1496 he made the first model for the shrine of S. Sebaldus in the church of that saint in Nuremberg, which was carried out by Peter Vischer (see Vischer).

Fäh, *Geschichte der Bildende Künste.*

STOUP. *A.* A basin for holy water, placed in a niche or against a wall or pillar near the entrance of a Roman Catholic church.

B. Same as Stoop.

STOVE. *A.* A heated room of any sort, as a greenhouse, in which an especially high temperature is maintained for tropical plants; a drying chamber used in various manufactures; a Laconicum, or sweat room.

B. A warming or cooking apparatus, generally of iron, and portable. In Germanic and other cold countries the stove is often a more important and permanent structure, built of glazed tiles, more or less decorative in character, and so situated, generally, as to warm contiguous rooms. (See Kang.)

STOWE, RICHARD DE; architect.

He built the Eleanor Cross (see Cross of Queen Eleanor) at Lincoln (England), and about 1306–1310 was employed as *cementarius* at Lincoln Cathedral. He contracted to continue the central tower.

Hunter, *On the Death of Queen Eleanor of Castille.*

STRACK, JOHANN HEINRICH; architect; b. July 24, 1805; d. June 13, 1880.

He studied architecture with Schinkel (see Schinkel), and in 1834 went to Italy. After his return he was made professor in the Academy of Berlin. In 1862 Strack went to Athens and superintended the excavation of the theater of Dionysos. He published *Das altgriechische Theatergebäude* (1843, folio); *Zeigel Bauwerke des Mittelalters und der Renaissance in Italien* (Berlin, 1889, folio); *Baudenkmäler Roms des XV.–XVI. Jahrhunderts: ergänzung zu Letarouilly* (Berlin, 1891, folio) etc.

Allgemeine deutsche Biographie.

STRAIGHTEDGE. *A.* A ruler used by draughtsmen for ruling long lines for which the T square cannot be conveniently employed; *e.g.* the converging lines of a large perspective drawing. It is usually of light, hard wood, but hard rubber and celluloid are also used.

B. An implement used in building, for various purposes. For laying off long lines and for testing the evenness of a plane surface of plaster or stone, a thoroughly seasoned board with an edge planed perfectly true is employed. For testing levels a long, wide board is used, having the lower edge perfectly true and the middle part of the back or upper edge parallel to it; from this part the back tapers somewhat to either end. It is used by setting the lower edge on the surface or surfaces to be tested, and applying the spirit-level to the middle of the back.

—A. D. F. HAMLIN.

STRAIGHT LINE PEN. Same as Drawing Pen, *B* (which see under Pen).

STRAIN. The deformation or change of shape of a body as the result of a Stress (which see).

Breaking Strain. A strain so great that the body subjected to it is ruptured.

STRAIN DIAGRAM; POLYGON. A geometrical diagram used in the graphical method of determining the strains in a framed structure, such as a truss. The given loads or other outer forces are represented in amount and direction by a series of lines; other lines are plotted to the same scale corresponding in direction to the respective members of the structure. On completion of the polygon, these latter may be directly measured by scale on the drawing. The process is similar to that employed in the Polygon, and the Parallelogram, of Forces.

STRAINING ARCH. (See under Arch.)

STRAINING BEAM. (See under Beam.)

STRAINING PIECE. Same as Straining Beam (which see under Beam).

STRAP ORNAMENT; WORK. A method of ornamentation, especially characteristic of the time of Elizabeth in England, composed of a capricious interlacing, folding, and interpenetration of bands or fillets, sometimes represented as cut with foliations.

PLATE XXVI

STREET ARCHITECTURE

At Rouen, in Normandy. Two fronts of private houses dating from the sixteenth century. The ground story with the shop-fronts has been too much modified to be of interest, but the rest of the façade is in each case fairly well preserved. The strongly marked central feature carried through the whole front, from the lowest story to the dormer, is remarkable as showing the indifference the designer felt with regard to the relative narrowness of his façade.

STRAW HOUSE. (See Grass House.)

STREET. A public way in a village, town, or city; the continuation of a road through a district thickly covered with houses and upon which the houses face. The term may be considered as including the actual surface of the ground with the pavements, or other covering and preparation of the ground to bear travel, together with the gutters and similar conveniences; or it may include the soil below and the air space above, as when an exercise of the legal right of a community to carry out repairs or the like is in question; or, finally, it may even be considered as including the houses facing upon the roadway, and their gardens and approaches. (See Alley; Calle; Fondamenta; Galleria; Gallery in senses *F* and *G;* Mews; Passage (II), pronounced as in French; Rio Terrà; Riva; Wynd.) Also under the general head come such terms as *avenue; place,* in the sense of a limited part of longer street; *road,* in the sense used in London for long streets, until lately suburban; *terrace,* in nearly the same sense as place, above; and local terms such as *chaussée, circle, cité, court, crescent, gasse,* each of which is capable of distinct explanation.

STREET, GEORGE EDMUND, R.A., F. S.A.; architect; b. June 20, 1824; d. Dec. 18, 1881.

In 1844 he entered the atelier of Sir George Gilbert Scott (see Scott, G. G.). In 1852 he was appointed diocesan architect at Oxford, England, and afterward held the same office for the dioceses of York, Ripon, and Winchester. In 1856 he established his office in London. He restored a large number of mediæval monuments, the cathedrals of York, Carlisle, Bristol, and Dublin, the church of S. Peter Mancroft at Norwich, the church at Hythe, etc. He built a very large number of new churches in the Gothic styles, being especially successful in the smaller designs. In 1867 he entered the memorable competition for the new Courts of Justice in London, and in 1868 was appointed architect of that work. A list of his works is given in the *Builder,* Vol. XLI. (1881), p. 779. Street was made a member of the Royal Academy in 1871, and was afterward elected president of the Royal Institute of British Architects. He published *Brick and Marble Architecture in Northern Italy* (1855, 1 vol. 8vo), *Gothic Architecture in Spain* (1865, 1 vol. 8vo), and numerous contributions to periodicals, especially the *Ecclesiologist* and the *Transactions of the Royal Institute of British Architects.* His notes on the sepulchral monuments of Italy were published by the Arundel Society (1 vol. folio, 1883).

A. E. Street, *Memoir of George Edmund Street;* Obituary in *Builder,* 1881, Vol. XLI., p. 777.

STREET ARCHITECTURE. That pre-pared to face the street, and, in a more general sense, city architecture generally.

The cities of antiquity seem to have had a street architecture of which the moderns can form but little conception. This is the arrangement of numerous covered galleries, porticoes, and buildings open to all comers, which, in the more sumptuous towns, occupied a great deal of space. Antioch, Palmyra, Gerasa, and other cities of Syria were remarkable for their long and straight avenues flanked by double colonnades supporting roofs, so that for considerable distances the footway was roofed and formed a continuous portico. What the city of Rome possessed were the splendid Imperial Fora, which were added to the Roman Forum, by different emperors, on the north and also eastward of the Capitol. Meanwhile, the exteriors of private houses were probably of minor importance, and even great public monuments were more commonly low and plain in their outside appearance, temples only having an effective external architecture. For the modern city, then, the consideration of street architecture begins with the Middle Ages, going back to antiquity only for lessons in landscape architecture. It is with the improvement of those crowded mediæval cities, too, that the legal aspect of street architecture demands attention. Overhanging upper stories had to be forbidden; private owners had to be checked when their fronts encroached upon the roadway; dangerous cellar steps had to be guarded; narrow and dark alleys had to be closed with gates: and little by little the modern city has grown up, sacrificing picturesqueness and often seemliness to sanitary conditions and the appearance of uniform ordonnance. — R. S.

STRENGTH. In building, commonly in the phrase **STRENGTH OF MATERIALS.** The power of solid bodies to resist forces which tend to change their shape, position, or consistency. This power is developed in their resistance to the various stresses to which they are subjected, viz., stresses of compression, of tension, of shear, of torsion, and transverse stresses. The science of the resistance of materials has for its object to determine the internal stresses developed in the different parts of a structure, and to enable its parts to be proportioned with economy. It is in part theoretical and partly experimental.

Nearly all the solid materials used in construction possess a greater or less degree of elasticity, a property which tends to cause a body to return to its original shape upon the removal of the external force by which it has been deformed. If by reason of the application of an excessive force the body does not resume its original shape, its elasticity has been impaired, the elastic limit has been exceeded. Within the elastic limit the deformations are proportional to the applied forces. The elongation or shortening of a bar under tension or compression (l) is proportional to the applied force (P), and to the length of the bar (L), and inversely to its cross-sectional area (A), and to a specific constant called the "Modulus of Elasticity" of the material, represented by the letter (E); we have therefore the relations:

$$P = \frac{E \, A \, l}{L} \text{ and } l = \frac{P \, L}{E \, A}.$$

As the ratio $\frac{l}{L}$ is very small, E is generally a very large number. If A is made $= 1$, and $\frac{l}{L} = 1$, then $E = P$. E therefore is the imaginary force which would double the length of the rod under tension, or reduce it to zero under compression. These forces are imaginary because the formula assumes them applicable to all elongations and compressions, whereas this is only true within the elastic limit of the material.

Compression tends to reduce the length of the body subjected to it, and is accompanied by lateral expansion. If carried to the limit, it destroys the body by crushing it. This, however, applies to short blocks three or four diameters in height. When the length is twelve times the thickness or more, the tendency to bend modifies the distribution of the compression on the section, and in very long columns produces rupture by bending. Short bodies when crushed act differently according to their structure. Granular bodies, as brick, stone, cast iron, fail by the separation of cones or pyramids which slide down along the slopes of a central cone or pyramid. If the body is four or five times as long as its thickness, two cones remain upon the upper and lower bases, and the sides flake off between them. If fibrous, as wood, the fibres will buckle and the block will split endwise under pressure; if the fibres cohere strongly as in wrought iron and steel, the body will bulge, in the shape of a barrel. This bulging varies with the hardness of the material. In a recent experiment with steel from the head of a rail, the side next to the surface, which had been hardened by the hammering of the wheels, bulged very little; most of the deformation was on the side of the specimen most remote from the head of the rail. Under tension a body elongates and contracts laterally, a feature which becomes very marked as the specimen approaches rupture.

Shear is a stress acting upon any section of a body parallel to the plane of section, tending to make the parts slide upon each other. Resistance to the shearing stress is the molecular force developed in the section equal and contrary to the shear. In a beam loaded with detached weights, the reaction of the supports being forces acting upward, the shear at any point is equal to the reaction at one end less the sum of all weights between the point and the support considered, and is uniform from one weight to the next. It becomes zero at the point where the sum of the weights is equal to the reaction on the same side of the section. If the load is continuous, the shear will diminish gradually from either support to its zero point. In a system of detached weights, the shear at any point by its distance from the next weight between it and the support, is the increase in bending moment, to be added to the bending moment at the weight considered.

Transverse Stress. Assume a prismatic bar or beam resting upon two supports and loaded with a weight. The reactions of the supports are forces acting upward. Consider a section between the weight and one support. This portion is acted upon by the force P, which tends to cause it to slide upward at the plane of section. This is the shearing stress. The resistance to shear is a molecular force developed in the section equal and opposite to the shearing stress. Under the same conditions the force P, multiplied by its distance from the section, is the bending moment about that section. It tends to bend that portion of the beam upward, compressing the fibres in the upper half of the beam, and extending those in the lower half. If we had considered the other portion of the beam, the part carrying the weight, the treatment would have been the same, only the shear from the reaction of the support would be reduced at the position of the weight, which acts downward, making the shear between the weight and the section equal to the difference between the weight and the reaction. The bending moment also would be reduced by the moment of the weight, that is, the weight multiplied by its distance from the section considered. The moment of resistance of the fibres to compression and extension, that is, the sum of the resistance of all the fibres, each by its distance from the centre line which is neither extended nor compressed, must be equal and contrary to the bending caused by the external forces. The stresses upon the fibres are proportional to their distance from the centre line (the neutral axis), the outermost fibres are therefore the most strained, and rupture begins with them. By a principle of mechanics a shearing stress in one plane is accompanied by a shearing stress of equal intensity in a plane at right angles to the first. The vertical shearing force therefore at any section causes an equal horizontal shearing force distributed over the section and greatest at the neutral axis. This horizontal shear is familiarly shown by the fact that two equal beams placed one on top of the other will bear only half as great a load as a single beam of the joint depth of the two, unless these be prevented from sliding upon each other by means of keys and bolts. The two resist bending as $2\,h^2$, h being the depth of each ; the single (or the compound) beam resists as $(2\,h)^2 = 4\,h^2$.

Torsion is produced when a bar fixed at one end is subjected to forces forming a couple in a plane perpendicular to the axis of the bar. It tends to revolve in their own plane the transverse sections of the bar, and to change the straight fibres into spirals.

Of the materials commonly used in building, cast iron is generally the least reliable, where exposed to bending stresses. Its resistance to compression is four or five times as great as its tensile strength. Wrought iron and mild steel have about the same strength to resist tension and compression, their resistance to shear is about two-thirds of their tensile strength. Wood varies greatly in strength. Its resistance to tension is, as a rule, considerably greater than its resistance to compression. Its resistance to shear across the grain is also slight, though very much greater than its resistance to horizontal shear (shear along the grain) which is very small, varying from 200 to 300 pounds to the square inch for the softer woods, to 600 or even 1000 for the harder and tougher kinds. It is difficult to develop the full tensile strength of timber because to connect it in such manner as to apply tension, notches or gains must be cut into it which weaken the stick.

The horizontal shear from the key to the end of the timber must be equal to the compression of the key upon the fibre of the beam. Consequently the deeper the key seat the greater must be its distance from the end. The depth of the key seat also diminishes the section of the timber. This may be made less if long timbers are to be connected by not placing the keys opposite to each other.

Breaking Strength; Crushing Strength; Shearing Strength; Tensile Strength; Torsional Strength ; Transverse Strength ; same as Ultimate Strength in resistance to a force tending to cause rupture ; crushing ; shearing (see Shearing Weight) ; tension ; twisting ; cross breakage, — respectively. This use of the term strength is familiar, but erroneous.

Ultimate Strength. The last and greatest strength in a piece of material as noted by testing in it the extreme power of resistance observed just before it gives way.

Working Strength. The strength which in practice it is considered safe to depend on, in any given material or member. It was formerly determined by dividing the ultimate strength of the material (the Breaking Load) by a " factor of safety " which expressed a ratio determined by experience to provide for unseen contingencies. At this day, however, it is

usual to refer the working stress to the elastic limit of the material, — the stress at which permanent deformation takes place. This cannot be exceeded ; and the allowed stress is generally limited to one-third or one-half of the elastic limit, or in extreme cases to two-thirds. Allowance is made for impact if the structure is exposed to shock, and for variable stresses according to the conditions of the case.

Middleton, *Strains in structures, a text-book for students*, London, 1887, 1 vol. 12mo.; Kent, *The Strength of Materials*, New York, 1890, 1 vol. 12mo.; Tarn, *The Mechanics of Architecture*, London, 1892, 1 vol. 12mo.; Philbrick, *Beams and Girders: Practical Formulas for their Resistance*, New York. Van Nostrand, 1886, 1 vol. 16mo.

— W. R. HUTTON.

STRESS. The mutual action caused at the surface of contact between two bodies, whereby each exerts a force upon the other. Also the similar force between two imaginary parts of a body, as on the opposite sides of an imaginary section taken at any point of the body under consideration. Thus, a column exerts by its weight a downward force on its foundation, which reacts upward on the column : each of these bodies is said to be in a state of stress. And, in like manner, at any part of the column, the parts on each side of an imaginary plane passed through the column react upon one another, and are in a state of stress.

The effect of a stress on a body is to produce a change of shape, which deformation is called strain. Thus, in the above case, each of the two bodies is compressed or shortened vertically. These definitions are those maintained by Rankine[1] and other scientific men, although the distinction made has not yet received universal acceptance, and the terms are in common usage confused and often taken as synonymous. — D. N. B. S.

STRESS DIAGRAM. (See Strain Diagram.)

STRETCHER. In masonry, a solid, as a brick or stone laid lengthwise in the wall. (Compare Binder ; Header ; Through Stone.)

STRETCHING. Laying lengthwise, as bricks in a wall.

STRETCHING COURSE. In masonry, a course of stretchers, in contradistinction to one of headers, which would be a Bond Course.

STRETCHING PIECE. Properly, a tie ; frequently a strut or brace, a term more common in furniture making than in building.

STRIGIL ORNAMENT. In Roman architecture, a decoration of a flat member, as a fascia, with a repetition of slightly curved vertical flutings or reedings, supposed to resemble the strigil or scraper used after anointing.

[1] Rankine, William John Macquorn (1820–1872), civil engineer and discoverer in physical science.

STRIKE. *A.* To dress and smooth, as the outer edge of a joint of mortar between two bricks or stones. Struck joints are those which have been shaped either with a trowel or

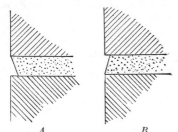

STRIKE: STRUCK JOINTS IN BRICK OR STONE FACING. *A* IS EASY TO MAKE BUT LEAVES A SHOULDER TO HOLD WATER. *B* SHEDS WATER WELL, THE MORTAR PROTECTS THE BRICK BELOW AND IS ALSO LESS VISIBLE, SO THAT THE WALL REMAINS OF A MORE UNIFORM COLOUR.

a special instrument, and the striking of the joints is usually called for in the specifications of the mason work.

B. To take down and remove, as a temporary structure, especially of a centre, as of an arch or vault.

STRIKER. A slightly bevelled metal plate set in the jamb of a door to receive and guide the door latch to its socket in closing.

STRING. One of the sloping members of a stair, usually a thick plank, which supports the steps and landings. Hence, by extension, the Ramp or side piece of a stone or other solid-built stair, if not so high as to be a parapet.

Bracketed String. An Open String having bracket-shaped pieces secured to its face in the angle between each tread and the riser below; the bracket mitreing with the end of the riser and seeming to support the end of the tread.

Close or Closed String. A string having its upper edge straight, and in general parallel with the lower edge, so that the outer ends of the treads and risers butt against it and are concealed. (Compare Open String.)

Curb String. Same as Close String.

Cut String. When of wood, the same as Open String; the upper edge being cut into notches to receive the treads and risers.

Cut and Mitred String. A Cut String of which the vertical edges of the notches are made to mitre with the ends of the risers.

Face String. The string at the outer and exposed edge of a stair as distinguished from the wall and the rough strings. It may be a part of the actual construction, or merely a piece of better material or finish applied to the face of the supporting member.

Horsed-out String. (See Horse, v.)

Housed String. (See House, v.)

Open String. A String which has its upper edge notched, or otherwise worked to the shape

of the steps, so that the treads and risers are supported by and overlap the step-shaped edge. (Compare Close String.)

Rough String. In a wooden stair, any one of the strings behind and concealed by the Face String, and which is intended to be covered by the plaster or other finish applied to the soffit of the stairs.

Wreathed String. (See Wreath.)

           —D. N. B. S.

STRING BOARD. Any board or plank, or facing of thin pieces glued together, serving in a building to cover the ends of steps in a stair, as when hiding the true string, or to cover the edge of a floor where a wellhole is cut through it. Often called Bridge Board.

STRING COURSE. A horizontal course on the face of a building. When continuous with a row of window sills or lintels, it is called a Sill Course or Lintel Course.

STRINGER. *A.* Same as String, as in a stair.

B. Same as Stringpiece.

STRINGPIECE. Any long, continuous, and solid member—usually horizontal—of a frame, as in a pier or bridge. Also a smaller piece not forming part of the frame, but used temporarily, as in moving or raising a building. (See description of such work under Shoring.) Stringpieces are almost always of heavy timber.

STROKED WORK. The tooling of stone so as to produce a finely fluted surface, often produced by the Drove Chisel. (See Stone Dressing.)

STRUT (n.). In a truss or other frame, a rigid piece acting as a brace or supporter, but differing from a post in being commonly set in a diagonal position.

STRUTTING PIECE. *A.* Same as Straining Beam (which see under Beam).

B. Same as Strut.

STUART, JAMES, F. R. S., F. S. A.; painter and architect; b. 1713; d. February, 1788.

He studied painting, and in 1742 visited Italy. His *De Obelisco Cæsaris Augusti* was published at the expense of Pope Benedict XIV. (1 vol. folio, 1750). January, 1751, with Nicholas Revett (see Revett) and W. Pars, a painter, he visited Greece and made a careful examination and measurements of the ruins at Athens. He returned to England in 1752. The first volume of Stuart and Revett's monumental *Antiquities of Athens* (folio) was published in 1762, the second in 1788 (the year of his death), the third, edited by W. Reveley, appeared in 1794, and the fourth, edited by J. Woods, in 1816. A supplementary volume, *Antiquities of Athens and Other Places in Greece, Sicily, etc.,* was published by C. R. Cockerell (see Cockerell, C. R.), W. Kinnard, T. L. Donaldson (see Donaldson), and

W. Railton (1830). From 1758 until his death Stuart held the office of surveyor at Greenwich Hospital.

J. Woods, Memoir in *Antiquities of Athens,* Vol. IV., 1816.

STUCCO. Any material used as a covering for walls and the like, put on wet and drying hard and durable. Plaster when applied to walls in the usual way (see Plastering) is a kind of stucco, and the hard finish is almost exactly like fine Roman stucco except that it is applied in only one thin coat instead of many. Vitruvius (VII., 3) speaks of three coats mixed with sand and three coats mixed with marble dust, but does not give the thickness of the coats, nor, what would answer the same purpose, how wet the mixture was made. He speaks of well-finished stucco shining so as to reflect the images falling upon it, and states that persons used to get slabs of plaster from ancient walls and used them for tables, the material being so beautiful in itself.

The term is generally applied to out-of-door work. Even in modern fireproof buildings the decorative use of fine plastering to replace woodwork, as for dadoes and the like, is not in the United States called stucco, but takes the name of the material used, generally a proprietary name.

The term is used commonly for rough finish of outer walls (see Rough Cast). The practical value of stucco is very great as being so nearly impervious to water ; thus, an excellent wall three stories high, or even higher, may be built with 8 inches of brick on the inner side, 4 inches of brick on the outer side, an air space of 2 or 4 inches across which the outer and the inner walls are well tied, and two coats of well-mixed and well-laid stucco on the exterior, this being finally painted with oil paint. — R. S.

Bastard Stucco. Plastering applied to walls according to a process considered inferior. A term probably not used in the United States.

STUD (I.). A relatively small projecting member as a boss, a small knob, a salient nail-head ; either for ornamental or mechanical purpose.

STUD (II.). A small slender post used in the framing of partitions and the lighter portions of wooden houses. Usually about 2 or 3 inches by 4 or 5 inches in lateral dimensions. (Compare Joist, *B.*)

STUD AND MUD. Same as Wattle and Dab.

STUDIO. *A.* The working room of an artist, preferably arranged — in north latitude, — to receive north light and especially free from cross lights.

B. By extension from the above, any large apartment fitted as a working room, especially for more or less artistic employments, as photography and designing of all sorts.

STUDY. In a household, a room preferably apart and remote, for reading, writing, or any similar use.

STUDY OF ARCHITECTURE. *A.* That which is required by the architect, either in preparation for the practice of his profession, or as required to keep his intelligence fresh and his ability at the highest point.

B. That necessary for the proper understanding and enjoyment of works of architectural art, on the part of those who are not expecting to practice the art or the profession.

The course of study pursued by architectural students in different parts of the European world is considered under the headings Architect ; Architect, The, in England ; — France ; — Italy ; School of Architecture ; Societies of Architects. It may be noted here, however, that the art of free-hand drawing, in the sense of accurate delineation and of accurate setting down of visible forms, is not taught or insisted on with sufficient emphasis, even in the great Paris school, while it is still less a matter of careful consideration in the great majority of the architectural schools existing. If, however, anything serious is to be gained by the study of the past, it can only be had by one who has the habit of continual drawing from the ancient buildings. If it were possible for every practising architect to spend some weeks of every year among the monuments of art which most interest him, and most closely appeal to his sense of what should be done in the present, his work would be kept from the otherwise almost inevitable lapse into commonplace, and his practice from becoming an inartistic professional service, giving to clients that which they asked for, but nothing further or more exalted than that.

STUFF. Carpenters' and plasterers' materials taken in the mass ; thus clear stuff means boards free from such imperfections as knots, shakes, etc. ; inch stuff, boards of that thickness ; merchantable stuff, boards, and the like, inferior to clear stuff, but still fit for use.

STUNNING. *A.* The deep scoring of marble surfaces, caused in cutting slabs by coarse particles of sand getting between the saw blade and the saw-kerf.

B. The injuring of the surface of stone by a bruise, which is often caused by careless cutting, especially in marble.

STUPA. In Indian architecture, a building erected to contain a Chaitya (see Chaitya Cave), and usually of a towerlike form, with no more interior subdivisions than are sufficient to afford an adequate shrine ; depending entirely upon its exterior effect. (See India, Architecture of ; Tope.)

STURM, LEONHARD CHRISTOPH ; architect ; b. about 1669 ; d. 1719.

A mathematician and architect who was professor in the Ritter Academy at Wolfenbüttel, and afterward at the University of Frankfort an der Oder, Germany. He was later made *Oberbaudirector* in Schwerin, and was *Baudirector* in Braunschweig when he died. Sturm is best known by his many important works on civil and military architecture, published at Augsburg between 1714 and 1720.

Füssli, *Allgemeines Kunstler-lexicon.*

STY; **STYE**. A pen for hogs; applied only to small shelters of the kind, as on ordinary farms.

STYLE (I.). Character; the sum of many peculiarities, as when it is said that a certain building is in a spirited style. By extension, significance, individuality; especially in a good sense and imputed as a merit, as in the expression, "Such a building has style."

STYLE (II.). A peculiar type of building, of ornament, or the like, and constituting a strongly marked and easily distinguished group or epoch in the history of art; thus we say that in Europe the Romanesque style prevailed from the fall of the Western Empire until the rise of the Gothic style; but we also say that during that Romanesque period such minor styles as the Latin style, the Rhenish or West German style, the Norman Romanesque style, more vigorous in England than even in the country of its origin, and the Tuscan round-arched style, as in the church of Samminiato al Monte, were all in existence successively, or at the same time. So it is an open question whether the Byzantine style is properly one form of the Romanesque style. Moreover, it is often said that there are but two styles of architecture, the Trabeated and the Arcuated (see those terms); but this is forcing the word "style" out of its usual meaning, and we should rather say there are but two principal Ways of Building. For a style to exist, there must be a recognized artistic treatment common to all the buildings of an epoch, or of a group, while those buildings have also their individual peculiarities.

Going back now to the earliest buildings known to us, we find that the Egyptian style is characterized by an absolute rejection of arched forms for all ornamental and decorative building, although it appears that the arch was known; by the absence of any visible roof; by the character of great permanence, although this is not quite as essential to the style as has been often assumed, for many of the features of the work contradict it, as where columns have the lower part of the shaft rounded, thus standing upon a base much smaller than they might easily have received; by a very free use of surface sculpture, usually in concavo-convex relief (see Relief); by a free use of polychromy applied to such reliefs, and also to flat surfaces, the latter taking the two shapes of purely dec-

orative effect, and of elaborate representative painting with landscapes, figures, legends, histories of battle, of siege, and of ceremonies of peace.

The Chaldean and the Assyrian styles (see Mesopotamia, Architecture of) are hard for us to realize perfectly. Until it is absolutely settled whether the palace halls were vaulted, or finished with flat roofs, and a modification of columnar architecture, we cannot be said to know what any of the styles of Mesopotamia and the neighbourhood really were. The Persian style of the early times is better understood (see Persian Architecture, Part I.). The numerous styles of India are to be discriminated one from another as Buddhist, Jaina, Hindu, and the like (see India, Architecture of); but there cannot be said to be an Indian style. On the other hand, the architecture of Japan is a national architecture, which has endured through many centuries, and in a single style; for the unchanging life of a people without the invasion of foreign influence, and renewing their impressions at the same source where they received their original civilization, has allowed the beautiful post-and-beam architecture of the ninth century A.D. to continue down to the latter half of the nineteenth century, when European ideas invaded the land. (See Japan, Architecture of.)

In Europe there have been the following important styles: The classical Grecian is marked by an absence of arcuation as complete as that of the Egyptian; by an extreme simplicity of structure; by the absence of a general interest in large and monumental interiors — the one or two instances of such interiors, which we know something of, being local and caused by special conditions (see Greece; Grecian Architecture; Sicily; Thersilium); by a use of highly realized and perfected sculpture of human subject, contrasting boldly with other sculpture of the most severe and conventional sort, with hardly any representative meaning; and, finally, by a free use of polychromatic painting, applied not in the way of story and representation, but in the way of coloured adornment of the architecture. There was, of course, mural painting, but, so far as we are informed, it hardly told upon the architecture, except as certain interiors were especially arranged for the reception of such painting. An extreme solicitude about details, extending to the profiles of simple mouldings, and the almost invisible curves of the entasis, marks all the finer work.

The Greco-Roman style is the style built up under the Roman Empire by the Italian structure of arch and vault, especially when made of solid mortar masonry, invested with the Greek orders or modifications of them, these orders being used sometimes as a mere decoration, but sometimes for screens, colonnades, porticoes, and the like, so that a large building might be partly arcuated and partly altogether columnar. In Syria, and to a large extent in northern Africa, the stone-built and stone-vaulted buildings, both of imperial civic purpose and of the early centuries of the Christian church, form a style by themselves, neither Greco-Roman on one side, nor Byzantine on the other, and as their interesting remains are more carefully studied, a name especially fitted to them will be brought into use.

In the East, the Byzantine style succeeded the Roman Imperial way of building, and in the West, what we call the Latin style was introduced into Italy. (See Latin Architecture.) But the term Romanesque must of necessity be used to include the Latin (even if not the Byzantine) ; and must be held to describe all those buildings of as yet immature artistic quality which were erected during seven centuries. In France, in the twelfth century, and at a still later time in Germany, a highly developed and richly ornamented style had taken shape, and this undoubtedly would have received a name separating it from the other Romanesque work, except for the sudden appearance of the Gothic system of vaulting with its necessary results, which grew out of this later Romanesque.

The Gothic style is that of ribbed vaulting, with the pointed arch as an almost inevitable result, and with an elaborate system of decoration based partly upon the pointed arch, with its cusps and resulting tracery, and partly upon a very free study of leafage, with a constantly growing introduction of animal and human form.

Romanesque and Gothic in all their forms and at all epochs, as well as the Byzantine of the Eastern Empire, with its resulting more recent styles in Russia, Moldavia, and Armenia, are all arcuate styles of the most marked character. Nothing in antiquity is so wholly dependent upon the arch, and its extension, the vault, as are the Byzantine buildings and those of the whole of Western Europe. In the East, brick and abundant mortar is more used; in the West, stone from the nearest quarry, in relatively small pieces, cut with a constantly growing skill, and always with a great sense of the best method to follow for lightness and durability, is the one material used; except that timber, in the forest-covered regions, gives rise to a style of framed building obviously very different from the Gothic structure, which is absolutely a masonry style, but partaking of its decoration and echoing its general forms.

The most noticeable thing about architectural styles is the spontaneity of their growth, developing from the obvious conditions of building, and also developing one out of another, according to what we now see to have been an inevitable succession of processes and resulting forms.

There is, indeed, the self-conscious element in architectural work, and a certain amount of deliberate imitation of previous styles, these recurring at intervals when a community is comparatively learned and literary, and begins to study and consider the works of other epochs. Thus, there can be no doubt that the forms of Roman Imperial architecture were modified by deliberate imitation of Greek art, and in like manner the domed buildings of western France were imitated from the far distant Byzantine models, imitated in shape and design, if not in the system of building adopted. In general, however, the growth of important architectural styles is found to be as natural as that of a plant. When the classical Renaissance of the fifteenth century began in Italy, although the purpose of the first architectural artists was a return to Roman forms and Roman principles of design, they were by no means consistent in that resolve, or else there were but few of them who were so determined, while others adopted only a certain amount of anti-mediæval feeling derived from a study of the Roman monuments, but wholly without care for the Roman details. In this way a style took shape in Italy, which developed itself in as natural a growth, from 1430 to 1500, as if it had not originated in a deliberate imitation of classical antiquity. This succession was stopped by the classical study, first of the Renaissance artists, and then of the later men ; and it is for this reason that the Italian writers, and we, following them, stop the Italian Renaissance with the beginning of the cinque cento, and speak of all the work of the sixteenth century, the seventeenth century, and even a later epoch, together as of the Classicismo, or of the Decadenza (see these terms). At almost the same time, however, that the Italian Renaissance stopped, the French Renaissance, the German Renaissance, and the Flemish Renaissance took their rise, beginning about eighty-five years after the first appearance of the classical Renaissance in Italy ; and each of these styles began its own evolution much as had been the case under the Italian Renaissance, each retaining much of the spirit of mediæval work while abandoning its forms. Here, again, in the North, the growth of style was interfered with by deliberately renewed study of Roman Imperial building ; and there was also a deliberate imitation of Italy. At this period, intercourse between the nations of Europe was freer than it had been, and it was possible for learned men and artists to visit Italy, and remain there in safety and comfort, pursuing their studies. The result is seen in the fact that soon after the beginning of the seventeenth century, the architecture of Western Europe is more alike in all the different nations than it had been at any previous time. There are often found existing, side by side, a formal classical style, encouraged by the nobles of the court, and a simpler style existing in the country; but it is the stately manner of building based upon that of Italy which generally prevails. So that, although we are now considering the epoch recognized as studious, scholarly, self-conscious, deliberate, rather than spontaneous, we have yet a consistent and uniform growth from the seventeenth and eighteenth centuries as obvious as that in the Gothic style itself.

The feeling of students of the second half of the nineteenth century has been generally hostile to these later neoclassic styles, as being founded upon bad taste, without harmony or charm, but this feeling is gradually giving way to a perception of the greater relative value of these late styles, and especially of their inevitableness, coming as they do from the efforts of men determined to be classical, and yet seeking something fresh and original, at least in detail.

(See Byzantine Architecture; Cinque Cento; Classicismo; Decadenza; Dravidian Architecture; Grecian Architecture; Greco-Roman; Henri Deux; Henri Quatre; Latin Architecture; Louis Quatorze; Louis Quinze; Louis Seize; Louis Treize; Pig Tail and Periwig; Quattro Cento; Renaissance; Rococo; Romanesque; Roman Imperial; Sei Cento; Style Empire; Tre Cento; Zopf; also geographical terms.)   — R. S.

STYLE EMPIRE. In French, and always pronounced as in French, the style of the Napoleonic empire; an elaboration of the style of the later part of the reign of Louis XVI. in which the severe and classically inspired design of about 1780 is overlaid by rather incongruous ornamentation, and loses much of its charm. This style had, however, so brief a reign, that it is impossible to judge of what its development might have been. It is the last of the naturally developed styles of Western Europe, and has been succeeded by the chaos of modern times.

STYLOBATE. In Greek architecture, that part of the Stereobate upon which the peristyle stands; by extension, any continuous base, plinth, or pedestal, upon which a row of columns are set.

SUABIAN ARCHITECTURE. That carried on or inspired by the house of Suabia, especially in other lands than in the German kingdom (Holy Roman Empire) immediately under its control. Thus, the Suabian architecture of southern Italy is a style of recognized peculiarities, but the architecture of the Suabian emperors in Germany, in the twelfth and thirteenth centuries, is hardly to be distinguished from the general current of mediæval architecture in that country.

SUARDI BARTOLOMMEO (BRAMANTINO). Milanese painter and architect; b. about 1455; d. after 1536.

He was practising painting in Milan when Bramante came there about 1472 (see Bramante), and seems to have become his pupil and assistant. Sept. 28, 1513, he was in Milan, and made a contract for pictures with the monks of the Certosa of Chiaravalle, in which he is mentioned as *domino Bartholomeo dicto Bramantino de Suardis filio Alberti.* A volume of drawings in the Bibliotheca Ambrosiana at Milan is ascribed to him, and has been published in facsimile by Giuseppe Mongeri: *Le Rovine di Roma al principio del Secolo XVI., Studi del Bramantino* (Milan, 1880).

Giuseppe Mongeri, *Il Bramantino,* in his edition of *Rovine di Roma,* Milan, 1880; Seidlitz, *Bramante in Mailand;* Crowe and Cavalcaselle, *History of Painting in North Italy.*

SUBSELLIUM. Same as Miserere.

SUBSTRUCTION; SUBSTRUCTURE. A mass of building below and supporting another; especially referring to foundations, and plainer and heavier work, such as the retaining walls of a platform and the like.

SUBSURFACE IRRIGATION. A system of sewage disposal adapted for isolated country houses and institutions not within reach of sewers, in which the sewage is distributed under the top soil by means of a flush tank and tile or absorption drains. (See Drainage; Irrigation.) — W. P. G.

SUBWAY. An accessible underground passage, especially in cities, for street cars and other public conveyances, to relieve congestion of surface traffic in the street above, also to contain gas and water mains, telegraph wires, etc.

SUDATIO. An apartment in the Roman bath or gymnasium between the laconicum, sudatorium, or stove, and the caldarium or warm bath, where athletes retired to remove the sweat from their bodies.

SUDATORY. A chamber used for the sweat bath. (For the structure built by the American Indians, see Sweat Lodge under Lodge.) — F. S. D.

SUGER (SUGGER); abbot and builder. Suger, abbot of S. Denis, near Paris, rebuilt the church of his abbey about 1137–1140. This contains much of the earliest existing proto-Gothic work in France. Suger was also minister to Charles VI. of France.

Bauchal, *Dictionnaire;* Moore, *Gothic Architecture.*

SUITE. A succession of connected rooms, generally on one floor. The term carries with it the double meaning of a common purpose being served by these rooms, and of their forming a sort of continuous gallery by opening into one another freely.

En Suite. In French, forming a series; in English, especially said of rooms opening into one another with doors carefully placed opposite

SUBSTRUCTURE OF CHOIR OF CATHEDRAL: ERFURT, SAXONY, GERMANY.

one another. (See En Axe; En Enfilade, under the principal terms.)

SUMMER (I.). A principal beam; the first or principal member in a piece of framing, as a floor. The term "girder" is now used for such primary pieces, especially in the United States; but in old English practice the girder was a secondary piece which rested upon or was more commonly framed into the summer. Spelled also Somer. (See Breast Summer.)

SUMMER (II.). (Probably the French *sommier*.) A stone forming the top of a pier, or of that part of a wall at the jamb of an opening which supports a lintel, arch, or corbel. Called also summer stone. Where the barge stones of a gable start from the summer it is sometimes called Skew Table.

SUMMERHOUSE. An open ornamental pavilion in a park or garden for out-of-door rest or retirement. (See Casino, *A*; Kiosk; Pavilion, *B*.)

SUMMER TREE. Same as summer, especially in the sense of a wooden lintel over an aperture; also called Breast Summer, Bressummer, Dormant Tree.

SUNDIAL. A device for indicating the time of day by means of the shadow cast by the sloping edge of a projecting point, or *gnomon*, set in a surface upon which the hours of the day are set forth on points radiating from the gnomon. It is sometimes in the form of a table in a garden, and sometimes it is placed conspicuously as an ornament on a wall or gable.

SUNK. Having the surface lowered or cut away, as a panel in sense *A*. A sunk square is usually an ornamental feature (see Caisson, II.; Lacunar). Sunk work is usually decoration in relief upon a sunken panel, but may be incised or impressed.

Double Sunk. Recessed or lowered in two degrees or steps, as when a panel is sunk below the surface of a larger panel.

SUNLIGHT BURNER. In artificial lighting by gas or electricity, the concentration of many lights or burners around a powerful circular reflector placed in or against the ceiling, often in connection with a ventilator, and covered by an inverted half globe of glass. (Called also Sunburner.)

SUN POLE. A sacred pole made from the "mystery tree" with much ceremony, for use in the "mystery" lodge during the sun dance of the Sioux Indians. The devotees are attached to the sun pole by thongs fastened to skewers which are passed through their flesh.

— F. S. D.

SUN PRINT. In photography, a print made by some chemical process and by a direct exposure of a chemically prepared surface to the light; especially a reproduction of a mechanical drawing in the work of architects and

engineers. Cyanotypes or "blue prints" are the most common, but there is also a process which gives blue lines on white ground, and those which give black or brown lines on a white or light gray ground.

SUN ROOM. An exposed room or gallery enclosed toward the sun by a glass partition or continuous window, generally for the use of invalids in a hospital; sometimes called Solar and sun bath.

SUOVETAURILIA. In Roman antiquity, a sacrifice consisting of a swine, a sheep, and a bull; the word being compounded of the Latin names of the three beasts. Hence, in modern archæology, a representation, as in relief sculpture, of the three creatures together.

SUPERCAPITAL. (Called also Impost.) A piece of stone above the capital proper of a column, perhaps recalling the ancient use of the entablature, as in Roman Imperial practice, even above isolated columns; perhaps intended rather as a constructional device to enable the capital to receive a still larger superimposed mass. The use of supercapitals is characteristic of Byzantine art and all its imitations.

SUPERCILIUM. In Roman architecture, the fillet above the Cymatium, forming the topmost member of the cornice. Also, sometimes, referring to the fillets above and below the Scotia of an attic base.

SUPERCOLUMNIATION. Superimposition in columnar architecture, with special reference to the disposition of the orders. The more elaborate orders are at the top; but where there are four or five stories the Composite in some form is commonly placed above the Corinthian. (See Superimposition.)

SUPERIMPOSITION. In building, the placing of solids, as piers or pillars, in certain relations to one another vertically. Thus, the main constructional uprights of a Gothic building were continued through from foundation to spring of vault, and that because of the necessity of securing the most perfect verticality or continuity in supports, which were by the very nature of the structure light and slender in comparison with the work they had to do. On the other hand, many buildings in which the strength of the structure is sufficient are naturally arranged on a different plan. The fenestration of the front having two or three large openings below and perhaps twice as many in each story above, is often more effective if the openings, whether arched or closed with lintels, are arranged without reference to the axes of the openings and solids below; and this in many different styles of architecture.

Artistically, the propriety of such arrangements depends entirely upon the style employed, and the effect proposed, and the general harmony and charm of proportion which the designer finds within his reach. Constructionally, it is entirely a matter of the strength and perfectness of the work. — R. S.

SUPERINTENDENCE. The act or process of examining the materials and watching the work of a building; especially such services when rendered by the architect or his representative. As nearly all building is now done by contract, it is as carrying out of a part of the contract that superintendence demands special notice.

In contract work, the architect, acting as superintendent, has large powers given him by the terms of the contract. His remuneration for the work involved in superintending is usually one and one-half per cent, or three-tenths of the whole Commission. (See that term; also Superintendent; Surveyor.)

The person who watches a piece of day's work or piece work is not conducting superintendence in the above sense. Thus, if, in his absence, a pier or arch is built not in accordance with drawings furnished, the expense of taking down and rebuilding, in most cases, will fall upon the employer — the owner of the building. On the other hand, in superintendence properly so-called (*i.e.* in contract work) the architect coming to the building has the power to order such errors repaired at the builder's expense. On this account a day's work job will be watched hour by hour by some competent person, while the contract work need not be visited more than perhaps once a week; and the last-named kind of supervision is superintendence in the technical sense.

Several attempts have been made to introduce distinctive terms for the two kinds of care and watching described above, but none has been accepted as yet (see Supervision). It will be found necessary to agree upon such definite words or phrases, because there is a certain tendency towards day's work in the most important buildings. When a very costly structure is to be hurried to completion, as when a steel-cage building is to be finished in ten months, contract work is found hardly available.

SUPERINTENDENT. The person who examines officially, as required by the contract or agreement, the work and materials of a building. This is usually the architect or his representative. (See Superintendence.)

The requirements of the superintendent are extremely numerous and varied. His personal characteristics are of much importance, and his usefulness increases in proportion to his power of controlling men. Unfailing good temper, combined with firmness, based upon an accurate knowledge of the subject at hand and wide experience, are qualities that make the ideal superintendent. He must keep himself perfectly familiar with the plans and specifications of the building under his charge by frequently comparing the work in progress with the draw-

ings, and he must constantly check all measurements to avoid errors. He must carefully note the adjoining buildings and their condition, also the grades, levels, sewers, and water courses. After the excavation is finished, he should examine minutely all the ground before any foundations are laid, as unexpected qualities of the soil require special provision in the foundations. Many problems present themselves in this connection, and additional spread of concrete or stone footings may be needed; and the discovery of quicksand, springs, or water courses will necessitate arching, piling, or grillage. Where buildings come in contact with each other, as they do in overcrowded cities, questions of party walls, neighbours' rights or encroachments, errors in surveyors' measurements, etc., must be considered, and conditions arise not to be reasonably expected, and which severely tax the ingenuity of the superintendent.

The various materials used must be carefully examined as they are delivered, and their quality and condition scrutinized. The sand must be clean and sharp, the broken stone also clean and of proper size, the cement of the brand specified and unspoiled by air or water. The bricks must be of good form, well baked, and hard enough to ring when sharply struck together. Terra cotta should be hard burnt, straight, and not warped or discoloured. The composition of the mortar, concrete, and plaster is of much importance, and the proportion of the ingredients and manner of mixing must be exactly as specified. The mixing must always be done in a trough, never on the bare ground. No plastering should be done and no masonry laid when the temperature is below freezing point, and in winter all walls should be protected at night during construction.

The tooling of stonework must be according to specifications and the arrises true and straight, and all stone free from oil or iron stains, sand holes, and quarry marks.

Iron castings must be of full thickness, and all columns should be bored as a test. Columns should have level beds, and bearings of beams must be as specified and always on iron plates or capstones. Tie-rods for arches, anchors, and shutter eyes must be built in the masonry as required. All iron must be delivered at the building, and inspected before being painted. Loose rivets must not be permitted, and all connections must be carefully made.

There must be no large or loose knots in the lumber. Framing must be compared continually with the ground plans. All headers over 4 feet in length should be hung in bridle irons. Woodwork for interiors, trims, etc. (see Inside Finish, under Finish), must be painted on the back. Gutters and roofs should be tested by water to ascertain their pitch. Tin flashing must be painted on both sides. All woodwork not to be varnished should be primed or have a coat of oil as soon as it is delivered at the building. It is important to insist on sufficient nailing for cross-bridging and for clapboards and shingles.

Gas pipes must grade to the rising lines, and must be tested without the use of water, which rusts the joints. Drain pipes in cellar must have proper fall and the main trap be accessible. All the plumbing fixtures must be trapped and vent pipes run to roof. The hot and cold water supply pipes must be separated or be covered with non-conducting material. Steam pipes must have proper fall, and metal shields not omitted where they pass through floors or partitions.

These items, selected at random from the great mass of instructions necessary for the various contractors, will serve to indicate a few of the innumerable considerations that demand the attention of the superintendent, and the nature of his services. (For more detailed information, see Iron Construction ; Masonry ; Wood, Construction in.)

The materials that enter into the construction of a building are so varied, and the branches of work so diverse, that it is difficult to insist upon a uniform standard of excellence, but this must be the superintendent's endeavour, and his duty is to supplement and interpret the specifications. He must also strive to make the work of these different trades harmonize with each other, and foresight and watchfulness will prevent many future annoyances. He must see that openings in the walls for pipes and sewers are not forgotten, and that chases and recesses, which even if shown on the plans are often overlooked, are provided for plumbing and steam pipes and heating flues. Framing in floors for plumbing fixtures, and spaces in partitions for ventilation flues and hot air ducts, accommodation for electric and mechanical appliances, require provision made for them long before their special work is to be performed.

The position of gas and electric outlets, and the location of radiators, registers, bells, and speaking tubes, must be verified, and similar matters which seem of lesser importance require careful attention. The success of a building depends largely upon the care with which these details are arranged.

Workmen must be prevented from recklessly cutting wooden beams and masonry, and from injuring each other's work. As a rule, mechanics employed in a building exhibit no interest whatever in anything beyond their immediate tasks, the general result being a matter of no moment to them. It is even difficult to induce them to protect properly their own work from injury by taking the most

obvious and simple precautions against accidental defacement.

The rubbish that accumulates in a building and all rejected material should be properly removed to prevent finished work being damaged, and to reduce the risk of fire.

Constant tests of materials are advisable, and the knowledge that these tests will be made do much to induce the builder to maintain a high standard of excellence.

It would seem that plans and specifications made by a competent architect would ordinarily be correct, and the superintendent's duty would be limited to interpreting them and insisting upon their faithful performance ; but errors will creep in, and unexpected emergencies arise which must be met and promptly decided. There are many points which are perforce left unstudied in the plans for a complicated building, and these must be determined on the spot. This is especially apt to be true where buildings are altered or additions are made to them, when the most careful written specifications will fail to cover all the work required. It is, in fact, impossible to specify exactly in these cases, as so much depends upon conditions not known until the building operations are actually in progress ; and faulty construction which must be remedied, weak spots in walls, defective framing, and other unwelcome discoveries only come to light after the work has reached a certain stage.

Delinquencies of contractors and the failure of supplies, which necessitate the adoption of other materials, and even the deterioration of well-known materials, are matters that require immediate adjustment. The failure of contractors to provide the work and materials demanded by the specifications is the principal difficulty that the superintendent is obliged to meet, but when this neglect is wilful he has no option but to enforce the stipulations of the contract as far as lies in his power. The possibility of delay often forces the superintendent to accept an inferior material or a poorer method of construction. The speed with which a building can be erected is now nearly always an important factor, and demands for concessions or changes in the method of carrying on the work are most frequently based on the plea of delay. These demands must be carefully weighed, and it is often the wisest course to permit modifications in the construction : the superintendent, therefore, must have a certain discretion allowed him. Where there is telephonic communication difficult questions may be referred back to the architect's office for settlement, but emergencies arise where this is not possible, and a decision must be made on the spot to avoid delay.

It must always be borne in mind that no amount of superintendence will insure good work from a poor builder. If a builder is not equipped for good work and in the habit of constructing first-class buildings, mere desire on his part is not sufficient, and neither persuasion, threats, nor promises will make him raise his standard. This is generally understood where the element of art is involved, and no one supposes that entreaties or advice will make a poor carver, modeller, or decorator produce artistic results. The same is true of masonry, carpentry, and of all mechanical work. The superintendent may reject bad workmanship, and repeatedly refuse to accept it; but he is powerless to compel the contractor to furnish the quality desired if he is unfamiliar with it and unwilling to furnish it.

A merely careless builder, or one whose business is not well organized, may to a certain extent be kept up to a fair standard by faithful superintendence; but watching a dishonest or incompetent contractor is a fruitless task, and for the former, nothing short of a complete detective system will insure even an approximate adherence to the plans and specifications.

The superintendence given by architects or their representatives to the buildings in their charge should not be understood to mean constant supervision. This can only be obtained by the employment of a clerk of the works, who will be in attendance at the building at all times. Accordingly, it is important for the superintendent to time his visits so that they will be of the greatest value.

— ARNOLD W. BRUNNER.

SUPERSTRUCTURE. A structure raised upon another structure, as a building upon a foundation, basement, or substructure.

SUPERVISION. Same as Superintendence. The schedule of charges of the American Institute of Architects, 1901, contains the following clause, " The supervision or superintendence of an architect (as distinguished from the continuous personal superintendence which may be secured by the employment of a clerk of the works) means," etc.

SUPPLY TANK. (See Supply Cistern, under Cistern.)

SURBASE. The moulding or group of mouldings forming the crowning member of a basement story, a plinth, dado, base course, or the like.

SURVEY. A plan, map, or plotting, made from measurements and angles taken, and lines run, as described under Surveying; also the whole operation of surveying a piece of ground or the like, and recording the results in such a map.

SURVEYING. That branch of engineering which has for its object the location and measurement of the lines surrounding any portion of the earth's surface, and from which the area of any such portion can be determined, and sub-

sequently plotted in the form of a map; also, more particularly, the locating of points on the earth's surface relatively to one another.

Broadly, the measurements of surveying consist in determining the horizontal angle included between any two intersecting courses, and in measuring the lengths of these courses, — a course being a line as "run" (determined or laid out). By continuing in this way along the entire perimeter of any piece of ground, however irregular in shape it be, sufficient data may be obtained for the computation of the area of this piece of ground. Also from these data, obtained in the field, the survey can be accurately plotted on paper, to any convenient scale, the horizontal angles being laid off with the aid of a protractor. However, in case greater accuracy is desired, the different corners of the survey may be referred, by means of rectangular coördinates, to a common point of origin, — the horizontal angles and the lengths of courses being necessary in the computation of these coördinates.

In most cases it is also necessary to determine the *true* bearings of each and every course, as distinguished from the magnetic bearings, in order that the survey shall be completely located. If the true bearing of any one course is known, the bearings of the other courses can easily be calculated with the aid of the horizontal angles already determined; but when this is not the case, and when reference to prior surveys is not possible, it will be necessary to establish a line of true Meridian, and to determine the angle which some one course makes with this line. When, however, a surveyor's compass is employed, the *magnetic* bearings of the different courses are read direct, and from them, the variation between the magnetic and true meridians being known or determined, the true bearings may be computed with only a small remaining error of angle. This correction does not, however, include errors of angle due to local magnetic attraction, such as is found in ferruginous districts.

The foregoing is an outlined description of the art of surveying; in addition, however, there is much important detail, some of which will be mentioned in connection with the description of instruments included below.

The *engineer's transit* is the instrument now commonly used for the measurement of angles in the best engineering practice in the United States; it appears to be the same instrument as the transit theodolite in Great Britain. It is the most important of surveying instruments, and the one by which the most accurate work can be done. For these reasons the transit is the instrument best adapted for those surveys necessary to the architect or the builder. In the surveying of city or town lots, and especially in those cities in which real estate has a high market value, the very greatest accuracy is required, as a conflict or error in the lines bounding adjoining properties might be the source of considerable litigation and heavy damages. Also in the laying out of foundation lines, or the setting out of individual piers, great care is necessary that these shall be accurately located.

The engineer's transit consists of a telescope mounted upon a horizontal axis supported by two vertical standards which are, in turn, carried by the upper of two horizontal circular plates. This, called the vernier plate, also carries a compass box, two verniers, and two spirit levels. Immediately below and completely concealed by the vernier plate, except for openings at the verniers, is a second plate called the horizontal limb, whose circumference is divided into degrees of the circle and subdivisions. These two plates are arranged so that they will rotate about the vertical axis of the instrument independently of one another. Thus, by clamping the lower plate to the vertical axis, and by directing the telescope in two successive and different directions, the vernier plate will have passed through an angle whose magnitude may be measured upon the lower plate.

Below these horizontal plates and detachable from them, there is still another horizontal plate to which are connected four levelling screws resting upon a levelling plate. By means of the levelling plate and screws the instrument can be made truly horizontal, as shown by the spirit levels attached to the vernier plate.

A vertical circle graduated in degrees is attached to the horizontal axis of the instrument, and this axis with its telescope being free to revolve, angles of inclination can be read by means of a vernier fixed to one of the standards.

Enclosed in the barrel of the telescope two cross hairs at right angles to each other enable an object to be accurately bisected. Attached to the telescope there is a spirit level or " long bubble," in order that the telescope may be made truly horizontal.

The transit is placed usually upon a tripod, and by means of a plummet or plumb bob, suspended from the centre of the instrument, the transit may be centred upon any desired point.

The *surveyor's compass* may be used when no great amount of accuracy in the survey is required. It has two open sights through which any distant object can be seen, and, when seen, the magnetic bearing of the curve between the distant object and the point of sight will be indicated upon a graduated dial by the point of the compass needle. A *circumferentor* [1] differs

from the compass only in that the compass box is free to rotate upon the brass plate carrying the sights. In this way, by means of an attached vernier, the measurement of horizontal angles is possible independently of the needle ; that is to say, the needle is held stationary or fixed. The circumferentor also often carries an attachment by which angles of inclination may be determined.

Both the surveyor's compass and the circumferentor are levelled, and shown to be level, in a manner similar to that of the transit. Also, as in the case of the transit, these instruments are generally mounted upon tripods, a so-called *Jacob's staff* being, however, occasionally employed. This is simply a single staff, pointed at the lower end, and to the top of which the compass or circumferentor may be attached.

The *demicircle* is for measuring and indicating angles, and is not unlike an ordinary protractor, with a revolving bar mounted on a pivot at the centre of the circle, and a compass set firmly in the plane of the graduated arc. It may have a telescope in place of, or attached to, the revolving bar. It may be levelled approximately by being laid or set on the plane table, and is used only as a rough substitute for the theodolite or transit.

The only other angle-measuring instrument that needs mention is the *surveyor's cross*. Very simple in construction, it comprises two horizontal bars at right angles to each other, each bar supporting an open sight at either end. Obviously, the use of this instrument is limited to the laying out of right angles ; it is now rarely seen.

There are two methods, other than that of triangulation, commonly employed in the measurement of lengths or distances.

By the first method the distance between any two points is determined by stretching a chain or tape of known length between these points. The telescope of the transit, or of other instruments, equipped with stadia or micrometer wires, is the means by which distances can be measured under the second method.

Gunter's chain, for so long in universal use, has a length of 66 feet, divided into 100 links of 7.92 inches, every tenth link having some distinguishing mark. Steel pins are employed for marking the end of chain lengths where the distance to be measured is greater than 66 feet. This chain has, to a large extent, been replaced by the engineer's chain of 100 feet in length, divided into links of 1 foot.

The *tape* is a very thin steel ribbon, usually from $\frac{1}{8}$ to $\frac{3}{8}$ inches in width, and ranging between 100 to 500 feet in length, subdivisions being designated by some convenient mark.

[1] The term " circumferentor " is applied sometimes to the " perambulator " or wheel measurer, in which a wheel is simply run along a road, recording its revo-

lutions by means of a cyclometer, and so furnishing a rough measurement of distances.

The result obtained by measuring distances with the tape is the most exact of all methods now commonly in use.

In measuring distance by telescope, two horizontal or stadia wires, one above and one below the horizontal cross hair alluded to in the description of the transit, are placed at such a distance apart that when sighting at a vertical rod 100 feet away the wires will include 1 foot (or some other convenient constant) of vertical height of rod, and will include proportional spaces for other distances.

In the operation of surveying, and in the subsequent mapping, that part of the earth's surface upon which the operations are conducted is considered to be a horizontal plane, correction for the curvature of the earth being neglected in the case of small surveys. For this reason it is necessary to reduce inclined measurements to horizontal lines. When the inclined distance and the angle of inclination, determined by the vertical circle of the transit between any two points, are known, this correction can readily be made. If the inclined distance and the difference in elevation between the two points are known, this will answer the same purpose.

To insure greater accuracy in taping or chaining, corrections also for temperature and for the catenary curve, due to imperfect stretching, must be made.

The art of Levelling is also to be included under the general head surveying. It consists in determining the difference in elevation between any two points, or in determining the elevation of one or more points above or below a datum line or bench mark, the level of which may be assumed, if not known. In extensive surveys the datum line is assumed, whenever possible, to be the level of mean high tide. The operation of levelling may be conducted by means of instruments especially devised for this purpose, or by the use of the transit. If the latter is employed, the angle of inclination and the inclined distance between any two points are determined, and from them the height of one point above the other is calculated.

Of the instruments in use for levelling, the only two that need mention here are the Y level and the hand level.

The Y level has two standards, or Y's (from which the instrument derives its name), attached to either end of a levelling bar, itself connected by a spindle and socket joint to the levelling plates and screws below it. The levelling arrangement is in all respects similar to that of the transit. The Y's support a telescope, and by means of clamps hold it rigidly in a position parallel to the levelling bar. Suspended below the telescope there is a spirit level, or long bubble. This bubble will show whether or not the telescope and levelling bar

have been made truly horizontal by means of the levelling screws. As in the case of the transit, the telescope of the level is supplied with cross hairs, and also, as with the transit, the level is supported by a tripod.

The principle of levelling with this instrument consists simply in the prolonging of a known horizontal line, and in measuring the height of this imaginary line above any two points, and from which the difference in elevation, if any, between these points can be easily determined. To insure accuracy in reading heights a *levelling rod* has been devised. It consists of a wooden rod, one side of which is graduated into feet, which are in turn subdivided into tenths and hundredths of a foot. A circular target divided horizontally and vertically into quadrants alternating red and white in colour is free to slide upon the rod, and by means of these quadrants the points at which a given horizontal line intersects the rod can be determined. An opening in the target, to the edge of which a vernier is attached, allows the graduations to be read to a thousandth of a foot. In general, the levelling rod is constructed of two intersliding pieces, in order that it may be conveniently lengthened.

The *hand level*, as its name denotes, is a telescope which, by holding in the hand and sighting through it, the height of the eye above any point can be found. The barrel of the telescope is divided in such a way that any object may be freely seen through one side, whereas on the other side the reflection, by mirror, of cross hairs and the bubble of a spirit level are brought to view. When the horizontal cross hair is shown to bisect the bubble, the level is horizontal. The method of levelling with the hand level is in all respects the same as with the Y level, but the same amount of accuracy cannot be expected. — D. N. B. S.

NOTE. — For assistance in the preparation of this article the writer is indebted to Mr. Edward B. Sturgis.

SURVEYOR. *A.* One who makes surveys, as of land. (See Surveying.)

B. One who examines anything to ascertain its quality or condition — or, more technically, in connection with architectural practice, one who estimates or examines, measures, and tests the extent and condition of lands and buildings and their accessories, and the materials and work expended upon them, or to be so expended.

This word has, in the specialization provoked by modern industrialism, still retained many of its old wide meanings and general uses, and consequent indefiniteness. Hence the necessity for the explanatory prefix which frequently accompanies it. Land Surveyor, City Surveyor, and Quantity Surveyor are modern forms, in use in the practice of and preparation for building.

Until recently the designation "surveyor" was borne by an individual who performed many or all functions implied by it. But now the tendency is to break up and divide such labours into various groups; and further, in America, the weaker influence of tradition in such professions has encouraged other new lines of development.

Much of the work formerly done by surveyors is in modern practice allotted to civil engineers, and many functions of which a "surveyor" was the depositary before the study and practice of art became systematized have naturally come to be considered as belonging to the architectural profession. It is recorded that Inigo Jones was appointed and paid as "surveyor" of his Majesty's works. Now he would be designated "architect," or "architect and surveyor," since that conjunction of terms is still quite usual.

In the United States the occupation of surveyor has been entirely separated from that of architect, and further clearly differentiated into special kinds of surveying. In connection with architecture and real estate, the old general title, "surveyor," was understood to mean one competent to measure and map existing buildings and lands, and to compare same with title deeds; and to estimate and supervise repairs required by covenants and titles upon their commencement and expiration, and to make valuations and appraisements of all such things. The great frequency in English real estate custom of holdings by lease and other transitory title makes this a very important profession in that country and its dependencies, while in the United States it is little known. In America, even in places where leaseholds prevail, they do not much modify the usual custom, under which the real estate agent and the experienced builder, oftener than the surveyor, negotiate such matters as the repair and restoration of buildings for delivery to the landlord, which in former times would have been scheduled under the special term of a Survey of Dilapidations. An architect is occasionally called upon to perform duties properly those of a surveyor, and in England one who does such work frequently will call himself "Architect and Surveyor."

The professional work most likely to arise in this way is the examination of existing buildings to determine their safety, or strength, or value, or the consideration of their possible improvement. Also, in case of damages by fire or accident, the questions for and against their restoration are such as are understood to be surveying rather than architecture, and the architect's inspection of unsafe buildings in New York is officially designated as a "survey."

The City Surveyor is one who does the necessary work of measuring and plotting the dimensions and levels of property and examining municipal and other records, and prepares the plans necessary to define the boundaries of properties and thoroughfares, in cities and other densely populated communities; but those calling themselves city surveyors generally claim no knowledge of the building processes or their values, or the real estate appraisements, for which the general surveyor was qualified.

The Quantity Surveyor renders important services to architecture and building in British practice, which has no counterpart in the United States, under this or any other designation. These duties consist chiefly in the preparation of elaborately detailed bills of quantities of materials and labour required for the construction of certain buildings, for which drawings and specifications have been prepared by the architects. The bills of quantities are multiplied, and a copy is given to each of the builders who are to make proposals for the execution of the work, in order that the labour of "taking off" such quantities may be performed once only, for all of them, and may be for all alike, uniform, and systematic. This work naturally allies itself with that of measuring up building materials and labour after construction, and to some extent with the functions of appraiser and valuer. But the occupation in its customary designation of "quantity surveying" expresses the main part of its duties. It is somewhat surprising that in the United States there is little or no recognition of this office. Occasionally there have been efforts to fill the want, and men of English training have assisted estimators in their accustomed way. But the system has not found favour, and is not in use, and the occupation is still unknown.

Part of the duties of quantity surveyor are, however, sometimes performed by engineers (and more rarely by architects), when engaged upon public works, for which, with the design, they are called upon to furnish a schedule of materials, giving also quantity of each. But this usually takes no note of labour except as implied in the descriptive title, and does not profess to enumerate all finishings and accessories other than by a blanket clause, and it is doubtful whether it is ever used by those tendering proposals as a reliable basis for their estimates, and is consequently not in any sense a substitute for the work of the quantity surveyor.

There is probably a field for the reëstablishment of this ancient profession in the necessity of expert appraisements of real estate and improvements thereon, and in valuations for rents and insurance and similar things, which are now performed unsystematically by persons with whom they are only incidental to some other occupation. (See Bill of Quantities.) — ROBERT W. GIBSON.

SUTH DOOR. One of the doors of a parish church, and generally the most important one. The word " suth " is most probably the old form of south, and refers to the fact that the southern door was that for the entrance of the congregation, and that where persons accused of crime might take oath that they were innocent, as well as that where notices of ecclesiastical ceremonials, feast days, and the like, were put up.

SUYS, T. F. ; architect.

He was a Belgian by birth and came to Paris in 1807. He studied with Percier (see Percier) and at the *École des Beaux Arts*. In 1812 he won the *Grand Prix de Rome* in architecture. On his return from Rome he was extensively employed in Belgium and Holland. Suys assisted Haudebourt in the preparation of his work on the *Palais Massimi à Rome*, and published himself *Le Panthéon de Rome* (Brussels, 1838 ; grand folio).

Lance, *Dictionnaire*.

SWAG. A festoon ; the common English name for that form which is very heavy in the middle and slight at the points of support.

SWAGE. A tool or die used in imparting à given shape to hot metal in a stamping press or rolling mill, or on an anvil, or to sheets of cold metal, as in galvanized iron or copper work.

SWALLOWTAIL. Same as Dovetail.

SWAMP DWELLING. (See Pile Dwelling.)

SWAMP VILLAGE. (See Pile Dwelling.)

SWAN NECK. In stair building, a ramp terminating in a knee, as where a hand rail curves near a newel so as to be about vertical, and is then continued a short distance horizontally, entering the newel at right angles.

SWEAT HOUSE. (See Sweat Lodge, under Lodge.)

SWEATING ROOM. A room for sweating bathers in a Turkish bath. (See Laconicum ; Sudatory ; Stove.)

SWIMMING BATH. An artificial pool, tank, or basin of water, either open to the sky or covered, intended for bathing, particularly for swimmers.

Generally, we may distinguish open and enclosed swimming baths, the former being available only during the summer, the latter capable of being kept open the year round (swimming baths in bath houses).

Excellent as rain baths (see Bath House) are for personal cleanliness and hygiene, the need of well-arranged swimming baths for pleasure and general health in cities should also be recognized. In this respect even small European cities are far better off than large American cities. Many persons bathe together in swimming baths, which should therefore be supplied with water flowing through them continuously. Salt water baths are preferably located outside of harbours, in places where the sea water is purer than in the harbour. The pollution of the neighbouring beach, either by drain outfalls from seashore hotels, or from city garbage, dumped into the sea and cast up by the waves and tides, must be prevented. River baths likewise must be carefully located, preferably above the outfalls of the city sewers, away from garbage dumps, and not too near to manufacturing establishments. The immense one at Vienna is on the new canalized stream, two miles from the city proper ; those in Paris are safe from sewerage because this is all discharged several miles down stream, below the city.

River and sea baths generally require the simplest kind of architectural structures, though there are some examples of more pretentious buildings, such as the Sutro Baths near San Francisco. There are some ocean baths which have both the dressing pavilions and the swimming place enclosed. Such structures are erected either on piles, or on floats, or pontoons. The river swimming baths are built on a floating dock, or pontoon, anchored in the stream, with the cabins arranged on the four sides.

City swimming baths which are to be kept open the entire year must be suitably warmed in winter.

The swimming basin may be oblong, or circular, or its plan is a rectangle with one or two semicircular ends. One or more series of steps are provided to enter the bath. The dimensions of swimming basins vary from 30 to 75 feet in length, 15 to 30 feet in width, and from 2 to 7 feet in depth of water. Even the last-named depth of water is hardly sufficient for diving, and none but experienced divers should attempt it in the ordinary swimming basin. In European baths about 24 square feet of water surface are provided for each swimmer, and 10 to 12 square feet for each non-swimmer.

The basin is built of brick or cement masonry, the walls are constructed with due regard to stability and water tightness. The outer shell of the smaller basins consists sometimes of iron, lined inside with asbestos paper or other waterproof material. The surface of the bottom and of the side walls is finished in enamelled brick, glazed tiles, or with white marble slabs. Due attention should be given to the bottom, which, in the basins for non-swimmers, should not be too slippery. Where one basin answers both for swimmers and non-swimmers, the bottom is made sloping, and a net or line indicates the division. Overflow and emptying pipes must be provided, also openings on the side above the water line for spitting. There are needed also jumping boards, a rail around the basin for tired swimmers, hook poles, life preservers, and life lines in case of accidents. The gangway directly around the swimming basin is made 3 to 5 feet wide, and often projects about 18 inches in width over the basin, the water level in the basin being from 2 to 4 feet below the level of the gangway. Along this inner gangway are located the dressing rooms, which are about 4 feet wide and deep, 7 or 8 feet high, and of which there are sometimes several tiers. In the best plans there is another outer gangway from which bathers enter the dressing room, while they are permitted to walk along the inner gangway only after undressing. This precaution avoids the soiling of the inner gangway by dirty shoes, etc.

The swimming basin must be well lighted, side light from high windows being preferable to overhead lights on account of the glare and heat of the sun.

The water in the basin must be suitably warmed and maintained at a uniform temperature of about 70° Fahr. The water is warmed either by direct introduction of steam, or by suitably protected steam coils in the bottom or along the sides of the basin, or else water is heated in hot water tanks and mixed with the cold water flowing into the basin. Sometimes the water is warmed by continued circulation, though this is not so desirable. The swimming basin must be completely emptied, cleaned, and refilled with fresh water once or twice a week. There should be, when the basin is full, a continuous admission of pure water, the amount being calculated to entirely renew the contents once every twenty-four or thirty-six hours.

A very desirable precaution consists in arranging cleansing or preparatory baths (foot and douche baths), where each bather must go to soap and clean himself thoroughly, before he is admitted to the swimming basin.

Notwithstanding all such precautions, the surface of the water in the basin may become slightly polluted by abrasions from the skin, by oily secretions of the body, etc., hence it is important that the water be kept artificially stirred and in constant motion, as by fountains, cascades, or douches. It is also important that suitable water-closets and urinals be provided near the dressing rooms.

Klinger, *Die Bade-Anstalt;* Runge, *Die öffentliche Badeanstalt in Bremen;* Kabierske, *Das Hallenschwimmbad in Breslau;* Schultze, *Bau und Betrieb von Volks-Badeanstalten;* Vetter, *Das Stuttgarter Schwimmbad;* Marggraff, *Moderne Stadtbäder;* Osthoff, *Bäder und Badeanstalten;* *Handbuch der Architektur,* Part IV., Vol. 5. 3 Genzmer, *Bade-und-Schwimmanstalten;* *Fortschritte der Architektur, Heft XI., Das Schwimmbad zu Frankfurt-am-Main;* Farrar, *Baths and Bathing;* Kane, *New System of Public Baths;* R. Owen Allsop, *Public Baths and Washhouses.* — W. P. GERHARD.

SWISS HUT. (See Hut, *B.*)

SWITCH; SWITCH BOARD. (See Electrical Appliances.)

SWITZERLAND, ARCHITECTURE OF. That of the modern republic as it has existed since 1815. Three different races, French, German, and Italian, occupy the country; hence the impossibility of a single and unmixed style of architecture. Besides, in the past. Switzerland was smaller, and in 1200 contained only the three small primitive cantons. So a number of monuments, that are now Swiss, did not belong to Switzerland six centuries ago, but were Savoyard, Burgundian, or German.

The country that is now French Switzerland was under the Burgundian influence at the Romanesque and Gothic period, and the greater number of the monuments were built by the large religious communities of Clairvaux, Cluny, and Cîteaux. The principal among them are the churches of Romainmotier, Payerne, Saint Sulpice, Grandson (Vaud), Saint Imier (Berne); they belong to the Romanesque period of the eleventh and twelfth centuries.

In German Switzerland at the same period : the Allerheiligen minster at Schaffhausen, Schöntal (Bâle), the chapel of S. George, near Wallenstadt. A little later, and still Romanesque, is the minster at Zurich, one of the important monuments of that epoch. In civil architecture, the castle of Kyburg (eleventh century) and Hapsburg (the original seat of the Austrian imperial house); parts of the castle of Burgdorf (Berne); in French Switzerland, a part of the celebrated castle of Chillon and the castle of Blonay (Vaud).

During the Gothic period, the Burgundian influence of the Cistercian Order prevailed : S. Pierre at Geneva with admirable capitals ; the cathedral of Lausanne whose nave and double pillars are exceedingly interesting, and which has a porch of the Apostles of the purest effect, the collegiate church at Neuchâtel, and numerous other churches of lesser importance. The cathedral of Fribourg is of the fourteenth century, with a fifteenth century tower. In German Switzerland, the cathedral of Bâle, with one Romanesque door (twelfth century), the Cistercian monastery of Wettingen, and the cathedral at Berne are of importance. The castles in both parts of Switzerland are numerous; the finest are those of Vufflens (Vaud) of the fourteenth century ; and those of Champvent, Aigle, and Lausanne, generally of the fifteenth. The Hôtel de Ville of Bâle is also of interest.

Then comes the Renaissance. As everywhere we find the influence of the Italian monuments of the sixteenth century. The Maison Turretini at Geneva ; the palace Stockalper at Brieg (interior court), and many houses and churches at Bâle, Lucerne, and Geneva, in which the Italian influence is clearly marked.

SWITZERLAND, ARCHITECTURE OF: HOUSE AT WOLFENSCHIESSEN; A CHÂLET OF THE
LARGEST SIZE AND GREATEST ELABORATION.

SWITZERLAND, ARCHITECTURE OF: MINSTER AT BÂLE; WEST FRONT AND TOWERS
COMPLETED ABOUT 1500.

But there is another point to note as important in Swiss architecture, and that is, the long resistance that it made to the new spirit, not in the details, that became rapidly classical, but in the construction itself, in which we find an evident disposition to the picturesque, which is clearly the popular Swiss element in architecture.

We see, from the sixteenth century up to our time, high roofs, gable ends, turrets, projecting windows, exterior staircases on corbels surmounted by acute pinnacles; and notwithstanding the Renaissance, its flat roofs, and Italian galleries. Notwithstanding the fashion of horizontal lines, Swiss architecture, as a whole, persists in profiling on the sky the slender steeples of its roofs. Instances are to be seen in the castle of Avenches (sixteenth century), that of Nyon, the Hôtel de Ville de Lucerne, and innumerable other buildings in all parts of Switzerland.

During the eighteenth century a great number of country houses, called châteaux, were built in a simple neoclassic style, without any ornamentation; but generally the roof is widespreading, and gives an air of grandeur and comfort to the construction. Such a building is the Château de l'Isle, near Lausanne, built in 1697.

Wooden building has always been common in Switzerland, and the primitive log house long ago passed into the solid timber-built châlet. Since the sixteenth century the true originality of Swiss art manifests itself especially in wooden buildings.

—JEAN SCHOPFER.

Freeman, *History and Architecture of Switzerland*; Gladbach, *Der Schweizer Holzstyl*; Hochstetter, *Schweizerische Architectur in Perspek.*, etc.; Varin, *Architecture Pittoresque en Suisse*.

SYENE GRANITE. Egyptian Syenite; *granito rosso*. A coarse, red granite occurring at Syene, in Egypt, and much used by the ancient Egyptians in the monoliths and temples. The various obelisks, like those in Paris and New York, are of this material.
—G. P. M.

SYENITE. A rock of the nature of granite, but differing in containing no appreciable amount of quartz. Not a common stone.
—G. P. M.

SYLE. One of a pair of Crutches, straight instead of curved like the gavel forks. (See Wood, Construction in, Part I.)

SYMBOLOGY. The art of determining the signification and right use of symbols and emblems. A symbol is a picture, sign, or character by which something other than that portrayed is suggested to the mind; and it may signify a person, a fact, a virtue, a mystery, a spiritual idea, or it may be manifold in its meaning and stand for all of these types. The cross, for example, is primarily and essentially the symbol of the Christian faith, but it is also the symbolic sign of a person, Christ; of an event, the Sacrifice of Calvary; of a

SWITZERLAND, ARCHITECTURE OF: TOWN HALL OF ZURICH; c. 1700.

virtue, Hope; of a mystery, The Passion; and it is the Standard of Salvation, and thus symbolizes a spiritual idea. An Emblem, in Christian symbology, is a device or object belonging to some particular person, and is employed to distinguish that person from all other persons; in this sense it is also an attribute. The Keys form the emblem of S. Peter, because Christ said to him, "I will give unto thee the keys of the kingdom of heaven" (S. Matthew xvi. 19); a cross in the form of the letter X is the emblem of S. Andrew, because it was the instrument of his passion; and a pot of ointment, that of Mary Magdalen. Sometimes a symbol is an emblem, and an emblem a symbol: the sword is one of the symbols of faith, because Christ said, "I came not to send peace, but a sword." The sword is also the emblem of S. Paul, because he was decapitated with a sword.

Colour. The symbolism of colour is much the same in all religions and all forms of religious art; light, represented symbolically by white, is the source of every colour, and stands for truth and for purity; and when represented by red (because the colour of fire is red) is symbolic of divine love and wisdom, and of the Holy Spirit. It has also a sinister symbolism, and the devil is clothed in black and red, red becoming the symbol of hatred and egotism. Yellow is the symbolic colour of faith, but, if it is a dirty yellow mixed with black, it stands for inconstancy, jealousy, and deceit. Blue is the symbol of truth, fidelity, and immortality; green, of life in action, hope, charity, abundance, and victory; purple, of a love of truth; and violet, of the manifestation of divine love.

In Christian symbology there are a number of fixed forms and devices which have a symbolical signification, apart from their particular iconographic application, viz., the halo, the aureole, the crown, the sword, the palm, the rose, the lily, the olive, and the vine, together with a number of beasts, birds, and fishes (see Aureole, Cross, Glory, Halo). The four evangelical symbols are taken from the vision of Ezekiel (i. 10), and from the words of the Book of Revelation (iv. 7). The beast with the face of the man is the symbol of Matthew, because his gospel is largely about the humanity of Christ; the lion stands for Mark, because it was believed that a lion was born dead and did not come to life until the father breathed upon it, and Mark's gospel has much to say about the resurrection; the calf belongs to Luke, because it is a sacrificial beast, and he writes of the priesthood of Christ; and the eagle, who can gaze unflinchingly upon the sun, is the symbol of John, because his writings make plain to man the glory of the Sun of Righteousness, which he looked upon with the eye of an eagle.

X. Barbier de Montault, *Traité d'Iconographie Chrétienne*, 2 vols. 8vo (Paris, 1890); H. Detzel, *Christliche Ikonographie*, 2 vols. 8vo (Freiburg, 1896); William Durandus, *The Symbolism of Churches and Church Ornaments* (New York, 1893); E. P. Evans, *Animal Symbolism in Ecclesiastical Architecture*; F. C. Husenbeth, *Emblems of Saints*; Raffaels Garrucci, *Storia delle Arte Christiana*; J. R. Allen, *Christian Symbolism in Great Britain.*

— Caryl Coleman.

SYMMETRY. In architecture and decorative art, the balance of part by part; a balance which may be precise repetition, or repetition in counterpart, or may deviate very widely from that, as it involves merely the supposed equivalent value of one part to another.

Thus, if buildings be considered with reference to their axes, a Greek temple will generally be found to be exactly alike, one half to the other half, but in counterpart, that is to say, the one half of the front is as if it had been revolved about the axis, from the other. The sculpture of this same temple would, however, be not exactly the same, although similar, on both sides: that is to say, the recumbent figure in the northern angle of the pediment would be balanced by another recumbent figure in the south angle, but one a little different from the first; and in like manner the sculpture of the metopes to the north and to the south of the axis would be wholly different in subject, although equivalent in mass and in general treatment. Moreover, many instances exist showing that the Greeks cared little for exactness in grouping several buildings. The human mind seems to find it easier to balance part by part, very exactly, than to produce the equivalent in one set of forms to a totally different set of forms. On this account, where no inconvenience exists in planning a building or a group evenly balanced about an axis, where there is plenty of room and no immediate call for diversity, a long building will be planned uniformly, like the splendid façades by Gabriel on the north side of the Place de la Concorde, in Paris. So, when, in 1878, it became desirable to build a vast structure on the hill opposite the Champ de Mars, to adorn and also to bound and limit the great exposition of 1878, although the design was cast in a very free modification of Romanesque, and although the building stretches a quarter of a mile from end to end, the building is still as exactly symmetrical as any Greek temple. But in the Louvre it has never occurred to any of the monarchs, nor to any of the architects who have worked at its gradual extension, to build another great court at the western end, and to have the buildings between exactly alike in design in the whole length of either or each to the other. It is accepted as a series of designs rather than as one design; and the designers' love of accurate symmetry is gratified by the balance of part with part within each single façade of a hundred or two hundred feet. — R. S.

SYNAGOGUE. A place of assembly for Jewish instruction and prayer.

It is difficult to prove the existence of the synagogue prior to the Babylonian captivity of the Jews. It is referred to in the New Testament as a fixed institution, and there were many established in Jerusalem and throughout Palestine.

While originally intended as a place for religious and moral instruction only, the synagogue soon became a house of prayer for those who lived at too great a distance to go to the

Temple at Jerusalem, and since the dispersion of the Jews it has been their customary place of worship. As far as possible the early synagogue in its interior arrangement represented the temple, and that in itself was but an enlarged type of the tabernacle. The building was always rectangular in form and of great simplicity. At the extreme eastern end was erected the holy ark or sanctuary, in which were deposited the scrolls of the law. These were written on parchment rolled from both ends, and were generally ornamented and covered with rich stuffs.

The ark was placed on a raised platform reached by steps, with seats for the elders of

uniformly obeyed, but the main traditions, the simplicity of plan, the position of the ark with its ever-burning light, the separation of the sexes (a custom dating back to the Temple, where there was a separate court for women), were invariably rigidly followed.

The exteriors of the ancient synagogues appear to have possessed but little architectural interest, and of interior decoration, as we understand it, there was none. Remains of synagogues found in Galilee show that a stone porch ornamented with carving of plant forms was generally the only important feature. Sculpture and painting were never encouraged, and representations of the human face were strictly for-

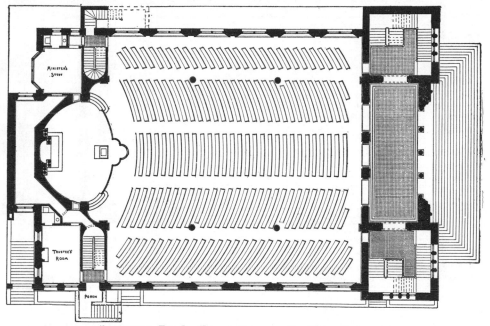

SYNAGOGUE, FIG. I.: TEMPLE BETH–EL, NEW YORK CITY; 1892.

the congregation, either in front or at the sides, and before it hung the perpetual lamp.

In the centre of the building, also raised above the level of the floor, was a desk from which the law was read aloud.

The women were always separated from the men, and the worshippers faced the east during prayer.

The site of the building was, whenever possible, to be near the seashore or a running stream. The structure itself, or some part of it, was to overtop the surrounding buildings, and there were Talmudic instructions regulating the number of windows, the position and size of entrances, and other details. It was even supposed to be desirable to have the floor of the synagogue on a lower level than the entrances and vestibules. These commands were not

bidden. Nevertheless a certain amount of symbolism was permitted, and the form of flowers, the grape, the pomegranate, etc., were sometimes employed for decorative purposes, and the lion, the ancient emblem of Judah, appeared frequently. Gold and silver lamps were profusely used, and were often of great beauty. (See Syria, Architecture of.)

The synagogue at Worms, in Germany, is the oldest now existing in Europe; and we find in Frankfort-on-the-Main and in Prague interesting Gothic synagogues, dating from the thirteenth century, which contain excellent examples of vaulting. These were built at the time when galleries for women first came into use.

These galleries were placed at a considerable height above the main floor, and the occupants were shielded from the view of the men by a close lattice.

During the Middle Ages the synagogues were always unpretentious, as it was not safe for Jewish buildings to attract too much attention. The interiors, however, were often rich and handsomely finished and equipped.

In Spain two noted synagogues built in the

and the main decoration of its walls is an ornamented arcade, over which is a sculptured frieze of great beauty and delicacy of design.

The synagogues of Europe, as we find them to-day, have in their interior arrangement generally followed the traditional lines of antiquity. The position of the ark is retained and the plan is rectangular, the transept being invariably

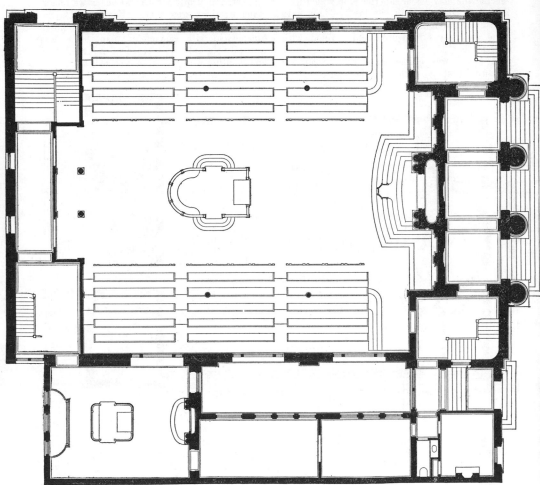

SYNAGOGUE, FIG. II.: WEST SEVENTIETH STREET, NEW YORK. AS THE ARK MUST BE AT THE EAST END, IT IS SET AGAINST THE INNER WALL OF THE GREAT VESTIBULE, FROM WHICH THE GROUND STORY IS ENTERED AT RIGHT AND LEFT.

fourteenth century still remain, and both are in Toledo. One is known as La Transito, so called from a picture of the Ascension it contains; the other is S. Maria la Blanca, both now being used as churches. They are good examples of Moorish architecture, and contain evidences of much former beauty. S. Maria la Blanca is divided by long lines of octagonal columns with floriated capitals, from which spring horseshoe arches supporting the roof. La Transito is an unbroken rectangle in plan,

avoided, and galleries are provided for women. The most notable change, which, however, is seldom found in English synagogues, but often on the Continent and in America, is the removal of the reading desk from its position in the centre of the building and its combination with the platform in front of the ark. This plan is now frequently adopted in the newer buildings, as it not only secures a concentration of the service, but it renders the entire floor space available for seating purposes.

Since the expulsion of the Jews from Spain the Moorish style of architecture has frequently been employed by synagogue builders. This is, however, by no means the rule. Synagogues were commonly built in the same style as the contemporary churches, and there exist innumerable buildings for Jewish worship designed in all the styles of architecture. Many of the synagogues in London suggest Sir Christopher Wren's churches, those in Paris are in the prevailing French style of church architecture, and there are good specimens of Classic, Gothic, Romanesque, and the various periods of Renaissance scattered throughout Europe. In America we find the little synagogue at Newport, Rhode Island, built by Spanish Jews in 1763, quite similar in expression to the architecture of its period, thoroughly "colonial" or Georgian in detail, and distinctively Jewish only in its plan and interior disposition.

It appears strange that, while there is so little scope for variations in plan, synagogues have no traditional lines of architectural expression, and that no distinct style has been developed. A vague but unmistakable Oriental feeling is nearly always evident, and this, notwithstanding the lack of an acknowledged style, produces a remarkable general likeness. The modern freedom that characterizes the architecture of to-day has affected the synagogue as it has the church, and a still greater latitude of expression is becoming evident in the latest examples.

The plans herewith given are of the two most important synagogues built in New York City within recent years.

Figure I. is a plan of the Temple Beth-El, erected in the year 1892. The main entrance vestibule, which faces Fifth Avenue and is reached by a broad flight of steps, is flanked by two towers containing staircases leading up to the galleries and down to the Sunday-school rooms, which occupy the entire basement. The ark is placed in a semicircular recess at the eastern end of the building, and is reached by steps from the platform, on which are seats for the officers of the congregation. On the platform is the reading desk, with the pulpit directly in front of it. There is a marble colonnade above the ark, and in the space behind the columns are placed the choir and organ. The galleries are on three sides of the auditorium, and a second gallery extends across the end facing the ark. The pews or seats cover the entire floor space, and there is accommodation for twenty-two hundred worshippers. The trustees' room and minister's study are at the eastern corners of the main floor, and are reached by a separate entrance from the street. The building is constructed entirely of limestone and is designed in the Romanesque style. In the interior marble, bronze, and mosaic are largely used. This may be considered as a typical plan for a modern synagogue for what are known as Reformed Jews.

The type of building for the Orthodox Jews, who in their worship strictly follow the traditions of the past, is shown in Fig. II., which is the Synagogue Shearith Israel, erected in 1897. The dimensions of the main building are 78 feet by 115 feet, and on the main floor there are also a small synagogue for special services, a minister's study, class rooms, and an open court to be used for the Feast of Tabernacles. The entire basement is devoted to school purposes. On account of the position of the lot, and as it was necessary to place the ark on the eastern end of the building, the auditorium is not entered directly from the main porch, but access to it is gained through the two side vestibules, which also contain the staircases leading to the women's gallery. There is an additional entrance on the northwest corner of the building. The ark is built against the wall of the main vestibule, and the platform in front is reached by a broad flight of marble steps, upon which stands the pulpit. The chairs for the officers of the congregation are placed on platforms in front of the screen which flanks the ark. The seats for worshippers are parallel to the sides of the building, leaving the central portion of the auditorium entirely free, and occupied only by the reading desk. The building is of limestone and designed in the classic style, with pilasters and arches, and the front is enriched by four Corinthian columns surmounted by an ornamented pediment.

— Arnold W. Brunner.

SYNODAL HALL (French *salle synodale*). A hall in which the synod of a diocese was accustomed to meet. It differs from the chapter house (in French *salle capitulaire*) in that the synod is a general gathering of the clergy of the whole diocese, and of representatives duly appointed. The hall was, therefore, of necessity large. The Synodal Hall at Paris has perished, but is known by ancient prints. That at Sens (Yonne), built in the middle of the thirteenth century, is perfect, and has been restored with much discretion. Viollet-le-Duc, who has given drawings of this noble building, states that it will hold nine hundred persons.

SYRIA, ARCHITECTURE OF. That of the country stretching from the eastern coast of the Mediterranean eastward to the Euphrates. This region can scarcely be said to possess an indigenous architectural style, possibly owing to the fact that the Semitic tribes who peopled it were not a building race, and never aspired to the erection of monuments which should exist as records of their greatness. In all the earlier work of the country, down to the Mohammedan invasion in the seventh century, there are two special characteristics not found elsewhere.

Early Characteristics: *Monolithism.* The first is that which Renan describes as "monolithism," viz., the employment of immense blocks of masonry, essentially Phœnician, not only in its origin, but in its continuance through-

the great labour involved in detaching them, as it were, from the main block. In Roman work, capitals, shafts, and bases, and in the case of pilasters, portions of the wall itself, were all cut out of the same block, and in the early Christian work, the arches themselves would, with their archivolt, be treated in the same way.

SYRIA, ARCHITECTURE OF: THE SO-CALLED PRETORIUM AT MUSMIGEH, BUILT ABOUT 170 A.D.

out the early periods. From this characteristic the native builders seem never to have emancipated themselves, and throughout the Jewish, the Roman, and the early Christian periods, they employed in their building blocks of stone of great size, in which were produced decorative features copied from other styles, regardless of the origin or meaning of those features, or of

Early Characteristics: *Drafted Masonry.* The second characteristic is that which was originally considered to be of Phœnician origin, but of which there are no genuine examples in Syria prior to the period of Herod, viz., what is known as *drafted masonry.* In order to obtain a fine and accurate joint, the masons worked round the edge of each stone a draft of from 3 to 6 inches in width, leaving the central portion in relief, thus constituting what is known as rusticated masonry. The projection of this rustication varied from 2 to 3 inches for exposed work, to 12 or 14 inches in the foundation courses. The draft was worked vertically with a chisel, in which there were eight teeth to the inch. Subsequently, in the finished work, the rustication was worked off with a pick to within half an inch from the drafted surface, and constituted what was accepted as an architectural embellishment. The finest examples of this work are found on the wall of the Jews' wailing place, on the west side of the Haram, or second enclosure, at Jeru-

Herod at Jerusalem was devised and carried out as an architectural embellishment, and must not be confused with the unfinished work of the Phœnicians in the tombs of Amrit or of the palace of Hyrcanus at Arak-el-Emir,[1] in which the rustication is only found on some of the stones, and the draft is not of equal width all round. The palace of Hyrcanus at Arak-el-Emir is the earliest dated (171 B.C.) building known in Palestine. It is built on a platform about 320 feet square, and consisted of a rectangular building measuring 126 feet by 62 feet, of which a portion only of the eastern wall remains and the foundations of internal walls. The wall is about 22 feet high and consists of a

TEMPLE AT BAALBEC; 2ND CENTURY.

salem. In the working off of this rustication, the first step taken was to form a second draft within the first, examples of which are found in the tower of David. This type of work is the chief characteristic of Syrian masonry, and was adopted afterward by the Romans, the Byzantines, and the Crusaders, each having his own method of finish. In the masonry of the Crusaders, the chisel was always used in a diagonal direction, and many of the castles and enclosed walls formerly attributed to the Phœnicians, as at Tortosa, for instance, have of late, owing to this special method of working, been ascribed to their proper builders, the Crusaders.

It should be clearly recognized from the first that the system of drafting as employed by

lower course or plinth in one course 8 feet high, constituting the frieze on which there are carvings of lines. This was probably crowned by a cornice of some kind. One of the stones of the centre course is 17 feet 4 inches long, which shows the Phœnician influence. The dentil course and the frieze are Persian in character, though executed probably by Greek artists. Various capitals of Greek style were found in

[1] M. De Vogüé's drawing, published in the *Temple of Jerusalem* is incorrect. The 6-inch draft shown above the middle stone in his drawing is a part of the course out of which the dentil course is cut. The joint is shown in the drawing 5 inches above its real position, as proved by photographs. The middle stone referred to has a draft 4 inches to 6 inches wide at the bottom, 2 inches on the left-hand side, 1 inch at the top, and no draft at the right-hand side. This is not drafted masonry.

the interior, and these probably belonged to an atrium at the north or entrance end.

Herodian and Roman Work. Of Herod's work in the rebuilding of the Temple of Jerusa-

DOOR OF A TOMB IN SYRIA.

lem only the lower portions of the walls enclosing the Haram enclosure (to which we have already referred) remain. In addition to the architectural embellishment given by the drafting of the masonry, much of the monumental character is due to the immense size of the masonry. One of the courses, that which runs on a level with the sills of the double and triple gate on the south side, is 6 feet high. The foundations of this wall were put at the southeast corner, 80 feet below the present level. The upper portions of this sunken wall, those which enclose the Portico of Herod, were, it is supposed, decorated with flat pilasters about 5 feet wide and from 6 inches to 9 inches projection, similar to those still existing at Hebron. The bases of two such pilasters were found at the northeast end of the Haram enclosure. This method of breaking up the wall surface with wide projecting pilaster strips might be regarded as a third Syrian characteristic, except that it is confined to early work. The Roman pilasters have Corinthian capitals. There are known one or two examples with cavetto capitals, one at Byblos and a second in the great western porticus of the temple of Damascus, the south end of which forms now the foundation of one of the min-

arets. The pilaster strips at Helm are 5 feet wide, 25 feet high, 9 inches projection, and rest on a plinth 15 feet high. They are crowned by an ogee moulding which returns and forms also the upper string course of the main wall. The spaces between the pilasters measure about 8 feet.

Whilst courting popularity with the Jews by rebuilding the Temple of Jerusalem, Herod erected temples to Augustus and to the Phœnician god, Baal-Samin, one of which exists at Siah in the Hauran and has been measured and illustrated in De Vogüé's *Syrie Centrale*. The cella was so much encumbered with ruins of subsequent buildings erected within it that its original plan was not determinable. Its façade consisted of a portico of two columns in antis between wings, probably carried up as towers in imitation of the Temple of Jerusalem, and to which allusion is made in one of the inscriptions which speaks of "the lofty buildings" erected. (De Vogüé's restoration in a pen perspective sketch in no way suggests the probable design.) The temple was preceded by an atrium with porticoes round a great portal. The other temple with triple archways would seem to have been added in later times by the Romans. The capitals of the columns of the portico, though Greek in the execution of their foliage, suggest an Oriental origin. The epistyle carried by these columns and the lintel of the entrance door to the cella are carved with the vine leaves and grapes, essentially Jewish features. Similar capitals and bases

DETAILS OF THE CHURCH OF S. SIMEON STYLITES AT KALAT SEMÁN.

are found at Souideh, close by, and referred to the same period.

The tombs in the Kedron valley and others near Jerusalem are mixed in style. The cavetto cornice which crowns the so-called tombs of Zachariah and of Absalom, and the pyramid among the former, is Egyptian. The semi-detached columns with Ionic capitals and responds and the Doric epistyles are Syro-Greek. To the same artists must be ascribed the frontispieces of the tombs of the Kings and of the Judges, who by the introduction of the vine and grapes and the pot of manna show that they were working for the Hebrew race. The date of all these tombs is now generally accepted as belonging to the period of Herod and down to the siege of Jerusalem by Titus.

exact date, some claiming them to be the buildings erected by Simeon Bar Yochai, who, about 120 A.D., is recorded to have built twenty-four synagogues in Galilee, whilst others, among whom is Renan, ascribe them to the end of the second century. They all face the south and are always rectangular. With one exception (the small synagogue at Kefr Birim, which has two rows only) they are all divided into five aisles by four rows of columns, carrying a timber roof of joists 8 inches deep, set close together and covered over with earth. On account of the weight of the roof the columns were set

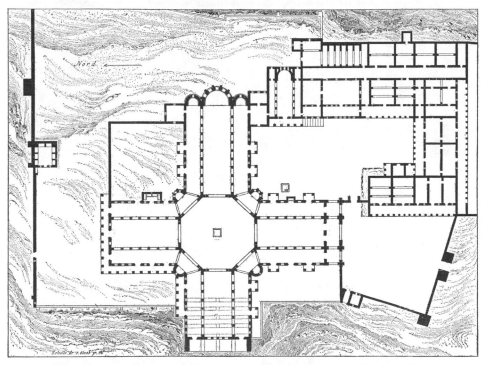

CHURCH AND CONVENT OF S. SIMEON STYLITES: 6TH CENTURY. KALAT SEMÁN.

Synagogues. Though of much later date than the tombs just quoted, the synagogues of Galilee are best mentioned here. In the porticoes preceding them and in the design of the doorways and niches, they are evidently based on Roman examples, but the contour of their moulding shows they were probably executed by Greek workmen. They are neither sufficiently numerous nor important enough to have had much influence on the development of the Byzantine style, but in the accentuation of the constituent features of the design and in the profiles of their mouldings they precede by more than three centuries the architecture of the time of Justinian. Though generally accepted as the work of the second century, there appears to be some difference of opinion as to their

close together with small intercolumniation. The two end supports of the outer rows always consisted of a square pier, with two responds, whether to carry a gallery or for what purpose is not known. The masonry is well built in courses of limestone, set without mortar and finely chiselled. They all have three entrances on the south side, a large central doorway, and two small ones leading into the outer aisles.

The most perfect example, which may be taken as the type of all the others, is the great synagogue at Kefr Birim. This was preceded by a porch, hexastyle prostyle. The columns have the moulded circular capital peculiar to some Syrian temples, carrying a square abacus, and are raised on two pedestals. The angle supports consist of square piers with responds. In

KALAT SEMÁN.

APSE OF CHURCH OF S. SIMEON STYLITES: 6TH CENTURY; KALAT SEMAN.

the great central doorway the lintel projects 8 inches beyond the side jambs (as found in early Greek work, such as in Beule's doorway entering the Acropolis at Athens), and carried round it is a strongly profiled moulding which returns down the door jambs. Within these the ordinary fascia mouldings of the Roman prototype are carried round the door panel, but with sharply accentuated profiles, the inner mouldings not bent behind the main fascia. The cushion frieze, carved with the vine and grapes, and the lintel are, in accordance with the style of the country, in one stone. This is crowned with a simple ogee moulding. The relieving arch is semicircular with seven voussoirs about 2 feet deep, and in its design includes all the subdivisions of a complete entablature, viz., architrave, frieze, and cornice. To the two smaller doorways there is no relieving arch, and the lintel does not project beyond the door jambs. The synagogue measures 60 feet 6 inches by 46 feet 6 inches without the portico. Internally there are four rows of columns 2 feet 2 inches in diameter, the intercolumniation being 6 feet 9 inches, and the height of shaft with capital 12 feet.

Roman Work, Second Century and Later. With the exception of Baalbec and Palmyra, all the best-preserved Roman remains lie on the east side of the Jordan and in the Hauran. Through all these districts the Romans ran their roads (some of which are used down to the present day), bringing into connection the ancient cities of Moab and Bashan. These they apparently rebuilt, for, with the exception of a few tombs, there are no vestiges of any earlier architectural work than that of the beginning of the second century of our era. The preservation of the Roman work is due mainly to the desertion of those towns in the Mohammedan invasion in the seventh century, and their subsequent occupation by wandering tribes, who contented themselves with the temporary shelter of the existing buildings, and such additional protection as could be obtained from the erection of enclosures built with the smaller materials thrown down by earthquakes. In some of the large towns, such as Gerasa, Gadara, and Pelle, for instance, there is no trace whatever of Mohammedan occupation at any period, and though from time immemorial there have been constant strifes between tribes, the destruction of the Roman work is mainly due to frequent earthquakes. At one time or another, temples, basilicas, colonnades, theatres, and tombs have nearly all been thrown down by earthquakes, and remain in that condition to the present day, the beautiful sculpture of the capitals and of the enrichments of the cornices, doorways, and niches being as sharp and fresh as if carved only yesterday.

The temples, theatres, basilicas, baths, and other structures built by the Romans in Syria do not materially differ from those erected in other parts of the Empire, except in a somewhat freer treatment. At the same time, owing to a strong Greek influence, the sculpture of the capitals and the profile of the mouldings is far purer than that found even in Rome. This remark does not apply to the work in some of the larger towns, as Palmyra, Baalbec, and Gerasa, where, from the importance and extent of the monuments erected, artists would seem to have been sent over from Rome; but even in these towns some of the capitals and the enrichment of the entablature show in the execution of their foliage the Greek rather than the Roman chisel.

Colonnaded Streets. There is, however, one architectural feature of importance, which exists, so far as we know, only in Syria and in one or two towns of Asia Minor, viz., the colonnaded streets. As a rule, the principal colonnaded street ran from east to west, and was crossed by one or more streets, also sometimes with colonnades, running at right angles to the main street. In the case of a cross street, having also colonnades, their junction was afforded by means of a tetrapylon, a vaulted structure, having great archways on each of the four sides. For the main streets an archway, 20 to 22 feet wide, intercepted the colonnade, the entablature running through unbroken. Another characteristic feature in these Syrian towns, and these are found not only in the colonnades, but in the porticoes of the temples and the porticoes of the great enclosure courts, is the employment of stone brackets projecting from the column and forming part of the shaft about two thirds up, to carry statues or busts. None of these pieces of sculpture remain *in situ*, but the numerous inscriptions show that these statues or busts were erected in honour of distinguished citizens, who had contributed to the adornment of the town by erecting important public buildings at their own expense.

The principal colonnaded streets in Syria are, first, that at Palmyra, 3154 feet long, with a central avenue, 37 feet wide, flanked by a row of columns, 31 feet high on each side. Exclusive of the tetrapylon (in this case not a vaulted one) and the eight archways, there were 454 columns in this street, of which over 100 still stand erect. Second, the Via Recta at Damascus, 1550 feet long, and running through the town from gate to gate; excepting the two gateways, the last vestiges above ground of this were destroyed at the time of the massacre of 1860, when the Christian quarter was destroyed. Third, that of Gerasa, 1880 feet long, terminating at the west end in a circular piazza of 300 feet diameter, surrounded with Ionic columns; for about 600 feet at the east end of this colonnaded street the columns had also

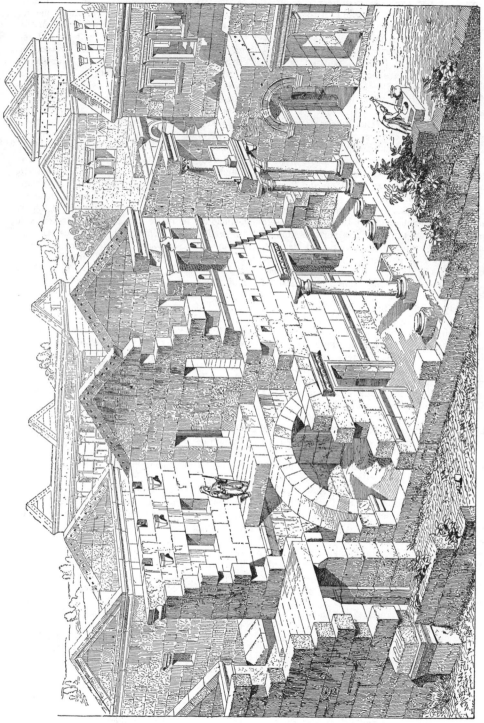

TYPES OF HOUSES IN THE CITY OF DJCHEL RIHA.

Ionic capitals, the remainder being Corinthian. A vaulted tetrapylon existed here. Amman, Kunawat, Bosra in the Houran (with two tetrapylons), Gadara, Pella, Apamea, and other towns are referred to by travellers. The most ancient colonnaded street of which remains exist is that found at Samaria, which was built by Herod. There are no remains of the celebrated streets erected by Antiochus Epiphanes, B.C. 170, at Antioch, which extended over two miles in length.

Roman Temples. The Roman temples in Syria always face the east, even though occasionally, by such orientation, they were placed at an angle with the colonnaded streets or other buildings. In Rome they were looked upon as the principal features of the fora, and face all points of the compass.

Four of the great temples, those of Palmyra, Gerasa, Husn-Suleiman, and Damascus, were enclosed in great courts with a porticus around, and one, the temple of Jupiter Sol, at Baalbec, was preceded by two great courts. Three of the temples in Rome had similar courts, but none of the dimensions approached those of either Damascus or Palmyra.

Nearly all the temples in Syria, as in Rome, were raised on stylobate platforms, the exceptions being the two temples of Palmyra and the second temple at Gerasa, where there were steps only. Flights of steps built between pedestals, in which the cornice and base of the stylobate are continued, precede the more important temples, but in all the minor examples the stylobate runs close up to the east portico. Access to the cella, therefore, would seem to have been confined to the priests, who entered by small doors in the stylobate to chambers under the sanctuary at the west end, which was raised from six to eight feet above the floor of the cella, and thence through side doors into the cella. The most important of these internal raised platforms is found at Baalbec in the temple of Jupiter, and here a flight of steps, no longer in existence, is said to have led down into the cella. A similar arrangement is found in the temple of Isis in Pompeii, with secret approach, which enabled the priests to enter unperceived to deliver the oracle from the statue which we may assume was placed on each of these platforms.

We have already referred to the stone brackets which project from the columns, to carry busts or statues, and which form, each of them, a part of one of the drums of the shaft (for, with one or two exceptions, the shafts of the temples and colonnades are found to be of three or four drums, and not monolithic as in Rome). A second peculiarity in these Syrian temples is the raising of the column on square pedestals. A third peculiarity, found in some of the temples, even of an early date, is the wide inter-

columniation of the two central columns of the portico, which necessitated the use of the arch, with its entablature complete, carried round it. The earliest dated example known is that of the temple of Atil in the Hauran, built by Antoninus Pius, 151 A.D. This precedes by about a century and a half the well-known example in Diocletian's palace at Spalato. The Syrian coins had already suggested the existence of this feature, but it has hitherto been assumed to be a conventional representation of the shrine in the rear of the temple, and this is doubtless the case in many Roman coins; but in the Syrian coins, the mouldings of the architrave, which is all they attempt to show, are clearly carried round the central arch. De Vogüé refers to this peculiarity on many occasions, but only in two cases, we think, gives examples, namely, that of the temple palace at Kunawat (spelt Qennaouât in his work, *Syrie Centrale*), and the well-known archway at Damascus, the inner or court elevation of the western propylæa of the great temple court. The profiles of the mouldings, and the sculpture of the capitals and other ornaments, are of the same pure style as that existing in the temple of Atil, so that we may assume it as being also the work of Antoninus Pius. In both the temples of Baalbec, the central intercolumniation is much wider than that of the other columns, and another coin of the portico leading to the great court of Baalbec indicates an arch in the centre. The same coin shows the two wings carried up as towers, which suggests a much more probable design than that given in Wood and Dawkins's work.

Although the great temple of the Sun at Palmyra belongs to the decadent period of Roman art, and, situated as it is far away from the centre of Roman culture, shows inequalities of design which would not have been countenanced in Rome, it nevertheless, with its magnificent court and porticus, must be looked upon as one of the great monuments of Imperial Roman architecture. The outer court, with its enclosure walls, 730 feet wide and 720 feet deep, is raised on a stylobate, 18 feet high. In the centre of the principal front, facing the west, was a flight of steps leading up to the portico of the propylon, 120 feet wide. The portico and steps are no longer in existence, but Dawkins's plan shows a wide intercolumniation in the centre of 13.6, as against 11.6 in the other and coupled columns, which suggest also that an arch was thrown across. The same columniation is shown in the inner propylon, facing the court, and on the farthest side of the court, the intercolumniation of that column of the porticus is also 13.6. There would have been no necessity for this unless it were to display an arch. The temple itself, octostyle prostyle, raised on a stylobate of three steps, runs north and south, and is not placed in the axis of the propylon. The principal doorway, which faces west and lies in the axis of the propylon, has six columns of the peristyle on one side and eight on the other. At a later period, probably during the Restoration after the destruction of the town by Aurelian, the attached semicolumns were added, and door jambs and lintel fitted in between the attached columns, all showing a great decadence in style. The porticus on the west side, including the propylon, had one row of columns, 48 feet high, including capital and base. The three other sides had a double range of columns, 32 feet high. Externally, the enclosure wall was broken by Corinthian pilasters of the same height in each case as the column of the porticus inside. That which would seem to have been a pronaos and posticum in the first temple built, had a portico in antis (now walled up), with capitals of the Ionic order, all the columns being Corinthian. Of the capitals of the temple itself, only the bells remain, the leaves and volutes being probably in metal.

The temple of the Sun at Gerasa, hexastyle peristyle, was also enclosed in a porticus, with enclosure wall measuring about 300 by 150 feet. The temple at Husn Soleiman, near Tartus, discovered by the American Palestine Exploration Fund, was hexastyle pseudoperipteral, and of the Ionic order, with enclosure walls, 442 by 252 feet, the date being given as 253 A.D. The dimensions of all these three temples known would seem to be far exceeded by those at Damascus, where the enclosure measured 1300 feet from east to west, and 1000 feet from north to south. Owing to the continued occupation of the time, and the subsequent rebuilding at various epochs, it is difficult to trace out the original plan. Small portions of the enclosure wall only exist, decorated with broad pilaster strips. The eastern side of the western propylon, already referred to, 40 feet wide, with its central archway — the triple doorway of the eastern propylæa; the walls of an internal porticus, 320 feet long and 38 feet wide, which now form the west enclosure of the great mosque (this was decorated with broad pilasters, surrounded by cavetto moulded cap, carrying an architrave with dentil cornice) ; and the triple doorway of the great temple, 70 feet wide, which is enclosed in, and forms part of, the south wall of the mosque, — all exist. The great doorway of the temple and the remains of the two propylons, one of the same style of work as the temple of Jupiter at Baalbec, are ascribed to Antoninus Pius, but the porticus and the great enclosure would seem to be of an earlier date, to judge by the pilaster strips which are employed to decorate the wall surface.

The great temple of Jupiter Sol at Baalbec was built on the site of the Phœnician temple of Baal already raised on a lofty platform, the

walls of which, on the north and west sides, were too close to allow of a porticus round. The great courts therefore precede it. The entrance to the enclosure was through a portico in antis of twelve columns 180 feet long and 37 feet deep, originally preceded by a flight of steps. The portico was in antis between two wings, which were probably carried up as towers ; of the upper story the pedestals only of the pilasters remain. A coin published in Donaldson's *Numismatica* gives a superstructure of this portico, with a pediment in the middle on the four central columns and an arch on the two centre ones. The columns of the portico all rested on square pedestals. The first court is hexagonal, the second court square. The courts are surrounded, not by a porticus, but by a series of rectangular and semicircular recesses, with an enclosure of columns in front not altogether dissimilar to those in the Pantheon at Rome, combined, however, for another purpose, within the thickness of the wall. The rectangular recesses are 25 feet deep, and vary from 50 feet to 75 feet wide. The hemicycles were 30 feet in diameter and roofed over with stone, the wall decoration of both, inside, consisting of two rows of niches for statues, one above the other. This scheme of decoration is one which seems to be universal in all the Roman work in Syria. The decorative carving of the niches of the hemicycles is so free in its treatment as to resemble that of the early Italian Renaissance. The great temple of Jupiter Sol was decastyle peripteral, with a wide intercolumniation in the centre, also found in the smaller temple of Jupiter close by. This latter is by far the best preserved in Syria, and, allowing for the distance from Rome and the period of its erection, is one of the finest examples of Roman Imperial architecture. It still preserves part of the stone ceiling of the peristyle. This peristyle was 9 feet in the clear, and was covered over with stone slabs, cut to a segmental form underneath, and sunk with deep coffers, alternately diamond-shape and hexagonal, showing a complete departure from the ordinary stone beams and flat-coffered slabs of the Greeks. The entrance portal to the cella was 21 feet wide and 42 feet high, the largest in Syria. Its lintel was formed of five voussoirs, the centre one of which having slipped, is now carried by a pier. The cella was decorated with three-quarter detached, engaged columns of Corinthian style, each relieved upon a shallow pier, six on each side, with responds, and between them niches in two ranges, one above the other. The fallen masses of stone in the interior show that these shafts were coupled together and carried broken pediments. The slight thickness of the wall, only 4 feet without the piers, the absence of any portion of a vault, and the fact that none of the walls have ever been pushed out, render it extremely improbable that it could have been vaulted over with stone, the internal width between the shafts being 60 feet. The raised platform or sanctuary, reduced to about 28 feet in width between piers, was vaulted over. Although the decoration is of a somewhat florid type with redundance of ornament, some of the capitals are of very pure design, evidently carved by Greek artists. This characteristic is found throughout in the Roman temples of Syria, some of the carving of the capitals and door jambs being quite equal to the purest work of the time of Augustus. On the other hand, in the outlying districts, away from strict Roman influence, the carving is of the most primitive or most decadent type. There is a series of temples of the Ionic order, with porticoes of two columns in antis, as at Hibberiyeh, Deir el Ashayir, Thelthatha (Neby Sufa), and Ain Hammul, with the Ionic capital also carved on the responds, and these are of the most primitive type. In these four temples the raised platform or sanctuary still exists ; in the two former the pavement of the raised platform is carried on vaults ; in the two others, it consists of slabs carried on corbel strings and brackets.

Roman Tombs. The tombs in Syria of Roman style are of two types, those erected in masonry and those which are cut in the face of the rock. Of the former, the earliest are those which are built in the form of a tower, 20 to 30 feet square in plan and from 60 to 100 feet in height, of which a very large number still exist in Palmyra.

In other parts of Syria the Roman tombs are decorated with Corinthian pilasters. Internally they are covered with barrel vaults, or domes carried on pendentives or stone slabs placed across the angles.

Some of the Roman tombs in central Syria are sunk in the rock, and over them are built groups of two or more columns held together by their entablatures.

Of the tombs excavated in the rock, a large number follow the arrangement typified by that of the Tombs of the Kings at Jerusalem, viz., a portico in antis with two or more columns, surmounted by an entablature and occasionally by a pediment.

The most important of the rock-cut tombs are the magnificent examples at Petra. Cut in the vertical sides of a cliff, and rising sometimes to over 100 feet in height, the artist was freed from the trammels of ordinary construction, and was able to realize his conceptions much in the same way as a painter produces a theatrical scene. The most perfect of the tombs is that known as the Khusneh, or the Treasury of Pharaoh, and it is evident that the perfection of its realization is due to many earlier trials. There are others of similar design showing incomplete and abortive attempts. As evidence of originality of design and richness of concep-

tion, these tombs are remarkable examples of the Roman Imperial style, but the absence of any constructive character takes them out of the range of serious architectural developments.

Theatres. The Roman theatres in Syria were all excavated in the sides of a hill, and seem to have existed in most of the important towns, except in Palmyra. The largest is that at Amman, 228 feet in diameter with forty-two rows of seats. The large theatre of Gerasa had twenty-eight rows of seats, and retains portions of the proscenium, which was decorated with Corinthian columns coupled together, and niches alternating with the three doorways. The best-preserved is the theatre of Akud el Beisan, 197 feet in diameter. At Bozrah, in the Hauran, there still remain (the only example of its kind existing in Syria) portions of the colonnade gallery surrounding the upper row of the theatre, the order employed being the Doric.

There are numerous other Roman buildings, such as thermæ and basilicas, but too little is known of them as yet to be able to determine either their plans or architectural design.

Sassanian or Doubtful Buildings. Two other interesting buildings exist in Syria, to which it is difficult to assign an exact date. The first is the palace of Mashita, in Moab, discovered by Canon Tristram and assigned by Fergusson to Chosroes, the Sassanian king, 614 A.D. The elaborate carving of the lower portion of the walls suggests an earlier date, the design resembling the work of Justinian. Perrot and Chipiez (Vol. V., *La Perse*) point out, however, that a Byzantine author, Theophylactus Simocatta, mentions the construction of this palace, which he ascribes to Chosroes, and states that he employed Greek artists to build and decorate it.

The other example is a building in the citadel of Amman, which consists of a central square court open to the sky, with four great recesses on either side, two carried with barrel vaults, and two with hemispherical vaults on clumsy pendentives. The walls are richly decorated with blind arcades enriched with flowing ornament, evidently sculptured by Greek workmen, and their string courses and arch moulds were carried with the zigzag fret, a decoration which owes its origin to brick construction, where bricks are placed anglewise to support a projecting string. This is found in nearly all the Sassanian palaces ; so that we are safe in ascribing this building also to Chosroes II. in his triumphal march to Jerusalem. The great arches are also of the same elliptical form as those found in Sassanian buildings.

Christian Buildings: Earliest Churches. Prior to the "Peace of the Church," the Christians in Syria would seem to have contented themselves with simple erections suited to their faith, and the earliest church of importance now existing is the great basilica, the church of the Nativity at Bethlehem, built by Constantine. This consisted of nave, with double aisles on each side, transept, and choir built over the chapel of the Nativity. The eastern apse is probably also Constantine's work, but the transept apses were added by Justinian. Except for the wall which now cuts off the transept from the nave — the subsequent decoration of the walls of the nave with mosaics executed in the twelfth century — and a reconstruction of the roof, this church remains practically the same as when built by Constantine, and may be looked upon as the best example existing of an early Christian basilica. The great basilica erected at Jerusalem in front of the Holy Sepulchre and Justinian's church of S. Mary have disappeared ; and we have now to take up the most important architectural development of Christian architecture in Syria, only within a few years made known to us by the important work of M. de Vogüé on central Syria. Some attempt has been made by De Vogüé and Viollet-le-Duc to show a connection between the churches of central Syria and the Romanesque work of Europe ; but although in the plans and designs of the early Christian churches we recognize very similar arrangements, none of their more salient features can be traced in the Romanesque work of Europe prior to the Crusaders, and if they had been known to the Crusaders, it is evident that the first attempts at reproduction would be found in their work in Syria. This, as we shall hereafter see, is far from being the case. Almost the only Oriental features found in the Crusaders' churches (apart from the domes or pendentives, which are distinctly French in design) are the polygonal exteriors given to the apses ; but these are found in numerous examples in western Syria and throughout Greece, so that the models in this case were much nearer at hand than in the deserted towns of the Hauran and north Syria. It is extremely doubtful whether the Crusaders ever penetrated so far as the Hauran in the west, or Kalat Semán in the north, but, at all events, a distinct Romanesque style had already been developed in France, Italy, and Germany prior to the Crusades ; and the churches in Syria are clear evidence that it is mainly to the two former countries that we owe the design of the Crusaders' work of the twelfth century.

Syrian Round-arched Style. The style developed in Syria from the fourth century to the Mohammedan invasion, made known to us by M. de Vogüé's remarkable work, *La Syrie Centrale*, is by far the most interesting, as it virtually contains the elements of a distinct architectural style, which, though based in its origin on the monuments erected under Roman rule, would seem to have been able to throw off their trammels and to have evolved a homogene-

ous development, founded on the special requirements of the Christian religion, with a simple and rational constructional use of the materials at hand. The subject divides itself into two sections : the development in the Hauran, and that of the north of Syria between Antioch and Aleppo and about 100 miles south of these towns.

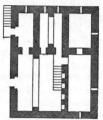

PLAN OF THE STONE HOUSE AT DOUMA: 2ND–3RD CENTURY.

In the Hauran the principal material was the basaltic rock of the district, which, on account of its hardness, allowed little decorative carving. The absence of timber also necessitated an entirely different system of design, both roofs and floors being constructed with stone slabs. The bearing of these was limited, so that when the area to be carried exceeded 6 or 8 feet, intermediate supports in the form of arches had to be thrown across the same. The earliest building of this type at Shakha (Chaqqa in De Vogüé) belongs to the Roman period anterior to the fourth century, and is assumed by De Vogüé to have constituted the reception halls of a Roman præfect. The principal hall measured 115 feet by 30 feet wide, and across it were thrown ten arches ; each bay therefore measured about 11 feet wide, centre to centre of arch ; the thickness of the arch is 2 feet 2 inches, and the wall it carries is surmounted by a corbel string of two courses projecting 1 foot 2 inches on each side ; on this corbel string the slabs, 6 inches thick, rest, their bearing being thereby lessened to 6 feet 6 inches. The piers carrying these arches project 1 foot 6 inches from the wall, and on the outside are buttresses of the same projection, *the earliest examples known.* All the doorways and windows in this part of Syria are fitted with stone doors and shutters working on pivots. In the same town is a Roman basilica with central hall, aisles, and galleries above, in which the supporting arches receive a further development. The intermediate support here may be said to consist of a screen wall with a great arch thrown across the central hall, its thrust being counteracted by carrying the screen to the outer walls ; smaller arches on two levels are pierced on each side in this wall, the lower arches forming the aisle passage, the upper ones those of the gallery. The whole work is carried out with well-worked masonry in courses and regular voussoirs to the arches, all laid without mortar.

The churches built in the fifth and sixth centuries were based on the Roman basilica described, and architecturally do not differ except that there is less carving, limited in fact almost to that of a cross in a circle. There are two churches of exceptional form : the church of S. George at Ezra, 510 A.D. (erroneously called Edrei in Murray and Fergusson), has an octagonal nave covered with a lofty elliptical dome, built probably without centring. In Bosrah, 512 A.D., are the external walls only of an apparently similar building, but of much larger size.

In domestic work the same method of construction obtains : the floors of the upper story and the roofs are all constructed with stone slabs, the large rooms having arches thrown across.

7 feet from the ground. The apses are semi-circular, there being three exceptions, viz., at Hass (fourth century) and Behioh, where they are square, and at Tourmanin, where there are polygonal externally as well as internally. In the majority of cases the apse and the diaconicon and prothesis are enclosed within a square external east wall (all the churches are orientated). At Baqouza the apse alone is circular externally, being built in between the square end of the diaconicon and prothesis ; and in Kalat Semán, where there are apses at the termination of the aisles as well, all three are developed as circular externally. In this latter case the diaconicon and prothesis are on the north and south sides of the aisles. This latter church is of considerable dimensions, being 330 feet east to west, with transepts and porch

STONE HOUSE AT CHAQQA: 2ND–3RD CENTURY.

We now turn to the north of Syria, where there was less difficulty in procuring timber, and where the construction, except in certain local peculiarities, followed very much on the same lines as those of the Romanesque style in Europe. In some of the towns, as at El Barah, the system of employing arches to carry the stone floor of the upper story is still retained in houses and in monastic establishments, as also in the tombs, to which we shall refer again.

The plans of all the principal churches are more or less uniform in their arrangement, consisting of nave and aisles, an apse, and, on either side of same, two chambers called the Diaconicon and Prothesis, the former reserved for the clergy only, the latter destined for the offerings of the faithful. In the majority of cases the separation of nave from aisles is by arcades of from six to eleven bays carried on monolithic shafts with capitals of classic type, and without either the dosseret or the abacus moulding found in Byzantine or Romanesque work ; the arcades are high in proportion to their width (about one to three), and the columns are sometimes raised on low pedestals. The two exceptions are Ruweiha and Kalb Louzy, where the nave and aisles are separated by three wide arches carried on piers with impost mouldings,

300 feet long. It was built to enclose the pillar on which S. Simeon Stylites spent forty years of his life. It consists of nave and transept, both with aisles, and, in the crossing, an immense octagonal central space (the same width as nave and aisles together), open to the sky, in the centre of which remains the original base of the pillar. The west end of the nave, being on the side of a hill, is carried on a crypt, and the principal entrance was on the south side, consisting of a porch with three doorways and extending the whole width of transept and aisles. There are besides these no fewer than twenty-one other entrance doorways, so that the pilgrims could stream in on all sides. The church was built at the beginning of the fifth century, and yet its porch might well have been designed and carried out by the architect of S. Trophime of Arles, so close is the general resemblance. Many of the west porches of these churches are adaptations of the classic portico, but there are some in which the central entrance, consisting of a single arch flanked by towers of three stories rising to the level of the nave, might, if raised higher and surmounted by belfries, pass for eleventh or twelfth century French work. In the church of Tourmanin a flight of steps leads up to the porch, which con-

sists of a single archway flanked by small
arched openings on either side. Above the
porch was a balcony of four columns and responds covered with a flat stone roof, beyond
which are the three west windows lighting the
nave. The rooms in wings probably contained
timber staircases to ascend to the balcony. The
roofs of all these churches were in timber, with
trusses over the nave carried on stone corbels.
The recesses in the end walls show the position
of other timbers, both in nave and aisles; the
support of those in the aisles is not clear in
De Vogüé's drawings.

In the architectural design of these churches
there are two characteristics to be noted: first,
the extremely original treatment of details,
evidently borrowed from Roman sources, but
adapted so as to constitute a new style;
secondly, the acceptance of the semicircular
arch with its archivolt mouldings, but without
the logical sequence involved in the construction
of these features. The arch is rarely, if ever,
constructed with regular voussoirs; sometimes
it is cut out of a single stone, as in the small
church of Moudjeleia, or in two horizontal
courses, as in the large church in the same
place; and even when, as in the wide arcade
of the nave of Kalb Louzy, there are nineteen
voussoirs, each voussoir is more than twice the
length of its own archivolt moulding, the outer
label of which projected some 4 inches. The
entire disregard, in fact, which, in the decoration, is paid to the real meaning of the feature
introduced and the origin of its development,
would incline us to suppose that masonry was
constructed *en bloc* and carved or worked down

PLAN OF DOOR OF A TOMB IN SYRIA.

afterward. It is only from this point of view
that the conception of the peculiar winding
terminations of the labels of the window jambs
can be understood; which, instead of descending vertically on the sills, are carried round to
an adjoining window or door, or terminate in

large circular rosaces. In the decoration of the
exterior of their apses, the Christian architects
of Syria adopted very much the same design as
those of the Romanesque style of Europe, except that the semidetached columns are in
Syria usually in two stories, superimposed.

STONE DOOR IN THE BASILICA OF TAFKHA.

The object of these attached shafts (sometimes
carried on corbels) would appear to have been
to give support to a boldly projecting corbel
table carrying the gutter, with intermediate
corbels between.

Many of the tombs in north Syria, especially
the examples excavated in the rock, do not
differ from those of Roman times, consisting
of porticoes in antis forming the entrance to the
tomb. There are, however, many instances
which only in their inscriptions and in the
Byzantine style of carving show their late date,
as otherwise they might be taken for small
Roman temples. There is one type known in
which the tomb, square in plan and built in
either one or two stories, is surmounted by a
lofty pyramid with small projecting bosses in
the centre of each stone, giving the appearance
of a pine cone. The Roman origin of these
tombs is shown in the enrichments of the
string courses, the door architraves and cornices,
and the angle pilasters and capitals; the pyramidal covering was probably derived from these
tombs already described, at Jerusalem, to which
we have assigned an Egyptian origin.

To give an adequate description of the domestic architecture of the early Christians in
north Syria, whether ecclesiastical or civil,
would be beyond the scope of this article, and
we must refer our readers to the interesting
series of drawings given by De Vogüé in his
Syrie Centrale. The most remarkable development is found in the group of houses at El
Barah, all based on the same and very staple
plan, consisting of two to four rooms side by
side, measuring about 20 feet by 14 feet, with
an arch thrown across to carry the floor of a
first story, and, on the south side, a portico of

columns on two floors, characteristic rather of a public monument than of a private residence. One of these houses, with four rooms on each floor and with a frontage of about 90 feet, had twenty-two columns to the ground story and a similar number above, the quarrying, working, and carving of which would cost a fortune at the present day, especially as capital, shaft, and base are all carved out of the same block of stone. At El Barah, in an area of about 250 by 150 feet, as shown in De Vogüé, there are nine houses with an aggregate of one hundred columns 12 feet high on the ground story alone, which shows considerable wealth and revenue in these towns, seeing that these columns were not taken from ancient buildings, but specially worked for the houses in question. All these porticoes face the south, with a court in front with lofty walls.

Crusaders' Work. Nearly all the Crusaders' churches are built on the same plan, consisting of three bays of nave and aisles (the width of the aisles being about two thirds of that of nave), both vaulted and with flat roofs, a transept with dome on pendentives over the crossing, and three apses in the axes of nave and aisles respectively, circular inside and polygonal outside. They were all built between 1120 and 1185. The vaults are intersecting, groined vaults, built with comparatively large stones, and have transverse ribs. All the arches are pointed, including those of the windows, and all have keystones. The external stonework is in fine-dressed ashlar. With the exception of the polygonal exterior of apses (a Byzantine characteristic), the general design is of French or Italian origin, and the mason's marks belong to these two countries only. The interiors are of the greatest simplicity; the nave arches are of two orders, slightly recessed only, one behind the other, which, with the centre keystone, denotes Italian or Sicilian influence. The dome, or pendentive, is built on the French system of Périgord and Angoumois, and the pointed barrel vault of the churches at Beyrout and Byblos, erected possibly about 1130, and that of Tortosa, of later date, are all of French origin. The western portals are the only highly decorated portions of the churches; they have from three to four orders elaborately moulded, and in their decoration, as well as in that of the capitals carrying them, show a mixture of French, Italian, Sicilian, and Byzantine Greek carving, the latter predominating, which suggests that the Crusaders availed themselves of the services of those artists who hitherto had worked for the Mohammedans.

The churches of S. Anne, S. Mary the Great, S. Mary Magdalene, and S. James the Great, all in Jerusalem, are examples of the general type above described.

The churches at Beyrout, Byblos, and Tortosa have pointed barrel vaults over the nave, the aisles being covered with intersecting groined vaults, and no domes. Whether owing to the difficulty of procuring suitable timber, or to the Crusaders having recognized the custom of the country, all the Crusaders' churches have flat roofs over the nave and aisles. The triforium, therefore, is non-existent, and the churches are lighted by clearstory windows above the aisle roofs.

The most important example built by the Crusaders in the Holy Land was the church of the Holy Sepulchre, and as this was attached to the rotunda containing the Holy Sepulchre, and had to include additional chapels, its plan differs somewhat from other examples, but the architecture is all of the same type. The only portion of the exterior which has any architectural pretensions is the south front of the transept, in the lower portion of which is a double portal with arches of two orders and a hood mould. The hood mould is enriched with Byzantine carving, the outer order has the cushion voussoir peculiar to the Norman work in Sicily, and the stone lintels carrying the tympana (now plastered over), and carved with figure sculpture and conventional foliage, are evidently the work of French sculptors.

Moslem Work. The earliest Mohammedan building in Syria of importance is the so-called mosque of Omar, the Dome of the Rock (Kubbet-es-Sakkra), built by the Sultan Abd-el-Melik in 686, over the sacred rock on the summit of Mount Moriah in Jerusalem. Though constructed partly with materials taken from more ancient buildings, the building is, architecturally, one of the most beautiful structures in the world, being admirably adapted to its purposes, and enriched, both externally and internally, with the most beautiful coloured materials. Some of these are due to the restorations of the sixteenth century by Sultan Soleiman, who redecorated the dome, filled the windows with stained glass, relined the walls with marble and mosaic, and covered the exterior with Persian porcelain tiles. Already, however, in the time of the Crusaders, it was looked upon as a most beautiful type of building, and led, after the Crusades, to its imitation in the numerous Templars' churches through Christendom. In the mosque of El Aksa (to the south of the mosque of Omar) Abd-el-Melik utilized the materials of the church of S. Mary, erected by Justinian at the southeast angle of the Hauran enclosure, and destroyed by the Sassanian monarch, Chosroes II. The pointed arches of the nave are probably restorations of the latter end of the eighth century, but even then they antedate by nearly a century those found in Egypt. Architecturally, the mosque has few pretensions, and is completely overshadowed by the adjoining structure, the Dome of the Rock. The great mosque of the Omeiyades at Damascus, built by Al Walid, 705–713, and almost entirely destroyed by fire in 1893, owed its great fame to the richness of the marble and mosaic decorations with which the walls were covered both externally and internally. Whilst the arches of the transept carrying the central dome are slightly pointed, those of the arcades of the triple aisles to east and west of the transept, and of all the windows, are semicircular, showing, at all events, that at that period the pointed arch was not always accepted. The mosaics were executed by Greek artists sent over from Byzantium, and as the employment of figure subjects was prohibited by the Mohammedan religion, the conventional representation of towns of note formed the chief subjects ; some of them still existed on the north transept wall prior to the fire. The minarets at the southwest and southeast corners of the mosque are additions of a much later date ; the former was built by Sultan Kaitbey, and is similar to the numerous examples in Cairo. The dissimilarity of the three buildings just cited, and the dearth of any other architectural structure of note, suggests that there was scarcely any development of the style in Syria itself, and that it is to Cairo, Bagdad, or Constantinople that we should look for the original models. The Khan Assad-Pacha at Damascus, said to have been built in the commencement of the last century, has a magnificent portal, which shows the same style in its design as that found in Constantinople due to the Seljukian dynasty. The interior, covered with nine domes or pendentives on pointed arches, carried by four central piers and their responds, is built in alternate layers of white and dark green stone. There is no carved ornament of any kind, but in its proportion and simplicity it is one of the most pleasing buildings in Syria. Compared with Cairo and Constantinople, Mohammedan street architecture in Syria is barren in the extreme, and it is chiefly in the interiors of the houses and the courtyards that we find any attempt at architectural display. This, however, seems to be confined to inlays of black and white marble for the walls, and richly painted and gilded ceilings in the Persian style. In this century a singular rococo style has crept in with a tendency to bastard Italian work.

Burchardt, *Travels in Syria*, London, 1822 ; Cassas, *Voyage pittoresque de la Syrie*, Paris, 1799 ; Conder, *Syrian Stone-lore*, London, 1896 ; Fergusson, *History of Architecture*, 3d ed., London, 1893 ; Laborde, *Journey through Arabia Petræa*, London, 1836 ; *Voyages en Orient*, Paris, 1858 ; Lewis, *The Holy Places of Jerusalem*, London, 1888 ; Longfellow, *Encyclopædia of Works of Architecture in Italy, Greece, and the Levant*, New York, 1895 ; Palestine Exploration Fund, various publications and photographs ; Perrot et Chipiez, *Histoire de l'Art dans l'Antiquité*, Vols. III. and IV. ; Porter, *Five Years in Damascus*, London, 1855 ; Renan, *Mission en Phœnicie*, Paris, 1864 ; Saulcy, *Voyage en Terre-Sainte*, Paris, 1865 ; Strange, *Palestine under the Moslems*, London, 1890 ; Vogüé, *Les églises de la Terre-Sainte*, Paris, 1860 ; *Temple de Jérusalem*, *Haram-ech-cherif*, Paris, 1864 ; *Syrie Centrale*, Paris, 1867 ; Willis, *Architectural History of the Church of the Holy Sepulchre at Jerusalem*, London, 1849 ; Wood, *Ruins of Palmyra*, London, 1753 ; *Ruins of Baalbec*, London, 1757 ; Baedeker, *Guide to Syria*, 1894 ; Murray, *Handbook, Syria, Palestine*, 1892.

— R. PHENÈ SPIERS.

SYRINX. In Greek archæology, anything tubular in form ; in architecture, especially a tunnel-shaped, rock-cut tomb belonging to that epoch in Egyptian antiquity which succeeded the age of the Mastaba. (See Egypt, Architecture of ; Tunnel Tomb, under Tomb.)

SYSTYLE. A close arrangement of columns in a peristyle, the usual systyle intercolumniation measuring two diameters from centre to centre of shafts. (See Columnar Architecture.)

T

TAA. Same as Paoh-Tah.

TABERNACLE. *A.* The portable place of worship and religious ceremonial used by the Israelites during their wanderings, as described in Exodus.

TABERNACLE: HADDISCOL CHURCH, NORFOLKSHIRE ; ABOUT 1160.

B. A house of worship, especially a building for Christian worship, but so planned and arranged as to differ from the ordinary church, as where seats for a very large congregation are provided.

C. In the Roman Catholic Church, a cupboard with doors, or similar shrine, used for keeping the consecrated bread. The use of the tabernacle is recent, dating probably from the seventeenth century; the name may, by extension, be given, as in France, to the metal

TABERNACLE: LADY CHAPEL, EXETER CATHE-
DRAL; c. 1280.
From this and the Kiddington example figures have been re-
moved.

vase or hollow dove used for the same purpose, or even the suspended pyx, when made decora-

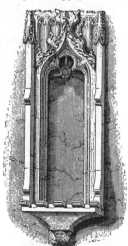

TABERNACLE: KIDDINGTON CHURCH, OXFORD-
SHIRE; c. 1450.

tive in itself and kept permanently in sight. (Compare Peristerium.)

D. A decorated recess, as a niche, or a framed space (see Tabernacle Frame), especially

when filled with figures of religious or ecclesiastical character. In this sense, any one of the niches with statues of saints, in a mediæval church porch, or the canopied open part of a pinnacle, as in Reims cathedral, or the Eleanor Cross at Northampton. (See cut.)

TABERNACLE FRAME. The frame for a door, window, or other opening, when treated as a complete design with columns or pilasters and an entablature, and also, when the opening is high in the wall, with an ornamental pendant below the window sill. Also a similar frame for a permanent work of art. (See Tabernacle, D.)

TABERNACLE: QUEEN ELEANOR'S CROSS AT
NORTHAMPTON; 1294.

TABERNACLE WORK. In mediæval architecture : —

A. An arcade or series of niches, highly decorated, with jamb shafts supporting carved overhanging canopies, and containing corbels for the support of figures or groups of figures.

B. By extension, any combination of delicate ornamental tracery, such as is peculiar to canopies of tabernacles, whether applied to choir stalls, sedilia, altars, ciboria, or any other fixtures of a church, or to furniture and vessels, whether in wood, stone, metal, or fine jewellery. (See Canopy; Niche; Tabernacle.)

TABLE. A. A flat, distinctive, rectangular surface on a wall, often charged with inscriptions, painting, or sculpture; if raised, it is called a raised or projecting table; if rusticated in any way, a rusticated table; if raking, a raking table, etc.

B. A string course, or other horizontal band of some size and weight. (Compare Corbel Table, Skew Table, below.)

C. In mediæval architecture, the frontal on the face of an altar; the painted or carved panel behind and over an altar. (See Retable.)

D. A slab set horizontally and carried on supports at a height of from 2 to 3 feet. In architectural treatment especially, (1) That used for the communion service when for any reason the altar is not in use, as at the time of the Puritan revolution in England, and as kept in usage by many sects of Christians; called Communion Table; Holy Table. (2) One of those used by the wealthier people of Roman antiquity for out-of-door service, composed usually of a slab of fine marble set upon carved marble supports. (See Monopodium.) (3) One of those used in modern times for ornament rather than for use, as in the halls of the Pitti Palace at Florence, the tops of those being composed of great slabs of Florentine mosaic, or of some costly and rare natural material, such as one which is entirely of lapis lazuli, and one which is veneered with malachite; the frames of these being of carved and often gilded wood.

Earth Table. The lowest course or courses of a stone wall visible above the ground, especially when forming a projecting member for the purpose of a water table. (Called also Ledgement Table.)

Grass Table. (Same as Earth Table.)

Ground Table. (Same as Earth Table.)

Ledgement Table. A band or belt course, usually moulded, especially one carried along the lower portion of a building, and which projects so as to form an Earth Table.

Skew Table. A stone set at right angles to the coping of a gable wall at its foot, and built into the masonry, to prevent the coping stones from sliding, and to serve as a stop for the eaves, the gutter, etc., of the side wall. When it projects, corbel-wise, beyond the angle of the building, it is called a Skew Corbel. The terms Kneeler and Summer Stone are also used, no perfect distinction being preserved.

Water Table. A string course or other projecting member, with a weathering, and otherwise so devised as to guide water away from the face of the wall.

TABLE STONE. (Same as Dolmen.)

TABLET. *A.* A small slab or panel, usually a separate piece, set into or attached to a wall or other larger mass, usually intended to receive an inscription.

B. A horizontal coping or capping of a wall, sometimes called Tabling.

TABLING. (Same as Coping.)

TABLINUM. In Roman architecture, a room, generally at the farther end of the atrium, in which were kept the family archives recorded upon tablets. Applied by modern archæologists to a large and very open room in a Roman house connected with the atrium, and often serving as a passage from it to the peristyle or garden. (See House.)

TABULARIUM. At Rome, a building of the time of the Republic standing on the extreme southeastern edge of the Capitoline Hill. The upper stories have been replaced by the Palace of the Senator, but the lower stories remain almost unaltered. The building must have had one high story on the side of the Capitol, where is now the square of the Campidoglio, and two high stories crowning a very lofty basement on the side toward the Forum.

TABLET IN THE VON DER LINDE HOUSE; STOCKHOLM, SWEDEN.

TADDEO GADDI. (See Gaddi, Taddeo.)

TAENIA. In a Doric entablature, the fillet which separates the frieze from the architrave.

TAH. (Same as Paoh-tah.)

TAIL. *A.* The exposed part of a slate or tile in roofing.

B. (Same as Tailing.)

TAIL BAY. (See Case Bay.)

TAIL BEAM. (Same as Tail Piece.)

TAILING. That portion of a projecting stone or series of stones, as in a cornice, which is built into the wall, and which, by its superior weight, is intended to prevent the stone from toppling over.

TAILLOIR. In French, the Abacus of a capital.

TAILPIECE. A short joist or rafter fitted into the Header. (See also Trimmer.)

TAIL TRIMMER. In floor framing, a trimmer, set clear of the brickwork of a chimney and parallel thereto, to receive the ends of the floor joists, thus avoiding flues.

TAJ MAHAL. At Agra in India, a tomb built in the seventeenth century, of great size and of the most elaborate and refined design, especially in the details. It is a typical building of the Moslem style in the far East. (See India, Architecture of.)

TALAVERA, JUAN DE; sculptor.

In 1514 he was employed on the decoration of the cathedral of Toledo (Spain).

Viñaza, *Adiciones.*

TALAYOT. (See *Balearic Islands*, under Mediterranean Islands.)

TALENTI, FRANCESCO; architect and sculptor; d. after 1369.

The Talenti came from Ponte-a-Lieve, near Florence. Francesco is mentioned among the sculptors working on the Duomo of Orvieto in 1329 (Della Valle, op. cit., p. 272, doc. XXIV.). His name next appears in an inventory of marble for the campanile of the Florentine cathedral, dated 1351. This marble was for four windows. The three upper stories of the campanile are probably his work. (See Giotto and Andrea da Pisa). He is last mentioned in the records of the campanile in 1357. May 29, 1355, Talenti was commissioned to make a model for the cathedral (S. Maria del Fiore), which should determine the position of the windows of the nave. At this time it was decided to make the four vaults of the nave square instead of oblong, as designed by Arnolfo di Cambio, thus increasing the length of the nave to its present dimensions. In 1358 Giovanni di Lapo Ghini (see Ghini) was associated with him as *capomaestro*. Dec. 20, 1364, Talenti was discharged, but July 22, 1366, appears again in a position subordinate to Ghini. His salary was stopped in 1369, which is probably about the date of his death. The nave was then nearly completed. (For the history of the cathedral at this time, see Ghini, Giovanni di Lapo.)

Guasti, *S. M. del Fiore*; Del Moro, *S. M. del Fiori*; Rohault de Fleury, *Toscane*; Della Valle, *Duomo di Orvieto*; L. Runge, *Glockenthurm zu Florenz.*

TALENTI, SIMONE; sculptor and architect.

The son of Francesco Talenti (see Talenti, Fr.). He assisted his father at the Duomo (Florence), and in 1366 presented a model for that building. In 1375 he succeeded Francesco Salvetti as *capomaestro* of the Duomo. In 1376 Benci di Cione (see Benci di Cione) was associated with him, and they, with the assistance of Taddeo Ristoro, designed and began the building now called the Loggia dei Lanzi (Florence). In June, 1377, the three architects were superseded both at the Duomo and the Loggia. Talenti afterward returned to the Loggia and executed all the carvings on the piers and brackets, finished Nov. 29, 1379.

(See Loggia dei Lanzi for the common attribution.) About 1378 Simone filled in the lower arches of Or S. Michele (Florence), and decorated them with tracery.

Karl Frey, *Loggia dei Lanzi*; Guasti, *S. M. del Fiore.*

TALL BOY. A chimney pot of long and slender form, intended to improve the draught by lengthening the flue.

TALMAN, WILLIAM; architect; d. probably about 1700.

His principal work was Chatsworth House in Derbyshire, England, built, in 1681, for William Cavendish, Earl, and afterward Duke, of Devonshire. He built Thoresby House (1671, burned before 1762). In 1694 he was appointed by King William III. comptroller of the works in progress at Hampton Court. Sir Christopher Wren (see Wren) was surveyor at Hampton Court at the same time, and was much disturbed by Talman's interference.

Blomfield, *Renaissance in England.*

TALON. (Same as Ogee.)

TAMBOUR. *A.* Same as Drum, as of a cupola, *B.*

B. Same as Bell, as of a capital.

This is the French term often used in English; the original signifies also a drum of a column.

TAMIL. Same as Dravidian.

TAMP (v.). To ram an earth surface, so as to harden it and form a floor, or the bottom of a trench to make it fit to receive foundations.

TANK. A large vessel, reservoir, or cistern, of wood or metal, intended for the storage of a fluid, usually water. (See Plumbing; Water Supply.) — W. P. G.

Supply Tank. (See under Cistern.)

TAP. *A.* A faucet or cock through which liquor can be drawn from a tank or cask. (Rare in the United States.)

B. A steel screw bolt, the threads of which are cutting edges, used to screw into the smooth hole of a nut to form an internal or female screw therein.

TAPER. The slope or diminishing of a spire, or of a conical or pyramidal roof. Also the diminishing of a shaft of a column; but as this is very nearly always curved, it is not often called Taper. (See Entasis.)

TAPESTRY. A fabric made by a process somewhat unlike weaving; and, therefore, not a textile fabric. It is used for wall hangings. Anciently it was the most available covering for the stone walls of halls and chambers of a strong castle or other residence of the nobility, and was usually hung from tenterhooks by means of which it was suspended at a distance of at least some inches from the face of the masonry. It was often allowed to cover the door openings in such a way that even when the door was thrown open the person entering had still no view of the interior, a parting or division between two pieces of tapestry alone serving as the entrance. In modern times, tapestry is used only for its beauty of surface, and is too often stretched upon frames, partly on account of the small size of modern rooms, and their crowd of furniture and other objects, and partly on account of the modern taste for extreme accuracy and smoothness. This practice is, however, ruinous to the best effect of the material.

TAPIA. A material like Pisé used in many parts of Spanish America. A superior kind has lime mixed with the fat earth; this is sometimes called *Tapia Real* or Royal Tapia.

TAPROOM. In Great Britain, the same as Barroom, as being the place where liquors are drawn from the tap.

TAR. A product formed by the destructive distillation, mainly of resinous woods, extensively used, in combination with gravel and paper, as a watertight roofing material; or, alone, as a damp-proof course.

TARISEL (TARISSEL), PIERRE; architect.

Maître d'œuvre (architect) of the city and cathedral of Amiens (Somme, France). In 1470 he designed the tower of La Haye at Amiens, and in 1479 planned the new line of fortifications of that city. In 1483 Tarisel made the great altar of the cathedral of Amiens. He designed also the main portal of that cathedral and the central window.

Nodier-Taylor-Cailleux, *Voyages; Picardie*, v. 1; Jourdain-Duval, *Portail de la Cathédrale d'Amiens;* Bauchal, *Dictionnaire.*

TARKIBEH. (See Gravestone.)

TARRAS. *A.* An ancient spelling of Terrace.

B. A strong cement formerly used in hydraulic engineering.

TARSIA. The Italian inlaying of wood, usually light upon dark, common in the fifteenth century. The patterns were usually Renaissance scrollwork and arabesques, but also curious pictures with perspective effects were introduced into the larger panels. (See Inlaid Work.)

An imitation of the inlay was very commonly made by painting, as in the celebrated cupboards of S. Maria delle Grazie at Milan, known as *Lo Scaffale*, which have been well reproduced in a book bearing the same title.

TARTARY, ARCHITECTURE OF. (See Turkistan.)

TASMANIA, ARCHITECTURE OF. The native inhabitants, now extinct, were savages of the same type as those of Australia, and had no buildings, not even roofed and walled huts. The white inhabitants are as yet less than 200,000 in number, nearly all of British

descent, and have erected no buildings of importance. The cathedral of Port Arthur, the abandoned convict station, has gone almost entirely to ruin. This was one of the few stone buildings on the island, but it was almost devoid of architectural interest. The model prison, at the same point, was open, low in the walls, a mere series of utilitarian buildings. The towns of Hobart and Launceston are of about 20,000 and 30,000 inhabitants respectively, and in spite of excellent roads and much comfort in the better classes of dwellings, little of architectural interest is to be found. The free settlers are of but recent arrival, and there has not yet been time for that development of interest in decorative treatment of a town which, unless in the rare case of individual enterprise taking that direction, is necessary to growth of decorative art of any kind (compare Australia). There are, however, a parliament house and a city hall in Hobart; and a monument to Sir John Franklin, who was at one time governor of Tasmania, stands in the square. In each of the towns named there are churches of different sects. — R. S.

TASSEL. Same as Torsel.

TASSO, GIOVANNI BATTISTA DEL; woodworker (*intarsiatore*) and architect; b. 1500; d. May 8, 1555.

Battista belonged to a famous family of wood carvers which flourished during the fifteenth and sixteenth centuries in Italy. He was a *protégé* of Pier-Francesco Riccio, majordomo of Duke Cosmo I. dei' Medici, and was much employed in the improvement of the Palazzo Vecchio. There is a ceiling by him in the second story of the palazzo on the side toward the Uffizi. The curious door which he built for the church of S. Romolo is preserved by Ruggieri (op. cit.). His most important work is the loggia of the Mercato Nuovo of Florence, which was begun by the order of Duke Cosmo I., Aug. 26, 1547.

Hans Stegmann in Geymüller-Stegmann, *Die Arch. der Ren. in Toscana;* Ruggieri, *Studio d'Architettura.*

TATTI, JACOPO. (See Sansovino, Jacopo.)

TAURISCUS OF TRALLES.

Apollonios and Tauriscus of Tralles made the group of sculpture called the "Farnese Bull" at Naples.

Collignon, *Histoire de la Sculpture Grecque.*

TAVERN. *A.* A public house; properly such a house used for temporary visits only and for the sale of wine and other refreshments, excluding cooked food.

B. By extension, a small inn of any sort.

C. Formally, or locally, in Great Britain, a small shop at the front of a house, either on the ground floor or in a cellar, and usually not communicating with the rest of the building.

TAYLOR, ISIDORE JUSTIN SÉVERIN; baron; French author and artist; b. 1789 (at Brussels); d. 1879.

Taylor was the son of an Englishman naturalized in France. He was educated in Paris, and in 1811 began his artistic voyages. He served in the army in 1813, and was *commissaire royal* at the Théâtre Français in 1824. In 1838 he was created *inspecteur général des beaux arts*. He travelled extensively in Europe and the East, and published a series of monumental topographical works, the most important of which is the *Voyages pittoresques et romantiques de l'ancienne France* (Paris, 1820–1863, 24 vols. folio). This work was never finished. The innumerable lithographic illustrations are extraordinarily fine, drawn by Isabey, Géricault, Ingres, Horace Vernet, Fragonard, Viollet-le-Duc, Ciceri, Duzats, and Baron Taylor himself. In the editorial work he was assisted by Charles Nodier and A. de Cailleux. He published *Voyage pittoresque en Espagne, en Portugal, etc.* (Paris, 1826–1832, 3 vols. 4to); *Syrie, l'Égypte, la Palestine et la Judée* (Paris, 1835–1839, 3 vols. 4to); *Pélerinage à Jérusalem* (Paris, 1841); *Voyage en Suisse* (Paris, 1843); *Les Pyrénées* (Paris, 1843, 8vo).

Larousse, *Dictionnaire.*

TAYLOR, GEORGE LEDWALL; architect; b. 1780; d. April, 1873.

In 1817–1819, and again in 1857–1868, he visited France, Italy, Greece, and Sicily. June 3, 1818, he discovered the monumental lion which commemorates the battle of Chæronea (338 B.C.). Taylor published numerous architectural works, and is best known by his *Autobiography*, which contains descriptions and illustrations of many important monuments.

Taylor, *Autobiography of an Octogenarian Architect.*

TAYLOR, SIR ROBERT; sculptor and architect; b. 1714; d. Sept. 27, 1788.

The son of a stone mason of London. He visited Rome, and on his return executed, among other works, two monuments in Westminster Abbey, a statue at the Bank, and the sculpture of the pediment of the Mansion House, London. He had a large practice in England, and succeeded James Stuart (see Stuart, J.) as surveyor of Greenwich Hospital.

Redgrave, *Dictionary.*

TAZZA. A vase having the form of a flat and shallow cup, with a high foot or stand. The term is applied to the basin of a fountain when supported by a pillar; and some fountains have two, or even three, tazzas, vertically arranged, and growing smaller as they ascend.

T BAR. (See special noun.)

T BEAM. (See special noun.)

TCHISH. The Klamath term for settlement, camp, wigwam, lodge, village, town. (See Latchash.)

TEAGLE POST. In timber framing, a post supporting one end of a tie-beam; that is to say, one of the lower angles of a roof truss.

TEBI. In Egyptian building, brick made of the mud of the Nile, mixed with fragments of pottery, chopped straw, or the like. (See Brick, n.)

TECASSIR. In Mohammedan architecture, a gallery in a mosque, especially one for the use of women.

TECCIZCALLI. (See Calli.)

TECPAN. The Aztec (Nahuatl) council house, or official house. — F. S. D.

TEDESCO, GIROLAMO. (See Girolamo Tedesco.)

TEE (adjectival term). Having the shape of a capital T. Compound terms beginning with this word are used to describe many objects, of which sometimes only the section suggests the capital T. The same fancied resemblance has caused the use of the word, substantively, for the Burmese royal symbol, generally appearing as a crowning ornament, as upon the spire of a pagoda.

TEEPEE. Same as Tipi.

TEE SQUARE. (See under Square.)

TEGULA. A tile; the Latin term, and used in English for tiles of unusual shape or material, such as the marble tiles of some Greek temples. (See Tile and subtitles.)

TEL. A mound; the modern Arabic term, which enters into many compound names of sites, as in Egypt and Mesopotamia. (Also written Tell.)

TELAMON (pl. **TELAMONES**). A male statue serving to support an entablature, impost, corbel, or the like, and forming an important part of an architectural design. Telamones are generally considered the same as Atlantes, which word is more usual in classical archæology. In the elaborate architecture of the eighteenth century, half figures of men, usually bearded, and of exaggerated muscular development and extravagant pose, are used as supports of porches, and the like. The name "telamones" may be extended to apply to these.

TELEPHONE. (See Electrical Appliances.)

TELESTERION. A place for initiation; especially the temple at Eleusis, in which were held the initiatory rites to the Eleusinian Mysteries. The building was of unusual character for a Greek temple, having twelve columns in the front, the only dodecastyle portico known in antiquity; and the interior was hypostyle, with forty-two columns in six rows. Seats cut in the rock were arranged on all four sides of the building. The interior measured about 170 by 175 feet. The manner of its roofing and lighting is not known. (Compare Thersillium and the Zeus temple at Akragas, described under Sicily, for Grecian halls and interior architecture.)

TELFORD, THOMAS ; engineer ; b. Aug. 9, 1757 (in Scotland) ; d. Sept. 2, 1834.

He was apprenticed to a stone mason, and in 1780 went to Edinburgh. After 1782 he was employed on Somerset House in London. Between 1795 and 1805 he constructed the Ellesmere canal, with its great aqueduct, and between 1773 and 1823 the Caledonian canal in Scotland. He made the roads in the highlands of Scotland, with about twelve hundred bridges. His name is associated with a peculiar form of pavement for roads.

Rickman, *Life of Telford.*

TELLTALE PIPE. A small overflow pipe, attached to a tank or cistern, to show, by dripping, when the receptacle is full.

TEMANZA, TOMASO ; architect, and writer on architecture ; b. 1705 (at Venice) ; d. 1789.

The son of an architect, a nephew of G. Scalfarotti, and a pupil of Niccolò Comini and the Marquis Poleni (see Poleni). In 1726 he entered the commission of engineers at Venice, of which he became chief in 1742. Among the few buildings constructed by him are the church of S. Maria Maddalena in Venice (Cicognara, op. cit.), the façade of Margherita at Padua, and the Rotondo of Piazzolo. He is best known by his books : *Dell' Antichità di Rimino, libri due, traccolta di Antichi inscrizioni* (Venice, 1741) ; *Dissertazione sopra l'antichissimo territorio di Sant' Ilario nella diocesi d' Oliveto* (Venice, 1761, folio); *Vite de' più celebri architetti e scultori Veneziani che fiorirono nel secolo decimosesto* (Venice, 1778, folio) ; *Antica pianta del inclita città di Venezia delineata circa la meta del XII. secolo,* etc. (Venice, 1781, 4to). The *Degli Archi e delle volte,* etc., was not published until 1811. Temanza's *Vite* is one of the most important books of its class.

Comolli, *Bibliografia Storico-critica ;* Paoletti, *Rinascimento ;* Larousse, *Dictionnaire;* Cicognara, *Fabbriche di Venezia.*

TEMASCALE ; TEMAZCALLI. A little adobe hut, built by Indians in Mexico as a Sweat Lodge. — F. S. D.

TEMENOS. In Greek antiquity, a piece of ground specially reserved and enclosed, as for sacred purposes, corresponding nearly to the Latin *templum* in its original signification. In some cases the temenos contains but a single shrine, or temple, in the modern sense, while in others, as in the celebrated cases of Olympia and Epidauros, many important buildings, including several temples of considerable size, are arranged within the enclosure. (See Delubrum.) Cut, column 755.

TEMPER. *A.* To mix, moisten, and knead clay, so as to bring it to proper consistency to form bricks, pottery, terra cotta, etc., preliminary to hardening by fire.

B. To bring a metal, as steel, to a proper degree of hardness and elasticity, by alternately heating and suddenly cooling the metal, its colour, by those processes, gradually changing from light yellow to dark blue, the metal becoming harder at each stage.

C. To toughen and harden glass by plunging it at a high temperature into an oleaginous bath, under the process invented by M. de la Bastie, or by heating and suddenly cooling it, according to the Siemen process.

D. To mix and knead lime and sand and water, in such proportions as to make mortar for masonry or plastering.

TEMPERA (L. *temperare* = to mix in due proportion).

A water-colour process. It is also called in these days Kalsomine (which see) or Calcimine. The medium is water mixed with some binding substance, such as the white and yolk of egg, or the yolk alone, gum tragacanth, glue, honey, glycerine, milk, or the like. Unless mixed with, or protected by, some insoluble material, it is not suited to surfaces exposed to moisture. The Egyptians used tempera both on the outside and inside of their buildings. It was the national method. The Greeks and Romans occasionally used it for interior decorations, and very frequently in combination with other processes. For instance, the author's investigations have led him to the conclusion that the ground of the panel or mural painting was often true fresco, and that the applied ornament or figure composition was in tempera. Tempera was much employed by the mediæval artists for the interior decoration of buildings, and occasionally by the Renaissance painters, whose process *par excellence* was fresco, though all retouches in this latter process were made in tempera. It is much used in modern times. (See Kalsomine.) The Italians use it to-day on the exterior of buildings, the milk with which the colour is mixed preventing its dissolution. Sometimes a touch of oil or a little glue is mixed with the first coat, but the last coat is generally a simple mixture of milk, water, and colour. If these coats are applied to fresh plaster, so much the better. (See Fresco Painting.) For the special qualities of milk as a medium the reader is referred to Casein. Cennino Cennini, who is the mouthpiece of Giotto's followers, gives two recipes (preferring the latter) for tempera on interior walls : (1) the colours to be mixed with egg and the milky juice of the fig tree ; (2) the colours to be mixed with the yolk of egg alone. All water-colour paintings, if protected from moisture and sunlight, are relatively durable. They fade slightly if exposed to an excess of light; but, on the other hand, they do not darken, as oil or varnish paintings darken, with time. Moreover, they have a dead or flat finish. Dampness, of course, is fatal to them. They

(See Thermostat; Temperature Regulator; both in the article Electrical Appliances.)

TEMPERATURE REGULATOR, ELECTRIC. (See Electrical Appliances.)

TEMPIETTO. In Rome, a small circular

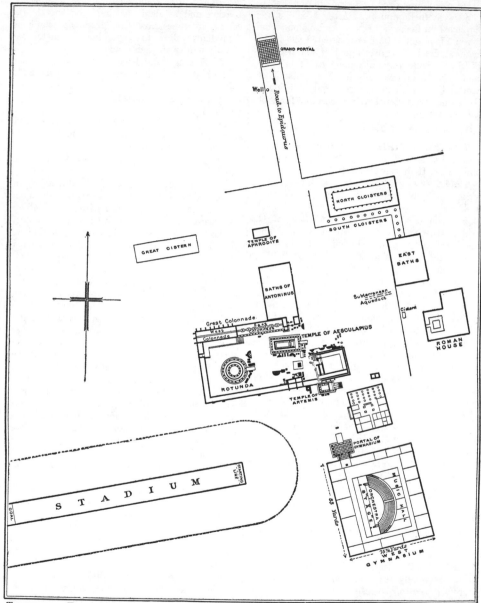

TEMENOS AT EPIDAURUS: THE BOUNDARIES HAVE NOT BEEN DETERMINED THROUGHOUT; THE STADIUM WAS OUTSIDE THE SACRED ENCLOSURE.

cannot be washed, and for that reason are not suited to walls requiring constant cleaning. (Also called Distemper.)

— FREDERIC CROWNINSHIELD.

TEMPERATURE, REGULATION OF.

building designed by Bramante, and erected in 1502. It stands in the cloister court of S. Pietro in Montorio.

TEMPIO MALATESTIANO. The church of S. Francesco, the cathedral, at Rimini, on the east coast of Italy ; an ancient Gothic church which was altered by Leon Battista Alberti at the command of the lords of Mala-testa, who governed the district. This was one of the earliest pieces of work done under the classical revival ; for Alberti undertook to cover the old building with detail studied from the antique, and began the erection of a west front

not ordinarily applied to buildings erected by Christians (but see definition *B*) nor by Moham-medans ; by the modern Jews it is used in a somewhat special sense, as part of a proper name, given to an individual synagogue in con-nection with other words usually of Hebrew origin ; as the Temple Beth-El in New York.

B. A building erected for Christian worship

TEMPLE, FIG. 1: THAT OF KHUNSU, BUILT BY RAMSES III. AT KARNAK; THE HYPÆTHRAL COURT.

studied from the Roman triumphal arch at Rimini.

TEMPLATE. Same as Templet.

TEMPLE, THE. In London. (For Inner Temple, Middle Temple, see Inns of Court ; see also Temple Church, and Church, col. 568.)

TEMPLE. *A.* An edifice dedicated to the service of a deity or deities ; more especially a building used for such purposes as worship and the performance of sacred rites, or the keeping of objects of veneration. The word is

other than that especially recognized by or pre-vailing in a given state ; as especially in France, a place of Protestant worship, and in England, in the sense of a proper name, nearly like the usage of the modern Jews mentioned above, especially a building of the nonconformists or dissenters, and intended to receive a large con-gregation. (Compare Tabernacle.)

C. An establishment of the Knights Templars ; a mediæval and modern term re-placing the full title of commandery or preceptory; especially in Paris, the important establishment, some of the buildings of which remained until after the French Revolution. In this sense, in French history, the temple was the building used as the prison in which King Louis XVI. and his family were confined.

(For other places of worship, see Chapel; Church; Synagogue.)

General. In most languages the temple bears a name indicating that it is the dwelling place of the deity. The word *templum* (derived from the same root as the Greek *temenos, i.e.,* cut off or separated) was, with the Romans, originally used to designate the space of earth and sky marked off by an augur for divination. Later it was used of consecrated spaces generally, and it was probably not till the end of the republic that its use as applied to the house of a god (superseding the older *œdes* or *œdes sacra*) became general.

sacred rites, it is thought by some writers to have also been in early times a fortress in which the god and his people defended themselves against foes who sought to conquer the country and destroy the local deity. Through the conservatism so characteristic of the Egyptians, its defensive character was maintained even after the consolidation of the empire had checked local warfare, and after the establishment of a national pantheon had placed the temples of the gods beyond frequent danger from attack.

As a typical plan of an Egyptian temple we may take that of the south temple at Karnak. Often, as in this instance, a great ceremonial gateway (see Vol. I., pl. XXX.) dominated the approach, while beyond a roadway, flanked by rows of sphinxes or of images of the temple's sacred animal, led up to the real entrance of the temple. Sometimes the avenue of sphinxes

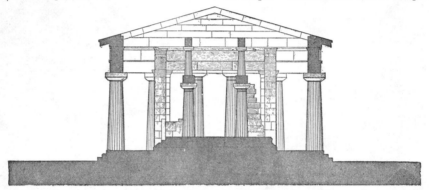

TEMPLE, FIG. 2: THAT OF NEPTUNE AT PÆSTUM; SECTION SHOWING TWO STORIED COLONNADES DIVIDING NAOS.

The temple is common to religions which have reached a certain stage of advancement, having generally passed beyond the worship of natural objects and reached a point at which an image of the god needs the protection of walls and a roof. Thus the Cultos image is the *raison d'être* of the temple.

The religious ceremonies of the ancients were largely centred around the altar, which, although it was not within the temple, was of more moment to them than the image of the god. Thus a temple is not necessarily a place of public worship, many temples being open to the priests only. In providing for the needs of both worship and ritual, a temple generally has, first, either in or near it, a place for the meeting of the worshippers (as around the altar in the Greek and Roman temple or in the great forecourt in the Egyptian temple); second, an important chamber (as the naos of the Greek or the hypostyle hall of the Egyptian temple); third, a sanctuary, adytum, or holy of holies.

Egypt. While in Egypt the temple was always a place suited to the performance of

terminated in obelisks which stood before the wall which enclosed the temple proper. The front of this wall consisted of two colossal pylons or wide towers, each with its four sides sloping slightly inward and crowned by a characteristic cornice, made of a roll and a great hollow moulding. The passage between the towers was narrow, and, being fitted with a wooden door, plated with metal, it was easily defended. There were also, as a rule, some small posterns piercing the great wall.

Passing between the pylons, one entered a courtyard enclosed by the temple wall and colonnaded on two or three sides. This part of the temple is called the hypæthral court. It was without a roof except over the colonnades. (See Fig. I., though this is of a much smaller court.) Beyond the courtyard one reached the hypostyle hall, architecturally most imposing part of the temple. Its roof was carried by many columns. Light was admitted by a clearstory, or, in later times, over a low screen wall between the columns of the front. (See Vol. I., pl. XXXI., for the exterior

of a hypostyle hall and the screen wall.)
Beyond the hypostyle hall lay the sanctuary,
the part of the temple of greatest religious
significance. Within it was a rectangular
structure, serving in some cases as the cage
of the sacred animal, and in others to contain
whatever other object was supposed to be the
incorporation of the god. The sanctuary was
more or less surrounded by chambers, generally
dark, which served as storerooms for furniture,

a gate directly opposite the pylons. Sacred
ways, flanked by sphinxes or animals, led from
one temple to another or to the Nile, where
barks for the service of the temple or of the
dead were moored.

The Egyptian temple seems always to have
been regarded as open to additions. Its
growth was gradual. The temple with the
normal plan is seized upon by a new king,
who converts its courts into covered halls,

TEMPLE, FIG. 3: THAT OF NEPTUNE AT PÆSTUM; SEE THE SECTION, FIG. 2.

sacred garments, processional objects, standards,
and the like.

The inner walls of the temple, from pylon to
sanctuary, were adorned with scenes representing religious ceremonies. The front walls of
the pylons were sculptured with scenes of victory over the enemies of the king and of the
god. The walls and their sculpture were
generally covered with fine plaster and finished
in brilliant colours. The sacred enclosure,
which frequently contained groves, lakes, and
the dwellings of the priests, was surrounded
occasionally by a wall, and more frequently by
an earthwork, the only access being through

builds new courts before the old, new pylons in
front of all. Another sovereign repeats the
process, until at length we have vast areas
covered with buildings, as at Luxor and at
Karnak.

There were some departures from the typical
plan, and among these the most marked were
temples excavated from the mountain side, as
that at Ipsamboul, with its colossal, seated,
rock-cut figures guarding its entrance; or
those others partly built upon the plain and
partly within the mountain, as that at Deir-el-
Bahri, where the temple stands on a series of
terraces. The plans of small temples are quite

variable. At Elephantine there is one of unusual beauty, the plan of which, a cella surrounded by a colonnade, strongly suggests the Greek type. (See Egypt, Architecture of.)

Mesopotamia. The plain of the Tigris and Euphrates, similar in many ways to the valley of the Nile, produced, however, a temple system strongly in contrast with that of Egypt. In Egypt the temple overshadows in importance all other structures. In Mesopotamia it is the palace which puts the temple in a secondary place. The temples of Egypt, built for the most part of enduring materials, are so well preserved that our knowledge of them is almost complete. In Mesopotamia the temples, built as a rule of unburnt bricks, have melted into shapeless mounds. In spite, how-

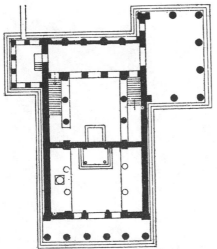

Temple, Fig. 4: the Erechtheum at Athens; containing at least Three separate Shrines. Hexastyle Ionic Portico partly indicated by the Three Porticoes; Tetrastyle Ionic Portico with Two Columns in return; and below, Tetrastyle Portico of Caryatides with Two Figures in return.

ever, of the unfavourable condition of the ruins, we have learned from them, and from ancient reliefs and texts, certain fundamental facts. Certain Assyriologists maintain that the plain-inhabiting races of Mesopotamia regarded their gods as mountain-born and as dwellers upon mountain tops, and that, therefore, in erecting dwelling places for them, they sought to reproduce their mountain homes. Certain it is that a mound of earth was piled up and formed into a terrace for the temple, which, both in Babylonia and Assyria, took the form of a square tower, known as the zikkurat, which rose in successive stages, forming a stepped pyramid. (See cut under Mesopotamia.) This tower was ascended either by steps leading from story to story, or by an inclined way running around it, by which access was had to

the platform at the top, where stood, according to Herodotus, a mystic shrine, the dwelling place of the god. Hugeness and especially height were the criteria of excellence in the zikkurat. The number of stories varied. Three or four were usual, but in some cases there were seven. The mound grew by accretions, a new ruler raising it to form his terrace at a level higher than those of his predecessors, a method clearly demonstrated in the excavations of the temple of Bel at Nippur. While the mass of the zikkurat was of unbaked brick, one or more of the outer wall faces were generally of burned bricks, while in some cases enamelled bricks of yellow and blue were used for facings. Within the temple there seem to have been certain chambers. At Nimroud two temples have been found showing a long hall and a small room containing the statue of the god. This was the Papakhu, the most sacred part of the temple, to which but few had access. One of these temples had, in addition to these two chambers, a small hall in front of the larger, and thus we have the usual three-fold division. Within the temple area were smaller shrines, and in front of the zikkurat was a large open space where the faithful congregated. Sacrifices were offered, not at the top of the tower, but on altars at its base. Clustered about the temple were dwelling places for the priests, schools, observatories, halls of judgment, and other buildings. (See Mesopotamia, Architecture of.)

Phœnicia. The Phœnicians, who carried the arts of Egypt and Mesopotamia to all the shores of the Mediterranean, were undoubtedly builders of great temples. So scanty are the actual remains, however, that we can do scarcely more than approximate the general type. There is sufficient evidence to show that a monumental enclosure surrounded a great platform (as at Baalbec), on which stood a sanctuary. Of the sanctuary itself, our knowledge, derived chiefly from certain medals, is very slight.

Judæa. The architecture of ancient Judæa was Phœnician in character. The temple of Solomon was largely of Phœnician workmanship. Its actual remains are most scanty, consisting of certain foundations, the megalithic aspect of which recalls similar work at Baalbec. Among the many restorations of the temple based upon Biblical texts, great discrepancies exist. None of them bear such an air of inherent probability as to be really convincing. From the texts it is easily seen that the Temple of Solomon had an entrance porch, a rectangular chamber lighted by narrow windows, and called the holy part, and a cubical sanctuary, the holy of holies. All these, excepting the porch, were surrounded by many small chambers, three stories in height, apparently in the

PLATE XXVII

TEMPLE

That of Poseidon, at Paestum (in Greek, Poseidonia) in Campania. This gives the typical interior of a Doric temple of the fifth century, and should be compared with the Plate of the Theseion.

thickness of the exterior wall. Although the arrangement of the plan is clear, the manner in which the exterior was treated is not known.

The very detailed description of the temple seen by Ezekiel in a vision is partly a memory of the earlier structure and partly a fabric of the imagination. Ezekiel shows us a temple with surroundings far larger and more complete than those of the earlier temple. The temple as actually reconstructed by Zerubbabel was certainly less splendid than that of Solomon, but was probably larger.

consisting of a double enclosure, of the hearth or altar, have recently been discovered. Their plan is closely similar to that of Greek houses of the Homeric age, where the hearth had a sacred character. (See Persian Architecture.)

Greece. The planning and construction of Greek temples having been so fully discussed in other articles (see Grecian ; Greco-Roman ; Greece, Architecture of; Roman Imperial) the origin of the temple among the Greeks and the relation of its parts to their worship will alone be considered here.

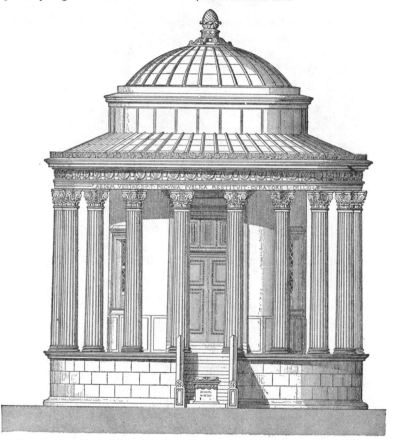

TEMPLE, FIG. 5: THAT OF VESTA AT TIVOLI; RESTORATION OF J. A. LEVEIL.

Of the temple built by Herod on the site of Solomon's temple, several ancient descriptions exist, throwing some light upon it and much upon its surroundings. The state of the evidence, however, is not such as to allow a plan of the temple itself to be made with certainty. Its architectural treatment was influenced by the use of classic orders. (See Syria, Architecture of.)

Persia. The ancient Persians were both star and fire worshippers. Remains of a staged tower similar to those of Mesopotamia have been found at Djour, and sanctuaries for fire worship,

From the earliest times there seem to have been plots of land in Greece set apart for certain deities and consecrated to their uses. A sanctity was associated with caves or mountain tops or groves of trees. Even the Mycenæan age reveals no structure which is definitely a temple, although such an arrangement as the Megaron of the palace at Tiryns, a porch preceding a room containing a hearth, was undoubtedly the archetype of the Greek temple, the simplest forms of which approximate it closely (see plan of amphiprostyle temple, under Columnar Architecture). Though Homer makes some slight mention of the temples of the gods, he gives no description of them as he does of the palaces of his heroes, whom we see sacrificing upon the altars in their forecourts. Indeed, it is highly improbable that such structures as we designate by the word "temple" ex-

general stimulus to temple building was felt in Greece. The Greek temple, properly so called, scarcely reaches an earlier period than the seventh century B.C.

Among the Greeks the temple was not a

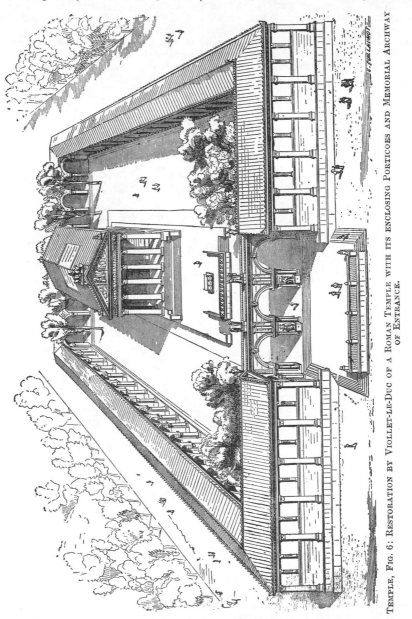

TEMPLE, FIG. 6: RESTORATION BY VIOLLET-LE-DUC OF A ROMAN TEMPLE WITH ITS ENCLOSING PORTICOES AND MEMORIAL ARCHWAY OF ENTRANCE.

isted at all at the time of Homer. It was not till anthropomorphic ideas of divinity, necessitating the use of images, came into vogue, that some form of artificial shelter for such images, i.e., a temple, became necessary. Centuries elapsed after the Dorian invasion before any

building in which a congregation met and worshipped. It was regarded as a place where the god might favourably be invoked, though not necessarily his dwelling place. It thus happened that many temples were kept closed except on special occasions, some being opened but once a year.

The perfected Greek temple was ordinarily divided into pronaos, naos, and opisthodomos. (See plan of Parthenon under Columnar Architecture.) Passing through the pronaos, in which stood statues or votive offerings, one entered the naos or cella, which occupied the central part of the building. In the larger temples the naos consisted of three longitudinal divisions, those on the sides being separated from the central by rows of columns. (See Figs. 2 and 3.) In the central division and at the end farthest from the entrance stood the chief object of veneration, in early times a rude image and at last a splendid statue of the deity. Beyond the naos, at the extreme end of the temple, was the opisthodomos or treasury, the proximity of which to the sacred image served as a special protection to the wealth of votive offerings stored within it. These offerings, very varied in character, frequently of great value, were in certain cases so numerous that special storehouses or treasuries, as at Olympia, had to be provided for them.

Not infrequently the temple contained an adytum or place to which access was prohibited, a secret chamber in which sacred or mysterious objects were hidden. These adyta were sometimes under ground, and to them were generally removed the older and more sacred images when they were replaced by more splendid statues of the gods.

The Greek temple stood within a sacred enclosure or Temenos (which see), within which may have been temples, treasuries, tombs, altars, monuments, and even groves, the whole enclosure being marked out by boundary stones, or enclosed within a wall and entered through a great gateway or propylæon.

Rome. As the primitive religion of the Romans was essentially that of the Etruscans, it is natural that their early temples should have been based directly upon Etruscan models. In its early form the Etruscan temple seems to have been a wooden structure with columns widely spaced and with decorations of terra cotta and bronze. Its portico, of unusual depth, was divided into three parts, by two rows of columns, and its cella, similarly divided, usually had at its extremity the shrines of three deities. One important example of such a temple, that of Jupiter Capitolinus, survived until the time of the Empire. On this, Vitruvius based his account of the Tuscan temple.

The Romans seem to have been far less impressed by the splendid groups of temples, such as those at Pæstum, erected at an early date by Greek colonists in Magna Græcia, than one would have imagined. Indeed, it was not until after the conquest of Greece itself that the temples of the Romans were deeply influenced by those of the Greeks. Certain well-marked

differences were, however, well maintained. The Roman temple differed from the Greek : 1st, in the greater depth of its portico ; 2d, in the greater proportional width of the cella and the omission of its interior rows of columns ; 3d, in the relatively infrequent use of a peristyle ; 4th, in the placing of the temple, not on a stylobate

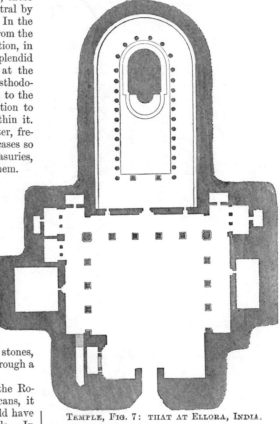

TEMPLE, FIG. 7: THAT AT ELLORA, INDIA.

of steps, but on a lofty base or podium, with plinth and cornice of its own. (See Vol. II., pl. XII.)

The Romans, from the earliest to the latest times, showed a fondness for the circle in their temple plans. In the Temple of Vesta, in the Forum Romanum, one of the earliest of Roman temples (compare that at Tivoli, Fig. 5) ; in the Pantheon of Hadrian, the noblest of circular buildings ; even in such late examples as those of Spalato and Baalbec, this fondness manifests itself.

The altar stood before the Roman temple, and its treasury was usually formed under the floor within the podium on which the temple was built. (See preface to Vol. II.)

India. Of the temples of the first Brahminical period in India, the age anterior to the third century B.C., but little is known.

Of the Buddhistic period, beginning about the third century B.C., and extending to the fifth century of our era, abundant remains of temples, both above and below ground, exist. The general form of the tope or tumulus raised over a sacred relic is a hemisphere carried on a circular basement, while that of the cave temple is a basilica with two aisles and a nave, at the end of which stands a sanctuary in the form of a tope. (See Fig. 7.) The façade, ornamented with columns, was cut like the rest of the temple from the rock. The cells of a monastery usually surround the Buddhist temple.

TEMPLE OF THE WINDS, AT ATHENS.

eral form of the tope or tumulus raised over a sacred relic is a hemisphere carried on a circular basement, while that of the cave temple is a basilica with two aisles and a nave, at the end of which stands a sanctuary in the form of a

The second Brahminical period, beginning about the fifth century and reaching to the present time, developed new temple types, of which the pagoda is the most striking and important. The pagoda is in some instances a building of

PLATE XXVIII

TEMPLE

The Tannoji Temple and Pagoda at Osaka, Japan; the Hondo and To of a great religious establishment. Originally of a very ancient epoch, they have been often rebuilt, and are now nearly of pure Tokugawa style, seventeenth or eighteenth century. Compare plates and text illustrations under Japan and Pagoda.

two stories (as at Ellora) or more commonly a tower of many stories. Two types exist. In one the walls are vertical, and each story is slightly smaller than the one below it, *i.e.*, a staged tower. In the other, the faces of the tower curving inward, produce highly interesting and characteristic masses. Though it is difficult to summarize the types of Indian temples, it will be well to point out that in some instances great halls appear, the roofs of which are carried by columns, while in others dome-covered areas are found. The ordinary accompaniments of Brahminical temples are gateways, covered halls for pilgrims, and sacred lakes surrounded by porticoes. At times the gateway takes the form of the stepped tower, giving access to a columned hall which is the temple. In other instances the columned hall is the gateway, and the tower plays the rôle of temple. Sometimes the entire group of temple and accessories was cut from the living rock. As in the case of Egyptian temples, the principal Brahminical temples were formed by successive growths around an earlier sanctuary. (See India, Architecture of.)

China and Japan. In so brief a summary the religious architecture of China and Japan may be reduced to a description of the Buddhist temple. Its type is a building of two stories, of which the lower is open in front but surrounded by a veranda, while the upper is covered by an ornate roof. The sanctuary is enclosed by a sort of cloister, behind which are rooms for pilgrims and cells for bonzes. At the entrance to the enclosure is a porch before which stands a gateway without doors. Pagodas, which it must be remembered are not necessarily temples, often stand within the enclosure. As in Egypt and India, the temple group is often the result of successive growths. In China the arrangement of temples is generally a symmetrical one. In Japan, where the picturesque prevails, the sacred enclosure is often treated as an informal park. In China the temple has an hieratic stamp; in Japan it is a personal and living work. (See China, Architecture of; Japan, Architecture of.)

Mexico; Yucatan; Peru. A similarity exists between the temples of Mesopotamia and those of Mexico, Yucatan, and Peru. In these countries the temple is usually set on a platform or terrace. Its typical form, called a Teocalli, was a pyramid or cone, up the sides of which ran straight flights of steps, leading to a sanctuary on the summit. In some examples the slopes are continuous as in a true pyramid, in others they rise by stages, forming a stepped tower. (See Mexico, § I. ; South America.)
      — FRANK MILES DAY.

TEMPLE BAR. (See Bar.)

TEMPLE CHURCH. In general, a church belonging, or which has belonged, to a post or fortress of the Knights Templars; especially a very interesting and beautiful structure in London consisting of two parts, a circular Romanesque church of the twelfth century, and a choir with nave and aisle, built in the thirteenth century. The building is valuable architecturally, and contains some beautiful altar tombs and other monuments.

TEMPLE MOUND. *A.* A mound with level summit, supposed to have supported a temple. The most noteworthy of these is at Cahokia, Illinois. It is 90 feet high with a summit area of 200 by 450 feet.

B. The Teocalli of Mexico and adjacent regions. (See Mound; Teocalli.) — F. S. D.

TEMPLE OF ANTONINUS AND FAUSTINA. In Rome, fronting on the Forum on the northeast side; hexastyle, Corinthian, but with shafts of rich marble, and not fluted. The cella is used as a church.

TEMPLE OF APOLLO DIDYMÆUS. At Miletus, in Asia Minor ; an Ionic building of great splendour, dipteral, the outer colonnade decastyle, with twenty-one columns on the flank.

TEMPLE OF APOLLO EPICURIUS. At Bassæ, near Phigalæa in the Peloponnesus ; Doric peristylar hexastyle, with fifteen columns on the flank, the naos divided in a very unusual manner, and for purposes not well understood, the unusual length of the building also requiring explanation.

TEMPLE OF ARTEMIS. At Ephesus, in Asia Minor ; commonly called, after the English translation of the New Testament (Acts xix. 27), Temple of Diana of the Ephesians ; a magnificent Ionic building, dipteral, the outer colonnade octostyle, with twenty columns on the flank ; the naos had a portico distyle in antis, and this and the inner chambers are divided by a double row of columns. (For the unique feature of this building, see Columna Cælata.)

TEMPLE OF ATHENA NIKE. At Athens ; a very small tetrastyle Ionic building on the Acropolis. When the Turkish fortifications were demolished the fragments of this temple were discovered, and the whole was put together in 1836 by German architects, in what is probably a correct reproduction, though the exact ancient site cannot be determined. There is a parapet of slabs of marble exquisitely sculptured in relief.

TEMPLE OF ATHENA POLIAS. One of the shrines contained in the Erechtheum (which see).

TEMPLE OF BASSÆ. (See Temple of Apollo Epicurius.)

TEMPLE OF CASTOR. In Rome; properly of the Dioscuri, Castor and Pollux, on the southerly side of the Forum. The partly existing building dates from the reign of Augustus; three Corinthian columns are in place.

TEMPLE OF CONCORD. At Rome; a very curious building at the extreme northwest of the Forum. It was oblong, with the main entrance in one of the long sides; but it is so entirely ruined that its original character is largely matter of conjecture. It is considered in Lanciani's *Ruins and Excavations*.

TEMPLE OF FAUSTINA. Same as Temple of Antoninus and Faustina.

TEMPLE OF FORTUNA VIRILIS. (See Temple of Fortune.)

TEMPLE OF FORTUNE. At Rome, in the Forum Boarium; a very ancient Ionic temple, probably rebuilt in its present form in the third century.

TEMPLE OF HEROD. At Jerusalem. (See the article Temple; *Judœa*.)

TEMPLE OF JUPITER CAPITOLINUS. At Rome; more properly, of Jupiter Optimus Maximus on the Capitoline, the most revered of the shrines of Rome, standing on the southern peak of the Capitoline Hill. Originally of Etruscan type, with columns in front only and wooden entablatures, afterward rebuilt, and finally by Domitian, but nearly on the old plan.

TEMPLE OF JUPITER OLYMPIUS. At Athens. (See Temple of Zeus.)

TEMPLE OF JUPITER STATOR. At Rome, near the Arch of Titus, but wholly ruined, and named here only because the name has been erroneously given to buildings in other quarters.

TEMPLE OF MARS ULTOR. In Rome; a building of the time of Augustus, in the Forum Augustum, northeast of the Forum Romanum. Three columns are erect, and a part of the cella wall.

TEMPLE OF MINERVA MEDICA. In Rome; a large decagonal hall covered by a cupola; not a temple in the usual sense, though considered by Lanciani a "nymphæum."

TEMPLE OF NIKE APTEROS. Same as Temple of Athena Nike.

TEMPLE OF SATURN. In Rome, at the extreme eastern corner of the Forum; a remarkable ruin with a modified Ionic order.

TEMPLE OF THE SUN. In Baalbec. On the site of a very ancient Temple of Baal, a colossal structure of Roman Imperial architecture, but probably never completed. A very large square court, an outer hexagonal court, and an outermost portico lead up to this temple.

In Palmyra. Of the third century A.D., surrounded by a great court, which is enclosed by a high wall. This was one of the most gigantic of the buildings of Imperial Roman style, the Oriental modifications of which are less obvious than is sometimes asserted.

In Rome. On the Quirinal Hill, built by the Emperor Aurelian after his Palmyrene War; a colossal structure, now known by its founda-tions, by fragments only of the superstructure, and by mediæval drawings.

TEMPLE OF THE WINDS. An octagonal building in Athens used to hold a Clepsydra. The name is derived from the sculptured representations of the different winds on its surfaces.

TEMPLE OF VENUS AND ROME. At Rome, northeast of the Forum, in part existing behind the church of S. Francesca; once an immense double temple with two apses back to back and a great peristyle, and surrounded by a court, an outer wall, and colonnade.

TEMPLE OF VESPASIAN. At Rome, close to the Temple of Concord, and, like it, built close against the lofty wall of the Tabularium. Three Corinthian columns are still in place.

TEMPLE OF VESTA. In Rome; a circular building in the Forum, the ruins of which have been rediscovered since 1875, and are described in Lanciani's *Ruins and Excavations*. It was circular, with a peristyle and a conical, or dome-shaped, roof over the naos.

Other round temples are often called temples of Vesta, generally without sufficient authority.

TEMPLE OF ZEUS. At Athens; often called temple of the Olympian Zeus. The immense temple whose Corinthian columns still stand east of the Acropolis. It was begun in the very early days of historical Greece, but its existing remains probably date from the time of Hadrian, who is known to have worked upon it.

At Olympia; Doric hexastyle, with thirteen columns on the flank, the cella divided by two rows of columns.

TEMPLE, RAYMOND DU. (See Raymond du Temple.)

TEMPLET (I.). A pattern to secure accuracy and uniformity in shaping parts, and in repeating dimensions. It is made usually of wood or of sheet metal. In stone-cutting it gives the shape of the end or joint of the stone, showing the profile of such mouldings as it may have. The templet may be used on plastic material as a tool to give the body its shape. In boiler work and other riveted work, a templet formed of a strip of metal with holes at the proper distances is used to mark the position of the rivet holes, and thus secure accuracy.

— W. R. H.

TEMPLET (II.). A piece of stone, metal, or timber placed in a wall to receive the bearing of a girder, beam or truss, so as to distribute the weight, or over an aperture, to sustain floor joists and transfer their burden to the piers. (Sometimes written Template.)

— H. V. B.

TEMPLE WIGWAM. An American Indian house or wigwam devoted to religious uses.

— F. S. D.

TEMPLUM. In Roman antiquity, a space reserved; practically the same as temenos. The idea of a building is hardly included in the term in Latin until the later times of the Republic. (See Ædes; Delubrum.)

TENACITY. The power of resisting a pull, that is to say, strength against breaking by means of a pull. The extraordinary tenacity of iron wire is at the bottom of the use of that material for suspension bridges. Tie rods and tie beams are used because of their tenacity, and the strength of the metal in tie rods determines their size; but tie beams are commonly made, for architectural effect or for convenience, very much thicker than is required for tenacity alone.

TENDER. The offer made by any one to do certain work at a certain price, especially the offer of a builder with whom it is proposed to make a contract, if the tender is considered favourable. More common in England; in the United States offer or bid is more frequently used.

TENEMENT. A piece of ground, a building, or similar piece of property held either in fee simple or by the payment of rent by any one tenant; especially a residence, in the sense of a house, or room, or set of rooms, or even a house with grounds and appurtenances. The use of the term as meaning especially a hired place of residence seems to have come from the general sense of holding implied by the word itself, as distinguished from ownership in fee simple. In some American cities the term is extended to mean a Tenement House (which see). In New York City, the distinction between a tenement, as part of a Tenement House, and an apartment in an Apartment House, is very difficult to establish. The New York State law gives no help, as all such buildings are classed together. The most usual distinction (apart from amount of rental, for which see Apartment House and Tenement House) is in the presence of a private hall or passage from which the rooms of the apartment open. The term "flat" (which see) is entirely general, and applies to any domicile in one story of a larger building.

TENEMENT HOUSE. A building occupied by more than one family and usually having suites of rooms, a public stairway, dumbwaiter, and toilet room common to two or more families on each floor, each suite consisting of a living room, with one or more bedrooms opening therefrom, and furnished with cold water supply and a chimney flue, and renting for less than $300 a year. (See Apartment House.)

Historical. With the growth of a town, the first tenements have always been abandoned houses of the wealthier classes, but these are ultimately replaced by houses divided into sep-arate suites and occupied by many tenants. The tenement house was undoubtedly an early result of ancient city life, coming as an inevitable consequence of the increase of population within circumscribing defensive walls. Rome is known to have had tenements many stories in height, and the crowded cities of mediæval Europe housed their poor under steep gables and in high buildings. The conditions of life under these circumstances are always very objectionable, in both a sanitary and moral sense, and the menace which such crowding constitutes has become well recognized by legislators and philanthropists.

The Modern Tenement House. This is the result of conditions which are different in different localities and times. These are briefly:

(*a*) The size of the lot in Europe is large and approximately square, and the building is erected about a central court with an open passageway to the street on the first floor; in America long narrow lots are in vogue, resulting in buildings with small air shafts.

(*b*) The amount of capital employed limits the building to a certain size and character; in Europe the investors represent wealth, in America they commonly represent small capitalists who erect buildings on small lots.

(*c*) Legal restrictions which have generally resulted from a struggle between forces allied to vested interests on the one side and those associated with sanitary requirements on the other.

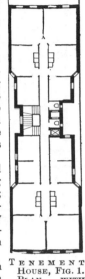

TENEMENT HOUSE, FIG. 1. PLAN WITH FOUR TENEMENTS IN A STORY. SITTING ROOMS AT FRONT AND REAR.

The New York Tenement House. This being built under what are probably the most severe conditions in the world, small lot, small capital, and stringent laws, is commonly erected on a unit lot of 25 feet by 100 feet. The law limits the percentage of the lot that can be occupied, requires an open rear and courts of a certain size, and regulates the plumbing, ventilation, construction, etc. The commonest type produced under these conditions is the "dumbbell" plan (Fig. 1), and the modified form of this plan which provides narrow courts along the party lines and open at the rear. Three or four families are accommodated on each floor, each family having a living room looking upon the street or upon the open yard, and bedrooms on the air shafts. Public halls are long and narrow, lighted only at the middle point, if at all. The chief advantages of this plan are cheapness and simplicity of construction, and small running expense; the chief disadvantages are wasted room in public halls, narrow air

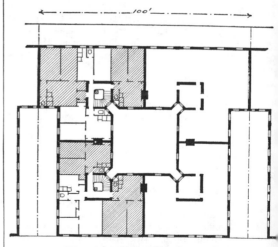

TENEMENT HOUSE ON A PLOT 100 FEET SQUARE, WITH NARROW OUTER RESERVATIONS FOR LIGHT AND AIR, AND A CENTRAL COURT; SIXTEEN TENEMENTS IN EACH STORY. FIG. 2.

shafts giving little light or air below the top story and rendering privacy in summer almost an impossibility, public water closets, and the like. Other types of plan have been used on wider lots which have a much better disposition of area and arrangement of courts. An absolute departure from old lines has been made lately (Fig. 2) by building companies which have erected tenements upon large plots of ground, generally on a unit lot of 100 feet square. This type of building has a large square court in the middle with broad courts open at the street or yard along the party lines. The advantages of avoiding the long, dark, public hall, the public toilet room, and the dark, narrow air shaft are evident. The chief disadvantages are the many living rooms which have no outlook upon the street or yard, the amount of capital required to erect, the fewer number of suites on a given area than are provided by the "dumb-bell" plan, and the smaller income from the capital invested.

Requirements. The living room is the largest room and must accommodate laundry tubs, table, range, sink, and dresser, the minimum area being 120 square feet. The other rooms should have a capacity of at least 600 cubic feet with direct access to outer air by means of a window of at least 12 square feet of area. The living room must be accessible from the public hall either directly or through a private entry. The bedrooms must be entered

either from the living room or from a hall. It is very desirable that each suite should have a short private hall, stand for refrigerators, private toilet opening off private hall, windows on narrow courts not opposite each other, and a closet in each bedroom. The laundry tubs frequently have a removable partition so that they can be used for bathing. It is desirable to have the cross partition set so as to divide them unequally, making one tub larger than the other. The sink and the back of the laundry tubs may be of metal. Gas should be provided for lighting with rising mains for the supply of each row of apartments and branches taken off so that metres can be placed in each suite, using either the old type or the new prepay system. Each suite of rooms should have a second exit by means of a fire escape. The drying of clothes must be provided for by a drying frame on the roof or by means of tall poles with pulleys thereon set on the rear lot line, and each suite must have a locked coal box or room in the yard or cellar. Halls are lighted and cared for by the owner. Lighting of halls may be furthered by setting wire glass in the upper half of doors opening upon them. It is very desirable to provide for the safe use of the roof by the tenants in hot weather by

TENEMENT HOUSE, FIG. 3.

A model plan approved by reform committees in New York, 1900. It is adapted to plots 100 feet square, each plot containing fourteen tenements, and the deep and narrow courts (about 20 by 60 feet) are open in every case to the street, while a reserved space 10 feet wide is left between the rear wall and the centre line of the block.

means of slat platforms and proper railings and guards at front and rear and around courts.

Shower baths are sometimes provided in the basement. The walls and ceiling of the passage-way from the entrance doorway to the public staircase should be fireproofed and have the floor concreted and the walls tiled or cemented to a height of five feet.

Construction. A complete fireproof con-struction is much the best from every point of view except that of expense. It is feasible only when the only restriction on the builder is safe construction. In any case the stairways, stair landings, and dumbwaiter shafts with all open-ings therein must be fireproofed. The ceilings should be wire-lathed and plastered, both being carried completely across all floors to prevent the communication of fire between stories. The first tier of beams should be of iron with fire-proof floor construction. All toilet rooms should have water tight floors and impervious side walls to a height of at least two feet.
— George Hill.

TEN–FOOT ROD. A device commonly used by carpenters in setting up their work. (See Rod.)

TENIA. Same as Tænia.

TENNIS COURT. A room arranged for the ancient game of tenis, which is very nearly the French *Jeu de Paume;* one third as wide as long, thirty or more feet high, receiving its light from windows high in the wall. On one of the long sides there is a high gallery for spectators. In order that the white balls may be the more easily seen, the walls are sometimes black; or, if the walls are made white for cool-ness, as is said to be the case in India, the balls are black.

TENON. The cutting of the end of a rail, mullion, sill, or beam to form a projection of smaller transverse section than the piece, with a shoulder, so that it may be fitted into a corresponding hole or mortise in another piece. (See Mortice; Shoulder; Teaze Tenon, below; Tusk; also Framing, Braced Fram-ing.)

Teaze Tenon. A double tenon, one tenon above another, with a double shoulder, wrought on the top of a post, to receive two horizontal timbers at right angles to each other. (Written also Tease Tenon.)

TENPIN ALLEY. (See Bowling Alley.)

TENSILE STRENGTH. The strength of a member or material to resist a tensile force, *i.e.,* a force tending to separate or break by stretching; an abbreviated and erroneous term. (See Resistance; Strength of Materials.)

TENSION. The opposite of compression; the force which operates by stretching, as in a tie beam, a tie rod, a suspension piece of any sort.

TENSION BAR. A bar or rod to which a strain of tension is applied, or by which it is resisted.

TENSION MEMBER — PIECE. In a framework, truss, or the like, a piece calculated to resist strains of tension; as a tie.

TEOCALLI. The worship mound of the Aztecs. (See Mound.) — F. S. D.

TEOPAN. An Aztec building similar to the Teocalli, and like that devoted to the ser-vice of the gods. — F. S. D.

TEOSCOPOLI. (See Theotocopuli.)

TEPIDARIUM. In ancient Roman baths, a room of intermediate temperature between the Frigidarium and the Calidarium and fitted with baths to correspond.

TERM. A terminal figure, especially one of the sort called by the Greeks Hermes (which see ; see also Terminal; Terminus).

TERMINAL (n.). The ornamental finish, or termination, of an object, corresponding some-times nearly to Finial or to Acroterium, but applied to minor and subordinate uses. Thus, the carved end of a bench, as in a church, is called by this name. (Compare Knob; Hip Knob.)

TERMINAL (adj.). In Latin, having to do with the Roman god Terminus.

A Terminal Figure is a decorative figure in which a head, or a head and bust, or the human figure to the waist and including the arms, is finished by a block, prism-like, or shaped like a reversed truncated cone, and either plain or decorated severely (See Gaine; Scabellum.) These figures are thought to have been used originally for statues of Hermes as god of roads and boundaries corresponding to the Roman Terminus. Ancient Greco-Roman examples are sometimes arranged for two heads attached at the back and facing in opposite directions.

A Terminal Pedestal is a pedestal prepared for a bust, so that the two together would be a terminal figure.

It is to be noted, with regard to Terminal Bust and Terminal Pedestal, that the whole must be designed together as if one statue, and of such height that, when the bust is set upon the pedestal, the two together shall have a height from the floor proportional to the size of the bust itself.

TERMINUS. In Latin, the ancient Italian god of landmarks, the guardian of property in land; hence the figure of that god, represented without legs and feet to express the irremovable nature of the landmarks, the lower limbs being replaced by a solid prism or inverted truncated cone (see Terminal).

TERN PLATE; TERNE PLATE. A kind of roofing plate in which the alloy coating the sheet iron is composed of tin and lead.

TERRACE. An embankment or prepared and artificially levelled mass of earth, as where in a garden the natural inequalities of the ground have been regulated, or wholly artificially raised surfaces have been prepared. Formal gardens depend very largely for their effect upon the proper use of terraces, perrons being used to communicate from the level of one terrace to that of another; and, especially in a hilly country, the whole design may be based upon the succession of these horizontal levels marked by their stone parapets. By extension (1) the roof of a house when flat and very solid, inviting the use of it in warm climates as a place to sit after sundown; (2) a balcony, but this use of it seems to have been abandoned; (3) a paved or floored out-of-door platform, as if the floor of a veranda without its roof and partial enclosure; often used in the United States for so much of the veranda as extends beyond the roof.   — R. S.

TERRA COTTA. Hard baked pottery, especially that which is used in architecture or in decorative art of large scale. It may be left with its natural brown surface unglazed and uncoloured, or it may be painted as was customary among the Greeks (see Antefix; Grecian Architecture; Polychromy), or it may be covered with a solid enamel of grave or brilliant colours.

In parts of Italy the architecture of the later Gothic style and of the early Renaissance is marked by the free use of terra cotta (see Keramics; Robbia Work). In the nineteenth century its use was largely revived, and in England from 1860, and in the United States from about 1880, it has been freely employed in connection with bricks of similar or agreeably contrasting colour for the exterior of buildings, almost to the exclusion of cut stone.

Gruner, *Terra-cotta Architecture of North Italy, 12th–15th Centuries;* Paravicini, *Die Architektur der Lombardei;* Strack, *Ziegelbauwerke des Mittelalters und der Renaissance in Italien.* (See also bibliography for Keramics.)

TERRA–COTTA LUMBER. A light porous terra cotta which can be readily shaped with rough carpenter's tools, will hold nails well, and can be used instead of boards for fireproof sheathing, and the like. (See Fireproofing, cols. 25, 36.)

TERRASS. Same as Trass.

TERRAZZO VENEZIANO. An inexpensive concrete pavement used for floors in the province of Venetia, even in houses of some pretentions to elegance. Lime-mortar made unusually dry is the principal material; in this are inlaid small pieces of marble, usually not too large to pass through a ring an inch and a half in diameter. The whole is beaten hard, rubbed down, and polished. Fine examples are given, full size, in Gruner's *Specimens of Ornamental Art.*

TERRE PLEINE. In French, a level platform of earth; used in English in fortification, rarely elsewhere.

TERRONES WORK. (From Spanish, *terron,* a clod of earth.) A wall or building

constructed of earth, mud, adobe, or similar compact and uniform material which hardens as it dries. (See Adobe; Cajon; Pisé.) — F. S. D.

TESSELLAR. Made up of Tesseræ; after the fashion of mosaic work.

TESSELLATE (v.). To make an inlay or mosaic of tesserae. Tessellated work is an inlay of square pieces, generally small.

TESSERA (plural Tesseræ), a small, approximately cubical piece of marble, glass, or other hard material, used in mosaic.

TESSIN, NICODEMUS (I.); architect. Little is known of his life. He studied in Italy and in 1645 succeeded Simon de Lavallée as architect of the Swedish court. Among his principal works in Sweden are the palace of Drottningsholm, finished by his son, the royal villa of Stroemsholm, and the mausoleum of Charles Gustav.

Larousse, *Dictionnaire;* Seubert, *Künstler-Lexicon.*

TESSIN, NICODEMUS (II.); court architect; b. 1654; d. 1728.

He was the son of Nicodemus Tessin (I.) and was educated at the universities of Stockholm and Upsala, Sweden, and learned architecture from his father. He visited Italy and worked four years under Bernini (see Bernini) and Carlo Fontana (see Fontana). In 1669 Tessin was appointed royal architect in Sweden. The royal palace in Stockholm, burned in 1667, was rebuilt by him. He finished the palace of Drottningsholm, begun by his father, designed the parks of Drottningsholm and Ulriksdal, and made plans for the reconstruction of the palace in Copenhagen, Denmark. He took an important part in public and political affairs.

Larousse, *Dictionnaire;* Seubert, *Künstler-Lexicon.*

TEST (v.). To ascertain the quality, especially the strength, of material by trial. For building materials, such as stone, metal, and timber of all sorts, powerful testing machines are employed to ascertain their greatest endurance under specific strains.

TESTER. A flat canopy, as over a bed, throne, pulpit, or tomb.

TESTING. (See Test (v.).)

TESTUDO. In Roman architecture, an arched vault or ceiling, especially when surbased or flattened.

TETRAPYLON. Something characterized by having four gateways as a building with a nearly equal gateway in each of four sides. Such a building is the well-known arch of Janus near the church of S. Giorgio in Velabro, Rome, and in a somewhat similar building at Constantine in Algeria. (See North Africa, Architecture of.)

TETRASTOON. *A.* Having a porch or portico on each of its four sides, as a cloister.

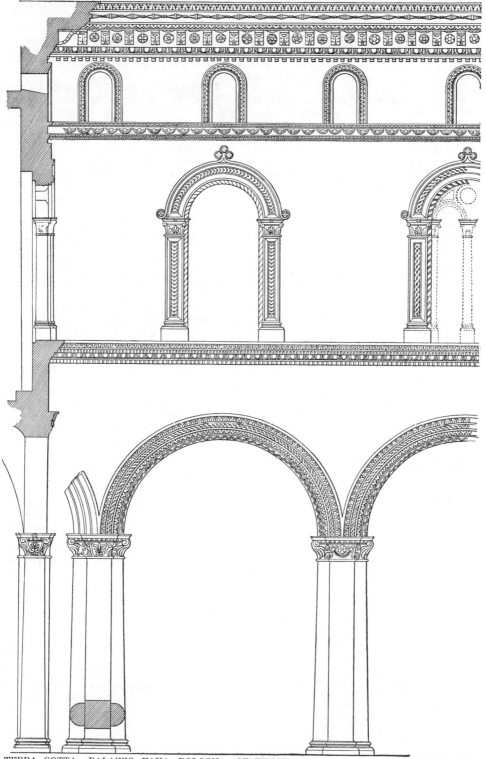

TERRA COTTA: PALAZZO FAVA, BOLOGNA, OF WHICH THE DECORATIVE FEATURES ARE
ALL MOULDED IN CLAY AND FIRED.

785   786

B. Having four porticoes ; said of any building. (Rare in either sense.)

TETRASTYLE (adj.). Having four columns in the front or end row; consisting of a row or rows of four columns. (See Columnar Architecture, and the terms given there.)

TEXIER, CHARLES FÉLIX MARIE; architect and archæologist ; b. Aug. 22, 1802 ; d. 1871.

In 1823 he entered the École des Beaux Arts and was appointed inspector of the public works of Paris in 1827. In 1833 he went to Asia Minor and made extensive explorations of antique monuments. Returning to France in 1837 he presented the results of his investigations to the Académie and published *Description de l'Asie Mineure faite par ordre du Gouvernement français* (Paris, 2 vols. folio, 1839–1849). In 1839 he visited Persia, Armenia, and Mesopotamia, and published the results of his explorations in *Description de l'Arménie, la Perse et la Mesopotamie,* (Paris, 1842–1849, 3 vols. folio). In 1840 Texier was appointed professor *suppléant* in Archæology at the Collège de France, Paris. July 8, 1845, he was sent to Algeria as *inspecteur général des bâtiments civils.* He published also *Mémoires sur les ports antiques situés à l'embouchure du Tibre,* 1858, 8 vo, *L'Architecture Byzantine,* London, 1865, folio, translated by R. P. Pullan, and in collaboration with Pullan, *The Principal Ruins of Asia Minor,* London, 1865, 1 vol. folio.

Revue Générale, Vol. 28 ; *Nouvelle Biographie générale.*

TEXIER, JEAN LE (JEAN DE BEAUCE); architect and sculptor.

Le Texier was employed in the construction of the church of La Trinité at Vendôme (Loir et Cher). Nov. 11, 1506, he contracted with the chapter of the cathedral of Chartres to rebuild the northern spire of that edifice, according to a design on parchment which he that day exhibited. This new spire (*clocher neuf*), entirely of stone and one of the most splendid examples of the Flamboyant Gothic style in France, was completed in 1513. In 1514 Le Texier commenced the beautiful sculptured screen which surrounds the choir of the cathedral. This work, on which many sculptors were employed, was not finished at his death. Before 1510 he enlarged the church of S. Aignan at Chartres, by means of an arch with a span of fourteen metres thrown across the river Eure, on which he built the new choir of the church. Le Texier and Martin Chambiges (see Chambiges, M.) were the last great champions of the Gothic style in France.

Gonse, *L'Art Gothique;* Gilbert, *Église cathédrale de Notre Dame de Chartres ;* L'Abbé Bulteau, *Description de la Cathédrale de Chartres ; Monographie de la Cathédrale de Chartres.*

TEZCACOAC. An Aztec arsenal.

TEZCALLI. (See Calli.)

THALAMIUM. In Greek architecture, an inner room or chamber ; especially, the women's apartment.

THALAMUS. Same as Thalamium.

THATCH. Roof covering of straw or reeds. Such a covering was generally 12 inches thick in England, and is said to have been better when several inches thicker. Wheat straw carefully combed and cleared of short pieces was considered the best material, except where good rushes were available. Thatch was often whitewashed as a partial preventive against fire, and even plastering or clay applied in a thick coat was used for the same purpose.

THEATRE. A building prepared for performances on the stage with some attempt by means of scenery and costume to represent special epochs and places as well as the special personages of the drama. It is, however, supposed by many archæologists following Dr. Dörpfeld, that the Greek theatre of the pre-Roman time had no raised stage — that the performers occupied a part of the pavement not raised above that of the orchestra. Where the ruins of Greek theatres are known to contain raised stages these are thought additions of Roman Imperial times. The Greek theatres, moreover, were rarely elaborate in their architectural arrangement ; it was usual to take advantage of the slope of a hill and to conform the arrangement of the seats to that natural slope with but little alteration, while the skene, or stage, with its surroundings and architectural background, was rarely of much pretension. The theatre at Epidauros is perhaps the easiest to trace in all its parts of all the theatres of purely Greek design, as the stone steps forming the seats are generally in place, and large fragments of the proscenium remain within reach. This also is known to history as the most important and splendid of the theatres of Greece, the circular space occupied by the orchestra was forty feet in diameter, with a fountain in the middle evidently for the altar of Dionysos. The low building back of the stage is probably of Roman time, but its design is as severe and almost as pure in detail as if it had been Greek of the great period, so that we may infer that the fame of the original theatre ascribed to Polyclitos (see Polyclitos) still controlled the Roman architects.

The Roman theatre, modelled upon that of the Greeks and consisting like it of a nearly semicircular funnel-shaped auditorium with seats either of wood or stone, differed from its prototype in having a semicircular space reserved for the chorus, and a stage much enlarged, raised high above the floor of the orchestra, and backed by somewhat elaborate architectural structures, often a two-story or three-story colonnaded building. The lavish way in which the Roman pro-consuls and prætors built is exemplified by the comparative indifference shown to taking advantage of the ground, as well as by the costly architectural work of the stage and proscenium. Where there was no convenient hillside the relief necessary was got by structures of wood, under the Republic, and by structures of stone toward the close of the Republic and under the Empire ; the system often involving very elaborate series of vaults, sometimes cylindrical, sometimes conical in shape, and supporting the cuneus or half cone of seats. The theatre of Marcellus, at Rome, has preserved for us more of the exterior of the auditorium than any other (see the cut under Alette), but the wall behind the stage and the other structures there can best be judged from the theatre at Orange (Vaucluse) in the south of France, where the great wall forming the back or outside of the proscenium stands almost intact, 140 feet high. The colonnades of the stage, which in this case was roofed and open on one side only, can be partly understood.

The modern theatre differs from the ancient in being always an enclosed building, one which so far from being a public monument with a semi-religious purpose, is devoted to pure amusement or to the dramatic art in its higher sense combined with amusement, and maintained by private persons for gain. The only exceptions to this rule are the subventions to theatres which are paid by certain European states ; thus in Paris, four theatres are separately aided by the state, the *Théâtre Français* being one. A modern theatre, then, consists properly of two buildings closely attached each to the other. The one of these contains the scenery and the galleries and passages for its arrangement and its easy management, together with the Dressing Rooms for actors, a Foyer or more foyers than one, and some few private rooms and offices. This building may be extremely simple, four-square, and roofed with an ordinary low-pitch roof, as nothing is needed but a large, safe, unobstructed interior in which the theatrical engineer and machinists can do their work. The architect cannot be said to have anything to do with the interior of such a building as we are describing, except on the side toward the auditorium, where the great arch of the proscenium must be built into the wall, and must be so arranged as to show with a decorative effect or to be compatible with other decorative arrangements on the side turned toward the public.

The stage projects at this point some distance beyond the proscenium arch except in some few instances, as where, in the great theatre of Bordeaux, the whole arrangement of the proscenium wall is unusual and includes towers of masonry which are utilized for boxes.

In the design of the opera house at Paris, *Théâtre de l'Opéra,* the building of the stage as described above rises high above the auditorium, the general lines of the design being extremely realistic and logical.

The other building, that which contains the auditorium, contains so much else in addition to this that frequently the auditorium seems in plan to be but a minor consideration. In any large modern theatre, vastly more superficial space on any one horizontal plane is occupied by lobbies, staircases, the foyer for the public,

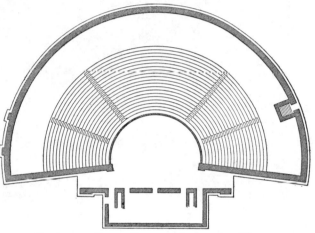

THEATRE OF ROMAN STYLE AT IASSUS, ASIA MINOR.

ticket offices, corridors, and the like, than for the mere seating of the spectators. All this has resulted from a natural evolution of the central idea, which is to make a certain limited number of people very comfortable during certain hours of the evening; and to provide for their exit from the building in a very short space of time, either in case of necessity, as of an alarm of fire, or for more convenience both to visitors and attendants. This matter of exit is especially important and is not adequately met by the providing of certain doorways which can be thrown open in case of need. The requisite is that the doorways known to the public and in daily use shall themselves be sufficient, allowing of unencumbered exit by the mere withdrawing or throwing down of slight temporary barriers. The number of seatings is generally kept down from considerations of acoustics, of easy view of the stage from all parts of the house, and of reluctance to have an auditorium so large that it will be but rarely filled. Thus, the opera house at Paris above alluded to, though built at lavish cost between 1865 and 1875, provides for only 2156 spectators; and the famous *Théâtre Français*, largely supported by the state, which supplies the house as well as an annual income, seats but 1520 persons. The famous *Odéon*, standing free on all sides and forming an architectural monument of some importance, has 1650 seatings. If this is expedient in the case of theatres for ordinary dramatic performances, it is still more desirable in the case of buildings for especially careful and serious musical entertainments (see Music Hall). — R. S.

Defrasse et Lechat, *Epidaure*.

THEOLOGEION. In the Greek theatre, the place where persons representing the deities of Olympos stood and spoke.

THEOPHILUS (Rugerus); monk and writer on art.

Theophilus, supposed to have been a German or Italian "priest and monk," wrote the mediæval technical manual of the arts entitled *Diversum artium schedula*. It was probably written late in the twelfth century, although the date is conjectured variously from the tenth to the thirteenth. The work is divided into

THEATRE: RUINS OF THE LARGER ONE AT POMPEII.

THEODORUS OF SAMOS; architect and artisan.

Flourished during the early part of the sixth century B.C., and was one of the principal artists of the earliest Greek school. In much of his work he was associated with Rhœkos and Smilis. Theodorus, Rhœkos, and Smilis built the labyrinth at Lemnos. According to Herodotus, Rhœkos built the Temple of Hera at Samos, a description of which was written by Theodorus. Theodorus was consulted about the construction of the temple of Artemis at Ephesos, begun about 576 B.C., and advised laying the foundations in charcoal. Theodorus designed the building called the Skias, at Sparta. Numerous temple statues and works in the precious metals were attributed to him, among others the famous ring of the tyrant Polykrates of Samos, and the silver wine cooler which was sent by Crœsus to Delphi.

Brunn, *Geschichte der griechischen Künstler*.

THEODOTOS; architect.

According to an inscription, Theodotos was architect of the temple of Æsculapius at Epidauros, Greece, built between 380 and 375 B.C.

three parts. The first part is on painting, the second on the manufacture and painting of glass, and the third on metal work. It was first noticed in the last century by Lessing, who discovered the manuscript in the library at Wolfenbüttel, Germany, of which he was librarian. There are manuscripts also in the libraries of Leipzig, Paris, Cambridge (Trinity College), and Venice. The first part was published by Raspe in his *Critical Essay on Oil Painting* in 1781, and the entire treatise by Leiste and Lessing in the same year. A Latin and French edition was published by Count de l'Escalopier in 1843. Another French edition with notes by Bourassé was published by J. P. Migne in *Nouvelle encyclopédie théologique*, Vol. 12, 1851. An English translation by Robert Hendrie was published in 1847 (see bibliography). A translation of the second book (on glass), from the French of de l'Escalopier, was published by Winston in his *Hints* (see bibliography). The manuscripts have been collated and the Latin text published with a German translation and appendix by A. Ilg (see bibliography).

Theophilus, ed. Ilg; Theophilus, ed. Hendrie;

A. Entrance to rear of stage.
B. Staircase to dressing rooms.
C. Service staircase.
D. Dwelling of the janitor.
E. Entrance for the musicians.
F. Foyer for the supernumeraries.
G. Foyer for stage carpenters.
H. Post of the firemen.
I. Passage for scenery.
J. Open court.
K. Passageway with stairs to stage.
L. Stage.
M. Room for direction of rehearsals.
N. Storeroom.
 1. Public vestibule.
 2 and 3. Ticket offices.
 4. Receipt of tickets.
 5. Office of commissary of police.
 6. Police officers.
 7. Staircase to the boxes.
 8. Open courts with toilet.
 9. Entrance for the chief of the state.
10. Entrance for persons alighting from carriages.
11. Staircase leading to box of chief of state.
12. Stairs for the audience.
13. Auditorium.
14. Communications between the auditorium and the stage.

The parts not referred to are shops opening on the street with private apartments in the *entresol*.

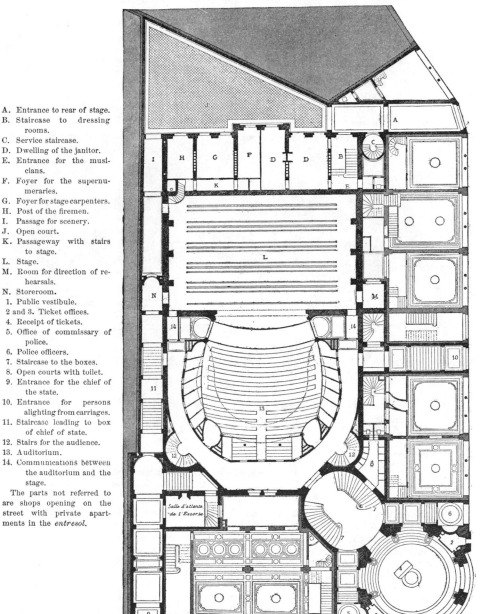

THEATRE: PLAN OF THE THÉÂTRE DU VAUDEVILLE, PARIS.

Winston, *Hints on Glass Painting;* Westlake, *History of Design in Painted Glass.*

THEOTOCOPULI, JORGE MANUEL; sculptor and architect; d. March 29, 1631.

A son and pupil of Domenico Theotocopuli (El Greco). March 10, 1625, he was made architect and sculptor of the cathedral of Toledo in Spain. In 1626 he began the cupola of the Capilla Muzarafe in this cathedral, and finished it in 1631.

THEOTOCOPULI (TEOSCOPOLI) DO-MENICO (EL GRECO); painter, sculptor, and architect; b. 1548 (in Greece, or perhaps in Venice); d. 1625.

thermæ in Rome in the reign of Diocletian, after the completion of the establishment bearing the name of that emperor, which was by far the largest; and over nine hundred smaller ones under the control of private citizens.

The peculiarity of the architectural plan is so great that it can be compared to that of no other class of buildings. The outer enclosure of the thermæ of Diocletian measured 1100 feet northeast and southwest, and nearly 1200 feet in the opposite direction, without including certain projections, as of exedræ and decorative alcoves and the like, of unknown use, one of which, a rotunda, retaining its ancient cupola,

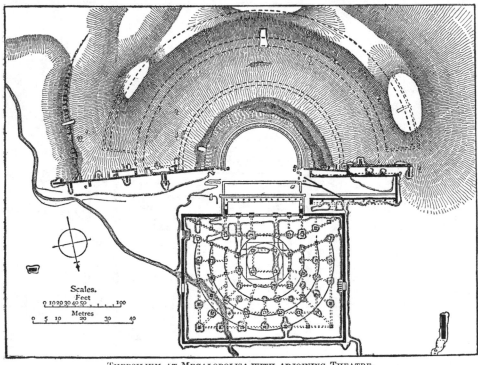

THERSILIUM AT MEGALOPOLIS; WITH ADJOINING THEATRE.

A pupil of Titian in Venice, and in 1577 was in Spain painting altar pieces in the style of Titian. He designed the church of the Caridad and the city hall at Toledo, Spain, the church of the college of Doña Maria de Arragon at Madrid, the church of the Franciscan Monastery at Illescas, with the marble tombs of its founders which have been destroyed.

Stirling-Maxwell, *Annals of the Artists of Spain.*

Bermudez, *Diccionario.*

THERMÆ. (Latin, hot baths; a plural noun.) An establishment for bathing, of which there are many in the different cities of the Roman Empire, some of extraordinary size and importance as works of elaborate architecture. According to Lanciani there were eleven large

is now the church of S. Bernardo. Within this and surrounded by open spaces the great block of the thermæ proper was about 480 by 750 feet, and included a vaulted hall (the Tepidarium) 80 feet wide, a part of which is now the nave of the church of S. Maria degli Angeli.

Here, as in the other thermæ, the tepid baths were small basins arranged around the edge of the great hall of the tepidarium. The caldarium or warm bath gave its name in like manner to the halls in which such baths were contained, which were in the large thermæ circular and crowned with a cupola; but this form is not to be supposed especially fitted for that purpose, for in the Stabian baths at Pompeii the frigidarium is circular, the caldarium a rectangle with an apse, and the tepidarium a simple rec-

PLATE XXIX

THESEION

The so-called temple of Theseus at Athens; a perfect example of Doric hexastyle temple, and the best-preserved one. Such repairs as were made in connection with its use as a mediæval church have not defaced the monument.

tangle, while another cold bath, the swimming basin, is entirely out of doors in this and in the other public thermæ of Pompeii, an arrangement which suits the much warmer climate of that city. The laconicum or sweat bath differs greatly in different establishments as to size, form, and connection with the other rooms, indicating a natural difference in the habits of the people. The vast extent of the thermæ is to be accounted for only by noting the palestræ or grounds for running and for exercise, lecture rooms, libraries, rooms, and porticoes for conversation, all of which were provided within the walls, and were elaborately built and richly adorned. (For a description of the Thermæ of Caracalla see Roman Imperial architecture; see also Italy, part IX.) — R. S.

Geymuller, *Documents Inédits sur les Thermes d'Agrippa, le Panthéon et les Thermes de Dioclétien;* Nispi-Landi, *M. A. e i suoi tempi; le terme ed il Pantheon;* Mau, *Pompeii, Its Life and Art;* also *Restaurations des Monuments Antiques* (Firmin-Didot), Vol. for 1825, *Thermes de Caracalla;* for 1841, *Thermes de Dioclétien;* for 1871–1872, *Thermes de Titus.*

THERMOSTAT. (See Electrical Appliances.)

THERSILIUM. A building at Megalopolis in Greece, described by Pausanias (VIII., XXXII.) as already in ruins, and as a council house for the Arcadian Ten Thousand. Recent excavations show that it was a hypostyle hall, 3500 square feet in area. It is fully discussed by Fraser, op. cit.

J. G. Fraser, *Pausanias's Description of Greece.*

THESEION. A temple or sanctuary dedicated to Theseus; especially a hexastyle peripteral Doric temple remaining at Athens, and long known by that name; but now ascertained to be a temple of Hephæstus (Vulcan).

THESILIUM. Same as Thersilium, probably a mistaken reading.

THICKNESS (v.). To bring to a uniform thickness; thus, it is common in specifications to state that the planks, as of a floor, must be accurately thicknessed. (See Match, v.)

THOLOBATE. The circular substructure of a dome.

THOLOS. In Greek and Greco-Roman architecture, a round building. The Tholos of Epidauros in the Morea, near the eastern coast, is the most celebrated; for, although entirely in ruins, it has been theoretically restored with great appearance of authenticity, and was evidently a building of extraordinary beauty. The interior order was Corinthian, and this affords, probably, the earliest instance which we have of fine Corinthian capitals in a building of pure Greek style. One capital was found in a kind of crypt or cell, underground, and was worked with the leafage differently subdivided in different parts, as if experimentally, the capital having served to all appearance

as a guide to the workmen who carved the others. (See cut, Vol. I., cols. 679, 680.) Besides the articles in archæological periodicals, the student should consult the work by Defrasse and Lechat, *Épidaure, Restauration et Description,* Paris, 1895. These writers think that the tholos was a spring house built over a sacred well which is known to have existed at Epidauros and to have been dedicated to the tutelary deity Asklepios. — R. S.

THOLOS OF ATREUS. (See Treasury of Atreus.)

THOMAS DE CORMONT. (See Cormont, Thomas de.)

THOMPSON, SIR BENJAMIN; Count Rumford; b. March 26, 1753 (at Woburn, Massachusetts); d. 1802 (at Paris); soldier and scientist.

The famous Benjamin Thompson who received from Charles Theodore, Elector of Bavaria, the title of Count Rumford, laid out the *Englischer Garten,* in Munich, Bavaria. (See Skell, F. L.)

Renwick, *Life of Count Rumford; American Architect,* Vol. XXII., 303.

THOMSON, ALEXANDER ("Greek Thomson"); architect; b. 1817 (at Balfron, Scotland); d. 1875.

He began life in a lawyer's office, where he was discovered by the architect, Robert Foote. About 1834 he entered the office of John Baird in Glasgow. Thomson made a special study of Greek architecture, and was famous for his successful adaptation of Greek motives. Among his many works in Glasgow are the churches in Caledonia Road, Vincent Street, and Queen's Park, the Egyptian Hall in Union Street, and many buildings in Gordon Street.

Obituary in *British Architect,* Vol. III., 1875; Stephen-Lee, *Dictionary of National Biography.*

THORNTON, DR. WILLIAM; architect.

The first advertisements in the competition for the Capitol at Washington were published in March, 1792. In October of that year Dr. William Thornton of the island of Tortola in the West Indies wrote to the commissioners asking permission to compete. His plans were submitted early in 1793, were much admired by the commissioners, and April 5th were approved by President Washington. The designs which were considered second in point of merit were those of Stephen Hallet, who was placed in charge of the construction of Thornton's design under the general direction of James Hoban (see Hoban), architect of the White House. Hallet was discharged Nov. 15, 1794. Sept. 12, 1794, the President appointed Thornton to be one of the commissioners in charge of the District of Columbia, and he had general supervision of the Capitol until his office was abolished in 1802. At this time the north wing of the older part of the

Capitol, now occupied by the Supreme Court, was complete, and the foundations and basement story of the south wing were partially laid. The exterior of this part of the building

THOROUGH STONE. Same as Through Stone.

THORPE, JOHN; architect.

The author of an architectural sketch book

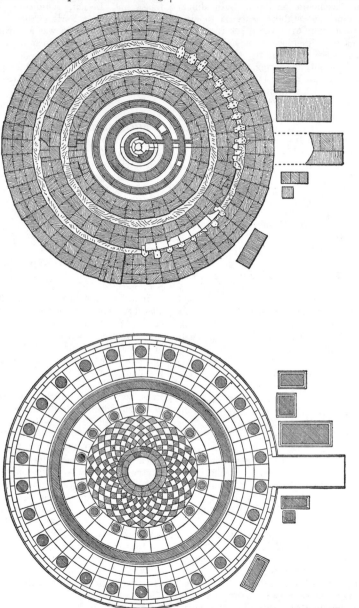

THOLOS AT EPIDAURUS AS IT EXISTS, AND AS RESTORED. THE OUTER ORDER IS DORIC; THAT WITHIN CORINTHIAN.

is still much as Thornton left it. After retiring Thornton was placed in charge of the Pension office and remained there until his death.

 Glenn Brown, *History of the United States Capitol;* Glenn Brown, *Dr. William Thornton* in *Architectural Record.*

preserved in the museum founded by Sir John Soane (see Soane, Sir J.). It is a folio volume of 282 pages, containing drawings of about 140 different buildings of the early sixteenth century in England. Many of these represent buildings in course of construction, others are sketches of existing buildings, others are copied from French works on architecture, especially those of Jacques Androuet Du Cerceau (see Androuet Du Cerceau, J. (I.)). There is also a record of a payment made to him in the issues of the Exchequer.

Gotch, *John Thorpe* in *Building News*, 1884, Vol. XLVI. ; Gotch and Brown, *Renaissance in England.*

THREE-CENTRED. Drawn from three centres ; constructed on three centres. (See Basket-handle Arch under Arch.)

THREE-COAT WORK. Plastering put on in three coats ; superior to two-coat work. Ordinarily, in three-coat work the first coat is rough mortar, the second is scratched, that is to say, scored with the trowel so as to enable the finishing coat to hold to it more firmly, and the third is the finishing coat, which may be of sand finish or white finish.

THREE PAIR. (See Two Pair.)

THRESHOLD. The sill of a door. The word is hardly used in connection with modern buildings, and has gained a rather poetical signification, being used in a general rather than in a particular sense. (See Saddle, A. ; Sill.)

THROAT. In a chimney, the passage from the fireplace to the flue. (See Chimney.)

THRONE. A chair of state, especially one appropriated to a monarch, or in ecclesiology, to a bishop (see Bishop's Throne). The throne of modern European sovereigns is merely an elaborately decorated armchair distinguished by its position on a raised platform and beneath a canopy with hangings, upon which emblems, heraldic devices, and the like may be embroidered. Eastern princes, whose position when seated is usually cross-legged or sitting upon the heels, have thrones which allow of a different treatment, and the throne in Persia, and anciently in other lands east of the Mediterranean, is a very splendid structure four or five feet wide and of twice the depth, supported by a number of columns, and covered with rich decoration and often with applications of costly materials. On the other hand, the Mikado of Japan seems not to have occupied a throne of any sort before the change in the government, but a raised platform only ; and the Shogun in ancient times, and the Tenno to-day, like the princes of China, seem to have used a highly decorated armchair, or in some cases a camp-stool curiously recalling the use of the curule chair by ancient Roman magistrates.

THRONE ROOM. A chief room of state containing the throne upon a dais and under a canopy.

THROUGH. In masonry, same as Perpend. (Compare Bond.)

THROUGH STONE. A bond stone passing through the wall and showing on both faces, as distinguished from a Stretcher. (Also Thorough Stone.)

THRUST. A force which pushes and tends to compress, crush, displace, or overturn a body ; as the thrust of an arch is the force tending to push back or overturn the pier or abutment. In an arch it may also be defined as the horizontal component of the reaction of the abutment, and, therefore, uniform throughout the arch. — W. R. H.

THULITE STONE. A red or pink manganese epidote of a fine granular texture and pleasing colour. As yet but little used. Found at Hinderheim, Norway. — G. P. M.

THUMB PIN ; THUMB TACK. A short, sharp pin with a large, flat head, designed to be thrust in by the pressure of the thumb ; used by draughtsmen.

THYMELE. In Greek architecture, an altar ; specifically, the altar of Dionysus, standing in the centre of the orchestra of a Greek theatre, and around which the chorus performed their evolutions.

TIBALDI, DOMENICO; architect ; b. 1541 ; d. 1583.

A younger brother of Pellegrino Tibaldi, whom he assisted in many of his undertakings. He built the choir of the church of S. Pietro, the archbishop's palace (1575–1577), the Palazzo Magnani Giadotti in the Piazza Rossini (one of his best works), the Palazzo Matteo, and the court of the Palazzo di Giustizia, all at Bologna. Although in the baroque style, his work shows much classical refinement.

(For bibliography, see Pellegrino Tibaldi.)

TIBALDI, PELLEGRINO; painter and architect ; b. 1527 ; d. 1598.

Tibaldi began as a painter, the pupil of Danielo da Volterra (see Ricciarelli). He was especially patronized by San Carlo Borromeo at Milan. Tibaldi applied the principles of Vignola (see Barozzio, G.) to a large number of churches and palaces. In 1560 he began the reconstruction of the façade of the cathedral of Milan. Of this work five doors and five windows remain. He built the fine church of S. Fidele, Milan, begun 1569, the court of the archbishop's palace, Milan, 1570, the Palazzo della Sapienza, Pavia, 1562, the church of S. Gaudenzio, Novara, 1577, the church of S. Francesco da Paola, Turin, and the court of the University, Bologna, 1570.

Müntz, *Renaissance;* Gurlitt, *Geschichte des Barockstiles in Italien;* Ebe, *Spät-Renaissance.*

TICPLANTLACALLI. (See Calli.)

TIE. Anything which is used to resist a pull, as to prevent the spreading of the two sides of a roof, the separating of the two solid parts of a hollow wall, the collapsing of a trussed beam, and the like. Much used in composition. (See Tie Beam and other titles below.)

Chain Tie. An iron tie to connect and hold securely the columns and piers in arched construction, or other parts of masonry buildings, by means of tie bars or rods having an eye at each end set upon the hooked ends, or pins, of other bars set in the masonry. Chain ties of many-linked bars were used to excess in French buildings of the last century, and are still used in Paris to tie the walls together through the floors, even where iron beams are used for the latter. Chain ties are also employed as belts about the bases of domes, and in consolidating defective masonry. (See Chain.)

Land Tie. A tie rod or chain tie used to hold a retaining wall, or out-of-door flight of stairs, or the like, against the pressure of the earth, as after rain. It is built into the wall and may be secured to a massive pier, or simply held to the earth by means of timbers or stone beams set crosswise.

TIJOU, JEAN; ironworker.

Tijou, a French ironworker, was employed by Sir Christopher Wren to make the iron screens in S. Paul's cathedral. He made the fine gates on the north side of the Long Walk at Hampton Court, which are now in the South Kensington Museum. He published *Nouveau livre de desseins* (1 vol. folio, 1693).

Blomfield, *Renaissance in England.*

TIKI. (See New Zealand, Architecture of.)

TILE. *A.* Primarily, a piece of solid material used for ·covering a roof of a building. Roof tiles may be either flat or may be of different sections, so as to produce ridges and valleys, and so that one form covers the joints between tiles of another form, as will be explained below.

B. Any slab of hard material, large or small, but especially one of many rather small pieces, used together to form roofing, flooring,

TILES OF BAKED CLAY FOR HOLDING TOGETHER THE PARTS OF A HOLLOW WALL; THE SLOPE COMING IN THE AIR SPACE.

TIE BEAM. In common wooden framed construction, especially in roofing, the large horizontal piece which crosses from wall to wall, or between any points of support, forming the lowest member of a truss, and into which the rafters are framed, its centre being often kept from sagging by a king-post. (See Roof; Truss.)

TIE ROD. A rod, usually of iron, used as a tie to prevent the spreading of an arch, or of a piece of framing in wood or iron. In the commonest form it replaces the tie beam, the king-post, or other simple member intended to resist tension.

TIEPOLO, GIOVANNI BATTISTA; painter; b. 1693; d. 1770.

By a sympathetic study of the great decorators of the sixteenth century, Tiepolo succeeded in reviving their methods and traditions. He painted an extraordinary series of frescoes in Venice, Würzburg, and Madrid.

Urbani de Gheltof, *Tiepolo;* J. E. Wessely, *Tiepolo;* Zanetti, *Pittura Veneziana;* Molmenti, *La Villa Valmarana;* Lanzi, *Storia Pittorica;* Orlandi, *Abecedario.*

TIERCE POINT. (See Tiers Point.)

TIERCERON. In later mediæval vaulting, a secondary or intermediate rib springing from the pier on either side of the diagonal ribs or arcs doubleaux.

TIERS POINT. In French, the point where the two determining arcs of a pointed arch meet, the apex. The term means originally the third or culminating point of a triangle.

Arc en Tiers Point. A pointed arch.

wall facing, or the like. Much the greater number of tiles have always been made of baked clay in some form; but marble, stone, and other materials are used.

C. By extension, and because of the application of the name to all pieces of baked clay used for accessories to building, a piece of drain pipe; one section of a continuous tube. In this sense often called Draining Tile or Drain Tile.

D. A piece of hard material, especially of baked clay, used for any purpose whatever, even for the preserving of written records, as in the case of those libraries entirely composed of inscribed tiles which have been found in Mesopotamia. (See, for the manufacture of Tiles, Keramics.)

Amé, *Les carrelages émaillés du moyen âge et de la renaissance;* Bourgoin, *Les Arts Arabes;* Brenci and Lessing, *Majolika-Fliesen aus Siena, 1500–1550;* Jacobsthal, *Süd-italienische Fliesenornamente, nach Originalaufnahmen;* Prisse d'Avennes, *L'Art Arabe d'après les monuments du Kaire;* Rossi, *Musaici Cristiani e saggi dei pavimenti delle chiese di Roma* (for pavements of marble, etc.).

Book Tile. In the United States, a hollow terra-cotta tile for light fireproof roofs and ceilings; so called from its having the form of a closed book. When laid, the convex edge of one fits into the concave edge of the next, the other, plane edges being supported by light T irons, or the like.

Covering Tile. Same as Tegula.

Crest Tile. One made to form part of a cresting or ridge covering, as of a roof. It may form part of a very elaborate cresting.

Crown Tile. A flat roofing tile, called also in England "plain," "thack," or "roof" tile. The size has varied under different royal or parliamentary acts; $5\frac{3}{4}$ by $9\frac{1}{2}$ inches and $6\frac{1}{2}$ by $12\frac{1}{2}$ inches, $\frac{5}{8}$ inch thick, are common sizes. They are laid like slates with two nailings upon laths or battens, with or without mortar. The term is also applied to a Ridge Tile.

Dutch Tile. A wall tile of enamelled and painted earthenware; the term was applied originally to those made at Delft and elsewhere in the Netherlands, and used for the facing of chimney pieces and the like. They are generally painted in dark blue on a white ground.

Encaustic Tile. In English keramic work, a tile decorated with a painted pattern, as distinguished from one of a uniform colour, which is called a mosaic tile. The term "encaustic" is inaccurate as used here, and is to be considered a trade name.

Foot Tile. A paving tile 12 inches square.

Gutter Tile. Same as Imbrex.

Hip Tile. A Ridge Tile so formed as to serve for the covering of a hip; each tile lapping over the one next below.

Hollow Tile. Same as Hollow Brick (which see under Brick).

Pan Tile. *A.* A roofing tile having a concave surface, distinguished as an Imbrex or Gutter Tile, alternating with one having a convex surface, distinguished as a Tegula or Covering Tile; the joint between two of the former is covered by one of the latter, so that when laid, the surface of the roof presents a series of ridges and furrows running continuously from the ridge to the eaves; hence, this species of tiling is sometimes called ridge and furrow tiling.

B. A roofing tile made with a ridge and furrow in each piece, or with a double curvature, so that, when laid, the upturned edge of the concave part of one tile is fitted to the downward-turned edge of the adjoining tile, making a water-tight joint, with the same general effect as is secured by the first-named system. — H. V. B.

Plane Tile. A flat roofing tile, usually about the size of a small slate.

Ridge Tile. A tile of arched form made to fit over a ridge and to correspond with the pan tiles or flat tiles of the roof. Somewhat similar tiles are laid over the hips. Otherwise called crown tiles. In some cases the raised arched ridge is a part of the same tile with the flat covering part. The whole is then called a ridge tile.

Roll Roofing Tile. One of which the joints are covered by overlap, or of separate gutter-shaped pieces inverted. When laid such tiles form a series of continuous ridges alternating with furrows running at right angles or diagonally to the ridge pole. (See Pan Tile.)

Wall Tile. Tile, thinner than floor tile, especially adapted to the facing of a wall, as in the lining of a passage or in a bathroom.

Weather Tile. A tile used as a substitute for shingles, slates, or weatherboards in covering the walls or roof of a frame building; such tiles are thin, pierced with holes for nailing, arranged to overlap, and often cut with round or polygonal-shaped tails.

TILE CREASING. (See Creasing.)

TILE PIN. A pin of hard wood passing through a hole in a roof tile and into the wood beneath to keep the tile in place.

TILING. *A.* The art and the practice of laying tile of any description.

B. A quantity of tile taken together and acting as one covering, facing, or the like, as in the phrase, a floor covered with tiling. (See Keramics; Tile.)

TILTING FILLET; TILTING PIECE. Same as Arris Fillet.

TILT YARD. A place reserved for the joust and the tournament, and in later times for riding at the ring, and similar exercises. Such grounds were not always mere lists enclosed from the open country, but were sometimes reserved in the courts of castles; indeed, the outer court, or *Basse Cour*, was often arranged for this purpose. (See List.)

TIMBER. Wood, whether growing or cut, of such quality and size as fit it for use in building; excluding that which has been cut up into planks or boards, and, in the United States, that cut smaller than about 6 by 6 inches. (See Scantling.)

TIMOTHEOS; sculptor.

According to an inscription of about 375 B.C., Timotheos made the sketches from which the sculptural decoration of the temple of Æsculapius at Epidaurus in Greece was executed. The inscription gives the names of the sculptors who carried out the work. He was also associated with Bryaxis (see Bryaxis), Leochares (see Leochares), and Scopas (see Scopas), in the decoration of the mausoleum at Halicarnassus.

Defrasse et Lechat, *Epidaure;* Cavvadias, *Epidaure.*

TIN. Same as Tin Plate; the abbreviated commercial term.

TINO DI CAMAINO; architect and sculptor.

A pupil of Giovanni da Pisa (see Giovanni da Pisa) who was employed on the cathedral of Siena after 1300. He made several monuments in Florence, the most important of which is that of the Emperor Henry VII. In the will of Maria, widow of Charles II. of Naples, Tino is chosen to construct her tomb. He is mentioned in other documents as architect of several buildings in the vicinity of Naples.

Reymond, *Sculpture Florentine;* Perkins, *Tuscan Sculptors.*

TIN PLATE. Sheet-iron plates coated with tin, after having been cleaned, toughened, and annealed by various mechanical processes. It is largely used for the covering of roofs of very low pitch; and also for flashing in connection with slate and shingles.

TINTORETTO (JACOPO ROBUSTI); painter.

Ridolfi's *Maraviglie* is the principal source of information about Tintoretto. He served a short apprenticeship with Titian and Schiavone. Tintoretto was a most prolific painter, and the greater part of his work is to be found in Venice. The most important of his mural pictures are in the church of S. Maria del' Orto, the Scuola di S. Rocco, and the Doge's Palace.

Ridolfi, *Le Maraviglie dell' Arte;* Janitschek, *Tintoret* in *Dohme Series;* Berenson, *Venetian Painters of the Renaissance;* Lanzi, *Storia Pittorica.*

TI'PI. (tee'-pee). [From the Dakota "ti," a house. As "pi" is a common plural ending, it is probable that in the beginning the form "tipi," applied to a single structure, grew out of our mistaking plural for singular.] (See "ti" and "pi" in the *Dakota-English Dictionary,* Vol. VII.; *Contributions to N. A. Ethnology,* U. S. G. S., pp. 421, 467.) The Dakota special name for skin tent is *wa-ke'-ya* ⟨wah-kay'-ah⟩, and for any shelter, *wo'-ke-ya.*

TIPI OF BUFFALO HIDE; DAKOTA TYPE.

A conical Indian tent composed of a number of poles, with their upper ends tied together near the top, spread into a circle on the ground, and covered with skins, or in recent times with canvas. Primarily the portable tipi is a Dakota structure, belonging to the Plains, but the same thing is in wide use among other Indian tribes, and the term now has an equal range. The tipi has also been copied with modifications in the United States army "Sibley" tent. As a *portable* skin tent it seems to have been perfected by the Dakotas, but it should be noted that other tribes (as well as the Dakotas) made bark-covered tents, and the Iroquois constructed a triangular one with bark covering, on similar principles. The poles of the tipi are 7 to 20 or 30 in number, and 15 to 18 feet long, tied together near the small ends, while the large ends enclose a circle 10 or 15 feet in diameter. According to Morgan the proper number of poles is 13. The cover, being drawn around the poles, is pinned together by sticks thrust crosswise through holes, or laced, for about the middle third of the distance from top to bottom, leaving the lower third open for a doorway and the upper third for a smoke outlet. The door was protected by an extra skin fastened, only by the top, to the tent outside, and spread by a stick fixed transversely near its upper end. Sometimes a loose skin was adjusted outside to the apex of the tent to form a hood that could be turned according to the wind direction; but the usual practice was to place long outside poles in pockets provided in each of the two triangular ends of the skin cover, by means of which these flaps could be arranged from below. If there was no wind, they were both left open; but otherwise they were adjusted accordingly, the windward flap being set high, while the leeward one was drawn down close to the frame, leaving only hole enough for the exit of smoke. The tipi was fastened to the ground by pegs through holes in the edges of the skins made for the purpose, and in high winds stones or other weights were laid on the bottom portions. In travelling the poles were attached to the sides of horses; and the long ends, trailing on the ground, furnished a vehicle for various articles of baggage. — F. S. DELLENBAUGH.

TIPPLE HOUSE. A rough shed or house to protect the tipples or dumps of a coal mine.

TIRANT. A tie rod or tie beam. (Anciently tiraunt.)

T IRON. In Iron Construction, a member approximating in section to the form of the Roman letter T (compare I Bar, etc.).

TITIAN. (See Vecelli, Tiziano.)

TIYOTIPI. Among the Dakota Indians, a soldier's lodge. A sort of council tent, as well as a feasting and lounging place. Regulations for the camp, and especially for the hunt, were made in it and published by means of a crier. (See Tipi.) — F. S. D.

TLILLANCALLI. An Aztec building used for a military school. — F. S. D.

TOIL. In a hinge, the same as Flap. — (A. P. S.)

TOILET ROOM. *A.* Same as Lavatory.

B. In a hotel, railway station, theatre, or the like, a room for washing, usually having water-closets, etc., connected with it, and often having in connection with it a place for the storage of out-of-door garments. (Compare Cloakroom; Coatroom.)

TOLEDO, JUAN BAUTISTA. (See Juan Bautista di Toledo.)

TOLLBOOTH. A stall or office where tolls in any sense are to be paid; hence, by extension, in a way variously explained, a jail, especially in Scotland.

TOLLHOUSE. Same as Tollbooth in its original sense; in the United States a house near the tollgate of a turnpike or bridge where tolls are paid, and serving as the residence of the keeper.

TOLMEN. Same as Dolmen; but some attempt has been made to apply the term to a stone pierced by a hole, of prehistoric or unknown date.

TOLOMEI. (See Federighi.)

TOLSA, MANUEL; architect, engineer, and sculptor; b. about 1750 (at Valencia, Spain); d. about 1810 (in Mexico).

In 1781 he went to Mexico as government architect. He directed the erection of the towers of the cathedral of the city of Mexico, 1787–1791, designed the College of Mines in Mexico, 1797, and other buildings. In 1798 he was appointed director of the Academy of S. Carlos, city of Mexico. His chief work is the fine equestrian statue of Carlos IV., now in the *Pasco de Bucareli*, city of Mexico.

Appleton, *Cyclopædia of American Biography*.

TOLTEC ARCHITECTURE. That of the pre-Aztec inhabitants of Mexico and contiguous country, attributed to a race called Toltec. (See Mexico, Architecture of, § I.) — F. S. D.

TOMASO DI ANDREA PISANO; sculptor.

According to Vasari (*Vita di Andrea Pisano*), he completed the Campo Santo and Campanile at Pisa. Documents of 1368 discovered by Professor Bonaini prove that he was the son of Andrea da Pisa (see Andrea da Pisa).

Vasari, Milanesi ed.; Vasari, Blashfield-Hopkins ed.

TOMB. Primarily, a grave, perhaps a hollow in a rock or a natural cave used for this purpose rather than an excavation in the earth. More usually, a monument of some importance, but always placed at a grave or erected for the purpose of forming the burial place within itself. Thus, the tombs in many churches and some of those erected out of doors during the Middle Ages contain each a sarcophagus in which the body was really laid, the lid being usually very heavy, and commonly secured as strongly as possible. The Cenotaph is sometimes, but improperly, called a tomb.

A tomb of the most magnificent sort is often called a Mausoleum; one of the simplest sort is called Gravestone, burial slab, or the like.

Difference in custom is extremely marked in the matter of tombs, as of all burial arrangements. The tower-like structures on the hillsides above Palmyra seem all to be of Roman date. They have but little ornamentation, and their comparatively great size (one of them is 80 feet high and nearly 30 feet square) and their striking composition, are all that call attention to them; but these are rather close copies of Greek tombs certainly four hundred years earlier, of which some still remain on the hillsides of Asia Minor, and some have been removed bodily to European museums. The famous Harpy Tomb (which see, below) is one of these. Other Greek tombs exist on the main-

land of Greece and in the colonies (for those which are merely slabs, however rich, see Gravestone; Stele). Large ones are the Nereid Tomb (which see, below); the Heroön, so called, of Gjolbaschi (which see, under Heroum); the Lion Tomb at Cnidus (Knidos) (see Lion Tomb, II., below); and of irregular work, the extraordinary tombs, partly rock-cut and partly built, recently discovered in the hill country of Asia Minor (for one of which see Lion Tomb, I., below). The Romans of the Empire, although using cremation rather than sepulture, and placing the cinerary urns in Columbaria, yet made these receptacles into decorative structures; moreover, sepulture was never entirely abandoned. The result is that the Campagna of

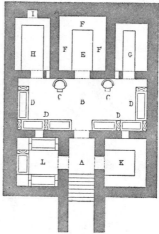

TOMB, FIG. 1, OF THE TWO SEATS, CERVETRI, ITALY; PLAN.

A, entrance. B, outer chamber with the two seats, C, and later sarcophagi, D. E, G, H, K, Tombal chambers with platforms, F, on which bodies were laid. L, chamber with sarcophagi.

Rome contains many tombal structures; and ruins of a vast number can be traced. These were commonly arranged outside the gates of towns, as in the well-known case of Pompeii, and on the Via Appia, south of Rome; but also in what seem to have been private plots of ground, probably not often reserved for the express purpose of a tomb, but rather forming part of the gardens, etc., accompanying a place of residence. The tomb of Cecilia Metella, and several others named in the subtitles, are instances of these. The pyramid of Caius Cestius and the sarcophagus of the Scipios are earlier instances of the same sort of decorative treatment.

The tombs of Moslems generally take the form of a nearly square vaulted structure of brick with a small dome. The vaulted chamber above ground has a door of entrance, and it is customary to resort there at certain times. The actual grave is usually a vaulted chamber beneath. The most magnificent tombs among the

TOMB, FIG. 2, OF THE TWO SEATS, AT CERVETRI, ITALY. SEE PLAN.

TOMB, FIG. 3, THAT OF CÆCILIA METELLA, NEAR ROME, 1ST CENTURY, B.C. THE BATTLEMENTS ARE
MEDIÆVAL, THE TOWER HAVING BEEN INCLUDED IN A CASTLE. SEE FIG. 4.

Moslems are those buildings outside the walls of Cairo, generally called tomb mosques. These are really places of worship, and might perfectly well be compared with the mosques of the city itself, or of other centres of the worship of Islam. There are a number of these buildings, larger and smaller, some of them adorned with minarets of extraordinary beauty, and they form

Tombs of the neoclassic period in Europe have been generally set up in churches. Even those of princes have seldom been large mausoleums, especial memorials taking generally other forms, as votive chapels, or monuments, unconnected with the grave itself. The same tendency existed throughout the nineteenth century. The tomb of the private person of wealth is apt

TOMB, FIG. 4, SECTION (SEE FIG. 3). THE SOLID CORE OF MASONRY FACED WITH BLOCKS OF CUT STONE WAS ORIGINALLY CROWNED BY A CONICAL OR STEPPED ROOF-LIKE COVERING.

almost a town outside the eastern gate of Cairo, which is known by the common name of Karafa, or the cemetery. Among the Christian nations of Europe the tomb took many forms, which are best described under the subtitles : Altar Tomb ; Wall Tomb ; and the like. The most important out-of-door structures of the Middle Ages are those at Verona (for which see Scala Tomb, below).

to be a family monument (compare Grave Monument), and in connection with this, the family tombs of American cemeteries should be mentioned, which have usually a chamber for the access of the living, and separate receptacles for coffins opening out of it on one side or on many sides, or opening upon a burial chamber beneath the pavement. These "family vaults," as they are popularly called, are sometimes of great size and cost ; one near New York city is octagonal and of general Byzantine form, vaulted and very

TOMB, FIG. 5, THAT OF IAMLICHUS, PALMYRA, A.D. 83.

massive, each side of the octagon having three receptacles for coffins opening sidewise into the

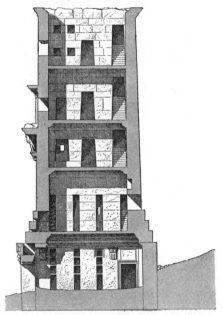

TOMB, FIG. 6, THAT OF IAMLICHUS ; SECTION, SEE FIG. 5.

central chamber. The more usual form is, however, a parallelogram with some reference to the

815

form of a Greek temple, and this, although entirely above ground or built upon a hillside from which it seems to emerge. — R. S.

Altar Tomb. A tomb built in the general form of an altar. This kind of sepulchre originated from the custom the early Christians had of placing beneath or within their altars the bodies of the martyrs. Upon many altar tombs

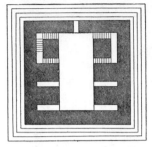

TOMB, FIG. 7, THAT OF IAMLICHUS ; PLAN ; SEE FIG. 5.

erected during the Middle Ages and the Renaissance there are recumbent effigies of the deceased, accompanied with heraldic devices.
— C. C.

Harpy Tomb. An ancient tomb discovered at Xanthos in Asia Minor, and decorated with a remarkable frieze at the top of the square vertical shaft, and set about 18 feet above the site. The sculptured parts are now in the British Museum.

TOMB, FIG. 8, 4TH CENTURY A.D., AT DANA, IN SYRIA.

High Tomb. One raised from the floor instead of being a mere slab inlaid in the pavement. Usually an Altar Tomb.

Lion Tomb (I.). A tomb adorned by the effigy of a lion. Of these there are several

816

PLATE XXX

TOMB. PLATE I

That of Leonardo Bruni in the church of S. Croce, at Florence. This is a masterpiece of Bernardo Rossellino. Bruni, the historian, died in 1444, and the tomb must have been erected almost immediately afterward.

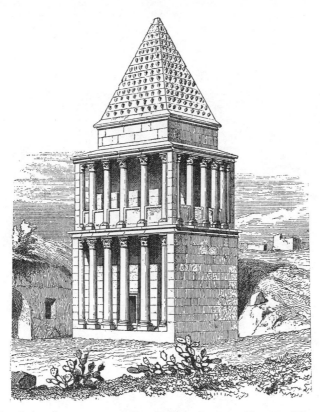

TOMB, FIG. 9, 4TH CENTURY A.D.; ABOUT 35 FEET SQUARE; KHURBET-HÂSS, IN SYRIA.

TOMB, FIG. 11, SURROUNDING A COURT OR CHURCHYARD AT MESCHUM, SYRIA.

TOMB, FIG. 10, THOSE AT KHURBET-HÂSS, IN SYRIA; SEE FIG. 9.

TOMB, FIG. 17, IN CLOISTER S. ANTONIO, PADUA; A MURAL PAINTING UNDER THE CANOPY.

among the ruins of primeval Greece and Western Asia. The full significance of the lion in

TOMB, FIG. 12, OF 6TH CENTURY, AT RONEIHA, SYRIA; SEVENTEEN FEET SQUARE WITHOUT THE LITTLE PORCH. THIS FORM, WITH CUPOLA, HAS BEEN COPIED BY THE MOSLEM PEOPLES FOR CENTURIES.

these compositions is not perfectly understood. At Ayazinn, in Asia Minor, is a tomb recently

TOMB, FIG. 19, IN THE PAVEMENT, CHURCH OF S. M. DEL POPOLO, ROME, 1479.

discovered, the front of which is decorated by two lions carved in the rock, their position

being similar to that of those on the Lion Gateway at Mycene. They are much larger, however, their size being apparently 18 feet long, and they are rudely carved in very high relief. As the tomb is almost wholly inaccessible, it has been drawn and described from a distance. Another tomb, with sculptures of

TOMB, FIG. 16, THAT OF MASINO II DELLA SCALA; c. 1351, A.D., AT VERONA.

better quality, exists near Beykeui, in Asia Minor, and this, which the explorer, Professor W. M. Ramsay, calls "The Broken Lion Tomb," is a very large rock-cut sepulchral chamber with the entrance 20 feet above the ground, and most interesting and curious proto-Ionic columns. The head only is left of the lion, but it is a powerful and vigorous piece of archaic sculpture. This tomb was also adorned by relief sculpture of warriors combatting, a precious and unique piece of archaic sculpture not wholly explained.

Lion Tomb (II.). One found at Cnidus by Sir Charles Newton of the British Museum, and now preserved in that institution, was adorned by a crouching lion 10 feet long, and

Scala Tomb. One of the monuments in the little churchyard of S. Maria Antica at Verona, all of which belong to the ruling family, Della Scala, powerful from 1260 to 1380. The monument of Can Grande is over the church door. This is of great beauty, and

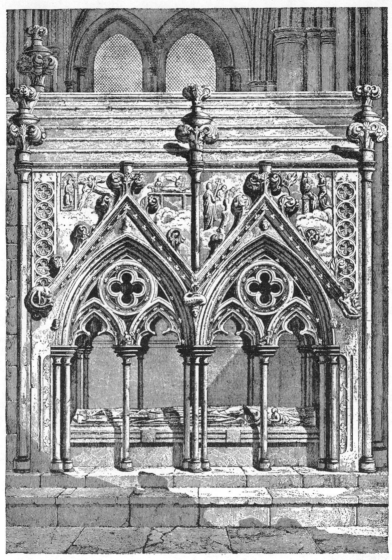

TOMB, FIG. 13, THAT OF BISHOP GILES OF BRIDPORT, 1262, A.D. CATHEDRAL AT SALISBURY, WILTSHIRE. ALTAR TOMB UNDER CANOPY.

this formed the apex or finial of a monument of great height. The conjectural restoration by Mr. Pullan shows an oblong basement carrying a superstructure of solid masonry decorated with engaged columns and entablature, and this crowned by a stepped pyramid, the lion and his own pedestal resting upon this, the whole about 63 feet high.

it is unusually severe and formal. The culminating point of the peculiar system of design, constituting almost an independent style, is in the monument of Mastino II., of which a cut is given. There is a larger and later tomb, still splendid, but of degenerate style.

Tunnel Tomb. In Egyptian archæology, a tomb excavated in the rock, usually of the

PLATE XXXI

TOMB. PLATE II

Monument in the church of S. Thomas at Strasburg, commemorating the Marshal Maurice de Saxe, who died in 1750. It is the work of the sculptor Jean Baptiste Pigalle, and perhaps his masterpiece. It is also the finest specimen in Europe of the descriptive and highly allegorical tomb of the eighteenth century. France personified tries to keep back Saxe from his open tomb, which he faces cheerfully, and to banish Death. Hercules appears as a Mourner, and the creatures emblematic of the Empire, England, and the United Provinces, are seen in terror and flight.

TOMB, FIG. 14, OF 14TH CENTURY, ASSISI, IN UMBRIA; CHURCH OF S. FRANCESCO.

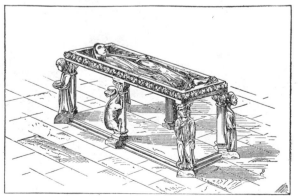

TOMB, FIG. 15, IN A CHURCH AT LIMBURG, GERMANY; 14TH CENTURY.

TOMB, FIG. 18, THAT OF KING LADISLAUS († 1414) IN CHURCH OF S. GIOVANNI
CARBONARA, NAPLES.

period of the Theban empire, and, therefore, of a time later than that of the Mastaba (which see). The general type is that of a tunnel leading horizontally into the rock from which a deep shaft leads to the burial chamber below. (See Egypt, Architecture of.)

TONDINO. A moulding of convex rounded section, especially a large one, such as a torus ; the Italian term sometimes used in English.

TONGUE. A projecting member, as a tenon ; a continuous ridge left on the edge of a board or plank, and intended to fit into a groove worked in the edge of another board or plank. The joint so made is in constant use in flooring, and is used occasionally in the siding of houses. Tongued and grooved flooring is objected to by some because, when heavy pressure comes at a point near the edge of a plank, one side of the groove may break away and the floor be permanently injured ; in this way, in the United States, the best floors in Boston are laid without this joint, and those in New York almost universally with it.

tenoned frame. On either side of the tenon a strip of hard wood is let in to the shoulder

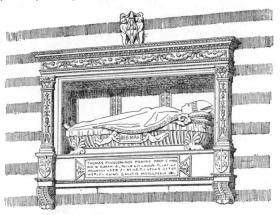

TOMB, FIG. 20, SIENA CATHEDRAL, c. 1483.

of the piece upon which the tenon is worked, and these strips fit into slots cut on either side of the mortise in the other piece, thus giving great additional stiffness.

Riley, *Building Construction.*

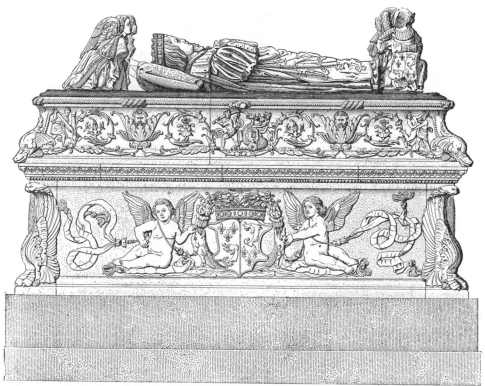

TOMB, FIG. 21, THAT OF THE SONS OF CHARLES VIII., AT TOURS.

Cross Tongue. A piece of the nature of a dowel used to give additional strength to a

Loose Tongue. A slender strip for securing the joint between two abutting parts by being driven into two corresponding grooves formed on their respective adjoining faces or edges. (Compare Dowel; Spline.)

TONGUED AND GROOVED. Finished with tongues and grooves, as the planks intended for flooring. Usually, each plank has

other material or the same material may be bonded into it and make a continuous surface. The jamb stones of an aperture are made long and short so as to tooth in with the general wall surface, whether of stone or brick.

TOOTHED CHISEL. A chisel of which

TOMB, FIG. 22, THAT OF BENEDETTO PESARO, CHURCH OF S. MARIA GLORIOSA DEI FRARI, VENICE.

one edge tongued and the other grooved. (See Tongue.)

TOOL (v.). To finish or dress a surface, especially of stone, so as to leave the marks of the tool; said especially of work with the Drove Chisel and the Toothed Chisel.

TOOL HOUSE. A house where tools are kept, especially farming tools.

TOOTH AXE. (See Axe, II.).

TOOTHING. Leaving projections or tenons on the end of a wall, so that when required an-

the cutting edge is indented, used to roughen regularly, give texture to, or dress a surface of masonry.

TOOTH ORNAMENT. In Romanesque and early Gothic architecture, an ornament consisting of a series of little pyramids often cut to form four-leaved flowers, projecting generally from a hollow moulding. Called also Dog Tooth Moulding.

TOPE. A Buddhist monument, common in India and Southeastern Asia, consisting of a tumulus of masonry, generally domical in form, for the preservation of relics, when it is distinguished as a Dagoba; or to commemorate an event, when it is called a Stupa. It is sometimes elevated on a square, cylindrical, or polygonal substructure built vertically or in terraces, and is nearly always crowned with a finial, called a Tee, shaped like an umbrella. (See India, Architecture of.)

TOPIARY. Relating to the clipping of trees and shrubs into regular or fantastic shapes, in a formal garden. This practice is called the topiary art.

TOP OUT (v.). To finish the top of anything, as of a chimney; to cap. In brickwork, such a finish is called the topping-out courses.

TORAN; TORANA. In Buddhist architecture, a gateway, composed of from one to three horizontal lintels, generally of wood, but sometimes of stone, placed one above another upon two posts, the whole being often elaborately carved. Similar gateways are, in Japan, called Torii, and are used to give dignity to the approach to a shrine or sacred place. (See India, Architecture of (*Buddhist Structural Monuments*); Japan, Architecture of.)

TORCH. In architectural decoration, an emblem founded upon sculptured representations; in Greco-Roman work, usually, of a bundle of strips held together by occasional withes or bands. This feature is generally repeated without a clear understanding of its significance. The torch inverted is used to symbolize death, probably because of the obvious idea of turning the burning torch downward in order to extinguish the flame against the ground.

TORCH HOLDER. (See Bracciale.)

Torch Holder; Bronze, 15th Century; Palazzo del Magnifico, Siena.

TORELLI, GIACOMO; painter and architect; b. 1608; d. 1678.

Torelli was especially associated with the rapid development of the construction and

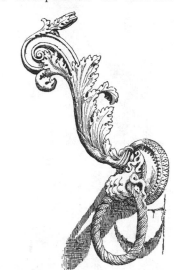

Torch Holder; Bronze, 15th Century; Palazzo del Magnifico, Siena.

decoration of theatres and scene painting in the seventeenth century. He made improvements in his native city, Fano, in Italy, which were engraved and attracted much attention. He was called to Venice, and at the theatre of SS. Giovanni e Paolo in that city invented a method of changing scenes which was universally adopted. Torelli was called to Paris by Louis XIV., and remained there until 1662. He arranged the theatre of the Petit Bourbon. The *Andromeda* of Corneille was first placed upon the stage by him. Returning to Fano, he built the still existing Teatro della Fortuna.

Gurlitt, *Geschichte des Barockstiles in Italien;* Milizia, *Memorie.*

TORII. (See Toran.)

TORREGIANO, PIETRO (PETER TORRYSANY); sculptor and architect; b. 1472; d. about 1522.

Torregiano was one of the boys selected by Lorenzo de' Medici to study in the Gardens of S. Marco, Florence, where he was associated with Michelangelo. Leaving Florence, he entered the army of Cæsar Borgia. About 1503 he drifted to England. In 1512 he made the contract for the monument to Henry VII. in Westminster Abbey. The monument to Margaret, Countess of Richmond, also in Westminster Abbey, is ascribed to him. The latter part of his life was spent at Seville in Spain. Some unimportant monuments in the churches of that city are supposed to be by him.

Perkins, *Tuscan Sculptors;* Müntz, *Renaissance;* George Gilbert Scott, *Gleanings from Westminster Abbey;* Neale, *Westminster Abbey.*

TOWER: CENTRAL TOWER OF CHURCH AT NOGENT LES VIERGES (OISE), FRANCE, 12TH CENTURY.

TORRYSANY, PETER. (See Torregiano, Pietro.)

TORSEL. A piece of solid material used to receive the end of a beam or girder and so distribute the weight over the masonry of the wall beneath. Stone, iron, and even hard wood are used for this purpose. (Compare Templet.)

TORSION. The act or result of twisting, as of a timber so distorted in drying or under some especial strain.

TORSIONAL STRENGTH. The strength of a member or material to resist a torsional force; *i.e.* a force tending to separate or break by twisting; an abbreviated and erroneous term. (See Resistance; Strength of Materials.)

TORSO. An imperfect statue, of which the body alone, or the body with parts of the limbs, is in place and tolerably perfect. By extension, the body of a complete statue. The adjectival term

835

applied to a twisted or spiral shaft is founded on confusion between a French and an Italian term of wholly different meanings, and should be avoided.

TORUS. A bold projecting moulding, convex in section, forming generally the lowest member of a base over the plinth, especially of a column or pilaster. When two tori are used, separated by a scotia with fillets, the parts being of normal relative size, the combination forms an Attic Base.

TOSH NAILING. Same as Blind Nailing (which see under Nailing).

TOTEM POST. A wooden post set up in front of a dwelling by some North American Indians, carved with totemic emblems. The most remarkable are those of the tribes of the Northwest coast, like the Haida. — F. S. D.

TOURELLE. In French, a turret; in English, especially one which is corbelled out from the wall or springing from a group of piers or buttresses, as on the angle of a larger building, and finishing with a steep conical roof.

TOWEL PATTERN. Same as Linen Pattern.

TOWER. A structure, of any form in plan, which is high in proportion to its lateral dimensions; or which is an isolated building with vertical sides and simple character, even if not high in proportion (see Tower of Silence); or a part of a structure higher than the rest, but always having vertical sides for a part of its separate and detached altitude; or, in buildings erected for defence, a projecting part, nearly equivalent to a bastion, often, but not always, higher than the curtain. Towers include the

TOWER; GROUP OF FIVE TOWERS; 10TH AND 11TH CENTURIES; TOURNAI, BELGIUM.

TOWER; RAVENSTHORPE, NORTHAMPTONSHIRE;
c. 1300.

TOWER; BRISLINGTON, SOMERSETSHIRE; c. 1500.

TOWER OF TOWN CHURCH, BOZEN, TYROL; c. 1590.
837

TOWER; TOWN CHURCH OF GRAZ, IN AUSTRIA;
c. 1780.
838

ancient Pharos and the modern Lighthouse; the Keep, the Gateway Tower, and other projecting breaks in the walls of mediæval castles (see Castle); the Pele Tower, and other isolated towers of defence, observation, or refuge of feudal times; the Round Tower in its limited and its more general senses; the Lat, Stamba, Vimana, Sikra, and the so-called Pagoda, in all its meanings, and often the Tope and Stupa; the Campanile of Italy; the Bell Tower of the

Tower; Cathedral of Laon; Northwest Tower.

Christian world, including the Central Tower (see below), the spire-topped tower or Steeple; the Minaret of Islam; the Shot Tower; the Water Tower; the Clock Tower in all its forms, and the Beffroi; and, in modern times, such engineering works as the uprights set to carry the anchorage of the suspension bridge; also, in fact though not in name, the high many-storied office buildings or sky scrapers of the United States, when assuming the form of a shaft of uniform width and depth, high in proportion to horizontal dimensions, and rising above surrounding structures.

The general rule is that towers stand upon

the ground, and rise from it without serious break in their verticality; but there are important exceptions. The whole class of Central Towers (see below) are without continuous vertical lines, except as the reëntrant angle of nave and transept is carried up by the projecting angle of the tower. The church towers of London city are, in some notable instances, set upon the roofs of the columnar porticoes of their fronts (see cut under Gibbs); and this, though an obvious anomaly, has been followed elsewhere, and makes an important feature of a subordinate style of neoclassic art. (For the gateway towers of India, in which a similar plan was followed in very early times, see Gopura; and for its reappearance in mediæval pseudo-Byzantine forms see Russia; see also Beffroi; Rococo and cuts; Turret; and cuts under Belgium, France, Germany.)

Sutter, *Thurmbuch*; *Thurmformen aller Stile und Länder*; C. A. Levi, *I. Campanili di Venezia.*

Bell Tower. (See under B.)

Butter Tower (in French, *Tour de Beurre*). A church tower supposed to have been built from funds raised by selling the privilege of using in Lent butter and other things not compatible with the fast. There are several towers called by this name, as one attached to the cathedral of Rouen.

Central Tower. In a special sense, that at the crossing of a church, and therefore resting upon open arches and detached piers. One of the most remarkable is that of the Creisker at Saint-Pol-de-Léon (see France, Part V.); another (much higher) is at Salisbury (see England); but many exist in all the mediæval styles, and many more have been ruined by the burning of the roofs of the churches. The towers named above are crowned by stone spires. Other central towers are finished as Lanterns, as in S. Ouen at Rouen (see France, Part III.). The cupola at the crossing of a Byzantine or a neoclassic church is to be compared with the central tower (see plates, Vol. I., frontispiece, xxix., xxxiv.; Vol. III., plates xv., xvi., xx.)

Eiffel Tower. A tower built of cast iron and wrought iron, in the Champ de Mars, Paris, as a decoration of the great exposition of 1889. It was constructed under the direction of A. G. Eiffel, an engineer, and is three hundred metres high, or nearly one thousand feet, being, therefore, much the highest building in the world.

Pele Tower. (See under Pele.)

Round Tower. (See under R; see also Bell House.)

Wall Tower. A tower built in connection with, and forming an essential part of, a wall;

TOWER; CHURCH OF S. ANNA AT VIENNA; C. 1747.

especially one of a series occurring in a mural fortification, as a city wall.

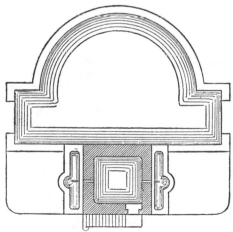

WATER TOWER FOR A FARM; PLAN, SHOWING TWO CATTLE TROUGHS AND LARGE BASIN FOR FILLING VESSELS. THE TOWER ITSELF IS A RESERVOIR.

Watch Tower. A lofty structure intended to enable the approach of enemies to be detected, as by sea or through a mountain pass. The

term is often applied loosely to any high building whose use is not known. (See Bell House; Echauguette; Noraghe; Talayot.)

Water Tower. A tower constructed to hold a column of water at a level high enough to supply fountains or to afford a head for the distribution of water through a system of pipes for fire service, etc.; sometimes movable, and even light enough to be dragged by horses to a conflagration. (See Stand-Pipe.)

WATER TOWER; SEE THE PLAN.

White Tower. The keep or donjon of the fortress called the Tower of London. (See that term.)

TOWER OF LONDON. In England, commonly called The Tower, as a building much identified with English history and romantic tradition. A very ancient castle on the north side of the Thames, now used for various purposes, as a museum, and a place of storage for valuable national possessions.

TOWER OF SILENCE. A tower used by the Parsees for the exposure of dead bodies. The buildings are about forty feet in height, and of large diameter; with smooth cylindrical wall, unbroken except by one doorway. They have a grated floor a few feet below the top of the wall, upon which bodies are laid exposed to birds of prey, the separated bones falling into pits below. Also Dahkme; Dokhma; Dokmeh.

TOWN. In ancient times, a collection of houses enclosed by a wall of defence, with mural towers and fortified gates. In modern times any collection of houses larger than a village. In the United States, a geographical subdivision of a county, a township; but in thickly populated countries, the town is the area occupied by an agglomeration of houses under a specific town or municipal government. (See City.) — H. V. B.

contrasted with any form of arched construction; hence, by extension, an entablature.

TRACERY. Decoration made up of lines or of narrow bands and fillets, or of more elaborately moulded strips, but always without, or with but little, representation of natural objects (but see Branch Tracery, below). By extension, and because the word became identified with the subdivisions of a window, design

TRABEATED CONSTRUCTION; CLOISTER OF S. M. DELLA PACE, ROME; UPPER STORY. ONE OF THE EARLIEST WORKS OF BRAMANTE; C. 1495.

TOWN, ITHIEL; architect; b. 1784; d. June 13, 1844.

In 1829 he formed a partnership with A. J. Davis and designed the State Capitol, the Episcopal church, and several residences in New Haven. He built also residences in Northampton, Massachusetts, the city hall in Hartford, Connecticut, churches in New York, the State Capitols of Indiana and of North Carolina, and several official buildings in Washington.

Dunlap, *Arts of Design; Arch. Pub. Soc. Dictionary.*

TOWNHOUSE. *A.* The same as Town Hall (which see under Hall); hence, by extension and often jocosely, the Jail, or the Poorhouse.

B. A mansion in town as distinguished from a country residence.

TRABEATED. Constructed with horizontal beams or lintels. (Compare Arcuate; Post and Lintel Construction.)

TRABEATION. Lintel construction as

in pierced patterns, in which the openings show dark on light from without and light on dark from within (see Bar Tracery, below). The term when used without qualification has come to mean Gothic window tracery exclusively; but precisely similar tracery was used contemporaneously in stone relief, in wood carving, as on doors and pieces of furniture, and in pierced, cast, and wrought metal. Tracery of totally different character is found in scrollwork of the simpler kinds, as in Roman so-called Arabesques, Strapwork, and Interlaced Ornament, and in Northern sculpture of the early Middle Ages (see Scandinavia, Architecture of).

It was customary in antiquity to fill a large window with screenwork or grating, often of bronze, sometimes of pierced marble slabs. These were not intended to hold glass, which was rare in the windows even of the later Roman Imperial epoch. In the earlier Middle Ages glass was also uncommon; and windows

TRACERY, FIG. 1; S. MARTIN DES CHAMPS, PARIS;
c. 1220.

TRACERY, FIG. 2; CHARTRES CATHEDRAL; c. 1220.

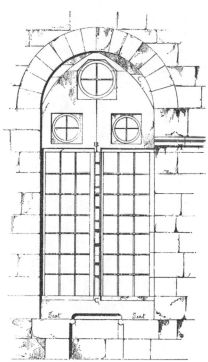

TRACERY, FIG. 4; ROUEN CATHEDRAL; UPPER
SACRISTY; INTERIOR ELEVATION.

TRACERY, FIG. 3; ROUEN CATHEDRAL, UPPER
SACRISTY; EXEMPLIFYING A TRANSITION FROM
PLATE TO BAR TRACERY, THOUGH OF A LATE
EPOCH.

filled with admirable tracery exist, in which there is no reference whatever to glass, but

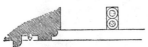

TRACERY, FIG. 5; S. ANDREA, MANTUA. EXAMPLE OF PLATE TRACERY WORKED IN BRICK.

where the tracery itself helps to keep from the interior too great a mass of rain or snow. In the simpler buildings of the Romanesque epoch the openings were small, and were left plain. With the earliest years of Gothic architecture, decorative glass, which was already in use, became more accessible as well as richer, and at the same time the introduction of cusping, within pointed arches and round and oval windows, made the pattern, the lights and darks, interesting. Here, then, was the commencement of window tracery. An upright mullion would carry a tympanum of plain cut stone walling, through which a circle was cut, and this circle, and the two pointed arches carried by the mullion and supporting the tympanum, would be filled with cusps. This earliest tracery was then plate tracery; and that of even the royal domain of France continued to be of this character as late as 1220 (see Figs. 1 and 2), or thereabout, although signs of a change were not unknown (see Fig. 3). In Italy plate tracery remained in use much later (see Fig. 5), and was in fact the prevailing manner of filling large windows until very late in the Gothic epoch, the middle of the fourteenth century or thereabout, when an attempt at bar tracery was seen.

Although glass was now the rule for win-

dows, and tracery was usually arranged for glass, some of the finest examples fill the openings of cloisters and the like, where no glass was intended to be used (see Fig. 6). There are even cases where tracery acts as a part of the construction elsewhere than in windows, as in Fig. 7; but these are generally late, and may be considered as fanciful variants of the Gothic structure. The possible structural value of tracery was, however, studied in Venice, and the celebrated second story arcade of the Ducal Palace (see Fig. 8) is an instance of perfectly balanced arcuated construction combined with perfectly harmonized decorative effect, carrying as it does a lofty wall of great thickness, and floors and roof of unusual weight, because of the great size of the halls enclosed. This system was copied in the fourteenth century Gothic palazzi, but none of the private buildings equalled the Ducal Palace in the perfect carrying out of the idea.

In England, window tracery was a favourite study of the Gothic architects. What is called Flowing Tracery begins with the fourteenth century (see Fig. 9), Net Tracery see (Fig. 10)

TRACERY, FIG. 7: TOMB IN THE ABBEY OF LAACK, RHENISH PRUSSIA.

is a variety of it. These varieties lasted in England until the advent of Perpendicular

TRACERY, FIG. 6; CATHEDRAL OF TOUL (FRANCE); CLOISTER.

TRACERY, FIG. 8; ARCADE OF THE DUCAL PALACE, VENICE.

849   850

Tracery late in the fourteenth century, Fig. 11 showing what is in a way transitional. Figures

TRACERY, FIG. 9; CARLISLE CATHEDRAL, NORTHUMBERLAND; c. 1300, A.D.

12 and 13 show the perfected Perpendicular style, which lasted longer than any other, and is more characteristically English.

Besides window tracery, that of the fourteenth century parapets, especially in France, is of great beauty (see Figs. 14 and 15).

Late Perpendicular work is sometimes enriched by floral sculpture, as in the church of Rushden (see Figs. 16 and 17). These specimens are not pierced; they are merely panels carved in low relief; but Fig. 18 shows similar decoration in window tracery.

TRACERY, FIG. 16; RUSHDEN CHURCH, NORTHAMPTONSHIRE; c. 1450.

Figure 19 is given to show the effectiveness of window tracery when the shape of the mullion and of the curved bars which spring from the mullions is what it should be, namely, thin on the face of the wall and very deep in the thickness of the wall. In this respect the earlier English work is less successful than the great mass of Continental work, but the example before us of late fourteenth century work is

worthy of study. Here also is an admirable instance of solid or panel tracery with which the stone ceiling is entirely filled.
—R. S.

Bar Tracery. That form of window tracery which, in Gothic architecture, succeeded the earliest Gothic tracery. At first the mullions consisted of one or more slender shafts with bases and capitals. In later bar tracery the mullions are merely vertical moulded bars of stone, the mouldings splitting and dividing to start the various branching elements which fill the window head.

Branch Tracery. A form of Gothic tracery occasionally seen in German churches of the end of the fifteenth century and beginning of the sixteenth, in which the tracery is made to imitate rustic work of boughs with the bark and knots, perhaps in imitation of the fancies of the German stained glass workers of the time. The portal of a church at Chemnitz is a noted example.

Fan Tracery. The peculiar decoration of fan-vaulted roofs, in which ribs are suggested, though the construction is no longer rib vaulting, but is solid in a single Shell of cut stone. (See under Vaulting.)

Flowing Tracery. Tracery in windows, gables, and surface panelling, which abounds in waving lines into which the mullions pass tangentially, as distinguished from Geometrical Tracery with its circles and foils or featherings, and "Perforated" Tracery. (See Flamboyant.)

Geometrical Tracery. That in which famil-

TRACERY, FIG. 17; RUSHDEN CHURCH, NORTHAMPTONSHIRE; c. 1450.

iar geometrical forms prevail, such as circles and triangles with curved sides, as distinguished from flowing or flamboyant tracery.

Net Tracery. Gothic tracery, as of windows, in which the openings are of nearly the same size and of approximately the same form.

Perforated Tracery. Same as Plate Tracery, below.

Plate Tracery. That which is composed of

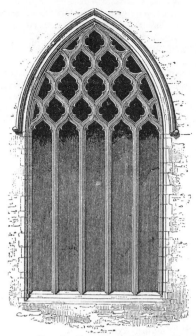

TRACERY, FIG. 10; CHURCH OF FRIARY, READING,
ENGLAND, A.D. 1306.

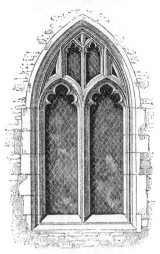

TRACERY, FIG. 12; MINSTER LOVEL, OXFORDSHIRE;
c. 1430.

TRACERY, FIG. 11; KINGSTHORPE, NORTHAMPTON-
SHIRE, c. 1350.

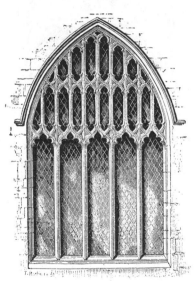

TRACERY, FIG. 13; SWINBROOK, OXON; c. 1500.

TRACERY, FIG. 14; PARAPET OF S. GERVAIS,
FALAISE, IN NORMANDY.

853

TRACERY, FIG. 15; PARAPET OF S. GERVAIS,
FALAISE, IN NORMANDY.

854

openings pierced usually in thin slabs of stone, the design being in the shape and disposition of the openings, not, as was the case with Bar Tracery, in the solid parts or moulded mullions dividing the openings. It was common in the late round-arched and early pointed styles, and originated in the circular opening which was pierced through the tympanum between the heads of coupled windows and under the label which covered and united them with a single arch. These openings were afterwards multiplied with beautiful effect, as in the famous rose window of Chartres and of the transept of Lincoln. Plate Tracery was characteristic of Italian architecture throughout the whole mediæval period.

TRACERY, FIG. 18; WINDOW TRACERY, RICHLY ADORNED, ENGLISH; ABOUT 1400.

Reticulated Tracery. Same as Net Tracery.

Stump Tracery. A kind of tracery characteristic of the decline of mediæval art in Germany in the sixteenth century, consisting of a sort of flamboyant tracery with frequent interpenetrations and truncated ends.

TRACHELIUM. In a Grecian Doric column that part of the necking which comes between the hypotrachelium and the capital proper. What it is exactly depends upon what the hypotrachelium is; thus, in Vol. II., cols. 295, 296 (Grecian Architecture), the horizontal lines at bottom indicate the groove or channel; if this be the hypotrachelium, then the trachelium is the whole space above this to the spreading out of the bell of the capital.

TRACING CLOTH. A smooth linen fabric coated with size to make it transparent and fit for tracing; used by draughtsmen for drawings because less destructible than tracing paper, and because it makes possible an indefinite number of repetitions of drawings made upon it by sun print and other processes.

TRAMMEL. An instrument for drawing arcs of large radii and ellipses. (See Beam Compass, under Compass; Ellipsograph.)

TRANSENNA. In early Christian archi-

tecture, a carved open lattice work, or screen of marble, or of fine metal work, used to enclose shrines.

TRANSEPT. Any large division of a building lying across, or in a direction contrary to, the main axis. In a Christian basilica the large and high structure immediately next the apse, on the side nearer the main entrance; usually so high that the nave and aisles stopped against its wall; and also more open and large within than any other part of the church. In a cruciform church the transept is commonly of the same section as the nave; it may have two aisles, like the nave, or one, or none. That part which is to the north when the sanctuary is at the east is the north arm of the transept, often called simply north transept, and that to the south, similarly, the south transept, the bay of the nave lying between being known as the Crossing. Occasionally, in England, there are two complete transepts, and the nomenclature then is, Northeast Transept, Southwest Transept, etc.

TRANSFORMER. (See Electrical Appliances.)

TRANSITION. In architectural style, the passing from one style to another. This process is always slow, and is marked by the designing of buildings, or parts of buildings, in which the new style is not yet fully in control. This will be more visible in buildings of secondary importance, though occasionally a monument of great size and cost will show the changing style.

The transition from Romanesque to Gothic is marked by the architectural style of domestic buildings throughout Europe, and that from Gothic to Renaissance includes the whole interesting florid Gothic of France and Germany; while in England the same changes go on at a still slower pace, that of the sixteenth century extending indefinitely into the time of the Stuart monarchs. (See Elizabethan; Gothic Architecture in England; Tudor.)

TRANSOM. A horizontal bar of stone, metal, or wood, as distinguished from a Mullion; especially one across a door or window opening near the top. (Compare Mullion.)

TRANSOM BAR. A comparatively slight and subordinate transom; especially, in modern usage, a bar separating a fanlight from the opening below.

TRANSOM LIGHT; WINDOW. The opening above a transom when fitted as a window, very commonly small, as in the doors of chambers in hotels and the like; more rarely large and architectural (compare Fanlight).

TRANSPORTATION. In architecture, the moving of building material, especially in large quantities or in single pieces of great size and weight. In modern building this has no difficulty, nor is it other than a question of appropriation of more or less money for the

TRACERY, FIG. 19; CARLISLE CATHEDRAL, THE CONFESSIONAL FROM THE PRIEST'S SEAT.

purpose. The old necessity commonly felt by builders of limiting their efforts to the material of the neighbouring quarry or the like, can hardly be said to exist. (See under Stone the constant mention of materials used in building, though drawn from a very distant source.)

Under the conditions prevalent in ancient times, without steam or other mechanical power of the sort, the moving of large masses must have involved the labour of many men and animals, and much time. The processes employed have been most carefully and ingeniously discussed by August Choisy in the opening chapters of his *Histoire de l'Architecture*.

TRANSVERSE STRENGTH. (See Strength of Materials.)

TRAP (I.). Same as Trap Door (which see under Door).

TRAP (II.). Igneous rocks like diorite and diabase. — G. P. M.

TRAP (III.). In plumbing, a device attached to a plumbing fixture, and consisting essentially of a bent or U-shaped part of a pipe (with or without enlargement), which, while it permits the discharge of water when the fixture is used, is intended to retain a sufficient quantity to form a water seal against the passage of air or gases from soil, sewer, or waste pipes. There are many kinds of traps, such as drain and sewer traps, waste-pipe traps, non-siphoning traps, and traps with anti-siphon vent attachments. (See House Drainage.) — W. P. G.

Bell Trap. A trap consisting of a bell or cup inverted over the mouth of the pipe, which rises under it from the bottom of a basin or cistern. It is so adjusted that the edge of the bell is submerged by the liquid which drains into the basin. Thus, the liquid can pass under the bell to the pipe, while the gas is prevented from rising by the bell.

D Trap. A trap having the general shape of the letter D, or, at least, one nearly semi-circular bend and no more, as a boxlike receptacle into which a soil pipe empties and another leads out. This form is not used in good modern work.

Grease Trap. A fixture or device for preventing the accumulation of kitchen grease in waste pipes, whereby they become stopped up. Grease traps retain the grease and permit it to solidify. Some forms made in iron or brass are attached directly under the kitchen or pantry sink. Sometimes grease traps of iron or stoneware are placed outside of the building, on the line of the kitchen drain. They are useful for kitchens of large institutions. — W. P. G.

S Trap. Any trap formed by a double or S curve in a pipe.

TRAP DOOR. (See under Door.)

TRASCORO. In Spanish church architecture, a part of the choir, or enclosed space for the clergy or choristers, which part is separated from the main choir, as by the open passage at the crossing of the nave and transept. This separation is made in Seville and Santiago cathedrals, where the names given are *coro* (choir) for the western half, and *capilla mayor* (greater chapel) for the eastern part; but sometimes the eastern part is called the *coro* and the western part the *trascoro*.

TRASS. A volcanic substance found in the valley of the Rhine and in Holland, which closely resembles the pozzuolanas of Italy, and, like them, is used to give hydraulic properties to common lime for building. It occurs generally in pulverulent lumps which require to be pulverized and mixed with lime. A good proportion to form hydraulic mortar is one part by volume each of lime, of trass, and of sand. (Also written Terrass.) — W. R. H.

TRAVE. *A.* A cross beam.

B. One of the divisions or bays, as in a ceiling, made by cross beams. In this sense also called travis, traviss, or trevis.

TRAVELLER. Same as Travelling Crane (which see under Crane). Properly, that part which travels only.

TRAVERSE. Any member, or structure, set or built across an interior or an opening; especially

A. A screen, railing, or other barrier, used to keep away intruders, to allow of passage from one place to another by an official or dignitary, or to conceal anything.

B. A Transom, or the horizontal member of a Chambranle. (Compare Ascendant.)

TRAVERTINE. A building stone, consisting of carbonate of lime deposited from solution in the waters of springs and streams. One of the most celebrated is the so-called *lapis Tiburtinus* of Tivoli, Italy, which was so largely used in the buildings of ancient Rome. The so-called onyx marbles are also travertines. — G. P. M.

TRAVIATED. Having a series of transverse divisions or bays, referring to ceilings.

TRAZZO. Same as Terrazzo Veneziano, as a trazzo floor.

TREAD. *A.* That part of a step in a stairway, of a doorsill, or the like, upon which the foot rests, as distinguished from the riser. The term applies equally to the upper surface alone, and to the plank, slab of marble or slate, or thin casting of iron, in those staircases where each step is not a solid mass. (See Stair.)

B. The horizontal distance from one riser to the next. Thus, a stair is said to have 12½ inch tread, that being the whole distance which a person moves horizontally in ascending one step. This distance is measured without regard to the nosing, which, where it exists, projects beyond the riser in each case. (See also Flier; Going; Winder.) — D. N. B. S.

TRANSITION; HOUSE FRONT OF THE ROMANESQUE STYLE PASSING INTO GOTHIC, COLOGNE, GERMANY.

TREASURY OF ATREUS. A building of unknown date at Mycenæ in Greece, now known to have been a grave chamber. (See the cuts under Stone Cutting.)

TRECENTISTI. In Italian art, the people of the fourteenth century, used especially of literary men, scholars, and artists. (See Tre Cento.)

TRE CENTO. In Italian art, the fourteenth century. (Compare Cinque Cento; Quattro Cento; Sei Cento.)

TREENAIL. *A.* A large pin of hard wood used in mediæval woodwork and in modern use, for fastening together timbers, as especially in shipbuilding. It is now little used in architecture, at least in the United States.

B. Same as Gutta, in Greek architecture, because of the theory that the guttæ represent the heads of nails, or pins.

TREE OF JESSE. (See under Jesse.)

TREFOIL. A panel, an opening, or a division of tracery, having three foliations, or lobes, separated by cusps. (See Foil.)

TRELLIS (n.). *A.* Screenwork made of strips crossing one another, either at right angles or in a more elaborate pattern. The most usual form is that made of thin laths of wood. By extension, —

B. An arbour, or framework, for the support of vines.

TRENAIL; TRENNEL. Same as Treenail.

TRENCHED. Inserted or let in, as the edge of a board or plank into the surface of another one, as described under Dado (v.) and House (v.). The term is mainly British in its use. A trenched joint may be either simply where the whole width of one board is let into a groove in the other; or tongued, where the groove is narrower, and the inserted board has to be cut with a tongue; or dovetailed trenched, where the groove is cut spreading as it enters, so that the tongue has to be shaped like a dovetail.

TRESGUERRAS, FRANCISCO EDUARDO; architect, sculptor, painter, musician, and poet; b. March 13, 1745 (at Celaya, Mexico); d. Aug. 3, 1833.

"The Michelangelo of Mexico." Tresguerras was a pupil of the painter Miguel Cabrera for a short time at the Academy of S. Carlos, in the city of Mexico. He did not have the advantage of European travel and study. His activity was confined to a group of cities in the vicinity of Celaya. He began as a painter and afterward took up wood carving, and acquired extraordinary skill in that art. He probably learned the elements of architecture from the Jesuits, who supplied him with a Vignola and other architectural works. Tresguerras's work as an architect is characterized by great originality and beauty of proportion, especially in domes and towers. His interiors are extremely rich. His best building is the church of Nuestra Señora del Carmen, at Celaya. Other important works are the convent churches of S. Rosa and S. Clara in Querétaro, the Alarson Theatre in San Luis Potosi, the bridge of La Laja, the beautiful church of La Conception in San Miguel de Allenda, and other works. His most important picture is the altarpiece of the church of S. Rosa in Querétaro. At the age of seventy he became an enthusiastic supporter of the Mexican revolution.

Sylvester Baxter, *A Great Mexican Architect* in *American Architect*, Vol. LV., 1897.

TRESHAM (TRESSAM), SIR THOMAS; amateur architect; b. about 1543; d. 1605.

In 1573–1574 he was sheriff of Northamptonshire. From 1581 to 1588 and again in 1597 and 1599 he was imprisoned as a Catholic. He built the market house at Rothwell, the "triangular lodge" at Rushton, and the new building at Lyveden.

Gotch, *A Complete Account of Buildings by Sir Thomas Tresham;* Gotch and Brown, *Renaissance in England.*

TRESTLE. A frame consisting usually of uprights with a crosspiece (commonly called a "horse"); the uprights set at an angle, so as to spread at the bottom; the whole used as a support, as for a table or for a scaffolding. Trestle work is a series of trestles braced in every direction, and often carried to a great height, or to a great length, unsupported, as in bridges; used in extensive scaffolding, and in railroad work. It is sometimes of iron or steel, but generally of timber.

TRIANGLE. A drawing instrument in the form of a mathematical right-angled triangle cut from a flat thin piece of wood, hard rubber, celluloid, or metal, or framed of three strips; used for drawing parallel lines at any given angle by sliding it along the fixed blade of a T-square, straight edge, or the like. The right-angled side serves for lines perpendicular to the blade, the oblique side for inclined lines. The commonest forms of triangle have acute angles both of 45° or one of 30° and one of 60°; but special forms are made with other angles for lettering and other special purposes. Called also Set Square. — A. D. F. H.

TRIAPSIDAL. Having three apses. The two more usual dispositions of a triapsidal church are, that with three apses at the eastern end, as one at the end of the choir and two terminating the side aisles; and that with three apses on the east, north, and south sides of a central tower, or central square, into which the nave and its aisles open on the western side. (See Latin Architecture; Romanesque Architecture.)

TRIBOLO (NICOLÒ DEI BRACCINI DEI PERICOLI); architect, landscape architect, sculptor, and painter; b. 1500; d. Sept. 5, 1550.

The nickname Tribolo (trouble) was given to him on account of his timidity. He entered the atelier of Nanni Unghero and later that of Jacopo Sansovino, then working in Florence. In 1525 he was invited to Bologna to continue the sculpture of the smaller portals of the façade of the church of S. Petronio. (See Giacomo della Quercia.) Two Sibyls on one of these portals and two statues in the Capella Zambeccari at S. Petronio, are by him. After the death of Andrea Sansovino, in 1529, Tribolo assisted Mosca, Montelupo, and others in completing the sculpture of the Casa Santa at Loreto. After the election of Cosimo I. de' Medici, Duke of Tuscany, in 1537, Tribolo was employed in laying out and embellishing the gardens of his villas and palaces. At the villa of Castello he made two fountains, to the larger of which Ammanati added the group of Hercules and Antæus (see Ammanati); at the villa of Petraio he constructed a fountain, and was engaged in laying out the Boboli Gardens, Florence, when he died.

Vasari, Milanesi ed.; Müntz, *Renaissance;* Perkins, *Tuscan Sculptors;* Anguillesi, *Palazzi e ville appartenenti alla R. Corona di Toscana;* Guizzardi, *Le sculpture delle porte di San Petronio in Bologna.*

TRIBUNAL. *A.* In Roman archæology, that part of a basilica used to receive the seat of the magistrates, and also, by extension, the raised seat or post of any person of authority.

B. A platform from which speeches are delivered, or where a presiding officer sits. In this sense used very loosely and applied also to the court or magistracy itself, or to any body or individual to which important matters are referred.

TRIBUNE. *A.* Same as Tribunal, in either sense.

B. Any place from which one speaks, a stage, or pulpit; especially in the French Chamber of Deputies, and generally in French legislatures of the past, since 1789, the raised desk or pulpit from which members addressed the house.

C. Any part of a church or public building, especially distinguished as if for the reception of a tribunal platform or desk, as an apse; in this sense used very loosely. By extension, any apsidal structure, even one not containing a platform for speakers, a pulpit, or a throne, or magistrate's chair. C. E. Norton, in *Church Building in the Middle Ages,* applies the term to all three of the great apses of the cathedral of Florence, east, north, and south. Beresford Pite, in the (London) *Architectural Review* for

January, 1899, applies it to the central apse of the same church, the one which is set on the axis of the principal nave, as distinguished from the two others of precisely similar plan; and, indeed, tribuna is the local (Italian) name.
— R. S.

TRICLINIUM. *A.* A couch upon which persons recline while at meals; the name implying the division of it into three parts, nearly separate, enclosing the table on three sides, the fourth side being left open for service.

B. By extension, a dining room in a Roman house, furnished with a low table, surrounded on three sides by couches. In general, each couch accommodated three guests reclining, the total number of guests being thus limited to nine.

TRICLINIUM FUNEBRE. In Roman archæology, an arrangement of three couches and a table in connection with a tomb, for the purpose of occasional banquets in honour of the dead. One such near Pompeii is an open-air structure of masonry, enclosed by a low wall, the interior of which is decorated as if in a private house.

TRIFORIUM. In mediæval church architecture, the space between the vaulting and the roof of an aisle, when opened into the nave over the nave arches and under the clearstory windows by an arch, or two arches, in each bay, or,

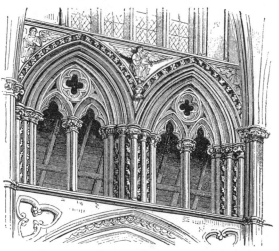

TRIFORIUM; LINCOLN CATHEDRAL, C. 1260.

more characteristically, by three arches (hence the name), the whole forming a gallery.

TRIGLYPH. In Greek architecture, one of the vertical blocks in a Doric frieze, suggesting, in stone, the outer ends of the ceiling beams of the primitive wooden construction; it has two vertical grooves or triangular channels with a corresponding chamfer on each side, behind which is a groove or rebate, into which are fitted thin slabs which fill the metopes, and often called by that name. One triglyph is set over and on the axis of each column, except those of the corners, which, however, are set nearer to the adjoining columns than the width of the regular intercolumniation; one over each intercolumniation on its axis, and one at each corner of the frieze, showing two faces. The arrangement in Roman Doric is nearly the same, but the last triglyph of each range is sometimes placed, like the rest, over the centre of the column and not on the corner. — H. V. B.

TRILITH; TRILITHON. A structure composed of three stones, especially, in prehis-

Trilith at St. Nazaire (Loire-Inférieure), France.

toric architecture, a monument or part of a larger structure so built up.

TRIM (n.). *A.* The visible wooden finish of a house (see Inside Finish, under Finish).

B. In the United States, sometimes the hardware of a house (see Builder's Hardware).

Cabinet Trim. Same as Cabinet Finish (which see under Finish).

TRIM (v. t.). *A.* To fit up and finish (see Trim (n.) in both senses).

B. To adjust closely, prepare for, and put into, a given place; said of a piece of material. Often with *in* or *out*, as a board may be trimmed in between joists, and a well-hole may be trimmed out with fascias or string boards.

C. To frame an opening, in a floor or roof especially.

TRIMMER. That timber, in framing around an opening in a floor for a staircase, a lift, a chimney, or the like, into which one of the ends of the Header is entered, the timbers which are framed into it being called Tailpieces. Except when the opening comes in a corner between two walls, there are two trimmers, between which the header is held in place.

TRIMMING; TRIMMINGS. Same as Trim.

TRINGLE. *A.* A bar, or rod, on which rings may run for curtains. Hence, by extension, —

B. A narrow straight moulding of any section.

TRINQUEAU. (See Nepveu, Pierre.)

TRIPLET. A group of three; especially, in mediæval architecture, such a group of windows; also in combination, as a triplet window.

TRIPOD. Any object standing on three legs, specifically a table, a seat, or a stand for a vase or caldron, such as were common in classical antiquity, when it was sometimes used as a sort of portable altar. It was used extensively as a decorative symbol.

TRIPOLI, ARCHITECTURE OF. (See North Africa, Architecture of.)

TRIUMPHAL. Having to do with triumph, victory, or remarkable achievement. The term is applied loosely to many monuments of the past, merely because of their size and grandeur.

TRIUMPHAL ARCH. *A.* A monumental structure; one variety of the Memorial Arch. Modern monumental buildings, taking the form of the Roman memorial arch, or simply of the arched gateway, are commonly spoken of as triumphal arches, and this in consequence of the general feeling that their purpose is the commemoration of military achievement, or the like. Ancient arches have been fully treated in the article, Memorial Arch; modern ones are of the last three centuries, for, although gateways leading into fortresses and fortified cities were sometimes made decorative, and that with deliberate memorial purpose, in the Middle Ages and in the earlier years of the Renaissance, those structures were hardly triumphal arches in the proper sense of the word (see Gateway). The Arch of Alfonso of Aragon (1470), and the Porta Capuana (1485), each in Naples, and the Gate of S. Maria at Burgos, are admirable instances of the decorative gateway; but they are in no respect to be considered in connection with the memorial arches of the Romans. Even when, in 1672, the Porte S. Denis was built, and when, in 1674, the Porte S. Martin was built, each by Louis XIV. at the height of his power, and with deliberate intention to commemorate the military triumphs of his reign, the true form of the Roman structure was so little understood that it was thought enough to build up a wall 14 or 15 feet thick, from 60 to 80 feet high, and pierced with one or three archways, exactly as if it had been one section of a city wall of defence which was under consideration. The true Roman monument, rather a great pedestal for statuary than a gateway, reappears first during the same century. Perhaps the most perfect early example is the Porte du Peyrou at Montpellier, which was built at the close of the seventeenth century, in memory of the Revocation of the Edict of Nantes by Louis XIV. This is in some respects a careful study from the antique, even in its placing reminding the student strongly of the placing of the arches in the Forum. The Brandenburger Thor, at Berlin, built at the close of the eighteenth century; the Sieges Thor (Gate of Victory), at Munich, built between 1843 and 1850; the "Marble Arch" in London, moved at a later time to the northeast corner of Hyde Park; the interesting arch, Della Pace, at Milan (called also The Gate of the Simplon (del Sempione), because intended by Napoleon to form the termination of the carriage road over the Simplon Pass); the Arc du Carroussel, in what was once the courtyard of the Tuileries in Paris, — are all triumphal arches in the proper sense of the word, that is to say, buildings standing free, usually in large open parks or promenades, intended to receive and display commemorative sculpture, and to be crowned with sculptured groups of great importance. Much the largest triumphal arch, modern or ancient, is the Arc de l'Étoile in Paris, undertaken by Napoleon in commemoration of his victories, and announcing itself as dedicated by him to his soldiers and sailors. This building is of the dimensions of a very large modern apartment house or business building, such as are rising in American cities. It is 160 feet high, nearly 150 feet wide, 72 feet thick or deep, and pierced by a single archway 47 feet wide, and rising 67 feet from the pavement to the crown. Similar arches pierce the ends or narrow sides; these are 27 feet wide and 60 feet high. No ancient Roman monument of the kind approached these dimensions.

B. The great archway leading from the body of an early Christian church, such as a basilica, into the presbytery or sanctuary. The term is a translation of the ecclesiastical and Latin term, *arcus triumphalis.* — R. S.

TRIUMPHAL AVENUE. One of the great central streets of some of the cities of the Roman Empire, as notably Palmyra, where the double colonnade of Corinthian columns is still partly in place, and Gerasa, where the somewhat similar colonnade is of the Ionic style. (See Syria.) — R. S.

TROCHILUS. Same as Scotia.

TROMPE. In French, a piece of vaulting of conical or partly spherical shape, or resembling one corner of a Cloistered Vault, the essential thing being that it supports a weight imposed upon it on one side or irregularly. Thus, if a projecting angle of a building is cut off below, the overhanging piece, triangular in plan, may be carried on corbelling; but if carried on an arched structure, that structure is a trompe. A turret-like building in a reëntrant angle may be carried in a similar way. A Pendentive is of the nature of a trompe.

TROPHY. Usually a group of arms and armour of the enemy, erected as a memorial of

victory. (See Monument, Historical Sketch.) In Greek and Latin lands it consisted primitively of the actual arms hung on the trunk and branches of an oak, cut to resemble the human frame, and either consecrated in a temple (*e.g.* Romulus, "Spolia opima") or other public structure erected conspicuously on a mound, and usually accompanied by an inscription. It was essentially a Dorian and not an Ionian custom, and most early examples were

TROMPE CARRYING PROJECTING ANGLES; HOUSE AT PÉRIGUEUX (DORDOGNE), FRANCE.

in the Peloponnesus, such as the trophies of Zeus Tropaios and Polydeukes at Sparta, of Herakles, near Sellasia, and those over the Corinthians, and over Laphaes at Argos. In course of time the idea prevailed of making such trophies permanent monuments of architecture and sculpture. Rising from a circular or quadrangular stepped basement, or a tower or column, was the group of trophies carved in marble or cast in bronze, in imitation of the original arms, and accompanied — even at times replaced — by figures of the same material, in relief or in the round, of historic, emblematic, or religious import. Part of the sculptures were on the basement. Sometimes the central crowning piece of sculpture was a "Victory," either armed (Aitolian trophy at Delphi), or unarmed (Paionios' "Nike" at Olympia). This type was also a creation of Dorian artists. The earliest belong to the sixth to fifth century; e.g. the bronze trophy of the Sikyonians, and that for the Peloponnesian War at Olympia, that of Thrasyllos, and that of the Messenians of Naupactos at Delphi. It is true that in commemoration of the victories over the Persians, two trophies were erected in Attica, — at Salamis a naval, and at Marathon a land, trophy, — but these were the offerings of all Greece, and probably by Dorian artists. Perhaps the most interesting for sculpture were the two nearly identical trophies designed by the great Paionios for Olympia and Delphi — the latter famous for its statue of Nike, now recovered. These and other monuments of the fifth and fourth centuries B.C. were not colossal. The round tower of the trophy of Epaminondas at Leuktra (371 B.C.) was only 11 feet in diameter. But some Hellenistic (third–second centuries B.C.) trophies appear to have been larger and more architectural, such as that of Artemisia at Rhodes, of Pyrrhos at Argos (marble, with reliefs), of Aratos at Mantineia, and of the Aitolians at Delphi. Now, also, came in the custom of introducing trophies of arms and armour in relief in the decoration of large monuments, such as the altar at Pergamon. The best source of information for all Greek trophies is Pausanias (Frazer's ed.).

The Romans gave to the trophy a truly monumental character, making it the greatest record of their wars. As an emblem the trophy of arms was used everywhere by a custom current since the foundation of Rome. At the close of the republic the entire city had become an arsenal of conquered arms, either consecrated in public structures or kept in private houses as family prizes, and trophies were set up on memorial arches (see Memorial Arch), carved on memorial columns (see Memorial Column), on temples, sarcophagi, and altars, and stamped on coins. But the trophy erected in a conquered land, both as a record and as a fear-compeller, became an *apotropaion*. Tacitus says that when, after a great victory, the soldiers of Germanicus erected a trophy, the Germans felt its disgrace more keenly than the defeat itself, and whenever possible the Germanic and other northern enemies of Rome would destroy these hated symbols.

Transitional between Greek and Roman was the recently discovered trophy of Paulus Æmilius, erected by the Roman general at Delphi for his victory over Perseus at Padna (Livy, xlv., 27). Its quadrangular base (2.15 by 1.05 m.), approached by a couple of steps, was decorated by a continuous frieze of Hellenistic

sculpture representing details of the Macedonian defeat with a Roman regard for exactitude. The earliest purely Roman examples recorded are those erected in 121 B.C. by Domitius Ahenobarbus and Fabius Maximus, after victories over the Allobroges and Arverni. They consisted mainly of marble towers sustaining the grouped arms. After Marius had saved Rome from the Cimbri and Teutones, in 101 B.C., he erected famous trophies in Rome, which were cast down by Sulla, but defiantly restored by Julius Cæsar, in 68 B.C. during the dictatorship of Sulla himself. Sulla, after his victory at Chæroneia (86 B.C.) in the Mithridatic War, erected two trophies with Greek inscriptions on the battlefield, one on the plain, the other on the heights, and Pausanias saw them more than two centuries after. He erected another after the battle of Orchomenos (85 B.C.). But it was Pompey who built, after the close of the Sertorian War (71 B.C.), the trophy most famous for the beauty of its execution and site. The inscription stated that he had subjected to Rome 876 cities from the Alps to the farther end of Spain. It stood in a commanding position along the great Roman military road at the west end of the Pyrenees. To Cæsar only a single trophy is attributed, after victory over Pharnakes at Ziela (47 B.C.). The exquisite marble trophies, still preserved and popularly called "Trofei di Mario," at Rome, are probably of the time of Cæsar or Augustus. A rival to Pompey's monument was set up by Augustus in 7–6 B.C. on the heights above Monaco, facing the Alps and the sea, on the Roman road connecting Italy and Gaul. It commemorated the submission of all the Alpine tribes from the Mediterranean to the Adriatic, and its remains are sufficient to show that it consisted of (a) a square platform, 130 feet each side, (b) a massive square basement of 110 feet, with flights of steps on the north and south ends, and (c) a circular tower, 100 feet in diameter and of considerable height, decorated with eleven pilasters, and surrounded by a two-storied marble peristyle of Doric and Ionic (or Corinthian) orders. On the tower stood the trophy, 18 feet high, at whose base on either side was a seated lamenting figure (man and woman) representing the subject peoples, very much as the group is often given on late Republican and Imperial coins reproducing such trophies. The inscription on the basement enumerated the subjected tribes. Ruins of other trophies of a similar type, and dating from the times of Cæsar and Augustus, remain in the south of France (e.g. Aix and Nîmes), and on the Rhine (e.g. Niederwald). Under Augustus, Drusus erected a tumulus with trophies on the Elbe, from the spoils of the Marcomanni, as did Germanicus on the Weser under Tiberius. But the best preserved of all these memorials is that restored by or built for Trajan in 109 A.D. at Tropæum Traiani, near the Danube and the Black Sea (modern Adam-Klissi). It appears to commemorate the conquest of Dacia after the two wars of 101–102 and 105–107, and to have been designed by Apollodorus of Damascus. It is in the form of a basement of steps, on which stands a great circular mound of masonry (diameter 30 m.) faced with marble, decorated with a frieze of triglyphs and sculptured metopes, framed by carved battlements and surmounted by a conical roof, from whose centre rises the pedestal of the central trophy (diameter 9.20 m.), with the group of prisoners at its feet. The total height was probably over 100 feet, with a diameter of about 150 feet. It will be seen that the older form of the tower was often superseded by that of the mound, making the structure resemble somewhat such funerary tumuli as the imperial mausoleums of Augustus and Hadrian at Rome. Thus the trophy was not only a memorial of victory and a deterrer of revolts, but a glorious funeral mound for the fallen victors. That the custom continued to the close of the Empire is shown by the remains of a trophy of Constantine at the gate of Tomi, not far from that of Trajan.

— A. L. FROTHINGHAM, JR.

TROUGH (n.). Any receptacle for fluids in the nature of an open channel or gutter with or without an outlet.

TROWEL. *A.* A mason's tool made of a thin plate of metal, approximately lozenge-shaped, always pointed at the end, and fitted with a handle ; used for spreading and otherwise manipulating mortar in laying up masonry, and for breaking and trimming bricks.

B. A plasterer's tool, generally a small parallelogram of thin wood, with a handle underneath ; used either like a pallet to hold putty or mortar, or to spread or float the last coat upon walls or ceilings. Masons use a tool of the same sort for kneading and mixing putty in pointing joints.

TRUCK HOUSE. In the United States, a building for housing a hook and ladder truck, together with the horses and men for its operation. The building is equipped similarly to an engine house.

TRUE (v.). To test for correctness in level, straightness, or the like, either by the eye alone (see Bone), or by means of instruments.

TRULLO. In Southern Italy, a rough stone building not unlike the Noraghe or trudheu of Sardinia. It is generally of cylindrical form with cupola-shaped roof. It appears that the poorer people, even at the present day, find them dry and not inconvenient habitations.

TRUMEAU. In French, a stone mullion or pier supporting the tympanum of a wide doorway, as in mediæval churches ; often character-

istically bearing on its face a figure of Christ, of the Virgin and Child, or of a saint.

TRUNK. *A.* Same as shaft ; that is, of a column ; obsolete or obsolescent.

B. A large and central or principal spout, conductor, or hollow shaft, as in ventilation, the delivery of grain, and the like.

TRUSS. A combination of rigid pieces, as posts and struts, with ties, so as to make a frame for spanning an opening or the like. Under Roof, Figs. 1 and 2 show a King-post Truss and a Queen-post Truss ; Fig. 3 is also of a King-post Truss, but is not well shown, and Fig. 10 is a Hammer Beam Truss, though not adequately framed ; but the other cuts are of roofs whose principals are not trusses, in a strict sense. A truss must be made up of triangles, as no other mathematical figure is fixed and immovable. The Howe, Pratt, and Warren trusses (see subtitles) are used in building to carry large roofs where supporting uprights are to be avoided, as in a music hall or large modern church.

Howe Truss. A bridge truss in which the struts are diagonal, crossing one another, and the chords are held together by vertical ties.

Pratt Truss. A bridge truss in which the struts are vertical and the ties diagonal.

Scissor Beam Truss. A roof truss in which the feet of the principal rafters are connected, each with a point on the upper half of the opposite rafter, by ties which cross at the middle like the two halves of a pair of scissors. It is a weak truss, fit for small spans only.

Warren Truss. One with parallel chords between which the braces and ties are set at the same angle, so as to form a series of isosceles triangles. — W. R. H.

TRUSS (v.). To fit with braces, struts, or ties, in such a way as to strengthen, as a beam or a stud partition. (See Trussed Partition, under Partition).

TRUSSEL. Same as Trestle.

TRUTH IN ARCHITECTURE. The expression, in design, of the essential facts of the plan and structure. The doctrine of Artistic Realism is of very ancient lineage ; so far as one can judge from collateral evidence, the modified form of it which Aristotle upheld was but a restatement of a doctrine current in his day, and which even then was not altogether acceptable, and required defence. To us it becomes self-evident that the doctrine of imitation, as it is usually interpreted, can only be upheld by narrowing the field of art in a thoroughly artificial way, which no modern philosopher would defend for a moment.

That the doctrine does express a half truth we shall see below ; but that it does not express a principle which is universally valid for the whole field of art appears clear when we note that in some directions it is inapplicable altogether, and, furthermore, that it must be modified in statement, or limited by definition, if it is to be made applicable to special fields.

The general doctrine of Artistic Realism may be stated thus : " Fine Art is the expression of the true essence, the real nature, of the subject presented by the artist." It is comparatively easy to apply this supposed principle to literature, to painting, and to sculpture, without arousing a natural demand for its qualification or limitation ; but it is evident that it is impossible to interpret our modern music in accord with any such formula ; and when we turn to architecture, we find it necessary to restate the principle altogether to give it any semblance of validity.

In order to make the supposititious principle applicable to the work of the artist-architect, it has been assumed by the defenders that the true essence of architecture lies in its practical and constructional worth, and that true architecture, therefore, consists in the expression in building of constructional values, and in the suggestion upon the exterior of the uses which buildings as wholes, or in their special parts, are intended to subserve.

But it is easy to show that these assumptions are entirely unwarranted. There can be no doubt, of course, that there is great æsthetic value in certain expressions of constructional function ; but to claim that the expression of constructional function is necessarily æsthetic is certainly impossible, for, were this true, all scientific engineering would have architectural value, which manifestly is not the case. Works of engineering must thrill us with their beauty if they are to lay claim to the possession of architectural value.

It is true, also, that certain indications upon the exterior of a building of the purposes for which the interior is to be used give satisfaction to the beholder, a satisfaction which often adds much to the æsthetic value of the whole mass ; but to hold that the indication upon the exterior of the purposes for which the parts of a building are to be used is necessarily æsthetic is manifestly absurd, for such a principle would involve, in an ideal building, the indication by appropriate forms, or decorations, of the existence of menial offices which we wish to forget, and which we must necessarily lose sight of if we are to enjoy the beauty of a building as a whole. The uses of a building, or of its parts, may be expressed in the forms employed, but the expression must be beautiful if it is to add to the æsthetic character of the building.

As a matter of fact we have in this principle of Truth, of Sincerity, of Veracity, as applied to architecture, but a half truth, as the doctrine of Artistic Realism in all its modifications teaches but a half truth. The truth which, half expressed, has led to so persistent a life for this

discredited realistic theory is this : that untruth, insincerity, lack of veracity, and pretence, are in general disturbing, unpleasant, and ugly ; if a work of art, therefore, is to have permanent value, it must avoid the expression of untruth and pretence ; and the easiest way to avoid this expression of untruth and pretence is to bear in mind, and to some extent to express, the truth. The mere expression of truth, however, will not make a work of man's hand æsthetic ; the æsthetic quality is something which must be superadded.

The aim of every artist should be to produce an object of perfect beauty, in whatever material he expresses his thought ; this he cannot well do if he shocks the observer with unreality ; and, if he be an architect, he cannot succeed in producing this effect of permanent beauty in his buildings if he persistently lies about the construction he adopts, and deceives us about the uses of the apartments he erects ; and this is due, not to the fact that where he succeeds the truth is expressed, but to the fact that lying and deception are in themselves anti-æsthetic. On the other hand, mere sincerity and lack of pretence in one's architectural work will not make it artistic ; to this lack of deceit must be added the quality of beauty which brings to the masses of cultivated beholders a permanent feeling of pleasure. The greatest sincerity, if unattractively presented, can have no permanent æsthetic value.

If the position thus taken be correct, then the architect may well make certain practical applications of the principles involved in the guidance of his artistic efforts. In the first place, he is taught that he should aim to avoid the pretence of constructional effects which evidently cannot exist ; but, having done this, he must equally avoid the expressions of constructional effects which are not beautiful. It may be true, to take an analogy from a kindred art by way of illustration, that the human frame is largely made up of bone and muscle, and the artist-sculptor will certainly not model his figure so that it will appear to be apparently unanatomical ; nevertheless, the most perfect reproduction of anatomical detail will not make a statue beautiful, nor would we consider the sculptor to be in any sense an artist who made it a principle to represent his human subjects as exceptionally thin in order to emphasize the position of bone and muscle which make their attitudes possible. Similarly is it true that buildings could not stand did there not exist certain balancing of forces, certain strains on material parts, certain lines of thrust and pressure ; but evidently, to strip a building of all beauty in order to express this balancing of strains and thrusts and pressures, would be manifestly absurd from an artistic standpoint ; the critic who so emphasizes the delight he obtains in the architect's expression of these physical forces that he finds in such expression alone the true essence of architecture, is as abnormally warped in his æsthetic development as is the surgeon who finds beauty in a skeleton, or in a fine piece of dissection, or in a skilful preparation of cancerous tissue.

The architect should aim at the production of a beautiful building; to this end he must avoid obvious constructional untruth, which for most intelligent men is ugly; and so far as in him lies he should aim to emphasize the con-structional and practical values of the parts of his structure; and this for the simple reason that such emphasis tends to be attractive to the intelligent observer: but he should never em-phasize these constructional and practical values at the expense of a loss of beauty, nor need he strive for this emphasis unless it is possible to gain it in a manner which will actually add to the permanent æsthetic value of the building as a whole.

But as the architect should avoid giving the observer the shock which constructional un-truth entails, so also should he avoid shocks of all sorts and kinds which involve more or less of ugliness; and not infrequently he finds that, by the adoption of some scheme which in-volves a minor inconsistency of construction, he may avoid other shocks of much greater im-portance. The ideal architect, to be sure, would of course be able to avoid all shocks of all kinds, but the poor human being all too often finds himself called upon to make a choice of the lesser evil; and surely the architect who is merely human should not be condemned if he ask us to overlook some inconsiderable untruth for the sake of the better æsthetic results he thus obtains. He may well argue that at best we can express but partial truth in any art. The truths the realist is wont to emphasize are only some of many which he chooses to con-sider, while he leaves out of sight many others which, but for mere convention, might as well be considered as those which he aims to express. The sculptor, for instance, actually assumes in general a conventional falsity of colourlessness which he asks us to overlook in order that he may the better express certain beauties that are independent of colour. So in architecture there are many other truths than those of structural thrust and strain, or practical use, which all artistic architects (and even those who labour to express constructional values) have come to overlook entirely, and this with perfect pro-priety in consideration of the fact that the end in view is the production of beauty; e.g. they overlook the nature of their foundations, of the filling in behind their finished protective and ornamental stone facings, of the masonry and furrings back of their plastered interior wall surfaces. If, then, it be permissible, in the

effort to build beautiful buildings, to forget some of many realities, why should not the architect occasionally ask us to pass over some slight structural disingenuousness, provided he is able by such means to produce a nobler type of beauty than were possible if he did not dis-regard this minor inconsistency?

We have inherited from a long line of artist ancestors many architectural forms which have arisen from constructional usage, all too often very faulty from a modern scientific stand-point; for instance, we should not be able to enjoy to-day the beauty of the maze of flying buttresses in the Gothic cathedrals had the mediæval architects understood how to calcu-late thrusts as accurately as we do, and had they expressed these thrusts logically. Thus it happens that inherited architectural forms, more or less logical, have been refined and beautified until they have become in them-selves æsthetic elements capable of employment for the purpose of adding artistic quality to buildings, as the artist in colour adds to the value of his painting by his technique; and there seems to be no manifest reason why the modern architect should not use such elements, as in fact his ancestors always have done, to beautify his work, without too great regard to their constructional worth, only provided he does not use them for purposes of intentional deceit.

Architecture, more than all the other arts, is replete with forced compromises. A symmetri-cal exterior, for instance, may produce æsthetic results which could not be gained were all the minor lack of symmetries in plan emphasized upon the exterior. The artist must trust to his genius to determine for him how far he can afford to sacrifice one element of beauty in his effort to gain another, and that he is an artist is attested by the fact that the truths he over-looks are forgotten by the observer in the beauty of the results attained.

It is thus that great architects have almost invariably used old constructional forms as merely decorative features, and if the beauty of the result is sufficient to arouse our en-thusiasm we do not hesitate to condone the inconsistency. It is thus that the Romans so often used the Greece-born orders, being con-tent to accept and adapt forms perfected by long use in other relations than those which were appropriate to their civilization, and in this adaptation adding elements of grandeur and proportion which lead us to overlook the illogical usage. It is thus that the Venetians used old constructional forms purely decoratively to add elements of beauty to their well-studied compositions, and we forget the inconsistency in the joy we gain from the entrancing group-ings in their waterside palaces.

It is, of course, to be conceded, as has been

suggested above, that the ideal architect or race of architects would avoid such inconsistencies, but even in the work of the Greeks, which reaches the highest grade of consistency, we find, *e.g.* in the triglyphs, the modillions, the dentils, of their masonry temples, the use of forms which had been perfected in wooden structures and which were used decoratively, but not as truthfully, in stone constructions. In the development of the Gothic cathedrals, which many think of as the only examples of an architecture of thoroughly logical construction, we can easily trace the same practice, when, for instance, we note the blundering steps by which the columns of the basilica, used first as mere columns, were gradually transformed into buttresses when engaged in the walls, or into piers where standing isolated and free.

In conclusion, then, it appears that the expression of constructional truth in architecture is only one element amongst many which are at the command of the artist-architect for use in the production of beautiful buildings, — a most important element, indeed, and one which, if skilfully used, must add great satisfaction to the trained observer, one, also, which cannot be disregarded without great risk of ruining the beauty of the building in which the architect is expressing his thought. But for all that, we are compelled to agree that in many cases this constructional and practical worth may quite properly be subordinated to other elements which are incompatible with it, provided the latter, without it, are capable of producing æsthetic results which with it would be impossible of achievement.
— HENRY RUTGERS MARSHALL.

T SQUARE. (See Tee Square, under Square.)

TUBULAR. Having a section like a tube of any shape ; thus a tubular girder is a built-up plate beam which is a tube of rectangular section.

TUDELLA ; sculptor and architect.

Studied sculpture in Italy, and in 1528 established himself in Zaragoza, Spain, and worked on the choir of the cathedral in that city.

Bermudez, *Diccionario ;* Viñaza, *Addiciones.*

TUDOR ARCH. (See under Arch.)

TUDOR ARCHITECTURE. The accession of Henry VII. to the throne of England marked the beginning of a period so distinct in the architectural history of England that it has been customary to describe it by the name of Henry's Welsh family, Tudor. No one period of English history is more interesting than this, covering the reigns of Henry VII., Henry VIII., Edward VI., Mary, and Elizabeth, a long and eventful period reaching from 1485 to 1600. The later work is often separately designated as Elizabethan, but there is hardly sufficient change in character to make a real division.

With Tudor times an enormous impetus was given to house-building by the general tendency toward more comfort and luxury, and this was further accelerated by the dissolution of the monasteries, which put land and wealth in the hands of the layman.

The great lord and landowner was not only the head of his family, but the head of a host of retainers of every description, from lesser nobles and knights down to the artificers in the various trades. The keeping up of such a retinue and establishment bred hospitality, and also led to a demand for private apartments for the family, where some retirement from the motley turmoil was possible.

The plan of the house had developed from two directions toward a similar end. The buildings grouped about the irregular castle court grew into the group which surrounded the regular quadrangle. The great hall of the manor or grange was extended laterally, and then at right angles on the two ends, until it also enclosed a quadrangle, or at least bounded it on three sides. Modifications of this plan gave the E and the H plans. These then, the quadrangle, the E, and the H, are the general types of Tudor house plans.

The climate called for substantial material, light on the south, shelter on the north, steep roofs, many fireplaces, and abundant admission of sun. Thus the English characteristics of Tudor work have their natural explanation, — buildings long and low, with steep roofs and gables, with many tall chimneys, and great glazed bays.

Of the rooms, the hall, although no longer so all-important as in early days, was still the most important feature, and the stairs, but recently mere squared logs going up between walls, were now an especial object of decoration. Oak was almost invariably the material. The stairs had close strings, and the balusters and panels forming the balustrade were often profusely carved in a manner which suggested the influence of the Italian Renaissance, and yet was distinctly English.[1]

Indeed, up to the time of Grinling Gibbons, there was no carving in England which approached in skill and dexterity the work of Italy and France. It was coarse, often grotesque, but generally well-placed, effective, and well understood in relation to the architecture (this latter an especially valuable quality, and one liable to be overlooked when the technical skill of the carver attracts too much attention).

Although Gothic work was now a thing of the past, in nothing is its influence so clearly seen as in the windows, which, throughout the Tudor period, remained subdivided by mullion and transom, and thus permitted the retention and development of the many-sided bay so char-

[1] For Italian influence under Henry VIII. see England, Architecture of.

PLATE XXXII

TUDOR ARCHITECTURE

The interior of the Chapel of Henry VII., Westminster Abbey, London. This is the typical building of those which can properly be called Tudor, for it was begun within fifteen years of the accession of the Tudor dynasty in the person of Henry VII. (1485), and it is the first important monument of the peaceful times succeeding the civil wars. The picture shows the south flank of the extraordinary brass screen which surrounds and almost hides the altar tomb of Henry VII. and his wife, Elizabeth of York. Through the central door is seen the ambulatory of the Abbey and the screen of Edward the Confessor's Chapel. The stalls are appropriated to the Order of the Bath.

acteristic of the English country house, both as an external feature and as a marked characteristic of the hall and dining room, in which it was most frequently found.

With the growth of the arts and the new learning more space was required for pictures and books, and this may have in part accounted for the long galleries which were so striking a feature. These rooms, or corridors, were generally on an upper floor, often running the length of the house under the roof, and of such size and importance that the English artist loved here to display fine panelling, marble mantles, and richly modelled ceilings.

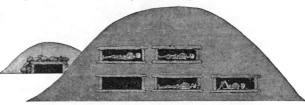

TUMULUS IN THE ORKNEY ISLANDS, SECTION SHOWING SEPARATE CHAMBERS FOR BURIAL MADE OF FLAT STONES.

In the reign of Elizabeth Italian influence was more clearly felt, and classic detail was pretty generally adopted, but the main lines were still Tudor. Under her successor, classic really began to rule, and a distinct style arose known from the Stuart family as Jacobean (which see).

(For ecclesiastical work in Tudor times see Gothic Architecture in England.)

— R. C. STURGIS.

TUDOR FLOWER. An ornament of late English Gothic art; a trefoil flower developed from the upright points of the crossing or the cusps of the foliated arch.

TUDOR ROSE. (See under Rose.)

TUILERIES, PALACE OF THE. In Paris; built originally outside the walls. It was added to by many succeeding princes, but never served as the principal royal residence until the Revolution, when Louis XVI., being brought into Paris by the mob, took up his quarters there. Napoleon, the kings of the Restoration, Louis Philippe, and Napoleon III. lived there, except when brief visits were made to Compiègne, Saint-Cloud, or Fontainebleau. The building was entirely destroyed by fire in 1871,

TUMULUS, ILE DE GAVR'INIS (MORBIHAN), FRANCE; SECTION SHOWING LONG CISTVAEN, THE SLABS INCISED WITH PATTERNS.

and its ruins cleared away in 1885. The original design of Jean Bullant is of incomparably more consequence than any of the later additions, and can be seen in Du Cerceau's *Bastiments de la France*. The garden of the Tuileries is one of the public parks of Paris, and contains some important pieces of sculpture. — R. S.

TUMULUS. An artificial mound of prehis-

toric or unknown antiquity; the work of uncivilized people; especially a barrow or grave mound; but applied, as the origin of the word warrants, to artificial hills intended for sacrificial purposes, the ruins of fortifications, and the like. (See Mound.)

TUNISIA, ARCHITECTURE OF. (See North Africa, Architecture of.)

TUNNEL. A passage or conduit excavated through solid rock or ground, or below the surface of the earth, or built under water in crossing a river, or the like, for a highway, for a railroad, or merely as a culvert, or for sewer, gas, or water pipes, or electric wires.

TUPIK. (Written also tupiq, tupic, tupek, and tupeck.) From the Eskimo; a tent. In the milder Arctic weather the Iglu and Iglugeak become uninhabitable, the former because of the dampness, and the latter because the dome melts and falls in. The Eskimo then resort to tents. Some of these resemble the ordinary Tipi, but have no smoke hole, the fire being built outside. while others are of a horseshoe shape, and still others are similar to our "A" tents, but with rounded ends. These variations belong to different localities. Skins are the usual covering. Sometimes two or more tents are placed together. (See also Karmang.)

Turner, *11th An. Bu. Eth.*; Murdoch, *9th An. Bu. Eth.*; Boas, *6th An. Bu. Eth.*; Peary, *Northward*; Nansen; Rink; Ross; Hall.

— F. S. D.

TURKEY, ARCHITECTURE OF. (See Moslem Architecture; Roman Imperial; also Asia Minor, Architecture of; Balkan Peninsula; Egypt; Syria.)

TURKISTAN, ARCHITECTURE OF. That of the country lying immediately north of the modern kingdom of Persia and state of Afghanistan, extending from the boundaries of the lofty table-land of Pamir on the east to the trans-Caspian provinces of the Russian empire on the west, and including the cities of Bokhara, Khiva, Merv, Samarcand, and Tashkand. The whole country is more or less dependent upon Russia since 1876, but the population is still thinly distributed, of mixed Asiatic origin, and is probably much smaller than it was in the sixteenth century of our era and previous to that time. The term Turkistan is more properly applied to this country than any other geographical expression, because the tendency of modern ethnological and geographical writing is to speak of the ruling races which originated here as "Turks," using that term in a general sense. The conquering Khans of the eleventh, twelfth, and thirteenth centuries of our era are considered Turks as much as the Seljuks or the Ottomans.

The country has been little visited by any European who has had a sense of architectural art, but recent travellers have at all events taken photographs which have been published in their volumes. One traveller in Turkistan had, however, a marked feeling for architectural fine art, Eugene Schuyler (d. July, 1890), who travelled in the country in 1875–6.

The fine arts of the country have been greatly influenced by Chinese example ; but it is not in architectural art that the Chinese influence could be most weighty. In the northeast, between Tashkand and Kuldja, there are the ruins of cities in which Chinese building had evidently controlled the design, and in Kuldja itself the ancient buildings have been ruined and this city, though close to the Chinese frontier, is almost wholly a Turki town. (See China, Architecture of.) It is a Persian influence which is the most visible in all the architectural art known to us ; but this not exclusively the influence of the Persian art of the fifteenth century and following years with its strong tendency toward decoration, both external and internal, by means of glazed tiles in brilliant colour. It is rather a more ancient Persian art dating from the early years of the Moslem control, or roughly speaking, from the eighth to the twelfth century inclusive. As has been pointed out in the articles on Persia that land has always been a centre of decorative art, its influence felt over the whole of Western Asia and thence by the whole Byzantine empire and indirectly Europe itself in the earlier Middle Ages. This exceptional mastery of artistic design was developed in a more strictly architectural sense after the beginning of the eleventh century of our era, and the buildings of the cities named in the first paragraph above, though none have been explored and studied of a certain date earlier than 1150, are all of a Persian type, giving distinct evidence of a still earlier influence coming from Persia and developing in the comparatively uncivilized northern country in a slightly different way from that of the Persian cities.

The four-centred pointed arch characterizes these buildings from the twelfth century to the latest epoch ; simple and unbroken masses of wall decorated with patterns in colored brickwork or in slight relief of bricks set horizontally,

vertically, and at various slopes in the outermost shell or face of the wall are common methods of decoration. The round minaret at Bokhara is a simple truncated cone with very steep sides, crowned by a cylindrical chamber like a belfry carried in slight projection by a system of corbelling ; and this structure from base to the springing of the corbel course is absolutely unbroken by window or visible door (the entry being from a small building adjoining) and is adorned merely by horizontal bands of colour sparingly and most judiciously applied. The mosques on the great square at Samarcand, called by Schuyler, The Medressehs, Shir-Dar, Tilla-Kari, and Ulug-Bek, have each a superb porch with a very lofty arch dividing the whole mass of the central pavilion into two heavy piers ; wings with much lower walls are flanked by conical minarets. The Medresseh Shir-Dar has lost the crowning chamber or gallery of its minaret, but has preserved the corbelling which once carried it, and a cupola with the lofty and circular drum concealed from the front by the lofty porch is attractive from the rear and side. A similar cupola crowns the celebrated Guramir, the supposed tomb of the conqueror Timur (d. 1405) in the neighborhood of Samarcand. The much later palace at Khokand retains some of the features of these older buildings, but is very inferior in dignity of mass or in grace of proportion. It is, moreover, covered by diaper patterns very ill-imagined, according to the too common tendency of modern Persian art, which seems to assume that there cannot be too much of such covering patterns. (See Decoration ; Diaper ; Polychromy.) At the city of Turkistan, in the far north, is the very ancient tomb said to have been begun by Timur, and there is also the mosque called Hazret, or the Divine Presence, which was certainly built by that conqueror. These buildings, dating from the last few years of the fourteenth century, still retain some part of their admirable tile sheathing.

Samarcand, in the fourteenth century, was certainly one of the most magnificent cities on earth, and carefully managed exploration in this town should result in a great enlargement of our knowledge of the principles of Asiatic architecture.

The simple buildings of the people and the relics of ancient architecture before the time of Moslem influence coming from Persia are alike unstudied and unknown except for the occasional evidence of photographs taken for another purpose. The opportunity for enlarged archæological research in the one case, and of social study in the second, with the architectural interest inherent in both would seem to be unsurpassed by that of any region in the world.

Bigham, *A Ride Through Western Asia*, 1897 ; Schuyler, *Turkistan, Notes of a Journey in Russian Turkistan, Khokand, Bukhara, and Kuldja*,

PLATE XXXIII

TURKISH ARCHITECTURE

Interior of the great Mosque of Sultan Suleiman I. (Suleimanieh). This is the most important piece of Turkish architecture, and was built in imitation of the church of S. Sophia, at least in so far as the cupola and pendentives are concerned. Stained glass is remarkable as the most important display of non-European work of the sort. The legend is that two pieces (not shown in this Plate) were taken in war with the Persians, and that the others were copied or studied from them. The building dates from the middle of the sixteenth century.

2 vols., 1877; Vambéry, *Bokhara*, 1873; *Central Asia*, 1864. —R. S.

TURN (v.). To lay up, as an arch, in brick or stone on a temporary centring.

TURNBOUT. Same as Turnbuckle.

TURNBUCKLE. A right and left screw coupling in the form of a link, both ends of which screw on the separated ends of a rod or bar, so that by turning the buckle the tension of the rod or bar may be increased or diminished at will. It is often used in setting up a truss.

TURNING PIECE. A piece of board cut to a curve to guide the mason in turning any small arch for which no centring is required.

TURRET; TOWER WITH STAIRCASE TURRET; GORING, OXFORDSHIRE; C. 1120.

TURPIN, JEAN; architect and sculptor.

With Antoine Avernier, Arnoul Boulin, and Alexandre Huet he made the stalls of the cathedral of Amiens (Somme, France), finished in 1522.

Gilbert, *Cathédrale d'Amiens.*

TURRET. A small tower; especially one attached to a larger tower, as where an échauguette or stair turret rises above the platform of a fortified tower, or where a circular stair is built at an angle of a church tower to lead to the belfry.

Pepper Box Turret. A turret circular in plan, and with some form of conical or domical roof.

TUSCAN ARCHITECTURE. *A.* That of the ancient Etruscans (see Etruscan Architecture).

B. That of modern Tuscany at any epoch, especially any style taking shape in this region

and not extending much beyond it. The most important of such styles is the round-arched

TURRET; GLASTONBURY ABBEY, C. 1200; IT COVERS THE HEAD OF A WINDING STAIR AND GIVES ACCESS TO THE ROOFS.

Gothic, exemplified by the Loggia dei Lanzi and the Bargello, or palace of the Podestà, both in Florence, and the cathedral of Lucca, and other buildings, a style which was mainly Gothic in

TURRET; S. MARY'S, BEVERLY; C. 1450.

structure with its system of building received from the North, but protested against the northern style as a decorative system.

TUSCAN ORDER. One of the three Roman orders of architecture according to Vitruvius; one of the five recognized by sixteenth century

TURRET; TOWN HALL OF SAUMUR, WITH TWO ANGLE TURRETS OR ECHAUGUETTES.

887   888

TUSCAN ARCHITECTURE; CATHEDRAL OF LUCCA, GOTHIC IN STRUCTURE
BUT ITALIAN IN DESIGN.

writers. It resembles the Roman Doric, but has fewer and bolder mouldings, no triglyphs, and no decorated details. In neoclassic work the shafts are sometimes built with rusticated bands, and, in a superimposition of orders, its place is in the basement.

TUSK. A bevelled shoulder on a tenon to give it additional strength, the mortise being cut to correspond.

TWO–PAIR (adjectival term). In a London lodging house, belonging to the third story, accessible by two flights of stairs. The two-pair front is the front room of the third story, counting from the street, or the second story in English usage.

TYMPAN. Same as Tympanum.

TYMPANUM OF A WINDOW IN EL-BARAH, SYRIA; 5TH TO 6TH CENTURY.

TYMPANUM. The triangular recessed space beneath the coping of a pediment and between the raking cornice of the roof and the horizontal geison below. Also the slab or piece of walling which is used to fill up the space between an arch and the square head of a door or window below. This may be a single stone, or, if of small parts, it may rest upon a lintel. It is often used for rich decoration, and in large Gothic churches it may receive the richest relief sculpture, as seen in Vol. II., Plates I. and IV., and cut col. 203. The term having merely the general significance of a smooth, thin plate or membrane is applied also to a panel by writers who take the word in this sense direct from Vitruvius, IV. 6. (Compare Lunette.)

TYROL, ARCHITECTURE OF. (See Austrian States.)

TZAPOTECO ARCHITECTURE. That of the American Indians of the Tzapoteco stock, whose country was south of the Aztec, and who rivalled the latter in their architectural works, still exhibited in the ruins of Mitla. (See Mexico, Architecture of, § I.)

TZOMPANTLI. An Aztec building erected for the purpose of receiving and executing prisoners of war, and for dividing their flesh among the proper recipients. (See Mexico, Architecture of, § I.) — F. S. D.

U

UCCELLO, PAOLO DI DONO; painter; b. 1397; d. 1475.

A mural painter at Pisa and Florence. (In the General Biography, Crowe and Cavalcaselle; Vasari; Nagler: also Müntz, *Renaissance.*)

UDINE, GIOVANNI DA. (See Ricamatori, Giovanni de'.)

UFFIZI. (In Italian, Gli Uffizi, "the offices.") A building in Florence of which the uppermost story is used for a museum, one of the most important in Europe.

ULPIAN BASILICA. (See Basilica of Trajan.)

ULRICH VON ENSINGEN; architect; d. 1429.

Ulrich from Ensingen, a village in Switzerland near Fribourg, was chief architect of the cathedral of Ulm (begun 1377) from 1390, when the most important part of the construction was actually undertaken, until his death in 1429. From 1410 to 1429 he was also employed in some capacity at the cathedral of Strasburg. In 1387 he was called to Milan to advise concerning the construction of the cathedral. He was succeeded by his sons, Gaspard and Mathias.

Hassler, *Ulms Kunstgeschichte im Mittelalter;* Gérard, *Les Artistes de l'Alsace;* Schneegans, *Les Architectes de Strassburg.*

UNBURNT. Not baked, or fired, in a kiln; said of articles of clay such as in most cases are so completed by exposure to heat. Unburnt bricks are very common in Egyptian and Syrian building.

UNCOURSED. Masonry not laid up in courses or layers with continuous horizontal joints, but irregularly. (See Ashlar; Course; Masonry.)

UNCTORIUM. In the Roman baths, an apartment used by the bathers for anointing the bodies with oil or some unguent, which was then scraped off with a strigil. (Called also Elæothesium.)

UNDERCROFT. Any vault or secret passage underground.

UNDERCUT. In carving, as in high reliefs, cut away behind; said of the background or of the whole carving, the figures standing clear, or nearly clear, from the background.

UNDERDRAWN. Closed beneath, as by lath and plaster, or by boarding, as when a floor previously of exposed timber is closed for greater warmth or prevention of sound. By extension, having the whole structure of a ceiling put in, as beneath the roof of a cottage, leaving a garret above.

UNDERPINNING. *A.* The rough walls or piers supporting the first floor timbers of a building without a cellar. The upper part of a foundation wall showing above the grade and under the water table, or ground sill. In New England often used for the masonry foundations, as in a house otherwise built of wood.

B. The material and labour used in replacing,

TYMPANUM OF DOOR; CHURCH OF S. JEAN-BAPTISTE DE BELLEVILLE, PARIS.

in whole or in part, an old or infirm foundation wall with a new wall, or in extending with new material a wall already built to a lower and more stable bottom. The terms also applied to labour and material employed in the reconstruction of an old wall, so as to furnish a new and permanent bed for a stone or bearing for a beam. (See Shoring.)

UNDERTHROATING. The cove of an outside cornice when so treated as to serve as a drip.

UNDERWRITERS' DOOR; FLOOR; etc. An appliance, or fitting, of the form and structure approved by the insurance companies as not calculated to burn readily or to help the spread of fire.

UNDULATED. Arranged with a wavelike form or movement, as in a guilloche, or in any other decorative feature.

UNGEWITTER, GEORG GOTTLOB; architect; b. 1820; d. 1864.

In 1837 he entered the academy in Munich. In 1842 he settled in Hamburg, and afterward practised in Lübeck and Leipzig. Ungewitter published *Lehrbuch der Gothischen Konstructionen* (Leipzig, 1890–1892, 2 vols. 4to); *Gothische Stadt und Landhaüser* (Berlin, 1889–1890); *Gothische Holzarchitektur* (Berlin, 1889–1890, folio). (See Statz.)

Reichensperger, *Georg Gottlob Ungewitter.*

UNITED STATES, ARCHITECTURE OF. That of the whole territory of the republic, as it was after the Gadsden Purchase in 1853.

§ I. *Pre-Columbian Era.* The architectural constructions of the aborigines of America

were, and are, exceedingly varied in form, location, material, and method. Almost every kind of position where a house or village might be established, according to expedience or necessity, was a opted, from the immediate shores of the sea to almost inaccessible ledges in mighty cliffs of the far interior. Almost every material available for building purposes, excepting metals, was utilized, from mere twigs and branches of trees to stone; even to snow and the bones of whales. And the structures were given almost every possible shape; square, round, semicircular, oval, triangular, rectangular, conical, and domed. The methods of erecting embraced framing, wattling, masonry, pisé, jacál, and others. Many structures were only of one story, but some were of four or five. From the rude bough wickyup of the Arizona Pai Ute, lightly abandoned on every change of camp, to the massive and elaborately ornamented stone buildings of the Maya of Yucatan, is an immense range, greater than can be elsewhere studied within our historic period. It is possible, therefore, in America to take up the study of house building where the thread is lost in Europe, and with both follow the line of development from the wickyup to the Parthenon. Examples of almost every form of dwelling possible for mankind to devise exist still in America, occupied or in ruins. Apparently the very beginning is in the sun shelter, of which there may yet be observed specimens in temporary use among American Indians. Passing into the wickyup type, then into the more substantial and permanent wigwam, the adobe house and the durable stone house were finally arrived at, all forms being determined by culture stage and by environment. Forest regions developed bark houses; polar regions, snow houses; treeless plains with large game, portable tents; arid regions, where disintegrating cliffs offer abundance of ready-made building material, stone houses; broad, dry valleys with little timber or stone, and no large game, mud or adobe houses, with a growth from isolated one-family structures to huge communal affairs, half fortress in character. No better exhibition can be found of the manner in which man in all stages of culture adapts himself to varying conditions, than in this wide range of American aboriginal architecture. Materials are moulded to his needs according to his degree of progress. With nothing better in the way of an axe than a broken stone, trees were felled for frames, or lintels, or rafters. Logs were split into planks by means of wooden or bone wedges, and dressed with adzes of jade, serpentine, obsidian, or similar stone. Elaborate carvings in wood and stone were executed with stone and shell chisels, and knives. Roofs were made of bark, of skins, of snow, of woven bark mats, or of timbers, reeds, earth, or stone. Within the limit of the United States are found examples of most of the methods of construction employed, culminating in such substantial buildings as may still be seen in the various occupied villages of the Pueblos, like Taos, Zuñi, and the towns of the Mokis, and in the numerous ruins scattered over the Southwest, like Casa Grande, the Cliff Dwellings (which see), and those of the Pecos and the Chaco, the latter representing the highest quality of masonry to be found north of Mexico. Metal tools were not used north of the Aztec country, and nowhere, prior to the European advent, was metal in any way a part of the construction. (See Mexico, Architecture of, § 1; Assembly House; Cajon; Communal Dwelling; Jacál; Kiva; Lodge; Mound; Pisé; Tipi; etc.) — F. S. DELLENBAUGH.

§ II. *Modern Era.* As a rule, the architecture of the territory comprised within the present limits of the United States was English in its origin, and the prevailing influence continued to be English down to the third quarter of the nineteenth century. The exceptions to this rule may be briefly noted. The Atlantic seaboard, which included all that there was of the United States when their independence was declared, included lands originally settled or claimed by Spain, Holland, Sweden, and France, as well as by Great Britain. The oldest settlement on the coast was the Spanish Saint Augustine; but Florida did not become a part of the United States until 1821. The principal relics of the Spanish domination are the cathedral of S. Augustine (1793), and the fort now called Marion (1756). In California, Arizona, and New Mexico, which were not acquired by the United States until 1848, there are no Spanish buildings comparable in extent or costliness with the churches of Old Mexico. The Spanish manner of building appears to have extended northward from Florida to South Carolina, in at least one noteworthy instance, that of S. James's Church, at Goose Creek, on the Cooper River, built about 1715. In this edifice the indications of Spanish workmanship are unmistakable. In its present condition, it shows that preparations had been made for surmounting its front with the curvilinear screen, or sham gable, which is a characteristic feature of Spanish ecclesiastical architecture; although it does not appear that this frontispiece was ever, in fact, added. The detail elsewhere is equally Spanish. Apart from a few detached churches, the principal remains of the Spanish domination, of what is now the Pacific slope of the United States, are the buildings of the Catholic missions, each group of which includes a church. (See California Mission, under Mission.)

The only relics of French colonization within the limits of the United States are in Louisiana, where there are traces of the successive occupations of France and Spain. Founded by Bienville, in 1718, New Orleans continued to be held by the French until 1769, when Spain took formal possession under a cession granted in 1762. In 1800, the French retook possession under the treaty of San Ildephonso, and, in 1803, Louisiana was acquired by the United States. Perhaps the only relic of the original French occupation is the Ursuline convent, now known as the Archbishop's Palace, which was erected under Bienville's administration, in 1727. It is a plain building of two stories, in stuccoed brick, with a central pavilion crowned with a low pediment; but in spite of its plainness, it has enough of architectural character to indicate the nationality of its builders. The most conspicuous monument of the Spanish domination is the cathe-

UNITED STATES: HOUSE AT PORTSMOUTH, N H.

dral, built in 1794, but named after the patron saint of France. Fronting an open square, and with the flanking municipal buildings of stuccoed brick, it makes a somewhat pretentious architectural composition for a colonial capital, of no more importance than New Orleans was when it was built. The mansard roofs of the flanking buildings are later additions; the original scheme having been that of the Ursuline convent, a nearly equal triple division into two wings, and a central pavilion crowned with a low pediment. These buildings also are of two stories only. They are very massively built of brick, and derive some importance from their size and solidity, if not from their design. The cathedral seems to have been originally designed in the Spanish, or Spanish-American manner, with a frontispiece, consisting of a free standing gable, and a lower roof behind. But the existing flanking and central towers, which are no more congruous with the front than admirable in themselves, were added in 1851, together with other alterations that obscure the original design. The domestic building of the New Orleans of the eighteenth century, so far as can be judged by its dilapidated remains, was much more Spanish than French, showing the heavy Spanish tiled roofs, and the deeply re-

stone, sparingly garnished with brick, or, more commonly, rectangles of stonework one story high, with roof gables of timber, and the eaves projecting beyond the walls, a protective device, which gave the building its only touch of picturesqueness. Specimens of these are still numerous in that part of New Jersey behind the Palisades. The Van Cortlandt

UNITED STATES: FARMHOUSE NEAR HINGHAM, MASS.

cessed upper galleries, suitable to a tropical climate, and also the massiveness of construction which has preserved dwellings originally humble, where they have not been demolished by fire, or by design.

The Dutch settlers on the Hudson, as well as the Swedish settlers on the Delaware, followed their native modes of building so far as possible.

manor house, on the east bank of the Hudson River, was built in 1681, and the Slip house, on Bergen Heights, in Jersey City, in 1666. The older part of the Philipse manor house, now the City Hall of Yonkers, was built in 1682, by Frederic Philipse, the richest merchant of his time; and the rudeness of its interior workmanship attests the absence from the colony of skilled carvers in wood. The brickwork of the period is very good, but both bricks and bricklayers were imported. But, upon the whole, the building of the Dutch settlers was so simple and humble, and so exclusively for the satisfaction of the bodily wants, that it cannot be called architecture. How simple it was may be judged from the fact that what was really a "specimen" of Dutch architecture, the so-called "Vanderheyden Palace" in Albany, built in 1725, was a building of two stories, measuring 50 feet by 20, and with but two rooms on

UNITED STATES: ROGER WILLIAMS HOUSE, SALEM, MASS., 1635.

It was not, however, until toward the close of the seventeenth century that they were able to build of substantial materials. It is not probable that there are a dozen buildings left standing in the region settled by the Dutch, which antedate the final British occupation of New York in 1674. The farmhouses built in the Dutch manner after that time were of rough

the ground floor. The churches were as plain as the dwellings, mere "meetinghouses," as may be seen in the only one that remains, that built at Sleepy Hollow, in 1699, by Philipse. This is a room of moderate size, enclosed in walls of rough stone, with window arches of yellow Holland brick, its ecclesiastical character being denoted by the tall undivided windows, and the apsidal end.

United States: Church at Hingham, Mass., 1681.

United States: The Royall Mansion, Medford, Mass.

Perhaps the only remaining buildings of the Swedish settlement upon the Delaware are two churches, almost exactly contemporary with the last mentioned, and with each other. The "Old Swedes" church, at Wilmington, was begun in 1698, and was consecrated on Trinity Sunday, 1699. It is a rectangle of rough stone, 66 feet long, 36 broad, and 20 high, with walls

English workmanship. The original building was plain to absolute baldness, for the few details that show a decorative intention are evidently of later application, and in wood.

The oldest church still standing upon the Atlantic seaboard is, undoubtedly, S. Luke's, near Smithfield, Virginia. To this local tradition assigns the date of 1632. It seems incredible that an erection, showing so high a degree of mechanical skill, and so considerable an expenditure, should have been made within twenty-five years after the settlement at Jamestown; and it is likely that tradition confuses the existing building with an earlier one upon the same site. However that may be, the church was doubtless built before the last quarter of the seventeenth century. It is a room of 50 feet by 20, with a tower 18 feet square by about 50 high, all in very substantial brickwork. Its ecclesiastical character is denoted not only by the rudely pointed arches, but by buttresses which seem to be without any architectural significance. The tower is heavily groined in brickwork, however, and the keystone of the round-arched doorway projects. Upon the whole, it is such a building as an English bricklayer, working with English bricks, from a recollection of current English church building, might have been expected to produce, during the reign either of Charles I. or of Charles II. That it is the oldest church in the United States

UNITED STATES: OLD STATE HOUSE, BOSTON, 1748.

varying in thickness from 2 to 3 feet, with openings arched and groined in brickwork. The existing porch, built mainly as a buttress for the walls, which had shown a dangerous weakness, was not added until 1762, nor the existing tower until 1802. Although the pastor of the church was a Swede, the workmen employed upon it were Englishmen from Philadelphia, and what of architectural character the building can be said to possess is English also. The "Old Swedes" church in Philadelphia was built in 1700. This is in brickwork, and very good brickwork; but is also an example of

is very probable, even if we deduct half a century from the duration assigned to it by tradition.

It was not until the eighteenth century was well advanced that any churches of architectural pretensions began to be erected in the European settlements in America, and these were all based upon English models. The earliest of them, S. Philip's, at Charleston, was built before 1733; and it is to this, doubtless, that Burke refers in the "European Settlements in America" (1757), as "a church executed in very handsome taste, exceeding any-

thing of that kind that we have in America."
This church was burned in 1835; but its successor is an execution of virtually the same
design, except that the spire has been elon
gated. The name of the architect is not known.
Of the other parish church of Charleston, S.
Michael's, it has been conjectured that the
" Mr. Gibson," from whose designs it was said
in the newspapers of the time to have been
erected, was, in fact, James Gibbs, then the

UNITED STATES: HOUSE ON LONG ISLAND.

most fashionable church architect in London.
S. Michael's was begun in 1752, and Gibbs
died in 1754. There were no churches of as
much architectural pretensions, nor in as pure
and scholarly a style, as these two in the more
northerly settlements for many years after they
were built. The Old South in Boston (1729),
and Christ church in Philadelphia (1727), were
practically contemporary with S. Philip's in
Charleston. The former, as an architectural
work, is entitled to no consideration. The
designer of the latter, a local amateur, Dr.
John Kearsley, had evidently studied the classic orders. The gallery is recognized and emphasized in the design, to the extent of dividing
the building into two distinct stories at the
sides. The end is undivided; and is converted
into a grandiose and very fairly successful
feature, a Palladian triple window, with the
central arch sprung from the entablature that
covers the lower openings of the sides, with
their order of pilasters, and, above a heavy
cornice, a blind attic and a pediment. All are
accurately proportioned and detailed. The lack
of available stonecutters compelled the construction of the more elaborate parts in wood, or, as
in the entablature of the front, in brick, the
body of the church being very good brickwork.
The steeple was not added until twenty years
after the completion of the church. It has
nothing admirable, excepting the stage of transition from the square brick shaft to the octagonal spire, which is a very well considered
piece of design. The interior, as " restored "
by Thomas U. Walter, in 1836, is a gram-
matical design in Roman Doric.

At this time, and for long afterward, there
was not a church in New York, nor in New
England, that showed any architectural training
on the part of its designer. Peter Harrison, a

pupil of Vanbrugh, was imported in 1747, to
design and superintend the building of King's
Chapel in Boston, which was executed according to his design, and is fairly representative
of the English architecture of the time; although
the spire has never been added, and the portico,
which is its most important feature, was built
in wood. The first piece of architecture incorporated in, or rather adjoined to, a church
in New York, was the portico, fronting Broad-
way, of S. Paul's church. The body of the
church was completed in 1766; but this portico
seems to have been added from the designs of
Major Charles L'Enfant, about 1789, when he
was employed to enlarge, embellish, and convert
into " Federal Hall," for the reception of Congress, the old City Hall, built in 1700. The
spire of S. Paul's was added in the nineteenth
century.

The secular public buildings erected during
the colonial period, were, for the most part,
cheaply and hastily built for their immediate
requirements, and it was only toward the close
of the period, politically colonial, that they took
on any architectural pretensions. The New
York City Hall, occupied in 1700, and afterward extended and embellished by L'Enfant,
as already explained, for a Federal Hall, stood
until it was demolished to make room for the
customhouse, now the subtreasury, in 1834.
It consisted of two wings and a recessed centre,
two stories high; and without other ornament
than the wooden brackets of the roof, and the
coats of arms of the governor and lieutenant-
governor. The State House of Pennsylvania,

UNITED STATES: VAN RENSSELAER HOUSE,
GREENBUSH, N.Y.

better known as Independence Hall, a generation later in date (1731–1735), like the contemporaneous Christ Church, had an amateur
architect, Andrew Hamilton, well known as a
lawyer. It is a sober, discreet, and still respectable edifice, especially notable for an employment of cut stone in the groins, panels,
string courses, and keystones, which was then
profuse. The State House of Virginia, at
Williamsburg, built before 1723, is now known

only from Jefferson's description, which represents its only architectural feature as a portico of two orders, which Jefferson criticises. This was doubtless of wood. The still standing capitol at Richmond was built from the design obtained by Jefferson in France of "M. Clarissault" (?), and its design was compounded of those of the Erechtheum, of the temple of Baalbec, and of the Maison Carrée at Nîmes; but the model most closely followed was the last named building, though the order, "on account of the expense," was changed from Corinthian to Doric, and Doric of the Italian Renaissance. The State House of Maryland is one of the civic buildings, the other being S. John's College, which combine with many private houses, which have been carefully preserved, to make Annapolis the most interesting museum of Georgian architecture in the United States. The college was built in 1744, by a Scotch architect, specially imported for the purpose. That is of slight architectural im-

portance. The State House was begun in 1772, under the direction of a native, or at least of a resident, architect. The chief feature of the exterior is a cupola, unduly and disproportionately elongated; but the central rotunda of the interior, though executed in wood, from want of money, or of artisans capable of executing it in stone, is one of the most elaborate, and monumental, as well as one of the most "elegant" examples of colonial architecture. It is really an admirable design competently carried out. The architecturally colonial period lasted nearly half a century after the political independence of the United States. Indeed, as has been said, American architecture continued for nearly a century to be a reflection of current English modes. The State House of Massachusetts (1795) is a typically colonial building, bearing, in some peculiarities of treatment, the marks of an American differentiation from the British Georgian, peculiarities which reappear in the work done in the Capitol of the United States by its author, Charles Bulfinch, apparently the first American who regularly studied the profession of architecture. The buildings of the University of Virginia (1819–1826), designed by Thomas

Jefferson, belong also to colonial architecture, though they form an exception to the rule that colonial building was English building. Jefferson's studies and travels had put him in architectural, as well as political, sympathy with France. As we have seen, he employed a French architect to design the Virginia State House; and his own work, though he intended it to be an accurate reproduction of the antique, is in a somewhat French version of classical. His plan for the university was really grandiose in scheme and scale, and, although want of means impaired the complete execution of it, what was done elicited general and angry protests upon the score of extravagance, $300,000 being spent upon it in Jefferson's lifetime.

The Capitol of the United States, excepting the wings and the dome, afterward added, is not only a typical, but the most considerable, example of colonial architecture. The original designer, Dr. Thornton, was a West Indian, and an amateur, and the main dispositions of the existing central building are his. His successors, Hallett, Hoban, Hadfield, Latrobe, and Bulfinch, carried the central building to the condition in which, excepting the cupola, it now appears; but the real designers were Thornton, Latrobe, and Bulfinch. The contributions of the latter two are important and distinguishable, though each respected the work of his predecessors.

Colonial domestic architecture did not become of much importance until the middle of the eighteenth century. The vernacular dwelling of all the colonies was the "frame house," the structure of beams covered with clapboards, which remains the vernacular dwelling of the States. The veranda, which is now thought an almost indispensable adjunct of every country house above the pretensions of a cabin, does not seem to have been introduced during the whole of the architecturally colonial period. The houses of the great tobacco planters of Virginia and Maryland were large and substantial mansions of brick; but the bricklayers, if not the bricks, were specially imported, and such decorative features as they present, even in wood, appear to have been constructed in England. "Brandon," on the lower James, was built about 1740, "the Grove," 1746, "Westover," 1749, "Whitehall," the seat of the governor of Maryland, between 1740 and 1750. They were rectangles of brick, without much architectural pretension, excepting the last named, which is a regular and effective composition of a centre and wings, the centre signalized by a wooden portico. A brick house of the same general character, and of great massiveness and solidity,

UNITED STATES: APTHORPE HOUSE, NEW YORK, N. Y.

UNITED STATES: CHURCH AT RICHMOND, VA., 1811.

was built at Portsmouth, New Hampshire, as early as 1718, at a cost of £6000; but this remained for nearly a quarter of a century unique, not only in Portsmouth, but in New England. Town mansions of successful pretensions, and in durable material, did not begin to be erected in the coast towns until after 1730. The Frankland, Hancock, and

UNITED STATES: UNIVERSITY OF VIRGINIA, CHARLOTTESVILLE, VA., 1817.

the Shirley houses, in Boston, date respectively from 1735, 1737, and 1748. The Walton House in New York, the so-called Arnold House in Philadelphia, and the Pringle House in Charleston are of later date, while the principal colonial house of Annapolis was built between 1740 and 1770. Almost without exception, these houses were designed and built by mechanics, without the supervision of an architect. They owe their undeniable charm, not only to the fact that the detail was for the most part accurately copied from the best examples of contemporary English architecture, of which Sir William Chambers was then the leading practitioner, but also to the fact that the studying and copying of this detail had inculcated a refinement and discretion which are equally seen in its scale and adjustment. It is not unusual to find in remote villages unpretentious houses, built about the beginning of the present century by local carpenters, which exhibit these attractive qualities in as much perfection as the better known and costlier examples of colonial architecture.

The effects upon American building of the publication of Stuart and Revett's work upon Athens, founded upon actual investigations and measurements of the architectural remains of Athens, were long delayed. Greek architecture had in the first place been modified and sophisticated, in Roman example and in Roman precept, and the Roman remains and the writings of Vitruvius were the source of the Italian Renaissance, which had spread over Europe, and held undisputed sway for three centuries. The architecture, thus extended and elaborated, was not easy to be suppressed by the exhibition of the simpler and more primitive types from which

it had been derived. It was scarcely before the beginning of the present century that the Athenian monuments began to influence European architecture, and nearly a quarter of a century later before their influence upon this side of the Atlantic. It may perhaps be detected in some of Latrobe's modifications of Thornton's design for the portico of the Capitol (about 1815). Other buildings by Latrobe are more distinctly products of the Greek revival, notably the United States, now the Girard, Bank, in Philadelphia. This was the first Grecian portico erected in the United States, with details correctly reproduced from the Athenian examples. The building was universally admired, and its influence was immediate and lasting. Strickland, a pupil of Latrobe, followed with others in the same style in Philadelphia, the Second Bank of the United States, and the United States Mint; and in the Merchants' Exchange, gave the first example in America of a Corinthian portico executed in carved stone. The building to which this portico is attached is treated with absolute plainness, excepting that the mullions of the

UNITED STATES: OLD NORTH CHURCH, NEW HAVEN, CONN.

openings are pilasters, the openings themselves being unmoulded. The semicircular portico is, however, an ingenious adaptation of the order of the choragic monument of Lysicrates, a reproduction of the monument itself, with openings between the columns surmounting the composition as a lantern. The Grecian became the official style of the country, and so remained, at least until 1860. The Treasury Department, and the Patent Office, and the General Post Office, were built in one or the other of its orders, as well as the customhouse and the buildings required by the government in different cities. The customhouse of New York, now the subtreasury, aimed at reproducing the Parthenon ; although it is amphiprostyle instead of peripteral, and the frieze is without sculpture. The present customhouse, built for the Merchants' Exchange, and completed in 1841, from the designs of Isaiah Rogers, shows, perhaps, the most effective Ionic colonnade in the United States. States and cities followed the lead of the Federal government, and for more than a generation, scarcely a public building was erected which was not at least supposed by its builders to be in the Grecian style. Doubtless, nothing could have been practically more inconvenient than the requirement that one or more parts of a building divided into offices should be darkened by the projecting portico. In many cases this difficulty was sought to be obviated by placing the main reliance for light in an opening at the centre of the roof, and converting the central space into a rotunda ; a wasteful arrangement, which was not, however, without some compensation in a grandiose effect. This is the disposition adopted in the former and in the present customhouse in New York. The style imposed itself also for private dwellings, both in town and country, the former being for the most part "rows," fronted with colonnades, and the latter temples, with a portico at one end consisting of a Grecian order, generally the Doric, for the most part accurately proportioned, but executed

UNITED STATES: LIBRARY, BOSTON, MASS.

in wood. This type established itself in all parts of the country, and was often employed, even for churches. Highly unsuitable as it was either for these or for dwellings, it served the purpose of familiarizing the public with an orderly and harmonious assemblage of studied

architectural forms, and it was the only agency by which this could then have been accomplished. For at about the time when the Greek revival set in, the tradition of the colonial or Georgian building had begun to die out among the mechanics, to whom the build-

UNITED STATES: FIRST CHURCH, NEW HAVEN, CONN.

ing of both town and country houses was almost universally confided. This tradition had issued in New York in a type of house of moderate size, two or, at the most, three stories high, with a half-sunk basement, a "high stoop," and a roof containing an attic lighted by dormer windows. These dormers and the doorway, which was commonly arched, though often lintelled, were the only parts treated with any elaboration, excepting the posts, if they may be called so, of open ironwork, against which the railing of the stoop ended. The houses were of brick, the doorway and the dormers commonly of wood, though, in the more pretentious houses, the former was of stone. Many examples of these houses may be seen, not only in New York, but in the towns of the Hudson River, and in the villages which arose along the "stage route" from Albany to Buffalo. They were not only carefully and successfully planned, and entirely suitable to their purpose, but the sparing ornament they bore was copied from examples so well chosen, and was so well adjusted in assemblage and in scale, as to give them an air of positive elegance. The typical dwellings of the other coast towns were by no means equally attractive, those of Philadelphia having almost absolutely plain fronts of very red and very smooth brick, with equally plain sills and lintels of white marble. Before 1860, the New York house described had given way to the "brown stone front," also a "high stoop" dwelling; but with no visible roof, with windows often framed in mouldings, the

UNITED STATES: HOUSE IN MARYLAND; TYPICAL MANSION WITH OUTHOUSES; 18TH CENTURY.

entrance commonly an arch, with a protruding keystone, and a round or triangular pediment carried, sometimes on a pair of columns, sometimes on consoles, the detail extreme and bloated in scale, as was also the modillioned cornice, commonly executed in wood or in sheet metal. Miles of these edifices may be seen in New York, and are still the most numerous class of private dwellings, at least in the middle part of the city which was built between 1850 and 1870. In country houses, the helplessness of the mechanic who had lost the wholesome traditions of his craft issued in the extreme of vulgarity. The introduction of the jig saw facilitated the production of crude and unstudied detail intended to be ornamental. Pretentious "towers" in clapboards were added to cottages, and the smaller American towns and villages came to have an aspect of complete repulsiveness. The Grecian temples and the Grecian colonnades were almost the only examples of studied design that were to be seen. And by the contrast which they offered to the recklessness and thoughtlessness of the common building, they must have had a beneficent influence. The latest example of the Greek revival was the most extensive and impressive. This was the addition of the wings to the Capitol at Washington. Their colonnades are worthy of the building which they flank, and add great stateliness to what was already, perhaps, the stateliest public building of the century. These wings were added by Thomas U. Walter, the pupil of Strickland, as Strickland had been of Latrobe. He had already designed in Girard College, in Philadelphia, finished in 1847, the most elaborate and substantial reproduction of Grecian architecture in the United States, an octostyle and peripteral Corinthian temple, on a scale ample enough to give the architecture its full effect, and carried out with perfect purity of detail and adequate mechanical execution. While Walter's wings to the Capitol are entirely successful, so much cannot be said

of his cupola, which is so exaggerated as to overpower the building beneath it, and to deprive itself of an architectural base, besides being executed in cast iron, a material to which the design does not at any point defer. Nevertheless, the Capitol is without dispute the most impressive public building in the United States.

During this period, commercial building shared the fate of domestic building. In the seaport towns, there were rows of solid warehouses of brick, or granite, with visible roof, with perfectly plain openings where they were practically needed, and most convenient for the builder, but without any attempt at grouping or diversification with reference to their architectural effect. Many of these buildings remain upon or near the water fronts of these towns. They can scarcely be classified as belonging to architecture; but their massive construction and the very absence of pretension make them inoffensive and respectable, and negatively attractive. On the other hand, the "shopping streets" of these towns came to be lined with buildings which were meant to be attractive, and which, being designed by builders, or even so-called architects, without architectural skill or training, were positively repulsive. The art of architecture has seldom sunk so low in any civilized country, as in the United

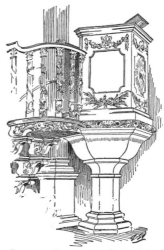

UNITED STATES: PULPIT IN S. PAUL'S CHAPEL, NEW YORK; CHURCH BUILT 1764-1766.

States at the middle of this century. The "commercial Renaissance" of the show streets of the principal cities was a series of stories of stone, or brick, or cast iron, apparently standing upon a wall of plate glass at the ground floor, surmounted by an exaggerated cornice in sheet metal, and usually offensive in direct proportion to its elaboration and pretentiousness.

UNITED STATES : HOUSE AT GREY'S FERRY, PHILADELPHIA, 1730.

These edifices were imitated with cheaper material in the smaller towns.

The United States had thus nothing to show in its current building but copies of a pure and refined architecture, of which the features were inextricably implicated with dispositions entirely unsuitable to almost all practical requirements, and the attempt to satisfy those requirements by means of buildings of which the dispositions were not studied with any view to their capabilities of expression, and of which the features and details intended for ornament were impure and coarse. It was upon this condition that the Gothic revival depended. It began very brilliantly with the erection of Trinity church in New York, completed and consecrated in

pioneer, of the Gothic revival in the United States. It may be questioned whether any subsequent work of that revival was more successful. The church differs from contemporary churches in England, in showing less of archæological scrupulosity. Details of different periods are employed together, but without compromising the artistic unity of the work. The success of Trinity was immediate and complete, and led to an effective demand, especially from the Protestant Episcopal church, for Gothic buildings, which were supplied by its designer, and by other architects of European birth and training, for the most part English, but in some cases German; and these architects and their American pupils did much to diffuse a knowl-

UNITED STATES: DWIGHT HOUSE, SPRINGFIELD, MASS., 1764.

1846. For half a century before, pointed arches had been introduced in churches as an ecclesiastical form, especially suitable to the Protestant Episcopal church, and distinguishing it from other denominations. We have seen that, two centuries before Trinity church was built, the builders of S. Luke's at Newport, in Virginia, working by tradition, and in a purely unschooled and vernacular fashion, had employed both pointed windows and useless buttresses to designate the purpose of their building. But Trinity was the first church on any considerable scale which was built in North America by an architect who was really schooled in Gothic architecture. The church is thus entitled to be regarded as the starting-point, and its architect, Richard Upjohn, as the

edge, or at least a recognition, of Gothic work. It cannot be said that they did much to raise the degraded standard of the common building of the country. The "mansard roof" had come in as a cheap and convenient device for securing an additional story, and the expressiveness which a visible roof had imparted, even to a wooden building of which the frame was concealed by clapboards, had melted away. In the Gothic work, too, there were apt to be survivals of forms which had lost their structural significance. But in almost every considerable town there came to be a church which was designed in tolerably correct Gothic, and which was recognized as more admirable than what it displaced. For some years the Gothic revival was confined to church building, and for the most part to monochromatic masonry. But the time had become ripe for the importation of what is specifically known as Victorian Gothic. This was very largely the result of Mr. Ruskin's admiration for the mediæval building of north Italy and of the eloquence with which he gave it expression. *The Seven Lamps of Architecture* appeared in 1849, three years after the completion of Trinity church in New York, and was followed ten years later by *The Stones of Venice*. The effect of these works upon building in Great Britain, already turned by "Anglican" considerations in the direction of the insular Gothic, was almost immediate. The adoption of an unquestionably English style for the Houses of Parliament, begun in 1840, had

can revivalists possessed the tact and discretion to employ different colours appropriately and harmoniously, or to refrain altogether from employing them, the result was some of the most interesting and successful architecture that had been produced in the United States, especially as the men who did it followed another precept of Ruskin, and betook themselves for ornament to the careful conventionalization of natural forms. The inexhaustible source of decoration thus opened, in comparison with the repetition of the very limited repertory of authorized classic detail, gave interest even to buildings that were not interesting in their general design. But where tact and discretion were wanting, the result was even wilder work than had been done before. As Victorian

UNITED STATES: MORRIS HOUSE, NEW YORK, N. Y., 1762.

given an impulse to the use of Gothic in secular buildings. But it is a very long stride from the House of Parliament to the Oxford Museum (1855), which was the first fruit of Mr. Ruskin's teachings. The young architects of England took to studying and reproducing the mediæval movements of France and north Italy as well as of England. About 1860 the revival had made its way across the Atlantic. By 1865 almost every American city had at least one example of "Victorian Gothic" to show in civic work, and for the next decade the most serious work that was done in architecture in the United States was done in this style. The external use of colour was one of the points in the architecture of north Italy upon which the revivalists had most insisted; but it is that in which most tact and discretion are imperatively required, and there is comparative safety in monochrome. Where the Ameri-

Gothic was applied to every kind of building, commercial and domestic as well as ecclesiastical, even controlling for a short period the government architecture; as it opened the whole field of mediæval architecture in Europe to the eclecticism of designers; as the studious and cultivated designers were everywhere in the minority; and as the bulk of the building continued to be done by men who were not architects at all, — the total result was discouraging.

Even the most thoughtful and artistic of the revivalists were apt to take mediæval architecture as a more or less literal model, rather than as a starting-point for modern work, and failed to divest their secular buildings, at least to the popular appreciation, of an ecclesiastical expression. Many architects began to revert with regret to the early part of the century and the decency of colonial building, and the time was ripe for the importation of the next

British fashion, that of "Queen Anne," comprising the Jacobean and Georgian periods, as well as that after which it was named, ultimately including even the Flemish Renaissance.

The vogue of "Queen Anne," specifically so-called, was very brief, but it assisted in a general reaction toward classic architecture. During the period of the Gothic revival, what was called the Renaissance had continued to be the prevailing mode for public and commercial buildings and for town houses, and it had been done with increasing knowledge under the influence of graduates of the Continental schools of architecture. The reaction was for a time interrupted by the appearance, in the person of Henry H. Richardson, of a very strong artistic individuality. A classic by training, he was a romantic by temperament, but he was prevented from joining in the Gothic revival by his dissatisfaction with the finical elaborateness which is apt to be its characteristic in unskilful hands, and by the additional restlessness which was imparted to the American phase of Victorian Gothic by the misapplication of colour. He reverted in his earliest characteristic work to the simpler, more massive, and more rudimentary Romanesque which preceded the development of vaulted architecture, and of which the Provençal variety especially appealed to him. His first work was Trinity church in Boston, completed in 1877, of which the central tower is very skilfully and successfully adapted from that of Salamanca cathedral, but of which the detail is for the most part in the style of the Romanesque of the south of France. The power of the design is, however, not in this detail, but in the success with which the body of the church was subordinated into a system of harmonious appendages to the central tower, which thus became the essential building. The effect of these dispositions was much enhanced by the singularly successful combination of colour, the fields of the wall being of rough, light granite, while the wrought work was of dark brown sandstone, the stress of colour being everywhere logically employed to add emphasis to the structural dispositions. The popular success of this work was immediate and great. The architect followed it up, during the decade that passed before his death, with a series of work which displayed the same striking power of simplification, and in which he aimed to show the adaptability of the style he had chosen to all descriptions of buildings. He designed Romanesque town halls, courthouses, exchanges, libraries, schools, warehouses, and dwellings, all characterized by simplicity and by a Cyclopean massiveness, and all of an interest which had a more rational basis than their mere novelty. The popular success of these works at once imposed upon a great number of the younger architects the style in which they were composed. It commended itself by the absence of the finical elaboration into which most of the Victorian Gothic had degenerated. On the other hand, the drawback of the style for modern purposes was its inherent rudeness. Richardson himself not only made no effort to mitigate this, but delighted in it, and added to it an exaggeration, commonly beyond reason, and sometimes violent, of the scale of the parts. In almost all his works he had a distinct motive, which was detached and made conspicuous by his treatment, and which was striking enough to carry off his extravagance of detail. But these extravagances were much easier of imitation than the essential merits of his work, and most of the imitators whom his success raised up confined themselves to the reproduction of them. There were others who really analyzed his work, who penetrated the sources of its power and availed themselves of them, and some of the buildings thus produced are among the most creditable achievements of American architecture. A very few of these practitioners even essayed, and with an encouraging measure of success, to mitigate the rudeness of the style as originally developed and as even exaggerated by the revivalist, and to demonstrate that it comprised elements which might be made flexible to all uses, and might become the basis of a true expression in architecture of modern life. It was evidently more eligible in this respect than the pointed Gothic, of which many even of the decorative forms and details were developed from a system of vaulted building, and lose their significance when separated from it. The Romanesque revival was thus the most promising beginning that had been made in the United States, if not in any country, toward the evolution of a living architecture. But this promise was destined to be broken, and the Romanesque revival did not long survive the revivalist. It cannot be said to have been developed, except in a very few instances, beyond the point to which he carried it, and in the hands of most of its practitioners it came far short of that point. But besides its intrinsic interest, it is noteworthy as having been the first architectural movement in the United States which was not a more or less belated importation of the current English mode. With the Romanesque revival American architecture ceased to be colonial.

During the period of the Romanesque revival the profession of architecture had come to appeal to a greatly increased number of educated Americans, as offering the probability of a livelihood, and the possibility of a career. Many of them availed themselves of the apparatus for technical education provided by the schools of architecture that had sprung up in the United States, and of which the curriculum was generally adapted from that of the School of Fine

Arts in Paris. Many others resorted to that institution itself, and upon their return to their own country devoted themselves to the reproduction of the contemporary French architecture which they had been taught to produce. They even established a concerted propaganda of the architecture of the school. Almost since the middle of the century there had been occasional American students at Paris, but these had used its curriculum only as a training in design, and had employed their discipline to entirely different results from those of the French architects. Richardson himself was one of these. But the later and more numerous graduates devoted themselves, not to developing, by means of their training, an architecture out of American conditions, but to domesticating current French work in the United States; to substituting, in fact, the French fashions for the English fashions which had prevailed from the beginning of the eighteenth century to the third quarter of the nineteenth. By far the most signal triumph which had been won in this endeavour was the architecture of the World's Fair in Chicago in 1893. A singularly judicious and fortunate landscape treatment of the strip of low shore selected for the exhibition, together with a largeness of scale almost without precedent, gave scope for a pompous architectural display, to which no approach had before been made in the United States, and to which, indeed, there is no parallel in real and durable building anywhere. The Greco-Roman architecture was imitated in façades of lath and plaster which had, in the chief and most admired buildings, no relation in their design, either to their own material and actual construction, or to the buildings which they masked and which were in fact modern engineering constructions in metal. Only in one of the great buildings was an attempt made at an architectural development of the facts of material and construction, and this building was the least admired of any. In only one other of the principal buildings was there any departure from Greco-Roman architecture, either in production of the antique forms or in the French version of them, and this was an essay in a Romanesque much lighter and more graceful in intention than that which had become known as Richardsonian, in a building which owed its success, however, chiefly to the skilful introduction of marine forms in its profuse decoration. The most admired building of all was the execution of an ideal project prepared some years before for a competition of the Paris school. The grandiose effect of the architectural display was naturally attributed by the public to the style employed, although there were other elements in it of even more importance. For the first time, a number of architects had been able to coöperate in the execution of a prearranged architectural scheme of great extent

and importance. For the first time sculpture and painting had been introduced upon a great scale, as integral parts of an architectural whole. But the popular success of the display was accepted without much analysis by architects as well as by the public as proof of the eligibility of the style, or styles, in which the façades fronting the so-called "Court of Honor" had been composed, and "classic," in one or another of its modes, was almost at once reëstablished as the most eligible style for public buildings. A more serious and durable work than of the theatrical and illusory buildings of the World's Fair was already under construction when those buildings were begun, but received, in its completion and embellishments, the benefit of the lesson inculcated by them. This was the Library of Congress, of which the style, the Italian Renaissance, was in effect dictated by its position confronting the Capitol, to which it virtually conforms in the scale of the order. Its large and simple plan enforced an exterior treatment which, if not wholly free from monotony, at least escapes frivolity, and by the sobriety and plainness of the design makes the most of unusually ample dimensions. The same simplicity of disposition secures in the interior spacious fields for pictorial decoration, while the domed octagon of the central reading room affords an opportunity for sculptural embellishment, by means both of symbolic figures and of portrait statues. Each of these opportunities was taken advantage of by the employment of those American artists who had most indicated their capability. The choice was, upon the whole, very skilfully made, and the result was surprising as well as gratifying. The library was the first government building to be adequately decorated, while the central reading room is without doubt the most impressive apartment, in virtue both of its architecture and its decoration, belonging to the United States.

The popular recognition of the merits of the library, which was not less immediate and of course much more lasting than that of the buildings of the World's Fair, tended to confirm the reëstablishment of the classic. The Parisian propaganda has been crowned with entire success, and no architect would now think of submitting in competition a design for a public building in any other style than that officially sanctioned in France. The admiration of the young architects for French architecture has in many cases taken the form of direct and specific imitation. Foreign buildings have been freely reproduced, and published designs not executed abroad have been executed in the United States, without any alteration that amounted to a disguise, not merely for temporary exigencies, as in the case of the Art Building at the World's Fair, but for durable and important buildings.

There is no longer any pretence, as there was in the Gothic and Romanesque revival, of using the selected style as a basis or a point of departure to be modified and developed in accordance with American needs and ways of thinking, and with the introduction of new material and new modes of construction. Architectural design is frankly imported even when it is not directly imitated. The new town hall of an American city is apt to be, architecturally, precisely what its architect would have designed for a similar edifice in France, and in its strange surroundings it necessarily appears incongruous and incapable of domestication. Gothic and Romanesque continue to be employed for Protestant churches, the style here being imposed by the employers, not as the most artistic, but as the most " churchly." But even in churches there are not wanting examples of the reversion to classic models. In civic buildings it may be said, as a rule, that there are no longer evidences even of an aspiration toward a national architecture.

In dwellings the classic reaction has by no means so exclusive possession of the field. It cannot even be said that there is any longer a typical American town house. The widest and freest eclecticism prevails, insomuch that the newest residential quarters of even the oldest American towns constitute an architectural museum, in which nearly every historical style is represented. The "specimens" are reproduced sometimes with crudity and recklessness, but often with scholarly accuracy and sometimes with successful originality of composition. The French Renaissance is a favourite style, and several American architects have wrought in it with success, in town houses as well as in the even more pretentious dwellings of watering places and summer resorts. There is scarcely such a thing in the United States as a country seat, in the European sense, an extensive and costly mansion detached by a spacious park and forming the central feature of an estate. "Biltmore," in North Carolina, is almost unique in this respect. There is, in fact, no country life in the European sense in the United States. Rich Americans are more gregarious in their social habits than rich Europeans, and build themselves country houses in proximity to those of their acquaintances. Hence, at such seaside resorts as Newport and Bar Harbor, and at such mountain resorts as Lenox and Tuxedo,—though this latter is rather an exclusive suburb than a resort, — very profuse expenditures have been made upon houses to which justice is not done by grounds ample enough to secure them proper detachment, and which can scarcely be seen by themselves. At Newport, where in extent and costliness many of the houses are on a really palatial scale, this is notably the case ; and Newport for this reason has, perhaps, more the air

of an architectural museum than any other American town. Some of the less pretentious summer resorts, and some of the suburbs of the chief cities, are really more representative and typical. In these the efforts of the architects of country houses have not been to present examples of historical styles, but to develop, out of given dispositions, materials, and methods of construction, their own appropriate architectural expression. The best of these houses have a familiar and vernacular and even autochthonous air. As the dispositions, materials, and modes of construction are the supply of real demands, when the architecture is simply the expression of the given facts, the result, in the case of an artistic designer, is a building which, being of no style, yet has style. Such works are the most creditable, and are among the most characteristic products thus far of architecture in the United States.

The most characteristic of these products cannot as yet be called the most creditable. This is the "tall building " which forms so conspicuous a feature of every large American city. This may be an apartment house or a warehouse, but it has reached its greatest development in the " office buildings," which are erected in the quarters in which land is the most valuable, and upon the altitude of which it is difficult to foresee any limit that may be set by self-interest, or otherwise than by legal regulation in the interest of the public. Such a regulation has been invoked in some cities, but none thus far in the most populous of all ; and it is accordingly in New York that the excesses of altitude are most marked. There are several office buildings in that city of more than twenty stories, and one which attains a height in general of twenty-seven, and, in the added towers, of thirty. The effect upon light and air and traffic of these huge and populous houses, in many cases fronting only upon streets which were laid out in contemplation of buildings not more than three stories high, has been so injurious as to induce an organized movement for limiting their altitude, as has already been done in Chicago, where the limit has been set at about ten stories. There have gone to the evolution of the tall building two principal factors of almost equal importance. The first was the passenger elevator, or lift, which came into use about 1870, and was at first introduced into existing buildings in order to make their upper stories more attractive to tenants. Within two or three years two buildings, expressly designed with reference to the elevator, and thence called "elevator buildings," were concurrently under construction in New York. These attained a height of ten stories. Before the end of the decade some scores of buildings of an equal height had been added, many of them office buildings, like the two pioneers, but many of them also apartment houses in the residential quarters. These ponderous edifices made, by reason of the enormous load imposed upon their foundations, a much greater demand upon the scientific capacity of their constructors than their predecessors, and this demand was, with a few exceptions, satisfactorily met, often by the employment of an engineer. They equally enlarged, by their novelty and by the lack of available precedents in historical architecture for their treatment, the demand made upon the artistic capacity of their constructors, and this cannot be said to have been so fully supplied. The analogy of the preceding buildings of half as many stories was for the most part followed, excepting that for a single story a group of stories were substituted as an integral part of the composition. This device, however, was so evidently arbitrary and factitious that the effect of it could not be completely successful. The success of it was still further obstructed by the practice of nearly all of the designers to aim at variety, to the prejudice of unity and homogeneousness, and to use a more ornate style than befitted a building so strictly utilitarian. In this respect the elevator buildings of Chicago, in which the elevator building made its appearance some years after it had become rife in New York, marked a decided advance. The commercial buildings were much plainer and more commercial of aspect than those of New York. They were also much taller. The design of getting the utmost out of a given area of very costly ground evidently defeats itself, when the altitude is carried beyond a certain point, and when real walls which carry themselves are employed, by the necessity of increasing the area of the supports in proportion to their height. In New York the limit was fixed by general consent at ten or twelve stories. In Chicago it was found commercially practicable to raise this limit to eighteen, which is the height of the so called Masonic Temple. The Monadnock, also in Chicago, is of sixteen. The model of this building is an Egyptian pylon. Although great and successful pains have been taken to give it an effective outline, and although the blankness of the walls is relieved by a succession of shallow oriels, it is absolutely devoid of ornament, and for fourteen stories the treatment of the openings is identical. Architecturally, it is perhaps the most successful and impressive of all the tall buildings which are built with real walls.

But, as has been said, there has been another factor at work in the evolution of the tall building scarcely less important than the elevator itself, and this is the "steel frame," "skeleton," or so-called "Chicago," construction, although it seems to have been introduced independently and almost simultaneously in more than one city, about 1889. The diminished cost of the production of steel, and the consequently in-

creased employment of it in interior and subordinate construction, naturally led to the use of it as the chief structure of the building. Cast iron had been extensively used twenty years before as the material of commercial buildings, which architecturally were for the most part mere imitation of stonework, although in a few instances attempts had been made to give the metal a characteristic treatment. But two great fires, those of Chicago and Boston, had entirely discredited the use of unprotected metal for the essential supports of a building, and it ceased to be employed except with a protective envelope of fire-resisting material. A demand for terra cotta arose for this purpose, which gave a great impulse to the manufacture, and within a few years this has been so extended and improved as to be equal to any demand made upon it by the architects for decorative as well as for purely constructional work. When it was seen to be feasible to make the essential structure of a building a steel skeleton, to dispense with structural walls altogether, and thus to evade the necessity of thickening them in proportion to their height, the limit upon the practicable altitude of buildings was removed, and edifices began to be erected which bore the same relation to their predecessors, in which the elevator was the only new factor, that these had borne to the commercial buildings in which stairways had provided the only means of ascent. The modern American tall building is thus a steel skeleton, with its floors and partitions also framed in steel, enclosed for protection against fire in baked clay, and with exterior walls of stonework, brick, or terra cotta, which are mere screens, hung to the structure, and which may be built from the top down, as well as from the bottom up, or begin at any intermediate stage, being carried upon the steel beams. In fact, it is not uncommon to see a tall building in course of erection, bearing a belt of its architectural envelope, with the steel cage showing above and below.

A new architectural treatment has been enforced by this vertical extension. It is scarcely practicable, and it is evidently not desirable, to distinguish and individualize each story, or even successive and nearly equal groups of stories. Recourse was made to an emphatic triple division, in which two or three stories at the bottom are set off and distinguished as a base, and two or three more at the top as a capital, the intermediate stories, no matter how numerous, being virtual or actual repetitions of each other, treated with plainness and severity, and together constituting the shaft of the tower. The analogy thus suggested of the classic column has been as closely followed as the conditions will allow, and may be said to have imposed itself upon most designers of tall buildings as a model upon which it is permissible to execute variations only in detail. It is allowable to speak of it as in some measure a new architectural type.

It is evident, however, that it cannot be regarded as final or satisfactory, or accepted as a true architectural type. It is the substitution of an arbitrary form for an expression of the facts. The actual structure is masked and obscured by the apparent structure. It is left to be inferred that the tall building is not an actual structure of masonry only because the piers are evidently inadequate to the work they appear to do, and the shallow reveals of the openings disclose that the wall is but a screen, except in those cases in which the designer has given it the factitious appearance of greater depth, in order to carry out the suggestion of other than the actual construction. Even if it were desirable, it would not be practicable, to make this elaborate imitation of another than the actual construction successful to the point of complete illusion.

Nevertheless, the elements of these buildings are all necessary, all the results of real requirements. The steel frame so economizes space that, after it had once been introduced, scarcely any architect would now propose to employ any other construction for commercial buildings where land is so costly and traffic so great as to make it worth while to double the number of stories that was practicable before the elevator was introduced. The fire-resisting envelope which covers this construction is also necessary to protect it from fire, and this envelope must, in some degree, mask the construction it covers. The correlation of structure and function must be expressed in the tall building under this condition. The arbitrary division almost universally adopted is irrelevant to the accumulation of tiers of similar cells, of which only the lowest and the uppermost can be said to be so far distinguished in function as to call for or admit of a distinguishing treatment. The protective envelope must be a clinging drapery, revealing the structure behind it, and indicating the anatomy of the structure. A few very interesting essays have been made upon these lines, and it may be hoped that they will be taken up and carried farther by architects who are too serious to be satisfied with that conventional solution of the problem of the tall building which contents the majority of practitioners. If this is done, the American commercial building may become as truthful an expression of one phase of American life as the country house already is, in many instances, of another; and out of the satisfaction of commonplace and general requirements may arise the beginnings of a national architecture. — MONTGOMERY SCHUYLER.

UNIVERSITY. An institution for the advancement of the higher learning, undertaking all branches of study, as its name implies, or at least aiming at such completeness. In Eng-

land, especially, a collection of separate colleges, as at Oxford and Cambridge, each college having its own organization and its own buildings, though the University of London is not so composed. The great universities of the Continent of Europe have but few important buildings, the students lodging anywhere about the town, and the lecture rooms, halls for examinations, libraries, and the like, having no especial collegiate treatment (see College). Some of the buildings are ancient palaces or the like, modified to meet their new requirements; thus, the University of Berlin is housed in the palace of Prince Henry, built in the eighteenth century.

UPHERS. Fir poles, 4 to 7 inches in diameter and 20 to 40 feet long, sometimes roughly hewn, used in England for scaffoldings, and occasionally, when split, for slight and common roofs.

UPJOHN, RICHARD; architect; b. Jan. 22, 1802, in Shaftesbury, England; d. Aug. 16, 1878.

He was apprenticed to a builder and cabinet-maker in 1829, came to the United States, and settled in New Bedford, Massachusetts. He went to Boston in 1833 and assisted in the construction of the city Court House. In 1839 he went to New York to take charge of proposed alterations in the old Trinity church. This scheme was abandoned, and Upjohn designed and constructed the present Trinity church, which was finished in 1846. He built also S. Thomas's church, Trinity Building, the Corn Exchange Bank, and other buildings in New York, several churches in Brooklyn, and other buildings. He was president of the *American Institute of Architects* from 1857 to 1876.

Appleton, *Cyclopædia of American Biography*.

UPPER CROFT. The triforium gallery or other upper gallery of a church, a term, perhaps, obsolete.

UPSTART. A stone set otherwise than on the quarry bed; local or obsolete.

URINAL. A toilet room convenience or plumbing fixture intended for men's use, and consisting of a trapped bowl, trough, or gutter, connected with a waste or drain pipe, and arranged with a flushing device similar to that for water-closets. By extension, the apartment in which this fixture is placed or fitted up. (See Plumbing.) — W. P. G.

URN. A receptacle for the ashes of the dead; usually a large vase with a rounded body and a foot. When of this special shape, it is employed as a symbolic decoration or finial in modern work, especially in mortuary monuments.

V

VAGA, PERINO DEL. (See Buonaccorsi, Pierino.)

VALDELVIRA, PEDRO DE; architect and sculptor.

A contemporary and rival of Berruguete (see Berruguete). He studied Michelangelo's works in Italy. In the town of Ubeda, Spain, he built the castle of Francisco de los Cobos, secretary of Charles V., and the church of S. Salvador.

Stirling-Maxwell, *Annals of the Artists of Spain;* Bermudez, *Diccionario.*

VALENCE, PIERRE DE; architect, engineer, and sculptor.

The chief member of a large family of French architects. In 1500 he was employed on the church of S. Gatien at Tours (Indre-et-Loire). January 11, 1503, Valence was called by the Cardinal Georges I. d'Amboise to inspect the works at the château of Gaillon, near Rouen, and in 1506 undertook the construction of the water works and fountains of that château. In 1507 he directed the construction of the fountain of Beaune in Tours. January 22, 1511, he made a contract for the fountains at Blois. His sons, Germain and Michel, succeeded him.

Deville, *Château de Gaillon;* Grandmaison, *Tours Archéologique;* Bauchal, *Dictionnaire.*

VALFENIÈRE. (See Royer de la Valfenière.)

VALLÉE, SIMON DE LA; architect.

He was called to Sweden by Queen Christina. At Stockholm he built the palace of the nobility (begun 1648), the church of S. Marie, S. Cathcrine, etc.

Dussieux, *Les Artistes français à l'étranger;* Bauchal, *Dictionnaire.*

VALLEY. The internal angle formed by the meeting of two roof slopes, the external angle formed by such a meeting being called a Hip or Ridge. The rafter under the valley is called the valley rafter, and the board fixed in the angle to receive the flashing or gutter is called the valley board.

VALUATION. Estimate; appraisement. As applied to the cost of a structure erected or to be erected, the valuation is approximated either by comparing it, according to its relative cubical area, with the known cost of another similar building, or, more accurately, by estimating it in detail, according to the quantity, character, and cost of material and labour involved in its erection.

VALVE. *A.* In a double door, French window, or the like, one of the two folds, or leaves.

B. A device for regulating the flow of water gas or other fluid (see Plumbing; House Drainage).

VALVE HOUSE. A building to cover the valves and valve chamber of the mains from a reservoir.

VANBRUGH, SIR JOHN; dramatist and architect; b. 1666; d. March 26, 1726.

Vanbrugh devoted the early part of his life to literature and distinguished himself as a dramatist. In 1702 he succeeded Talman (see Talman) as comptroller of the royal works. His first completed building was a theatre (1703–1705) in London, afterward destroyed. In 1701 he began for the Earl of Carlisle the palace called Castle Howard in Yorkshire, England. As a reward for the distinguished services of John Churchill, Duke of Marlborough, the royal manor of Woodstock (England) was granted to him and to his heirs by act of Parliament of March 14, 1705, with half a million pounds to build the great palace called Blenheim, which is Vanbrugh's most important and characteristic work. In 1716 he succeeded Sir Christopher Wren as surveyor of Greenwich Hospital (London). Among the residences built by Vanbrugh are Eastbury in Dorsetshire (1716–1718), Seaton Delaval (1720), portions of Audley End (1721), Grimsthorpe (1722–1724), etc.

Bloomfield, *Renaissance in England;* Mavor, *A New Description of Blenheim;* Neale, *Seats of Noblemen and Gentlemen;* Campbell, *Vitruvius Britannicus.*

VAN CAMPEN. (See Campen.)

VAN DER NULL. (See Null, Edward van der.)

VANE. A contrivance by which a bannerlike plate, as of thin metal, is moved by the wind around a pivot, so that a point on the opposite side of the pivot points always toward the quarter whence the wind comes. Called also Weathercock.

Banner Vane. A vane in the form of a banner or flag.

VANISHING POINT. In Perspective, a point toward which any series of parallel lines seems to converge.

VAN RIEL. (See Riel.)

VANUCCI, PIETRO (**PERUGINO**); painter; b. 1446; d. 1524.

For Sixtus IV. (Pope 1471–1484) he painted a series of frescoes in the Sistine Chapel, some of which were destroyed to make room for Michelangelo's *Last Judgment.* In 1499 and 1500 Perugino painted the decorations of the Sala del Cambio (Exchange) of Perugia, Italy, one of the most perfect examples of the decorative work of the fifteenth century. (See Santi, R.)

Müntz, *Renaissance;* Crowe and Cavalcaselle, *History of Painting in Italy;* Vasari, Milanesi ed.;

VANE FROM STOCKHOLM, SWEDEN.

Vasari, Blashfield-Hopkins ed.; Morelli, *Italian Painters.*

VANVITELLI (VAN WITEL), LUIGI; painter and architect; b. 1700; d. 1773.

Vanvitelli was the son of one Kaspar van Witel, a Dutch painter, and spent his entire life in Italy. He was a pupil of Philippo Juvara (see Juvara). At the age of twenty-six he was made supervising architect of S. Peter's in Rome. He conducted the works at the harbour of Ancona and built the campanile of the church of La Casa Santa at Loretto. He built the convent of S. Agostino at Rome, and designed a chapel for the church of the Jesuits at Lisbon. About 1749 he remodelled Michelangelo's church of S. Maria degli Angeli (the great hall of the Baths of Diocletian in Rome). Vanvitelli's chief monument is the immense Palazzo di Caserta in Naples. This building is described in a monograph by Vanvitelli, *Dichiarazione del reale Palazzo di Caserta* (1 vol. folio, Naples, 1756).

Gurlitt, *Geschichte des Barockstiles in Italien;* Ebe, *Spät-Renaissance;* Milizia, *Memorie.*

VAN WITEL. (See Vanvitelli.)

VAPOR-TIGHT GLOBE. (See Electrical Appliances.)

VARDY, JOHN; architect.

A pupil of W. Kent (see Kent). He succeeded H. Joynes as clerk of the works at Kensington Palace, London, between 1748 and 1754. February 13, 1746, he was appointed clerk of the works at Chelsea Hospital.

Arch. Pub. Soc. Dictionary.

VARELLA. A pagoda; apparently the Italian term in the sixteenth century, used in English by Purchas.

Hart, *Picturesque Burma.*

VARNISH. A solution of amber, copal, rosin, mastic, shellac, or other resinous substance mixed with a solvent, generally of linseed oil, turpentine, or alcohol, so as to form a transparent fluid capable of hardening and of a certain resistance to the influence of air and moisture. Some kind of varnish is used by painters to form a permanent decorative and protective glazing coat over the work.

VASALETO. (See Vassallectus.)

VASARI, GIORGIO; painter and architect; b. 1511; d. July 27, 1574.

Giorgio Vasari was born at Arezzo (Italy), a kinsman of Luca Signorelli (see Signorelli). His first teacher in painting appears to have been Guillaume de Marcillat (see Guillaume de Marcillat). His literary training was superintended by the Aretine poet Giovanni Pollastra. About 1523 he went to Florence, and entered the service of Ottaviano de' Medici and the Duke Alessandro de' Medici. He went to Rome afterwards with the Cardinal Ippolito de' Medici. From 1555 to the end of his life he was court painter to Cosimo I. de' Medici, duke

of Florence. The most important of his undertakings are the frescoes of the Cancelleria in Rome and those of the Palazzo Vecchio in Florence. As architect he prepared in 1536 the decorations of the triumphal entry of the Emperor Charles V. into Florence. He made the original plans of the Vigna di Papa Giulio (Julius III., Pope 1550–1555) in Rome (see Barozzio, G.). He remodelled the Palazzo Vecchio and built the Palazzo degli Uffizi in Florence. At Pistoia he built the cupola of the church of the Madonna dell' Umiltà (see Vitoni), and at Pisa the Palazzo dei Cavalieri da S. Stefano. He built the Badia and the "Loggie Vasari" at Arezzo.

Vasari's most important work is his series of biographies of artists; *Le Vite de' più eccellenti Architetti, Pittori e Scultori.* The first edition appeared in 1550. The second, in 1568, was more complete. The standard edition of Vasari is that of Gaetano Milanese, which was published in Florence between 1878 and 1885. A new comprehensive Italian edition is now in progress under the supervision of A. Venturi. The *Vite* were translated into English by Mrs. Foster in 1888. A selection of seventy of the *Lives* from Mrs. Foster's translation, with introduction, annotation, and bibliography by E. H. and E. W. Blashfield and A. A. Hopkins was published in New York in 1896.

Vasari, Blashfield-Hopkins ed.; Vasari, Milanesi ed.; Redtenbacher *Architektur der Italienischen Renaissance;* Müntz, *Renaissance;* H. Mosler, *Sansovino u. s. w.;* Ruggieri, *Studio d'Architettura civile.*

VASE. A hollow vessel of decorative character and various form, with or without ears or handles; hence the resemblance of such a vessel, in solid material, as marble, much used in the art of the Renaissance to decorate balustrades, pedestals, gate posts, and monuments of all sorts.

VASISTAS. (A corruption of the German words Was ist das; a common term in French for that which the Germans call rather Guckfenster or Schiebefenster.) A small opening in, or by the side of, a door of entrance; usually fitted with a wicket to shut and a fixed grating or the like through which to look or to speak. Its purpose is to ascertain, before the door is opened, the character of the person asking for admission.

VASSALLECTUS (VASALETO); architect, sculptor, and mosaicist.

The name Vassallectus, variously spelled, appears in inscriptions on several monuments of the thirteenth century in the vicinity of Rome. The most important of these, the cloister of S. Giovanni in Laterano, which was probably built about 1230, bears this inscription, discovered by Count Vespignani in 1887 (De Rossi, op. cit., p. 128): NOBILIS ET DOC-

PLATE XXXIV

VATICAN

View of the southeast corner of the palace with the north wing
of Bernini's colonnade (Piazza di S. Pietro) in the foreground, and,
on the left, an obelisk 85 feet high. That part of the palace which
is seen is the chief residential part, surrounding on three sides the
Cortile di S. Damaso. The glazed arcade on the left is that of the
Loggie di Raffaelo.

TUS HAC VASSALLETTUS IN ARTE, CUM PATRE CŒPIT OPUS QUOD SOLUS PERFECIT IPSE. The inscription indicates that the sculptor belonged to a family of *marmorarii* (marble workers). A throne with lions, which was made about 1263 for the Abbot Lando, and is now in the museum of the cathedral of Anagni, Italy, is signed *Vasaleto de Roma me fecit.* The name appears also on an *œdicula* for holy oil in the church of S. Francesco at Viterbo. It is supposed by Frothingham (op. cit.) that the fine monument of the Pope Adrian V. in this church was made by the same person. Less important works are a lion before the church of SS. Apostoli (Rome), and a candelabrum in the church of S. Paolo fuori le Mura (Rome). There is also an inscription which belonged to a monument which stood in the old basilica of S. Peter's (Rome). These works may be by one person or several. De Rossi supposes that there were four. A screen in the cathedral of Segni, dated 1185, and a canopy in the church of SS. Cosmo e Damiano (Rome) appear to be by an earlier member of the family.

Frothingham, *Roman Artists of the Middle Ages;* G. B. de Rossi, *Delle altre famiglie di marmorarii Romani,* etc.; Lanciani, *Pagan and Christian Rome;* Perkins, *Italian Sculptors;* Rohault de Fleury, *Le Latran.*

VASE, MARBLE; AT CHÂTEAU OF FONTAINEBLEAU, FRANCE.

VASSALLETO. (See Vassallectus.)
VAST. (See Wast.)

VAUDOYER, ANTOINE LAURENT THOMAS; architect; b. Dec. 20, 1756 (at Paris); d. May 27, 1846.

VASE, MARBLE; ANCIENT ROMAN WORK IN THE MUSEUM OF THE VATICAN, ROME.

He studied with A. F. Peyre (see Peyre, A. F.) and at the *École royale d'Architecture,* and won the *Grand Prix de Rome* in architecture in 1783. In 1793 he established with David Leroy an atelier of architecture at the Louvre. August 25, 1795, when the Institute was created, Vaudoyer became voluntary secretary of the *Commission d'Architecture.* In 1800 he was appointed architect of the Collège de France and the Sorbonne (Paris), and made extensive additions to those monuments. In 1804 he had charge of the installation of the Institute at the Palais des Quatre Nations (see Levanu). He was associated with Destournelles (see Destournelles) and L. P. Baltard (see Baltard, L. P.) in publishing *Grands Prix d'Architecture,* 1804–1831 (Paris, 1818–1834, 2 vols. folio).

Bauchal, *Dictionnaire.*

VAUDOYER, LÉON; architect; b. June 7, 1803 (at Paris); d. Feb. 9, 1872.

A son of A. L. T. Vaudoyer (see Vaudoyer, A. L. T.). He studied architecture with his father and Lebas (see Lebas) and at the *École des Beaux Arts* (Paris). In 1826 he won the *Premier Grand Prix de Rome.* While in Rome he made the monument to Poussin at the church of S. Lorenzo-in-Lucina. In 1853 he was appointed *inspecteur général des édifices diocésains*, and in 1855 architect of the cathedral of Marseilles, which had been begun in 1852. He won a medal of the first class at the Salon of 1855.

Lance, *Dictionnaire*.

VAULT. *A.* An arch or a combination of arches used to cover a space. It is primarily a

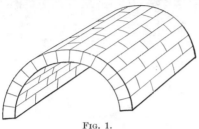

Fig. 1.

ceiling, but may be also a roof; or it may carry a roof, or a floor, or stairs.

B. A room or enclosed space of any kind which is covered by a vault; in this sense,

Fig. 2.

popular and applying to cellars and underground places of safety.

C. By extension, any strong place or place of safety, as a Safe Deposit Vault.

Fig. 3.

D. The semblance in some light material of a true vault. In this sense, the beautiful ceilings of rooms in certain civic buildings of Belgium are notable; they are wholly decorative, without attempt to deceive the spectator, as the boarding is distinctly marked and the construction is obviously inadequate to a masonry vault. The famous Octagon of the cathedral of Ely is, on the contrary, a wooden imitation apparently intended to be taken for stone vaulting. In

modern churches and in some civic and semi-public and private buildings vaulting of a classic sort is produced in plaster with a support of lathing or the like.

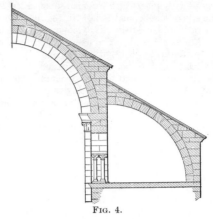

Fig. 4.

Vaults may be classified thus: —
As to form, Simple and Compound or Intersecting;
As to construction, Solid and Ribbed.

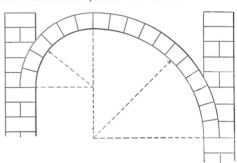

Fig. 5.

Solid Vaulting — Simple. The most ancient form of vault is that known as the barrel, tunnel, wagon, or cradle vault. Its cross section

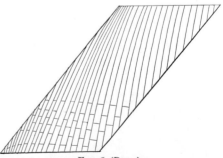

Fig. 6 (Plan).

may be semicircular (Fig. 1), semielliptical, segmental, or pointed (Fig. 2). The semicircular form is known also as the cylindrical. When it is of stone or brick the leading, or

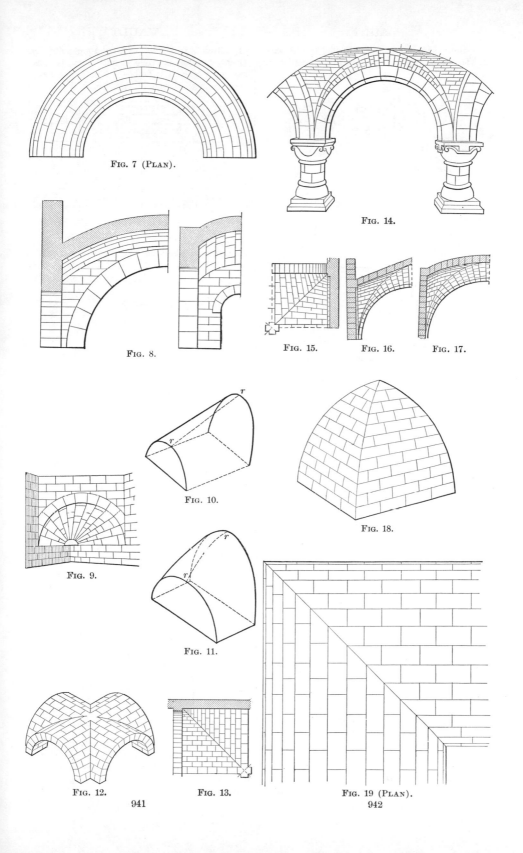

FIG. 7 (PLAN).

FIG. 14.

FIG. 8.

FIG. 15. FIG. 16. FIG. 17.

FIG. 10.

FIG. 9.

FIG. 18.

FIG. 11.

FIG. 12. FIG. 13. FIG. 19 (PLAN).

coursing, joints are usually parallel to the axis, and the cross joints in planes perpendicular to

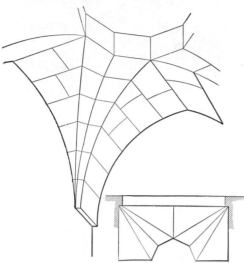

FIG. 20 (PLAN AND VIEW).

it. The oldest well-authenticated example of a barrel vault is one at Nimroud (see Mesopota-

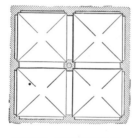

FIG. 21 (PLAN AND SECTION).

mia, Architecture of), of pointed section, covering a drain, and carrying a load of earth. In

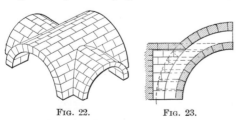

FIG. 22.   FIG. 23.

the pyramids at Meroë, not later than 800 B.C., cylindrical and pointed forms occur. There is a very perfect example, covering the chamber

of a tomb, at Gizeh, dating about 600 B.C. (Fig. 3). It is of stone, in four rings, that is to say, four concentric arches. The angular structure beneath it, which is the ceiling of the

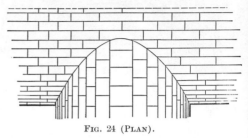

FIG. 24 (PLAN).

tomb, the vault being the roof, may be termed a vault with plane surfaces. The Cloaca Maxima at Rome is a well-known example, of stone, in three rings, probably of the fourth century

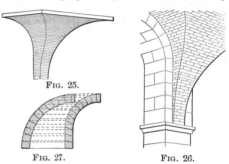

FIG. 25.

FIG. 27.   FIG. 26.

B.C. In the above cases the vault was merely a mechanical device for covering spaces with materials of small size instead of slabs of stone. It was used in places where it could not be seen,

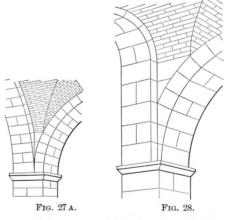

FIG. 27 A.   FIG. 28.

and therefore had no architectural character. The Romans seem to have been the first to adopt it as a visible structure, worthy of ornamentation, and of recognition for its æsthetic value.

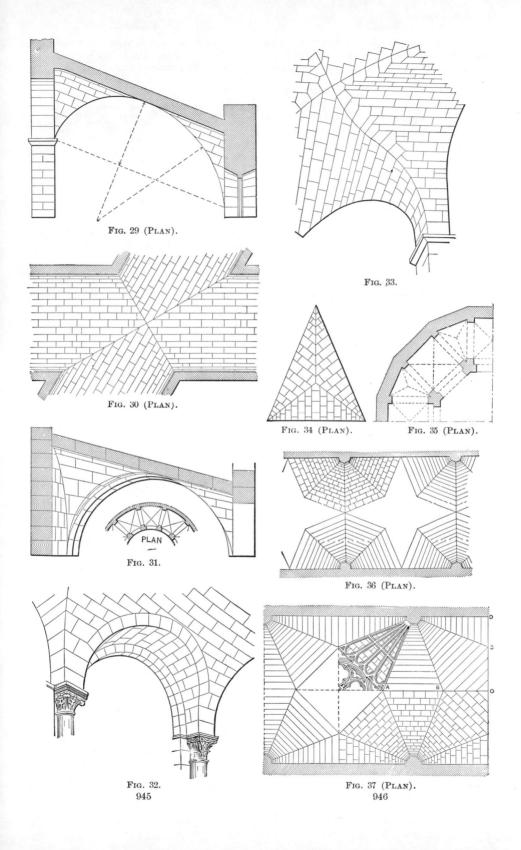

FIG. 29 (PLAN).

FIG. 33.

FIG. 30 (PLAN).

FIG. 34 (PLAN).   FIG. 35 (PLAN).

PLAN

FIG. 31.

FIG. 36 (PLAN).

FIG. 32.
945

FIG. 37 (PLAN).
946

A barrel vault usually covers a rectangular space, but sometimes a triangular, or trapezoidal. Its axis and ridge are commonly horizontal, but sometimes inclined, as when it covers or carries a stair. Figure 4 shows the use of half barrel vaults, over aisles, or triforia, of churches, carrying solid stone roofs, and serving

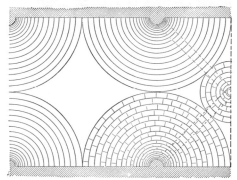

FIG. 38 (PLAN).

also as continuous flying buttresses resisting the outward thrust of the nave vaults. They are common in southeastern France, in the eleventh and twelfth centuries.

Figure 5 shows a rampant vault.

Figure 6 is a soffit plan of what is known as a skew arch, often used for bridges but rare in architectural work. Its ends are in planes

FIG. 39 (PLAN).

oblique to the axis. The cross section is semicircular or semielliptical. The joints are warped surfaces, usually, and run spirally.

An annular vault (Fig. 7) is a barrel vault with a curved axis. Its intrados is a portion of the surface of a cylindrical ring. An annular vault may also be used with its axis in a vertical plane (Fig. 8).

A spiral vault may be described as an annular vault with a spiral axis. It is used for supporting the steps of a spiral stair.

Expanding Vaults. These are larger at one end than at the other, and usually have inclined ridges. The common forms are : —

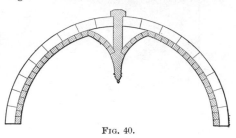

FIG. 40.

A. Conical (Fig. 9), used in pendentives for reducing a square to an octagon. Frustra of cones also cover trapezoidal spaces.

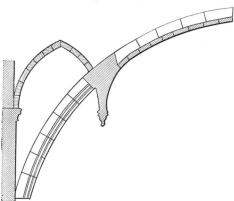

FIG. 41.

B. Conoidal, the smaller base semicircular, the larger semielliptical (Fig. 10); rr is the ridge line.

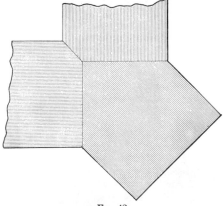

FIG. 42.

C. In the form shown in Fig. 11, the bases are as in Fig. 10, and the elements of the surface at the springing are straight lines parallel to the axis, but the ridge is curved, the expansion being in a vertical direction only. The surface, not being generated by the movement of any line, cannot be mathematically defined;

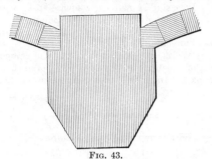

FIG. 43.

but such vaults may be termed convex-conoidal. They rarely occur except as parts of a compound vault.

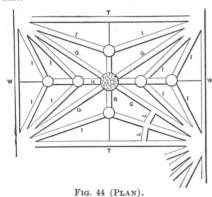

FIG. 44 (PLAN).

Solid Vaulting — Compound. Compound vaults are formed by the intersection of two or

ties, which may properly be classified as follows: —

A. Quadripartite, formed by the intersection of two barrel vaults, or by expanding vaults instead.

I. *For covering a square compartment.*

(*a*) The common groined vault, formed by the intersection, at right angles, of two equal barrel vaults, of any cross section. The angle

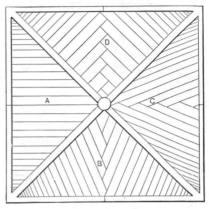

FIG. 45 (PLAN).

of the groin is 90° at the springing, widens as it goes up, and disappears in a straight line at the ridges. The horizontal projection of the groin edge is straight, and the edge itself lies in a vertical plane, and is elliptical. Figure 12 is an external view, and Fig. 13 is a quarter plan. The compartments to be covered are shown in Fig. 13 as separated by cross bands, which in Romanesque work are often deepened

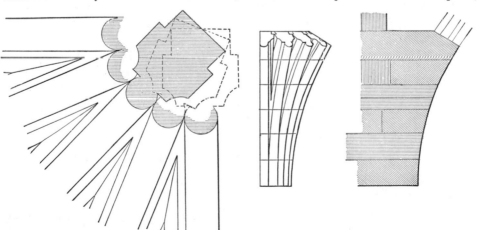

FIG. 46 (PLAN, ELEVATION, AND SECTION).

more simple ones, and are generally known as Groined Vaults, the groin being the salient angle made by two intersecting surfaces; or as Cloistered Vaults. There are numerous varie-

so as to become distinct arches, as in Fig. 14.

(*b*) Domical vaults. In these the centre or apex is raised above the level of the crown of the cross arch, so that the ridges rise toward it. They are formed, over square spaces, by the intersection of four equal expanding vaults, conical or conoidal. The groin edge is straight on

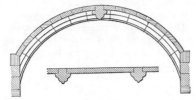

FIG. 47.

the plan. Its curve is elliptical if the composing vaults are conical; otherwise it is indefinable (Figs. 15, 16, 17).

(c) The so-called cloistered arch, or square dome (Fig. 18), is composed of four parts of

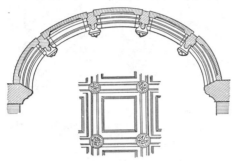

FIG. 48 (PLAN AND SECTION).

equal barrel vaults, but is just the reverse of the groined, the internal angles being reëntrant.

(d) A square space at the corner of a cloister is often covered by two intersecting barrel

FIG. 49 (PLAN).

vaults, the inner quarter being groined and the outer cloistered (Fig. 19).

(e) Figure 20 shows a method of covering a square space by a combination of groined and cloistered vaulting, occurring in a mosque at Ephesus.

(f) A square room may be covered by four

951

quadripartite vaults, each springing at one of its corners from a central pillar, as in Fig. 21. In a similar manner, a square space may be covered by nine vaults on four pillars.

II. *For covering an oblong rectangular compartment.*

(a) Welsh, or underpitch vaults, the components of which are usually cylindrical, of unequal widths, the transverse vault being narrower than

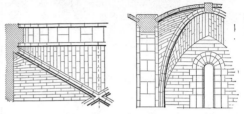

FIG. 50 (PLAN AND SECTION).

the main vault, but both springing from the same level, so that the intersection is not complete (Figs. 22, 23, 24). The horizontal projection of the groin line is a hyperbola. Welsh vaults are unknown in Roman work, but are common in Romanesque and the later neoclassic.

(b) Stilted vaults, in which the components are cylindrical, the transverse narrower than the main and springing from a higher level, so that the ridges are on the same level. The groin

FIG. 51 (PLAN AND SECTION).

line is of double curvature. The Romans used this form on a grand scale, and it is quite common in French Romanesque (Figs. 25, 26).

(c) In segmental vaulting (Fig. 27), the components may be equal or unequal.

(d) Figure 28. A segmental main vault, intersected by a semicircular transverse vault.

(e) Figure 29. A rampant barrel vault intersected by an inclined barrel vault. The radius of the upper part of the rampant is the same as that of the inclined vault, so that the upper part of the compound is an ordinary groined vault. The example is from S. Fidele, Como, Italy.

952

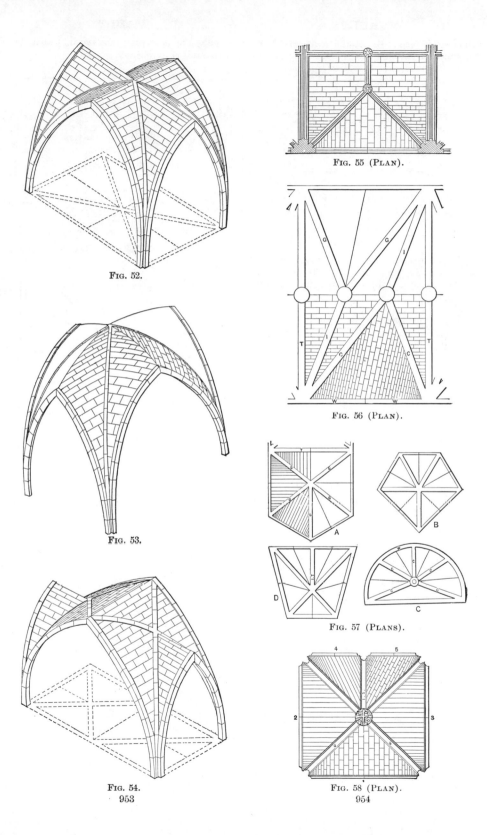

FIG. 52.

FIG. 53.

FIG. 54.

FIG. 55 (PLAN).

FIG. 56 (PLAN).

FIG. 57 (PLANS).

FIG. 58 (PLAN).

The form is used in the capitol at Albany, N.Y., for supporting stairs.

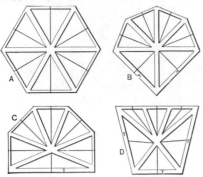

FIG. 59 (PLANS).

(*f*) One component is semicircular and the other semielliptical, but of wider span, the heights being equal; or both may be semi-elliptical.

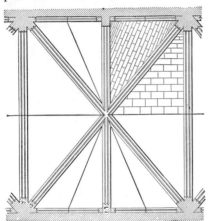

FIG. 60 (PLAN).

III. *Oblique Vaults.*

(*a*) Figure 30. With straight axes and composed of equal barrel vaults, or of unequal, one being semicircular and the other semielliptical.

FIG. 61.

(*b*) An annular vault intersected by a conical vault, the centre of the annulus being the apex of the cone (Fig. 31).

(*c*) An annular vault intersected by an under-pitch vault (Fig. 32).

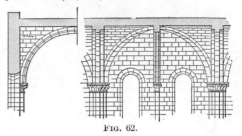

FIG. 62.

(*d*) An annular vault intersected by a stilted cylindrical vault (Fig. 33).

IV. *Tripartite Vaults,* covering triangular

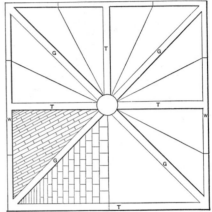

FIG. 63 (PLAN).

spaces and formed by the intersection of three barrel or three expanding vaults (Fig. 34). They occur in Romanesque buildings, alter-

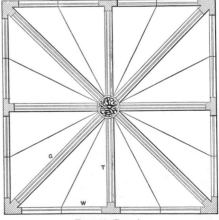

FIG. 64 (PLAN).

nately with quadripartite vaults, over the aisles of polygonal apses, as in Fig. 35.

V. *Polygonal Vaults.* These are mostly

octagonal on the plan, and are of the nature of the cupola.

VI. *Fancy Tracery Vaulting.* This is a variety of solid vaulting, although it was developed from the ribbed vaulting of the Gothic style, to the later period of which, in England, nearly all of the examples belong. There are two kinds.

(*a*) Pyramidoidal, the surface being that of a half of a pyramid with concave sides. A

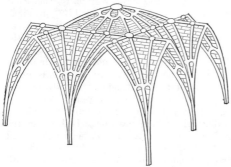

FIG. 65.

square space may be partly covered by two halves of the pyramidoid inverted and set opposite to each other. The bases are octagonal. The halves may meet at points, Fig. 36, leaving a star-shaped ridge space uncovered; or by sides, Fig. 37, leaving a square. If the non-cardinal sides of the pyramidoid be continued on to the centre, as in the right-hand end of Fig. 37, the square will be covered. The surfaces are carved into panels with mullions and tracery, but these are merely ornamental.

(*b*) Conoidal, made of halves, or less, of concave-sided cones.

FIG. 66 (PLAN).   FIG. 67 (PLAN).

1. For covering a square space. The half conoids have their bases tangent to each other on the ridge levels, and leave a large part of the space uncovered. They must, therefore, be supplemented by a flat, or slightly domical, ceiling connecting them (Fig. 38).

2. For covering an oblong space (Fig. 39). The conoids intersect at the sides. In this kind of vaulting pendents often occur: partly occupying the central space, as in the right-hand side of Fig. 38 and in Fig. 40; or placed at the sides, as in Fig. 41. They are supported by arches which are usually concealed. The

great examples of fan tracery vaulting are in Henry the Seventh's Chapel, Westminster Abbey; King's College, Cambridge; and St. George's Chapel, Windsor.

FIG. 68 (PLAN).

Rib Vaulting. In rib vaulting the surfaces, called panels, are sustained by a skeleton structure of ribs, which are usually of stone, while

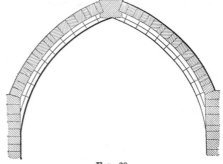

FIG. 69.

the panels may be of a lighter kind of stone, such as tufa or pumice, or even of brick. The pieces that form the panels may run straight

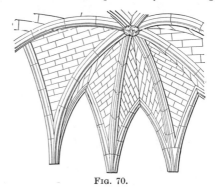

FIG. 70.

from rib to rib, in which case the surfaces are cylindrical, conical, or conoidal; or they may be arched from rib to rib, the surfaces then being spheroidal or convex-conoidal. The ribs are of circular or elliptical curvature, forming semicircular, semielliptical, pointed, three-centred, or four-centred arches. They lie, as a rule, in vertical planes.

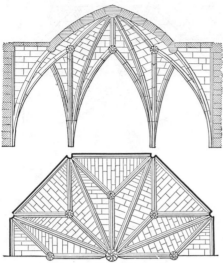

FIG. 71 (PLAN AND SECTION).

The first step in the development of the rib system of vaulting is often said to be the increase of the depth of the cross band in barrel vaults, making it an independent arch, with the vaulting above it. But such a rib, if it is properly so called, does not sustain the vault, which would stand just as well without it. It is true that there are several Roman vaults which are apparently thin and rest by the ends of their pieces on cross ribs; but there are no such in the Romanesque period. The begin-

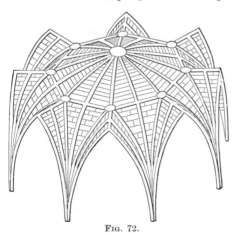

FIG. 72.

ning of the rib system will doubtless be found in the substitution of a square-cornered arch for the groin stones of a solid compound vault, as in Fig. 42, from S. Ambrogio, Milan. This

is a great advance in ease of construction. The shaping of groin stones is quite a problem in stereotomy, no two pieces being alike, but the rib at the groin is perfectly simple.[1] By degrees it becomes larger and the vault itself thinner, until finally the latter depends upon the former for support, and the result is true rib vaulting. The next step was the conversion of the heavy cross arch of the Romanesque vault into the light transverse rib of the Gothic. The process was slow on the Continent of Europe, as in France from 1130 to 1180, but apparently immediate in England (as at Canterbury, 1175), and there all ribs are of the same size and section. Then follows the wall rib, which shows a little more than half of the full section, and is built into the wall, or forms the head of a great window. It is really the transverse rib of the side vault. The next, existing only in complicated vaults, is the intermediate rib, which lies obliquely between the groin rib and the transverse, or the groin and wall. With it comes the ridge rib, which at first connects the apex of the intermediate with the apex of the groin rib, being then a structural necessity, as without it the two halves of the intermediate rib, not being in the same plane, would fall toward the centre, unless the panelling were inserted when they were laid. It is afterward continued to the transverse rib and the wall. Liernes, or cross ribs, run from one rib to another, dividing the panels. They are commonly of no practical use; but in some cases they are continuations of groin ribs, and are then necessary to the completion of the structure. They occur in late and florid work. In France the term "lierne" was applied to the ridge rib. Figure 44 is a plan of a fully developed rib vault. The following table gives the names and positions of the ribs. (Ridges without ribs are indicated by single lines.)

Position	English Names	French Names	Marks
Diagonal . . .	Groin Rib Diagonal Rib . .	Ogive . .	G.
Across the main axis	Transverse Rib . .	Arc doubleau. .	T.
Between the groin and transverse, or between the groin and wall ribs	Intermediate Rib	Tierceron	I.
Against the walls, parallel to the main axis . .	Wall Rib .	Formeret	W.
At the ridges . .	Ridge Rib	Lierne .	R.
From one rib to another, not at the ridges . .	Cross Rib, or Lierne		L.

[1] See Vol. II., cols. 97–99.

At the points where the ribs meet there are usually keystones, called bosses, ornamented by carving. They receive the ends of the ribs and thus avoid the mitring of the mouldings. Ribs

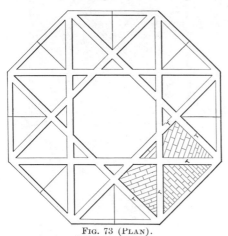

FIG. 73 (PLAN).

are decorated by mouldings such as chamfers, coves, and bowtells.

The methods of jointing panels are shown in Fig. 45.

In early examples only groin and transverse ribs are used, and each starts with its full section, but later on they are bunched together, each starting with only its soffit roll visible, as in Fig. 46. As they rise the section develops until the ribs separate. The structure up to this point is known as the springer. It is a solid mass, often with horizontal joints, a great corbel really, bonded into the wall, and forming no part of the vault proper.

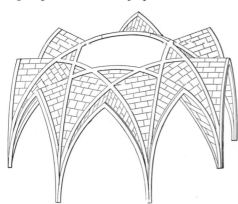

FIG. 74.

Analysis of Rib Vaulting. A. Simple.
Fig. 47. From Castle Campbell, Scotland.
Fig. 48. The panel vaulting of the " After Gothic " in France.
B. Compound. It will be best to classify these according to the number of cells.

1. Tripartite. These cover a triangular space, which usually occurs in an apsidal aisle, as in Fig. 35. The ribs meeting at the centre are halves of groin ribs, the others are either transverse or wall ribs.

2. Quadripartite.

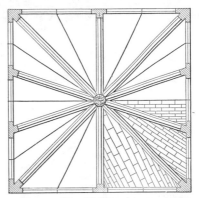

FIG. 75 (PLAN).

(*a*) With groin ribs only (Fig. 49).
(*b*) With groin ribs and transverse arches (Fig. 50). From Gerland, France; one of the earliest examples. Both ribs and arches are semicircular, and the vaulting is therefore domical.
(*c*) Groin and wall ribs only (Fig. 51).
(*d*) Groin, transverse, and wall ribs, with level ridges (Fig. 52). The same with curved ridges, the vault domical, and panels spheroidal (Fig. 53).
(*e*) Welsh vaults (Fig. 54). The groin ribs cross each other before reaching the main ridge, and are continued as liernes; or they

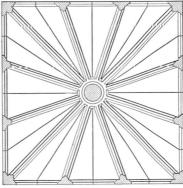

FIG. 76 (PLAN).

may stop at the crossing and be connected with the centre by a single lierne (Fig. 55).
(*f*) Groin, transverse, intermediate, and ridge ribs (Fig. 44).
(*g*) Side vaults oblique (Fig. 56), choir of Lincoln cathedral. The half groin ribs on

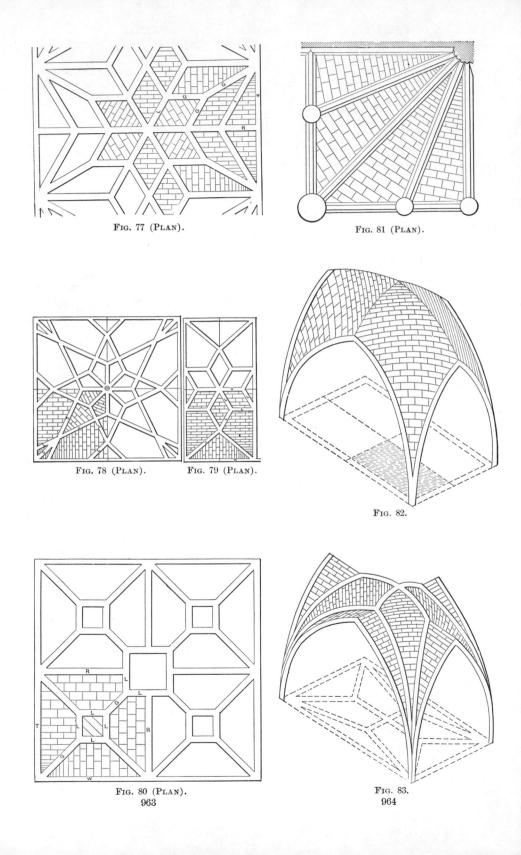

FIG. 77 (PLAN).

FIG. 81 (PLAN).

FIG. 78 (PLAN).   FIG. 79 (PLAN).

FIG. 82.

FIG. 80 (PLAN).
963

FIG. 83.
964

each side are met at the centre, not by their other halves, but by an intermediate rib.

3. Quinquepartite.

(*a*) For covering a pentagonal space. Two forms are shown in Fig. 57, and also one covering a semicircle, and one a trapezoid.

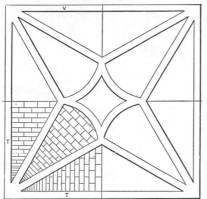

FIG. 84 (PLAN).

(*b*) Covering a rectangle (Fig. 58). It is composed of three quarters of a quadripartite vault and one quarter of a sexpartite.

4. Sexpartite. Figure 59 shows plans of vaults with six cells, and Figs. 60, 61, show the form known as sexpartite, or hexapartite, found in late Romanesque and early Gothic work. The side vaults are double and oblique, separated by an intermediate transverse rib. Figure 62 gives a form known as bisected. It is a quadripartite vault with the transverse components cut in two by intermediate transverse ribs carrying spandrel walls. It looks as though it were the predecessor of the sexpar-

FIG. 85 (PLAN).

tite vault, but it is not. There are four examples, all near Caen in Normandy.

5. Septempartite (Fig. 63). It is made up of half a quadripartite and half a sexpartite.

6. Octopartite.

(*a*) For covering a square space enclosed by

965

walls, as in towers (Fig. 64). There are eight oblique cells. The construction is on the prin-

FIG. 86 (PLAN).

ciple of a sexpartite vault. Figure 65 is a unique example, from Lincoln cathedral, covering the

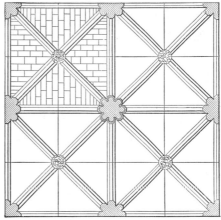

FIG. 87 (PLAN).

intersection of nave and transepts. The ridges enclose a central square which is covered by

FIG. 88 (SEE FIG. 87).

extending the groin and transverse ribs to the centre.

966

(*b*) Figures 66, 67, show how irregular spaces may be covered by vaults with eight cells.

(*c*) Covering an octagonal space. Figure 68 is a plan, and 69 a section, of an octagonal vault whose internal angles are reëntrant.

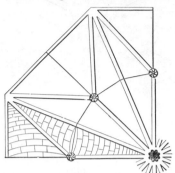

FIG. 89 (PLAN).

(*d*) Figure 70 has the same ribs as (*c*), but they are groin ribs, and there are sixteen cells.

(*e*) Figure 71, Welsh vaulting.

(*f*) Figure 72, groin ribs not meeting at the centre, but terminating at the angles of an octagon — York cathedral.

(*g*) Figures 73, 74, eight semicircular transverse, or rather groin ribs. The central octagon is not covered.

7. Decapartite (Fig. 75).

8. Dodecapartite (Fig 76). The central open circle is a common feature in some other varieties, especially quadripartite.

9. Groin ribs interrupted, or diverted and branched.

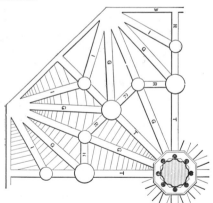

FIG. 90 (PLAN).

(*a*) Star vaulting (Figs. 77, 78, 79).

(*b*) Panel vaulting is the name given to this form in England (Fig. 80).

10. Vaults whose ribs, except at ridges, are all arcs of the same circle, differing only in length, and all properly groin ribs. Such vaults are necessarily domical. Figure 81 is a quarter plan.

11. Diagonal ribs omitted (Figs. 82 to 86).

12. Vaulting of rooms with a central shaft (Figs. 87, 88, square; 89, 90, octagonal).

13. Pendant rib vaults (Figs. 91, 92) from

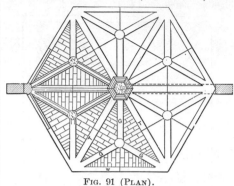

FIG. 91 (PLAN).

the Lady Chapel at Caudebec, France. (See Vaulting and subtitles; also France, Pt. I.; Gothic Architecture; Pendant; Roman Imperial Architecture, cols. 341–343.)

— CHARLES BABCOCK.

Barrel Vault. A vault having everywhere a uniform section, semicircular, or nearly so, a form of Tunnel Vault (Fig. 1, Vault).

Cloistered Vault. Same as Coved Vault.

Coved Vault. A vault composed of four quarter-cylindrical surfaces or coves, meeting in vertical diagonal planes, the axial sections of the vault being arched, and the horizontal courses diminishing in length from spring to crown; called also Cloistered Vault. (See Fig. 18, Vault.)

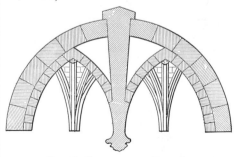

FIG. 92 (SECTION, SEE FIG. 91).

Cradle Vault. Same as Barrel Vault.

Fan Vault. (See Fan Vaulting under Vaulting.)

Green Vault; Vaults. (See Grüne Gewölbe.)

Groin Vault; Groined Vault. A compound vault in which tunnel vaults intersect, forming arrises which are called groins. The Roman Imperial practice in this respect was to use only tunnel vaults of nearly semicircular section (barrel vaults) and of the same size and height. When the tunnel vaults are of different heights, so that the groins do not meet at the crown of the vault, the structure is called a Welsh vault. It is not strictly accurate to class ribbed vaults as groined vaults.

Lierne Vault. A ribbed vault in which there are many secondary ribs. (See Lierne.)

Octopartite Vault. (See Vault.)

Rib Vault; Ribbed Vault. One built with ribs as the principal structure. (See Ribbed Vaulting; also Rib, Gothic Architecture, and the general article Vault.)

Sexpartite Vault. (See Vault.)

Six Part Vault. Same as Sexpartite Vault.

Tunnel Vault. A vault having everywhere a uniform section; either nearly semicircular, as in cradle, or barrel vault, or pointed at the top, as in some Romanesque churches of the south of France, and very rarely in Byzantine construction.

Wagon Vault. Same as Barrel Vault.

Welsh Vault. A construction in which a central higher vault is crossed or intersected by vaults of lower pitch. The form usually so called is that shown in Fig. 22 of the article above, and in the view of the church of S. Roch (which see under Church). The Romans never used such vaults, but attempts were made during the Romanesque period; and the neoclassic builders of the sixteenth century vaulted cloisters and the corridors of palaces, etc., in this way. For the use of the term in connection with ribbed vaulting see the article Vault.

VAULTED. *A.* Constructed as a vault; said of a roof, the supporting member of a stone staircase, or the like.

B. Covered or closed by a vault, as in the phrase a "vaulted aisle."

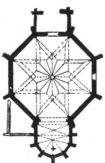

VAULTING OF THE KARLSHOFER CHURCH, PRAGUE, BOHEMIA; ALL SPRINGING FROM THE ANGLES OF THE OUTER OCTAGON, MAKING WHAT IS CALLED A GOTHIC DOME.

VAULTING. The art and practice of building vaults and of closing or finishing rooms, passages, or entire buildings, by means of vaults.

(For the subtitles, Barrel Vaulting, etc., see generally, Barrel Vault, etc.)

Cross Vaulting. Vaulting in which two or more simple vaults intersect one another as described under Groined Vault, Welsh Vault, and generally in the account of Ribbed Vaults in the article Vault.

Fan Vaulting. A species of stone vaulting in which the intrados of the vault, made up of constantly repeated surfaces of revolution,

FAN VAULTING; CLOISTERS GLOUCESTER CATHEDRAL, C. 1450.

each generated by a curved line, revolved horizontally about a fixed point, the apex of the vault being in plan an arc of a circle tangent to the opposing vault sprung from the opposite support, the horizontal spaces left between the tangent circles being filled with flat slabs, or keys of very slight curvature. The convex surfaces are formed with radial ribs of uniform curvature spaced closely together, giving the appearance of a folding fan bent to a curve, and butting at the crown against a horizontal circular ring. This species of vaulting is peculiar to the late English Gothic, finding its highest development in the chapel of King's College, Cambridge, and in Henry the Seventh's Chapel, Westminster Abbey. There are only about twenty-five examples of this construction in England and none fully developed on the Continent. In the English examples the vaulting springs from engaged shafts on the side walls, with one instance only of radiation from a central pillar. The lines of the curves are tangent to each other at the apex of the vault, in the centre, and between the engaged columns, leaving horizontal spandrels which are filled in by flagging or flat archings. A somewhat similar species of construction covers the small chapel of the monastery at Belem, near Lisbon; but in the Portuguese example the fans make complete circuits about slender isolated pillars, meeting half vaultings from the side walls, but not touching each other, and at the apex the lines of the fans, which are separated by a con- | cealed arch which spans the whole chapel, a single voussoir being extended several feet be-

VAULTING, NEOCLASSIC; CHURCH OF S. PETER, ROME; INTERIOR.

siderable space, are connected by very flat, ribbed, domical vaultings. The elaboration of the vault of Henry the Seventh's Chapel is greatly complicated by a series of drops from | low the line of the arch to form the drop and serve as a support for the inverted fans. (See Vault, VI., also England, Architecture of.)
— C. H. BLACKALL.

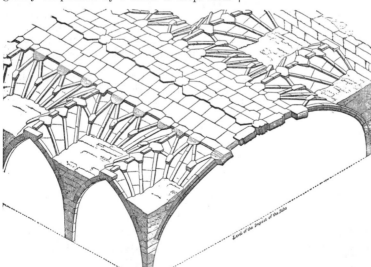

Ribbed Vaulting. A construction in which arched ribs are built from point to point over the space to be vaulted, the smaller and usually triangular spaces between the ribs being filled with lighter masonry. (See the article Vault, and Gothic Architecture.)

Stellar Vaulting. A late development of English fan vaulting as exhibited especially in the choir roof of Oxford cathedral, where the spaces between the intersections of the characteristic inverted polygonal pyramids of the vaulting are made by tracery to assume star-shaped forms. — H. V. B.

FAN VAULTING; CONSTRUCTION OF CHOIR ROOF, S. GEORGE'S CHAPEL, WINDSOR CASTLE. THE MIDDLE SECTION IS NOT RIBBED AT ALL BUT VAULTED IN SOLID BLOCKS. THE HAUNCHES ARE KEPT IN PLACE BY FILLING OF ROUGH MASONRY.

which springs a secondary system of fan vaulting. These drops are really a part of a con-

VAULTING CELL. One compartment of a vault which is so planned that one part can be built at a time, as in ribbed vaulting.

VAULTING COURSE. A horizontal course made up of the abutments or springers of a vaulted roof; generally made of stones set in projection or corbelled out, with horizontal beds.

VAULTING RIB. (See Rib.)

VAULTING SHAFT. In ribbed vaulting, the vertical upright, in one or several rounded members, which leads to the springer of a rib

VAULTING SHAFT; MÜNSTERMAIFELD, RHENISH PRUSSIA. THE SHAFTS PROPER SPRING FROM CULS-DE-LAMPE AND ARE ONLY TWO FEET LONG.

or group of ribs. This shaft may rise from the ground, or from a corbel at a greater height in the face of the masonry.

VAULTING TILE. A light piece of baked clay, intended to serve as a part of the filling of a vaulted cell, or of a groined vault built on centres.

VAULT LIGHT. (See under Light.)

VAUX, CALVERT; landscape architect; b. Dec. 20, 1824 (in London); d. November, 1895.

He studied architecture under Lewis N. Cottingham. He became the assistant of A. J. Downing, and later formed a partnership with him. The firm of Downing and Vaux laid out the grounds of the Capitol and of the Smithsonian Institution in Washington. In association with Frederick Law Olmsted, Vaux made the plans according to which Central Park in New York was laid out, and retained his posi-

tion as consulting landscape architect of the department of parks in New York until his death. Olmsted and Vaux designed Prospect Park, Brooklyn, the parks of Chicago and Buffalo, the State Reservation at Niagara Falls, and the Riverside and Morningside parks in New York.

Obituary in *American Architect*, Vol. L., p. 93.

VECELLI, TIZIANO (TITIAN); painter; b. 1477; d. 1576.

A mural painter of great power.

Crowe and Cavalcaselle, *Life of Titian*, also in general bibliography, Berenson, *Venetian Painters*.

VELARIUM. In the roofless Roman theatre and amphitheatre, a great awning which was often spread to protect the spectators from the sun or rain.

VELLANO. (See Bellano.)

VENEER. A thin facing of hard wood, which has desirable ornamental qualities under polish, glued upon a more common wood, usually pine, as in doors, wainscoting, cabinet work, etc. An extension of this meaning, used in house carpenters' trade, is described under Wood, Construction in, Part II.

VENETIAN BLIND; DENTIL; DOOR; PAVEMENT, etc. (See under special nouns.)

VENT. Any opening provided for the escape of smoke or foul air.

VENTIDUCT. A passage or duct for the conveyance of air, and to control and direct its movements in ventilation or heating.

VENTILATION. The process and art of supplying fresh air to the interiors of buildings, to mines, large vehicles of transportation, and the like, so as to maintain a constant acceptable standard of purity.

Anything short of the above can hardly be called ventilation, and it must be noted that movements of confined air, which simply produce a sense of cooling, must not be confounded with ventilation.

The savage made a hole in the roof of his house to let the smoke out. This was the first attempt at ventilation, and very little improvement was made on this primitive method until about six hundred years ago, when the fireplace and chimney appeared; and this sufficed for dwellings until about Franklin's time, when he invented an aspirating stove, the waste heat of which drew a measure of air out of the room, which air was renewed the best way possible, through window and door cracks and porous building materials. The early chimney was as a general thing so large that when the doors and windows were closed the air to supply the fire came down one side of the chimney, while the smoke went up the other side; and this circulation went on even after the fire was out, though in a subdued measure, thus securing incidental ventilation.

In the latter part of the seventeenth century systematic ventilation was undertaken by Sir Christopher Wren in the British Houses of

Mr. Clarence B. Young appeared in the annual reports of the Board of Regents of the Smithsonian Institute for the year 1873 and 1874. He recommended as the amount of air to be changed every hour to preserve the healthful condition of the room as follows : —

VAULTING SHAFT; THE NEAR ANGLE, BETWEEN CHOIR AND TRANSEPT, HAS A SHAFT FOR EACH GREAT GROUP OF RIBS, FIVE IN ALL.

Parliament, London. It was little better than "some holes in the ceilings." About 1723 Desaguliers improved the system by connecting the holes or tubes with heated chimneys. This is the first well-authenticated account of ventilation by "heat aspiration." In about the year 1736 Desaguliers again improved the ventilation of the British House of Parliament by the use of centrifugal fans, which were very similar to the housed pressure fan of to-day. This is probably the first well-authenticated account of the use of "pressure" and "exhaust" fans to buildings.

It is only within the last forty years, however, that a great and well-defined stride has been made in the development of systematic ventilation for habitations. The little that had been done by persons previous to that was in special cases and only in notable buildings, such as the Capitol at Washington and some hospitals and asylums; and it is probable that General Arthur Morin, director of the Conservatory of Arts and Trades, Paris, was the first to disseminate and give a clear understanding in his writings of the true principles of modern systematic ventilation, and a translation of his work on *Warming and Ventilating Occupied Buildings* is suggested for the consideration of all students. A translation of this work by

	Cubic Feet.
Hospitals :	
For ordinary cases of sickness	2119–2472
For surgical and lying-in cases	3532
During epidemics	3709
Prisons	1766
Workshops :	
Ordinary occupations . . .	2119
Unhealthful occupations . .	3532
Barracks :	
During the day	1059
At night	1413–1766
Theatres	1413–1766
Assembly rooms and halls for long receptions	2119
Halls for brief receptions ; lecture rooms	1059
Primary schools	4200–4530
Adult schools	833–1059
Stables	6357–7063

and it will be noticed that they do not fall so far below what is considered very fair practice of the present day. It is not quite apparent why he provides so high a proportion for stables, and does not say whether it is per man or per horse.

Morin is probably the first to point out the importance of keeping the quantity of air admitted to a building *constant* while making its temperature *variable*, the variations to suit the changes in the outside temperature. The only method in vogue previous to about twenty years ago was to close the register when the room was sufficiently warm; which of course not only cut off the heat supply, but the air supply as well, interrupting ventilation. This, however, is changed now in most buildings that are systematically ventilated, except, perhaps, private houses, where the change of air with indirect apparatus is generally sufficient for the limited number of persons present. General Morin called attention to the necessity of the " mixing valve," in the following words : —

" During the period of artificial heating, it is proper to reserve means of mixing with the warm air supplied by the heating apparatus, cool air, the amount of which may be regulated by convenient registers. For this purpose the warm air supplied by the heating apparatus

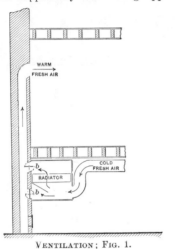

VENTILATION; FIG. 1.

should be received in a special register or mixing chamber, into which the cold air also enters, before passing into the distributing pipes."

The usual method of accomplishing the foregoing, now followed in the United States, is shown in the cut (Fig. 1). The dampers b, b are connected with a rod and operated from the room by hand pulls, or automatically operated by pneumatic pressure controlled by a thermostat. Many modifications of this method of mixing are shown in Dr. John S. Billings's work, *Ventilation and Heating.* Mixing systems, however, have been carried to a greater extent than this in some of the great modern buildings in the United States. In the new College of Physicians and Surgeons, built by Mr. William H. Vanderbilt, and which has since become a part of Columbia University, was first introduced the hot and cold air system in which parallel pipes conveyed both warm and cold air to the registers in the room, the parallel air ducts starting from a common cold air

supply, one duct being warmed to 120° and called the hot duct, and the other warmed to 60° and called the cold duct. This is shown by the diagram (Fig. 2), and the figure is typical of all the important points of the most modern warming and ventilating apparatus.

The cold air is taken in at I, which is called the cold air inlet. At G is a strainer of copper wire to intercept leaves, birds, mice, etc., but no dust, as the latter is practically impossible, unless with elaborate apparatus. The coils p are called primary heating coils, as they give the first increment of heat to the air — 60° or less. S is a settling chamber, the floor of which is flooded with an inch or so of water W, into which a very large percentage of the dust falls. F is a pressure fan capable of 1 oz. of pressure without extraordinary speed. C is the heating chamber, in which are located two sets of secondary heating coils, each capable of warming the air to 120° Fahr. or higher. These coils are divided into sections, as well as the primary coils, so that various graduations of heat can be obtained. The secondary coils upper SH are called "hot coils," while the coils lower SH are, for the sake of distinction, called "the cold coils." They are both, however, equal in all respects, only that under normal usage a large percentage of the hot coils are in use, while a small percentage of the cold coils are in use. From the heating chamber both the hot and cold air ducts start, and run one above the other (the warm one of preference being on top) to the various points of distribution about the building. The hot air duct, of course, is connected with the housing of the " hot coil," while the cold duct connects with the housing of the " cold coil," lower SH. The air and pressure in the heating chamber is common to both sets of ducts, so that, if one duct does not take it, the other does, the same quantity of air always reaching the rooms of the separate building, regardless of the temperature. From the horizontal ducts parallel vertical flues are carried to the register head, one " hot " and one " cold." In the register head, inside the face of the register, there is a simple slide valve just large enough to cover one entire pipe only. A simple mechanism attached to this slide valve serves as a handle to move it across the head of the hot and cold air pipes. It also indicates its position, so that the occupant of the room is enabled to mix the hot and cold air to any desired range of temperature between 60° and 120° Fahr.

A feature of this style of apparatus is that, should the main secondary coils upper SH get out of order, it is only necessary to shut them off and let on the lower SH, thus converting the cold air duct into a hot one, and *vice versa,* and run the apparatus reversed, securing equal results until the other is repaired. This is a feature of this style of apparatus that makes it particularly adapted to hospital use, so that it was carried out in both the old and new Sloane Maternity Hospitals, the Vanderbilt Clinic, and the Wm. J. Syms Operating Theatre of Roosevelt Hospital, all of New York City.

In the Sloane Maternity Hospital, 8000 cubic feet of air per bed per hour is admitted in this manner, and every ward is treated in the simple manner shown in the illustration, there being nothing but an air inlet and air outlet in each room. This is the minimum of possibilities for a hospital ward in a cold climate, doing away entirely with coils and dust catches in the room, and securing results that are uniform even in the coldest weather. The lower edge of the heat register is placed 7 to 8 feet from the floor, the lower ventilating register, which is only a face (easily removable for cleaning the flue), being only 4 inches from the floor, so as to finish on the marble, coved corner of the room and be as near the floor as possible, so as to take off the air at the lowest stratum possible ; while the upper vent is a full register placed as near the cove of the ceiling as possible, to take off the upper stratum of air when it is found necessary. These registers, however, are in the power of the nurses or occupants to close. In the first part of the Sloane Maternity Hospital to be built the ceiling registers were omitted, and all the air drawn off at the floor, but it was found that, when anæsthetics were used, it was necessary to have ceiling registers.

All the rooms of the College of Physicians and Surgeons, and the entire group of buildings including the Vanderbilt Clinic and the Sloane Maternity Hospital, are treated as above shown. The auditoriums of these buildings and the dissecting rooms of the college have different treatment, the details of which are given, as they also are typical of the most advanced practice in this regard. Figure 3 shows the amphitheatre of the College of Physicians and Surgeons, with the lecture room, and fan and heating chambers underneath. The centre heating chamber supplies heat and air to both the amphitheatre and the lecture room. In the case of the amphitheatre, the air is carried to a plenum underneath the raised steps, through

flues f, f, and thence it is passed out through the rises of the steps, on which the seats are arranged (small arrows), and delivered through long slots under the feet of the occupants. The slots are covered with iron flaps, as shown in the detail, so as to make the air impinge on the floor, and spread evenly and not strike on the backs of the legs. A quantity of air equal to 600,000 cubic feet per hour can be admitted to this hall without inconvenience by the method shown. The outgoing air of the room is entirely at the top, as shown by the large arrows, and all indication of smoking will disappear almost as quickly as the audience can retire, and the

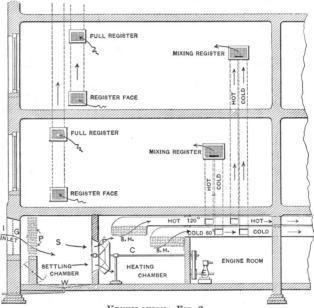

VENTILATION; FIG. 2.

lecturer is not affected by it. This is a case of the direct passage of the air of a room in a single upward direction, no part of the air returning to the person again.

The lecture room (just below) has the same treatment so far as the inlet of air is concerned, but the method of drawing it out differs on account of the construction of the building. The air is drawn out at opposite ends in central walls at floor and ceiling. There are registers r, r at both floor and ceiling, and a peculiarity of the system is that both floor and ceiling registers have separate flues without means of closing them, so that about one half the air goes off at the floor line and the remainder at the ceiling. The results are found to be good. In other rooms of the building, both the floor and ceiling registers are in the same flue. The dissecting room of this building, which contains about eighty tables, has a distinct treatment. The air is admitted through a perforated cornice or air box running around the entire ceiling, and it is drawn out at registers in the baseboard; the object being to secure a downward current of air within the room, and, if possible, make emanations fall to the floor. The general results are good, about 500,000 cubic feet of air being passed through the room in an hour. The dissecting room fan chamber is shown in Fig. 3 at A. It is a single flue system, the

admitting 2,000,000 cubic feet of air per hour is provided, which allows 666 cubic feet per person per hour, and, though low compared to hospital ventilation, is still a generous allowance of fresh air. The fresh air supply to this building is taken from a colonnade or open gallery on the south side of the building at a distance of about 75 feet above the ground. The air is then carried down through a shaft to a fan chamber, where it is warmed and forced into the plenum through the fan F, shown in the drawing. The plenum is formed by the entire basement underneath the main floor. The construction is entirely iron and masonry, and fireproof. Under every third seat both on the main floor and on the balcony floor air is admitted through a mushroom-like cap, shown in the detail. This cap is capable of three

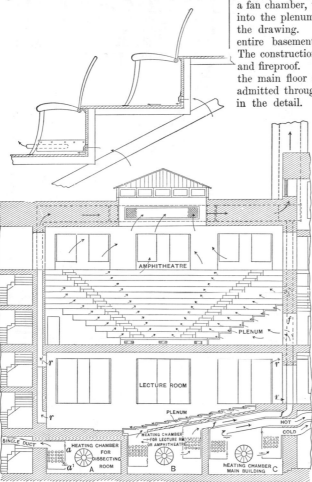

VENTILATION; FIG. 3.

adjustments, but it is so arranged that it never can be closed entirely. From the main plenum air is carried through a system of ducts, which are shown, into the space formed between floor and ceiling of the first balcony. The gallery receives no heat or ventilation, except that which comes through the house generally. The method of withdrawing the air from the house is through a large central dome which connects with the main aspirating shaft on the roof. This dome is covered with a bell that is capable of adjustment, the controlling mechanism running down to the engineer's department. The ventilation from underneath the balcony and gallery is by an entirely different system of flues, that cannot be closed. A study of the drawing will show these flues running up separately in the rear wall, and connecting into a separate vent pipe placed within the main aspirating shaft. The object of

temperature being regulated by the engineer in the heat chamber by the mixing valves a and a; the upper one for warm air and the lower one for cold air, the adjustment of each securing the temperature required.

The American Theatre, New York (Fig. 4), is a good example of theatre ventilation and warming. The system is "forced ventilation," that is, a fan is used. Flues, etc., are, however, sufficiently ample to allow of warming without the fan. The seating capacity of the building is about 3000 persons, and means of

the separate set of vent ducts is to provide for drawing away the accumulations of hot air that usually form underneath the steep galleries. When the bell or valve in the central dome is partially closed the pressure of the outgoing air is increased underneath the balcony and gallery, so that the proportion of air forced to go out at these points can be increased or diminished by lessening or increasing the amount allowed to escape in the centre.

The stage is warmed entirely by direct radiation, large coils being hung on the rear wall

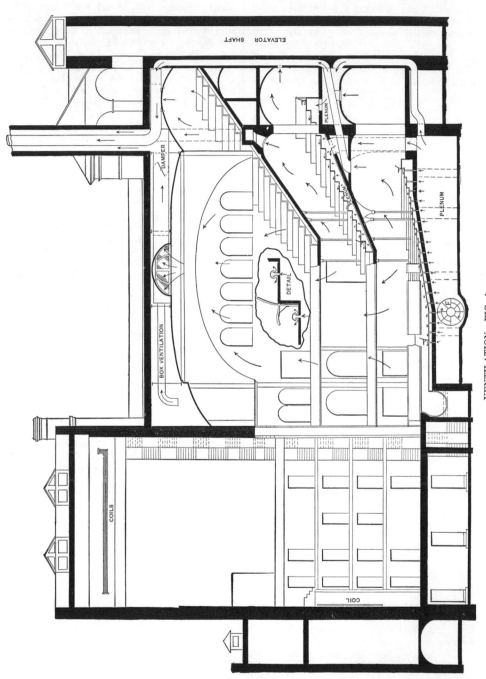

VENTILATION; FIG. 4.

ELEVATOR SHAFT

PLENUM

PLENUM

DAMPER

BOX VENTILATION

DETAIL

COILS

COIL

983   984

PLATE XXXV

VERA DA POZZO

The upper figure shows that in the Court of the Palazzo Vendramin Calergi, on the grand Canal, and is of that peculiar Venetian Romanesque which shows a strong influence of Byzantine models. It is of the twelfth century. That below is of the close of the fourteenth century, and designed, as many were, in the semblance of a capital for a column. The escutcheon on one side has very intelligible armorial bearings, which might reveal the name of the original owner and the original locality. The vera is now in an ancient cloister, that of the *Abbazia della Misericordia.*

and others suspended high so as to prevent a downfall of cold air, which is so often found to flow out into the body of the house upon the rise of the curtain. The temperature maintained in the plenum is about 65° Fahr., and the switch valve is used so that the engineer can keep the plenum at any desired temperature.

The usual school for from forty to fifty scholars, as now commonly designed, has a floor space of about 24 feet by 32 feet, with light on at least two sides of the room, the general endeavour being to have the sitting so arranged that the light will come in over the left shoulder of the scholar. Provision should be made for the admission of at least 100,000 cubic feet of fresh air to one such room in an hour. The admission of this air should be above the head line, and one inlet register is sufficient. Experiments have demonstrated that the necessary flue for such a room should have a cross section of not less than 3 feet in its smallest part, and that 4 feet is probably the limit required, the latter being the size now adopted by the engineers of the New York Board of Education. It is the custom in New York to reënforce the warm air system by a direct system, the object being to maintain the heat of the room by direct radiation when the fans are not running, such as at night, etc. It has been found, however, that when a quantity of air equal to 100,000 cubic feet is admitted to an ordinary schoolroom in an hour, that this amount can be admitted and withdrawn without appreciable draughts, and at a temperature sufficiently low to prevent the room from being overheated. Under this condition of quantity and low temperature it has been found, except in exceedingly cold parts of the United States, that direct radiation can be dispensed with, and still give comfortable conditions at all parts of the room. It is not desirable, however, from a point of economy of maintenance to admit such large quantities of air when the school is not in session; therefore, in the construction of a heating and ventilating apparatus for a school it is desirable either to provide a reasonable quantity of direct radiation, or to design the flues and the indirect portion of the heating apparatus in such a manner that sufficient air will pass through the flues by natural draught to maintain the heat, but with a greatly reduced quantity of air and with an increased temperature from that necessary when the school is in session. A register of 50 per cent greater area than the flue when placed above the head line, the lower edge being 7 or 8 feet from the floor, will not cause inconvenience, although the velocity of the air may be 4 or 5 feet per second.

In the matter of withdrawing air from a schoolroom the air should be drawn from as near the floor line as possible, and preference should be given to a register that will be low and wide rather than the reverse. Building construction, however, sometimes interferes with the proper shaped flue to secure the best results. The architect, however, should endeavour to make the flues wide so that the register can be low, and no objection should be made to having the register cut through the baseboard, as appearance should be set aside to utility. The vent registers can be in the same wall or group as the heat registers when the outlet is at the floor. The question of ceiling ventilation in a schoolroom is very unsettled. In winter time it is probably unnecessary, although this does not always satisfy, and for this reason it is customary to place another ventilating register in the same flue near the ceiling. This brings the ceiling outlet too close to the inlet or heat register, resulting in robbing the room of its heat, and the short-circuiting of the pure air current. For this reason, perhaps, it would be well to have a double set of vent registers and vent flues to each room when possible, the vent registers being placed near the floor in the group near the heat flues, and near the ceiling in the opposite group. This will permit of both floor and ceiling ventilation. It will also prevent the floor vent from being interfered with when the upper vent is opened, and it will still further prevent a considerable loss of heat by short-circuiting. All schools designed for forced ventilation should also be arranged so that, in case the forcing mechanism gets out of order, air and heat enough will still enter the rooms by natural methods to keep them comfortably warm, so that it will not be necessary to dismiss the school through temporary injury to the fan or motor.

— WILLIAM J. BALDWIN.

VENTILATOR. Any device for replacing foul by pure air; as a hood or cap at the top of the vent shaft or flue, contrived to prevent down draughts and to create up draughts; or an open lantern at the top of a building, provided with louver boarding, and connected with the exhaust system of ventilation.

VENT PIPE. A pipe carried from a house to the outer air, intended for the ventilation of a system of waste pipes, for the removal of foul gases, and also for the prevention of trap siphonage or back pressure; in general, an escape or relief pipe for steam, sewer, air, etc. (See House Drainage.)

VERA DA POZZO. A cistern curb; one of the parapets strongly resembling well curbs which abound in Venice, in public places and in the courts of large private houses. In the courtyard of the Ducal Palace two of these vere da pozzo exist, of bronze, and of very elaborate design. These date from 1556 and 1559. With these exceptions the cistern heads in Venice are all of stone; in most cases, Istrian stone. They vary in date from early Byzantine work, perhaps as early as the tenth century, to work of the Post-Renaissance time. The simplest are cylindrical or of reversed conical shape; but a very large number are extremely rich and elegant in design, and these are often designed like capitals of columns, with four angle projections of leafage. A valuable work has been devoted to them by the publisher, Ferdinando Ongania, of Venice, the title of which is *Raccolta delle Vere da Pozzo in Venetia.* — R. S.

With Viollet-le-Duc (see Viollet-le-Duc) he was architect of the diocesan buildings of Amiens and Beauvais (France). With Dr. Cattois he published *L'Architecture civile et domestique au Moyen âge et à la Renaissance* (Paris, 2 vols. 4to., 1855).

Bauchal, *Dictionnaire.*

VERGARA, FRANCISCO (I.); b. 1681 (at Valencia, Spain); d. 1753.

He studied sculpture under Rodulfo and Aliprandi, two Germans employed in the decoration of the cathedral of Valencia. Vergara made the statues of cardinal virtues and por-

VERA DA POZZO OF BRONZE, IN COURT OF DUCAL PALACE, VENICE.

VERANDA; VERANDAH. An open gallery or portico covered by a roof supported by pillars, and attached to the exterior of a building. It is often extended across one or more fronts of the building, or entirely around it, and is occasionally enlarged or otherwise so planned as to form an outside room, more or less protected by screens of vine or lattice. The conditions of climate in the United States render the veranda a necessary feature of life in the country, and especially at places of summer resort in the cottages and hotels. This local necessity has been a very important element in conferring distinctive character on structures of this kind in America.

VERDE ANTICO. (Same as Verdantique Marble, under Marble.)

VERDANTIQUE. (Same as Verdantique Marble, under Marble.)

VERDIER, PIERRE AYNARD; b. Nov. 19, 1819 (at Tours, Indre-et-Loire, France).

Verdier was a pupil of Labrouste (see Labrouste) and at the *École des Beaux Arts.*

traits of Valencian popes over the main portal of the cathedral, the high altar of the church of S. Augustine, the figures of S. Domingo and S. Catalina for the church of S. Domingo, etc., all at Valencia.

Stirling-Maxwell, *Annals of the Artists of Spain;* Bermudez, *Diccionario.*

VERGARA, FRANCISCO (II.); sculptor; b. 1713 (in Spain); d. July 30, 1761 (in Rome).

A nephew and pupil of Francisco (I.) Vergara (see Vergara, Fr., I.) of Valencia. He went to Madrid and made statues of S. Francisco de Paolo and S. Antonio in the church of S. Ildefonso. Vergara went to Rome and entered the school of Filippo Valle. He executed statues and bas-reliefs for the altar of S. Julian in the cathedral of Cuença (Spain), which was designed by the architect Ventura Rodriguez. For the church of S. Peter's in Rome he made a statue of S. Pedro Alcantara. Bermudez (op. cit.) praises his statues for their grand character and for the breadth and freedom of their draperies.

Stirling-Maxwell, *Annals of the Artists of Spain;* Bermudez, *Diccionario.*

VERGARA, IGNACIO; sculptor; b. 1715 (at Valencia, Spain); d. April 13, 1776.

A son and pupil of Francisco (I.) Vergara (see Vergara, Fr., I.). He enjoyed a high reputation in Valencia, and left many works there. Among the best of these is a group of angels in the façade of the cathedral. With his brother, Josef Vergara, he established the *Real Academia de S. Carlos* in Valencia, of which he became director in 1773.

Stirling-Maxwell, *Annals of the Artists of Spain;* Bermudez, *Diccionario.*

VERGARA, NICOLAS DE; sculptor, painter, and architect; d. 1606.

A son and pupil of Nicolas de Vergara, a painter and sculptor. In 1573 he succeeded his father as sculptor and painter of the cathedral of Toledo (Spain). He made the fine bronze and iron lateral lecterns of the choir, and designed the new Sagrario, or chapel of the Host, which was finished by Monegro. In 1575 he designed the church of the Bernardine nuns at Toledo, and in 1595 a chapel for the relics of the Jeronymites of Guadalupe (Spain).

Stirling-Maxwell, *Annals of the Artists of Spain;* Bermudez, *Diccionario.*

VERGAZ, ALFONSO GIRALDO; sculptor; b. Jan. 23, 1744 (at Murcia, Spain); d. Nov. 19, 1812.

He studied sculpture under Felipe de Castro in Madrid, and April 15, 1797, was made director of the *Academia de S. Fernando* in that city. Among his works are a statue of Don Carlos III. in the plaza publica of Burgos, a statue of Juan Sebastian Elcano at Guetaria, three angels in the cathedral of Jaen, and various works in Madrid.

Viñaza, *Adiciones.*

VERGE (1). A shaft, as of a column or colonnette; the French general term, occasionally used in English in this especial sense; perhaps generally with the French pronunciation, as in the case of Passage (II.).

VERGE (II.). That part of a sloping roof which projects beyond a gable or half-gable (as of a pent house). Verge and the terms compounded with it are used in contrast to *eaves* and its compounds. This term is hardly technical; but the supposed connection between it and Barge in certain combinations has given it an accidental importance.

VERGE BOARD. Same as Barge Board; there is, however, no etymological connection between the two phrases.

VERMICULATED WORK (also, but improperly, vermicular work). A sort of rusticated stonework so wrought as to appear thickly indented with worm tracks. (See Rus-

tic Work.) This device is used to roughen a surface regularly so as to create a marked contrast with smooth surfaces.

VERMICULATION. The act or art of producing vermiculated ornament; the roughening so produced.

VERONESE (PAOLO CALIARI); painter; b. 1528; d. 1588.

A mural painter of great power.

Charles Yriarte, *Paul Véronèse;* Charles Blanc, *Véronèse au Château de Masère;* Berenson, *Venetian Painters of the Renaissance.*

VERROCCHIO (ANDREA DI MICHELE DE' CIONE); sculptor, painter, and goldsmith; b. 1435; d. 1488.

Andrea was apprenticed to a goldsmith, Verrocchio, by whose name he was known. Of his work as goldsmith nothing remains except a bas-relief in the silver retable at the baptistery in Florence (1478–1480). In 1467 he assisted Luca della Robbia (see Robbia, Luca della) in casting the bronze doors of the sacristy of the cathedral of Florence About 1471–1472 he made the monument of Piero and Giovanni de' Medici in the church of S. Lorenzo at Florence. He visited Rome during the pontificate of Sixtus IV. (Pope 1471–1484), and made there the tomb of Francesca Tornabuoni, some bas-reliefs from which are now in the Museo Nazionale (Florence). The charming fountain (boy with dolphin), now in the court of the Palazzo Vecchio (Florence), was intended for the Medici villa at Careggi. Verrocchio's greatest work is the equestrian statue of the general, Bartolomeo Colleone, at Venice (begun 1479). The work was left incomplete at the death of Verrocchio. It passed through the hands of Lorenzo di Credi to Alessandro Leopardi, who cast the statue in 1496 and signed his name on the saddle girth. (See Leopardi, A.)

Vasari, Milanesi ed.; Vasari, Blashfield-Hopkins ed.; Müntz, *Renaissance;* Perkins, *Tuscan Sculptors;* Bode, *Italienische Bildhauer der Renaissance.*

VERTE ISLAND STONE. A hard red sandstone from Verte Island, Lake Superior.

VESICA PISCIS. A Glory of the long and sometimes pointed oval form supposed to be that of a fish bladder, whence the name. (See also Symbology.)

VESTIARY. A room or place for the keeping of vestments, garments, or clothes; a wardrobe.

VESTIBULE. A lobby or passage intermediate between the entrance and the interior of a building; a place of shelter or accommodation to those awaiting entrance to a building; and in northern climates the area between outer, storm, or front doors and inner, or vestibule doors, by which the house is protected from the cold draughts. (Compare Storm

Door, *B,* and Wind Porch.) Less properly, an anteroom to a larger apartment or suite. (See Lobby.)

VESTIBULE OF A HOUSE NEAR THE CHURCH S. M. DELLA PACE, ROME.

VESTIBULUM. In Roman archæology, the outer vestibule, a recess or sheltered place outside of the outer doors of a building, as distinguished from the Fauces. It was sometimes large and adorned with columns, forming an important architectural member, and a place where many persons could find shelter; but this must have been unusual, as only one of any elaborateness has been found in Pompeii. The Villa of the Papyri at Herculaneum seems to have had a perfectly plain, square vestibule within an outer columnar portico; it is possible that some allusions in ancient writers may be explained in this way.

VESTRY. A sacristy. A room adjoining the choir of a church, and sometimes behind the main altar, where the sacred vessels and vestments were kept, and where the priest put on his robes. In Protestant churches, a waiting room, next the chancel or pulpit, for the accommodation of the clergy. A choir vestry is a robing room for the choir. (See Diaconicon.)

VESTRY HALL. In England and in some of the English colonies, a hall in which the inhabitants or ratepayers of a parish, or their representatives, meet for the despatch of the official business of the parish. — (A. P. S.)

VESUVIAN DISTRICT, ARCHITECTURE OF, THE: That of a region of Italy lying southeast of Naples, and reaching from Naples to Castellamare, thus occupying the innermost coast of the Bay of Naples. The buildings which belong to this subject are those which have been overwhelmed by eruptions of Mt. Vesuvius, and which have been brought to light in recent times, or are in the way of being so explored. The considerable town of Pompeii has been about half uncovered; this labour having been much less difficult, because the original bed of ashes cannot have exceeded seven or eight feet in depth, and the subsequent deposits were still so slight that the upper stories of the houses were frequently left uncovered. The town of Herculaneum, however, is covered by a tufa formed of volcanic sand, which has solidified under the eruptions and subsequent rains into a porous stone; and this is sixty feet deep in some places, and nearly everywhere thirty-five to forty feet deep. Here only a few hundred square feet have been opened to the sky, the digging having been done in forty feet of soft rock; but two other important discoveries have been made. These are, first, that of a theatre, which is kept open and can be visited by descending through a well and passing along underground passages; and that of the celebrated Villa of the Papyri, called also the Villa Ercolanese, in which were found not only the great store of papyrus rolls which give it its common name, but also a large number of bronze statues, statuettes, busts, and groups, by means of which the Museum of Naples has been made richer in the matter of antique bronze sculpture than all the rest of Europe together. Other minor explorations have been made at different points south and southwest of Mt. Vesuvius, and valuable objects have been found. The architectural interest of this region is, however, almost entirely centred in the city of Pompeii, where, though the houses were visited by their owners and by plunderers, who dug down through the soft ashes of the first eruption, and, although the wooden upper stories, roofs, etc., have disappeared, and the masonry and decorative work of the lower story have disappeared altogether or suffered severely, there is still the material for a very valuable study of the Roman Imperial epoch.

The excavations of Pompeii are continued steadily and with care; and a more strict archæological influence has controlled these for the last twenty-five years. Nothing is being done at Herculaneum; and it will require elaborate preparations and a considerable expenditure of money to reveal the treasures that are below the surface in that neighbourhood. It is altogether probable that many such villas are buried under the soft rock, and that as many ancient works of art exist there, accessible to us, as are now contained in the museums of Europe. (See Comparetti's book mentioned below for the extraordinary art treasures discovered in the celebrated villa. The preface of Mau's book gives a number of titles.) — R. S.

Comparetti, *La Villa Ercolanese dei Pisoni i suoi monumenti e la sua biblioteca*, 1883; Mau, *Pompeii, Its Life and Art*, 1899.

B. The benefice and office or functions of a vicar.

VICAR'S CLOSE. (See Close.)

VICTOR, LOUIS. (See Louis, Louis Nicholas Victor.)

VICTORIAN ARCHITECTURE. That of the reign of Queen Victoria; the term may be applied, therefore, to any building commenced or planned since the accesssion of the queen, but is used more especially for buildings of any

VESTIBULE IN PALAZZO MACCARANI, ROME.

VIADUCT. An elevated roadway supported by arches of masonry, or by trestles of iron or wood, carried over a valley or any low-lying district where an embankment would be inexpedient or impracticable. (Compare Aqueduct.)

VIART, CHARLES; architect; d. about 1537.

He completed, in 1526, the Hôtel de Ville of Beaugency (Loiret, France), and in that year was called to Orléans (Loiret) to build the Renaissance portion of the Hôtel de Ville, now a museum. He was employed on the Hôtel de Ville of Montargis and on the château of Blois.

Herluison, *Artistes Orléanais;* Lance, *Dictionnaire.*

VICARAGE. *A.* In England, the home or residence of a vicar.

characteristic style unknown previous to the year 1837. During the reign the Gothic Revival began, culminated, and declined; and there were several other important movements, fashions, or attempts at creating a new style, such as the revived style of Queen Anne, in which Mr. Norman Shaw was active and which had great success at one time; also of late years a new ultra-classic revival, to which it has been attempted to give a purely Palladian character. Buildings, such as those which, belonging to the later years of the Gothic Revival, contain French and Italian elements freely used in connection with English, together with a free use of party-coloured materials, are commonly called Victorian Gothic. (See the articles, England, Architecture of; Gothic Revival; and a history of the Gothic Revival by Charles L. Eastlake, London, 1872.) — R. S.

VICTORIA STONE. A variety of artificial stone introduced in 1868.

VIGARNY, FELIPE DE (FELIPE DE BORGONA); sculptor and architect.

For the Cardinal Ximenes de Cisneros he made the great retable of the cathedral of Toledo (Spain), with its sculpture (1502). He afterward went to Granada to execute the royal chapel in the cathedral, and the fine monuments of Ferdinand and Isabella which it contains.

Stirling-Maxwell, *Annals of the Artists of Spain;* Bermudez, *Diccionario.*

VIGNOLA. (See Barozzio, Jacopo.)

and all the appurtenances which may be brought into direct connection with the design. Such is the Italian significance of the word, which, when adopted in English, had the same meaning. In the United States it has come to imply merely a suburban dwelling with small grounds, and there is left no term so comprehensive in its scope as *villa* in its original meaning. Therefore, it is to be hoped that, with the renewed interest in formal design of country places, the original use of the word may again come into use. According to this, the house should be considered as merely a part of the whole scheme, and not as the villa itself.

The villa is usually, though not necessarily, designed especially for occupancy during the

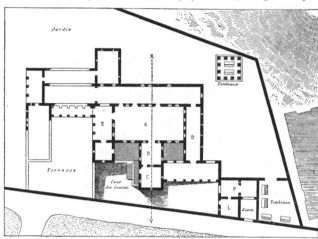

A. Great hall, with one or two stories over.

B, C. Lower buildings ; C is probably a kitchen.

D. Chief corridor of entrance.

E. Portico, where was probably the principal staircase.

L. Porter's lodge.

P. Entrance to the villa indirect, leading through three vestibules which could be closed.

VILLA, EL-BARAH, SYRIA; PLAN PARTLY RESTORED.

VIGNON, BARTHÉLEMY; architect; b. 1762 at Lyon; d. May 1, 1828.

A pupil of David Leroy and of De Gisors. In 1806 he won second prize in the competition for the transformation of the church of the Madeleine (Paris) into the Temple de la Gloire. His design was, however, preferred by the Emperor Napoleon. He undertook the work, and had charge of the building until his death, when he was succeeded by Huvé. (See Huvé.) The present classical form of the Madeleine is his design. (See Contant d'Ivry, and Couture.)

Paris dans sa Splendeur; Bauchal, *Dictionnaire.*

VIHARA. A Buddhist monastery. Structures of this sort were often excavated from the solid rock ; the halls, the ceilings of which were supported by sculptured pillars, being surrounded by small sleeping cells. (See India, Architecture of.)

VILLA. A country residence designed particularly with a view of affording all the enjoyments of country life, consisting of a house and surroundings, such as gardens, terraces, groves,

summer. The site is selected on account of the beauty and healthfulness of the situation, and the arrangement of the grounds is such as to give the occupants all the advantages of the country. The villa is, therefore, more distinctly the country place of a man from the city, as opposed to that of a continued country resident, or farmer, who gains his livelihood from tilling the land. And its requirements are aptly suggested in the French title for this sort of place, *"Maison de Plaisance"* (pleasure house). A villa is not "a lodge in some vast wilderness," or a summer cottage by the wayside, but the country seat of a highly civilized person who feels the necessity of being surrounded by those forms of art which may tend in any way to enhance or bring in relief the beauties of nature.

The villa, as we know it, in its typical form, is a product of Italian soil and of Italian art. Each country has its own method of arranging country places, varying with the character of the people, the climate, and local conditions ; but the fundamental principles which govern the design of such places as may be properly termed villas are on the same lines as those of the

VILLA; RESTORED VIEW OF THAT AT EL-BARAH; SEE PLAN.

997

998

Italians. Some of the finest examples of the Renaissance villa exist in Italy, with hardly a change which affects their main features. Their treatment is strictly formal. The grounds are laid out in architectural relation to the house. The paths, alleys, and roads are *en axe* with the principal openings of the house, and the whole arrangement of gardens, terraces, groves, etc., is usually enclosed within walls or some lines of a formal character which may give one a sense of privacy. The hand of the artist is frankly in evidence, and under that hand the place becomes the fitting seat of the man of culture.

The origin of the villa may be traced to the earliest movements of civilization. The Hanging Gardens of Babylon, those of the Pharaohs in Egypt, the Greek villas, these are all treated in literature by the writers of the time. But the villa could flourish only at a time of high civilization, when the security of property permitted men to live at a distance from cities or fortified towns. Therefore, it is not until we reach the time of the villas of ancient Rome, that anything like the modern villa came into existence. The ancient Romans were great lovers of country life, and the subject of the villa was treated extensively by many writers on architecture and agriculture. The letters of Pliny the Younger give very exact descriptions of three of his own villas, and from these and the writings of contemporary authors, very exact rules may be laid down for the arrangement of country places according to the style of the ancient Romans. The more important of their villas were divided into three parts: the Villa Urbana, the pleasure house and grounds of the master; the Villa Rustica, buildings and grounds set apart for the farmer, servants, cattle, etc.; and the Fructuria, or purely agricultural department. Sometimes the more common of these villas were composed of the Villa Urbana alone, being situated near Rome or near some town which could supply the necessaries, and so simply a place of retirement for the owner. It was the custom of the more important Romans to have several of these places in different parts of Italy suited to the different seasons; one near the sea, one in the hills.

Pliny's Villa of Laurentum, in Latium, known from the descriptions in his letters, was a place which should be classed with the most important villas of the Renaissance, or with the country residences of the English noblemen of our day, and it gives a very accurate idea of the type and of the style of the principal features of the Roman villa. It will be noted that architecture and sculpture played a very important part in the decoration of the grounds. Marble, porphyry, and bronze were contrasted with cypress, laurel, and box. Large parterres were laid out in various forms; and while the ancient Roman had a comparatively limited number of plants from

which to compose his garden, as compared with modern times, the main characteristics of the modern Renaissance garden would probably have been observed in that of the ancient Roman. It seems probable that in later times the architectural side of the Roman garden played too important a part. This is always a sign of decadence in formal villas, perfection in this kind of work meaning that a very nice sense of proportion should be observed in combining these two component parts. Under the Barbarian invasion the gardens of ancient Rome disappeared entirely, and it was not until the fifteenth century that they were born again under the Renaissance movement, the renewal of ancient art. It was under Lorenzo de' Medici, at Florence, that this movement commenced. Little but the traces of the original gardens remain at present, but enough to show (and particularly in the gardens which followed them) that they were inspired by the spirit of the villas of the ancient Romans. Symmetrical forms and architectural lines and sculptural decorations played the same part.

Founded upon these beginnings are the famous villas so well known: the Villa Medici, the Villa Borghese, Pamfili Doria, and Colonna, in Rome, the Villa d'Este in Tivoli, and Mondragone, Aldobrandini, and others, in Frascati. These were the residences of the most important families of that time, and their scale and scope were so important that they have remained more or less intact since. Traces of some of the Medici villas are to be found in the suburbs of Florence; the Villa Castello, however, is the only important one in a good state of preservation to-day.

The Villa Pamfili, near Rome, has been selected from many others as containing the main features and the best of them. More importance is, perhaps, given here to the flower garden and the parterre than is to be found in some of the others, but the skill of the architect is always shown by giving such importance to one part or another as the lay of the land seems to suggest, carefully disposing the terraces, groves, and gardens, so as to make a complete composition in relation to the house. Thus the site of the Villa d'Este in Tivoli, and the Frascati villas, required very extensive terracing. The artistic value of these terraces, forming a foreground for the distant views of the Campagna, is very great, and perhaps the main characteristic which distinguishes them from other villas. The situation of the bosquet, in the Villa Medici, distinguishes it from that of any other bosquet. The Villa Albani is remarkable for the simplicity of its design, admirably adapted to showing the beautiful collection of sculptures of the owner. Besides the wonderful terraces of the Villa d'Este, it is remarkable for the extraordinary variety of its fountains. The architect has taken advantage of the unlimited supply of water furnished by the cascades above the villa, and has run this supply through the villa in hundreds of fountains of every variety and form.   The flower gardens in the Villa Lante, the Villa Pamfili, and the Villa Castello are their most distinctive features.

and guarding the works of art contained within it.   Whatever may have been the cause, the result was, undoubtedly, to produce a very perfect work of art, every inch of ground within the enclosure being taken advantage of to produce some interesting effect, and a very delightful sense of privacy almost similar to

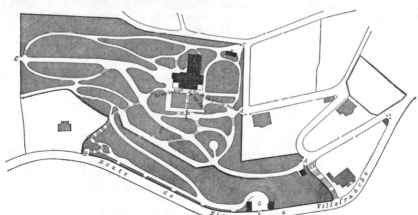

VILLA; AT MONTBORON, NEAR NICE (ALPES-MARITIMES), FRANCE.

A. Principal entrances; vehicles mounting by roads which pass beyond the house, and from which flights of steps ascend the hill.
B. Entrance for pedestrians by continuous path, partly a stair *a cordoni.*
C. Service entrances; that on the right below passing through the stable yard and thence by another wagon road to the level of that on the left which is on a level with the house.

D. Dwelling house.
E. Gardener's cottage.
F. Porter's lodge.
G. Stables and carriage house fronting on stable yard.
    The unshaded parts are not included in the estate. The staircase *a cordoni* on the right above the word Villefranche is public, or at least common to several properties.

One characteristic of all these villas, and the one lost sight of in the work of the later period in Italy, and also in Europe, is the limitation of the formal grounds within a comparatively small compass.   This may originally have been necessary on account of the frequency of wars, and the impossibility of protecting a larger area

that enjoyed within the walls of the house itself.

The first European country to feel the influence of the classic villa of the Italian Renaissance, aside from Spain, was France, where, under Francis I., Fontainebleau was started, entirely on the lines of this school.   But here, even in the beginning, the vast importance of the villa of the king of France made the scale upon which the usual features of the villa were laid out much larger than anything that had been done in Italy. The idea of carrying formal symmetrical lines to a greater distance from the house was started. In France, naturally, very different conditions governed the form which the country house and its grounds took, because those of most importance were not, as in Italy, *maisons de plaisance*, occupied by the owners for recreation and pleasure, but were the permanent seats of their owners and situated in the midst of their vast estates. In feudal times, of course, the house was a castle, and fortified; and though, under Francis I., they gradually assumed a less forbidding aspect, they were still so arranged as to be in a position to defend themselves if need be. At the same time, wherever it was possible, a sufficient amount of ground was enclosed within the fortified region to permit of the arrangement of gardens, restricted in size, but similar in character and design to those of the Italian villa. Plans of some of these châteaux, with their surroundings, may be seen in the work of J. Androuet Du Cerceau.[1] These places do not properly come under the heading of villa, but should be mentioned as having had their effect in the villa design which was developed later in France.

Under Henry IV. the French method merely indicated in the original designs of Fontainebleau was extended, the scale of work increased, and the idea introduced of extending formal lines through a vast forest. The style reached its perfection later under Le Nôtre, whose genius expressed itself in vast proportions, and may be seen to-day, having been preserved almost in its entire perfection at Versailles. It seems as if the impossible had been accomplished, and one can scarcely conceive of a work of this magnitude having been accomplished in the lifetime of one man.

With the perfection, however, of Le Nôtre's style, the logical conclusion of the extent to which formal work could be applied out of doors was reached. No further step could be taken. The time was indeed ripe for a reaction. The imitators and followers of Le Nôtre, by their lack of talent and merely strict following of rules deduced from his method, brought formality into disrepute. The result was to produce a revolution in villa design throughout Europe.

The influence of classic and Italian style had been strongly felt in England, beginning rather later than in France, the first important example being Hampton Court, done under the inspiration of Wolsey. The style spread through the estates of the principal noblemen and courtiers, and resulted in the creation of many beautiful

places. These places, however, although their style was on the lines of the villa, cannot properly come under this heading, being the seats of permanent residence of the owners rather than their pleasure houses. The large extent of the estate itself surrounding the house, and the temptation to include too much of it within the lines of formal treatment, caused the methods of Le Nôtre to be carried to a very great extreme here. This may be particularly well seen upon looking at the plan of Badminton,[1] which has the appearance of a vast geometrical problem worked out in alleys, vistas, etc., to an extent fatiguing in the extreme, completely obliterating the natural beauties.

The reaction against this sort of thing was inevitable. The work of the artist had ceased.

It does not come within the scope of this paper to treat of the school of villa design in England and in Europe, which was the result of this reaction. Treating the word "villa," and villa itself, as of Italian origin, and the design as being on the original lines of the Italian villa, those places created under the hand of the landscape gardener and his influences should be classified under another term. Suffice it to say, that the architect now ceased to design the grounds, his work ending with the house. The landscape gardener here took it up, and it will be seen that the reverse of formality was his theme, his object being, rather, to make a contrast to the necessarily formal lines of the house, and his desire to produce a picturesque effect, reproducing as far as possible natural effects. It may be safely said that the result of this method has not been beneficial to architecture, no distinct style having resulted. The desire to produce a picturesque building line, and a structure which might not call too loudly for corresponding style in the grounds, has resulted in buildings being made up of several styles, — towers and gables, the individual fancies of the architect and owner, playing a large part.

It seems now that a reaction against this method of design, the landscape gardening school, is on foot, and that the direction this reaction is taking is a return to the old Italian school.

The habit of life of the people in the United States is distinctly congenial to the villa idea. The winters are spent in the city and the summers in the country. Men go to the country for recreation, health, and pleasure, while in the city they leave their real interests, business, etc. Climate leads them to be as much as possible out of doors in summer. The country houses should be extended, and the scheme of gardens, terraces, etc., which does this in the Italian villas can be applied here. It seems not improbable that within the next generation or so this country may be the centre of development in villa design.

---

[1] *Des plus excellents Bâtiments de France*, Paris, 1576–1579.

[1] Kip's *Views.*

VILLA ADRIANA. Near Tivoli, east of Rome. A great accumulation of buildings over a mile of country measured from north to south, and including two theatres and grounds for exercise, swimming-tanks, and libraries, in addition to buildings of residence. Sculptures have been found there, but no organized system of exploration has yet made possible a perfect comprehension of the structure.

VILLA HADRIANA. (See Villa Adriana.)

VILLA MADAMA. Near Rome, on the north; a very beautiful building of the later years of the Renaissance, always ascribed to Raphael as designer, though built by Giulio Romano (see Pippi).

VILLA MEDICI. In Rome, on the Pincian Hill; buildings mostly of the sixteenth century, but altered for the use of the French Academy and School of Fine Art (see Prize of Rome).

VILLA MONDRAGONE. Near Frascati, in the Alban Hills; an enormous building, in part of the sixteenth century, and ascribed to Vignola.

VILLA PAMFILI DORIA. At Rome, close to the walls on the western side. The buildings are not of special importance, but the grounds are very extensive and magnificent.

VILLA PIA. At Rome, a small private house in the gardens of the Vatican palace, built in the sixteenth century.

VILLA ROTONDA. Near Vicenza in Venetia; one of the most famous works of Andrea Palladio.

VILLAGE. A small collection of houses; in the United States, forming part of a township and having but little independent existence.

Tribes and subtribes of American Indians, in all parts of the New World, congregated, for at least a part of the year, in fixed habitations, that were grouped together in a village. Among forest tribes these habitations were of poles covered with bark or mats, and were generally surrounded with high palisades of poles or logs set up vertically and sharpened at the top. Sometimes three or four rows of these logs were planted around a village. Among the Plain tribes the village was a cluster of tipis, or skin tents, arranged, according to a formula, in a circle. In the Southwestern United States the villages were sometimes, in early days, made up of detached stone or adobe houses; but more commonly they were groups of great communal dwellings, and often a whole village was comprised in one single, huge structure, like an immense honeycomb. In the Northwestern United States the villages were of two or more blocks of slab houses, with four or five communal houses in a block. (See Aboriginal American Architecture.) — F. S. D.

VILLALPANDO, FRANCISCO DE; sculptor and architect.

About 1540, in association with others, he executed much of the sculpture of the great chapel and choir of the cathedral of Toledo. The pulpits in gilded bronze in this cathedral are also ascribed to him.

Bermudez, *Diccionario.*

VILLARD DE HONNECOURT. (See Wilars de Honnecort.)

VILLEDIEU, RAOUL DE; abbot and architect.

Abbot of Mont Saint Michel from 1225 to 1236. He built the cloister of that abbey about 1226.

Le Héricher, *Mont Saint Michel.*

VIMANA. Same as Sikra.

VINCI, LEONARDO DA. (See Leonardo da Vinci.)

VINERY. Same as Grapery.

VINGBOOMS, PHILIPPUS; architect.

An architect of Amsterdam, who erected many important buildings in Holland, and in 1715 published two folio volumes on architecture.

Immerzeel, *Hollandsche en Vlaamsche Kunstenaars.*

VIOLLET-LE-DUC, EUGÈNE EMANUEL; architect and archæologist; b. Jan. 21, 1814 (at Paris); d. Sept. 17, 1879 (at Lausanne, Switzerland).

He was educated at the Collège Bourbon (Paris) and in the atelier of Achille Leclère (see Leclère). At the suggestion of his father, who was employed in the conservation of public buildings, he made a journey through France, studying and sketching the monuments. He travelled through Italy in the same way. Returning to France, in 1840, he undertook the restoration of the abbey church of Vézelay (Yonne, France) and the church of S. Père-Sous-Vézelay. About this time he restored the Hôtel de Ville at Narbonne (Aude, France), and was appointed *auditor* of the *Conseil des bâtiments civils.* He was associated with Lassus (see Lassus) in the restoration of the Sainte-Chapelle in Paris. In 1842 Lassus and Viollet-le-Duc were commissioned to superintend the restoration of the cathedral of Notre Dame (Paris). At the death of Lassus, in 1857, Viollet-le-Duc retained sole charge of that work, and designed the central spire and great altar, as well as the new sacristy and treasury adjoining the south flank. In 1846 he began the restoration of the abbey church of S. Denis, near Paris, and had charge of that building until his death. From 1849 to 1874 he was architect of the diocesan buildings of Reims and Amiens. In 1852 he took charge of the restoration of the *cité* of Carcassonne (France), with the ancient fortifications, and in 1853 was appointed *inspecteur général des édifices diocésains.* In 1858 he began the reconstruction of the château of Pierrefonds (Oise, France).

In 1862 he restored the church of S. Sernin, at Toulouse, and in 1863 the château de Coucy.

In 1863 he was appointed professor of æsthetics at the *École des Beaux Arts* (Paris). As his lectures were not in agreement with the traditions of the school, the students refused

and erected many new buildings throughout France. Among his many publications, the most important are *L'Art Russe: Les Origines*, etc. (Paris, 1877, 1 vol. 4to); *Comment on Construit une maison* (4th ed., Paris, 1883, 1 vol. 12mo); *Description et histoire du*

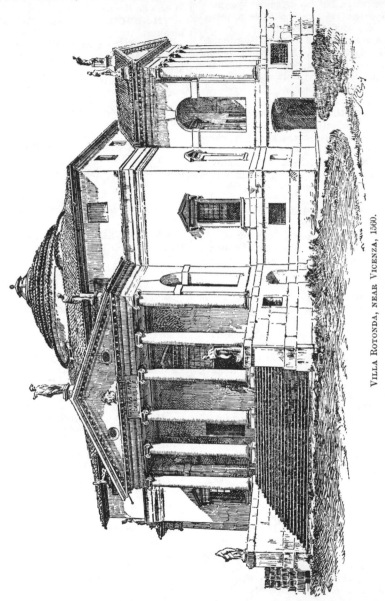

VILLA ROTONDA, NEAR VICENZA, 1560.

to listen to him. He resigned his position the following year, and published the material which he had prepared as the *Entretiens sur l'Architecture*. In 1873 he began the restoration of the cathedral of Lausanne (Switzerland), and built the fine spire of that church. Viollet-le-Duc restored many less important monuments,

château de Pierrefonds (8th ed., Paris, 1876, 1 vol. 8vo), *Dictionnaire raisonné de l'Architecture français* (Paris, 1854–1868, 10 vols. 8vo); *Dictionnaire raisonné du Mobilier français* (Paris, 1858–1875, 6 vols. 4to); *Entretiens sur l'Architecture* (Paris, 1863–1872, 2 vols. 8vo and atlas), *Essai sur l'Architecture Militaire au Moyen Âge* (Paris, 1854, 1 vol. 4to); *Habitations modernes* (Paris, 1875–1877, 2 vols. folio); *Histoire d'un Hôtel de Ville et d'une Cathédrale* (Paris, 1878, 1 vol. 8vo), *Histoire d'une forteresse* (Paris, 1874, 1 vol. 4to); *Peintures murales des chapelles de Notre Dame* (Paris, 1870, 1 vol. folio), and with Lassus, *Monographie de Notre Dame* (Paris, no date, 1 vol. folio).

Saint-Paul, *Viollet-le-Duc et son système archéologique;* Sauvageot, *Viollet-le-Duc et son œuvre dessiné;* Viollet-le-Duc, *Compositions et dessins;* Bauchal, *Dictionnaire; Avery Architectural Library, Catalogue.*

VIS. A screw; the French term used in English attributively. A spiral staircase is sometimes called a staircase *à vis.*

VISCHER, HERMANN; sculptor and bronze caster; d. 1487.

Hermann received the citizenship of Nürnberg (Germany) in 1453. A font in the parish church of Wittenberg bears his name and the date 1457. By him, also, are two monuments of bishops in the cathedral of Meissen (Saxony).

Allgemeine deutsche Biographie; Schadow, *Wittenberg's Denkmäler.*

VISCHER, PETER; sculptor and bronze founder; b. probably between 1460 and 1470; d. Jan. 7, 1529.

A son of Hermann Vischer (see Vischer, H.); he received the title of *Meister* in 1489, and was probably twenty-five or thirty years old at that time. He was intimately associated with Adam Kraft (see Kraft) and the bronze worker Sebastian Lindenast. His five sons, Hermann, Peter, Hans, Paul, and Jakob, assisted him in his work. The elder sons, Hermann and Peter, were most skilful. From their atelier came the statue of Otto IV., Henneberg in the Stiftskirche of Römhild, the monuments of the bishops Heinrich III., Veit II., and Georg II. in the cathedral of Bamberg (Bavaria), five monuments in the Fürstenkapelle at Meissen (Saxony), the monument of the Bishop Johann IV. in the cathedral of Breslau (about 1496), the monument of the Cardinal Friedrich in the cathedral of Krakau (Poland), the monument of Archbishop Ernst in the cathedral of Magdeburg (about 1497), etc. Peter Vischer's most important work is the great shrine of S. Sebaldus in the church of S. Sebaldus in Nürnberg (1508–1519). The first sketches for this work were made by Veit Stoss (see Stoss, V.).

Neudorfer, *Nachrichten von Künstlern und Werkleuten in Nürnberg;* Fah, *Geschichte der Bild. Künste; Allgemeine deutsche Biographie;* Lübke, Introduction to *Peter Vischer Werke.*

VISCONTI, LOUIS TULLIUS JOACHIM; architect; b. Feb. 11, 1791 (at Rome); d. Dec. 29, 1853.

A son of Ennius Quirinus Visconti, the archæologist, who came to Paris in 1798.

Between 1808 and 1817 Louis studied architecture at the *École des Beaux Arts* and with Charles Percier (see Percier). In 1814 he won second *Grand Prix* and the *Prix Départmental.* In 1822 he was employed as under inspector under Destailleur. He replaced Delannoy in 1825 as architect of the *Bibliothèque Royale.* His projects for this building were not carried out. Visconti was appointed in 1832 *conservateur* of the eighth section of the Monuments of the City of Paris. 1835–1839 he built the Fontaine Louvois (Paris). He arranged the ceremony of the reception of the remains of the Emperor Napoleon I., Dec. 15, 1840, and in 1842 was commissioned to construct the monument of the emperor in the church of the *Invalides.* In 1842 he completed the Fontaine Molière (Paris), and in 1846 commenced the Fontaine of the place Saint-Sulpice (Paris). In 1850 he was appointed architect of Napoleon III., and in 1851 made the plans for the completion of the Louvre and the gallery uniting the Louvre and Tuileries on the north. This work was begun July 25, 1852. After the death of Visconti, in 1853, it was continued by Lefuel (see Lefuel) according to his designs. He built numerous residences in Paris, and the monuments of the Marshals Lauriston, Saint-Cyr, Soult, and Souchet.

Charles Lucas in Planat, *Cyclopédie;* Bauchal, *Dictionnaire;* Lance, *Dictionnaire;* Babeau, *Le Louvre.*

VISCOUNTESS. (See Slate.)

VISTA. A view or prospect provided by nature or art, as through an avenue of trees in a park, or through a series of arches or other openings in a building. One of the leading *motifs* of design in the planning of important works, as palaces, temples, or gardens, especially in classic or Renaissance architecture, is the establishment of continuous centre lines through openings in adjacent halls and chambers, or through corridors or alleys, by which vistas are obtained terminating in some feature of especial interest, such as a statue, fountain, etc. This device tends to order, symmetry, and coherence in architectural composition.

VITECOQ, SYMON; architect.

June 29, 1527, he succeeded Roullant Leroux (see Leroux, R.) as *maître de l'œuvre architect* of the cathedral of Rouen (France). With Guillaume Dodemont he completed the church of S. Jean at Rouen in 1547.

Deville, *Architectes de la Cathédrale de Rouen;* Lance, *Dictionnaire.*

VITONI, VENTURA; architect; b. Aug. 20, 1442 (at Pistoia); d. after 1522.

He was brought up as a carpenter and, according to Vasari, was a pupil of Bramante (see Bramante). All the buildings which are attributed to him are in Pistoia (Italy). The earliest is the church of S. Maria delle Grazie (begun 1484). That of S. Giovanni Battista was begun 1495 and completed in 1513. Parts of the church of S. Chiara may also be by him. Vitoni's great work is the church of S. Maria dell' Umiltà, a combination in plan of the Pazzi chapel and the sacristy of S. Spirito at Florence. The large closed atrium and the choir were begun in 1494 and the central octagonal portion in 1509. That date is inscribed on the building. At his death he had carried the church to the windows of the third story. The dome is much later. (See Vasari.) His will is dated March 11, 1522.

Geymüller-Stegmann, *Die Arch. der Ren. in Toscana;* Müntz, *Renaissance;* Giuseppe Tigri, *Nuova Guida di Pistoia.*

VITRIFIED BRICK. Brick burned to a hard, glassy consistency so as to be impermeable to water and fit for damp-proof work, paving, or other purposes where such qualities are necessary.

VITRIFIED WORK. Masonry, especially of silicious stone, converted into hard glassy substance by fire and thus greatly solidified, as in certain early defensive works found in Scotland, France, etc. Argillaceous earth is sometimes so converted and used for ballast in railroad work to solidify the backing between the ties, and in paving. It is called *gumbo.*

VITRUVIAN. Of or pertaining to Marcus Vitruvius Pollio, a Roman architect of the first century B.C., the author of an important treatise which preserves much that is valuable in regard to Greek and Roman art, and is our principal authority for facts and practice in the building arts of the classic period. The term "Vitruvian" is used to distinguish principles and practices of the architecture of ancient Rome as revealed to us by this author.

VITRUVIUS (POLLIO), M. C. L.; architect and writer on architecture; b. about 83–73 B.C.

The author of a Latin work in ten books on architecture, the earliest existing manual on that subject, dating from about 30 B.C. Considerable portions of his book are quoted by Pliny in his *Historia Naturalis* without acknowledgment, and he is mentioned by Frontinus (see Frontinus) in his work on aqueducts. The little basilica at Fano described in his book is the only building which can be attributed to him. Among the many sources from which he derived information are the writings of Anaxagoras, Ctesiphon, Ictinus (see Ictinus), Theodorus (see Theodorus), etc. In a letter of the Councillor C. F. L. Schultz to the poet Goethe, the theory was first brought forward that Vitruvius' work was really a compilation made in the reign of the Emperor Theodosius, and afterward ascribed to Vitruvius, a well-known architect of the time of Augustus. This theory, with some changes, has

been developed by Dr. Ussing (op. cit.), and the arguments against it presented by Brown (op. cit.). Leake (*Peloponnesiaca,* 1846, pp. 128–129) supposes "that we possess no more than parts of the original work of Vitruvius, blended with productions of a later age." The work was highly esteemed during the Middle Ages and frequently transcribed. The manuscript of S. John's College, Oxford, was made as late as 1316 and belonged to the Abbey of Canterbury. There was a manuscript of Vitruvius in the palace of the popes at Avignon, which was carried to Spain in the fifteenth century. The *editio princeps* was published by Johannes Sulpitius Verulanus about 1486. During the reign of Julius II. (Pope 1503–1513) Fra Giocondo (see Giocondo) published his critical edition, which he dedicated to that Pope. The most important editions of the text are that of Poleni (see Poleni), 1825–1830, 4 vols. 4to., and the standard edition of Marini (Rome, 1836, 4 vols. folio). There are English translations by Newton (1791), Wilkins (London, 1872), and Gwilt (1826).

Brunn, *Geschichte der griechischen Kunstler;* Marini, Biography, in his edition of *Vitruvius;* Poleni, Biography, in his edition of *Vitruvius;* Müntz, *Renaissance;* Aldrich, *Elements of Civil Architecture;* Viollet-le-Duc, *Entretiens sur l'Architecture;* Ussing, *Observations on Vitruvius;* Schultz, *Briefwechsel;* Brown, *Ussing on Vitruvius.*

VITTORIA (DELLA VOLPE), JACOPO ALESSANDRE; sculptor and architect; b. 1524; d. 1608.

The autograph notes of Vittoria, preserved in the state archives at the convent of S. Maria Gloriosa dei Frari in Venice, are the most important source of information about his life. He was born at Trente in the Tyrol, and received his first training in his native city. He went to Venice in 1543, and entered the atelier of Jacopo Sansovino (see Sansovino, J.) in the *Procuratie Vecchie.* In 1547 he went to Vicenza and assisted Palladio (see Palladio) on the basilica and other buildings until 1553, when he returned to Venice. Much of the sculpture on the façade and the stucco of the interior of Sansovino's *Libreria* is the work of Vittoria. Especially fine are the two caryatides of the main door. The famous stucco decoration of the *Scala d'Oro* in the Doges' Palace is ascribed to him by Temanza without corroboration. He was also associated with Michele Sammichele (see Sammichele, M.), for whom, with the assistance of Pietro da Salo and Danese Cattaneo, he made the sculpture of the monument of the Admiral Contarini in the church of S. Antonio at Padua. In 1556–1558 he made the sculpture of the monument to Francesco Venier at S. Salvatore (Venice), designed by Sansovino. About 1568 he superintended the sculptural decoration of the Villa

Barbaro at Maser (Yriarte, op. cit.), built by Palladio and painted by Paolo Veronese (see Veronese). Vittoria built the *Scuola di San Fantino* (now Ateneo, Venice) after 1562. He devoted the last years of his life to the construction and decoration of the *Capella del Rosario* at the church of SS. Giovanni e Paolo (Venice). This chapel, which commemorated the battle of Lepanto (Oct. 7, 1571), and contained the picture of Peter Martyr by Titian, was burned Aug. 16, 1867. Vittoria's tomb at S. Zaccaria (Venice) was erected partly by himself from his own designs. A list of his works is published by Moschini (op. cit.).

Victor Ceresole, *Alessandro Vittoria;* Temanza-Moschini, *Vita di A. Vittoria;* Giovanelli, *Vita di Vittoria;* Müntz, *Renaissance;* Selvatico, *Arch. e Sculp. in Venezia;* Yriarte, *La Vie d'un Patricien*, etc.

VIVARIUM. A place where animals are kept alive, and as far as practicable in their natural state, as a zoölogical garden. When adapted especially to fish, it is called an *aquarium;* to birds, an *aviary;* to frogs, a *ranarium*, etc.

VOLCANIC STONE. Stone which has been formed by volcanic agency, including lava, peperino, pumice, tufa, tufo, etc.

VOLTAIC CELL. (See Electrical Appliances.)

VOLTERRA, DANIELLO DA. (See Ricciarelli, Daniello.)

VOLUTE. A spiral scroll; especially that which forms the distinctive feature of the Ionic

capital, which is repeated in the horns of the Corinthian and Composite capitals.

VOMITORIUM. One of the passages arranged to give direct ingress to, or egress from, the various tiers of seats in a Roman theatre or amphitheatre.

VOUSSOIR. One of the stones used to form an arch or vault, being cut on two opposite sides to converging planes, in what is generally a wedge shape, though in some forms of vault four faces converge as in a truncated pyramid.

VREDEMAN DE VRIES, HANS (JAN); painter and architect; b. 1527 (at Leeuwarden, Holland); d. 1588.

A pupil of Reijer Gerritszen, glass painter, of Amsterdam. In 1569 he assisted in the erection of the triumphal arch in honour of the entry of Charles V. into Antwerp. De Vries painted many perspective decorations in Mechlin, Frankfurt, Braunschweig, Prague, Hamburg, Danzig, and elsewhere, and made many designs for buildings, furniture, monuments, etc. He published works on Perspective and Architecture.

Immerzeel, *Hollandsche en Vlaamsche Kunstenaars.*

VOUSSOIR; CHURCH AT ARNSTEIN, RHENISH PRUSSIA. ARCH COMPOSED OF THREE VOUSSOIRS AND TWO SKEW BACKS OR IMPOST BLOCKS, EACH STONE CUT AWAY TO GIVE THE DECEITIVE APPEARANCE OF A TRIPLE ARCH UNDER AN ENCLOSING ARCH.

VREDEMAN DE VRIES, PAUL; architect and painter; b. 1567 (at Antwerp, Holland).

A son and pupil of Hans Vredeman de Vries (see Vredeman de Vries, H.). He attached himself to the court at Prague (Bohemia), and returned to Amsterdam (Holland) about 1600. In 1639 he was appointed city architect at The Hague (Holland).

Galland, *Hollandische Baukunst.*

VRIENDT, CORNELIS DE. (See Floris, Cornelis de.)

VRIES. (See Vredeman de Vries.)

W

WAGON-HEADED. Having a continuous round arched vault or ceiling, as in barrel vaulting.

WAGON ROOF. Same as Wagon Vault (which see under Vault).

WAGT, CONRAD; architect.

In 1472 he succeeded Jost Dotzinger (see Dotzinger, J.) as architect of the cathedral of Strasburg (Elsass, Germany). Some time after 1481 he was invited to visit Milan (Italy) by the Duke Galeazzo Sforza.

Gérard, *Les Artistes de l'Alsace.*

WAILLY, CHARLES DE; architect and painter; b. Nov. 9, 1729; d. Nov. 2, 1798.

De Wailly entered the school of Jacques François Blondel (see Blondel, J. F.) and was associated also with Legeay (see Legeay) and Servandoni (see Servandoni). In 1752 he won the *Grand Prix d'Architecture* and visited Rome. In 1767 he entered the *première classe* of the Académie d'Architecture in Paris and in 1771 the Académie de Peinture. In 1779–1782, in collaboration with Marie Joseph Peyre (see Peyre, M. J.), he built the theatre of the Odéon (Paris). He enlarged the choir of the church of S. Leu (Paris), and built a chapel in the Rue Hoche at Versailles. The plans which he made for the embellishment of the city of Cassel (Germany) are in the library at Cassel. He had an atelier in the palace of the Louvre and died there.

Lance, *Dictionnaire;* Leroy, *Rues de Versailles.*

WAINSCOT. *A.* In British usage, a superior quality of oak imported for fine panel work; hence, panel work of that material, usually applied as a covering to interior walls.

B. By extension, any wooden covering or facing of an interior wall face, especially when of somewhat elaborate workmanship. The use of the term, common in the United States as equivalent to dado, and applied to any material, is erroneous.

WAINSCOTING. Same as Wainscot, *B.*

WAITING ROOM. A room for the use of persons waiting, as at a railway station or other public place, fitted with seats and other conveniences.

WALES, ARCHITECTURE OF. That of the ancient principality, including thirteen counties. In two departments of archæological study Wales is rich, namely, in prehistoric or undated remains, such as, in the first place, rude stone monuments, camps, and dikes, and, in the second place, strong castles of mediæval and later date. The early remains seldom reach much interest in the strictly architectural sense; but the cistvaens are still numerous, though many have been destroyed; and it is probable that two or three centuries ago there were more cromlechs and similar monuments in Wales than in any part of Europe of the same extent. There are inscribed stones also which are important. (Compare what is said under Cathstone.) The Roman occupation was so long disputed by the natives, and that occupation was so purely military for a long time, that archæological research would undoubtedly lead to the identification of many of the rude traces of fortresses and intrenchments as belonging to Roman permanent encampments. But others are unquestionably native, and are of generally unknown date. Circular huts of rude stone are found in connection with these early "camps," which were undoubtedly in most cases hill forts of the native tribes.

The mediæval castles are numerous and of the best period, because they were built either by Edward I., as the means of securing his conquest of Wales, or at later times, either afresh or on the Edwardian foundations. Conway Castle and Cærnarvon Castle are celebrated in the north, and the castles of Kidwelly, Caerphilly, and Raglan are equally well known in the south of Wales; but some of these, and especially the last named, have kept little of their mediæval character. Raglan is an extraordinary structure, much ruined, yet retaining so much of its character that it may be studied as the best example in Great Britain of a fortress residence of the earliest Tudor time; for it appears to have been begun during the brief reign of Henry V., and to have been continued at intervals during succeeding reigns.

The cathedral of S. David's and that of Llandaff are the two most important churches of Wales; but the priory church at Brecon, partly Norman, partly transitional Gothic, and partly perfected Gothic, is also a large church, and was of special interest before it was restored. The restoration was, however, very complete, taking away much of the original charm and introducing a certain regularity into a building, much of whose charm was its picturesque roughness of structure. Llandaff cathedral has been even more hardly treated by succeeding generations, for it was almost in ruins at the beginning of the eighteenth century, and, during the nineteenth century, was almost completely built. It is, in short, an interesting modern Gothic church, in which the old lines of the building have been consciously followed as far as they could be perfectly understood. It is a plain structure with but little sculpture and of no great pretensions as to size. S. David's cathedral has been much more fortunate, and if it is not all in repair this is rather because of the smallness and poverty of the community than from any neglect. The church is, indeed, though small for a cathedral, yet large for the little town and its thinly settled neighbourhood; nearly 300 feet long, and with a transept 120 feet long. The lady chapel and the chapels flanking the choir are roofless, but are not otherwise ruined, and the church is otherwise in good repair. The interior is much more interesting than the outside, for the nave is one of the most beautiful pieces of unaltered

Romanesque in Great Britain, and a very late flat wooden ceiling is spirited in its design and so boldly divergent from the style of the arcades which support it that it challenges admiration as a separate entity. There are interesting late Gothic stalls. Close to the building, at the northwest, are the ruins of S. Mary's College and a bishop's palace, the latter being a most picturesque building and giving evidence of a former splendour which is well worthy the careful conjectural restoration of some competent student.

S. Asaph's cathedral, in the north of the principality, is, in size and architectural treatment, only a very small and unpretending parish church; and it has been almost entirely modernized, though retaining its interesting window tracery and other details.

Apart from these buildings, the churches of Wales are not very important. There are, of course, attractive parish churches, some as yet unrestored. A church at Holyhead retains very curious fifteenth century sculpture. — R. S.

WALHALLA. In Bavaria, on a hill above the Danube and near Ratisbon (Regensburg); a Hall of Fame built by King Ludwig I. about 1830. The exterior is like that of a Grecian Doric temple, but of granite.

WALL. A structure of stone, brick, or other materials, serving to enclose a room, house, or other space, and in most cases, to carry the floors and roof. A framed structure, as of wood or iron, serving the same purposes, is called a wall as soon as it is sheathed or covered in so as to look solid.

    Cavity Wall. A wall built with an Air Space (which see).

    Hollow Wall. Same as Cavity Wall, above.

    Partition Wall. Same as Partition, but often used with the sense of a partition of importance, as of solid material or between large divisions of a building.

    Party Wall. A wall built upon the division line of adjoining properties, the owner of each having equal right to use it. It may belong to one owner, or partly to each; but what characterizes it as a party wall is the easement which both owners have in what belongs absolutely to neither. Party walls are built under party wall agreements reciting the character of the wall itself and the privileges and limitations of use which each owner may have in it.

    Springing Wall. A buttress wall; a wall built to withstand the thrust of an arch.

    Sustaining Wall. A bearing wall, or retaining wall, in contradistinction to one serving merely as a partition or screen.

    WALL (v.). *A.* To form a division or partition between rooms.

B. To support a superincumbent weight.

C. To afford defence, shelter, or security, as a rampart, a fortification, or a solid fence around

a garden or park. (See sub-titles under Wall, n.)

    WALL CHAMBER. A chamber built in the thickness or mass of a wall, as often in a mediæval castle in the upper stories.

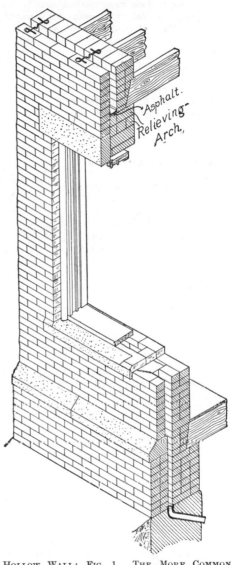

HOLLOW WALL; FIG. 1. THE MORE COMMON FORM, USED FOR TWO-STORY AND THREE-STORY BUILDINGS.

    WALL PAINTING. The painting of the surface of a wall with ornamental designs or figure subjects, as decoration. It is usually classified as Encaustic, Fresco, or Tempera painting. (See those terms and Mural Painting.)

    WALL PAPER. Paper, usually decorated in colours, used for pasting on walls or ceilings of rooms. The term includes plain papers in single colours, or printed in many colours, often with gilded or bronzed patterns, often imitating stuffs, tiles, wood, leather, and other hangings, or with pictorial, architectural, or historic effects. Various surface effects are also obtained, as satin finish, flock paper (called also velvet paper), and watered, embossed, and stamped patterns. Thick cartridge papers and papier-maché are used, deeply stamped with diapers and other patterns, and prepared for painting. The designing and manufacture of wall paper are important branches of decorative art.

WALL PIECE. A decorative painting with figures especially adjusted to the shape, position, and other local conditions of a wall.

WALL PLATE. (See under Plate.)

WALL RIB. (See under Rib.)

WALL SPACE. That part of the superficial area of a wall unoccupied by doors, windows, or other features; the clear area of a wall.

WALL STRING. That one of the string pieces of a staircase which is set next the wall.

WALSINGHAM, ALAN DE; ecclesiastic and architect.

Alan de Walsingham, *Vir venerabilis et artificiosus frater*, was subprior of Ely in 1321 and prior in 1341. As subprior he is supposed to have designed S. Mary's chapel in Ely cathedral. After the fall of the central tower he built the present beautiful octagonal tower and lantern. Alan was a skilful "fabricator" in gold and silver.

Redgrave, *Dictionary of Artists.*

WALTER, THOMAS USTICK; architect; b. Sept. 4, 1804; d. Oct. 30, 1887.

In 1819 he entered the office of William Strickland as a student in architecture. In 1831 he designed the Philadelphia County Prison, and in 1833 the fine building of Girard College (Philadelphia), which was built entirely under his direction. In 1851 he was appointed architect of the Capitol in Washington, superseding Robert Mills (see Mills). The old Capitol was completed according to the designs of Charles Bulfinch (see Bulfinch) when he left it in 1829, and remained practically unchanged until 1850, when Walter presented his scheme for the addition of two wings containing accommodations for the Senate and House of Representatives. The cornerstone of the new work was laid by Daniel Webster, July 4, 1851. Walter rebuilt the western front, which had been destroyed by fire, and added the library.

At the close of 1854 the walls of the wings had reached the height of the ceiling. In 1855 the old dome was removed and the new dome begun. Both wings were covered in 1856. The House of Representatives first met in its new quarters Dec. 16, 1857, and the Senate Jan. 4, 1859. The government ordered the suspension of the work in 1861, but through the patriotism of the contractors operations were continued during the entire Civil War. The exterior of

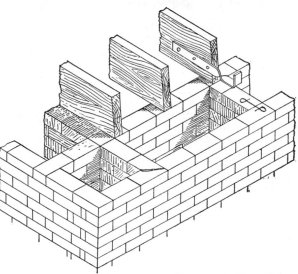

HOLLOW WALL, BUILT WITH LARGE CHAMBERS, A RARE FORM BECAUSE MUCH GROUND SPACE IS USED.

the dome was completed in 1863 and the entire work in 1865, when Walter retired from office.

Howard, *Architects of the United States Capitol.*

WALTHAM CROSS. (See Cross of Queen Eleanor.)

WANE. The bevel or feather edge on a board or plank sawn from an unsquared log, the bevel being a part of the natural curvature of its surface.

WARD. *A.* The outer defences of a castle.

B. A division or quarter of a town separated from other quarters to facilitate the transaction of public business, and for the sake of proper representation in the town government.

C. One of the apartments into which a hospital is divided; as a *convalescent ward*, a *fever ward*, *casualty ward*, etc.

D. A curved ridge of metal inside of a lock, forming an obstacle to the passage of a key which has not a notch in the web or bit of the key corresponding with the ridge; hence, one of the open notches or slits in the web of the key.

WARDROBE. *A.* A room or large closet, provided with presses, shelves, and hanging spaces, generally enclosed by doors, for the convenient keeping of wearing apparel; and where in former times the making and repairing of clothes were done.

B. A piece of furniture, fixed or movable, enclosed by doors, and often with drawers below, for the convenient keeping of wearing apparel, either hung from hooks or folded.

C. A cloak room, as in a schoolhouse or other public building.

WARDROBE ROOM. (Same as Wardrobe, *A.*)

WARE, ISAAC; architect; d. Jan. 5, 1766.

Ware is said to have begun life as a chimney sweeper. He attracted the attention of a wealthy patron, who educated him and sent him to Italy. October 4, 1728, he was appointed clerk of the works at the Tower of London, and Oct. 14, 1729, to the same office at Windsor Castle. He is known by his *Complete Body of Architecture* (1 vol. folio, 1756).

Redgrave, *Dictionary of Architecture.*

WAREHOUSE. A storehouse; especially one in which goods of some value are kept, either by the owner or occupier of the building, as when a large shop or store is spoken of popularly as a warehouse, or for the safe keeping of the property of persons who hire a room or a safe in the building, or who leave goods on deposit. (See subtitles.)

Bonded Warehouse. In countries where a customs tariff is placed upon merchandise, a building in which such goods may be left for a certain length of time without paying the duty, which becomes due only on their withdrawal " from bond." According to the law of different nations, greater or less privileges are allowed to the owner of such goods; thus, he may be allowed to exhibit his goods in bond to possible purchasers, or may be allowed to change the form of their packages, as by bottling liquors which arrive in casks, or the like.

Storage Warehouse. In many modern cities, a building supposed to be fireproof and to be watched at all times, in which space is rented for the deposit of private property. Persons giving up their homes are supposed to leave " in storage " furniture and other valuables, and rooms of different sizes can be secured in storage warehouses for such deposit. The more precious and compact articles, as jewellery, securities, and the like, are generally put in safe deposit vaults (for which see the article Safe).

— R. S.

WARING, JOHN BURLEY; artist and writer on art; b. 1823; d. March, 1875.

In 1843 Waring travelled in Italy and later in Spain. He published with Macquoid *Examples of Architectural Art in Italy and Spain* (folio, 1850), *Architectural Studies in Burgos and Miraflores* (folio, 1852). He was associated with M. D. Wyatt in preparing the handbooks for the Crystal Palace (8vo, 1854). He published also *The Arts connected with Architec-*

ture: *Central Italy XIII to XVII centuries* (1 vol. folio, 1858); *Notes of an Architect in Spain* (1 vol. 8vo, 1852); etc.

Waring, *A Record of My Artistic Life; Avery Architectural Library, Catalogue.*

WARMING. In tropical countries, even at the present day, houses large and small are built without any means whatever of affording warmth, whether by raising the temperature of the atmosphere within or by affording radiant heat to persons sitting near a source of heat. The houses, often of wealthy men, in regions where the thermometer never goes below 60° Fahr., are usually open on either side to the wind; and lamps, gas flames, and the like have to be sheltered with peculiar care on this account.

In the remote past, and in classical antiquity, there seems to have been a comparative disregard of what we now consider necessary to comfort; and even in the comparatively northern climate of Greece and Italy the preparations for warming were what would now be considered very slight. Even at the present day, many persons living in the cities of Italy spend the winter without the use of fires in stoves or otherwise; a physician of high standing in an Italian city told the writer in 1883 that he needed a little fire in a plaster stove for his consultation room, but that the waiting room for his patients could not have a fire, as it would give persons sitting there headaches and cold feet, and keep his patients away. So, in Pompeii, there has been found but one house which has any arrangements for warming, except in the heating of baths. The same difference in habit is seen in the slight warming of English interiors as compared with that in use in the United States. As a general thing it appears that the colder the climate the hotter the interiors may be kept with comfort, partly because the body seems to require a perfectly comfortable temperature (about 70° Fahr.) if it has to face an exceedingly low temperature when in the open air. The high degree of warmth considered necessary for interiors in Russia, north Germany, and parts of the United States, is easy to maintain if no great thought is given to ventilation; but if a great deal of fresh air is called for, then the warming of such interiors becomes expensive and troublesome.

In the megaron of a Greek house a fire on the hearth in the middle of a large room, the smoke of which escaped through the opening in the roof, would be thought sufficient even in winter. In the women's apartment one or more small fires would be kept up. The dwellings of the poor were probably altogether without fire except for cooking. The same conditions existed in the houses of the German farmers (see House), in which a single fire served for cooking and for such warmth as was expected in winter, and the smoke circulating through the building is thought to have been found hygienic and even agreeable, as counteracting odours from the cattle lodged under the same roof. Such a fire may, however, have been kept up night and day without difficulty, owing to the abundant forests of Central Europe in the Middle Ages. The first chimneys would be a mere extension of the above described "fire on the hearth," as providing a more direct passage outward for the smoke, and as placing the fire against one side of the large room instead of in the middle. Great waste of heat accompanied this change, but convenience, and perhaps a rudimentary notion of elegance, dictated it. The chimney in the Middle Ages, as now in many farmhouses, had a very open throat and flue, so that a person standing beside the fire of logs could see the sky above, and feel the rush of cold air downward besides the warm air ascending. The warmth of such a fire is merely that derived from radiant heat in the most pleasant and wholesome, but also the least economical way. The chimney in this way grew to be an important architectural member, both within and without. The "middle chimney" of a New England wood-framed house is a hillock of rough masonry, in which fireplaces are opened, and around which the rooms of the house are clustered ; and the chimneys of the French or German châteaux are the most conspicuous parts of the whole structure, adorning the roofs outside and the walls within. In some cases two or three fireplaces side by side fill one end or side of a great hall ; by which system one or more fires of logs could be kept burning, and on occasion a great amount of heat provided.

The Stove (which see) undoubtedly preceded any attempt at increasing the convenience and economy of the open fireplace, partly because it would be readily seen that the economy of fuel was very great. This also supplies radiant heat. Another form of providing warmth by radiation was in the use of the Hypocaust (which see). The warmth of the floor would in this case raise the temperature of the air in the room slightly ; but the direct warming of the person of any one standing upon such a floor would be more important. Some attempts at a like system in modern schemes for warming have been based on the theory that a low temperature in the surrounding air, but a greater heat radiated directly to the body, is a more healthful condition of things. The immediate tendency, however, of any warming of an interior, whether by stoves or by heated flues or other system of direct radiation, is found in the demand that the temperature of the room shall be always kept at what is thought a comfortable point — sometimes 68° Fahr., sometimes 70°, sometimes at an even higher point.

The use of furnaces, which seems to have begun in the United States about 1830, involved the admission into each room of warmed air taken directly from a chamber in the cellar, which immediately adjoined the iron of the furnace proper, a kind of stove built in with brickwork. In this way the use of radiant heat was almost ignored, but the immediate successors of the hot air furnace, the steam heating, and the hot water heating apparatus, allowed of either or of both methods of warming. Thus, a radiator or a stack of radiators would be filled by the steam or hot water, and would warm a hall by direct radiation, while other rooms in the same building would be heated by warmed air rising from boxes in the cellar, in each of which boxes was a coil of pipe, or the like, filled with the steam or hot water. The hot water apparatus was in some respects the most simple, because when used in conservatories the pipes could be very large and the water would flow naturally and could easily be returned to the boiler, and no elaborate system of stopcocks and the like was requisite. Many houses on the Continent of Europe are warmed in this simple way, the iron pipes running from room to room upstairs and down, and the hot water circulating through them everywhere. American practice has usually demanded a very elaborate system of control, doubling the cost of the apparatus. Some hot water heaters are filled with a strong brine, and that with the purpose of avoiding freezing in the case of sudden changes of temperature. Such an apparatus as this marks the highest elaboration of the scheme of heating interiors previous to the introduction of modern plants of combined warming and ventilation (for which see Ventilation).

— R. S.

WARMING, ELECTRIC. The production of heat by means of the electric current. Energy is necessary to force an electric current through resistance, and this energy is all transformed into heat. All conductors offer more or less resistance to the passage of electric current, and the amount of heat generated is proportional to the resistance if the current remains the same. When the production of heat is the end to be attained, a comparatively great resistance is confined to a small space, so that there will not be conduction and radiation except in the direction wished. In electric smoothing irons, for instance, a coil of fine wire is placed inside the iron and the current is led to this coil through flexible conductors. The heat generated in the coil raises the temperature of the iron till the heat that is radiated and conducted from the outside of the iron just balances the amount generated in the coil. When this point is reached the temperature remains constant. If the current is doubled, the heat generated is increased four times, and if the current is halved the heat generated is one fourth as much. By means of proper appliances the current can be increased or diminished with the greatest refinement, so that the heat is under perfect control. Electric heaters have been made for a great variety of uses, but owing to the cost of generating and distributing electric energy most of the heaters have been used where the amount of heat can be small if applied directly to the purpose intended. Small portable stoves, foot warmers, smoothing irons, soldering irons, chafing dishes, glue pots, and similar appliances have been the ones most commonly used. The advantages of electric heating are evident. It is under perfect control. The heat can be applied in the most direct way, and the temperature can easily be kept constant. There is no combustion, and consequently no vitiation of the air. It is perfectly clean, and the heat almost instantly available. Except in special cases where the advantages just mentioned have a considerable pecuniary value, heating by electricity is more expensive than heating by means of combustion. Electricity is usually generated by dynamo-electric machines that are driven by steam engines, and these in turn are driven by steam that is generated in steam boilers by the combustion of fuel. Owing to the losses in boilers, piping, steam engine, dynamos, wiring, etc., only a very small proportion of the energy of the coal is available at the electric heater, and to get this small proportion an elaborate system of appliances must be kept in repair. For this reason the mere production of heat is of course much more cheaply accomplished directly by combustion of fuel. However, in most cases heat is wanted only for a definite time that is often short, and usually one wishes to apply the heat to a particular object. Stoves and other appliances for getting useful heat from combustion must often generate an enormous amount of heat for the sake of a small amount made use of. A large proportion of the heat generated by electric heaters can be made effective if care is used, and on this account they sometimes compete successfully with other heaters in spite of the losses in generating electricity. — RUSSELL ROBB.

WARNER, OLIN L.; sculptor; b. 1844 (at Suffield, Connecticut); d. August, 1896.

At the age of twenty-two he entered the atelier of François Jouffray at the *École des Beaux Arts* in Paris. He remained in Paris three years. Among his most important works are the statue of W. Lloyd Garrison in Boston, the statue of Governor Buckingham in the Capitol at Washington, a fountain at Portland, Oregon. He carried out some important sculpture of strictly architectural character, as at the Congressional Library Building.

Obituary in *American Architect*, Aug. 22, 1896.

WASH. A thin layer of water colour put on with the brush while in a very liquid state.

WASHBOARD. Generally the same as Baseboard. Sometimes, specifically, a similar member, especially disposed so as to retain or throw off water and direct its flow to a drain.

WASHER. An annular piece of leather, rubber, metal, or other substance strung on a screw joint of a pipe or faucet to secure tight fitting and prevent leakage, or over a bolt so as to make a tight joint, or enlarge the bearing surface when a nut is screwed over it. Washers often serve as cushions or packing in the joints of machinery and constructional iron-work, or in metal are used at the ends of the rods to give them a more secure hold on the points to be tied.

WASHHOUSE. *A.* That part of a laundry in which the actual washing is done.

B. A public laundry or lavatory. In this sense not common in the United States.

WASHTUB. In plumbing, a wooden, metallic, porcelain, slate, or soapstone vessel or fixture, rectangular in form, connected by a trapped waste pipe with a soil or sewer pipe, supplied with hot and cold water, and intended for cleaning and rinsing the wash of the household. — W. P. G.

WAS IST DAS. Same as Vasistas.

WAST (VAST), JEAN (I.); architect; d. 1524.

Maître d'œuvre of the cathedral of Beauvais (Oise, France). May 21, 1500, he was associated with Martin Chambiges (see Chambiges) in the construction of the transept of the cathedral of Beauvais. He was also employed on the cathedral of Amiens.

Nodier-Taylor-Cailleux, *Picardie*, Vol. III.; Desjardins, *Cathédrale de Beauvais;* Benouville, *Cathédrale de Beauvais; Revue Universelle des Arts*, Vol. XIV., 876.

WAST, JEAN (II.); architect; d. Oct. 8, 1581.

At the death of his father Jean (I.), he succeeded him as *maître en second* in the construction of the cathedral of Beauvais, serving under Martin Chambiges until his death in 1532, and after that under Michel Lalye (see Lalye). In 1557 he had succeeded Lalye as chief architect. Wast made the plans of the famous central tower of the cathedral of Beauvais, and built the lower stories, which were of stone. The wooden spire was added by Florent Dailly. This tower fell in 1573.

(For bibliography, see that of Wast, Jean, I.)

WASTE PIPE. A pipe intended for the conveyance of waste water from all kinds of plumbing fixtures, except water closets. (See House Drainage.) — W. P. G.

WASTING. The process of rough dressing a block of stone with a pick or hammer so as to secure approximately plane surfaces.

Stone so worked is said to be wasted off. (See Boast, v.)

WATCHHOUSE. A police station; a lockup; the headquarters of a police force, especially of night watchmen, provided with cells for the temporary safe keeping of offenders against the peace.

WATCHING LOFT. A lookout chamber in a tower, steeple, or other high building for police or military purposes, or for fire service.

WATCHMAN'S REGISTER. (See Electrical Appliances.)

WATER BACK. In plumbing, a coil of pipes, generally cast in one piece, adjusted to the back of a fireplace in constant use, as a stove or cooking range, and connected with the circulation of the hot water service pipes of a house, the contact of the water back with the fire furnishing the heat for this purpose.

WATER BAR. In British usage, a small strip, usually of metal, applied to a sill so that a door or casement will shut against it, thus preventing the entrance of water. — (A. P. S.)

WATER BUTT. In a fountain, lavatory, or architectural structure of any kind involving the storage or free use of water, the receptacle for water of whatever form and material.

WATER CHECK. Same as Water Bar.

WATER-CLOSET. The apartment in which plumbing fixtures are placed which are intended to receive and remove the alvine discharges by means of water (see Latrine; Privy). More specifically, the plumbing appliance used for this purpose, usually consisting of a metal or porcelain bowl with flushing rim, connection to a soil pipe, hardwood seat, and flushing cistern. (See House Drainage; Plumbing.)

WATER COLOUR. In painting, any work done with water as the vehicle, though some viscous or adhesive medium must be added. The varieties of this method used in architectural practice are calcimine (or kalsomine), distemper (or tempera).

WATER HAMMER. (See Hydraulic Jar.)

WATER LEAF. A peculiar leaf observed in Greek ornament, probably a kind of ivy. The term was introduced by the archæologists of the eighteenth century.

WATERPROOF. Impermeable to water, as any structural device or covering for roofs, walls, or floors, to keep water from penetrating; or any application of tar, asphaltum, or other material to the face of foundation walls to keep the basement dry, or interposed in the courses of an underpinning to prevent damp from rising in the walls. (Compare Damp Course.)

WATERPROOFING. The process of preparing and applying material to render roofs, walls, or floors impermeable to water.

WATER RAM. (See under Ram.)

WATER SEAL. A body of water in a trap unchanging in quantity, though constantly supplied and overflowed, which prevents, by reason of its depth, the passage of sewer air through the same. (See House Drainage; Trap, III.)

WATERSPOUT. A spout, pipe, or duct for the conveyance of water from a roof gutter to the ground or to a cistern. (See Conductor; Leader.)

WATER SUPPLY. An artificially constructed system designed to furnish water to cities or buildings, comprising means for collection of water, storage in reservoirs, tanks, or standpipes; distribution mains and services; valves, hydrants, and faucets, and sometimes a pumping plant.

The water supply of buildings varies according to source of supply and available pressure. In cities it is derived from the network of street mains; but for country houses it is often necessary to install a special supply, derived from wells, cisterns, springs, rivers, or lakes.

Plumbing fixtures are supplied either from direct street pressure, or from house tanks, or by a combination of both. Where the pressure in city street mains is sufficient, house tanks are unnecessary, but country houses usually require them to store the water pumped. A combination of both methods becomes necessary in districts of cities where the day pressure is insufficient to reach the upper floors. Sometimes tanks fill from the street main during the heavier pressure at night; but in some city houses, and nearly always for country residences, water must be pumped. For this purpose hand pumps, hot air engines, gas, steam, and electric pumps, and, in the country, windmills and hydraulic rams, are employed. Drinking water is best supplied from direct street pressure. House tanks are also used where the pressure in the main is very heavy, for this wears out piping and faucets quicker.

House storage tanks are made in round shape of wooden staves, or oblong and square in shape of narrow boards; in the latter case the inside is lined with tinned copper. Lead-lined and galvanized iron tanks are unsafe, owing to danger from the water coming in contact with these metals. Wrought iron riveted tanks, painted, are much used. All tanks, except roof tanks, require safes, and iron tanks particularly, because they sweat in summer, owing to condensation. The tank overflow should discharge on the roof or into a sink in the lower part of the house; it must not connect with a soil pipe. Emptying pipes are provided for cleaning out the tanks. All tanks should be covered to exclude dust and germs; ventilation is desirable, also precautions against freezing.

Street mains are of cast iron, and service pipes of heavy lead or galvanized wrought iron pipe. Brass $\frac{1}{2}$ and $\frac{5}{8}$ inch taps or corporation stops connect service pipes with the main. Larger buildings are supplied from ¾ inch and 1 inch services, through water meters. Public buildings should have supply pipes varying from 2 to 4 inches, and theatres 6-inch mains, for fire protection. Water pipes in houses are of different material. (See Pipe.) Table I. gives the size of pipes used in dwellings for plumbing fixtures: —

TABLE I.

Main supply service	1¼ to 2″
Supply to house tank	1¼ to 1½″
Pump rinsers	1½″
Supply to kitchen boiler	1 to 1¼″
Supply to laundry boiler	¾ to 1″
Supply rinsers for a bathroom, hot and cold water	1″
Branch supply to a water-closet flushing cistern	½″
Branch supply to a bathtub	¾″
Branch supply to a basin	½″
Branch supply to a pantry sink	½″
Branch supply to a kitchen, scullery, and slop sink	¾″
Branch supply to a urinal cistern	½″
Branch supply to a needle and shower bath	1 to 1¼″
Branch supply to a sitz or foot bath	½″
Water-closet flush pipes	1¼ to 1½″
Urinal flush pipes	¾ to 1″

Supply pipes are run so they may be completely emptied when water is shut off; lines are usually kept exposed and not placed in outside walls or plastered partitions. Where required, pipes are protected against freezing. Branches are provided with shut-off valves and air chambers. Special devices are used for governing the flow of water through house pipes, such as ball cocks for cistern and tank supplies; stopcocks in the line of pipes regulating the flow of water through same, and faucets or bib-cocks at the ends of branches for supplying fixtures. These are constructed either as ground key work with all-metal tapering plugs, or as compression work with compressible washers. Roundway cocks give more water than ordinary cocks. Compression cocks are either hand-closing or self-closing.

By Table II. the amount of water in United States gallons per minute delivered by supply pipes of different diameters, under various heads of pressure and length of lines, can be determined. (*H* equals head of water in feet; *L* equals length of service in feet.)

TABLE II.

Diameter of Pipe in Inches.	United States Gallons Delivered per Minute.												
	H=10 L.	H=8 L.	H=6 L.	H=4 L.	H=2 L.	H=1½ L.	H=L.	H=¾ L.	H=½ L.	H=⅓ L.	H=¼ L.	H=⅕ L.	H=$\frac{1}{10}$ L.
½″	1.98	17.7	15.8	12.5	8.8	7.7	6.3	5.4	4.4	3.6	3.1	2.8	2.0
⅝″	34.5	30.1	26.5	21.8	15.4	13.4	10.9	9.5	7.7	6.3	5.5	4.8	3.5
¾″	54.4	48.7	42.2	34.4	24.3	21.1	17.2	14.9	12.2	9.9	8.6	7.7	5.4
1″	111.8	100.0	86.6	70.7	50.0	43.2	35.3	30.6	25.0	20.4	17.7	15.8	11.2
1¼″	195.2	174.6	151.2	123.4	87.3	75.6	61.7	53.5	43.7	35.6	30.9	27.6	19.5
1½″	308.0	275.4	238.5	194.8	137.7	119.3	97.4	84.3	68.7	56.2	48.7	43.9	30.8
2″	632.2	566.4	488.1	399.8	282.7	248.8	199.9	173.1	141.4	115.4	100.0	89.4	63.2

Where water pressure is very heavy, pressure regulators are used. Water meters control consumption of water and check waste, particularly in manufacturing establishments and large buildings.

The quantity needed for domestic supply varies in different cities and is larger in the United States than in Europe. In London 37 gallons is a standard allowance per head per day. In America it is 60 gallons, which includes water for drinking, cooking, washing, bathing, laundry, stable, flushing water-closets, and ordinary manufacturing purposes. In Washington the consumption reaches the enormous amount of 172 gallons per capita daily. In cities using water meters the amount is much less. In New York City (Manhattan and Bronx), with one fifth of the water taps metered, the consumption was 116 gallons in 1899; in Lowell, one third metered, it is 80; in Providence, three fourths metered, it is 57; in Morristown, N. J., where all supplies are metered, it is only 40 gallons.

Bayles, *House and Drainage and Water Service; Deutsches Bauhandbuch;* Folwell, *Water Supply;* Gerhard, *Sanitary Engineering of Buildings*, Vol. 2; *Handbuch der Architectur*, Part III., Vol. 4.

— W. P. GERHARD.

WATER-TIGHT. Impenetrable by water. (See Waterproof.)

WATERWORK; WATER WORKS. A construction, or engine, for conducting, forcing, distributing, or otherwise disposing of water. The aggregate of constructions and appliances for the collection, storage, and distribution of water for domestic service, for the working of machinery, or otherwise for the practical use of a community, or for the purpose of maintaining fountains, waterfalls, and other similar ornamental features of a park or garden.

WATTLE. Basket work; a framework composed of interwoven rods or twigs.

WATTLE AND DAB; WATTLE AND DAUB. Building with wattle work plastered with clay or mud.

WATTLING. A method of construction by the interweaving of boughs, rods, canes, withes, vines, etc.

WAX PAINTING. That done with a medium composed of wax dissolved in an essential oil, such as turpentine; although this may be modified, if desired, by other ingredients. The following medium has been used successfully for more than twenty years in America:—

4 oz. apothecary's white wax. ½ lb. Venice turpentine. 1 qt. spirits of turpentine. The wax and turpentine to be melted together, then the spirits of turpentine to be stirred in gradually and the whole made to boil.

If the medium be too stiff, add spirits of turpentine. It can be kept for an indefinite time without injury. The unctuous nature of Venice turpentine — an oleo-resinous substance — facilitates the working of the colours and ultimately hardens them. This medium combines perfectly well with the ordinary oil colours; but experience counsels the avoidance of oil, or, at least, its reduction to a mimimum. If the wall to be painted is of a porous nature, such as stone, plaster, unprimed wood, or canvas, saturate it with the medium and let it dry for a day or two. Were the picture to be painted directly on stone, the "burning in" of the medium would be desirable. When the picture is to be painted on a previously existing ground of oil paint, the addition of a small amount of linseed oil to the medium is advisable for the first painting — not subsequently — to prevent possible scaling. The advantages of wax painting for mural decoration may be summarized as follows:—

(1) Its durability. Wax resists moisture and the action of acids and sulphuretted hydrogen gas.

(2) Its flat surface and exquisite airy tones. It has low-toned and transparent capabilities too; may be polished, burnt in by means of the brazier, and even varnished.

(3) Its impasto, equalling that of oils without the latter's tendency to darken.

(4) Its quick-drying qualities, that enable the painter to complete the work in hand at a sit-ting, or to continue it without fear of subsequent cracks. — FREDERIC CROWNINSHIELD.

WEATHER (v. t.). To slope or cut or build with a slope, as the upper surface of any projecting buttress, moulding, window head, sill, or other exposed feature, so as to shed the water. (See Weathering.)

WEATHER (v. i.). To suffer change (not always deterioration) by exposure to the weather. A stone weathers better if laid in its natural bed, and wood if painted. Stone is often much improved in appearance by Weathering (which see).

WEATHER BACK. Any application to or treatment of the back of a wall to render it more impervious to wind or water, as back plastering, coats of tar or asphaltum, layers of sheathing paper, etc.

WEATHER BOARD. A board which, when laid horizontally over any construction, its thinner edge overlapping the thicker edge of a corresponding board above, protects the surface so covered from the weather. (See Clapboard; Novelty Siding, under Siding.)

WEATHERCOCK. A vane; especially a vane in the form of a cock, as an emblem of vigilance, often associated with a horizontal cross bearing on the ends of its arms the letters N. S. E. and W., to denote the points of the compass. (See Vane.)

WEATHERING. *A.* The inclination given to any upper surface, as in Weather (v. t.). (See Amortisement.)

B. The process of undergoing change which is caused by the action of the weather. In this respect stone, brick masonry, unpainted wood, and the like, are to be very carefully studied, the different kinds and qualities of each of these materials being very different in the character of their weathering. In some materials the effect of time on a building is almost wholly beneficial, giving to the surface a beauty of tint which nothing else can imitate, and which is entirely destroyed by "restoration," or by cleansing or scraping of the surface. Weathering is often modified by smoke, as in London, and by exhalations from salt water, as in Venice; but apart from these influences it should be welcomed, and materials should be chosen with express reference to the favourable change in their colour resulting from continued exposure. Painted exteriors are generally unsusceptible to this influence, for the injury done to painting by the weather is repaired by other painting. The cast-iron fronts of American cities are kept freshly painted, the colour often changing. We have no means of judging whether the polychromatic decoration of Greek and Greco-Roman buildings was constantly renewed, but it may be assumed that it was kept in what appeared to the custodians good and fresh condition. The picturesqueness caused by weathering seems not to have appealed to the peoples of antiquity. Painted surfaces of wood, like those of old clapboarded and shingled houses in America, often receive a very effective weathering when the paint has not been renewed for many years and that which clings to the wooden surface has become dim. In this way, houses seventy years old, or more, are sometimes as beautiful as if they had never been painted. The weathering of unpainted wood, as in the case of shingled roofs, differs greatly according to the kind of wood employed ; thus, some shingles receive an exquisite pearly gray which no stain or paint can equal for beauty; (see col. 637). — R. S.

WEATHER STRIP. A slender strip of wood or metal, sometimes moulded, to which a strip of cloth, or more properly of rubber, is attached, so that when secured to the jambs of a door or window, and adjusted so as to bear against the door or sash closely, the weather is effectually excluded.

WEATHERVANE. Same as Vane, *A* (compare Weathercock).

WEB. *A.* The vertical plate connecting the two horizontal plates or flanges of a steel or iron beam or girder, as in an **I** beam.

B. The blade of a saw.

C. The flat part of a key which enters the lock.

WEBB, JOHN; architect; b. 1611 (in London) ; d. Oct. 24, 1672.

Webb was a nephew and pupil of Inigo Jones (see Jones, I.), whose only daughter he married. He carried out many buildings from Jones's designs.

Redgrave, *Dictionary of Artists.*

WEDGE. A solid body bounded by two planes, which meet at a very acute plane angle, and by at least three other planes. The perfect wedge is used only as a tool, but truncated wedges are used for arch solids (see Arch ; Voussoir), and the Lewis consists of such wedges acting together.

Foxtail Wedge. (See under F.)

WEIGHT (I.). The force of gravity acting vertically, as in the case of a pillar or horizontal lintel, or diagonally, as along the line of a rafter. (See Stress.)

Breaking Weight. The weight which is just sufficient to break a bar, beam, or the like.

Crushing Weight. The weight which is found sufficient to crush a solid, as a prism or cube, of known dimensions.

Shearing Weight. (See under Shearing.)

WEIGHT (II.). For a window. (See Sash Weight.)

WELDING. The process of uniting or consolidating two pieces of metal by hammering or compression, with or without previous softening by heat. With most metals this process is accomplished just before the actual fusing point of the surfaces to be united is reached, the fusing being done in the forge, by blow pipe, by a hot iron, or by a current of electricity, and the union of the abutting points so treated being obtained by compression, by percussion, or by both, according to the nature of the metal.

WELL. *A.* Primarily a spring which *wells* up from the earth.

B. More usually a deep pit, usually cylindrical in form, and comparatively small in diameter, by means of which access is given to a spring deep in the earth. Ordinarily the water is drawn from such a well by means of a bucket ; but there are a few cases in which access to the water is gained by more elaborate means. Thus, in the remarkable well at Orvieto, called Pozzo di San Patrizio, the cylinder is 180 feet deep and nearly 50 feet in diameter, and this is filled with a tower or shaft of masonry, double-walled, containing between the walls two continuous spiral staircases, which occupy the same space in the tower, that is to say, a person ascending or descending by one of the spirals has the other above him and also below him. The water, filling a cylindrical cistern at the bottom, is reached in this way, and is brought to the surface on the backs of asses, and by similar means. Illustrations of this well can be seen in the book entitled *Stampe del Duomo di Orvieto*, published at Rome, 1791. (Compare Well Curb.)

C. An open space, more or less enclosed, and commonly of small dimensions as compared to its height. Thus, the open space between walls in which a stair or elevator is placed may be spoken of as a well, while the term is equally applicable to a wellhole in its more specific meaning. — R. S.

Absorbing Well. A well sunk through impervious strata to enable surface water to reach an absorbent stratum and so be carried away. Called also Drain Well ; Waste Well.

Drain Well. Same as Absorbing Well.

Waste Well. Same as Absorbing Well.

WELL CURB. A parapet or low wall built at the mouth of a well to prevent persons or beasts from falling into it, and so arranged as to allow of drawing of the water under proper conditions. The term may be taken to cover also the appliances for drawing the water, so far as they are constructive in character and not mere pieces of machinery. The well curb of common wells at farmhouses in America and largely in England is of wood, and often has a slight roof overhead. This is sometimes enlarged into a decorative piece of architecture, especially for a well on the village green, or the like, or when a memorial purpose is attached to it.

The well curbs of the Middle Ages have generally perished. There are, however, some elaborate wrought-iron canopies and herses existing, as notably in Nuremberg and cities of Belgium, some of which have come down but little altered from the fifteenth century. Very splendid well curbs of architectural character

WELL CURB, RATISBON CATHEDRAL, BAVARIA, 15TH CENTURY.

exist in some towns of Italy. Thus, one in Pienza, attached to the Palazzo Piccolomini, has two columns upon which rests a trabeated structure treated on either side like a classical entablature, and from the under surface or soffit of this trabeation is suspended the wheel and other machinery for the buckets of the well. Another at San Gimignano in Tuscany is much more simple and probably earlier. In character it is still somewhat mediæval and probably dates from the early fifteenth century. The horizontal beam of stone in this case is supported on simple uprights which are carried

out on the inner side with corbels, so as to diminish the free bearing of the lintel, which is loaded with a small ornamental superstructure. (See Vera da Pozzo.) — R. S.

WILLENS, FRANTZ; engineer; d. Dec. 6, 1897.

A Belgian engineer. He was vice-president of the jury of Classe 66 (civil engineering) at the Paris Exposition of 1878. For a long time he directed the works at the Palais de Justice at Brussels (Belgium).

Nécrologie in *Construction Moderne*, Dec. 18, 1897.

WELLHOLE. Any open area of which the vertical dimensions generally predominate over the horizontal, and in this general sense not to be distinguished from Well, *C*, except as being smaller. In its most specific use, the clear vertical space about which a stair turns, or between a stair and a landing or passage parallel to it; usually limited by the hand rail; but not the hole in any one floor as commonly as the vertical space left open through two or more stories.

WELL CURB; PIAZZA DEI SIGNORI, VERONA. THE CURB PROPER AND THE COLUMNS AND CROSS-BEAM ARE OF MARBLE; THE BOX WITH WICKET IS OF WOOD, AND TEMPORARY.

WELL HOUSE. A small house or pavilion built over a well.

WERWE, CLAUX DE. (See Claus de Werwe.)

WEST END. (See Orientation.)

WELL CURB IN THE OLD MARKET, MAYENCE, DATED 1526.

WEST INDIES, ARCHITECTURE OF. That of the islands, their country districts and their towns, some of which latter are of ancient establishment and contain buildings of the sixteenth century, and those which have immediately succeeded them, while others are in architectural character entirely of the nineteenth century, and not of its earliest years. The number of communities is so great and they are individually so petty, the number of nationalities and of national influences represented by these communities is so large, that nothing can be done here more than to call attention to a few of those marked peculiarities which make the architecture of the islands interesting to the student of planning and design.

It will readily be understood that the churches are not strongly differentiated from those of Europe. The cathedrals and larger churches of Cuba, Santo Domingo, and Puerto Rico are, like those of Mexico, reflexes of the buildings of Spain of slightly earlier date, nor are there, as sometimes in Mexico, any novel principles inherent in their design. The Anglican church of the comparatively wealthy town of Port of Spain, Trinidad, is, in its plan, its general appearance, and its location among trees, a slighter and less cared for English parish church, and that is all. The proclivities of men of the south of Europe are seen in the solid masonry of the Spanish buildings, and those of the English builders of the first half of the nineteenth century are equally visible in the slight structure last named. The Spanish feeling for design is well shown in the cathedral at Cienfuegos in Cuba, and something of it is visible in the church of Guadaloupe in the same island, as also in the cupola and its arrangement at Guayama, Puerto Rico. On the other hand, there is here and there among the British colonies a small attempt at modern Victorian Gothic church building, but it is never of importance. The British settler, even in the oldest colonies, seldom thinks that he has come to stay; the permanent resident, "the West Indian," exists, but there are not enough of him to make a church building community.

The public buildings are impossible to classify. There is here one of considerable importance; and, again, in another colony, equally large and rich, there is nothing which deserves remark on account of its plan or disposition, or which, in its exterior design, differs from a private house somewhat enlarged, or from two or three private houses side by side. Thus, in the great British colony of Trinidad, the governor lived in a cottage which was nothing more than the Lodge attached to the Botanical Garden near Port of Spain, until about 1876, when a new house was finished which has since been the gubernatorial palace. Even the new house is small compared with an English country mansion, but it is still

a national or, at least, a provincial building of some dignity. So the Captain General's palace at Havana — long and low, with only one story above the ground floor arcade — has not a very imposing character, but its patio within is dignified; and so, to an even greater degree, is the court of the Club House, which our newspaper writers call the "Spanish Casino," at Havana. At Mayaguez, Puerto Rico, is a town hall not badly designed, with an order of pilasters in the principal story and large open arches between, and this fronts upon a plaza which is laid out with a really imposing disposition of pilasters and terraces, though on a small scale.

There must here be mentioned some of the curious conditions which obtain in a climate where there has never been frost in the memory of man, and where the range of temperature is very moderate indeed. Thus, where there is no frost, the conditions which govern masonry are radically different. Water is hardly to be feared by brickwork, even when only fairly well laid, where the thermometer never goes below 65°. If one walks through the streets of Charlotte Amalia, the one town of Saint Thomas and a busy free port, as soon as the streets begin to climb the steep hillsides back of the town, it will be noted that the whole street, carriage way, foot way, street gutters, and all, are arranged to take a sudden and overwhelming flood of water. In the same town a great deal has been done of late years in the building of comfortable small houses, and in the dressing up and fitting with pretty garden walls, and the like, of these and of the older dwellings; and all these accessory structures are built of masonry — of good average brickwork laid in lime mortar and rather prettily and fantastically adorned with the material itself. No precautions are taken against the "heaving" or "lifting" or "creeping" of these copings, or of the foundations; nor, indeed, is it necessary to guard your foundation against anything except the direct rush of a summer flood. Every one who knows our New England towns is somewhat familiar with that curious coping which is made of large boulders, roughly dressed on one side so as to form a bed, and then laid upon the top of a wall, their great mass preventing for a few years any disturbance from frosts, and the spaces between them, triangular or otherwise, being covered as best may be for one season at a time. It is precisely in the other way that the Danish mason works in the tropics. He will set a flight of steps the whole width of the street, alternating with the slopes above and below, — providing, in short, a stairway a *cordone* where the grade is too steep for a ramp; and he builds these steps of brick set on their edges, so that each tread is composed of the face or narrower surface of the bricks set close together with a small mortar joint. This is found to wear perfectly well, for the narrow joint and the fairly well-mixed and well-laid mortar defy the rush of the warm rains even when these have accumulated in the hillside above and rush down in torrents.

Now, the dwelling houses of olden time seem to have taken little note of these peculiarities of climate, and still less of those requirements of life in the tropics which the older lands of the sun — India, North Africa, and Java — have studied. The houses of even sixty years ago are European houses, differing in little except their somewhat inferior construction from the house of the mother country — Spain, Great Britain, Holland, Denmark. The town of Willemstadt, at Curaçao, presents on its harbour fronts just·such rows of gabled houses as, in the seventeenth century and to day, faced and still face the canals of Amsterdam. The dwelling house on a village street in Cuba, as in the towns of the Spanish Main (Puerto Cabello, Cumana, Caracas, Ciudad Bolivar), is Spanish in character, low, with but few openings on the front, and those heavily fenced, the monstrous cage of stout wooden bars built out a foot or more from the face of the wall, so that the inhabitant leaning on the sill can look up and down the street through the bars which form the flanks of each cage. If few of these houses are built in the orthodox way around a patio, it is because the simplicity of life and the small amount of money spent upon each residence has, in most cases, prevented this. Instead of a court surrounded on every side with a colonnade with rooms opening from this, quite like a Roman peristyle and its adjoining apartments, a Spanish colonial house of medium size is apt to consist of a building on the street in front, another building on the street or alley in the rear, and an open yard between, divided from the neighbouring property by a high masonry wall on each side, and affording in one corner of its breezy extent the most comfortable place for the family meals, served at a table beneath an awning. These houses are built directly upon the ground, with but seldom any cellarage below the principal floor, which, indeed, is laid with bricks or tiles upon a prepared surface — with nothing else to separate it from the natural soil.

In the above, and in similar ways, the European house has become adapted to tropical requirements ; but this change is more marked in the recent dwellings, that is to say in those of the last thirty-five years, than in those of any previous epoch. Thus, it has been customary during those years to alter the town houses from their original aspect, as of town houses in Southern Europe, by building, outside of their stone walls, long stretches of wooden galleries which are enclosed on the outer face by jalousies. This involves great changes in the internal economy. Suppose a house standing at the corner of two streets ; on each side fronting upon the street and its own garden, however small the latter may be, you build a gallery, like a veranda, but enclosed everywhere with light woodwork with slats like those of the Venetian blind, but broader. These slats are generally fixed, but every now and then there is a panel which opens on hinges, and every now and then there is a glass window set into the slatted wall, the purpose of that window being to give a free outlook during the torrential summer rains, when all jalousies must be kept tightly closed. The floor of this veranda is on the level of the floor of your rooms within ; therefore, you cut the window-back or *allège* away, you remove the glazed sash entirely, and leave free exit from the rooms within to the gallery. This gallery increases the size of your house by just so much. There is no longer any provision for shutting out the external air. The pretence of the necessity of shutting casements or sash like those of Europe is dismissed. Some centuries of experience have proved to the inhabitants that there is no day in the year when a thorough draft is not desirable, and, therefore, one ceases to shut out the winds of heaven, and resorts instead to various devices for protecting the flames of kerosene lamps or candles from too direct sweep of the wind. Nothing else is to be feared, for there are no fires nor any fireplaces in the house, and dust must needs be allowed to come in freely and settle, even in the course of a few hours, visibly upon floors and furniture. These galleries are never on the street level, nor, in the country houses, are they very often as near the ground as the verandas in the United States. In the city the sidewalk is left beneath the gallery, which is supported on posts, and in the country the better houses have the family rooms raised a half story, or even a whole story, above the ground level, and the first gallery is also at that height, level with the floor to which it corresponds.

The effect of all this upon the architectural appearance of the streets is very great. The street of a prosperous town in a colony of modernized tendencies shows an almost unbroken row of what seem to be large wooden houses walled entirely with window shutters. The fact that there is a stone or a brick house inside of this outer shell concerns no one. As for the larger dwellings in town or country, where the structure is newly arranged or rearranged, and where there has been money enough to do things in a fairly convenient way, the marked peculiarity is the opening up of all partitions so that the trade wind may search out every corner of the dwelling. Thus, in a merchant's dwelling house of Barbados, Trinidad, or Jamaica, to name the British islands only, the drawing-rooms and sitting rooms open into each other and into the entrance passage or staircase hall by doorways set close together — 4 feet 8 inches of doorway to 2 feet 4 inches of pier ; and these doorways are not filled by doors, either sliding or hinged, nor have they, in most cases, *portières*, unless those of the most absolutely movable quality, easy to put up and easy to take down and put away. In like manner, partitions dividing the bedrooms are very often kept to the height of 8 feet or thereabouts, the remaining space below the ceiling left open with the slightest railing of wood filling up the space between the solid partition and the ceiling. Whatever inconvenience this may cause, as not preventing the free transmission of sound from room to room, is put up with for the sake of the free admission of air. And in this connection we are reminded of the great hospital at Port of Spain, and the boast of the physician in charge concerning its perfect ventilation. The ventilation consists of the admission of the winds as they blow, freely, throughout the rooms, above a height of about 7 feet. The 7-foot screen shelters the patients' beds, the space above that and to the ceiling is the opening for " ventilation." Slowly the northern European mind has reached the conclusion that conditions are different in the heavenly climate of the West Indies, and has accepted the novel situation.

The above are the marked peculiarities of building among the West Indian islands. The conditions of the time are not favourable to the development of a new style of architecture. In an architectural epoch these new principles of planning and building might be expected to develop something very interesting in an artistic way, and that before many years had passed.

— R. S.

WESTMINSTER HALL. (See under Hall.)

WESTMINSTER PALACE. In London ; originally an irregular group of buildings of many epochs, which was nearly all destroyed by fire in 1834. Since that time the new palace at Westminster has been built, which is nothing more than the legislative palace of the United Kingdom of Great Britain and Ireland, or, as it is more commonly called, the Houses of Parliament. This building was designed by Charles Barry, who was knighted after the completion of the work. Westminster Hall forms the public entrance to the building, and this disposition has saved that important structure from serious alteration, the taking down and the repairing of the southern wall being the only change made. The building encloses eleven principal courts. The official residence of the Speaker, the Sergeant-at-Arms, Librarian, and other officers of the House of Commons, and of similar officers of the House of Peers, are included in the structure. The whole building is an elaborate piece of Tudor Gothic,

rather successfully maintained throughout, but the exterior is a rather monotonous piece of panelling, similar in all its parts, and there is not much satisfaction for the enthusiast in fine art, except in the study of a few of the large and important wall paintings.

The greatest peculiarity is the arrangement of the two legislative chambers. The House of Commons affords sittings for only about two-thirds of its members, and this on benches which have no divisions, and are like the pews in a church. There are no desks or other conveniences for papers or for writing. The accommodation for strangers, too, is extremely limited, for the galleries on both sides of the House are for members, and the lower gallery over the Speaker is for reporters. Strangers, then, are admitted to two galleries at the end opposite the Speaker, containing in all about two hundred sittings, and women are admitted only to the gallery behind the Speaker and above the reporters ; which is fitted with a grating in front and resembles a cage. The chamber is, indeed, very small, its dimensions being given generally as 45 by 70, and 41 feet high, and the retention of it in this form, so that all speakers can be easily heard and all debates be kept conversational and easy, seems to be the reason for the anomalies above mentioned. The House of Peers is larger, a little wider and higher, and nearly 100 feet long. It is also much more elaborately fitted.

— R. S.

WESTON, WILLIAM DE ; architect. William de Weston built S. Stephen's Chapel, Westminster, in the reign of Edward III.

Redgrave, *Dictionary of Artists.*

WHEELING STEP. (Same as Winder.)

WHISPERING GALLERY. A room, natural or artificial, so shaped that a whisper or other faint sound, produced at a particular point, can be heard at some distant point with remarkable loudness.

Whispering galleries are usually accidental, but may without difficulty be predetermined. They are of two general types — focussing and conducting. In the one the sound diverging from the source is received upon some concave reflecting surface, and is concentrated again at the conjugate focus. One of the best and most accessible examples of this type is the Statue Hall — the old chamber of the House of Representatives — in the Capitol at Washington. The ceiling of this is a very considerable portion of the surface of a sphere whose centre is near the floor. Standing at the centre of this sphere, one can hear his own whisper returned to him. Standing at one side of this point, he can whisper, especially if he turn his face toward the ceiling, to a person standing at an equal distance on the other side of the centre.

PLATE XXXVI

WESTMINSTER HALL; IN LONDON

A building which in its present form is thought to have been built by Richard II., and there is no doubt that the wooden roof has remained in place since that reign. This is the most important decorative piece in wood which exists in Europe. The building is nearly 78 feet wide within the walls, and 92 feet high to the peak of the roof. The door on the left leads up a passage, reserved to members of the House of Commons, straight to the Commons' Lobby.

For any position of the speaker there is a corresponding point at which the whisper is more or less accurately focussed. The ceiling, painted so that it appears deeply panelled, is smooth. Had the ceiling been panelled, the reflection would have been irregular and the effect very much reduced. The most accurate form for a whispering gallery is that in which the reflecting surface is a considerable portion of the surface of an ellipsoid, that has for its foci the two points between which there is to be a communication.

The second type of whispering gallery is best illustrated in the dome of S. Paul's cathedral, London. A whisper close to and along the smooth concave wall is continually deflected inward upon itself by the wall, is prevented from spreading, and is thus conducted with but slightly diminished intensity to the other side of the dome. The sound, travelling from the source by great circles, concentrates again at the opposite end of the diameter on which the sound is produced. The spherical form is, therefore, in this case the best.

The essential difference between the two types is : that in the first the sound is brought to a focus after a single reflection ; in the second it is brought from the one point to the other by a series of reflections at short intervals, and it is in this sense that it is spoken of as conducted. In the second case, the convergence of the great circle paths of successive reflection might be regarded as focussing the sound. — W. C. Sabine.

WHITE. *A*. Having a surface which reflects light as it is received, without change in its spectral quality ; hence, having a surface nearly or approximately perfect in this respect. In the arts and trades white wood is almost any wood of pale colour, yellowish, brownish, or of a greenish gray ; the white coat in plastering is the finishing coat even if much speckled, or even of a generally gray hue ; white armour in the fifteenth century and later was brightly burnished steel, as distinguished from that of blackened, browned, or reddened surface.

B. In many trades and arts, devoid of colour, or nearly so ; transparent, or nearly so. Thus, white glass is clear glass, such as is used for common windows and tableware.

WHITE FINISH. (See Plastering.)

WHITE HOUSE. In Washington, capital of the United States ; the official residence of the President, finished in its present form in 1818.

WHITE LEAD. A mixture of the carbonate and hydrated oxide of lead in about the proportion of three quarters of the former to one quarter of the latter. In manufacture the resultant pure white carbonate is seldom more than 65 per cent ; mixed with 10 per cent of

linseed oil it forms the paint known as white lead and oil.

WHITEWASH. A composition of quicklime and water, or of a whiting size and water, used for whitening woodwork, brickwork, the plaster surface of walls, etc., especially in cellars. A superior kind of whitewash, often tinted, is called calcimine, or Kalsomine.

WHITING. A preparation of dried and ground chalk, used in fine whitewashing and in distemper painting, also as an adulterant in making putties for modelling and gilding.

WICKEEUP. Same as Wickyup.

WICKER. A pliant twig, osier, or withe used in making wickerwork or basketwork, also work done and any fabric made in this way. As applied to the making of closures with mud or clay, wickerwork is generally called wattle (see Wattle and Dab).

WICKET. A small door, gate, window, or trap ; especially a small door or gate forming part of a large one, usually specified as wicket door, wicket gate, etc., according to use.

WICKYUP. (Written also wickiup and wickeeup. Wikiup is the form adopted by the United States Bureau of American Ethnology, in accordance with the system used there.)

A. An American Indian hut or shelter composed of brush, rushes, boughs, or bark ; especially one of the dwellings of the Pai Ute, which are built of tule rushes woven over a conical framework of poles 8 or 10 feet high, and also in some localities of rough cedar (juniper) or pine branches covered with boughs and twigs from the same trees, and open to the sun for a third of their circumference.

B. Throughout the Western United States any rude, temporary shelter or habitation.

The derivation is from the Algonquin, though Dorsey suggested (p. 275, 13th *An. Rep. Bu. Eth.*) an origin in the Dakota word *wakeyapi*, the plural of *wakeya*, a form of skin tent. The word is found in many of the Algonquin dialects. In the Sac-and-Fox-Algonquin it occurs as wigiap and wikiapi, being, according to Gatschet, their form of the word "wigwam." In the Menomini-Algonquin it is wikiop, a habitation of bark, brush, or wood. According to Hoffman (14th *An. Rep. Bu. Eth.*) it is a corruption of wikomik, which in turn he derives from wigiwam (wigwam). It would appear, however, that inasmuch as *wiki* is a word for home and *wekop* is basswood bark, that a probable derivation is from a compound of these two, *wiki-wekop*, denoting a home covered with basswood bark (or with mats of basswood bark) as distinguished from one covered with another material. This would be contracted according to Indian habit into wikiop. (See Communal Dwelling; Wigwam; Tipi.) — F. S. DELLEN-BAUGH.

WIGWAM (pron. wig'-wahm). (From the Algonquin, *wigiwam, wekiwam,* and *wigewam.*) Hoffman derives *wikomik*, another Algonquin name for a house, also from wigiwam, but this would appear rather to be contracted from something like *wikimatik;* "*wiki*," home, and "*matik*," tree or wood, and meaning a house of wood or logs, as distinguished from wigiwam, derived from wigi (wigwas), birch bark, a house of birch bark. The American languages differentiated and eliminated in this manner, and it is probable that the variation in the Algonquin terms for house arose, at least partly, by differentiations, combinations, and contractions (see Wickyup). The derivation of wigwam is also given from *wek*, his house, or *wekowan*, their house. When the dialects of Algonquin have been more thoroughly studied, the confusion now existing as to the derivation of wigwam, and other terms, will disappear.

A. An Algonquin house, built of poles and bark or mats, varying in size and shape according to locality and tribe. It was generally either circular or a flattened ellipse. It was made by planting poles in the ground and bringing their tops together. The Ojibwa brought them to a point with a curve outward, that is each pole was bow-shaped, the convex side out. The Menomini form was a flattened ellipse with the poles forming an arched roof; and when the wigwam was quadrilateral its roof was arched. The covering was of various kinds of bark, and also mats of woven basswood bark, and skins. The covering was held in place by a second series of poles tied through to the first; and on the inside horizontal poles were added for bracing. A hole was left in the top for a smoke-outlet. The size on the ground was about 10 by 14 feet for the oblong, and 10 to 16 feet for the circular. The height was from 6 to 10 feet. The quadrilateral were much larger, being sometimes 50 or more feet long.

B. In popular use, any Redskin habitation, except the stone and adobe houses.

C. In the United States a large building, more or less permanently constructed, used for political meetings. These were originally rude board structures of a temporary nature, but

some substantial buildings are now so called, as Tammany Hall, New York, which is often spoken of as the "Wigwam." (See Lodge; Long House; Tipi.) — F. S. DELLENBAUGH.

WIKOMIK. An Indian habitation made of logs, bark, or other material; probably originally meaning specifically a house of logs; a wigwam. (See Wigwam and Wickyup.)

WILARS DE HONECORT; architect.
Wilars, thought to have belonged to Honnecourt, a village near Cambrai (Nord, France), is known by an album of sketches preserved in the collection of manuscripts taken from the Abbey of S. Germain des Prés, which are now in the Bibliothèque Nationale, Paris. In the fifteenth century the volume contained forty-one leaves of vellum. There are now but thirty-three. The drawings are made with lead or silver point, sometimes inked in. The book contains numerous figures probably taken from sculpture or glass, sketches of architectural details, such as the plan of the towers of Laon, the rose window at Chartres, the rose window at Lausanne, and many mechanical devices. From internal evidence contained in his book, it is supposed that he was one of the leaders in the development of Gothic architecture in the thirteenth century, and that he built, between 1227 and 1251, the choir of the cathedral of Cambrai, which was destroyed during the French Revolution. About 1244 he visited Hungary. The apse of the church at Meaux and the church at Vaucelles, also some buildings in Hungary which show French influence, have been attributed to him by different writers.

Villard de Honnecourt, *Album* (edition Lassus-Darcel); Wilars de Honecourt, *Sketchbook* (translation by Willis, with essay by Quicherat); Garling, *Remarks on the Album of Villard de Honnecourt.*

WILDERNESS. In ornamental gardening, of the formal sort, a part of the grounds less regular in treatment, and supposed to have some of the wildness of nature.

WILKINS, WILLIAM, M.A., R.A.; architect; b. 1778; d. Aug. 31, 1839.
The eldest son of Henry Wilkins, the author of a book on Pompeii, published in Rome in 1819. In 1800 he graduated at Caius College, Cambridge. In 1801 he won a travelling scholarship, and spent four years in Greece, Asia Minor, and Italy. He erected various buildings in imitation of Greek architecture. Among the many works published by him are *The Civil Architecture of Vitruvius*, a translation, prefaced by a *History of the Rise and Progress of Grecian Architecture* (folio, 1812–1817), and *Prolusiones Architectonicæ* (4to, 1827).

Redgrave, *Dictionary of Artists.*

WILLIAM OF SENS; architect.
In 1175 the chapter of the cathedral of Canterbury (England) undertook the reconstruc-

tion of that building, which had been destroyed by fire in 1174. William of Sens (Yonne, France) was employed as architect, and built the walls, pillars, triforium, and clearstory of the choir, and completed the vaulting of the choir aisles. He was preparing to turn the great vault of the choir, when (about Sept. 13, 1178) he was thrown from a scaffold, receiving injuries from which he died two years later. It is supposed by Viollet-le-Duc and others that he built a considerable part of the cathedral of Sens before he went to England.

G. S., *Chronological History of Canterbury Cathedral;* Willis, *Canterbury Cathedral;* Viollet-le-Duc, *Dictionnaire.*

WILLIAM OF WYKEHAM; architect; b. 1324; d. Sept. 27, 1404.

He was born at the village of Wickham near Winchester (England), and was educated at the priory school at Winchester. He early became known to Bishop Edingdon of Winchester, who employed him on the cathedral and recommended him to the king. In 1349 he was appointed king's chaplain. October 30, 1356, he was appointed surveyor of the works at Windsor Castle. July 10 he was made chief warden and surveyor of the royal castles of Windsor, Leeds, Dover, and Hadleigh. Wykeham made important additions to Windsor Castle. In 1361–1367 he built Queensborough Castle. He was made keeper of the Privy Seal and king's secretary in 1364. According to Froissart (*Chronicles*) he had at this time attained such power " that by him everything was done, and without him they did nothing." October 17, 1367, he was made chancellor of the kingdom, and October 10 of the same year was consecrated bishop of Winchester. March 5, 1380, he laid the foundations of New College, Oxford, and March 26, 1387, commenced S. Mary's College at Winchester. In 1394 he commenced alterations at Winchester cathedral. He began the reconstruction of the nave and aisles, which was not completed until after his death. In rebuilding the church Wykeham used the existing Norman masonry, transforming it into the perpendicular style of the time.

Lowth, *William of Wykeham;* Moberly, *William of Wykeham;* Willis, *Architectural History of Winchester Cathedral.*

WILLIAM THE ENGLISHMAN; architect.

He succeeded William of Sens (see William of Sens) as architect of Canterbury cathedral, and in much of his work simply carried out the designs of his predecessor. The new Trinity chapel or chapel of Becket was built entirely under his direction.

Willis, *Canterbury Cathedral.*

WIND (pronounced to rhyme with mind). A bend, twist, or crook, such as occurs in some timber in drying.

Out of Wind. Free from bends, twists, or crooks; perfectly straight and true, referring to timber, boards, panel work, or any artificial surface, as a plaster wall, etc.

WIND-BREAK. An arrangement of vertical poles, bushes, boughs, bundled rushes, or of stones, in a semicircle or in a straight line, as a shelter from wind. Used by American Indians also to protect tent entrances. The wind-break in winter is often extended entirely around the Tipi.

WINDER. A step, more or less wedge-shaped in plan, adjusted to the angle or curve of a turn in a stair, as described under Step. As a winder cannot conform in width to the size assumed for the fliers, this regular spacing is usually — in good work — measured on the curve naturally followed by a person ascending with his hand on the rail along the well or newel side. This is usually taken as a curve parallel to the rail, and from 15 to 18 inches from it. The risers of such steps should not, in good work, radiate from a common centre except in the case of a winding stair. It is more convenient, as well as safer, to cause them to converge somewhat before the actual turning place is reached, so that the fliers pass almost insensibly into the winders. The common plan in an ordinary stair, and one to be generally condemned, is to permit three, or even four, steps to occupy a quarter-pace (see Pace), with risers radiating from a common point. (See Balanced Step, under Step.) — D. N. B. S.

WIND-GUARD. A cowl for a chimney.

WIND-LOAD. (See Wind Pressure.)

WINDOW. An opening for the admission of light and sometimes of air into the interior of a building; and, by extension, the filling of this opening with glass, as usual in modern times, with the frame and sash, or casement, and their accessories. The term is usually confined to openings in vertical or nearly vertical surfaces, as walls. It is impracticable to distinguish in terms between the opening and the filling, as can be done between Doorway and Door.

Windows are of comparatively little consequence in countries where the habits of the people are based upon life in the open air. Such countries are, in modern times, only those of the tropical zone; but in antiquity, for reasons that are not wholly clear, the people of the Mediterranean lands lived as if their climate were tropical and without a winter. Hence windows are not known to have existed in Greece in classical times; they were rare in Grecian lands elsewhere; and although the window was certainly in use among the Romans of the later Republic, there are almost no instances known to us of windows in the usual modern sense, either in Pompeii or among the ruins of monuments elsewhere in the West,

previous to the fifth century A.D. Rooms of
private houses opened on courts (see Atrium;
House; Peristyle), and generally received light
and air only through doorways of greater or
smaller dimensions, the sitting rooms of diffcr-
ent kinds having high and wide openings, with
little but curtains and low screens to separate
them from the court or garden. The sleeping
rooms (see Cubiculum; House) were very small,
and had besides the door of entrance merely one
or two very narrow loopholes high in the wall.
There is found in Pompeii an arrangement by
which a cubiculum had a small door as well as
a large one, which latter could be barricaded

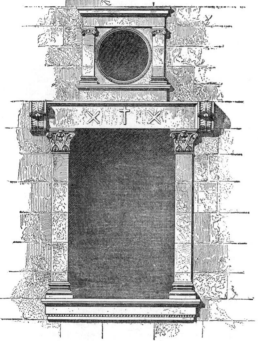

WINDOW, FIG. 1: IN THE PALACE AT CHAQQA OR
SHAKKA; 3D CENTURY A.D.

and left open in warm weather; but nowhere
is a window of the usual modern sort known to
exist. The Romans, moreover, used glass for
windows but rarely, though it is known that
they understood the glazing of sash.

WINDOW, PART I. *The Architectural
Treatment of the Opening.* This depends
chiefly upon the character of the wall, though
where a permanent framework divides up the
window opening, this may have great influence
upon the general design. Thus, where slabs
of plaster or of marble, pierced with larger or
smaller openings, fill up the whole window
space (as in some Byzantine and some modern
buildings), or where bronze gratings, with
square openings set diagonally, are used, or a
copy of these in marble, as in some Roman

Imperial buildings, it became easy to open very
large spaces, such as the lunettes under the
intersection of vaults with walls, and this without losing a severe architectural character.

The private buildings of the third and subsequent centuries down to the twelfth century
have disappeared, leaving behind them no important trace. Only in the deserted towns of
Syria have the stone-built edifices kept their
shape and ordonnance. Figure 1 shows a very
early Greco-Roman window, probably of the
third century, and we need not doubt that such
openings as this were somewhat common in
Roman country houses. This window is in the
second story, the larger opening nearly 6 feet
wide. Figure 2 is a much smaller window, and
is very like many which existed thirty years ago
in the earliest still existing Romanesque houses
of Western Europe. It will be noted that here

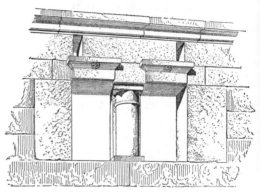

WINDOW, FIG. 2: PRIVATE HOUSE AT KHURBET-HASS.

the spanning of the opening by a lintel, and the
supporting of that lintel by uprights, as well as
the apparent serving of pilasters for the same
purpose, are the essential characteristics. The
window is here what it became so commonly in
later times, a chief element in the design. The
form of a lintel supported by a column existed
even into the Gothic period in Belgium and
other Northern lands. In general, however, the
earliest Romanesque windows were single lights,
and these had semicircular arched heads except
in the commonest work. The lancet windows
of early French and English Gothic (see Figs. 3
and 4) show the same type, with merely the
substitute of a pointed for a round arch. These
two figures show the outside and the inside of
very similar single lights in churches. The
fact of the interior being much more highly
adorned than the exterior is not merely because
the one church is larger than the other; it is a
marked peculiarity of the early mediæval architecture that the interior is always richer, and
this applies especially to the window and door
openings. Figure 5 is also the interior of a lancet
window, and this time almost devoid of orna-

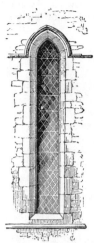

WINDOW, FIG. 3: WITNEY CHURCH,
OXFORDSHIRE; C. 1220.

WINDOW, FIG. 5: WITNEY CHURCH, OXFORDSHIRE;
C. 1220.

WINDOW, FIG. 6: SALISBURY CATHEDRAL; C. 1225.

WINDOW, FIG. 4: CHURCH AT SAINT OUEN
(CALVADOS); C. 1225.

ment. In all these cases the glass in small quarrels is modern, though the ancient work was probably like it.

WINDOW, FIG. 7: SALISBURY CATHEDRAL, NORTH TRANSEPT; C. 1225.

For the beginnings of the traceried window see Tracery, Figs. 1 and 2, in which two pointed lights with but a narrow pier between them are surmounted by a rondel enclosing a

the openings below are widened until they fill the whole space between two buttresses, having but a narrow monolithic mullion to separate

them. Figure 6 (Window) shows the same influences at work with somewhat less elaboration, and with a larger sense of the importance of the bounding and enclosing arch, for in the

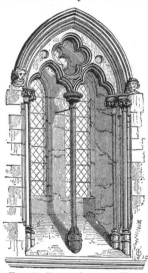

WINDOW, FIG. 8: STONE CHURCH, KENT; C. 1240.

WINDOW, FIG. 9: THE DEANERY, NORWICH; C. 1250.

cusped quatrefoil. It is easy to see that the enlargement of all these three openings from what they are in Fig. 1 gives us the tracery shown in Fig. 2 (Tracery), where the rondel above puts on the form of a rose window, and

Chartres window (Fig. 2, Tracery), that arch has not interested the builder much, while in Fig. 6 of the present article it is seen that the architect has cared more for the generally pointed shape of his window than for the details of its subdivision. In Figs. 7 and 8 is shown a very curious system resulting naturally from the heavier walls of the early English Gothic work. In France, at the same time, the

WINDOW, FIG. 10: BOYTON CHURCH, WILTSHIRE; 1250.

vaulting principle had come to control the whole design, and the space beneath each wall arch and between two buttresses was treated like a great opening to be filled with glass; but in England the wall still interested the builders, and a natural way to make a window in a very thick wall was (Fig. 7) to make an outer arcade with four arches filled with glass, and an inner arcade with six arches with very slender col-

WINDOW, FIG. 12: THE BROLETTO, MONZA; C. 1270.

umns and with no filling of any sort between them. Figure 8 shows the same principle, of somewhat later date and with still more refined forms.

About the middle of the thirteenth century the traceried window had assumed the most important place, and Fig. 9 compared with Fig. 6 will show how this tracery itself had been refined and made more delicate as well as more logical. Figure 10 is a single light of the same

epoch, showing in an interesting way how the feeling for cusping, so important in all tracery, finds expression even in a single opening. In domestic work at the same time windows were becoming larger, and were getting to be filled with more elaborately finished casements. It was, therefore, natural to make the actual window heads square; and in a building of pointed style this could be included beneath a pointed arch with advantage both in construction and in utility (see Fig. 11). Figure 12, however, shows a window which, though taken from a building of civic purpose, is as badly arranged as possible for the convenience of handling casements. This, however, was in north Italy, where conditions of life were very different. Figure 13 shows a French Gothic window in which the preparation for the woodwork has

WINDOW, FIG. 14: THURNING CHURCH, HUNTINGDONSHIRE; C. 1300.

been carried so far that the stone mullions are cut with a deep blade in which a bolt hole is made. The arch is a mere simulacrum, each arched head, including the cusp, consisting of two pieces only. In Fig. 14 the simplest tracery of the close of the thirteenth century is shown as it appeared in the simpler English churches, and in Fig. 15 is shown that which replaced at the same period the earlier lancet window. The form, resulting from a flat lintel partly supported by two corbels of slight projection, and the head thus resulting modelled with simple splay or with more elaborate cutting, but always mitring at each angle and carried around each curve, remains, from that time, a favourite form, more especially in England.

In the middle of the fourteenth century the square-headed window becomes very common, and in elaborate buildings is filled with tracery

WINDOW, FIG. 11: RUE BRICONNET, TOURS; C. 1260.

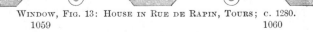

WINDOW, FIG. 13: HOUSE IN RUE DE RAPIN, TOURS; C. 1280.

in accordance with the style set for the larger and pointed openings.   Great ingenuity is shown in the arranging of this tracery, and the forms resulting are sometimes very beautiful (see Figs.

side window" is sometimes applied to such windows as this, but without sufficient cause.

WINDOW, FIG. 15: THANINGTON CHURCH, KENT; c. 1300.

WINDOW, FIG. 17: DENFORD CHURCH, NORTH-AMPTONSHIRE; c. 1350.

16, 17).   Figure 18 is a single light of the same epoch.   Figure 19 is the exterior view of a manor house of about 1375, the fenestration of which is very interesting.   Figure 20 shows the small

The windows of the Renaissance in Italy, of the Renaissance in the North a century later, and of the subsequent neoclassic styles, are so varied in the character of their design that it

WINDOW, FIG. 16: ARDLEY CHURCH, OXFORD-SHIRE; c. 1350.

WINDOW, FIG. 18: APPLEFORD CHURCH, BERK-SHIRE; c. 1350.

square window near the ground (see Fig. 19) immediately below the sill of a larger one, this latter view being taken from within, which accounts for the discrepancies in the arrangement of the head and sill.   The term "low

would be hard to give them in sequence.   (See, for the Italian Renaissance, Vol. I., cols. 50, 223, 225; and Plates XI., XIII.   For the French Renaissance, Vol. I., col. 11; Vol. II., cols. 150, 349, and Plate XV.; Vol. III., cols.

186, 273, 277, 279. For later neoclassic, Vol. I., cols. 603, 806, and Plate XXVI.; Vol. II., cols. 21, 241, 373, 801, 807, and Plates VII., XVI., XVII., XXII. In Vol. III., cols. 51, 303. For modern work, see Vol. I., Plates III., XIX., XXXVI.; Vol. II.,

WINDOW, FIG. 19: SUTTON COURTENAY MANOR HOUSE, BERKSHIRE.

cols. 417, 819.) The simpler form of window in which some neoclassic decoration is attempted may be instanced by Fig. 21. — R. S.

WINDOW, PART II. *The Fitting of the Window Opening with a Frame to receive the Glass.* This may be wholly architectural in

WINDOW, FIG. 20.

character, as in the case of the Roman bronze gratings and the mediæval tracery (for which see Part I. and Tracery). It may be slight and altogether temporary. as where a wooden hinged shutter fills the whole space when closed, or as where temporary sash or white cotton cloth is

put into window openings of a building not yet completed. It may be slight and rough, though more permanent, as in stables and various factories (see Hit and Miss Window, below). Again the Casement or Sash (see those terms) may be very elaborate in make and fittings. Figure 22 is an elaborate Swiss window in a wood-built house, with hinged casement, bull's-eye lights in simple metal frames, and a wicket. The arrangement still existing in north Germany involves double windows with an air space between them during the winter, the permanent casement usually opening inward and the temporary sash put up nearly flush with the outer wall. In this temporary sash a wicket opens, usually one to each window, and this is all the chance for ventilation during the four or five months of cold weather. Such double windows are comparatively rare in the United States; but it is to be desired that window frames should be planned with special reference to putting them up, and fitting them so that they can be opened wide upon occasion.

WINDOW, FIG. 21: WADSTENA, PROVINCE OF OESTERGÖTLAND, SWEDEN.

The usual form of a window in a dwelling house, hotel, business building, or public building is an oblong, with its length set vertically; but there are exceptions, involving peculiar treatment of frame and sash or casement. Thus in English country houses, ancient (see cuts, Bargeboard ; Half Timbered ; and Plate XIV. of Vol. II.) and modern, it is not infrequent to open one side of the room into a single wide and low window (the sill about 3 feet 4 inches from the floor, the head about 3 feet higher, the whole width 7 or 8 feet), divided into several lights each of the whole height of the window, and each fitted with a single casement of light ironwork. So in recent American work windows have been built nearly as follows : opening in wall, 10 feet wide, 7 feet high, with the sill 2 feet 8 inches above the floor ; one heavy transom, about 4 feet above sill ; the space above the transom filled with two or three swinging casements between mullions ; the space below the transom fitted with a fixed frame holding a single sheet of plate glass. Many modifications of this arrangement will suggest themselves.

In public buildings, where adequate systems of forced ventilation are in use, fixed sash are preferred as allowing no interference with the regular supply of air ; and this will tend to become the rule in such cases. It is probable that, in the case of any one room or hall, the choice will be made between full forced ventilation with fixed window frames and sash, and movable sash or casement with no system of ventilation.

Part III. is devoted to the consideration of decorative glass, usually coloured, and the filling of windows so as to make them architectural in the highest sense. The more ordinary glazing of windows may be treated here.

The high cost of glass during all periods previous to the first improvement, introduced about 1830, caused the general adoption of small lights, which, even when involving much labour in glazing, whether with wooden or metal sash bars, was cheaper than paying for larger sheets of glass, and, moreover, provided that, if a piece were broken, the loss would be comparatively slight. In the country houses of moderate cost throughout France and England glass was used in small quarrels (not exceeding eight inches in greatest dimension) ; in the cities window glass hardly exceeded under any circumstances what is now a small light, about 10 by 12 inches ; as late as the close of the seventeenth century even the superb halls of Versailles could not have mirrors of a size greater than twice the above in each dimension. The consequence of this was the inevitable appearance of the window from the outside as being in great measure part of the wall. A closed window could not be like the open window, a positive hole made in the wall substance. This fortunate circumstance, of great value in domestic external architecture, was done away with by the introduction of large lights, not merely of plate glass (see under Glass) but of

large sheets of window glass at no great cost. In the cities of Europe, even shops of considerable display previous to 1820 hardly possessed any show windows in the modern sense. The bow windows (see Bow Window, and under Bay Window) were indeed filled with glass, but the lights were small and the sash bars heavy. It was not until a time within the memory of living man that the first large plate glass shop windows appeared, and these were usually made up of four or six lights ; the single light show window with a single piece of plate glass containing 120 square feet or more having been very rare until long after the middle of the nineteenth century.

The unarchitectural effect produced by these vast sheets of material, which are at once nearly

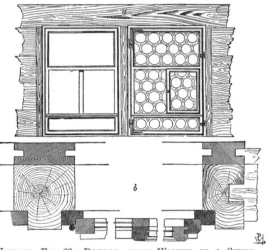

WINDOW, FIG. 22: DOUBLE, WITH WICKET, IN A SWISS CHALET.

A, elevation ; B, plan at a scale four times as great ; the clear width of each half is about 2′ 8″ : the wicket about 1′ 2″.

transparent and with a surface so brilliant that it reflects external objects if any dark surface be arranged behind it, has brought about the attempt, repeated in many forms, to fill a part, at least, of the window opening with glass of a very different appearance — with leaded sash and coloured, or, at least, obscured glass, which will give an architectural and somewhat decorative effect — leaving the perfectly transparent plate glass to the show window proper next above the sill. As yet no very successful result has followed.

Another modification of the glass filling of windows is seen in the prismatic lights used for mills and factories of different sorts. By means of this glass the rays of light are thrown horizontally into the room, and thus workmen at the greatest possible distance from the window, 18 or 20 feet, may be expected to receive daylight nearly as abundant as that which is to be had nearer the window opening. Different patent arrangements have been proposed to cover the use of this kind of glass, and the business houses controlling these are proposing to introduce them into business buildings and dwellings.

Rough plate glass, corrugated, marbleized, and ribbed glass are rarely used in windows, perhaps only when the window looks into some light court or illuminates a closet, bathing room, or similar office. — R. S.

WINDOW, PART III. *The Translucent Filling of the Lights.* In the following paragraphs the word "glass," used simply, means glass coloured in the mass, except in the case of design in uncoloured glass or *en grisaille.* Glass which is coloured in its body, while molten, is called Pot metal (which see), and it is to this division, especially, that the word "stained glass" is inaccurately applied in ordinary phrase. Properly it refers to a transparent colour, which is fastened to the surface of glass by the action of heat, but differs from painting with enamel colour in being fastened by cementation and incorporated with the glass. This manner is *almost* entirely confined to one colour, yellow, made from silver — hence called yellow stain (see Silver Stain under Stain). Painted glass means glass that has had paints made of enamels fused to the surface of the glass by means of heat, whether that glass be coloured in substance or relatively white.

The breaking of surfaces, either dark or light, by opposing divisions, that is to say, of light on dark and dark on light, has always been a pleasure to the instinct of man. The necessary openings in objects of use, either buildings or utensils, have been filled in by various modes of ornament ; perhaps first based on utility, but continued for pleasure. The artistic ingenuity has been exercised to make these divisions unite handsomely with the edges of the openings. This we see distinctly in the divisions of windows that we call tracery (see Tracery and Window, Part I.).

It is not only the division which abstractedly gives pleasure to its shape, but also the sizes and shapes through which light passes, thus modifying the quality of the light, and themselves affected by the light, so as to present differences of light and dark, and simulate gradation, making what the artist calls values. It is upon these general considerations that the successful artistic filling of windows is based. In certain countries of little development in methods, but of sensitiveness to beauty, mother-of-pearl shells have been used, for instance, to give a pleasant value of light by the irregular breaking of the same. At a great distance this irregular semiopacity connects with the definite forms of such divisions as tracery and bars and leading. In the same way, at various epochs, semitransparent slabs of stone have been used

for the purpose of tempering the light in a handsome manner. When glass was first made and used, in remote antiquity, it would seem natural that it should have been used in some such way as above described. But we have no trace so far of a very remote use of glass in openings of buildings.

Glass slabs have been found, and, as before said, translucent stones were certainly used. Here and there we find descriptions that may mean a great deal. In Ceylon there is uncertain record (in the *Mahavansa*), of the date 306 B.C., mentioning "windows with ornaments like jewels, which were as bright as eyes," indicating, perhaps, such methods of decoration as were formerly in use in Europe, and still in the East, by which means small pieces of glass, coloured or uncoloured, are fixed in frames of marble, stone, or stucco, so perforated as to form patterns.

We know that, far back as we can go into antiquity, we find glass made for ornamental purposes ; and the skill and taste shown in every ancient example implies already a preceding industry long established.

The Egyptian remains indicate great mastery over glass, and the Egyptian records refer to it in a remote antiquity. We know enough from the extraordinary fragments of glass made in Roman times to feel quite certain that the men of that day were consummate masters in countless variations of process. Their materials, also, are not essentially different from those that we are especially using here to-day.

Our imagination, therefore, can be indulged in making images for ourselves of possible wall openings and wall spaces filled with beautiful glass, used by the Roman, the Byzantine, the Gaulish, or the Eastern artist.

In the Western world, when we come to the twelfth century, we have remaining examples implying that they are made in succession of earlier work. But whether we have any hesitation in admitting that the Western world of an early date — the Greco-Roman period — employed coloured glass for openings, such as windows, we certainly can admit that the Eastern world indulged in modes of translucid decoration of buildings at a remote period. It would appear that with the first relations of Rome with Asia there came into Italy mosaics composed of coloured glass paste, again not essentially different from what we are using here to-day. When the empire was established in Byzantium, came vases of coloured glass highly valued in the West already in the seventh century. The East is more or less unchangeable ; and the openings, filled in with stucco, or with marble, either translucent or opaque, into which are fitted bits of glass of various colours, and which we see in buildings of the thirteenth and fourteenth centuries in Asia or in Egypt, must belong to a very ancient tradition, whose origin may perhaps be toward Persia.

The use of glass in the Arabic windows is ancient and points to previous similar uses. There are typical windows in Egypt going back to the fourteenth century. Some are merely of one tint, carefully chosen. Others are described by Mr. Gayet (*L'Art Arabe*), as follows : " The window is merely a frame of plaster in which the design is cut out. Little pieces of glass, rudely shaped, are incrusted in each opening of the network. When in place these perforated panels produce a singularly artistic effect. The theme of the decoration is that of the larger decorations of pottery — a bunch of flowers and a cypress. The decoration is symbolical : the bouquet of flowers is a prayer rising with its perfume to Allah. As to the cypress, it is to the Arab the tree to which Satan was chained, an emblem of life and delivery ; for the Persian, the image of a soul tending to heaven. Smaller windows have hardly more than a flower pattern or an arrangement of polygons. But, owing to the idea of the nature of the window, the full spaces are more important than the empty ones ; and under the light of the east the rays of the sun, filtered through the red of tulips, the violet of jacinths, the yellow of pansies, the white of anemones, the green of the cypress, drop into the building in a powdering of opal, of gold, of purple, of sapphire, and of emerald, in a light dim and melancholy. From the narrowness of the openings the light seems to come from afar. Under the domes of the tombs its charm is strangely sweet and sad, and one regrets that the architects have not closed more bays that he might light them in with similar glazed openings." The most beautiful windows of the Arabs are those of the Baharite period. Similar use of glass occurs in India, in Persia, and in the mosques of Jerusalem.

We can see that all this resembles the use of cloisonné enamels, whose existence quite far back, and certainly common in the Byzantine period, would be but one step from the joining of glass by heavy lead or heavy metal instead of the divisions of gold or copper.

It is a question whether it is worth while to indicate the various accounts of glazed ornamental windows, prior to those that we know in the West. It is evident from the make of the first ones that exist, whose date is certain, that they represent a result of much previous experience.

The precision of the work shows no hesitation or trial of the means employed. Already as far back as the fourth century, windows of magnificent colour adorned the Basilica of S. Peter, according to Anastasius the Librarian, and earlier than that Lactantius speaks of coloured windows being frequent. S. John Chrys-

ostom and S. Jerome have mentioned coloured glass of chapels in the churches. Prudentius at the beginning of the fifth century says of the windows of S. Paul beyond the Walls, " In the arcaded windows are various coloured glasses ; thus glitter the meadows adorned by the flowers of spring." Sidonius Apollinaris describes the filling of the windows with brilliant and many-coloured glass in a chapel erected at Lyons by Patiens, bishop in 450. Fortunatus compliments the Holy Bishops who fill the basilicas with glass, and sings of the first lights of dawn through the illumined bays of the cathedral of Paris, whose expenses were paid by King Childebert. He also celebrates the seventy-two windows which lit the church of S. Martin, rebuilt by Gregory of Tours after the fire of 525. Gregory of Tours himself speaks of the windows of the church of Izeure, which were detached from their openings by a thief who thought that their splendour might be the result of gold and silver, and hence tried to melt them. S. Bennet Biscop brought to Wearmouth, from France, toward 680, men skilful in the art of glass. Hincmar, Archbishop of Reims, in the month of April, 845, placed coloured glass in the cathedral which he had completed. In 863 Charles the Bald grants residence with income to the glass workers, Ragenulf and Baldenc. It is said of Adalbern, Archbishop of Reims in 969, that he adorned his cathedral with windows representing historical subjects. Roger and Herbert, clergymen of Reims, famous in their art, executed, about 1060, windows for the Abbey of S. Hubert in Ardennes, ordered by the Countess Adelaide. The cathedral of Le Mans was filled with stained glass by Hoel, bishop in 1081. Eraclius wrote on the painting of glass a treatise, in the tenth or beginning of the eleventh century. Desiderius, Abbot of Monte Casino, orders the colouring of the windows of the Capitular Hall and Chapel, 1058–1066, and Leo of Ostia in the next century describes the making of these windows in a manner that shows the similarity of methods to those later employed.

About Theophilus and his essay we speak elsewhere. Nor is it to be forgotten that S. Bernard, in the severity of his monastic building, forbade decorated windows of colour. The general chapter of the order in 1134 decides that they shall be white without any cross and any colour.

With this we come to the twelfth century, whose windows remain in part to us with those of the thirteenth century, and represent the beginning of the great period of mediæval art in glass. For one of the windows of the cathedral of Chartres, a claim is made that it may have been executed before 1113, having escaped the fires of 1120 and 1194. This is known as " Our Lady of the Beautiful Glass." It would not be far in date from the beautiful panel of Vendôme, also representing the Virgin and her Son, and executed somewhere about 1170 or 1180.

The glass of the twelfth century and beginning of the thirteenth in Western Europe is at once a perfect model of its kind, and as it is applied to architectural decoration, an example and a lesson for all artists. Then, again, whether from accumulated tradition, or from that accurate reasoning which intense interest in art brings on, the principles upon which all this decorative stained glass work is constructed are fundamental ones, carrying the result as far as the knowledge and the materials of that day allowed. Later things may be as interesting, or more interesting as being nearer to our feelings and notions. But in the older stained glass windows, such for example as the glorious west windows of Chartres, all the principles of work in glass are stated, though in an archaic form. A clear understanding or apprehension of the difficulties of colour radiation and its effects from one colour upon another, the opposing or harmonizing effect of the use of complementary colours, and design arising from an adjustment of these difficulties, — these points can be seen stated there as in a grammar.

Certain points of the machinery or mechanism of the technique which met these difficulties and made use of them as points of beauty are worth referring to, though I must repeat that the subject is too complicated and too technical for a proper analysis within our brief space. In decoration by glass, whether painted or not, we meet with a well-known phenomenon, less known, less visible to the painter who paints pictures on canvas or on walls. The artist who uses a piece of blue glass, for instance, where the painter in oil uses a touch or more of blue paint, will find his piece of blue glass change its size and shape at a distance, as opaque colour would not. If he uses other colours, their shapes and sizes, their distinctness and their tones, are all modified by distance. Naturally, too, placed alongside of each other, they not only change in themselves, but they change the appearance of their neighbours.

In some old work, for instance, the shape and the painting of a hand, will be elongated and narrowed because with the glass that they used, and more or less with all glass, the real shape would look too large and too broad. The painting of the older work was arranged to meet these difficulties. We may notice that the idea of representing natural forms, or of making ornament more or less natural, that is to say, to look like a modelled thing, like a thing that is to delude you, is one of the inevitable directions of art. The mere pattern which satisfied the older Eastern workman, such as that of carpets and stuffs, has always passed

into attempts at representing nature. By painting upon pieces of coloured glass the older men could both *simulate* a certain *imitation* of the modelling of real things, and at the same time, by a judicious conventional method of painting, varying according to each different colour, sacrificing very often the real shape, they made a certain picture effect, and they also met the troubles of irradiation. With a greater development of painting with other materials (opaque painting, which is what we usually call painting), came a time when the methods of opaque painting were more or less transplanted to the transparent painting of glass, and necessitated a weaker, less powerful effect, which last tradition has been continued down to our day, into the English windows, for instance.

The lead used to join the pieces of glass together is an important part of the design of the older windows, and their decorative pattern persists even into the Renaissance, so long as the tradition of glass is unbroken. Therefore, this intelligent use of leads persists longer in Northern Europe than in Italy, where even the work of such a consummate designer as John of Udine is meant to do without leads, so that they are merely an ugly necessity. Though the mediæval work, at its best moment, is much painted, it is so in strict connection with the leads which help to form a background. As in all high forms of art, the edge or outline is the part most taken care of. The necessity of the leads was also turned into a beauty by helping to connect the representations or patterns of the design with the edges of the window itself. In many of the earlier and more splendid examples the impression of connection of the window with the wall is so great that the window gives the impression of the wall being translucent and coloured. Later mediæval art insists more distinctly on the edges of the window repeating the shapes of tracery and edges. The fact that, in the representations of nature by painting, things were detached one from another by values and lines, and not by cast shadows, or later by what is called chiaroscuro, is repeated in the picture in glass. The study of shadows by later pictorial art was antagonistic to the representation by values, and in so far destroyed the tendency to use glass as a material for pictures.

The abandonment of mediæval tendencies by the Renaissance implied, at that moment, the abandonment of mediæval methods, and quite logically the latest work of the Renaissance in glass is typified by a light or clear opening in which subjects coloured and painted are hung. Some of it is quite admirable in its way, but is no longer of any importance as affecting the wall.

In the older way the method of laying on the

enamel paint upon the coloured glass was calculated so as not to make the glass dirty or dingy, and thereby detract from the pleasure the eye has in receiving a frank, luminous expression through a crystal medium. The older artists, perhaps from necessity, worked with a small number of principal colours of glass, modifying their tones by relation so as to make more of them to the eye, if not in fact, and using these limitations as a source of that power which attaches to simplicity and repetition.

With the early mediæval artist his picture, as we would call it to-day, that is to say, his intention of making an illustration, will not have been different from his decorative work. He will, like the Chinaman, make a horse blue or red, if thereby the decorative space or picture attains the necessary balance of effect, and patterns keep their place, from the colour values representing, as in nature, atmosphere and modelling.

Later the same general methods were followed, but they were followed with less conviction. Changes were made in methods of execution, probably with a certain notion of improvement, often, from the unfortunate tendency of all art — I might say of all things — to fall into the domain of trade. In that way mechanisms, which have had a reason in their solutions of difficulties, merely become trade recipes; and if the difficulties remain great, the cause of the difficulty is eliminated absolutely by some change of material.

At various times in the later Middle Ages, with changes of style, new departures, not very grave ones, were made; until at the end, in imitation of supposed classical building, such as it was understood in Italy, the stained glass became more or less pale and weak, even when helped, as it was occasionally and very handsomely sometimes, by the use of patches of solid colour, and the beautiful innovation of the yellow stain.

Grisaille Glass. As shown elsewhere, the name " grisaille " is the same as that of " griset," which is the name of the neutral coloured enamel paint, used to model and draw upon the surfaces of glass. There are windows, and very beautiful ones, with no colour, or very little, which belong to this class. There are some very celebrated ones. As I state elsewhere, there are cases of a window being partly in full pot metal colour and the balance in grisaille. The examples and the subdivisions of the subject are too numerous to do more than to mention this separate class, and to point out how originally the grisaille window may have been nothing but the white or colourless glass, joined together by leads. Then patterns of pleasing shapes are placed between leads; and leads and patterns make the design of the window. It was a possible desire for

more light, as a practical question, also a matter of great economy; and lastly, the effect of the tempered white light, passing over the coloured light, adds the veiling which makes the colours of the deeper glass more mysterious. At certain moments the monotony of the absence of colour was relieved by spaces filled with colour. The method has persisted more or less through all the ages of glass painting. In its best example its principle is that first stated in this notice, of the joining of the borders of the window by interlacing of patterns of dark on light; and the more successful pieces are dependent for their beauty upon the combination of pattern which will produce a series of values that fill the space, and avoid, thereby, the monotony of continuous repeated ornaments. That monotony is very much felt in many grisaille windows, to the extent of making them extremely fatiguing to the eye. This annoyance is, as I have just stated, much lessened in those windows in which the arrangement of colourless values has been well understood.

We know that the end of the eighteenth century saw the almost entire disappearance of the art, which had been preceded by attempts at painting on windows in what was thought to be a parallel to painting in oils. The story of the disappointment of Sir Joshua Reynolds, when he had a picture copied upon glass by Jervas, is historical, but may not be, for all that, thoroughly understood.

" I had frequently," said Sir Joshua, " pleased myself with reflecting, after I had produced what I thought a brilliant effect of light and shadow on my canvas, how greatly that effect would be heightened by the transparency which the painting on glass would be sure to produce. It turned out quite the reverse."

To-day one might say, " Well, he should have known better." Nevertheless the principle of the mistake is not, I think, usually grasped. Sir Joshua, like most of us artists, found life too short to make analyses of the principles of light and colour; which even now the scientific man, with all his engines of observation, is only beginning to accomplish for us. Sir Joshua saw indistinctly the ideas belonging to his own art of painting, which is the representation of coloured appearances that we see about us by coloured surfaces, which we make by applying opaque colours to wall or canvas. He confused these fundamental ideas with his own methods of work, his trade recipes, all derived from the practice of painting with oil colour in opaque surfaces, which makes more or less the representation of the shading of things, — that is to say, the dulling of things, — and as it were taking away colour to make shadow. The shadows of things are also colours, and in such a material as glass, which gives a full intensity of lights, and which allows one, in fact, to paint with light, the proper gradation and representation of shading is by other colours of glass to represent the shadows. Consequently his painting on glass, done by the increasing of what he would have called shadows, that is to say, by adding more opaqueness and more dirt, was not the brilliant translation of his painting that he had hoped for. I use Sir Joshua's example — which is not, perhaps, absolutely fair — that we may understand the disappointing effect of transplanting to a transparent surface the exact methods that are meant for an opaque one. Whether Sir Joshua went into an analysis, and whether I have attributed too much or too little to him, is of no consequence as to the facts of that case or similar ones.

The second quarter of the century saw in England a revival of ancient methods, which has continued with laudable results to the present day. I shall make no reference to what was done in a similar way in France and in Germany, especially because one important side which the English tried for was not properly cared for on the Continent, and that is the making of glass fairly similar to the ancient material of the Middle Ages.

Making of Windows. A colour study is made at each moment, as he prefers, of the system of chromatic decoration to be employed by the designer. A full-size drawing is also made, in which the outlines of the figures, pieces of landscape, decorative patterns, etc., are carefully drawn, all of the full size of the intended pieces of glass, and sometimes coloured. Upon this "cartoon," as it is generally called, the pieces of the leads are marked with accuracy, or this is done on separate drawing. The lines of this cartoon are transferred to other sheets of paper, several such transfers being made. One of these transfers is cut up into pieces representing the pieces of glass which are to be cut. Upon another of these transfers the lead lines must be accurately marked, if they have not already been so transferred from the cartoon. Now, as in mediæval times, a drawing or cartoon has to have the lead lines distinctly indicated before the work upon the glass is begun. In the early mediæval directions which we have, the lead lines alone are mentioned. It may even be supposed that in many of the earlier and finer windows there was little indicated in the cartoon besides the lead lines, the painting of the actual pieces of glass being left to the skill and knowledge of the artist, who would probably be the same man who had made the cartoon or transfer upon which the leads were marked. Of course, fragmentary cartoons of parts may be made of one single detail. Upon a large sheet of plate glass, commonly called a *glass easel*, the divided pieces of the transfer, above described, are arranged together, and the artist having previously decided upon the colour of some one of

the pieces of glass in the future window, lays this piece upon the paper pattern at the point where that particular colour is to be used. The piece of paper which has hitherto represented the piece of glass is removed, so that the effect of the glass may be judged by transmitted light. The piece of glass being in this way finally decided, the workman marks upon the glass what he is to cut out, or else places the paper pattern immediately upon it and follows the edges with a diamond. Before the introduction of this use of the diamond, the glass was cut with a hot iron. It should be said, however, that in a good deal of simple work and in much of the work which the English do to-day, the indication of the colour of glass is made on the cartoon, or on some other drawing, by the mere use of letter and number. In very special glass, like the American opalescent glass, there is an unlimited choice, and such simple methods are only for cheap work.

The piece of glass, cut to the right shape, is secured to the glass easel by some cohesive matter, such as wax. The replacing of pieces of paper by pieces of glass of the same size and shape is continued until the entire window, or so much of it as the easel will accommodate, is in place upon the easel, but, of course, without its leads. This process enables the artist to change or modify the colour scheme to almost any extent. If needed, upon these pieces he then paints in enamel colour, which pieces are separately placed in the kiln and fired until the enamel is fixed.

Plating is also used to alter the effect of colour. This means the superposition of one piece of glass upon one or more others, so as to vary the colour or its depth, or the modelling of the gradations of colour contained in it.

After the pieces of glass have all been cut, they are joined together by a lead ribbon, with flanges, having nearly the section of a capital I. The pieces of glass used in plating, which may be two or three thick, are held by lead bars of similar character, especially soldered to the lead of the main surface of the window, or a wider grooved lead is used. The leads are finally secured to iron bars and armatures, by which the window is kept in place in the window opening.

The essential mechanism for stained glass windows is, therefore, of a very simple, almost childish, character. It is more difficult — it is harder work than using a brush with ink to draw with, or a lead pencil, but it is of a similar infantile nature. That does not make it easier.

Let us see how near the description of the method of the monk Theophilus, the oldest document we have on the making of stained glass windows, corresponds with the description just made. Judging by certain parts of the texts, Theophilus may have lived in the second part of the twelfth century. This is his way of making a window : "First," he says, "make a table of wood, level and of such width and length that you may trace upon it two panels of each window." This table is covered with a coat of chalk mixed with water and rubbed with a cloth. On this preparation, when quite dry, the artist traces subjects or ornaments with a stylus of lead or tin. Then, when his line is determined on, he makes it over again, with a red and black outline, put on with a brush between these lines. The colours are marked for each piece by means of a sign or letter. Suitable pieces of glass are placed upon the table, and these lines, which are those of the leads, are traced upon the glass ; after which they are cut with a hot iron and nippers.

Theophilus does not clearly indicate whether he draws on his table what we now would call a cartoon — the complete modelling of figures or ornaments ; he speaks only of an outline. However, when he speaks of painting, that is to say, of putting on enamel paint-work, indicating modelling, on the pieces of already coloured cut glass, he says that one should follow carefully the lines which are on the drawing. This passage, however, relating to such early work, may merely refer to the fact that on these pieces of coloured glass, in very early work, the modelling is little more than certain lines traced in the direction of a form. Though wherever there was a gradation in the glass which the artist could use as modelling, he took advantage of it.

In the gradual attempt to model more delicately, which has slowly gone on through all these centuries, the modelling of the forms represented in the window has come at length to be merely a copying of a delicate, usually a very weak, drawing. This is not to say that in many cases, especially in those which were imitations of archaic work, or continued to be so, there is not some use of hard, firm lines ; but they usually do not connect with the leads in a successful way. These windows are either, as I say, archaic imitations, or are distinctly the representation of a drawing on paper transposed to glass ; and I mean by *transposed*, carried over, not properly translated, as they should be when made in another material. To meet this halfway, the original cartoons are prepared already so as to miss some of the great qualities of drawing on paper, and the weakness is at both ends. Hence we may see in some interesting window, by a superior English artist, a surface of mere drawing, with tints here and there of colour, which is glass, while the intensity and richness of that same artist's work is kept for his paintings in oil or distemper, materials which in their essential nature are less rich, less powerful, than the material of glass.

American Art of Glass. Some account of

the renewal of the art of glass in the United States will be in place, because it has involved an attempt at bringing back into the art of glass the ancient principles which allowed the mediæval artists to make of their windows, monuments as important as those of sculpture and painting, and to use the most splendid way of carrying out the full strength of colour and the strongest expressions of line. An analysis of its origin will serve again as a method of explaining the capacities of the art, which however great in the past, yet offers possibilities not yet attained.

When the American artist first turned his attention to the art of glass and the making of pictured windows, he had one foremost difficulty : the best glass, meaning the material itself, was imported. Even then only poorer samples came here, the better being carefully culled by good European workers. European manufacturers even objected to accepting orders for better material, as injuring the possible sale of the more common sent over. In limited quantities and in limited choice, colour, and substance, some was made here to supplement this need, with the advantage that the making of a few varieties showed that in such a simple manufacture anything could be obtained in small quantity if needed. The imported material seemed to be intimately connected with foreign methods of using it. There were no inferior artists or superior artisans here to copy the cartoons of designers and supply smaller details indicated in the general plan. In Europe such and such men were employed for such a part of the work on a window ; some for ornament, some for figures, and some for drapery, etc.,— all strictly non-individual, and all their ways based on a well-known convention which has reached its furthest limit of development. No *improvement* then could be made on that line.

The first attempts were made with considerable novelty of design and with great attention to the importance of line and composition ; but all the more did the material betray by its thinness the representation of line made by the connecting leads. Nor were there fairly skilled painters to paint upon this poor material of glass, though some artists of higher grade might occasionally attempt it.

Designs were therefore made, which were strictly designs in lead. Here, again, came the difficulty that the cuts, that is to say, the shapes which the glass could assume under the use of the cutting diamond in the mechanic's hand, were extremely limited, and any considerable refinement was too difficult to carry out into anything like practice ; but the idea persisted of drawing with the leads, which, though at first a failure for mechanical reasons, was in itself a novelty for modern times. This development of design, therefore, was one of the first impulses. But, as usual, design cannot be separated in the decorative arts from colour, even in its simplest form of light and shade. The colour of the inadequate material of the glass was not of sufficient *quality* to join harsh edges of glass without the adjoining of painting on glass ; for which, as said before, there were no expert artisans, and only professional artists, too costly to employ often.

The so-called mosaic work implied the necessity of considerable range of what are called values, to be defined as degrees of depth and tone in the quality of the glass ; but this was almost impossible from lack of material.

Hence arose the use of what is called plating, superposing one colour on another so as to increase its depth and richness, to modify its transparency, or to change its tone ; as, for instance, when we plate a colour with its complementary colour, or variation of that complementary. Yet there seemed to be a possible future in a strictly logical order ; that is to say, the use of glass in its purity, untouched by pigment, or added colour, and joined together by leads which should be as carefully designed as the choice of glass itself.

It was at this time that it occurred to the writer that opal glass, then made in this country and used for the imitation of porcelain, but often so badly made as to be more than translucent, suggested a means of meeting the defects of thinness of texture and flatness of colour, and of securing a permanent recall of the necessary complementary colour. The deficient pieces, which were translucent, exhibited that peculiar effect of two contrasting colours, which we call opaline. The making of such glass seems to have been known for an indefinite period, though it does not appear that this glass has been used in this way in window work. After many experiments in having it coloured, in testing its variations in density, the material seemed to be the proper basis for a fair venture into the use of free colour in windows, even when it was used only in small patches, alongside of the English glass, whose flatness was relieved by the opal's suggestion of complementary colour,— that mysterious quality it has of showing a golden yellow, associated with a violet ; a pink flush brought out on a ground of green.

From this moment began a long series of experiments in the making of opal glass, either to recall the tones of mediæval glass, or to increase the number of shades and tones. All the various firms of makers of glass for artistic use in windows have grown out of these first demands and struggles of the first American artists in glass, whose number could be counted twice on a single hand.

With the use of these new materials, necessitating a different handling by the cutter, a finer training and a habit of doing more difficult work became characteristic of the American workshop. The everyday acquirements in that way would have been some twenty-five years ago merely pieces of work such as a master workman might do to show his best skill occasionally. Hence came the possibility of taking up greater refinements of the lead line, — refinements increased by the casting of glass into shapes already laid out, cutting out similar shapes with acid, stamping and moulding the glass into shapes, etc.

With these improvements came the widening and narrowing of leads, the shaping of the leads into irregular forms, so as to imitate the touch of the brush or the different widths of lines. Moreover, the infinite variety of modulations of the opal glass allowed a degree of light and shade for each piece, which not only gave modelling, but also increased the depth sufficiently to allow the darker spaces to melt softly into the harsh lead line.

Painting was almost wholly dispensed with, and the work became a form of translucent mosaic, held together by lead instead of cement. Only the heads, hands, faces — what the trade calls flesh — still continued to be painted, especially because with them expression, an element of design and not of colour, would always be the principal aim.

However, in the anxiety for a thoroughly logical system of doing without any painting, a method was invented by the writer of joining glass without lead, by melting, or of joining exceedingly minute divisions of glass, small as those cut by the jeweller, with threads of finer metal, so that these should become almost invisible at a distance. But the costliness of the process and the great risk involved in firing, with the rude appliances of the American workshop, prevented this method from going further than a few examples. The architects, also, and clients, had not enough experience and knowledge of decorative building to appreciate such a refinement, and there still remains an entire division of this great art of glass to be explored.

It would then seem that the theory of window decoration is that of painting in air with a material carrying coloured light. The first attempts are those we know of the Middle Ages, which *expressed* all that can be done. But they were obliged to work within a narrow limit of material and size of material ; and they had neither the knowledge of representation of form of their classic predecessors, nor their successors of the Renaissance. The later mediævalists fell away in the weakening of all their intentions, and by the methods becoming more commercial. The Italians at the beginning of the Renaissance made a few attempts in the right direction, embodying the general principle of the past work, and introducing some of the results of their study of nature. But the study of form in nature had become so important as to carry even the arts of painting and sculpture with it. The art of glass would logically be one of the very first ones to be neglected, as not being a proper field for such studies ; and indeed all that side of art which we call decoration suffered through its impersonality, and has never again been in complete union with the other side, either experimental art or art as considered as the expression of sentiment. The painters, anxious to express their feeling through the human face, for instance, would wish some method adjusted to delicate fluctuation. And they gradually turned more and more from monumental work.

Historical Styles in Glass. All varieties of art are properly in the state of transition ; so that the division into periods must always have a certain arbitrariness. This is especially so in the case of the art of stained glass, which has covered only a small part of the general history of art. For convenience, it may be well to assume the thirteenth century glass as so connected with the previous work of the twelfth century that we may run them in together as possessing similar characteristics, which are merely extended by practice.

There were stained glass windows, apparently, by the year 1000 at Tegernsee, the earliest example claimed as existing ; and there are a few undecided cases up to the time of the twelfth century, when, toward the middle, we have the glass of the Abbey of St. Denis in France, whose history we know, and which remains to us, but unfortunately subjected to rearrangements. The difference of date of others, a little earlier and a little later, is unimportant. Part of the three great windows above the doors of Chartres, some at Angers, an extraordinarily beautiful one at Vendôme (perhaps 1172), may be cited. In the earlier glass, the most important feature is its deep rich colour, recalling jewels. Notwithstanding, however, there are cases of silvery grayness. There are also grisaille of ornamental pattern. Medallion windows, that is to say, subjects on small scale within medallion shapes set in ornament, are characteristic.

The strong iron bars are, except in the earliest, bent to follow the outline of the medallion. Rose windows occur mostly in French churches. They are mainly circular arrangements of the medallion. Figure and canopy windows are frequently placed in the clearstory and triforium. The protection of the figure by being placed in a sort of niche, which is an ingenious way of connecting the edge of the window with the centre so as to recall architecture, develops later into what are called canopy windows, and in the next centuries, and up to the very end of the Gothic period, become extraordinary features. The border in the early glass was very important, and frequently very broad. In certain cases, as

at Chartres, it is used to tie the design to the wall in such a way that at certain hours of the day the window looks like the wall becoming transparent. This is an example of the principle stated in the beginning of this notice. The ornamental detail is, of course, very conventional, beginning with the Romanesque tradition which in Germany lingers far into the thirteenth century, as at S. Kunibert in Cologne. Heraldry and the personality of the donor are very modestly represented. The glass is very uneven in substance and in colour. The glazing is distinctly of the mosaic type, even if much painted. No large pieces of glass occur. Sometimes masses of one colour are made of many pieces, whence great richness in tone. The painting is of one pigment, strongly marked, as if in the way of a sketch ; and in the more important cases, this manner of suggesting form and expression has a value which more than rivals all possible delicate modulations and recalls the extraordinary charm which the sketches of the great masters had, such as we see in the abbreviations of Rembrandt's drawings or even of Raphael's sketches.

Leads indicate the movement in the same manner of synthesis. Of course this implies, in the greater examples, the existence of remarkable artists, and is not to be given to the date ; for it is impossible to smaller minds.

The early palette consists of white, greenish, and rather clouded ; red, often streaky and ruby-like ; blue, a deep sapphire, and even inclining to violet, down to palest blue. A turquoise blue, which in many of the French windows is still distinctly on the blue ; yellow, quite strong but not reddish ; green, very pure, like emerald, or deep and low in tone, sometimes inclining to olive ; purple, brown-reddish or brownish ; a flesh tint, apparently lighter, and pinker shades of the same colours. Violet does not come until later. Though the palette must have been restricted, accident might have produced almost any colour. It is well to be remembered that from one source alone, iron, any of the colours can be obtained ; and also, in the same connection, that greater fire will vary a colour from red to green or gray.

In the early glass, the painting is thus described by Theophilus, who was supposed to represent the middle of the twelfth century. Bontemps, who has translated him, and who has written on the manufacture of glass and of the making of windows, puts him in the eleventh century. He indicates the composition of a grisaille or enamel colour made of equal parts of oxide of copper and of burnt green and blue glass. This, in powder, is put on with a brush, reserving the lights. Theophilus advises three distinct values, "so that they may seem to be three colours brought near one another" ; this is spoken of with regard to flesh. These gradations should be placed under eye-brows, around eyes, nose, chin, and so forth. We can observe the same process in the printing of the Japanese colour prints, which, indeed, in other tones contain the whole grammar of the early glass colour-scheme.

On these half tints the painter drew with a brush his outlines and shadows. A point was used to take out some lights. After the shadows, an intermediate coating was placed between the lighter shadows and the general clear tone. The painter again took out lights with a point and edged his darkest stroke by a fine line of white. The glass, thus prepared, was placed in the oven in an iron tray, covered with ashes or unslaked lime. They were placed in the oven according to the resisting power of their make. The pieces of glass were placed in lead "cams," joined together by tin soldering; all this differing little from our present methods.

Theophilus gives some recommendation as to the arrangement of colours, such as recommending a white ground if the draperies are coloured; on the contrary, white drapery if the ground is red or blue or coloured. We must remember, continually, that the harmony of colours remained until the sixteenth century a constant preoccupation of the artist; all the more in the earlier period when traditions were most alive. The local colour, or natural colour, is changed, if necessary; as, for instance, the Christ of the Passion, in the great window in Patois, has blue hair. The artist in glass studied, before everything, the values as translated by colour. It may be well to note that Theophilus speaks of France as being specially a home of stained glass, using these words, "whatever in the precious variety of their windows is loved by France."

The glass was cut with a hot iron. The use of the diamond is quite late, perhaps not anterior to the beginning of the sixteenth century. The shape was completed by the use of "grosing," that is to say, breaking off the edges with a kind of nippers. There was some advantage in this over the clean cut of the diamond, as taking a better hold of the cement put into the leads.

With the fourteenth century, or intermediate period, the colour may be described as more lively, and does not divide so distinctly into colour and grisaille. Thus, both are used together in the same window (S. Pierre, Chartres). There are more panels than medallions in the compositions; decorated canopies begin to come into use, at first in flat elevation, and often as the most conspicuous point of the window. The windows have borders, as a rule narrower than before the Tracery lights, which now form an important part of the construction, having borders of their own. There is also a marginal line of white as a natural insistence upon the

shape of the division. This persists to-day in what is called "the white line."

The use of this white line marks a distinct view of the problem of treating an opening, as stated in the first paragraphs of this notice.

Sometimes the white line was broad enough to have a pattern painted on it, or to be broken by ornament or colour. The yellow stain which gives its name to stained glass comes in at this period. It was an important invention, and its complete sinking into the glass separates it from painting by enamels. It is more delicate than pot metal, and helps to brighten these later windows and to do away with the necessity of lead in certain cases. However graceful the figures may be, they are less natural than in the early work, and posed more. There is much use of diaper pattern in background; ornament inevitably becomes more naturalistic; the glass material is more even, sometimes lighter; flesh tint becomes white, and white glass, which before had always been more or less coloured, is now almost white; the painting becomes more delicate; stippling begins to be used at the end of the period.

More green is introduced, and more yellow, and there are combinations of yellow and green. Green is used for background. There is much more olive green. In some German windows, green, yellow, purple, and brown are the main colours. Occasionally pale blue is made green by the yellow stain.

With the fifteenth century, glass is made in larger sheets, is lighter in fact as well as in effect, and white is more used. Canopies become more and more important; the screens behind figures are more and more used, and, of course, the yellow stain becomes more important. Armorial bearings, and the donors of windows, are on a larger scale. Borders are often left out in the canopy designs. Naturally, there is a more curious use of material. The graded glass is used to suggest shading or local colour, or to imitate marble, for instance. Glasses, first blue and later red, are abraded for a white pattern; attempts at landscape and atmospheric effects are made, and occasionally the picture runs through several lights. The colours are higher and sometimes grayer. Red glass is less crimson.

As with the fifteenth century comes the development of the art of painting, the drawing is no longer archaic, and is sometimes excellent. Painting is still more delicate; stippling is used; figures and ornament carefully shaded. Naturally, too, with this development, the lead lines tend to be less a part of the design, and finally do not even convey it; but there remains, even in the sixteenth century, a manner of arranging the leading in a handsome way. This dies out gradually, and is one of the grave deficiencies of modern work. It is to be remembered that there is still a close connection between the painter in distemper or oil, beginning to feel the possibilities of his art, and the artist in glass.

Of this we shall speak later as we pass into the sixteenth century, which brings in the Renaissance of the North. In what we have been considering, we have not brought in the Italian as subject to these styles. The Italian glass does not express its date as does Northern glass. The persistence of the classical feeling is seen in Italian work even of an early date, whose manner recalls the earlier Northern manners, that is to say, a strict mosaic treatment of glass and a scorning of small modelling and detail. It also happens that often the painting upon the glass has been worn away, so that the exact effect of its use cannot be determined. Yet we know that the Italians used paint to attenuate or affect certain crudities of their material.

However unimportant the Italian glass is in quantity, it has carried out almost to the end some of the better principles and finer ways. We do not expect it in such quantities as in the North, for the development of the fresco, and afterward of the painting to be placed in churches, was not favourable to closing out light or modifying it extremely by colour. There are certain points which are what might be expected of the Italian : a certain colouring of such parts as canopy and its frame, which is less bald and obvious than the Northern one. The design is also simpler, and recalls the architectural work of the frescoes. With the development of painting on wall and canvas, it could not be expected that the more difficult material, glass, should equally continue its development, especially with no accumulation of tradition. And it is obvious that the greater artists would inevitably turn to those manners in which they could best and most easily express themselves, as well as continue the study of external nature, of which the art of painting was but one form.

The art of glass, however stupendous in its possible results, is not favourable to the expression of delicate sentiment. Its very power is in its way. As, for instance, in music, the instruments used to express fine shades of meaning are developed singly for that purpose. And yet what few specimens there are of later Italian glass of the fourteenth century are sufficient to show what could be done in glass upon the lines of the development of that period and in a manner connecting thoroughly with the earliest and best work. We can see, also, how completely the painting of the Italian Quattro Cento could be translated into glass. But it would have needed men of the same power as those who worked on wall or canvas. Along such lines there might have been a full continuation, and it is on such lines that the future serious work must go. It is impossible to ask of the artist who is abreast of his time to turn

back and forget the materials of his knowledge. He may insist upon some more than upon others, but that he does in whatever department of technique he works.

In the North the very fact of the existence of a previous method of glass, already somewhat degraded, seems to have interfered with the full expression of the few painters who undertook to work in glass. We shall see this later in the case of Van Orley, at Brussels. He abandons in his glass some of the best developments of the art of painting,

In the sixteenth century, in the North, Gothic traditions survive, even in the furthest Renaissance, perhaps in many cases helping to injure the new style by cramping it, and also by opposing, through tradition, an application of the general principles of painting. It must be owned, however, that the Italian influence in the Renaissance of the North was not of the better kind, and was more or less a side development of painting, destined to destroy it later in its own country. For example, we see how, in that remarkable book, the first treatise on Decoration, the *Hypnerotomachia of Poliphilus*, the beautiful, easy designs of the Venetian artist (which give figures not strictly within the canon of proportion, and ornament largely treated) are changed for the worse in the French edition published soon after. The misunderstood Italian influence on the French draughtsman, traditionally a famous one, J. Cousin, has made him design these small figures over again, so as to give them the requisite "number of heads," and, in general restudy, their anatomy and the probability of their drapery. This is a type of what happened in most of the foreign applications of the new departure in design.

As the separate study of various naturalistic points, perspective, anatomy, etc., became more advanced, certain principles of general design were less noticed. This was the case with all forms of art. The development of the picture as a representation of nature, involving a loosening of the subject in the frame, detached artists more and more from that one principle which I first noted, — the connection with the border. In painting, as we now understand it, this deficiency, if it be one, is not felt, because of the question of tone and chiaroscuro, supplementing our need for line and construction. The decorators, influenced by those Italians whose methods were followed outside of Italy, forgot the traditions and the study of the *values* of colour, which were still carefully kept by the painters of northern Italy and Spain. They therefore abandoned the great principles of decoration that had held in all the decoration of the past, and which, we notice, have been so carefully kept by the Orientals, notably the Japanese. The separation of decorative painting from the art of painting had begun. These general considerations establish the main reasons for what happened, and to them we must add the social and religious disturbances that filled the end of the sixteenth century and a large part of the seventeenth, which necessarily broke up continually the industrial conditions. In the traditions of glass, destruction of windows by religious fanaticism is one of the notes of the change. The gradual wish for more light, which had begun at once with the end of the fifteenth century, and continued increasing, made the practical difficulty of a continued system of design still greater, and as we get into the dry settling of the Renaissance the absence of Roman tradition for window decoration tended to prevent serious attempts at ornamenting windows in the new style.

The increasing division between the artist and artisan is also a sufficient factor for any change or decadence. We are thus prepared to see that the glass work of the sixteenth and seventeenth centuries was neither true to the best principles of previous glass work nor of the best contemporaneous painting. At the same time, a curious attempt at realism involved the trying to imitate the appearance of seeing through the window into a reality — an attempt which was carefully avoided by the great schools of painting. One of the most splendid of these attempts, typifying some of the best late Renaissance work, is the great window of S. Gudule in Brussels. A huge monumental structure fills the greater part of the window, not making a canopy over the subject. Figures stand against it or against the sky, beyond which is a delicate painting on gray blue, giving a considerable effect of reality. This is increased by the shadow of the architectural part. But the result is what it might be in painting : the figures look as if cut out and set up against the distance. This is one of the splendid examples, and a great work of art, notwithstanding the mistakes. It gives the characteristics of Renaissance glass, — monumental work with figures in front, strong contrasts of light and shade, an attempt at accurate perspective, and an attempt at atmospheric effect in the distance, not continued into the foreground. In the early part of the sixteenth century, and in many pieces of more intelligent work later, the shadows are obtained by separate glass and not by mere painting. But the tendency to paint as much as possible was inseparable from the tendency to obtain modelling. The use of enamel colour is also a mark of the period, and probably did not reach its possible results from the fact of the separation of the art of the artist designer from that of the craftsman. Occasionally, in certain places, these two connected, perhaps owing to the tradition of certain families of artists and artisans.

Certain details of style may be indicated : canopy and sometimes a rich frieze and cornice

occasionally filled with subjects. Occasionally the figures are seen *through* the monumental ornamentation. Naturally, the portraits of the donors, sometimes of great beauty of execution, occupied important parts of the window. The spaces of the window above the architectural ornamentation are often merely of clear glass glazed in squares or diamonds, as in S. Gudule above mentioned. Earlier windows have a coloured ground above the Renaissance canopy. The pot metal colours are used for the figures, while white glass is used for the architecture. The delicate distance is painted in landscape, in architecture, and sometimes in figures. This is painted sometimes on white, sometimes on faintly coloured glass. The tracery lights often contain figure subjects. The detail of ornament abandons the Gothic leafage. Screens and draperies have patterns in white and yellow stain, or on ruby or other coloured grounds, produced by abrading the colour and painting and staining the white. Other patterns are stained on the coloured glass, yellow on blue making green, and so forth. The pieces of glass become larger and larger.

In the seventeenth century the art of the sixteenth continues, more and more in the same direction, with more painting instead of coloured glass, with a heavier use of it, and usually less skill, so that its lastingness is less great than that of earlier monuments, and more especially the lead line is in the way, and looks ugly and unnecessary. This, of course, is felt more in the smaller work than in the very large windows.

In the famous windows of Gouda, in Holland, the end of the sixteenth century saw the carrying out of an attempt at realistic rendering, which still preserved a great many traditions of mechanism. They cannot be described in our small space ; but though very deficient in the greater elements of art, that is to say, in line, composition, colour, and moral elevation of character or purpose, they remain examples of what might have been done had their makers been men of genius instead of excellent traditional artisans. Their effect is much enhanced by whitewashed wall, and we must consider also that greater lighting and whitewash had much to do with later windows. The Gouda windows are attempts at using great masses of architecture and landscape, and their reputation is deserved so far as the extraordinary courage with which the artists have carried out the project of what might be called big pictures. But they are distinctly the work of inferior minds. Perhaps had many excellent designers who worked for the Renaissance windows found such men as the Crabeths and their pupils and assistants to carry out their intentions, a more adequate representation of what the Renaissance ideas were capable of might be found. The French draughtsmen of the sixteenth century, and many of the Germans of very high grade, have made designs for glass in themselves extremely beautiful. The names of Aldegrever, of Holbein, of Dürer, of Baldung Grün, and of Jean Cousin are sufficiently important to show how slowly the artists detached themselves from the workman; but though we have many designs remaining, we have no equivalent representations. Occasionally in some of the French windows, notably those attributed to Jean Cousin, one can recognize in actual execution the hand of a better artist retouching the inferior work. Mere mention can be made, but it is essential, of the windows used for private dwellings, as distinguished from churches, wherein, during the sixteenth and seventeenth centuries, the window had merely a space in it reserved for coloured glass. Many of these designs are remarkably successful, both in their intention and in their execution; and even to a very late date in Holland the treatment of these windows is perfectly well adapted to the intention of private dwellings.

In Germany and Switzerland especially, these panels, carrying coats of arms and supporters, or figures acting as such, are very often pleasant works of art and thoroughly well understood in their design and execution.

The painting and enamel which occupies part of them is relieved by the intelligent use of pot metal colours, to give character. The designs of Holbein or Dürer, of Manuel Deutsch, of Baldung Grün, for similar subjects, are the types of that special class of work of which extraordinary examples can be seen at Basle.

The eighteenth century has little to tell us. Leaded glass is still much used. Already with the seventeenth century the making of coloured glass had so declined as to make it occasionally difficult to obtain. The great dislike for the earlier work, or anything that recalled the Gothic, and for splendour of colour, had increased to such an extent that a very intelligent admirer of art, President de Brosses (in his *Journey in Italy*), uses the example of the mosaics of S. Mark as a type of all that is abominable in art. The word "Gothic" became, as we know, a term of reproach. The tendency of religious services to depend on preaching increased to such an extent that the most sacred, from national and religious reasons, of the great windows of Chartres — a window placed by St. Louis, king of France, was taken down so as to allow the preacher of the day to be seen in a clear light. It is true that other reasons of lighting certain modern works of art were also given, and that frequently.

The whole tendency of the temper of the time, in and out of decoration, was one of avoidance of the more solemn sides of art. Perhaps something might have been done had not the end of the seventeenth century already broken

the traditions. Le Vieil, perhaps the only and last of the artists in glass in France in the middle of the century, and the author of an important treatise, remarks that "there are still coats of arms placed in the windows, and through their use we keep up the only practical acquaintance we have with the art of glass painting." At any rate, England alone seems to have kept some intention of trying the effects of glass. The famous windows for which Sir Joshua painted the studies I have referred to elsewhere.

The details of the resuscitation of stained glass, owing to the interest in Gothic art, I shall not go into further than to state that they came to a point of considerable importance about the middle of the nineteenth century.

Before that, in various places, attempts at imitation of older work were made; one of the main difficulties in the way of getting back at the meaning of the old work being in the make of glass itself. The resuscitations were all troubled by the fact that painting on the glass was still considered an obligation, and filled the mind of the artist and his encouragers.

It should be noted that Chevreul, the eminent scientist, called the attention of the architects and designers for glass to the main principles of mediæval work somewhere in the thirties. He explained that they had not understood the questions of the material as affecting colour and light, and that they paid no attention to the use of the complementary colours, which were one of the most important of the ancient factors in use of colour. Also, that they treated the work as they might a drawing more or less tinted. It was, therefore, by no want of warning that the modern artist in glass did not succeed in recalling the principal merits of ancient work. This misunderstanding persists to this day, wherever, even in fairly good work, the whole effect is really translatable into black and white, or gradations of the same. The use of glass as translucent mosaic was not perceived as the main method of getting back to the first principles; and though many imitations and restorations were accomplished, they were, like most restorations and imitations, mechanically done. But a great deal of intelligent imitation was done in England, and still more or less persists. When varied, it has the difficulty of bringing in the newer habits of representation with older habits of design. Some remarkable men have devoted some effort to the art; but those efforts have been limited by the separation of the draughtsmen from the executants in the glass, so that the most famous of these, Burne-Jones, complained to the writer of this article, in 1873, that his designs assumed a commercial shape when translated into glass, though made through the firm of a sympathetic manufacturer and a very intelligent designer himself, Mr. Morris.

The difficulty still persists, and must continue as long as the drawing and cartoon are the main points, and the execution made so easy that, as Burne-Jones noticed, each work could be repeated indefinitely, thereby becoming strictly commercial.

The possible future of the use of glass in windows as decoration is much larger than would seem even yet at present. The general development of its make points to a number of new uses : when the wall itself will be of glass and a large part of the construction. However fitted together, the window may become all the richer. But these considerations are not historical, nor would an appreciation of present or late work, which can be found described in print or is within easy access. Personal motives of proper courtesy also prevent my formulating any judgment.

— JOHN LA FARGE.

Émile Amé, *Recherches sur les vitraux incolores de l' Yonne*, 1854 ; Appert and Henlivaux, *Verre et Verreries*, 1894 ; *La Verrerie depuis vingt ans*, 1895 ; Albert Babeau, *Linard Goutier et ses fils, peintres verriers*, 1888 ; Troyes ; Belhomme, *Status des peintres verriers de Toulouse au XVIe siècle*, 1843, Toulouse ; L'Abbé Blanquart, *Notice sur les vitraux de Gisors, première partie, les peintres verriers*, 1884, Pontoise, imp. de A. Paris (extrait des Mémoires de la Société historique du Vexin, Tome III.) ; G. Bontemps, *Guide du verrier ; traité historique et pratique de la fabrication des verres, cristaux, vitraux*, 1868 ; *Peinture sur verre au XIXe siècle. Les secrets de cet art sont-ils retrouvés ? Quelques réflexions sur ce sujet adressées aux savants et artistes*, Paris, 1845; Bulteau, *Vitraux de N. D. de Chartres ;* Cahier, *Caractéristique des saints*, 1867 ; Cahier and Martin, *Monographie de la cathédrale de Bourges ;* Capronnier, *Vitraux de la cathédrale de Tournay*, 1848, Bruxelles ; L. Charles, *Atelier de verrier à la Ferté-Bernard à la fin du XVe siècle et au XVIe*, Le Mans, 1851 ; L'Abbé Coffinet, *Les peintres verriers de Troyes*, 1858 ; L'Abbé Crosnier, *Vocabulaire des symboles et attributs, Tome XIV du Bulletin monumental ;* E. de Coussemaker, *Vitraux peints et incolores des églises de la Flandre maritime*, 1860, Lille ; L. F. Day, *Windows*, 1897 ; André Félibien, *Des principes de l'architecture, de la sculpture et de la peinture*, 1676, Paris (Chapitre XXI, *Principaux modes d'assemblages usités à cette époque pour le verre blanc)* ; A. Fournier, *La verrerie de Portieux (Lorraine)*, 1886, Paris ; Gessert, *Geschichte der Glasmalerei*, 1839, Stuttgart and Tübingen ; De Grandmaison, *Documents inédits pour servir à l'histoire des arts en Touraine (généalogie des Pinaigrier)*, 1870, Tours ; L'Abbé V. Guerber, *Essai sur les vitraux de la cathédrale de Strasbourg*, 1848, Strasbourg ; Docteur Hafner, *Les chefs-d'œuvre de la peinture suisse sur verre, publiés par la Société d'histoire et d'antiquité de Winterthur, photographiés d'après les peintures originales sur verre, existantes en différents lieux*, 1892, Berlin ; Herberger, *Die ältesten Glasgemälde im Dom zu Augsburg*, 1860, in *Der Himmerschen Buchdruckerei*, Augsburg ; Holbein, le jeune, *L'œuvre de Hans*, photographs of drawings for glass by Braun ; Henry Holiday, *Stained Glass as an Art*, London, 1897 ; Eugène Hucher, *Vitraux de la cathédrale du Mans*, Le Mans, 1864 ; Ingres, *Vitraux de la chapelle Saint-Ferdinand*, 1845 (planches) ; Kunkel, *Glasmacherkunst*, 1756 ; Paul Lacroix, *Peinture sur verre*, in Volume V. of *Moyen Âge et de la Renaissance*, 1848, Paris ; J. La Farge, *The American Art of Glass*, 1893 ; Hyacinthe Langlois, *Essai sur la peinture sur verre*, 1832, Rouen ; Ferdinand de Lasteyrie, *Histoire de la peinture sur verre, d'après les monuments français de France*, 1843, Paris ; M. A. Lenoir, *Traité historique de la peinture sur verre, et description de vitraux anciens et modernes, pour servir à l'histoire de l'art en France*, 1856 ; Pierre Le Vieil, *L'art de la peinture sur verre (dans les arts et métiers de l'Académie)*, 1774, Paris ; Edmond Lévy, *Histoire de la peinture sur verre en Europe*, 1860, Bruxelles ; Lucien Magne, *L'œuvre des peintres verriers français. Verrières de Montmorency, d'Écouen et de Chantilly*, 1885, Paris ; Marchand et les abbés Bourassé et Manceau, *Verrières du chœur de l'église métropolitaine de Tours*, 1848, Tours ; L'Abbé L. Marsaux, *Vitraux de l'église Saint-Martin, de Groslay*, 1889, Paris ; Albert de Méloizes, *Les vitraux de la cathédrale de Bourges, postérieurs au XIIIe siècle*, Bourges ; F. de Mély, *Études iconographiques sur les vitraux du XIIIe siècle de la cathédrale de Chartres*, 1888, Bruges *(extrait de l'Art Chrétien)* ; Mrs. Merrifield, *Original Treatises*, 1849; Oliver Merson, *Les Vitraux*, Paris, 1895 ; L'Abbé Michaud, *Notice sur l'église de Saint-Nicolas de Chatillon-sur-Seine, son origine, son architecture, ses verrières*, Dijon, 1870 ; Aubin Louis Millin, *Antiquités nationales ou recueil des monuments pour servir à l'histoire générale et particulière de l'empire français, tels que tombeaux, inscriptions, statues, vitraux, fresques tirées des abbayes, monastères, châteaux et autres lieux devenus domaines nationaux*, 1790, Paris ; Rondot Natalis, *Peintres sur verre de Troyes, du XIVe et du XVe siècle*, 1887, Nogent-le-Rotrou ; Alexander Nesbitt, *Glass*, South Kensington Handbooks, 1888 ; L. Ottin, *L'art de faire un vitrail*, Paris, 1892 ; Pierre Pelletier, *Les verriers dans le Lyonnais et le Forez*, 1886, Paris ; L'Abbé Perdreau *Guide du visiteur et du pèlerin à l'église Saint-Étienne-du-Mont*, brochure in 16, Paris ; J. P. Schmidt, *Monuments religieux*, 1859 ; C. Schoefer et A. Rossteucher, *L'ornement dans les vitraux du Moyen Âge et de la Renaissance. Vitraux allemands provenant de Marburg, Alterberg, Immenhausen, Nordelhausen, Lingen, Ulm, Augsburg, Strasbourg, etc.* ; R. Sturgis, *Decorative Windows in England and America*, 1896-7 ; L'Abbé Texier, *Histoire de la peinture sur verre dans le Limousin*, 1847, Paris ; *Histoire de la peinture sur verre*, 1850 ; Lemoine Théophile' *Diversarum artium Schedula*, traduit par le comte de Lescalopier, Toulouse, 1843 ; Émile Thibaud, *Considérations historiques et critiques sur les vitraux anciens et modernes et sur la peinture sur verre*, 1842 ; L. C. Tiffany, *American Art Supreme in Coloured Glass*, Forum, XV., 621, July, 1893 ; Villard de Honnecourt, *Reproduction exacte de l'album de V. de Honnecourt*, 1858 ; Viollet-le-Duc, article, *Vitraux*, in the *Dictionnaire raisonné d'architecture ;* John Weale, *Divers Works of Early Masters in Christian Decoration*, London, 1846 ; N. H. I. Westlake, *History of Design in Painted Glass*, London, 1881–1886 ; Charles Winston, *An Enquiry into the Difference of Style observable in Ancient Glass Paintings, especially in England, with Hints on Glass Painting by an Amateur*, Oxford, 1847.

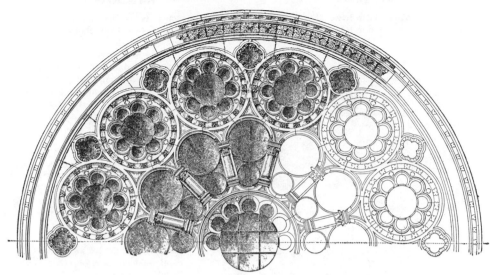

WINDOW, FIG. 23: ROSE WINDOW, CATHEDRAL OF CHARTRES, WEST FRONT, C. 1225.

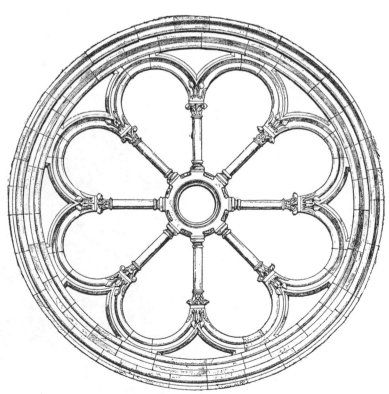

WINDOW, FIG. 24: ROSE WINDOW, WEST FRONT OF CHURCH, MONTRÉAL (YONNE), BURGUNDY; C. 1250.

Catherine Wheel Window. Same as Rose Window (which see under R).

WINDOW, FIG. 25: ROSE WINDOW, BARFRESTON, KENT, C. 1180.

Compass Window. In England, a bay-window of a semicircular or otherwise curved plan ; rare or obsolete in the United States.

Diocletian Window. Same as Venetian Window.

Hit and Miss Window. A window used in stables, the upper sash being fixed and glazed, while the lower half of the window is filled in with two wood gratings, the outer one being stationary, the inner one moving in a groove. The bars of the movable grating are made wider than the openings of the stationary one, so that these openings are completely covered when the inner sash is closed down. — (A. P. S.)

Lancet Window. (See Lancet Arch, under Arch.)

Lowside Window. A window, usually very small, set much below the level of the larger windows, especially in a church, principally English. There is much dispute about the purpose of a lowside window in a church ; all the ecclesiologists agree that it was not originally glazed, but closed probably by solid shutters, and it has been noted that a seat of solid material is often placed immediately within the opening. When the lowside window is very near the chancel, it may have been intended to afford a view of the altar from without; but these openings are found in all parts of the church.

Offertory Window. Same as Lowside Window.

Palladian Window. Same as Venetian Window.

Pede Window. A window in such a posi-

tion with regard to another and larger window above as to be supposed to symbolize one of the feet of Christ.

Rose Window. A circular window divided into compartments by mullions, forming tracery radiating from, or having more or less geometrical relations with, the centre. They are especially frequent in French mediæval architecture, where they occur as the characteristic central feature of the western fronts and transept, fronts which allow great size. They are distinguished by great beauty of detail, geometrical or flamboyant, according to the period of their construction. Some circular windows of the later mediæval cathedrals of France hardly recognize the centre as a generative point for the tracery. (See Wheel Window, below.)

Transom Window. *A.* A window divided by a transom into an upper and lower part.

B. A window above a transom, as in a doorway.

Venetian Window. A window characteristic of the neoclassic styles having an arched aper-

WINDOW, FIG. 27: ROSE WINDOW, BEAUVAIS CATHEDRAL ; C. 1450.

ture, flanked by a narrow, square-headed aperture on either side, separated by columns or pilasters.

WINDOW, FIG. 26: ROSE WINDOW, BEVERLEY MINSTER, YORKSHIRE, C. 1220.

WINDOW, FIG. 28: ROSE WINDOW, CATHEDRAL OF AUCH (GERS), FRANCE; C. 1250. THE SUBJECT OF THE GLASS PAINTING (A GLORY OF ANGELS) IS INDICATED, BUT THE DRAWING IS NOT TRUSTWORTHY.

Wheel Window. A large circular window on which the radiation of tracery from the centre is more or less distinctly suggested. It may be considered a variety of the Rose Window, in which the tracery is more distinctly committed to a spokelike arrangement. Also called Catherine Wheel Window.

Wyatt Window. In Ireland, a square-headed Venetian Window, or a wide window divided into three openings by two mullions.

WINDOW BACK. The ceiling or panelling occurring under a window, between the stool and the floor, and covering the inner face of the breast (see Breast). This is so commonly a piece of panelling that the term "panelled back" is in use.

WINDOW BAR. *A.* A muntin; a division of wood, lead, or iron between the panes or lights of a sash.

B. A bar of wood or iron for securing a casement or the shutters of any window when closed.

C. Same as Guard Bar.

WINDOW BOARD. An inner sill, usually light and thin; a mere covering for the top of a dwarf wall below the window opening.

WINDOW FASTENER. (See Espagnolette ; Sash Fastener.)

WINDOW FRAME. The frame, boxed for sliding sash, or solid and rebated for casement, which is set in a wall to receive and hold the window.

WINDOW GUARD. Same as Guard Bar.

WINDOW LEAD. A slender bar or rod of lead cast with grooves to receive the glass (see Came).

WINDOW LEDGE. The narrow shelf formed by the stool on the inside, or the sill on the outside, of a window.

WINDOW LIFT. A handle secured to the lower rail of a sliding sash to facilitate the raising of the sash ; commonly called sash lift.

WINDOW OPENER. A rod by which a window sash, otherwise inaccessible, may be opened or closed.

WINDOW PANE. (See Pane, *B.*)

WINDOW POST. In framed building, one of the solid uprights between which the Window Frame is set. In the United States it is customary to nail together two studs to make each window post (compare Door Post under Post).

WINDOW SASH. The sash or light frame, generally movable, in which the panes or lights of glass are set.

WINDOW SCREEN. *A.* Any device, especially if ornamental, as the pierced lattice of the Hindus and Arabs, used for filling in all or a part of a window opening ; it usually replaces glass and sash or casement of any sort.

B. Any form of closure, of wire or other material, to prevent insects from entering, or

to obstruct the view of an interior from the outside.

WINDOW SEAT. A seat in the recess of a window between the inner jambs.

WINDOW SEAT IN ALNWICK CASTLE, NORTHUMBERLAND; c. 1310.

WINDOW SHUTTER. A shutter used to darken or secure a window, generally panelled, and hung on each side of the aperture, outside or inside, in one or more folds. When formed of frames with open slats, it is called in the United States a Blind.

WINDOW SILL. The bottom or sill of a window opening ; often the wooden sill of the window frame, as distinguished from the stone or terra cotta sill of the opening.

WINDOW STOOL. (See Stool.)

WIND PORCH. A small vestibule, often temporary, planned to allow the opening of the outer doors of a building without admitting much cold air. (Compare Weather Door, under Door.)

WIND PRESSURE. The force exerted by wind upon any part of a building. This is, generally, matter of inquiry and precaution only in the matter of high roofs, or spires ; as the walls of an ordinary building when built in the common way are not affected by any winds but tornadoes or tropical hurricanes. The force of wind upon a roof is generally considered as a horizontal force, tending to push the roof over ; but it really acts along a line normal to the sloping surface. The tables of pressure are made up in this way ; and, as observation has shown that the winds of the north temperate zone hardly exceed fifty pounds per square foot of a surface normal to their direction (*i.e.*

vertical), the extreme pressures are given as follows by Du Bois, *The Strains in Framed Structures.*

Angle of roof with horizon, 5°; pressure in pounds, 6.6.
Angle of roof with horizon, 30°; pressure in pounds, 33.1.
Angle of roof with horizon, 45°; pressure in pounds, 44.
Angle of roof with horizon, 60°; pressure in pounds, 50.6.

WINE VAULT. Same as Wine Cellar, under Cellar.

WING. *A.* A part of a building, or any feature of a building, projecting from and subordinate to the central or main part.

B. One of the folds of a double door or screen.

WING WALL. In bridge building, a wall carried from one side of one extremity of the bridge proper to retain the earth of the approach. In ancient bridges in flat country, in which the roadway of the bridge itself was carried up a steep incline from either extremity toward the centre, the wing walls were unnecessary, or were small and low.

WINLIN, HANS. (See Erwin, I., von Steinbach.)

WINTER GARDEN. (See Greenhouse.)

WIPE (v.). In plumbing, to apply and smooth off solder when in a semi-fluid condition, by wiping it over the part to be soldered with a pad of leather or cloth.

WIRE CLOTH. A fabric woven of wire, the coarser grades being nettings used for meat safes, strainers, etc., and as lathing for fireproof plastering, and the finer grades being of gauze used for window screens.

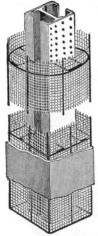

WIRE CLOTH USED FOR LATHING, IN FIREPROOF COVERING OF A STEEL COLUMN.

WIRE GAUZE. Wire cloth of fine texture.

WIRE GLASS. (See under Glass.)

WIRE LATHING. A wire netting, coarser than wire cloth, and used for lathing. (See Metallic Lath, under Lath.)

WIRING. The process of fitting and placing wires in buildings, as for bells. (For Wiring, Electric, see Electrical Appliances.)

WITEL, VAN. (See Vanvitelli.)

WITH; WITHE. A wall dividing two flues in a chimney stack, generally composed of a single thickness of brick.

WITNESS LINE. In drawing, same as Reference Line.

WITNESS POINT. Same as Reference Point.

WITTE, PIETER DE (PETER CANDID); painter, sculptor, and architect; b. 1548 (at Bruges, in Belgium); d. 1628.

Peter's father, Elio Candido, was a Belgian bronze caster associated with Jean Bologne (see Bologne). The family name, de Witte (White), was translated into Candido in Italy, and became Candid in Germany. Peter Candid appears first in 1572, associated with Georgio Vasari (see Vasari) in his decorative work in Rome and afterward in Florence. In 1586 he attached himself to the court of the dukes of Bavaria at Munich, and was one of the chief movers in the introduction of Italian art into Bavaria, which followed the admission of the Jesuits in 1559. He was especially employed upon the extensive improvements undertaken by the Elector Maximilian I. at the *Residenz* in Munich. He continued the decorations of the old *Residenz*, and built and decorated the new palace which was added by Maximilian I. between 1607 and 1617. In 1619 Candid made designs for the decoration of the ceiling of the Golden Hall of the *Rathhaus* in Augsburg, which was actually executed by Mathias Kager. The designs are still in the cabinet of engravings at Munich. He painted altarpieces in the Jesuit church of S. Michael, at Munich, and designed the statue of S. Michael on the façade of that building. In 1604 the Elector Maximilian I. established a manufactory of tapestry, which was placed in charge of Peter Candid.

Dr. P. J. Ree, *Peter Candid sein Leben und sein Werke*; Lübke, *Geschichte der Renaissance in Deutschland*; *Allgemeine deutsche Biographie*; Seidel, *Königliche Residenz in München*.

WOGT, CONRAD; architect.

In 1480 he succeeded Jost Dotzingor (see Dotzinger, J.) as architect of the cathedral of Strasburg (Elsass, Germany), and held that office until 1484.

Gérard, *Les Artistes de l'Alsace.*

WOLLATON HALL. In Nottinghamshire, and close to the town of Nottingham; an Elizabethan house, little altered, and having one feature very remarkable among English country houses. Wollaton has a lofty central tower, rising, like the donjon of a mediæval strong castle, above the lower buildings. This tower is occupied within by a great hall which is 60 feet high and about the same length. The original timber-framed roof is preserved, and the lighting of the hall is by large windows high up beneath the arches of the roof.

WOOD. That part of the substance of the trunks and branches of exogenous trees which is inside of the bark and the soft alburnum which comes next to the bark, and outside of the pith. Those trunks or branches in which there is much pith or soft central body hardly furnish wood, in the ordinary sense, for in most trees the pith becomes unimportant and almost unnoticeable by the time the dimensions are sufficient to allow of cutting for timber. By extension, the trunks of certain palms (endogenous trees), when used to replace wood in the more usual sense : they make excellent posts, beams, bars, and the like, when used intact or nearly so, as is common in many tropical lands. Bamboo (a grass), and rattan (a peculiar variety of palm) in its many varieties, are also used for purposes to which their peculiar lightness and great comparative strength fit them well.

Wood is to be considered as a solid substance capable of being cut and shaped to almost any extent without losing its strength by such treatment, provided the grain is kept continuous for a sufficiently great distance. As the fibres which give strength to the material lie almost altogether in the direction of the length of the trunk or branch, and as the adherence

FIG. 1.

between these fibres in the opposite direction is limited, the workman who cuts away too much or cuts too deeply into one part of the stick risks the strength of the whole, because he greatly increases the danger of partial splitting. A familiar example is the ordinary axe helve, which must be rived out of the solid plank, and only carved into its peculiar shape, with care taken to preserve intact the full strength of the stick measured by its smallest cross-section ; axe helves which are turned or cut by machinery out of the solid are altogether untrustworthy, because many of them have the grain running diagonally across the finished helve, which therefore will break almost at a touch.

In consequence of these characteristics, wood, when used for engineering purposes and for the ordinary framing of houses, when this is to be concealed by sheathing and plastering, is selected with a view to the straightness of the grain. There is, of course, no object in cutting away any part of the piece of timber, sill, post, stud, brace, plate, or the like, for in the case of the engineer's work, there is no appeal to architectural effect, and in the case of the ordinary frame building the construction is concealed. It is enough to see to it that the pieces which take the weight and resist the strains to which the structure is to be exposed shall have no

interruption in the regular run of the grain from end to end of each piece. If a piece come on the ground which is seen to have the grain running diagonally across it so as to make it easily breakable, it will be rejected, or cut short and used for exceptional purposes, as for jack

FIG. 2.

rafters, or short diagonal braces. Knots are objectionable, chiefly because of the twisted grain which accompanies and surrounds them. In some woods, as in the different yellow pines of the Southern states of the United States, the grain is very visible, forming narrow stripes of darker and lighter colour ; and these, when parallel and nearly straight, form what is called Comb Grain, considered a mark of sound material.

On the other hand, what are called knees, less common in house carpentry than in shipbuilding, are cut from wood taken at the place where a branch leaves the trunk (see Knee, A ; also Vol. I., col. 779). If enough of the wood be left to hold the knotted and twisted parts well together, these pieces have great strength.

In view of these requirements and limitations, the preparation of the wood for the workmen is important. In the illustration (Fig. 1) the piece of plank is badly cut and badly laid, because there is a strong tendency for the whole face, which is turned toward the

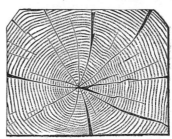

FIG. 2A: A PIECE OF HEWN TIMBER WHICH HAS CHECKED IN DRYING.

middle of the trunk and which here is turned uppermost, to split away in large flakes. This plank would be better if laid with the other side up, but it is a poor piece of wood. In ordinary flooring the planks which show comb grain in narrow, nearly parallel, stripes, are good, and will keep their consistency for centuries, because they are the pieces which have been cut with their sides in the direction of the medullary rays, as explained below ; while those in which a broad piece lies flat on the surface have no endurance, the broad piece, as in the plank in Fig. 1, splitting off with the greatest ease, and sometimes by the mere action of shrinkage, so as first to form long splinters and then to break away. This is the reason why Quarter-sawed Wood is preferred (see that term). Let Fig. 2 be the section of a trunk sawed in the usual way ; of this only those boards or planks which lie upon or near the middle of the trunk are good, because in the

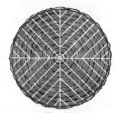

FIG. 3.

others the tendency before spoken of, to split or separate, is very great, and also because the tendency of all logs is to check from drying, the checks opening in the direction of lines radiating from the centre. Quarter-sawing (see that term ; also Clapboard) is resorted to, therefore, as shown in Fig. 3, and the planks are taken out as nearly as possible in the direction of the possible checks. This, which gives beauty to wood used for joinery, marquetry, and the like, gives strength also to timber and planks which are to undergo severe strains. The silver

FIG. 3A: A METHOD OF SAWING BY WHICH WIDER PLANKS OR BOARDS ARE GOT THAN IN FIG. 3 — BUT SLOW AND AWKWARD ; USED FOR VERY PRECIOUS WOOD.

grain, which is caused by what botanists call the medullary rays, is not often visible in soft woods ; it is more seen in hard wood trees, and most of all in oak, in which it is a special characteristic.

For ornamental work in joinery and furniture, the wood which is unfit for framing may be the best. A twisted grain, making an untrustworthy post or joist, may be so beautiful that the piece is saved for careful seasoning and for the finest cabinet work. This is especially true of veneers, which are cut out of knots, roots, and even excrescences caused by disease or injury to the trunk.

Soft wood is usually considered as that of a

certain number of coniferous trees, as white pine, larch, fir, spruce, and hemlock, in their many varieties ; but the wood of certain coniferous trees, as the Georgia pine (called also long-leafed pine — *Pinus australis* and *Pinus palustris*) and several other varieties, are hard, giving as much trouble to the workman as the nut trees and the oak. Hard wood generally, however, is that of the broad leaf trees, most of which are deciduous, just as most of the coniferous trees are evergreen.

It is so common to build with wood by ordinary rule of thumb and without close calculation, that the framing of walls, partitions, roofs, floors, and the like hardly differs at all in principle, and differs but slightly in the size of timbers used, whatever wood is to be employed. The log cabins of Russia and the solid built châlets of Switzerland (see Châlet ; Log House) are indeed of soft wood, but those of the Northwestern states of America and Canada are commonly of hard word, and the treatment is nearly the same. It is noticeable, too, that while the soft larch, so abundant in Switzerland, was used for the solid-built timber houses alluded to, the extremely hard oak of the Jura and Vosges mountains and of the forests which once existed in many regions of the north of France was used in the very complex framing of the fifteenth and sixteenth centuries. (See Pan de Bois ; Wood, Construction in, Part I. ; also illustrations, Half-timbered and House, where Fig. 11 is the simple Swiss work, and Fig. 9 the complex and elaborate French work, involving a great amount of skilled manual labour put into the hardest wood.) It is, therefore, useless to seek any immediate influence exercised upon the architectural design by the kind of timber used. The general tendency to use sticks a little greater in either transverse dimension is all that is traceable to the use of softer or weaker material.

In carpenter work wood is not often seasoned as well as it should be. In the United States it is hardly seasoned at all, the stuff being cut and piled up for a few months or weeks until an order comes for its shipment. The seasoning needed for ordinary framing is that of the open air, where the boards or scantling are usually piled with small strips between the pieces to allow the air to circulate. The absence of such seasoning is the great cause of the sudden settling of floors, disturbances in the equilibrium of walls, and cracks in the plastering of partitions within. For when a stick shrinks it, of course, releases to that extent the pieces which abut upon it, either at right angles to its length or diagonally, as in the case of braces ; and a whole partition, even if carefully framed, may lose its integrity by the shrinking of its separate pieces.

For joinery and ornamental work of all kinds

it is customary to season wood by artificial drying, a process usually described as kiln-drying. It is customary to shape the piece of wood approximately according to its future size, then to glue a piece of paper over each end in order that the drying shall not proceed more rapidly where the end grain is exposed, and finally, to put the whole into a chamber heated to 150 or 175° Fahr., which chamber should, if possible, be ventilated so that a slight current of air may be kept up. Wood dried in this way is, of course, very ready to absorb moisture, and it commonly happens in our hasty building that the benefits of the thorough seasoning are lost by the bringing of the wood into a damp unfinished house, where the plastering has not yet lost its moisture. One sees a stout plank, as of oak, which has been thoroughly kiln-dried and which is so secured in a massive piece of framing that it is no longer free to expand, bent to a curve like that of a bow, with perhaps 3 inches of versed sine in a length of 2 feet, by exposure "over Sunday" in a damp building. It is, however, almost impracticable to prevent this; the owner is always urging on the speed of the work, nor is he often willing to admit that it is worth three months' delay to let his seasoned joinery work lie until the house is reasonably free from moisture.

As regards the kinds of wood most in use: in the United States white pine (*Pinus strobus*) has always been the favourite wood from the Great Lakes and the Mississippi southward and eastward, but since the great rise in the price of that wood, spruce (*Abies* of several species) and hemlock (*Abies canadensis*) are used for all kinds of framing, and white pine is reserved for inside finish; while siding, clapboards, and the like, though best of pine, are passable when made of spruce. Shingles have been made at different times of all the soft woods of coniferous trees, the preference being generally for cypress (*Taxodium*), since that wood has been cut in the Southern states. In Great Britain fir (*Pinus sylvestris*) is used, and is brought from Scandinavia, eastern Prussia, and western Russia. Larch (*Abies larix*), which grows freely in the Alps and in the northern Apennines, is used freely in Switzerland and the Tyrol, where wooden building has always prevailed. Cypress has only recently come into use in the United States, and that at a time when chosen wood was already in such demand and so costly that there have been but few frames built of it in the North. It is curiously durable under circumstances which destroy most woods rapidly, that is to say, in cellars and the like, where there is dampness and especially variable quantities of moisture present in the air. Redwood is very soft and is fit for every purpose that white pine is good for. It has even certain advantages over white pine, as in being less liable to great swelling and shrinkage. Selected qualities of redwood are brought to the East for purposes of joinery.

As to the hard woods, they are used for framing when soft wood is not easily obtainable. Thus, previous to 1865, and throughout the Western states from Iowa and Wisconsin west, hickory or walnut or chestnut were used for framing, and also for flooring and siding almost exclusively. Chestnut is the most durable of the hard woods commonly in use, and as it is also less hard than oak and ash it is a favourite for some kinds of rough work; thus, it is used for railway sleepers, and in the same manner for sleepers in cellar floors and the like. Locust, however, is the best of all woods for this purpose, and is almost imperishable; but it is rarely found of great size, and is scarce in most parts of the country. Black walnut was so much in favour from 1855 to 1875 that nearly all the interior finishing of costly houses, doors, trim, sideboards, and the like, were made of it, and good qualities reached a very high price. It is now out of fashion in the United States, and oak has taken its place. White oak is by far the most common, but red oak, which has a beautiful colour, is as suitable for interior finish, except where very delicate work with carving and minute mouldings are required. Maple and birch are always in use in a moderate way, as they are called for by persons who desire light-coloured wood for furniture or interior fittings; and butternut, which is softer and has a pretty light brown colour, is used in the same way, the difference of cost being considerable when the work is complete. Ash, which is seldom used for delicate joinery in the United States, is in constant demand to help out work in oak; thus, if a contract is for a staircase of oak, it is very probable that the balusters will be made of white ash in the hope that the superintendent will not discover the difference. — R. S.

Bass Wood. That of the lime tree (*Tilia*); so called because of the use of the fibrous inner bark under the name of bass. It is not much used in framing. Its peculiar merit is in its close grain, and in its permanence when once seasoned, as it does not warp or shrink.

Bay Wood. That of the laurel tree; and as this is seldom used in building, a light red wood supposed to resemble laurel wood, and brought from different tropical countries and used in the United States to replace mahogany. It is softer than mahogany, and is thought by some to be a variety of cedar.

Brazil Wood. That of the tree *Brauna* or *Garauna*; brought from South America and used for veneer, which is of brownish red colour, and very beautiful in its veining.

Heart Wood. The duramen, the matured and solid wood of the trunk between the pith and the alburnum. (See definition of Wood, above.)

Sap Wood. The alburnum; the as yet immature wood of recent growth, immediately within the bark.

Satin Wood. A brilliant yellow wood with a beautiful grain of which veneers are made for delicate furniture. It is the product of several tropical trees belonging to different genera, and brought from India, the West Indies, and recently from Australia and New Zealand.

Teak Wood. That of the tree *Tectona* ; indigenous to Burmah and neighbouring countries. It was the favourite timber for shipbuilding in the British navy, and more anciently in the fleet of the English East India Company. If the forests are allowed to grow up now that the shipbuilding is largely of iron, this wood might become cheap enough for use in all parts of the world for superior joinery, as it has a very pretty light brown colour of various shades, and is singularly durable.

White Wood. In the United States, the wood of certain kinds of poplar, especially the tulip tree. Also, by extension, of the bass wood and other kinds of linden or lime tree. In the former sense it is the wood of greenish white colour having little visible grain, moderate softness, and considerable endurance, which is largely used for the inner parts of well-made furniture. The drawers, shelves, and lining of such pieces of furniture are often composed entirely of white wood when the exterior is to be of richer coloured woods, either solid or veneered upon the white wood itself.

WOOD BRICK. A piece of wood of the dimensions of a brick, built into a brick wall to afford a nailing for furring or wood finish.

WOOD CARVING. (See Carving; Sculpture.)

WOOD, CONSTRUCTION IN. Building with wood, usually in solid timber, and in Europe, usually by some of the processes included under Framing. Apart from the European methods and their results, the most important development is that found in the ancient temples of Japan. (See Japan, Architecture of; Switzerland, Architecture of.)

Part I. The woodwork of the Romans is only known to us indirectly through the evidences contained in painted wall decorations, in such sculptured bas-reliefs as occur on the column of Trajan, and more especially through the descriptions of Vitruvius (see, also, Choisy, op. cit., Chap. III.). Their vast erections of mortar masonry in rubble and brick, the remains of which are to us the chief visible indications of their genius in construction, have naturally so preoccupied our minds, that we are not accustomed to regard them as equally skil-

ful in the production of more perishable, but probably hardly less important and interesting, work in timber and carpentry. The immense domains covered by primeval forests which were added by conquest to their Empire, gave them an abundance of timber, which they knew how to shape and use in bridges and military works of great extent ; and the detailed descriptions by Vitruvius of the construction of his own basilica of Fano show, not only that they often used wood in the construction of their entablatures and epistyles, but were familiar with difficult problems of roof framing, and knew how to make them an effective part of an architectural scheme. We have evidence also that a large part of their cities was originally of wood construction, and that even their public monuments, such as amphitheatres and bridges, were primitively of this material ; and the temporary wooden centrings, upon which their immense vaults and domes of masonry were built, could not have been framed and supported without a knowledge of carpentry at least equal to that required in the construction of visible timber roofs over their unvaulted halls. It is probable that the general characteristics of these roofs survived in those of the early Christian basilicas of Rome, which were composed of a series of massive trussed rafters of the simplest character, with little or no attempt at decoration, sometimes left open and naked, and sometimes concealed by panelled ceilings with deep coffers and embellished with carving and colour. It is evident that the constructive character of all these roofs was fundamentally controlled by the degree of inclination of the slope, which never materially varied from that of the classic gable. This traditional low inclination of the roof was maintained with no essential variation through the Romanesque period, until imperative exigencies of construction which developed in the mediæval period, as we shall presently note, forced the roof to assume a steeper pitch.

But meanwhile, in Oriental countries and in the states of North Africa, traditions much more ancient than those of Greece or Rome created the flat or terraced roof, which remains the characteristic form in all regions where a hot and dry climate prevails. This form necessitated a construction of wooden posts and horizontal beams supporting terraces of earth, clay, tiles, asphaltum, etc., with parapets, the external walls alone being of durable and monumental material. In Syria, Egypt, and the Barbary States, in Spain, and in the Spanish colonies of America and the tropics, this persistent type still gives to the modern, as it did to the ancient city, its distinctive horizontal sky lines, broken only by the domes, the minarets, or campaniles of its religious buildings, and still upon the terraced roofs the .household life, as among all Oriental peoples, swarms to enjoy the coolness of the evening.

Among the most characteristic forms of Roman constructions in wood which survived through the Romanesque period, probably with little change, were buildings framed with heavy, squared timbers, generally of oak, the showing in relief against the plaster filling or parquetting of the panels, where these were not left open for windows or latticed casements. In the cities these buildings were often framed with the successive stories overhanging those below, with supports of moulded corbels. These visible timbers were frequently richly carved

WOOD, CONSTRUCTION IN, PART I., FIG. 1: INTERIOR HALL OF NURSTED COURT, KENT; 13TH CENTURY.

From the stone pillars there start uprights to support purlins, and diagonal braces which help support purlins and also carry transverse beams. From the centre of the transverse beams slender posts carry a plate upon which the collar beams rest. Except for the free use of diagonal braces this construction is very unscientific, but heavy timber and thick walls carry it through.

interstices being filled with some form of beton or coarse white plastering. This method of building in wood was brought to perfection in the half-timbered houses of the Middle Ages (see Pan de Bois). It consisted of massive horizontal beams or plates bearing the floor framing, supported at frequent intervals by vertical posts and braced with straight or curved braces. This framing was always visible, with mouldings and chamfers wrought in the solid. The conspicuous panelling thus formed was infinitely varied by the disposition of curved or arched braces. Sometimes, especially in Elizabethan houses in England, these panels were formed in a succession of trefoils and other foliated patterns or arabesques more or less capricious, and the plastered or rough-cast spaces between the timbers were often stamped, while plastic, with decorations of diapers or ornamental strap work (see Parget ; Parget Work). The timbers were framed with mortise and tenon, the joints being fitted together with great precision and secured by oak pins, never by spikes or bolts. The old towns of Europe, up to the end of the Elizabethan era in England, were composed almost exclusively of half-timbered houses, the successive stories,

Old Hall (see Cut II., Col. 345) in Cheshire, often presented framework of elaborate decoration with wide bays filled with casement windows. Often these structural frames were visible in the interior, and the floors, constructed of heavy squared timber, were framed to form panelled ceilings, frequently richly carved. The concealment of these structural frames by plaster and panelled wainscots or

WOOD, CONSTRUCTION IN, PART I., FIG. 2; MAISON DU POIDS ROYAL; SAINT LO, FRANCE.

crowned with gables, overhanging the narrow streets. Many of these interesting structures still remain in Rouen, Lisieux, Bruges, Ulm, Louvain, Antwerp, Brussels, Nuremberg, and Strasburg, on the Continent, and the counties of Salop, Chester, and Stafford, in England. The gables were often decorated with deep barge boards, profusely enriched and carved, and the corbellings were frequently wrought in grotesque forms. The Elizabethan half-timbered manor house, as, for instance, Moreton

ceilings in interiors, and by plastering, tiling, or other forms of covering on the exteriors, rarely occurred before the close of the sixteenth century, when the era of the Renaissance introduced new ideals of architecture, in which structural decoration ceased to play a dominant part. Traditions of honest carpentry in visible timbering lingered among the builders of Northern Europe even to the end of the seventeenth century. In fact, the vital energy of the mediæval spirit, which developed a true architecture from construction in stone, was hardly less successful in creating characteristic style from wooden framing.

By far the most brilliant demonstration of the mediæval spirit in wood construction is exhibited in the framing of the roofs. In Romanesque and mediæval architecture the construction of roofs may be divided into two classes: viz., those which were intended to cover stone vaulting and were unseen from below; and those which were intended to be visible and to form an essential part of the architectural scheme. In the latter class may be included roofs of which the structural supports are wholly or partly concealed by flat ceilings, often panelled in wood, as in the basilica of S. Maria Maggiore, at Rome.

Most of the Romanesque work remaining to us reveals the preoccupation of the builders to recall in the roof structure the main characteristics of Romanesque stone vaulting. This was accomplished in many cases by making the tie beams massive enough to support the feet of curved braces so disposed as to give, in the succession of the trusses, an arched effect. The various members were decorated with chamfers, chamfer stops, and mouldings wrought in the solid, not applied, and often were treated with colours, as in the restored basilica of S. Lorenzo fuori le Mura at Rome. As the proper function of the tie beam is not to bear weight, but simply to prevent the principals from spreading, this system was unstructural and was only practicable in roofs of small span. An example of this primitive and unscientific method is exhibited in many of the cuts given under Roof. In later constructions, especially in the great halls of feudal buildings, where the span was so considerable that it became impracticable, even with the resources of the virgin forests at command, to make the tie beam massive enough to support the arched braces, which seemed to be indispensable to the mediæval builders, they made the roof much steeper, so that the arched braces could start more properly from near the wall ends of the tie beam, thus relieving that member and giving a wider span to the arch. It is apparent that the steep roofs of the thirteenth century owe their origin in great part to this structural condition.

The next step in the evolution of the arched truss of the Middle Ages was evidently suggested by the fact that the extreme steepness of the roof, by reducing the tendency of the rafters to spread, rendered less necessary the tie beam connecting the feet of the principals; accordingly, in the latter part of the fourteenth century, the builders began to cut away the central part of the tie beam, leaving the two ends in the form of short horizontal beams projecting from the top of the wall. Into the outer end of this beam was framed the foot

of the principal rafter; from the inner end sprang the great arched brace, the full development of which was the principal formative element in the truss and beneath it a smaller arched brace, starting from a corbel built into the wall below, or from a wall shaft, enabled the beam to do its important work of support. This member was often carved in the form of a winged angel bearing an escutcheon. One of the boldest and most beautiful examples of this early use of the hammer beam occurs in the nave and transepts of the cathedral of Ely; and the English carried the system of hammer beam construction to its highest development in the fifteenth century. Important specimens of this characteristic English carpentry are in the roof of Eltham Palace hall, 36 feet span; of Hampton Court, 40 feet span, and of Westminster Hall, 68 feet span. The latter is an example of the boldest, most elaborate, and most beautiful carpentry of the Middle Ages. (See Plate XXXVI.: Hammer Beam, under Beam.)

The covering of stone vaulting with wooden roofs for protection from the weather presented to the carpenters of the Middle Ages a different problem. At first the protective covering was laid directly upon the upper surface of the vault, but on account of the rapid deterioration of the masonry through the infiltration of water, it was soon found necessary to build timber roofs over them independent of the vault. The inconvenience of constructing these roofs with tie beams, requiring the building of the walls to the height of the crown of the vault, soon became apparent, and the total abolition of the tie beam in such cases and the construction of a roof frame, which should envelop the vault, and yet be independent of it, presented to the builders a practical problem which they proceeded to solve in various ways. Though the various devices employed to accomplish this object in covering the nave vaulting of the great cathedral were sometimes, from the point of view of modern carpentry, unscientific and clumsy, the builders generally displayed great boldness, skill, and practical efficiency in the work, and they met the constantly varying conditions of the problem with an ingenuity which modern carpentry with its greater resources and experiences could hardly excel.

The distinctive methods of wood construction in the Oriental countries, in Scandinavia, Russia, Switzerland, and the Tyrol, all derived from ancient traditions, are treated under the proper geographical terms, and under Châlet; Log House.

Since the Renaissance the principles of the king-post and queen-post truss, as briefly described under Roof, have been indefinitely expanded and adapted to an infinite variety of uses (see Cuts 1 and 2 under Roof). Elaborate

WOOD, CONSTRUCTION IN, PART I., FIG. 3: HOUSE AT RUETI. SOLID BUILDING OF SQUARED TIMBER OR THICK PLANK, SIMILAR TO A LOG HOUSE. THE VERTICAL RIDGE IN THE MIDDLE OF THE GABLE WALL DENOTES A PARTITION. OUTSIDE SHUTTERS SLIDE HORIZONTALLY.

and sometimes complicated variations of those types have been used in the wide spans of churches and public halls, of theatres, markets, railway stations, and in Mansard roofs. Sir

WOOD, CONSTRUCTION IN, PART I., FIG. 4.

Christopher Wren and his followers in the eighteenth century showed great skill and ingenuity in adapting the principle of the king or queen post truss to the framing of church roofs, in which the visible ceilings were flat, arched, or vaulted in plaster. A characteristic example of these adaptations may be seen in the roof of the church of S. Martin's in the Fields, Westminster, designed by Gibbs, and in the roof of old Drury Lane Theatre, built at the close of the eighteenth century. The work of Philibert de l'Orme, named below, may be consulted for information concerning the characteristic carpentry of the French builders in the sixteenth century, their method of framing domes or curvilinear roofs, with rafters built up with several thicknesses of shaped plank and bolted or spiked together, being especially noteworthy for simplicity and strength.

In modern work constructions in carpentry are rarely used in the trusswork of wide spans, framings of iron and steel being substituted.

Choisy, *L'Art de Bâtir chez les Romains;* Philibert de l'Orme, *Nouvelles Inventions pour bien bâtir à petits Frais*, Paris, 1561; Gwilt's *Encyclopædia of Architecture;* Viollet-le-Duc, *Dictionnaire;* Articles Charpente,*Pau de Bois;* Rondelet, *Traité de l'Art de Bâtir*, 8th ed. 1838–1855, and Supplement; Bötticher, *Holzarchitectur des Mittelalters;* Sanders, *Carved Oak in Houses and Furniture;* see also Bibliography of Switzerland.

WOOD, CONSTRUCTION IN; PART II.

The log house of the early settlers of North America was, with the advance of civilization, succeeded by massive framed constructions of squared and hewn oak timber, following, as closely as the conditions of the New World would permit, the contemporary or recent traditions of the mother country. These constructions gave to the old colonial domestic architecture of America an aspect of dignity and permanence, not readily secured in the lighter, less spacious, and more economical methods of building which have since been developed. In fact, the difference between the old and new methods is largely responsible for a distinct evolution of style. This difference resulted mainly from the discovery that increased strength of construction could be obtained with a far smaller expenditure of material and labor; thus, in floor construction especially, it was found that far greater stability could be secured by using thin planks set on edge and regularly spaced as joists and connected by bridging, than was obtained by our forefathers in their laborious and costly framed constructions of heavy squared and hewn girders, supporting smaller squared tim-

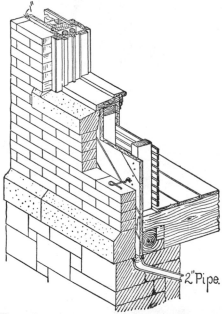

WOOD, CONSTRUCTION IN, PART I., FIG. 5. STRUCTURE OF A FRAME HOUSE FACED WITH FOUR INCHES OF BRICKWORK AS DESCRIBED IN TEXT.

bers mortised into them at right angles six or eight feet apart, these spacings in turn being subdivided by still lighter squared scantlings, upon which complex the wide flooring boards of our ancestral homes found at last a fairly substantial bearing.

When the improved machinery of the saw-mills began economically to convert forest timber into heavy scantlings of any desired dimensions for sills, girders, posts, plates, purlines, and truss timbers ; into studs 2 inches by 4 inches and 2 inches by 6 inches ; into planks from 2 to 4 inches thick and from 6 to 14 inches wide for joists and rafters ; into inch boards of various widths for the covering of house frames ; into thin shingles for roofs or walls ; into clapboards or sidings for the outer covering of walls alone ; and into light laths to form a good key for plastering,— the builders were furnished with an abundance of cheap material admirably adapted to economical wooden structures, suited for every condition and scale of living, for storage and shelter of every sort, including even churches and public buildings. As the system of construction which was presently developed from these conditions imposed practically no limit of shape or size, and was very inexpensive, it was more elastic for the expression of any caprice of the builders, or of any prevailing whim of design, than any other system known. But on the whole, though thus peculiarly subject to architectural aberrations, and to temporary fashions, more or less whimsical and unreasonable, it has, through the efforts of trained architects, become so well disciplined by its application to conditions of comfort and use and decent living, that its results may be considered as an illustration of a healthy evolution of style consistent with an infinite variety in form.

The usual specifications for this structure include a sill varying from 6 by 6 inches to 6 by 8 inches, bedded solidly near the outer edge of the foundation walls, bolted or rebated together and pinned with oak pins at the joints and angles. Girders of various dimensions according to service, corresponding with the main divisions of the plan and crossing the area of the basement or cellar, are carried upon intermediate piers, or posts of brick or wood ; upon these girders and upon the inner edge of the foundation walls bears the framing of the first floor, composed of joists 2 inches thick, and from 8 or 10 inches to 12 or 14 inches deep, equally spaced, and stiffened every 6 or 8 feet by a bridging composed of narrow strips of wood, nailed crosswise between each pair of joists in continuous lines, to distribute the floor strains and to provide against the twisting of the timber. When the distance between bearings is considerable, these joists are dressed upon their upper edge in the form of a very flat rising curve to correct the level of the floor in the case of sagging. Where stairs or chimneys are to be provided for, the necessary openings in the floor framing are made by enclosing the open area with heavier joists, those parallel with the common joists being called *trimmers* and those

at right angles being called *headers*, the latter being either framed into the former, or, preferably, hung to them by wrought-iron stirrups.

Flush with the outer edge of the sill and tenoned into it are vertical posts, 4 inches by 6 inches or 6 inches by 8 inches, extending the whole height of the walls. These occur at the corners, and, where the character or extent of the plan requires, at one or more intermediate points on each wall. If there is to be a third floor, the joists of the intermediate, or second, floor, which is framed practically like the first, but with such modifications in detail as the plan requires, have their outer bearings upon the top of horizontal timbers, called *girts*, or perhaps more properly *girths*, which have the thickness of the frame (4 inches or 6 inches) and a depth of 6 inches or 8 inches ; these are mortised into the posts. The girts, which run parallel with the joists, are in the best constructions set flatwise and flush with the upper surface of the floor framing, projecting inward to receive the nailings of the ends of the flooring boards. The posts are connected at the top by a horizontal member, called the *wall plate*, 4 inches by 6 inches or 6 inches by 6 inches, the principal function of which is to receive the lower end of the sloping rafters. These horizontal and vertical members of the wall-frame are braced at all their intersections by diagonal braces tenoned and treenailed.

The main skeleton of the walls being thus obtained, the open spaces between the posts are occupied by smaller vertical posts, called *studs*, 2 inches wide, and the thickness of the frame (4 inches or 6 inches) mortised at top and bottom, regularly spaced, set edgewise, and flush with the frame ; those for the first story are set between the sill and the girt, and those for the second, between the girt and the wall plate. Similar vertical studs form the frames for the interior partitions, each stud being spiked at top and bottom to horizontal pieces and stiffened at one or more intermediate points by lines of bridging, composed of short pieces of studs cut in between the vertical members and thoroughly nailed. Apertures for doors and windows are framed by thicker or double studs at the sides and at top and bottom, the former being trussed when they bear weight.

The third floor joists for the roof chambers are often less deep than those of the first or second. Like the other joists, they bear upon the heads of the main partitions, but at their outer ends they bear either upon the wall plate, or, if more space is required in the third story under the lower part of the slope of the rafters, they are notched over the upper edge of a board about 6 inches wide, let flush into the back of the outside studs a foot or more below the wall plate ; this is called a *ledger board* or *ribbon strip;* it is nailed to each stud, and plays a very important part in binding and stiffening the entire fabric.

The spacing of floor joists and studs, except where cross furring is used (see below), is governed by the length of the laths. These are roughly sawn strips, about $\frac{2}{8}$ or $\frac{3}{8}$ of an inch thick, $1\frac{3}{8}$ inches wide, and 4 feet long, set about half an inch apart, so as to afford a key for the plaster to hold by. They require each either four or five nailings, the former calling for a spacing of joists or studs 16 inches on centres, and the latter, 12 inches on centres. They are nailed to the inner surfaces of the outside studs and to both surfaces of the inside or partition studs, to receive the wall finish, and to the under surface of the joists, to receive the ceiling finish; but in the better class of work, cross furrings, composed of strips of $\frac{7}{8}$-inch boards, about $1\frac{1}{2}$ inches wide, are first nailed to the under side of the joists and rafters, and at right angles to them, to correct irregularities of level, and these receive the lath nailings. The thickness of the lathing and plastering is from $\frac{3}{4}$ to $\frac{7}{8}$ of an inch. In order that the surface of the plastering may be true and level, it is worked to grounds $\frac{3}{4}$ or $\frac{7}{8}$ of an inch thick, respectively placed at points to be covered by the interior wood finish.

Roofs are framed with rafters 2 inches wide and from 6 inches to 12 inches deep, according to service, and generally 20 inches on centres, having a bearing at bottom upon the wall plate, and at top, for simple constructions, against a ridge pole, which is often formed by an inch board; or, if the character of the design is such as to require a roof of double slope, the upper ends of the rafters are notched to support a *curb*, or upper plate, 6 inches to 8 inches square, upon which rests the joists of the flat or upper roof slope. The hips are generally constructed with timber 2 inches to 4 inches thick, and somewhat deeper than the rafters.

The dormers are framed with light studs or rafters spiked to the rafters of the lower roof-slope, which are doubled or increased in size at all roof openings.

The stability of this light cagelike structure depends, not only upon the mortising together of its principal members, with thorough nailing and spiking, and pinning at all the intersections, with bracing as described, and with the effective stiffening secured by the construction of its floors,—but also upon an envelope of rough boarding or sheathing, $\frac{7}{8}$ of an inch thick and from 6 inches to 10 inches wide, generally tongued and grooved together, which is nailed over the entire outer surface of the wall framing, over the upper surface of the rafters for the roof closure and of the joists for the flooring. This sheathing is sometimes applied diagonally to the surface of the frame to afford greater stiffness and stability. Often the rafters, instead of being covered with close boarding, receive narrow strips, spaced so as to afford nailing for the shingles, which, by this method, have the advantage of ventilation from beneath, and consequently greater security against decay.

The exterior finish, or siding, of the walls, is composed of narrow boards, called clapboards (see Clapboard; Weather Board), which are sawn and planed by machinery to a thin upper edge and a thick lower edge, and nailed horizontally through the rough boarding or sheathing to the studs, overlapping in successive regular courses, and showing from 4 inches to 6 inches to the weather; or of sidings (see Siding), which are regular courses of boards planed with a bevel at top and bottom and tongued and grooved together; or of vertical boards nailed to horizontal pieces cut in between the studs at each height of 2 feet, the joints being covered by narrow bevelled battens, hollowed slightly on the under side to secure closer joints; or of shingles showing from 4 inches to 6 inches to the weather, sometimes of equal widths, and laid in patterns or shaped with tools in the form of tiles or scales.

All this exterior finish is laid over stout weatherproof building paper, thoroughly lapped and nailed, sometimes in two or more layers, over the entire surface of the sheathing boards. The same treatment is applied under the shingles of the roof. Sometimes the whole frame is filled in with bricks laid in mortar between the studding; or it receives a closure of back plastering laid upon laths cut in between the studs; or a double system of lathing and plastering is used, the first being secured to the back of the studs, and the second to a system of furring pieces nailed through the first plastering and coinciding with the studs. By any of these systems a warm weatherproof house is obtained.

The mouldings of the exterior cornices, string courses, window and door frames, etc., are wrought out of boards and thin plank at the planing mills, where they are often kept in stock, and, with the assistance of furrings, can be put together so as to obtain any desired effect of solidity, or to meet any of the conventional exigencies of design. Thus most of the more important decorative projections are hollow and made of thin stock, not wrought in the solid like the timber work of mediæval constructions. Columns, with all the appearance, but none of the reality, of solidity, are built up with glue upon furring pieces around a hollow core in forms following classic, mediæval, or any other formulas. The turning lathe contributes its share to this phantasm of architecture, and balusters, vases, spindles, and finials of any desired shape and in any desired quantity can be cheaply obtained at the woodworking factories.

For this characteristic system of obtaining

decorative effects in wood construction some practical advantages are reasonably claimed. In the climate of America, dry and wet by turns, a solid timber construction would not only be costly, but would be subject to twists, cracks, checks, and interior decay; while the better ventilated hollow and furred construction, when kept well protected by paint and by flashings of tin or zinc on its weathered parts, withstands the vicissitudes of time for indefinite periods. The facilities of the planing mills have tempted the builder to many unfruitful experiments in design, to many imitations of forms never intended to be expressed in wood, and to many unspeakable inventions of more vernacular type.

When the production of nails was cheapened by machinery, and cut nails of steel and iron and nails made of wire could be furnished of excellent quality and at a cost much less than the old-fashioned wrought-iron nails, the laborious and comparatively expensive method of house framing with mortise and tenon began to be supplanted by a more economical system dependent entirely upon the efficacy of nailing. This involves the complete abandonment of braces and girts and mortise joints, and the substitution of long studs extending continuously through two, or even more, stories from the sill to the wall plate, the second and third floor joists being notched over flush ledger boards or ribbon strips let into the back of the studs, the whole system being secured by nails at every point of junction, and made stable by the nailing of covering or sheathing boards over the outside of the wall, studs, and rafters, and by the nailing of flooring boards over the joists. This is called Balloon Framing (which see).

The established merchantable lengths of joists and studs exercise a marked influence over the ordinary shape and size of the balloon-framed building, as "cutting to waste" is repugnant to the principle of economy on which this system is founded. This structure, though cheap, apparently frail, and suited only to temporary or provisional purposes, has been found by experience to be stable against ordinary wind pressure, and to afford at least as safe, as comfortable, and as commodious a shelter as any other construction of its class and grade. Indeed, it is claimed by Western builders that balloon framing, as it has fewer points for dislocation and no mortise holes subject to rot, is a more rigid and permanent structure than any dependent upon girts, timber braces, and mortise framing.

In the development of these systems it must be recognized that certain new and distinct ideals of design, in strong contrast to those evolved from the half-timbered buildings of the Old World, as described in Wood, Construction in, Part I., have gradually grown out of these peculiar conditions of structure. Con-

spicuous among those is an ideal of neatness, a mechanical precision and workmanlike cleanliness and squareness of outline and smoothness of surface, eliminating to some degree many of the picturesque accidents of effect and much of the softness and roundness of outline, which have been derived from other conditions of material and are associated with all Old World traditions which we have inherited and which we admire. It has been a part of the duty of the American architect in some way to elevate this new, uncompromising condition of structure into a virtue of design.

In the wooden buildings of the Old World, as indicated in Part I. of this essay, the timber frame is commonly visible, and is vitally essential to their expression as works of architecture. In the wooden buildings of the New World the frame, by a purely scientific and reasonable process, is reduced in dignity of proportion and use. As in the high commercial buildings of modern America, the light steel frame, which does all the work, is nevertheless necessarily concealed under a thin protective envelope of masonry, so in the wooden buildings the light timber frame must be covered by a thin sheathing of wood. Both systems are thus deprived of the noble privilege of treating the frame as architecture, and are constrained to elevate the mere integument to this high function. Under this important limitation the wooden buildings of the United States must depend for architectural effect upon the disposition of masses and outline, upon fenestration, upon the wide porches, verandas, and loggias, which the conditions of climate and of social life invite, and more especially upon the texture and colour of the surface. In the effort to obtain reasonable variety in this latter respect, the board sheathing, instead of being covered by clapboards, sidings, or shingles, — by each or all of these weatherings sometimes in the same building, — requiring staining or painting, and thus introducing contrasts of artificial colour as a vital element in the decorative scheme, receives sometimes a veneer of one thickness of brickwork, or a thin ashlar facing of stone, laid upon a ledge of the foundation, and secured to the boarding through its covering of sheathing paper by nails driven in the joints of the masonry; a permanent structural colour is thus given to the exterior, and a more effectual closure secured. This device, though of course open to certain palpable objections as a base imitation of real masonry, a deceit, and a vain pretence, is not without its defensible points. The veneered building is a comfortable building to live in, it dispenses with the necessity of paint, substitutes a natural or structural colour for an applied colour, it enlarges the scope of design, especially when combined with a second story covered with wood finish painted or stained, and it affords another example of the audacity with which any new device of method, appliance, or material, which may commend itself to common sense for economical or practical reasons, is adopted, however revolutionary may be its consequences.

George Collings, *Circular Work in Carpentry and Joinery, a Practical Treatise on Circular Work of Single and Double Curvature*, London, 1890, 1 vol. 8vo; *Roof Carpentry, Practical Lessons in the Framing of Wood Roofs for the Use of Working Carpenters*, London, 1893, 1 vol. 12mo; John Thomas Hurst, *Elementary Principles of Carpentry*, 8th ed., London, 1892, 1 vol. 12mo; James Newlands, *The Carpenter and Joiner's Assistant*, London, 1840.
— HENRY VAN BRUNT.

WOODHOUSE. An outhouse in which firewood may be stored for use.

WOODWORKING MACHINERY. Power machinery for shaping and finishing wood. It includes sawing and turning machines of every description, planers, moulders, jointers; boring, mortising, and tenoning machines; sanders, filers, and polishers; machines for the manufacture of flooring, boxes, sashes, blinds, and doors, and panelling of all sorts; and combination machines called universal woodworkers, adapted for a great variety of carpenter's work, formerly done entirely by hand.

The substitution of machine labour for hand labour in every department of industry has had much to do with the increase of material prosperity during the nineteenth century. It has given to the people many things essential to their comfort and well-being, which, under the old conditions of hand labour, would have been far out of their reach. It has given them food for mind and body, clothing, easy transportation, and decent shelter. To the last, woodworking machinery has largely contributed in supplying them with cheap timber, cheap shingles and sidings, cheap flooring and interior finish, cheap sashes and doors. Thus, the same class, whose fathers a century ago lived sordidly and meanly, but picturesquely, in thatched cottages of one or two poor rooms, with latticed casements, mud floors, and rough walls rudely plastered or whitewashed, now finds itself decently installed in houses which, though often hard and square in outline, basely mechanical in detail, and with but few elements of grace or beauty, at least afford them spacious, comfortable, if not luxurious, lodgment, encourage clean and decent living, and a wholesome self-respect. But while woodworking machinery in general has thus accomplished large results in increasing the sum of human happiness, this facility of production has had a tendency to create a cheap architecture of imitation, pretence, and show — a tendency which has presented serious obstacles to the development of forms of art properly

adjusted to these difficult mechanical conditions; for it has been proved by a thousand failures that the old ideals, based upon hand labour, and upon an unscientific and prodigal use of heavy timber, cannot do honest service in modern, economical wood construction.
— HENRY VAN BRUNT.

WORKHOUSE. A house in which work is carried on; especially a house in which able-bodied paupers or vagrants are compelled to work; a poorhouse.

WORKING DRAWING. A detail drawing, made either to a rather large scale or at full size, exhibiting the structure of the whole or a part of a building, so as to form a guide for the workmen in the actual construction of the object so represented.

WORKING STRENGTH. (See Strength.)

WORKMANSHIP. *A.* The skill of a workman as shown in his work.

B. The quality imparted to anything made by man by the actual process of its making; the character given to it by the work put into it, apart from the excellence of its material or the value of the original conception. The workmanship of an object may be fine, although its design, in an artistic sense, or its planning, shape, or arrangement may be very bad. Workmanship may even be noticeably good in a thing which is not solidly put together or likely to be permanent; thus, a piece of building may be so badly conceived by the engineer or builder who planned it, that it will not stand long, and yet the workmanship, as of stonecutting, joinery, and the like, may be excellent. Good workmanship of certain kinds can generally be had by demand backed by willingness to spend money, especially if this is long continued; thus, no better workmanship is to be found anywhere in countries of European stock than in the house fittings, furniture, and the like, of wealthy Englishmen, that class having been, for many years and until quite recent times, much the most freely spending class of people in Europe. Houses in London, and country houses built under the same general influences, fifty years ago as now, would show floors of such perfect level, and doors so perfectly hung that saddles might be dispensed with; it was quite common to see the carpets brought into the recess of a door and fitted together edge to edge without any break in the uniformity of the level; the doors swinging easily, grazing the pile of the carpet, but never pressing it, and shutting perfectly true, the bolts of the latch and lock going home without noise or shock. The decorative woodwork of the same house, that which was fitted to the house, and that which was put into movable articles alike, would be perfectly jointed and truly worked, the mitres faultless, the mouldings worked with absolute uniformity. And yet all this would be found in a house whose seemingly vaulted roofs in the halls, etc., were the merest shams of wood and plaster, whose external roof had no gutters overhanging the walls, but shed off the water of rain and snow into lead gutters, which at every moment threatened the interiors of the house with the results of leakage, and whose flues threatened, and sometimes not in vain, to allow the ignition of the wooden structure near. This means that all the workmanship which the owner and his family and their guests were in the way of seeing was very perfect, whereas that which they disregarded, belonging to a class not greatly interested in architecture or building of any sort, was neglected, being kept in working order by constant repairs. In France, on the other hand, the building is of much greater solidity: stairs of stone, hand rails of wrought iron, floors without wood, and wholly incombustible; nothing to shrink or settle; the vaults of cellar or corridor, or, in a church, of the nave and aisles, all of solid masonry; and yet the sash and doors do not always fit tightly, nor is there as uniformly neat an aspect given to interior work.

In its largest sense, workmanship includes selection and care of material. Thus, it is proper to say that no pieces of workmanship known to us are more perfect than fine Japanese lacquers, for the boxes, trays, dwarf writing-tables, and cabinets of drawers, which come within that category, were made with a lavish employment of time and patience in the preparation, by the father, of the wood which not he, but his sons, would cut up and utilize, the most extraordinary precautions taken in the way of seasoning the wood, and causing the drying of the varnish to go on slowly and at a measured rate. Material in this sense is not perfectly good until workmanship in a certain sense has been applied to it, but the workmanship which the collector knows best is that of the laying on of the external coats of the varnish, and the staining, painting, inlaying, and applying of other materials in which the decorative design of the piece is conveyed.

In architecture, care is to be taken not to allow good workmanship to be mistaken for that which merely appears delicate; thus, it is a very common fault in modern building to demand that brickwork shall be laid up with very thin joints — whereas every brickmason knows that thin joints mean bad work. Good workmanship is as possible, and good building is far more easy, with joints $\frac{3}{4}$ of an inch thick than with invisible ones. So, in cut stone facing, the smooth slabs of stone set on edge which are commonly considered necessary to the finished look of a street front are not nearly as good building as if the same stone were laid upon its quarry bed, with the result that the

whole would be less uniform in colour and less absolutely smooth in appearance; but workmanship may be equally good in either case.

— R. S.

WORKSHOP. An atelier; a place equipped for the carrying on of any specific work, whether mechanical or artistic.

WORONICHIN, ANDREI NIKIFORO-WITSCH; architect; b. 1760; d. March 5, 1814 (in Saint Petersburg).

He studied at the Academy of Saint Petersburg, and was sent by Catherine II. to Germany and Italy. In 1791 he was appointed architect to the court of Saint Petersburg. His most important work is the church of Notre Dame in Kasan, Saint Petersburg. He built numerous palaces.

Seubert, *Künstler-lexicon.*

WORSHIP MOUND. (See Mound.)

WOTTON, SIR HENRY; poet, diplomatist, and writer on architecture; b. March 21, 1568; d. Dec. 5, 1639.

The brilliant Elizabethan poet and diplomatist represented England in Venice for twenty years. On his return to England in 1524 he prepared a tract on architecture, *The Elements of Architecture, collected by Henry Wotton, Knight, from the Best Authors and Examples.* The book seems to have been first published in 1651 in the collection of Wotton's miscellaneous productions, with a sketch of his life by his friend Isaak Walton. It is based on Vitruvius and the old Italian writers. It has many quaint and interesting practical suggestions. A reprint was issued in 1901.

Builder, Nov. 24, 1883, p. 677.

WREATH. *A.* A twisted band, garland, or chaplet made of flowers, fruits, leaves, or other material, or representing such material, often used in decoration.

B. The curved portion of the string or hand rail which follows a turn in a geometrical stair. In plan, a wreath usually follows the curve of a quarter-circle, and therefore corresponds to a portion of the surface of a vertical cylinder.

WREN, SIR CHRISTOPHER; architect and astronomer; b. Oct. 20, 1632 (at East Knowle, Wiltshire, England); d. Feb. 27, 1723.

He was a student at Oxford (B.A., 1650, M.A., 1653), and afterward a fellow, and in 1660 was appointed Savilian Professor of Astronomy in that university. His scientific work was known throughout Europe. He was an original member of the Royal Society at its foundation in 1662, and was elected president of that body in 1681. Having gained a great reputation as a mathematician, he was consulted in architectural matters during the confused times of the Restoration. In 1661 he was made a member of the commission in charge of the restoration of old S. Paul's cathedral in London. The first building which Wren actually designed and superintended was the chapel of Pembroke Hall, Cambridge. He began the fine library of Trinity College, Cambridge, in 1676. His Sheldonian Theatre at

WREN, SIR CHRISTOPHER: STEEPLE OF S. MARY-LE-BOW, 1677.

Oxford was opened July 9, 1669. He visited Paris in 1665 and met Bernini (see Bernini), then occupied with his design for the façade of the Louvre. Wren never visited Italy. The Great Fire of London occurred Sept. 2, 1666. Immediately afterward Wren made a plan for the reconstruction of the burned district, which

was not followed. He also began to make designs for the reconstruction of S. Paul's cathedral, which had been burned, and in 1673 was commissioned to prepare the fine model which is now in the South Kensington Museum. This model, being in the form of a Greek cross, did not satisfy the ritualistic tendencies of the court, which required a long nave for processions. A design in the form of a Latin cross was finally accepted May 14, 1675. The cathedral was begun on the site of the old cathedral, and finished in 1710. It was paid for by a tax on the coal brought to London by sea. The " Monument " in commemoration of the Great Fire was begun by Wren in 1671. In 1675, with the assistance of the Astronomer Flamsteed, he built the observatory at Greenwich, London. About 1695 he took charge of the reconstruction of the old Greenwich palace, and was instrumental in having it transformed into a seaman's hospital. The double colonnade of coupled columns at Greenwich is one of his finest works. Wren repaired the spire of Salisbury cathedral. He began the construction of Chelsea hospital in 1682. He made a fine design for a mausoleum to Charles I. which was not executed. On the accession of William and Mary in 1689 he began the enlargement of Hampton Court palace, one of his most characteristic works. In 1708 the erection of fifty new churches in London was ordered by act of Parliament. Wren actually designed fifty-three. Of these buildings ten have been recently destroyed. Among the most important of those still standing are S. Mary-le-Bow, S. Stephen, Walbrook, S. Bride, Fleet Street, S. Lawrence, Jewry, S. Michael, Cornhill, etc. He sat in Parliament for many years. There is a collection of his drawings in the library of All Souls' College, Oxford.

Wren, *Parentalia;* Loftie, *Inigo Jones and Wren;* Elmes, *Sir Christopher Wren;* Lucy Philimore, *Sir Christopher Wren;* Stratton, *Sir Christopher Wren;* Longman, *Three Cathedrals of St. Paul;* Macmurdo, *Wren's City Churches;* Clayton, *Churches of Sir Christopher Wren;* Taylor, *Towers and Steeples of Sir Christopher Wren;* Law, *Hampton Court Palace;* Blomfield, *Renaissance in England;* Dugdale, *St. Paul's Cathedral.*

WROUGHT IRON. (See Metal Work.)

WYATT, JAMES; architect; b. Aug. 3, 1748; d. Sept. 5, 1813.

A brother of Samuel Wyatt (see Wyatt, S.). Wyatt was taken to Rome at the age of fourteen by·Lord Bagot, ambassador to Italy. He studied also for two years in Venice with Visentini. In 1770 he made considerable reputation by adapting the old Pantheon in Oxford Street, London, for dramatic performances (burned 1792). Working originally in the classic style, he afterward imitated Gothic architecture, and built in that style Fonthill Abbey, Wiltshire, for W. Beckford, and other important works. March 16, 1796, he was appointed surveyor general and comptroller of his Majesty's office of works, succeeding Sir William Chambers (see Chambers), and held that office until it was dropped in 1815. He was made a member of the Royal Academy in 1785, and temporary president in 1805. He built the royal military academy of Woolwich, and restored Salisbury and Lincoln cathedrals.

Redgrave, *Dictionary of Artists; Arch. Pub. Soc. Dictionary; Dict. of National Biography.*

WYATT, JEFFREY. (See Wyatville, Sir Jeffrey.)

WYATT, SIR MATTHEW, DIGBY; architect; b. July 28, 1820; d. May 21, 1877.

The youngest son of Matthew Wyatt, an English barrister. In 1844–1846 he travelled on the Continent. He was secretary of the executive committee of the great exhibition of 1851, and assisted in making the plans for it. In 1855 he was appointed surveyor of the East India Company. He was honorary secretary of the Royal Institute of British Architects from 1855 to 1859. Wyatt published *An Architect's Note-book in Spain* (London, 1872, 1 vol. 4to); *Specimens of Ornamental Art Workmanship in Gold, Silver, Iron, Brass and Bronze from the Twelfth to the Nineteenth Centuries* (London, 1852, large folio); *Specimens of the Geometrical Mosaic of the Middle Ages* (London, 1848, folio), etc.

Arch. Pub. Soc. Dictionary; Avery Architectural Library, Catalogue.

WYATT, SAMUEL; architect; b. Sept. 8, 1737; d. Feb. 8, 1807.

An elder brother of James Wyatt (see Wyatt, J.). In 1782 he was employed at Somerset House, London, under Sir William Chambers (see Chambers). He built numerous residences in England, and March 5, 1792, was appointed clerk of the works at Chelsea hospital (London).

Redgrave, *Dictionary of Artists ; Arch. Pub. Soc. Dictionary.*

WYATVILLE (WYATT) SIR JEFFREY; architect; b. Aug. 3, 1766; d. Feb. 18, 1840.

His name was originally Wyatt, a son of Samuel Wyatt (see Wyatt, Samuel). He exhibited at the Royal Academy after 1786, was created associate in 1823, and royal academician in 1826. From 1784 to 1799 he worked with his father and his uncle, James Wyatt (see Wyatt, J.). In 1799 he went into partnership with a builder and engaged in extensive government contracts. He enlarged Wollaton Hall, Nottinghamshire (1804), Woburn Abbey, Bedfordshire (1818–1820), Chatsworth in Derbyshire, and other residences. From 1824 until his death he was architect in charge of Windsor Castle. He completed the quadrangle and staircase of George III., rebuilt

the Brunswick Tower, etc. August 12, 1824, his name was changed to Wyatville by royal license. December 9, 1828, he was knighted. His *Illustrations of Windsor Castle*, edited by Henry Ashton, was published in 1841 (2 vols. folio). A list of his works is given in the *Architectural Publication Society's Dictionary.*

Redgrave, *Dictionary of Artists; Arch. Pub. Soc. Dictionary.*

WYND. In Scotland, an alley, a lane ; especially a narrow alley in a town forming a passage from street to street.

X

XAINTES. (See Isenbert de Xaintes.)

XAMETE; sculptor and architect.

An important master working in Spain in the early sixteenth century. In 1537 he made the candelabra of the Capilla de la Torre in the cathedral of Toledo. He also executed the fine portal of the cloister of the cathedral of Cuença.

Bermudez, *Diccionario.*

XAT. A carved post in North American Indian art. (See Canada, Architecture of.)

XENAIOS; architect.

The walls of Antiochia in Asia Minor were built under his direction when that city was founded by Seleukos in 296 B.C.

Brunn, *Geschichte der griechischen Künstler.*

XENODOCHEUM ; XENODOCHEION. In classic architecture, a room or building devoted to the reception and accommodation of strangers or guests.

XYST; XYSTUS. In Greek and Roman architecture, a long covered portico for exercise in bad weather. In Roman villas, a garden walk or avenue planted with trees. Vitruvius (V., 11) says expressly that the Romans had misapplied the term in the latter sense.

Y

YALI. A Turkish summer mansion. (See Konak.)

YAMUN. The official residence of a Chinese mandarin ; also, the office or court where a mandarin transacts the business of the department under his care.

YARD. *A.* A piece of enclosed ground of moderate size, especially one adjoining a residence; as in the terms, front yard, dooryard, barnyard, inn yard.

B. An enclosure for labour and traffic ; as, brickyard, woodyard, stockyard, dockyard, railway yard, vineyard.

YBL, NIKOLAUS VON; architect ; d. 1891.

A distinguished architect of Hungary. He was a pupil of Pollak in Pesth and afterward of Gärtner (see Gärtner) in Munich. He was constantly engaged on important works, was raised to noble rank, and made a member of the upper house of the Hungarian Parliament.

American Architect, Vol. XXXI., p. 130.

YELLOW METAL (called also Muntz's Metal.) An alloy of three parts of copper and two of zinc, malleable when hot. It has taken the place of copper for sheathing, because cheaper and more easily rolled.

YILDIZ KIOSK. (See under Kiosk.)

YOKE. The horizontal piece forming the head of a frame for double hung sash.

YOURT. A term sometimes applied to the permanent or winter houses of the Alaska Eskimos and Aleuts. (See Iglu.) Also any house or hut of the natives of Siberia. (Written also yurt, youret, yourta, jurt.)

YRIARTE, CHARLES; editor and writer on art; d. April 7, 1898.

He was editor in chief of Le Monde Illustré in Paris, and published many important works on the Italian Renaissance, Florence, Venise, Paul Véronèse (in Les Artistes célèbres); Matteo Civitale (Paris, 1886, folio); La vie d'un patricien de Venise au 16e Siècle (Paris, 1874, 8vo); Un Condottiere au XVe siècle, Rimini (Paris, 1882, 4to); etc.

A. Kämpfen in Gaz. d. Beaux Arts (1898, Vol. 82).

YUAN MING YUAN. The summer palace of the emperor of China, which was plundered and partly destroyed, with immense destruction of precious artistic treasures, by the French and British invading army, 1860.

YUCATAN, ARCHITECTURE OF. (See Mexico, Architecture of, § I.)

YURT. (See Yourt.)

Z

ZACCAB. An earth used in ancient and modern times by the natives of Yucatan as stucco, plaster, etc. It is mixed with lime in place of sand. The colour is white, and it occurs abundantly in pockets. The cement used by the ancient Mayas is said to have been composed of one part slacked lime to two parts zaccab, but it is doubtful if they understood the process of making quicklime. (See Memoirs Peabody Museum, Vol. I., No. 3, E. H. Thompson.) — F. S. D.

ZAHCAB. Same as Zaccab.

ZAMPIERI, DOMENICO (DOMENICHINO); painter and architect; b. 1581 (at Bologna); d. 1641 (at Naples).

The celebrated painter, Domenichino, was much employed in the construction of villas. He assisted at the Villa Negroni, Rome, and designed the Villa Belvidere at Frascati and the

Villa Ludovisi in Rome. His most important architectural undertaking was the design of the church of S. Ignazio in Rome (begun 1626).

Gurlitt, Geschichte des Barockstiles in Italien; Ebe, Spät-Renaissance.

ZANTH, LUDWIG VON; architect; b. about 1798; d. Oct. 7, 1857.

He was educated at Cassel, Germany, and Paris. After 1810 he was associated with Hittorff (see Hittorff), and in 1823 went with him to Sicily. They published together Architecture antique de la Sicile (Paris, 1825, folio); and Architecture moderne de la Sicile (Paris, 1835, folio).

Arch. Pub. Soc. Dictionary.

ZAPOTEC ARCHITECTURE.. (See Tzapoteco Architecture.)

ZARCELLO Y ALCAREZ, FRANCISCO; sculptor; b. May 12, 1707; d. 1781.

His father, Nicolas, also a sculptor, came from Capua (Italy) to Murcia (Spain) at the end of the seventeenth century. After making a statue for the Dominican church at Murcia, Francisco went to Rome to study. Returning to Spain, he made the statues of the Spanish kings which decorate the new palace, Madrid. He finally settled in Murcia, where he founded a school.

Bermudez, Diccionario.

ZAX. An implement used for cutting and pressing slates. It is usually a kind of hatchet, with a sharp point on the pole for perforating slate to receive a nail or pin.

ZECCA. In Italian, a mint; of especial interest is that at Venice, behind the library of S. Mark and fronting on the sea; the work of Jacopo Sansovino, and built about 1536.

ZEHUTER, HEINRICH. (See Egl, Andreas.)

ZENANA. In India, that part of a house in which the women are secluded; an East Indian Haram.

ZETA. A closed or small chamber; a room over a church porch where documents were kept.

ZIEBLAND, GEORG FRIEDRICH; architect; b. Feb. 7, 1800; d. July 24, 1873.

He was sent to Italy by the king of Bavaria, and on his return was charged with the design and construction of the basilica in Munich.

Raczynski, L'Art moderne en Allemagne.

ZIGURAT; ZIKHURAT. A stepped pyramid, as in the sacred architecture of the people of Western Asia in antiquity. (See Mesopotamia, Architecture of; Temple.)

ZIGZAG (adj.). Making short and sharp turns; in architecture said especially of the mouldings in arched door heads and the like of Romanesque style. (See Bâtons Rompus.)

ZOÖPHORIC. Carrying the figure of an animal.

ZOÖPHORIC COLUMN (or **PILLAR**). A pillar supporting the figure of a beast, usually symbolical, like that which carries the Lion of S. Mark in the Piazzetta at Venice, and the similar one in the Piazza Signoria at Verona. Such columns were set up by the Venetian Republic in some, at least, of the cities subject to its rule.

ZOÖPHORUS; ZOPHORUS. A representation of living things; in classical archæology, a frieze or other band or panel filled with figures of men and animals; especially the cella frieze of the Parthenon.

ZOPF STYLE. (See Pigtail and Periwig Style.)

ZOTHECA. *A.* A niche or alcove.

B. A living room or day room as opposed to a sleeping room or dormitory.

Z PLAN; or **Z-SHAPED PLAN.** A plan composed of three wings joined somewhat like the letter Z. Occasionally used in hospitals to obtain certain advantages of aspect.

ZUNIAN ARCHITECTURE (pron. zoon'- yee-an). That of the Zuñi Indians of western New Mexico. The Zuñis are Pueblos, and their architecture is the same as that of the other tribes of this class. (See Adobe; Communal Dwelling; Kiva; Pueblo.)

ZWINGER. In old German, a fortress or strong place in or adjoining a city; also an outer court or Bailey; a popular term, from which, by extension, comes the modern name of several palaces, or parts of palaces, in German cities. That at Dresden is a very important and interesting specimen of the florid style of the eighteenth century.

ZWIRNER, ERNST FRIEDRICH; architect; b. Feb. 28, 1802; d. Sept. 22, 1861 (at Cologne).

He studied architecture in Breslau in 1821, and with Schinkel (see Schinkel) in Berlin in 1824. He devoted himself especially to the revival of Gothic architecture in Germany. In 1833 he was appointed inspector of the construction of the cathedral of Cologne, and in 1853 architect of that building. The completion of this work was largely due to his efforts in interesting the people of Germany, and especially Freidrich Wilhelm IV., king of Prussia, in it. Many leading German architects were educated by him and assisted him in his work. Zwirner built also the castle of Herdringen (1844–1852) for the Count of Fürstenberg, the church of S. Apollinaris at Ramagen, near Bonn, etc.

Seubert, *Künstler-lexicon.*

BIBLIOGRAPHY

Titles of most of the books consulted in the preparation of the Dictionary. Those from which illustrations have been drawn are indicated by an asterisk.

The reader is reminded that a classification of the titles is furnished by the separate bibliographies throughout the Dictionary.

The articles named below have been illustrated, wholly or in part, from original drawings or reproductions of drawings.

Apartment House, drawings furnished by author, and by Messrs. H. J. Hardenbergh and Ernest Flagg.
Arch (Figs. 1 and 3), drawings furnished by author.
Bath House, drawing furnished by author.
Bath Tub, drawings furnished by author.
Brace, drawing furnished by author.
Cliff Dwelling, drawings furnished by author.
Club House, drawings furnished by Messrs. McKim, Mead & White.
Figuring, drawings furnished by author.
Germany, drawings furnished by author.
House Drainage, drawings furnished by author.
Lath, drawings furnished by Bostwick Steel Lath Co., Niles, O.
Log House, drawings furnished by author.
Masonry, drawing furnished by author.

Mexico, drawings furnished by author.
Office Building, drawing furnished by author and by Mr. Bruce Price.
Parallelogram of Forces, drawing furnished by author.
Pendentive, drawings furnished by author.
Polygon of Forces, drawing furnished by author.
Pot Chimney, drawing furnished by author.
Round Tower, drawing furnished by author.
Shoring, drawings furnished by author.
Synagogue, drawings furnished by author.
Tenement House, drawings furnished by author.
Tipi, drawing furnished by author.
Vault, drawings furnished by author.
Ventilation, drawings furnished by author.
Wickyup, drawing furnished by author.

Abel, Lothar.
Asthetik der Gartenkunst. Vienna, 1877.
Ackermann, Rudolph.
History of the University of Oxford. London, 1814.
Adam, Robert.
Ruins of the Palace of the Emperor Diocletian at Spalatro in Dalmatia. 1764.
Adamy, Rudolf.
Architektonik des Muhamedanischen und Romanischen Stils : forms a part of Architektonik auf Historischer und Aesthetischer Grundlage. Hanover, 1883–1889.
Addy, Sidney Oldall.
The Evolution of the English House. London, 1898.
Adler, Friedrich.
Mittelalterliche Backstein-Bauwerke des Preussischen Staates. 2 vols. Berlin, 1898.
Die Stoa des Königs Attalos II. zu Athen. Berlin, 1875.
Advanced Building Construction. London, 1892. (One of Longmans' Advanced Science Manuals.)
Agincourt, Seroux d'.
Histoire de l'Art par les Monuments depuis sa Décadence au 5me siècle jusqu'à son Renouvellement au 15me siècle. 3 vols. in folio with 325 plates, but usually bound in 6 vols. Finished 1823.
Aiken, Edmund.
An Essay toward a History and Description of the Cathedral Church of S. Paul, London ; in Britton, Fine Arts of the English School.
Allan, W.
Theory of Arches. New York, 1890.
Allen, John Romilly.
Early Christian Symbolism in Great Britain and Ireland before the Thirteenth Century. London, 1887.
Allgemeine Bauzeitung mit Abbildungen [Periodical]. Vienna, 1836.
Allgemeine Deutsche Biographie. Leipzig, 1875–1900.
Allgemeines Künstlerlexicon. (See Füssli, J. R.)
Allmers, Hermann.
Die altchristliche Basilika als Vorbild des Protestantischen Kirchenbaues. Oldenburg, 1870.
Allsop, R. Owen.
Public Baths and Wash-houses. London and New York, 1894.
Amé, Émile.
Recherches sur les Vitraux Incolores de l'Yonne. 1854.
Les Carrelages émaillés du Moyen Âge et de la Renaissance. Paris, 1859.
American Architect and Building News [Periodical]. Boston, 1876–1884 ; in one form only ; 1885 to 1901 in a regular edition, and also a larger edition, with many additional plates ; two such larger editions 1890–1899. Still in publication.
American Journal of Archaeology [Periodical].

Baltimore and New York, 1885, 1—1. (Published by Archaeological Institute of America.)

American Journal of Philology [Periodical].

American Public Health Association, Transactions.

Amorini, Marchese Antonio Bolognini.
Elogio di Sebastiano Serlio, Architetto Bolognese, dedicato alla Pontificia Accademia di Belle Arti in Bologna, 1823.

Anderson, Sir John.
The Strength of Materials and Structures. London, 1887.

Anderson, Joseph.
Scotland in Early Christian Times . . . Edinburgh, 1881.

Anderson, William.
Pictorial Arts of Japan, with . . . remarks upon the Pictorial Arts of the Chinese and Koreans. London, 1886.

Anderson, William J.
The Architecture of the Renaissance in Italy. London, 1896.

André, Édouard.
L'Art des Jardins.
Traité général des Parcs et des Jardins. Paris, 1879.

Anguillesi, Giovanni Domenico.
Notizie storiche dei Palazzi e Ville appertenanti alla R. Corona di Toscana. Pisa, 1815.

Annales Archéologiques ; ed. by A. N. Didron and later by E. A. Didron [Periodical]. Paris, 1844–1870. There is a volume of tables by Barbier de Montault.

Annali della Fabbrica del Duomo di Milano dall' Origine fino al presente. 9 vols. 1877–1885.

Antiquities of Athens. (See Stuart and Revett.)

Antiquities of Ionia. Published by the Society of Dilettanti. 4 parts in 4 vols. London, 1821, 1797, 1840, 1881. (See Ionian Antiquities, of which work the above Part I (dated 1821) is a new edition, much modified.)

Antoine, J. D.
Hôtel des Monnaies à Paris (plans, etc.). Paris, 1826.

Appert and Henlivaux.
Verre et Verrerie. Paris, 1894.
La Verrerie depuis vingt ans. Paris, 1895.

Archaeologia ; or Miscellaneous Tracts relating to Antiquity [Periodical]. London, 1770–1794.

Archaeological Institute of America. (See American Journal of Archaeology.)

Archäologische Zeitung [Periodical]. Berlin, 1843–1885.

Archeografo Triestino, Raccolta di opusculi e notizie per Trieste e per l'Istria. Trieste, 1829–1837.

Architectural Association of London. Visit to the Domed Churches of Charente. (See Visit.)

Architectural Publication Society. Dictionary of Architecture. 8 vols. London (n.d.).

Architectural Record ; published quarterly, with illustrations [Periodical]. New York, 1891–.

Architectural Review [Periodical]. London, 1896–1901.

Architecture and Building [Periodical]. New York, 1883–.

L'Architecture, ; Journal Hebdomadaire de la Société centrale des Architectes français [Periodical]. Paris, 1888–.

* Architecture Toscane ou Palais, Maisons, et autres Édifices de la Toscane. 1 vol. folio (n.d.).

Architekten und Ingenieur-Verein für Niederrhein und Westfalen : Notizblatt. Cologne, 1876.

Archives des Missions scientifiques et littéraires ; choix de Rapports et Instructions. Paris, 1850–. Continued as Nouvelles Archives.

Archives . . . Monuments historiques. (See Commission.)

Archivio Storico dell' Arte [Periodical]. Rome, 1889–.

Archivio Storico Lombardo. Giornale della Società Storica Lombarda [Periodical]. Milan, 1874–.

Archivio Veneto, Nuovo [Periodical]. 1871–.

Arco, Carlo d'.
Delle Arti e degli Artifici di Mantova. Mantua, 1857.
Istoria della vita e delle opere di Giulio Pippi Romano. Mantua, 1842.

Armstrong, Robert.
Chimneys for Furnaces, Fireplaces, and Steam Boilers. New York, 1883.

Armstrong, Walter.
Alfred Stevens ; a Biographical Study. Paris, 1881.

Arnold, Friedrich.
Der Herzogliche Palast von Urbino . . . mit erläuterndem Texte. Leipzig, 1857.

*L'Art pour Tous, Encyclopédie de l'art industriel et décoratif. Paris, 1861–. (Publication continued.)

L'Art, (Beaux-Arts, Archéologie, Littérature). Revue mensuelle illustrée [Periodical]. Paris, 1874–.

Artistes Belges à l'Étranger, Les. Études Biographiques, Historiques, et Critiques. Brussels, 1857 and 1865.

Artistes Célèbres, Les. A series edited by P. Leroi. Paris (n.d.).

Arundel Society. London, 1854–1882. Various publications. (See Ruskin.)

Assier, Alexandre.
Les Arts et les Artistes dans l'ancienne Capitale de la Champagne. Paris, 1876.
Comptes de l'Œuvre de l'Église de Troyes. 1855.
Les Arts et les Artistes de Troies. (See Les Arts et les Artistes de l'ancienne Capitale de la Champagne.)

*Astrophysical Journal [Periodical].

Athenæum, The [Periodical]. London.

Atti Memoriale della Reale Deputazione di Storia patrice per le Provincie dell' Emilia [Periodical]. Nuova Serie, 1877–.

Auer und Lange.
Monuments de Vienne.

Aufleger, Otto, und Trautmann, K.
Münchener Architektur des XVIII Jahrhunderts. Munich, 1892.

Avery Architectural Library, Catalogue of. New York, 1895.

Babeau, Albert.
Linard Goutier et ses fils, peintres verriers. Troyes, 1888.
Le Louvre et son histoire. Paris, 1895.

Babelon, Ernest.
Manuel d'Archéologie Orientale. Chaldée — Assyrie — Perse — Syrie — Judée — Phénicie Carthage. Paris, 1888.

Baedeker, Karl.
Palestine and Syria Handbook for Travellers. Leipzig, 1876–1894.

Bailey, John Denton.
Sanitary Engineering . . . Lectures before the School of Military Engineering at Chatham. 1876. London, 1877.

Baker, M. N., and Rafter, George W.
Sewerage and Sewage Disposal. New York and London, 1893.

Baldi, Bernardino.
Memorie Concernenti la Citta di Urbino. Rome, 1727.

Baldinucci, Filippo.
Notizie dei Professore del Disegno da Cimabue in Qua. Florence, 1767.

Baldus, Édouard Denis.
Monuments Principaux de la France. Paris, 1875.

Baltard, Victor (Institut de France).
Notice sur Caristie. Paris, 1863.
Villa Médicis à Rome. Paris, 1847.

Bancroft, Hubert Howe.
Native Races of the Pacific States. 1875–1876.
History of Central America. 1882–1883.

Bancroft, Robert M., and Bancroft, F. J.
Tall Chimney Construction; a Practical Treatise on the Construction of Tall Chimney Shafts. Manchester, 1885.

Bandelier, Adolph Francis Alphonse.
Final Report of Investigations among the Indians of the Southwestern United States, 1880–1885. Part II. 1892.
Report of an Archaeological Tour in Mexico in 1881. Boston, 1884. (See Archaeological Institute of America). Papers Amer. Ser., 1884, Vol. II.

Barbier de Montault, Xavier.
Traité pratique de la Construction, de l'Ameublement et de la Décoration des Églises avec un appendice sur le Costume Ecclésiastique. Paris, 1878.

Bari : Nella terrà di Bari.
Ricordi di Arte Medioevale. (Published by a committee of the Turin Exposition.) Trani, 1898.

Barqui, F.
L'Architecture Moderne en France. Paris 1865–1871.

Barry, Alfred.
Memoir of the Life and Works of Sir Charles Barry, Architect. London, 1870.

Bauchal, Ch.
Notre-Dame et ses Premiers Architectes: Notices Historiques et Antiques. Paris, 1882.
Dictionnaire des Architectes français. Paris, 1887.

Baudecour, P. de.
Le Peintre-Graveur français continué ; Ouvrage faisant suite au Peintre-Graveur français de M. Robert-Dumesnil. 1859.

Baudot, Joseph Eugène Anatole de.
Églises de Bourgs et Villages. Paris, 1867.

Baudri, Fr. editor.
Organ für Christliche Kunst, herausgegeben und redigirt von F. Baudri. Cologne, 1851–1873.

Baukunde des Architekten unter Mitwirkung von Fachmännern der Verschiedenen Einzelgebiete, bearbeitet von den herausgebern, der Deutschen Bauzeitung und des Deutschen Baukalenders. Berlin, 1890.

Baumeister, Karl August.
Denkmäler des Klassischen Alterthums, zur erläuterung des Lebens der Griechen und Römer in Religion, Kunst und Sitte. Munich and Leipzig, 1885–1888.

Bayet, C.
L'Art Byzantin. Paris, 1883. (See Bibliothèque de l'enseignement des Beaux-Arts.)

Bayles, J. C.
House and Drainage and Water Supply. New York.

Bayley, John.
The History and Antiquities of the Tower of London, etc. 2 pts. London, 1821–1825. 2d ed., 1830.

Becker, Max.
Allgemeine Baukunde des Ingenieurs. Leipzig, 1882.

Begule, Lucien, and Guigue, C.
Monographie de la Cathédrale de Lyon. Lyons, 1880.

Belcher, John, and Macartney, Warren E.
Later Renaissance Architecture in England. 1897, 1901.

Behnke, Gustav.
Die Markthalle in Frankfurt. Berlin, 1880.

Beitrage zur Kunstgeschichte [Periodical]. Leipzig, 1878–1892.

Belhomme, ——.
Status des Peintres Verriers de Toulouse au XVIe siècle. Toulouse, 1843.

Bellier de la Chavignerie, Emile.
Dictionnaire général des Artistes de l'École française depuis l'origine des Arts du Dessin jusqu'à nos jours ; Architectes, Peintres, Sculpteurs, Graveurs, et Lithographes. Paris, 1882–1885.

Bellori, Giovanni Pietro.
Le vite dei Pittori, Scultori et Architetti Moderni. Parte prima. Rome, 1672. A second part was left by the author, but appears not to have been published.

Beltrami, Luca.
Soncini e Torre Pallavicina. Milan, 1898.
Bramante Poeta. Milan, 1884.

Bender, Hermann.
Rom und Römisches Leben im Alterthum. Tübingen, 1879.

Benjamin, Samuel Greene Wheeler.
Persia and the Persians. 1886.
The Story of Persia. 1887.

Benndorf, O.
Travels in Asia Minor. (See Reisen im Südwestlichen Kleinasien).

Benndorf, Otto, and Niemann, George.
* Reisen in Lykien und Karien. Vienna, 1884.

Benoit, François.
L'Art français sous la Révolution et l'Empire. Paris, 1897.

Benouville, Léon.
Étude sur la Cathédrale de Beauvais ; Concours pour les Fonctions d'Architecture Diocésain. Paris, 1892.

Bentham, Rev. James.
History and Antiquities of the Cathedral Church of Ely, from the Foundation of the Monastery, A.D. 673–1771. Cambridge, 1771.

Berenson, Bernhard.
The Florentine Painters of the Renaissance. New York, 1896.
Central Italian Painters of the Renaissance. New York, 1897.
The Venetian Painters of the Renaissance. New York, 1894.

Bermúdez, Juan Agustin Cean.
Diccionario de los Mas Illustres Professores de las Bellas Artes en España. Madrid, 1800.

Bernasconi, ——.
Cenni intorno la Vita e le Opere di Antonio Rizzo, architetto e scultore Veronese. Verona, 1859. Appendix, 1863.

Berry, William.
Encyclopedia Heraldica ; or Complete Dictionary of Heraldry by William Berry ; 1828–1840.

Bertolotti, A.
Artisti Lombardi a Roma nei secoli XV, XVI,

XVII. Studi e Recherche negli Archivi Romani. 1881–1890.
Nuovi documenti, intorno all' architetto Antonio Sangallo ed alla sua famiglia. Rome, 1892.

Bertrand, Édouard.
Études sur la Peinture et la Critique d'Art dans l'Antiquité. Paris, 1898.

Berty, Adolphe.
Topographie historique du vieux Paris. (Louvre and the Tuileries form Part I.) Paris, 1886–1887.
Les Grands Architectes Français de la Renaissance, P. Lescot ; Ph. de l'Orme ; J. Goujon ; J. Bullant ; les Du Cerceau ; les Métezeau ; les Chambiges . . . Paris, 1860.
* La Renaissance Monumentale en France. Paris, 1864.

Beulé, Charles Ernest.
L'Acropole d'Athènes. Paris, 1862.

Bibliothèque de l'École des Chartes. Paris.

Bibliothèque de l'Enseignement des Beaux-Arts. Paris, 1892–1893. (Many volumes, some of which are named separately in this list.)

Bibliothèque Internationale de l'Art. Paris, 1882–1893.

Bigot, Charles.
Raphaël et la Farnésine. Paris, 1884.
Translated into English as : Raphael and the Villa Farnesina, by Mary Healy (Madame C. Bigot). London, 1884.

Billings, Robert William.
* Architectural Illustrations and Description of the Cathedral Church at Durham. London, 1843.
Architectural Illustrations and Account of the Temple Church, London. London, 1838.
* Architectural Illustrations, History, and Description of Carlisle Cathedral. London, 1840.
Baronial and Ecclesiastical Antiquities of Scotland. 4 vols. Edinburgh, 1845–1852.
* Illustrations of the Architectural Antiquities of the County of Durham. Durham, 1846.

Biographie Nationale, publiée par l'Académie Royale des Sciences des Lettres et des Beaux-Arts de la Belgique.

Birch, George H.
London Churches of the 17th and 18th Centuries : a Selection of the most remarkable Ecclesiastical Buildings . . . erected . . . between 1630 and 1730 from the designs of Inigo Jones and Sir Christopher Wren, Nicholas Hawksmoor and James Gibbs, with Historical and Descriptive Accounts. London, 1896.

Birkmire, William H.
Architectural Iron and Steel. New York, 1891.
Skeleton Construction in Buildings. New York, 1893.
Compound Riveted Girders. New York, 1893.
Planning and Construction of High Office Buildings. New York, 1893.

Blanc, Charles.
Les Artistes de mon Temps. Paris, 1876.
Histoire de la Renaissance en Italie. Paris, 1889.
Les Fresques de Véronèse au Château de Masère près de Trévise ; in Gazette des Beaux Arts, second series ; Paris, 1878.

Blanquart, L'Abbé.
Notice sur les Vitraux de Gisors ; première partie, les Peintres Verriers. 1884.

Blashfield-Hopkins. (See Vasari.)

Blätter für Architektur und Kunsthandwerk [Periodical]. Berlin, 1800–.

Blomfield, Reginald.
A History of Renaissance Architecture in England. 1500–1800. London, 1897.

Blomfield, R., and Thomas, F. Inigo.
The Formal Garden in England. London, 1892. Abridged edition, 1900.

Blondel, J. F., and Patte.
Cours d'architecture ou Traité de la décoration, distribution et construction des bâtiments, etc. 1771–1778.

Bocchi-Cinelli. (See Cinelli.)

Bock, Fr.
*Rheinlands Baudenkmale des Mittelalters. Cologne and Neuss (n.d.).

Bode, Wilhelm.
Italienischen Bildhauer der Renaissance. 1887.

Boetticher, Karl.
* Die Tektonik der Hellenen. Berlin, 1874–1881. 2 vols. octavo, and atlas.
Die Holzarchitektur des Mittelalters mit Anschluss der Schönsten in dieser Epoche Entwickelten Produkte der Gewerblichen Industrie. Berlin, 1856.

Bohn, Richard.
Die Propylaeen der Akropolis zu Athen. Stuttgart, 1882.

Boisserée [Johann].
Geschichte und Beschreibung des Doms von Köln. Munich, 1842.
Denkmale der Baukunst von 7ten bis zum 13ten Jahrhundert am Niederrhein. 1842.

Boito, Camillo.
Il Duomo di Milano. Milan, 1889.
Architettura del Medio Evo in Italia. Milan, 1880.
Architettura Cosmatesca. Milan, 1860.
Andrea Palladio. Milan, 1883.

Boito, Camillo, Editor.
The Basilica of S. Mark in Venice ; illustrated from the points of view of art and history ; (different authors). Venice, 1888, 1889.

Bokelberg, G., und Rowald, P.
Die städtische Markthalle zu Hannover. Hannover, 1894.

Bolognini, Amorini Antonio.
Vite dei Pittori ed Artifici Bolognese. Bologna, 1841–1843.

Bon, Gustave le.
Les Monuments de l'Inde. Paris, 1893.
Les Civilisations de l'Inde. Paris, 1887.
La Civilisation des Arabes. Paris, 1884.

Bonnar, Thomas.
Biographical Sketch of George Meikle Kemp. Edinburgh, 1892.

Bontemps, G.
Peinture sur Verre au XIXe Siècle. Les Secrets de cet Art sont ils Retrouvés ? Quelques Réflexions sur ce Sujet adressées aux Savants et Artistes. Paris, 1845.
Guide du Verrier ; Traité Historique et Pratique de la Fabrication des Verres, Cristaux, Vitraux. 1868.

Borghini, Raffaello.
Il Riposo. Florence, 1730.

Borrmann, Richard.
Die Bau- und Kunstdenkmäler von Berlin. Berlin, 1893.
Die Keramik in der Baukunst (forms part of the Handbuch der Architektur).

Borrmann, Richard ; Kolb, H. ; Vorlaender, O.
Aufnahmen Mittelalterlicher in Deutschland. Berlin, 1897.

Bosc, Ernest.
*Dictionnaire Raisonné d'Architecture. 4 vols. Paris, 1883.

Bottani, Giovanni.
Descrizione storica delle pitture del Regio-Ducale Palazzo del Te. Mantua, 1783.
Bottari, Giovanni Gaetano.
Raccolta di Lettere sulla Pittura, Scultura ed Architettura, scritte da più Celebri Professori, etc. 1754–1768. (See Ticozzi, Stefano, for later edition.)
Bötticher, Gustav Adolf.
Der Hypäthraltempel, auf Grund des Vitruvischen Zeugnisses gegen L. Ross. Berlin (n.d.).
Bouchet, Jules Frédéric.
La Villa Pia des Jardins du Vatican, Architecture de Pirro Ligorio avec une Notice sur l'Auteur de ce Monument . . . et Texte . . . par Raoul-Rochette. Paris, 1837.
Bourassé, l'Abbé J. J.
Les Résidences Royales et Impériales de France. Tours, 1864.
Les Cathédrales de France. Tours, 1843.
Bourgoin, Jules.
Les Arts Arabes; Architecture . . . Paris, 1873.
Boutell, Charles.
Heraldry, Historical and Popular. London, 1864.
English Heraldry. London, 1871.
Boutmy, Émile.
Le Parthénon et le Génie grec. (Originally issued as: Philosophie de l'Architecture en Grèce.) Paris, 1870.
Boyden.
Public Libraries, see R. I. B. A. Journal, 1899.
Boyle (Richard, Lord Burlington).
Ed. of Palladio (Andrea), Fabbriche antiche designate da A. Palladio date in luceda R., Conte di Burlington. London, 1730.
Bramantino, Bartolommeo Suardi, il.
Le Rovine di Roma al Principio del Secolo XVI . . . fotocromo-litografate da A. della Croce, con . . . note di G. Mongeri. Milan, 1880.
Branche, Dominique.
L'Auvergne au Moyen Âge. Paris, 1842.
Brandon, J. A., and Brandon, J. R.
Parish Churches. London, 1848.
Brandt, E.
Lehrbuch der Eisen-Constructionen mit besonderer Anwendung auf den Hochbau. Berlin, 1876.
Brasseur de Bourbourg, Charles Étienne.
Histoire des Nations Civilisées du Mexique et de l'Amérique Centrale durant les Siècles antérieurs à Christophe Colomb. Paris, 1857–1859.
Brayley, E. W., and Neale, J. P.
Historical and Architectural Account of Henry Seventh's Chapel at Westminster. London, 1856.
History and Antiquities of the Abbey Church of S. Peter, Westminster. 1818–1823.
Brehm, Reinhold Bernard, M.D.
Das Inka-Reich: Beitrage zur Staats-und Sittens Geschichte des Kaiserthums Tahuantinsuyu. Jena, 1885.
Brenci, Gusmano, and Lessing, Julius.
Majolika-Fliesen aus Siena 1500–1550. Berlin, 1884.
Brentano, Giuseppe.
Concorso per la Nuova Facciata del Duomo di Milano. Milan, 1888.
Breyman, G. A., und Lang, H.
Allgemeine Bau Constructionenslehre mit besonderer Beziehung auf das Hochbauwesen. Leipzig, 1881.

Brice, Germain.
Description Nouvelle de ce qu'il y a de plus remarquable dans la Ville de Paris. Paris, 1687.
Brinton, Daniel Garrison.
Essays of an Americanist. Philadelphia, 1890.
Brinton, Selwyn.
The Renaissance in Italian Art; three Parts. London, 1900.
British Museum Library, Catalogue of Printed Books. London.
Britton, John.
Chronological History and Graphic Illustrations of Christian Architecture in England (a supplementary volume to Architectural Antiquities of Great Britain), 1818–1826.
Cathedral Antiquities of England. 14 vols., usually bound in 5, 1814–1835.
History and Description of the Ancient Palace and House of Parliament at Westminster. 1834–1836.
* Architectural Antiquities of Great Britain, represented and illustrated . . . Views . . . of various Ancient English Edifices, with . . . Accounts of Each. 5 vols. London, 1806–1821.
Picturesque Antiquities of the English Cities. London, 1836.
History and Antiquities of Bath Abbey Church, London, 1825.
Autobiography. London, 1849.
The Fine Arts of the English School. London, 1812.
Britton, John, and Brayley, E. W.
Memoirs of the Tower of London. London, 1830.
Britton, John, and Pugin, A.
Illustrations of the Public Buildings of London, etc. London, 1825–1828.
Brochure Series of Architectural Illustration, The [Periodical]. Boston, 1895–.
Brockhaus, A. A., Publisher.
Brockhaus' Konversations-Lexikon. 14th edition, 16 vols. Berlin, 1892–1897.
Brown, G. Baldwin.
Dr. Ussing on Vitruvius, R. I. B. A. Journal, 1899.
Brown, Glenn.
Healthy Foundations for Houses (reprinted from Sanitary Engineer). New York, 1885.
History of the United States Capitol. 1900.
Browne, John.
History of the Metropolitan Church of S. Peter, York. London, 1847.
Brownell, William Crary.
French Art; Classic and Contemporary Painting and Sculpture. 1892. New edition, ill. 1901.
Brugsch, Heinrich Karl.
Geschichte Aegyptens unter den Pharaonen. Leipzig, 1877.
Egypt under the Pharaohs. Translated by M. Brodrick. London, 1880; revised edition, 1891.
Brunn, Dr. Heinrich.
Ueber die Sogenannte Leukothea in der Glyptothek Sr. Majestät König Ludwig I. Pamphlet. Munich, 1867.
Geschichte der Griechischen Künstler. Stuttgart, 1889.
Bryan, Michael.
Dictionary of Painters and Engravers, Biographical and Critical. New Edition, revised and enlarged, edited by Robert Edmund Graves, B.A., of the British Museum. London, 1886.

Budge, E. A. Wallis.
The Mummy ; Chapters on Egyptian Funereal Archæology. Cambridge, 1894.
Builder [Periodical]. An Illustrated Weekly Magazine for the Architect, Engineer, Archæologist, Constructor, Sanitary Reformer, and Art Lover. Vol. I. London, 1843 ; current.
"Builder" Series, The. The Cathedrals of England and Wales. London, 1894.
Building Construction, Notes on. London, 1875. (Issued for the South Kensington Schools.)
Building News [Periodical]. London, 1854-.
Building News and Engineering Journal [Periodical]. London, 1857-.
Buisson, J.
Puvis de Chavannes ; in Gazette des Beaux-Arts, 1899.
Bulfinch, Ellen S.
Life and Letters of Charles Bulfinch, Architect, with other Family Papers. Edited by his granddaughter. Boston, 1896.
Bulletin Monumental [Periodical]. Paris, 1834-.
Bulletino dell Instituto di correspondenza archeologica. Rome, 1829-1885 [volumes for '54, '55, published with the Monumenti, etc.].
Bülau, Theodor.
Les Trois Âges de l'Architecture Gothique . . . examples choisis à Ratisbonne. Paris, 1841.
Bulletino di Archeologia Cristiana [Periodical]. Rome, 1863-1889.
Bulteau, M. T.
Description de la Cathédrale de Chartres. Chartres, 1850.
Monographie de la Cathédrale de Chartres. Chartres, 1887-1888.
Vitraux de N. D. de Chartres. Chartres, ——
Bunsen, Christian Karl Josias (originally Gutensohn and Knapp).
*Die basiliken des Christlichen Roms, nach ihrem Zusammenhange mit Idee und Geschichte der Kirchenbaukunst. Munich [pref. 1842].
Burckhardt, Jacob.
Cicerone, or Art Guide to Painting in Italy. London, 1873.
Civilization of the Period of the Renaissance. London, 1878.
Geschichte der Renaissance in Italien, forms part of Geschichte der Neueren Baukunst. (See Burckhardt, Jacob, and Lübke, Wilhelm.)
Burckhardt, Jacob, and Lübke, Wilhelm.
Geschichte der Neueren Baukunst. Stuttgart, 1882-1891.
Burckhardt, John Lewis.
Travels in Syria and the Holy Land. London, 1822.
Burdett, Henry Charles.
Hospitals and Asylums of the World. London, 1891-1893.
Burgoyne, Frank J.
Library Construction, Architecture, Fittings, and Furniture. London, 1897.
Burlington (Lord). (See Boyle, Richard, Lord Burlington.)
Burr, William H.
A Course on the Stresses in Bridge and Roof Trusses, Arched Ribs, and Suspension Bridges. New York, 1893.
Burton, Sir Richard Francis.
Etruscan Bologna ; a Study. London, 1876.
Butler, Alfred Joshua.
*The Ancient Coptic Churches of Egypt. Oxford, 1884.

Butler, Howard Crosby.
*Scotland's Ruined Abbeys. New York and London, 1899.
Buzonnière, Léon de.
Histoire Architecturale de la Ville d'Orléans. Paris, 1849.

Cahier et Martin.
Monographie de la Cathédrale de Bourges.
Cahier, J.
Caractéristiques des Saints. 1867.
Cain, William C. E.
Voussoir Arches applied to Stone Bridges, Tunnels, Domes, and Groined Arches. 1 vol. New York, 1879.
Callet, ——.
Notice Historique sur la Vie . . . et les Ouvrages de quelques Architectes français du Seizième Siècle. Paris, 1843.
Calliat, Victor, and Leroux de Lincy, A. J. V.
Église S. Eustache à Paris. Paris, 1850.
Hôtel-de-Ville de Paris. Liège, 1846.
Calvi, Girolamo Luigi.
La Fondazione del Tempio della Certosa. (A Pamphlet published in Milan, 1862.)
Notizie sulla Vita e sulle Opere dei Principali Architetti, Scultori e Pittori fiorivono in Milano durante il Governo de' Visconti e degli Sforza. Milan, 1859.
Cameron, Charles.
The Baths of the Romans explained and illustrated : with the Restorations of Palladio Corrected and Improved. London, 1772.
Campbell, Colin.
Vitruvius Britannicus. London, 1717-1725.
Canéto, François.
Sainte-Marie d'Auch. Atlas Monographique. Paris, 1857.
Canetta, Carlo.
Aristotele da Bologna, in Archivio Storico Lombardo, Anno IX. 1882.
Canina, Cav. Luigi.
Ricerche sull' Architettura dei Tempi Christiani. Rome, 1846.
Capronnier. (See Descamps.)
Carderera y Solano, Valentin.
Iconografia Española ; Coleccion de Retratos, Estatuas, Mausoleos y demas. . . . Madrid, 1855-1864.
Casati, Dr. Carlo.
Leone Leoni d' Arezzo, Scultore e Giov. Paolo Lomazzo, Pittore Milanese. Milan, 1884.
I Capi d' Arte di Bramante nel Milanesi. Milan, 1870.
Cassas, Louis François.
Voyage Pittoresque de la Syrie, de la Phénicie, de la Palestine et de la Basse Égypte. . . . Paris, 1799.
Cassina, Ferdinando.
Le Fabbriche più Cospicue di Milano. Milan, 1840.
Castell, Robert.
Villas of the Ancients Illustrated. London, 1728.
Castelazzi, Guiseppe.
Il Palazzo detto di Or San Michele. Florence, 1887.
Castiglione, Fra.
Ricordi. Venice, 1584.
Cathedrals of England and Wales, The. (See "Builder" Series.)
Cattaneo, Raffaele.
L' Architettura in Italia dal Secolo VI al Mille circa. Venice, 1888.
Architecture in Italy (translation of the above by Contessa Isabel Curtis-Cholmeley in Bermani). London, 1896.

Cavvadias. (See Kavvadias, P.)
Cellesi, Donato.
    Sei Fabbriche di Firenze. Florence, 1851.
Cellini, Benvenuto.
    Œuvres Complètes ; translated by Leopold
        Leclanché. Paris, 1847.
    Vita di Benvenuto Cellini . . . del Dottor F.
        Tassi. Florence, 1829.
    Autobiography ; translated into English by J.
        A. Symonds as Autobiography of Benvenuto
        Cellini. London, 1887.
Century Guild Hobby Horse, The [Periodical].
    Orpington, England, 1864–.
Ceresole, Victor.
    Alessandro Vittoria ; in L'Art. 1885.
Cerf, Charles.
    Histoire et Description de Notre Dame de
        Reims. Reims, 1861.
Chabat, Pierre.
    Dictionnaire des Termes employés dans la Con-
        struction. 2 vols. Paris, 1881.
Chabeuf, Henri.
    Dijon, Monuments et Souvenirs. Dijon, 1894.
    Jean de la Huerta, Antoine le Moiturier, et le
        Tombeau de Jean Sans Peur. 1891.
Champeaux, Alfred de.
    Des Fondeurs, Ciseleurs, Modeleurs en Bronze
        et Doreurs, etc. Paris, 1886.
    L'Art Décoratif dans le Vieux Paris. Paris, 1888.
    Le Meuble. Paris, 1888.
Champeaux et Gauchery.
    Les Travaux d'Art exécutés pour Jean de
        France, duc de Berry, avec une Étude Bio-
        graphique sur les Artistes employés par ce
        Prince. Paris, 1894.
Champollion-Figeac, Jean Joseph.
    Monographie du Palais de Fontainebleau.
        Paris, 1863.
Chandler, Joseph Everett.
    Colonial Architecture of Maryland, Pennsylva-
        nia, and Virginia. Boston, 1892.
Chandler, R ; Revett, N. ; Pars, W.
    (See Ionian Antiquities.)
Chapuy, Nicolas Marie Joseph.
    Vues Pittoresques de la Cathédrale d'Amiens.
        Paris, 1826.
Charles, L.
    Atelier de Verrier à la Ferté-Bernard à la fin
        du XVe siècle et au XVIe. Le Mans, 1851.
Charnay, Désiré.
    Les Anciennes Villes du Nouveau Monde ;
        Voyages d'Exploration au Mexique et dans
        l'Amérique Centrale (1857–1882). Paris,
        1884.
    Translated as Ancient Cities of the New
        World by J. Conino and H. S. Conant.
        London, 1887.
    Le Mexique : Impressions et Souvenirs. (See
        also Viollet-le-Duc, Cités et Ruines.) Paris,
        1863.
Charvet, Étienne Léon Gabriel.
    Lyon Artistique ; Architectes ; Notices Bio-
        graphiques et Bibliographiques avec une
        Table des Édifices et la Liste Chronologique
        des Noms. Lyons, 1899.
    Architectes Lyonnais.
        (See Charvet, Lyon Artistique.)
    Biographie d'Architectes : Les de Royers de la
        Valfenière. Lyons, 1870.
Chateau, Léon.
    Histoire et Caractères de l'Architecture en
        France. Paris, 1864.
Chateau, Théodore.
    Technologie du Bâtiment, ou Étude Complète
        des Matériaux de toute Espèce employés
        dans les Constructions. Paris, 1880.

Cheney, Mrs. Ednah Dow Littlehale.
    Life of Christian Daniel Rauch, drawn from
        German Authorities. Boston, 1893.
Chennevières-Pointel, Charles Philippe de.
    Archives de l'Art Français. Paris, 1851–1860.
Chesneau, Ernest.
    La Peinture Française au 19e Siècle. Paris,
        1862.
    Le Statuaire J. B. Carpeaux, sa Vie et son
        Œuvre. Paris, 1879.
Chevalier, Casimir.
    Le Château de Chenonceau. Tours, 1869.
    Archives Royales de Chenonceau. 1864.
Chipiez, Charles.
    Histoire Critique des Origines et de la Forma-
        tion des Ordres Grecs. Paris, 1876.
Choisy, François Auguste.
    * L'Art de Bâtir chez les Romains. Paris, 1873.
    Histoire de l'Architecture. Paris, 1899.
    * L'Art de Bâtir chez les Byzantins. Paris,
        1883.
    Études Épigraphiques sur l'Architecture
        Grecque. Paris, 1884.
Christine de Pisan.
    Le Livre des Faits et bonnes Mœurs du Sage
        roi Charles ; Mémoires relatifs à l'Histoire
        de France. Paris, 1854.
Chronique des Arts et de la Curiosité, supplé-
    ment à la Gazette des Beaux-Arts. Paris,
    1875–.
Chrysander, Wilhelm Christian Justus.
    Hist. Nachricht von Kirchen-Glocken. Rin-
        teln, 1755.
Church, Albert E.
    Elements of Descriptive Geometry. New
        York, 1865.
Church, A. H.
    The Chemistry of Paints and Painting. Lon-
        don, 1890.
Cicognara, Leopoldo, conte da.
    * Le Fabbriche più Cospicue di Venezia. 2
        vols. Venice, 1815–1820.
    Catalogo ragionato dei libri d' Arte e d' Anti-
        chità. Pisa, 1821.
    Storia della Scultura dal suo Risorgimento in
        Italia . . . 2d edition. Prato, 1823–1824.
Cicognara, Leopoldo ; Selva, G. A. ; and Diedo
    Antonio.
    Monumenti Sepolcrali Cospicui . . . Turin,
        1858.
Cinelli (Bocchi-Cinelli).
    Belleze delle Citta di Firenze. 1677.
Cittadella, Luigi Napoleone.
    Notizie relative a Ferrara. Ferrara, 1864.
Claretie, Jules.
    Peintres et Sculpteurs contemporains. Pre-
        mière Série, Artistes décédés de 1870 à 1880.
        Paris, 1882.
    Deuxième Série ; Artistes vivants en Janvier,
        1881. Paris, 1884.
Clark, Hugh.
    An Introduction to Heraldry. London, 1884.
Clarke, Joseph Thacher.
    The Hypæthral Question ; An Attempt to deter-
        mine the Mode in which the Interior of a
        Greek Temple was lighted. Cambridge,
        1879.
Clausse, Gustave.
    Les Monuments du Christianisme au Moyen-
        Âge ; Basiliques et Mosaïques Chrétiennes ;
        Italie, Sicile. Paris, 1893.
Clayton, John.
    The Dimensions, Plans, Elevations, and Sec-
        tions of the Parochial Churches of Sir
        Christopher Wren, erected in the Cities of
        London and Westminster. London, 1848.

Clemen, Paul (editor).
Die Kunstdenkmäler der Rheinprovinz. 5 volumes. Dusseldorf, 1899–1901.
Cockerel, C. R.
Antiquities of Athens. (See Stuart and Revett.)
Coëtlosquet, le Comte Charles de.
Notice sur la Cathédrale de Metz. Metz, 1877.
Coffinet (L'Abbé).
Les Peintres Verriers de Troyes. 1858.
Cole, Henry Hardy.
(See India, Archæological Survey.) Illustrations of Ancient Buildings in Kashmir. London, 1869 ; and, Illustrations of Buildings near Muttra and Agra. London, 1873.
Coleman, Caryl.
Christian Altars and their Accessories. Architectural Record, Vol. IV. New York, 1895.
Collignon, Maxime.
Mythologie Figurée de la Grèce. Paris, 1883.
Histoire de la Sculpture Grecque. Paris, 1897.
Manuel d'Archéologie Grecque. Paris. Translated into English as Manual of Greek Archeology, by J. H. Wright. London, 1886.
Phidias [forms part of series Les Artistes Célèbres]. Paris (n.d.).
Collings, George.
Circular Work in Carpentry and Joinery ; a Practical Treatise on Circular Work of Single and Double Curvature. (See Weale's Rudimentary Series.) London, 1890.
Roof Carpentry, Practical Lessons in the Framing of Wood Roofs for the Use of Working Carpenters. (See Weale's Rudimentary Series.) London, 1893.
Colvin, Sidney.
Jacopo della Quercia, in Portfolio. 1883.
The History of a Pavement ; in Fortnightly Review, Vol. 24, 1875.
Colyer, Frederick.
Treatise on the Modern Sanitary Appliances. London.
Public Institutions ; their Engineering and Sanitary and other Appliances, with the Construction of Several Departments. London, 1889.
Commission des Monuments Historiques.
Archives. 4 vols. Paris, 1855–1872.
Archives. Paris (n.d.). Publication begun 1898 unfinished ; wholly separate from the earlier publication.
Comolli, Angelo.
Bibliografia Storico-Critica dell' Architettura Civile ed Arte subalterne. Rome, 1788–1792.
Comparetti, Domenico, and Petra, Giulio de.
La Villa Ercolanese dei Pisoni ; i suoi Monumenti e la sua Biblioteca. Turin, 1883.
Conder, Claude Reignier.
Syrian Stone-Lore. London, 1896.
Conder, Josiah.
Landscape Gardening in Japan. Tokio, 1893.
Condivi, Ascanio.
Vita di Michelangelo Buonarroti. Pisa, 1823.
Construction Moderne, La ; Journal Hebdomadaire Illustré [Periodical]. Paris, 1st vol., 1885, current.
Contarini, Domenico.
The Basilica of S. Mark in Venice, translated by F. Horne Rosenberg.
Corfield, William Henry.
Sanitary Construction of Dwellings. 1880.
Cornelius, Carl.
Jacopo della Quercia. Halle, 1896.
Corner, James M., and Soderholtz, E. E.
Examples of Domestic Colonial Architecture in Maryland and Virginia. Boston, 1892.

Examples of Domestic and Colonial Architecture in New England. Boston, 1891.
Corroyer, Édouard.
Description de l'Abbaye du Mont S. Michel. Paris, 1877.
L'Architecture Gothique. Paris.
L'Architecture Romaine. Paris.
(See Bibliothèque de l'enseignement des Beaux-Arts.)
Coste, Pascal.
Monuments modernes de la Perse. Paris, [1865]–1867.
Couchaud, A.
Choix d'Églises Byzantines en Grèce. Paris, 1837, 1842.
Courajod, Louis.
Alexandre Lenoir, son Journal, et le Musée des Monuments Français. Paris, 1878.
Leçons professées à l'École du Louvre.
I. Origines de l'Art Roman et Gothique.
II. Origines de la Renaissance. Paris, 1899, 1901.
Cousin de Contamine.
Eloge de Coustou, sculpteur ordinaire du Roy. Paris, 1737.
Coussemaker, E. de.
Vitraux Peints et Incolores des Églises de la Flandre Maritime. Lille, 1860.
Crane, Edward A., and Soderholtz, E. E.
Examples of Colonial Architecture in South Carolina and Georgia. Berlin.
Cresy, Edward.
Practical Treatise on Bridge-Building and on the Equilibrium of Vaults and Arches, with the . . . Life and Selections from the Works of Rennie. London, 1839.
Cresy, Mrs. Eliza Taylor.
Lives of Celebrated Architects, Ancient and Modern, translated from the Italian. (See Milizia, Francesco.)
Crosnier (L'Abbé).
Vocabulaire des Symboles et Attributs. Tome XIV. du Bulletin Monumental.
Crowe, J. A., and Cavalcaselle, G. B.
A New History of Painting in Italy. 3 vols. London, 1864–1866.
A History of Painting in North Italy. London, 1871.
The Early Flemish Painters. London, 2d ed. 1872 ; 3d ed. 1879.
Titian, His Life and Times. London, 1877.
Raphael, His Life and Works. 2 vols. London, 1882–1885.
Crowninshield, Frederic.
Mural Painting. New York and Boston, 1887.
Crystal Palace. The Fine Arts Courts. London, 1854.
Cummings, Thomas Seir.
Historical Annals of the National Academy of Design. New York, 1865.
Cunningham, Sir Alexander.
Mahabodi, or the Great Buddhist Temple at Buddha-Gayâ. London, 1892.
Cunningham, Sir Alexander (compiler). (See India, Archæological Survey Reports, 1871.)
Cunningham, Allan.
Lives of the Most Eminent British Painters, Sculptors, and Architects. London, 1830–1833.
Life of Inigo Jones.
Curtis, William Eleroy.
Capitals of Spanish America. New York, 1888.
Curtius, Ernst, and Adler, Friedrich.
Olympia ; die Ergebnisse der von dem Deutschen Reich veranstalteten Ausgrabung. Berlin, 1890.

Curzon, Hon. Robert.
    Visits to Monasteries in the Levant. London, 1849.
Cussans, John E.
    Handbook of Heraldry. London, 1882.
Cyclopedia of American Biography (Appleton).

Dahl, Johan Christian Clausen.
    Denkmale einer sehr Ausgebildeten Holzbaukunst aus den Frühesten Jahrhunderten in den inneren Landschaften Norwegens. Dresden, 1837.
Daly, César.
    Funérailles de Félix Duban, Architecte du Gouvernement. Paris, 1871.
Daniell, A. E.
    London City Churches. New York, 1896.
Danti, Ignatio.
    Vita di Jacopo Barozzi da Vignola: in Barozzi da Vignola; Le due Regole della Prospettiva pratica. Rome, 1583.
Darcel, Alfred.
    Les Autels de Pistoia et de Florence; in Gazette des Beaux-Arts, 1883.
Daremberg, Ch., and Saglio, Edm.
    Dictionnaire des Antiquités Grecques et Romaines. Paris, 1873–. Not yet complete.
D'Argenville, Antoine Joseph. (See Dezallier.)
Darmstadt Handbuch. (See Handbuch der Architektur.)
Dartein, F. de.
    * Étude sur l'Architecture Lombarde. Paris, 1865–1882.
Daun, Berthold.
    Adam Kraft und die Künstler seiner Zeit; ein Beitrag zur Kunstgeschichte Nürnbergs. Berlin, 1897.
Davie, W. Galsworthy.
    Architectural Studies in France. London, 1877.
Deck, Joseph Théodore.
    La Faïence. Paris, 1887.
Decloux and Doury.
    * Histoire de la Sainte Chapelle du Palais. Paris, 1865.
De Forest, Lockwood.
    Indian Architecture and Ornament. Boston, 1887.
    Indian Domestic Architecture.
Defrasse, Alphonse; Lechat, Henri.
    Épidaure, Restauration et Description. Paris, 1895.
Degen, Ludwig.
    Der Bau der Krankenhäuser. Munich, 1862.
Dehio, Georg, und Bezold, Gustav.
    Die Kirchliche Baukunst des Abendlandes. Stuttgart, 1887.
Dehli, Arne, and Chamberlin, George.
    Norman Monuments of Palermo and Environs; a Study. Boston, 1893.
Delaporte, Louis Marie Joseph.
    Voyage au Cambodge; l'Architecture Khmer. 1880.
Delisle, Dom Joseph.
    Histoire de l'Ancienne Abbaye de Saint Mihiel. Nancy, 1758.
Delisle, Leopold Victor.
    Le Cabinet des Manuscrits de la Bibliothèque Impériale (Nationale). Paris. 1865.
De l'Orme, Philibert.
    Nouvelle Invention pour bien bâtir et à petits frais. Paris, 1561, 1568, or 1576. Included in Œuvres d'Architecture. 2 vols. Paris, 1626, or Rouen, 1648.
Demidoff, Anatoli Nikolaivich, Knyaz San Donato.
    Voyage Pittoresque et Archéologique en Rus-

sie; Dessins faits d'après Nature, et Lithographiés par André Durand et Raffet. Paris, 1840–1847.
Dennis, George.
    The Cities and Cemeteries of Etruria. 2 vols. London, 1878–1883.
Denton, John Bailey.
    Farm Homesteads of England. London, 1864.
Department of Agriculture, Washington, D. C.
    Circulars.
De Quincy. (See Quatremère de Quincy.)
Descamps, Henri Philibert Valentin, and Le Maistre d'Anstaing, J.
    Les Vitraux de la Cathédrale de Tournai, dessinés par J. B. Capronnier et mis sur pierre par J. de Keghel. Brussels, 1848.
Description de l'Egypte, 1809–1813. 25 vols (2d edition, 1821–1830). [The great work on Egypt resulting from Bonaparte's Expedition.]
Deshaisnes.
    Histoire de l'Art dans la Flandre, l'Artois et le Hainault, avant le XVe Siècle. Lille, 1868.
Desjardins, Gustave Adolphe.
    Histoire de la Cathédrale de Beauvais. Paris, 1865.
Desjardins, J. J. Abel.
    La Vie et l'Œuvre de Jean Bologne. Paris, 1883.
Destailleur, Hippolyte.
    Notice sur quelques Artistes français. Paris, 1893.
Detcheverry, Arnaud.
    Histoire des Théâtres de Bordeaux, depuis leur Origine dans cette Ville jusqu'à nos Jours. Bordeaux, 1860–1880.
Detzel, H.
    Christliche Ikonographie. Freiburg, 1896.
Deutsche Bauzeitung; Verkündigungsblatt des Verbandes deutscher Architekten- und Ingenieur-Vereine. Berlin, 1867.
Deutsches Archaeologisches Institut; Athenische Abtheilung. (Previous to 1886 known as Deutsches Archaeologisches Institut in Athen.)
    Mittheilungen. Athens, 1876–.
Deutsches Bauhandbuch.
    Berlin. (New edition published about 1894.)
Deville, Jean Achille.
    Revue des Architectes de la Cathédrale de Rouen, jusqu'à la fin du XVIe Siècle. Rouen, 1848.
    Comptes des dépenses de la Construction du Château de Gaillon. Paris, 1851.
    Tombeaux de la Cathédrale de Rouen. Paris, 1881.
Devillez, Barthélemy Adolphe.
    Éléments de Constructions Civiles, Art de Bâtir, Composition des Édifices. Paris, 1882.
Dezallier d'Argenville, Antoine Nicolas.
    Vie des Fameux Sculpteurs depuis la Renaissance des Arts, avec la Descriptions de leurs Ouvrages. Paris, 1788.
Dictionary, The, of Architecture; issued by the Architectural Publication Society. London (n.d.).
Dictionary of National Biography. Edited by Leslie Stephen, by him and by Sidney Lee, and by Sidney Lee. 64 vols., 1885–1900. (3 vols. supplementary, 1901.)
Dictionary of Painters and Engravers, biographical and critical. (See Bryan, Michael.)
Dictionnaire Critique. Paris, 1872. (See Jal, A.)
Dictionnaire de l'Ameublement et de la Décoration. (See Havard, Henry.)

Dictionnaire des Antiquités chrétiennes. (See Martigny, Joseph Alexandre.) Paris, 1865.

Dictionnaire des Architectes français. Paris, 1872. (See Lance, Adolphe.)

Dictionnaire des Sculpteurs français. Paris, 1898. (See Lami, Stanislas.)

Dictionnaire Historique d'Architecture. Paris, 1832. (See Quatremère de Quincy, A. C.)

Didot, Ambroise Firmin.
Étude sur Jean Cousin. Paris, 1872.

Die Mittelalterlichen Baudenkmäler Niedersachsens. Hanover, 1856.

Dietrichson, Dr. L., und Munthe, H.
Die Holzbaukunst Norwegens in Vergangenheit und Gegenwart. Berlin, 1893. Dresden (n.d.).

Dieulafoy, Marcel Auguste.
L'Art antique de la Perse, Achéménides, Parthes, Sassanides. Paris, 1884.

Dilettanti, Society of.
Unedited antiquities of Attica, comprising the architectural remains of Eleusis, Rhamnus, Sunium, and Thoricus, by the Society of the Dilettanti [Forms a 2d supplement to Stuart and Revett; cf. Cockerell et al., under Stuart and Revett.]
Antiquities of Ionia. (See Antiquities.)
Ionian Antiquities. (See Ionian.)

Dilke, Lady.
French Painters of the Eighteenth Century. London, 1899.
French Architects and Sculptors of the Eighteenth Century. London, 1900.

Discorso per l'Inaugurazione del Monumento a Michele Sanmicheli, eretto in Verona li 7 Giugno, 1874 [per G. Camuzzoni], e Publicazione di Suoi Scritti Inediti e di Altri Documenti Tratti dal R. archivio Generale di Venezia [da A. Bertoldi]. Verona, 1874.

Dohme, Robert.
Barock- und Rococo-Architektur. Berlin, 1892.
Geschichte der Deutschen Baukunst. Berlin, 1887.
Die Masken Sterbender Krieger im Hofe des ehemaligen Zeughauses zu Berlin von Andreas Schlüter: text von Dr. R. H. Dome. Berlin (n.d.).

Dohme Series. (See Kunst und Kunstler des Mittelalters und der Neuzeit.)

Dollman, F. T., and Jobbins, J. R.
Examples of Ancient Domestic Architecture. London, 1861–63.

*Domestic Architecture in England, Some Account of. 3 vols. in 4. (Vol. I. by Dawson Turner, the others "by the editor of the Glossary of Architecture.") Oxford, 1851–1859.

Donati, ——.
Elogio di Baldassare Peruzzi. Siena, 1879.

Doolitle, Justus.
Social Life of the Chinese ; with some Account of their Religious, Governmental, Educational, and Business Customs and Opinions. New York, 1867.

Du Cerceau, Jacques Androuet.
Les plus excellents Bastiments de France. Paris, 1579. Reprinted, 1868.

Dublin Builder, The. A monthly journal devoted to architecture, engineering, and sanitary improvement, vols. 1–8. (Continued as The Irish Builder.) Dublin, 1859–1866.

Dubois, A. Jay.
The Strains of Framed Structures, with numerous Practical Applications to Cranes — Bridge, Roof, and Suspension Trusses —

Braced Arches — Pivot and Draw Spans — Continuous Girders, etc. New York, 1892.

Duchesne, Jean.
Notice historique sur la vie et les ouvrages de Jules Hardouin-Mansart. Reprinted from Magazin Encylopédique. 1805.

Dugdale, Sir William.
Monasticon Anglicanum; a History of the Abbies and other Monasteries, Hospitals, and Churches in England and Wales. London, 1817–1830.
History of St. Paul's Cathedral in London. London, 1658, 1716, 1818.

Dumesnil, Antoine Jules.
Histoire des Plus Célèbres Amateurs Français. Paris, 1856–1858.

Dumont, A. L.
Discours prononcés aux funérailles de M. le Baron Bosio. Paris, 1845.

Dunraven, Edwin Richard Windham Quin, Earl of.
Notes on Irish Architecture. London, 1875–1877.

Dupasquier, Louis.
Monographie de Notre Dame de Brou. Paris, 1842.

Duplais, Léonie.
Étude sur les Anguier (Français et Michel), Célèbres Sculpteurs du 17e siècle . . . 2e ed.

Duppa, Richard.
Life and Literary Works of Michelangelo Buonarroti. London, 1806.

Durand, J. N. L.
Notice Historique sur la vie et les Ouvrages d'Antoine Rondelet. 1835.

Durandus, William.
The Symbolism of Churches and Church Ornaments. New York, 1893.

Durelli, Gaetano e Francesco.
*La Certosa di Pavia descritta . . . Milan, 1863.

Durm, Josef.
Constructive and Polychrome Details der Griechischen Baukunst. Berlin, 1880.
Die Baukunst der Etrusker . . . der Römer ; in Handbuch der Architektur.

Duruy, Jean Victor.
Histoire des Romains depuis les Temps les Plus Reculés jusqu'à la Mort de Theodose. 7 vols., 1876–1885, and later editions.
Histoire de la Grèce ancienne. 1862.

Dusevel.
Recherches Historiques sur les Ouvrages exécutés dans la ville d'Amiens, par les Maitres de l'Œuvre, etc. Amiens, 1858.

Dussieux, Louis Étienne.
Le château de Versailles. Versailles, 1881.
Les Artistes Français à l'Etranger. 1852.

Duthilleul, Hippolite Romain Joseph.
Éloge de Jean Bologne. Douai, 1820.

Dyer, Louis.
Studies of the Gods in Greece at certain Sanctuaries recently excavated. London and New York, 1891.

Eastlake, C. L.
A history of the Gothic Revival. London and New York, 1872.

Ebe, Gustav.
Die Spät-Renaissance ; Kunst-Geschichte der Europäischen Länder von der mitte des 16. bis zum ende des 18. Jahrhunderts. Berlin, 1886.
Die Schmuckformen der Monumentalbauten. Leipzig, 1896.

Ecclesiologist, The. Published by the Cambridge Camden Society. Cambridge, 1842–1868.

Edhem-Pacha.
L'Architecture Ottomane ; ouvrage autorisé par iradé-impériale. Constantinople, 1873. Also in German.

Edwards, Miss Amelia Blandford.
Egyptian Archæology (translation of Maspero's Archæologie Égyptienne). London, 1887.

Eggers, ——.
De Origine et Nomine Campanarum. Jena, 1684.

Eggers, Hartwig Karl Friedrich.
Christian Daniel Rauch. (Edited and continued by K. F. P. Eggers.) Berlin, 1873–1887.

Ehret, George.
Twenty-five years of Brewing, with an Illustrated History of American Beer. New York, 1891.

Eitelberger von Edelberg, Rudolph von, und Heider, G. A., und Hieser, Joseph, compilers.
Mittelalterliche Kunstdenkmale des Oesterreichischen Kaiserstaates. Stuttgart, 1858, 1860.

Elis, Carl.
Der Dom zu Halberstadt. Berlin, 1883.

Elmes, James.
Sir Christopher Wren and his Times, with . . . sketches and anecdotes of . . . distinguished personages in the seventeenth century. London, 1852.

Emerson, William Ralph.
The Architecture and Furniture of the Spanish Colonies during the seventeenth and eighteenth Centuries. Boston (n.d.).

Emulation (L') : Publication Mensuelle de la Société Centrale d'Architecture de Belgique [Periodical]. Brussels, 1891–1893.

Encyclopedia of Architecture. (See Gwilt, Joseph.)

Encyclopédie d'Architecture et des arts qui s'y rattachent. Paris, 1888.

*Encyclopédie d'Architecture. Journal Mensuel. Paris, 1851–1862. [Periodical.]

Encyclopédie de l'Architecture et de la Construction. Paris (n.d.). (See Planat.)

Encyclopédie des Travaux Publics. C. Lechalas, editor. Paris, 1893.

Engineering Record [Periodical], New York. (Formerly the Sanitary Engineer.)

Enlart, C.
Origines Françaises de l'Architecture Gothique en Italie. Paris, 1894.

Ephrussi, Charles.
Albrecht Dürer et ses Dessins. Paris, 1881.
Paul Baudry, sa Vie et son Œuvre. Paris, 1878.

Ernouf de Verclives, A. A., and Alphand, T. C.
L'Art des Jardins. Paris, 1868.

Ernst, Leopold, and Oscher, L.
Baudenkmale des Mittelalters in Erzherzogthum Oesterreich ; Algemeine Bauzeitung (about 30 vols.).

Essenwein, August.
Die romanische und die gothische Baukunst (forms part of Handbuch der Architektur ; only Parts I. and II., military and domestic building). Darmstadt, 1889–1892.

Ethnology, Bureau of American. (See United States.)

Evans, Edward Payson.
Animal Symbolism in Ecclesiastical Architecture. 1896.

Evelyn, John.
Diary. London, 1818.

Eyriès, Gustave.
Châteaux Historiques de France. Poitiers, 1880.

Fabricius, M. P.
Le Kremlin de Moscou, Esquisses et Tableaux, autrefois et aujourd'hui. Moscow, 1883.

Fabriczy, C. von.
Giuliano da Maiano architetto del Duomo di Faenza ; in Archivio Storico dell' Arte, vol. 3 (1890).
Filippo Brunelleschi. Stuttgart, 1893.

Facco de Lagarda, Professor Eduardo, and Sacconi, Conte Giuseppe.
Loreto, Monografia Storico-Artistica. Rome, 1895.

Fagan, Louis.
The Works of Correggio at Parma. London, 1873.

Fah, Dr. Rudolf.
Grundriss der Geschichte der Bildenen Künste. Freiburg im Breisgau, 1897.

Fahne, Anton.
Diplomatische Beiträge zur Geschichte der Baumeister des Kölner Domes und der bei diesem werke thätig gewesenen künstler. Cologne, 1843.

Falda, Giovanni Battista.
Le Fontane di Roma. Rome, 1680.

Falkener, Edward.
Ephesus and the Temple of Diana. London, 1862.

Fantozzi, Federigo.
Nuova Guida di Firenze. 1844.

Farish, ——.
Isometrical Perspective. Cambridge, 1820.

Farrar, Joseph.
Baths and Bathing. Bristol (Eng.) and London, 1890.

Farrow, Frederic Richard.
The Recent Development of Vienna ; in R. I. B. A., Transactions, 1887–1888.

Fauré, P.
Théorie des Proportions en Architecture, d' après l'analyse des monuments. Paris, 1893.

Feasey, Henry John.
*Westminster Abbey historically described. London, 1899.

Félibien, André.
Des principes de l'Architecture de la Sculpture et de la Peinture. Paris, 1676. (Chapitre XXI, principaux modes d'assemblages usités à cette époque pour le verre blanc.)
Entretiens sur les Vies et les Ouvrages des plus excellents Peintres, anciens et modernes, avec la Vie des Architectes. Paris, 1685–88.
Mémoires pour servir à l'histoire des Maisons Royales et Bâtiments de France. Paris, 1874.

Fellows, Charles.
A Journal written . . . in Asia Minor. London, 1839.
An Account of Discoveries in Lycia. London, 1841.
Lycia, Caria, Lydia, illustrated by G. Scharf. London, 1847. Part I., all published.

Fergus, Andrew.
The Sewage Question, with Remarks and Experiments showing the Inefficiency of Water Traps. Glasgow, Edinburgh, printed 1874.

Fergusson, James.
History of the Modern Styles of Architecture. 2d ed. London, 1873.
The History of Indian and Eastern Architecture. London, 1876.

Rude Stone Monuments in all Countries; their Age and Uses. London, 1872.

Illustrations of the Rock-cut Temples of India. London, 1845.

Picturesque Illustrations of Ancient Architecture in Hindostan. London, 1848.

A History of Architecture in all Countries. 3d ed. edited by R. P. Spiers. 5 vols. London, 1876, 1891, 1893. (This includes The History of Modern Architecture, which is edited by Robert Kerr, and The History of Indian and Eastern Architecture, as above.)

Palaces of Nineveh and Persepolis Restored. London, 1851.

Fergusson, James, and Burgess, James.
Cave Temples in India. London, 1880.

Fermelhuis, ——.
Éloge Funèbre de Coysevox Sculpteur du Roy, prononcé à l'Académie. Paris, 1721.

Ferrari, Luigi.
Palladio e Venezia. Venice, 1880.

Ferree, Barr.
The Chronology of the Cathedral Churches of France. New York, 1894.

Ferrero, Ermanno.
L'Arche d'Auguste à Suse. Turin, 1901.

Ferrey, Benjamin.
Recollections of A. N. Welby Pugin and his father, Augustus Pugin, with notices of their Works; with an appendix by E. S. Purcell. London, 1861.

Fewkes, Jesse Walker.
Preliminary Account of an Expedition to the Cliff Villages of the Red Rock Country and the Tusayan Ruins of Siknatki and Arvatobi, Arizona, in 1895; in Smithsonian Institution Annual Report, 1895.

Preliminary Account of an Expedition to the Pueblo Ruins near Winslow, Arizona, in 1896. Smithsonian Institution Annual Report for 1896.

A Preliminary Account of Archæological Field Work in Arizona, 1897. Smithsonian Institution Annual Report for 1897.

Archæological Expedition to Arizona in 1895. Illustrated, 82 pl., 4 maps. United States Bureau of American Ethnology Annual Report. Washington, D.C., 1898.

Fillon, Benjamin, and Rochebrune, O. G. de.
Poitou et Vendée. Fontenay-le-Comte, 1862–1865.

Firmin-Didot, Ambroise.
Œuvres choisies de Jean Cousin. Paris, 1872.

Flandin, Eugène Napoléon et Coste, X. P.
Voyage en Perse pendant les Années 1840 et 1841, entrepris par ordre de M. le Ministre des Affaires Étrangères d'après les instructions dressées par l'Institut. Paris, 1843–1854.

Fletcher, Banister.
Quantities, a Text-book for Surveyors, in Tabulated Form. London, 1880.

Dilapidations; a Text-book for Architects and Surveyors, in Tabulated Form. London, 1891.

Fletcher, Banister, and Fletcher, Banister F.
A History of Architecture. London and New York, 1896.

Folchi, Clemente.
Discorso . . . in Encomio . . . del Commendatore Luigi Canina.

Folwell, Amory Prescott.
Water Supply Engineering; the Designing, Construction, and Maintenance of Water Supply Systems, both City and Irrigation. New York, 1800.

Ford, Richard.
A Handbook for Travellers in Spain. London, 1882.
(This, or a modification of it, published as Murray's Handbook for Spain.)

Förster, Ernst.
*Denkmale Deutscher Baukunst, Bildnerei und Malerei von Einführung des Christenthums bis auf die neueste Zeit. Leipzig, 1855–1869.
Translated into French as: Monuments d'Architecture de Sculpture et de Peinture de Allemagne; by W. and E. de Suckau. Paris, 1866.

Fourcaud, L. de.
François Rude; in Gazette des Beaux-Arts 1888–1890.

Fournier, A.
La Verrerie de Portieux (Lorraine). Paris, 1886.

Fournier, Édouard.
Paris à travers les Âges; aspects successifs des Monuments et Quartiers historiques de Paris depuis le XIIIe siècle jusqu'à nos jours. Texte par MM. E. Fournier, A. de Montaiglon, etc. Paris, Mesnil (Eure), 1875.

Frazer, J. G.
*Pausanias's Description of Greece. Translated with a commentary by J. G. Frazer. 6 vols. London and New York, 1898.

Freitag, Joseph Kendall.
Architectural Engineering; with special reference to High Building Construction . . New York, 1895.

French, Henry F.
Farm Drainage. The Principles and Effects of Draining Land, etc. New York, 1879.

Frey, Karl.
Loggia dei Lanzi zu Florence. Berlin, 1885.

Friederichs, Karl Heinrich F. W.
Der Doryphores des Polyklet. Berlin, 1863.

Friedlaender, Julius.
Gottfried Schadow, aufsätze und briefe nebst einem verzeichniss Seiner Werke . . . Düsseldorf, 1864.

Friedmann.
Entwurfe für den Bau von Hallen Markten und Lagerhaüsen.

Friedrich, Karl.
Augustin Hirsvogel als Toepfer. Nuremberg, 1885.
Die Essenbeinreliefs an der Kanzel des Doms zu Aachen. Nuremberg, 1883.

Fritsch, K. E. O.
Denkmaler Deutscher Renaissance. Berlin, 1891.

Froebel, Julius.
Seven Years' Travel in Central America, Northern Mexico, and the far West of the United States. With illustrations. [Translated from the German.]

Frontinus, Sextus Julius.
De Aquæductibus Urbis Romæ, Libri II. Translated into English as: The Two Books on the Water Supply of the City of Rome of Sextus Julius Frontinus. A Photographic Reproduction. Explanatory chapters by Clemens Herschel. Boston, 1899.

Frothingham, A. L., Jr. Notes on Roman Artists of the Middle Ages; in American Journal of Archaeology, Vols. V., VI., 1889–1890.

Fuentes, Don Manuel Atanasio.
Guia historico-descriptiva, administrativa, judicial y de domicilio de Lima. Lima, 1860.

Fumagalli, Carlo.
Il Castello di Malpaga. Milan, 1894.

Fumi, Luigi.
    Il Duomo di Orvieto e i suoi restauri . . . Rome,
        1891.
Furtwängler, Adolf.
    Meisterwerke der Griechischen Plastik ; Kunst-
        geschichtliche untersuchungen.   Leipsic,
        1893.
    Translated as : Masterpiece of Greek Sculpture.
        A series of Essays on the History of Art.
        Edited by Eugénie Sellers.   With 19 full
        page plates and 200 text illustrations.   New
        York, 1895.
Füssli, Johann Rudolf.
    Allgemeines   Künstlerlexicon ;   oder   Kurze
        Nachricht von den Leben und den Werken
        der Mahler, Bildhauer, Baumeister, Kup-
        ferstecher.   Zurich, 1779-1821.

Gailhabaud, Jules.
    * Monuments Anciens et Modernes.   Paris,
        1849-1858.
    * L'Art dans ses diverses branches. Paris, 1863.
    * L'Architecture du Vme au XVIIme siècle et les
        Arts qui en dependent.   Paris, 1858.
Galland, Georg.
    Geschichte der holländischen Baukunst und
        Bildnerei im Zeitalter der Renaissance, der
        nationalen Blüte und des Klassicismus.
        Frankfurt a. M., 1890.
Galton, Sir Douglas Strutt.
    Healthy Hospitals : Observations on Some
        Points connected with Hospital Construc-
        tion.   Oxford, 1893.
Galvani, Dr. F. A.
    Il Re d' Armi di Sebenico.   Venice, 1884.
Gandon, James, Jr.
    Life of James Gandon . . . prepared for pub-
        lication by Th. J. Mulvany.   Dublin, 1846.
Gardner, Ernest Arthur.
    A Handbook of Greek Sculpture.   London,
        1897.
Gardner, Percy.
    Sculptured Tombs of Hellas. London, 1896.
    New Chapters in Greek History ; Historical
        Results of recent Excavations in Greece and
        Asia Minor.   New York, 1892.
    The Types of Greek Coins ; an Archæological
        Essay.   Cambridge, 1883.
Garnier, Charles.
    Michel-Ange, architecte (first published in the
        Gazette des Beaux-Arts).
    Le Nouvel Opéra de Paris.   Paris, 1875-1881.
Garnier, E.
    Voyages dans l'Hindoustan, l'Indo-Chine, le
        Sindhy, à Lahore, à Caboul et dans l'Af-
        ghanistan.   Tours, 1857.
Garrucci, Raffaele.
    Storia della Arte cristiana nei primi otto secoli
        della chiesa . . .   Prato, 1873-1881.
Gasset, Alphonse.
    Les Coupoles d'Orient et d'Occident.   Paris,
        1889.
Gatty, Alfred.
    The Bell, its Origin, History, and Uses. Lon-
        don, 1847.
Gaucherel, Léon.
    * Exemples de Décoration Appliqués à l'Archi-
        tecture et à la Peinture.   1st pt. ; 2d pt.
        never published. Paris, 1857.
Gaudard, Jules.
    Foundations ; translated by L. F. Vernon Har-
        court. New York, 1891.
Gauthier, Martin Pierre.
    Les plus beaux Édifices de la Ville de Gênes et
        de ses Environs.   Paris, 1830-1832.

Gavard, Jacques Dominique Charles.
    Galeries historiques de Versailles. Paris, 1838.
Gaye, Johann Wilhelm.
    Carteggio inedito d' arteggio dei secoli 14, 1516.
        Florence, 1839-1840.
Gazette des Beaux-Arts [Periodical].   Paris, 1859
        and following years.
Geier, Franz, und Garz, R.
    Denkmale Romanischer Baukunst am Rhein.
        Frankfurt am Main, 1846-1847.
Gélis-Didot, P.
    La Peinture décorative en France du XIe au
        XVIe siècle. Paris (n.d.).
    La Peinture décorative en France du XVIe au
        XVIIIe siècle. Paris.
Genevay, Antoine.
    Le Style Louis XIV., Ch. Lebrun, ses Œuvres,
        etc. Paris, 1886.
Genouillac, H. Gourdon de.
    L'Art héraldique. Paris.
Genuys, Charles.
    Construction Maçonnerie. Paris, 1885.
* "Georgian   Period,   The," being   measured
        Drawings of Colonial Work.   American
        Architect and Building News Co.   (8 parts
        published, 1901.)
Gérard, Charles.
    Les Artistes de l'Alsace pendant le Moyen-
        Âge. Colmar, 1872-1873.
Gerhard, William Paul.
    Disposal of Household Waste.   New York,
        1890.
    House Drainage and Sanitary Plumbing. New
        York, 1890.
    Sanitary Engineering of Buildings. New York,
        1899.
    Recent Practice in the Sanitary Drainage of
        Buildings.   1890.
    Sanitary House Inspection.   1885-1887.
    Entwaesserungs-Anlagen amerikanischer Ge-
        baüde [an extra number (Fortschritte
        No. 10) of the Handbuch der Architektur].
        Stuttgart, 1897.
    Haus Entwaesserungen, eine bauhygienische
        Skizze.
German Architectural Pocket Library.   Deutsche
        Bautetechnische Taschenbibliothek. Leip-
        zig, 1875-.
Gerspach, Édouard.
    L'Art de la Verrerie. Paris, 1885.
    La Mosaïque. Paris, 1833. (Forms part of
        Bibliothèque de l'enseignement des Beaux-
        Arts.)
Gessert, ——.
    Geschichte der Glasmalerei.   Stuttgart and
        Tübingen, 1839.
Geymüller, Baron Heinrich von.
    Les Projets primitifs pour la Basilique de S.
        Pierre de Rome par Bramante, Raphaël
        Sanzio, etc. Paris, 1880.
    Documents inédits sur les Manuscrits et les
        œuvres d'architecture de la famille des
        San Gallo ; in Mémoires de la Société
        nationale des Antiquaires de France. 1884.
    Les du Cerceau. Paris and London, 1887.
    Raffaello Sanzio come architetto, con l' aiuto
        di nuovi documenti. Milan, 1884.
    Documents inédits sur les thermes d'Agrippa,
        le Panthéon et les thermes de Dioclétien.
        Lausanne, 1883.
Geymüller-Stegmann.
    Die Architektur der Renaissance in Toscana
        (originally supported by the Gesellschaft
        San Giorgio in Florence), parts 1-36 ; 1885-
        1896.   Four more parts, completing the
        work, had not appeared August, 1901.

Giannuizzi, Pietro.
　Giorgio da Sebenico, Architetto e scultore vissuto nel secolo XV. ; in Archivio Storico dell' Arte, 1894.
Gilbert, A. P. M.
　Description historique de l'Église Cathédrale de Notre Dame de Chartres. Chartres ; Paris, 1824.
　Description historique de l'Église Cathédrale de Notre Dame d'Amiens. Amiens, 1833.
Gillespie, William Mitchell.
　Elements of Perpendicular Projection. 1897.
Gindriez, Charles.
　François Rude ; in L'Art [Periodical] for 1881.
Giovanelli, Conte Benedetto dei.
　Vita di Alessandro Vittoria, scultore trentino. Trent, 1858.
Girard, Paul.
　La Peinture Antique. Paris, 1892.
Giraudet, Eugène.
　Les artistes Tourangeaux. Notes et documents inédits. Tours, 1885.
Girault de Prangey, ——.
　Essai sur l'Architecture des Arabes. 1842.
Gisors, Alphonse de.
　Le Palais du Luxembourg. Paris, 1847.
Gladbach, Ernst.
　* Les Constructions en Bois de la Suisse. Paris, 1870.
　Die Schweizer Holzstyle. Zurich, 1882.
* Glossary (A) of Terms used in Grecian, Roman, Italian, and Gothic Architecture. Oxford, 1850.
Gnoli, Domenico.
　La Cancelleria ed altri Palazzi attribute a Bramante ; in Archivio Storico dell' Arte, 1892.
　Le Opere di Mino da Fiesole in Roma ; in Archivio Storico dell' Arte, Vol. II., 1889.
Gomez, Camillo A.
　Historia de la America Central Guatemale, Tipografia Nacional. 1895–1897.
Goncourt, Édmond et Jules de.
　L'Art de la dix-huitième siècle. Paris, 1874.
Gonse, Louis.
　L'Art Gothique : L'Architecture, La Peinture, La Sculpture, Le Décor. Paris, 1890.
　La Sculpture française. Paris, 1895.
Gonzati, Bernardo.
　Basilica di Sant' Antonio di Padova. Padua, 1852, 1853.
Goodyear, William Henry.
　The Grammar of the Lotus. New York, 1890.
Gorringe, Lt.-Commander Henry H., U. S. N.
　Egyptian Obelisks . . . (illustrated). New York, 1882.
Gosset, Alphonse.
　Les Coupoles d'Orient et d'Occident. Paris, 1889.
Gotch, John Alfred.
　Complete Account of the buildings erected in Northamptonshire by Sir Thomas Tresham . . . 1575–1605. Northampton, 1883.
Gotch, John Alfred, and Brown, Walter Talbot.
　Architecture of the Renaissance in England. London, 1894.
Gotti, Aurelio.
　Vita di Michelangelo Buonarroti. Florence, 1875.
Gouffé, Jules.
　Le Livre de Cuisine. Paris, 1867.
Gourlier, Charles Pierre ; Biet, Léon Marie Dieudonné ; and others.
　Choix d'édifices publics. Paris, 1825–1850.

Goze, A.
　Nouvelle description de la Cathédrale d'Amiens, suivie des descriptions du beffroi et de l'Hôtel-de-Ville par M. H. Dusevel. Amiens, 1847.
Grand Dictionnaire Universel. (See Larousse, P.) Paris, 1866.
Grande Encyclopédie, La ; Inventaire Raisonné des Sciences, des Lettres, et des Arts . . . sous la direction de M. Berthelot, and others. Paris, n.d. (unfinished, 1901).
Crandidier, Philippe André.
　Essais historiques et topographiques sur l'Église Cathédrale de Strasbourg. Strasburg, 1872.
Grandmaison, De.
　Documents inédits pour servir à l'histoire des arts en Touraine. (Généalogie des Pinaigrier.) Tours, 1870.
Granet, Jean Joseph.
　Histoire de l'Hôtel Royal des Invalides. Paris, 1736.
Grangaret de Lagrange.
　Les Arabes en Espagne. Paris, 1824.
Gravina, Domenico Benedetto.
　Il Duomo di Monreale. Palermo, 1859.
Gregorovius, Ferdinand.
　Geschichte der Stadt Rom in Mittelalter vom V bis zum XVI Jahrhundert. Stuttgart, 1874.
Griffin, Sir Lepel.
　Famous Monuments of Central India. London (n.d.).
Griggs, William.
　India ; Photographs and Drawings of Historical Buildings. London, 1896.
Grimm, Hermann.
　Das Leben Michelangelo's. Berlin, 1879 ; Hanover, 1860–1863.
　Translated by F. E. Bunnett as Life of Michael Angelo. London, 1865.
Grothe, Hermann.
　Katechismus der Wäscherei, Reinigung und Bleicherei. 2d ed. (with 41 illustrations). Leipzig, 1884.
Grüneisen, Karl von, and Mauch, F. E.
　Ulm's Kunstleben im Mittelalter. Ulm, 1840.
Gruner, L.
　"Lo Scaffale" or Presses in the Sacristy of S. Maria Grazie at Milan. London, 1860.
　Terracotta Architecture of North Italy. London, 1865.
　Specimens of Ornamental Art, selected from the best Models of the Classical Epochs. London, 1850.
Gruyer, François Anatole.
　Essai sur les Fresques de Raphaël au Vatican. Paris, 1859.
Gsell-Fels, Dr. Theodor.
　Ober-Italien und die Riviera. 6th ed. Leipzig, 1898.
　Mittel-Italien. 4th ed. 1886.
　Rom und die Campagna. 5th ed. 1901.
　Unter-Italien und Sizilien. 3d ed. Leipzig, 1889.
　(This is the current edition of the Italian volumes of Meyer's Reisebücher.)
Gualdus, Paolus.
　Vita di Andrea Palladio, first published in Montenari, Teatro Olimpico di Palladio. 2d ed. 1749. (See Montenari.)
Guastavino, R.
　Essay on the Theory and History of Cohesive Construction. Boston, 1893.
Guasti, Cesare.
　La Cupola di Santa Maria del Fiore, illustrata con i documenti del archivio, dell' opera secolari. Florence, 1887.

Santa Maria del Fiore. La Construzione della chiesa e del Campanile. Florence, 1857.
Il Pergamo di Donatello del duomo del Prato. Florence, 1887.

Guerber (L'Abbé).
Essai sur les Vitraux de la Cathédrale de Strasbourg. Strasburg, 1848.

Guhl, Ernst, und Koner, Wilhelm Weh.
Das Leben der Griechen und Römer nach antiken bildwerken dargestellt. Berlin, 1882.

Guicciardini, Lodovico.
Description de touts les Pais-Bas. Antwerp, 1582.

Guidicini, Giuseppe.
Cose Mirabili di Bologna. Bologna, 1868.

Guiffrey, Jules Marie Joseph.
Comptes des Bâtiments sous Louis XIV. et sous Louis XV. Paris, 1879.

Guilbert, Pierre (Abbé).
Description historique des Château, Bourg et Forest de Fontainebleau . . . Paris, 1731.

Guilhermy, Roch François Marie Nolasque, Baron de, et Viollet-le-Duc.
Description de Notre Dame de Paris. Paris, 1856.

Guilmard, Désiré.
Les Maîtres Ornementistes. Paris, 1880-1881.

Guizzardi, Giuseppe, and Davia, Marchese V.
Le Sculture delle Porte della Basilica di San Petronio. Bologna, 1834.

Gurlitt, Cornelius.
Die Baukunst Frankreichs. Dresden (n.d.).
Geschichte des Barockstiles in Italien . . . Stuttgart, 1887.
Geschichte des Barockstiles und des Rococo in Deutschland. Berlin, 1899.

Gutensohn, Johann Gottfried, und Knapp, J. M.
Denkmale der Christlichen Religion. Rome, 1822.
Published later as Die Basiliken des christlichen Roms. (See Bunsen, C. K. J.)

Gwilt, Joseph ; Papworth Wyatt.
Encyclopedia of Architecture. London, 1881.

Hafner (Docteur).
Les chefs-d'œuvre de la Peinture suisse sur Verre, publiés par la société d'histoire et d'antiquité de Winterthur, photographiés d'après les peintures originales sur verre, existantes en differents lieux. Berlin, 1892.

Halsted, Byron David.
Barn Plans and Outbuildings. New York, 1882.

Hamerton, Philip Gilbert.
The Mount and Autun. Boston, 1897.

Hamilton, William Richard.
Memorandum on the Subject of the Earl of Elgin's Pursuits in Greece. London, 1815.

Hamlin, A. D. F.
A Text-book of the History of Architecture. New York, London, and Bombay, 1896.

Hampel, W.
Die Moderne Teppichgärtnerei. Berlin, 1880-1887.

Handbook for Use in Private and Public Laundries. Including descriptive accounts of modern machinery and appliances for laundry work. By the editor of The Laundry Journal. With numerous illustrations. London.

* Handbuch der Architektur ; about 35 volumes published, 1883 to 1901 ; there is no uniformity of size except of the page. The volumes of Dr. Josef Durm, Die Baukunst

der Griechen, Die Baukunst der Etrusker . . . der Römer, and those by Dr. August von Essenwein on Mediæval Art (though this subject is far from complete) have been referred to in the text. Darmstadt.

Händke, Berthold, and Müller, August.
Des Münster in Bern. Bern, 1894.

Hardouin, Michel.
Livre de tous les Plans, Profils et Élévations du Château de Clagny. Paris, 1680.

Hardwick, Thomas.
Memoir of the Life of Sir William Chambers. London, 1825-1862.

Harford, John Scandrett.
Life of Michael Angelo Buonarroti, with translations of many of his Poems and Letters. London, 1857.

Harrison, Frederic.
Annals of an Old Manor House, Sutton Place, Guildford. London and New York, 1893.

Harrison, Miss Jane Ellen.
Mythology and Monuments of Ancient Athens. 1890.

Hart, Mrs. Ernest.
Picturesque Burma, Past and Present. London and Philadelphia, 1897.

Hartwig, J.
Die Auflage von Lustgebieten und Blumengärten. Weimar, 1861.

Hasenauer, Karl, Freiherr von.
Das K. K. Hofburgtheater in Wien.

Hassler, Konrad Dietrich.
Ulms Kunstgeschichte im Mittelalter. Stuttgart, 1864.

Haswell, Charles H.
Mechanics' and Engineers' Pocket Book of Tables, Rules, and Formulas, etc. New York, 1891.

Hauk, G.
Die subjective Perspective und die horizontalen Curven des Dorischen Styls. Stuttgart, 1879.

Haupt.
Backstein Bauten der Renaissance. Frankfurt a. M., 1899.

Haussmann, Georges Eugène.
Mémoires. Paris, 1890-1893.

Havard, Henry.
* La France Artistique et Monumentale. 6 vols. 4to. Paris (n.d.).
L'Œuvre de P. V. Galland. Paris, 1895.
*Dictionnaire de l'Ameublement et de la Décoration. Depuis le 13e siècle jusqu'à nos jours. Paris, 1887-1891.

Heaton, John Aldam (editor).
Furniture and Decoration in England. London, 1889-1892.

Heidelberg, Karl.
Die Ornementik des Mittelalters ; translated into French as Les Ornements du Moyen-Âge. Nuremberg, 1838-1855.

Heideloff, Karl Alexander von.
Die Bauhütte des Mittelalters in Deutschland. Nuremberg, 1844.

Heideloff, Karl Alexander, und Müller, Friedrich.
Die Kunst des Mittelalters in Schwaben. Stuttgart, 1855.

Heiss, Aloïss.
Les Médailleurs de la Renaissance ; Francesco Laurana, Pietro da Milano. Paris, 1882.

Heiss, Philipp.
Die Bierbrauerei mit besonderer Berücksichtigung der dickmaisch Brauerei. Munich, 1853.

Helbig, Karl Friedrich Wolfgang.
Die Italiker in der Poebene. Leipzig, 1879.

Helms, Jacob.
   The Churches of Sallingland. Copenhagen, 1884, and following years.
   Ribe Dom-Kirke. Copenhagen, 1870.
Hennicke, Julius.
   Mittheilungen über Markthallen in Deutschland, England, Frankreich, Belgien und Italien. Berlin, 1881.
Henzen, Wilhelm.
   Zu den Fälschungen des Pirro Ligorio (in Commentationes Philologæ in Honorem Theodori Mommseni . . .). Berlin and Leipzig, 1877.
Herberger, ——.
   Die ältesten Glas gemälde im Dom zu Augsburg. Augsburg, 1860.
Herdman, William Gawin.
   A Treatise on the Curvilinear Perspective of Nature. London (n.d.).
Herluison, Henri.
   Actes de l'État Civil d'Artistes français, Peintres Graveurs, Architectes, etc. Extraits des Régistres de l'Hôtel de Ville de Paris. Orléans, 1873–1880.
   Artistes Orléanais. Orléans, 1863.
Herrera, Antonio de.
   The General History of the Vast Continent and Islands of America. Translated into English by Captain John Stevens. London, 1725–1726.
Herschel, Clemens.
   See Frontinus.
Hittorff, J. Ignace.
   Notice sur la Vie et les Œuvres de Sir Charles Barry. Paris, 1860.
   Restitution du Temple d'Empédocle à Sélinonte ; l'Architecture polychrome chez les Grecs. Paris, 1851.
Hittorff, and Zanth, L.
   Architecture antique de la Sicile. Paris, 1827 (never completed).
   Architecture moderne de la Sicile. 1835.
Hochstetter, J.
   Schweizerische Architektur . . . Erste Abtheilung. Holzbauten des Berner Oberlandes aufgenommen von C. Weinbrenner und J. Durm. Hfte. 1–6. Carlsruhe, 1857–1858.
Hoffbauer, Joseph Hubert Isidor (editor).
   Paris à travers les Âges. Paris, 1885.
Holbein, Hans le jeune.
   Photographs of Drawings for Glass, by Braun.
Holiday, Henry.
   Stained Glass as an Art. London, 1896.
Holl, Elias.
   Die Selbstbiographie des Elias Holl, Baumeisters der Stadt Augsburg, 1573–1646 ; hrsg. von Dr. Christian Meyer . . . Augsburg, 1873.
Holm, C. F. ; Hansen, Heinrich ; etc.
   Danske Mindesmaerker. Copenhagen, 1869.
Holmes, W. H.
   Archæological Studies among the Ancient Cities of Mexico. Chicago, 1895.
Holtzinger, Dr. Heinrich.
   Über den Ursprung und die Beudeutung der Doppelchöre. Leipzig, 1882.
Honecourt or Honnecourt.
   See Villard and Wilars.
Hope, E. W.
   Slaughter Houses, an article in 5th and 6th Annual Reports, Massachusetts State Board of Health.
   Slaughter Houses, article in Stevenson and Murphy Treatise, (which see).
Hope, Sir Theodore Cracraft.
   Architecture at Ahmedabad, the capital of

   Goozerat (with architectural note by J. Fergusson). London, 1866.
Hotzen, Adelbert.
   Das Kaiserhaus zu Goslar. Halle, 1872.
Howard, James Q.
   History of American Architects of the National Capitol, in International Review, Vol. I., 1874.
Hübsch, Heinrich.
   Die altchristlichen Kirchen. Carlsruhe, 1862–1863.
Hucher, Eugène.
   Calques des Vitraux Peints de la Cathédrale du Mans. Le Mans and Paris, 1864.
Hughes, John Arthur.
   Garden Architecture and Landscape Gardening. London, 1886.
Huillard-Bréholles, Jean Louis.
   Recherches sur les Monuments et l'Histoire des Normands et de la Maison de Souabe dans l'Italie méridionale. Paris, 1844.
Humann, K. and Puchstein, O.
   Reisen in Kleinasien und nord Syrien. Berlin, 1890.
Humboldt, Alex. von.
   Personal Narrative of Travels to the Equinoctial Regions of America during the years of 1799–1804. Translated and edited by Thomasina Ross. London, 1852–1853.
Hunter, Joseph.
   On the Death of Queen Eleanor of Castille . . . in Archæologia, 1842.
Hurst, John Thomas.
   Elementary Principles of Carpentry. London, 1892.
Husenbeth, Rev. Frederick Charles.
   Emblems of Saints, by which they are distinguished in Works of Art. London, 1860.
Huss, G. M.
   Rational Building. Translated from article "Construction" in Viollet-le-Duc's Dictionnaire Raisonnée de l'Architecture Française. New York, 1895.
Husson, Jean Christophe Armand.
   Étude sur les Hôpitaux. Paris, 1862.
Hutchinson, Thomas Joseph, M.D.
   Two Years in Peru, with Exploration of its Antiquities. London, 1873.

Immerzeel, C. H.
   De Levens en Werken der Hollandsche en Vlaamsche Kunstschilders, Beeldhouwers Graveurs en Bouwmeester's . . . Amsterdam, 1842–1843.
India, Archæological Survey of.
   Cunningham, Hope, and others, forming an extensive series.
Ingres, Jean Dominique Auguste.
   Vitraux de la Chapelle Saint-Ferdinand (planches). 1845.
Inkersley, Thomas.
   Inquiry into the Chronological Succession of the Styles of Romanesque and Pointed Architecture in France with notice of some of the . . . buildings on which it is founded. London, 1850.
International Monthly [Periodical]. New York, afterwards Burlington, 1898-.
International Review [Periodical]. New York, 1874-.
Inventaire général des Œuvres d'Art apartenant à la ville de Parjs dressé par le Service des Beaux-Arts ; Édifices religieux. Paris, 1878–1886.
Inventaire général des Richesses d'Art de la France.

Paris, Monuments Religieux, 1876–1888.
Paris, Monuments Civils, 1879–1889. Published by Ministère de l'Instruction Publique et des Beaux-Arts (France).
Ionian Antiquities ; published with permission of the Society of Dilettanti by R. Chandler, N. Revett, W. Pars. (See Antiquities of Ionia.) London, 1769.
Irish Builder, The, and Engineering Record, Vol. IX, etc. (See the Dublin Builder.) Dublin, 1867–.
Isabelle, M. E.
* Les Édifices circulaires et les Dômes. Paris, 1855.
Parallèle des salles rondes de l'Italie. Paris, 1863.
Isham, Norman M., and Brown, Albert F.
Early Rhode Island Houses. Providence, R. I., 1895.
Early Connecticut Houses. Providence, 1900.

Jackson, Thomas Graham.
Dalmatia, the Quarnero and Istria, with Cettigne in Montenegro and the Island of Grado. Oxford, 1887.
Modern Gothic Architecture. London, 1873.
Jacob, Lt.-Col. Samuel Swinton.
Jeypore Portfolio of Architectural Details. London, 1890.
Jacobsthal, Johann Eduard.
Sud-italienische Fliesen-Ornamente ; Original-aufnahmen. Berlin, 1886.
Jahrbuch der Kunsthistorischen Sammlungen des Oesterreichischen Kaiserhauses. [Annual volumes.] 21 vols. Vienna, 1883–.
Jahrbuch der Königlich Preussischen Kunstsammlungen. Berlin, 1880–. (Four parts forming a large volume are published each year.)
Jal, A.
Dictionnaire critique de Biographie et d'Histoire. Paris, 1872.
Janitschek, Dr. Hubert.
Leone Battista Alberti's Kleinere Kunst. Vienna, 1877. — In R. Eitelberger von Edelberg ; Quellenschriften für Kunstgeschichte.
Japan Society. London (Eng.)
Transactions and Proceedings. London, 1893.
Jenkins, R. C.
Heraldry, English and Foreign. London, 1880.
Jevons, Frank Byron. Translated by Schrader, O.
Prehistoric Antiquities of the Aryan Peoples : a Manual of Comparative Philology and the Earliest Culture. New York, 1890.
Joanne, Paul.
Itinéraire général de la France. Many volumes. Paris, different dates.
Guides à l'Étranger. Many volumes. Paris, different dates.
Johansen, P.
Copenhagen, in Blätter für Architektur und Kunst Handwerk for Aug. 1, 1895.
Johnson, Robert J.
Specimens of Early French Architecture. Newcastle-on-Tyne, 1864.
Johnson's Universal Cyclopedia.
New York, 1893–1895 (a second and much revised edition).
Jolimont, François Gabriel T. B. de.
Les Principaux Édifices de la Ville de Rouen en 1525, dessinés à cette époque sur les plans d'un MS. . . . appelé, Le Livre des Fontaines. . . . Rouen, 1845.
Monuments les plus remarquables de la Ville de Rouen. Paris, 1822.
Joly, Jules de.
Plans, Coupes, Élévations et Détails de la Res-

tauration de la Chambre des Députés. Paris, 1840.
Jomard, Edme François.
Description de l'Égypte, Antiquités (forms part of the great work, Description de l'Égypte, which see).
Jones, H. Stuart.
Select Passages from Ancient Writers illustrative of the History of Greek Sculpture. London and New York, 1895.
Jones, Inigo.
Designs, consisting of Plans . . . for Public and Private Buildings, published by W. Kent with some additional Designs. London, 1727.
London Churches of the 17th and 18th Centuries. London, 1896.
Jones, Owen.
The Grammar of Ornament. London, 1856. (A smaller edition. London, 1865.)
Alhambra Court in the Crystal Palace . . . London, 1854.
Jopling, ——.
Practice of Isometrical Perspective. London, 1835.
Jouffroy d'Eschavannes.
Armorial universel, précédé d'un Traité complet de la Science du Blazon, et suivi d'un Supplément. Paris, 1844–1848.
Jouin, Henri.
Charles Lebrun et les Arts sous Louis XIV. Paris, 1889.
Antoine Coysevox, sa Vie et son Œuvre. Paris, 1883.
David d'Angers ; in Revue des Arts décoratifs.
Jourdain-Duval.
Portail de la Cathédrale d'Amiens ; in Bulletin Monumental.
Journal of Hellenic Studies, The.
London, 1880 (publication continued).
Junghändel, Max, und Gurlitt, Cornelius.
Baukunst Spaniens. Dresden, 1891–1893.
Justi, Carl.
Diego Velasquez and his Times. London, 1889. (Translation from the German by A. S. Keane.)

Kabierske, Dr.
Das Hallenschwimmbad in Breslau. Breslau (Germany), 1899.
Kaiserlich Deutsches Archaeologisches Institute
Antike Denkmäler. Berlin, 1891–.
Kandler, Pietro.
Cenni al forestiere che visita Pola. Trieste, 1845.
Cenni al forestiere che visita Parenzo. Trieste, 1845.
[MSS. cited in Jackson's Dalmatia.]
Kane, James.
New System of Public Baths. London (n.d.).
Kaufmann, A.
Der Gartenbau im Mittelalter und während der Periode der Renaissance. Berlin, 1892.
Kavvadias, P.
Fouilles d'Épidaure. Athens, 1891.
Keane, Marcus.
Towers and Temples of Ancient Ireland. Dublin, 1867.
Kempf, Rudolph, and Buff, Dr. A.
Alt-Augsburg : Eine Sammlung Architectonischer und Kunstgewerblicher Motive. Berlin, 1898.
Kent, William.
Strength of Materials. (Reprinted from Van Nostrand's Engineering Magazine.) New York, 1890.

Kerr, Robert.
　The Gentleman's House, or How to Plan English Residences. London, 1865.
Kidder, F. E.
　Architects' and Builders' Pocket Book. New York. Many editions.
　*Building Construction and Superintendence. New York, 1898, 1899.
　Part I, Mason's Work, 3d. ed.
　Part II, Carpenter's Work, 2d. ed.
King, Richard John.
　Handbooks of the Cathedrals of England. London, Oxford, 1864–1881.
King, Thomas H.
　*The Study-book of Mediaeval Architecture and Art. London, 1868.
Kingsborough (Lord).
　Antiquities of Mexico. 9 vols. folio. London, 1831–1848.
Kip, Johannes.
　Brittannia Illustrata ; or Views of all the Kings' Palaces, several Seats of the Nobility and Gentry ; all the Cathedrals of England and Wales. London, 1727.
Kiprianov, Valérian.
　Histoire Pittoresque de l'Architecture en Russie. St. Petersburg, 1864.
Kitchin, George William.
　Life of Pope Pius II., as illustrated by Pinturicchio's frescoes in the Piccolomini Library at Siena. Arundel Society. London, 1881.
Klasen, Ludwig.
　Grundriss vorbilder von Gebäuden aller art. Leipzig, 1884.
Klinger, J. H.
　Die Bade-Anstalt. Vienna and Leipsic, 1891.
Knackfuss, Kunstler Monographien. [Separate biographies of artists]. Leipzig, various dates.
Knight, Charles.
　London. London, 1841–1844.
　Old England, the Pictorial Museum of Regal, Ecclesiastical, . . . and Popular Antiquities. London, 1845.
　Pictorial Half Hours of London Topography. London, 1851.
Koch, Julius, and Seitz, Fritz.
　Das Heidelberger Schloss . . . Darmstadt, 1891.
Koldewey, Robert, and Puchstein, Otto.
　Die Griechischen Tempel in Unteritalien und Sicilien. Berlin, 1899.
Kramm, Christiaan.
　De Levens en Werken der Hollandsche en Vlaamsche Kunstschilders . . . Amsterdam, 1857–1864.
Krätschell, Johannes.
　Karl Friedrich Schinkel in seinem Verhältniss zur gothischen Baukunst. Berlin, 1892.
Krell, Paul Friedrich.
　Geschichte des Dorischen Styls. Stuttgart, 1870.
Kreuser, Johann Peter Balthasar.
　Der christliche Kirchenbau. Bonn, 1851.
Krouse, Louise B.
　Reading List on Library Buildings.
　Suggestive Plans for the New York Public Library Competition.
Kugler, F. T.
　Pommersche Kunstgeschichte Nach den erhaltenen Monumenten dargestellt, in Gesellschaft für Pommersche Geschichte, etc. in Baltische Studien. Jahrg. 8, Heft. 1. Stettin, 1832.
　Kleineschriften und Studien zur Kunstgeschichte. Stuttgart, 1853, 1854.

Handbuch der Kunstgeschichte. Stuttgart, 1842.
Handbook of Painting. The German, Flemish, and Dutch Schools, based on the handbook of Kugler remodelled by the late Dr. Waagen and thoroughly revised and in part rewritten by the late Sir Joseph Crowe. London, 1898.
Kuhn, Oswald.
　Krankenhäuser ; forms part of Handbuch der Architektur, Part IV.
Kumlien, H. J.
　Svenska Herrgårder och Villor af Svenska Arkitekter. Stockholm.
Kunkel, ——.
　Glassmacherkunst. Nuremberg, 1756.
Kunstchronik, wokenschrift für Kunst und Kunstgewerbe. [Supplement to Zeitschrift der Bildenden Kunst. A periodical in course of publication.] Berlin.
Kunstkronjik, uitgegeven ter aanmoediging en verspreiding der schoone Runsten [Periodical]. The Hague and Leyden, 1841, etc.
Kunstler Monographien.
　See Knackfuss Kunstler Monographien.
Kunst und Kunstler des Mittelalters und der Neuzeit. Biographien und Charakteristiken. R. Dohme (editor). Leipzig, 1875, etc.
Kutschmann, Theodor.
　Romanische Baukunst und Ornamentik in Deutschland. Berlin and New York.

Labarte, Jules.
　Le Palais Impérial de Constantinople, et ses abords, Sainte-Sophie, le Forum Augustéon et l'Hippodrome tels qu'ils existaient au dixième siècle. Paris, 1861.
Laborde, Léon, Marquis de.
　Les Contes des Bâtiments du Roi, 1528–1571, suivi de documents. Paris, 1877–1880.
　Les Ducs de Bourgogne. Paris, 1850.
　La Renaissance des Arts à la Cour de France. Paris, 1850–1855.
　Versailles, ancien et moderne. Paris, 1841.
　Les Archives de la France pendant la Révolution. Paris, 1866.
　Documents inédits ou peu connus sur l'Histoire et les Antiquités d'Athènes. Paris, 1854.
Laborde, Léon, Marquis de, and Linant de Bellefonds, M. A.
　Voyage de l'Arabie Pétrée . . . Paris, 1830.
Lachner, Carl.
　Geschichte der Holzbaukunst in Deutschland. Leipzig, 1887.
Lacroix, Paul.
　Peinture sur Verre ; in Volume V. of Le Moyen-Âge et de la Renaissance. Paris, 1848.
La Farge, John.
　The American Art of Glass. New York, 1893.
La Faye de l'Hôpital, Pierre de.
　Description archéologique et historique de la cathédrale de Clermont. Clermont-Ferrand, 1865.
Lagrange, Léon Marius.
　Pierre Puget, Peintre, Sculpteur, Architecte. Paris, 1868.
Laloux, Victor ; Monceaux, Paul.
　Restauration d'Olympie. Paris, 1889.
　L'Architecture Grecque. Paris, 1888.
Lambert (l'Abbé).
　Histoire littéraire du Règne de Louis XIV. Paris, 1751.
Lambert, André.
　Madonna di San Biagio, près Montepulciano, bâtie par Antonio di San Gallo de 1518 à 1528. Stuttgart, 1884.

BIBLIOGRAPHY

Lambert, André, et Rychner, Alfred.
L'Architecture en Suisse aux différentes Époques. Basle, 1883.
Lami, Stanislas.
Dictionnaire des Sculpteurs français de l'école française du Moyen-Âge au Règne de Louis XIV. Paris, 1898.
Lance, Adolphe Étienne.
Dictionnaire des Architectes Français. Paris, 1872.
Lanciani, Rodolfo.
Ancient Rome in the Light of Recent Discoveries ; with one hundred illustrations. Boston and New York. Cambridge, 1889.
Pagan and Christian Rome. Profusely illustrated. Boston and New York. Cambridge, 1893.
The Ruins and Excavations of Ancient Rome. Boston and New York. Cambridge, 1897.
The Destruction of Ancient Rome ; a Sketch of the History of the Monuments. New York ; London, 1899.
Forma Urbis Romæ, consilio et autoritate regiæ academiæ Lyncæorum formam dimensus est et ad modulum I : 1000 delineavit. (Plans of the city.) Milan, completed 1901.
Lanck, Léopold.
Traité pratique de la Construction Moderne et Description du Matériel employé par les Constructeurs. Paris, 1877.
Lanckorónski, K. ; Niemann, G. ; and Petersen, E.
Städte Pamphyliens und Pisidiens. Vienna and Prague, 1890, 1892.
Lane, Edward William.
An Account of the Manners and Customs of the Modern Egyptians. London, 1836.
Lange, Walther.
Das antike griechish-römische Wohnhaus. Leipzig, 1878.
Langhorne, John and William.
Plutarch's Lives. See Plutarch.
Langlois, Hyacinthe.
Essai sur la Peinture sur Verre. Rouen, 1832.
La Normandie Illustrée ; Monuments, Sites et Costumes de la Seine-Inférieure, de l'Eure, du Calvados, de l'Orne et de la Manche, dessinés d'après Nature par F. Benoist . . . texte par R. Bordeaux et A. Bosquet . . . sous la direction de A. Pottier pour la Haute Normandie. Nantes, 1852.
Lanzi, Abate Luigi Antonio.
Storia pittorica della Italia dal Risorgimento delle Belle Arti fin presso al fine del XVIII secolo, edizione terza . . . accresciuta dall' Anton. Bassano, 1809.
La Quérière, Eustache de.
Notice historique et descriptive sur l'ancien Hôtel de Ville, le Beffroi, et la Grosse Horloge de Rouen . . . Rouen, 1864.
Larousse, Pierre.
Grand Dictionnaire Universel du XIXᵉ Siècle. Paris, 1866.
Lasinio, Giovanni Paolo.
Le tre Porte del Battistero di San Giovanni di Firenze. Florence, 1821.
Laslett, Thomas.
*Timber and Timber Trees. London, 1875.
Laspeyres, Paul.
Die Bauwerke der Renaissance in Umbrien. Berlin, 1873.
*Die Kirchen der Renaissance in Mittel-Italien. Berlin and Stuttgart, 1882.
Lassus, J. B. A., and Quicherat, Jules.
See Villard de Honnecourt.

BIBLIOGRAPHY

Lassus and Viollet-le-Duc.
Monographie de Notre Dame de Paris. Paris (n.d.).
Lasteyrie, Ferdinand de.
Histoire de la Peinture sur Verre, d'après les Monuments français. Paris, 1843.
Latham, Baldwin.
Sanitary Engineering ; a Guide to the construction of Works of Sewerage and House Drainage, etc. London, 1873.
Laurière, Jules de.
Observations sur les Dessins de Giuliano de San Gallo in Mémoires de la Société National des Antiquaires de France. 1884.
Law, Ernest Philip Alphonso.
History of Hampton Court Palace. London, 1885–1888.
Layard, Austen H.
Discoveries in the Ruins of Nineveh and Babylon ; with travels in Armenia and Kurdistan and the Desert. London, 1853.
Nineveh and its Remains. London, 1849.
Monuments of Nineveh (two series), 1849 and 1853.
Lazare, Louis.
Dictionnaire des rues de Paris, etc. Paris, 1844.
Leake, William Martin.
Travels in Northern Greece. London, 1835.
Researches in Greece. London, 1814.
The Topography of Athens. London, 1821.
Travels in the Morea. London, 1830.
Peloponnesiaca (supplementary to Travels in the Morea). London, 1846.
Le Bris, Guy.
Les Constructions Métalliques ; Bibliothèque des sciences et de l'industrie. Paris, 1894.
Lechevallier-Chevignard, Edmond.
Les Styles Français. Paris, 1892.
Lecoy de la Marche, Albert.
Extraits des Comptes et Mémoriaux du roi René. Paris, 1873.
Le Héricher, Édouard.
Mont St. Michel, Avranches et Mortain. 1852 ; in La Normandie Illustreé.
Le Héricher, et Bouet, G.
Histoire et description du Mont Saint-Michel. Caen, 1848.
Leland, John.
Itinerary ; to which is prefixed The New Year's Gift. Oxford, 1710–1712.
Lenoir, Albert.
Statistique Monumentale de Paris. 2 vols. folio, 1 vol. 4to. Paris, 1867.
*Architecture Monastique, in 3 parts. Paris, 1852–1856.
Lenoir, M. A.
Traité Historique de la Peinture sur Verre, et description de vitraux anciens et modernes, pour servir à l'histoire de l'art en France. 1856.
Lenormant, François.
La Grande-Grèce. Paysages et Histoire. 3 vols. Paris, 1884.
Lepage, Henri.
Archives de Nancy ; ou documents inédits relatifs à l'histoire de cette ville, etc. Nancy, 1865.
Palais ducal de Nancy. Nancy, 1861.
Leroux de Lincy, A. J. V.
Recherches Historiques sur le Pont Notre Dame (Paris), in Bibliothèque de l'École des Chartes. 2d series, Vol. 2.
Lessing, Otto.
Schloss Ansbach ; Barock- und roccoco-dekorationen aus dem 18. Jahrhundert, mit erläuterndem vorwort. Berlin, 1892.
Supplement. Berlin, 1893.

Le Strange, Guy. Palestine under the Moslems. London, 1890.
Letarouilly, P. M.
    *Edifices de Rome moderne. 1 vol. text, 3 vols. plates. Paris, 1860.
    Le Vatican et la Basilique de S. Pierre de Rome, monographie mise en ordre et complétée par A. Simil. Paris, 1882.
Lethaby, W. R.
    Leadwork, Old and Ornamental, and for the most part English. London and New York, 1893.
    Architecture, Mysticism, and Myth. New York, 1892.
Lethaby, W. R., and Swainson, Harold.
    The Church of Sancta Sophia, Constantinople; a Study of Byzantine Building. London, 1894.
Levi, Cesare Augusto.
    *I Campanili di Venezia. Venice, 1890.
Le Vieil, Pierre.
    L'Art de la Peinture sur Verre, in Arts et Métiers de l'Académie. Paris, 1774.
Lévy, Edmond.
    Histoire de la Peinture sur Verre en Europe. Brussels, 1860.
Lewis, Thomas Hayter.
    The Holy Places of Jerusalem. London, 1888.
Leybold, Ludwig.
    Das Rathhaus der Stadt Augsburg. Berlin, 1886–1888.
Licht, Hugo.
    Architektur Deutschlands. Berlin, 1882.
    Architektur Berlins. Berlin, 1877.
Lindemann, A.
    Die Markthallen Berlins. Ihre baulichen Anlagen und Betriebseinrichtungen. Berlin, 1899.
Lodge, Oliver J.
    Lightning Conductors and Lightning Guards. London and New York, 1892.
Loftie, W. J.
    Inigo Jones and Wren, or the Rise and Decline of Modern Architecture in England. New York, 1893.
    History of London. London, 1884.
Loftus, Sir William Kenneth.
    Travels and Researches in Chaldea and Susiana. London, 1857.
Lohde, Ludwig.
    Die Architektonik der Hellenen nach C. Bötticher's Tektonik der Hellenen. Berlin, 1862.
Loiseleur, Jules.
    Résidences royales des bords de la Loire. Paris, 1863.
Longfellow, W. P. P.
    The Column and the Arch. New York, 1899.
Longfellow, W. P. P. (editor).
    A Cyclopedia of Works of Architecture in Italy, Greece, and the Levant. New York, 1895.
Longman, F. S. A.
    A History of the Three Cathedrals dedicated to S. Paul in London. London, 1873.
Loudon, John Claudius (editor).
    See Repton, Humphry (1752–1818), Landscape Gardening and Landscape Architecture.
Lowell, Percival.
    Chosön, the Land of the Morning Calm; a Sketch of Korea. Boston, 1886.
Lowth, Robert.
    Life of William of Wykeham. London, 1758.
Löwy, Emanuel.
    Inschriften Griechischer Bildhauer mit facsimiles. Leipzig, 1885.

    Lysipp und seine Stellung in der Griechischen Plastik. Hamburg, 1891.
Löwy, J.
    Wien vor 150 Jahren. Vienna, 1890.
Lübke, Wilhelm.
    Die Mittelalterliche Kunst in Westfalen. Leipzig, 1853.
    Vorschule zur Geschichte der Kirchenbaukunst des Mittelalters.
    Introduction to Peter Vischer, Werke. Nuremberg, 1875.
    Geschichte der Renaissance in Deutschland. Stuttgart, 1882.
Lübker, Friedrich.
    Reallexikon des Classischen Alterthums. Leipzig, 1877.
Lucianus (Lucian) of Samosata.
    Διάλογοι — Dialogues. No complete English translation; one partial by Franklin. London, 1781.
Lucioli, G. (See Sanmichele, Michele.)
Lüdecke, Carl.
    Das Rathhaus zu Breslau. Berlin and Breslau, 1868.
Luschan, F.
    Travels in Asia Minor. (See Reisen im S. W. Kleinasien.)
Lussault, N.
    Éloge d'Antoine, Jacques Denis. Paris, 1801.
    Notice historique sur le défunt Antoine, architecte. Paris, 1804.
Luthmer, Ferdinand.
    Sammlung von Innenräumen, Möbeln und Geräthen im Louis-Seize und Empire-Stil. Frankfurt am Main, 1897.
Lützow, Carl F. A. von.
    Die Meisterwerke der Kirchenbaukunst. Leipzig, 1871.
Luzi, Lodovico.
    Il Duomo di Orvieto, descritto ed illustrato. Florence, 1866.

Maccari, Enrico.
    Il Palazzo di Caprarola. Rome, 1876.
Macgibbon, David.
    The Architecture of Provence and the Riviera. Edinburgh, 1888.
Macgibbon, David, and Ross, Thomas.
    Castellated and Domestic Architecture of Scotland from the 12th to the 18th century. Edinburgh, 1887–1892.
    The Ecclesiastical Architecture of Scotland. Edinburgh, 1896.
Macklin, Herbert W.
    Monumental Brasses. London, 1890.
Macmurdo, Arthur Heygate.
    Wren's City Churches. Sunnyside, (Kent, England), 1883.
Magne, Lucien.
    L'Œuvre des Peintres Verriers français par M. Lucien Magne; Verrières des Monuments élevés par les Montmorency : Montmorency-Écouen-Chantilly. Paris, 1885.
Magrini, Antonio.
    Memorie intorno la vita e le opere di Andrea Palladio. Padua, 1845.
A Magyar Mérnok Egyles Heti Ertesitöje. Budapest.
A Magyar Mérnok (— Épitész) — Egyesület Közlönze . . . Szerkeszté Szily Kálmán [Krusper István, Ambrozovics Béla, and others]. Budapest, 1867–1891.
Malagola, Carlo.
    See, Atti e memoriale Reale Deputazione di Storia patria per le provincie dell' Emilia.

Malaspina di Sannazaro, Luigi, Marquis.
    Memorie Storiche delle Fabbriche della Catte-
    drale di Pavia.   Milan, 1816.
Malcolm, Sir John.
    Sketches in Persia.   London, 1827.
Mallay, A.
    *Essai sur les Églises Romanes, et Romano-
    Byzantines, du département du Puy-de-
    Dôme.   Moulins, 1841.
Mallet, L'Abbé J.
    Cours d'Archéologie Religieuse.
    Architecture, with illustrations.
    Mobilier, with illustrations.   Paris, 1887.
Mancini, Girolamo.
    Vita di Leon Battista Alberti.   Florence, 1882.
Manetti, Antonio.
    " Vita di Filippo di Ser Brunellesco : " manu-
    script first published by Moreni at Florence
    in 1812 ; republished at Berlin in 1887 by C.
    Frey in his Sammlung ausgewaehlter Bio-
    graphien Vasaris ; again by Holtzinger in
    his " Filippo Brunellesco die Antonio di
    Tuccio Manetti," and again by Milanesi in
    his " Opere istoriche di Antonio Manetti."
    Florence.
Mangin, Arthur.
    Les Jardins.   Histoire et Description.   Tours,
    1857.
Maniago, Fabio di (count).
    Storia delle Belle Arti Friulane . . . Edizione
    seconda . . . accresciuta.   Udine, 1823.
Maquet, Auguste Jules.
    Paris sous Louis XIV ; Monuments et Vues.
    Paris, 1883.
Marchand et les Abbés Bourassé et Manceau.
    Verrières du Chœur de l'Église métropolitaine
    de Tours.   Tours, 1848.
Marchese, Vincenzo Fortunato.
    Memorie dei piu insigni Pittori, Scultori e
    Architetti Domenicani.   Florence, 1845-
    1846.
Marggraff, Hugo.
    Moderne Stadtbäder.   Berlin, 1882.
Mariette, Pierre Jean.
    Abecedario, et autres notes inédites de cet
    amateur sur les Arts et les Artistes.   Paris,
    1851-1859.
Marionneau, Claude Charles.
    Douze lettres de Victor Louis, architecte du
    roi de Pologne et du duc de Chartres.
    1776-1777.   Paris, 1858.
    Victor Louis   . sa Vie, ses Travaux et sa
    Correspondence.   1731-1800.   Bordeaux,
    1881.
Markham, Clements Robert.
    History of Peru.   London, 1893.
Marot, Jean, and Marot, Daniel.
    L'Architecture française ; ou Recueil des Plans,
    Élévations, Coupes et Profils des Églises,
    Palais, Hôtels et Maisons . . . de Paris et
    . . . de France . . .   Paris, 1827.
Marquand, Allan.
    Hunting della Robbias in Italy ; in American
    Journal of Archaeology.
Marquez, Pietro Giuseppe.
    Della ville di Plinio il giovane.   Rome, 1796.
Marsaux (L'Abbé L.).
    Vitraux de l'Église Saint Martin de Groslay.
    Paris, 1889.
Martha, Jules.
    * Manuel d'archéologie Étrusque et Romaine.
    1884.
    L'Art Étrusque : illustré de 4 Planches en cou-
    leurs et de 400 Gravures dans le Texte,
    d'après les Originaux, ou d'après les Docu-
    ments les plus Authentiques.   Paris, 1889.

Martigny, Joseph Alexandre.
    Dictionnaire des Antiquités Chrétiennes
    contenant . . .   I. Étude des Mœurs et
    Coutumes des premiers Chrétiens . . .
    II. Étude des Monuments Figurés . . .
    III. Vêtements et Meubles, etc.   Paris, 1865.
Martinow, Alexis.
    Anciens Monuments des Environs de Moscou.
    1889.
Marzo, Gioacchino di.
    I Gagini e la scultura in Sicilia.   Palermo,
    1880-1883.
Maspero, G.
    L'Archéologie Égyptienne.   Paris, 1887.
Massachusetts State Board of Health : Annual
    Reports.
Massari e Vermiglioli.
    Le Scultore di Nicolo e Giovanni da Pisa e di
    Arnolfo Fiorentino . . . la fontana di
    Perugia.   Perugia, 1834.
Mau, August.
    *Pompeii, its Life and Art.   Translated by
    Francis W. Kelsey.   New York and Lon-
    don, 1899.
Mauch, Johann Matthäus von.
    Vergleichende darstellung der architecto-
    nischen ordnungen der Griechen und Rö-
    mer . . .   Potsdam, 1832.
Mavor, William Fordyce.
    New Description of Blenheim.   1789.   (Many
    subsequent editions.)
Mayeux, Henri.
    La Composition décorative.   Paris, 1885.
Mazois, Charles François.
    Les Ruines de Pompéi.   Paris, 1824-1838.
Mazzanti, Riccardo, and Badia, Jodoco del.
    Raccolta delle Migliori Fabbriche antiche e
    moderne di Firenze ; text by del Badia.
    Florence, 1876.
Mediæval Towns.   A Series by Different Authors.
    London, 1899-1901.
Mélanges d'Archéologie et d'Histoire [Periodi-
    cal].   1884-.
Melani, Alfredo.
    Architettura Italiana.   I. Architettura Pelas-
    gica, Etrusca, Italo-Greca, Romana.   II.
    Architettura Medievale del Rinascimento,
    del Cinquecento, del Seicento, del Sette-
    cento, e Moderna.   Milan, 1887.
    Manuale di Scultura Italiana Antica e Mo-
    derna.   Milan,
    Andrea Palladio, sa vie et son œuvre, in l'Art.
    1890.
Méloizes, Albert de.
    Les Vitraux de la Cathédrale de Bourges, pos-
    térieurs au XIIIe Siècle.   Bourges.
Mély, F. de.
    Études iconographiques sur les Vitraux du
    XIIIe Siècle de la Cathédrale de Chartres.
    Bruges, 1888.   (Extrait de l'Art Chrétien.)
Mémoires de la Société National des Antiquaires
    de France.   (See Société nationale [royale]
    des antiquaires de France.)
Mémoires Relatifs à l'histoire de France.   Paris,
    1854.
Ménard, René.
    L'Art en Alsace-Lorraine.   Paris, 1876.
Merrifield, Mrs. Mary Philadelphia.
    Ancient Practice of Painting in Oil, Miniature,
    Mosaic, and on Glass, etc.   London, 1849.
Merrill, George P.
    Stones for Building and Decorations.   New
    York, 1891.
Merriman, Mansfield.
    Elements of Sanitary Engineering.   New York,
    1898.

Merson, Oliver.
Les Vitraux. Paris, 1895.
Mertens, Franz, and Lohde, Ludwig.
Die gründung des Cölner Domes und der erste
Dombaumeister, in Zeitschrift für Bau-
wesen.
Messager des Sciences historiques; ou, Archives
des arts et de la bibliographie de Belgique
[Periodical]. Ghent, 1823–1886.
Messmer, Joseph Anton.
Über den ursprung, die Entwickelung und Be-
deutung der Basilika in der Christlichen
Baukunst. Leipzig, 1854.
Meyer, Alfred Gotthold.
Das Venezianische Grabdenkmal der Frühre-
naissance, in Jahrbuch der Königlich Preus-
sischen Kunstsammlungen. 1889.
Meyer, Christian (editor). (See Holl, Elias.)
Meyer (publisher).
Konversations-Lexikon. Leipzig and Vienna,
several editions.
Italian Guide-Books. (See Gsell-Fels.)
Michaelis, Adolf Theodor Friedrich.
Der Parthenon. Leipzig, 1870–1871.
Michelangelo's Plan zum Capitol, in Zeitschrift
für bildende Kunst.
Michaud (L'Abbé).
Notice sur l'Église de Saint Nicolas de Chatil-
lon-sur-Seine, son Origine, son Architecture,
ses Verriers. Dijon, 1870.
Michel, Emil.
Rubens, sa Vie, son Œuvre et son Temps.
Paris, 1899.
Michel, Nicolas Leopold.
Recueil des Fondations et Établissements faits
par le Roi de Pologne, duc de Lorraine et
de Bar. Lunéville, 1762.
Michon, Jean Hippolyte.
Statistique Monumentale de la Charente. Paris,
1844.
Middleton, George Alexander Thomas.
Strains in Structures: a Text-book for Stu-
dents. London, 1889.
Middleton, J. H.
The Remains of Ancient Rome, 2 vols. (many
editions; first published as Ancient Rome
in 1885).
Mignaty, Madame.
Le Corrège. Paris, 1881.
Milanesi, Gaetano.
Documenti per la storia dell arte Senese. Siena,
1854–1856.
Lettere di Michelangelo Buonarroti, con i
ricordi e documenti artistici. Siena, 1875.
Milanesi, Gaetano (editor). (See Vasari.)
Milizia, Francesco.
Le Vite dei più celebri Architetti d' ogni Nazione
e d' ogni Tempo. Rome, 1768. Later edi-
tions take the title Memorie degli Architetti
antichi e moderne.
Translated into English by Mrs. Edward Cresy
as: The Lives of Celebrated Architects,
Ancient and Modern. London, 1826.
Memorie degli Architetti antichi e moderne.
(Title of later editions of Le Vite dei più
celebri Architetti d' ogni Nazione e d' ogni
Tempo.)
Millar, Alexander H.
Historical Castles and Mansions of Scotland;
Perthshire and Farfarshire. London, 1890.
Miller, J. B.
Elements of Descriptive Geometry. London,
1878.
Millin, A. L.
Antiquités Nationales ou Recueil des Monu-
ments pour servir à l'histoire général et

particulière de l'empire français. Paris,
1790–1798.
Milman, Henry Hart, D.D.
Annals of S. Paul's Cathedral. London, 1868.
Milner, Henry Ernest.
The Art and Practice of Landscape Gardening.
London, 1890.
Minutoli, Alexander, freiherr von.
Der Dom zu Drontheim und die mittelalter-
liche christliche Baukunst der Scandina-
vischen Normannen. Berlin, 1853.
Mitchell, Lucy M.
A History of Ancient Sculpture. New York,
1883.
Mithoff, H. Wilh. H.
Kunstdenkmale und Alterthümer im Hanno-
verschen. Hanover, 1871.
Mittelalterliche Kunstdenkmale des Oesterreichi-
schen Kaiserstaates. Stuttgart, 1858. (See
Eitelberger von Edelberg.)
Mittheilungen des Heidelberger Schlosses. 1890.
Moberly, George Herbert.
Life of William of Wykeham. Winchester,
1887.
Moisè, Filippo.
Santa Croce di Firenze: illustrazione storico-
artistica, con note e copiosi documenti ine-
diti. Florence, 1845.
Molinier, Charles Louis Émile.
Benvenuto Cellini. Paris, 1894. Forms part
of series, Les Artistes Célèbres.
Molinier, Charles Louis Marie Émile, and Caval-
lucci, C. J.
Les della Robbia. 1884.
Moller, Georg.
Denkmäler der deutschen Baukunst. 4. ver-
schönerte, verbesserte Auflage, 2 vols. folio.
Frankfurt a. M., 1854.
Molmenti, Pompeo Gherardo.
Tiepolo et la Villa Valmarana. Venice, 1880.
Monfalcon, Jean Baptiste.
Histoire Monumentale de la ville de Lyon.
Paris, 1866.
Mongeri, Giuseppe. (See Bramantino, Bartolom-
meo Suardi.)
Moniteur des Architectes, Le: revue mensuelle
de l'art architectural ancien et moderne
[Periodical]. Paris, 1866–1893.
Monroe, Harriet.
John Welborn Root, A Study of his Life and
Work. Boston, 1896.
Montaiglon, Anatole de Courde de.
Sur l'ancienne statue équestre ouvrage de
Daniello Ricciarelli et de Biard le fils.
Paris, 1851.
Montenari, Giovanni.
Del Teatro Olimpico di Andrea Palladio in
Vicenza. Padua, 1749.
Montfaucon, Bernard de.
L'Antiquité Expliquée et Representée en Fig-
ures. Paris, 1719.
Montferrand, A. Ricard de.
Église Cathédrale de Saint-Isaac; description
architectural . . . et historique de ce monu-
ment . . . Saint Petersburg, 1845.
Montigny, A. H. V. Grandjean de, et Famin, A.
Architecture Toscane; ou Palais, Maisons, et
autres Édifices de la Toscane. Paris,
1815.
Monumente des Mittelalters und der Renaissance
aus dem Saechsischen Erzgebirge. Dresden
and Leipzig.
Moore, Charles Herbert.
Development and Character of Gothic Architecture. 2nd ed. rewritten and enlarged.
New York and London, 1899.

Morelli, Giovanni.
Italian Painters ; critical studies of their works. London, 1892. Vol. I., the Borghese and Doria-Pamphili galleries in Rome. Vol. II., the galleries of Munich and Dresden. London, 1893.

Morgan, Lewis Henry.
Houses and House Life of the American Aborigines. Geographical and Geological Survey of the Rocky Mountain Region. Contributions to North American Ethnology. Washington, D. C., 1877.

Morrona, Alessandro da.
Pisa antica e moderna. Pisa, 1821.

Moschini, Giovanni Antonio.
Guida per la Città di Venezia. Venice, 1815.

Mosler, H.
Sansovino und seine Werke. Leipzig, (n.d.).

Mothes, Oscar.
Die Baukunst des Mittelalters in Italien. Jena, 1884.
Die Basilikenform bei den Christen. Leipzig, 1859.

Mouhot, Henri.
Travels in the Central Parts of Indo-China, Cambodia, and Laos during the years 1858, 1859, and 1860. London, 1864.

Moutié, Auguste.
Notre-Dame de la Roche. Paris, 1862.

Mowat, William and Alexander.
A Treatise on Stairbuilding and Handrailing. London, 1900.

Müller, Franz Hubert.
Beiträge zur teutschen Kunst- und Geschichtskunde durch Kunstdenkmale. Leipzig and Darmstadt, 1837.

Müller-Walde, Paul.
Leonardo da Vinci, Lebenskizze und Forschungen. Munich, 1889.

Mulvany, Thomas J. (editor). (See Gandon.)

Munch, P. A., and Schirmer, H. E.
Throndhjems domkirke [The Cathedral of Throndheim]. Title-page and text in Norwegian and English. Christiania, 1859.

Müntz, Eugène.
La Renaissance en Italie et en France à l'époque de Charles VIII. Paris, 1885.
Histoire de l'Art pendant la Renaissance. 3 vols. Paris, 1889–1891.
Florence et la Toscane. Paris, 1897.
Les Précurseurs de la Renaissance. Paris and London, 1882.
Guide de l'École Nationale des Beaux-Arts. Paris, 1899.
Histoire de la Tapisserie en Italie, en Allemagne, en Angleterre, en Espagne, en Danemark, en Hongrie, en Pologne, en Russie, et en Turquie. Paris, 1889.
Raphaël, sa Vie, son Œuvre et son Temps . . . Paris, 1881. Nouvelle édition, entièrement refondue. Paris, 1886. Translated into English as : Raphael, his Life, Works, and Times . . . Illustrated . . . Edited by Walter Armstrong. London, 1882 [1881].
Giuliano da San Gallo et les monuments du midi de France au XVe siècle, in Mémoires de la Société Nationale des Antiquaires de France. 1884.

Murphy, James Cavanah.
Arabian Antiquities of Spain. London, 1813.

Murray, A. S.
A History of Greek Sculpture from the Earliest Times down to the Age of Pheidias. London, 1880.

A History of Greek Sculpture under Pheidias and his Successors. London, 1883.
Handbook of Greek Archæology. New York, 1892.

Musée, Le, de Sculpture comparée du Palais du Trocadéro. Paris.

Mylne, Rev. Robert Scott.
Master Masons to the Crown of Scotland and their Works. Edinburgh, 1893.

Myskovsky, Viktor.
Kunstdenkmale des Mittelalters und den Renaissance in Ungarn. Vienna, 1885.

Nadaillac, Jean François.
Prehistoric America ; translated by N. D'Anvers. New York, 1884.

Nagler, Georg Caspar.
Allgemeines Künstler-Lexikon ; 22 vols. Munich, 1835–1852.

Nagler-Meyer.
Allgemeines Künstler-Lexikon. Leipzig, 1872 and following years. (This is a second enlarged and revised edition of Nagler. It is far from being complete.)

Nardini Despotti Mospignotti, Aristide.
Il Campanile di Santa Maria del Fiore. Leghorn, 1885.
Filippo di Ser Brunellesco e la Cupola del Duomo di Firenze. Leghorn, 1885.
Giovanni di Lapo Ghino, Il Duomo del 1360. Appendix to his Filippo di Ser Brunellesco di Firenze.

Narjoux, Félix.
Notes de Voyage d'un Architecte dans le nord-ouest de l'Europe. Paris, 1876.
* Histoire d'une Ferme. Paris, 1882.
Paris ; Monuments élevés par la Ville 1850–1880. Paris, 1880–1883.

Nash, Joseph.
Mansions of England in the Olden Time. London, 1839–1849.
Architecture of the Middle Ages drawn from Nature. London, 1838.

Natalis, Rondot.
Peintres sur Verre de Troyes, du XIVe et du XVe siècle. Nogent-le-Rotrou, 1887.

Neale, John Preston.
The History and Antiquities of Westminster Abbey and Henry the Seventh's Chapel. London, 1856.
Views of the Seats of Noblemen and Gentlemen in England, Wales, Scotland, and Ireland. London, 1818–1823.

Neckelmann, Fred. Skjold, and Meldahl, F.
Denkmaeler der Renaissance in Dänemark. Berlin, 1888.

Neitner, T.
Gärtnerisches Skizzenbuch. Berlin, 1883.

Nesbitt, Alex.
Glass. South Kensington Handbooks. 1888.

Nesfield, William Eden.
* Specimens of Mediæval Architecture. London, 1862.

Neudörffer, Johann.
Nachrichten von den Vornehmsten Künstlern und Werkleuten . . . Nuremberg, 1828.

Neuwirth, Josef.
Die Wochenrechnungen des Prager Dombaues. Prague, 1890.

Nevill, Ralph.
Old Cottage and Domestic Architecture in Southwest Surrey. Guildford, 1891.

Newlands, James.
Carpenter and Joiner's Assistant . . . A . . . Treatise on . . . Materials and . . . Framing . . . Glasgow, 1860.

Newton, C. T., and Pullan, R. P.
A History of Discoveries at Halicarnassus, Cnidus, and Branchidæ. London, 1863.
Newton, M. A.
Travels and Discoveries in the Levant. London, 1865.
Nicolai, F.
Beschreibung der Königlichen Residenzstädte Berlin und Potsdam. Berlin, 1786.
Nicoletti, Abate Giuseppe.
Illustrazione della Chiesa e Scuola di S. Rocco. Venice, 1885.
Niedermayer, Andreas.
Künstler und Kunstwerke der stadt Regensburg ; ein beitrag zur Kunstgeschichte Altbayerns. Landshut, 1857.
Niemann, G.
Travels in Asia Minor. (See Reisen im S. W. Kleinasien.)
Niemann, Georg, and Feldegg, Ferd. v.
Theophilos Hansen und seine Werke. Vienna, 1893.
Nineteenth Century [Periodical]. London.
Nispi-Landi, Ciro.
Le Terme ed il Pantheon. 2d ed. Rome, 1883.
Storia dell' antichissima Città di Sutri . . . Colla descrizione de' suoi Monumenti Massime della Anfiteatro Etrusco, etc. Rome, 1887.
Nissen, Heinrich.
Pompejanische Studien zur Städte Kunde des Alterthums. Leipzig, 1877.
Noback, Gustav.
Bier, Malz, sowie Maschinen und Apparat für Brauerein und Malzerein. Vienna, 1874.
Nodier, J. C. A. ; Taylor, I. J. S., baron ; Cailleux, A. A. de.
Voyages pittoresques et romantiques dans l'ancienne France. Paris, 1820–1878.
Nöhring, J., und Löwis of Menar, C. von.
Die Städtische Profanarchitektur der Gothik, der Renaissance und des Barocco in Riga, Revel und Narva. Lubeck, 1892.
Normand, Charles Pierre Joseph.
Nouveau Parallèle des Ordres d'Architecture des Grecs, des Romains et des Auteurs Modernes. Paris, 1819.
Translated into German by J. M. Mauch, as : Vergleichende Darstellung der Architechtonischen Ordnungen der Griechen und Römer. Potsdam, 1832.
Norton, Charles Eliot.
Historical Studies of Church-building in the Middle Ages. New York, 1880.
Urkunden zur Geschichte des Doms von Siena. In Jahrbuch für Kunst-wissenschaft, 1873.
Nouvelle Biographie Générale depuis les temps les plus reculés jusqu'à nos jours. Published originally as Biographie Universelle. Paris, completed about 1866.
* Nouvelles Annales de la Construction [Periodical]. Paris.
Nouvelles Archives de l'Art Français ; recueil de documents inédits publiés par la Société de l'Histoire de l'Art français. 1872–1885.
Nouvelles Archives des Missions scientifiques.
(See Archives des Missions scientifiques.)

Ocagne, Maurice, d'.
Cours de Géométrie Descriptive et de Géométrie Infinitesimale. Paris, 1896.
Odrzywolski, Slawomir.
Die Renaissance in Polen, Kunstdenkmale des XVI. und XVII. Jahrhunderts. Vienna, 1899. Title also in Polish.

Oettingen, Wolfgang von.
Über das Leben und Werke des Antonio Averlino. Leipzig, 1888.
Okely, W. Sebastian.
Development of Christian Architecture in Italy. London, 1860.
Ongania, Ferdinando (editor).
La Basilica di San Marco in Venezia . . . Venice, 1881–1888. (See Boito.)
Raccolta delle Vere da Pozzo in Venezia. 1889.
Oppert, Franz.
Hospitals, Infirmaries, and Dispensaries. London, 1867.
Orlandi, Pellegrino Antonio.
Abecedario Pittorico, nel quale . . . sono descritte le patrie, i maestri, ed i tempi, nei quali fiorirono, circa quattro mila. Bologna, 1704.
Orti, G. G. conte di Manara.
Dei Lavori Architettonici di Fra Giocondo in Verona. Verona, 1853.
Osten, Friedrich.
Die Bauwerke in der Lombardei. Frankfort, 1847.
Osthoff, George, and Schmitt, Eduard.
Schlachthöfe und Viehmärkte : Märkte für Lebensmittel, Getreide, Pferde, und Hornvieh. Darmstadt, 1891.
(Forms part of Handbuch der Architektur, 1891.)
Die Bäder und Bade-Anstalten der Neuzeit, unter besonderer Berüsichtigung der Schwimm-, Wannen-, Douche-, Dampf-, und Heisseluft-Bäder. Leipzig, 1887.
Otte, Heinrich.
Handbuch der Kirchlichen Kunst-Archäologie. Leipzig, 1868.
Geschichte der Romanischen Baukunst. Leipzig, 1874.
Ottin, L.
L'Art de faire un Vitrail. Paris, 1892.
Le Vitrail ; son Histoire, ses Manifestations a travers les Âges et les Peuples. Paris (n.d.).
Ouseley, Sir William.
Travels in Various Countries of the East, more particularly Persia. London, 1819, 1821, 1823.
Epitome of the Ancient History of Persia extracted from the Jehan Ara of Ahmad el Kazwini, the author of the Nigâristân. London, 1799.
Overbeck, Johannes.
Die Antiken Schriftquellen zur Geschichte der bildenden Künste bei den Griechen. Leipzig, 1868.
Geschichte der Griechischen Plastik. Leipzig, 1882.
Pompeii in seinen Gebäuden Alterthümern und Kunstwerken. 3d ed. Leipzig, 1875.

Pagrave, Venanzio de ; e Casati, Carlo.
Vita di Cesare Cesariano. Milan, 1870.
Palestine Exploration Fund. London, 1869–.
Various publications.
Paley, Frederick Apthorpe.
Illustrations of Baptismal Fonts by Thomas Combe. London, 1844.
Palladio, Andrea.
Le Fabbriche e i Disegni, raccolti ed illustrati da O. B. Scamozzi. Vicenza, 1776–1783, 1786.
Palustre, L.
La Renaissance en France. 3 vols. 1885 and previous years (all published).
L'Architecture de la Renaissance. Paris, 1892.
Paoletti, Pietro.
L'Architettura e la Scultura del Rinascimento

in Venezia; ricerche storico-artistiche. Venice, 1893.

Papworth, Wyatt.
John B. Papworth; a Brief Record of his Life and Works. London, 1879.

Paravicini, Tito Vespasiano.
Die Renaissance-Architektur der Lombardei. (Translated into German by R. Koppel. Title-page also in Italian and French.) Dresden, 1877–1878.

Parcerisa, F. I.
Recuerdos y Bellezas de España ... En laminas dibujadas del natural y litografiadas por F. I. Parcerisa.

Paris dans sa Splendeur, Monuments, Vues, Scènes Historiques, description Dessins et Lithographes par Philippe Benoist, texte par MM. Audiganne . . . Paris, 1861.

Paris, Pierre.
La Sculpture Antique. Paris, 1889.

Parker, John Henry (publisher).
Glossary of Architecture. (See Glossary.)
Domestic Architecture of the Middle Ages. (See Domestic.)

Parthey, Gustav Friedrich Constantin.
Wenzel Hollar. Berlin, 1835.

Parvillée, L.
L'Architecture et Décoration Turques au XVe siècle. Paris, 1874.

Passavant, J. D.
Raphael von Urbino und sein Vater Giovanni Santi. Leipzig, 1839.

Passerini, Luigi.
Gli Alberti di Firenze. Florence, 1870.
La Bibliografia di Michelangelo Buonarroti e gli incisori delle sur opere. Florence, 1875.

Pattison, Mrs. Mark.
Renaissance of Art in France. London, 1879.

Paulus, Dr. Eduard.
Die Kunst und Alterthums-Denkmale im Königreich Württemberg. Stuttgart, 1893.
* Die Cisterzienzer-Abtei Maulbronn. Stuttgart, 1879.

Pauly-Wissowa.
Pauly's Real-Encyclopädie der Classischen Altertumswissenschaft. Ed. by Georg Wissowa. 4 vols. issued, A-Cor. Stuttgart, 1894-1900.
(The original work by Pauly was completed in 6 vols. in 1852.)

Pausanias.
* Description of Greece. Translated with a Commentary by J. A. Frazer. 6 vols. London, 1898.

Peabody Museum of American Archæology and Ethnology. Harvard University Memoirs. Cambridge, 1897–1898 —.

Pegge, Samuel (the elder).
The Life of Robert Grosseteste, Bishop of Lincoln . . . with an account of the Bishop's Works and an Appendix. London, 1893.

Pelcel, Frantisek Martin.
Abbildungen Bohnischer und Mährischer Gelehrten und Künstler. Prague, 1773–1777.

Pelletier, Pierre.
Les Verriers dans le Lyonnais et le Forez. Paris, 1886.

Penanrun, David de; Roux, L. F.; Delaire, E. A.
Les Architectes Élèves de l'École des Beaux-Arts. Paris, 1895.

Pennethorne, John.
The Geometry and Optics of Ancient Architecture. London and Edinburgh, 1878.

Penrose, F. C.
An Investigation of the Principles of Athenian

Architecture (Society of Dilettanti). London and New York, 1888.

Pératé, André.
L'Archéologie Chrétienne. Paris, 1892.

Pérau, Gabriel Louis Calabre.
Description historique de l'Hôtel Royal des Invalides . . . Paris, 1756.

Percier, Charles, and Fontaine, P. F. L.
Palais, Maisons, et autres Édifices modernes dessinés à Rome. Paris, 1798.

Perdreau (L'Abbé).
Guide du Visiteur et du Pélerin à l'Église Saint-Étienne du Mont. Paris.

Perger, Anton, Ritter von.
Der Dom zu S. Stephan in Wien. Trieste, 1854.

Perkins, Charles C.
Historical Handbook of Italian Sculpture. London, 1883.
Tuscan Sculptors, their Lives, Works, and Times. London, 1864.
Italian Sculptors, 1868.
Ghiberti et son École. Paris (n.d.).

Perrault, Charles.
Les Hommes illustres qui ont paru en France pendant ce siècle. Paris, 1896.

Perrot, Georges, et Chipiez, Ch.
* Histoire de l'Art dans l'Antiquité, vols. issued Paris 1882–1898. I. L'Égypte. II. Chaldée et Assyrie. III. Phénicie et Cypre. IV. Judée, Sardaigne, Syrie, Cappadoce. V. Perse, Phrygie, Lydie et Carie, Lycie. VI. La Grèce primitive, l'art Mycénien. VII. Grèce de l'épopée, Grèce archaïque. Translated into English under different titles, the translations having different degrees of merit.

Perry, Walter Copland.
Greek and Roman Sculpture. London and New York, 1882.

Petersen, E.
* Travels in Asia Minor. (See Reisen im S. W. Kleinasien.)
Die Kunst des Pheidias am Parthenon und zu Olympia. Berlin, 1873.

Petersen, Eugen Adolf Hermann; and Domazewski, Alfred von; and Calderini, Guglielmo.
Die Marcus-Saüle auf Piazza Colonna in Rom. Munich, 1896.

Petit, Victor.
Châteaux de la Vallée de la Loire. Paris, 1861.
Petits Édifices historiques recueillis par A. Raguenet [Periodical]. Paris, 1891–[1894].

Petrie, George.
Ecclesiastical Architecture of Ireland anterior to the Anglo-Norman Invasion. Dublin, 1845.

Petrie, W. M. Flinders.
History of Egypt during the XVII. and XVIII. dynasties. London, 1899.
Egyptian Decorative Art. New York and London, 1895.
Ten Years' Digging in Egypt. New York, Chicago, London, 1892.

Pfnor, Rodolphe.
Monographie du Château d'Anet. Paris, 1867.
Monographie du Château de Heidelberg. Paris, 1859.
Le Château de Vaux-le-Vicomte. Paris, 1889.
Histoire et Guide artistique au Palais de Fontainebleau; préface par Anatole France. Paris, 1889.

Pfnor, Rodolphe, et Champollion-Figeac.
Monographie du Palais de Fontainebleau. Paris, 1863.

Philbrick, Edward S.
American Sanitary Engineering (in the Sani-

tary Engineering; now Engineering Record). New York, 1881.

Disposal of Sewage in Suburban Residences. New York, 1885.

Philbrick, Philetus H.
Beams and Girders; Practical Formulas for their Resistance. New York, 1886.

Philimore, Lucy.
Sir Christopher Wren; his Family and his Times; with Original Letters and a Discourse on Architecture, hitherto unpublished. London, 1883.

Phipson, Emma.
Choir Stalls and their Carvings. London, 1896.

Pingeron, Jean Claude.
Vies des Architectes anciens et modernes . . . Traduites de l'Italien (of T. Milizia) et enrichies de notes. Paris, 1771.

Piolin, Dom. Paul L.
Histoire de l'Église du Mans (l'église du Mans durant la Révolution . . . complément de l'histoire). Le Mans, 1851-71.

Planat, Paul (editor).
Encyclopédie de l'Architecture et de la Construction. Paris (n.d.).

Planché, J. R.
The Pursuivant of Arms; or Heraldry founded upon Facts . . . 3d ed. London [pref. 1873].

Plarr, Victor G. Men and Women of the Time. 14th ed. London, 1895.

Platt, Charles Adams.
Italian Gardens. New York, 1894.

Plinius [Secundus], Caius (Pliny the Elder).
Historia Naturalis. English translation by Holland. London, 1601.

Pliny the Elder, translated by K. Jex-Blake.
The Elder Pliny's Chapters on the History of Art (text and translation on opposite pages, notes by Sellers and Urlichs). London, 1896.

Plon, Eugène.
Benvenuto Cellini. Paris, 1883.
Leone Leoni et Pompeo Leoni. 1886.

Plutarch's Lives. Translated from the original Greek, with notes critical and historical, by John and William Langhorne. London, 1770; New York, 1822 (many other editions).

Plutarch's Lives: the translation called Dryden's, corrected from the Greek and revised by A. H. Clough. Boston, 1859.

Pontani, C.
Opere architettoniche di Raffaello Sanzio. Rome, 1845.

Pontremoli, Emmanuel, and Collignon, Maxime.
Pergame, Restauration et Description. Paris, 1900.

Poole, George Ayliffe.
History of Ecclesiastical Architecture in England. London, 1848.

Poole, William Frederick.
Notes on Library Construction; the Organization and Management of Libraries; and other papers, chiefly in the publications of the U. S. Bureau of Education.

Popp, Justus, and Bülau, Theodor.
Die Architektur des Mittelalters in Regensburg. Ratisbon, 1839.
Les trois Âges de l'Architecture Gothique, son origine, sa théorie, demontrés et représentés par des exemples choisis à Ratisbonne . . . tr. de l'Allemand. Paris, 1841.

Porter, Dwight.
The Removal of Roof Water from Buildings, reprinted in American Architect, Aug. 31, 1889.

Porter, Josias Leslie.
Five Years in Damascus. London, 1855.

Portfolio, The.
Monographs on Artistic Subjects. London, 1894, —.

Post, Pieter.
Les Ouvrages d'Architecture. Leyden, 1715.

Pottier, E., and Reinasch, S.
École Française d'Athènes. Recherches archéologiques, etc. Paris, 1887, and other dates.

Pouvourville, Albert de.
L'Art Indo-Chine. Paris, 1894.

Powell, George T.
Foundations and Foundation Walls for all Classes of Buildings. New York, 1889.

Prentice, Andrew N.
* Renaissance Architecture and Ornament in Spain; a series of examples selected from the purest works executed between the years 1500-1560. London (n.d.).

Prescott, William H.
Conquest of Peru. Boston, 1847, and many subsequent editions.

Pressel, Friedrich.
Ulm und sein Münster. Ulm, 1877.

Presuhn, Emil.
Pompeii; die neuesten Ausgrabungen. Leipzig, 1882.

Price, John.
Historical and Topographical Account of Leominster and its Vicinity, with an Appendix. Ludlow, 1795.
Historical Account of the City of Hereford, with some remarks on the river Wye. Hereford, 1796.

Prime, William Cowper.
Pottery and Porcelain of all Times and Nations. With tables of Factory and Artist's Marks for the use of Collectors. New York, 1878.

Prior, Edward S.
A History of Gothic Art in England. London, 1900.

Prisse d'Avennes.
Histoire de l'Art Égyptien. Paris, 1878.
L'Art Arabe d'après les Monuments du Kaire depuis le VIIe siècle jusqu'à la fin du XVIIIe. Paris, 1877.

Procopius of Cæsarea.
De Ædificiis Justiniani.
[English Translation of the Buildings of Justinian. Translated by Colonel Sir C. W. Wilson and Professor Hayter Lewis. London, 1888.]

Promis, Carlo.
Gli Ingegneri e gli Scrittori Militari Bolognese del XV e XVI secolo. Turin, 1863.

Pugin, Augustus Charles.
Specimens of Gothic Architecture. London, 1821-1823.

Pugin, A. Welby.
The Present State of Ecclesiastical Architecture in England. London, 1843.

Pugin, A. N. W., and Le Keux, Henry.
Specimens of the Architectural Antiquities of Normandy. 1827.

Pungileoni, Luigi.
Memoria intorno alla Vita ed alle Opere di Donato o Donnino Bramante. Rome, 1836.

Puttrich, Ludwig.
Denkmale der Baukunst des Mittelalters in Sachsen. 4 vols. Leipzig, 1844-1850.

Quantin, Albert Marie Jérôme (publisher).
Bibliothèque de l'enseignement des Beaux-Arts; about 30 vols., many of which have special reference here.

(Publishing-house continued as Librairies-Im primeries Réunies.)

Quast, Alexander Ferdinand von.
Das Erechtheion zu Athen. Berlin, 1862.
Die Entwicklung des christlichen Kirchenbaues. Berlin, 1858.
Über Form, Einrichtung und Ausschmückung. Berlin, 1853.
Die alt-christlichen Bauwerke von Ravenna. Berlin, 1842.
Denkmäler der Baukunst in Ermland.

Quatremère de Quincy, Antoine Chrysostome.
Dictionnaire d'Architecture, in l'Encyclopédie Méthodique. Paris, 1795–1825.
Dictionnaire Historique d'Architecture. Paris, 1832.
Histoire des Vies et des ouvrages des plus célèbres Architectes du XIᵉ siècle jusqu'à la fin du XVIIIᵉ.
Canova et ses ouvrages. Paris, 1834.
Notice Historique sur la vie et les ouvrages de M. Gondouin. Paris, 1816.
Notice Historique sur la vie et les ouvrages de M. Chalgrin. Paris, 1821.

Quilter, Harry.
Life of Giotto. London, 1880.

Quincy, Josiah.
Municipal History of the Town and City of Boston during two centuries from Sept. 17, 1630, to Sept. 17, 1830. Boston, 1852.

Raczynski, Atanazy (count).
Histoire de l'Art Moderne en Allemagne. Paris, 1836–1841.

Raggi, Oreste.
Della Vita e delle Opere di Luigi Canina. Casal-Monferrato, 1857.

Rahn, Johann Rudolf.
Ueber den Ursprung und die Entwickelung des Christlichen Central- und Kuppelbaues. Leipzlg, 1866.

Ramée, Daniel.
Histoire générale de l'Architecture. Paris, 1860.

Rām Rāj.
Essay on the Architecture of the Hindus. . . . London, 1834. (Oriental Translation Fund of Great Britain and Ireland.)

Ramsay, William.
A Manual of Roman Antiquities. Revised and partly rewritten by Rodolfo Lanciani. New York, 1895.

Ramsay, W. M.
A Study of Phrygian Art. Reprinted from the Journal of Hellenic Studies.

Raoul-Rochette, Désiré.
Notice Historique sur Pirro Ligorio in Jules Bouchet, La Villa Pia, 1837.

Raschdorff, J. C.
Toscana. Berlin, 1888. (In Palast-architektur von Ober-Italien und Toscana, Vol. 2.)

Ravioli, Camillo.
Notizie sui Lavori d' Architettura militare, sugli scritte o Disegni editi ed inediti dei Nove da San Gallo. Rome, 1863.

Rawlinson, Professor, The Rev. George.
The Five Great Monarchies of the Eastern World. New York, 1881.
The Sixth Great Oriental Monarchy; or the Geography, History, and Antiquities of Parthia. New York, 1873.
The Seventh Great Oriental Monarchy; or the Geography, History, and Antiquities of the Sassanian or new Persian Empire. New York, 1882.

Rayet, O.
Monuments de l'Art Antique. Paris, 1884.

Rayet, Olivier, et Collignon, Maxime.
Histoire de la Céramique Grecque. Paris, 1888.

Reber, Franz.
Geschichte der Baukunst im Alterthum. Leipzig, 1886.
*Kuntsgeschichte des Mittelalters. Leipzig, 1886.
Translation of the above by J. T. Clarke, History of Mediæval Art. New York, 1887

Réclus, Jean Jacques Élisée.
The Earth and its Inhabitants. Edited by E. G. Ravenstein. London, 1878, etc.

Redgrave, Samuel.
Dictionary of Artists of the English School. London, 1874.
A Century of Painters of the English School. London, 2d ed., 1890. A first and fuller edition exists.

Redtenbacher, Rudolf.
Baldassare Peruzzi und seine Werke. (See Mittheilungen aus der Sammlung Architektonischer Handzeichnungen in der Galleria der Uffizien zu Florenz. Carlsruhe, 1875.)
Architektur der Italienischen Renaissance. Frankfurt a. M., 1886.

Reichensperger, August.
Zur Characteristik des Baumeister Friedrich, Freiherr von Schmidt. Dusseldorf, 1891.

Reid, Henry.
A Practical Treatise on Natural and Artificial Concrete. London, 1879.

Reid, John.
Turkey and the Turks; or the Ottoman Empire. 1840.

Reinhardt, Robert.
Genua. (In Palast-Architektur von Ober-Italien und Toscana vom XV. bis XVII. Jahrhundert.) Berlin, 1886.
Reisen im Südwestlichen Kleinasien.
*Vol. I. by Benndorf, O., and Niemann, G. Vienna, 1884.
Vol. II. by Petersen, E., and von Luschan, F. Vienna, 1899.

Remusat, Jean Pierre Abel.
Nouveaux Mélanges Asiatiques, ou Recueil de morceaux de critique et de mémoires relatifs aux Religions, aux Sciences aux Coutumes, à l'Histoire et à la Géographie des Nations Orientales. Paris, 1829.

Renan, Joseph Ernest.
Mission de Phénicie. Paris, 1864.

Rennie, Sir John.
Autobiography. 1875.

Renouvier, Jules.
Histoire de l'Art pendant la Révolution. Paris, 1863.

Renouvier, Jules, et Ricard, Ad.
Des Maîtres de Pierre de Montpellier, et des autres artistes gothiques de Montpellier. Montpellier, 1844.

Renwick, James.
Life of Count Rumford (in Jared Sparks, Library of American Biography; second series). Boston, 1853.

Repton, Humphry.
Landscape Gardening and Landscape Architecture, being his entire works on these subjects. New edition with an . . . introduction . . . a biographical notice . . . and a copious . . . index, by J. C. Loudon . . . London, 1840.

Restaurations des Monuments Antiques, par les architectes pensionnaires de l'Académie de

France à Rome, depuis 1788 jusqu'à nos jours. A series. Thermæ, Trajan Col., etc. (Thermes de Caracalla, 1825 ; Thermes de Dioclétien, 1841 ; Thermes de Titus, 1871–1872.) Paris, 1877–1890.

Reumont, Alfred von.
Lorenzo dei Medici, il Magnifico. Leipzig, 1874.

Réunion des Sociétés des Beaux-Arts des Départements, published by Ministère de l'Instruction publique des Beaux-Arts. Vol. 14, of 1900.

Révoil, Henry.
Architecture Romane du midi de la France. Paris, 1873.

Revue Archéologique, ou Recueil de Documents et de Mémoires relatifs à l'étude des Monuments et à la Philologie de l'Antiquité et du Moyen Âge, publiée par les principaux Archéologues français et Etrangers, etc. [Periodical]. Paris, 3 series ; 1844–1883.

Revue de l'Art Chrétien ; recueil mensuel d'archéologie religieuse, dirigé par M. l'abbé J. Carblet. 17 tom. [Periodical]. Paris, Amiens, Tournai, Arras, 1857–1874.

Revue des Arts décoratifs [Periodical]. 1871–1880.

Revue générale de l'Architecture et des Travaux publics ; journal des architectes, des ingénieurs, des archéologues, des industriels et des propriétaires. Sous la direction de C. Daly, architecte [Periodical]. Paris, 1840–.

Revue Universelle des Arts [Periodical]. Paris ; Brussels, 1855–1866.

Reymond, Marcel.
La Sainte Cécile de Stéphane Maderna (in Gazette des Beaux-Arts, 1872).
Lorenzo Ghiberti (in Gazette des Beaux-Arts, 1896).
La Sculpture Florentine (4 parts, each of a separate epoch). Florence, 1898–1899.
Les della Robbia. Florence, 1897.

Rhys, Ernest.
Sir Frederick Leighton. 4to, 1895 (3d edition, 8vo, 1900, entitled Frederick, Lord Leighton, His Life and Works).

R. I. B. A. (See Royal Institute of British Architects.)

Ricci, Amico.
Storia dell Architettura in Italia. Modena, 1857–1859.

Ricci, Corrado.
Antonio Allegri da Correggio ; his Life, his Friends, and his Time. London and New York, 1896.

Riccio, Minieri.
Gli Artisti ed artifici che lavarono Castel Nuovo. Naples, 1876.

Richardson, George.
The New Vitruvius Britannicus, consisting of plans and elevations of modern buildings . . . in Great Britain, etc. London, 1802–1808.

Richter, Jean Paul.
Der Ursprung der abendländischen Kirchengebäude. Vienna, 1878.
The Literary Works of Leonardo da Vinci. London, 1883.

Rickmann, Fr. W. J.
Die Domkirche zu Ratzeburg. Ratzeburg, 1881.

Rickman, John (editor). (See Telford, Thomas.)

Rickman, Thomas.
An Attempt to discriminate the Styles of Architecture in England from the Conquest to the Reformation. London, 1817, 1819.

Ricordi di Architettura [Periodical]. Florence, 1878–1893.

Ridolfi, Carlo.
Le Maraviglio dell' Arte overo le vite de gl' illustri Pittori Veneti. Venice, 1648.

Rigato, Andrea (editor).
Osservazioni sopra Andrea Palladio. Padua, 1811.

Rikliter, Fedor.
Pamyatniki drevnyavo russkavo zodchestva . . . Moscow, 1850.
Translated into English as : Monuments of Ancient Russian Architecture . . . 1850.

Riley, J. W.
Building Construction for Beginners. London and New York, 1899.

Robb, Russell.
Electric Wiring, for the use of Architects, Underwriters, and the Owners of Buildings. New York and London, 1896.

Robert-Dumesnil, A. P. F.
Le Peintre-graveur Français. Paris, 1855–1871.

Robertson, Alexander.
A History of S. Mark's Church, Venice. New York, 1898.

Robertson, T. S.
The Progress of Art in English Church Architecture. London, 1897.

Robinson, John Beverly.
Principles of Architectural Composition ; an Attempt to order and phrase Ideas which have hitherto been only felt by the Instinctive Taste of Designers. New York, 1899.

Robinson, J. C.
Italian Sculpture of the Middle Ages and Period of the Revival of Art. London, 1862.

Robinson, Robert.
The History of Baptism, etc. London, 1790.

Robinson, William, F. L. S.
Garden Design and Architect's Gardens. London, 1892.
Parks, Promenades, and Gardens of Paris. London, 1869.

Robinson, William.
The English Flower Garden ; Style, Position and Arrangement. London, 1884, 1893.

Robuchon, Jules César.
Paysages et Monuments du Poitou photographiés . . . avec notices publiées sous les auspices de. la Société des Antiquaires de l'Ouest. Paris, 1884–1895.

Rocchi, E.
Baccio Pontelli e la Rocca d'Ostia, in Archivio Storico dell' Arte. 1898.

Rogers, W. G.
Remarks upon Grinling Gibbons, in R. I. B. A. Papers. 1866–1867.

Rohault de Fleury, Charles.
La Messe ; études archéologiques sur ses monuments, continuées par son fils (G. Rohault de Fleury). 8 vols. Paris, 1883–1889.

Rohault de Fleury, Georges.
* La Toscane au Moyen-Âge ; architecture civile et militaire. Paris, 1870–1873.
Le Latran au Moyen-Âge. Paris, 1877.
* Les Monuments de Pise au Moyen-Âge. Paris, 1866.

Romstorfer, Carl A.
* Die Moldauisch-Byzantinische Baukunst.

Ronchini, Amadeo.
I due Vignole Modena, 1860 [incomplete]. Vienna, 1896.

Rondelet, Antoine.
  Essai historique sur le Pont de Rialto. Paris, 1837.
Rondelet, Jean.
  Traité théorique et pratique de l'Art de Bâtir. Paris, 1838–1855. Supplément par G. A. Blouet. Paris, 1855–1868.
Ronzani-Lucioli.
  (See Sanmichele, Michele.)
Rosenberg, Marc.
  Quellen zur Geschichte des Heidelberger Schlosses. Heidelberg, 1882.
Rosengarten, A.
  Die Architektonischen Stylarten. Brunswick, 1874.
Ross, Ludwig; Schaubert, Eduard; and Hansen, Christian.
  Die Akropolis von Athen. Berlin, 1836.
Rossi, Gio. Battista de.
  Musaici Cristiani saggi dei Pavimenti delle Chiese di Roma anteriori al secolo XV. Rome, 1882.
  Delle alte famiglie di Marmorarii Romani, in Bulletino di Archeologia Christiana, 1875. (Vol. VI.)
Roulliet, A.
  Michel Colombe et son Œuvre. Tours, 1884.
Roussel, Pierre Désiré.
  Histoire et Description du Château d'Anet. Paris, 1875.
Rouyer, Jean Eugène, and Darcel, A.
  L'Art Architectural en France depuis François I jusqu'à Louis XIV. Paris, 1863–1866.
Royal Asiatic Society of Great Britain and Ireland, Reports and Transactions.
Royal Institute of the British Architects, Transactions. 1835–1892 [Periodical]. Journal of proceedings, 1885–1894.
  Kalendar, 1886 and the following years.
  Sessional papers, 1875 and the following years.
  Papers by H. W. Brewer on Central and Southern Germany. 1867–1868.
Rubens, Sir Peter Paul.
  Palazzi di Genova, con le loro piante ed alzati. Antwerp, 1622.
Rudde, ——.
  Monuments de Bruges. 1824.
Ruggieri, Ferdinando.
  Studio d'Architettura Civile sopra gli ornamente di porte e finestre, colle misure, piante . . . e profile, tratte da alcune fabbriche insigni di Firenzi . . . Florence, 1722–1728.
Runge, G.
  Die öffentliche Badeanstadt in Bremen. Bremen, 1878.
Runge, L.
  Der Glockenthurm des Doms zu Florenz, nebst entwurf zur West-Façade des doms. Berlin, 1853.
Rupin, Ernest.
  L'Abbaye et les Cloîtres de Moissac. Paris, 1897.
Ruprich-Robert, V.
  * L'Architecture Normande, aux XIᵉ et XIIᵉ siècles. Paris, 1885–1887.
  L'Église et le Monastère du Val-de-Grâce. Paris, 1875.
Rusca, Luigi.
  Recueil des Dessins de differens batimens construits à Saint-Pétersbourg; translation of Raccolta dei disegni di diverse fabbriche costrutte in Pietroburgo. St. Petersburg, 1810.
Ruskin, John.
  * The Stones of Venice. 3 vols. London, 1853.

Seven Lamps of Architecture. 1849. (New edition, Sunnyside (Kent, England). 1880.)
  Giotto and his works in Padua, published by the Arundel Society. London, 1854–1860. (In three parts, collected into one vol., 1877.)
Rymer, Thomas.
  Fœdera conventiones, litteræ et cujuscunque generis acta publica inter reges angliæ et alios quosvis imperatores reges ab ingressu Gulielmi I. in Angliam A.D. 1066 ad nostra usque tempora . . . accurantibus. Adamo Clarke, F. Holbrook, and J. Caliy. 3 vols. in 6, 15 pl. Folio. (Gt. Br. Record Com.) London, 1816–1830.

Sacken, Edward, Baron von.
  Katechismus der Heraldik. 4th ed. Leipzig, 1885.
Sahagun, Bernardino de.
  Historia General de las Cosas de Nueva España. Mexico, 1829–1830.
Saint Paul, Anthyme.
  Histoire Monumentale de la France. Paris, 1888.
Salazaro, Demetrio.
  Studi sui Monumenti della Italia Meridionale dal IVᵒ al XIIIᵒ secolo. 2 vols. Naples, 1877.
  L' Arte Romana al Medio Evo; appendice agli studi sui Monumenti della Italia Meridionale dal IVᵒ al XIIIᵒ secolo. Naples, 1881.
Salva, ——.
  Elogio di Michele Sammicheli. Rome, 1814.
Salvisberg, Paul.
  Die deutsche Kriegs-Architektur von der Urzeit bis auf die Renaissance in his Kunsthistorische Studien; Heft 3–4. Stuttgart, 1887.
Salzenberg, W.
  * Alt-christliche Baudenkmale von Constantinopel vom 5. bis 12. Jahrhundert . . . Berlin, 1854.
Sandby, William.
  The History of the Royal Academy of Arts from its foundation in 1768 to the present time, with biographical notices of all the members. London, 1862.
Sanders, William Bliss.
  Examples of carved Oak Wood-Work in the Houses and Furniture of the 16th and 17th Centuries. London, 1883.
Sanitary Engineer [Periodical]. New York. (Now the Engineering Record.)
Sanmichele, [Sammicheli] Michele.
  Le Fabbriche Civile Ecclesiastiche e Militari, disegnate ed incise da F. Ronzani e G. Lucioli, con testo . . . da F. Zanotto. Genoa (n.d.).
  Another ed. Venice, 1832.
Sansovino, Francesco.
  Venetia Citta nobilissima et Singolare. Venice, 1663.
Sant' Ambrogio, Diego.
  Castiglione Olona. Milan, 1894.
  Lodi Vecchio, S. Bastiano. Milan, 1895.
  Il Castello di Pandino. Milan, 1895.
  Gra Car. Carpiano Vigano-Certosino e Selvanesco. Milan, 1894.
  Negative ed Eliotipie di Calzolari and Ferrario. Il Tempio della B.ᴬ Vergine Incoronata di Lodi. Milan, 1892.
Sarre, Friedrich.
  Denkmäler Persischer Baukunst. Berlin, 1901.
  Der Fürstenhof zu Wismar und die norddeutsche Terrakotta-Architektur. Berlin, 1890.

Sasso, Camillo Napoleone.
Storia dei Monumenti di Napoli. Naples, 1856–1858.
Saulcy, L. F. J. Caignart de.
Voyage en Terre Sainte. Paris, 1865.
Saussaye, Louis de la.
Le Château de Chambord. Blois and Paris, 1861.
Sauvageot, Claude.
Monographie de Notre-Dame de la Roche (n.d.).
Monographie de Chevreuse. Paris, 1874.
*Palais, Châteaux, Hôtels et Maisons de France. Paris, 1867.
Viollet-le-Duc et son Œuvre Dessinée. Paris, 1880.
Sauval, Henri.
Histoire et recherches des Antiquités de la Ville de Paris. Paris, 1724.
Scamozzi, Vincenzo.
L'Idea dell Architettura universale . . . publicata per Cura di Stefano Ticozzi (which see). Milan, 1838.
Scamozzi, O. Bertotti (editor). (See Palladio, Andrea.)
Le Fabbriche e i Disegni, 1776–1783. Vicenza, 1786.
Schadow, Johann Gottfried.
Wittenberg's Denkmäler der Bildnerei, Baukunst und Malerei, mit historischen und artistischen Erläuterungen. Wittenberg, 1825.
Schäfer, Carl.
Mustergiltigen Kirchenbauten des Mittelalters in Deutschland. Berlin, 1886.
Schaubert, Eduard ; Ross, Ludwig ; and Hansen, Christian.
Die Akropolis von Athen nach den Neuesten Ausgrabungen. Berlin, 1839.
Schliemann, Heinrich.
Troy, 1869. Trojan Antiquities, 1874. Ilios, 1880. Orchomenos, 1882. Troja, 1884. Ilios, ville et pays des Troyens [a combination of the original Ilios and the Troja] 1885. Tiryns, 1885. Mycenæ, 1877.
Most of these works were published simultaneously in German and French, or German and English, or in all.
Schmarsow, August.
Meister Andrea. In Jahrbuch der Königlich preussischen Kunstsammlungen, 1883.
Nuovi Studi intorno a Michelozzo, in Archivio Storico dell' Arte, 1893 (Vol. VI.). Donatello. Breslau, 1896.
Schmidt, Christian Wilhelm.
Baudenkmale der romischen Periode und des Mittelalters in Trier und seiner Umgebung. Treves, 1836–1845.
Schmidt, J. P.
Monuments Religieux, etc. Paris, 1859.
Schmidt, Karl, and Schildbach, Moritz.
Der Königliche Zwinger in Dresden. Hamburg, 1892.
Schnaase, Carl ; Eisenmann, O. ; Lübke, W.
Geschichte der bildenden Künste im 15, Jahrhundert. Forms Vol. VIII. of Schnaase's Geschichte der bildenden Künste. Düsseldorf, 1866 to 1876.
Schoefer, C., and Rossteucher, A.
L'ornement dans les vitraux du Moyen Âge et de la Renaissance. Reproduction en chromolithographie de vitraux allemands provenant de Marburg (1266), Alterberg, Immenhausen, Nordelhausen, Lingen, Ulm (arbre de Jessé), Augsbourg, Strasbourg, etc.

Schönfeld, Paul.
Andrea Sansovino und seine Schule . . . Stuttgart, 1881.
Schuchardt, Dr. Carl.
Schliemann's Excavations : translated from the German by Eugenie Sellers. London and New York, 1891.
Schultz, Christoph Ludwig Friedrich, and Goethe.
Briefwechsel zwischen Goethe und Staatsrath Schultz. Leipzig, 1853.
Schultz, Johann Karl.
Danzig und seine Bauwerke. Berlin, 1872.
Schultz, Robert Weir, and Barnsley, S. H.
The Monastery of Saint Luke of Stiris, in Phocis : and the dependent monastery of Saint Nicolas in the Fields, near Skripou, in Bœotia. London, 1901.
Schultze, Rudolph.
Bau und Betrieb von Volks-Badeanstalten. Bonn, 1893.
Schultze, Victor.
Die Katakomben. Die Altchristlichen Grabstätten. Leipzig, 1882.
Schumann, P. T.
Barock und Rococo ; Studien sur Baugeschichte. Leipzig, 1885.
Schütz, Alexander.
Die Renaissance in Italien ; eine Sammlung der werthvollsten erhaltenen Monumente. Hamburg, 1886.
Schuyler, Eugene.
Turkistan : notes of a Journey in Russian Turkistan, Khokand, Bukhara, and Kuldja. London, 1877.
Schuyler, Montgomery.
American Architecture. New York, 1892.
Schwartz, Oscar, M.D.
Bau, Einrichtung und Betrieb öffentlicher Schlachthäuser und Viehhöfe. 2d ed. Berlin, 1898.
Scott, George Gilbert.
Remarks on Secular and Domestic Architecture, Present and Future. London, 1858.
Lectures on the Development of Mediæval Architecture. 2 vols. London, 1879.
Personal and Professional Recollections. London, 1879.
Gleanings from Westminster Abbey, with appendices . . . completing the history of the Abbey Buildings, by W. Burges, J. Burtt, G. Corner . . . [and others]. Oxford, 1864.
Seidel, G. F.
Die Königliche Residenz in München. Leipzig, 1880–1883.
Seidlitz, W. V.
Bramante in Mailand ; in Jahrbuch der Königlich preussischen Kunstsammlungen. Vol. III.
Selvatico, Pietro Estense, marchese.
Sulla Architettura e sulla Scultura in Venezia dal medio evo sino ai nostri giorni . . . Venice, 1847.
Sulla capellina degli Scrovegni. Padua, 1836.
Semper, Hans.
Hervoragende Bildhauer-Architekten der Renaissance. Dresden [pref. 1880].
Donatello, seine Zeit und Schule. Vienna, 1875.
Semper, H. ; Schulze, F. O. ; Barth, W.
Carpi. Ein Furstensitz der Renaissance. Dresden, 1882.
Semper, Die Söhne Sempers.
Die K. K. Hofmusen in Wien and Gottfried Semper. Drei Denkschriften Gottfried Semper's herausgegeben von seinen Söhnen. Innsbruck, 1892.

Seubert, Adolf Friedrich.
Allgemeines Künstler-lexicon. 3 vols. Frankfurt a. M., 1882.
S. G., Chronological History of Canterbury Cathedral. Canterbury, 1883.
Sharpe, Edmund.
The Ornamentation of the Transitional Period in Central Germany. London, 1874–1876.
On Lincoln Cathedral, in Associated Architectural Societies, Reports and Papers, Vol. 9.
* Architectural Parallels ; or the Progress of Ecclesiastical Architecture in England through the Twelfth and Thirteenth Centuries exhibited in a series of parallel examples. London, 1848.
Domed Churches of the Charente. (See A Visit to the Domed Churches of Charente, etc.)
Shaw, Henry.
Details of Elizabethan Architecture. London, 1839.
Shaw, Richard Norman.
* Architectural Studies from the Continent. London, 1858.
Sheraton, Thomas.
Cabinet-maker and Upholsterer's Drawing Book. London, 1794.
Sighart, Joachim.
Die mittelalterliche Kunst in der Erzdiöcese München-Freising, dargestelt in ihren Denkmälern. Freising, 1855.
Simakoff, N.
L'Art de l'Asie Centrale. S. Petersburg, 1883.
(Title-page in Russian and French.)
Simpson, William.
Architecture in the Himalayas. In R. I. B. A. Transactions, 1882–1883.
Buddhist Architecture in the Jellalabad Valley. In R. I. B. A. Transactions, 1879–1880.
Skene, William Forbes.
Celtic Scotland : a History of Ancient Alban. 1876–1880.
Smiles, Samuel.
Lives of the Engineers. 5 vols. London, 1861.
Smith, John Thomas.
Antiquarian Ramble in the streets of London. London, 1846.
Smith, William
Dictionary of Greek and Roman Biography and Mythology. 3 vols. London, 1844–1849.
Dictionary of Greek and Roman Geography. 2 vols. London, 1854–1887.
Dictionary of Greek and Roman Antiquities. 2 vols., 3d ed., 1890–1891.
Smithsonian Institution, Annual Reports. Washington, D.C.
Snell, Henry Saxon.
Charitable and Parochial Establishments. London, 1881.
Société Académique d'Architecture de Lyon, Annales [Periodical]. Lyons, 1869–1887.
Société Archéologique de Bordeaux. Comptes rendus et mémoires [Periodical]. Bordeaux, 1879—.
Société Nationale [royale] des Antiquaires de France, Mémoires et dissertations sur les antiquités nationales et étrangères [Periodical]. Paris, 1817–1834.
Atlas de tome 9. Paris, 1831.
Nouvelle série. Paris, 1835.
Troisième série. Paris, 1852–1863.
Quatrième série. Paris, 1869–1879.
Cinquième série. Paris, 1880, etc., in progress.
Annuaire de la Société. Paris, 1848–1855.

Bulletin, etc. Paris, 1857–1860.
Society of Antiquaries of London.
(See Archæologia.)
Vetusta Monumenta [Periodical]. London, 1747 —.
Sopwith, Thomas.
Treatise on Isometrical Drawing. London, 1834.
Souhaut, L'abbé.
Les Richiers et leurs Œuvres. 1883.
Sousa, Fr. Luis de.
Plans, Elevations, Sections, and Views of the Church of Batalha. 1836.
Souslow, W.
Monuments de l'ancienne Architecture Russe. Edition de l'Académie impériale des beaux-arts. Title-page in Russian and French, text in Russian. S. Petersburg, 1895–1898.
South Kensington Museum.
Catalogue of the Special Exhibition of Works of Art. London, 1863.
A Descriptive Catalogue of the Maiolica . . . with Historical Notices, Marks, and Monograms. London, 1873.
Ancient and Modern Furniture and Woodwork . . . with an Introduction by John Hungerford Pollen. London, 1874.
A Descriptive Catalogue of the Bronzes of European Origin . . . with an Introductory Notice by C. Drury E. Fortnum. London, 1876.
Spratt, Thomas Abel Bremage, and Forbes, Edward.
Travels in Lycia, Milyas, and the Cibyratis, in company with the late Rev. E. T. Daniell. London, 1847.
Springer, Anton Heinrich.
Raffael und Michel Angelo. Leipzig, 1878.
Squier, Ephraim George.
Nicaragua ; its People, Scenery, Monuments, and the proposed interoceanic Canal, with numerous original maps and illustrations. New York, 1852.
Peru ; incidents of Travel and Exploration in the Land of the Incas. London, 1876–1877.
Notes on Central America — particularly the Notes of Honduras and San Salvador, their geography, topography, climate, population, etc. New York, 1855.
Stabenrath, le Baron Charles de.
Le palais de justice de Rouen. Rouen, 1843.
Stahr, Adolf Wilhelm Theodor.
Torso ; Kunst, Kunstler, und Kunstwerke des griechischen und römischen Alterthums. Brunswick, 1878.
Stannus, Hugh.
Alfred Stevens and his Work : being a Collection of fifty-seven Autotypes, with a brief Memoir and Account of his principal Productions, so far as they are known. London, 1891.
Stappaerts, Félix, and Moke, H. G.
La Belgique Monumentale . . . 1840.
Statham, H. Heathcote.
Modern Architecture, a Book for Architects and the Public. London and New York, 1898.
Architecture for General Readers : a short Treatise on the Principles and Motives of Architectural Design, with a historical sketch. New York, 1895.
Steam Laundries and Public Health, issued by the London Sanitary Publishing Co. London, 1895.

Stegmann, Carl von.
Die Architektur der Renaissance in Toscana. (See Geymüller-Stegmann.) .

Stegmann, Dr. Hans.
Die Bildhauerfamilie della Robbia, in Geymüller-Stegmann, Die Architektur der Renaissance in Toscana.

Stephen-Lee.
(See Dictionary of National Biography.)

Stephen, Leslie, and Lee, Sidney.
(See Dictionary of National Biography.)

Stephens, John L.
Incidents of Travel in Central America, Chiapas, and Yucatan . . . London, 1841.

Stephens, Rev. W. R. W.
Life and Letters of E. A. Freeman. London, 1895.

Stevenson, Thomas, and Murphy, Shirley F.
Treatise on Hygiene and Public Health. 3 vols. Philadelphia, 1892.

Stirling-Maxwell, William.
Annals of the Artists of Spain. 2d ed. London, 1891.

Stockbauer, Jacob.
Der christliche Kirchenbau in den ersten sechs Jahrhunderten. Ratisbon, 1874.

Stokes, Miss Margaret MacNair.
* Early Christian Architecture in Ireland. London, 1878.

Stolze, F.
Persepolis; Denkmaler und inschriften von Persepolis Istakhr, Pasargadae-Shâhpûr. Berlin, 1882.

Storelli, André.
Notice Historique et Chronologique sur les Châteaux du Blaisois. Paris, 1884.

Storer, James Sargant.
Graphic and Historical Description of the Cathedrals of Great Britain. 4 vols. London, 1814-1819. A separate monograph is devoted to each cathedral.

Storico dell' Arte.
(See Archivio Storico dell' Arte.)

Story, W. W.
Phidias and the Elgin Marbles, in the author's Excursions in Art and Letters. Boston, 1891.

Stothard, C. A.
The Monumental Effigies of Great Britain. London, 1817.

Stout, Peter F.
Nicaragua, Past, Present, and Future. Philadelphia, 1859.

Stow, John.
Survey of London, written in . . . 1598. London, 1842.

Strack, Heinrich.
Ziegelbauwerke des Mittelalters und der Renaissance in Italien. Berlin, 1889.
Baudenkmäler Roms des 15–19 Jahrhunderts. Berlin, 1891.

Stratton, Arthur.
The Life, Work, and Influence of Sir Christopher Wren; an Essay. Liverpool, 1897.

Street, Arthur Edmund.
Memoir of George Edmund Street. London, 1888.

Street, George Edmund.
* Some Account of Gothic Architecture in Spain. London, 1865.
* Brick and Marble in the Middle Ages. Notes of Tours in the North of Italy. 2nd ed. London, 1874.

Struve, Emil.
Die Entwickelung des Bayerischen Braugewerbes im neunzehnten Jahrhundert. Leipzig, 1893.

Stuart, James, and Revett, Nicholas.
*Antiquities of Athens, measured and delineated. 4 vols. London, 1762–1816.
Antiquities of Athens and other Places in Greece, Sicily, etc. ; supplementary to the Antiquities of Athens by . . . Stuart and Revett, delineated and illustrated by C. R. Cockerell . . . and others. London, 1830. (See also Dilettanti Society.)

Stubel, Alphons, and Uhle, Max.
Die ruinenstätte von Tiahuanaco im Hochlande des alten Perú. Breslau, 1892.

Sturgis, Russell.
Bibliography of Fine Art. Boston : The Library Bureau, 1897. Part III.
* European Architecture ; a Historical Study. New York and London, 1896.
Decorative Windows in England and America ; in Architectural Record, Vol. VI, 1896, 1897.
Ruskin on Architecture, an introduction to the Ruskin volume of The World's Great Books, a series ; New York, 1898.
Michelangelo ; in Johnson's Universal Cyclopedia, 2d ed.

Sturgis, Russell, and others.
Homes in City and Country. New York, 1893.

Supervising Architect to the Secretary of the Treasury. Annual Report for the year ending September 30, 1896. Washington, D. C., 1897. The same for all the years since the creation of the office.

Sutter, Conrad, and Schneider, Fr.
* Thurmbuch, Thurmformen aller style und Laender. Berlin, 1895.

Suys, Tilman Frans, and Haudebourt, L. P.
Palais Massimi à Rome. Paris, 1818.

Sybel, Ludwig von.
Katalog der Sculpturen zu Athen. Marburg, 1881.

Sykes, W. J. M. D.
Principles and Practice of Brewing ; Short Account of Allsopp's Breweries. Burton-on-Trent (n.d.).

Symonds, John Addington.
Life of Michaelangelo Buonarroti. London, 1892.
Renaissance in Italy. London, 1875, and following years.

Tarbé, Louis Hardouin Prosper.
Notre-Dame de Reims. Reims, 1852.

Tarbell, F. B.
A History of Greek Art. Meadville, Pa., 1896.

Tarn, Edward Wyndham.
Mechanics of Architecture ; a Treatise on Applied Mechanics, especially adapted to the Use of Architects. London, 1892.

Taylor, Andrew Thomas.
Towers and Steeples designed by Sir Christopher Wren ; a Descriptive, Historical, and Critical Essay. London, 1881.

Taylor, George Ledwell.
Autobiography of an Octogenarian Architect ; being a record of his studies at home and abroad during sixty-five years . . . London, 1870-1872.

Taylor, George Ledwell, and Cresy, Edward.
Architectural Antiquities of Rome. London, 1821-1822.

Taylor, Isidore Justin Séverin (baron).
Voyage pittoresque en Espagne, en Portugal, et sur la côte d'Afrique de Tanger à Tétouan. Paris, 1832.

Telford, Thomas.
Life of Thomas Telford, Civil Engineer, writ-

ten by himself, containing a Descriptive Narrative of his Professional Labours, with a Folio Atlas and Copper Plates, edited by John Rickman, one of his Executors, with a Preface, Supplement, Annotations, and Index. London, 1838.

Temanza, Tommaso.
Vite dei piu celebri Architetti e Scultori Veneziani. Venice, 1762, 1768.
Vita di Jacopo Sansovino. Venice, 1752.
Vita di Andrea Palladio Vincentino, egregio architetto. Venice, 1872.

Temanza, Tommaso, and Moschini, Giovanni Antonio.
Vita di A. Vittoria, scritta e publicata da Tommaso Temanza, ora reprodotta con note ed emende, dell Abate Gio. Antonio Moschini. Venice, 1827.

Testolini, Marco.
Ricerche intorno ad Alessandro Leopardi; in Archivio Veneto, Vol. III. 1872.

Texier, Charles Félix Marie.
Description de l'Arménie, la Perse, et la Mésopotamie. Paris, 1842–1852.
Monuments Arabes du Caire.
Asie Mineure. Description Géographique, Historique et Archéologique des Provinces et des Villes de la Chersonnèse d'Asie. Paris, 1882.

Texier, Charles, et Pullan, R. Popplewell.
Architecture Byzantine ou Recueil de Monuments des Premiers temps du Christianisme en Orient. London, 1864.

Texier, L'Abbé, Jacques Rémy Antoine.
Histoire de la Peinture sur Verre en Limousin. Paris, 1847.
Histoire de la Peinture sur Verre. 1850.

Theophilus (Rugerus).
Diversarum artium schedula: translated into French by the comte de Lescalopier. Toulouse, 1843. Translated into English as An Essay upon Various Arts, in 3 books, by Theophilus . . . with notes by Robert Hendrie. London, 1847.

Thibaud, Émile.
Considerations historiques et critiques sur les Vitraux anciens et modernes et sur la Peinture sur Verre. 1842.

Thierry, Jules D.
Arc de Triomphe de l'Étoile. Paris, 1845.

Thiers, Jean Baptiste.
Dissertation sur les principaux autels, etc. Paris, 1688.

Thirion, H.
Les Adam et Clodion. Paris, 1885.

Thomas, Cyrus.
Mound Explorations. (See Bureau of Ethnology.)
Burial Mounds of the Northern Sections of the United States.
Prehistoric Works east of the Rocky Mountains.
Introduction to American Archæology.

Thomson, Richard.
Chronicles of London Bridge by an Antiquary. London, 1827.

Ticozzi, Stefano.
Raccolta di lettere sulla Pittura, Scultura ed Architettura, scritte da piu celebri personali dei secoli XV, XVI, e XVIII, publicata da G. Bottari e continuata fino ai nostri giorni da S. Ticozzi. 1833. (See Bottari, Giovanni Gaetano, for earlier edition.)

Ticozzi, Stefano, ed.
Vita di Scamozzi, introduction to: Scamozzi, l'Idea dell' Architettura universale (which see).

Tiffany, L. C.
American Art Supreme in Coloured Glass. (In the Forum, New York, XV, 621.) July, 1893.

Tigri, Giuseppi.
Nuova guida di Pistoia. 1881.

Tipaldo, ——.
Elogio di Fra Giovanni Giocondo. Venice, 1840.

Tonini, Luigi.
Guida illustrata di Rimini. Rimini, 1893.

Tosi, Francesco Maria, and Becchio, Alessandro.
Altars, Tabernacles, and Sepulchral Monuments of the 14th and 15th centuries: descriptions in Italian, English, and French by Mrs. S. Bartlet. Lagny, 1843.

Tourneur, Victor (abbé).
Histoire et description des vitraux et des statues de l'intérieur de la Cathédrale de Reims. Reims, 1857.

Tower, F. W.
Plumber's Text-book. Published by the Springfield (Mass.) Industrial Institute. 1897.

Tozer, Henry Fanshawe.
Researches in the Highlands of Turkey. London, 1869.
Lectures on the Geography of Greece. London, 1873.
The Islands of the Ægean. London, 1890.

Tremblaye, R. P. dom, de la.
Solesmes. Les Sculptures de l'Église Abbatiale 1496–1553. Solesmes (Sarthe), France, 1892.

Troche, N. M.
L'Architecte Lassus (pamphlet). 1857.

Trotter, Alys Fane.
Old Colonial Houses of the Cape of Good Hope. London and New York, 1900.

Trou, Denis.
Recherches historiques sur la ville de Pontoise. Pontoise, 1841.

Tschudi, Hugo von.
Donatello e la Critica moderna. Turin, 1877.

Tsountas, Chreston, and Manatt, James Irving.
The Mycenæan Age: a Study of the Monuments and Culture of pre-Homeric Greece. London and Cambridge, Mass., 1897.

Tuckerman, Henry T.
Book of the Artists, American Artist's Life. Comprising biographical and critical sketches of American artists. New York, 1867.

Tuker, M. A. R., and Malleson, Hope.
Handbook to Christian and Ecclesiastical Rome. New York and London, 1900.

Uhde, Constantin.
*Baudenkmaeler in Spanien und Portugal. Berlin, 1889.

Ungewitter, G.
Lehrbuch der Gotischen Konstruktionen. 3d ed. Leipzig, 1892.

United States Bureau of American Ethnology, Annual Reports. Washington, D. C.

United States Bureau of Education, Circulars of Information.

Upmark, Gustav.
* Die Architektur der Renaissance in Schweden (1530–1760). Dresden, 1899—.

Urbani de Gheltof, G. M.
*Les Arts industriels a Venise. Venice, 1885.
*Venezia dall' Alto: I Camini. Venice, 1892.
Tiepolo e la sua Famiglia. Venice, 1879.

Urlichs, Karl Ludwig von.
Skopas, leben und werke. Greifwald, 1863.

BIBLIOGRAPHY

Ussing, J. L.
Observations on Vitruvius di Architettura Libri Decem ; with special regard to the time at which this work was written. London, 1898.

Vachon, Marius.
L'Ancien Hôtel de Ville de Paris. Paris, 1882.
Philibert de l'Orme. Paris, 1887.
Puvis de Chavannes. Paris, 1895.
Vacquet, Th.
Le Bois de Boulogne architectural. Paris, 1860. 2d ed. 1875.
Valabrègue, Antony.
See Jean Bérain in Revue des Arts décoratifs. 1871–1880.
Abraham Bosse. Paris, 1892.
Valle, Guglielmo della.
Storia del Duomo di Orvieto. Rome, 1791.
Vambéry, Arminius.
Travels and Adventures in Central Asia. London, 1864.
History of Bokhara from the earliest Period down to the Present, 1873.
Van Campen, Jacob.
Afbeelding van't Stadt Huys van Amsterdam. Amsterdam (n.d.).
Van Mander, Carel.
Het Leven der doorluchtige Nederlandsche en eenige Hoogduitsche Schilders. Amsterdam, 1764.
Van Nostrand.
Science Series. New York, 1873–1891.
Van Rensselaer, Mrs. Mariana Griswold.
Henry Hobson Richardson and his Works. Boston, 1888.
Van Ysendyck, Jules Jacques.
Documents classés de l'art dans les Pays bas. Antwerp, 1889.
Vapereau, Louis Gustave.
Dictionnaire universel des Contemporains. Paris, different eds., the latest in 1893.
Dictionnaire universel des Littérateurs. Paris, 1876.
Varin, Eugène, et Varin, A.
Architecture pittoresque en Suisse. 1861.
Vasari.
Delle Vite dei più excellenti Pittori, Scultori, et Architetti ; ed. by Milanesi. 1878–1885.
Lives of the Most Eminent Painters and Sculptors and Architects ; translated from the Italian of Giorgio Vasari by Mrs. Jonathan Forster. London, 1858.
Lives of Seventy of the Most Eminent Painters and Sculptors and Architects, by Giorgio Vasari ; edited and annotated by E. H. and E. W. Blashfield and A. A. Hopkins. New York, 1896.
Vasselot, Jean-Joseph M. A. Marquet de.
Histoire des Sculpteurs Français de Charles VIII à Henri III. Paris, 1888.
Velt'man, Aleksandr Theodorovich.
Description du Nouveau Palais impérial du Kreml de Moscou traduit du Russe par le Baron L. de Bode. Moscow, 1851.
Venetian Painting.
Della Pittura Veneziana e delle Opere pubblicha dei Veneziani Maestri ; libri ; v. Venice, 1771. Edizone seconda. 2 pt. Venice, 1792. (See Zanetti, A. M.)
Venturi, Adolfo.
The Farnesina ; Italian and English Editions. 1891.
Verneilh, Felix de.
L'Architecture Byzantine en France : S. Front

de Périgueux et les églises à coupoles de l'Aquitaine. Paris, 1851.
Verrall, Margaret de G., and Harrison, Jane E.
Mythology and Monuments of Ancient Athens. London and New York, 1890.
Verschelde, Charles.
*The Ancient Domestic Edifices of Bruges. Bruges, 1875.
Vetter, Leo.
Das Stuttgarter Schwimmbad. Stuttgart, 1889.
Vetusta Monumenta. (See Society of Antiquaries of London.)
Vigo, Pietro.
L'Architetto Giovanni di Lapo ed il duomo di Firenze, studio. Leghorn, 1887.
Villa-amil, Genaro Perez de, and Escosura, Patricio de la.
España Artistica y Monumental. Paris, 1842–1850.
Villa-amil and Castro.
Antigüedades prehistoricas de Galicia. Madrid, 1868.
Villani, Filippo.
Cronica, 1846. Collezione di storici e cronisti Italiani, etc. Florence, 1844–1849.
Villard de Honnecourt, Architecte du XIIIe siècle.
Album ; Manuscrit publié en fac-simile annoté . . . par J. B. A. Lassus . . . ouvrage mis au jour . . . après la mort de Lassus . . . par Alfred Darcel. Paris, 1858. (See Wilars de Honecourt.)
Viñaza, El conte de la.
Addiciones al Diccionairio histórico de los más ilustres profesores de las bellas artes en España de Juan Agustin Cean Bermúdez. Madrid, 1889–1894.
Viollet-le-Duc.
* Dictionnaire Raisonné de l'Architecture Française du XIe au XVIe Siècle. 10 Vols. Paris, 1858–1868. (See also Huss.)
Église abbatiale de Vézelay (reprint from archives de la commission).
Compositions et dessins, publiés sous le patronage du Comité de l'œuvre du maitre. Paris, 1884.
Histoire de l'Habitation humaine depuis les temps préhistoriques jusqu'à nos jours. Paris (n.d.).
L'Art Russe. Paris, 1887.
*Entretiens sur l'Architecture. Paris, 1863–1872.
Visit, A, to the Domed Churches of the Charente, France ; by the Architectural Association of London, in the year 1875. London.
Vitet, Ludovic.
Le Louvre. Paris, 1853.
Vitruvius.
M. Vitruvii Pollionis de Architectura Libri Decem. Many editions ; that by Marini, Rome, 1836, is cited in text.
English translation : The Architecture of Marcus Vitruvius Pollio, in ten books. Translated from the Latin by Joseph Gwilt. London, 1826.
Vogüé, Charles Jean Melchior, comte de.
Les Églises de la Terre Sainte. Paris, 1860.
Le Temple de Jérusalem ; monographie du Haram-Ech-Cherif. Paris, 1864.
*Syrie Centrale : Architecture civile et religieuse du Ie au VIIe Siècle. Paris, 1865–1877.
Volpini, S.
Appartimento Borgia nel Vaticano. Rome, 1887.
Von Hammer, I.
Constantinopolis und der Bosporus, örtlich und geschichtlich beschrieben. Budapest, 1822.

BIBLIOGRAPHY

Waagen, Gustav Friedrich.
Treasures of Art in Great Britain, . . . the chief collections of Paintings, Drawings, Sculptures, etc. London, 1854.

Wade, W. M.
Walks in Oxford ; an . . . Account of the Colleges, Halls, and Public Buildings of the University . . . [and] a . . . History and Description of the City. . . . Oxford, 1817.

Waldstein, Charles.
Excavations of the American School of Athens at the Heraion of Argos, 1892. London and New York, 1892.
Essays on the Art of Pheidias. Cambridge and New York, 1885.

Wallis, Frank.
Old Colonial Architecture and Furniture. Boston, Mass., 1887.

Walpole, Horace.
Anecdotes of Painting in England (from Vertue's MSS.). 4 vols. 1762-1771 [1780].

Wanderer, Fr.
Adam Krafft und seine Schule, 1490-1507. Nuremberg [pref. 1869].

Waring, George E.
Draining for Profit and Draining for Health. New York, 1867.
The Elements of Agriculture. Montpelier, U. S., 1855.
Sewerage and Land Drainage. Illustrated with woodcuts in the text, and full page and folding plates. Quarto. 3d ed. New York, 1898.
Modern Methods of Sewage ; disposal for towns, public institutions, and isolated houses. 2d ed., revised and enlarged. 260 pages. Illustrated. New York, 1896.
How to Drain a House. Practical information for householders. 2d ed. Illustrated. 12mo. New York, 1895.

Waring, J. B.
* The Arts connected with Architecture ; illustrated by examples in Central Italy, of Stained Glass, Fresco, Ornaments, Marble and Enamel Inlay, Wood Inlay, etc. London, 1858.
* Stone Monuments, Tumuli and Ornaments of Remote Ages. London, 1870.
Record of my Artistic Life. London, 1870.

Waring and Macquoid.
* Examples of Architectural Art in Italy and Spain, chiefly of the 13th and 16th centuries. London, 1850.

Warner, Charles Dudley.
Our Italy. New York, 1891.

Wasmuth, (publisher). ——.
Architektur der Gegenwart. Berlin (publication still proceeding).

Watkins, Charles F.
The Basilica or Palatial Hall of Justice and Sacred Temple, and a description of the Basilican Church of Brixworth. 1867.

Watson, William.
Course in Descriptive Geometry for the use of Colleges and Scientific Schools. London, 1880.

Weale, John.
Divers Works of Early Masters in Christian Decoration. London, 1846.
Rudimentary Series. London, 1859-1893.

Weichardt, C.
Pompeji vor der Zerstoerung. Leipzig (n.d.).
Motive zu Garten-Architektur. Weimar, 1879.

Weilbach, Philip.
Nyt Dansk Kunstnerlexikon (Dictionary of Danish Artists). 2 vols. Copenhagen, 1896-1897.

Weltmann, A. (See Velt'mann, Aleksandr Theodorovich.)

Wessely, Joseph Eduard.
Giovanni Battista Tiepolo (in Kunst und Kunstler series).

Westlake, N. H. F.
History of Design in Painted Glass. London, 1881-1886.

Weyermann, Jacob Campo.
De Levens-Beschryvingen der Nederlandsche. Dordregt, 1729-1769.

Weyl, Dr. Theodor.
Handbuch der Hygiène, Vol. VI., Markthallen.

Wharton, Henry.
Anglia Sacra. London, 1691.

Wheatley, Henry Benjamin.
The Adelphi and its Site. London, 1885.

Whewell, Rev. William.
Architectural Notes on German Churches. Cambridge, 1835.

Wickhoff, Franz.
Roman Art. New York, 1900.

Wiener Bauzeitung. (See Allgemeine Bauzeitung.)

Wilars de Honecourt.
Facsimile of the Sketch-Book of——, illustrated by commentaries and descriptions, and published by Alfred Darcel from the MSS. of J. B. A. Lassus ; translated by Rev. Robert Willis, with an essay by J. Quicherat. London, 1859. (See Villard de Honnecourt.)

Wild, Charles.
The History and Antiquities of the Cathedral Church of Lincoln. 2d edition revised by John Britton. London, 1837.

Wilkinson, George.
Practical Geology and Ancient Architecture of Ireland. London, 1845.

Wilkinson, Robert.
Londina Illustrata ; Graphic and Historic Memorials of Monasteries, Churches, Chapels, Schools.

Williams, Rev. George.
The Holy City ; Historical, Topographical and Antiquarian Notices of Jerusalem. 2d edition enlarged, including An Architectural History of the Church of the Holy Sepulchre by Rev. R. Willis. London, 1849.

Williams, J. Haynes.
Fontainebleau. Fifteen photogravures, with an introduction by Frederick Wedmore. London, 1890.

Williamson, Édouard.
Les Meubles d'Art du Mobilier National. Paris, 1883-1885.

Willis, Robert.
The Architectural History of Canterbury Cathedral. London, 1845.
Architectural History of Glastonbury Abbey. Cambridge, 1866.
* On the Construction of the Vaults of the Middle Ages (Trans. R. I. B. A.). Vol. I., Part II. 1842.
Architectural History of the Church of the Holy Sepulchre. (See Williams, Rev. G., Holy City.) London, 1849.
Architectural History of Winchester Cathedral. London, 1846.

Wilson, Charles Heath.
Life and Works of Michelangelo. London and Florence, 1876.

Wilson, Sir Daniel.
Archæology and Prehistoric Annals of Scotland. Edinburgh, 1851.

Winkles, Benjamin.
Historical and Descriptive Account of the Cathedral Church of Gloucester. Gloucester (n.d.).
Winkles, Henry, and Winkles, Benjamin.
Winkles's Architectural and Picturesque Illustrations of the Cathedral Churches of England and Wales . . . London, 1836–1838.
Winsor, Justin.
Memorial History of Boston, including Suffolk County, Mass., 1630–1880. Boston, 1880–1881.
Narrative and Critical History of the United States. Boston, 1884–1889.
Winston, Charles.
An inquiry into the difference of Style observable in Ancient Glass Paintings, especially in England ; with hints on Glass Painting, by an Amateur. Oxford, 1847.
Winter, M.
Die Dach Constructionen verschiedenartigsten Formen und Bedingungen. Berlin, 1862.
Wochenschrift des österreichischen Ingenieur-und Architekten-Vereines. Vienna, 1876–1891.
Wolff, Carl, Dr.
Städtische das Schwimmbad in Frankfurt a. M. [an extra number (Fortschritte, No. 11), of the Handbuch der Architektur]. Stuttgart, 1897.
Wolff, J. G., and Mayer, Dr. Friedrich.
Nürnberg's Gedenkbuch, 1843–1850.
Wolsogen, Alfred Freiherr von.
Schinkel als Architect, Maler und Kunstphilosoph, ein Vortrag gehalten im 'Verein für Geschichte der Bildende Künste zu Breslau. Berlin, 1864.
Woltmann, Dr. Alfred.
Geschichte der Deutschen Kunst im Elsass. Leipzig, 1876.
Woltmann, Alfred Friedrich, and Woermann, K.
Geschichte der Malerei. Leipzig, 1878.
Wood, Anthony A.
The History and Antiquities of the Colleges and Halls in the University of Oxford. Oxford, 1786–1790.
Wood, J. T.
Reply to Mr. Fergusson, etc. (See Trans. R. I. B. A., 1883–1884.)
Discoveries at Ephesos [by J. Wood]. London, 1877.
Wood, Robert.
The Ruins of Palmyra and Balbec. London, 1827.
Ruins of Palmyra, otherwise Tedmor, in the Desart. London, 1753.
Ruins of Balbec, otherwise Heliopolis, in Cælosyria. London, 1757.
Woodhouse, William J.
Ætolia, its Geography, Topography, and Antiquities. Oxford, 1897.
Woodward, Rev. John, and Burnett, George.
A Treatise on Heraldry, British and Foreign, published by W. and A. K. Johnson. 2 vols. Edinburgh and London, 1892.
Wren, Christopher.

Parentalia, or Memoirs of the Family of . . . Wrens. London, 1750.
Wurzbach, Dr. Constant von.
Biographisches Lexikon des Kaiserthums Oesterreich, etc. Vienna, 1856.
Wyatt, Sir Matthew Digby.
Architect's Note-book in Spain. London, 1872.
Specimens of Ornamental Art, Workmanship in Gold, Silver, Iron, Brass and Bronze from the 12th to the 19th centuries. London, 1852.
Specimens of the Geometrical Mosaic of the Middle Ages. London, 1848.
Wyttenbach, J. H.
Translated by Dawson Turner, The Stranger's Guide to the Roman Antiquities of the City of Treves.

Yriarte, Charles Émile.
Un Condottière au XVe siècle, Rimini. Paris, 1882.
La Vie d'un Patricien de Venise. 1874, 1885.
Paul Véronèse. Paris, 1888. [Forms part of series Les Artistes Célèbres.]
Florence ; l'histoire des Médicis. Venice, 1877.
Matteo Civitale. Paris, 1886.
Yule, Captain Henry.
A Narrative of the Mission sent by the Governor-General of India to the Court of Ava in 1855, with notices of the country, government, and people. London, 1858.

Zamboni, Baldassare.
Memorie intorne alle pubbliche Fabbriche della città di Brescia. Brescia, 1778.
Zanella, Giacomo.
Vita di Andrea Palladio. Milan, 1880.
Zanetti, Antonio Maria, the Younger. (See Venetian Painting.)
Della Pittura Veneziana, etc. [By A. M. Z.] 1771, 1797.
Zanetti, Antonio Maria Erasmus, conte ; Zanetti, G. F. ; and Zanetti, Alessandro.
Delle antiche Statue greche e romane che nell' antisala della Libreria di San Marco, e in altri luoghi pubblici di Venezia ei trovano. Venice, 1740–1743.
Zanotto, François.
Edifices et monuments remarquables de Venise. Venice, 1858.
Il Palazzo Ducale di Venezia. Venice, 1841–1861.
Text to Sanmichele. (See Sanmichele.)
Zanth, Ludwig von.
(See Hittorff.)
Zeitschrift des Österreichischen Ingenieur und Architekten-Vereines [Periodical].
Zeitschrift für Bauwesen. Berlin, 1851–1894.
Zeitschrift für bildende Kunst, mit dem Beiblatt Kunstchronik, (which see). Leipzig, 1866–1893.
Zestermann, August and Christian Adolf.
Die antiken und die christlichen Basiliken nach ihrer Entstehung. Leipzig, 1847.

A CATALOG OF SELECTED
DOVER BOOKS
IN ALL FIELDS OF INTEREST

A CATALOG OF SELECTED DOVER
BOOKS IN ALL FIELDS OF INTEREST

DRAWINGS OF REMBRANDT, edited by Seymour Slive. Updated Lippmann, Hofstede de Groot edition, with definitive scholarly apparatus. All portraits, biblical sketches, landscapes, nudes. Oriental figures, classical studies, together with selection of work by followers. 550 illustrations. Total of 630pp. 9⅛ × 12¼.
21485-0, 21486-9 Pa., Two-vol. set $25.00

GHOST AND HORROR STORIES OF AMBROSE BIERCE, Ambrose Bierce. 24 tales vividly imagined, strangely prophetic, and decades ahead of their time in technical skill: "The Damned Thing," "An Inhabitant of Carcosa," "The Eyes of the Panther," "Moxon's Master," and 20 more. 199pp. 5⅜ × 8½. 20767-6 Pa. $3.95

ETHICAL WRITINGS OF MAIMONIDES, Maimonides. Most significant ethical works of great medieval sage, newly translated for utmost precision, readability. Laws Concerning Character Traits, Eight Chapters, more. 192pp. 5⅜ × 8½.
24522-5 Pa. $4.50

THE EXPLORATION OF THE COLORADO RIVER AND ITS CANYONS, J. W. Powell. Full text of Powell's 1,000-mile expedition down the fabled Colorado in 1869. Superb account of terrain, geology, vegetation, Indians, famine, mutiny, treacherous rapids, mighty canyons, during exploration of last unknown part of continental U.S. 400pp. 5⅜ × 8½. 20094-9 Pa. $6.95

HISTORY OF PHILOSOPHY, Julián Marías. Clearest one-volume history on the market. Every major philosopher and dozens of others, to Existentialism and later. 505pp. 5⅜ × 8½. 21739-6 Pa. $8.50

ALL ABOUT LIGHTNING, Martin A. Uman. Highly readable non-technical survey of nature and causes of lightning, thunderstorms, ball lightning, St. Elmo's Fire, much more. Illustrated. 192pp. 5⅜ × 8½. 25237-X Pa. $5.95

SAILING ALONE AROUND THE WORLD, Captain Joshua Slocum. First man to sail around the world, alone, in small boat. One of great feats of seamanship told in delightful manner. 67 illustrations. 294pp. 5⅜ × 8½. 20326-3 Pa. $4.95

LETTERS AND NOTES ON THE MANNERS, CUSTOMS AND CONDITIONS OF THE NORTH AMERICAN INDIANS, George Catlin. Classic account of life among Plains Indians: ceremonies, hunt, warfare, etc. 312 plates. 572pp. of text. 6⅛ × 9¼. 22118-0, 22119-9 Pa. Two-vol. set $15.90

ALASKA: The Harriman Expedition, 1899, John Burroughs, John Muir, et al. Informative, engrossing accounts of two-month, 9,000-mile expedition. Native peoples, wildlife, forests, geography, salmon industry, glaciers, more. Profusely illustrated. 240 black-and-white line drawings. 124 black-and-white photographs. 3 maps. Index. 576pp. 5⅜ × 8½. 25109-8 Pa. $11.95

CATALOG OF DOVER BOOKS

THE BOOK OF BEASTS: Being a Translation from a Latin Bestiary of the Twelfth Century, T. H. White. Wonderful catalog real and fanciful beasts: manticore, griffin, phoenix, amphivius, jaculus, many more. White's witty erudite commentary on scientific, historical aspects. Fascinating glimpse of medieval mind. Illustrated. 296pp. 5⅜ × 8¼. (Available in U.S. only) 24609-4 Pa. $5.95

FRANK LLOYD WRIGHT: ARCHITECTURE AND NATURE With 160 Illustrations, Donald Hoffmann. Profusely illustrated study of influence of nature—especially prairie—on Wright's designs for Fallingwater, Robie House, Guggenheim Museum, other masterpieces. 96pp. 9¼ × 10¾. 25098-9 Pa. $7.95

FRANK LLOYD WRIGHT'S FALLINGWATER, Donald Hoffmann. Wright's famous waterfall house: planning and construction of organic idea. History of site, owners, Wright's personal involvement. Photographs of various stages of building. Preface by Edgar Kaufmann, Jr. 100 illustrations. 112pp. 9¼ × 10.
23671-4 Pa. $7.95

YEARS WITH FRANK LLOYD WRIGHT: Apprentice to Genius, Edgar Tafel. Insightful memoir by a former apprentice presents a revealing portrait of Wright the man, the inspired teacher, the greatest American architect. 372 black-and-white illustrations. Preface. Index. vi + 228pp. 8¼ × 11. 24801-1 Pa. $9.95

THE STORY OF KING ARTHUR AND HIS KNIGHTS, Howard Pyle. Enchanting version of King Arthur fable has delighted generations with imaginative narratives of exciting adventures and unforgettable illustrations by the author. 41 illustrations. xviii + 313pp. 6⅛ × 9¼. 21445-1 Pa. $5.95

THE GODS OF THE EGYPTIANS, E. A. Wallis Budge. Thorough coverage of numerous gods of ancient Egypt by foremost Egyptologist. Information on evolution of cults, rites and gods; the cult of Osiris; the Book of the Dead and its rites; the sacred animals and birds; Heaven and Hell; and more. 956pp. 6⅛ × 9¼.
22055-9, 22056-7 Pa., Two-vol. set $21.90

A THEOLOGICO-POLITICAL TREATISE, Benedict Spinoza. Also contains unfinished *Political Treatise*. Great classic on religious liberty, theory of government on common consent. R. Elwes translation. Total of 421pp. 5⅜ × 8½.
20249-6 Pa. $6.95

INCIDENTS OF TRAVEL IN CENTRAL AMERICA, CHIAPAS, AND YUCATAN, John L. Stephens. Almost single-handed discovery of Maya culture; exploration of ruined cities, monuments, temples; customs of Indians. 115 drawings. 892pp. 5⅜ × 8½. 22404-X, 22405-8 Pa., Two-vol. set $15.90

LOS CAPRICHOS, Francisco Goya. 80 plates of wild, grotesque monsters and caricatures. Prado manuscript included. 183pp. 6⅝ × 9⅝. 22384-1 Pa. $4.95

AUTOBIOGRAPHY: The Story of My Experiments with Truth, Mohandas K. Gandhi. Not hagiography, but Gandhi in his own words. Boyhood, legal studies, purification, the growth of the Satyagraha (nonviolent protest) movement. Critical, inspiring work of the man who freed India. 480pp. 5⅜ × 8½. (Available in U.S. only)
24593-4 Pa. $6.95

ILLUSTRATED DICTIONARY OF HISTORIC ARCHITECTURE, edited by Cyril M. Harris. Extraordinary compendium of clear, concise definitions for over 5,000 important architectural terms complemented by over 2,000 line drawings. Covers full spectrum of architecture from ancient ruins to 20th-century Modernism. Preface. 592pp. 7½ × 9⅝. 24444-X Pa. $14.95

THE NIGHT BEFORE CHRISTMAS, Clement Moore. Full text, and woodcuts from original 1848 book. Also critical, historical material. 19 illustrations. 40pp. 4⅝ × 6. 22797-9 Pa. $2.50

THE LESSON OF JAPANESE ARCHITECTURE: 165 Photographs, Jiro Harada. Memorable gallery of 165 photographs taken in the 1930's of exquisite Japanese homes of the well-to-do and historic buildings. 13 line diagrams. 192pp. 8⅜ × 11¼. 24778-3 Pa. $8.95

THE AUTOBIOGRAPHY OF CHARLES DARWIN AND SELECTED LETTERS, edited by Francis Darwin. The fascinating life of eccentric genius composed of an intimate memoir by Darwin (intended for his children); commentary by his son, Francis; hundreds of fragments from notebooks, journals, papers; and letters to and from Lyell, Hooker, Huxley, Wallace and Henslow. xi + 365pp. 5⅜ × 8. 20479-0 Pa. $5.95

WONDERS OF THE SKY: Observing Rainbows, Comets, Eclipses, the Stars and Other Phenomena, Fred Schaaf. Charming, easy-to-read poetic guide to all manner of celestial events visible to the naked eye. Mock suns, glories, Belt of Venus, more. Illustrated. 299pp. 5¼ × 8¼. 24402-4 Pa. $7.95

BURNHAM'S CELESTIAL HANDBOOK, Robert Burnham, Jr. Thorough guide to the stars beyond our solar system. Exhaustive treatment. Alphabetical by constellation: Andromeda to Cetus in Vol. 1; Chamaeleon to Orion in Vol. 2; and Pavo to Vulpecula in Vol. 3. Hundreds of illustrations. Index in Vol. 3. 2,000pp. 6½ × 9¼. 23567-X, 23568-8, 23673-0 Pa., Three-vol. set $37.85

STAR NAMES: Their Lore and Meaning, Richard Hinckley Allen. Fascinating history of names various cultures have given to constellations and literary and folkloristic uses that have been made of stars. Indexes to subjects. Arabic and Greek names. Biblical references. Bibliography. 563pp. 5⅜ × 8½. 21079-0 Pa. $7.95

THIRTY YEARS THAT SHOOK PHYSICS: The Story of Quantum Theory, George Gamow. Lucid, accessible introduction to influential theory of energy and matter. Careful explanations of Dirac's anti-particles, Bohr's model of the atom, much more. 12 plates. Numerous drawings. 240pp. 5⅜ × 8½. 24895-X Pa. $4.95

CHINESE DOMESTIC FURNITURE IN PHOTOGRAPHS AND MEASURED DRAWINGS, Gustav Ecke. A rare volume, now affordably priced for antique collectors, furniture buffs and art historians. Detailed review of styles ranging from early Shang to late Ming. Unabridged republication. 161 black-and-white drawings, photos. Total of 224pp. 8⅜ × 11¼. (Available in U.S. only) 25171-3 Pa. $12.95

VINCENT VAN GOGH: A Biography, Julius Meier-Graefe. Dynamic, penetrating study of artist's life, relationship with brother, Theo, painting techniques, travels, more. Readable, engrossing. 160pp. 5⅜ × 8½. (Available in U.S. only) 25253-1 Pa. $3.95

HOW TO WRITE, Gertrude Stein. Gertrude Stein claimed anyone could understand her unconventional writing—here are clues to help. Fascinating improvisations, language experiments, explanations illuminate Stein's craft and the art of writing. Total of 414pp. 4⅝ × 6⅜.   23144-5 Pa. $5.95

ADVENTURES AT SEA IN THE GREAT AGE OF SAIL: Five Firsthand Narratives, edited by Elliot Snow. Rare true accounts of exploration, whaling, shipwreck, fierce natives, trade, shipboard life, more. 33 illustrations. Introduction. 353pp. 5⅜ × 8½.   25177-2 Pa. $7.95

THE HERBAL OR GENERAL HISTORY OF PLANTS, John Gerard. Classic descriptions of about 2,850 plants—with over 2,700 illustrations—includes Latin and English names, physical descriptions, varieties, time and place of growth, more. 2,706 illustrations. xlv + 1,678pp. 8½ × 12¼.   23147-X Cloth. $75.00

DOROTHY AND THE WIZARD IN OZ, L. Frank Baum. Dorothy and the Wizard visit the center of the Earth, where people are vegetables, glass houses grow and Oz characters reappear. Classic sequel to *Wizard of Oz.* 256pp. 5⅜ × 8.
                                   24714-7 Pa. $4.95

SONGS OF EXPERIENCE: Facsimile Reproduction with 26 Plates in Full Color, William Blake. This facsimile of Blake's original "Illuminated Book" reproduces 26 full-color plates from a rare 1826 edition. Includes "The Tyger," "London," "Holy Thursday," and other immortal poems. 26 color plates. Printed text of poems. 48pp. 5¼ × 7.   24636-1 Pa. $3.50

SONGS OF INNOCENCE, William Blake. The first and most popular of Blake's famous "Illuminated Books," in a facsimile edition reproducing all 31 brightly colored plates. Additional printed text of each poem. 64pp. 5¼ × 7.
                                   22764-2 Pa. $3.50

PRECIOUS STONES, Max Bauer. Classic, thorough study of diamonds, rubies, emeralds, garnets, etc.: physical character, occurrence, properties, use, similar topics. 20 plates, 8 in color. 94 figures. 659pp. 6⅛ × 9¼.
                                   21910-0, 21911-9 Pa., Two-vol. set $15.90

ENCYCLOPEDIA OF VICTORIAN NEEDLEWORK, S. F. A. Caulfeild and Blanche Saward. Full, precise descriptions of stitches, techniques for dozens of needlecrafts—most exhaustive reference of its kind. Over 800 figures. Total of 679pp. 8⅜ × 11. Two volumes.   Vol. 1 22800-2 Pa. $11.95
                                   Vol. 2 22801-0 Pa. $11.95

THE MARVELOUS LAND OF OZ, L. Frank Baum. Second Oz book, the Scarecrow and Tin Woodman are back with hero named Tip, Oz magic. 136 illustrations. 287pp. 5⅜ × 8½.   20692-0 Pa. $5.95

WILD FOWL DECOYS, Joel Barber. Basic book on the subject, by foremost authority and collector. Reveals history of decoy making and rigging, place in American culture, different kinds of decoys, how to make them, and how to use them. 140 plates. 156pp. 7⅞ × 10¾.   20011-6 Pa. $8.95

HISTORY OF LACE, Mrs. Bury Palliser. Definitive, profusely illustrated chronicle of lace from earliest times to late 19th century. Laces of Italy, Greece, England, France, Belgium, etc. Landmark of needlework scholarship. 266 illustrations. 672pp. 6⅛ × 9¼.   24742-2 Pa. $14.95

ILLUSTRATED GUIDE TO SHAKER FURNITURE, Robert Meader. All furniture and appurtenances, with much on unknown local styles. 235 photos. 146pp. 9 × 12. 22819-3 Pa. $7.95

WHALE SHIPS AND WHALING: A Pictorial Survey, George Francis Dow. Over 200 vintage engravings, drawings, photographs of barks, brigs, cutters, other vessels. Also harpoons, lances, whaling guns, many other artifacts. Comprehensive text by foremost authority. 207 black-and-white illustrations. 288pp. 6 × 9. 24808-9 Pa. $8.95

THE BERTRAMS, Anthony Trollope. Powerful portrayal of blind self-will and thwarted ambition includes one of Trollope's most heartrending love stories. 497pp. 5⅜ × 8½. 25119-5 Pa. $8.95

ADVENTURES WITH A HAND LENS, Richard Headstrom. Clearly written guide to observing and studying flowers and grasses, fish scales, moth and insect wings, egg cases, buds, feathers, seeds, leaf scars, moss, molds, ferns, common crystals, etc.—all with an ordinary, inexpensive magnifying glass. 209 exact line drawings aid in your discoveries. 220pp. 5⅜ × 8½. 23330-8 Pa. $4.50

RODIN ON ART AND ARTISTS, Auguste Rodin. Great sculptor's candid, wide-ranging comments on meaning of art; great artists; relation of sculpture to poetry, painting, music; philosophy of life, more. 76 superb black-and-white illustrations of Rodin's sculpture, drawings and prints. 119pp. 8⅜ × 11¼. 24487-3 Pa. $6.95

FIFTY CLASSIC FRENCH FILMS, 1912–1982: A Pictorial Record, Anthony Slide. Memorable stills from Grand Illusion, Beauty and the Beast, Hiroshima, Mon Amour, many more. Credits, plot synopses, reviews, etc. 160pp. 8¼ × 11. 25256-6 Pa. $11.95

THE PRINCIPLES OF PSYCHOLOGY, William James. Famous long course complete, unabridged. Stream of thought, time perception, memory, experimental methods; great work decades ahead of its time. 94 figures. 1,391pp. 5⅜ × 8½. 20381-6, 20382-4 Pa., Two-vol. set $19.90

BODIES IN A BOOKSHOP, R. T. Campbell. Challenging mystery of blackmail and murder with ingenious plot and superbly drawn characters. In the best tradition of British suspense fiction. 192pp. 5⅜ × 8½. 24720-1 Pa. $3.95

CALLAS: PORTRAIT OF A PRIMA DONNA, George Jellinek. Renowned commentator on the musical scene chronicles incredible career and life of the most controversial, fascinating, influential operatic personality of our time. 64 black-and-white photographs. 416pp. 5⅜ × 8¼. 25047-4 Pa. $7.95

GEOMETRY, RELATIVITY AND THE FOURTH DIMENSION, Rudolph Rucker. Exposition of fourth dimension, concepts of relativity as Flatland characters continue adventures. Popular, easily followed yet accurate, profound. 141 illustrations. 133pp. 5⅜ × 8½. 23400-2 Pa. $3.50

HOUSEHOLD STORIES BY THE BROTHERS GRIMM, with pictures by Walter Crane. 53 classic stories—Rumpelstiltskin, Rapunzel, Hansel and Gretel, the Fisherman and his Wife, Snow White, Tom Thumb, Sleeping Beauty, Cinderella, and so much more—lavishly illustrated with original 19th century drawings. 114 illustrations. x + 269pp. 5⅜ × 8½. 21080-4 Pa. $4.50

SUNDIALS, Albert Waugh. Far and away the best, most thorough coverage of ideas, mathematics concerned, types, construction, adjusting anywhere. Over 100 illustrations. 230pp. 5⅜ × 8½. 22947-5 Pa. $4.50

PICTURE HISTORY OF THE NORMANDIE: With 190 Illustrations, Frank O. Braynard. Full story of legendary French ocean liner: Art Deco interiors, design innovations, furnishings, celebrities, maiden voyage, tragic fire, much more. Extensive text. 144pp. 8⅜ × 11¾. 25257-4 Pa. $9.95

THE FIRST AMERICAN COOKBOOK: A Facsimile of "American Cookery," 1796, Amelia Simmons. Facsimile of the first American-written cookbook published in the United States contains authentic recipes for colonial favorites—pumpkin pudding, winter squash pudding, spruce beer, Indian slapjacks, and more. Introductory Essay and Glossary of colonial cooking terms. 80pp. 5⅜ × 8½. 24710-4 Pa. $3.50

101 PUZZLES IN THOUGHT AND LOGIC, C. R. Wylie, Jr. Solve murders and robberies, find out which fishermen are liars, how a blind man could possibly identify a color—purely by your own reasoning! 107pp. 5⅜ × 8½. 20367-0 Pa. $2.50

THE BOOK OF WORLD-FAMOUS MUSIC—CLASSICAL, POPULAR AND FOLK, James J. Fuld. Revised and enlarged republication of landmark work in musico-bibliography. Full information about nearly 1,000 songs and compositions including first lines of music and lyrics. New supplement. Index. 800pp. 5⅜ × 8¼. 24857-7 Pa. $14.95

ANTHROPOLOGY AND MODERN LIFE, Franz Boas. Great anthropologist's classic treatise on race and culture. Introduction by Ruth Bunzel. Only inexpensive paperback edition. 255pp. 5⅜ × 8½. 25245-0 Pa. $5.95

THE TALE OF PETER RABBIT, Beatrix Potter. The inimitable Peter's terrifying adventure in Mr. McGregor's garden, with all 27 wonderful, full-color Potter illustrations. 55pp. 4¼ × 5½. (Available in U.S. only) 22827-4 Pa. $1.75

THREE PROPHETIC SCIENCE FICTION NOVELS, H. G. Wells. *When the Sleeper Wakes, A Story of the Days to Come* and *The Time Machine* (full version). 335pp. 5⅜ × 8½. (Available in U.S. only) 20605-X Pa. $5.95

APICIUS COOKERY AND DINING IN IMPERIAL ROME, edited and translated by Joseph Dommers Vehling. Oldest known cookbook in existence offers readers a clear picture of what foods Romans ate, how they prepared them, etc. 49 illustrations. 301pp. 6⅛ × 9¼. 23563-7 Pa. $6.50

SHAKESPEARE LEXICON AND QUOTATION DICTIONARY, Alexander Schmidt. Full definitions, locations, shades of meaning of every word in plays and poems. More than 50,000 exact quotations. 1,485pp. 6½ × 9¼. 22726-X, 22727-8 Pa., Two-vol. set $27.90

THE WORLD'S GREAT SPEECHES, edited by Lewis Copeland and Lawrence W. Lamm. Vast collection of 278 speeches from Greeks to 1970. Powerful and effective models; unique look at history. 842pp. 5⅜ × 8½. 20468-5 Pa. $11.95

THE BLUE FAIRY BOOK, Andrew Lang. The first, most famous collection, with many familiar tales: Little Red Riding Hood, Aladdin and the Wonderful Lamp, Puss in Boots, Sleeping Beauty, Hansel and Gretel, Rumpelstiltskin; 37 in all. 138 illustrations. 390pp. 5⅜ × 8½. 21437-0 Pa. $5.95

THE STORY OF THE CHAMPIONS OF THE ROUND TABLE, Howard Pyle. Sir Launcelot, Sir Tristram and Sir Percival in spirited adventures of love and triumph retold in Pyle's inimitable style. 50 drawings, 31 full-page. xviii + 329pp. 6½ × 9¼. 21883-X Pa. $6.95

AUDUBON AND HIS JOURNALS, Maria Audubon. Unmatched two-volume portrait of the great artist, naturalist and author contains his journals, an excellent biography by his granddaughter, expert annotations by the noted ornithologist, Dr. Elliott Coues, and 37 superb illustrations. Total of 1,200pp. 5⅜ × 8.

Vol. I 25143-8 Pa. $8.95
Vol. II 25144-6 Pa. $8.95

GREAT DINOSAUR HUNTERS AND THEIR DISCOVERIES, Edwin H. Colbert. Fascinating, lavishly illustrated chronicle of dinosaur research, 1820's to 1960. Achievements of Cope, Marsh, Brown, Buckland, Mantell, Huxley, many others. 384pp. 5¼ × 8¼. 24701-5 Pa. $6.95

THE TASTEMAKERS, Russell Lynes. Informal, illustrated social history of American taste 1850's–1950's. First popularized categories Highbrow, Lowbrow, Middlebrow. 129 illustrations. New (1979) afterword. 384pp. 6 × 9.

23993-4 Pa. $6.95

DOUBLE CROSS PURPOSES, Ronald A. Knox. A treasure hunt in the Scottish Highlands, an old map, unidentified corpse, surprise discoveries keep reader guessing in this cleverly intricate tale of financial skullduggery. 2 black-and-white maps. 320pp. 5⅜ × 8½. (Available in U.S. only) 25032-6 Pa. $5.95

AUTHENTIC VICTORIAN DECORATION AND ORNAMENTATION IN FULL COLOR: 46 Plates from "Studies in Design," Christopher Dresser. Superb full-color lithographs reproduced from rare original portfolio of a major Victorian designer. 48pp. 9¼ × 12¼. 25083-0 Pa. $7.95

PRIMITIVE ART, Franz Boas. Remains the best text ever prepared on subject, thoroughly discussing Indian, African, Asian, Australian, and, especially, Northern American primitive art. Over 950 illustrations show ceramics, masks, totem poles, weapons, textiles, paintings, much more. 376pp. 5⅜ × 8. 20025-6 Pa. $6.95

SIDELIGHTS ON RELATIVITY, Albert Einstein. Unabridged republication of two lectures delivered by the great physicist in 1920–21. *Ether and Relativity* and *Geometry and Experience*. Elegant ideas in non-mathematical form, accessible to intelligent layman. vi + 56pp. 5⅜ × 8½. 24511-X Pa. $2.95

THE WIT AND HUMOR OF OSCAR WILDE, edited by Alvin Redman. More than 1,000 ripostes, paradoxes, wisecracks: Work is the curse of the drinking classes, I can resist everything except temptation, etc. 258pp. 5⅜ × 8½. 20602-5 Pa. $4.50

ADVENTURES WITH A MICROSCOPE, Richard Headstrom. 59 adventures with clothing fibers, protozoa, ferns and lichens, roots and leaves, much more. 142 illustrations. 232pp. 5⅜ × 8½. 23471-1 Pa. $3.95

PLANTS OF THE BIBLE, Harold N. Moldenke and Alma L. Moldenke. Standard reference to all 230 plants mentioned in Scriptures. Latin name, biblical reference, uses, modern identity, much more. Unsurpassed encyclopedic resource for scholars, botanists, nature lovers, students of Bible. Bibliography. Indexes. 123 black-and-white illustrations. 384pp. 6 × 9. 25069-5 Pa. $8.95

FAMOUS AMERICAN WOMEN: A Biographical Dictionary from Colonial Times to the Present, Robert McHenry, ed. From Pocahontas to Rosa Parks, 1,035 distinguished American women documented in separate biographical entries. Accurate, up-to-date data, numerous categories, spans 400 years. Indices. 493pp. 6½ × 9¼. 24523-3 Pa. $9.95

THE FABULOUS INTERIORS OF THE GREAT OCEAN LINERS IN HISTORIC PHOTOGRAPHS, William H. Miller, Jr. Some 200 superb photographs capture exquisite interiors of world's great "floating palaces"—1890's to 1980's: *Titanic, Ile de France, Queen Elizabeth, United States, Europa*, more. Approx. 200 black-and-white photographs. Captions. Text. Introduction. 160pp. 8⅜ × 11¼. 24756-2 Pa. $9.95

THE GREAT LUXURY LINERS, 1927–1954: A Photographic Record, William H. Miller, Jr. Nostalgic tribute to heyday of ocean liners. 186 photos of Ile de France, Normandie, Leviathan, Queen Elizabeth, United States, many others. Interior and exterior views. Introduction. Captions. 160pp. 9 × 12. 24056-8 Pa. $9.95

A NATURAL HISTORY OF THE DUCKS, John Charles Phillips. Great landmark of ornithology offers complete detailed coverage of nearly 200 species and subspecies of ducks: gadwall, sheldrake, merganser, pintail, many more. 74 full-color plates, 102 black-and-white. Bibliography. Total of 1,920pp. 8⅜ × 11¼. 25141-1, 25142-X Cloth. Two-vol. set $100.00

THE SEAWEED HANDBOOK: An Illustrated Guide to Seaweeds from North Carolina to Canada, Thomas F. Lee. Concise reference covers 78 species. Scientific and common names, habitat, distribution, more. Finding keys for easy identification. 224pp. 5⅜ × 8½. 25215-9 Pa. $5.95

THE TEN BOOKS OF ARCHITECTURE: The 1755 Leoni Edition, Leon Battista Alberti. Rare classic helped introduce the glories of ancient architecture to the Renaissance. 68 black-and-white plates. 336pp. 8⅜ × 11¼. 25239-6 Pa. $14.95

MISS MACKENZIE, Anthony Trollope. Minor masterpieces by Victorian master unmasks many truths about life in 19th-century England. First inexpensive edition in years. 392pp. 5⅜ × 8½. 25201-9 Pa. $7.95

THE RIME OF THE ANCIENT MARINER, Gustave Doré, Samuel Taylor Coleridge. Dramatic engravings considered by many to be his greatest work. The terrifying space of the open sea, the storms and whirlpools of an unknown ocean, the ice of Antarctica, more—all rendered in a powerful, chilling manner. Full text. 38 plates. 77pp. 9¼ × 12. 22305-1 Pa. $4.95

THE EXPEDITIONS OF ZEBULON MONTGOMERY PIKE, Zebulon Montgomery Pike. Fascinating first-hand accounts (1805-6) of exploration of Mississippi River, Indian wars, capture by Spanish dragoons, much more. 1,088pp. 5⅜ × 8½. 25254-X, 25255-8 Pa. Two-vol. set $23.90

CATALOG OF DOVER BOOKS

A CONCISE HISTORY OF PHOTOGRAPHY: Third Revised Edition, Helmut Gernsheim. Best one-volume history—camera obscura, photochemistry, daguerreotypes, evolution of cameras, film, more. Also artistic aspects—landscape, portraits, fine art, etc. 281 black-and-white photographs. 26 in color. 176pp. 8⅜ × 11¼. 25128-4 Pa. $12.95

THE DORÉ BIBLE ILLUSTRATIONS, Gustave Doré. 241 detailed plates from the Bible: the Creation scenes, Adam and Eve, Flood, Babylon, battle sequences, life of Jesus, etc. Each plate is accompanied by the verses from the King James version of the Bible. 241pp. 9 × 12. 23004-X Pa. $8.95

HUGGER-MUGGER IN THE LOUVRE, Elliot Paul. Second Homer Evans mystery-comedy. Theft at the Louvre involves sleuth in hilarious, madcap caper. "A knockout."—Books. 336pp. 5⅜ × 8½. 25185-3 Pa. $5.95

FLATLAND, E. A. Abbott. Intriguing and enormously popular science-fiction classic explores the complexities of trying to survive as a two-dimensional being in a three-dimensional world. Amusingly illustrated by the author. 16 illustrations. 103pp. 5⅜ × 8½. 20001-9 Pa. $2.25

THE HISTORY OF THE LEWIS AND CLARK EXPEDITION, Meriwether Lewis and William Clark, edited by Elliott Coues. Classic edition of Lewis and Clark's day-by-day journals that later became the basis for U.S. claims to Oregon and the West. Accurate and invaluable geographical, botanical, biological, meteorological and anthropological material. Total of 1,508pp. 5⅜ × 8½.
21268-8, 21269-6, 21270-X Pa. Three-vol. set $25.50

LANGUAGE, TRUTH AND LOGIC, Alfred J. Ayer. Famous, clear introduction to Vienna, Cambridge schools of Logical Positivism. Role of philosophy, elimination of metaphysics, nature of analysis, etc. 160pp. 5⅜ × 8½. (Available in U.S. and Canada only) 20010-8 Pa. $2.95

MATHEMATICS FOR THE NONMATHEMATICIAN, Morris Kline. Detailed, college-level treatment of mathematics in cultural and historical context, with numerous exercises. For liberal arts students. Preface. Recommended Reading Lists. Tables. Index. Numerous black-and-white figures. xvi + 641pp. 5⅜ × 8½.
24823-2 Pa. $11.95

28 SCIENCE FICTION STORIES, H. G. Wells. Novels, *Star Begotten* and *Men Like Gods,* plus 26 short stories: "Empire of the Ants," "A Story of the Stone Age," "The Stolen Bacillus," "In the Abyss," etc. 915pp. 5⅜ × 8½. (Available in U.S. only)
20265-8 Cloth. $10.95

HANDBOOK OF PICTORIAL SYMBOLS, Rudolph Modley. 3,250 signs and symbols, many systems in full; official or heavy commercial use. Arranged by subject. Most in Pictorial Archive series. 143pp. 8⅛ × 11. 23357-X Pa. $5.95

INCIDENTS OF TRAVEL IN YUCATAN, John L. Stephens. Classic (1843) exploration of jungles of Yucatan, looking for evidences of Maya civilization. Travel adventures, Mexican and Indian culture, etc. Total of 669pp. 5⅜ × 8½.
20926-1, 20927-X Pa., Two-vol. set $9.90

DEGAS: An Intimate Portrait, Ambroise Vollard. Charming, anecdotal memoir by famous art dealer of one of the greatest 19th-century French painters. 14 black-and-white illustrations. Introduction by Harold L. Van Doren. 96pp. 5⅜ × 8½.
25131-4 Pa. $3.95

PERSONAL NARRATIVE OF A PILGRIMAGE TO ALMANDINAH AND MECCAH, Richard Burton. Great travel classic by remarkably colorful personality. Burton, disguised as a Moroccan, visited sacred shrines of Islam, narrowly escaping death. 47 illustrations. 959pp. 5⅜ × 8½.   21217-3, 21218-1 Pa., Two-vol. set $17.90

PHRASE AND WORD ORIGINS, A. H. Holt. Entertaining, reliable, modern study of more than 1,200 colorful words, phrases, origins and histories. Much unexpected information. 254pp. 5⅜ × 8½.   20758-7 Pa. $5.95

THE RED THUMB MARK, R. Austin Freeman. In this first Dr. Thorndyke case, the great scientific detective draws fascinating conclusions from the nature of a single fingerprint. Exciting story, authentic science. 320pp. 5⅜ × 8½. (Available in U.S. only)   25210-8 Pa. $5.95

AN EGYPTIAN HIEROGLYPHIC DICTIONARY, E. A. Wallis Budge. Monumental work containing about 25,000 words or terms that occur in texts ranging from 3000 B.C. to 600 A.D. Each entry consists of a transliteration of the word, the word in hieroglyphs, and the meaning in English. 1,314pp. 6⅝ × 10.
23615-3, 23616-1 Pa., Two-vol. set $27.90

THE COMPLEAT STRATEGYST: Being a Primer on the Theory of Games of Strategy, J. D. Williams. Highly entertaining classic describes, with many illustrated examples, how to select best strategies in conflict situations. Prefaces. Appendices. xvi + 268pp. 5⅜ × 8½.   25101-2 Pa. $5.95

THE ROAD TO OZ, L. Frank Baum. Dorothy meets the Shaggy Man, little Button-Bright and the Rainbow's beautiful daughter in this delightful trip to the magical Land of Oz. 272pp. 5⅜ × 8.   25208-6 Pa. $4.95

POINT AND LINE TO PLANE, Wassily Kandinsky. Seminal exposition of role of point, line, other elements in non-objective painting. Essential to understanding 20th-century art. 127 illustrations. 192pp. 6½ × 9¼.   23808-3 Pa. $4.50

LADY ANNA, Anthony Trollope. Moving chronicle of Countess Lovel's bitter struggle to win for herself and daughter Anna their rightful rank and fortune—perhaps at cost of sanity itself. 384pp. 5⅜ × 8½.   24669-8 Pa. $6.95

EGYPTIAN MAGIC, E. A. Wallis Budge. Sums up all that is known about magic in Ancient Egypt: the role of magic in controlling the gods, powerful amulets that warded off evil spirits, scarabs of immortality, use of wax images, formulas and spells, the secret name, much more. 253pp. 5⅜ × 8½.   22681-6 Pa. $4.50

THE DANCE OF SIVA, Ananda Coomaraswamy. Preeminent authority unfolds the vast metaphysic of India: the revelation of her art, conception of the universe, social organization, etc. 27 reproductions of art masterpieces. 192pp. 5⅜ × 8½.
24817-8 Pa. $5.95

CHRISTMAS CUSTOMS AND TRADITIONS, Clement A. Miles. Origin, evolution, significance of religious, secular practices. Caroling, gifts, yule logs, much more. Full, scholarly yet fascinating; non-sectarian. 400pp. 5⅜ × 8½.
23354-5 Pa. $6.50

THE HUMAN FIGURE IN MOTION, Eadweard Muybridge. More than 4,500 stopped-action photos, in action series, showing undraped men, women, children jumping, lying down, throwing, sitting, wrestling, carrying, etc. 390pp. 7⅞ × 10⅝.
20204-6 Cloth. $19.95

THE MAN WHO WAS THURSDAY, Gilbert Keith Chesterton. Witty, fast-paced novel about a club of anarchists in turn-of-the-century London. Brilliant social, religious, philosophical speculations. 128pp. 5⅜ × 8½.
25121-7 Pa. $3.95

A CEZANNE SKETCHBOOK: Figures, Portraits, Landscapes and Still Lifes, Paul Cezanne. Great artist experiments with tonal effects, light, mass, other qualities in over 100 drawings. A revealing view of developing master painter, precursor of Cubism. 102 black-and-white illustrations. 144pp. 8¾ × 6⅜.
24790-2 Pa. $5.95

AN ENCYCLOPEDIA OF BATTLES: Accounts of Over 1,560 Battles from 1479 B.C. to the Present, David Eggenberger. Presents essential details of every major battle in recorded history, from the first battle of Megiddo in 1479 B.C. to Grenada in 1984. List of Battle Maps. New Appendix covering the years 1967–1984. Index. 99 illustrations. 544pp. 6½ × 9¼.
24913-1 Pa. $14.95

AN ETYMOLOGICAL DICTIONARY OF MODERN ENGLISH, Ernest Weekley. Richest, fullest work, by foremost British lexicographer. Detailed word histories. Inexhaustible. Total of 856pp. 6½ × 9¼.
21873-2, 21874-0 Pa., Two-vol. set $17.00

WEBSTER'S AMERICAN MILITARY BIOGRAPHIES, edited by Robert McHenry. Over 1,000 figures who shaped 3 centuries of American military history. Detailed biographies of Nathan Hale, Douglas MacArthur, Mary Hallaren, others. Chronologies of engagements, more. Introduction. Addenda. 1,033 entries in alphabetical order. xi + 548pp. 6½ × 9¼. (Available in U.S. only)
24758-9 Pa. $11.95

LIFE IN ANCIENT EGYPT, Adolf Erman. Detailed older account, with much not in more recent books: domestic life, religion, magic, medicine, commerce, and whatever else needed for complete picture. Many illustrations. 597pp. 5⅜ × 8½.
22632-8 Pa. $8.95

HISTORIC COSTUME IN PICTURES, Braun & Schneider. Over 1,450 costumed figures shown, covering a wide variety of peoples: kings, emperors, nobles, priests, servants, soldiers, scholars, townsfolk, peasants, merchants, courtiers, cavaliers, and more. 256pp. 8⅜ × 11¼.
23150-X Pa. $7.95

THE NOTEBOOKS OF LEONARDO DA VINCI, edited by J. P. Richter. Extracts from manuscripts reveal great genius; on painting, sculpture, anatomy, sciences, geography, etc. Both Italian and English. 186 ms. pages reproduced, plus 500 additional drawings, including studies for *Last Supper, Sforza* monument, etc. 860pp. 7⅞ × 10¾. (Available in U.S. only) 22572-0, 22573-9 Pa., Two-vol. set $25.90

AMERICAN CLIPPER SHIPS: 1833–1858, Octavius T. Howe & Frederick C. Matthews. Fully-illustrated, encyclopedic review of 352 clipper ships from the period of America's greatest maritime supremacy. Introduction. 109 halftones. 5 black-and-white line illustrations. Index. Total of 928pp. 5⅜ × 8½.
25115-2, 25116-0 Pa., Two-vol. set $17.90

TOWARDS A NEW ARCHITECTURE, Le Corbusier. Pioneering manifesto by great architect, near legendary founder of "International School." Technical and aesthetic theories, views on industry, economics, relation of form to function, "mass-production spirit," much more. Profusely illustrated. Unabridged translation of 13th French edition. Introduction by Frederick Etchells. 320pp. 6⅛ × 9¼. (Available in U.S. only)
25023-7 Pa. $8.95

THE BOOK OF KELLS, edited by Blanche Cirker. Inexpensive collection of 32 full-color, full-page plates from the greatest illuminated manuscript of the Middle Ages, painstakingly reproduced from rare facsimile edition. Publisher's Note. Captions. 32pp. 9⅜ × 12¼.
24345-1 Pa. $4.95

BEST SCIENCE FICTION STORIES OF H. G. WELLS, H. G. Wells. Full novel The Invisible Man, plus 17 short stories: "The Crystal Egg," "Aepyornis Island," "The Strange Orchid," etc. 303pp. 5⅜ × 8½. (Available in U.S. only)
21531-8 Pa. $4.95

AMERICAN SAILING SHIPS: Their Plans and History, Charles G. Davis. Photos, construction details of schooners, frigates, clippers, other sailcraft of 18th to early 20th centuries—plus entertaining discourse on design, rigging, nautical lore, much more. 137 black-and-white illustrations. 240pp. 6⅛ × 9¼.
24658-2 Pa. $5.95

ENTERTAINING MATHEMATICAL PUZZLES, Martin Gardner. Selection of author's favorite conundrums involving arithmetic, money, speed, etc., with lively commentary. Complete solutions. 112pp. 5⅜ × 8½.
25211-6 Pa. $2.95

THE WILL TO BELIEVE, HUMAN IMMORTALITY, William James. Two books bound together. Effect of irrational on logical, and arguments for human immortality. 402pp. 5⅜ × 8½.
20291-7 Pa. $7.50

THE HAUNTED MONASTERY and THE CHINESE MAZE MURDERS, Robert Van Gulik. 2 full novels by Van Gulik continue adventures of Judge Dee and his companions. An evil Taoist monastery, seemingly supernatural events; overgrown topiary maze that hides strange crimes. Set in 7th-century China. 27 illustrations. 328pp. 5⅜ × 8½.
23502-5 Pa. $5.95

CELEBRATED CASES OF JUDGE DEE (DEE GOONG AN), translated by Robert Van Gulik. Authentic 18th-century Chinese detective novel; Dee and associates solve three interlocked cases. Led to Van Gulik's own stories with same characters. Extensive introduction. 9 illustrations. 237pp. 5⅜ × 8½.
23337-5 Pa. $4.95

Prices subject to change without notice.
Available at your book dealer or write for free catalog to Dept. GI, Dover Publications, Inc., 31 East 2nd St., Mineola, N.Y. 11501. Dover publishes more than 175 books each year on science, elementary and advanced mathematics, biology, music, art, literary history, social sciences and other areas.